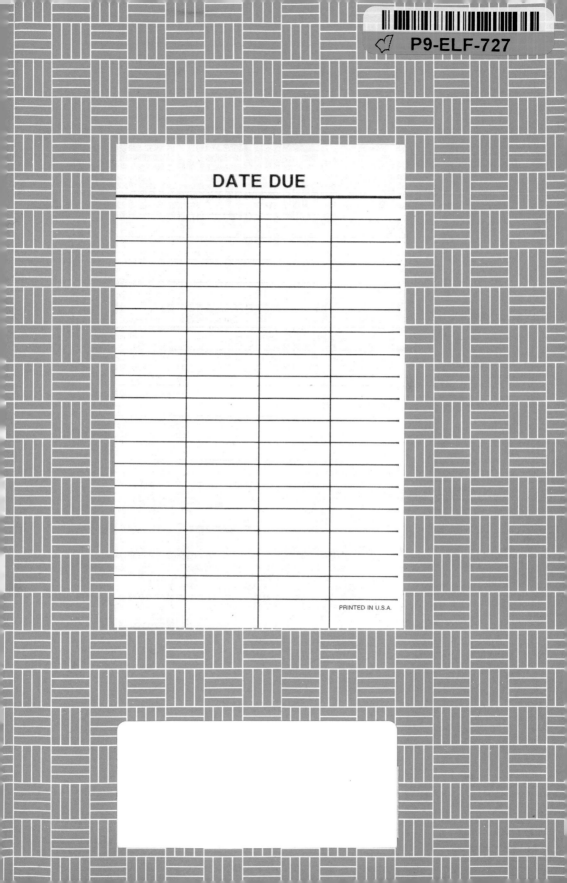

COMPANION ENCYCLOPEDIA
OF ANTHROPOLOGY

COMPANION
ENCYCLOPEDIA
OF
ANTHROPOLOGY

EDITED BY

TIM INGOLD

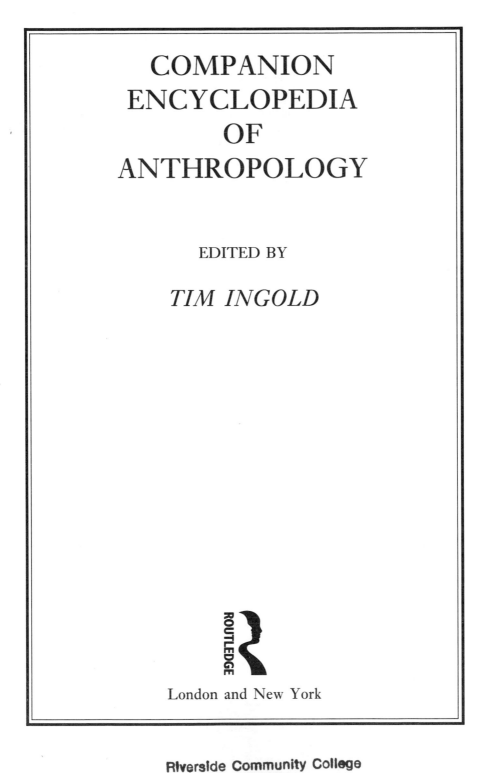

London and New York

First published in 1994
by Routledge
11 New Fetter Lane, London EC4P 4EE

Simultaneously published in the USA and Canada
by Routledge, Inc.
29 West 35th Street, New York, NY 10001

Typeset in 10½/12 pt Ehrhardt, Compugraphic by MCS Ltd, Salisbury
Printed in Great Britain by Clays Ltd, St Ives plc

British Library Cataloguing in Publication Data

A catalogue record for this book is available from the British Library.

Library of Congress Cataloging-in-Publication Data

A catalog record for this book is available on request.

ISBN 0–415–02137–5

CONTENTS

PREFACE

This volume started life on the initiative of Jonathan Price, at that time Reference Books Editor at Croom Helm. His idea was for an *Encyclopedia of Human Society* whose subject would span the disciplines of anthropology, sociology and archaeology. We first met to discuss the project in August 1986, and it was then that he charmed me into agreeing to become the volume's editor. It has been a big job, to put it mildly. In hindsight, it seems to me that I must have been mad to take it on at all, let alone single-handed. No doubt my motives were in part honourable, since I was strongly committed to the idea of anthropology as a bridging discipline, capable of spanning the many divisions of the human sciences. I wanted to prove that the possibility of synthesis existed not just as an ideal, but as something that could be realized in practice. No doubt, too, I was motivated by a certain vanity: if a synthesis was to be built, I wanted to be the one to build it, and to reap the credit! Seven years on, I am both older and perhaps a little wiser − no less committed to the ideal of synthesis, but a great deal more aware of the complexities involved, and rather less confident about my own abilities to bring it about.

Following my initial meeting with Jonathan Price, over a year passed before I was able to begin serious work on the project, which we had decided to call *Humanity, Culture and Social Life*. In October 1987 I drew up a prospectus for the entire volume, which included a complete list of forty articles, divided between the three parts spelled out in the title, and a rough breakdown of the contents for each. Then, during the first half of 1988, I set about recruiting authors for each of the articles. Meanwhile, Croom Helm had been subsumed under Routledge, from whose offices Jonathan continued to oversee the project.

My original schedule had been for authors to write their first drafts during 1989, allowing a further nine months for consultation and editorial comment, with a deadline for final versions of September 1990 and a projected publication date of April 1992. As always, things did not go entirely according to schedule, and I soon found that I was receiving final drafts of some articles while a pile of first drafts of others were awaiting editorial attention, and while for yet others I was still trying to fill the gaps in my list of contributors. To my great embarrassment, I found that I was quite unable to keep to my own deadlines. The inexorable growth of other commitments meant that drafts, dutifully submitted by their authors at the appointed time, languished for many months – and in some cases for more than a year – before I could get to work on them. During the academic year 1990–1, pressures of teaching and administration, coupled with my assumption of the Editorship of the journal *Man*, grew so heavy that progress on the project more or less ground to a halt, and my deadline for submitting the whole volume to the publishers – set for the end of April, 1991 – passed quietly by with most of the articles still at the first draft stage.

The project was rescued by my good fortune in securing one whole year and two subsequent terms of research leave from the University of Manchester. The first year (1991–2) was made possible in part by a grant from the University of Manchester Research Support Fund, for which I acknowledge my profound thanks. The two following terms were taken as sabbatical leave, and I should like to thank all my colleagues in the Manchester Department of Social Anthropology for covering my teaching and administrative duties in my absence. Shortly before his departure from Routledge to join the staff at Edinburgh University Press, the ever-patient Jonathan Price was finally rewarded for his forbearance. At noon on 14 October 1992, he arrived in my office to collect the entire, edited manuscript, and to carry it off to London. I had completed work on the manuscript only two hours before! But the editorial introductions had still to be written, and it was not until well into the following spring that they were eventually finished. Meanwhile, Mark Hendy was hard at work on the Herculean task of sub-editing the whole volume, which he completed by the beginning of May. I owe him a debt of gratitude for his efforts. Since Jonathan left for Edinburgh, responsibility for guiding the volume through the press passed to Michelle Darraugh, who has been wonderfully supportive, efficient and understanding. Most of all, however, this book belongs to Jonathan, without whom it would never have been conceived in the first place, and whose unflagging enthusiasm kept the project on the rails even during the most difficult of times.

Looking back, I am surprised how closely the book, in its final form, resembles the original plan drawn up so many years ago. Only four of the projected articles have been lost, and the titles and ordering of the majority have been changed little, if at all. There have been a few changes in the list of contributors along the way: in particular, I should like to put on record the sad loss of John Blacking, who died before he could begin work on his projected article, 'Music and dance'; and I should also like to thank Anthony Seeger for stepping into the breach at very short notice. There have also been some changes in the volume's title. All along, I wanted it to be a book to be *read*, and not merely consulted as a work of reference, and for that reason I was inclined to relegate the phrase *An Encyclopedia of Anthropology* to the subtitle. In many ways, the book is more akin to what might conventionally be called a handbook or a reader, rather than an encyclopedia. Be that as it may, after much discussion it was eventually decided to call it a *Companion Encyclopedia*, a phrase which nicely combines the notion of encompassing a whole field of knowledge with that of guiding and accompanying the reader in his or her journey through it. The original working title, *Humanity, Culture and Social Life*, accordingly became the volume's subtitle.

I would like to take this opportunity to extend my personal thanks to all the many contributors to this book. They have put up patiently with endless delays, and responded graciously to my many and sometimes inordinate editorial demands. I have, moreover, learned a tremendous amount from working through their articles. But for maintaining my sanity over all these years, my greatest debt of gratitude is to my wife, Anna, and my children, Christopher, Nicholas and Jonathan. Their support has been magnificent, and it is not something that I shall ever be able to repay.

Tim Ingold
Manchester
September 1993

GENERAL INTRODUCTION

THE SCOPE OF ANTHROPOLOGY

Anthropologists study people. They do not study stars, rocks, plants or the weather. But whilst we may have little difficulty in separating out the field of anthropological inquiry from those of astronomy, geology, botany or meteorology, it is not so obvious how − if at all − anthropology may be distinguished from the many other branches of the human sciences, all of which could claim to be studying people in one way or another. Medicine is concerned with the workings of the human body, psychology with those of the mind; history studies people's activities in the past, sociology their institutional arrangements in the present, and so on. The list could be extended almost indefinitely. What, then, is the distinctively *anthropological* way of studying people?

Part of the difficulty we have in answering this question is attributable to the fact that there is not one way of doing anthropology, but many. There are two facets to this diversity, the first having to do with the circumstances of the discipline's historical development, the second lying in its contemporary subdisciplinary divisions. I begin with a few words about anthropology's history.

In a sense, of course, anthropology can be traced to the earliest antiquity, when human beings first began to speculate about their own nature, origins and diversity. But as an explicitly defined field of academic inquiry, it is a creature of the last two centuries of thought in that region of the world conventionally known as 'the West'. Western thought, however, is not a monolithic edifice but a complex interweaving of often opposing currents, and this is no less true of the career of anthropology. Moreover, these currents did not flow in an historical vacuum, but at every moment responded to dominant moral, political and economic concerns of the time. Thus British anthropology developed alongside the growth of empire; its preoccupations were fuelled by the need of the colonial administration to take the measure of its presumed superiority over administered nations, and to turn a knowledge of their social organizations and cultural traditions to the service of indirect rule. In many countries of Continental Europe, by contrast, the growth of anthropology (more commonly known as 'ethnology') was linked to emergent nationalist movements of the late nineteenth and early twentieth centuries, and to the efforts, on the part of adherents of each movement, to discover a national heritage in the traditions of local folk or peasant culture. In North America the situation was different again: the United States and Canada had their indigenous Indian populations, and the first priority of many American anthropologists was to record as much as possible about the physical features, material artefacts, languages and cultures of extant Amerindian groups before it was too late. This was a kind of salvage anthropology.

The second facet to the diversity of anthropological approaches lies in the fact that anthropology, as it exists today, is not a single field, but is rather a somewhat contingent and unstable amalgam of subfields, each encumbered with its own history, theoretical agenda and methodological preoccupations. In the American tradition of scholarship, it has long been customary to distinguish four such subfields of anthropology, namely physical, archaeological, cultural and linguistic. In the British tradition, by contrast, there are only three subfields, of physical anthropology, archaeology and social (rather than cultural) anthropology. The exclusion of linguistics from British anthropology is a curious and somewhat scandalous anomaly to which I return below. The more immediate question is: why these fields in particular? What brought the study of physical types, ancient artefacts and supposedly 'primitive' ways of life under the umbrella of a single discipline of anthropology?

Most academic disciplines and their boundaries are, in fact, the fossilized shells of burnt-out theories, and in this, anthropology is no exception. The theory which, more than any other, established anthropology as a comprehensive science of humankind held that people the world over are undergoing a gradual, evolutionary ascent from primitive origins to advanced civilization, and that the differences between societies can be explained in terms of the stages they have reached in this progression. Anthropology, then, emerged as the study of human evolution – conceived in this progressive sense – through the reconstruction of its earlier stages. Physical anthropology studied the evolution of human anatomy, archaeology studied the evolution of material artefacts, and social and cultural anthropology studied the evolution of beliefs and practices – on the assumption that the ways of life of contemporary 'primitives' afford a window on the former condition of the more 'civilized' nations.

In short, it was progressive evolutionism that unified the study of human anatomy, artefacts and traditions as subfields of a single discipline. Yet this kind of evolutionary theory belongs essentially to the formative period of anthropology in the nineteenth century and is, today, almost universally discredited. So what, if anything, still holds the sublfields together? To the extent that contemporary anthropologists concern themselves with this question, their opinions differ greatly. Some argue that their continued combination, for example within University Departments, is an anachronism for which there is no longer any rational justification. Thus many cultural anthropologists, concerned as they are with the manifold ways in which the peoples among whom they have worked make sense of the world around them, find more common ground with students of philosophy, language, literature and the arts than with their colleagues in other fields of anthropology. Social anthropologists, who would regard their project as a comparative study of the generation, patterning and transformation of relationships among persons and groups, profess a close affinity – amounting almost to identity – to sociologists and historians, but have little time for archaeology (despite the obvious links between archaeology and history). For their part, physical anthropologists (or 'biological anthropologists', as many now prefer to be known) remain committed to the project of understanding human evolution, but their evolutionary theory is of a modern, neo-Darwinian variety, quite at odds with the progressive evolutionism of the nineteenth century. Having vigorously repudiated the racist doctrines of the turn of the century, which cast such a shadow over the early history of the discipline, anthropologists of all complexions now recognize that social and cultural variation is quite independent of biogenetic constraint. Thus physical anthropology, cut loose from the study of society and culture, has virtually become a subfield of evolutionary biology, devoted specifically to the evolution of our own kind.

Yet despite these tendencies towards the fragmentation of anthropology, along the lines of the heavily institutionalized division of academic labour between the humanities and social sciences on the one hand, and the natural sciences on the other, many anthropologists remain convinced that there is more to their discipline than the sum of its parts. What is distinctive about the anthropological perspective, they argue, is a commitment to *holism*, to the idea that it should be possible – at least in principle – to establish the *interconnections* between the biological, social, historical and cultural dimensions of human life that are otherwise parcelled up among different disciplines for separate study. It was, of course, just such a synthesis that the nineteenth century founders of anthropology claimed to have achieved with their theory of evolution. But the fact that the theory is now judged, in hindsight, to have been wrong does not mean that the project that gave rise to it was entirely misconceived (although aspects of it – such as its assumption of Euro-American superiority and its racist undertones – undoubtedly were). My own view, which also furnishes the rationale for the present volume, is that a synthesis of our knowledge of the conditions of human life in the world, in all its aspects, is something worth striving for, and that working towards such a synthesis is the essence of doing anthropology.

The obstacles, however, are formidable. Biological and cultural anthropologists, for example, are divided not simply by their attention to different kinds of facts, but by a more fundamental difference in their respective understandings of the relations between fact and theory. True, the data of observation in every branch of anthropology have one thing in common: they are not derived by experiment, but arc gathered through the conduct of fieldwork. But ethnographic fieldwork, as it is carried out by social and cultural anthropologists in the settings of everyday life, is very different from the kind of fieldwork that might be conducted by an archaeologist or physical anthropologist in searching, say, for the fossilized remains of early hominids or for evidence, in the form of preserved artefacts, of their activities. Fossils and artefacts can be treated, to all intents and purposes, as inert objects of investigation: they may be examined for every ounce of information they will yield, but they are not themselves party to its interpretation. Living people, however, cannot be treated as objects in this sense. In the field, ethnographers engage in a continuous dialogue with their informants, who provide instruction in the skills and knowledge that are entailed in their particular form of life. It has been said, with some justification, that ethnographers do not so much study people, as go to study *among* or *with* people, and the results of such study emerge as the products of this mutual, dialogic encounter. Indeed much so-called 'ethnographic data' is in fact autobiographical, describing the ways in which the fieldworker experienced those events in which he or she participated.

Under these circumstances, a clear distinction between observation and interpretation, between the collection of data in the field and their placement within a theoretical framework, cannot readily be sustained. This did not, however, prevent the first generation of British social anthropologists – pioneers of the kind of long-term, intensive field study that is now considered indispensable to competent ethnographic work – from pretending that it could, apparently in an effort to secure recognition for their discipline as a true science of society. This goes some way to explaining the curious neglect, by social anthropologists of this generation, of language and its uses. Knowledge of the native language was considered a prerequisite for ethnographic inquiry; as such, however, it was regarded as a tool of the anthropologist's trade rather than something to be investigated in its own right. One was to use language to probe the details of culture and social organization much as a botanist uses a microscope to examine the fine structure of plants. Only subsequently, as anthropologists became more reflexive, more sensitive to the epistemological conditions of their own inquiry, did language use re-emerge as a key focus of attention. Even in North America, where linguistic anthropology has always occupied its place among the four subfields of the discipline, its practitioners have long been in the minority, often drawn into the anthropological camp through their reaction against the excessive formalism of mainstream linguistics, and its insensitivity to the social and cultural contexts in which language is put to work.

But the challenge posed by ethnographic study among people whose backgrounds and sensibilities are situated in environments very different from those of the 'West' goes far beyond showing how the seemingly strange or irrational 'makes sense' when placed in its proper context. For the knowledge and wisdom that these people impart to the fieldworker, sharpened as it is by their practical experience of everyday involvement in the world, strikes at the heart of some of the most basic presuppositions of Western thought itself. To take this knowledge seriously, and to be the wiser for it, means bringing it to bear in a critical engagement with these presuppositions. In this engagement, every single one of the key concepts of Western civilization — concepts like society, culture, nature, language, technology, individuality and personhood, equality and inequality, even humanity itself — becomes essentially contestable. Theoretical work, in social and cultural anthropology, is largely a matter of opening up these concepts for inspection and unpacking their contents, thereby revealing the often hidden baggage that we carry with us into our encounters with unfamiliar realities. If we are ever to reach a level of understanding that breaks the barriers between Western and non-Western worlds of life and thought, such work is indispensable. Yet it also leaves anthropology perilously poised on a knife-edge. For how can a discipline whose project is rooted in the intellectual history of the Western world meet the challenge presented by non-Western understandings of humanity, culture and social life without undercutting its own epistemological foundations?

Perhaps uniquely among academic disciplines, anthropology thrives on the art of its own perpetual deconstruction. Caught at the intersection of two cross-cutting tensions, between the humanities and natural sciences on the one hand, and between theoretical speculation and lived experience on the other, it leaves little room for intellectual complacency. Like philosophy, the remit of anthropology is not confined to a delimited segment within a wider division of academic labour; rather it exists to subvert any such tidy division, rendering problematic the very foundations on which it rests. The best anthropological writing is distinguished by its receptiveness to ideas springing from work in subjects far beyond its conventional boundaries, and by its ability to connect these ideas in ways that would not have occurred to their originators, who may be more enclosed by their particular disciplinary frameworks. But to this connecting enterprise it brings something more, namely the attempt to engage our abstract ideas about what human beings might be like with an empirically grounded knowledge of (certain) human beings as they really are, and of what for them everyday life is all about. This engagement not only provides the primary motivation — apart from that of sheer curiosity — for ethnographic inquiry, but also carries anthropology beyond the closeted realms of speculative philosophy. Anthropology, if you will, is philosophy with the people in.

No more today than in the past, however, is anthropological work conducted in an historical vacuum. Just as much as the people they study, anthropologists are participants in the one world which we all inhabit, and therefore carry their share of the responsibility for what goes on in it. In many parts of the world, people currently face appalling deprivations, whether due to poverty, famine, disease, war, or some combination of these. There is no doubt that anthropological knowledge, tempered as it is by an awareness of the practical realities of life 'on the ground' in real human communities, has a vital contribution to make in the alleviation of human suffering. Moreover, to an increasing extent, anthropologists have involved themselves as advocates on behalf of the peoples among whom they have worked – for example in the struggle for recognition of indigenous rights to land – or as advisers or consultants in various projects of development. In view of such involvements, it has sometimes been suggested that a field of 'applied anthropology' should be recognized, alongside those branches of the discipline that are already well established.

If this suggestion has not met with wholehearted approval, the reason does not lie in any desire to keep anthropology 'pure', nor does it indicate that anthropologists prefer to wash their hands of the moral and political entailments of their involvement with local communities. It is rather that in the conduct of anthropological work it is practically impossible to separate the acquisition of knowledge from its application. The distinction between pure and applied science rests on a premiss of *detachment*, the assumption that scientists can know the world without having to involve themselves in it. But anthropology rests on exactly the opposite premiss, that it is only by immersing ourselves in the life-world of our fellow human beings that we shall ever understand what it means to them – and to us. Thus whatever else it may be, anthropology is a science of *engagement*. Indeed it may be said that in anthropology we study ourselves, precisely because it requires us to change our conception of who 'we' are, from an exclusive, Western 'we' to an inclusive, global one. To adopt an anthropological attitude is to drop the pretence of our belonging to a select association of Westerners, uniquely privileged to look in upon the inhabitants of 'other cultures', and to recognize that along with the others whose company we share (albeit temporarily), we are all fellow travellers in the same world. By comparing experience – 'sharing notes' – we can reach a better understanding of what such journeying entails, where we have come from, and where we are going.

HUMANITY, CULTURE AND SOCIAL LIFE

This is an encyclopedia *of* anthropology, it is not an encyclopedia *about* anthropology. The distinction is critical, and underwrites both the content of the articles that follow and the structure of the volume as a whole. There is a tendency, common to many branches of scholarship, for specialists to become so absorbed in debates internal to the discipline that they lose sight of their original purpose, namely to extend the scope of our knowledge of the world. The debates become an object of study in themselves. Though there must be a place in every discipline for a consideration of its history and its methods, I believe it is important to resist the inclination to detach such consideration from the primary objective of enlarging human understanding. In the case of anthropology, this means that however much we may tangle with the details of particular arguments, we should never forget that the pursuit of anthropological knowledge is for the benefit of people, and not the other way round. The tapestry of human life, in other words, has not been woven for the purpose of providing research opportunities for anthropologists; however, anthropological research can help us to unravel the strands and to reveal the subtleties of their patterning. This volume, then, is about human life in all its aspects, and each article, focusing on some specific aspect, sets out what current studies in anthropology (and in several cases, in contingent disciplines) have to say about it.

The same principle informs the division of the volume into its three parts, respectively entitled 'humanity', 'culture' and 'social life'. The emphasis, in the first, is on human beings as members of a species, on how that species differs from others, on how it has evolved, and on how human populations have adapted to – and in turn transformed – their environments. The second part focuses on the origination, structure, transmission and material expression of the symbolically constituted forms of human culture, and on the role of culture in action, perception and cognition. The third part examines the various facets – familial, economic, political, and so on – of the relationships and processes that are carried on by persons and groups, through the medium of cultural forms, in the historical process of social life. Each part begins with an introductory article that sets out the substantive areas to be covered in greater depth, and places the articles that follow in their wider anthropological context.

Of course any division of the entire field of human life is bound to be artificial, and there are perhaps as many common themes linking articles in different parts as within each part of the volume. The point I wish to stress, however, is that the division is not based on, nor does it correspond with, any of the conventional divisions of the field of anthropology. It is true that the work of archaeologists and physical (or biological) anthropologists figures relatively prominently in the first part, and that work in cultural and social anthropology predominates in the second and third parts. But if there is one thing that the volume establishes, beyond any reasonable doubt, it is that the issues of our common humanity, of cultural variation and of social process can be adequately tackled only through the collaboration of scholars working in *all* the conventional subfields of anthropology – biological, archaeological, cultural, social, linguistic – and of others besides, whose backgrounds lie in fields as diverse as medicine, ecology, psychology, cognitive science, history, sociology, comparative religion, political science, law, philosophy, architecture, drama, folklore and ethnomusicology. Indeed, practitioners of several of these latter fields number among the contributors to this book.

To attempt to compress all of human life within two covers may seem a hopelessly ambitious undertaking. For every topic included in the contents, a thousand others could have been selected; for every discussion of a given topic, a thousand others could have been presented, each drawing on different material and with a different orientation. Though the overall conception of the volume – including the definition of issues to be covered by individual articles, their ordering and arrangement into parts – is my own, contributors have been given a free hand to develop their ideas along whatever lines they find most productive and congenial. The result is something of a pot-pourri of approaches which, whilst they may accurately reflect the diversity of voices currently to be heard within the discipline, hardly add up to any consistent direction. So what possible justification can there be for collecting them all together under the grandiose and all-encompassing rubric of an *Encyclopedia*? To my mind, there are three good reasons for doing so.

The first, and most important, is to counteract the dangers of overspecialization. One of the more worrying consequences of the exponential growth in the volume of research and publication during the latter part of this century is that we know more and more about less and less. It is hard enough for any scholar to keep abreast of developments within a relatively narrow field, let alone to follow what is going on in even closely related specialisms. What is lost, in this process, is an awareness of the interconnectedness of phenomena, of their positioning within wider fields of relationships. Knowledge is fragmented, its objects treated in isolation from the contexts in which they occur. Yet it is only thanks to our ability to *connect* that knowledge is rendered significant. Thus, paradoxically, does the growth of knowledge breed ignorance, for the more we know, the less we understand of what that knowledge *means*. Despite its holistic aspirations, anthropology has suffered its own fragmentation, which some indeed have welcomed as testimony to the rapid advance of anthropological scholarship in recent years, on a wide range of fronts. Gone are the days, it is said, when anthropologists could read and contribute – as did the founders of the discipline – across the entire spectrum of its concerns. I do not personally believe this is the case, and if it is, I certainly do not welcome it. But there is no doubt that the proliferation of interests and approaches threatens the coherence of anthropology as a discipline, and that the need for integration and synthesis is urgent. This volume exists to meet that need.

The second reason for an encyclopedic compilation of this kind is that it serves to establish a baseline of anthropological knowledge upon which subsequent generations can build. This is not merely to embark on a stock-taking exercise, a survey of achievements to date in the various areas covered. Indeed, little is to be gained from attempts to recapitulate or paraphrase all that has been written on this or that topic: to do so leads at best to the sterile rehearsal of obsolete arguments, at worst to the contrivance of artificial 'schools of thought', each of which then becomes the subject of a separate story. Contributors to this volume were asked *not* to write articles of this sort, but were rather challenged to break new ground, not only by presenting their own versions of the 'state of play' in their respective fields of study, but by charting out new directions of inquiry hitherto unexplored. They have, without exception, risen to the challenge, and the result is a volume that takes anthropology *beyond* existing frontiers and that points unequivocally and sometimes provocatively towards the future. Many contributors, moreover, deal with issues that lie on the evolving interface between anthropology and other disciplines in the human sciences, from biology and psychology to linguistics, history and sociology, and herein lies the third *raison d'être* for the volume. For besides bringing out the connections within the discipline of anthropology, the articles collected here amply demonstrate the relevance of anthropological insights to work in a host of related fields, and the capacity of the discipline to build bridges across the frontiers between otherwise divided and mutually impenetrable intellectual territories.

Let me conclude with a few words about what this Encyclopedia is *not*. I have already pointed out that its subject is not anthropology but human life, and that its orientation is to the future rather than the past. For this reason, there are no articles dealing specifically with the history of anthropology. This is not to say that no space is devoted to historical themes. However it has been left to the discretion of individual contributors to dwell on the history of approaches to the topical issues that concern them, in so far as it is conducive to the elucidation of these issues themselves. The emphasis, in other words, is on learning *from* the history of the discipline rather than on learning *about* it. The same goes for questions of anthropological research method. With the reformulation of such questions as problems of 'methodology', they have tended to become objects of investigation in their own right, rather than questions whose resolution is but a means to the greater goal of enlarging human understanding. In this volume, matters of method are not made into the subjects of separate articles, but are rather introduced where they belong, in the context of inquiries into substantive anthropological topics. Finally, this is an encyclopedia of anthropology, not of ethnography. It does not aim to catalogue the range of human cultural variation, or to review the findings of anthropological research in particular regions of the world. Each article has a thematic rather than a regional focus, and authors have been free to draw on illustrative material from whatever region or period best suits the purposes of their exposition.

Though the volume qualifies as an encyclopedia, in that it encompasses the full circle of current anthropological knowledge, it is also a book that is designed not just to be consulted but to be *read*. While conceived as a work of reference, its aims go far beyond that: namely to lay the foundations for an integrated and synoptic perspective on the conditions of human life that is appropriate to the challenges of the next century. For an encyclopedia, the number of articles is relatively small, but by the same token, authors have had the opportunity to develop their ideas and arguments at some length. Each article, indeed, stands as a major contribution, an innovative synthesis at the cutting edge of the discipline. Moreover, the ordering of articles is not arbitrary, but has been carefully designed to bring out to best advantage the connections between them, and to weld the volume into a coherent whole. The resulting combination of breadth of coverage and depth in the treatment of individual topics is, I believe, unparalleled in contemporary anthropological literature.

I expect this book to be read primarily by students, teachers and academics working in fields of anthropology or related disciplines, who need to turn to a significant overview of current thinking to supplement their existing specialist knowledge. But I hope it will also offer a source of ideas and inspiration to the enthusiastic and informed 'general reader' who, once having encountered anthropology, wishes to find out more about various aspects of the subject. To cater for this wide readership, the articles are written so as to be both authoritative and yet readily comprehensible to professionals, students and lay persons alike. Each article is followed by a comprehensive list of references detailing works cited in the text, and by a selected list of 'further reading' recommended for those who wish to pursue the themes of the article in greater depth. Naturally, there is often a good deal of overlap between items included under 'further reading' and those listed in the references; however the costs of duplication were felt to be outweighed by the advantages of presenting the 'further reading' as a single, integral list.

What lies ahead is a journey through some of the most exciting and challenging domains of contemporary scholarship. I wish the reader *bon voyage* while, with the merciful relief of a marathon completed, I lay down my own pen.

THE CONTRIBUTORS

BARBARA ADAM received her Ph.D. from the University of Wales, and is currently Lecturer in Social Theory at the University of Wales, Cardiff. She is the founder editor of the journal *Time and Society*. She has written extensively on the subject of social time, and her book, *Time and Social Theory* (1990), won the Philip Abrams Memorial Prize in 1991, awarded by the British Sociological Association for the best first book.

ALAN BARNARD is Senior Lecturer in Social Anthropology at the University of Edinburgh. He was educated at the George Washington University, McMaster University and the University of London, receiving his Ph.D. in 1976. Before moving to Edinburgh in 1978, he taught at the University of Cape Town (1972–3) and at University College London (1976–8). He has carried out fieldwork with the Nharo and other Khoisan peoples of Botswana and Namibia and his research interests include kinship theory, hunter-gatherer studies, and regional comparison. He is the author, with Anthony Good, of *Research Practices in the Study of Kinship* (1984), and of *Hunters and Herders in Southern Africa* (1992). He is co-editor of *Kinship and Cosmology* (1989), and was editor of the journal *Edinburgh Anthropology* for 1988. Alan Barnard has published numerous articles on kinship, hunter-gatherers and the Khoisan peoples of southern Africa, as well as a wordlist and grammar of the Nharo language (1985) and a children's book on the Bushmen (1993). His recent interests include the early history of social anthropology and the relation between anthropology and popular literature.

NIKO BESNIER gained his Ph.D. from the University of Southern California in 1986, and is now Associate Professor in the Department of Anthropology at Yale University. He has conducted research in various locations in Western Polynesia and Melanesia, principally on Nukulaelae Atoll, Tuvalu. His published works deal with literacy, emotional life and the cultural construction of the person, political rhetoric, gossip, and the relationship between verbal accounts and social action.

ANDRÉ BÉTEILLE is Professor of Sociology at the University of Delhi where he has taught since 1959. He was Simon Fellow at the University of Manchester (1965–6), Commonwealth Visiting Professor at the University of Cambridge (1978–9), held the Tinbergen Chair at Erasmus University, Rotterdam (1984), was Visiting Professor at the London School of Economics (1986), Visiting Scholar in Residence at the University of California, Santa Barbara (1988), Fulbright Distinguished Lecturer (1989) and a Fellow of the Institute of Advanced Study, Berlin (1989–90). He has delivered the Auguste Comte Memorial Lecture at the London School of Economics (1979), the Kingsley Martin Memorial Lecture (1979) and the Commonwealth Lectures (1985) at the University of Cambridge, and the Ambedkar Lectures at the University of Bombay (1980). His research interests include stratification and social class, equality and social justice, and race, caste and ethnicity. In addition to many papers in scholarly journals, Béteille is the author of *Caste, Class and Power* (1965), *Castes: Old and New* (1969), *Studies in Agrarian Social Structure* (1974), *Inequality among Men* (1977), *Ideologies and Intellectuals* (1980), *The Idea of Natural Inequality and Other Essays* (1983), *Essays in Comparative Sociology* (1987), *Society and Politics in India* (1991) and *The Backward Classes in Contemporary India* (1992) . He is the editor of *Social Inequality* (1969) and *Equality and Inequality* (1983).

MARK COHEN graduated from Harvard College and Columbia University with degrees in anthropology. He has carried out archaeological fieldwork in North, South and Central America, in southern Europe and in East Africa. He is author of *The Food Crisis in Prehistory* (1977) and *Health and the Rise of Civilization* (1989), and senior editor of *Paleopathology at the Origins of Agriculture* (1984). He has been a Fellow of the Center for Advanced Study in the Behavioral Sciences, Stanford University (1978–9), a Fellow of the John Simon Guggenheim Memorial Foundation and Visiting Scholar at Cambridge University (1985–6), and a Fulbright Lecturer at the Hebrew University, Jerusalem (1989–90). Mark Cohen is currently Distinguished Teaching Professor of Anthropology at the State University of New York College at Plattsburgh, where he is working to reconstruct patterns of health in a sixteenth century Christian Maya population.

JEAN DEBERNARDI was educated at Stanford University and at the University of Oxford, and received her Ph.D. from the University of Chicago in 1986. She has carried out fieldwork in Penang, Malaysia (1979–81), and in Taiwan and Fujian Province of the People's Republic of China (1987). DeBernardi has taught at Beloit College, the University of Michigan and Bryn Mawr College, and is presently Assistant Professor in the Department of Anthropology, University of Alberta at Edmonton, Canada. Her research interests include Chinese popular religious culture, the use of anti-languages in Chinese secret societies, and linguistic nationalism in Taiwan. She is currently working on a book entitled *Empire over Imagination: Chinese Popular Religious Culture in Colonial and Post-Colonial Malaysia.*

ROBIN DUNBAR was educated at Oxford University and at the University of Bristol, where he received his Ph.D. in 1974. He has subsequently held research posts at Cambridge, Stockholm and Liverpool Universities. He is now Professor of Biological Anthropology at University College London. His research has been concerned mainly with the evolution of mammalian social systems and has involved field studies of primates and ungulates in Africa and Scotland. He is the author of *Reproductive Decisions: An Economic Analysis of Gelada Baboon Social Strategies* (1984) and *Primate Social Systems* (1988), and has published numerous articles in books and journals on themes in primatology, sociobiology and human evolution.

TIMOTHY K. EARLE is Professor of Anthropology at the University of California, Los Angeles. He received his Ph.D. in Anthropology from the University of Michigan in 1973. His research interests include the evolution of pre-industrial complex societies, institutional finance and prehistoric economies. He has carried out field research on the Hawaiian Islands and in Andean South America, and is presently involved in a long-term investigation of Danish Neolithic and Bronze Age chiefdoms. Earle is the editor or co-editor of a number of volumes, including *Exchange Systems in Prehistory* (1977), *Modeling Change in Prehistoric Subsistence Economies* (1980), *Contexts for Prehistoric Exchange* (1982) and *Specialization, Exchange and Complex Society* (1987). He is the author of *Economic and Social Organization of a Complex Chiefdom: the Halelea District, Kauai, Hawaii* (1978), and (with A. Johnson) of *The Evolution of Human Society* (1987).

ROY ELLEN was educated at the London School of Economics, where he received his B.Sc. in 1968, and his Ph.D. in 1972. He was Lecturer in Social Anthropology at the LSE in 1972–3, and thereafter Lecturer, Senior Lecturer and Reader at the University of Kent at Canterbury, England. Since 1988 he has been Professor of Anthropology and Human Ecology at the University of Kent. He has carried out several periods of social anthropological fieldwork among the Nuaulu of Seram, Eastern Indonesia, as well as in Sulawesi and Java, and in the Gorom archipelago. His interests include ecological anthropology (especially of rain forest environments), regional organization of trade, ethnobiology and classification, and anthropological research methods. He is the author of *Nuaulu Settlement and Ecology* (1978), *Environment, Subsistence and System* (1982) and *The Cultural Relations of Classification* (1993). He has also edited or co-edited a number of collections, including *Social and Ecological Systems* (1979), *Classifications in their Social Context* (1979), *Ethnographic Research* (1984) and *Malinowski Between Two Worlds* (1988). He was the Royal Anthropological Institute's Curl Lecturer for 1987.

CLIVE GAMBLE was born in 1951 and educated at Cambridge (MA and Ph.D.). He is now Reader in Archaeology at the University of Southampton. He has carried out extensive fieldwork in Palaeolithic Archaeology both in

Europe and in Australia. He is the author of *The Palaeolithic Settlement of Europe* (1986), *Timewalkers: the Prehistory of Global Colonization* (1993) and (with C. B. Stringer) *In Search of the Neanderthals* (1993), as well as numerous articles. He is editor, with O. Soffer, of *The World at 18,000 B.P.* (1990), and, with W. A. Boismier, of *Ethnoarchaeological Approaches to Mobile Campsites* (1991). He has broadcast on the fate of the Neanderthals and lectured in many countries on themes in Palaeolithic Archaeology.

IGOR DE GARINE was educated at the Sorbonne, Paris, and received his Doctorate in Ethnology in 1962 for a thesis on the economic and social life of the Massa of Cameroon. Since 1953 he has carried out fieldwork in numerous countries of Africa (Cameroon, Chad, Senegal, Niger), South America (Brazil, Argentina, Chile, Paraguay) and in South and South-east Asia (India, Nepal, the Philippines). He has made eleven films and authored over a hundred publications. Most recently, he was co-editor of *Coping with Uncertainty in Food Supply* (1988) and *Food and Nutrition in the African Rain Forest* (1990). He currently directs a 20-member research team of the Centre National de la Recherche Scientifique, which is investigating the influence of seasonality on food and nutrition in a number of African societies and in Nepal. In addition, de Garine is Regional Commissioner for Europe of the International Committee on the Anthropology of Food (ICAF), and Head of the Group on the Anthropology of Food of the Maison Des Sciences de l'Homme, Paris. His present research interests lie in the ethnology of the Plains populations of North Cameroon and Chad, and he has books in preparation on the social and religious organizations of these peoples, as well as on theoretical and methodological aspects of the anthropology of food.

CHRIS GREGORY studied Economics at the University of New South Wales and the Australian National University. After spending three years lecturing in Economics at the University of Papua New Guinea, where he developed an interest in economic anthropology, he went on to obtain his doctorate in Social Anthropology at the University of Cambridge in 1980. He subsequently carried out anthropological fieldwork on rural marketing in a tribal area of central India in 1982–3; his current ethnographic work in this region has focused on material culture and mythology. Chris Gregory is currently Senior Lecturer in the Department of Archaeology and Anthropology, Australian National University. He is the author of *Gifts and Commodities* (1982) and (with J. C. Altman) *Observing the Economy* (1989), as well as of numerous articles and reviews.

TIM INGOLD is Professor of Social Anthropology at the University of Manchester, England. After completing his first degree in Social Anthropology at the University of Cambridge (1970), he carried out fieldwork among Saami people in north-eastern Finland, leading to his Ph.D. and his first book, *The Skolt Lapps Today* (1976) . As well as pursuing this ethnographic interest, with further fieldwork among northern Finnish farmers, he has written extensively on comparative questions of hunting and pastoralism in the circumpolar North (*Hunters, Pastoralists and Ranchers*, 1980), on evolutionary theory in anthropology, biology and history (*Evolution and Social Life*, 1986), and on human ecology (*The Appropriation of Nature*, 1986). He is a co-editor of the two-volume work, *Hunters and Gatherers* (1988), and editor of *What is an Animal?* (1988). His current research interests are in the anthropology of technology (he is editor, with Kathleen Gibson, of *Tools, Language and Cognition in Human Evolution*, 1993), and in issues of environmental perception. Tim Ingold was the Malinowski Memorial Lecturer for 1982, and the Royal Anthropological Institute's Curl Lecturer for 1989. From 1990–2, he was editor of *Man* (the Journal of the Royal Anthropological Institute). In 1989 he was awarded the Rivers Memorial Medal.

STEPHEN KUNITZ is a physician and holds a Ph.D. in Sociology. He is professor in the Department of Community and Preventitive Medicine at the University of Rochester Medical Center, Rochester, NY, USA, as well as a Visiting Fellow (part-time, 1990–4) at the National Centre for Epidemiology and Population Health, Australian National University, Canberra. He has carried out most of his fieldwork among Indian peoples of the American South-west. Stephen Kunitz is author of *Disease Change and the Role of Medicine: the Navajo Experience* (1983) and *Diversity and Disease: the Impact of European Contact on the Health of the Indigenous Peoples of North America and Oceania* (1994). With J. E. Levy, he has also published *Indian Drinking: Navajo Practices and Anglo-American Theories* (1974), *Navajo Aging* (1991) and *Navajo Drinking Careers: a Twenty-five Year Follow-up* (1994), as well as several articles on population and health among the Navajo and Hopi Indians.

MARY LECRON FOSTER is a full-time researcher at the Department of Anthropology, University of California, Berkeley. She received her Ph.D. in linguistics from that University in 1965, and has initiated and taught programmes in social and cultural linguistics and in symbolic anthropology at California State University, Hayward. She has carried out extensive research in Mexico on indigenous languages and cultures, and has published grammars of two Mexican languages and many articles on language evolution and aspects of cultural symbolism. She is editor (with Stanley H. Brandes) of *Symbol as Sense* (1980), and (with Lucy J. Botscharow) of *The Life of Symbols* (1990).

GILBERT LEWIS initially studied Medicine at the Universities of Oxford and London, and held hospital medical posts in London between 1962 and 1965. He then went on to study Social Anthropology, and was Research Officer at the London School of Economics from 1967–71. Following anthropological fieldwork in West Sepik Province, Papua New Guinea, in 1968–70, Lewis gained a Ph.D. in 1972. He is presently Lecturer in Social Anthropology at the University of Cambridge. His books include *Knowledge of Illness in a Sepik*

Society (1975) and *Day of Shining Red* (1980). Lewis is currently engaged in medical anthropological research in West Africa (Guinea-Bissau).

PHILIP LIEBERMAN received his initial training in Electrical Engineering, at the Massachusetts Institute of Technology, but his Ph.D., completed in 1966, was in Linguistics. He was Associate Professor in Linguistics and Electrical Engineering, and subsequently Professor of Linguistics, at the University of Connecticut, from 1967–74. In 1974, he joined the Faculty at Brown University, where he is now the George Hazard Crooker University Professor and Professor of Cognitive and Linguistic Sciences. He has carried out research on the perception and production of speech, and on the innate foundations and evolution of human linguistic competence. He is the author of *Intonation, Speech and Language* (1967), *The Speech of Primates* (1972), *On the Origins of Language* (1975), *Speech Acoustics and Perception* (1976), *The Biology and Evolution of Language* (1984) and *Uniquely Human: The Evolution of Speech, Thought and Selfless Behavior* (1991), as well as of numerous articles and reviews.

DANIEL MILLER studied archaeology at the University of Cambridge, and received his Ph.D. in 1983. Since 1981 he has worked in the Department of Anthropology, University College London, where he is now Reader in Anthropology. His principal research interests are in material culture and mass consumption, and he has carried out fieldwork in Indonesia, the Solomon Islands, India, London and, most recently, Trinidad. He is the author of *Artefacts as Categories* (1985), *Material Culture and Mass Consumption* (1987) and *Modernity: an Ethnographic Aproach* (1994). He is editor, with C. Tilley, of *Ideology and Power in Prehistory* (1984), and with M. Rowlands and C. Tilley, of *Domination and Resistance* (1989). He is also sole editor of *Unwrapping Christmas* (1993).

HENRIETTA MOORE was educated at the University of Cambridge, receiving her Ph.D. in 1983. She has taught at the Universities of Kent and Cambridge, and is currently Reader in Anthropology at the London School of Economics. She has carried out fieldwork in Kenya, Burkino Faso, Sierra Leone and Zambia, and her major research interests include economic anthropology and development, gender and feminist studies, and contemporary issues in anthropological theory. She is the author of *Space, Text and Gender: An Anthropological Analysis of the Marakwet of Kenya* (1986) and *Feminism and Anthropology* (1988), as well as of numerous articles in books and journals.

HOWARD MORPHY studied Anthropology at the University of London and at the Australian National University, receiving his Ph.D. in 1977. He was Lecturer and subsequently Senior Lecturer in the Department of Prehistory and Anthropology, Australian National University, from 1978–86. He is currently Curator of Anthropology at the Pitt-Rivers Museum and Lecturer in Ethnology at the University of Oxford. He has carried out anthropological fieldwork over many years among the Yolngu, an Aboriginal people of Arnhem Land, northern Australia, and has collaborated with the film-maker Ian Dunlop on several films dealing with art and religion in Arnhem Land, including the Narritjin Series and a film ethnography entitled *Djungguwan*. He is the author of *Journey to the Crocodile's Nest* (1984) and *Ancestral Connections* (1991), and editor of *Animals into Art* (1989). He has also published extensively on themes in the anthropology of art and material culture, visual anthropology, and Australian Aboriginal ethnography. Howard Morphy was awarded the Stanner Prize for Aboriginal Studies in 1985 and 1992, and the J. B. Donne Prize for the Anthropology of Art in 1988. He was Malinowski Memorial Lecturer for 1993.

JOHN ODLING-SMEE holds a joint lectureship in the Departments of Biology and Biochemistry and of Human Sciences at Brunel University, West London. After taking his first degree in Psychology, and a subsequent period spent studying animal learning at the Medical Research Council's Neural Mechanisms Unit, both at University College London, Odling-Smee received his Ph.D. in 1973. He has worked extensively on animal behaviour and evolutionary theory, and has published numerous articles, many of them in collaboration with Henry C. Plotkin, in *Behavioral and Brain Sciences*, *Advances in the Study of Behaviour*, and in the volumes (edited by H. C. Plotkin) *Learning, Development and Culture* (1982) and *The Role of Behaviour in Evolution* (1988). In 1993 he was appointed to a five-year Research Fellowship at the Institute of Biological Anthropology, University of Oxford.

SUTTI ORTIZ studied at the University of London and received her Ph.D. from the London School of Economics in 1963. She is currently Associate Professor of Anthropology at Boston University. She has carried out several periods of fieldwork in Colombia, and has recently completed a study of labour markets in Colombian coffee production. She is the author of *Uncertainties in Peasant Farming* (1973), and of numerous articles on themes in economic anthropology and development, agrarian change, peasant sociopolitical organization and decision making, and rural labour markets. Sutti Ortiz is former president of the Society for Economic Anthropology, and editor of the proceedings of its first conference, *Economic Anthropology: Topics and Theories* (1983). With Susan Lees, she has also edited the proceedings of the Society's decennial conference, *Economy as Process* (1992).

FITZ JOHN PORTER POOLE is Associate Professor of Anthropology at the University of California, San Diego. His undergraduate studies were undertaken at several institutions in the United States and Europe, and were completed at New York University with a BA in Anthropology, Biology and Philosophy. He received his doctorate in Anthropology and Social Psychology from Cornell University in 1976, and went on to hold a position in the Department of Anthropology at the University of Rochester. His theoretical interests have focused primarily on the confluence of socialization and enculturation, the formation of identity, gender and ritual experience. His ethnographic research among the Bimin-Kuskusmin of Papua New Guinea is represented in numerous articles and in a forthcoming book, *The Rites of Childhood.*

ANN JAMES PREMACK graduated from the University of Minnesota, and is now a distinguished science writer whose work has appeared in many magazines and journals, including *Scientific American, La Recherche, La Debat, National Geographic* and *Geo.* Her book, *Why Chimps Can Read* (1975), has appeared in four foreign-language translations. With David Premack, she has published *The Mind of an Ape* (1983). She is also editor, with David Premack and Dan Sperber, of *Causal Understanding in Cognition and Culture*, to be published in 1994.

DAVID PREMACK gained his Ph.D. from the University of Minnesota in 1955. He taught at the University of Missouri, Columbia, from 1956 to 1964 and at the University of California, Santa Barbara, from 1965 to 1975. Since 1975 he has been Professor of Psychology at the University of Pennsylvania, and is currently affiliated to the Laboratoire de Psycho-Biologie de l'Enfant in Paris. He has also held visiting posts at Harvard University, the Van Leer Jerusalem Institute and the Institute for Advanced Study, Berlin, and is a recipient of the International Prize of the Fyssen Foundation. David Premack was one of the pioneers of experimental research on the linguistic capabilities of great apes, and has written extensively on comparative questions of ape and human language, learning and intelligence. His more recent work has been concerned with acquisition of 'theories of mind' and related problems of cognition. He is the author of *Intelligence in Ape and Man* (1976) and *Gavagai! Or the Future History of the Animal Language Controversy* (1986), as well as numerous articles in books and journals.

AMOS RAPOPORT has taught at the University of Melbourne, the University of California at Berkeley, University College London and the University of Sydney. Since 1972 he has been at the University of Wisconsin at Milwaukee, first jointly in Architecture and Anthropology and subsequently, from 1979, as Distinguished Professor of Architecture in the School of Architecture and Urban Planning. He is one of the founders of Environment-Behaviour Studies, and is the author of over two hundred articles in journals and edited collections. Amos Rapoport's books include *House Form and Culture* (1969), *Human Aspects of Urban Form* (1977), *The Meaning of the Built Environment* (1982, revised edition 1990) and *History and Precedent in Environmental Design* (1990). He has also edited or co-edited a number of collections, including *The Mutual Interaction of People and their Built Environment* (1976), *Environment and Culture* (1980) and *Human and Energy Factors in Urban Planning* (1982).

His work has been translated into many languages, including French, Spanish, Greek, Chinese, Korean and Japanese.

SIMON ROBERTS studied at the London School of Economics, and first taught at the Law School, Institute of Public Administration, near Blantyre, Malawi. He subsequently carried out two years of field research in Botswana. He is currently Professor of Law at the London School of Economics, and General Editor of *The Modern Law Review*. He is the author or co-author of *Order and Dispute* (1979), *Rules and Processes* (1981) and *Understanding Property Law* (1987). He is presently engaged in a field study of a London divorce counselling and mediation agency.

ROBERT A. RUBINSTEIN received his Ph.D. in Anthropology from the State University of New York at Binghamton. He also holds a Master's degree in public health from the University of Illinois at Chicago. He has carried out research in Egypt, Belize, Mexico, and in the United States. Robert Rubinstein is currently Associate Research Medical Anthropologist with the Francis I. Proctor Foundation at the University of California, San Francisco. He is co-chair of the Commission on the Study of Peace of the International Union of Anthropological and Ethnological Sciences. He is the editor or co-editor of *Epistemology and Process* (1984), *Peace and War* (1986), *The Social Dynamics of Peace and Conflict* (1988) and *Fieldwork: The Correspondence of Robert Redfield and Sol Tax* (1991). With C. D. Laughlin and J. McManus, he is a co-author of *Science as Cognitive Process* (1984).

RICHARD SCHECHNER holds a Chair at New York University and also teaches in the Performance Studies Department at the Tisch School of the Arts. He is editor of *TDR: A Journal of Performance Studies*. In 1967, Schechner founded The Performance Group with whom he has directed many plays, including *Dionysus in 69*, *Mother Courage and her Children*, *Oedipus*, *The Tooth of Crime* and *The Balcony*. Since 1980, Schechner has staged works and conducted performance workshops in several countries of Europe, Asia, Africa and the Americas. In 1992 he founded and became artistic director of the East Coast Artists, for which he directed *Faust/Gastronome*. Schechner's many books include *Environmental Theater* (1973), *Between Theater and Anthropology* (1985), *Performance Theory* (1988) and *The Future of Ritual* (1993). Schechner is also editor of various books including (with M. Schuman) *Ritual, Play and Performance* (1976) and (with W. Appel) *By Means of Performance* (1990). He is General Editor of the book series, *Worlds of Performance*. He has been awarded numerous Fellowships and Prizes, and has lectured and taught at Princeton University, Florida State University, Ball State University, and the School of Art Institute of Chicago.

ANTHONY SEEGER received his BA in Social Relations from Harvard University and his MA and Ph.D. in Anthropology from the University of Chicago. His research has focused on the social organization, cosmology and music of Brazilian Indians as well as on issues of land and cultural equity. He is the author of *Nature and Society in Central Brazil* (1981), *Why Suyá Sing* (1987), two other books and many articles and reviews. He has taught at the Museu Nacional in Rio de Janeiro (1975–82), and at Indiana University where he also served as Director of the Archives of Traditional Music (1982–8). Anthony Seeger is currently Curator of the Folkways Collection and Director of the Smithsonian Institution in Washington, DC, in connection with which he has directed the production of over fifty audio recordings.

FRANÇOIS SIGAUT was first trained in agronomy and received his degree from the Institut National Agronomique, Paris, in 1964. After a few years of professional work, he turned to the social sciences and received his Ph.D. in Ethnology in 1975 for a dissertation on the relation between agriculture and fire. His main field of research remains in the technology of pre-industrial European agriculture. Since 1985, his interests have widened to include the basic concepts and methods of technology, understood as the study of technics considered as an integral part of social life. He joined the Ecole des Hautes Etudes en Sciences Sociales, Paris, in 1978, where he is now Professor. He has co-edited four volumes on *Les Techniques de Conservation des Grains* (1979–85), has acted as guest editor for two issues of the journal *Techniques et Culture*, and is the author of numerous publications on technological, ethnological and historical topics.

ANTHONY D. SMITH received his first degree in Classics and Philosophy from the University of Oxford, going on to take a Master's Degree and Ph.D. in Sociology at the London School of Economics. He has taught at the Universities of York and Reading, and is currently Professor of Sociology at the London School of Economics . His many books include *Theories of Nationalism* (1971, 1983), *The Concept of Social Change* (1973), *Social Change* (1976), *Nationalism in the Twentieth Century* (1979), *The Ethnic Revival* (1981), *State and Nation in the Third World* (1983), *The Ethnic Origin of Nations* (1986) and *National Identity* (1991). He is the editor of *Nationalist Movements* (1976). His main interests are in ethnic identity and nationalism, but he also holds a Doctorate in the History of Art and maintains a further interest in the sociology of development. He is presently working on a study of the revival of ethno-nationalism in a global era.

BRIAN STREET is Senior Lecturer in Social Anthropology at the University of Sussex, England. After undertaking anthropological fieldwork in Iran during the 1970s, he has written and lectured extensively on literacy practices from both a theoretical and an applied perspective. He is best known for *Literacy in Theory and Practice* (1984); more recent works include an edited volume on *Cross-Cultural Approaches to Literacy* (1993) and a forthcoming collection of articles entitled *Social Literacies*. He has been active in applying theory to practice, both in relation to adult literacy programmes in the UK and in connection with development programmes. His latest research involves the investigation of everyday writing practices in the UK, focusing on self-selected adults who have written responses to questions on social and personal issues for the Mass-Observation Archive at the University of Sussex. Other research interests have included popular and literary representations of 'other' peoples. His study, *The Savage in the Literature*, appeared in 1975.

PHILLIP TOBIAS has recently retired from the headship of the Department of Anatomy and Human Biology at the University of the Witwatersrand, Johannesburg, South Africa, having held the position for thirty-two years. He has been elected to two Honorary Professorships at the same University, in Palaeoanthropology and in Zoology. His researches have focused mainly on the present and past inhabitants of Africa and he has written or edited nineteen books and published approximately 850 articles. Since 1959 he has been responsible for the description and evaluation of the fossil hominid remains from Olduvai Gorge and other sites in Tanzania and Kenya. With L. S. B. Leakey and J. R. Napier, he recognized and named a new hominid species, *Homo habilis*, in 1964; the appraisal of *Homo habilis* is the subject of his 2-volume work on the species, published in 1991. He has been in charge of excavations at two famous South African sites of early hominid discoveries, Sterkfontein (since 1966) and Taung (since the 1980s), and at the former site his team has brought to light some 550 new specimens of *Australopithecus africanus* and *Homo habilis*. Eight honorary degrees have been conferred upon Professor Tobias, and in 1987 he was awarded the Balzan International Prize (the first time this prize had been given for achievements in Physical Anthropology).

JAMES WEINER studied at the University of Chicago and at the Australian National University, and gained his Ph.D. from the ANU in 1984. He held a Lectureship in the Department of Prehistory and Anthropology, Australian National University, from 1986–9, and from 1990 has been Lecturer in Social Anthropology at the University of Manchester, England. Weiner has carried out a total of two and a half years of fieldwork among the Foi people of Papua New Guinea, on the basis of which he has published many articles and two books, *The Heart of the Pearlshell* (1988) and *The Empty Place* (1991). He is also the editor of *Mountain Papuans* (1988). He is currently working on a book on Australian and Papuan myth, and is carrying out further work on Foi Christianity.

PETER WORSLEY obtained his first degree in Anthropology and Archaeology at the University of Cambridge in 1947, and went on to read for an MA in Social Anthropology at the University of Manchester. From 1956–64 he taught in the Department of Sociology at the University of Hull, and from 1964 until his retirement in 1982 he was Professor of Sociology at the University of Manchester. He is now Professor Emeritus at that University. In 1955

Worsley received the Curl Bequest Essay Prize of the Royal Anthropological Institute, and from 1971–4 he was President of the British Sociological Association. He is the author of many books, including *The Trumpet Shall Sound* (1957), *The Third World* (1964), *Introducing Sociology* (1970, 1977), *Marx and Marxism* (1982) and *The Three Worlds: Culture and World Development* (1984).

THOMAS WYNN received his Ph.D. in anthropology at the University of Illinois, Urbana, in 1977. His research has centred on the application of theory in developmental psychology, especially that of Jean Piaget, to the archaeological record of prehistoric artefacts. He has recently published *The Evolution of Spatial Competence* (1989), and has written numerous articles for professional journals, including *Journal of Human Evolution*, *World Archaeology*, *Man*, *Cambridge Archaeological Journal*, *Journal of Anthropological Archaeology* and *American Anthropologist*. He is currently Professor of Anthropology, University of Colorado at Colorado Springs, USA.

1 HUMANITY

1

INTRODUCTION TO HUMANITY

Tim Ingold

THE HUMAN SPECIES

All people around the world belong to a single species, designated *sapiens*, the only extant species of the genus *Homo*. Indeed, many anthropologists argue that human beings of a biologically 'modern' form all belong to one subspecies, *Homo sapiens sapiens*, which long ago replaced the more 'archaic' subspecific forms – notoriously the so-called Neanderthals (*Homo sapiens neanderthalensis*). Be that as it may, by regarding human beings as members of a species we are led to ask the kinds of questions about them that we might ask of any other species in the animal kingdom. How did they evolve? What are the most distinctive morphological and behavioural characteristics marking them off from those species to which they are most closely related? From what sources in their environments, and by what means, do they obtain their food? And what factors govern the balance in their populations of fertility and mortality, and hence their rate of increase? It is of course impossible to treat each question independently of the others: to understand how a species evolves, for example, we need to know how it relates to its environment in the quest for food, and how variations in morphology and behaviour contribute to reproductive success. Nevertheless, these questions can be distinguished as major foci of inquiry and, taken together, they serve to establish a broad agenda which is followed by the articles making up the first part of this volume in their attempts to find answers for the human species.

To summarize very briefly: Articles 3 and 4 are principally concerned with the problems of human evolution – 3 with the conditions under which the line of descent leading to humankind diverged from those leading to present-day apes, 4 with the emergence, during a much later period, of the human species from pre-human, ancestral hominids. Articles 5 and 6 deal, respectively, with the two characteristics of human beings which have most commonly been taken to distinguish them from other animal species, above all from non-human primates: spoken language and the habitual use of tools. Articles

8 and 9 turn to consider the ways in which human beings draw a subsistence from their environments, reviewing on the one hand the social and ecological relations entailed in the exploitation of plant and animal resources, and on the other hand the nutritional and cultural significance of these diverse foods for human groups. Finally, Articles 10 and 11 are concerned with overall demographic trends: 10 with the dynamics of human population growth throughout prehistory; 11 with more recent historical trends – especially in the wake of European colonization – focusing on disease as the major agent of mortality.

I have omitted two articles from this topical summary: these are Articles 2 and 7. They differ from the others in that they deal primarily with conceptual rather than substantive issues. Article 2 sets the stage by considering what it means to ask questions about humanity as a *species* rather than as a *condition* – for it is this, above all, that has traditionally distinguished approaches in biological anthropology from those in the social and cultural branches of the discipline. And Article 7 addresses in a novel way the vexed question of how to integrate what is usually regarded as the defining characteristic of the human condition – namely *culture* – within an encompassing theory of evolution. Focusing as it does on the ways in which animals (including humans), in their activities, modify or transform their own environments, and on how these environments are in turn 'passed on' to subsequent generations in the form of altered pressures of selection, this article serves as an effective bridgehead between the evolutionary concerns of those preceding it and the more ecological orientation of those that follow.

By way of introduction, I now take the four questions from which I began as my guide and, in commenting on them, highlight some of the principal issues – whether of agreement or contention – that are raised by the articles of this part. First, however, a note is called for regarding the peculiar status of the human species as an object of scientific enquiry. A fact on which both Ingold (Article 2) and Tobias (Article 3) remark is that Linnaeus, in proposing the separate genus *Homo* for humankind, chose to characterize it by means of the single, cryptic expression *Nosce te ipsum* ('Know for yourself'). Now two interpretations can be placed on this. One, which Tobias puts forward, is that Linnaeus was taking the bold and unorthodox step of deposing humans from their pedestal of assumed uniqueness and supremacy over the natural world, to place them four-square among the animals. Indeed Linnaeus declared himself hard-pressed to find *any* definitive criterion whereby human beings could be distinguished anatomically from the apes. On the other hand, as Ingold observes, the demonstration of the anatomical similarity between apes and humans provided the foundation upon which Linnaeus could claim that humans are set apart by a criterion of a quite different order from the criteria that may be used to distinguish non-human species from one another in nature. It is in our wisdom, Linnaeus thought, not in our bodily form, that we differ essentially from apes. In other words the human distinction lies in the unique possession of the intellectual faculty of reason, which makes of us the

4

only beings who can seek to know, through our own powers of observation and analysis, what kinds of beings we are. There are no scientists among the animals.

I dwell on this point since it highlights a contradiction that is still with us today, and which continues to act as a stumbling block in our deliberations on the nature of humanity as a biological species. It is now generally accepted that this species has evolved, like any other, through a Darwinian process of variation under natural selection. And unlike Linnaeus, contemporary students of human evolution are able to point with some precision to a whole cluster of anatomical features by which human beings may be distinguished not only from extant, non-human primates but also from their prehuman, hominid forebears. It has become conventional in palaeoanthropology to classify individuals possessing this suite of features as 'anatomically modern humans'. But these humans did not evolve as scientists, let alone with a ready-made theory of evolution. Science and its theories are widely understood to be the products of a cultural or civilizational process quite separate from the process of biological evolution: a cumulative growth of knowledge that has left our basic natures unaffected. And this is where the contradiction reveals itself, for such a process − which purports to raise humanity onto a level of existence above the purely biophysical − is presupposed by science as providing the platform from which its practitioners, who are of course humans too, can launch their declarations to the effect that the human is just another species of nature. Why else do they find it necessary to refer to individuals of the species, in qualified terms, as *anatomically* modern humans? The implication is that the earliest human populations, though biologically pre-equipped with all the requisites for modern life, yet stood on the threshold of culture. Somewhere along the line leading from these early people to contemporary scientists (who are inclined to regard themselves as the arch-representatives of rational modernity) the process of culture must have 'started up', gradually gaining the upper hand in the direction of human affairs. History appears as the progressive realization of the latent capacities of our ancestors, biologically 'fixed' in the course of evolution.

EVOLUTION AND BEHAVIOUR

Until recently, palaeoanthropologists could base their reconstructions of human evolution on two sources of information: first, the fossilized remains of skeletal material; and second, the artefactual evidence, principally in the form of stone implements. To these, a third source has lately been added, based on biomolecular surveys of living populations. The aim of the latter is to measure the degree of difference between populations in their genetic material and, assuming a constant mutation rate, to estimate the time that has elapsed since their divergence from a common, ancestral population. The results of studies employing these different sources have not always been

5

consistent. This could be put down to the paucity of fossil or artefactual material, or to ambiguities in its interpretation, or alternatively to the artificiality of the assumptions entailed in the method of molecular dating. But there is a more serious problem that goes to the heart of the conceptualization of evolution in modern biology. Palaeontologists who work with fossils naturally think of evolution in terms of gradual changes of form, or of skeletal architecture. Archaeologists who work with artefacts are alert to what they reveal about changes in behaviour. Molecular biologists, for their part, assume that evolutionary change ultimately comes down to changes in the relative frequencies of genes. However, granting the facts of morphological, behavioural and genetic change, can we assume that they always take place in step, as though change in any one respect necessarily entailed corresponding change in the other two?

This question is critical both to Tobias's account, in Article 3, of the earliest phases of hominid evolution, and to Gamble's discussion, in Article 4, of the replacement by 'anatomically modern' humans of their 'archaic' predecessors. As regards the former, biomolecular studies at present indicate that the lines of descent leading respectively to chimpanzees and human beings diverged at some time between 6.4 and 4.9 million years ago. This point of divergence is taken to mark the origin of the hominids, of the genus *Australopithecus*, and subsequently *Homo*. Yet Tobias warns that while it may indeed mark the emergence of the *molecular* genetic constellation of the hominids, we cannot assume that the distinguishing *anatomical* features would have emerged at the same time. What evidence there is suggests that these features appeared somewhat later, and in a piecemeal or 'mosaic' fashion rather than all at once. Thus the genetic divergence does not translate, automatically and immediately, into a morphological one. Nor does it have any inevitable behavioural correlate.

Turning to the problem of the origin of 'modern humans', molecular dating places this between 140 and 290 thousand years ago, while the oldest fossils of an anatomically modern form are dated to 130 thousand years ago. Though these dates are in reasonable agreement, Gamble counsels against any hasty inference that genetically modern humans were modern in their behaviour as well. Evidence for the technical, linguistic and cultural characteristics that are generally taken as the hallmarks of modern human behaviour does not appear until some 40 thousand years ago. In other words, it seems that for the greater part of their time on earth so far, human beings – though genetically and anatomically within the contemporary range of variation of the species – *lacked* the essential behavioural capacities by which they are distinguished today!

To understand why this is such a problem, we have to return to a question to which I have already alluded. What *is* a 'modern human'? The simple but facile answer is to say that the label is merely shorthand for 'a member of the sub-species *Homo sapiens sapiens*'. Modern humans, it is often claimed, are 'people like us'. Yet it might reasonably be objected that the human beings of 40 thousand years ago were not like us at all, whoever 'we' may be. Not even

6

contemporary hunting and gathering societies can be regarded as Palaeolithic survivals. The conventional response to this kind of objection is to point out that they were like us *biologically* but not *culturally*: while biologically modern, they were culturally primitive. And the process which took humanity from its Palaeolithic origins to modern science and civilization was one not of evolution but of history.

But these dichotomies – between biology and culture, evolution and history – are sorely troublesome. For they set us in search of a baseline of universal human capacities, such as the capacity for language, or the capacity for culture, which must be amenable to specification independently of the diverse contexts of development in which human beings may grow up speaking this or that language, or skilled in this or that repertoire of cultural practices. Now a context-independent specification of an organism is, by definition, genetic. The definitive capacities of humanity must therefore be separately 'packaged' as properties of the modern human genotype. But if this genotype was already in place some 130 thousand years ago, why did it take another 90 thousand years for its phenotypic effects to appear in the archaeological record, in the form of such things as regionally specific tool traditions, structured camp sites, exotic trade goods, art and ornamentation, ritualistic burial, and so on?

Wynn's discussion of human tool-using and tool-making, in Article 6, brings us up against the same problem. Contrasting what he calls the 'natural history tradition' and the 'sociocultural tradition' in research on tool behaviour, he points out that the former is unable to countenance any change in tools or ways of using them, save as reflections of evolutionary changes in the capacities of the species concerned. The latter, by contrast, is inclined to attribute tools and their uses to an autonomous cultural subsystem, a technology, that undergoes a progressive development of its own without requiring any further restructuring of the biological equipment of its operators. The first tradition is predominant in ethological studies of non-human animals, the second in anthropological studies of human beings. But it is also true that in the study of human evolution, tools and tool behaviour are commonly treated as indices of the evolving capacities of their makers-cum-users, up to the point at which 'modern' capacities were established.

From that point on, it is imagined that technology 'took off', following a historical trajectory thenceforth effectively decoupled from the process of evolution. Thus Palaeolithic hunter–gatherers are supposed to have had the *capacity* to read and write, to ride bicycles, even to fly a spacecraft to the moon – that they failed to do so is not because they were constitutionally incapable of such activities but merely because the technical prerequisites for carrying them out, in the forms of knowledge and equipment, took time to develop. A prehistorian of the future, surveying the material remains of our present, technologically based civilization, would be making a fatal mistake were he to infer that its people were considerably more advanced in their innate capacities than their predecessors of earlier millennia. Yet comparing the tools of 'modern humans' with those of pre-modern hominids we do not hesitate to make such inferences. Somewhere, it seems, a line has to be drawn, beyond which we are no longer dealing with the evolution of a capacity but the history of its realization. But how do we know where to draw it?

What goes for tools and technology also goes for that other pre-eminent marker of human distinctiveness, spoken language. In arguing that human tool-use is fundamentally unlike language in the way it constructs sequences, which he believes is through simple 'string-of-beads' chaining rather than the application of syntactic rules, Wynn takes one side of a currently vigorous controversy. The other side is represented in this volume by Lieberman (Article 5), who argues that Broca's area, the region of the brain most directly implicated in the production and comprehension of syntax, is not only specific to anatomically modern *Homo sapiens*, but also involved in the control and sequencing of precise movements of the dominant hand, of a kind regularly entailed in skilled manual work. Broca's area is not, then, the brain's 'language organ'; rather, the capacity for language emerged thanks to the linking up, in an entirely novel way, of various neural mechanisms and anatomical structures that would each have undergone prior adaptation for non-linguistic functions: Broca's area for precise manual operations; the pre-frontal cortex for the storage and retrieval of information useful in foraging; the structures of the lungs, larynx and supralaryngeal tract for breathing, swallowing and vocalization. But Lieberman's view that the neural and anatomical foundations for speech and syntax are unique to anatomically modern humans has not gone undisputed. Tobias, in Article 3, presents the contrary argument, that these foundations were already in place some two million years ago with the emergence of the first hominine species, *Homo habilis*, from its Australopithecine predecessors. Both would agree that human beings are the only *living* animals that can talk: the issue is whether this capacity emerged early or late in human evolution.

The controversy should not be overstated. Even advocates of a late date for the origin of language accept that *Homo habilis* may have had some incipient linguistic abilities beyond those of present-day apes; and even those who propose an early origin accept that the speech of pre-human hominines would have differed substantially from that of modern humans. Thus we are brought back to the same question as before: at what point can we say that a 'capacity for language' has become established, such that subsequent developments belong to the history of language, not to its evolution? To resolve this issue we may have to look again at the very notion of 'capacity'. Does it make sense to ascribe specific capacities to the human genotype? Surely the abilities to talk, to use tools and so on *develop* in the early life history of every individual: they are not given ready-formed at the point of conception. And they will only develop if the appropriate conditions are present, not only in the genes but also in the surrounding environment. In other words, capacities are the properties of developmental systems, not of genes, and every developmental system consists in a nexus of relations between manifold reactants both within the individual (including the genome) and beyond it, in relevant aspects of its environment. Such systems can continue to evolve, and with them the capacities specified therein, even without significant genotypic modification, simply because – through their own activities – organisms change their environments and thereby alter the conditions of development for successor generations.

This is the major import of Odling-Smee's revision of evolutionary theory in Article 7. Many attempts have been made in recent years to bring human cultural variation within the scope of the so-called 'modern synthesis' of neo-Darwinian evolutionary biology. The strategy, in all these attempts, has been to treat the synthesis as a *fait accompli*, but to suggest the possibility of an alternative unit of inheritance to the gene, namely the culture trait (otherwise known as 'culturgen' or 'meme'), which is likewise subject to mutation and selective retention within populations of individuals. This approach has given rise to a variety of theories of so-called 'gene-culture co-evolution'. Odling-Smee's approach is quite different. He argues that the 'modern synthesis' is seriously incomplete, in that it presents us with only one hemicycle of what is in reality a cyclical or two-way interrelation between organisms and their environments. It shows how pressures of selection in the environment have consequences in terms of the differential replication of inherited genes, but it leaves out the reverse process, whereby the behaviour of organisms affects the environment – which is also bequeathed to the next generation via what Odling-Smee calls 'ecological inheritance'. One way in which organisms can change the environment for future generations is by colonizing new regions, and there is no doubt – as Gamble shows in Article 4 – that colonization has been a major force in human evolution. Another way is through its cultural reconstruction.

But human culture is just one instance, albeit of a rather special kind, of the general capacity of organisms to 'construct' their environments, and it can only be incorporated within an overarching theory of evolution if that theory is 'completed' through the addition of the part that is missing from the modern synthesis, thereby closing the cycle of organism–environment relations. In the model developed by Odling-Smee, evolution is a complex, multi-level process, of which the natural selection of inherited genes is just one level. While this both affects and is affected by processes at the other levels, of individual development, social learning and culture, these latter also have a certain autonomy. History, then, is not separate from evolution; it is, rather, a 'top-down' view of the process, as opposed to the 'bottom-up' view of evolutionary biology. From this it follows that it is pointless to seek the moment when history 'began', or to attribute certain embodied capacities – such as speech or bipedal locomotion – to evolution while relegating others – such as the ability to read and write, or to ride a bicycle – to history. For human history is but the continuation of the evolutionary process by another name.

9

SUBSISTENCE AND DEMOGRAPHY

Having addressed the issues surrounding the evolution, and distinctive behavioural capacities, of modern human beings, let me now turn to the question of subsistence − that is, of the procurement and consumption of food. Perhaps in no other area do cultural considerations bear more immediately on human biology. As de Garine shows in Article 9, human feeding behaviour differs markedly from that of other animals in at least four respects. First, human beings are highly selective in their choice of food, and these selections are not based merely on differential responses to sensory stimuli but are significantly structured by acquired cognitive schemata. Second, humans are the only animals to cook their food, which they are able to do thanks to their unique mastery of fire. Third, human feeding is neither continuous nor solitary, but takes place in clearly demarcated bouts, at regular times of each day, within the framework of groups of determinate composition. Finally, a very large proportion of the food that human beings eat comes from species that are not native to the regions in which they are consumed. This is particularly true of major staples, such as potatoes in Europe and maize in Africa. Staples apart, the range of plant and animal species consumed by human populations is truly vast − and if one adds non-food uses, such as for clothing, building material, ornamentation and medicinal purposes, the list is even longer.

It is also commonly asserted that human beings are the only animals to have domesticated their food resources or, to use another terminology, to have made the transition from food collecting to food production. Indeed the causes and consequences of this transition have assumed an importance on the agenda of archaeological inquiry fully equal to that attributed to the emergence, in an earlier period, of the 'modern human' way of life. Yet there is growing dissatisfaction with the conventional distinctions between hunting, gathering and fishing on the one hand, and agriculture and pastoralism on the other. Gamble, in Article 4, suggests that the selection of certain plants and animals for domestication, far from ushering in a new stage in human social evolution, was but one of many strategies by which human populations were able to extend their range of settlement. De Garine, in Article 9, makes the point that many − if not most − peoples around the world practise a mixed mode of subsistence, in which hunting, gathering and fishing, as well as plant and animal husbandry, all play a part. Food collecting did not disappear with the coming of agriculture, and is still practised 'on the side' even in modern industrial societies. And given the diversity of regimes of both food collecting and food production, or, as Ellen (Article 8) prefers to call them, 'extractive' and 'regulative' systems, the scope for generalization about the causes and mechanisms of transition from one to the other seems correspondingly limited. However it may be possible, Ellen suggests, to generalize about the dynamics of the process in particular regions.

In attempting such generalizations it is crucial to bear two distinctions in mind, and both are central to Ellen's argument. The first is between mode of production and mode of subsistence. A mode of production is specified by the social relations that govern the division of labour, access to productive resources, and the distribution of produce. A mode of subsistence, by contrast, is characterized by a particular ensemble of technical practices geared towards the management and extraction of environmental resources. Since we may encounter similar modes of subsistence within the contexts of diverse relations of production, and since, conversely, the same relations of production may frame diverse modes of subsistence, it is clearly necessary to hold these concepts distinct for the purposes of comparative analysis. The second key distinction is between husbandry and domestication. Husbandry refers to a kind of close ecological association between a human population and a plant or animal species, such that the former seeks to establish the conditions for the latter's reproduction. Domestication refers to a Darwinian process of species modification by variation under selection which may be more or less intentionally exercised by human agents. To understand the dynamics of the origins and development of agriculture or pastoralism, it is necessary to focus on how the association of a resource species with the human population that uses it affects the selective pressures to which it is subjected, and how the resulting adaptive modifications rebound in turn on the human–plant or human–animal association.

As a rule, agricultural regimes support greater populations than do regimes of hunting and gathering in the same environment (with pastoralism the contrast is not so clear). Prehistorians and anthropologists are agreed that population growth is somehow implicated in the origins and spread of agriculture, but whether as cause, consequence or both is a matter of contention. The arguments are reviewed by Cohen in Article 10. The case for population growth as a causative factor rests in particular on the supposition that the more land-intensive the system of production, the less efficient it is in terms of the yield of food relative to the labour invested in producing it. Thus it is claimed that people will not adopt agriculture in favour of hunting and gathering, or a more intensive system of agriculture in favour of a less intensive one, unless forced to do so by the increasing demands of a growing population on a circumscribed land base. Critics of this argument maintain, to the contrary, that agricultural production is just as efficient as hunting and gathering, if not more so. But as Cohen points out, whether hunting and gathering is more or less efficient than agriculture depends on the kind of hunting-gathering (and indeed of agriculture) in question. Economies dominated by hunting in game-rich environments may be considerably more efficient. In many environments, however, even before the adoption of agriculture, hunter–gatherers gradually shifted – under pressure of increasing numbers – towards a pattern of exploiting a 'broad spectrum' of small game animals, fish and vegetable foods. Broad-spectrum foraging, it appears, is somewhat *less* efficient than agriculture. Thus it comes as no surprise to find that it was in regions where this kind

11

of foraging was practised that agriculture was most readily adopted in its place.

The results of palaeopathological studies of prehistoric populations show that health and nutrition have tended to *decline* with increasing numbers, most especially after the transition to life in sedentary agricultural – and later urban – settlements. But why, then, despite the consequently higher mortality, did the overall rate of growth of the human population continue to rise? After considering the possible reasons, Cohen comes down in favour of the view that the rise is due to increased fertility rather than reduced mortality, and that this owes much to conscious decision-making on the part of parents seeking to counteract the effects of higher expected losses of progeny in childhood. Further light on this issue is shed by Kunitz's discussion, in Article 11, of the impact of disease on post-contact populations. As both he and Cohen point out, acute infectious diseases such as measles and influenza can only persist for any length of time in large host populations. Thus so long as people lived in small local communities, infectious disease was chronic rather than acute. The pandemics that swept through the major centres of civilization in Europe and Asia during historical times (while leaving the peoples of the New World untouched) owed their persistence to the massive growth of population in these centres, which offered a continual supply of new victims. As the impact of these acute infections has waned, partly due to more effective medical treatment, a residue of chronic infectious disease has remained, the effects of which are often amplified by malnutrition. But in regions where nutrition and living conditions have improved, these diseases have been replaced by various non-infectious and 'man-made' afflictions, from diabetes and hypertension to pollution-induced cancers, alcoholism and traffic accidents. De Garine's prediction, in Article 9, that alcohol abuse is likely to become, on a global scale, a more serious problem than malnutrition, is also noteworthy in this regard.

De Garine's discussion of nutrition and Kunitz's of disease are also linked in another way. Both stress the point that the ways people eat on the one hand, and the ways they sicken and die on the other, are crucially conditioned by the kinds of social relations in which they are involved and the sorts of cultural values that they hold. To anthropologists, this point may seem obvious, but it is not one that is always understood by medical and nutritional scientists from other academic backgrounds, who are inclined to evaluate what people eat in purely energetic and chemical terms, and to regard susceptibility to disease simply as a result of bodily malfunctioning or the lack of innate resistance. But human beings are not mere survival machines, chemical converters geared to the reproduction of their genes. They are *persons*, with specific social and cultural identities. What they eat, up to a point, makes them who they are, and their involvement in social support networks allows them to cope with disease and other afflictions, when they strike, in a way that they otherwise could not. In the study of such coping mechanisms, and how they work, biological

12

anthropology stands to make a vital contribution not only to theory, but also to the practical well-being of future generations.

FURTHER READING

Aiello, L. C. and Dean, M. C. (1990) *An Introduction to Human Evolutionary Anatomy*, London: Academic Press.

Bickerton, D. (1990) *Language and Species*, Chicago: University of Chicago Press.

Boyd, P. and Richerson, P. J. (1985) *Culture and the Evolutionary Process*, Chicago: University of Chicago Press.

Cohen, M. N. (1989) *Health and the Rise of Civilization*, New Haven: Yale University Press.

Durham, W. H. (1991) *Coevolution: Genes, Culture and Human Diversity*, Stanford, Cal.: Stanford University Press.

Ellen, R. F. (1982) *Environment, Subsistence and System: the Ecology of Small-scale Social Formations*, Cambridge: Cambridge University Press.

Foley, R. A. (1987) *Another Unique Species: Patterns in Human Evolutionary Ecology*, Harlow: Longmans.

Garine, I. de and Harrison, G. A. (eds) (1988) *Coping with Uncertainty in Food Supply*, Oxford: Clarendon Press.

Gibson, K. R. and Ingold, T. (eds) (1993) *Tools, Language and Cognition in Human Evolution*, Cambridge: Cambridge University Press.

Gould, S. J. (1987) *The Mismeasure of Man*, Harmondsworth: Penguin.

Harding, R. and Teleki, G. (eds) (1981) *Omnivorous Primates: Gathering and Hunting in Human Evolution*, New York: Columbia University Press.

Klein, R. G. (1989) *The Human Career: Human Biological and Cultural Origins*, Chicago: University of Chicago Press.

Lieberman, P. (1991) *Uniquely Human: the Evolution of Speech, Thought and Selfless Behavior*, Cambridge, Mass.: Harvard University Press.

Mascie-Taylor, C. G. N. and Lasker, G. W. (eds) (1991) *Applications of Biological Anthropology to Human Affairs*, Cambridge: Cambridge University Press.

McNeill, W. H. (1976) *Plagues and Peoples*, Harmondsworth: Penguin.

Mellars, P. and Stringer, C. (eds) (1989) *The Human Revolution: Behavioural and Biological Perspectives in the Origins of Modern Humans*, Edinburgh: Edinburgh University Press.

Reynolds, P. C. (1981) *On the Evolution of Human Behavior: the Argument from Animals to Man*, Berkeley: University of California Press.

Richards, G. (1987) *Human Evolution: an Introduction for the Behavioural Sciences*, London: Routledge & Kegan Paul.

Rindos, D. (1984) *The Origins of Agriculture: an Evolutionary Perspective*, Orlando: Academic Press.

Smith, E. A. and Winterhalder, B. (eds) (1992) *Evolutionary Ecology and Human Behavior*, New York: Aldine de Gruyter.

Tanner, N. M. (1981) *On Becoming Human*, Cambridge: Cambridge University Press.

2

HUMANITY AND ANIMALITY

Tim Ingold

The proper subject of anthropology is humanity. That much is easily stated, but it is more difficult to envision how such a science of humanity should be constructed. This article is an attempt to show how we might go about it. Perhaps you will think the project absurdly narrow, or on the other hand impossibly broad. Supposing you held the former view, you might respond as follows: 'Science of humanity? Don't be ridiculous. *Homo sapiens* is just one species among hundreds of thousands, and a relatively recent one at that. Do we have to have a separate science for every species?' If you were an advocate of the latter view, however, these particular objections would seem to miss the point. To study humanity, you would say, is not just to probe the idiosyncrasies of a particular species, of one minute segment of the world of nature. It is rather to lay open for investigation that world interminably multiplied in the exuberantly creative minds and activities of people everywhere. The task is impossible because the subject matter is forever exploding beyond our limited compass. Human beings ourselves, our problem is not that we have failed to cut humanity down to size, but rather that we shall never be able to catch up with it.

These alternative positions rest, in fact, on radically different notions of what humanity is, or might be. The best way to demonstrate this difference is by looking at the ways in which ideas about humanity and human beings have shaped, and been shaped by, ideas about animals. For those of us reared in the tradition of Western thought, 'human' and 'animal' are terms rich in association, fraught with ambiguity, and heavily laden with both intellectual and emotional bias. From classical times to the present day, animals have figured centrally in the Western construction of 'man' – and we might add, of Western man's image of woman. Every generation has recreated its own view of animality as a deficiency in everything that we humans are uniquely supposed to have, including language, reason, intellect and moral conscience. And in every generation we have been reminded, as though it were some startling new discovery, that human beings are animals too, and that it is by comparison with other animals that we can best reach an understanding of ourselves.

This article is divided into three parts. In the first I consider the definition of humanity as a *species* of animal, encompassing all individuals belonging to the biological taxon *Homo sapiens*. How do we recognize what is, or is not, a human being? This is a question that scarcely troubles us nowadays, for with a world now fully opened up to travel and communication, we think we know the full range of human variation. But it sorely troubled our predecessors during the early days of colonial exploration, and if we bother to ask it we may find it no easier than they did to come up with an answer that will withstand rigorous critical scrutiny. In the second part of the article I introduce a contrasting sense of humanity, as a *condition* opposed to the animal. This is the condition of being human, revealed in a seemingly inexhaustible richness and diversity of cultural forms fully equal to the diversity of organic forms in nature. In the final part I show how the popular identification of these two notions of humanity, of the species with the condition, has given rise to a peculiar view of human uniqueness. Far from being different from all other animals as the latter are from one another, the difference is attributed to qualities in respect of which all other animals are perceived as essentially the same. In order to overcome the anthropocentrism inherent in this view, we must think again. It is one thing to ask what a human being is, quite another to ask what it means to be human. I begin with the former.

A QUESTION OF TAILS

In the year 1647, a Swedish naval lieutenant by the name of Nicolas Köping was serving aboard a Dutch East-Indiaman in the Bay of Bengal. One day the ship approached an island whose naked inhabitants, according to Köping's account, had tails like those of cats, and a similarly feline comportment. Coming alongside in their canoes, these natives − evidently bent on trade − threatened to swarm the ship and had to be frightened off with a round of cannon-shot. The ship's pilot subsequently took ashore a landing party of five of the Dutch crew, to scour the island for provisions. They never returned, and a search mounted on the following morning revealed only their bones discarded beside a still smouldering fire, and their boat systematically stripped of its iron bolts.

Köping's story was later revived in a treatise of Linnaeus, recited by his pupil, Hoppius, in 1760. The tailed men were classed as a species of ape, appropriately named *Lucifer*, and illustrated by a picture that Linnaeus had gleaned from another source (Figure 1).[1] One of those who read Hoppius's oration was the learned but eccentric Scottish judge James Burnet, otherwise known as Lord Monboddo. In the first of six volumes entitled *Of the origin and progress of language*, and published between 1773 and 1792, Monboddo set out

Figure 1 'Anthropomorpha', from C. E. Hoppius, *Amoenitates academicae* (Linné), Erlangae 1760. *Lucifer* is the second figure from the left

to establish the continuities and contrasts between humans and other animals, and to characterize the condition of humankind in its original, 'natural' or 'brutish' state. Much intrigued to read of humans with tails, his first concern – quite properly – was to check the veracity of the account. Through personal correspondence with Linnaeus he ascertained Köping's credentials as a truthful and honest reporter, whose descriptions of the animal and plant life encountered on his voyage had proved accurate in every other respect. That the island's inhabitants did indeed possess tails, then, was not to be doubted. But were they actually humans? Of this, again, Monboddo reckoned there could be little doubt, for Köping's account reveals that they knew the arts of navigation, were accustomed to trade, and made use of iron (Burnet 1773: 234–9).

It is easy for us, with the benefit of hindsight, to recognize the element of fantasy in Köping's story, and to think Monboddo a fool for allowing himself to be taken in by it. Yet perhaps he was wrong for the right reasons. Anticipating the incredulity of his readers, Monboddo deftly turned the tables on conventional belief:

> I am sensible, however, that those who believe that men are, and always have been, the same in all ages and nations of the world, and such as we see them in Europe, will think this story quite incredible; but for my own part I am convinced, that we have not yet discovered all the variety of nature, not even in our own species; and the most incredible thing, in my apprehension, that could be told, even if there were no facts to contradict it, would be, that all men in the different parts of the earth were the same in size, figure, shape and colour.

16

It is no good your discounting the evidence for tailed people with the remark that 'humans just aren't like that'. If some populations have white skins and others black, if some are immensely tall and others of diminutive stature, why should not some have tails and others not? Monboddo was clearly of the opinion that there was nothing more extraordinary about having a tail than having a black skin, and that neither character furnishes a valid criterion for placing its possessors beyond the pale of humanity. We should not be deceived by limited, Eurocentric notions of the kind of thing that a human being is. For humankind, Monboddo insisted, is not fixed and immutable, rather it is both geographically and historically variable. Such variability is the hallmark of animal species, indeed of all of living nature, and in this the human is surely no exception (Burnet 1773).[2]

Modern biology, radically restructured in the wake of Darwin's revelations in *The Origin of Species* (1872; first published in 1859), is on Monboddo's side: not perhaps on the matter of tails, but certainly in its outright rejection of the idea that there exists an essential form of humanity of which all actual human beings, past, present and future, are more or less perfect embodiments. Let us agree, with Monboddo and against many of his contemporaries, that humans are not everywhere the same 'in size, figure, shape and colour'. Should we then conclude that they come in a wide variety of standard sizes, figures, shapes and colours, as do ready-to-wear coats at the tailor's – large, medium and small, black and white, with tails and without? A notion has persisted well into this century, and in some circles still persists, that one could construct a chart of distinctive 'human types'. This notion is fundamentally wrong. Individual human beings are no more embodiments of 'types' than they are of a unitary, species-specific essence. In biological terms, humanity presents itself as a continuous field of variation, compounded of a myriad of finely graded differences. Any divisions of the field are of our own making, artificial products of our penchant for classification and stereotyping. Real humans cannot be accommodated within artificial categories: for precisely this reason the ready-to-wear coat, designed to clothe a type rather than a particular customer, is never a perfect fit.

Individuals of the species *Homo sapiens* do display a remarkable degree of variability. Nevertheless, what holds for our species holds for all others: namely, that they are not classes of entities distinguished by the possession, by every member of each class, of a unique attribute or cluster of attributes. In other words, biological species are not natural kinds (Clark 1988: 20–1). Grains of salt constitute a natural kind, since every grain has the molecular composition and crystalline structure of sodium chloride. But the molecules that orchestrate the constitution of living things are vastly more complex, the most important of these molecules being deoxyribonucleic acid (DNA). As we now know, it is in the structure of DNA that genes, the basic units of heredity, are encoded. And although species vary in the diversity of their genetic material, for no species is there a single structure underwriting the

17

development of every individual of the class. On the contrary, the uniqueness of the individual most clearly distinguishes living organisms from lifeless objects (Medawar 1957). Like crystals, organisms grow, and like crystals they appear to be endowed with an invariant structure that underlies their surface transformations. But whereas for every crystal of some inorganic element or compound this structure is the same, for every organism of a species it is different. Every crystal is a replica, every organism a novelty.

How, then, are we to decide to which species a particular organism belongs? More to the point, on what grounds might we include one animal within *Homo sapiens*, and exclude another? Was the Lucifer of Linnaeus a man or a monkey? Such questions as these have fuelled centuries of bitter controversy, and although all of us nowadays might claim to be able to recognize a fellow human being when we see one, arguments still rage over how the principles of biological taxonomy should be properly applied. For our purposes, it is sufficient to note that these principles are basically genealogical. Organisms are grouped in the same class not because of their formal, surface resemblance, but because of their relatively close genealogical connection. As a rule, human beings do resemble one another rather more than they resemble apes, and in their lack of tails they resemble apes rather more than other primates. These resemblances, however, are indices of genealogical proximity, not of any prescribed conformity to type.

The more closely related individuals are in terms of descent, the more genes they are likely to have in common. Sometimes, when a conspicuous character is controlled by only one or a few genes, the slightest variations in the underlying genetic structure (or genotype) can have major consequences for the outward appearance of the mature individual (or phenotype), so that even closely related individuals can look very different. Other characters, even less conspicuous ones, may be controlled by a very large number of genes, so that the same amount of genotypic variation would be virtually imperceptible in the phenotype. Doubtless if humans had tails, varying from stumpy to pendulous as skin colour varies from white to black, some at least would have cause to wonder which is easier to hide: tail or skin. Fortunately perhaps, we do not have that problem, but for reasons that neither Monboddo nor his contemporary critics could have known. The amount of genetic modification needed to turn black skins into white (or vice versa) is minute compared with the amount needed to lose or gain a tail. The genetic difference between tailed and tailless primates implies a degree of genealogical unrelatedness that is simply incommensurate with their membership of a single species. Thus it is not necessary to invoke an essential form of humanity, or a priori notions of what human beings are like, in order to discount the existence of tailed individuals of the species *Homo sapiens*, or, more strictly, to regard the probability of their occurrence as vanishingly small.

The first tailless primate (barring cases of accidental mutilation) was not a hopeful monster, a bizarre mutant cavorting in the midst of a band of identically long-tailed relatives, upon whom fortune smiled, preserving its kind in future generations. Like every other significant evolutionary modification, tails became shorter by degrees, through an accumulation − over very many generations − of minute differences. Nature, according to a venerable maxim much favoured by Darwin, does not make leaps (*Natura non facit saltum*; see Darwin 1872: 146, 156). Nor, however, does it proceed along a fixed, preordained course. That ancient, tailless ape, which numbers among its descendants both humans and chimpanzees, was no more on its way to becoming a human than it was to becoming a chimpanzee. It was, purely and simply, being itself. An ape is an ape, not a botched or half-successful attempt at humanity. And though it may be true that only one possible route can connect the ancestral ape to the modern human being, that route was only one of any number of possible routes that could equally well have been taken. Humans did not *have* to evolve.

In relation to the evolution of life as a whole, the human lineage amounts to but one short and rather insignificant twig of an immense, sprawling bush. Each twig is tracing out a path that has never been traced before, and will never be traced again. The chimpanzees of the future may be a lot cleverer than we are today, but they will not be human beings. Humans are animals that, for all I know, could turn out to be the co-ancestors of my future descendants. Of what these descendants will actually be like a few million years hence, that is if we do not blow up the earth with ourselves, no-one has the slightest idea. In the meantime, like Monboddo, we continue to speculate on the variety of our species, in startlingly similar terms. 'As late as 1942,' recalls the anthropologist Edmund Leach, 'I was myself assured most positively, by an otherwise sane Englishman, that, in an inaccessible valley just the other side of a visible range of mountains, he himself had encountered men with tails' (Leach 1982: 64).

HUMAN BEINGS, AND BEING HUMAN

By and large, philosophers have sought to discover the essence of humanity in men's heads rather than in their tails (or lack thereof). But in seeking this essence, they did not ask: 'What makes humans animals of a particular kind?' Instead they turned the question around, asking: 'What makes humans different in kind from animals?' This inversion completely alters the terms of the inquiry. For once the question is posed in the latter form; humanity no longer appears as a species of animality, or as one small province of the animal kingdom. It refers rather to a principle that, infused into the animal frame, lifts its possessors onto an altogether higher level of existence than that of the 'mere animal'. Humanity, in short, ceases to mean the sum total of human beings, members of the animal species *Homo sapiens*, and becomes the state or condition of being human, one radically opposed to the condition of animality (Ingold 1988: 4). The relation between the human and the animal is thus turned from the inclusive (a province within a kingdom) to the exclusive (one state of being rather than another).

The great French naturalist, Count de Buffon, writing in 1749, was in no doubt as to the immensity of the chasm that separates the most primitive human from the ape, 'because the former is endowed with the faculties of thought and speech' whereas the latter is not. Yet in bodily form they are not very much different, and 'if our judgement were limited to figure alone, I acknowledge that the ape might be regarded as a variety of the human species' (Buffon 1866, 2: 43). Lord Monboddo, having read Buffon's *Histoire naturelle*, was of precisely this opinion. At that time the anthropoid apes were generally known as orang-utans – the term is of Malay origin, meaning 'man of the woods', and nowadays denotes a particular species (*Pongo pygmaeus*) native to Borneo and Sumatra (on the past significance and contemporary taxonomic status of the orang-utan, see Tobias's discussion in Article 3). Monboddo was firmly convinced that orang-utans were human:

> They are exactly of the human form; walking erect, not upon all-four, like the savages that have been found in Europe; they use sticks for weapons; they live in society; they make huts of branches of trees; and they carry off negroe girls, whom they make slaves of, and use both for work and pleasure.... But though from the particulars above mentioned it appears certain, that they are of our species, and though they have made some progress in the arts of life, they have not come the length of language. (Burnet 1773: 174–5)

Unlike Buffon, Monboddo believed that man's humanity was not installed from the start by an act of divine intervention, but was acquired by degrees, and was only completed with the emergence of reason and intellect, the twin foundations for that uniquely human achievement, the faculty of language. Apart from occasional discoveries of solitary 'wild men' – the quadrupedal savages of his account – orang-utans furnished Monboddo with as close a living approximation as he could find to an entire human population existing in an original state of nature. Lacking language and intellect, orang-utans were human beings that had not yet reached the stage of being human. They belonged to our species, yet had advanced only a little way towards the condition of humanity.

Primordial human beings, of which Monboddo could find no direct evidence but whose nature could easily be inferred through a backward extrapolation, would have been wholly 'without arts or civility', governed in their actions by instinct rather than custom, existing in a state that 'is no other than that of the mere animal' (Burnet 1773: 218, 291; see also Bock 1980: 19–26). The same, of course, might be said of the human infant, supporting an analogy that has a long pedigree in Western thought, between the maturation of the particular human being and the passage of humanity at large from savagery to civilization. 'Savages', as Sir John Lubbock declared in 1865, 'have often been likened to children, and the comparison is not only correct but also highly instructive... The life of each individual is an epitome of the history of the race, and the gradual development of the child illustrates that of the species . . . Savages, like children, have no steadiness of purpose' (1865: 570).

As a condition opposed to humanity, animality conveys an idea of the quality of life in the state of nature, where we encounter human beings 'in the raw', impelled in their conduct by brute passion rather than rational deliberation, and totally unconstrained by moral or customary regulation. This view of animal life and of 'human animality' is an extraordinarily pervasive one in the history of Western thought, which even today colours much ostensibly scientific discussion in the study of animal and human behaviour. A prominent feature of the Western tradition is a propensity to think in parallel dichotomies, so that the opposition between animality and humanity is aligned with those between nature and culture, body and mind, emotion and reason, instinct and art, and so on. It is even enshrined in the academic division of labour between the natural sciences, in their concern with the composition and structures of the material world (including human organisms), and the humanities, embracing the study of language, history and civilization. And it underlies the continuing arguments between scholars on both sides of this academic fence about the meaning of 'human nature'.

The trouble arises because the legacy of dualistic thinking invades our very conception of what a human being is, for it has given us the vocabulary for expressing it. We are, according to this conception, constitutionally divided creatures, one part immersed in the physical condition of animality, the other in the moral condition of humanity. In which of these two parts, you may ask, does human nature reside? It all depends on what you mean by 'nature', a term that is perhaps one of the most multivalent in the English language. Of its many meanings we need at this point to distinguish just two (for these and other meanings, see Williams 1976: 184–9). First, the nature of a thing may be some essential quality that all and only things of its kind may be expected to possess. As such it is a 'lowest common denominator' for the kind, what is universal rather than particular to each of its constituent individuals. Second, nature connotes the material world, the macrocosm of physical entities as distinct from their microcosmic representation on the level of ideas. It is in this sense that nature stands classically opposed to culture, the former an external reality, the latter a reality only as it exists 'inside people's heads'.

Now to return to our question – does human nature reside in our humanity or in our animality? – we find that the two senses of nature adduced above give us conflicting answers. Recall Buffon's view, fairly representative of its time, that it is in their possession of the faculty of mind rather than in bodily form that humans are distinguished from apes. What is essential to human beings, then, is their humanity: the component which, following orthodox Christian dogma, they owe to God's preferential bestowal of divine spirit. On the other hand, human beings also partake of the material world – or of nature in the second sense – in their bodily organs, comprehended by the Creator along with the bodies of every animal species (as Buffon put it) 'under one general plan'. Accordingly, human beings may be revealed in their material generation as biological organisms, by stripping away their essential humanity to leave an innate residue that they have in common with other animals. This is the layer of 'human animality' to which Monboddo and many others, both previously and subsequently, have referred as the 'brutish state' of humankind, supposedly representing an original and universal baseline for all social and cultural evolution.

Despite the theological upheavals that followed in the wake of Darwin's theory of human evolution, which of course had no place for mind or spirit except as the output of a material organ (the brain), the terms of the contemporary debate between 'scientists' and 'humanists' on the question of human nature are still very much the same as they were in the days of Buffon and Monboddo. Ethologists and sociobiologists, working within a natural science paradigm, explicitly identify human nature with what is animal in us, something normally so overlain with cultural accretions that it is more directly observable in species other than our own. They have made it their business to discover the prototypes for universal human dispositions in the behavioural repertoire most notably of non-human primates, though the search for parallels often takes them much further afield. Indeed much of the intense popular interest in ethological work stems from the belief that by studying the behaviour of other animals we can learn something important about ourselves. This is certainly true, yet when taken to excess it can lead us to rest our account of human nature on an amalgam of traits drawn from the repertoire of practically any species *except* our own. The readiness with which some sociobiologists are inclined to pronounce upon the human predicament on the basis of studies of such social insects as ants and bees puts one in mind of Will Cuppy's quip, in *How to Tell Your Friends from the Apes*, that 'the psychology of the Orang-utan has been thoroughly described by scientists from their observations of the Sea-urchin' (Cuppy 1931: 38).[3]

Anthropologists and others of a more humanist bent have naturally been concerned to recover the 'human essence' that is missing from sociobiological and ethological accounts. To adopt Eisenberg's (1972) phrase, they emphasize 'the *human* nature of human nature', replacing the ancient notion of spirit with what has come to be called 'the capacity for culture'. Just what this means is a matter of interminable dispute. Suffice to note, at this point, that in locating the distinguishing quality of human beings on the moral plane of culture, as distinct from the physical plane of nature, the eighteenth-century conception of man – as torn between the conditions of humanity and animality – is reproduced in all its essentials. Only when they are 'being human', it seems, do human beings show themselves for what they really are.

However there is not only one way of being human. Whatever else it may be, the capacity for culture is a capacity for generating difference. In and through that creative, generative process, played out in the ordinary course of social life, the essence of humanity is revealed as cultural diversity. For any particular individual, caught up in the process, 'becoming human' entails becoming different from other humans who speak different languages or dialects, practise different arts, hold different beliefs, and so on. If it is in their thus differentiating themselves from one another that human beings are essentially distinguished from animals, it follows, of course, that human animality is revealed as the absence of such differentiation, in sameness. Each one of us comes into the world as a creature born of man and woman, a biologically human organism whose physical constitution is entirely indifferent to his or her subsequent education into the code of conduct of one culture or another. As far as my existence as a member of the human species is concerned, the fact that I happen to be English rather than, say, French or Japanese is quite incidental. But with regard to the expression of my humanity, it is vital. It makes me some*one*, rather than just some*thing*. Or to put the same point in general terms, culture underwrites the identity of the human being, not as a biological organism but as a moral subject. In this latter capacity, we regard every man or woman as a person. My personhood is therefore inseparable from my belonging to a culture, and both are crucial ingredients of my being human.

We are now in a position to resolve a paradox at the heart of Western thought, which insists with equal assurance both that humans are animals and that animality is the very obverse of humanity. A human being is an individual of a species; being human is to exist as a person. In the first sense humanity refers to a biological taxon (*Homo sapiens*), in the second it refers to a moral condition (personhood). The fact that we use the same word 'human' for both reflects a deep-seated conviction that all and only those individuals belonging to the human species can be persons, or in other words that personhood is conditional upon membership of the taxon. 'All human beings', as Article 1 of the Universal Declaration of Human Rights states, 'are endowed with reason and conscience'. By implication, all non-human animals are not (Clark 1988: 23).

If we accept this tenet as an article of faith, then certain questions cannot be asked, at least not without compromising the principles of genealogical classification generally adopted in the definition of biological species. We cannot ask, as Monboddo did, how reason and speech were acquired in the history of human populations, or how these faculties may be lacking or deficient in particular individuals of human parentage. Nor can we ask whether, or to what extent, animals of other species may be endowed with the faculties of language and thought. Yet these are legitimate questions that cannot be resolved a priori but only through empirical investigation. It is perfectly reasonable to enquire, for example, whether chimpanzees or dolphins have language, or whether they engage in rational deliberation. It may turn out that they do not, except perhaps under quite artificial conditions, and that these capacities are indeed possessed only by biologically human animals. But who is to say that they will not eventually evolve, in future times, among species descended from the chimpanzees and dolphins of today? If this comes to pass, we would have grounds for treating such thinking and speaking animals as persons. They could not, however, be regarded as members of the human species, since they would not be of human descent.

Rigid adherence to the doctrine that only human beings can be persons would therefore lead us to the absurd situation of having to deny the possibility of an evolution that we cannot, at this stage, know anything about. Once again, in his discussion of the humanity of the orang-utan, Monboddo was wrong for the right reasons: wrong because anthropoid apes do not belong to the human species; right because although he lacked the vocabulary to express the point without contradiction, he recognized that membership of the taxon we now call *Homo sapiens* does not automatically confer qualities of personhood. This conclusion immediately opens up a field of inquiry of potentially inexhaustible scope, into the personhood of non-human animals or, if you will, into animal humanity rather than human animality. It suggests that the boundary between human and other animal species does not run alongside, but actually crosscuts the boundary between humanity and animality as states of being. And by the same token, we cannot just assume that approaches from the humanities are appropriate only to understanding the affairs of human beings, and that the lives and worlds of nonhuman animals can be fully comprehended within a natural science paradigm (Ingold 1989: 496).

One consequence of this assumption is that whereas human actions are generally interpreted as the products of intentional design, the actions of other animals – even when ostensibly similar in their nature and consequences – are typically explained as the automatic output of a 'wired-in' behavioural programme (Ingold 1988: 6). Of course, when it comes to those few animals with which we have close and enduring relationships, such as our domestic cats and dogs, we are quick to make exceptions, attributing to them intentions and purposes just as we do to other humans. For people of many non-Western cultures, whose practical involvement with other species vastly exceeds our own, our exceptions may very well be their rule. For example, among the Ojibwa, native hunters of subarctic Canada, personhood is envisaged as an inner essence, embracing the powers of sentience, volition, memory and speech, which is quite indifferent to the particular species form it may outwardly assume. The human form is merely one of the many guises in which persons may materially manifest themselves, and anyone can change his or her form for that of an animal more or less at will. When you see an animal, and particularly an animal that is behaving in an unusual way, you wonder *who* it is, for it may be somebody you know. Thus for the Ojibwa, there is nothing especially 'human' about being a person (Hallowell 1960).

My purpose in presenting this example is to emphasize that our conventional notion of personhood as a prerogative of human beings is just as much embedded in the Western worldview as is the contrary notion of the Ojibwa in theirs, and we have no more cause to attribute any absolute validity to the

24

former than to the latter. In his *Critique of Judgement* of 1790, the German philosopher Immanuel Kant summed up Western orthodoxy in the following words: 'As the single being on earth that possesses understanding, [man] is certainly titular lord of nature, and...is born to be its ultimate end' (Kant 1952, II S431). This imperialistic conception of 'man's place in nature,' with its dogmatic denial (accompanied by no evidence at all) of non-human forms of understanding, has done a great deal of damage in its time. Pragmatically, the Ojibwa level-pegging of humans and animals in relations of mutual interdependence enshrines a sound ecological wisdom, and with regard to the long-term survival of our species it has much to commend it. Scientifically, the investigation of the real nature of the similarities and differences between ourselves and other animals remains in its infancy, and should not be foreclosed by a priori assumptions about human pre-eminence. Such investigation, which anthropologists have tended to treat as somewhat marginal to their concerns, is in fact of crucial significance, since it strikes at the heart of the dominant conception of human uniqueness. It is to this that we now turn.

ON HUMAN UNIQUENESS

The human species is biologically unique. So is every other species on the face of the earth (Foley 1987: 274). This uniqueness, as we have seen, does not consist in some one or more essential attributes that all individuals of the species have in common, and that no individuals of any other species possess. Rather it lies in the present composition of the total pool of genetic traits of which every individual of the species, by virtue of its descent, represents a particular combination. The gene pools of different species may overlap a good deal, especially when they are phylogenetically close − for example, human beings and chimpanzees have been found to be about 99 per cent the same, genetically − but they are never precisely congruent. Moreover the composition of the pool for any species is changing all the time, which is simply another way of saying that it evolves. With regard to species other than our own, these facts are well-established and uncontentious. But when it comes to humans, they meet with obdurate resistance. As one eminent philosopher of biology notes, with scarcely concealed exasperation, 'the desire to find some trait that all human beings possess and no non-humans possess is all but overwhelming. But no matter the trait chosen, either some people do not exhibit it or else members of some other species do' (Hull 1984: 35). Why, then, do we go on searching? Whence comes the compulsion to discover that unique attribute?

Let us take a look at some of the attributes that have been proposed as candidates for the human distinction. Every author has a favourite word or phrase to fill the vacant space in the statement 'man is defined as a ——— animal', insisting that it denotes the single key to the essence of humanity. Yet should we attempt to compile a catalogue of such keys, it would soon become very long indeed. Undoubtedly 'language-using' and 'rational' would top the list. Equipped with language, human beings describe, speculate, argue, joke and deceive. They can lie, conjuring up things and events that have never been, and so they are peculiarly bothered by questions of truth and falsity. Reasoning about the world and their actions in it they also make mistakes: man is said to be an errant animal. He is moreover self-conscious or self-interpreting, and is consequently also aware of the passage of time and the transience of his own life. He seeks, therefore, to accommodate the facts of birth, ageing and death within a timeless order: man is a religious animal. And he is a designer, imposing symbolic schemes of his own devising upon the world of inanimate objects in the making of tools and artefacts, upon animals and plants in the production (as distinct from collection) of food, and upon fellow humans in the construction of the rules and institutions of social life.

All these things can, of course, be said equally of either sex, and though it is to be conventionally understood that in comparisons with other animals the word 'man' includes both male and female members of the human species, the structural bias of the English language has taken its toll in a rather pernicious tendency to attribute to the male all those qualities that are supposed to have made us human, and to characterize femininity either by their absence or by their relatively weak development. Nowhere is this tendency more evident than in the prevalent origin myth of 'man the hunter', according to which an exclusively male activity – the pursuit of big game – is supposed to have placed a selective premium on the concurrent emergence of toolmaking, language and rational intelligence, thereby putting males at the cutting edge of human evolution (e.g. Laughlin 1968). I do not intend to pursue this theme here, but raise it in order to alert the reader to the lingering resonance of an ancient doctrine to the effect that men's superiority over women is a natural and proper reflection of the superiority of humanity over animality.

Of more immediate concern is the objection commonly levelled against attempts to establish a Rubicon that would separate human beings from the rest of the animal kingdom, namely that whatever differences exist are of degree rather than kind. Advocates of this view, whom we can call gradualists, argue that although human language may be supremely versatile, it does not differ fundamentally from the systems of communication employed by other animals, and therefore that it is perfectly legitimate to refer to the latter as 'animal languages'. Likewise, while agreeing that humans are highly intelligent, gradualists warn against underestimating the intelligence of other animals – which moreover are rather less inclined than we are to make mistakes. And though recognizing the unparalleled range and complexity of human designs, they point out that the constructional abilities of non-human animals are by no means negligible. To insist, against all the evidence for animal language, intelligence and manufacture, that humans nevertheless differ in kind, is – say the gradualists – to adopt an attitude of unreflecting anthropocentrism that should have no place in rational scientific inquiry (Griffin 1976).

This accusation of anthropocentrism needs to be examined rather carefully. There is nothing in the least anthropocentric about asserting the uniqueness of the human species, for as I have shown, every biological species is unique in its way. But in assembling the various key attributes of humanity that I have mentioned – including language, reason, self-awareness and symbolic design – do we arrive at a description of a unique species that would satisfy the canons of natural history? Surely not. For they convey no information at all about the kinds of morphological or behavioural idiosyncrasies that otherwise enable naturalists to recognize individuals as belonging to one species or another. Reason, for example, cannot be considered as a 'trait' on a par with bipedalism, opposable thumb, year-round sexual receptivity and taillessness. The search for definitive attributes of humanity has not in fact been motivated by a concern to describe what human beings are like, along the same lines as we might seek to describe – say – elephants or beavers. It has stemmed rather from a desire to establish what is commonly known as the human *condition*. Bipedalism, opposable thumb and the rest are typical properties possessed by the vast majority of human beings, just as elephants have trunks and beavers build dams. Reason and self-awareness, by contrast, are essential qualities of *being human*. The former are based on the data of empirical observation, the latter are derived entirely from a process of introspection.

The anthropocentrism to which gradualists object is one that takes the 'human condition' to be an all-or-nothing state of existence open only to members of the human species and consequently denied to all other animals. We find a precedent for this view in the taxonomy of Linnaeus, set out in his *Systema Naturae* of 1735, where the genus *Homo* is placed within a classification of animals resting on such observable features as numbers of fingers and toes, but distinguished by the injunction *Nosce te ipsum*, 'know for yourself' (Bendyshe 1865: 422). Cast your attention inward, to your own soul, not outward onto nature, and there – says Linnaeus – you will discover the essence of human beings. This is clearly to envisage human uniqueness in a form that is not at all comparable to the uniqueness of other species. It is to claim that human beings are not different from elephants as elephants are different from beavers, for whereas the latter is a difference within animality, the former also – and more significantly – places humans altogether beyond the bounds of animality, so that the distinction between elephants (or beavers) and humans appears only as a particular instance of the general distinction between animality and humanity.[4]

We can now appreciate why, in the face of modern biological wisdom, intelligent people in the West continue to appeal to the essential attributes of humanity in order to establish the uniqueness of *Homo sapiens*. It is simply because of the popular identification, noted earlier in this chapter, of the human *species* with the human *condition*, an identification that rests in turn upon an ideological conflation of the biological individual with the moral subject or person. Once these are properly distinguished, the human species may be defined, just like any other species, in genealogical terms, without resort to essential qualities; and the human condition may be defined in terms of such qualities without prejudging the extent to which biologically human beings or other animals actually partake of it. It is this extent that the gradualists are concerned to estimate when they assert that humans differ from other animals in degree and not in kind. Instead of seeing humanity as an all-or-nothing state, they see it as a continuous scale against which the actual performance of human and animal populations can be gauged. It is not a question of either having or lacking language, reason and self-awareness: these, according to gradualists, are capacities with which animals may be either *more* or *less* endowed.

On this scale, chimpanzees are generally reckoned to come closest to humans in their level of attainment. An extraordinary amount of effort has been put into coaxing chimpanzees to demonstrate insightful problem-solving capacities, nascent self-awareness, and some rudimentary competence in language use. Up to a point the animals have obliged, enough to generate surprise and occasional consternation among human observers, as well as a good measure of scepticism about the validity of the experimental results. But even the most prodigal of chimpanzees are no match for adult humans. By comparison with ourselves, chimpanzees are (hardly surprisingly) not very good at being human, yet the likeness is such that we are inclined to regard them − as Monboddo regarded the orang-utan − as incomplete humans rather than complete apes. We see the human infant in every mature chimpanzee, and treat it accordingly as a case of arrested development.

Of this perception, many anthropologists are justifiably suspicious (e.g. Tapper 1988: 57−9). They point out, first, that not so long ago, 'primitive' humans were perceived in very much the same way, as beings whose humanity was as yet little developed: whose languages were relatively impoverished, whose intelligence was pre-rational and whose powers of self-control were extremely limited. Second, they observe that the 'we' who compare other animals with 'ourselves' are not representative of humanity at large, but only of a small and historically rather atypical section of humanity, namely urban and predominantly middle-class members of what we like to call 'modern Western society'. From the days when Thomas Huxley (1894) first popularized the view that the superiority of the modern European over the savage was akin to that of the savage over the ape, and therefore that there was no radical discontinuity in the passage from animal to human, the gradualist thesis has been loaded with a strong bias of ethnocentrism, that is by an assumption that the only true and universally applicable standards are those appropriate in one's own society. Somewhere far back along the scale of degrees culminating in 'Western civilized man' − supremely intelligent, scientifically enlightened, self-consciously liberated and (of course) male − the most excellent of apes were supposed to jostle for precedence with the most primitive of people. Even today, as we dream of discovering intelligent life on other planets, it is assumed that the extraterrestrials' standards of progress will be ours as well, even if they have so overtaken us as to make us appear primitive by comparison.

Alert to the facts of cultural diversity, anthropologists stress that there are as many standards of humanity as there are different ways of being human, and that there are no grounds – apart from sheer prejudice – for investing any one set of standards with universal authority. Yet they hold that this very diversity manifests a human essence, the capacity for culture, which sets humans radically apart from animals. The anthropologists' cultural relativism, their view that the conduct of any group of human beings can only be comprehended in relation to standards appropriate to the particular culture to which they belong, seems to rest on just that kind of anthropocentric conception of human uniqueness to which gradualists are opposed.

There is a serious dilemma here, for it appears that we cannot defeat ethnocentrism without taking refuge in anthropocentrism, and vice versa. Gradualism, in asserting differences of degree, cannot avoid positing a universal scale

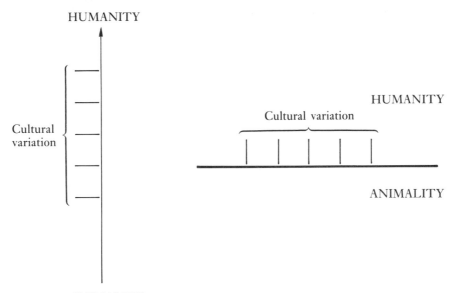

Figure 2 Ethnocentrism and anthropocentrism in views of animal–human differences. The diagram on the left shows the gradualist thesis: a single scale of absolute advance leads from apes, through 'primitive' humans, to modern civilization. On the right is depicted the counter-thesis of cultural relativism: diverse cultural forms, none of which can be judged more advanced than any other, are superimposed upon a universal substrate of animality

29

of progress, in terms of which humans and other animals may be judged 'more' or 'less'. If however we reject such a scale on the grounds of the ethnocentricity of its criteria of advance, then we are once more left with an anthropocentric view of humanity as an all-or-nothing condition, which admits of no variation in degree but is boundlessly variable in the manner of its expression. This dilemma, illustrated schematically in Figure 2, underlies much of the current debate between evolutionary biologists, who stress the continuity between humans and other animals and are reluctant to admit to differences in kind, and anthropologists, who remain committed to a dualistic conception of humankind − one part nature, the other part culture.

Our central problem, I believe, is to resolve the dilemma, to reconcile the continuity of the evolutionary process with the awareness we have of ourselves as living a life beyond that of the 'merely animal'. This cannot be done by limiting the study of humanity either to an investigation of the nature and evolution of the species *Homo sapiens* or to an investigation of the human condition as it is revealed in culture and history. Our ultimate objective should be to transcend the opposition that divides these alternatives, which have traditionally fallen into the respective domains of natural science and the humanities. That is to say, we have to comprehend the relation between the species and the condition, between human beings and being human. In this article I have shown not only how this relation is anything but a simple one, but also how we have been prevented from asking relevant questions about it by an assumption that the two notions of humanity are essentially the same, that the condition defines the species. To explore a relation, one must begin by distinguishing the terms which it connects. Our science of humanity must therefore be rephrased, more precisely, as a science of the relationship between two humanities, between a peculiar biological species and its social and cultural conditions of existence.

NOTES

1 The relevant passages from Hoppius's *Anthropomorpha* are reproduced, in English translation, in Bendyshe (1865: 448–58).
2 For an excellent account of Monboddo's ideas, in relation to those of his contemporaries, see Reynolds (1981: 38–42).
3 I am grateful to the late Nancy Tanner for drawing my attention to this marvellous book.
4 In the following article, Tobias discusses Linnaeus's conception of the genus *Homo* at greater length, but advances a somewhat different interpretation.

REFERENCES

Bendyshe, T. (1865) 'The history of anthropology', *Memoirs of the Anthropological Society of London*, vol. I (1863–4): 335–458.

Bock, K. (1980) *Human Nature and History: a Response to Sociobiology*, New York: Columbia University Press.

Buffon, Count (Georges Louis Leclerc) (1866) *Natural history* (2 vols), trans. W. Smellie, London: Thomas Kelly.

Burnett, J. (Lord Monboddo) (1773) *Of the origin and progress of language*, vol. I, Edinburgh: Kincaid and Creech [Facsimile reprint, Menston: Scolar Press, 1967].

Clark, S. R. L. (1988) 'Is humanity a natural kind?', in T. Ingold (ed.) *What is an Animal?*, London: Unwin Hyman.

Cuppy, W. (1931) *How to Tell Your Friends from the Apes*, New York: Horace Liveright.

Darwin, C. (1872) *The Origin of Species*, 6th edn, London: John Murray.

Eisenberg, L. (1972) 'The *human* nature of human nature', *Science* 176: 123–8.

Foley, R. A. (1987) *Another Unique Species: Patterns in Human Evolutionary Ecology*, Harlow: Longmans.

Griffin, D. R. (1976) *The Question of Animal Awareness: Evolutionary Continuity of Mental Experience*, New York: Rockefeller University Press.

Hallowell, I. (1960) 'Ojibwa ontology, behavior and world view', in S. Diamond (ed.) *Culture in History: Essays in Honor of Paul Radin*, New York: Columbia University Press.

Hull, D. (1984) 'Historical entities and historical narratives', in C. Hookway (ed.) *Minds, Machines and Evolution*, Cambridge: Cambridge University Press.

Huxley, T. H. (1894) *Man's Place in Nature, and Other Essays*, London: Macmillan.

Ingold, T. (1988) 'Introduction', in T. Ingold (ed.) *What is an Animal?*, London: Unwin Hyman.

—— (1989) 'The social and environmental relations of human beings and other animals', in V. Standen and R. A. Foley (eds) *Comparative Socioecology: the Behavioural Ecology of Humans and Other Mammals*, Oxford: Blackwell Scientific.

Kant, I. (1952) *Critique of Judgement*, trans. J. C. Meredith, Oxford: Clarendon Press.

Laughlin, W. (1968) 'Hunting: an integrating biobehavior system and its evolutionary importance', in R. B. Lee and I. DeVore (eds) *Man the Hunter*, Chicago: Aldine.

Leach, E. R. (1982) *Social Anthropology*, London: Fontana.

Lubbock, Sir J. (1865) *Prehistoric Times as Illustrated by Ancient Remains and the Manners and Customs of Modern Savages*. London: Williams & Norgate.

Medawar, P. B. (1957) *The Uniqueness of the Individual*, London: Methuen.

Reynolds, P. C. (1981) *On the Evolution of Human Behavior: the Argument from Animals to Man*, Berkeley: University of California Press.

Tapper, R. (1988) 'Animality, humanity, morality, society', in T. Ingold (ed.) *What is an Animal?*, London: Unwin Hyman.

Williams, R. (1976) *Keywords: a Vocabulary of Culture and Society*, London: Fontana.

FURTHER READING

Bock, K. E. (1980) *Human Nature and History: a Response to Sociobiology*, New York: Columbia University Press.

Clark, S. R. L. (1982) *The Nature of the Beast: Are Animals Moral?* Oxford: Oxford University Press.

Eisenberg, J. F. and Dillon, W. S. (eds) (1971) *Man and Beast: Comparative Social Behavior*, Washington, DC: Smithsonian Institution.

Griffin, D. R. (1976) *The Question of Animal Awareness: Evolutionary Continuity of Mental Experience*, New York: Rockefeller University Press.

Hirst, P. and Woolley, P. (1982) *Social Relations and Human Attributes*, pt I, 'Biology and Culture', London: Tavistock.

Horigan, S. (1988) *Nature and Culture in Western Discourses*, London: Routledge.

Ingold, T. (ed.) (1988) *What is an Animal?*, London: Unwin Hyman.

Leach, E. R. (1982) *Social Anthropology*, ch. 3, 'Humanity and animality', London: Fontana.

Leeds, A. and Vayda, A. P. (eds) (1965) *Man, Culture and Animals*, Washington, DC: American Association for the Advancement of Science.

Manning, A. and Serpell, J. (eds) (1993) *Animals and Society: Changing Perspectives*, London: Routledge.

Midgley, M. (1979) *Beast and Man: the Roots of Human Nature*, Brighton: Harvester Press.

—— (1983) *Animals and Why They Matter: a Journey Around the Species Barrier*, Harmondsworth: Penguin.

Reynolds, P. C. (1981) *On the Evolution of Human Behavior: the Argument from Animals to Man*, Berkeley: University of California Press.

Sebeok, T. A. and Umiker-Sebeok, J. (eds) (1980) *Speaking of Apes: a Critical Anthology of Two-way Communication with Man*, New York: Plenum Press.

Serpell, J. (1986) *In the Company of Animals*, Oxford: Blackwell.

Tanner, N. M. (1981) *On Becoming Human: a Model of the Transition from Ape to Human and the Reconstruction of Early Human Social Life*, Cambridge: Cambridge University Press.

Walker, S. (1983). *Animal Thought*, London: Routledge & Kegan Paul.

Willis, R. G. (1974) *Man and Beast*, London: Hart-Davis, MacGibbon.

—— (ed.) (1990) *Signifying Animals: Human Meaning in the Natural World*, London: Unwin Hyman.

3

THE EVOLUTION OF EARLY HOMINIDS

Phillip V. Tobias

What is an early hominid? To seek out an answer it is necessary to compare indisputable hominids, namely, modern human beings, with close relatives which are unquestionably not hominid – and these are the modern great apes.

THE PLACE OF THE HOMINIDS IN NATURE

We may accept that hominids are members of the animal kingdom. Not long ago this notion was considered revolutionary and outrageous. When, in his *Systema Naturae* of 1735, the Swedish naturalist Linnaeus classified man as a part of the *Regnum Animale*, the French biologist Buffon described the Linnaean system as *'une verité humiliante pour l'homme'*. It was indeed a cardinal contribution of Linnaeus – at the age of twenty-eight and over 250 years ago – to have demoted humans from our previous celestial separateness and to have placed us among the other animals. Linnaeus had to brave ostracism to assert that whatever rules applied to the classification of other animals should also apply to that of human beings. Charles Darwin, in *The Origin of Species* (1859), did not say as much: humankind earned only one hesitant sentence on the last page of Darwin's book. In a sense, Linnaeus brought people down from the angels to join the apes.

In *Systema Naturae* we find Linnaeus reacting so strongly to the prevailing view, which put humankind alone on a pedestal, as to declare his inability to discover characters by which people could be distinguished from apes: 'It is wonderful how little the most foolish ape differs from the wisest man, so that we have still to seek for that measurer of nature, who is to define their boundaries'. Again, in the preface to his *Fauna Suecica* of 1745 he states: 'It is a matter for the most arduous investigation wherein the peculiar and specific difference of man consists'.

BLURRING THE DISTINCTION BETWEEN HUMANS AND APES

How could Linnaeus have missed such obvious distinctions between humans and apes as habitual bipedalism and relative hairlessness in the former? When we look more closely, we are forced to conclude that he came up with the right idea for the wrong reasons. There is no doubt that Linnaeus used a much wider definition of apes than we nowadays accept, and that he even included some living human populations in his concept of the ape. Thus, he believed 'that there were apes which walked with body erect on two feet like man', and also 'that there are some regions where there are apes less hairy than man' (Tobias 1978).

These notions, as Ingold has described in the previous article, stemmed from the accounts which sailors and travellers were bringing back to Europe from remote parts of Africa and Asia. Their tales blurred the distinctions between some human hunting and food-gathering populations, like Pygmies and San (Bushmen), whose way of life was styled 'primitive', and the great apes of Africa and Asia. Even the name of the Asian great ape, orang-utan, betrays the confusion, or the perceived resemblance: for it means 'forest man' or 'wild man' in Malayan. That name was also given to an African ape that was dissected by Edward Tyson in 1699. Tyson's work bore the revealing title, 'Orang-Outang, sive *Homo sylvestris*: or the Anatomy of a Pygmie'. What he was describing was a juvenile chimpanzee! Yet his chosen title rendered synonymous the name of an Asian ape, a race of human beings and the Latin term for 'man of the woods'. Tyson went on to declare that the pygmies of the ancients were apes and not humans.

This linguistic and conceptual confusion also besets the word gorilla, which is thought to be derived from an African word meaning 'wild man', or a member of a tribe of hairy people, though the precise source of the word is unknown. It is interesting, too, that the zoological name given to the chimpanzee by Oken in 1816 was *Pan* — for Pan was the theriomorphic Grecian deity, part human, part animal.

We see that Linnaeus blurred the distinction between what were perceived as 'lowly' or 'primitive' human beings and non-human primates. In this blurring of the human-ape interface, there may reside at least some roots of the idea of racial superiority and inferiority which preoccupied the minds of many scholars and some societies in the nineteenth and twentieth centuries, and ultimately led to institutionalized racism in several parts of the world.

The tenth edition of *Systema Naturae* (1758) is accepted as the starting point for modern classification and nomenclature. Linnaeus proposed a separate genus, *Homo*, for human beings. He summarized its generic characteristics under the simple but striking definition, *Nosce te ipsum* ('Know for yourself'). Some of the implications of this definition have already been touched upon by Ingold in the last article.

THE SORTING OF APES AND HUMANS

Within the Animal Kingdom, human beings are set within the phylum Chordata, the subphylum Vertebrata, the class Mammalia, the subclass Theria and the infraclass Eutheria (Rothschild 1961). The eutherian or placental mammals are divided into a number of orders. In deference to human self-conceit, Linnaeus placed *Homo sapiens* within an order to which he gave the name 'Primates' — of the first rank among the mammals. As Simpson (1945: 180) put it, 'The primates are inevitably the most interesting of mammals to an egocentric species that belongs to this order.'

Within the order Primates, two suborders are recognized, the Prosimii (such as lemurs and tarsiers), so called by Illiger in 1811, and the Anthropoidea (such as monkeys and apes), a name conferred by Mivart in 1864 (anthropoid means 'having the form of human beings'). Within the suborder Anthropoidea, humans, gibbons, siamangs and great apes are considered to form a natural unit, the superfamily Hominoidea (or, less formally, the hominoids). The overall classification may be summarized as follows (modified from Simpson 1945):

Phylum Chordata Balfour, 1880
  Subphylum Vertebrata Cuvier, 1828
    Class Mammalia Linnaeus, 1758
      Subclass Theria Parker and Haswell, 1897
        Infraclass Eutheria Gill, 1872
          Cohort Unguiculata Linnaeus, 1766
            Order Primates Linnaeus, 1758
              Suborder I Prosimii Illiger, 1811
                Infraorder 1 Lemuriformes Gregory, 1915
                  Superfamily i Lemuroidea Mivart, 1864
                          ii Daubentonioidea Gill, 1872
                Infraorder 2 Lorisiformes Gregory, 1915
                      3 Tarsiiformes Gregory, 1915

              Suborder II Anthropoidea Mivart, 1864
                Superfamily   i Ceboidea Simpson, 1931
                          ii Cercopithecoidea Simpson, 1931
                          iii Hominoidea Simpson, 1931

Some of the major criteria by which the primates are differentiated are listed below (modified and amplified after Clark 1955, 1964):

1 Elaboration of the brain — especially cerebral cortex; relatively large and complicated brains.
2 Elaboration of vision — development of binocular vision.
3 Reduction of the apparatus of smell.

4 Loss of certain elements of primitive mammalian dentition and retention of simple molar cusp pattern.
5 Shortening of the muzzle.
6 Preservation of generalized limb structure, retention of the clavicle and pentadactyly (the possession of five fingers and toes).
7 Enhanced mobility of the digits, opposability of either the thumb or big toe or both; hands and/or feet prehensile or clearly derived from the prehensile type.
8 Flattened nails instead of claws on some or all of the fingers and/or toes; development of tactile pads on the digits.
9 Development of truncal uprightness.
10 Elaboration of processes to nourish the foetus before birth.
11 Prolongation of the post-natal life period.

In 1825, John Edward Gray proposed to place man in a separate primate family which he called Hominidae, a practice followed by most biologists and anthropologists to this day. At that time, early in the nineteenth century, the known members of the family comprised the living populations of the human species, *Homo sapiens*. The question of earlier and extinct members of the family had not entered the picture, because the discovery and recognition of fossil hominids came only somewhat later in the nineteenth century. Without this palaeontological and deep-time dimension, it was possible to offer a zoological definition of the hominids that was based exclusively on the features of modern humans, as contrasted with those of modern apes.

Most investigators, down to the present day, have continued to recognize humankind as a distinct primate family. Two factors have however forced a recent re-examination of the status of the hominids: one is the discovery and appraisal of fossil hominids, and the other is the startling result of biomolecular evolutionary studies in pointing to an unexpectedly close relationship between humans and the African great apes.

A rethink based on fossils

The margin of distinctness that was once supposed to separate humans from apes has been eroded by the accumulation, since the middle of the nineteenth century, of many fossil hominids. First came the discovery of Neanderthal men, then of *Pithecanthropus* (now called *Homo erectus*) late in the nineteenth century and, most dramatically, of the yet lowlier *Australopithecus* since 1925.

Late in 1925, or early in 1926, very soon after the announcement by Dart (1925) of the discovery of *Australopithecus* in southern Africa, an American zoologist, Harrison Hawthorne Wilder, prefaced his (undated) book, *The Pedigree of the Human Race*, with these words:

> In essaying to write of the Pedigree of the Human Race the author feels that he must write only as a professional zoologist, investigating the history of a single animal

species which has become universally distributed and which, in the matter of the nervous system, has far surpassed the powers of all other species.

(Wilder n.d.: v)

Wilder's concept of humankind was wider than that of Linnaeus, in that the former included fossil hominids. Hence, we find Wilder asserting that 'there are certainly no structural differences sufficient to make a different Family of them [man past and present]'. Accordingly, Wilder tries to see the diverse higher primates as a hypothetical scientist visiting from the planet Mars might observe them: he makes the radical proposal that the family Hominidae should include, along with humans, 'the tailless anthropoid apes and the various related species that have been recently unearthed in the soil'. As a compromise proposal, Wilder suggests that 'It may be useful to make a Sub-Family Homininae, to include man past and present'. This hominine subfamily would be of comparable status, in our classificatory system, to the subfamilies proposed for gibbons (*Hylobatinae*) and great apes (*Pongiinae*). Nevertheless, Wilder adds, 'Even a definite separation of Sub-Families is hard to accomplish, and the distinctions between these may be eventually lessened when the returns are all in' (Wilder n.d.: v).

Gregory and Hellman (1938, 1939a, b), after their detailed studies of the teeth and jaws of the South African fossil ape-men, supported Wilder's view. They proposed to add another subfamily, the Australopithecinae, to accommodate the various kinds of ape-man from Taung, Sterkfontein and Kromdraai. In its colloquial form, australopithecines, the term is still widely used today.

However, the proposal to accommodate apes in the same family as humans suffered a major setback, if not a near-fatal blow, when in 1945 Simpson produced his masterful classification of mammals. He placed all apes, including gibbons, extinct dryomorphs and, in his view, the australopithecines, in one family, for which he accepted Elliot's (1913) name of Pongidae. Simpson assigned the past and present members of the genus *Homo*, as well as *Pithecanthropus* (now *Homo erectus*) and *Eoanthropus* (later exposed as the forged remains of Piltdown), to a separate family, the Hominidae.

The enormous authority of Simpson's classification, and his supporting enunciation of the principles of taxonomy, ensured that apes and hominids were kept apart in two different families by most scholars for a long time afterwards. This position became entrenched with the publication of Clark's *The Fossil Evidence for Human Evolution* (1955, 1964). He offered clear and extensive zoological definitions of the two families Hominidae and Pongidae. Although early members of the two families were more alike than their later, derived descendants, including those living today, it was still possible for Clark to define the morphological trends characterizing the two families in such a manner that even early fossil hominoids could be assigned to one or other family.

This, then, has represented the formal position in hominid and ape systematics for about the last half-century:

ORDER   Primates
SUBORDER   Anthropoidea
SUPERFAMILY   Hominoidea
FAMILIES   Hominidae, Pongidae

This classification is based on the structural affinities and differences between the present-day and earlier forms of the two groups. Even Wilder's assault on the system was founded on the morphology of these higher primates. More recent challenges to it have been fuelled by the unforeseen and arresting results of molecular evolutionary studies.

A rethink based on molecules

At one time, the anatomy of creatures, present and past, enlivened by insights from comparative anatomy, constituted practically the entire basis for statements about biological affinities and descent. Since the early 1960s, however, hominid origins have engaged the attention of molecular biologists. Their approach has been founded, in the main, on the biochemical makeup of living organisms. These studies have shown that there is a far closer biomolecular affinity between humans and the African great apes than one might have predicted from their comparative anatomy alone. Indeed, at the molecular level, gorilla, chimpanzee and human beings are more closely related to each other than any one of these is to the Asian great ape, the orang-utan. This is forcing a realignment of the hominoids.

If at the genetic level the African apes are closer to humans than they are to the orang-utan, it makes little sense to continue sorting all of the great apes, Asian and African, into one family, and humans into another. It would seem more logical to place humans and the African great apes in one family (for which the name Hominidae may be suitable), and the Asian great ape, the orang-utan, in another family, the Pongidae. Such a re-sorting of the hominoids has been proposed by several scholars.

The classification of hominoids is therefore, at the present time, in a state of flux. Challenges to the orthodox systematics of Simpson and Clark have come not only from the differing thrusts of palaeontologists and molecular biologists, but also from the emergence of two major competing philosophies of taxonomy, following the work of Hennig (1950, 1966). Which of the two hominoid assortments to accept depends not only upon the weighting one attaches to different categories of evidence, but also upon the evolutionary philosophy one follows. *Evolutionary systematists* take into account the unique morphological and behavioural features of *Homo* that distinguish it from the great apes: thus they classify *Homo*, its ancestors and collaterals, in the Hominidae, and the great apes, African and Asian, in the Pongidae. The *cladists*, on the other hand, classify groups according to the sequence of divergences or branchings into 'sister groups'. Since the evidence points to an ancient branching time for the orang-utan from the African hominoids, cladists would place the former in Pongidae, and denote its sister-group — comprising humans, chimpanzees and gorillas — by the term Hominidae (Mayr 1981, Conroy 1990).

We need a new systematics that will satisfy both the fossil evidence and the molecular interpretations, the evolutionary systematists and the cladists. In the meantime, pending a consensus, we continue to use the term hominid to refer exclusively to the family of human beings and their Plio-Pleistocene ancestors and collaterals. In this article I follow the same convention.

ESSENTIAL MORPHOLOGICAL FEATURES OF THE HOMINIDS

Among the more important, commonly recognized differences between the extant non-human primates and *Homo sapiens*, are anatomical features and functional or behavioural traits. The principal features in each category — morphological and functional — are as follows:

A Morphological
1 habitual fully erect posture;
2 bipedal locomotion marked by striding gait and running (see Figure 1);
3 lower limbs much longer than upper limbs;
4 comparatively vertical face;
5 great reduction in the projection of jaws;
6 great reduction of the canine teeth;
7 absence of a bony diastema in the upper jaw for the reception of the tip of the lower canine;
8 prominent nose with elongated tip;
9 median furrow or philtrum of the upper lip;
10 outwardly rolled mucous membrane of the lips;
11 well-marked bony chin;
12 a forward lumbar convexity or 'hollow back' (see Figure 2);
13 non-opposable great toe, set in line with other toes;
14 foot arched transversely, and from front to back;
15 relative hairlessness of body;
16 absence of tactile hairs;
17 brain much larger than the largest non-human primate brains, both absolutely and relative to body size;
18 occiput of the cranium projects backwards;
19 highly rolled margin or helix of the ear;
20 absence of premaxillary bone from anterior aspect of face;
21 iliac fossae or pelvic blades face each other (see Figure 3);
22 longer post-natal growth period.

B Functional, cultural and social
1   articulate speech and language;
2   implements – the development of a complex culture;
3   dependence for survival primarily on cultural adjustments;
4   potentialities for development of intelligence;
5   capacity for symbolic thought – abstract thinking, substitute activity.

I shall concentrate in this section on morphological features.

Clark (1964) listed nineteen defining processes or morphological complexes of the family Hominidae. All of these were such that their presence or absence could be ascertained from fossilized skeletal remains. Sixteen were cranial and dental; three were postcranial (relating to parts of the upright human skeleton that lie below the skull). Pilbeam (1968) simplified the list to two principal sets of criteria: evidence of habitual bipedalism as the chief mode of locomotion and the presence of teeth of an essentially human form. Between these two extremes, Tobias (1983b) specified seven major aspects of the hominid structural pattern. The fossil record preserves evidence of all of these seven clusters of traits.

The seven sets of characteristics relate to (1) upright posture and habitual bipedal locomotion; (2) restructuring and redeployment of the upper limb so that it is no longer employed for locomotion, but becomes an instrument for carrying and for manipulating; (3) dental changes, most notably reduction of the canine teeth; (4) enlargement of the brain and its receptacle, the neuro-cranium, out of proportion to changes in body size; (5) differential enlargement of certain, well-defined areas of the brain; (6) remodelling of the cranium and the mandible; and (7) the development, at least in some more advanced hominids, of the structural basis of language and speech, both the peripheral mechanism of the vocal tract and the central, controlling mechanism of the cerebral motor speech areas.

The brain features may be inferred from fossil remains because of the happy circumstance that the endocranial cast (that is, the cast of the interior of the brain-case), whether a natural endocast or an artificial one, faithfully reflects impressions that the brain, in life, imprinted upon the inner surface of the cranial bones. This, in turn, permits us to infer the size and form of the brain that once was protected within the braincase.

Uprightness and bipedalism

The attainment of habitual and prolonged upright posture and habitual bipedal locomotion involves a number of skeletal adjustments (see Figures 1, 2, 3 and 6). These include (1) alterations in the base of the cranium and the head–neck (cranio-vertebral) alignment; (2) the development of structural mechanisms for the transmission of body weight down the spinal column, through the upper part of the sacrum, and through the ilium of the hip-bone; (3) substantial modification of the pelvis so as to make the new locomotor mechanism possible without the impairment of the other primal function of the pelvis, namely to serve as the birth canal; (4) adjustments in the head and neck, length, curvature and form of the thigh-bone (femur), in the structure and mechanism of the knee-joint, and in the ankle, foot and toes.

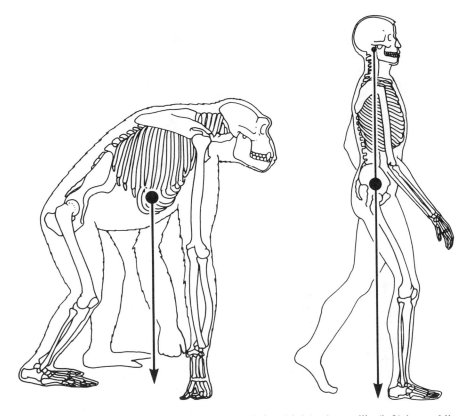

Figure 1 In contrast with the bipedal human being (right), the gorilla (left) is an obliquely quadrupedal animal. When a gorilla stands on all fours, its spinal column is at an oblique angle to the ground, not parallel to the ground as in most completely quadrupedal animals. In this position the gorilla's weight-line falls between the fore-limbs and the hind-limbs. When the human being stands and walks in the upright position, the axis of the body mass (or the 'centre of gravity') passes from the joint on the base of the cranium, close to the vertebral column, through left and right hip-joints, and so down the lower limbs to the feet. Although various forms of bipedalism occur in primates other than humans, the peculiarly human form of bipedalism is a distinctive adaptation that seems to have been acquired early in the process of hominization. Accompanying this adaptation are anatomical adjustments in most parts of the skeleton and the locomotor apparatus from the cranial base to the feet

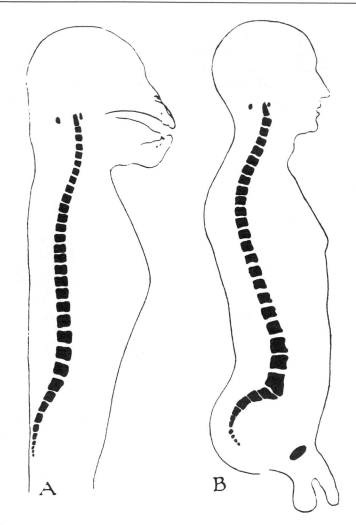

Figure 2 Median sagittal sections through the head and trunk of a chimpanzee (A) and of a man (B). The sections show the differences in the curvatures of the vertebral columns of ape and human, the cervical, lumbar and sacral curves being more marked in the upright human being. The sequence of vertebral body sizes from above downwards is another distinguishing feature: in an upright human, the sizes increase more markedly towards the lower lumbar vertebrae, since each vertebra regularly supports a greater mass than the one above it

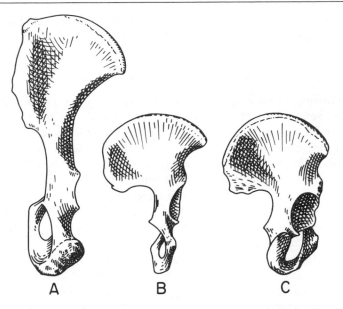

Figure 3 Right *ossa coxae* (pelvic bones) of chimpanzee (A), *Australopithecus africanus* (B) and a modern human (C). In each illustration, the bone is oriented with the plane of the ilium at right angles to the line of sight, and with the anterior superior iliac spine pointing to the viewer's right. The transversely expanded ilia of man and *Australopithecus* contrast with the narrow, vertically expanded ilium of the ape

The fossil evidence indicates that elements of this bipedal complex were developed at an early stage in hominization.

Restructuring of the upper limb

The restructuring of the upper limb has converted it from an organ involved in weight bearing, standing, walking or running in a quadrupedal gait, or in hanging from branches overhead and travelling by hand over hand movement (brachiation), to a limb freed to a large extent, or completely, from locomotor activities. With this emancipation of the limb from a postural and locomotor role, it has become redeployed and specialized for such functions as carrying (for example, food) and manipulation. These changes have involved the shortening of the whole limb, the straightening of the finger-bones, relative elongation of the thumb and the development of the function of opposition (the ability to move the thumb so that its pulp can be placed against the pulp of each of the four other fingers).

These changes are evident in fossil hominids, but some of them developed later in geological time than did the specializations connected with uprightness and bipedalism. Thus, hominids fairly advanced in some respects retained certain upper limb features that were not specific to hominids but could be described as primitive traits, shared with apes.

The hominization of teeth

The most conspicuous single dental feature is that whereas the canine teeth of apes are relatively large and have tips that protrude beyond the surfaces of adjacent tooth crowns, those of hominids are generally relatively small and have tips protruding only slightly, or not at all, beyond the level of adjacent tooth crowns. If the condition in apes represents the ancestral state of the canines, we must assume that a reduction occurred during hominid evolution. The fossil evidence indicates that canine reduction was achieved early in the evolving hominids, possibly as early as the attainment of habitual uprightness. It seems that these two features are the earliest morphological indicators of the emergence of the Hominidae so far attested.

The transformations of the other teeth affected the form, structure, shape, cusp pattern and enamel thickness of the tooth crowns, the absolute and relative crown sizes (including dental step-index values − i.e. the sizes of some teeth in relationship to those of other teeth), the extent of the pulp cavity (or the 'nerve' of the tooth), the number of roots and their form and structure, the patterns of occlusion between maxillary (upper) and mandibular (lower) teeth, and the nature of the masticatory functions. Overall tooth size followed two different trends within the hominids: in some species the cheek-teeth (premolars and molars) underwent enlargement, while in others, including those on the direct lineage of modern humans, there was a marked and long-continuing reduction in size (see Figure 4).

Brain enlargement

The capacity of the brain-case of the early hominids was, in absolute terms, no bigger than that of the extant great apes. Later hominids (from about 2.0 million years ago (Myr) onwards) showed a strong enlargement of endocranial capacity, and this increase was out of proportion to changes in body size. There was thus an evolutionary trend towards increasing both absolute and relative endocranial capacity. This trend was sustained until, in modern humans, the average endocranial capacity is in absolute terms some three times that of great apes (see Figure 5). Since the brain accounts for a large percentage of the total endocranial capacity, it may be inferred that not merely the capacity, but the brain itself trebled in absolute size, and showed a marked increment in relative size, between early and later hominids.

Selective encephalization

The surfaces of the brains or endocranial casts of hominids reveal that the

44

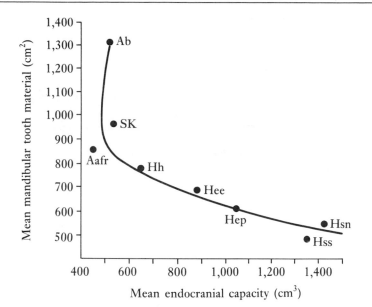

Figure 4 Brains and teeth of hominids. In this graph, the average tooth size and the average endocranial capacity are plotted for each of a series of hominid taxa (species or subspecies). The tooth size or 'tooth material' is calculated as the sum of the 'crown areas' of the cheek-teeth (the two premolars and the three molars) for each taxon. The earlier hominids lie on the left and the more recent hominids on the right of the graph.

Broadly, the graph shows that, from an early presumptive ancestor (Aafr=*A. africanus*), with small endocranial capacity and moderate tooth size, two lines of change may be recognized. In the upper line from *A. africanus* to SK (Swartkrans=*A. robustus crassidens*) and Ab (*A. boisei*), there occurred a marked enlargement of the teeth with a very small increase in brain size. This line became extinct between 1.5 and 1.0 Myr BP. The lower line covers various species and subspecies of *Homo*: as compared with *A. africanus*, this line is characterized by marked increase in endocranial capacity and a progressive diminution in tooth size, culminating in the extraordinarily large brains and diminutive teeth of modern humans

Key: Aafr, *Australopithecus africanus*; SK, Swartkrans (the site containing *A. robustus crassidens*); Ab, *A. boisei* (the 'hyper-robust' australopithecine); Hh, *Homo habilis*; Hee, *H. erectus erectus* (subspecies of *H. erectus* from Java, Indonesia); Hep, *H. erectus pekinensis* (subspecies of *H. erectus* from China); Hsn, *H. sapiens neanderthalensis* (Neanderthal Man); Hss, *H. sapiens sapiens* (the modern subspecies of *H. sapiens*)

enlargement did not affect all areas to the same degree. Selectively enlarged areas include the frontal and especially the parietal lobes of the cerebrum. These changes had the effect, in more advanced hominids, of expanding the brain transversely in these two regions. Moderate to marked asymmetry of some areas of the cerebral hemispheres became apparent, particularly of the post-rolandic part of the lateral (Sylvian) fissure: the resulting degree of asymmetry probably exceeded that in ape brains.

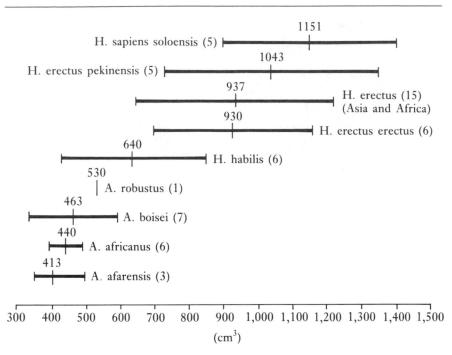

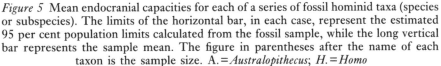

Figure 5 Mean endocranial capacities for each of a series of fossil hominid taxa (species or subspecies). The limits of the horizontal bar, in each case, represent the estimated 95 per cent population limits calculated from the fossil sample, while the long vertical bar represents the sample mean. The figure in parentheses after the name of each taxon is the sample size. A.=*Australopithecus*; H.=*Homo*

Remodelling of the skull

Because of all the other changes at the head end of the body, it was inevitable that the skull would be remodelled to accommodate and adapt to these transformations. The cranial remodelling was in accordance with (1) the repositioning of the head upon an upright trunk, involving changes in the cranial base and the poise of the cranium (see Figure 6); (2) alterations in the size of the dentition and in masticatory habit and vigour; (3) the enlargement, transverse expansion and refashioning of the brain; and (4) the development of the vocal tract above the larynx, and of a highly mobile tongue.

Development of spoken language

Language and articulate speech have a dual structural underlay. Their development requires both the emergence of the speech areas of the cerebrum, and peripheral changes in the airway and the food way, so as to form a vocal tract capable of producing vowel and consonant sounds. The

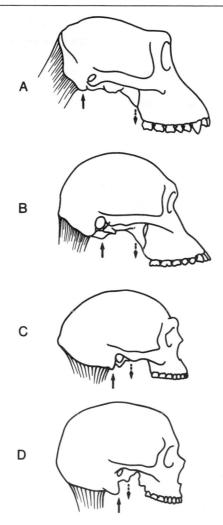

Figure 6 The crania of four higher primates, brought to the same length of the brain-case, to show important features of the poise and support of the cranium. The diagrams illustrate the varying degrees of development of the nuchal muscles (muscles of the nape of the neck) and the direction of the pull of their fibres. The downward-directed, dashed arrow indicates the approximate position of the centre of gravity of each skull; the upward-directed, solid arrow represents the position of the supporting occipital condyles. Note that, while the condyles have changed to a progressively more anterior position, from ape (A) through *Australopithecus africanus* (B) and *Homo erectus* (C) to the modern human (D), the position of the cranial centre of gravity has moved posteriorly, as the brain case has enlarged and the teeth and jaws diminished – until in the modern human, the weight-line and the condyles are almost coincident. It is inferred that these adjustments have been accompanied by progressive diminution of the bulk of the nuchal muscles and of the area of their purchase on the cranium and neck vertebrae, and by changes in the relative direction of the pull of their fibres

central basis of spoken language lies in the expansion of specific cerebral areas, namely Broca's area in the lower lateral part of the frontal lobe, Wernicke's area in the lower part of the parietal and the upper part of the temporal lobes, and the supplementary motor area on the medial surface of the cerebral hemisphere.

Some of the chief changes in the upper part of the respiratory tract, which helped to change it into a vocal tract, were: (1) the loss of intimate contact between the epiglottis and soft palate, (2) a change in the orientation of the entrance to the larynx, so that it comes to face posteriorly, (3) the midline interruption by the food way of continuity between the nasal cavities and the larynx, (4) the supplementation of the nasal airway by an oral airway, (5) the appearance and expansion of the nasal part of the pharynx (nasopharynx) and (6) the 'descent' of the larynx (see Article 5).

HOMINIDS AND THE FOSSIL RECORD

With these hallmarks of hominid status in mind it is possible to detect, in various early hominoid fossils, or fossil 'populations', the presence or absence of hominid features. In this enquiry, we recognize two broad stages. The first is that of hominid origins, by which we mean the first emergence of the Hominidae. The second refers to the further evolution of established hominids. Not only do these two stages follow each other in chronological sequence, but their study also requires profoundly differing strategies of research.

Strategy one: the phase of hominid emergence

Formerly, the anatomy and dating of the fossils, along with the comparative anatomy of related living forms, provided the only basis for statements about the origins and evolution of hominids. Within the last three decades, however, molecular biologists have shed new light on hominid origins.

The study of molecular systematics and evolution is based on immunological distances, protein sequencing and DNA hybridization data in living organisms. This approach was founded upon the concept of the molecular clock, according to which the closer the 'distance' between two species or populations of living organisms, the more recent was their divergence from their latest common ancestors, and the greater the distance, the more ancient their point of ancestral divergence. It has thus proved possible to compile a hierarchy of divergence times among various species. Granted the assumptions inherent in the notion of the 'molecular clock', and given one or more well-dated palaeontological milestones, 'absolute dates' may be postulated for the origins of groups whose relative divergence times have been established from molecular data.

Since the discovery of the structure of the DNA molecule and the deciphering of the genetic code, new molecular technologies have been applied to evolutionary problems. These are based on the sequencing of proteins, nuclear DNA and mitochondrial DNA, and on DNA hybridization experiments. Biomolecular specialists applied these methods to the problem of hominid origins, though at first with scant regard for palaeontological or anatomical facts. For their part, students of fossils initially paid little attention to the new molecular information. Though the two groups of scholars were probing the same set of evolutionary events, they did not appear to speak the same language.

By 1975, contradictions had emerged between inferences drawn by investigators of the fossil record and those based on molecular studies. At risk of over-simplification, the resulting controversy could be characterized as 'fossils versus molecules'. The critical bone of contention at that stage related directly to the dating of hominid origins. The controversy revolved around (1) the belief that some fossil evidence pointed to the emergence of the Hominidae some 15 to 20 million years before the present (Myr BP), and (2) an interpretation of molecular evidence as pointing to the late separation of Hominidae from apes, between 4 and 10 Myr BP. The two standpoints were epitomized by such assertions as 'Fossils are more important, because they provide the hard facts of evolution', and 'Molecules are more important, because they are close to the genes − and it is gene-complexes that have evolved.'

At a symposium held in 1974 (Salzano 1975), a plea was made for a synthesis of these two approaches to human evolution. At that time I argued that 'The fossil data bearing on hominid evolution are reconcilable with the evidence of close molecular similarities between living pongids and *Homo sapiens*' (Tobias 1975: 114). Palaeontologists have since examined their fossils more critically, while molecular biologists have looked more closely at their concepts and assumptions. As a result, the desired synthesis between the palaeontological and molecular results has been largely achieved. The synthesis was presaged in the volume edited by Salzano (1975), announced in a symposium organised in 1982 by Ciochon and Corrucini, and consummated in the same year (Chagas 1983).

Today, the major research strategies in the study of hominid origins comprise (1) the palaeoanatomy of fossils, (2) the comparative morphology of related living forms, including cytogenetic (chromosomal) data, and (3) the molecular biological study of living hominids (*Homo sapiens*) and non-hominid primates.

Strategy two: the further evolution of established hominids

To study hominids, after their separation from the apes, a different strategy is employed. In research on the patterns of hominid evolution from about 4 to about 1 Myr BP, molecular data play little if any part. Rather, the major focus is upon the palaeoanatomy of hominid fossils. This is supplemented by data from three essential sources: studies in dating, in palaeoecology and – from about 2.5 Myr onwards – in archaeology. Thus the palaeoanatomy of fossils is complemented and enriched by the parallel testimony of material culture and by ecological insights, from which may be drawn inferences concerning such matters as group size, distribution, diet, technical and social intelligence, linguistic ability and ideational forms.

THE EMERGENCE OF THE HOMINIDS

Molecular studies agree in showing that humans, chimpanzees and gorillas, taken together, are clearly distinct, in a number of genetic features, from orang-utans. This sorting of the four major living hominoids points to a

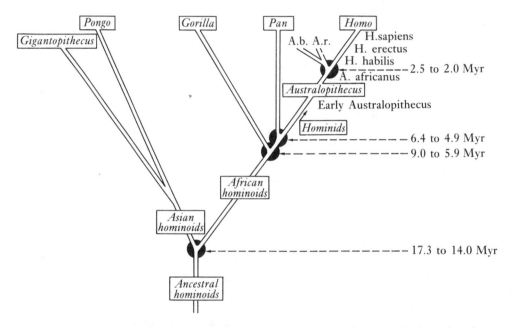

Figure 7 Schema of the main divergences in the evolution of the Hominoidea, based on molecular data for the earlier three divergences, and on palaeontological and geological evidence for the latest one at 2.5 to 2.0 Myr (millions of years before the present). The diagram shows estimated dates for the divergences leading to *Pongo* (orang-utan), *Gorilla* (gorilla) and *Pan* (chimpanzee). In this schema, it is accepted that the molecular evidence indicates a somewhat earlier divergence of *Gorilla* from the African hominoids and a somewhat later *Pan*–hominid divergence. However, some molecular biologists consider that the evidence points to a virtually simultaneous origin of *Gorilla*, *Pan*, and the Hominidae (in the narrow sense). On the other hand, the schema indicates a three-fold splitting (trifurcation) of the hominid lineage to give rise to *A. boisei*, *A. robustus* and *H. habilis*, at 2.5 to 2.0 Myr BP. It is possible, however, that an earlier split might have generated *A. boisei* and a somewhat later split, *A. robustus* and *H. habilis*. Further research and the discovery of more fossil specimens are necessary to resolve the differences between these interpretations

relatively ancient separation of the Asian great ape from the other three. The point of divergence is calculated by various methods as having been situated in Miocene times, between 17.3 and 14.0 Myr BP (see Figure 7).

Furthermore, molecular studies reveal that humans and chimpanzees are somewhat more closely related than are humans and gorillas. It is inferred that the gorilla separated from the remaining African hominoids (chimpanzees and humans) a little earlier than humans and chimpanzees parted company. The gorilla divergence has been variously set at as early a date as 9.0 Myr, or as late as 5.9 Myr BP (see Figure 7). The range of dates reflects the various methods employed for calibrating the 'molecular clock'. Some studies use a linear and others a non-linear scale, some a single, well-dated palaeontological divergence and others several divergences, in order to calibrate the clock (Gingerich 1985). There is no consensus on the right approach to adopt in molecular evolutionary studies; nor is there any agreement as to which nucleotide sequences, or which combinations of them, provide the most reliable results. Suffice it to say that, as more molecular approaches are tested, the posited relationships among living hominoids and the sequence of inferred divergence times have been increasingly confirmed. It is to be hoped that progressive refinement of the techniques will narrow the range of dates proposed for each major divergence, and thus enable us to decide which of the many possible interpretations of the molecular data, illustrated schematically in Figure 8, is correct.

After the divergence of the gorilla line from that of the African early hominoids, the human and chimpanzee lineages shared a common phylogenetic pathway for a further period variously estimated as of one to several million years. The chimpanzee–human divergence was the most recent of the major hominoid divergences. The date for this event is estimated as 6.4 to 4.9 Myr BP (Raza *et al.* 1983, Wu *et al.* 1983, Sibley and Ahlquist 1984, Andrews 1985, Pickford 1985, Thomas 1985, Sakoyama *et al.* 1987, Ueda *et al.* 1989). These last dates are considered to mark the origin of the Hominidae. Perhaps we should be more cautious and say that they mark the emergence of the *molecular* genetic constellation of the hominids.

May we assume that the earliest anatomical features distinguishing the hominids emerged at the same time as the critical molecular traits? Among the features assumed to have characterized the earliest phases of hominid evolution are the development of the anatomical basis of erect posture and bipedal gait and the emergence of distinctive hominid dental traits, most notably the reduction of canine teeth. There is no incontrovertible evidence that derived features of the brain, whether of size or of surface morphology, were present in the very early hominids. Nor is there evidence in the earliest hominids of a cultural life reflected in stone or bone tools. In other words, some features that are widely accepted as hallmarks of the hominids appeared later than others. For example, the enlargement of the brain, from an average size similar to those in modern apes, towards the expanded state shown by later

51

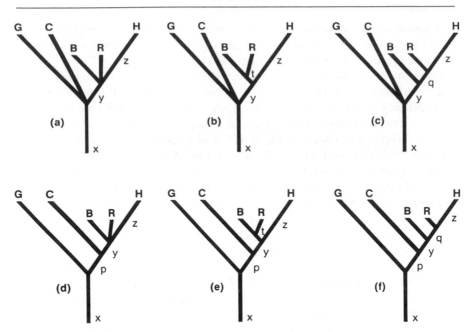

Figure 8 Six of the possible patterns of hominoid evolution. The divergences between African apes and hominids are based on molecular data and show two principal alternative patterns. The diagrams in the lower row reflect a common interpretation of the molecular data, namely that ancestral gorillas diverged from the other early African hominoids before the line leading to the chimpanzees diverged from the Hominidae *sensu stricto*. The diagrams in the upper row reflect another interpretation, namely that the gorilla and chimpanzee lineages diverged from the hominid line at virtually the same time. In each row three different patterns of further hominid diversification are shown. On the basis of fossil data, some hold that the robust (R) and hyper-robust (B) australopithecines diverged from the line of the genus *Homo* at virtually the same time (a, d). Another view has it that there was a common R–B stem, which first diverged from the *Homo* line, and some time later underwent a further divergence into *A. boisei* (B) and *A. robustus* (R), as in (b) and (e). Yet a third possible interpretation of the available fossil data suggests that *A. boisei* (B) diverged from the other contemporary hominids, and that this was followed some time later by another hominid divergence, that of *A. robustus* (R) from the *Homo* lineage, as in (c) and (f). The six diagrams reveal varying numbers of evolutionary branchings: two branchings in (a); three branchings in (b), (c), and (d); four branchings in (e) and (f). Two different kinds of branchings are shown: dichotomous and trichotomous. The choice among these six patterns, and even further possible schemata, will ultimately depend on the attainment of consensus among molecular evolutionists and on the discovery of more, and better-dated, hominoid fossils.

Key: G, gorilla; C, chimpanzee; B, *Australopithecus boisei*; R, *Australopithecus robustus*; H, *Homo*. x, pre-split African hominoids; y, early Hominidae (post-split); z, the lineage of *Homo*; p, last common ancestor of chimpanzee and Hominidae; q, last common ancestor of *A. robustus* and *Homo*; t, last common ancestor of *A. robustus* and *A. boisei* hominids, did not become evident until *Homo habilis* arrived on the scene just over 2 Myr BP.

If we accept that the features of modern humans are end-results of hominization, the fossil record shows that they appeared in a mosaic fashion: some early, some late. Hence, it may be difficult to detect demonstrable hominid anatomical features in all of the earliest claimants for hominid status. It is very likely that mosaicism also characterized the *molecular* evolution of the Hominoidea. Moreover, the appearance of the earliest *anatomical* features of the hominids was not necessarily synchronous with the emergence of the *molecular* constitution of the hominids, although assumptions to the contrary are often made.

What, then, does the fossil record tell us about hominid emergence?

FOSSIL CLAIMANTS TO EARLIEST HOMINID STATUS

The molecular data suggest that we should look for the earliest possible hominids in the period between 6.4 and 4.9 Myr BP. Unfortunately, however, we have very few apposite hominoid fossils from within this time range. Some of those we do possess do not include anatomical parts that would permit one to say whether the bones belonged to early hominids, or to early members of the chimpanzee lineage, or even to the last common ancestral population of chimpanzees and hominids.

The remains (see Figure 9 for locations) include a lower molar crown from Lukeino in the Tugen Hills, south of Lake Turkana in northern Kenya. It is dated to about 6.0 Myr BP. Although originally claimed to be a hominid molar, it would seem judicious to regard it as an indeterminate hominoid molar (Andrews, cited by Hill and Ward 1988). As its morphology has been said to include chimpanzee-like features, these may relate it to the last common ancestor of chimpanzees and humans, or it may represent a post-divergence proto-chimpanzee (Kramer 1986).

From Lothagam, south-west of Lake Turkana, Kenya, has come part of a mandible with the first molar and roots of the second and third molars. Discovered in 1967, the mandible has long been regarded as hominid and australopithecine. Recent studies relate it to the early East African hominids assigned to *Australopithecus afarensis* (Kramer 1986, Hill and Ward 1988). Dated to about 5.5 to 5.0 Myr BP, the Lothagam jaw is thus the earliest specimen to show hominid structure. Conroy (1990) describes it as 'the oldest *undisputed* hominid specimen from Africa'.

The second oldest specimen, whose hominid status is agreed upon by those who have studied it, is the Tabarin jaw fragment found in 1984 in the Chemeron Formation north of Lake Baringo in Kenya. Its date is between 4.9 and 4.15 Myr BP and this specimen, like that of Lothagam, is considered likely to belong to *A. afarensis*. Although mandibles are not the most suitable bones from which to identify the genus and species among hominoids, fine

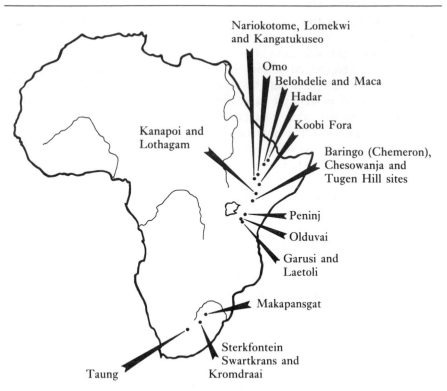

Figure 9 Map of Africa showing the approximate positions of the principal sites at which early hominid fossils have been discovered

analysis of the features of the jaw does seem to indicate that it is an early hominid (Hill 1985, Ward and Hill 1987, Hill and Ward 1988).

A fragment of the proximal end of a left humerus was found in the Chemeron Formation of the Tugen Hills, Kenya, in 1973. It shows features that appear to mark it as a hominoid humerus, though whether it is hominid or not remains problematical (Pickford *et al.* 1983, Senut 1983, Hill and Ward 1988). The specimen falls into the time range we are considering here: it was derived from a layer which is over 4.15 Myr but less than 5.07 Myr in age. This specimen illustrates that not all early hominoid specimens show enough distinctive features to diagnose them as hominid.

From Sahabi in Libya have come several specimens for which hominoid status has been claimed: these comprise a disputed partial left clavicle, the distal part of a left fibula and a fragment of a right parietal bone. Although the latter two specimens show anatomically interesting features, their claimed hominoid status is not yet proven (Boaz 1980, 1987, Boaz and Meikle 1982, Hill and Ward 1988). They are dated to approximately 5.0 Myr BP.

A well-preserved portion of the distal end of a humerus was discovered at

Kanapoi in Kenya in 1965. It shows seemingly hominid features, though on anatomy alone it is virtually impossible to determine its genus and species. The specimen is probably about 4.0 Myr in age, and Hill and Ward (1988) have suggested that it quite probably belonged to *A. afarensis*.

Two specimens about 4.0 Myr old were found in 1981 in the Middle Awash Valley, some 75 km south of Hadar in Ethiopia. From Belohdelie came a number of fragments, three of which have been joined to form much of an adult hominid frontal bone. It is part of a small cranium and the endocranial capacity would evidently have been low, as in apes and in early hominid specimens of the genus *Australopithecus*. It may represent a population of early *A. afarensis* (Clark *et al.* 1984, White 1984, Asfaw 1987). Some 700 metres to the south-west, at Maca, was found the proximal part of a left femur which is identified as having belonged to an adolescent hominid (Clark *et al.* 1984, White 1984). By modern human standards the bone would have been attributed to a youth of 16 or 17 years (White 1984). White has pointed out the presence of two anatomical features that 'appear to represent adaptations to a habitually bipedal mode of locomotion'. If his interpretation is correct, this specimen, which is dated to 4.0 to 3.5 Myr BP, would seem to provide the oldest evidence of habitual uprightness yet unearthed.

Lothagam, Tabarin, Kanapoi and Belohdelie form a scanty cluster of specimens that appear to possess some features that are recognizably hominid. This sample is dated to between 5.5 and 4.0 Myr BP. The specimens therefore seemingly confirm what the molecular information has suggested: namely, that anatomically recognizable hominids were in existence by the terminal Miocene and early Pliocene epochs. These fossils appear to represent one or more post-divergence, early hominid populations. The six-million-year-old Lukeino molar would seem to have belonged either to the postulated last common ancestors of chimpanzees and hominids, that is, to the pre-divergence population, or to the post-divergence, proto-chimpanzee lineage.

Hence, several of the most crucial gaps in the fossil hominoid record remain to be filled. We need to discover and diagnose adequate physical remains representing three postulated populations: the pre-divergence common ancestors of the human and chimpanzee lineages, the post-divergence, proto-chimpanzee populations, and the post-divergence, earliest populations of the hominid lineage.

Similarly, from earlier deposits, we have yet to recover and identify fossils representing the previous divergence, namely the pre-divergence, common ancestors of gorilla–chimpanzee–human, the post-divergence, proto-gorilla lineage, and the post-divergence, chimpanzee–human lineage. Deposits of the appropriate age (9.0 to 5.9 Myr BP) are known in Africa and some have yielded fragmentary hominoid specimens, for example the Samburu Hills maxilla from Kenya (about 8.0 Myr BP) and the Lukeino molar (about 6.0 Myr BP). The yet older remains of a partial talus from the Muruyur Beds in the Tugen Hills of Kenya (older than 13 Myr) and of two cheek-teeth from

Ngorora in the same area of Kenya (about 11.0 Myr) have been identified as hominoid, but their morphology does not permit a more precise taxonomic assignment. Even on the earliest date proposed for the gorilla divergence (9.0 Myr BP), these specimens represent populations that seemingly preceded it.

Here, then, are two hypothesized nodes of divergence where the palaeontologist still has to catch up with the molecular biologist, or − it may be fairer to say − where the hypotheses of the molecular evolutionists have not yet been confirmed by well-dated and well-identified fossil discoveries. In the light of these deficiencies, the search for the postulated common ancestral and derivative lineages at these Mio-Pliocene depths has become more urgent, and is likely to be intensified in coming years.

PLIO-PLEISTOCENE FOSSIL HOMINIDS FROM AFRICA

Historical and geographical note

In the last sixty-five years Africa has yielded a veritable hoard of fossil specimens that have been assigned to the Hominidae (see Figure 9 for site locations). In the second quarter of the twentieth century South Africa was the scene of critical discoveries. The Buxton Limeworks at Taung (1924), then in the northern Cape Province, and the sites of Sterkfontein (1936−) and Kromdraai (1938−) in the southern Transvaal, furnished the first remains of ancient hominids. Up to the outbreak of the Second World War, only one East African site, Garusi, near Lake Eyasi in northern Tanganyika, had yielded a single hominid fragment, but the outbreak of war delayed publication.

Immediately after the war, two further South African caves, Makapansgat (1947−) and Swartkrans (1948−), both in the Transvaal, yielded hominid fossils. In the ensuing forty years, although hundreds of further hominid specimens emerged from four of the five South African sites, only one new early hominid-bearing locality, Gladysvale, has come to light in the Transvaal and one, Uraha, in Malawi. The paucity of new southern African, Plio-Pleistocene sites has recently led a few investigators to search for additional fossil localities in the Transvaal. Opportunities in this direction are extensive.

In the last thirty-five years an immense series of discoveries has flowed from Tanzania (from 1955), Kenya (from 1965) and Ethiopia (from 1967). At least sixteen East African hominid-bearing sites, including the oldest thus far found, have added immeasurably to the knowledge of hominid evolution between 4.0 and 1.0 Myr BP. Table 1 lists the most important sites bearing fossil hominid remains within these time limits, and the dates when discoveries were made at each site.

Table 1 African sites of early hominid discoveries
(Pliocene to early Middle Pleistocene)

Site	Dates
SOUTH AFRICA	
Taung (Bophuthatswana)	1924
Sterkfontein (Transvaal)	1936–93
Kromdraai (Transvaal)	1938–80
Makapansgat (Transvaal)	1947–83
Swartkrans (Transvaal)	1948–87
Gladysvale (Transvaal)	1992–3
MALAWI	
Uraha	1991
TANZANIA	
Garusi	1939
Olduvai	1955–86
Peninj (Lake Natron)	1964
Laetoli	1974–9
KENYA	
Around Lake Baringo	
Chemeron (West Baringo)	1965–84
Chesowanja (East Baringo)	1970–8
Around Lake Turkana	
Kanapoi (south-west)	1965
Lothagam (south-west)	1967
Koobi Fora (east)	1968–90
Nariokotome (west)	1984–8
Lomekwi (west)	1985
Kangatukuseo (west)	1985
Kangaki (west)	1985
ETHIOPIA	
Omo	1967–74
Hadar	1973–92
Middle Awash	1981–90
CHAD	
Yayo (Koro-Toro)	1961

The dates given for each site are those for the first hominid
discovery made at that site and, where applicable, for the
most recently made hominid discovery known to the
compiler.

Some issues in classification

The problem of how to classify the African hominid fossils, representing hundreds of individuals, has provided much food for thought and argument. An accepted procedure is to recognize several categories within a family. The major subdivisions are:

> Family
> > Genus
> > > Species

Today, tens of millions of species of living things are known to exist. This diversity has led to the recognition of many more rankings within a family. For example, a more complete hierarchy embraces the following:

> Family
> > Subfamily
> > > Tribe
> > > > Subtribe
> > > > > Genus
> > > > > > Subgenus
> > > > > > > Species
> > > > > > > > Subspecies

It is not proposed here to review the lengthy controversies concerning the classification of the Hominidae. Probably far too much time and energy have been expended on this topic. Nowhere in biology is the division into 'splitters' and 'lumpers' more acute than in palaeoanthropology. The splitters tend to emphasize diagnosis (distinguishing between things) and analysis (separating things into their components); the lumpers incline towards definition (setting limits to things) and synthesis (putting things together into larger units). Thus, splitters are disposed to make very small units and many species or genera; as Simpson (1945: 23) delightfully puts it, 'their opponents say that if they can tell two animals apart, they place them in different genera, and if they cannot tell them apart, they place them in different species'! Lumpers lean towards large units: 'their opponents say that if a carnivore is neither a dog nor a bear they call it a cat'.

Hominid systematics have oscillated from splitting to lumping and now, it seems, back to splitting. The various genera that have been proposed within the Hominidae during this century are listed in Table 2. The list of eleven proposed genera is not exhaustive. However, for the last twenty-five or more years, most scholars found that their classificatory needs were satisfied by the recognition of two hominid genera, *Australopithecus* and *Homo*. This is still the view of many investigators.

In recent years, several investigators have resurrected the previously 'sunk' genus, *Paranthropus* (see summary in Grine 1988, Aiello and Dean 1990).

Table 2   Proposed genera within the hominidae

Proposed genus	Widely accepted later designation	Recent appellation
Atlanthropus	*Homo erectus*	n.c.
Australopithecus	n.c.	n.c.
Australanthropus	*Australopithecus*	n.c.
Eoanthropus	*Homo sapiens* (+*Pongo pygmaeus*)	n.c.
Meganthropus	*Homo erectus*	n.c.
Palaeanthropus	*Homo erectus*	n.c.
Paranthropus	*Australopithecus*	*Paranthropus*
Pithecanthropus	*Homo erectus*	n.c.
Plesianthropus	*Australopithecus*	n.c.
Praeanthropus	*Australopithecus*	n.c.
Sinanthropus	*Homo erectus*	n.c.
Zinjanthropus	*Australopithecus*	*Paranthropus*
11 genera	2 genera	3 genera

n.c. = no change.

This reversion to a trigeneric scheme (*Australopithecus*, *Paranthropus* and *Homo*) appears to be based on the supposed pattern of descent of early hominids and on notions about the systematic status of presumptive sister groups following evolutionary divergences. No up-to-date diagnosis of the generic distinctions between those forms placed in *Paranthropus* and in *Australopithecus* has, to the author's knowledge, been published, though Aiello and Dean (1990) have recently proposed that 'there is sufficient difference between these hominids [two species of *Paranthropus*] and those included in *Australopithecus*, particularly in the anatomy of the skull and dentition, to justify distinction at the generic (genus) level' (Aiello and Dean 1990: 12). There is thus no consensus at present among scholars engaged in studying the early hominids. Some espouse a bigeneric and some a trigeneric classification.

In this regard, it may be worthwhile to consider the use of the subgenus category, where fairly substantial differences between species are present. At one time I was inclined, along with L. S. B. Leakey, to retain (*Paranthropus*) and (*Zinjanthropus*) as subgenera within *Australopithecus*. However, following my own comparative study of early hominid remains, I abandoned even subgeneric distinction between the species of *Australopithecus* (Tobias 1967: 232). The accumulation of many new hominid fossils since that time, and the recognition of more variants, might well have created the need to reconsider and revive hominid subgenera. This approach may offer a solution to the current conflict on the number of hominid genera. It is well to recall the words of Simpson (1945: 24):

> the subgenus is perhaps the most notably neglected rank. When students recognize a definable group of species within what has been called a genus, they too often propose calling the group a separate genus when it could perfectly well and far more conveniently be called a subgenus if it really needs formal designation within the hierarchy.

Other differences of opinion revolve around the number of species within the hominid genera. In the third quarter of the century, most investigators found that six species sufficed, three in *Australopithecus* and three in *Homo*. Recently, a new wave of splitting has overtaken the field, and as many as sixteen hominid species have been proposed.

The differences are more than in the mere number of labels assigned. They betray different approaches to classification, and varying philosophies on the patterns of evolutionary change. These differences also reveal markedly contrasting ideas on the amount of variation within a species. The splitters are inclined to underestimate the permissible degree of intraspecific variability, whereas lumpers recognize broader tolerance limits of variation before they deem that a set of specimens has transgressed the reasonable boundaries of a species. Modern humans are extraordinarily variable; nevertheless, we have no difficulty in accommodating such diverse populations as Australian Aborigines, Alpine Europeans, San Bushmen, Greenland Inuit, Koreans, Nilotic Negroes, American Indians and Andamanese Pygmies, within one species of *Homo sapiens*. We know, too, that *Homo erectus* from China, Indonesia, north-west Africa, East Africa and (possibly) Europe, varied greatly. With these hominid analogues in mind, one might expect earlier hominids, such as *Homo habilis*, *Australopithecus africanus* and *Australopithecus boisei*, to have exhibited strong intraspecific variation. Such differences within a species are especially to be expected when the species concerned is widely dispersed geographically and occurs in the fossil record over a fairly long period. These considerations should support the arguments for marked intraspecific variability and for a lumping of fossil hominid populations into a minimal, not a maximal, number of species.

For the purposes of this chapter, the following simplified, 'lumped' classification will be employed:

GENUS	*Australopithecus*	
SPECIES	?	*afarensis*
SPECIES		*africanus*
SPECIES		*robustus*
SPECIES		*boisei*
GENUS	*Homo*	
SPECIES		*habilis*
SPECIES		*erectus*
SPECIES		*sapiens*

Biological features

The morphological trends of the hominids have already been set out (see pp. 39–48). In the direct human lineage, biological equipment progressively approached the modern form over the last three million years. The skeletal structure showed adaptations to uprightness and bipedalism, even though a capacity for erect posture was seemingly present early in hominid emergence. These skeletal adjustments involved the balance of the cranium on the cervical end of the spinal column, modifications in the vertebrae themselves the better to transmit body weight down through the pelvis to *two* weight-bearing limbs, the restructuring of the pelvis and alteration of virtually all parts of the lower limb. Even in as late a stage as that of *Homo erectus*, the pelvis and thigh-bones had not attained fully modern human morphology.

The upper limbs seem to have retained primitive hominoid traits for a longer time than did the lower limbs. Arms, forearms and hands attained their modern human form later, exemplifying the pattern of mosaic evolution.

The early reduction of the front teeth was rather slight in degree, but from *Australopithecus africanus* onwards, in the direct line of human descent, we find a reduction of the canine teeth, followed, at the stage of *Homo habilis*, by the onset of reduction of the cheek-teeth (molars and premolars). This trend continued up to the appearance of modern *Homo sapiens*.

While dentition and the supporting masticatory apparatus declined, brains were augmented. At the stage of *Australopithecus*, for all four species listed above, the endocranial capacity was small, being comparable in size to the mean capacities of the great apes. At the stage of *Homo habilis*, from 2.3 to 1.6 Myr BP, the first signs of a dramatic increase in brain-size became apparent. As compared with *A. africanus*, the average capacity of *H. habilis* was over 40 per cent greater. From estimates of body size obtained from vertebrae and limb-bones, it is clear that this was not only an absolute, but also a relative increase in brain size.

This trend of encephalization was sustained throughout the next phase, that of *H. erectus*, into that of the earlier populations of *H. sapiens*. It is one of the most unremitting evolutionary tendencies in the development of the modern human species. It has been suggested that its very degree and persistence must have made possible a marked increase in one or more of the following: adaptive capacity, sustained memory, social bonding mechanisms, intelligence, complexity and quality of the feeding-niche, home-range area, group size, and social cognition in the face of ever more complex sociality. One further functional modality emerged as part of selective encephalization: endocasts reveal prominent swellings in those parts of the brain related to the motor speech areas of Broca and Wernicke (see Figure 10).

Broca's cap, the bulge over Broca's area, is not a feature of ape brains or endocasts, but it is represented on the endocasts of *A. africanus* (Schepers 1946, 1950, Tobias, 1983a). It is also revealed in the endocasts of *H. habilis*, *H. erectus* and early *H. sapiens*. In the modern human brain, the inferior parietal lobule, comprising the supramarginal and angular gyri, is considered part of Wernicke's area, which is the second motor speech area of the cerebrum. The corresponding part of the brain or endocast of an ape is not protuberant or bulbous (Bailey *et al.* 1950, Critchley 1953, Geschwind 1965). The endocasts of *A. africanus* resemble those of apes in lacking a regional fullness of the inferior parietal lobule. In other words, there is no surface expression of Wernicke's area in apes or australopithecines; it is however present in *H. habilis*, as it is in *H. sapiens*. (Note that the superior motor speech area lies in the supplementary motor area, Ms II, which is on the *medial* surface of the cerebral hemisphere and is thus not detectable on an endocast.)

Falk (1983) has shown that, as well as in respect of Broca's area, the sulcal

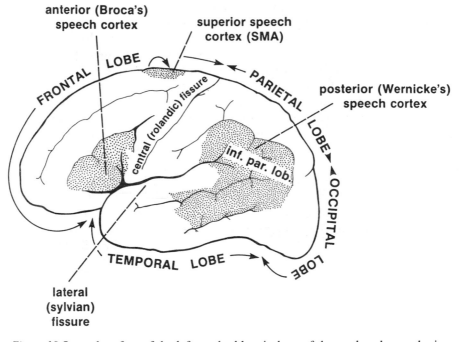

Figure 10 Lateral surface of the left cerebral hemisphere of the modern human brain, showing the lobes of the hemisphere, a few important fissures and the positions of the three cardinal areas concerned with spoken language. Inf. par. lob., inferior parietal lobule (part of Wernicke's area); SMA, supplementary motor area

pattern of the frontal lobe of the brain differs appreciably between modern humans and modern apes. She finds that the frontal lobe impression of *A. africanus* closely resembles that of apes, whereas that of *H. habilis* is nearly identical to that of modern *H. sapiens* (cf. Holloway 1978). Thus, on the evidence of both the sulcal pattern and Broca and Wernicke protrusions, the brain represented by the endocast of *H. habilis* closely resembles that of the modern human.

The representation of these motor speech areas on the endocasts of *H. habilis* led me to propose in 1980 that *H. habilis* possessed the neurological basis for spoken language (Tobias 1980, 1981, 1983a). When this evidence was considered along with the evidence of a complex and diversified stone tool culture (which Mary Leakey (1971) and Glynn Isaac (1978) had revealed), I proposed the hypothesis that *H. habilis* was a speaking primate (Tobias 1983a). Although some have doubted whether even such recent relatives as the Neanderthals could speak properly (Lieberman and Crelin 1971), the proposal, if accepted, would take the frontier of spoken language back from 40 000 years to some 2 million years ago! The range of habiline speech sounds might not have been as great as in the varieties of modern human languages, nor need the linguistic complexities have been so intricate. Nevertheless, it was apparently no coincidence that the dramatic enlargement of the brain and the appearance of the motor speech centres nearly coincided in the phylogenetic history of humankind; nor can it be any accident that these two neurological phenomena coincide with the behavioural evidence that *H. habilis* was dependent on implemental activities.

The author's proposal that *H. habilis* was capable of spoken language has been supported by Falk (1983) and Eccles (1989). As Eccles puts it, 'The increase in the putative speech areas of *Homo habilis* indicates their usage' (1989: 23). Moreover, Lieberman (1988) now appears to accept that *H. habilis* showed the first signs of development towards what he calls the human supralaryngeal vocal tract (see below, and Article 5), so that the earlier argument against a speaking *H. habilis* seems to have fallen away.

Thoughts on language

There are various ways in which language has been considered in relation to hominid evolution:

1 Some scholars have supported the view that the first hominid language was primarily *gestural*, carried on with hand and arm signals rather than vocal sounds. Hewes (1973) amassed much new evidence in support of this hypothesis. The new data have emanated from studies of communication among chimpanzees and other non-human primates (e.g. Gardner and Gardner 1969, 1971, 1978, Premack 1970a, b, 1971, 1976, Menzel 1973).

2 A second approach supports the view that spoken language was preceded

by vocal but non-verbal communication. Livingstone (1973) stressed the capacity to sing. He has argued that anthropoid apes are capable of producing the vocalizations which he calls singing and Westcott (1973) calls humming, and that early hominids might have developed a complex system of calls based primarily on pitch differences. However, several investigators have suggested that the parallels between the biology of bird song and human speech represent analogies rather than homologies, and are irrelevant to the evolution of human speech (Marler 1970, Steklis and Raleigh 1973).

3 A third view builds human speech directly from primate calls. The blending hypothesis of Hockett and Ascher (1964) provides one possible route by which this might have been achieved. According to their hypothesis a call system, such as that of the gibbon, began to 'open' by the blending of various calls. Westcott (1973) agrees that the blending of calls is an important language-generating mechanism, but he does not accept that it is the only such mechanism.

Steklis (1981, 1985) has reviewed the evidence favouring, respectively, the gestural and 'vocal continuity' models of human language origins. He draws attention to similarities in communicative abilities and their neural bases between humans and other Old World primates. In so far as these similarities have arisen through common ancestry and therefore represent homologies, this evidence suggests that the earliest hominids already possessed significantly developed *anlagen*, at the behavioural and neural levels, to make possible the development of a primordial speech system. Gestural language, Steklis concludes, need not have preceded vocal language and probably never played more than a secondary role in hominid propositional communication. Attractive as the signing and singing hypotheses may be, a number of other investigators have emphasized the idea of continuity between the communicative systems of hominids and other Old World primates (Falk 1978, 1980, Holloway 1969, Steklis 1981, Ragir 1985), and have stressed the probable early origin of human speech (Tobias 1980, 1981, 1983a, b, Falk 1983, Eccles 1989).

Buhler (1934), followed and developed by Popper (1972) and Popper and Eccles (1977), recognized two lower levels of language (expressive and signalling), which animal and human languages have in common, and two higher levels (descriptive and argumentative) that may be uniquely human – though this has been contested (see the discussion in Eccles, 1989). Despite numerous experiments to teach language to apes, it does seem that none of them has achieved linguistic prowess beyond the two lower levels (Chomsky 1980, Eccles 1989). The essential features of human language, taking the accomplishment to the third and fourth levels of the Buhler–Popper–Eccles model, seem to have emerged around the time of the splitting of the hominid lineage at 2.6 to 2.5 Myr, against the background of a deteriorating African environment.

Note on the vocal tract

Studies of the flexure of the cranial base led several investigators to attempt to reconstruct the morphology of the hominid vocal tract (Laitman and colleagues 1977, 1978, 1979, 1982, 1985), while Lieberman and Crelin (1971) based inferences about the anatomy of the vocal tract on the angle or position of the styloid process of the temporal bone. Both groups of workers inferred that the part of the pharynx above the larynx, mainly the nasal part of the pharynx (nasopharynx), was small in early hominids, from which they concluded that pre-modern hominids, up to and including the Neanderthals of a mere 40,000 years ago, were capable of only a relatively narrow range of speech sounds (for a comprehensive presentation of this argument, see Lieberman in this volume, Article 5).

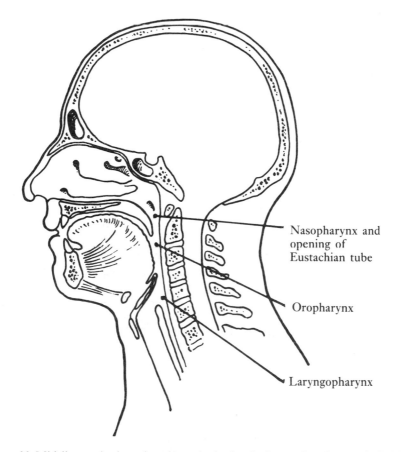

Figure 11 Mid-line sagittal section through the head of a modern human individual. The diagram shows the three parts of the pharynx, one of which − the nasopharynx − plays an important part in the making of some of the sounds of speech

65

Even if the basis of these inferences were valid, a smaller number of speech sounds would not, on its own, suffice to exclude the vocalizations from the status of spoken language. It should not be forgotten that there is an enormous diversity in the degree of phonetic complexity in modern human languages. For example, Traill (1978: 139) has characterized the languages of the San or Bushmen as being, from a phonetic point of view, *the world's most complex languages*. Yet it would be absurd to deny the phonetically simpler languages of Europeans or Asians their identity or status as spoken languages! Moreover, Goodenough (1992) reminds us that Hawaiian and Gilbertese, both of which qualify as fully functioning languages, have only 11 and 12 phonemes respectively.

Quite apart from this consideration, several investigators have questioned the validity of the inferences cited above. Limber (1980) is wary of claims that the essence of human language lies in the morphology of the vocal tract. He adds, 'a normal human vocal tract in itself is neither necessary nor sufficient to account for the linguistic ability of humans'. Tobias (1983a), and Aiello and Dean (1990: 242), doubt that the form of the cranial base is, on its own, a reliable guide to the structure of the upper respiratory tract of fossil hominids, while Duchin (1990) has stressed that human speech sounds are produced in the oral cavity and cannot be predicted from the morphology of the pharynx. It is relevant also that, well before the larynx reaches its adult position during ontogenetic development, human children are able to articulate [i], [a] and [u] vowel sounds (Goodenough 1992).

It may be concluded that the claim for a reduced range of speech sounds in early hominids has not been proven and that, even if it were valid, it would not refute the hypothesis that *H. habilis* not only possessed, but also used, the putative motor speech areas of its brain. The American anatomist, George Washington Corner, jocularly expressed a profound truth on the relationship between spoken language, brain and culture, when he declared that the only reason that an ape does not speak is that he has nothing to speak about. To turn the question around, what did *H. habilis* speak about? This brings us to the role of culture in hominid evolution.

CULTURE IN THE EARLY HOMINIDS

Before we examine the role of culture in the earlier history of humankind, it may be helpful to glance at its place among the human populations of today. To what relative extents do biological and cultural factors contribute towards adaptation in different populations of recent humans under varying environmental conditions? One way of looking at the problem is to try to determine the respective roles of morphological change, genetic differentiation, functional response and cultural adaptability in the accommodation of different human populations to their diverse ecological niches.

Studies of modern human populations have indicated that *Homo sapiens* appears to be virtually unique in the degree to which its adjustment to environmental conditions is made possible by cultural factors, quite apart from biological and other considerations. Thus, studies of the Kalahari San or Bushmen (Tobias 1957, 1964, Lee 1979, Tanaka 1980), and of other disadvantaged peoples of Southern Africa (Tobias, 1975, 1985, 1986a, 1988, Price et al. 1987), as well as of those groups surveyed by Watts et al. (1975), have shown how subtly and inextricably the cultural and biological modes of adaptation are interwoven in recent humankind.

Logically, this raises further questions. Do different kinds of environment elicit different patterns of response in modern human beings? That is, do some kinds of ecological challenge evoke predominantly cultural adaptation, with little or no morphological or physiological change? Do others again elicit functional responses with few morphological or cultural adjustments? If we postulate the existence of a spectrum of possible patterns of adjustment among recent human populations, what are the ecological and other circumstances that condition the 'choice' of any particular band of the spectrum, in a specific population's adaptation to its present milieu? To what extent does the mode of adaptation depend upon a group's *contemporary* environment, and to what extent upon the historical *duration* of the population's exposure to those conditions? This brings us face to face with the dimension of time.

If we plumb the depths to geological time levels, we reach the realm of adaptation in evolution. We confront another kind of question: if there are varying modes of adaptation among recent populations, were similarly diverse adaptive mechanisms available in the distant past? Was a particular band of the adaptational spectrum, or a limited range of bands, 'favoured' among earlier hominids? Is there evidence of a change, over time, in the 'preferred' mode of adjustment to the environment? Did the increasing intensity of the cultural dimension in hominid life, as revealed by the archaeological record, bring in its wake changes in the relative importance of cultural devices in adaptation?

The challenge for palaeoanthropologists is to determine whether the palaeontological and archaeological records enable us to infer patterns of adaptation in earlier forms of Hominidae. More particularly, when and how did ancient hominoids start shifting from a purely biological mode of adjustment to a pattern that was both biological and cultural (see Figure 12)?

In a sense, all animal behaviour is biologically grounded. Even the most sophisticated cultural conduct is predicated upon structural and functional patterns of the central nervous system and depends on such peripheral instruments as the hands and the vocal tract. These patterns and instruments are inherited genetically. However, given adequate neurological competence, an alternative mode of inter-generational transmission becomes possible, whereby information is passed on in the normal course of social life – by word of mouth, or by education – rather than by genetic inheritance (the uniqueness of human education, or 'pedagogy', is discussed by D. and A. Premack in this

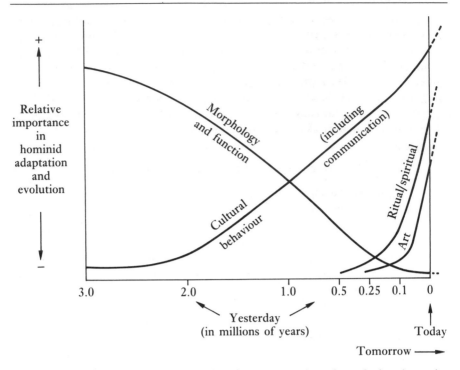

Figure 12 Graphs showing the relative importance, at various times during the evolutionary adaptation of the hominids, of changes inherited by the genetic mechanism (labelled as 'morphology' and 'function'), and of changes whose transmission down the generations is effected by cultural means (shown as 'cultural behaviour', 'ritual/spiritual' and 'art'). Although it is impossible to offer precise measurements of the relative importance of the various modalities, the graphs suggest that, during the past three million years, there have been changes in the relative importance of biological and cultural traits in hominid adaptation and evolution. Whereas it seems that morphological and functional factors were predominant determinants of survival at the time of *Australopithecus africanus*, 3.0 Myr BP, in subsequent hominization such factors, though still manifestly significant, played a relatively less important role, while cultural mechanisms of adaptation became progressively more significant from about 2.5 to 2.0 Myr BP. Gradually, it seems, the behavioural traits, including material culture and articulate speech, became of overwhelming importance in the determination of the adaptation and survival of the hominids, while anatomical and physiological adjustments played an ever-diminishing role. The diagram implies that, in recent humankind, such behavioural traits, including the newest acquisitions in ritual, spiritual and artistic spheres, have come to play the most prominent role as determinants of the present and future adaptation and evolution of human populations

volume; see Article 13). It should be noted, however, that culture may be considered not only as a part of human beings' adaptive equipment, but also as part of the environment to which they must perforce adapt. As Odling–Smee shows (this volume, Article 7), every human group inherits from its predecessors, besides a stock of genetically and culturally coded information, an environment that has itself been shaped and possibly transformed by past cultural practices. In adapting to a changing environment through their culture, human beings also change their environment in cultural ways.

Who were the earliest stone tool-makers?

A momentous period in the hominoid story is the final million years of the Pliocene Epoch, roughly 3 to 2 Myr BP. At least six series of climacteric events occurred during this period. These are summarized in Table 3. They culminate in the appearance of the earliest stone tools.

For many years some investigators, myself included, perceived a correlation between the earliest stone tools and the first appearance of *Homo habilis* (Leakey *et al.* 1964, M. Leakey 1967, 1971; Tobias 1971). Napier and Tobias (1964) used the association between *H. habilis* remains and early Oldowan tools as ethological evidence to support the then disputed assignment of the *habilis* bones to the genus *Homo*. At that time, there was no good evidence for the occurrence of stone tools earlier than the oldest fossil bones of *H. habilis*. I remain convinced that *H. habilis* was a confirmed toolmaker and a hominid that could be regarded as culture-bound. But was it the earliest hominid species to display lithicultural activities? Since 1976, an increasing body of evidence has pointed to hominid implemental activities earlier in the record than *H. habilis*.

The oldest skeletal remains attributed to *H. habilis* are dated to 2.2 to 2.0 Myr BP (Boaz 1979). These are the habiline remains from the Omo

Table 3 Some climacteric events in hominid evolution and ecology from 3.0 to 2.0 Myr BP

	Event	Approximate dating (Myr BP)
1	Cooling and aridification of Africa, with opening of woodland and increase of savanna	2.5 to 2.0
2	Many changes in mammalian fauna of Africa (baboons, elephants, pigs, bovids, hippopotami, sabre-toothed cats, rodents)	2.5 to 2.0
3	One or more splittings of hominid lineage	2.6 to 2.5
4	Emergence of *Homo habilis*	2.4 to 2.3
5	Acquisition of spoken language	2.5 to 2.0
6	Earliest stone cultural remains	*c.* 2.5

deposits in the south of Ethiopia. The oldest recorded occurrence of representatives of a species does not, of course, signify the date at which the species appeared; that date must be set at least a little earlier than 2.2 to 2.0 Myr BP.

Although it is not long since claims for the existence of stone tools older than 2.0 Myr BP were seriously disputed, it is clear that, in Ethiopia at least, stone tools appeared appreciably earlier. The most ancient traces of stone artefacts have come from the area west of the main hominid-bearing locations of Hadar, Ethiopia, where downcutting by the Gona river has exposed sections of the upper beds of the Hadar Formation. There, in the middle 1970s, Corvinus made the first discovery of stone artefacts in deposits which were subsequently dated to between 2.7 and 2.4 Myr BP (Corvinus 1976, Corvinus and Roche 1976, Taieb and Tiercelin 1979). The age determinations were based upon well-known dating techniques, namely potassium-argon dating, fission track studies, palaeomagnetic stratigraphy and stratigraphic correlation (Roche and Tiercelin 1977, Harris 1983). Further artefacts were obtained at Kada Gona 2-3-4 by Roche in 1976 and Harris in 1977, and at West Gona by Harris and Taieb in 1977, the latter site being accorded a preliminary date of 2.4 Myr BP (Harris 1983). Harris (1983) has stated that these stone tools are similar to later assemblages from Olduvai Bed I and from Koobi Fora in northern Kenya.

If these oldest tools are correctly dated, they are certainly older than the earliest recorded members of *H. habilis*. Some revision of these earlier claimed dates may be necessary, perhaps to a maximum antiquity of 2.5 Myr BP (J. W. K. Harris, personal communication). This would reduce the temporal priority of the earliest known tools over the oldest dated *H. habilis* remains to between 0.5 and 0.3 Myr. The argument that we may not have discovered the earliest *H. habilis* in the fossil record may apply equally, of course, to the earliest stone implements so far found. The margin of difference is moderate, when we take into account the limits of error of the dating methods used. Yet the available dates do suggest that toolmaking first appeared *prior to* (and *not* coincident with or subsequent to) the branching of the hominid lineage that generated, *inter alia*, *H. habilis*.

If further researches confirm these datings for the first occurrences of stone tools and of *H. habilis* remains, the development of stone tool-making would then have occurred in some hominid populations before the emergence of *H. habilis*. The most likely candidate as a fabricator of the oldest stone tools would be *A. africanus*. An advanced or 'derived' population (possibly subspecies) of *A. africanus*, postulated by Skelton *et al.* (1986), has been nominated as providing the earliest toolmakers (Tobias 1989, 1990a, b). This 'derived *A. africanus*' is considered by some to have been the last common ancestor of *Homo* and of the 'robust australopithecines' (*A. robustus* and *A. boisei*). Indeed, the acquisition of stone implemental activities by some populations of the 'derived *A. africanus*', but not by others, might have provided an evolutionary 'bottle-necking' mechanism which facilitated cladogenesis and branching speciation (Tobias, 1990a). Seen in this light, culture — as reflected initially by evidence of stone tool-making — played an important, probably a crucial role in the genesis of *Homo*, and of its earliest well-attested species, *H. habilis*.

Tool-making after the splitting of the hominid lineage

After the split or splits that occurred at about 2.6 to 2.5 Myr BP (Table 3), the tool-making habit would have persisted as the potential preserve of one, or both, or all of the daughter lineages. We cannot deny a tool-making capacity to *A. robustus* and *A. boisei* after the split; and it has been suggested that there may be evidence for such activities among *A. robustus crassidens* at Swartkrans (Brain *et al.*, 1988). However, it is the *Homo* lineage which seems to have made the culture of stone tool-making peculiarly its own. *H. habilis*, it seems, became *obligate* stone tool-makers and -users, whereas the late robust and hyper-robust australopithecines might have been only *facultative* tool-makers and tool-users.

From the time of the appearance of *H. habilis*, towards the end of the Pliocene Epoch, the archaeological evidence indicates that the cultural dimension came to play a very prominent part in the pattern of hominid life. Although I have stressed here the material cultural aspects, an essential component of human culture is its *cognitive* underpinning (Lowie 1937, Washburn and Benedict 1979). As the cultural component proliferated and diversified, with an inevitable deepening and widening of its cognitive basis, a considerable change in human adaptation must have been effected. Prior to the emergence of human cultural behaviour, hominid ecological adjustments must have been essentially biological and social in character. The acquisition of a cultural dimension added appreciably to the range of possible mechanisms of adaptation available to the evolving human organisms.

Critical cultural elements listed in Table 4 relate to the mastery of fire and to the emergence of modern human culture, but culture must have played a major role in the early to middle Pleistocene migrations of humankind, from Africa to Asia and to Europe. Culture might even have played a part in hastening the extinction of the last of Africa's australopithecines about a million years ago (Tobias 1986b).

In humanity's further evolution, biological and cultural events were concomitants. Indeed, it is often difficult to extricate the effects of one from those of the other. This dovetailing of biological and cultural mechanisms in human adaptation has persisted to the present day (Table 4). According to the spectrum of modes of adaptation envisaged above, the survival of the earliest hominids seems to have been predicated essentially upon biological factors. The survival and adaptation of the later Plio-Pleistocene hominids appear to have depended increasingly upon cultural capabilities, while many modern human populations have become largely or even totally culture-dependent in their survival strategies.

Table 4 Some climacteric events during hominid evolution in the Pleistocene Epoch

Event	Approximate dating (Myr BP)
1 Movement of hominids from Africa to Asia	2.0 to 1.5
2 Emergence of *Homo erectus*	1.6 to 1.5
3 Extinction of robust australopithecines	*c.* 1.3
4 Acquisition of control of fire	*c.* 1.3
5 Emergence of *Homo sapiens* (there are varied views on the nature, timing and indeed the very existence of an *erectus–sapiens* transition)	*c.* 0.5
6 Emergence of modern human culture	0.1 to 0.025

In a word, and as indicated schematically in Figure 12, there has been a change in the major emphasis during human evolution from mainly biological mechanisms at earlier stages to predominantly cultural mechanisms at later stages. In this transition spoken language has, from about 2 million years ago, played an ever more important role as a means for the transmission of cultural and social information. Thus has an 'animal hominid' been made over into 'a human hominid'. By the lower Pleistocene (1.8 to 0.7 Myr BP), humanity was becoming language-bound and culture-dependent. Armed with these qualities the hominids broke the geographical bounds of their African origins and moved into Asia and Europe.

ACKNOWLEDGEMENTS

I would like to thank Val Strong and Heather White for their assistance in the preparation of this chapter.

REFERENCES

Aiello, L. and Dean, C. (1990) *An Introduction to Human Evolutionary Anatomy*, London: Academic Press.

Andrews, P. (1985) 'Family group systematics and evolution among catarrhine primates', in E. Delson (ed.) *Ancestors: The Hard Evidence*, New York: Alan R. Liss.

Asfaw, B. (1987) 'The Belohdelie frontal: new evidence of early hominid cranial morphology from the Afar of Ethiopia', *Journal of Human Evolution* 16: 612–24.

Bailey, P., von Bonin, G. and McCulloch, W. C. (1950) *The Isocortex of the Chimpanzee*, Urbana: University of Illinois Press.

Boaz, N. T. (1979) 'Hominid evolution in eastern Africa during the Pliocene and early Pleistocene', *Annual Review of Anthropology* 8: 71–85.

—— (1980) 'A hominid clavicle from the Mio-Pliocene of Sahabi, Libya', *American Journal of Physical Anthropology* 53: 49–54.

—— (1987) 'Sahabi and Neogene hominoid evolution', in N. T. Boaz, A. El-Arnauti,

A. W. Gaziry, J. de Heinzelin and D. D. Boaz (eds) *Neogene Paleontology and Geology of Sahabi*, New York: Alan R. Liss.

Boaz, N. T. and Meikle, W. E. (1982) 'Fossil remains of primates from the Sahabi Formation', *Garyounis Science Bulletin*, special issue 4: 1–48.

Brain, C. K., Churcher, C. S., Clark, J. D., Grine, F. E., Shipman, P., Susman, R. L., Turner, A. and Watson, V. (1988) 'New evidence of early hominids, their culture and environment from the Swartkrans Cave', *South African Journal of Science* 84: 828–35.

Buhler, K. (1934) *Sprachtheorie: die Darstellungsfunktion der Sprache*, Jena: Gustav Fischer.

Chagas, C. (ed.) (1983) *Recent Advances in the Evolution of Primates, Pontificiae Academiae Scientiarum Scripta Varia* 50: 1–204.

Chomsky, N. (1980) 'Human language and other semiotic systems', in G. A. Miller and E. Lenneberg (eds) *Psychology and Biology of Language and Thought*, New York: Academic Press.

Ciochin, R. L. and Corruccini, R. S. (1982) 'Miocene hominoids and new interpretations of ape and human ancestry', VIII Congress of the International Primatological Society, Italy, July 1982.

Clark, LeGros, W. E. (1955) *The Fossil Evidence for Human Evolution: an Introduction to the Study of Paleoanthropology*, 1st edn, Chicago: University of Chicago Press.

—— (1964) *The Fossil Evidence for Human Evolution: an Introduction to the Study of Paleoanthropology*, 2nd edn, Chicago: University of Chicago Press.

Clark, J. D., Asfaw, B., Assefa, G., Harris, J. W. K., Kurashina, H., Walter, R. C., White, T. D. and Williams M. A. J. (1984) 'Palaeoanthropological discoveries in the Middle Awash Valley, Ethiopia', *Nature* 307: 423–8.

Conroy, G. C. (1990) *Primate Evolution*, New York and London: W. W. Norton.

Corvinus, G. (1976) 'Prehistoric exploration at Hadar, Ethiopia', *Nature* 261: 571–2.

Corvinus, G. and Roche, H. (1976) 'La préhistoire dans la région d'Hadar (Bassin de l'Awash Afar, Éthiopie): premiers résultats', *L'Anthropologie* 80: 315–24.

Critchley, M. (1953) *The Parietal Lobes*, London: Edward Arnold.

Dart, R. A. (1925) 'Australopithecus africanus: the man ape of South Africa', *Nature* 115: 195–9.

Darwin, C. (1859) *The Origin of Species*, 1st edn, London: John Murray.

Duchin, L. E. (1990) 'The evolution of articulate speech; comparative anatomy of the oral cavity in *Pan* and *Homo*', *Journal of Human Evolution* 19: 684–95.

Eccles, J. C. (1989) *Evolution of the Brain: Creation of the Self*, London and New York: Routledge.

Elliot, D. G. (1913) 'A review of the primates', *Monographs of American Museum of Natural History* 1: vols 1–3.

Falk, D. (1978) 'Brain evolution in Old World Monkeys', *American Journal of Physical Anthropology* 48: 315–20.

—— (1980) 'Language, handedness and primate brains: did the australopithecines sign?', *American Anthropologist* 82: 72–8.

—— (1983) 'Cerebral cortices of East African early hominids', *Science* 222: 1072–4.

Gardner, R. A. and Gardner, B. T. (1969) 'Teaching sign language to a chimpanzee', *Science* 15: 664–72.

Gardner, R. A. and Gardner, B. T. (1971) 'Two-way communication with an infant chimpanzee', in A. M. Schrier and F. Stollnitz (eds) *Behavior of Non-human Primates*, New York: Academic Press.

—— (1978) 'Comparative psychology and language acquisition', *Annals of the New York Academy of Sciences* 309: 37–76.

Geschwind, N. (1965) 'Disconnexion syndromes in animals and man', *Brain* 88: 237–94, 585–644.

Gingerich, P. D. (1985) 'Nonlinear molecular clocks and ape-human divergence times', in P. V. Tobias (ed.) *Hominid Evolution: Past, Present and Future*, New York: Alan R. Liss.

Goodenough, W. H. (1992) 'Language origin' (review of P. Lieberman, *Uniquely Human*), *Language and Society* 20: 145–7.

Gregory, W. K. and Hellman, M. (1938) 'Evidence of the australopithecine man-apes on the origin of man', *Science* 88: 615–16.

—— (1939a) 'The dentition of the extinct South African man-ape *Australopithecus (Plesianthropus) transvaalensis* Broom. A comparative and phylogenetic study', *Annals of the Transvaal Museum* 19: 339–73.

—— (1939b) 'Fossil man-apes of South Africa', *Nature* 143: 25–6.

Grine, F. (1988) 'Evolutionary history of the "robust" australopithecines: a summary and historical perspective', in F. Grine (ed.) *The Evolutionary History of the 'Robust' Australopithecines*, New York: Aldine.

Harris, J. W. K. (1983) 'Cultural beginnings: Plio-Pleistocene archaeological occurrences from the Afar, Ethiopia', *African Archaeological Review* 1: 3–31.

Hennig, W. (1950) *Grundzuge einer Theorie von Phylogenetischen Systematik*, Berlin: Deutscher Zentralverlag.

—— (1966) *Phylogenetic Systematics*, Urbana: University of Illinois Press.

Hewes, G. W. (1973) 'Primate communication and the gestural origin of language', *Current Anthropology* 14: 5–24.

Hill, A. (1985) 'Early hominid from Baringo, Kenya', *Nature* 315: 222–4.

Hill, A. and Ward, S. (1988) 'Origin of the Hominidae: the record of African large hominoid evolution between 14 My and 4 My', *Yearbook of Physical Anthropology* 31: 49–83.

Hockett, C. L. F. and Ascher, R. (1964) 'The human revolution', *Current Anthropology* 5: 135–68.

Holloway, R. L. (1969) 'Culture: a human domain', *Current Anthropology* 10: 395–412.

—— (1978) 'Problems of brain endocast interpretation and African hominid evolution', in C. J. Jolly (ed.) *Early Hominids of Africa*, London: Duckworth.

Isaac, G. (1978) 'The archaeological evidence for the activities of early African hominids', in C. J. Jolly (ed.) *Early Hominids of Africa*, London: Duckworth.

Kramer, A. (1986) 'Hominid–pongid distinctiveness in the Miocene–Pliocene fossil record: the Lothagam mandible', *American Journal of Physical Anthropology* 31: 49–83.

Laitman, J. T. (1977) 'The ontogenetic and phylogenetic development of the upper respiratory system and basicranium in man', unpublished Ph.D. thesis, Yale University.

—— (1985) 'Evolution of the hominid upper respiratory tract: the fossil evidence', in P. V. Tobias (ed.) *Hominid Evolution: Past, Present and Future*, New York: Alan R. Liss.

Laitman, J. T. and Heimbuch, R. C. (1982) 'The basicranium of Plio-Pleistocene hominids as an indicator of their upper respiratory systems', *American Journal of Physical Anthropology* 59: 323–43.

Laitman, J. T., Heimbuch, R. C. and Crelin, E. S. (1978) 'Developmental change in a basicranial line and its relationship to the upper respiratory system in living primates', *American Journal of Anatomy* 152: 467–83.

—— (1979) 'The basicranium of fossil hominids as an indicator of their upper respiratory systems', *American Journal of Physical Anthropology* 51: 15–34.

74

Leakey, L. S. B., Tobias, P. V. and Napier, J. R. (1964) 'A new species of the genus *Homo* from Olduvai Gorge', *Nature* 202: 7–9.

Leakey, M. D. (1967) 'Preliminary survey of the cultural material from Beds I and II, Olduvai Gorge, Tanzania', in W. W. Bishop and J. D. Clark (eds) *Background to Evolution in Africa*, Chicago: University of Chicago Press.

—— (1971) *Olduvai Gorge*, vol. III, 'Excavations in Beds I and II, 1960–1963', Cambridge: Cambridge University Press.

Lee, R. B. (1979) *The !Kung San: Men, Women, and Work in a Foraging Society*, Cambridge: Cambridge University Press.

Lieberman, P. (1988) 'Language, intelligence, and rule-governed behavior', in H. J. Jerison and I. Jerison (eds) *Intelligence and Evolutionary Biology*, Berlin: Springer.

Lieberman, P. and Crelin, E. S. (1971) 'On the speech of Neanderthal Man', *Linguistic Inquiry* 11: 203–22.

Limber, J. (1980) 'Language in child and chimp', in T. A. Sebeok and J. Umiker-Sebeok (eds) *Speaking of Apes*, New York: Plenum Press.

Livingstone, F. G. (1973) 'Did the australopithecines sing?', *Current Anthropology* 14: 25–6.

Lowie, R. H. (1937) *The History of Ethnological Theory*, New York: Farrar & Rinehart.

Marler, P. (1970) 'Birdsong and speech development: could there be parallels?', *American Scientist* 58: 669–73.

Mayr, E. (1981) 'Biological classification: toward a synthesis of opposing methodologies', *Science* 214: 510–16.

Menzel, E. W. (1973) 'Leadership and communication in young chimpanzees', in E. W. Menzel (ed.) *Precultural Primate Behavior*, Basel: S. Karger.

Napier, J. and Tobias, P. V. (1964) 'The case for *Homo habilis*', *The Times*, London, 5 June 1964.

Pickford, M. (1985) '*Kenyapithecus*: A review of its status based on newly discovered fossils from Kenya', in P. V. Tobias (ed.) *Human Evolution: Past, Present and Future*, New York: Alan R. Liss.

Pickford, M., Johanson, D. C., Lovejoy, C. O., White, T. D. and Aronson, J. L. (1983) 'A hominoid humeral fragment from the Pliocene of Kenya', *American Journal of Physical Anthropology* 60: 337–46.

Pilbeam, D. (1968) *The Earliest Hominids*, New York, Toronto, London: Bantam Books.

Popper, K. R. (1972) *Objective Knowledge. An Evolutionary Approach*, Oxford: Clarendon Press.

Popper, K. R. and Eccles, J. C. (1977) *The Self and its Brain*, Berlin, Heidelberg, London, New York: Springer.

Premack, D. (1970a) 'The education of Sarah, a chimp', *Psychology Today* 4 (4): 55–8.

—— (1970b) 'A functional analysis of language', *Journal of the Experimental Analysis of Behavior* 14: 107–25.

—— (1971) 'Language in chimpanzee?', *Science* 172: 808–22.

—— (1976) *Intelligence in Ape and Man*, Hillside, New Jersey: Lawrence Erlbaum.

Price, B., Cameron, N. and Tobias, P. V. (1987) 'A further search for a secular trend of adult body size in South African Blacks: evidence from the femur and tibia', *Human Biology* 59: 467–75.

Ragir, S. (1985) 'Retarded development: the evolutionary mechanism underlying the emergence of the human capacity for language', *The Journal of Mind and Behavior* 6 (4): 451–67.

Raza, S. M., Barry, J. C., Pilbeam, D., Rose, M. D., Ibrahim Shah, S. M. and Ward, S. (1983) 'New hominoid primates from the Middle Miocene Chinji Formation, Potwar Plateau, Pakistan', *Nature* 306: 52–4.

Roche, H. and Tiercelin, J. J. (1977) 'Découverte d'une industrie lithique ancienne in situ dans la formation d'Hadar, Afar, central Éthiopie', *C. R. Acad. Sci. Paris* D284: 1871–4.

Rothschild, Lord (1961) *A Classification of Living Animals*, London: Longmans.

Sakoyama, Y., Hong, K.-J., Byun, S.M., Hisajima, H., Ueda, S., Yaoita, Y., Hayashida, H., Miyata, T. and Honjo, T. (1987) 'Nucleotide sequences of immunoglobulin genes of chimpanzee and orangutan: DNA molecular clock and hominoid evolution', *Proceedings of the National Academy of Science USA* 84: 1080–4.

Salzano, F. M. (1975) (ed.) *The Role of Natural Selection in Human Evolution*, Amsterdam, Oxford: North Holland.

Schepers, G. W. H. (1946) 'The endocranial casts of the South African ape-men', in R. Broom and G. W. H. Schepers, *The South African Fossil Ape-Men: the Australopithecinae, Transvaal Museum Memoirs* 2: 153–272.

—— (1950) 'The brain casts of the recently discovered *Plesianthropus*, skulls', in R. Broom, J. T. Robinson and G. W. H. Schepers, *Sterkfontein Ape-man, Plesianthropus, Transvaal Museum Memoirs* 4: 85–117.

Senut, B. (1983) 'Quelques remarques à propos d'un humerus d'hominoide pliocène provenant de Chemeron (bassin du lac Baringo, Kenya)', *Folia Primatologia* 41: 267–76.

Sibley, C. G. and Ahlquist, J. E. (1984) 'The phylogeny of hominoid primates, as indicated by DNA–DNA hybridization', *Journal of Molecular Evolution* 20: 2–15.

Simpson, G. G. (1931) 'A new classification of mammals', *Bulletin of the American Museum of Natural History* 59: 259–93.

—— (1945) 'The principles of classification and a classification of mammals', *Bulletin of the American Museum of Natural History* 85: 1–350.

Skelton, R. R., McHenry, H. M. and Drawhorn, G. M. (1986) 'Phylogenetic analysis of early hominids', *Current Anthropology* 27: 21–43.

Steklis, H. D. (1981) 'The relative merits of the "vocal continuity" and "gestural" models of human language origins', abstract, Transdisciplinary Symposium on Glossogenetics, August 1981, Paris, France.

—— (1985) 'Primate communication, comparative neurology, and the origin of language re-examined', *Journal of Human Evolution* 14: 157–73.

Steklis, H. D. and Raleigh, M. J. (1973) 'Comment on "Did the australopithecines sing?"', *Current Anthropology* 14: 27.

Taieb, M. and Tiercelin, J-J. (1979) 'Sedimentation pliocène et paléoenvironments de rift: Exemple de la formation a hominides d'Hadar (Afar, Éthiopie)', *Bulletin de Société Géologique, France* 21: 243–53.

Tanaka, J. (1980) *The San, Hunter Gatherers of the Kalahari*, Tokyo: University of Tokyo Press.

Thomas, H. (1985) 'The early and middle Miocene land connection of the Afro-Arabian plate and Asia: a major event for hominoid dispersal', in E. Delson (ed.) *Ancestors: The Hard Evidence*, New York: Alan R. Liss.

Tobias, P. V. (1957) 'Bushmen of the Kalahari', *Man* 57: 33–40.

—— (1964) 'Bushman hunter-gatherers: a study in human ecology', in D. H. S. Davis (ed.) *Ecological Studies in Southern Africa, Monographiae Biologicae* XIV: 67–86.

—— (1967) *Olduvai Gorge*, vol. 2, 'The Cranium and Maxillary Dentition of *Australopithecus (Zinjanthropus) boisei*', Cambridge: Cambridge University Press.

—— (1971) *The Brain in Hominid Evolution*, New York, London: Columbia University Press.

—— (1975) 'Long or short hominid phylogenies? Paleontological and molecular evidences', in F. M. Salzano (ed.) *The Role of Natural Selection in Human Evolution*, Amsterdam, Oxford: North Holland.

—— (1978) 'The life and work of Linnaeus', *South African Journal of Science* 74 (12): 457–62.

—— (1980) 'L'Évolution du cerveau humain', *La Recherche* 11: 282–92.

—— (1981) *The Evolution of the Human Brain, Intellect and Spirit*, 1st Andrew Abbie Memorial Lecture, Adelaide, Australia: University of Adelaide Press.

—— (1983a) 'Recent advances in the evolution of the hominids with especial reference to brain and speech', *Pontificiae Academiae Scientiarum Scripta Varia* 50: 85–140.

—— (1983b) 'Hominid evolution in Africa', *Canadian Journal of Anthropology* 3: 163–90.

—— (1985) 'Negative secular trend', *Journal of Human Evolution* 14: 347–56.

—— (1986a) 'Physical stature in disadvantaged communities: Johannesburg blacks have *not* grown taller this century', *South African Journal of Science* 82 (10): 585–8.

—— (1986b) 'The last million years in Southern Africa', in T. Cameron and S. B. Spies (eds) *An Illustrated History of South Africa*, Johannesburg: Jonathan Ball Publishers.

—— (1988) 'War and the negative secular trend of South African blacks with observations on the relative sensitivity of cadaveric and non-cadaveric populations to secular effects', in *Proceedings, 5th Congress of the European Anthropological Association* 1, Lisbon.

—— (1989) 'The status of *Homo habilis* in 1987 and some outstanding problems', in G. Giacobini (ed.) *Hominidae*, Milan: Jaca Book.

—— (1990a) 'Some critical steps in the evolution of the hominid brain', *Pontificiae Academiae Scientiarum Scripta Varia* 78: 1–23.

—— (1990b) *Olduvai Gorge*, vols 4A and 4B, 'The Skulls, Endocasts and Teeth of *Homo habilis*', Cambridge: University Press.

Traill, A. (1978) 'The languages of the Bushmen', in P. V. Tobias (ed.) *The Bushmen: San Hunters and Herders of Southern Africa*, Cape Town, Pretoria: Human & Rousseau.

Ueda, S., Watanabe, Y., Saitou, N., Omoto, K., Hayashida, H., Miyata, T., Hisajima, H. and Honjo, T. (1989) 'Nucleotide sequences of immunoglobulin-epsilon pseudogenes in man and apes and their phylogenetic relationships', *Journal of Molecular Biology* 205: 85–90.

Ward, S. and Hill, A. (1987) 'Pliocene hominid partial mandible from Tabarin, Baringo, Kenya', *American Journal of Physical Anthropology* 72: 21–37.

Washburn, S. L. and Benedict, B. (1979) 'Non-human primate culture', *Man* 14 (1): 163–4.

Watts, E. S., Johnston, F. E. and Lasker, F. W. (eds) (1975) *Biosocial Interrelations in Population Adaptation*, The Hague: Mouton Publishers.

Westcott, R. W. (1973) 'Comment on "Did the australopithecines sing?"', *Current Anthropology* 14: 27.

White, T. D. (1984) 'Fossil hominids from the Middle Awash, Ethiopia', *Courier Forschungsinstitut Senckenberg* 69: 57–69.

Wilder, H. H. (n.d. – probably 1926) *The Pedigree of the Human Race*, London, Calcutta, Sydney: George G. Harrap.

Wu, R., Xu, Q. and Lu, Q. (1983) *Acta Anthropologica Sinica* 2 (1): 1–10 (cited by S. Ueda *et al.* (q.v.)).

FURTHER READING

Aiello, L. and Dean, C. (1990) *An Introduction to Human Evolutionary Anatomy*, London: Academic Press.

Binford, L. R. (1981) *Bones: Ancient Men and Modern Myths*, New York: Academic Press.

Cann, R. L. (1988) 'DNA and human origins', *Annual Review of Anthropology* 17: 127–43.

Clark, Legros, W. E. (1978) *The Fossil Evidence for Human Evolution*, 3rd edn, Chicago: University of Chicago Press.

Day, M. H. (1986) *Guide to Fossil Man*, 4th edn, London: Cassell.

Delson, E. (ed.) (1985) *Ancestors: the Hard Evidence*, New York: Alan R. Liss.

Eccles, J. C. (1989) *Evolution of the Brain: Creation of the Self*, London: Routledge.

Geertz, C. (1973) 'The growth of culture and the evolution of mind', in C. Geertz, *The Interpretation of Cultures*, New York: Basic Books.

Isaac, G. L. (1983) 'Aspects of human evolution', in D. S. Bendall (ed.) *Evolution from Molecules to Men*, Cambridge: Cambridge University Press.

Leakey, M. D. (1971) *Olduvai Gorge*, vol. 3, 'Excavations in beds I and II, 1960–1963', Cambridge: Cambridge University Press.

Potts, R. (1988) *Early Hominid Activities at Olduvai*, New York: Aldine de Gruyter.

Pilbeam, D. (1968) *The Earliest Hominids*, New York: Bantam Books.

Reader, J. (1980) *Missing Links*, Boston: Little Brown.

Richards, G. (1987) *Human Evolution: an Introduction for the Behavioural Sciences*, London: Routledge & Kegan Paul.

Tanner, N. M. (1981) *On Becoming Human*, Cambridge: Cambridge University Press.

Tobias, P. V. (1971) *The Brain in Hominid Evolution*, New York: Columbia University Press.

—— (1981) 'The emergence of man in Africa and beyond', *Philosophical Transactions of the Royal Society of London*, ser. B 292: 43–56.

—— (ed.) (1985) *Hominid Evolution: Past, Present and Future*, New York: Alan R. Liss.

Washburn, S. L. and Moore, R. (1980) *Ape into Human*, 2nd edn, Boston: Little Brown.

4

HUMAN EVOLUTION: THE LAST ONE MILLION YEARS

Clive Gamble

During the last million years hominids established themselves as the only globally distributed species. The period saw the dispersal and evolution of *Homo erectus*, which first appeared in Africa, into a number of regional populations of so-called 'archaic' *Homo sapiens*. Among these the European and Near Eastern Neanderthals formed a distinctive group. At a much later date, perhaps one hundred and fifty thousand years ago, both anatomical and genetic data point to Africa as the source for modern-looking humans. These early moderns did not, however, appear straight away with all the hallmarks of modern behaviour – art, ritual, symbolism, extensive social networking and, by inference, fully-fledged language. The archaeological evidence points to a later date again, some forty thousand years ago, for this subsequent human revolution. One of its consequences was the rapid colonization, after this date, of much of the habitable world. While the replacement of archaic by anatomically modern populations provides the most parsimonious explanation for the timing and scale of these changes, strong claims are still made by many scholars for continuity between the regional archaic populations, such as the Neanderthals, and ourselves.

THE HUMAN DRIFT

One million years ago, *Homo erectus* expanded out of sub-Saharan Africa. This has been seen by some as a momentous step, for, as Carleton Coon once claimed, Africa 'was only an indifferent kindergarten. Europe and Asia were our principal schools' (1962: 656).

The notion that hominids became humans in the challenging environments of more northerly latitudes has a long history in anthropology and archaeology. During the last two centuries the cradle of human origins has been moved

79

about the globe, more as a result of the way the world and its peoples have been judged than on the grounds of hard evidence for fossil ancestors. The main contenders have always been Asia and Africa, but some support can be found for many other regions including Australia, the Americas, the Arctic, and sunken islands in the Indian Ocean.

Europe, however, has rarely figured in such movements of the human cradle, owing no doubt, to the role of Europeans as definers and discoverers of the world and its past. But while humankind has been allowed to arise in another place, and current evidence – reviewed in the previous article – points overwhelmingly to sub-Saharan Africa, recent humanity, as Coon's comment indicates, has often been attributed with a European origin. For example Hrdlicka, writing in 1922, was less concerned with deciding where hominids originated, because there was so little evidence to go on, and instead singled out south-western Europe as the cradle of humanity, whence, he argued, the peopling of the rest of the earth had taken place comparatively recently. In keeping with the times he regarded this recency as due to the 'insufficient effectiveness' of Stone Age peoples which only expanded after certain mental and cultural thresholds had been passed. These, in his view, led to control over the environment and to population increase, so that humans were forced to people the earth. Necessity rather than desire governed the process, and the spread – or as others called it the drift – followed three great laws:

1 movement in the direction of least resistance;
2 movement in the direction of the greatest prospects;
3 movement due to a force from behind, to compulsion (Hrdlicka 1922: 545).

It is now possible to challenge both the factual basis for such geographical reconstructions and the assumptions behind these notions of the pace and character of the human drift. I argue here that our humanity emerged as part of the process of world colonization in prehistory rather than as an attribute which was exported from one centre by dominant forms and which Darwin, in *The Origin of Species*, memorably described as having been generated in the 'more efficient workshops of the north' (1859: 371).

GRADUAL OR PUNCTUATED?

World colonization proceeded in bursts, as shown in Table 1. The idea of a human drift whereby, given *enough* time, all habitable places would be reached by a slow continuous spread, can no longer be supported. Though Hrdlicka was correct in arguing for a recent peopling of much of the globe, the pattern throughout the Old World for much of the last million years has been one of population ebb and flow. This has been controlled by repeated, long-term climatic cycles each with a warm (interglacial) and cold (glacial) phase. These cycles form the internal divisions of the Pleistocene period beginning some 1.6 million years ago (Myr BP). Initially the cycles took about fifty thousand years

Table 1 A chronology for the peopling of the world

Period	Area	Hominids
5 Myr to 1 Myr	Sub-Saharan Africa	*Australopithecus*, early *Homo*, *Homo erectus*
1 Myr to 40 kyr	Old World mid-latitudes	*Homo erectus*, archaic *Homo sapiens*, Neanderthals, early anatomically modern humans
60 kyr	Australia	Anatomically modern humans
40 kyr to Present	Old World high latitudes, Pacific islands, New World, deserts, rain forests.	Late Neanderthals, anatomically modern humans

(50 kyr) to complete. The duration of the last four, however, was extended to 100 kyr. During the last million years there were some marginal geographical gains, notably after 200 kyr BP on the northern plains, before the recent, massive colonization that began with the settlement of Australia about 60 kyr BP. At this time sea levels were low, owing to the presence of large ice-caps, and Australia, New Guinea and Tasmania formed a single land mass known as Sahul. In earlier glacial phases large areas of the continental shelf in south-east Asia and Europe would also have been exposed. The distribution of early populations was determined by the effect of climate on food resources, often resulting in the abandonment of formerly settled regions for several millennia.

HOMO ERECTUS AS A COLONIZING SPECIES

Homo erectus spent almost as long in sub-Saharan Africa as outside it. The earliest fossils from East Africa date to 1.6 Myr and include a nearly complete skeleton of a twelve-year-old boy from West Turkana (specimen WT 15000) and more fragmentary material from Olduvai Gorge. This coincides at Olduvai with the first appearance of stone tools of the kind known as 'handaxes' and grouped under the Acheulean culture (after the French type site of St Acheul where comparable finds were first made). The appearance of large-brained *Homo erectus*, together with stone tools whose manufacture by flaking required a multi-stage reduction procedure, has often been interpreted as evidence for a link between encephalization and technology.

Such an association is more difficult to sustain when we consider that *Homo erectus*, with this apparently advanced technology, then continued to occupy *only* sub-Saharan Africa for the next 600 kyr. It is also the case that the earliest evidence outside of this region points to the use of less complex reduction techniques to produce stone tools, as for example at the Jordan Valley site of

'Ubeidiya (Bar-Yosef 1980) dated to between 1 and 0.7 Myr BP. Many of the stone tools from this complex Lower Pleistocene landscape were made on the spot and are comparable to the simply flaked, Oldowan pebble tools from sub-Saharan Africa, the oldest of which are from about 2.5 Myr BP.

A similar age to the finds at 'Ubeidiya is now agreed for the finds of fossil material in the complex sequences along the Solo River in eastern Java. It was here at Trinil, in 1891, that Dubois made the important discovery of a flat-headed skull. First called *Pithecanthropus*, it is now placed in the *Homo erectus* group. For many years this was the find which supported the idea of an Asian cradle for humankind. Stone tools were also claimed in association with further finds of *Homo erectus* on the Solo River at Sangiran. These skulls are now dated to the Middle Pleistocene and are younger than 730 kyr. The great antiquity of the stone tools has since been discounted and geographical expansion in this region apparently took place without them. It has been suggested that bamboo, which would not survive, formed the raw material for knives, digging sticks and possibly containers.

Five and a half thousand kilometres to the north the cave complex at Zhoukoudian, outside Beijing, has also produced a large collection of fossil skulls dated to the early Middle Pleistocene, 700 kyr BP. These *Homo erectus* are very definitely associated with stone tools, but bifacially worked handaxes are absent. Roughly flaked pebble and chopping tools, and smaller flakes with retouched edges, make up the excavated assemblages.

Small numbers of cores and simple struck flakes have been excavated from palaeosoils within the huge accumulations of loess in post-Soviet Central Asia in the region of Dushanbe. These wind-blown sediments result from erosion under cold conditions with little vegetation cover. The palaeosoils were formed during warmer, wetter, periods in the Pleistocene. The sediments can be dated by palaeomagnetic techniques and these show that the earliest tools are from 800 kyr BP (Ranov 1991). The recent discovery of a mandible of *Homo erectus*, from Dmanisi in the Caucasus mountains (Dzaparidze *et al.* 1989), has pushed back the antiquity of settlement in this region to well over a million years.

Some of the best-dated finds in the Old World come from a relict lakeside setting at Isernia La Pineta, south-east of Rome. Although no hominid material has yet been found, several thousand stone flakes, often with irregular or denticulate (notched) edges, as well as pebble tools, are stratified just beneath a volcanic horizon dated absolutely to 730 kyr BP. Furthermore, the sediments at this level switch from reversed to normal magnetic polarity. This switch is now recognized as a worldwide marker of the onset of the Middle Pleistocene. Pebble tools of similar age are also found in the lowest levels of coastal sites in North Africa such as the quarry of Sidi Abderrahman south-west of Casablanca.

THE ARCHAEOLOGY OF *HOMO ERECTUS* AND ARCHAIC *HOMO SAPIENS*

The wide distribution of locations in which artefactual and fossil remains dating between 1 and 0.7 Myr BP have been found points to three conclusions. First, technology does not seem to have been that important as a facilitator of colonization. Not only did 600 kyr pass after the appearance in East Africa of *Homo erectus* and the Acheulean, before the colonization of other regions began, but also we find that at the earliest Old World sites, in a variety of settings – cave, coastal, riverine and lake – Acheulean technology, which many have claimed was a significant advance on previous flake and pebble tools, was not consistently used. While claims regarding the use of bamboo are intriguing, but unverified, what we can point to is the complete lack of tools fashioned from materials that stand a good chance of survival such as bone, ivory and antler.

The second conclusion concerns the layout and organization of the sites themselves. Indeed to call them 'sites' is hardly appropriate since at many of the localities the artifacts have been redeposited by rivers or slumped into valleys by periglacial action. It would be more accurate, following Isaac (1981), to treat the archaeological traces as scatters and patches across landscapes. The patches of artifacts can be very dense, as at Kilombe and Olorgesailie in East Africa, dated to between 700 and 500 kyr BP, where many thousands of flakes and handaxes have been either excavated or recovered from erosion gullies. But these are not sites in the sense of places in the landscape where individuals or groups came together for any appreciable length of time during a seasonal round, or where highly specific tasks were carried out by designated work parties in an extended settlement system. Instead the repeated visits coincided more with the general distribution and abundance of food resources, so that over long periods of time the deposited artifacts gradually built up into the archaeological signature of a patch rather than a scatter on the landscape. But even so, what is most striking is the lack of structure and identifiable pattern left behind in the form of piles of debris.

This is also a feature of well-preserved sites prior to 1 Myr BP in East Africa. Isaac's excavations at Koobi Fora showed, by reassembling stone flakes to the nodules from which they had been struck, and by reconstructing bones from their scattered splinters, that materials had only been moved a few metres at most and that much of this dispersal was caused by hominids rather than due to fluvial redeposition (Isaac 1981). At this and other sites what is lacking are well-built hearths and the distinctive circular patterns of debris that grow around them as a result of their use for cooking and as centres of conversation. Traces of burning are found, but not as concentrations. Nor are there any postholes that might have carried tents or windbreaks, or interruptions in the spatial distribution of bone and stone that might also point to their previous existence.

In short, the most that can be said about these locations is that fires were lit, stone was knapped, bones smashed open for marrow and meat scraped off their surfaces. Indeed the same is true for early sites throughout the Old World. Fireplaces, as opposed to burnt areas, are absent, while traces of camp sites as we understand them, and as they appear much later in the archaeological record of the Upper Pleistocene, are entirely lacking. This is strikingly exemplified by open sites such as Boxgrove, Clacton, Hoxne and Swanscombe, all in southern England. These sites, with their fine-grained sediments, are dated to between 500 and 300 kyr BP and have excellent preservation. Here, if anywhere, features such as pits and hearths or site structure in the form of dumps would have been found, had they ever existed.

Third, from 1 to 0.2 Myr BP the archaeological record is very standardized and shows few regional differences that might be interpreted as adaptations to local habitat and resources. There appears to have been no significant change during this period either in the organization of technology or in the layout of living spaces. The evidence from raw materials used to fashion stone tools shows that local sources were invariably used. Materials might be carried 5 or 10 km, a day's journey, and in exceptional circumstances up to 50 km from a known source. Paddayya's survey (1982) of Acheulean sites in the Hunsgi Valley of the Indian peninsula confirms the local use of raw material, while from one undisturbed context he recovered a small piece of red ochre (iron oxide) which had been transported a distance of 25 km. Such objects are rare, and there are no traces throughout the Old World of ornaments, art of any description or intentional burial. Invariably, food resources and other raw materials are associated together in the immediate environment.

The fossil evidence is fragmentary, but points to the regional evolution of archaic *Homo sapiens* from the *Homo erectus* pioneers. In Europe there is a dearth of fossils from 730 to 300 kyr BP, by which time the transition to archaic *Homo sapiens*, as shown by the skulls from Steinheim, Petralona, Arago and Swanscombe, had already taken place. The robust Mauer mandible found near Heidelberg may be as old as 600 kyr BP and is still regarded by some palaeoanthropologists as an example of *Homo erectus*. In Java the material at Ngandong, which may be as recent as 100 kyr BP, still retains features of the earlier Solo river *Homo erectus*, while developments towards archaic *Homo sapiens* have been traced with the later Chinese material prior to 200 kyr BP.

NEW TECHNIQUES AND THE NEANDERTHALS

After 200 kyr BP in Europe and Africa there are some changes in the archaeological and fossil records. We have already mentioned the marginal territorial gains on the northern plains of Europe, as seen at open sites around Hamburg and Hanover. There was also the widespread appearance of a new technique for knapping long flakes, known as blades, and triangular points from stone nodules. Named after the Paris suburb of Levallois, where artifacts were found from which the technique was first identified, its essence lies in the predetermination of the shape of the flake or blade during the knapping process, rather than in taking what comes. The Levallois technique is often interpreted as entailing sequencing and forethought. It has been put forward as evidence for a cognitive advance over earlier techniques of producing flakes and knapping nodules into handaxes.

In Europe, where the fossil record after 200 kyr BP is richest, we find a distinctive population of *Homo sapiens* known as Neanderthals – after the original find in 1856. They had long, low skulls, with massive brow ridges, huge noses, large teeth and no chins. Their skeletons were extremely powerful and their limb bones had very thick cross-sections. They were descended from the archaic *Homo sapiens* of Europe such as those represented at the sites of Steinheim and Swanscombe. At a later date they possibly migrated to the Near East where a number of well-preserved skeletons at the caves of Amud, Shanidar and Tabun have been found. Neanderthals led a bruising lifestyle, as indicated by the many healed fractures on their skeletons. The size of their brains, which is well within and often at the upper end of the range of brain size for modern populations, has provoked spirited controversy concerning their role in later human evolution (Stringer and Gamble 1993). Neanderthals have not been found outside Europe, the Near East and parts of Central Asia. In these areas they are normally associated with Middle Palaeolithic stone tools, characterized by many different types of flakes, sometimes using the Levallois technique, and chipped into forms described as scrapers, points, knives, borers, notches and on occasion small handaxes. The last Neanderthal comes from Saint Césaire in France, dated to 36 kyr BP.

BIG-GAME HUNTING: WAS IT PRACTISED?

The colonization of northern environments by *Homo erectus* after 1 Myr BP has often been attributed to their proficiency in hunting. The association of handaxes and flint flakes with the bones of large northern animals such as woolly mammoth, bison and woolly rhinoceros has fostered the belief that the tool-makers engaged in big-game hunting. At the Italian site of Isernia large numbers of bison bones have been interpreted as evidence of big-game hunting, as have lakeside deposits at Bilzingsleben in eastern Germany, where pebble tools and bison have been found together. At the Spanish meseta sites of Torralba and Ambrona the practice of hunting has been inferred from finds of elephant bones and Acheulean handaxes in marsh deposits. Earlier reconstructions had favoured the idea that the animals were first mired in the swamp before being butchered and dismembered (Howell 1965). However, closer examination of the evidence shows that considerable sorting by river action has taken place, so that the association of bones and tools is an accident of post–depositional processes. In this as in all other cases, the deposits suggest other interpretations than the favoured one that the hominids were killing megafauna. At those English sites with deposits *in situ* the evidence from flint cut-marks on the bones indicates that pieces of animals rather than whole carcasses were being dismembered. A more parsimonious interpretation of the data is that hominids were scavenging or foraging for meat and marrow from natural mortalities and carnivore kills.

At the granite headland fissure of La Cotte de St Brelade on the island of Jersey two piles of mammoth and rhino skulls and their partial skeletons have been found in deposits dating to 180 kyr BP. The excavators (Callow and Cornford 1986) believe that there were two separate episodes when small herds were driven over the cliff (Jersey having been joined at this time by low sea levels to France) and then selected parts dragged up beneath the protective overhang. Such driving would have produced, respectively, 25 and 16 tonnes of meat. It is difficult to see how the use of handaxes, together with simple flakes with a variety of different retouched edges, could either have enhanced such behaviour or justified its characterization as big-game hunting.

HUNTING, PLANNING DEPTH AND HUMAN EVOLUTION

Once-popular notions that modern hunters were living relics of prehistory and, on the basis of their toolkits (Sollas 1911), representative of the Lower, Middle and Upper Palaeolithic stages of culture, have long been discarded. The Kalahari San (Yellen 1977) and the Alaskan Inuit (Binford 1978) still provide a point of departure, from contrasting habitats, for the prehistoric study of mobile, low-density populations, but this is now qualified by the widespread recognition that these peoples have their own histories (Leacock and Lee 1982, Schrire 1984, Mazel 1989, Gamble 1992), and are not Palaeolithic survivals.

Alongside these changed views about modern hunters and gatherers has come a reassessment of the importance of hunting in human evolution. No longer is it sufficient to say that meat eating and killing animals made us human, permitting the colonization of northerly latitudes by *Homo erectus* and, at a later date, most of the globe by anatomically modern humans. Hunting certainly involves killing animals, as so graphically portrayed in many popular works by supporters of the big-game hunting hypothesis. But in an evolutionary context the ability to plan ahead, either organizing people to be there at the right time and place for a successful hunt, or setting up stores of food to get through a lean season, is much more important. Such planning may not always result in killing animals. It would also have assisted survival when hominids foraged either for plant foods or for animals that died a natural death, so presenting an opportunity for scavenging.

If this is the case then a major distinction between ourselves, as modern humans, and ancestors such as *Homo erectus* will be expressed in what

Binford (1985) has referred to as an increase in planning depth. This notion is currently central to the investigation of how behaviour evolved during the Palaeolithic. As Binford asks, 'is it possible that hunting and all that it implies in terms of planning may well be a part of the emergence of our humanness in a modern sense?' (1984: 254).

Three examples of what is meant by relative levels of planning depth may be mentioned. First, we have already seen for hominids such as *Homo erectus* and archaic *Homo sapiens* that their camp sites lack evidence for structures and accumulated spatial patterns of bone and stone debris. The contrast with camp sites associated with anatomically modern humans after 40 kyr is dramatic. Here we have huts, postholes indicating tents, storage pits and very obvious circular patterns of debris arising from the repeated use of well-built fireplaces. The archaeological evidence points to a very different use both of living areas and of landscapes. Structures are built to be re-used, and food and raw materials are now being stored for future use. From these differences between the archaeology of the Upper Palaeolithic, beginning in Europe 40,000 years ago, and that of earlier hominids, it may be inferred that profound social changes had taken place.

The second line of evidence for planning extends this argument for a change in the form of social life. It is very noticeable that there is no evidence, in the archaeological record of *Homo erectus* and archaic *Homo sapiens*, for personal ornamentation – jewellery, beads – or for art forms such as figurines, paintings or engravings. These items are all found, worldwide, after 40 kyr BP. The personal ornaments are of interest because they were occasionally manufactured from raw materials whose sources we can identify. When, as in sites on the central Russian plain (Soffer 1985), the Upper Palaeolithic peoples used fossil amber or marine shells it is possible to reconstruct patterns of circulation, and to measure the distances over which the materials travelled. In the Russian examples distances of between 200 and 400 km were common, while some items travelled 600 km from their source. The inference to be drawn from these patterns of circulation is that social networks had now expanded to encompass peoples who were both socially and geographically remote. Servicing such networks required both planning and an elaborate memory for storing the history of social relationships. These larger networks must also have served as one means of overcoming local famines and periodic resource crises. This would have been accomplished by using alliances, partnerships and kin networks as a regional insurance policy. A group could admit its allies or partners at times of local resource abundance, in the knowledge that, at any future time of shortage, such hospitality would be reciprocated. The result can be described as social storage – spreading the risks of failure among and between populations by negotiating and maintaining ties and commitments. The exchange items that survive are evidence for a necessary but entirely commonplace behaviour among modern humans – behaviour whose first convincing appearance in the archaeological record dates to 40 kyr BP.

The third example concerns the process of colonization. The pattern of global colonization, as we have seen, was punctuated. A long pause followed the colonization by *Homo erectus* of the Old World mid-latitude open grasslands and broken woodlands. During the various warm interglacial stages of the Pleistocene hominids had several opportunities to move into the boreal forests of north-eastern Siberia, and thence to the New World, or into the thick deciduous forests of northern Europe (Gamble 1984, 1986), or the tropical rain forests of Africa (Brooks and Robertshaw 1990) and South-east Asia (Bailey *et al.* 1989). However, we find no archaeological evidence for such expansion until some time after 40 kyr BP.

What needs to be explained, therefore, is why populations of a large-brained, tool-using species such as *Homo erectus* never reached Australia or the New World, and why they seem to have been pushed out of many of the Old World habitats as climatic factors turned against them. The answer is that colonization is a social process, aided by technology and tempered by climate. Where environments are highly seasonal, social storage becomes as important for survival as does warm clothing or adequate housing. Ocean-going craft are obviously important when long voyages are involved, but so too are the social networks that provide the framework which allows people to return. Until such social structures were in place, there was little pressure for the invention of appropriate technology or for the peopling of new, potentially difficult, environments.

The implication of the archaeological evidence of artefacts and distributions is that earlier hominid populations, such as those of *Homo erectus*, had more limited capacities for planning and – by inference – smaller and less complex societies.

THE HUMAN REVOLUTION: CONTINUITY OR REPLACEMENT?

The changes that have taken place over the last 40 kyr, compared with the previous million years of relative inertia, have led some to see this date as marking a worldwide revolution (Mellars and Stringer 1989). Dramatic changes in anatomy and behaviour have been documented (Table 2). More recently the evidence from molecular biology has added support to the picture of rapid and recent change, resulting in humans that are not only genetically but also behaviourally and anatomically modern. The evidence is interpreted as indicating an African centre for the origins of modern humans. As they dispersed, these modern populations would then have *replaced*, by a variety of means, the more archaic populations of the Old World.

Table 2 A comparison of the anatomy and archaeology of archaic and modern humans

(a) Anatomy

Archaic humans including Neanderthals	*Modern humans*
Heavy musculature	Lighter musculature
Robust skeleton	More gracile skeleton
Thick cranial bones	Thinner cranial bones
Long, low crania	High and rounded cranial vault
Moderate to large brain	Large brain
Large face and dentition	Reduced face and dentition

(b) Archaeology

Before 40 kyr BP	*After 40 kyr BP*
Widespread and stable stone-tool assemblages	Varied and rapidly changing tool assemblages
Repetitive tool assemblages	Structured tool assemblages
Simple tools, spears, knives, scrapers	Composite and hafted tools, bows, boats, houses, sleds, use of bone and antler
No domestic animals	Domestic dogs
Lack of formal camp sites	Structured camps, villages with storage pits
Use of natural stores	Social storage
No art or ornament	Art, ornament, jewellery
Corpse disposal	Burial and ritual
Short distance transport of materials	Long-distance transport of raw material and prestige items
Limited language ability	Full language ability
Occupation of open environments with predictable animal and plant resources; low seasonal differences	Occupation of habitats with high risk resources; greater seasonal differences
Small, face-to-face societies, narrow band of tolerated population densities	Intensification of social life, expansion of networks to cope with high and very low population densities

Source: Foley (1989), with additions.

However others argue, equally strongly, that far from marking a human revolution, the genetic, anatomical and cultural changes can be explained in terms of *continuity* within the regions previously occupied by archaic populations (Figure 1). Fossils and artifacts have been assembled from China, South-east Asia and Australia, Africa and Eurasia to make the case for gradual change rather than replacement (Clark and Lindly 1989, Clark 1992, Wolpoff *et al.* 1988, Wolpoff 1989).

The debate between advocates of the replacement and continuity hypotheses has been conducted mainly with reference to data from Europe and the Near East, which are the regions most richly documented. Those who favour the idea of the replacement, around 40 kyr BP, of anatomically archaic Neanderthals by anatomically modern populations, and of Middle by Upper Palaeolithic technology, were roundly criticized by Brace (1964) for invoking ideas of catastrophism. The French palaeontologist Boule is regarded as the main culprit, following his detailed description in 1912 of the Neanderthal

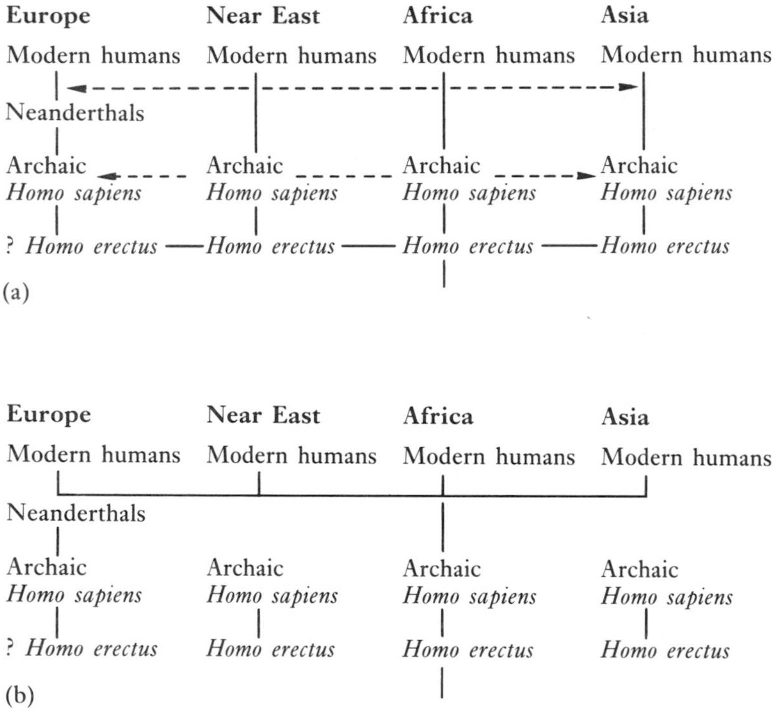

Figure 1 Two models for the appearance of modern humans. (a) Multi-regional continuity in later hominid evolution and the local appearance, aided by inter-regional gene flow, of modern populations. (b) An out-of-Africa origin for anatomically modern human populations that replaced regional populations of archaic hominids

skeleton from La Chapelle-aux-Saints. As both Brace, and later Hammond (1982), pointed out, this report unduly stressed the differences between modern and archaic populations, to the extent that Neanderthals were placed outside the evolution of humanity – an exclusion based on a misreading of the symptoms of old age and osteoarthritis as indicators of specific anatomical differences.

The same suspicion of catastrophism is now attached to the arguments that credit Neanderthals, and archaic hominids more generally, with only small-scale social organization and limited planning depth. The supporters of the regional continuity model stress instead the claims for Neanderthal burials in Europe and the Near East – and in particular the recent find from St Césaire, dated to 36 kyr BP, which occurs in direct association with the earliest Upper Palaeolithic stone tools – as evidence for more advanced forms of behaviour that foreshadow the modern pattern.

Evidence for technological developments *in situ* has been found at the multi-level site of Boker Tachtit in the Negev Desert. In a single sequence the transition is recorded from Middle Palaeolithic techniques of flake and blade production to Upper Palaeolithic blade production (Marks 1983). This occurs in the context of the manufacture of identical projectile points by the two different technical means. The levels date between 47 and 40 kyr BP. No fossils have been found. As we shall see below, it is no longer possible to predict, from the shape of the stone tools, which hominid – Neanderthal or modern human – was making them in this critical period of the human revolution.

Summing up what they see as the continuity in hominid evolution, Clark and Lindly regard it as lying in the adoption of 'solutions that depended upon behavioural changes and linked technological dependencies that, over the long run, replaced sheer strength and endurance' (1989: 660). Far from indicating revolutionary change, this implies that Neanderthals and modern humans behaved in very similar ways, with the former having all the potential of the latter but none of the need for change – which did not come until climatic deterioration forced the adoption of novel strategies. Anatomical and cultural changes were then accelerated. Brace (1979), among others, has referred to this as a 'culinary revolution'. He argues that developments in stone knife technology, cooking and food preparation meant that large teeth were no longer needed to tear food from the bone. Smaller tooth size resulted in a shortening of the face and a reduction in cranial robusticity, so that by the end of the process the modern face emerged from its archaic regional prototype. Hence, too, the large Neanderthal nose, which was so well adapted to warming cold air (Brose and Wolpoff 1971), shrank in size on the earliest modern-looking Europeans, even though they first appeared 35 kyr ago during a cold phase of the last climatic cycle.

Indeed from 30 to 20 kyr BP there occurred a dramatic cooling in climate which resulted in the last glacial maximum at 18 kyr BP (Soffer and Gamble

1990, Gamble and Soffer 1990). Yet the direction of the anatomical changes from archaic to modern forms is quite contrary to what would be expected, given this climatic nadir. For this reason, supporters of the continuity thesis, such as Brace and Wolpoff, have had to look to other factors than selective pressures from the physical environment to account for these changes. They have suggested a more dominant role for cultural adaptations in shaping biology, within the framework of a model of gradual modification.

However, the anatomical evidence speaks much more strongly in favour of advocates of the replacement model. Trinkaus (1982) has pointed out that the Neanderthal physique, with its short, powerful limbs and long body, is well adapted to cold climates, whereas the long-legged, short-bodied early modern humans in Europe display anatomical proportions more suited to warmer climates such as those of Africa. Moreover, if behaviour acts as a buffer against physical change, then why was such a dramatic redesign of northern populations required when behavioural changes should have sufficed? Our inability to provide satisfactory answers to these questions counts strongly in favour of the contrary thesis of the replacement of archaic by incoming modern populations. This would have taken place not only in Europe and the Near East but also throughout those regions of the Old World occupied by archaic hominids.

The anatomical evidence for replacement is supported by widespread archaeological evidence. The Saint-Césaire finds can be explained as imitation rather than innovation, since the earliest Upper Palaeolithic in Europe has a Near Eastern origin and appears in Bulgaria and Spain over 40 kyr BP. The European Upper Palaeolithic also included art, ornament and display. Sewn skin clothing, open-air shelters and stone-built fireplaces are just some of the innovations that appear after 40 kyr BP (Stringer and Gamble 1993). As a result the camp sites from this period are much more elaborate and were habitually re-used. In Europe their scale is such that they can best be described as villages, for example at Kostenki on the Don where lines of open hearths and dumps of mammoth bone coal are surrounded by subterranean pit dwellings and storage pits filled with bone, stone tools, ochre and figurines (Praslov and Rogachev 1982). These date to 23 Kyr BP, while later on the plains of Russia and the Ukraine we find circular footings of stacked mammoth bones at Mezhirich, Mezin and Yudinovo (Soffer 1985).

GENETIC MIGRATION FROM AFRICA

Cavalli-Sforza *et al.* (1988) have argued that what needs explaining in this human revolution is the very rapid colonization by modern humans of the whole world. Their conclusions are based on the measurement of genetic distances between contemporary human populations. Though these distances are never great, measurement of 120 alleles in 42 geographical populations confirms earlier work using mitochondrial DNA, and other measures using gene frequencies. The studies repeatedly isolate Africans from the rest of the world's aboriginal populations. In Cavalli-Sforza's analysis, the remainder form two super-clusters centred respectively on northern Eurasia (subdivided into Caucasoids, north-east Asians and Amerindians) and South-east Asia (which also includes Pacific islanders and Australoids).

The African populations show higher genetic diversity, which is interpreted as indicating that a longer period of time elapsed during which the modern genetic pattern evolved there, pointing to an origin for genetically modern humans in sub-Saharan Africa. More controversial are the estimates, based on mutation rates, of when they might have appeared. Using mitochondrial DNA (mtDNA), which is only inherited by females and is apparently not under selection, Cann et al. (1987) estimate that at a constant mutation rate of between 2 and 4 per cent every million years, the first African female with modern mtDNA, and from whom all subsequent forms are derived, was living between 140 and 290 kyr BP, which is in reasonable agreement with the earliest known anatomically modern skulls from Omo Kibish in East Africa, dated to 130 kyr BP.

EARLY MODERNS AND ARCHAIC BEHAVIOUR

Though the molecular data might indicate a geographical pattern for genetic history, it would be wrong to infer that genetically modern humans were modern in their behaviour as well. This point has been most clearly demonstrated as a result of the absolute dating of a series of important fossil skulls in the Near East. It has long been recognized from excavations in Israel that anatomically modern skulls and skeletons at the cave sites of Qafzeh and Skhul were associated with standard Middle Palaeolithic stone tools. With the advent of thermoluminescence dating on burnt flint the gap in dates between those obtainable by radiocarbon and potassium argon isotope dating techniques has been plugged, and the question of the absolute ages of the moderns and Neanderthals in the same region partially resolved. At Kebara cave in Israel a Neanderthal skeleton has been dated to 60 kyr BP, while at Qafzeh the age for the moderns is now set at 92 kyr BP. The Skhul dates are less precise but point to the bracket between 101 and 81 kyr BP, and are thus consistent with the dates for the modern-looking Qafzeh material which the Skhul fossils so closely resemble. Since the technological and cultural transition to the Upper Palaeolithic in the region is set at 40 to 35 kyr BP, it is immediately apparent that the appearance of anatomically modern humans precedes this revolution by at least 50 kyr. The assumption that modern-looking people were necessarily associated with modern behaviour, as characterized by greater planning depth, is called into question not only by these data, but also by the pattern of global colonization whereby Australia was not colonized until 55 kyr BP and the Americas, the Pacific and the tropical forests not until some time after 40 kyr.

TECHNOLOGY AND COLONIZATION

It is also noticeable that once again lithic technology played a secondary role in colonization. Two examples will suffice. The stone technology associated with the earliest occupation of Australia after 55 kyr BP has all the characteristics of the earlier, Middle Palaeolithic core and flake traditions of the Old World. In western New South Wales encampments dating to 30 kyr BP around the former Lake Mungo contain burials and cremations of anatomically modern humans along with thick, so-called 'horse-hoof cores', and stone flakes. The earliest dates for the colonization of the Pacific are now 32 kyr BP from Matenkupkum cave on the island of New Ireland (Allen and Gosden 1991), while an age of 28 kyr BP has come from excavated levels in sites from Buka in the Solomons (Wickler and Spriggs 1988). The excavated stone tools are pebble tools, flakes and — on the Solomons — cores. Yet the Pleistocene super-continent of Sahul (comprising New Guinea, Australia and Tasmania) could not have been reached, nor could the colonization of western Melanesia have commenced, without the use of ocean-going boats or rafts.

The pebble tools, cores and flakes may have been excellent for woodworking, but since wood rarely survives it has been on the evidence of their stone artefacts alone, described only twenty years ago as 'crude and rather colourless' (Clark 1967), that the placement of the Australians on a low rung of the prehistoric cultural ladder has been traditionally based. Our conclusion, to the contrary, must be that stone tools are poor indicators of modern behaviour, which is better measured by the signature of range extension and continental colonization.

My second example concerns the advanced technologies of the Late Stone Age of Africa and of the Upper Palaeolithic of Europe, which were based on long, thin, parallel-sided stone blanks (known as blades) struck from carefully prepared cores. For all their sophistication, these technologies did not become permanently established. At the western Cape site of Klasies River Mouth in South Africa, thick deposits containing Middle Palaeolithic artefacts sandwich a stratigraphic level containing a completely different stone industry known as the Howiesons Poort (Singer and Wymer 1982). This employed Upper Palaeolithic technology and used non-local fine-grained stone, unlike the Middle Stone Age, which exclusively used coarse-grained local rocks. In the Howiesons Poort industry, microlithic pieces classified as lunates and crescents are common. These must have been hafted in series to form cutting edges for knives, and tips and barbs for arrows. The age of this assemblage lies between 75 and 65 kyr BP. Comparable pre-Upper Palaeolithic technologies also appear at the other end of the continent in the Cyrenaican cave of the Haua Fteah and at the caves of Tabun and Amud in Israel (McBurney 1967). In all cases this technology gives way to further levels of Middle Palaeolithic flakes struck using the Levallois technique. In no instances are there any hints of art or bone tools. Nor, unfortunately, are there any associated fossils. It is impossible to trace a gradual transition, as at Boker Tachtit (Marks 1983), from one technology to another. As a result this technological pulse has often been explained as due to the incursion of a different people with a distinctive lithic technology, followed by their local replacement.

TECHNOLOGY, TYPOLOGY AND PREHISTORIC PEOPLES

Explanations of this kind, for apparent interruptions in sequences of unilinear development in the archaeological record, presuppose the notion of an archaeological culture as an assemblage of artefacts which, recurring in time and place, is taken to be representative of a prehistoric people (Childe 1935). It is claimed that such associations between particular human cultures and particular assemblages first appear on a regional scale after 200 kyr BP with the Middle Palaeolithic, marking a clear difference from the million years before (Ronen 1982). One noticeable feature both in Europe (Bordes 1968, Mellars 1969, Binford and Binford 1966), Africa (Clark 1982) and Asia (Wu and Olsen 1985) is the appearance of patterning in the shape and numerical composition of excavated assemblages of stone tools. Far from haphazard variation, it is common to find regional differences as measured by distinctive tool types (points, scrapers, picks and triangular handaxes), as well as variation in the degree to which stone nodules were prepared before flakes of predetermined size and shape (as in the Levallois technique) were knapped. The use of such techniques is variable even within regions where high-quality stone, such as flint, is abundant.

In his pioneering work Bordes identified five principal Mousterian assemblages from the Middle Palaeolithic period in south-west France. He explained these as the lithic products of five Neanderthal tribes who inhabited the rock shelters such as Le Moustier (which gave its name to the Mousterian stone industries), La Ferrassie and Combe Grenal along the Périgord rivers. In a single cave section these assemblages would change, indicating to Bordes the fluctuating fortunes of the various groups that competed for such desirable residences in the local area.

This interpretation has however been criticized on a number of occasions. Mellars (1969, 1970) has demonstrated that the assemblages, far from being contemporaneous, are stratigraphically separated from one another, implying that they are linked by a developmental trajectory. Moreover, the hypothesis that particular assemblages are indices of particular cultures was questioned by the Binfords (1966), who argued that the variation between stone tool assemblages stemmed from the existence of different types of settlement, such as residential bases and work camps, at which different kinds of toolkits were needed.

The current debate about variability in the Mousterian focuses not so much on the *types* of tools found among these assemblages as on their *edges*. For example, Dibble (1987) has recently shown how, during its use-life, a stone tool can pass, due to resharpening, through a number of different shapes corresponding to some of the distinct types originally identified by Bordes (1961), and which he had assumed to be finished artefacts, each the realization of a pre-existent image in the mind of the knapper. We may thus suppose that the knapper focused for the most part on producing a particular working edge rather than a complete tool. The retouched edges vary from concave or convex and straight to notched or denticulate (gap-toothed) (Barton 1988). Microscopic analysis of these edges has made it possible to identify which parts were used, and in some instances on what types of material. Furthermore, such use-wear analysis has established that unretouched flakes of all shapes and sizes were regularly used as tools, and so should not be classified as waste-products of knapping, as has so often been the case (Keeley 1980).

NETWORKS, ART AND STYLE IN THE UPPER PALAEOLITHIC

The stone tools of the Late Stone Age of Africa and of the European Upper Palaeolithic have been frequently classified, on the basis of recurrent types, into cultural traditions. In many cases as much attention has been paid to distinctive type fossils as to the composition of assemblages. We now find tools of bone and antler as well as many types of recognizable stone projectile points. In the preceding period between 200 and 40 kyr BP, there are instances of similarly distinctive hafted projectile points from restricted geographical areas, such as the tanged Aterian points of North Africa (Clark 1982) and the large, flat, leaf-shaped points from southern Germany (Allsworth-Jones 1986). It is noticeable, however, that after 40 kyr BP, marking the boundary of the Upper Palaeolithic, such distinctive forms proliferate within well-defined geographical territories and chronological bands. Observations of style and design enable new discoveries to be assigned to well-dated archaeological cultures. This is not possible with the earlier Acheulean, and even with much of the Mousterian material, where dating by these means is only possible within the broadest limits.

The distances from which stone materials were obtained also increased in the Upper Palaeolithic. These could reach up to 400 km from known sources, while in addition, fossil shells, amber and marine molluscs were frequently transferred over distances of 700 km. These were often pierced and either sewn onto clothing or suspended as ornaments.

Multiple burials as at the open sites of Dolni Vestonice in Moravia (Klima 1988), Sunghir — north-east of Moscow (Bader 1978), or in the Grimaldi Caves on the Italian Riviera (Mussi 1990) now point to the elaborate disposal of the dead, which on occasion was accompanied by lavishly decorated caps and clothing (reconstructed from the distribution of thousands of ivory beads), ornaments and displays of hunting gear. Such burials are only found after 40 kyr BP. Indeed, the fact that Neanderthal 'burials' have never been found in open sites (Smirnov 1991) suggests that they do not represent instances of the ritual disposal of the dead, but are rather the earliest survivals, in the fossil record, of complete skeletons in caves (Gamble 1989). This is also the case for the finds of anatomically modern skeletons which predate 40 kyr BP. One of the anatomically modern skeletons from Qafzeh cave had a large deer antler lying across the upper torso. While this has been interpreted as a grave good (Vandermeersch 1981), beads and ornaments are lacking.

Burials younger than 40 kyr BP from other parts of the world, for example from Lake Mungo in Australia, are less elaborate as measured by grave goods but, significantly, also occur in the open where unless protected, disturbance by carnivores would be expected.

The arctic fringe of Palaeolithic Europe has produced nearly all the Pleistocene portable art. Small ivory figurines of animals and anthropo-morphs come from the caves of Vogelherd, Geissenklosterle and the Stadel Hohlenstein in southern Germany. These are all older than 30 kyr BP. A local style is apparent here, as also in south-west France where triangular engravings on limestone blocks excavated from the early Upper Palaeolithic levels at La Ferrassie and other rock shelters have been interpreted as vulvae.

At a later date, between 25 and 21 kyr BP, a widespread style in projectile points and associated female figurines came to link central and eastern Europe (Delporte 1979, Bosinski 1982). This occurred during a time of climatic cooling and is associated with the large village sites, for example Kostenki and Dolni Vestonice/Pavlov in Moravia. What is significant is that people should have been living at all in central Europe at this time of diminishing resources, increased seasonality and encroaching ice sheets onto the north European plain and out from the Alps. There is no evidence for the occupation of such a glacial corridor by archaic populations, such as the Neanderthals, so that this must count as an extension of the range of settlement, made possible by modern behaviour. The style and design, now so vivid with ornament, figu-rines and stone points, and the evidence for complex settlements with below ground storage facilities, are the archaeological signatures of modern human behaviour (see Table 2). However, it was not so much the utility of the new technology that made it possible to occupy such harsh environments as those in central Europe at that time, but rather the greatly increased range and intensity of social interaction, indicated by the scale of raw material transfers and stylistic networks (Gamble 1982, 1986).

Following the last glacial maximum in Europe (20–18 kyr BP) the practice of cave painting, concentrated in south-west France and Cantabrian Spain, made its first appearance. From this period are also a number of complex open and cave sites containing abundant carved antler and ivory objects and, on occasion, small engraved stone slabs. At Gönnersdorf, near Koblenz, the remains were excavated of a large, circular, presumably skin-covered tent. This was paved with many hundred small slate slabs which had been engraved with pictures of mammoths, horses, birds and schematic female figures. Similar rich plaque sites are known at La Marche in France, the Parpalló cave in south-east Spain and the cave of Enlène, which forms one of the three Volp caves in the Pyrenees. At this site bone, stone and walls were engraved, and in the case of the latter, painted with ochres. The art from these sites dates to the late glacial between 15 and 11 kyr BP.

In many other parts of the northern hemisphere such artistic abundance is rare or absent. The skeleton in the Upper Cave at Zhoukoudian is associated with some pierced shells and animal teeth, but India, the Near East and North Africa have produced very few ornaments and no art. In the southern hemisphere, by contrast, there is widespread evidence not only for a rich tradition of rock art, but also for its very great antiquity. The earliest rock art currently comes from Australia where engravings of animal tracks at Karolta in South Australia may be as old as 31 kyr BP (Dorn *et al.* 1988). Chaloupka (1985) has argued that rock art in the Northern Territory dates from 30 kyr BP, on the grounds of the relation between what was painted and the changes in this riverine and then coastal landscape. Recent work in the limestone caves of south-west Tasmania (Cosgrove *et al.* 1990; Jones 1990) has also found hand stencils in red ochre and blood which could be older than 14 kyr BP. In southern Africa small painted slabs from the Apollo XI rock shelter in Namibia are securely dated to 27.5 kyr BP. Lewis-Williams (1983) has argued that these depict humans and animals, and that they demonstrate a Pleistocene antiquity for curing and trance ceremonies that persisted among native San peoples into historical times. However, portable art, in the form of ostrich shell ornaments, does not become abundant in southern Africa until after 12 kyr BP (Deacon 1990).

The patchy distribution of art and display items, usually interpreted as symbolic, should not be taken to indicate that regions of the world differed at this time in their social complexity. This was the view of Hrdlicka, and of many both before (e.g., Lubbock 1865) and since, and it has caused western Europe to be ranked as one of the most impressive regions of complex hunting societies, whether past or present (Mellars 1985: 271).

The art does not, however, provide an objective measure of advance or complexity, either in subsistence organization or in social institutions. Evidently the geographical expansion in range after 40 kyr BP occurred at a time when – somewhere in the world – such symbolic artefacts were being made. However, as we have seen with the settlement of Australia and Melanesia between 55 and 30 kyr BP, the pioneers did not festoon their burials with elaborate goods, and throughout much of the northern hemisphere there was no art at all. The appearance of modern behaviour cannot therefore be identified against a checklist of 'firsts' in the archaeological record. Symbolic behaviour undoubtedly provided the framework for expanding the scale and intensity of society that resulted in such a dramatic extension of the range of habitation, but this was not generally translated into forms of material culture that have preserved. It is interesting to note that the rapid colonization of the Americas some 15 to 12 kyr BP, while marked by the distribution of highly stylized stone projectile points, was achieved without surviving art or ornament (Martin 1973).

ART AND LANGUAGE

Art and language are commonly linked in archaeological discussions of the emergence of modern humanity. The extra dimension of symbolism and abstraction, and the culturally constructed worlds that linguistic communication permits, are seen by many as marking a great divide and as standing at the base of the human revolution.

Persistent claims have however been made, notably by Marshack (1972, 1989), for the existence of symbolic systems much earlier than 40 kyr BP. The evidence is sparse and invariably equivocal. It consists of a polished lammella of mammoth ivory, deeply scored zigzags on bones and pierced phalanges. All of the material comes from Europe (Chase and Dibble 1987, Lindly and Clark 1990). While these objects certainly raise questions, their extreme rarity and the possibility of more prosaic explanations, such as that the marks were caused by butchery, tend to undermine claims to either the antiquity or the continuity of symbolic systems. Nor does the production of such a disparate group of objects over such a long period of time provide much evidence of language, which would be required to express such symbolic content (Davidson and Noble 1989).

The argument is once again over continuity versus replacement. Archaic hominids in the Old World are all credited with communication skills both verbal and visual. However, as Lieberman shows in the following article (see also 1989), the modern voice-box which produces verbal language, in the form in which we know it today, had to evolve. The restrictions on phonetic production, as revealed by his reconstructions of the shape and position of the Neanderthal tongue, mean that the facility of rapid speech transmission enjoyed by all modern humans would have been limited. While evidence for cortical asymmetry, and hence for the lateralization of brain functions, can be traced in endocasts from East African *Homo erectus*, and while Broca's area – which controls the sequencing of the vocal cords and is hence a precondition for advanced vocal skills (Passingham 1982) – is present in *Homo habilis* from Africa, the laryngeal tract or voice-box that can capitalize on such developments would seem to have been a feature of only the last 200 kyr and, more specifically, to be associated with anatomically modern skulls and mandibles. (The contrary argument, that even *Homo habilis* was capable of spoken language, is advanced by Tobias in the previous article of this volume.)

Taking the view that spoken language was recent, Davidson and Noble (1989) argue that its appearance was intimately connected with that of art, and therefore that the chronology of language cannot be extended back beyond the earliest forms of artistic depiction. The effect of depiction, they claim, is to freeze a significant gesture so that it outlives the transient context of its production, thus allowing viewers not merely to perceive its meaning, but to perceive that it *has* a meaning. It is this recognition of the meaningful quality of signs that, according to Davidson and Noble, marks the transition from simple communication to language. And this, in turn, underwrites the possibility of socially shared systems of meaning – that is, of culture. As they put it, 'there can be no such thing as culture without language and the socially determined sharing of meaning and value. It will therefore be misleading to talk of culture for any hominids before fully modern humans' (1989: 137). Such conclusions obviously support the replacement model for modern human origins.

However, there is of course a problem here in that anatomically modern humans are known from at least 130 kyr BP at Omo Kibish and Ngaloba in East Africa, and yet the earliest depictions are not encountered until after 40 kyr BP. Consequently, others have favoured the idea that there already existed a *palaeoculture* during this longer period. This would entail a simpler system of communication, one that did not depend so heavily on symbols for the infusion of meaning, and yet accommodated the repetition of design elements and stylistic traits found in stone tools from the Lower and Middle Palaeolithic. Palaeocultural hominids would have possessed speech but not full language. Whallon (1989) has argued that the critical tense-modality aspect of language, which confers the power of efficient memory, would have come last. Without this feature, the abilities to discuss the future and to use the knowledge of the past would have been limited. Such a view of hominid palaeoculture favours the idea that social and cultural evolution was a slow, accretional process (Lindly and Clark 1990).

LANGUAGE IN EVOLUTIONARY CONTEXT

In order to evaluate the two models we must return to the contexts in which selection for improved vocal apparatus and verbal language skills occurred. To consider the rate of evolution in just one aspect, such as the voice-box, is like asking how long it took to become fully bipedal or to develop the precision grip without investigating the contexts that required and so selected what, with hindsight, are such 'obviously sensible' developments.

The context to which I return is set by the scale of society and the extension of range by modern populations after 40 kyr BP. In the long term of the last million years the repetitive environmental cycles of the ice ages (every 50 kyr, then every 100 kyr) were such that behaviour which facilitated an extension of occupation in existing ranges would have been positively selected (Vrba 1985, Gamble 1993). The recurrent rhythms of these cycles, which controlled the distribution of population in such seasonal environments, could only be overcome by the construction of social mechanisms. These depended in turn upon organizational frameworks whose maintenance required a continuous supply of information. Language provides the means for efficient memory, which not only allows hunters to plan forward but also permits the elaboration of social networks which are the channels along which such planning flows. Before this aspect of language had developed, planning depth would have been restricted and, as we have seen, many environments would have remained uncolonized.

I have already shown that the association between art, in its broadest sense, and colonization is tenuous. I would therefore rephrase Davidson and Noble's contention so as to place less emphasis on the significance of art in determining when modern culture appeared. I would stress instead that the colonization of environments after 40 kyr BP could only have taken place thanks to language, which allowed for the symbolic constructions of society and of social networks, *some* (but not all) of which were depicted. I do however agree with Davidson and Noble that culture can only exist together with language. The notion of a palaeoculture with a reduced level of symbolic content is, I believe, untenable. Symbolism is not a quality of social life that can be turned up and down. Either all behaviour is symbolically constructed, or none of it can be. The transition would be punctuated, a revolution rather than a gradual process. The behavioural confusion which would result from variable levels of symbolic organization, or from the possibility of being able to represent some contexts but not others within a symbolic framework, would produce a creature too muddled to construct its own environment. Death by self-imposed culture shock could be the only verdict on such a hapless hominid.

COLONIZATION AND SETTLING DOWN

From the archaeological perspective of the last million years, humanity emerged as a consequence of global colonization. It is no longer adequate to follow Hrdlicka's view that given *enough time*, the human drift would reach all parts of the globe. Archaeological discussions of humanity are only just beginning to recover from the deliberate shelving by scientists such as Wallace (1880), over a century ago, of the question of human distribution. In the intervening period too much attention has been paid to identifying centres of origin and to constructing from them a unilinear view of human development signposted, as I have shown, by technology, ritual and art. These schemes have ignored the obvious fact that our ancestors must have been very different beings when they only occupied part of the globe. That this partial occupation occurred at a time when behaviour was not yet constructed symbolically should come as no surprise.

The implications are considerable for understanding later processes of prehistory, which capitalized on this platform of global humanity. From such a perspective we can begin to regard the selection of certain plants and animals for domestication as just another element in the extension of the range of human settlement. Childe's (1935) concept of a Neolithic revolution that ushered in the prehistory of the modern world is no longer tenable. From a longer, Pleistocene perspective, the regular use of tropical rain forests, deserts and islands depends not so much on the elaboration of technology as on the intensification of social life to surmount the recurrent problems of fission and of tethering to resources. While the Sahara and the Pacific as well as much of the rain forest were first settled by horticulturalists and pastoralists rather than by fisher-gatherer-hunters, my point is that these economic labels are no longer very informative. What is critical is the extension of social networks now supported by the intensification of production which they originally called forth. The divisions between hunter and herder and between forager and farmer are legacies from the last century, which are generally unhelpful in understanding the evolution of humanity.

Finally, as Graves (1991) has pointed out, every age defines what a modern human will be through diverse and different media, as they construct their worlds in a myriad of different social contexts. This makes the search for the point of origin of modern humans a quest after an illusion. What we can conclude, however, is that the 'insufficient effectiveness' which Hrdlicka attributed to prehistoric hunters, and his idea of a human drift driven by necessity towards a global humanity, must finally be laid to rest in the investigation of human diversity, past and present.

REFERENCES

Allen, J. and Gosden, C. (1991) *Report of the Lapita Homeland Project*, Canberra: Department of Prehistory, Research School of Pacific Studies, Australian National University.

Allsworth-Jones, P. (1986) *The Szeletian and the Transition from Middle to Upper Palaeolithic in Central Europe*, Oxford: Clarendon Press.

Bader, O. N. (1978) *Sunghir*, Moscow: Nauka.

Bailey, R. C., Head, G., Jenike, M., Owen, B., Retchman, R. and Zechenter, E. (1989) 'Hunting and gathering in the tropical rain forest: is it possible?', *American Anthropologist* 91: 59–82.

Bar-Yosef, O. (1980) 'Prehistory of the Levant', *Annual Review of Anthropology* 9: 101–33.

Barton, C. M. (1988) *Lithic Variability and Middle Palaeolithic Behaviour*, BAR International Series 408, Oxford.

Binford, L. R. (1978) *Nunamiut Ethnoarchaeology*, New York: Academic Press.

—— (1984) 'Butchering, sharing, and the archaeological record', *Journal of Anthropological Archaeology* 3: 235–57.

—— (1985) 'Human ancestors: changing views of their behaviour', *Journal of Anthropological Archaeology* 4: 292–327.

Binford, L. R. and Binford, S. R. (1966) 'A preliminary analysis of functional variability in the mousterian of levallois facies', *American Anthropologist* 68 (2): 238–95.

Bordes, F. (1961) 'Mousterian cultures in France', *Science* 134: 803–10.

—— (1968) *The Old Stone Age*, London: Weidenfeld & Nicolson.

Bosinski, G. (1982) *Die Kunst Der Eiszeit in Deutschland und in der Schweiz*, Bonn: Habelt.

Brace, C. L. (1964) 'The fate of the "classic" Neanderthals: a consideration of hominid catastrophism', *Current Anthropology* 5: 3–43.

—— (1979) 'Krapina, "Classic" Neanderthals, and the evolution of the European face', *Journal of Human Evolution* 8: 527–50.

Brooks, A. and Robertshaw, P. (1990) 'The glacial maximum in tropical Africa: 22,000–12,000 BP', in C. Gamble and O. Soffer (eds) *The World at 18,000 BP*, vol. 2, 'Low Latitudes', London: Unwin Hyman.

Brose, D. and Wolpoff, M. (1971) 'Early upper paleolithic man and late middle palaeolithic tools', *American Anthropologist* 73: 1156–94.

Callow, P. and Cornford, J. M. (eds) (1986) *La Cotte de St Brelade 1961–1978. Excavations by C. B. M. McBurney*, Norwich: Geo Books.

Cann, R., Stoneking, M. and Wilson, A. (1987). 'Mitochondrial DNA and human evolution', *Nature* 325: 31–6.

Cavalli-Sforza, L. L., Piazza, A., Menozzi, P. and Mountain, J. (1988) 'Reconstruction of human evolution: bringing together genetic, archaeological, and linguistic data', *Proceedings of the National Academy of Sciences of the USA* 85: 6002–6.

Chaloupka, G. (1985) 'Chronological sequence of Arnhem Land rock art', in R. Jones (ed.) *Archaeological Research in Kakadu National Park*, Canberra: Australian National Parks and Wildlife Service, Special Publication 13.

Chase, P. and Dibble, H. L. (1987) 'Middle palaeolithic symbolism: a review of current evidence and interpretations', *Journal of Anthropological Archaeology* 6: 263–96.

Childe, V. G. (1935) 'Changing methods and aims in prehistory', *Proceedings of the Prehistoric Society* 1: 1–15.

Clark, G. A. (1992) 'Continuity or replacement? Putting modern human origins in an evolutionary context', in H. L. Dibble and P. A. Mellars (eds) *The Middle Palaeolithic: Adaptation, Behaviour, and Variability*, Philadelphia: The University Museum.

Clark, G. A. and Lindly, J. (1989) 'The case for continuity: observations on the biocultural transition in Europe and western Asia', in P. Mellars and C. Stringer (eds) *The Human Revolution: Behavioural and Biological Perspectives on the Origins of Modern Humans*, Edinburgh: Edinburgh University Press.

Clark, J. D. (1982) 'The cultures of the Middle Palaeolithic/Middle Stone Age', in J. D. Clark (ed.) *The Cambridge History of Africa*, vol. I: 'From the earliest times to *c.*500 BC', Cambridge: Cambridge University Press.

Clark, J. G. D. (1967) *World Prehistory in New Perspective*, Cambridge: Cambridge University Press.

Coon, C. S. (1962) *The Origin of Races*, London: Cape.

Cosgrove, R., Allen, J. and Marshall, B. (1990) 'Palaeo-ecology and pleistocene human occupation in south central Tasmania', *Antiquity* 64: 59–87.

Darwin, C. (1859) *On the Origin of Species by Means of Natural Selection, or the Preservation of Favoured Races in the Struggle for Life*, [1968 edition], Harmondsworth: Penguin.

Davidson, I. and Noble, W. (1989) 'The archaeology of perception: traces of depiction and languages', *Current Anthropology* 30: 125–55.

Deacon, J. (1990) 'Changes in the archaeological record in South Africa at 18,000 BP', in C. Gamble and O. Soffer (eds) *The World at 18,000 BP*, vol. 2, 'Low Latitudes', London: Unwin Hyman.

Delporte, H. (1979) *L'Image de la femme dans l'art préhistorique*, Paris: Picard.

Dibble, H. L. (1987) 'The interpretation of middle palaeolithic scraper morphology', *American Antiquity* 52: 109–17.

Dorn, R. I., Nobbs, M. and Cahill, T. (1988) 'Cation-ratio dating of rock-engravings from the Olary Province of arid South Australia', *Antiquity* 62: 681–9.

Dzaparidze, V., Bosinski, G., Bugianisvili, T., Gabunia, L., Justus, A., Klopotovskaja, N., Kvavadze, E., Lordkipanidze, D., Majsuradze, G., Mgeladze, N., Nioradze, M., Pavelenisvili, E., Schmincke, H-U., Sologasvili, D., Tusabramisvili, D.,

Tvalcrelidze, M. and Vekua, A. (1989) 'Der altpaläolithische Fundplatz Dmanisi in Georgien (Kaukasus)', *Jahrbuch des Römisch-Germanischen Zentralmuseums Mainz* 36: 67–116.

Foley, R. (1989) 'The ecological conditions of speciation: a comparative approach to the origins of anatomically modern humans', in P. Mellars and C. Stringer (eds) *The Human Revolution: Behavioural and Biological Perspectives on the Origins of Modern Humans*, Edinburgh: Edinburgh University Press.

Gamble, C. S. (1982) 'Interaction and alliance in palaeolithic society', *Man* (N.S.) 17: 92–107.

—— (1984) 'Regional variation in hunter-gatherer strategy in the upper pleistocene of Europe', in R. Foley (ed.) *Hominid Evolution and Community Ecology*, London: Academic Press.

—— (1986) *The Palaeolithic Settlement of Europe*, Cambridge: Cambridge University Press.

—— (1989) 'Comment on R. Gargett, "Grave shortcomings: the evidence for Neanderthal burial"', *Current Anthropology* 30: 181–2.

—— (ed.) (1992) 'The uttermost ends of the earth' (special section), *Antiquity* 66.

—— (1993) *Timewalkers: the Prehistory of Global Colonization*, Harvard: Harvard University Press.

Gamble, C. S. and Soffer, O. (eds) (1990) *The World at 18,000 BP*, vol. 2, 'Low Latitudes', London: Unwin Hyman.

Graves, P. M. (1991) 'New models and metaphors for the Neanderthal debate', *Current Anthropology* 32: 513–41.

Hammond, M. (1982) 'The expulsion of the Neanderthals from human ancestry: Marcellin Boule and the social context of scientific research', *Social Studies of Science* 12: 1–36.

Howell, F. C. (1965) *Early Man*, London: Time Life Books.

Hrdlicka, A. (1922) 'The peopling of Asia', *Proceedings of the American Philosophical Society* 60: 535–45.

Isaac, G. L. (1981) 'Archaeological tests of alternative models of early hominid behaviour: excavations and experiments', *Philosophical Transactions of the Royal Society of London*, ser. B 292: 177–88.

Jones, R. (1990) 'From Kakadu to Kutikina: the southern continent at 18,000 years ago', in C. Gamble and O. Soffer (eds) *The World at 18,000 BP*, vol. 2, 'Low Latitudes', London: Unwin Hyman.

Keeley, L. H. (1980) *Experimental Determination of Stone Tool Use: a Microwear Analysis*, Chicago: University of Chicago Press.

Klima, B. (1988) 'A triple burial from the upper palaeolithic of Dolní Vestonice, Czechoslovakia', *Journal of Human Evolution* 16: 831–5.

Leacock, E. and Lee, R. B. (eds) (1982) *Politics and History in Band Societies*, Cambridge: Cambridge University Press.

Lewis-Williams, J. D. (1983) *The Rock Art of Southern Africa*, Cambridge: Cambridge University Press.

Lieberman, P. (1989) 'The origins of some aspects of human language and cognition', in P. Mellars and C. Stringer (eds) *The Human Revolution: Behavioural and Biological Perspectives on the Origins of Modern Humans*, Edinburgh: Edinburgh University Press.

Lindly, J. and Clark, G. A. (1990) 'Symbolism and modern human origins', *Current Anthropology* 31: 233–40.

Lubbock, J. (1865) *Pre-historic Times, as illustrated by Ancient Remains and the Manners and Customs of Modern Savages*, London: Williams and Norgate.

McBurney, C. B. M. (1967) *The Haua Fteah (Cyrenaica) and the Stone Age of the South East Mediterranean*, Cambridge: Cambridge University Press.

Marks, A. E. (1983) 'The middle to upper palaeolithic transition in the Levant', *Advances in World Archaeology* 2: 51–98.

Marshack, A. (1972) *The Roots of Civilization*, New York: McGraw-Hill.

—— (1989) 'Early hominid symbol and evolution of the human capacity', in P. Mellars (ed.) *The Emergence of Modern Humans: an Archaeological Perspective*, Edinburgh: Edinburgh University Press.

Martin, P. S. (1973) 'The discovery of America', *Science* 179: 969–74.

Mazel, A. D. (1989) 'People making history: the last ten thousand years of hunter-gatherer communities in the Thukela Basin', *Natal Museum Journal of Humanities* 1: 1–168.

Mellars, P. A. (1969) 'The chronology of mousterian industries in the Périgord region of south-west France', *Proceedings of the Prehistoric Society* 35: 134–71.

—— (1970) 'Some comments on the notion of "functional variability" in stone tool assemblages', *World Archaeology* 2: 74–89.

—— (1985) 'The ecological basis of social complexity in the Upper Palaeolithic of southwestern France', in T. D. Price and J. A. Brown (eds) *Prehistoric Hunter-Gatherers: the Emergence of Cultural Complexity*, Orlando: Academic Press.

Mellars, P. A. and Stringer, C. B. (eds) (1989) *The Human Revolution. Behavioural and Biological Perspectives on the Origins of Modern Humans*, Edinburgh: Edinburgh University Press.

Mussi, M. (1990) 'Continuity and change in Italy at the last glacial maximum', in O. Soffer and C. Gamble (eds) *The World at 18 000 BP*, vol. 1, 'High Latitudes', London: Unwin Hyman.

Paddayya, K. (1982) *The Acheulian Culture of the Hunsgi Valley (Peninsular India): a Settlement System Perspective*, Poona: Deccan College Postgraduate and Research Institute.

Passingham, R. E. (1982) *The Human Primate*, Oxford: W. H. Freeman.

Praslov, N. D. and Rogachev, A. N. (eds) (1982). *Palaeolithic of the Kostenki-Borshevo Area on the Don River, 1879–1979*, Leningrad: Nauka.

Ranov, V. A. (1991) 'Les sites très anciens de l'âge de la pierre en URSS', in E. Bonifay and B. Vandermeersch (eds) *Les Premiers Peuplements Humains de l'Europe*, Actes du 114e Congrès National de Sociétés Savantes, Paris.

Ronen, A. (ed.) (1982) *The Transition from Lower to Middle Palaeolithic and the Origin of Modern Man*, Oxford: BAR International Series 151.

Schrire, C. (ed.) (1984) *Past and Present in Hunter-Gatherer Studies*, London: Academic Press.

Singer, R. and Wymer, J. (1982) *The Middle Stone Age at Klasies River Mouth in South Africa*, Chicago: University of Chicago Press.

Smirnov, Y. A. (1991) *Middle Palaeolithic Burials* (in Russian), Moscow: Nauka.

Soffer, O. (1985) *The Upper Palaeolithic of the Central Russian Plain*, New York: Academic Press.

Soffer, O. and Gamble, C. S. (eds) (1990) *The World at 18,000 BP*, 2 vols, London: Unwin Hyman.

Sollas, W. J. (1911) *Ancient Hunters and their Modern Representatives*, London: Macmillan.

Stringer, C. B. and Gamble, C. S. (1993) *In Search of the Neanderthals*, London: Thames & Hudson.

Trinkaus, E. (1982) 'Evolutionary continuity among archaic *Homo sapiens*', in A. Ronen (ed.) *The Transition from Lower to Middle Palaeolithic and the Origin of Modern Man*, Oxford: BAR International Series 151.

Vandermeersch, B. (1981) *Les Hommes fossiles de Qafzeh (Israel)*, Paris: Centre National de la Recherche Scientifique.

Vrba, E. S. (1985) 'Ecological and adaptive changes associated with early hominid evolution', in E. Delson (ed.) *Ancestors: the Hard Evidence*, New York: Alan R.Liss.

Wallace, A. R. (1880) *Island Life: or the Phenomena and Causes of Insular Faunas and Floras, Including a Revision and Attempted Solution of the Problem of Geological Climates*, London: Macmillan.

Whallon, R. (1989). 'Elements of cultural change in the later palaeolithic', in P. Mellars and C. Stringer (eds) *The Human Revolution: Behavioural and Biological Perspectives on the Origins of Modern Humans*, Edinburgh: Edinburgh University Press.

Wickler, S. and Spriggs, M. (1988) 'Pleistocene human occupation of the Solomon Islands, Melanesia', *Antiquity* 62: 703–6.

Wolpoff, M. H. (1989) 'Multiregional evolution: the fossil alternative to Eden', in P. Mellars and C. Stringer (eds) *The Human Revolution: Behavioural and Biological Perspectives on the Origins of Modern Humans*, Edinburgh: Edinburgh University Press.

Wolpoff, M. H., Spuhler, J. N., Smith, F. H., Radovčić, J., Pope, G., Frayer, D. W., Eckhardt, R. and Clark, G. (1988) 'Modern human origins', *Science* 241: 772–3.

Wu Rukang and Olsen, J. W. (eds) (1985) *Palaeoanthropoloqy and Palaeolithic Archaeology in the People's Republic of China*, Orlando: Academic Press.

Yellen, J. E. (1977) *Archaeological Approaches to the Present. Models for Reconstructing the Past*, New York: Academic Press.

FURTHER READING

Binford, L. R. (1983) *In Pursuit of the Past*, London: Thames & Hudson.

Brace, C. L. (1984) 'The fate of the "classic" Neanderthals: a consideration of hominid catastrophism', *Current Anthropology* 5: 3–43.

Cann, R., Stoneking, M. and Wilson, A. (1987) 'Mitochondrial DNA and human evolution', *Nature* 325: 31–6.

Foley, R. (1987) *Another Unique Species*, London: Longmans.

Gamble, C. S. (1993) *Timewalkers: the Prehistory of Global Colonization*, Harvard: Harvard University Press.

—— (1986) *The Palaeolithic Settlement of Europe*, Cambridge: Cambridge University Press.

Graves, P. M. (1991) 'New models and metaphors for the Neanderthal debate', *Current Anthropology* 32: 513–41.

Klein, R. G. (1989) *The Human Career: Human Biological and Cultural Origins*, Chicago: University of Chicago Press.

Mellars, P. and Stringer, C. (eds) (1989) *The Human Revolution: Behavioural and Biological Perspectives on the Origins of Modern Humans*, Edinburgh: Edinburgh University Press.

Richards, G. (1987) *Human Evolution: an Introduction for the Behavioural Sciences*, London: Routledge & Kegan Paul.

Ronen, A. (ed.) (1982) *The Transition from Lower to Middle Palaeolithic and the Origin of Modern Man*, Oxford: BAR International Series 151.

Soffer, O. (1985) *The Upper Palaeolithic of the Central Russian Plain*, New York: Academic Press.

Soffer, O. and Gamble, C. (eds) (1990) *The World at 18,000 BP*, vol. 1: 'High Latitudes'; vol. 2: 'Low Latitudes', London: Unwin Hyman.

Stringer, C. B. and Gamble, C. S. (1993) *In Search of the Neanderthals*, London: Thames & Hudson.
Trinkaus, E. (ed.) (1989) *The Emergence of Modern Humans*, Cambridge: Cambridge University Press.

5

THE ORIGINS AND EVOLUTION OF LANGUAGE

Philip Lieberman

It has become apparent that human linguistic ability derives from a number of specialized neural and anatomical mechanisms. Though the particular language that a child acquires obviously depends on the child's particular cultural environment, the general properties of all human languages are structured by the characteristics of these biological mechanisms. These innate attributes are species-specific; they differentiate anatomically modern *Homo sapiens* from all other living animals. However, they act in concert with brain mechanisms and anatomical structures that we share with other related animals, to form the biological substrates of human language. It has also become clear that the various components of human linguistic ability are to a degree independent and derive from biological mechanisms that have different evolutionary histories.

Language thus seems to derive from a constellation of biological mechanisms – the neural mechanisms that are the bases of the brain's 'dictionary', for example, also appear to be involved in the way that we and other animals learn by association. The neural mechanisms that regulate the production of human speech, though they probably derive from mechanisms for fine manual motor control, appear to provide the basis for syntax. Their evolutionary history accounts for their particular properties. Knowledge of the origins and evolution of language can, therefore, provide fresh insights into the properties of human language and thought.

ANIMAL VERSUS HUMAN LANGUAGE

Human language obviously differs from the communication systems of other animals, even those of closely related animals like chimpanzees and gorillas. However, the precise nature of the distinction has, until very recently, eluded science. In the late 1960s it became apparent that chimpanzees are able to understand and communicate using words transmitted by means of manual sign language (Gardner and Gardner 1969). The number of words that a chimpanzee raised in a human-like environment is able to learn is very limited compared with a human child, but the chimpanzee's words, like those of human language, represent concepts rather than specific objects or actions. Thus the word *car* is a symbol not for any specific car, but for a class of vehicles. The chimpanzee's words, like the words that humans use, have 'fuzzy' conceptual references; their 'meanings' reflect real-world experiences and the conceptual framework derived from these experiences (Bronowski 1971, 1978, Lieberman 1984, 1989, 1991).

Chimpanzees, like human beings, coin new words to describe new experiences and transmit the words that they know to the next generation (Fouts *et al.* 1982). Analysis of the errors that chimpanzees make while communicating with manually signed words reveals that they seem to think in terms of the words that they know (Gardner and Gardner 1984). Informal observations of many other animals indicate that they, too, appear to understand a limited number of words; controlled experiments with cetaceans, dogs and parrots confirm that this is indeed the case (Herman and Tavolga 1980, Schusterman and Krieger 1984, Warden and Warner 1928, Pepperberg 1981).

It seems most likely that 'distributed neural networks', of the kind originally proposed by Hebb (1949), are responsible for the dictionaries that exist in the brains of human beings and other animals. Neural networks essentially integrate and store the responses of neurons to stimuli in the complex *pathways* that connect these neurons. A 'memory trace' of an event does not reside in a particular location but in the connections between the neurons. Neural networks have inherent properties that provide a 'mechanical' basis for learning by means of association; they have other properties that match the behaviour of animals as they learn to cope with new phenomena (Anderson 1988, Bear *et al.* 1987). Computer models that simulate distributed neural networks can derive the concepts that underlie rule-governed phenomena like the 'morphological' distinctions differentiating the plural and singular forms of English verbs (Sejnowski *et al.* 1988). The difference between the brains of humans and other animals is probably quantitative in this regard (Anderson 1988); the rudiments of the neural bases of the linguistic dictionary can be seen in such simple animals as molluscs (Lieberman 1984). In other words, the difference between the abilities of humans and other animals with respect to the lexicon – words and the concepts that they stand for – is one of degree. Animals that are phylogenetically closer to modern human beings appear to approximate more closely to human ability. However, the quantitative difference is extreme; chimpanzees never progress beyond the abilities of average three-year-old human children.

The qualitative distinctions between human language and the communication systems of other animals appear to lie in speech and syntax (Bickerton 1990, Lieberman 1991). Human beings are able to talk – no other living animal can do this. Moreover, comparative studies also demonstrate that language-trained apes are unable to attain the syntactic abilities of even three-year-old human children. Both speech and syntax appear to derive from our possession of species-specific brain mechanisms and anatomical structures. The fossil record indicates that these may have evolved in comparatively recent times, that is between one and two hundred thousand years ago, and may differentiate anatomically modern *Homo sapiens* from extinct archaic hominids.

HUMAN SPEECH

Until the 1960s it was not realized that speech is itself an important component of human linguistic ability. Linguists thought that any set of arbitrary sounds would suffice to transmit words. Research that was initially directed at making a machine that would read books to blind people demonstrated however that the sounds of speech had a special status (Liberman *et. al.* 1967). Speech allows us to transmit phonetic 'segments' (which correspond approximately to the letters of the alphabet) at an extremely rapid rate, up to 25 per second. By contrast, we are unable to identify non-speech sounds at rates that exceed 7 to 9 items per second. A short sentence such as this one, if read aloud, contains about fifty speech sounds. These sounds, or phonetic segments, can be uttered in two seconds, and human listeners have no particular difficulty in understanding what has been spoken. If this sentence were transmitted at the non-speech rate, it would take so long that a listener would forget the beginning of the sentence before hearing its end. The high transmission rate of human speech is thus an integral part of human linguistic ability, as it allows complex ideas to be transmitted within the constraints of short-term memory.

Although sign language can also achieve a high transmission rate, the signer's hands cannot be used at the same time for other tasks. Nor can viewers see the signer's hands, except under restricted conditions. The emergence of vocal language thus represents a continuation of the trend in hominid evolution towards freeing the hands for carrying and tool use, a trend that started with upright posture and bipedal locomotion. Some scholars have claimed that human language was at one time exclusively gestural (Hewes 1973). This is most unlikely, however, since many of the anatomical specializations for vocal communication are present in all primates (monkeys, apes and humans). The comparative anatomist Victor Negus (1949) showed that the larynges of primates are specialized for the production of vocal signals, even though the anatomical modifications entailed are at the expense of respiratory efficiency. Furthermore, as we shall see, the evolution of the human tongue and supralaryngeal airway could not have occurred unless vocal communication was not already an important factor in the communication systems or languages of archaic hominids. It is therefore likely that hominids always communicated by means of both vocal and gestural signals.

THE PHYSIOLOGY OF SPEECH

Research that started in the time of Johannes Muller (1848) shows that the production of speech is in many ways analogous to the performance of music on a woodwind instrument or pipe organ. Figure 1 shows the three basic anatomical components that are involved in speech. The lungs provide the motive power. During quiet respiration the phases of inspiration and expiration are roughly equal; the amount of air that passes into the lungs closely matches the oxygen requirements of a person's activity. A set of 'chemoreceptors' monitor oxygen requirements to meet 'vegetative' needs (the oxygen requirements of

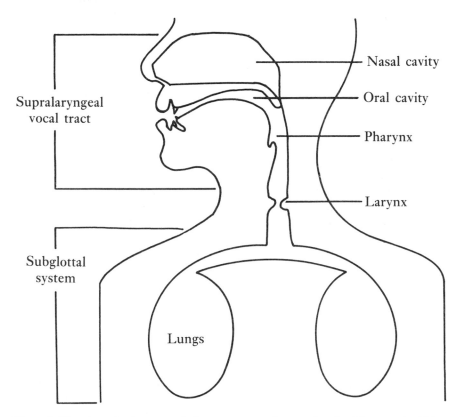

Figure 1 The three basic anatomical components that are involved in speech. (After Lieberman 1984)

the body); for example, we automatically breathe more air when we run. During the production of speech human beings deviate from these vegetative constraints — the airflow from the lungs is modified to conform to *linguistic* goals. The duration of expiration is usually keyed to the length of a sentence; the amount of air that we take into our lungs varies according to the length of the sentence that we *intend* to speak. We override the oxygen limits set by the chemoreceptors and typically hyperventilate when we talk. Moreover, as Darwin (1859) noted, the morphology of the human lungs which, like all lungs, evolved from the swim bladders of fish, produces an air pressure function that is keyed to their volume. In the absence of speech, the air pressure generated by the lungs during expiration is initially very high and falls as the lungs deflate. This would interfere with the operation of the larynx. A complex set of manoeuvres involving the muscles of the abdomen and chest must be executed whenever we talk or sing to produce a steady air pressure.

The human larynx evolved from a simple valve that sealed the lungs of lungfish while they swam. A series of adaptations has modified the larynx for the production of sound; the human larynx does not differ materially in this respect from the larynges of many other animals, such as dogs and non-human primates (Negus 1949). Its primary speech function is to convert efficiently the relatively steady airflow from the lungs into a source of acoustic energy by means of the process of *phonation*. Phonation occurs when sounds like the vowels of English, or consonants like [v] or [m], are produced. It involves the *vocal cords* of the larynx, which are a complex assemblage of muscles, cartilage and other soft tissue, rapidly opening and closing, and thereby interrupting the airflow out from the lungs.

The periodic laryngeal air 'pulses' constitute a rich source of acoustic energy. The larynx's role in the process of phonation is similar to that of the reed of a woodwind instrument. The perceived *pitch* of a person's voice reflects the average rate at which the laryngeal air pulses occur. This rate is the *fundamental frequency* of phonation (F0); the calls that many animals use for communication are differentiated by the fundamental frequency pattern. Our present knowledge of the vocal communications of animals is, however, extremely limited. Goodall (1986), for example, notes that chimpanzees in their natural habitat make dozens of different calls whose detailed acoustic structure or precise function is unknown.

Most human languages also make use of variations in the fundamental frequency pattern to convey different words. The 'tones' of Mandarin Chinese, for example, differentiate words: the syllable [ma] produced with a falling F0 pattern means 'scolding', when it is produced with a level F0 pattern it means 'mother'. The *intonation* or melody of speech also derives in part from the activity of the larynx. All human languages make use of intonation, which involves the F0 pattern and amplitude of the laryngeal source (and the relative duration of words) to signal which words constitute a sentence. The necessity for stabilizing the air pressure generated by the lungs, noted above, derives

from the fact that F0 is determined in part by air pressure. Controlled variations in the air pressure generated by the lungs are used by human speakers
to signal emphasis by placing linguistic *stress* on words.

The supralaryngeal vocal tract consists of the airway above the larynx.
Figure 2 shows a schematic cross-sectional view of the supralaryngeal vocal
tract of a normal adult human. The oral (mouth) and nasal (nose) cavities can
be seen, separated by the hard and soft palate which form the roof of the
mouth. The velum, which is the posterior (back) part of the roof of the mouth,
is a flap that can move upwards to seal the nasal cavity off from the rest of
the supralaryngeal airway. Nasal sounds, like the English consonants [m] and
[n], are produced when the velum is lowered. Most of the speech sounds of
English and other languages are 'oral' (that is, non-nasal) and are produced
with a raised velum. The contour of the human tongue seen in cross-section
is rounded. We can see only half of the tongue when we look into someone's
mouth; more than half is positioned in the pharynx, which runs down into the

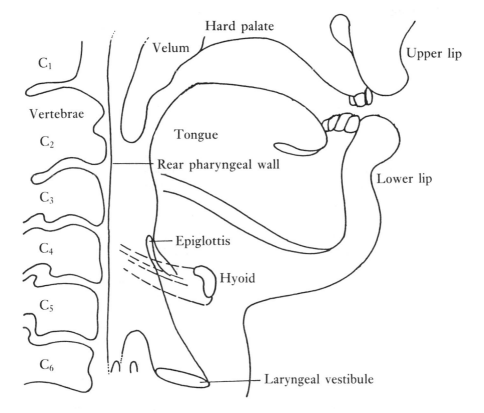

Figure 2 Schematized cross-sectional view of a normal adult human supralaryngeal
vocal tract. (After Lieberman 1984)

113

throat. Note the low position in the throat of the larynx and the 'epiglottis'. The epiglottis is another flap of soft tissue. Though some older anatomy texts claim that the epiglottis folds down to cover the entrance to the larynx when we swallow, this is not in fact the case. This can cause complications in swallowing since solid food and liquid must pass over the entrance to the larynx to get into the oesophagus (the entrance to the digestive system) which is positioned behind the larynx. Human beings must execute a complex manoeuvre in which they pull their larynx forward and upwards to safely swallow liquids and solid food (Negus 1949). The way that humans swallow differs dramatically from that of all other terrestrial mammals and, as we shall see, it reflects adaptations of the human supralaryngeal airway for speech production.

The role of the supralaryngeal vocal tract during speech is that of an *acoustic filter*. Sunglasses and stained-glass windows are perhaps more obvious examples of filters. These optical filters selectively absorb energy at different spectral frequencies. The colour or colours that we see through a pair of sunglasses or through a stained-glass window depend on the frequencies at which relatively more light energy passes through the filter. The source of light (the sun) obviously affects the colours that we see. If we look at a candle flame through a stained-glass window, the colours will shift to red, because the candlelight has more energy at lower (red) frequencies.

Woodwind instruments and pipe organs are examples of musical instruments that achieve their effects by means of analogous acoustic filtering. The *formant frequencies* of speech sounds are the frequencies at which maximum acoustic energy will get through the supralaryngeal airway, which acts in a similar fashion to the pipe organ or bassoon, in letting relatively more acoustic energy through at the formant frequencies. During the production of human speech we continually change the shape and length of the supralaryngeal airway by moving the tongue, lips, larynx and velum. This changes the filtering characteristics of the vocal tract, therefore continually changing the formant frequency pattern. The high transmission rate of human speech is achieved through the generation of rapidly changing formant-frequency patterns and rapid temporal and spectral cues by the species-specific human supralaryngeal airway.

Figure 3 illustrates the filtering effect of the supralaryngeal vocal tract. The uppermost graph shows the filter function for the vowel [i], the vowel of the word *bee*. The formant frequencies, F1, F2 and F3, are the frequencies at which maximum acoustic energy will get through the supralaryngeal airway. The plot in the centre shows the spectrum of the acoustic signal produced by the larynx. This is roughly similar to the sound that you would hear (a raspy buzz) if you held the reed of a woodwind instrument and blew through it. The acoustic energy at the fundamental frequency of phonation shows up at 500 Hz as the line furthest to the left in the graph. The laryngeal output also has energy at the harmonics of F0 (the multiples of 500 Hz): 1 kHz, 1.5 kHz, 2.0 kHz, etc. The lower plot shows the net effect of the filter on the glottal

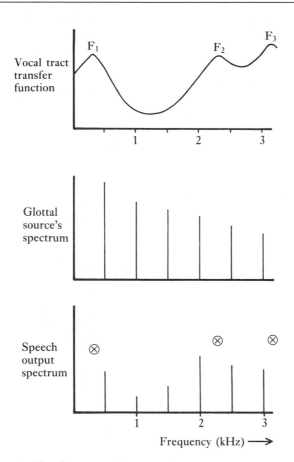

Vocal tract transfer function

Glottal source's spectrum

Speech output spectrum

Frequency (kHz) ⟶

Figure 3 Above: the filter function of the supralaryngeal vocal tract for the vowel [i]. Centre: the frequency spectrum of a possible glottal source that is generated by the larynx. Below: the net effect of the filter on the glottal source. The frequencies of the formants are marked by the encircled crosses. (After Lieberman 1984)

source. The frequencies of the formants are marked by the encircled crosses. Note that there is no energy present in the output signal at the exact frequencies of the formants. Human beings are equipped with brain mechanisms that, in effect, calculate these formant frequencies from the speech signal. We do this even when very little acoustic information is present, as is the case when listening to speech on a telephone.

Human listeners perform some other remarkable feats as they interpret the linguistic significance of different formant frequency patterns. We have to estimate the probable length of a speaker's supralaryngeal airway in order to assign a particular formant frequency pattern to a particular speech sound. The lengths of the airway differ greatly between different individuals. Those of young children are half the length of those of adults. The vocal tracts of adults also differ in length; this results in overlap between the formant frequency patterns that convey different speech sounds. For example, the word *bit* spoken by a large adult male speaker who has a long supralaryngeal vocal tract can have the same formant frequency pattern as the word *bet* produced by a smaller person. Although for each speaker the formant frequencies of *bit* are higher than those of *bet*, the longer supralaryngeal airway of the larger speaker produces lower formant frequencies for *bit* than those produced by the shorter airway of the smaller person, and the former's *bit* can match the latter's *bet*. When we listen to speech we are not aware of these complications; we hear the *bits* of both the long and the short supralaryngeal airways as *bit*, even though they have different absolute formant frequencies. Innate brain mechanisms appear to be present in human beings that automatically 'normalize' for different supralaryngeal vocal tract lengths.

BRAIN MECHANISMS FOR SPEECH PRODUCTION AND SYNTAX

The results of studies that have examined the effects of damage to the human brain demonstrate that it is equipped with neocortical mechanisms that allow us to produce the complex articulatory manoeuvres involved in speech production. However, recent data indicate that older parts of the brain also play an essential part in making language possible. The structure of the human brain reflects its evolutionary history. In a sense, the brain resembles an onion; its phylogenetically newer parts are layered over older parts. The innermost layers are derived from the brains of reptiles, the 'old' motor cortex which is found in simple mammals is the next layer, while the outer layer is the neocortex (MacLean 1973).

Figure 4 shows the surface of the left hemisphere of a human brain. *Broca's area* is located in the dominant (usually the left) hemisphere. It is connected to other parts of the brain by means of pathways that are similar to electrical 'circuits', in that they transmit information from one part of the brain to other parts. Broca's area appears to be a multi-purpose device that is used in the storage or 'accessing' of 'automatized' sequential activities. The process of automatization allows an animal to learn, store and execute a complex pattern of motor commands as a single entity (Evarts 1973). An analogous process in computer programming is writing and then executing a 'subroutine'. Broca's area is involved in the voluntary production of the automatized motor control patterns that are necessary to produce human speech. Broca's 'aphasia' can occur from the brain damage of a stroke when lesions cut subcortical pathways to the prefrontal cortex (Stuss and Benson, 1986). Recent studies show that the metabolic activity of the prefrontal cortex is diminished as a consequence of these interruptions. The patient may be unable to co-ordinate the muscles of the supralaryngeal vocal tract and larynx to produce the distinction between sounds like [b] and [p]. These sounds are distinguished by the lapse of time between the start of phonation and the emission of sound when the lips move apart. These must be separated by less than 25 ms (thousandths of a second) to produce a [b]. Patients suffering from Broca's aphasia may exhibit a number of such speech deficits. The problem may arise from the disruption of the pathways between Broca's area and the parts of the brain that also control

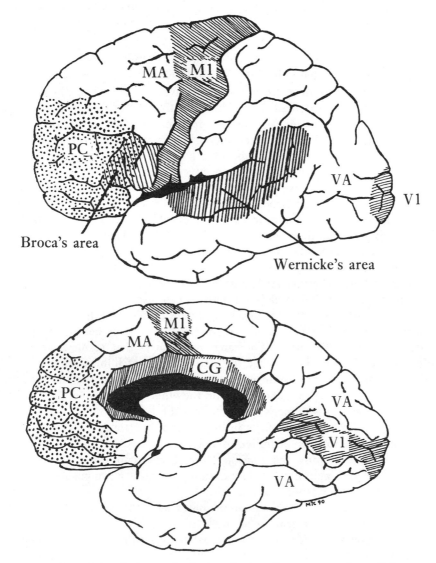

Figure 4 The left hemisphere of a human brain. Above: top surface of the cortex. Below: medial section. (After Lieberman 1991)

vocalization in non-human primates (the anterior cingulate gyrus in the old motor cortex). Similar speech production deficits can also occur in Parkinson's disease, when the subcortical pathways are disrupted because of a lack of the neurotransmitter dopamine.

Broca's aphasia can, moreover, result in deficits in the comprehension of syntax that also appear to follow from the disruption of pathways between Broca's area and the prefrontal cortex. Victims of strokes that have disrupted these pathways speak in a 'telegraphic' manner, omitting the words that convey grammatical distinctions in languages like English – such as articles, conjunctions and prepositions. Furthermore, access to words is often impeded; the meaning of a word may be intact but the sounds cannot be recalled. Broca's aphasics also have difficulty in comprehending sentences that have moderately complex syntax, for example 'passive' sentences like *The boy was kissed by the girl*, or sentences that include relative clauses like *The man who was sitting in the car saw the boy*. Similar grammatical deficits can also occur in diseases such as Parkinson's, when subcortical basal ganglia pathways to the prefrontal cortex are disrupted (Lieberman *et al.* 1990). The prefrontal cortex appears to be a general-purpose brain mechanism that is involved in all 'creative' or 'abstract' behaviour, including language (Stuss and Benson 1986).

It is thus apparent that Broca's area is *not*, in itself, the brain's 'language organ'. Not only does it appear to be involved as well in the control of manoeuvres of the dominant hand (the right hand for 90 per cent of humans), but also it cannot regulate speech production and syntax without being connected to prefrontal regions of the neocortex. Other parts of the human neocortex are also necessary for language. Traditional studies of aphasia show that damage to Wernicke's area (see Figure 4) can result in the use of inappropriate or invented words (neologisms). The victim's speech is fluent and syntactically correct, but is devoid of meaningful content because inappropriate words are being used. The language deficits that result from these different pathologies confirm that the neural bases of human language are highly complex. Different brain mechanisms appear to underlie the lexicon, on the one hand, and speech and syntax on the other. For example, the pathologies that result in Alzheimer's disease affect the lexicon, but do not appear to affect syntax or speech. Deficits in linguistic ability tend, moreover, to be accompanied by various cognitive deficits – particularly ones involving abstract reasoning (Stuss and Benson 1986, Lieberman 1991). These data indicate that the neurological foundations of human language are not independent of other aspects of cognition.

Comparative studies of non-human primates show that a functional Broca's area is a species-specific feature of modern *Homo sapiens*. Non-human primates are unable to produce voluntary vocalizations – their cries are triggered by affectual states. Goodall's (1986) field observations, for example, show that a chimpanzee cannot suppress a food bark even when it knows that the call will result in its being attacked by other chimpanzees. Laboratory studies in which the parts of the non-human primate brain homologous to Broca's area (or any other neocortical structures) are either electrically stimulated or ablated show that their vocalization is not affected, whereas similar damage or electrical stimulation in human beings has a pronounced effect on speech.

THE EVOLUTION OF HUMAN SPEECH ANATOMY AND THE BRAIN

The evolutionary history of human language is necessarily complex since the underlying biological structures have other, non-linguistic functions. Parts of the brain, like the prefrontal cortex that make human language possible, also contribute to virtually every other aspect of 'creative' behaviour. Comparative studies show that selection for a larger prefrontal cortex has taken place throughout the order of primates (Exner 1881). The human prefrontal cortex is proportionally two to three times larger than that of the chimpanzee (Deacons 1988). A larger prefrontal cortex would have contributed to the biological fitness of early hominids in foraging, hunting, tool-making, mate selection, social interaction, and indeed in virtually every other aspect of their behaviour including speaking. One cannot therefore rule out the possibility that selection favoured a larger and more complex prefrontal cortex on account of its functions in domains other than that of language. Likewise, Broca's area appears to be involved not just in speech but also in precise, lateralized manual manoeuvres involving the dominant hand (Kimura 1979, Stuss and Benson 1986). Since many animals besides *Homo sapiens* show hand or paw preferences, the origins of Broca's area may be found in the neurological entailments of these activities.

However, a totally functional Broca's area that makes it possible to produce the automatized articulatory manoeuvres of human speech appears to be a property exclusive to modern *Homo sapiens*. A hypothetical archaic hominid that was able to produce human speech would have to have had *both* a functional, human-like Broca's area and a human-like supralaryngeal vocal tract. The relationship here between anatomical structures and 'matching' brain mechanisms is analogous to the brain—body matches found both in other species such as frogs and electric eels (Lieberman 1984), and in connection with other unique human attributes. Upright bipedal locomotion, for example, involves both specialized skeletal morphology and the human brain's 'walking' reflex which facilitates our acquisition of the complex muscular manoeuvres that are necessary for locomotion.

The human supralaryngeal vocal tract would, in fact, *reduce* biological fitness were it not for brain mechanisms adapted for the voluntary control of the articulatory manoeuvres that underlie human speech. In contrast to the supralaryngeal airway typical of other living terrestrial mammals and extinct archaic hominids, modern human beings make use of a common supralaryngeal pathway when they ingest liquids and breathe air. As Negus (1949) showed, all other terrestrial mammals have a supralaryngeal airway similar to that sketched in Figure 5. The larynx is positioned high in the neck, close to the bottom of the skull. When the animal breathes the larynx moves up (like a submarine's periscope) and locks into the entrance to the nose. The velum and epiglottis act as a gasket to seal the air pathway from the nose through the larynx into the lungs from liquids and masticated solid food, which pass through channels to either side of the raised larynx into the pharynx to the oesophagus and digestive system. That is why horses, pigs, monkeys and newborn human beings (who have a similar supralaryngeal airway) can simultaneously drink and breath without choking.

In adult-like humans air, liquids, and solid food make use of the common pharyngeal pathway; food can fall into the larynx, obstructing the pathway into the lungs. This peculiar deficiency was first noted by Darwin (1859). The adult human configuration is also less efficient for chewing, because the length of the palate and of the mandible have been reduced compared with those of non-human primates and archaic hominids. The reduced length of the palate

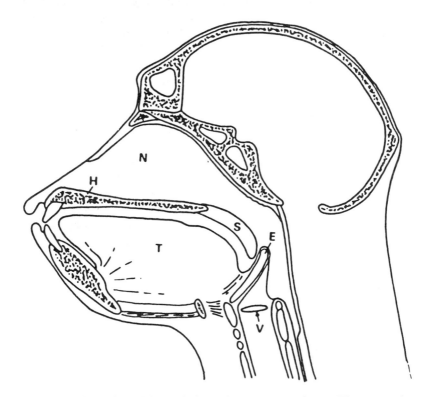

Figure 5 Midsagittal view of the typical non-human upper airway. The tongue is positioned entirely within the oral cavity. N, nasal cavity; H, hard palate; S, soft palate; E, epiglottis; T, tongue; V, vocal cords of larynx. (After Laitman and Heimbuch 1982)

and mandible also crowd our teeth, presenting the possibility of infection due to impaction – a potentially fatal condition until the advent of modern medicine. These deficiencies are only offset by the increased phonetic range of the human supralaryngeal airway, which can produce non-nasal sounds and the vowels [i] and [u] that facilitate the process of vocal tract 'normalization' noted earlier. In short, the selective advantages of the human supralaryngeal vocal tract lie in the capacity it confers to produce speech sounds that are less susceptible to confusion and better adapted to the formant frequency encoding process that makes possible the rapid transmission rate of human vocal communication. However, as noted above, both comparative studies of apes and clinical studies of brain damage and disease processes show that the production of speech is not possible without specialized brain mechanisms. In other words, a modern human supralaryngeal vocal tract is useless for speech unless the corresponding brain mechanisms are in place.

We can therefore infer from the presence of a modern supralaryngeal airway that these brain mechanisms are established: a hominid who had a human supralaryngeal vocal tract would have had the necessary brain mechanisms for speech production. The relationship is again like that between the skeletal morphology for upright bipedal locomotion and the brain mechanisms involved in walking.

RECONSTRUCTING SUPRALARYNGEAL VOCAL TRACTS

The supralaryngeal vocal tract consists of soft tissue and cartilages, so it is never present in a fossil. However, it can be reconstructed using the methods of comparative anatomy. This can be done since the base (bottom) of the skull and mandible (lower jaw) support the tongue and other parts of the supralaryngeal vocal tract. Qualitative (Lieberman 1968, Lieberman and Crelin 1971) and quantitative (Laitman and Heimbuch 1982, Laitman *et al.* 1979) methods have been used to reconstruct the supralaryngeal airways of a number of fossil hominids. Figure 6 shows some of the significant basicranial landmarks for the reconstruction of the supralaryngeal vocal tract. They are noted on a midsagittal (midplane side view) of a chimpanzee skull.

Many of the relationships between soft tissue and skeletal structure are quite direct. The relatively long distance between the end of the palate (the roof of the mouth) and the vertebral column – that is from staphylion to endobasion (points B and E in Figure 6) – provides space for a larynx positioned close to the entrance to the nose with a pharynx behind the larynx. In the nonhuman supralaryngeal airway the larynx is positioned high in the throat; the chimpanzee's pharynx is positioned behind its larynx. Therefore there has to be room for the larynx and the pharynx. The long palate likewise reflects the fact that a long thin tongue is positioned entirely within the oral cavity. The *basicranial line* (linking points A, B, C, D and E in Figure 6) captures many of these skeletal-to-soft tissue relationships. Laitman and his colleagues

Figure 6 Some of the significant basicranial landmarks for the reconstruction of the supralaryngeal vocal tract. They are noted on a midsagittal (midplane side view) of a chimpanzee skull. (After Laitman and Heimbuch 1982)

(1979, 1982) have charted the basicranial lines of living primates and fossil hominids; the change from an unflexed basicranial line to a flexed one corresponds to the change from the generalized non-human supralaryngeal airway, with a long, flat tongue within the mouth, to the bent, modern human supralaryngeal vocal tract with a round tongue positioned in the mouth and pharynx (Figure 2).

Figure 7 shows how the human tongue, moving in the right-angled space defined by the roof of the mouth and the spinal column, can make the abrupt, extreme changes in the cross-sectional area function of the supralaryngeal airway that are necessary to produce vowels like [i]. (The cross-sectional area of the pharynx is ten times greater than that of the oral cavity; the transition occurs abruptly at the mid-point of the supralaryngeal airway at the right-angle juncture of the pharynx and oral cavity.) Non-nasal sounds can be produced by the human airway because of the short distance spanned by the velum and the flexed basicranial line.

The human supralaryngeal vocal tract is necessary for the production of 'articulate' speech − speech that is as intelligible as that produced by the normal range of adult human speakers. Though some linguists still dispute this point, quantitative studies of the speech produced by patients suffering from

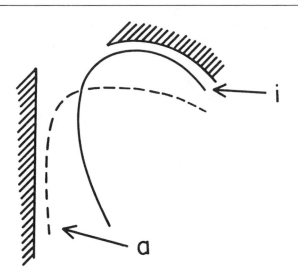

Figure 7 The human tongue moves in the right-angled space defined by the roof of the mouth and the spinal column, and therefore can make the abrupt changes in the cross-sectional area function of the supralaryngeal airway that are necessary to produce vowels like [i]. The curved lines show the contour of the tongue with respect to the hard palate and rear pharyngeal wall during the production of the vowels [i] (solid line) and [a] (dashed line). (After Nearey 1978)

craniofacial anomalies that deform the supralaryngeal vocal tract show that their speech is distorted and hard to understand. Anomalies that restrict tongue movements or deform the tongue make it impossible to produce the range of formant frequency patterns necessary for human speech. Speakers with such anomalies cannot produce vowels like [i] or [u]; listeners cannot identify most of the speech sounds that the speakers intend to communicate (Landahl and Gould 1986). The speech sounds produced by victims of craniofacial anomalies that prevent normal closure of the velum are likewise nasalized, again reducing the intelligibility of their speech (Pruzansky 1973).

Bearing in mind that less than half of the human tongue is in the mouth, it is readily apparent that a modern supralaryngeal vocal tract cannot be 'fitted' into many archaic hominids. The other half of the tongue (somewhat more for adult males who have a longer pharynx) falls into the throat. In Figure 8(a) the Neanderthal skull and mandible from La Chapelle-aux-Saints have been placed on a modern vertebral column. Figure 8(b) shows tongue contours recorded during the production of different vowels of English (Ladefoged *et al.* 1972). Note that the contours are almost circular and that the tongue does not change its shape in the production of these vowels. The movements of the round, undeformed human tongue in the right-angled space defined by the vertebral column and basicranium are necessary to generate the full range of

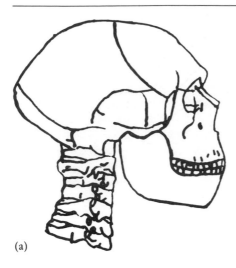

(a)

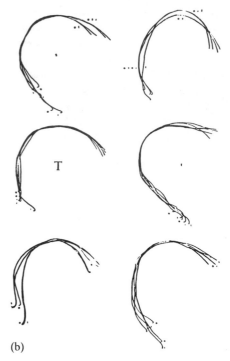

T

(b)

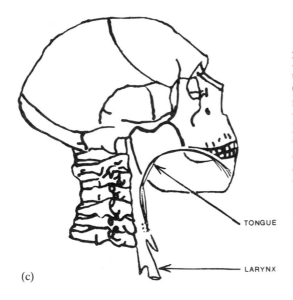

TONGUE

LARYNX

(c)

Figure 8 Giving a classic Neanderthal a modern human upper airway: (a) the La Chapelle-aux-Saints skull and mandible placed on a modern vertebral column; (b) Midsagittal views of human tongue contours recorded during the production of different vowels of English; (c) tongue 'T' from (b), making an [i] vowel within the Neanderthal skull; the larynx would have to be positioned in the chest – an impossible situation. (After Lieberman 1984 and Ladefoged *et al.* 1972)

sounds of human speech. In Figure 8(c) we have 'given' the Neanderthal of Figure 8(a) the tongue labelled 'T' from Figure 8(b). The modern human tongue must fill the long Neanderthal mouth – otherwise the reconstructed fossil would be unable to eat. Since the Neanderthal mouth is long, the radius of the human tongue that we have fitted to the Neanderthal skull must also be long. This results in the larynx lying at a correspondingly long distance down the throat. The larynx would in fact be *below* the throat, in the chest, if the Neanderthal fossil had had a normal human neck. The reconstruction yields an impossible creature; no mammal has its larynx in its chest. Though scholars (Arensberg *et al.* 1989) who insist that classic Neanderthal hominids had perfectly normal human supralaryngeal airways could claim that they also had extremely long necks, this is most unlikely. The Neanderthal neck was, if anything, probably shorter than that of modern human beings (Boule and Vallois 1957). The correct vocal tract reconstruction is one in which the long, unflexed Neanderthal basicranium matches a non-human supralaryngeal vocal tract.

The Neanderthal speech controversy, like many other such debates, usually misses some important points. For one thing, the question is not an all-or-nothing one of whether Neanderthals talked or not. They clearly would have had vocal abilities far in advance of present-day apes. In all likelihood they had the ability to produce voluntary speech sounds, given the complex nature of their stone tools and the probable link between Broca's area and the control of fine hand movements. Moreover, they clearly would have had the ability to communicate and think using words, since even present-day apes can do so. Their culture appears to have been quite complex. In short, *they undoubtedly possessed language* (Lieberman 1984), but we can see that in one respect, namely speech, their linguistic ability was not as developed as that of anatomically modern *Homo sapiens*.

In a celebrated passage in his *On the Origin of Species*, Darwin noted (1859: 61) that

> any variation, however slight and from whatever cause proceeding, if it be in any degree profitable to an individual of that species, in its infinitely complex relations to other organic beings and to external nature, will tend to the preservation of that individual, and will generally be inherited by its offspring.

Human speech confers a selective advantage if the medium of communication is already vocal. At the very least, a modern human supralaryngeal airway would yield speech that was 30 to 50 per cent more intelligible; that is, the probability of error in perceiving the words conveyed would be reduced by that amount. Since selective advantages of only 5 per cent demonstrably shift the course of evolution this, in itself, would constitute a significant contribution to biological fitness. To the degree that speech encoding is enhanced by the presence of vowels like [i] and [u], which facilitate normalization, the contribution to biological fitness would be further magnified.

Given the important contribution of human speech to language, the advantages conferred could have resulted in adaptations for speech in various 'Neanderthals' as well as in earlier hominids that may have been ancestral to both anatomically modern *Homo sapiens* and classic Neanderthals. Various transitional variations are apparent in the fossil record (Lieberman 1984). Australopithecines had supralaryngeal vocal tracts that closely resemble those of living apes. The flexure of the basicranium in *Homo erectus* fossils like KNM-ER-3733 from Lake Turkana, Kenya, is greater than that of living pongids or of Australopithecines, possibly indicating a lowering of the larynx to facilitate mouth-breathing. One of the earliest exemplars of the transition from *erectus* to *sapiens* is the fossil skull found at Broken Hill, Zambia, in 1921 (originally known as 'Rhodesia Man'). Probably at least 125,000 years old, the fossil has a modern basicranial flexure with a longer palate. Its vocal tract would appear to be functionally modern, though not optimal for the production of vowels like [i] and [u] (Stevens 1972).

By about 100,000 years ago, or soon after, we find completely modern supralaryngeal vocal tracts as represented in the fossil skulls of Jebel Qafzeh VI and Skhul V from Israel (on the question of the dating of this material, see Gamble's discussion in Article 4). These fossils, of anatomically modern *Homo sapiens*, could *not* support a non-human supralaryngeal airway; there is not enough room for a high larynx almost in line with the tongue and pharynx. The length of the palate is similar to that of present-day humans and their vocal tracts would have produced quantal speech sounds that were stable. As Gamble has shown in Article 4, recent theories propose that anatomically modern *Homo sapiens* originated in Africa somewhere between 100,000 and 200,000 years ago, and subsequently dispersed through the Middle East to Europe and Asia (Stringer and Andrews 1988). The presence of a functionally modern vocal tract in the African Broken Hill fossil, and its retention and elaboration in Jebel Qafzeh VI and Skhul V, are consistent with this theory.

The presence of Neanderthal hominids such as at Tabun, Shanidar, and Kebara, which lacked modern human supralaryngeal vocal tracts, in the same region of the Near East as anatomically modern humans, may seem puzzling. How could hominids whose linguistic capacities differ co-occur in the same region? The Shanidar and Kebara Neanderthal fossils lived about 60,000 to 50,000 years ago; the Tabun Neanderthals may have lived 100,000 years ago. Two possible explanations may account for these observations. The Neanderthal and human populations may have shared the same region at different periods; glacial periods in Europe would have forced the Neanderthals south, pushing modern humans back into Africa. In warmer periods the populations would have once more shifted northwards. However, the inherent phonetic limitation of the Neanderthal supralaryngeal vocal tract may itself have functioned as a powerful genetic isolating mechanism. Recent population-genetic studies show that the language affiliations of present European populations play a major role in maintaining and causing genetic differences. The effects are evident even for dialects (Barbujani and Sokal 1990, 1991). In other words, people tend to mate with those who have the same dialect or language. If this effect occurs for modern human beings who can learn any dialect, then its effect can only have been stronger a hundred thousand years ago, when Neanderthal hominids could not have produced the sounds of which contemporary modern human populations are capable. In other words, we cannot rule out the role of speech and language as isolating mechanisms that maintained the boundaries between separate human and Neanderthal populations.

THE EVOLUTION OF THE BRAIN MECHANISMS FOR SPEECH AND SYNTAX

Though the brain mechanisms that regulate speech and syntax in modern human beings are species-specific, they appear to have evolutionary antecedents in the mechanisms that facilitate lateralized hand and paw movements. Although non-human primates and other mammals do not have species-wide preferences for one hand or paw, individual animals show such preferences when they perform difficult tasks (Denenberg 1981, MacNeilage *et al.* 1987). Broca's area may have initially evolved to facilitate precise one-handed operations (Kimura 1979). The morphology of the motor control areas of the primate brain, in which the area that directly controls hand movements is above the areas regulating the facial and vocal tract muscles, would have provided the fortuitous, *preadaptive* basis for its role in speech production. The concept of preadaptation derives from Darwin, who noted that 'an organ originally constructed for one purpose ... may be converted into one for a wholly different purpose' (1859: 190). The initial purpose for the specialized neural mechanisms underlying speech production could, then, have lain in the performance of precise, lateralized hand movements. The fact that deficits in dominant hand manoeuvres often occur in Broca's aphasia supports this theory (Stuss and Benson 1986).

The role of Broca's region in the comprehension of syntax would, in turn, follow from its earlier functions in manual motor control and speech production (Lieberman 1985). It is important to note that Broca's area is part of a network of neural structures that work in concert to make speech and syntax possible. The human brain does not consist of a set of independent localized 'modules', each of which directly regulates one aspect of behaviour (Fodor 1983). Though various parts of the brain are specialized to perform particular operations (for example, sequential operations), they participate in different aspects of behaviour connected by different pathways (Stuss and Benson 1986). Broca's area of the brain appears to control speech motor activity and syntax through pathways to the phylogenetically 'older' cingulate (motor) cortex as well as to the prefrontal cortex. Though speech and language are perhaps the most recent, defining characteristics of modern human beings, the

127

relevant pathways involve still 'older' parts of the brain; the basal ganglia which ultimately derive from the brains of reptiles (MacLean 1973). However, we do not simply have reptilian basal ganglia; they have been greatly enlarged and restructured in the course of evolution (Parent 1986). As regards language, the distinction between the non-human primate brain and the human brain may rest, in part, in changes in these subcortical pathways.

Human language, as Gamble has argued in Article 4, is clearly essential for human culture. It is, for example, impossible even to state the concepts that are central to the world's religions without language. How could the concept of reincarnation, which is such an essential element of Buddhism, be formulated or communicated without language? Human 'moral sense' likewise depends on the prior existence of language. Though the 'altruistic' behaviour of animals in small bands of genetically related individuals can be explained by mechanistic models, in terms of the enhancement of biological fitness (Hamilton 1964), the selfless behaviour exemplified in the lives of Christian saints or Buddhist Bodhisattvas follows from concepts that cannot be stated or communicated without language.

To conclude, though human language (the complete linguistic system of anatomically modern *Homo sapiens*) involves phylogenetically recent components such as speech and syntax, it has a long evolutionary history. Clearly some form of language must have been present in the earliest hominids – though it was not the complete system that we find in modern human beings. The neural mechanisms that underlie the brain's lexicon likewise exist in reduced form in other living species, and are probably responsible for learning by association.

The complete linguistic system of modern human beings, including human speech and syntax, appears to be a comparatively recent development. The presence of the human supralaryngeal vocal tract in fossil hominids is an index of the establishment of the brain mechanisms that allow voluntary control of speech and execute the necessary rapid motor commands. The earliest stages of specialization for human speech could have been built up on a non-human primate anatomy, *if* voluntary neural control of vocalization was already in place. The initial increase in fitness stemming from more efficient vocal communication might possibly be derived without additional neural modifications for speech perception beyond the capabilities of present-day apes. Studies of the perception of human speech by chimpanzees (Savage-Rumbaugh *et al.* 1985) show that they can perceive such speech using formant transitions and fundamental frequency contours. Therefore, the initial contribution to biological fitness of the human supralaryngeal vocal tract could have been to produce more distinct, unnasalized, quantal sounds without the increase in data rate that follows from formant frequency encoding. However, we know that our speech, the end-point, *is* encoded for rapid data transmission. At some point, the brain mechanisms that allow automatized speech motor activity, vocal tract normalization and the 'decoding' of encoded speech must have evolved. The presence of a functionally modern human vocal tract 125,000 years ago, and its retention and elaboration, are consistent with the view that these brain mechanisms came to be established around this time. If present research on the preadaptive bases of the brain mechanisms for syntax is correct, this aspect of human language would also have evolved during this same period.

REFERENCES

Anderson, J. A. (1988) 'Concept formation in neural networks: implications for evolution of cognitive functions', *Human Evolution* 3: 83–100.

Arensberg, B., Tiller, A. M., Vandermeersch, B., Duday, H., Schepartz, L. A. and Rak, Y. (1989) 'A Middle Palaeolithic human hyoid bone', *Nature* 338: 758–60.

Barbujani, G. and Sokal, R. R. (1990) 'Zones of sharp genetic change in Europe are also linguistic boundaries', *Proceedings of the National Academy of Sciences USA* 187: 1816–19.

—— (1991) 'Genetic population structure of Italy, II: physical and cultural barriers to gene flow', *American Journal of Human Genetics* 48: 398–411.

Bear, M. F., Cooper, L. N. and Ebner, F. F. (1987) 'A physiological basis for a theory of synaptic modification', *Science* 237: 42–8.

Bickerton, D. (1990) *Language and Species*, Chicago: University of Chicago Press.

Boule, M. and Vallois, H. V. (1957) *Fossil Men*, New York: Dryden Press.

Bronowski, J. (1971) *The Identity of Man*, Garden City, NY: Natural History Press.

—— (1978) *The Origins of Knowledge and Imagination*, New Haven: Yale University Press.

Darwin, C. (1859) *On the Origin of Species*, [Facsimile edn 1964], Cambridge, Mass.: Harvard University Press.

Deacon, T. W. (1988) 'Human brain evolution, II: Embryology and brain allometry', in H. J. Jerison and I. Jerison (eds) *Intelligence and evolutionary biology*, NATO ASI Series, Berlin.

Denenberg, V. H. (1981) 'Hemispheric laterality in animals and the effects of early experience', *Behavioral and Brain Sciences* 4: 1–49.

Evarts, E. V. (1973) 'Motor cortex reflexes associated with learned movement', *Science* 179: 501–3.

Exner, S. (1881) *Untersuchungen über Localisation der Functionen in der Grosshirnrinde des Menschen*, Vienna: W. Braumuller.

Fodor, J. (1983) *Modularity of Mind*, Cambridge, Mass.: MIT Press.

Fouts, R. S., Hirsch, A. D. and Fouts, D. H. (1982) 'Cultural transmission of a human language in a chimpanzee mother–infant relationship', in H. E. Fitzgerald, J. A. Mullins and P. Gage (eds) *Child Nurturance*, vol 3, New York: Plenum Press.

Gardner, R. A. and Gardner, B. T. (1969) 'Teaching sign language to a chimpanzee', *Science* 165: 664–72.

—— (1984) 'A vocabulary test for chimpanzees (*Pan troglodytes*)', *Journal of Comparative Psychology* 4: 381–404.

—— (1988) 'Feedforward versus feedbackward: an ethological alternative to the law of effect', *Behavioral and Brain Sciences* 11: 429–93.

Goodall, J. (1986) *The Chimpanzees of Gombe: Patterns of Behavior*, Cambridge, Mass.: Harvard University Press.

Hamilton, W. D. (1964) 'The genetical evolution of social behavior', pts 1, 2, *Journal of Theoretical Biology* 7: 1–52.

Hebb, D. O. (1949) *The Organization of Behavior*, New York: John Wiley.

Herman, L. M. and Tavolga, W. N. (1980) 'The communication systems of cetaceans', in *Cetacean Behavior: Mechanisms and Functions*, New York: John Wiley.

Hewes, G. W. (1973) 'Primate communication and the gestural origin of language', *Current Anthropology* 14: 5–24.

Kimura, D. (1979) 'Neuromotor mechanisms in the evolution of human communication', in H. D. Steklis and M. J. Raleigh (eds) *Neurobiology of Social Communication in Primates*, New York: Academic Press.

Ladefoged, P., De Clerk, J., Lindau, M. and Papcun, G. (1972) 'An auditory-motor theory of speech production', *UCLA Working Papers in Phonetics* 22: 48–76.

Laitman, J. T. and Heimbuch, R. C. (1982) 'The basicranium of Plio-Pleistocene hominids as an indicator of their upper respiratory systems', *American Journal of Physical Anthropology* 59: 323–43.

Laitman, J. T., Heimbuch, R. C. and Crelin, E. S. (1979) 'The basicranium of fossil hominids as an indicator of their upper respiratory systems', *American Journal of Physical Anthropology* 51: 15–34.

Landahl, K. L. and Gould, H. J. (1986) 'Congenital malformation of the speech tract in humans and its developmental consequences', in R. J. Ruben, T. R. Van de Water and E. W. Rubel (eds) *The Biology of Change in Otolaryngology*, Amsterdam: Elsevier.

Liberman, A. M., Cooper, F. S., Shankweiler, D. P. and Studdert-Kennedy, M. (1967) 'Perception of the speech code', *Psychological Review* 74: 431–61.

Lieberman, P. (1968) 'Primate vocalizations and human linguistic ability', *Journal of the Acoustical Society of America* 44: 1574–84.

—— (1975) *On the Origins of Language: An Introduction to the Evolution of Speech*, New York: Macmillan.

—— (1984) *The Biology and Evolution of Language*, Cambridge, Mass.: Harvard University Press.

—— (1985) 'On the evolution of human syntactic ability: its preadaptive bases – motor control and speech', *Journal of Human Evolution* 14: 657–68.

—— (1989) 'The origins of some aspects of human language and cognition', in P. Mellars and C. B. Stringer (eds) *The Human Revolution: Behavioural and Biological Perspectives on the Origins of Modern Humans*, Edinburgh: Edinburgh University Press.

—— (1991) *Uniquely Human: The Evolution of Speech, Thought and Selfless Behavior*, Cambridge, Mass.: Harvard University Press.

Lieberman, P. and Crelin, E. S. (1971) 'On the speech of Neanderthal man', *Linguistic Inquiry* 2: 203–22.

Lieberman, P., Friedman, J. and Feldman, L. S. (1990) 'Syntactic deficits in Parkinson's disease', *Journal of Nervous and Mental Disease* 178: 360–5.

MacLean, P. D. (1973) 'A triune concept of the brain and behaviour', in T. Boag and D. Campbell (eds) *The Hincks Memorial Lectures*, Toronto: University of Toronto Press.

MacNeilage, P. F., Studdert-Kennedy, M. G. and Lindblom, B. (1987) 'Primate handedness reconsidered', *Behavioral and Brain Sciences* 10: 247–303.

Muller, J. (1848) *The Physiology of the Senses, Voice and Muscular Motion with the Mental Faculties*, trans. W. Baly, London: Walton & Maberly.

Nearey, T. (1978) *Phonetic Features for Vowels*, Bloomington: Indiana University Linguistics Club.

Negus, V. (1949) *The Comparative Anatomy and Physiology of the Larynx*, New York: Hafner.

Parent, A. (1986) *Comparative Neurobiology of the Basal Ganglia*, New York: John Wiley.

Pepperberg, I. M. (1981) 'Functional vocalizations by an African Grey Parrot (*Psittacus erithacus*)', *Zeitschrift für Tierpsychologie* 55: 139–60.

Pruzansky, S. (1973) 'Clinical investigations of the experiments of nature', in *Orofacial Anomalies; Clinical and Research Implications*', ASHA Report 8, Washington DC: American Speech and Hearing Association.

Savage-Rumbaugh, S., Rumbaugh, D. and McDonald, K. (1985) 'Language learning in two species of apes', *Neuroscience and Biobehavioral Reviews* 9: 653–65.

Schusterman, R. J. and Krieger, K. (1984) 'California sea lions are capable of semantic comprehension', *The Psychological Record* 34: 3–23.

Sejnowski, T. J., Koch, C. and Churchland, P. S. (1988) 'Computational neuroscience', *Nature* 241: 1299–1306.

Stevens, K. N. (1972) 'Quantal nature of speech', in E. E. David Jr and P. B. Denes (eds) *Human Communication: a Unified View*, New York: McGraw-Hill.

Stringer, C. B. and Andrews, P. (1988) 'Genetic and fossil evidence for the origin of modern humans', *Science* 239: 1263–8.

Stuss, D. T. and Benson, D. F. (1986) *The Frontal Lobes*, New York: Raven.

Warden, C. J. and Warner, L. H. (1928) 'The sensory capacities and intelligence of dogs, with a report on the ability of the noted dog "Fellow" to respond to verbal stimuli', *Quarterly Review of Biology* 3: 1–28.

FURTHER READING

Bickerton, D. (1990) *Language and Species*, Chicago: Chicago University Press.

Bronowski, J. (1978) *The Origins of Knowledge and Imagination*, New Haven: Yale University Press.

Falk, D. (1980) 'Language, handedness, and primate brains: did the australopithecines sign?', *American Anthropologist* 82: 72–8.

Gibson, K. R. and Ingold, T. (eds) (1992) *Tools, Language and Cognition in Human Evolution*, Cambridge: Cambridge University Press.

Goodall, J. (1986) *The Chimpanzees of Gombe: Patterns of Behavior*, Cambridge, Mass.: Harvard University Press.

Grolier, E. de (ed.) (1983) *Glossogenetics. The Origin and Evolution of Language*, New York: Harwood Academic.

Harnad, S. R., Steklis, H. D. and Lancaster, J. (eds) (1976) *Origins and Evolution of Language and Speech*, Annals of the New York Academy of Sciences, vol. 280.

Harré, R. and Reynolds, V. (eds) (1984) *The Meaning of Primate Signals*, Cambridge: Cambridge University Press.

Hewes, G. (1973) 'Primate communication and the gestural origin of language', *Current Anthropology* 14: 5–24.

Kendon, A. (1991) 'Some considerations for a theory of language origins', *Man* (N.S.) 26: 199–221.

Lenneberg, E. (1967) *The Biological Foundations of Language*, New York: John Wiley.

Lieberman, P. (1984) *The Biology and Evolution of Language*, Cambridge, Mass.: Harvard University Press.

—— (1991) *Uniquely Human: the Evolution of Speech, Thought and Selfless Behavior*, Cambridge, Mass.: Harvard University Press.

McNeil, D. (1979) 'Language origins', in M. von Cranach, K. Foppa, W. Lepenies and D. Ploog (eds) *Human Ethology*, Cambridge: Cambridge University Press.

Noble, W. and Davidson, I. (1991) 'The evolutionary emergence of modern human behaviour: language and its archaeology', *Man* (N.S.) 26: 223–53.

Parker, S. T. and Gibson, K. R. (1979) 'A developmental model for the evolution of language and intelligence in early hominids', *The Behavioral and Brain Sciences* 2: 367–408.

—— (eds) (1990) *'Language' and Intelligence in Monkeys and Apes*, Cambridge: Cambridge University Press.

Steklis, H. D. (1985) 'Primate communication, comparative neurology and the origin of language re-examined', *Journal of Human Evolution* 14: 157–73.

Wescott, R. W. (ed.) (1972) *Language Origins*, Silverspring, MD.: Linstok Press.

White, R. (1985) 'Thoughts on social relationships and language in hominid evolution', *Journal of Social and Personal Relationships* 2: 95–115.

6

TOOLS AND TOOL BEHAVIOUR

Thomas Wynn

INTRODUCTION

Use of a tool is a commonplace human behaviour; every day, everyone of us uses tools. Until fairly recently, tool-use and tool-making held a privileged place in definitions of humanness. Humans made and used tools, animals did not. Comparative evidence has effectively deflated this simple and comfortable distinction. Chimpanzees and other non-humans make and use tools. However, even in the face of this growing body of comparative examples, we generally believe human tool behaviour to be different and special. We have even used presumed tool skills in the naming of the earliest member of our genus – *Homo habilis*, 'Handy Man'. Just what is it about human tools, tool-use, and tool-making that sets us apart?

A problem of definition has long troubled discussions of tools, especially non-human tools, and while a common-sense understanding of the term would probably suffice for the following discussion, I will try to be more explicit. I will, in fact, use two definitions, one very broad and inclusive, the other narrower and exclusive.

Animals live in and modify their environments. It is to be expected that objects in those environments can come to play roles in animals' day-to-day lives. An inclusive definition of 'tool' encompasses any employment of an object in the environment for a useful end, so long as the object is not part of the individual's anatomy. Such a category includes nests, ornaments, camouflage, traps, and so on, as well as objects used to obtain food directly. Part of the human story is one of dramatic developments in the way we use objects to achieve ends, and this inclusive definition allows us to include such 'marginal' cases of tool-use as the citrus farmer who plants eucalyptus trees to act as a windbreak.

A more exclusive definition of 'tool' will predominate in the following article. A tool is a detached object that is controlled by the user to perform work (in the mechanical sense of transferring energy), usually as an extension

133

of the user's anatomy. This category is imprecise at the boundaries (it would exclude baits, for example), but encompasses most common-sense examples of tools. The definition does not include some features occasionally found in definitions of tools. For example, it contains no reference to design or authorship and no requirement that an object be modified. As such, it is not as exclusive as it might be. It is not, however, my intention to propose a definition of tool that would exclude all but humans. My definition does not in fact set humans apart, but it will allow us to discuss how humans use tools and how our tool-use differs from that of even our closest relatives.

Thirty years ago the distinction between tool-use and tool-making held the status of a significant evolutionary Rubicon. We now know that many species, including some birds, modify objects before use; the evolutionary significance of the difference has therefore faded. More telling for this article is the observation that using and making employ the same kinds of skill and knowledge in human action; the distinction does not identify separate domains of human endeavour. *How* a tool comes to be modified will be of interest to us, but the making–using distinction carries little significance in and of itself.

We also require a working definition of technology. This is a term encountered commonly in philosophy, history, and social science, where, as I shall show below, it usually implies more than just tool-use. There is also a tendency to apply it to humans, but not to non-humans. Such a usage would bias our examination of the distinctions between the two. Here I shall use technology as largely synonymous with tool behaviour, though with the added connotation that technology is a learned system of tool-use and tool-making, thereby excluding examples of innate or genetically coded tool behaviour, as well as isolated instances of tool-use.

While it is important to be clear as to what one means by a tool, it is also important not to place too much emphasis on definition. It is perhaps even misleading to grant tools the status of a separate ontological category. By doing so we focus our attention on one component of complex behaviours or actions. If we can identify a tool, we feel justified in lumping the behaviours together. In many cases the differences far outweigh this one tangible similarity. For example, there is a species of wasp that uses a pebble to tamp down the entrance to a subterranean nest. This, by many definitions (including mine), qualifies as tool-use (but not as technology). We humans, of course, also use tools to build our homes. What kind of understanding do we gain by lumping these instances together? Very little, I would say, beyond noting an interesting but superficial example of evolutionary convergence. The wasp tool-use and human tool-use have dramatically different sources (one is genetically determined; one is learned), and it is precisely such differences that should concern us.

The following discussion will focus on small-scale, skilled tool-use and tool-making. Most of my examples will come from skilled tool behaviour because here the characteristics stand out particularly clearly. These characteristics can, nevertheless, be identified in the less exciting world of driving to work, cooking, or mending a garden wall. Only a few examples will be drawn from industrial technology. While, arguably, such large-scale tool behaviour possesses some size-dependent qualities not found in small-scale tool behaviour, industrial technology is very recent and is restricted in its geographical distribution. It cannot be an element distinguishing human tool behaviour from that of non-humans, unless we wish to exclude from humanity such diverse peoples as classical Romans and modern Amazonian natives. Moreover, inclusion of industrial technology would tend to overwhelm discussion of the human characteristics of the tools that all of us use, every day.

I will begin with a brief consideration of non-human tool behaviour. Following this, I will go on to discuss two very different intellectual traditions that have been brought to bear on our understanding of tool-use. This forms a necessary preliminary to my attempt to characterize human tool behaviour in terms of human anatomy, human cognition, and human culture.

NON-HUMAN TOOLS

Humans are not the only tool-users and tool-makers. In New Guinea, for example, the satin bower bird makes a 'paintbrush' by nibbling a piece of bark into an appropriate shape and holds this tool in its bill to control the flow of a paint solution used to decorate its bower (van Lawick-Goodall 1970). Woodpecker finches use cactus spines to probe beneath bark for insects and even shorten spines that are too long (Beck 1980). While floating on their backs, sea otters balance stones on their chests to use as anvils for cracking open mussels. Many species of mammal and bird use objects to assist them with feeding, hygiene, and social encounters. Some species modify the objects and in this sense can be said to make tools. Indeed, tool-use and tool-making are found in such diverse groups of vertebrates that Beck (1980) concludes that tool behaviour carries no implications for the relatedness of species and is in most cases simply an opportunistic solution to a local adaptive problem. The mere presence of tool-use or tool-making does not make humans unique or remarkable.

Primates, more than animals of any other vertebrate order, turn to tools, especially in agonistic situations. This propensity may be a result of the primate grasping hand, which was initially selected for by the demands of locomotion in the tree-tops. Primates are anatomically equipped to manipulate objects, and most do. Chacma baboons, for example, throw stones at humans to discourage intrusion (Hamilton *et al.* 1975). Barbary macaques throw roof tiles, Japanese macaques throw pine cones, and Cebus monkeys throw fruit (Beck 1980). Gorillas, gibbons, and orang-utans shake, drop, and brandish vegetation as displays and to discourage intrusion (Beck 1980; van Lawick-Goodall 1970; Galdikas 1982). The use of tools in agonistic encounters is so common among anthropoids that it has few implications for relatedness within the suborder. Surprisingly, agonistic uses of tools are rarely mentioned in discussions of early hominid tool behaviour, where attention has been directed almost entirely towards the use of tools in foraging.

There are fewer primate examples of the use of tools in the narrower sense. Capuchins and crab-eating macaques have been observed to use stones to break open shellfish (Beck 1980), and several monkey species have been observed breaking open insect nests with sticks, after which the insects are gathered by hand (van Lawick-Goodall 1970). However, by far the most extensive and elaborate examples of making and using tools as mechanical aids for feeding are found among chimpanzees (*Pan troglodytes*). Several varieties of tool-assisted foraging have been observed. Some chimpanzees (but not all) use twigs or grass stems to probe for termites (McGrew *et al.* 1979; Teleki 1974). These probes are stripped of leaves, shortened to optimal length, and even repaired during use. Chimpanzees in Rio Muni use stout levers to break open the termite mound (Sabater Pi 1974). Some East African chimpanzees use long probes to 'fish' for driver ants (McGrew 1974). In the Tai forest of Ivory Coast chimpanzees use hammers to break open nuts. Moreover, they select stone hammers for the hard nuts and wooden hammers for the softer ones. They carry these hammers to nutting stations, which they re-use over and over again, producing impressive quantities of refuse (Boesch and Boesch 1984). Chimpanzees also make sponges of chewed leaves, which they use to extract brains from monkeys they have hunted and water from inaccessible spots (Teleki 1974). The variety of patterns of tool-assisted foraging, and the seriousness with which it is practised by some chimpanzee groups, indicates that it forms a significant, if minor, aspect of the chimpanzees' adaptive complex.

The above examples may appear trivial when placed beside a modern petrochemical plant or a personal computer (both of which count as tools under my inclusive definition). The power and complexity of modern human tools dwarf the accomplishments even of chimpanzees. People raised within Western culture often consider technology to represent a great evolutionary divide separating humans from animals. This is an opinion also held by many Western scholars. 'Thus tool modification by other primates does not erode the significance of human tool-making; it serves, if anything, to highlight how much further we have gone in that direction than any species' (Gowlett 1984: 175). This huge difference in power and complexity may, however, have kept scholarship from asking subtler questions about the nature of human tools. Does the difference between human and ape tools lie only in power and complexity? An affirmative answer would carry some troubling implications. The power and complexity of Neolithic tools may be closer to that of chimpanzees than to that of modern industrial technology, yet few would want to argue that Neolithic farmers were pre-human or sub-human (see McGrew 1987 for an interesting comparison of Tasmanian Aboriginal and chimpanzee tools). In order to understand what makes human tool behaviour different we need to examine both non-human and human tool behaviour more closely. After all, evolutionary theory argues that there should be some continuity between the two, especially in view of the close phylogenetic distance between humans and chimpanzees (we share over 98 per cent of our genes, for example). Unfortunately, sober comparisons have rarely been made. In part this is because the difference is apparently so large that serious comparison may seem an odd, almost pointless undertaking. However, comparison is also hampered by a fundamental mismatch between the theories and methods employed by natural scientists who study non-human tool behaviour, and those of social scientists who study human tool behaviour, including anthropologists who study early hominid culture. The former employ a 'natural history' perspective and the latter a 'socio-cultural' perspective. The two approaches study different phenomena and reach non-comparable conclusions. The result is an artificial chasm separating the tools of apes from those of humans.

THE NATURAL HISTORY TRADITION IN STUDIES OF TOOL BEHAVIOUR

Most studies of non-human tool-use and tool-making fall within the long-established tradition of natural history. Until recently, the emphasis in these studies was descriptive and anecdotal, with the tacit goal of documenting the range of tool behaviour encountered in natural populations. In the last thirty years or so, the emphasis has expanded to include systematic studies of the role of tool behaviour within specific adaptive niches (see Beck's comprehensive review (1980) of this literature).

Much of the literature on non-human primate tool behaviour remains anecdotal. Anecdotal accounts are not, as the term might imply, simply hearsay accounts. They are careful descriptions of behaviour observed in the field. They differ from more comprehensive studies in that they make little or no attempt to raise general or theoretical issues. For example, Brewer and McGrew (1990) describe a single incident of chimpanzee tool-use and tool-making in which a rehabituated (wild-born) female used a series of four separate tools to extract honey from the nest of a species of stingless bee. The initial tool was a 'stout tool' used to break away a layer of bitumen covering the opening leading to the nest. The second tool was shorter, thinner and 'sharper-pointed' and used with a different grip to widen the excavated hole. The third tool was a pointed 'bodkin' used forcefully to puncture the nest itself, after which the fourth tool, a flexible 'dip stick', was used to extract the honey. The report details the sizes of the tools and the durations of their use. It concludes with the observation that 'even if these were exceptional actions of an individual specialist, the skilful performance is impressive' (Brewer and McGrew 1990). This anecdote is important because it documents something unique and unexpected. However, in this report at least, the authors do not discuss the relevance of the behaviour for our overall understanding of

137

chimpanzee behaviour or of the evolution of tool behaviour. The report simply serves to expand the catalogue of known behaviours.

While many reports of tool behaviour are anecdotal, a few are more comprehensive. They analyse tool behaviour within an explicitly defined interpretive context, in effect using evidence of tool behaviour to advance our overall understanding of the animal in question. By far the most common interpretive context in the natural history tradition is that of the adaptive niche.

A fine example of this is Uehara's (1982) study of seasonal changes in the termiting techniques used by chimpanzees in the Mahale Mountains of Tanzania. Uehara observed two groups of chimpanzees and noted that termites constituted a higher proportion in the diet of one group than of the other. The chimpanzees in one of the groups used taste to determine whether a termite mound could be usefully exploited. Uehara noted an interesting seasonal difference. Prior to the termites' seasonal swarming, the chimpanzees used probes manufactured from plant stems to extract the termites from tunnels in the mounds. Later in the wet season, they simply broke open the mounds by hand and plucked the termites from the surface. These Mahale chimpanzees also 'fished' for ants all year round, manufacturing a different kind of probe for this task. Uehara's study includes descriptions of tool size, the grip used, and analyses of faecal samples to assess importance in the diet. He integrates tool behaviour into a more general account of chimpanzee foraging. Studies such as these differ from anecdotal reports in the number of observations recorded, the use of intraspecific comparison, and the adoption of an interpretive context, in this case that of foraging.

Yet even here, the questions of origin and evolutionary change are largely ignored. They are issues that are rarely raised in the natural history literature. Alcock (1972), in one of the few explicit treatments of evolution and tool-use, discusses the possible general mechanisms of origin and spread of feeding tools. He argues that the source of most tool-use lies in the novel application of pre-existing patterns of behaviour. For example, he speculates that a woodpecker finch, unable to reach a tasty grub under the bark, would have expressed its frustration by the displacement activity of nest building. In carrying out this activity, the bird might have fortuitously impaled the grub with a cactus spine, and might have eventually learned to repeat the performance, specifically as a way of obtaining food. The behaviour would then have spread by observational learning, especially observation of parents. Alcock also addresses the problem of 'subsequent evolution', that is, evolution after a pattern of tool behaviour has become established. Excepting the few cases in which tool-use is 'hard-wired' in the genome (sand-throwing ants, for example), Alcock sees subsequent evolution operating to adapt an organism *to* a specific variety of tool-use by optimizing its ability to learn that particular behavioural pattern. In Alcock's view, subsequent evolution does not appear to include any possible change in the behavioural pattern itself, or, more particularly, in the tools. 'However, it should be stressed that for many species tool-using is a rare event which probably is simply the by-product of selection for certain general abilities which underlie many different behaviour patterns' (Alcock 1972: 469).

Alcock's argument is echoed, with greater exemplary support, by Beck (1980). He devotes a chapter of his book to the question of the evolution of tool behaviour. Like Alcock, his discussion deals with the emergence of tool behaviour in taxa that had previously not used tools. He discusses, for example, the hypothesis that object manipulation leads to object use, the hypothesis that agonistic behaviour is a source of tool use, and the hypothesis that animals 'ill-adapted' to their current niche might adopt tools. He finds none of these hypotheses convincing. Indeed, Beck finds it difficult to explain tool behaviour in classic Darwinian terms.

> The evolution of a novel phenotype is disjunctive: the behaviour does not exist until the moment that a novel stimulus–response sequence incorporating an object is produced and reinforced. Such quantum changes are not easily accommodated within modern evolutionary theory. Perhaps only the general genetic determinants of learning, *and not the learned behaviour patterns per se*, can be said to evolve. [Emphasis mine]
>
> (Beck 1980: 183–4)

It is here that we encounter one of the characteristics of the natural history perspective on tool behaviour. In principle, there is no reason why patterns of tool behaviour could not themselves change, especially in cases where the behaviour is learned. By observation, problem solving, or even serendipity, a specific pattern of use could be transferred from one task to another. Alcock emphasizes this as a possible explanation for the origin of a tool behaviour, but not for its subsequent change. Such a process is, in fact, fairly common in evolution (Gould and Vrba (1982) use the term exaptation), that is when a structure or behaviour that has evolved for one use is co-opted or 'turned to account' for another. Repeated use of a particular tool could also, by similar processes, result in a change in the size or even the form of a tool (choice of an alternative raw material, for example) so as to make it better suited to its new use. Any such change over time could be regarded as evolutionary. Beck and Alcock do not grant importance to this kind of change. Instead, they argue that the capacity for learning (Beck's 'genetic determinants of learning') can and does evolve in classic Darwinian fashion, and that this is the central evolutionary process in animal tool behaviour. In a sense, they acknowledge a kind of evolutionary specialization – better and better learning – but do not consider the possibility of gradual change in the behavioural patterns themselves.

Huffman and Quiatt (1986) take this reasoning a step further. They do not merely ignore the possibility of evolution of the pattern of tool behaviour itself: they specifically deny its possibility. They base their argument on a discussion of stone handling by provisioned Japanese macaques. The macaques collect and manipulate stones and pebbles; they do not, however, use them as tools. Huffman and Quiatt discuss how such handling might lead to stone tool-use through 'environmental opportunity'. If this handling yielded certain adaptive advantages, then selection for competence might appear. Thus tool behaviour would evolve through environmental opportunity and niche transformation. Huffman and Quiatt rule out any alternative mechanism:

> It [stone handling] encourages us not to think of the invention of stone tools either as a serendipitous solution to problems set by nature or as the automatic end point of a natural chain of events: non-instrumental manipulation of stones → use of stones as tools → manufacture of stones.

(Huffman and Quiatt 1986: 422)

This is an explicit denial of any process of technical change or, to put it another way, a denial of progress as a factor in the evolution of tool behaviour.

What is missing in the natural historic literature is any discussion of change in the patterns of tool behaviour themselves. The evolution of tool behaviour is invariably couched in terms of environmental constraint and niche alteration. Competence in tool-use evolves in classic Darwinian fashion, and environmental opportunity or restriction determines whether a particular tool behaviour, whatever its origin, flourishes or disappears. Despite the close attention accorded to the biomechanics of grip, dimensions of the tools, raw materials, and even techniques of tool-making, neither the patterns of tool behaviour nor the tools themselves are seen to change. True, non-human tools have not been observed to change but, more to the point, natural scientists seem not to expect them to change, but only to appear or disappear as niches change. One kind of termite probe is not expected to lead to a another, better model. It is this omission that most clearly distinguishes natural historic approaches to tool behaviour from those of the 'socio-cultural tradition'.

THE SOCIO-CULTURAL TRADITION

Social scientists, including most social and cultural anthropologists, study tool behaviour from a very different perspective. Instead of emphasizing the role of tools in an adaptive niche, they emphasize the role played by tools in cultural and social systems. Tool behaviour becomes technology, a quasi-autonomous component in a complex web of cultural and social dynamics. Different schools of social theory and philosophy vary considerably in the importance they grant to technology. However, two threads run through the social science literature that may help us to understand why social scientific discussions of tools and tool behaviour are so incompatible with those of natural science. These are the idea that technology is a super-organic, autonomous force, and the idea of progress.

A major theme of philosophical literature is the idea that technology is an autonomous entity or force whose nature has profound consequences for human society. Jacques Ellul, one of the leading exponents of this view, goes so far as to argue that humans are now embedded in a technological milieu (something he terms 'technique') rather than a natural milieu (Ellul 1963). This milieu is internally consistent, like nature, and is self-determining in the sense that it is independent of human intervention. Social phenomena exist *within* this context, not in separate-but-equivalent domains of human behaviour. The technological milieu is value-neutral, neither necessarily benign nor necessarily evil. Nevertheless, it is the essential context within which such matters as human freedom must be addressed. Ellul's is perhaps an extreme position, but he makes explicit an idea tacitly held by many scholars in the history and philosophy of technology: that of technology as an autonomous force (not all philosophers agree, of course, as shown by the example of Lewis Mumford (1966)). The same idea appears in social theory as well, the most well-known theory being that of Marx, who argued that the economic base of a society sets the conditions for the other characteristics of that society. 'Material forces of production', including tools, techniques, and control of physical power, condition the 'relations of production', which are the relationships between persons with regard to access to, and control over, the means of production and distribution of produce. These then condition features of the 'superstructures', which include government, religion, ideology and so on. Changes in technology force accommodation in the relations of production and, in turn, in the superstructures (Somerville 1967). Exegesis of Marx is, of course, a factious field, and there are alternative interpretations of Marx's major points. What is important for us is that Marx emphasized production, tools, and techniques as central dynamic forces in human history. Moreover, Marx's ideas have been very influential in the development of social science.

More recent materialist theories take a similar tack, though they differ considerably in detail. In anthropology the best recent examples are the cultural evolutionism of Leslie White (1959) and the cultural materialism of Marvin Harris (1979). These view cultural adaptations, especially in technological and productive domains, as determining the major characteristics of other social and symbolic systems and as being the prime movers of change. While alternative theories of culture downplay or reject the deterministic role of technology, they often retain a perspective in which technology is treated as a self-contained, unitary system, independent of but affecting other domains.

A second thread in the social science literature is the idea of technological progress. This is an idea so pervasive in Western thought that it is difficult to find precise definitions. Skolimowski sees it as 'the ability to produce more and more diversified objects with more and more interesting features, in a more and more efficient way' (1966: 375), and this is a reasonable approximation to the common-sense notion. The idea of progress is very much a nineteenth-century one (Staudenmeier 1985), and indeed Mumford (1961) blames its scholarly popularity on anthropologists and archaeologists of the period, who devoted considerable energy to constructing classifications of artefacts and arranging the classes in sequences, based largely on the criterion of

141

complexity. The idea that animal species could be arranged into a sequence of increasing complexity, a 'great chain of being', was of course an old one. It was the basis for the ideas of several pre-Darwinian evolutionists, most notably Lamarck, who saw a definite order of progression in evolutionary change. Scholars such as Herbert Spencer and Edward Tylor, who were interested in the evolution of society and culture, tended to derive their concepts of evolution from this pre-Darwinian, progressive source. In the study of material culture, the most influential of these socio-cultural evolutionists was Lane Fox (1875), who subsequently wrote under the name of Pitt-Rivers.

Pitt-Rivers's primary concern was to describe and explain the evolution of material culture. His evidence consisted of an extensive collection of indigenous artefacts from all over the world. At the core of his analysis was a classification based on a direct analogy with biological classification, which, like the notion of progressive evolution, was pre-Darwinian. It was Pitt-Rivers's contention, unusual for the time, that a study of culture could be as scientific as a study of the natural world (Thompson 1977). Whereas previous classifications of artefacts had been based largely on criteria of geographic or ethnic origin, Pitt-Rivers classified exclusively on the basis of 'affinities' of form, disregarding context. In so doing he was able to establish formal series for throwing-sticks, bows, boats, and so on, each exemplar in a series sharing affinities with adjacent exemplars. Pitt-Rivers then argued, again on the basis of the biological analogy, that the formal series also represented gradual evolutionary sequences. Initially he drew on Darwin, but later on he turned to Herbert Spencer for his evolutionary mechanism. He was always careful to emphasize that artefacts do not reproduce, and attributed the increasing complexity of artefacts over a series to a 'succession of ideas' tied to the increasing utility of the artefact for its task. He argued, appealing largely to Spencer, that this succession of ideas would lead to selection for appropriate neural structures.

Pitt-Rivers enjoyed widespread influence at the time because he corroborated the Victorian notions of progress and the advance of technology. He played leading roles in the Ethnological Society and the International Congress of Prehistoric Archaeology and, even though he did not write extensively himself, his ideas received wide circulation (Thompson 1977). In part he simply formalized the 'progress' thinking of the times and combined it with the surge of enthusiasm for evolutionary reconstruction. But the ultimate result of his work was the establishment of the idea that artefacts have genealogies. His repeated insistence that tools do not reproduce faded into the background in favour of an emphasis on gradual sequences of form driven by the progressive force of increasing 'utility'.

Of the two ideas — technology as an autonomous force and the notion of progress — the former is the more pervasive in current social science. Even theoretical approaches that are not avowedly materialist acknowledge the

142

importance of technology. Thus Pfaffenberger, who regards technology as 'humanized nature', insists that

> it is a fundamentally *social* phenomenon: it is a social construction of the nature around us and within us, and once achieved, it expresses an embedded social vision, and it engages us in what Marx would call a form of life.
>
> (Pfaffenberger 1988: 244)

While Pfaffenberger explicitly argues against technological determinism, it is clear from this passage that he sees technology as something with ramifications throughout cultural systems. This is more in line with current fashion in social theory. For the most part, modern social theory deals with technology as a monolithic entity and rarely considers its components. Little attention is given to actual tool behaviour, so that we are remarkably naïve about how people actually use tools (Pfaffenberger 1988). There have been a few recent studies that take a cognitive approach to tool behaviour in modern contexts (e.g. Dougherty and Keller 1982; Gatewood 1985; Lemonnier 1986), but these are exceptional and not yet well developed. Social science appears to be interested in how technology drives, or constrains, or is in turn affected by, cultural context, but not very interested in how the tools themselves are used.

The idea of progress, on the other hand, has few active exponents on any level. The only recent one outside the historical and archaeological literature is Wendell Oswalt (1976), who has made a comparative study of food-getting technology that is very much in the tradition of Pitt-Rivers. Nevertheless, the idea of progress has not disappeared from social science, but has rather persisted as an implicit and rarely examined assumption. It has changed little in the last century, and is in fact a kind of 'survival' from the heyday of nineteenth-century evolutionism. As a consequence it does not fit well with modern biological notions of evolutionary dynamics. Indeed, socio-cultural conceptions of technology are not easily reconciled with important features of the modern synthetic theory of evolution. What is the source and nature of technological variation? How are tools selected? Although there have been relatively simplistic attempts to equate invention with mutation and utility with selection (Basalla (1988) is a good recent example), none has been very persuasive. The idea of gradual change in gene frequency just does not apply easily to tools. The natural historic and socio-cultural perspectives on tools *do* share the concept of evolution, but do *not* share a concept of evolutionary mechanism, and in the absence of a common understanding of the mechanism of change they have little of relevance to contribute to one another.

Let me summarize briefly the contrast between the natural historic and the socio-cultural approaches to tool behaviour.

The natural historic approach provides descriptions of tool behaviour, often detailed and exhaustive, and emphasizes its adaptive context. It does not attend to the ramifications that tool behaviour has outside of the specific contexts of use. Its interest in evolution extends to niche alteration and selection for competence in learning, but does not appear to consider the possibility that the learned behavioural patterns might change or that the tools might change. The natural historic approach falls squarely within the mainstream of ecological, neo-Darwinian ethology.

The socio-cultural approach emphasizes the role of technology within cultural systems, especially in its relationship with social behaviour. It sees technology as an autonomous force and as inherently progressive – one technical idea leading, as a matter of course, to another, better one. Despite this emphasis on progress, the socio-cultural approach is oddly uninterested in the details of tool behaviour. Its perspective is evolutionary, but more in the tradition of nineteenth-century evolutionism than in that of the synthetic theory of modern evolutionary biology.

The history of ideas does influence how we conceive a problem. In the case of tool behaviour two very different intellectual traditions have been brought to bear. These traditions do not just determine how we interpret specific evidence; they also influence the very questions we ask. Because the 'natural historic' and 'socio-cultural' traditions are so different, and because the former perspective is normally applied to non-human animals and the latter exclusively to humans, the question of continuity between non-human and human tool behaviour is rarely even posed. Social science (and folk knowledge) tends to think about tools in a way that precludes continuity. By focusing on the role of tools and, especially, technology as active agents in social systems, and by largely ignoring questions of how tools are made and used on a small scale, recent anthropology has made it difficult to formulate hypotheses about intermediate conditions. Almost all students of early hominid behaviour, for example, assume that tools are integrated within holistic cultural systems. This is a feature of modern human culture, but not of apes (see Tobias (1983) for a good example). On the other hand, the natural historic approach underplays or ignores all but the most basic, mechanical role of tools. They are treated much as any specific feature of anatomy or behaviour is treated. The possibility of behavioural change that is not genetically induced in the neo-Darwinian sense is not considered, nor is the idea that tools might, in their use, have ramifications beyond the contexts of foraging. Once again the question of continuity between non-human and human tools rarely arises.

If we want to understand the distinctiveness of human tool behaviour, we must examine the continuities and discontinuities with non-human tool behaviour directly, rather than ignoring them through a methodological and conceptual mismatch. One approach is to examine some of the individual components of tool behaviour. Many different behavioural components come together in an episode of tool behaviour – anatomy of limbs, neural circuitry, memory, problem solving abilities, social status of the artisan, the task to be accomplished, and so on. Human tool behaviour may be dramatically different from that of apes in one component, but very similar in another. Such an approach may fail to identify some general dynamic, but it has the advantage of emphasizing more easily identified components of behaviour.

In what follows I shall discuss several components of tool behaviour and attempt to identify what about each of them sets humans apart.

TOOLS AND HUMAN ANATOMY

Human tool behaviour appears to have selected for an appropriate anatomy and, perhaps, unique neural pathways. If true, *Homo sapiens* would be the only living primate to have evolved an anatomy specific to tool behaviour. The most important feature of this anatomy is the hand.

The human hand is without equal in its ability to deliver fine, precise movements. In its basic anatomy it is little different from that of an ape; it has the same bones, the same muscles, and the same tendons. However, in the course of evolution it has been modified into a structure of great precision and strength. Here, at a very basic level of anatomical constraint, we encounter a distinctiveness in human tool behaviour. The human hand allows more precision in tool-making and tool-use than does the hand of an ape.

There are five anatomical features that distinguish the human hand from that of apes (Marzke and Shackley 1986). First, humans have long thumbs relative to the fingers. Second, humans have structures in the centre of the palm that stabilize the palm against both external and internal forces. For example, there is a projection at the base of the third metacarpal (centre bone of the palm) that abuts against one of the wrist bones, making this joint more stable. Third, the muscles of the palm are positioned in such a way that they can turn the fingers slightly, allowing optimal gripping positions. Fourth, the thumb and first two fingers are relatively robust and operate as a unit. Fifth, the ends of the fingers are flattened and have broad pads, allowing a firm grasp with the finger tips. Marzke and Shackley argue that these anatomical features were selected by two motor patterns: maintenance of an effective grip, and stabilization of the palm for accommodating great external and internal forces (contraction of muscles when gripping a stone core receiving a blow, for example). Many of these distinctive features can be recognized in fossil hands from Bed I at Olduvai, almost two million years old, indicating that even at this relatively early date our presumed ancestors had evolved as tool-users and tool-makers.

Tool behaviour may have selected for distinctive neural structures as well. Almost all humans have a preference for one hand or the other, with the majority being preferentially right-handed. Handedness is tied to morphological asymmetries of the brain, in particular the slight relative expansion of the left occipital and right frontal lobes (Holloway 1981). Neither monkeys nor apes demonstrate unequivocal handedness (Falk 1980) and, though there is some evidence for brain asymmetry in these primates, it is not the left-occipital – right-frontal pattern seen in humans. Frost (1980) has argued that handedness and brain asymmetry were selected in the context of stone tool-use and tool-making. Because stone knapping is an asymmetrical behaviour (the two hands do different things) and because there is 'competition for neural space', the important neural structures and processes come to lie in only one half of the brain. This interpretation is controversial. Asymmetry is also tied to language and symbolic behaviour (see Lieberman's discussion in Article 5). Falk (1980) argues that primate vocalization led to asymmetry, with handedness as a secondary consequence. What we do know is that handedness and cortical asymmetry are linked. We cannot be certain whether tool-use or some other factor initially selected for brain lateralization. However, if Frost and others are correct, then not only human hands but human brains as well have evolved to be tool-using and tool-making organs.

TOOLS AND HUMAN COGNITION

Humans may think about tools in a unique way. The cognitive strategies and abilities we bring to bear on tool-use and tool-making may be very different from those exercised by apes. Indeed, a common hypothesis for the evolution of human intelligence grants considerable importance to the selective power of tool-use. Use of a tool is not inherently intelligent (Beck 1986), however, so we must look more closely at patterns of tool-use if we are to hope to identify distinctive features of cognition. Here I will explore two possibilities: that human tool-use is language-like and therefore unique, and that human problem solving with tools is somehow distinctive.

Human language differs from the communication systems of apes in its grammatical foundation. Using words and a set of rules for stringing them together, any normal human adult can produce a virtual infinity of understandable utterances. Apes, under natural conditions (that is, in the absence of human tuition), can do nothing of the sort because they do not employ syntactical rules to string vocalizations into sentences. Human language is so different from ape communication that it has acquired a special status in definitions of humanness. The source of this remarkable ability is a matter of controversy. Chomsky (1975), for example, argued that basic features of grammar are genetically innate. This is an extreme position, but even more conservative theories acknowledge some genetic component, even if it is merely a predisposition for human infants to acquire syntax.

Might not human tool behaviour also employ grammatical rules, or, if not grammar, then some similar, special organizational feature? If so, then human tool-use would stand apart from ape tool-use much as human language stands apart from ape communication. Because tool behaviour consists of sequences of acts, just as sentences are sequences of words, the first place to look would be at sequence construction. Does tool behaviour produce sequences in a syntactical fashion?

What little systematic evidence we can bring to bear on this question suggests that tool behaviour is rather different from language in the way it constructs sequences. Gatewood (1985), in a study of purse seining (a form of commercial salmon fishing employing complex tackle), concludes that technical skills are learned in a relatively primitive fashion. The novice purse seiner first learns the tasks by serial memorization with no clear idea of how each action relates to others or, indeed, of how all of the actions combine to accomplish a result.

> Typically, this understanding involves a simple memorization after the fashion, 'First I do job$_1$, then I do job$_2$, then I do job$_3$,..., then I am finished'. In other words, this first level of understanding is in the form of a string of beads.
>
> (Gatewood 1985: 206)

Gatewood found that such string-of-beads organization was used by all novices, at least initially. The novice does not learn hierarchies of routines and sub-routines. Instead he learns by chaining actions into longer and longer sequences by memorization. Later, after mastering the tasks, he may come to understand them as a hierarchy, but he does not learn them this way.

Because tool sequences are organized like strings of beads and learned by observation and memorization, apprenticeship is essential. This is clear from Gatewood's example, but the ethnographic record (and no doubt the reader's own experience) can supply numerous corroborating cases.

> Tom [a silversmith] said that the Navajo learn by watching and then doing, following as exactly as possible what they have seen their teachers do.
>
> (Adair 1944: 75)

> Marie [a Navajo weaver] doesn't 'tell' when teaching. She 'shows.' The Navajo word for 'teach' means 'show' and is absolutely literal.
>
> (Reichard 1934: 21)

> Copying, and trial and error, rather than explicit teaching are certainly the methods by which Duna men [in Papua New Guinea] learn about flaked stone.
>
> (White et al. 1977: 381)

During apprenticeship the novice learns sequences of tool use (often very many sequences) by repetition and rote memorization. These 'strings of beads' are organized by chaining one action to the next, using temporal or spatial contiguity to cue the next action in the sequence. The artisan builds long sequences by accretion, adding newly mastered actions (including muscle tensions, hand orientations, etc.) onto previously memorized sequences.

This form of sequence construction is not limited to the narrow domain of tool behaviour. It is commonly encountered in any human behaviour requiring precise motor co-ordination. Instrumental musicians, for example, use much the same technique in learning complex passages of music. It is also the essence of most sport. The 'motor memory' of the sports psychologist reminds one of Gatewood's strings of beads. Tactics in sports are not, of course, sequential, but the units of action, which are the pieces employed in the

147

tactical game, must be learned by repetition. Just as one cannot hope to beat a world-class fencer by reading a book about fencing, one cannot learn to build a fine violin by reading an instruction manual. One must practice, often for years, repeating basic actions and sequences until they have been learned at a very primitive cognitive level.

Strings of beads, motor memory, and chaining actions to one another by means of temporal contiguities constitute a very simple kind of thinking. It is, in fact, a kind of thinking that appears early in childhood. The developmental psychologist Jean Piaget termed this kind of thinking 'sensori-motor' intelligence, whose operation resembles 'a slow-motion film, in which all the pictures are seen in succession but without fusion, and so without the continuous vision for understanding the whole' (Piaget 1960: 121). Sensori-motor intelligence is the intelligence of infants, and is also a kind of intelligence found commonly in the animal world. It is true that the sequences constructed by adults in tool behaviour are longer, and employ more memory, than those of infants. Moreover, other kinds of thinking are used in tool-use. But the basic way in which the sequences are put together and learned is the same.

The primitive nature of tool sequences, and the way they are learned, indicate that there is no technological equivalent to syntax. In everyday speech, strings of words are not generated by accretion and memorization. They are generated by the rules of syntax, rules that allow the spontaneous production of *new* sequences that include such complex internal patterns as embedding and the reversal of subject–verb order. An active hierarchy is employed in syntax, with phrase structure and order within phrases, and this is present in the initial, spontaneous production of sentences. When language constructs sequences it uses complex organizing principles that are not found in other domains of behaviour.

Tool sequences, on the other hand, make use of a very common form of cognitive organization. Not only do humans of all ages use this kind of thinking in all skilled motor tasks, but it is also almost certainly the kind of thinking used by non-humans in tool behaviour. A chimpanzee learns termiting by observing its mother and repeating her actions; it constructs its own strings of beads through spatial and temporal contiguity. The style of thinking is the same as that used by humans when learning tool behaviour; what differs is the length of the sequences. This is a quantitative matter of memory capacity, not a qualitative difference in the way we think when using tools.

Because there is no syntax in human tool behaviour, it is not as dramatically distinct from ape tool behaviour as human language is from ape communication. Nevertheless, humans do seem to use tools more 'intelligently' than apes. The difference lies not in the way we build basic motor sequences, but in the way we solve problems.

There is more to tool-use and tool-making than building and learning motor sequences. Tool behaviour also entails problem solving, the ability to adjust behaviour to a specific task at hand and, for this, rote sequences are not

148

enough. It appears that when an artisan has a project to complete, he or she brings together a variety of relevant bits and pieces of information, including previously learned motor sequences.

Lévi-Strauss (1966) has described the thinking of the '*bricoleur*', a kind of handyman who can accomplish a wide range of projects using only a limited repertoire of tools and procedures. The *bricoleur*

> has to turn back to an already existent set of tools and materials, to consider or reconsider what it contains and, finally, to engage in a sort of dialogue with it and, before choosing between them, to index the possible answers which the whole set can offer his problem. He interrogates all the heterogeneous objects of which his treasury is composed to discover what each of them could 'signify' and so contribute to the definition of a set which has yet to materialize but which will ultimately differ from the instrumental set only in the internal disposition of its parts.
>
> (1966: 18)

While Lévi-Strauss mentions only tools and materials, procedures must also be part of this novel 'set'. His use of 'dialogue' to describe the style of thinking emphasizes the interplay between memory of past projects and plans for the current job. However, Lévi-Strauss specifically contrasts this kind of thinking with that of the craftsman (1966: 19) and the engineer, and here, I think, he misses the mark. The vast majority of human tool-use employs a similar kind of problem solving.

In a study of blacksmithing, a craft rather than a form of *bricolage*, the Kellers refer to 'constellations of conceptual units' (Dougherty and Keller 1982, Keller and Keller 1991). In making a fleur-de-lis, for example, the smith brings together ideas of appropriate process, materials, tools, time expenditure, and so on. This 'constellation' comes together at the time of use, and, while many of the elements may have existed as prior knowledge, the particular constellation is determined by this specific task at hand. There is also an important feedback between the image of the task and the actual actions. The goal must be constantly modified, however slightly, in the light of developments in the procedure. These modifications, in turn, affect other elements of the constellation. Artisans often repeat the same constellation over and over again – a blacksmith making an iron fence may produce scores of fleurs-de-lis – and as a task is repeated the original dynamic interplay of elements and goal is replaced by an almost unconscious recipe. 'When a production has become routine much of the detail of the task becomes "taken-for-granted" and is difficult or impossible to articulate' (Keller and Keller 1991). Because so much tool behaviour is repetitive and mundane, it consists largely of recipes. In attempting to describe a technique of candy making known as 'throwing', a candy maker remarked: 'I can't tell you how I know when it's ready. I just can feel it' (Weddell 1989).

'Constellation of knowledge' and 'recipe' are descriptive concepts that enable us to characterize the kind of everyday thinking employed in tool behaviour. Like many such concepts, they also allow us to pose more specific questions. One such question concerns the nature of problem solving employed in tool behaviour.

Constellations are plans of action that can have varying degrees of complexity. Modern tool behaviour incorporates two kinds of planning: trial-and-error and contingency planning. Trial-and-error planning begins with an idea or image of a desired result, which calls up ideas about appropriate materials, tools, procedures, and so on. The artisan then proceeds until some problem is encountered, or even complete failure, after which the plan is revised, begun again, and so on. The dynamic interplay between goal and constellation takes place in action. From the perspective of Piaget's work on intelligence, trial-and-error planning lacks 'reversibility', the ability to rehearse action in thought, to foresee a potential failure, and return to the starting point *in thought*, before actually committing the error. Reversibility is characteristic of the thinking used in contingency planning, where failures are anticipated and alternative procedures prepared ahead of time. In reality, modern tool behaviour incorporates both kinds of planning. Despite the capacity of reversibility, the artisan can rarely envision all of the possible problems and solutions of a new task.

Here we *do* encounter a difference between human tool behaviour and that of non-humans. While we can describe the chimpanzee opening the bee's nest (see p. 137) as forming constellations of knowledge in the general sense, these constellations are strictly trial-and-error affairs. No example of non-human tool behaviour requires reversibility and contingency planning. How significant is this as a distinguishing feature of human tool-use? Humans are more intelligent than chimpanzees, as has been amply demonstrated by their respective proficiencies in the many kinds of problem-solving tasks posed in laboratory research (Premack 1976, Passingham 1982). It should not be surprising that humans employ this greater intelligence in tool-use and tool-making. There is nothing specifically technological about human intelligence. Indeed, evolutionary developments in the hominid brain have few correlations with developments in tools (Wynn 1988); tools do not appear to have selected for human intelligence. The use of constellations of knowledge in tool behaviour is an interesting kind of problem solving, but it does not appear to be a 'domain-specific' kind of thinking. Rather, it is the application of generalized human problem solving abilities to specific technological tasks.

Use of string-of-beads motor sequences and constellations of knowledge in tool behaviour does not entail cognitive processes with any distinctive features not found in other fields of human behaviour. Unlike language, tool behaviour has apparently not evolved with its own restricted forms of organization and thinking.

TOOLS AND HUMAN CULTURE

The concept of culture is central to anthropology. While definitions and discussions of the term vary in emphasis, most include reference to knowledge that is learned (culture is not genetically transmitted) and shared (cultural knowledge is shared to some degree by more than one individual). Many definitions also include reference to symbolic behaviour, as both a prerequisite for the transmission of ideas and an element of cultural knowledge itself. All anthropologists include human tool behaviour within the boundaries of cultural practice and most acknowledge that it is crucial to human survival. It is therefore important to examine tool behaviour as cultural behaviour.

Most skilled tool behaviour is learned by apprenticeship. This is as true in modern industrial societies as it is among craftsmen in the contemporary non-industrial world or as it was in the Renaissance. There are social and economic reasons for apprenticeship, but these are not my central concern. The major reason for apprenticeship, from our present perspective, lies in the nature of technological learning.

Apprenticeship is necessary because practice is necessary. At the heart of any skilled tool-use is a body of string-of-beads style action sequences, consisting largely of patterns stored in motor memory. As we saw earlier, these sequences are learned largely by accretion – new actions are added on to previously mastered sequences. Despite the primitive nature of these patterns, they are not in any way genetically coded, and are entirely learned. However, because these essential skills are learned at a primitive, sensori-motor level of intelligence, they can be learned only by repetition. Many skilled tool behaviours such as cabinet-making require that a huge number of these strings of beads be learned. One cannot learn to plane a surface in a few sessions, and basic skills like planing are just the beginning. Modern power tools have not eliminated the need for repetitive learning; they have merely changed the tasks. In some instances, power tools have increased the tolerance for motor error (a drill press, for example), but in others this tolerance has been reduced (certain power sanders, for example). Practice is still necessary.

Artisans also learn their constellations of knowledge by apprenticeship. This is because constellations are largely non-linguistic and are rarely taught by more than cursory verbal instruction. Gatewood (1985) reports that on his first day on the purse seining boat:

> They did not bother naming parts of the hardware, nor did they explain the purpose of each task I was assigned. Rather, they just told me to do several things in a linguistic form similar to: 'Put that [point] through there [point].'
>
> (Gatewood 1985: 204)

Both Gatewood's study of purse seining and the Kellers' study of blacksmithing suggest that much of the knowledge acquired in tool behaviour is not lexical. As Gatewood puts it, 'one experiences visual imagery and muscular tensions appropriate to certain actions, but can only grope for words to express these inner thought–feeling flows' (Gatewood 1985: 206). Of course, technological learning is not entirely non-linguistic. Teachers can direct apprentices to proper tools, and apprentices in some modern technologies can even consult manuals. But these are far from being sufficient. As a candy maker said of his technique, 'You can't learn this out of any book. And you can only be told so much about how to do it. Mostly it's hands-on experience' (Weddell 1989). Apprentices learn almost entirely by observation and repetition. Readers who have ever tried to fix a piece of machinery by reading a manual will appreciate the inadequacy of linguistic instruction.

This non-linguistic character of technological learning has interesting implications for the understanding of culture in general. Some definitions of culture (e.g. White 1959), perhaps in another attempt to draw a sharp line between humans and apes, emphasize the criterion of symbolic transmission. However, since technological knowledge makes only minimal use of symbols in learning, symbolic learning cannot be seen as the key to all of cultural behaviour – unless, of course, one wants to exclude tool behaviour from 'real' culture.

As in other domains of cultural practice that require considerable memory, tool behaviour does employ short cuts and mnemonic devices. One way is through organization. Some technological knowledge is organized in such a way that the artisan learns a few basic elements and a set of rules for applying them and transforming them. Glassie (1975) presents an excellent account of this kind of knowledge in his discussion of house design and construction from the seventeenth to the nineteenth century in a small area on the eastern seaboard of North America. The local builders, who may well have been only semi-literate, did not use blueprints or graphic plans of any sort. Instead they possessed a knowledge of basic forms and dimensions. 'The plan of each house included a square, and all of the other dimensions of the house are determined by adding or subtracting units to or from the width of that square' (Glassie 1975: 22). The size of the square was determined by the length of the diagonal, which, interestingly, varied from builder to builder. Some used a $14\frac{1}{2}$-foot diagonal, others an 8-yard diagonal, and still others a 9-yard diagonal. After the initial square was laid out, the builder used a number of conventions to add additional rooms, the dimensions of which were regular 'transformations' of the dimensions of the initial room. Another series of conventions was used to locate windows, doors, fireplaces, and so on. Using this kind of approach the builder did not need to learn a large number of specific house designs. Instead, he employed one basic form and a relatively small number of conventions or rules.

Glassie's account of folk housing is more an example of how technological knowledge is applied than of how it is learned. Nevertheless, because the knowledge is organized in this fashion it is in fact easier to learn and retain. This structuring of technological knowledge (and Glassie is an avowed structuralist[1]) once again tempts us to draw a comparison with language. Are not Glassie's forms and transformations analogous to the kernel sentences and transformational rules of Chomskian linguistics? The forms Glassie records are not 'deep' structures, and they are certainly not innate. They were learned in each successive generation through apprenticeship. Moreover, as Glassie discusses at some length, the conventions changed over time under the influence of a new architectural style. This kind of organization of cultural knowledge is not limited to technology. It is a feature of myth as well, where a relatively small number of themes and motifs may be rearranged into a wide range of specific narratives (Littleton 1967). Lévi-Strauss (1966), for example, compares mythical thought to that of the *bricoleur* (see p. 149). Tool behaviour and myth may, at first glance, seem to have little in common, but especially in pre-literate societies, both rely entirely on the memory of the practitioner, who must learn and retain a large body of relevant information. The structured nature of this knowledge is, if nothing else, a distinct aid to learning.

One thing is clear about the way tool behaviour is learned. It is not learned in the way language is learned. Chomsky's argument for an innate grammar may be losing ground to the idea of a partly innate 'language acquisition device' (LAD) that guides a child to learn the rules of his or her language, operating in concert with a 'language acquisition support system' (LASS), also partly innate, that structures the way adults speak to children at various stages of learning (Bruner 1985). Even children raised in extremely impoverished environments learn their native languages without obvious instruction. Whether one favours the narrow Chomskian view or the less entailed LAD and LASS, something appears to be innate in the acquisition of language. The same cannot be said for tool behaviour. People raised in impoverished tool environments do *not* learn how to use tools. Very many people never acquire a competence in tools comparable to their mastery of language. There appears to be no 'technology acquisition device' coded somewhere in the genes. However, there do appear to be 'technology acquisition support systems'. These are not, however, even partly innate. They are, in fact, the systems of apprenticeship to which I have already drawn attention. Societies must supply the entire acquisition support system, and apprenticeship is often long and tedious, precisely because there is nothing innate about the knowledge of what to do or of how to learn it. Once again, tool behaviour is unlike language, but like other learned behaviour.

Tool behaviour may be unlike other aspects of culture, however, in the degree to which it is shared between individuals. During apprenticeship, the novice learns by observation, practice, and failure. Both the Kellers and Gatewood note an important consequence of apprenticeship. Each novice constructs his or her own constellations of knowledge; they are *not* shared. When Gatewood enquired about the 'cognitive segments' (Gatewood's term for constellations) employed by other seiners, he found that there were marked differences in content, even though the same words were used as labels (for example, 'pursing' or 'lifting rings' would evoke an idiosyncratic constellation of knowledge for each seiner). The primary reason why constellations are not shared is that each has been constructed by associations and correspondences individually recognized by each person while learning the task. Once again, other ethnographic descriptions corroborate the idiosyncratic nature of technological knowledge. Adair (1944), in his study of Navajo silversmiths, found that 'the way smiths learned was by finishing each piece' (p. 75). Regardless of even gross errors, the apprentice was made to complete every piece begun. If constellations of knowledge must be constructed by each individual, and if such constellations are not shared, then such a practice not only makes sense, it is also essential. Every artisan brings idiosyncratic ways of doing things, personal taste, and so on, to any task. Because of this, no two artisans truly share entire constellations of knowledge, even for the same task. Nevertheless, they can and do share some *elements* used in their construction of constellations.

Traditions and community standards constrain the range of choices an artisan can make, perhaps even more than does personal history. The artisan draws from a pool of solutions known by his or her own community, which tend to be very constraining. An interesting example of this comes from the Anga, a Papuan society whose material culture was studied by Lemonnier (1986). The Anga use a traditional style for the arrows they use in hunting. Some of their neighbours make a much deadlier kind of arrow, one that is better for hunting. The Anga know how to make this type of arrow but make their traditional design instead. The wood used and the game hunted are the same; the Anga simply choose not to make the deadlier arrow. In addition to exerting constraints on what an artisan is willing to produce, community standards can be very conservative, to the point of violating what would seem obvious 'functional' considerations. A well-known archaeological example is that of Chalcolithic copper axes, which for centuries were made to resemble the ground stone celts that preceded them (Basalla 1988).

From the perspective of the individual artisan, community standards consist of the range of appropriate forms (and acceptable deviations) from which the artisan can choose. In some cases this range encompasses all of the known technological solutions to a particular task. But often, as in the case of Anga arrows, community standards are a subset of the known solutions. It is here that we can speak of technological knowledge being shared. The bits and pieces of knowledge that make up community standards are presumably shared by all community artisans. However, they form only one set of considerations that an artisan brings to a specific task. They constrain the range of possible forms, sizes, decoration, and so on, but community standards alone cannot achieve any result. The artisan combines them with idiosyncratic knowledge, action sequences learned by rote, considerations of cost, and other such factors.

Thus far I have discussed learning and sharing of cultural knowledge as the critical factors behind tools and tool-use. But are not the essential features of tools determined by their 'functions', that is, by the tasks they are called upon

154

to perform? The idea that function determines form (or that it should do so) is a pervasive one and, indeed, is related to the ideas, which I have already reviewed, of progress and of an evolutionary sequence of increasing utility. However, it is almost certainly wrong to think that the nature of a task determines anything specific about the shapes and sizes of tools, or how they will be used. A very large number of possible tools, styles, and procedures will actually get the job done. The task does not specify which is to be adopted, because it is in no way tied directly to those tools and procedures. It is connected to the necessary means only through the mind of the artisan, who must choose what to do. 'The form of designed things is decided by choice or else by chance; but it is never actually entailed by anything whatsoever' (Pye 1964: 9). Pye, an authority in furniture design, seriously challenges the notion that function determines form. This is a theme taken up by the archaeologist Sackett (1982) and the ethnographer Lemonnier (1986). The array of tools and procedures that can successfully achieve a task at hand is, if not infinite, at least immense. Artisans draw on their own knowledge to make the choice. Some of this knowledge is idiosyncratic, some is shared with other artisans. The immediate task, the 'function', generates little or no new knowledge and so cannot be said to determine anything about the solution finally adopted. Of course, the task must be accomplished, but this is only a very broad constraining consideration.

Cultural behaviour includes semiotic behaviour, semiotics being the study of signs. Most of us think of tools as mundane objects used to get results, rather than as signs that stand for something else, or which carry information. Modern human tools, however, like other features of human culture, do participate in the semiotic domain, and in some very important ways.

Tools operate as signs in at least two ways. The most common semiotic role of a tool is as an index, which is a sign that signals its referent by physical contiguity (Casson 1981) or direct association. The choices an artisan makes when assembling constellations of knowledge can come to 'mark' that artisan. An idiosyncratic technological solution can act as an index of its maker; one can recognize a Stradivarius violin from the specific choices made during its manufacture. Because artisans also choose from a range of community standards, tools can also act as indices of social groups. Anasazi pots are a fine example. The range of vessel shapes, manufacturing techniques, and decorative motifs identify the pot as Anasazi even if it appears in a London auction house. The indexical quality of tools is largely an unintended consequence of people making choices. If function really did determine the form of tools, they would rarely or never act as unintended indices of anything other than the purposes for which they were used. Sometimes people use the indexical potential of tools to make public statements about their individual or group status; in these cases the choice is intentional. Rolex watches and Ferrari sports cars are obvious examples. The relative ease with which tools can 'index' status is commonly exploited in advertising, where the status implied by the tool is as important as its potential mechanical use (see Carrier 1990, for an interesting discussion of this point).

Tools can also come to stand for ideas and institutions. Here the symbolic meanings invariably exploit an iconic connection between the sign (in this case a tool) and its referent. An icon and its referent share certain features; unlike in the case of 'true' symbols, the connection is not completely arbitrary. A mason's trowel, for example, is a tool for building, but in another context it is a sign of the Masonic brotherhood. The iconic value derives in part from a presumed historical connection between modern Masons and the builders of Solomon's temple. Here, what was initially an unintentional index (trowel=mason) has been endowed with additional indexical value (trowel=Mason) and symbolic meaning (trowel=faith and dedication, as possessed by the builders of the temple). True, the iconic connection here is not as simple as that of a picture of fire representing an actual fire. Nevertheless, the mason's trowel has come to stand for something else by virtue of features shared with its referent. Interestingly, the shared features are largely indexical qualities. Occasionally, the symbolic value of a tool becomes the predominant consideration in its use and manufacture. In these cases mechanical considerations often fade and the 'tool' can no longer actually be used as a tool. However, the iconic connection – the 'toolness' – of the sign remains fundamental to its meaning. The Christian cross is an example. For the Romans it was a simple tool. Early Christians attached symbolic value to it because it was an icon for the passion of Christ. Today an artisan making a crucifix does not attend to its possible use as an instrument of execution, but does attend to its role as a symbol. Nevertheless, the relation between sign and referent is not arbitrary; there remains an iconic link between crucifixes and Roman crosses.

The indexical and iconic roles of tools are ubiquitous in human culture. A tool is rarely just a tool; it identifies its user in obvious or subtle ways, and can stand for ideas only remotely connected with the mechanical tasks it performs. Tools are not unique in this regard. Humans have a remarkable capacity and inclination to endow the objects in their environments with meaning. When the artisan makes or chooses a tool, these indexical and iconic considerations are part of the constellations of knowledge he or she brings to the task; they are incorporated into the very nature of the tool.

These kinds of semiotic roles are simply unknown in the case of non-human tools. One might argue that non-human primates are exploiting an indexical quality when they use tools in agonistic encounters. A good example comes from the chimpanzees of Gombe studied by Goodall. Mike, a sub-dominant male, serendipitously discovered that he could make an intimidating noise by banging together two paraffin tins. He then used this noisy display to ascend the dominance hierarchy. However, such an association between tools and dominance barely qualifies as indexical. While it is possible that the semiotic role of human tools evolved from such displays, they compare poorly with the rich symbolic role of human tools. Moreover, tools used by chimpanzees for display are used *only* for that purpose. Nowhere do we see the simultaneous, multiple roles played by human tools.

CONCLUSION

The preceding discussion suggests two important conclusions about human tool-use and tool-making. First, while there are several specific differences between human tool behaviour and that of non-humans, these differences should not be considered to represent an evolutionary gulf; and second, when compared to other domains of human behaviour, tool-use and tool-making do not seem unique.

It is possible to identify several features of human tool behaviour unknown in the tool behaviour of apes. (1) Humans have undergone anatomical and, probably, neurological adaptations to the skilled use of the hands. This is almost certainly a result of selection for tool-use and reflects the relative importance of tools in later hominid adaptations. (2) Modern humans sometimes use tools in ways that require a more sophisticated intelligence than any known for apes. Often this is simply a matter of greater memory, but occasionally human tool-use requires more complex organizing skills. (3) Human tools are employed as unintentional and intentional signs. Just as importantly, they fulfil these roles at the same time as assisting in the performance of more mundane mechanical tasks. Neither feature is known for the tool behaviour of apes. (4) The anatomical adaptations and the semiotic role of tools point to a fourth, obvious difference. Tools have come to saturate human life. They have not only selected for specific anatomies, but have also entered that most important of human domains, symbolic behaviour.

Despite these specific features, human tool behaviour is not as different from that of non-humans as social science has often supposed. Continuity between ape and human tools is easy to envisage. For example, apes almost certainly use strings-of-beads sequences and constellations of knowledge in their tool behaviour. The general pattern of thinking is shared with humans, but specific features differ. Human apprentices can learn longer sequences than those used by apes because their memory is greater. Humans use contingency plans in their constellations, apes do not. However, the common general cognitive pattern allows us to conceive of cognitive abilities intermediate between those of apes and those of humans, employing greater memory than that of which apes are capable, and slightly more complex plans of action.

Within the bounds of human behaviour, tool-use and tool-making do not appear especially unique. Unlike language, tool behaviour has no domain-specific features that cannot be found in other everyday pursuits. Apprenticeship for tool behaviour is well known and, as we have seen, is quite necessary to learn the many strings-of-beads sequences, and the constellations of non-lexical, partially shared knowledge. But apprenticeship is also necessary for the acquisition of skill in the fields of oral narrative, performing arts, and sport, to name just three, and is necessary for the same reasons. Tool behaviour taps into the same abilities used in other kinds of problem solving. Certain organizational features of technological knowledge are just as typical of myth and music. Semiotic content is a characteristic of almost all culture, not just of tools. In short, while tool-use and tool-making have played an important role in the human career, they have not as a consequence evolved distinctive features of their own.

NOTE

1   This aspect of Glassie's study is discussed by Miller in Article 15 of this volume.

REFERENCES

Adair, J. (1944) *The Navajo and Pueblo Silversmith*, Norman University of Oklahoma Press.

Alcock, J. (1972) 'The evolution of the use of tools by feeding animals', *Evolution* 26: 464–73.

Basalla, G. (1988) *The Evolution of Technology*, Cambridge: Cambridge University Press.

Beck, B. B. (1980) *Animal Tool Behavior*, New York: Garland Press.

—— (1986) 'Tools and intelligence', in R. J. Hoage and L. Goldman (eds) *Animal Intelligence*, Washington, DC: Smithsonian Institute Press.

Boesch, C. and Boesch, H. (1984) 'Mental map in wild chimpanzees: an analysis of hammer transports for nut cracking', *Primates* 25: 160–70.

Brewer, S. and McGrew, W. C. (1990) 'Chimpanzee use of a tool-set to get honey', *Folia Primatologica* 54: 100–4.

Bruner, J. (1985) 'Vygotsky: a historical and conceptual perspective', in J. Wertsch (ed.) *Culture, Communication and Cognition: Vygotskian Perspectives*, Cambridge: Cambridge University Press.

Carrier, J. (1990) 'The symbolism of possession in commodity advertising', *Man* (N.S.) 25: 693–706.

Casson, E. W. (1981) *Language, Culture, and Cognition*, New York: Macmillan.

Chomsky, N. (1975) *Reflections on Language*, New York: Pantheon Books.

Dougherty, J. and Keller, C. (1982) 'Taskonomy: a practical approach to knowledge structures', *American Ethnologist* 5: 763–74.

Ellul, J. (1963) 'The technological order', in C. Stover (ed.) *The Technological Order*, Detroit: Wayne State University Press.

Falk, D. (1980) 'Language, handedness, and primate brains: did the australopithecines sign?', *American Anthropologist* 82: 72–8.

Frost, G. T. (1980) 'Tool behavior and the origins of laterality', *Journal of Human Evolution* 9: 447–59.

Galdikas, B. (1982) 'Orang-utan tool-use at Tanjung Putang Reserve, Central Indonesian Borneo (Kalimantan Tengah)', *Journal of Human Evolution* 11: 19–33.

Gatewood, J. (1985) 'Actions speak louder than words', in J. W. D. Dougherty (ed.) *Directions in Cognitive Anthropology*, Urbana: University of Illinois Press.

Glassie, H. (1975) *Folk Housing in Middle Virginia*, Knoxville: University of Tennessee Press.

Gould, S. J. and Vrba, E. (1982) 'Exaptation – a missing term in the science of form', *Paleobiology* 8: 4–15.

Gowlett, J. (1984) 'Mental abilities of early man: a look at some hard evidence', in R. Foley (ed.) *Hominid Evolution and Community Ecology*, London: Academic Press.

Hamilton, W. J., Bushirk, R. E. and Bushirk, W. (1975) 'Defensive stoning by baboons', *Nature* 256: 488–89.

Harris, M. (1979) *Cultural Materialism*, New York: Random House.

Holloway, R. (1981) 'Cultural symbols and brain evolution: a synthesis', *Dialectical Anthropology* 5: 287–303.

Huffman, M. and Quiatt, D. (1986) 'Stone handling by Japanese macaques (*Macaca fuscata*): implications for tool use of stone', *Primates* 27: 413–24.

Keller, J. and Keller, C. (1991) 'Thinking and acting with iron', Beckman Institute Cognitive Science Technical Reports Cs–91–08, Champaign-Urbana, Ill.: Beckman Institute.

Lane Fox, A. (1875) 'On the principles of classification adopted in the arrangement of his anthropological collection', *Journal of the Royal Anthropological Institute of Great Britain and Ireland* 4: 293–308.

Lemonnier, P. (1986) 'The study of material culture today: toward an anthropology of technical systems', *Journal of Anthropological Archaeology* 5: 147–86.

Lévi-Strauss, C. (1966) *The Savage Mind*, Chicago: University of Chicago Press.

Littleton, C. (1967) *The New Comparative Mythology*, Los Angeles: University of California Press.

Marzke, M. and Shackley, M. (1986) 'Hominid hand use in the Pliocene and Pleistocene: evidence from experimental archaeology and comparative morphology', *Journal of Human Evolution* 15: 439–60.

McGrew, W. C. (1974) 'Tool use by wild chimpanzees in feeding upon driver ants', *Journal of Human Evolution* 3: 501–8.

—— (1987) 'Tools to get food: the subsistants of Tasmanian aborigines and Tanzanian chimpanzees compared', *Journal of Anthropological Research* 43: 247–58.

McGrew, W. C., Tutin, C. and Baldwin, P. (1979) 'Chimpanzees, tools, and termites: cross-cultural comparisons of Senegal, Tanzania, and Rio Muni', *Man* (N.S.) 14: 185–214.

Mumford, L. (1961) 'History: neglected clue to technological change', *Technology and Culture* 2: 230–6.

—— (1966) *The Myth of the Machine: Technics and Human Development*, New York: Harcourt Brace, Jovanovich.

Oswalt, W. (1976) *An Anthropological Analysis of Food-Getting Technology*, New York: John Wiley.

Passingham, R. (1982) *The Human Primate*, New York: W. H. Freeman.

Pfaffenberger, B. (1988) 'Fetishized objects and humanized nature: towards an anthropology of technology', *Man* (N.S.) 23: 236–52.

Piaget, J. (1960) *The Psychology of Intelligence*, trans. M. Piercy and D. Berlyne, Totowa, NJ: Littlefield, Adams.

Pye, D. (1964) *The Nature of Design*, London: Studio Vista.

Premack, D. (1976) *Intelligence in Ape and Man*, Hillsdale, NJ: Lawrence Erlbaum.

Reichard, G. (1934) *Spider Woman: A Story of Navajo Weavers and Chanters*, Glorietta, NM: Rio Grande Press.

Sabater Pi, J. (1974) 'An elementary industry of the chimpanzees in the Okorobiko mountains, Rio Muni (Republic of Equatorial Guinea), West Africa', *Primates* 15: 531–64.

Sackett, J. (1982) 'Approaches to style in lithic archaeology', *Journal of Anthropological Archaeology* 1: 59–112.

Skolimowski, H. (1966) 'The structure of thinking in technology', *Technology and Culture* 7: 371–83.

Somerville, J. (1967) *The Philosophy of Marxism: An Exposition*, New York: Random House.

Staudenmeier, J. (1985) *Technology's Storytellers: Reweaving the Human Fabric*, Cambridge, Mass.: MIT Press.

Teleki, G. (1974) 'Chimpanzee subsistence technology: materials and skills', *Journal of Human Evolution* 3: 575–94.

Thompson, M. (1977) *General Pitt-Rivers*, Bradford-on-Avon: Moonraker Press.

Tobias, P. (1983) 'Hominid evolution in Africa', *Canadian Journal of Anthropology* 3: 163–85.

Uehara, S. (1982) 'Seasonal changes in the techniques employed by wild chimpanzees in the Mahale mountains, Tanzania, to feed on termites (*Pseudocanthotermes spiniger*)', *Folia Primatologica* 37: 44–76.

van Lawick-Goodall, J. (1970) 'Tool-using in primates and other vertebrates', in D. Lehrman, R. Hinde and E. Shaw (eds) *Advances in the Study of Behavior*, vol. 3, New York: Academic Press.

Weddell, L. (1989) 'Head candy-maker has the pull it takes to make good treats', *Colorado Springs Gazette Telegraph* 11 December.

White, J., Modjeska, N. and Hipuya, I. (1977) 'Group definitions and mental templates', in R. V. S. Wright (ed.) *Stone Tools as Cultural Markers*, Atlantic Highlands, NJ: Humanities Press.

White, L. (1959) *The Evolution of Culture*, New York: McGraw-Hill.

Wynn, T. (1988) 'Tools and the evolution of human intelligence', in R. Byrne and A. Whiten (eds) *Machiavellian Intelligence: Social Expertise and the Evolution of Intellect in Monkeys, Apes, and Humans*, Oxford: Oxford University Press.

FURTHER READING

Adair, J. (1944) *The Navajo and Pueblo Silversmith*, Norman: University of Oklahoma Press.

Basalla, G. (1988) *The Evolution of Technology*, Cambridge: Cambridge University Press.

Beck, B. (1980) *Animal Tool Behavior*, New York: Garland Press.

Berthelet, A. and Chavaillon, J. (eds) 1993 *The Use of Tools by Human and Non-human Primates*, Oxford: Clarendon Press.

Boesch, C. and Boesch, H. (1984) 'Mental map in wild chimpanzees: An analysis of hammer transports for nut cracking', *Primates* 25: 160–70.

Dougherty, J. and Keller, C. (1982) 'Taskonomy: a practical approach to knowledge structures', *American Ethnologist* 5: 763–74.

Gatewood, J. (1985) 'Actions speak louder than words', in J. W. D. Dougherty (ed.) *Directions in Cognitive Anthropology*, Urbana: University of Illinois Press.

Glassie, H. (1975) *Folk Housing in Middle Virginia*, Knoxville: University of Tennessee Press.

Holloway, R. L. (1983) 'Human brain evolution: a search for units, models and synthesis', *Canadian Journal of Anthropology* 3(2): 215–30.

Ingold, T. (1987) *The Appropriation of Nature*, Iowa City: University of Iowa Press.

Lemonnier, P. (1986) 'The study of material culture today: toward an anthropology of technical systems', *Journal of Anthropological Archaeology* 5: 147–86.

—— (ed.) (1993) *Technological Choices: Transformation in Material Cultures since the Neolithic*, London: Routledge.

Lévi-Strauss, C. (1966) *The Savage Mind*, Chicago: University of Chicago Press.

McGrew, W. (1992) *Chimpanzee Material Culture*, Cambridge: Cambridge University Press.

Oswalt, W. (1976) *An Anthropological Analysis of Food-Getting Technology*, New York: John Wiley.

Pfaffenberger, B. (1988) 'Fetishized objects and humanized nature: towards an anthropology of technology', *Man* (N.S.) 23: 236–52.

Piaget, J. (1960) *The Psychology of Intelligence*, Totowa, NJ: Littlefield, Adams.

Pye, D. (1964) *The Nature of Design*, London: Studio Vista.

Staudenmeier, J. (1985) *Technology's Storytellers: Reweaving the Human Fabric*, Cambridge, Mass.: MIT Press.

Wynn, T. (1988) 'Tools and the evolution of human intelligence', in R. Byrne and A. Whiten (eds) *Machiavellian Intelligence: Social Expertise and the Evolution of Intellect in Monkeys, Apes, and Humans*, Oxford: Oxford University Press.

7

NICHE CONSTRUCTION, EVOLUTION AND CULTURE

F. J. Odling-Smee

What do phenotypes do in evolution? By 'phenotypes' in this article I mean those observable individual organisms which express their genotypes in environments, which carry genes for as long as they survive, which pass on genes to their offspring when they reproduce, but which die or divide in each generation. What are phenotypes for? The correct answer to this question ought to take us a long way towards establishing the true nature of the biological infrastructure that underlies the subject matter of all the human sciences, including anthropology. All of these sciences are primarily concerned with human phenotypes. So if we could first understand the role of phenotypes in general, we ought to achieve a better understanding of human phenotypes in particular. Let us start by taking another look at evolutionary theory.

THE MODERN SYNTHETIC THEORY OF EVOLUTION

Any theory of evolution, to use Darwin's apt phrase, must provide an account of 'descent with modification'. It has, therefore, to explain both how descent occurs, by specifying some principle of inheritance or intergenerational transmission, and how the composition of what is transmitted undergoes modification over time. For empirical purposes the theory also needs a currency so that the contributions of diverse organisms to the pool of inherited variation can be measured. This currency is generally known as 'fitness'.

Contemporary neo-Darwinism, the 'modern synthetic theory' of evolution, satisfies all of these requirements with considerable parsimony. It recognizes only one kind of inheritance, namely genetic inheritance, and it assumes that only one modifying process, natural selection, can influence the inheritance of genetic variants in a non-random fashion, and therefore in ways that sometimes lead to adapted organisms. Every other modifying process, such as genetic drift or mutation pressure, is supposed to work by chance. Hence fitness becomes a measure of the transmission of genes by organisms from one generation to the next in the presence of natural selection and chance.

This exclusively gene-based definition of fitness, however, not only determines how the modern synthesis treats genes and genotypes in evolution, but also how it must model phenotypes. If the only kind of descent is genetic descent, then the only way in which phenotypes can contribute to evolution must be by passing on their genes to their descendants via genetic inheritance. If, in addition, it is not possible for any parent organisms to change their own genes in the light of their own 'acquired' experiences before passing them on to their offspring, and the evidence indicates that Lamarck was wrong here (Maynard Smith 1986, Buss 1987), then there can only be one task left for phenotypes to perform in evolution. Phenotypes become just diverse gene-carrying 'vehicles' whose interactions with their environments either cause them to die prematurely or allow them to survive for long enough to reproduce, and to pass on their genes to their successors (Dawkins 1989).

But if the fundamental evolutionary role of phenotypes is as restricted as this, then the role of all the non-genetic processes that occur in phenotypes must be likewise restricted. These supplementary processes have to do with development (Bonner 1982, Campbell 1985, Buss 1987 Edelman 1989), immunology (Roitt 1980, Tonegawa 1985), behaviour, including imprinting and learning (Pulliam and Dunford 1980, Plotkin and Odling-Smee 1979, 1981, 1982), proto-cultural processes, including imitation and social enhancement (Galef 1988, Standen and Foley 1989) and, in ourselves, the whole battery of cultural processes (Boyd and Richerson 1985, Ingold 1986). The list is impressive, yet if the modern synthesis is right, if genetic descent is the only kind of descent which occurs in evolution, then the only evolutionary function which can be assigned to any of these other processes, including human culture, must be one of assisting phenotypes to carry out their basic gene-transmitting duties. Hence, all of these other processes become just the operation of 'proximate' mechanisms in phenotypes whose 'ultimate' contribution is limited to their statistical consequences as regards the transmission of genes by phenotypes from one generation to the next (e.g. Alcock 1989).

That is not to reduce phenotypes to nothing but genetically determined robots, as critics of the modern synthesis have sometimes suggested (e.g. Rose *et al.* 1984). Genetic determinism is not the issue which divides the human from the biological sciences (Dunbar 1989). The modern synthesis readily accepts that there are many phenotypic traits, especially in human beings, which are genetically 'underdetermined'. In practice, leading evolutionary biologists have, for years, acknowledged that phenotypes are typically left 'open' by their genes for eventual within-lifetime 'closure' by one or more of the non-genetic processes listed above (e.g. Mayr 1974). Instead, it merely implies that genetic inheritance is ultimately the only thing that matters in evolution, because it is the only route via which organisms can contribute anything to descent. So, if a phenotypic trait is to affect evolution at all, it can only do so via genetic inheritance, regardless of whether the trait itself is genetically determined or not. That is not genetic determinism, although it is an equally potent claim.

Another common mistake is to believe that the modern synthesis implies 'selfish phenotypes'. It does not (Dunbar 1989). The theory may insist on 'selfish genes', but it does not require exclusively competitive phenotypes (Axelrod 1984, Trivers 1985, Dawkins 1989). In fact it provides some commendably simple explanations for co-operation among phenotypes, and therefore for the existence of complex social life in many species. To cite the two most famous hypotheses: Hamilton's (1964) concept of inclusive fitness, sometimes called kin selection, recognizes that even 'neo-Darwinian' organisms, which in general must compete with each other to survive and reproduce, should still help other organisms which carry the same genes to do the same. Moreover, they should help each other in proportion to the number of genes they share in common (i.e. to their degree of genetic relatedness). Similarly Trivers's (1985) concept of reciprocal altruism recognizes that even genetically unrelated organisms should trade in mutually altruistic acts, provided that they associate regularly with each other in shared environments, and provided they can all increase their genetic fitness by doing so (see Article 27).

In spite of this flexibility it is, nevertheless, true that the modern synthesis confines arguments about the nature of the biology which underpins the phenomena of concern to the human sciences to some remarkably narrow limits. There are many different views about the relationship between genetic evolution and culture (Durham 1991). Richards (1987) recently listed nine of them. Yet, as long as the modern synthesis is held to be both a necessary and a sufficient theory of evolution, they are all logically reducible to only two broadly opposed alternatives.

The first is to suppose that the ultimate function of all cultural activity is to contribute to genetic descent, in which case all human cultures, past and present, are to be judged as adaptive devices whose relative success is to be measured in terms of the genetic fitness conferred on their bearers. This is the approach adopted by many sociobiologists, who hold that if we are to understand ourselves and our institutions properly, we had better admit, whether we like it or not, that they have an underlying genetic rationale (see for example Wilson 1975, Alexander, 1979, Lumsden and Wilson 1981, Trivers 1985). The alternative is to agree with critics of sociobiology (e.g. Sahlins, 1976, Rose et al. 1984, Kitcher 1988, Saunders 1988), who claim that even though contemporary human cultures are clearly products of prior biological evolution, they now demonstrate emergent properties which are so robust and potent as to cause them to be effectively decoupled from their biotic origins. The priority for people of the present day is to contribute to cultural and not to genetic evolution, and this makes biological evolution no longer relevant to contemporary human affairs. By way of a curious kind of reversal, this second approach sometimes ends up by placing biological evolution, and all of its products, at the disposal of human culture, turning the rest of nature into little more than human property. This is tantamount to permitting management of the earth's resources to proceed without much reference to ecology, and none at all to evolution (MacNeill 1989, Ruckelhaus 1989). Roughly speaking, these arguments represent opposing sides in the contemporary sociobiology debate.

There is another possibility, however. Maybe the modern synthesis is not yet a sufficient theory of evolution. Perhaps it is not yet complete. Surprisingly this alternative is not often considered, either by those who are convinced that the sociobiological view is too simplistic, or by those who are equally convinced that the idea that human culture has become separated from biological evolution is both factually untenable and exceedingly maladaptive in practice. Since the synthetic theory is known to suffer from a number of shortcomings (e.g. Gould 1980, Lewontin 1983, Vrba and Eldredge 1984, Depew and Weber 1985, Buss 1987, Ho and Fox 1988, Plotkin 1988, Endler and McLellan 1988, Crook 1989) this third alternative is worth looking at. I intend to consider it here.

NICHE-CONSTRUCTING PHENOTYPES IN EVOLUTION

Self-induced natural selection

One of the first scientists to raise a significant doubt about the sufficiency of the modern synthesis was a developmental biologist, Waddington (1959, 1960, 1969). Waddington was unhappy with the way the theory encourages us to think about the sources of natural selection in evolution. He pointed out that phenotypes are not just passive, physical objects which are forced to react with 'Newtonian'-like responses to whatever local selection pressures are impressed on them by their external environments. Instead they are living agents which routinely select and perturb their own niches and habitats. Hence phenotypes must select and change at least some of the natural selection pressures which occur in their own local environments. Subsequently these local selection pressures, which the phenotypes themselves have now changed, act back on the phenotypes, and on their offspring, and very likely on other related organisms too, with 'better' or 'worse' consequences for the genetic fitness of all these organisms.

In other words, there are some pressures of natural selection which are self-induced by phenotypes. So phenotypes do more in evolution than just survive, reproduce and pass on their genes to their descendants. Metaphorically speaking, phenotypes are not just 'throwaway survival machines' or 'vehicles' for their genes (Dawkins 1989). Rather they are positive 'interactors' (Hull 1988) which, to greatly varying extents, choose and change their own local habitats, and by doing so, exert a considerable influence over which particular selection pressures will later select their own and their descendants' genes. Waddington complained that this second kind of contribution from phenotypes is either ignored by the modern synthesis, or, when not ignored, is inadequately handled. He called it the 'exploitive system' and made a plea for its inclusion into evolutionary theory.

More recently, Lewontin (1983), a population geneticist, used a set of deliberately over-simplified equations to illustrate the same point:

$$dO/dt = f_1(O, E) \tag{1}$$

$$dE/dt = f_2(E) \tag{2}$$

$$dO/dt = f_1(O, E) \tag{3}$$

$$dE/dt = f_2(O, E) \tag{4}$$

Equations (1) and (2) are an uncoupled pair of differential equations which encapsulate the essence of the modern synthesis. They show how this theory inadvertently separates organisms from their environments. Equation (1) describes evolutionary change in organisms (O) over time (t) as a function of those organisms interacting with natural selection pressures in their environments (E); while equation (2) describes environmental change as being entirely due to autonomous events in those environments. Autonomous environmental events are then supposed to act as the source of changing natural selection pressures on organisms. There is therefore only a 'one-way', linear relationship linking organisms to their environments, by way of which the evolution of organisms is seen to be driven exclusively by independent events in their environments. Lewontin's second pair of equations, on the other hand, are coupled, and summarize what he thinks is actually happening in nature. Equation (3) is the same as Eq. (1), but Eq. (4) now shows environmental changes being caused both by independent environmental events (E), and by phenotypes (O) altering their own environments. Thus living organisms not only react to their local environments, but in addition, they partly construct and destroy them by their own activities. For this reason, Lewontin proposes that the relationship between organisms and the pressures of natural selection is reciprocal (Eqs (3) and (4)), rather than linear (equations (1) and (2)). Organisms and their environments co-evolve and co-determine each other by way of their mutual inputs and outputs. Like Waddington, Lewontin also calls for an extension of evolutionary theory to enable it to cope with this 'two-way' co-evolutionary process.

Some examples may help to illustrate how phenotypes can alter selection pressures in their own environments. Here I choose some celebrated ones. The first is an instance of the kind of phenomena which biologists often call cultural, much to the annoyance of anthropologists! This I call 'proto-cultural'. It is the innovative habit of opening milk bottles which has spread among blue tits and great tits in Britain during the last few decades (Fisher and Hinde 1949). Typically these milk bottles are left on the doorsteps of human households and are then raided by these songbirds, who open them by tearing off their foil caps. The birds then drink the cream from the tops of the bottles, thereby gaining a new resource. The habit seems to have spread 'proto-culturally' via some kind of social learning or social enhancement. In this example a novel and probably learned behaviour appears to have modified these birds' environments in ways which may have subsequently changed the selection pressures which act back on the birds themselves (Sherry and Galef 1984), for instance by encouraging them to exploit urban and suburban environments. As yet, no-one has demonstrated any genetic response to these altered selection pressures. Nevertheless, here is one scenario in which a genetic change is eventually likely to occur in response to a phenotypically induced feedback cycle between organisms and their environments.

My second example dispenses with any dependence on human artefacts (such as milk bottles). It is the habit of Galapagos woodpecker finches to use tools, consisting of twigs or cactus spines, to poke out grubs from the barks of trees (Alcock 1972). These birds conspicuously lack the specialized beaks and elongated tongues of more typical woodpeckers. Since they do their 'woodpecking' in such an unusual fashion, they appear to have cancelled out the selection pressures which, in more conventional woodpeckers, promote these unusual (anatomical) woodpecker adaptions. Instead, Galapagos wood-peckers are probably being selected for quite different phenotypic traits, their intelligence perhaps, or possibly their tool-using skills.

Two further examples come from anthropology, and extend the same logic to human cultures. In most mammals the enzyme 'lactase', which degrades 'lactose', and which is necessary for the digestion of milk, is synthesized by infants but not by adults. This makes sense because most mammals cease to drink milk after they are weaned. However, when our human ancestors first domesticated cattle and started to drink milk throughout their lives, they modified the natural selection pressures which acted back on themselves in favour of genes which continue to synthesize the lactase enzyme in adults as well as in infants (Bodmer and Cavalli-Sforza 1976, Kretchmer 1977, Potter et al. 1985). Durham (1991) has pointed out that the full story is more compli-cated than was originally supposed, since it involves calcium as well as lactose absorption. Nevertheless, the result is the same. Today, between 70 and 100 per cent of human adults whose ancestors came from long-term dairy-farming areas are lactose-tolerant, whereas the great majority of those who stem from non-dairy-farming areas remain lactose-intolerant. This differentiation must have occurred within the last 10,000 years, and must have been induced by human phenotypes changing their own environments. The other example has also been elaborated by Durham (1991). Traditional swidden agricultural practices among 'Kwa'-speaking peoples in tropical West Africa increased the breeding grounds for malaria-carrying mosquitoes. Hence these peoples inadvertently increased the intensity of their own natural selection by malaria. That in turn led to a prevalence of individuals who carry a gene which, in homozygous carriers, causes the fatal condition of sickle-cell anaemia. The high frequency of the sickle-cell gene is maintained because, in heterozygous carriers, it confers some protection against malaria (Livingstone 1958).

Human beings and non-human animals apart, other organisms also modify selection pressures in their environments. For example in autogenic ecological succession, successive plant species change their habitats by producing litter, or by changing their soil's moisture or acidity, or maybe just by altering the availability of light, and by doing so they make their own local environments untenable to themselves, but favourable to some other successor species. Collectively they thereby drive their own ecological succession (e.g. Begon *et al.* 1986). Another case, which works in the opposite direction, is the manner in which some plant species ensure the periodic outbreak of forest fires. For example, the vegetation of the Californian chaparral (a dwarf woodland community) is adapted to fire to such an extent that it probably could not exist without it. In the absence of fires it would be replaced by other, less fire-resistant species. Yet by various methods, for instance by regularly building up stacks of dry tinder beneath itself, the chaparral makes the periodic outbreak of brush fires a near-certainty. Each fire incident then resets the local 'succession clock' to an earlier stage, which allows the chaparral community to persist (Odum 1989, see also Romme and Despain 1989). Micro-organisms can also change their own environments. On a small scale, influenza viruses probably aid their own transmission from host to host by causing their hosts to sneeze! On a large scale, the cyanobacteria were almost certainly responsible for changing the earth's early oxygen-free atmosphere to its present composition, which contains about 21 per cent oxygen (Odum 1989).

The key points illustrated by all of these examples are, first, that the relationships between organisms and their environments are reciprocal and not linear; and second, that phenotypes make a dual contribution to these reciprocal relationships. They react to impinging natural selection pressures from their environments by surviving and reproducing differentially, thereby contributing to the *consequences* of natural selection. They also actively select and perturb their own local environments, thereby contributing to the *sources* of natural selection. The first of these contributions, to which I shall refer henceforth as 'the first role of phenotypes in evolution', comprises the classic, gene-carrying or 'vehicle' role of phenotypes, which is already comprehensively handled by the modern synthesis. The second contribution, henceforth referred to as 'the second role of phenotypes in evolution', encapsulates both Waddington's notion of the 'exploitive system', and Lewontin's of organism–environment co-evolution, but it is as yet barely recognized by the modern synthesis (Endler 1986), and is not adequately handled by it.

Organism–environment feedback cycles

Why not? The best way to answer this question is to take a closer look at how the modern synthesis currently explains the kinds of examples just presented. This may highlight the limitations of the modern synthesis, and point to where, if anywhere, the theory is still insufficient. Unavoidably this exercise requires a brief digression into population biology.

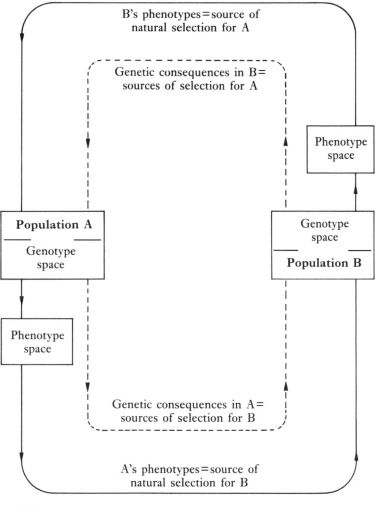

(a)

Figure 1 Feedback cycles between organisms and their environments; the solid line depicts what is happening in nature, the dotted line depicts how this is modelled by the modern synthetic theory of evolution. (a) Interactive relationship between two co-evolving populations (A and B). (b) Co-evolution between a population (A) and an abiotic component (X) of its environment. (c) Biogeochemical cycle including both biotic components (populations A and B) and an abiotic component (X)

Figure 1 shows some elementary examples of the principal kinds of feed-back cycles which can occur between organisms and their environments. It depicts three different scenarios, in each of which a population of organisms (population A) is both responding to natural selection from its environment and driving changes in those naturally selecting inputs by modifying either a living or a non-living component of its own environment. In each scenario the outer cycle (solid line) illustrates what is probably happening in nature, while the inner cycle (dotted line) shows how it is currently being modelled by the

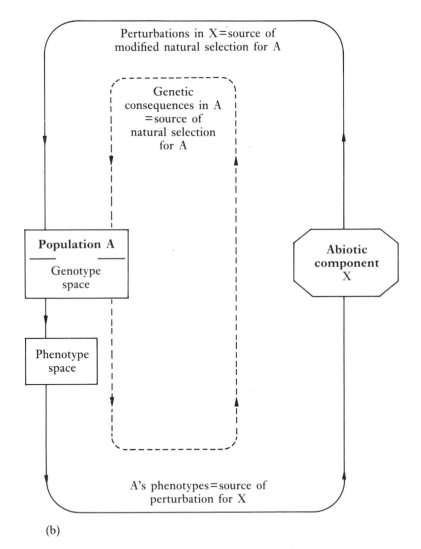

(b)

Figure 1 Continued

170

modern synthesis. Let us work through each scenario in turn by focusing on population A, and by considering how the actions of A's phenotypes affect A's genotypes once the consequences of these actions feed back to population A itself in the guise of modified selection pressures returning from A's environment.

Cycle 1 (Figure 1a) symbolizes any interactive relationship between two (or sometimes more) co-evolving populations. These relationships include predation, mutualism, commensalism, competition and parasitism. This is the

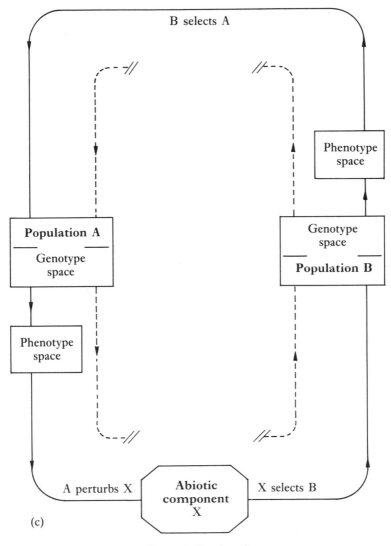

Figure 1 Continued

standard picture which lies at the heart both of modern co-evolutionary theory (Futuyma and Slatkin 1983) and, in an expanded multi-population form, of most contemporary models in population-community ecology as well (e.g. Maynard Smith 1974, May 1981, Begon *et al.* 1986, O'Neill *et al.* 1986). Let us suppose that it represents a simple interactive relationship between a single predator (population A), and its single prey (population B). Typically such a relationship promotes a scenario described as an 'arms race' by Dawkins and Krebs (1979), generating a sequence like this:

$$A \rightarrow B \rightarrow A' \rightarrow B' \rightarrow A'' \rightarrow B'' \rightarrow \text{etc.}$$

Thus, predators (foxes, A) run, but their prey (rabbits, B) run faster; so foxes (A') are naturally selected by their interactions with (B) to run a bit faster; the rabbits (B') are then naturally selected by their interactions with A' to run still faster, and so on.

This kind of co-evolution is already well modelled by the modern synthesis. The only reason why this is so, however, is that in this case both populations A and B incorporate a recognized inheritance system of their own, namely the genetic system. Hence the existence of population B's genes allows the outputs from population A's phenotypes to be redescribed not as phenotypic outputs from A which are changing a component (population B) in A's environment, but merely as natural selection pressures in B's environment which are selecting B's genes (and vice versa for A). This mutual translation of phenotypic outputs into naturally selecting inputs thereby converts *sources* of natural selection, which cannot be modelled, namely the activities of phenotypes in each of these two populations, into *consequences* which can be modelled, namely changing gene frequencies in each receiving population. In this way the second role of phenotypes is collapsed into the first. It is a neat solution, because it allows cycle 1 to be modelled exclusively in terms of reciprocal pressures of natural selection and reciprocal population genetics (the inner cycle in Figure 1a) without violating any of the conventional assumptions of the synthetic theory (Futuyma and Slatkin 1983).

The price paid for this solution is some unavoidable 'short circuiting' of the natural cycle. The one difference between the inner and the outer cycles in Figure 1a is that the translation from genotypes to phenotypes is omitted from the inner cycle. Hence, in so far as the outputs of phenotypes are not determined by their genotypes, but are co-determined by other supplementary processes such as learning, or by socio-cultural processes, these models are too simple. This is worrying from the point of view of social scientists, who are interested in these processes. However, it does not worry population geneticists, because they can usually afford to 'write off' these extra phenotypic contributions (the outer cycle in Figure 1a) as mere 'noise'. For their purposes models based exclusively on the inner cycle in Figure 1a are usually good enough, since they already allow the investigation of feedback cycles among co-evolving populations and communities.

Now let me turn to cycle 2 (Figure 1b). Again, the outer cycle (solid line) depicts what happens in nature. Here we have a population of organisms A, co-evolving with some abiotic component (X) of its environment. Suppose that A is a plant species whose phenotypes are causing a directional change in its own soil chemistry or soil moisture (corresponding to X), and that the changes in X, which are caused by A, eventually feed back to A in the form of modified natural selection pressures from X.

In this case the solution which suffices for cycle 1 does not work for cycle 2. This is because in cycle 2 there is no receiving genetic system in the abiotic environmental component (X). Nor is there any other kind of internal inheritance system in X in relation to which population A's phenotypic outputs might conceivably be relabelled as 'natural selection pressures' for X. To put it bluntly, it makes no sense to speak of the natural selection of X. Therefore in cycle 2 it is not possible to collapse the second role of phenotypes (their contribution to the *sources* of natural selection) into their first role (their contribution to the *consequences* of natural selection) in the same way as was done in cycle 1. Yet cycle 2 may still have to be modelled because the feedback from the abiotic X to population A, caused by the prior perturbation of X by A, may still have evolutionary consequences for population A.

For instance, a possible consequence might be an episode of ecological succession similar to that just described. This might lead to either the local disappearance, or even the global extinction, of population A. Another more interesting possibility is that the outputs from population A's phenotypes might initiate a positive feedback cycle between population A and the soil conditions X, similar to the 'arms race' cycle between foxes and rabbits of the kind depicted in Figure 1a, causing A to drive its own successive evolution like this:

$$A \rightarrow X \rightarrow A' \rightarrow X' \rightarrow A'' \rightarrow X'' \rightarrow \text{ etc.}$$

Suppose the plants (A) capture water (X) through their roots, thereby reducing the amount of moisture in the soil. The reduction in moisture then modifies the selection pressures which feed back from X to A, and select for different variants A'. But these A' variants are adapted to take still more water out of the soil, perhaps because they have more efficient roots. That, in turn, reduces the soil moisture still further, which changes X into X', and so on. Alternatively, if the variants A' in population A were adapted to need less water, rather than to gain more, perhaps by being drought-resistant, then a negative feedback cycle between A and X might develop, eventually settling down at some stable, self-regulated point.

The closest that the synthetic theory can get to modelling this type of cycle is in terms of an intraspecific competition between different individuals in population A for the resources available in X. The best-known models are those dealing with habitat selection (Wilson and Turelli 1986), and with density-dependent and frequency-dependent selection (Slatkin 1979; Hartl and Clark 1989). These models capture about half of these cycles. In effect they give up the struggle to model any kind of 'co-evolutionary' change in the abiotic component (X), and instead concentrate only on modelling the natural selection of population A, doing so in terms of putative selection pressures whose source is now assumed to lie within population A itself, rather than in X. In essence the rationale for this approach runs as follows:

> Any organism in Population A can potentially cause changes in X. Also any change in X potentially affects every organism in Population A. Therefore it is legitimate to treat any subset of organisms in A as a source of natural selection pressures for any other subset of organisms in A, relative to their mutual interactions with X.

By this device the 'reflection' of the abiotic component X (e.g. the soil moisture) can at least be caught in the 'mirror' provided by population A's genetic system (the plants). Thus the *sources* of the selection pressures which actually lie in X can once again be collapsed into genetic *consequences* in A. In this genetic form they can then be modelled in terms of the transmission of genes by organisms from one generation to the next in the usual way. Thus cycle 2 can also be modelled without violating the synthetic theory.

This time, however, the price is high. A very tight 'short circuit' is set up (compare the inner and outer cycles in Figure 1b) according to which the natural cycle between population A and the abiotic environmental component (X) is replaced by a 'pseudo'-cycle between A's genotypes (acting as the *sources* of natural selection) and A's genotypes (acting as the *consequences* of natural selection), without this cycle ever getting outside of population A at all. This solution is no longer neat. It distorts reality and discourages the investigation of X following X's perturbation by A. Instead, X is now placed firmly outside the scope of evolutionary theory, where it is left for the ecologists to deal with.

The problem crops up a third time in cycle 3 (Figure 1c). Here the natural cycle (the solid line in the figure) represents an elementary example of a bio-geochemical cycle which includes both biotic and abiotic components. In its expanded multi-component form, this is the kind of cycle studied by process ecologists, who seek to understand flows of energy and matter in ecosystems, such as the nitrogen cycle, or the carbon silicate cycle. The problem here is that the modern synthesis cannot provide sufficient mechanisms to model either the formation or the regulation of these cycles, because once again it cannot cope with the changes caused in the abiotic components, such as X, by the activities of phenotypes. In effect, this inability interrupts these cycles and rules out any possibility of their treatment in co-evolutionary terms (Patten 1982, O'Neill *et al.* 1986; Hagen 1989). For this reason no inner cycle can be shown in Figure 1c. It also forces process ecologists to look beyond the

174

modern synthesis, for instance to general systems theory (Patten and Auble 1981), for alternative ways of modelling biogeochemical cycles.

Finally, there is one further idea which potentially embraces all three of the cycles in Figure 1; this is Dawkins's (1982, 1989) concept of the 'extended phenotype'. This idea goes some way towards recognizing the true importance of the second role of phenotypes in evolution. Dawkins points out that genes frequently have phenotypic effects which extend well beyond the bodies of the particular organisms which carry them. For instance, they can affect the structure and function of other organisms, as in parasitism; or they can affect abiotic components in their own organisms' environments, such as the houses built by caddis fly larvae out of stones. Dawkins (1989) convincingly argues that caddis fly stone houses are as much a part of the phenotypic expression of caddis fly genes as the shells of snails are the phenotypic expression of snail genes.

The advance here is that the concept of extended phenotype recognizes that phenotypes do modify at least some of the pressures of natural selection in their local environments, and that when they do, they become sources of at least some phenotypically induced selection pressures for themselves, and for other organisms. However, in every other respect Dawkins's approach is identical to that enshrined in the models of intraspecific competition just discussed, because he maintains that the capacity of phenotypes to act as *sources* of self-induced selection need only be modelled in terms of the *consequences* of natural selection, and therefore along exactly the same lines as those illustrated by the inner cycles in Figure 1a and b. With that, the challenge of the 'extended phenotype' to conventional theory is neutralized, as it is reduced to the same role that has always been assigned to phenotypes by Dawkins, that of being 'survival machines', or 'vehicles' for their genes.

It is now possible to see why the modern synthesis has such difficulty with the second role of phenotypes in evolution. All of the feedback cycles in Figure 1 are cyclic only because phenotypes contribute to both the *sources* and the *consequences* of natural selection. Yet the preceding models can only cope directly with the contributions phenotypes make to the consequences of natural selection. They cannot handle the contributions phenotypes make to natural selection itself, except indirectly. Hence all these models are forced either to collapse those sources of selection, which are in fact induced by phenotypes, into natural selection's consequences (as in Figure 1a) or, when this is not possible (as in Figure 1b and c), to treat the sources of selection as lying outside the scope of evolutionary theory, as ecological events in a supposedly autonomous environment.

The root of the problem lies in the parsimony of the modern synthesis. Because this theory recognizes only one kind of evolutionary descent, the only currency it can provide is that of genetic fitness. Genes offer an entirely suitable currency for measuring the consequences of natural selection, which are changing gene frequencies in populations, but they do not provide a suitable currency for measuring the sources of natural selection in environments (Endler 1986), including those sources which are modified by phenotypes.

This brings us back to sociobiology because it is of course sociobiology's exclusive concern with genetic fitness that makes its attempt to establish an adequate evolutionary foundation for the human sciences so problematic. The issue has now cropped up again, but here in its more fundamental form. Assuming that this is the form in which we must tackle the issue, can we do anything about it?

Organism–environment co-evolution

The key requirement is to extend evolutionary theory to the point where it can model both the roles of phenotypes without constantly collapsing their second role into their first. This means finding some way of modelling the changes caused by phenotypes to selection pressures in their own environments which is indifferent to whether the changes themselves affect biotic or abiotic components. In practice it means deriving some supplementary, non-genetic, evolutionary currency, to measure those environmental events which are caused by organisms, and to differentiate these events from all the other environmental events which are not.

At present the currencies normally used to measure directly the conditions and resources in environments are ecological. With the single exception of the genetics of other co-evolving populations (Figure 1a), none of these currencies is evolutionary. None measures any kind of evolutionary descent. The question, therefore, is whether it is possible to turn any of these ecological currencies into currencies which are at least 'eco-evolutionary'.

Evolutionary currencies can be derived only from inheritance systems. Thus genetic fitness is a bona fide evolutionary currency because it is derived from the internal genetic inheritance of evolving populations. The trouble is that there is a conspicuous lack of any corresponding internal inheritance system among the abiotic components of environments which could possibly serve as the basis for a currency suitable for measuring phenotypically induced changes in co-evolving environments. At first glance this fact alone appears to rule out all attempts to extend evolutionary theory beyond its present limits.

Yet an alternative approach is conceivable. There is no reason why the inheritance system on which an evolutionary currency is based should necessarily be *internal*. Thus although it is impossible to model the changes which are caused by phenotypes in the abiotic components of their environments in terms of any kind of internal inheritance, it may well be possible to model exactly the same phenotypically induced changes in terms of a different kind of inheritance system, an *external* ecological inheritance. An eco-evolutionary currency might then be derived from this new external inheritance system relative to populations of evolving organisms.

176

Elsewhere I have suggested one way in which this might be done. Starting from Lewontin's (1983) position, I proposed the expansion of evolutionary theory into a general theory of organism–environment co-evolution (Odling-Smee 1988). The proposal explicitly involved the addition of a second kind of inheritance in evolution, supplementary to the genetic system, namely the inheritance by organisms of ancestrally chosen and modified environments. It also involved a second co-directing force in evolution in addition to natural selection, the non-random choice and perturbation of local environments by phenotypes.

The essence of the idea is summarized in Figure 2. On the left, genes are transmitted by parent organisms (O) to successor organisms (not shown) via genetic inheritance, and under the direction of natural selection. On the right, modified environments are also transmitted by these same parent organisms (O) to their successors via the external environment (E). This second inheritance system, called *ecological inheritance*, is partly directed by autonomous events (from the 'rest of E') which lie outside the influence of organisms. These could be cosmological, physical or chemical events, or possibly just unmodifiable biological events. However, it is also partly directed by the non-random, environmentally perturbing actions of phenotypes, including actions

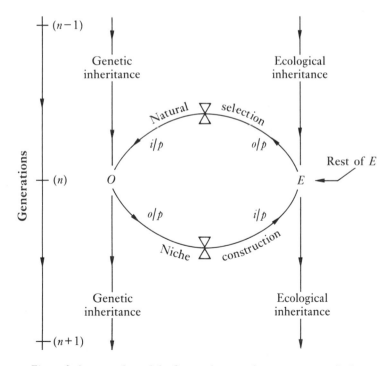

Figure 2 A general model of organism–environment co-evolution

which are not directly determined by genes, but which could be co-determined by other phenotypically based processes, including human culture. Collectively these actions constitute a second, phenotypically driven, co-directing force in evolution which I call *niche construction*.

Several points require amplification (see Odling-Smee 1988 for a fuller account), but I can only deal with two here.

1   These two kinds of inheritance work by way of different mechanisms. They therefore have different operating characteristics. Genetic inheritance depends on the mechanisms of reproduction. Hence (ignoring viruses and plasmids), genes can be inherited by organisms only once during their lifetimes, namely at the point of conception. They can only be inherited from parents, and they can only be transmitted in one direction, vertically, from parents to offspring. Ecological inheritance, on the other hand, involves the inheritance of modified natural selection pressures in environments. Since environments are modified by the activities of phenotypes, and since phenotypes are active throughout their lives, these modifications may be transmitted and received by organisms continuously. Ecological inheritance is also less strictly tied to the succession of generations. For example, parent organisms can modify the environments of their offspring, but so too can offspring modify those of their parents. Finally, modifications to any environment need not always be caused by genetic relatives. They are actually caused by 'neighbours' in shared ecosystems. Such neighbours must be ecologically related, but they need not be genetically related. Thus ecological inheritance may be vertical, horizontal or oblique (see Cavalli-Sforza and Feldman 1981).

2   Niche construction includes its opposite, niche destruction. For example, niche destruction occurs whenever organisms deplete their own or their successors' environments of vital resources, particularly when these are non-renewable, or, alternatively, if they overload their environments with polluting detritus.

The net result is a dual inheritance system, involving the inheritance both of genetically encoded information and of environmental resources. Active organisms inherit an 'information package' from their 'genetic ancestors' in the form of whatever information is encoded by their naturally selected genes. However, they also inherit a 'resource package', namely the resources of living space, energy and materials which are provided by their local habitats following the prior selection and perturbation of those habitats by their 'ecological ancestors'. Moreover, the fitness value of the contributions of organisms to each of these kinds of inheritance is strongly affected by their contributions to the other. Genes are only 'fit' (or unfit) relative to the particular habitats which are passed on to successor organisms by their 'ecological ancestors' (who may or may not also be their genetic ancestors). Conversely habitats are only useful relative to the particular adaptations which are expressed by particular organisms on the basis of the genes they inherit from their 'genetic ancestors'. This dual inheritance system then recurs, generation after generation, as a function of the co-evolution of organisms and their environments, under the direction of both naturally selecting inputs from environments to organisms, and niche–constructing outputs from organisms to their environments.

Even this expanded picture of inheritance falls short of what really happens, as a recent paper by two population geneticists, Kirkpatrick and Lande (1989), makes clear. There they describe several kinds of 'non-Mendelian inheritance' (i.e. which do not obey Mendel's genetic laws). One comprises an external environmental component which falls within the scope of what I am calling 'ecological inheritance'. However, another is a non-Mendelian maternal inheritance (for sexually reproducing organisms) consisting of the inheritance of cytoplasm, ribosomes, mitochondrial DNA and other cellular bits and pieces, from the maternal ovum, which I have not otherwise touched on here. When Kirkpatrick and Lande's scheme is combined with my own proposal, the complete inheritance system looks like that in Figure 3.

One significant new problem introduced by this richer view of inheritance is that it is no longer possible to describe evolution in terms of an elementary 'Newtonian' analogue. It is worth remembering that the modern synthesis is Newtonian as well as Darwinian in conception. It explains evolution, first by treating changing organisms as separate from changing environments, and

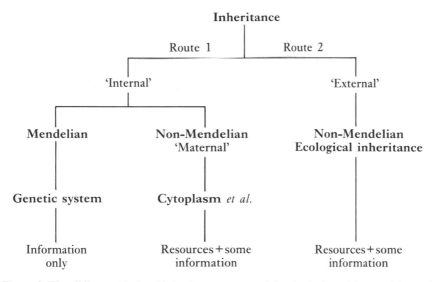

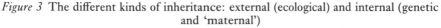

Figure 3 The different kinds of inheritance: external (ecological) and internal (genetic and 'maternal')

second by supposing that the evolution of organisms is just a 'reaction' to a 'force', natural selection, which is 'impressed' on organisms by their 'external' environments (Campbell 1982, Sober 1984). For the scheme shown in Figures 2 and 3, however, that simple description no longer works, because here the ultimate source of at least some of the selection pressures which act on organisms is the evolving organisms themselves.

A possible way around this difficulty (again see Odling-Smee 1988 for a full account) is summarized by equations (5), (6) and (7), which, between them, propose a fully relativistic, non-linear scheme:

$$d[OE]/dt=f_1(O, E, [OE]) \tag{5}$$

$$dO/dt=f_2(O, [OE]) \tag{6}$$

$$dE/dt=f_3(E, [OE]) \tag{7}$$

In this triplet of equations, OE represents the interactive organism–environment relationship, or the meeting point (Simon, 1982) which occurs between any organism or set of organisms (e.g. a population) and its co-evolving environment. It changes over time (equation 5) as a function of both inputs from its organisms (O) and inputs from the rest of the environment (E). The evolution of organisms then becomes a function both of changes in the organisms (O) themselves, and of their (OE) interactions with their co-evolving environments (equation 6). Conversely environmental change (equation 7) becomes a function of these same (OE) interactions, but also of events in the 'rest of the environment' (E). The scheme is fully relativistic because every time a new organism, or a new population (O), becomes the centre of attention, it immediately defines a new (OE) relationship. Its disadvantage is that it makes it impossible to talk about 'the environment' in an absolute sense. It is now only possible to talk about the relative habitats or environments of specified organisms (Lewontin 1982, 1983). However, its advantage is that the (OE) interactions can encapsulate as many feedback cycles for any given set of organisms (O) as is necessary, simply by reducing all such cycles to their essence, the (OE) relationship itself.

Relativistic schemes are always complicated, yet the basic ideas summarized by these three equations is simple. Since, in Figure 2, the source of the natural selection pressures which act on organisms (O) is no longer an autonomous environment (E), but is rather the mutual (OE) relationship, we need to model the evolution of organisms (O) relative to this (OE) relationship, instead of relative to a supposedly autonomous environment (E).

We are now in a position to consider how a second evolutionary currency might be derived from this external, ecological inheritance. If the source of natural selection is really a relationship (OE), and if this relationship subsumes two different kinds of selection pressures, (a) those which are due to genuinely autonomous events in the environment, and (b) those which are self-induced by phenotypes, then it should be possible to partition any specified selection pressure (S) into two distinct components,

$$(OE) \rightarrow S = (S_a + S_{nc}),\tag{8}$$

Where S_a is the autonomous component of natural selection which cannot be modified by organisms, while S_{nc} is that component which is self-induced by niche-constructing phenotypes. These two components may be separated experimentally by enhancing, blocking or cancelling out the niche-constructing acts of different groups of organisms, and comparing what happens to these groups, and to their offspring, with normal, unmanipulated controls.

The actual measures used could be any of the standard ecological measurements which are already employed by ecologists to monitor the states and perturbations of environments. The only difference is that in this general co-evolutionary scenario, any ecological measures of the S_{nc} component of selection will also become measurements of the contributions of niche-constructing phenotypes to their own ecological inheritance systems. Such measures should therefore be 'eco-evolutionary' and their units should establish a second, 'eco-evolutionary' currency of fitness.

That still leaves one major problem unresolved. It remains difficult to see how the contributions of phenotypes to an external ecological inheritance (their second role in evolution) relate to and combine with their contributions to the internal genetic inheritance of their populations (their first role of evolution). Ideally the concept of fitness needs to be stretched until it includes not only the transmission of genetically encoded information from genetic ancestors to their successors, but also the transmission of environmental resources from ecological ancestors to their successors, as shown in Figure 3. As yet this ideal is out of sight even though a few tentative and controversial steps have been taken (e.g. Weber *et al.* 1988, Odum 1989, Fox, 1988). Fortunately there is no need to wait for the resolution of this problem before admitting the significance of both niche construction and ecological inheritance in evolution. There is at least one famous precedent. For Darwin did not know about genes or genetic fitness when he introduced the idea of natural selection.

THE SUPPLEMENTARY PROCESSES

Multiple levels in evolution

Let me now return to the human sciences to see what difference this proposed extension to evolutionary theory may eventually make.

Its immediate effect is to alter the status of phenotypes in evolution by recognizing both their roles. Under this scheme phenotypes transmit both naturally selected genes and modified selection pressures from one generation to the next. This dual role not only affects genetic evolution itself, but also all those non-genetic processes which were listed at the beginning of this article, and which depend on phenotypes for their existence. These processes include human culture.

In a previous attempt to relate population genetics to culture, Plotkin and Odling-Smee (1979, 1981) developed a multiple-process model of evolution incorporating genes and culture, as well as what we and others, notably Boyd and Richerson (1985) and Durham (1991), consider to be the vital intervening processes of individual development and learning. This exercise was only partially successful because it was still rooted in the modern synthesis. What I would now like to do is to see what happens to this model if the present theory of organism–environment co-evolution is substituted, at its base, for the modern synthesis. I shall first summarize the model in its original form, before extending it by adding the mechanisms of niche construction and ecological inheritance.

The original model is illustrated in Figure 4. It shows evolution as a four-level hierarchy of processes for gaining information, or more accurately 'knowledge' (Holland *et al.* 1989), relative to different species of organisms. Here every species depends on level 1, and most depend on both levels 1 and 2. Animals typically depend on level 3 as well, and some animals, including ourselves, also depend on level 4. It should be noted that this is an unconventional hierarchy of *processes* rather than the more usual hierarchy of *units* (e.g. molecules, organelles, cells, organs, organisms, populations, etc.). Confusingly, these units are both (a) consequences of evolution and (b) the entities via which evolution continues to work. Confusingly, also, (c) each higher-level process is itself a consequence of underlying genetic evolution, as we see again later. There is therefore a complex relationship between these processes and their products which has to be grasped before the model itself can be understood (Odling-Smee and Plotkin 1984).

In this hierarchy each process is distinguished by its own mechanisms and units, and by its own 'knowledge-gaining' entity (previously called its 'referent'). Each process therefore has unique operating characteristics. For example, each works at a different rate. These rates may vary from the very slow (e.g. genetic evolution in long-lived species), to the rapid (e.g. individual learning). Because of their different operating characteristics each process also gains qualitatively different 'knowledge' from the interactions of its organisms with their environments, and it thereby assembles its own logically distinct 'knowledge base'. Physically, these 'knowledge bases' are not always distinguishable in the organisms themselves. For instance, genetically encoded 'knowledge' is physically separable from neurally encoded 'knowledge', but individually learned 'knowledge' and cultural 'knowledge' are probably inseparable in animal brains. Subsequently each process, at each level, contributes its different kind of 'knowledge' to the adaptations of organisms, such that in any given case, the expression of an adaptation by an organism is likely

182

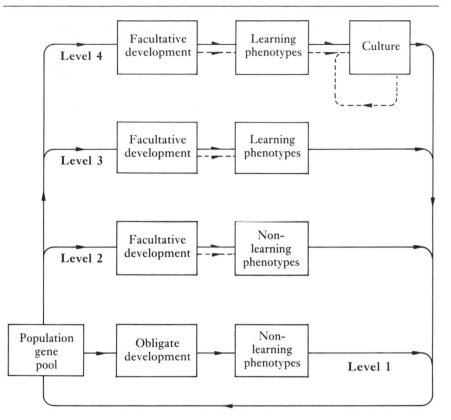

Figure 4 The alternative genetic inheritance cycles in multi-process evolution (solid arrows=genetic; dashed arrows=acquired)

to depend on the integration of 'instructions' from several processes and several 'knowledge bases'.

Level 1 is the basic process of genetic evolution we have just been looking at, and it refers exclusively to genetically encoded 'knowledge'. Because it is so heavily dependent on natural selection, and because natural selection only works on a between-individual and a between-generation basis, the only entities which can gain 'knowledge' at this level are populations. Individuals cannot gain any 'knowledge' here; they can only inherit it from their ancestors. Thus individuals always run the risk that their genetic 'knowledge' may be out of date. In spite of this limitation, genetic evolution is robust. It is the only process which affects every aspect of phenotypic expression. It is also the only process which can work independently of all the other processes, making it the fundamental process in evolution. This last point is indicated in Figure 4 by the arrows travelling from the gene pool of a population to the expression of elementary phenotypes, via 'closed' developmental pathways, labelled here

183

'obligate development'. These arrows simply demonstrate the limiting case where only level-1 evolution occurs, and where only genetic 'knowledge' is available.

Level 2 then introduces 'facultative' or 'open' development in lieu of the 'obligate' development shown at level 1. At level 2 some new, more up-to-date, and more locally relevant 'knowledge' may be 'acquired' by individual organisms during their lives via a variety of epigenetic processes (e.g. Bonner, 1982, Walbot and Holder 1987). Typically, organisms will then use this extra 'knowledge' to 'fine tune' their adaptations which would otherwise be based only on their genetic inheritance. Hence the 'knowledge' gaining entity at level 2 is no longer a population, but an individual organism.

Level 3 is little more than an extension of level 2, and likewise deals with 'knowledge' acquired by individual organisms. The difference is that at this level the knowledge is gained by specialized phenotypic subsystems which only process particular kinds of 'knowledge', and only serve restricted domains of adaptation. The two outstanding examples are the vertebrate immune system, and animal learning based on the central nervous system.

Finally, at level 4, 'knowledge' is gained by socio-cultural processes, and therefore, once again, by collections of organisms rather than by individuals. Level 4 processes include both animal proto-cultures and human cultures. To participate at level 4, each individual organism must be capable of level-3 type learning, and it must also be capable of transmitting and receiving previously learned 'knowledge' to and from other individuals, both within and between generations, via social learning or social enhancement (e.g. Galef 1988). The transmission of culturally acquired 'knowledge' therefore demands the existence of at least one non-genetic channel of communication between phenotypes. Human language is the supreme example.

The outputs from all these processes are shown on the right of Figure 4. Given that the model, as presented so far, still rests on the modern synthesis, at each level these outputs are the same. They comprise the naturally selected genes which are transmitted by phenotypes to the next generation of their population. The only influence which any of these higher processes exerts is statistical. They affect the probability that individual organisms will survive and reproduce, and will pass on their genes to the next generation, but that is all. Everything else is ruled out, (a) by the 'Weismann barrier', which buffers genes from the within-lifetime experiences of the individual organisms which carry them (e.g. Maynard Smith 1986), thereby ruling out the Lamarckian inheritance of acquired characteristics, and (b) by the absence of any other kind of non-genetic inheritance system in the modern synthesis. This accounts for the orthodox representation, in Figure 4, of the fate of the non-genetic 'knowledge' which is acquired by organisms at levels 2, 3 and 4. At levels 2 and 3 individually 'acquired' knowledge is erased in each generation by the deaths of organisms, while at level 4 cultural 'knowledge' may be transmitted to future generations via channels of cultural inheritance, but without culture having any influence over genetic evolution, except statistically.

A recursive heuristic in evolution

The other main feature of our original model was that we proposed that each process at each level is governed by a common inductive heuristic. This heuristic is characterized by three essential sub-processes: (a) a capacity (g) of the knowledge gaining entity to *generate* repertoires of variety embodied in units of variation; (b) some capacity (t) to *test* this variation and to select its units in the light of either direct or 'proxy' encounters with an environment; and (c) a capacity (r) to *regenerate* or propagate the selected variants differentially. In shorthand we referred to this as the g-t-r heuristic. Since similar proposals have often been made before (e.g. Childe 1951, Campbell 1974, Dennett 1975, Edelman 1989, Schull 1990), and just as often rejected (e.g. Piatelli-Palmarini 1990), this idea also needs some elaboration.

To start with, and contrary to what is held by its critics, the hypothesis never implies the 'simple mimicry' of the raw Darwinian (level 1) process by any other process. As Edelman (1989) puts it, there are 'enormous differences in detail' between each process, at each level. So the first requirement is always to spell out these differences in enough detail to support an empirical programme.

So far, the hypothesis has probably been most successful in respect of the now widely accepted theory of clonal selection (Burnet 1959) in immunology (level 3). This was eventually made possible by advances in molecular biology, which led to the discovery of both the sources of variety and the associated selective mechanisms in the immune system (e.g. Roitt 1980; Tonegawa 1985). A second provisional success is Edelman's (1989) own 'neural Darwinism'. Edelman proposed that animal brains are organized into 'populations' of cells, which form variant networks, whose structures and functions are selected during both development (level 2) and learning (level 3). Again, the main reason for Edelman's success has been his unequivocal demonstrations of both units of variety and molecular selective mechanisms in animal brains.

The hypothesis has fared less well at level 4. Units of cultural variation have been suggested (such as Dawkins's (1989) 'memes' or Lumsden and Wilson's (1981) 'culturgens'), but they have remained vague. Moreover, proposals for the entailed mechanisms of cultural selection have tended to proliferate without check. Yet some modest successes have been reported in studies of animal proto-cultures. One recent example comes from a study of chaffinch songs which was based on an unusually flexible definition of song units or 'memes', thus: 'a song composed of one syllable A, B, C and D in that sequence includes four memes of one syllable (A, B, C, D), three memes of two syllables (AB, BC, CD), two memes of three syllables (ABC, BCD), and one meme of four syllables (ABCD)' (Lynch *et al.* 1989: 638). The usefulness of this inclusive definition of song units was demonstrated by the results. These showed that, in at least one case, a system of cultural transmission which appears superficially to be based on 'blending inheritance' (i.e. song blending) can in fact be resolved into discrete 'mutations' and 're-combinations' of elementary song units, once the units themselves have been adequately defined.

A second frequent complaint against the *g-t-r* hypothesis is that at level 1 genetic evolution is 'blind', but that all the other processes shown in Figure 4 are not. They are 'purposive' or 'intentional'. Hence the whole idea of a recursive heuristic, at levels 2, 3 and 4, is flawed. But in fact, the hypothesis does not imply that any higher-level process need be 'blind', indeed quite the reverse.

This issue has been extensively discussed before (Plotkin and Odling-Smee 1979, 1981, 1982), and I will only reiterate the main point. The hierarchy in Figure 4 is a *nested* hierarchy. This means that the capacity of any organism to operate at any higher level ultimately depends on genetic evolution itself. This being so, there is no reason why an organism's genes should only supply it with '*tabula rasa*' higher-level capacities. Rather, the economics of adaptation make it far more likely that an organism's developmental, learning or cultural processes will be guided 'a priori' by as much innate 'knowledge' as is adaptive. Thus these higher-level processes should seldom, perhaps never, be 'blind'. To put this in a more concrete way, the units of variation generated by each higher-level process are seldom arbitrary. Usually they stem from repertoires of alternatives (e.g. behavioural repertoires in learners) which are already pointing in more or less adaptive directions. Similarly the ability of the immune system to select between 'self', 'not self' and 'infected self', or of a learner to select between rewarding and punishing outcomes among its own behaviours, is often grounded in, and guided by, innate 'a priori' knowledge that is already adaptive (e.g. Staddon 1983).

Finally, this *g-t-r* heuristic is meant to apply only to the gaining of 'new' knowledge, and not to the transmission or re-use of 'old' knowledge by any process. That may sound simple, but it can make the task of dissecting out the role of the *g-t-r* heuristic at any higher level extremely difficult. Only at level 1 and, oddly enough, at the other extreme, in scientific methodology (Kuhn 1970, Popper 1972, Holland *et al.* 1989), does the *g-t-r* heuristic stand out comparatively clearly. More often, at level 4 for instance, the processes of cultural selection and cultural instruction appear inextricably entwined. These issues are fast becoming the objects of empirical research in artificial intelligence (e.g. Rumelhart *et al.* 1986), and in cognitive science (e.g. Holland *et al.* 1989; Reeke and Edelman 1988), so there is hope that they may eventually be sorted out.

AN INFRASTRUCTURE FOR THE HUMAN SCIENCES

Within levels

That is about as far as we can take the original multiple-process model without going beyond the modern synthesis. The next step is to see what happens if we substitute, at the base of the model, the theory of organism–environment co-evolution for the modern synthesis. This at once adds ecological inheritance and niche construction to the model, with two major effects. One effect applies within levels, the other between them. I shall consider the within-level effect first.

We saw earlier that at level 1, phenotypes not only react to naturally selecting pressures from their environments, they also modify some of those selection pressures via their outputs (Figure 2). This implies that organisms are not just 'problem solvers' in evolution, which merely solve adaptive

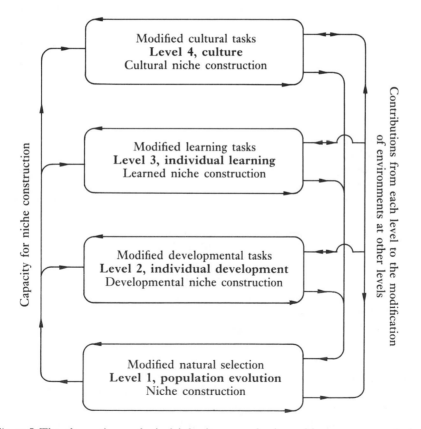

Figure 5 The alternative ecological inheritance cycles in multi-process co-evolution

187

problems imposed on them by their environments. They must also be 'problem setters' who are constantly setting themselves, and each other, new adaptive problems by virtue of their niche-constructing and niche-destroying acts. This means that the g-t-r heuristic at level 1 is not just a simple 'trial and error' process. Organisms do not just generate and propagate variety, and then passively submit that variety to independent test by an autonomous environment. Instead they also modify the test itself by actively changing at least some of the selection pressures in their own, and in their successors', environments.

However, if the g-t-r heuristic is cyclic at level 1, and if it is also recursive at levels 2, 3 and 4 (Figure 4), then individual development, learning, and culture should be cyclic too. Each of these higher-level processes should depend on two-way rather than one-way organism-environment interactions, and each should introduce some additional feedforward and feedback loops. Thus, at level 2 in Figure 5, prior niche-constructing outputs from developing phenotypes should modify their own subsequent individual development. At level 3, prior niche-constructing behaviours by phenotypes should modify their own subsequent learning tasks, while at level 4, prior collective niche-constructing activities by members of a culture should modify their own subsequent cultural tasks.

To a large extent this hypothesis merely catches up with critics who have already pointed out the 'two-way' or interactive nature of many of these processes (e.g. Lewontin (1982, 1983) and J. Campbell (1985) concerning levels 1 and 2; Plotkin and Odling-Smee (1982) concerning level 3; Richards (1987) and Ingold (1986) concerning level 4). Previously, it had been impossible to reconcile this point with the logic of the modern synthesis. However, when the theory of organism—environment co-evolution is substituted, the point readily falls into place.

A single example of the difference this may make at level 4 must suffice. One reason why units of cultural variation and cultural inheritance are, as noted above, so difficult to define, is that it is still not clear whether they refer to signs, symbols and ideas, or to physical artifacts, or all of these (e.g. Lumsden and Wilson 1981: 27). This issue may become less confusing when it is realized that there are two different inheritance systems in evolution, the inheritance of genetic instructions (which at the cultural level may be generalized to include all kinds of inherited 'knowledge'), and the inheritance of modified niches (which may be generalized to include the inheritance of all kinds of environmental resources, including human 'material culture'). Clearly, both ideas and artifacts can be inherited at level 4, but by different routes. Hence the attempt by sociobiologists to use the same units (e.g. memes) for both kinds of cultural inheritance is probably no more than a misplaced analogue of the genes-only view of inheritance at level 1. If this idea is accepted, then we should expect the two kinds of cultural inheritance − knowledge and artefacts − to drive and direct each other in a truly reciprocal fashion. An example occurs in science itself. Scientific knowledge is translated into new technological artefacts. New technological artefacts help us gain new scientific knowledge.

Between levels

The between-level innovation is more fundamental. Figure 4 illustrates how, based on a 'modern synthesis' model, all higher-level processes are linked to the basic genetic inheritance system at level 1 by way of a set of alternative genetic inheritance cycles. The between-level interactions were modelled by (a) a 'causal arrow' pointing up (on the left), indicating how the capacity of any species to operate at any higher level is ultimately based in its genes, and (b) by a second 'causal arrow' pointing down (on the right) showing how, at each level, genes are returned by 'fit' phenotypes to their populations' gene pools. Since all of these interactions are excluded by the Weismann barrier from encoding any 'acquired knowledge' in the next generation's genes, it follows that none of the extra 'knowledge' gained by organisms at levels 2, 3 or 4 can be transmitted to their successors at level 1 via any of these genetic cycles.

Figure 5 now shows how the same higher-level processes are linked to the proposed ecological inheritance system, by illustrating a set of alternative ecological inheritance cycles. Here the between-level interactions depend on (a) the same upwards causal arrow as in Figure 4, which in this case supplies organisms with their species-specific, niche-constructing capacities; and (b) on a new bidirectional causal arrow (on the right), in addition to the downward causal arrow depicted in Figure 4. This new bidirectional arrow refers to the fact that the niche constructing acts of organisms at each level not only modify the environment at that level, but potentially at every other level too. For example, cultural niche construction at level 4 may modify individual learning or developmental tasks at levels 3 and 2, as well as natural selection at level 1. Conversely learned niche construction at level 3 may eventually modify some cultural tasks at level 4.

The other major difference between Figures 4 and 5 is that in the latter there is nothing in ecological inheritance equivalent to the Weismann barrier in genetic inheritance, to stop organisms from contributing their 'acquired knowledge' to the co-direction of their population's evolution via any of these ecological inheritance cycles. If phenotypes modify selection pressures in their environments, it makes no difference to the logic of organism–environment co-evolution whether their niche-constructing acts are innately determined by their genes at level 1, or whether they are controlled by 'acquired knowledge' gained at levels 2, 3 or 4. In every case the consequences for genetic evolution should be the same. Modified selection pressures, which are induced by phenotypes acting at any level, should feed back to their populations at level 1, where they may then select for different genes in the population's gene pool.

The only difference that the higher-level processes may make is that they are likely to amplify the capacity of the phenotypes for niche construction. If this is so, then they will also amplify the capacity of the phenotypes to co-direct evolution.

So although 'acquired knowledge' cannot change 'innate knowledge' by changing the instructions encoded in individual genes at the molecular level, it may nevertheless change the 'knowledge base' contained in a population's gene pool as a whole, by modifying some of the pressures which select between different genes in a population's gene pool. In other words, even though the Weismann barrier cannot be broken by modifying genes, its effects may be bypassed by modifying natural selection pressures in environments. This is still not Lamarckism. 'Acquired knowledge' still does not travel via genetic inheritance. It only travels externally via ecological inheritance, via its impact on local environments, and therefore via Waddington's (1959) 'exploitive system'. Thus we end up with Waddingtonian, not Lamarckian, evolution.

It is now easy to account for such phenomena as lactose absorption in dairy farming communities, and potentially for much else besides. The acquisition of lactose tolerance is apparently just one instance of self-induced natural selection, caused by the niche-constructing activities of human beings in the human 'exploitive system', under the direction of cultural 'knowledge'.

CONCLUSION

When the within-level and between-level changes illustrated in Figure 5 are combined, they radically alter our picture of the relationship between genetic evolution and culture, forcing a basic revision of the sociobiological paradigm. The details of this revision go well beyond the scope of the present chapter, but I shall end with a provisional sketch of its principal implications.

The present theory envisages a relationship between genes and culture such that the capacity for culture has a genetically evolved basis, and such that culture reciprocates by co-directing genetic evolution. The theory's main novelty is its proposal that cultural phenotypes make a two-fold contribution to evolutionary inheritance. They bequeath naturally selected genes to the next generation via genetic inheritance. They also bequeath culturally modified selection pressures to the next generation via ecological inheritance, each kind of contribution being measured relative to each other.

If this is so, however, then it no longer makes sense to evaluate the cultural activities of phenotypes exclusively in terms of genetic inheritance and genetic fitness. The way in which culture co-directs genetic evolution is through the application of culturally acquired knowledge to the modification of natural selection at level 1. Yet culturally acquired knowledge can only travel non-genetically between phenotypes. It cannot travel via genetic inheritance. Hence, if we measure the cultural contribution to genetic fitness alone, we risk losing a complete hemicycle from the total cycle of gene–culture interactions.

And that would leave us with a sociobiology in which either cultural evolution is seen to run parallel to, yet separately from, genetic evolution (e.g. compare Durham 1982 with Durham 1991), or else an extremely limited gene–culture cycle is envisaged such that genes affect culture but culture cannot affect genes, except statistically (e.g. Lumsden and Wilson 1981).

Thus the first implication of this theory is that even if it is not yet possible to measure 'fitness' in units which can combine the genetic and the ecological contributions of phenotypes within a single measure, it is better to have two separate scores, respectively ecological and genetic, rather than to collapse everything into genes.

The second implication is that the recognition of this two-fold contribution of phenotypes to evolution may change our understanding of certain cultural phenomena within level 4, as well as our understanding of between-level gene and culture interactions. Social altruism is a case in point.

At present contemporary sociobiology provides two alternative bases for understanding human co-operation: Hamilton's (1964) notion of kin selection; and Trivers's (1985) of reciprocal altruism. Both these ideas are based on the calculus of genetic fitness. That now calls for two comments. First, the mechanisms by which kin selection and reciprocal altruism work to establish co-operative behaviour are not those of differential reproduction and genetic inheritance. Instead they are those of niche construction and ecological inheritance. Co-operation between organisms is actually achieved by altruists modifying selection pressures in other organisms' environments. Moreover at level 4, these modifications depend on culturally 'acquired knowledge' which cannot be transmitted by genes anyway. The genetic fitness scores of co-operating organisms are thus affected not only in the usual statistical sense, but also qualitatively by culturally modified selection pressures. Second, if cultural phenotypes are assessed for their contributions to both ecological inheritance and genetic inheritance, then that could also change the basis of our understanding of socio-cultural altruism. For instance, the transmission of human property from one generation to the next may prove to have as much of a bearing on the evolution of human altruism as the transmission of human genes from one generation to the next, a point already anticipated in social anthropology.

Finally, this revised sociobiology also raises the prospect of some new hypotheses which either have remained unnoticed or are ruled out by the modern synthesis. For example, interactions between genetic evolution and culture could act either constructively or destructively in relation to the evolutionary fate of the species. Constructive interactions might occur if a species's cultural activities at level 4 modified the natural selection pressures which selected its own genes at level 1 in such a way that they increasingly selected for, say, sociality among its own phenotypes (e.g. Caporael et al. 1989). Conversely, destructive interactions could involve cultural phenotypes changing their own natural selection pressures in directions, or at rates, which exceeded the capacity of the basic level 1 genetic process to track them. If so, a species could conceivably co-direct its own extinction. The important between-levels variables here are (a) the intergenerational turnover time at level 1, which decides the maximum rate at which the genetic process can operate, and (b) the variables which determine the potency of cultural niche construction. The human example is relevant because we are long-lived, and because of the unprecedented potency of our own niche-constructing and niche-destroying acts.

If this last idea sounds alarmist it does nevertheless suggest that the sociobiologists have always been right about one point. We must take evolutionary biology seriously if we want to understand ourselves.

ACKNOWLEDGEMENT

The preparation of this article was supported by Grant Number F275 N 5893153 from the Leverhulme Trust.

REFERENCES

Alcock, J. (1972) 'The evolution of the use of tools by feeding animals', *Evolution* 26: 464–73.
—— (1989) *Animal Behaviour*, 4th edn, Sunderland, Mass.: Sinauer.
Alexander, R. D. (1979) *Darwinism and Human Affairs*, Seattle: University of Washington Press.
Axelrod, R. (1984) *The Evolution of Co-operation*, New York: Basic Books.
Begon, M., Harper, J. L. and Townsend, C. R. (1986) *Ecology: Individuals, Populations and Communities*, Oxford: Blackwell.
Bodmer, W. F. and Cavalli-Sforza, L. L. (1976) *Genetics, Evolution and Man*, San Francisco: Freeman.
Bonner, J. T. (ed.) (1982) *Evolution and Development*, New York: Springer.
Boyd, R. and Richerson, P. J. (1985) *Culture and the Evolutionary Process*, Chicago: University of Chicago Press.
Burnet, F. M. (1959) *The Clonal Selection Theory of Acquired Immunity*, Nashville: Vanderbilt.
Buss, L. W. (1987) *The Evolution of Individuality*, Princeton, NJ: Princeton University Press.
Campbell, D. T. (1974) 'Evolutionary epistemology', in P. A. Schlipp (ed.) *The Philosophy of Karl Popper*, Chicago, Ill.: Open Court Publishers.
Campbell, J. H. (1982) 'Autonomy in evolution', in R. Milkman (ed.) *Perspective on Evolution*, Sunderland, Mass.: Sinauer.
—— (1985) 'An organizational interpretation of evolution', in D. J. Depew and B. H. Weber (eds) *Evolution at a Crossroads*, Cambridge, Mass.: MIT Press.
Caporael, L. R., Dawes, R. M., Orbell, J. M. and van de Kragt, A. J. C. (1989) 'Selfishness examined: co-operation in the absence of egoistic incentives', *Behavioral and Brain Sciences* 12: 683–739.
Cavalli-Sforza, L. L. and Feldman, M. W. (1981) *Cultural Transmission and Evolution: a Quantitative Approach*, Princeton, NJ: Princeton University Press.
Childe, G. (1951) *Social Evolution*, London: Collins.

Crook, J. H. (1989) 'Socioecological paradigms, evolution and history: perspectives for the 1990s', in V. Standen and R. A. Foley (eds) *Comparative Socioecology*, Oxford: Blackwell.

Dawkins, R. D. (1982) *The Extended Phenotype*, Oxford: W. H. Freeman.

—— (1989) *The Selfish Gene*, 2nd edn, Oxford: Oxford University Press.

Dawkins, R. D. and Krebs, J. R. (1979) 'Arms races between and within species', *Proceedings of the Royal Society of London*, ser. B 205: 489–511.

Dennett, D. C. (1975) 'Why the law of effect will not go away', *Journal of the Theory of Social Behaviour* 5: 169–87.

Depew, D. J. and Weber, B. H. (eds) (1985) *Evolution at a Crossroads*, Cambridge, Mass.: MIT Press.

Dunbar, R. I. M. (1989) 'Selfishness re-examined', *Behavioral and Brain Sciences* 12: 700–2.

Durham, W. H. (1982) 'Interactions of genetic and cultural evolution', *Human Ecology* 10: 289–323.

—— (1991) *Co-evolution: Genes, Culture, and Human Diversity*, Stanford, Cal.: Stanford University Press.

Edelman, G. M. (1989) *Neural Darwinism*, Oxford: Oxford University Press.

Endler, J. A. (1986) 'The newer synthesis? Some conceptual problems in evolutionary biology', in R. Dawkins and M. Ridley (eds) *Oxford Surveys in Evolutionary Biology*, vol. 3, Oxford: Oxford University Press.

Endler, J. A. and McLellan, T. (1988) 'The processes of evolution: toward a newer synthesis', *Annual Review of Ecology and Systematics* 19: 395–421.

Fisher, J. and Hinde, R. A. (1949) 'The opening of milk bottles by birds', *British Birds* 42: 347–57.

Fox, R. E. (1988) *Energy and the Evolution of Life*, San Francisco: Freeman.

Futuyma, D. J. and Slatkin, M. (eds) (1983) *Co-evolution*, Sunderland, Mass.: Sinauer.

Galef, B. G. (1988) 'Imitation in animals', in T. Zentall and B. G. Galef (eds) *Social Learning*, Hillsdale, NJ: Erlbaum.

Gould, S. J. (1980) 'Is a new and general theory of evolution emerging?', *Paleobiology* 6: 119–30.

Hagen, J. B. (1989) 'Research perspectives and the anomalous status of modern ecology', *Biology and Philosophy* 4: 433–55.

Hamilton, W. D. (1964) 'The genetical evolution of social behaviour', *Journal of Theoretical Biology* 7: 1–32.

Hartl, D. L. and Clark, A. G. (1989) *Principles of Population Genetics*, 2nd edn, Sunderland, Mass.: Sinauer.

Ho, M. W. and Fox, S. W. (1988) *Evolutionary Processes and Metaphors*, Chichester: John Wiley.

Holland, J. H., Holyoak, K. J., Nisbett, R. E. and Thagard, P. R. (1989) *Induction: Processes of Inference, Learning and Discovery*, Cambridge, Mass.: MIT Press.

Hull, D. L. (1988) 'Interactors versus vehicles', in H. C. Plotkin (ed.) *The Role of Behaviour in Evolution*, Cambridge, Mass.: MIT Press.

Ingold, T. (1986) *Evolution and Social Life*, Cambridge: Cambridge University Press.

Kirkpatrick, M. and Lande, R. (1989) 'The evolution of maternal characters', *Evolution* 43: 485–503.

Kitcher, P. (1988) 'Imitating selection', in M. W. Ho and S. W. Fox (eds) *Evolutionary Processes and Metaphors*, Chichester: John Wiley.

Kretchmer, N. (1977) 'The geography and biology of lactose digestion and malabsorption', *Postgraduate Medical Journal* 58: 65.

Kuhn, T. S. (1970) *The Structure of Scientific Revolutions*, 2nd edn, Chicago: University of Chicago Press.

Lewontin, R. C. (1982) 'Organism and environment', in H. C. Plotkin (ed.) *Learning, Development and Culture*, Chichester: John Wiley.

—— (1983) 'Gene, organism and environment', in D. S. Bendall (ed.) *Evolution from Molecules to Men*, Cambridge: Cambridge University Press.

Livingstone, F. B. (1958) 'Anthropological implications of sickle cell gene distribution in West Africa', *American Anthropologist* 60: 533–62.

Lumsden, C. J. and Wilson, E. O. (1981) *Genes, Mind, and Culture: the Co-evolutionary Process*, Cambridge, Mass.: Harvard University Press.

Lynch, A., Plunkett, G. M., Baker, A. J. and Jenkins, P. F. (1989) 'A model of cultural evolution of chaffinch song derived with the meme concept', *American Naturalist* 133: 634–53.

MacNeill, J. (1989) 'Strategies for sustainable economic development', *Scientific American* 261: 104–13.

May, R. M. (ed.) (1981) *Theoretical Ecology*, 2nd edn, Oxford: Blackwell.

Maynard Smith, J. (1974) *Models in Ecology*, Cambridge: Cambridge University Press.

—— (1986) *The Problems of Biology*, Oxford: Oxford University Press.

Mayr, E. (1974) 'Behaviour programmes and evolutionary strategies', *American Scientist* 62: 650–9.

Odling-Smee, F. J. (1988) 'Niche constructing phenotypes', in H. C. Plotkin (ed.) *The Role of Behaviour in Evolution*, Cambridge, Mass.: MIT Press.

Odling-Smee, F. J. and Plotkin, H. C. (1984) 'Evolution: its levels and its units', *Behavioral and Brain Sciences* 7: 318–20.

Odum, E. P. (1989) *Ecology and our Endangered Life-Support Systems*, Sunderland, Mass.: Sinauer.

Odum, H. T. (1988) 'Self-organisation, transformity, and information', *Science* 242: 1132–9.

O'Neill, R. V., DeAngelis, D. L., Waide, J. B. and Allen, T. F. H. (1986) *A Hierarchical Concept of Ecosystems*, Princeton, NJ: Princeton University Press.

Patten, B. C. (1982) 'Environs: relativistic elementary particles for ecology', *American Naturalist* 119: 179–219.

Patten, B. C. and Auble, G. T. (1981) 'System theory of the ecological niche', *American Naturalist* 117: 893–922.

Piatelli-Palmarini, M. (1990) 'Which came first, the egg problem or the hen solution?', *Behavioral and Brain Sciences* 13: 84–6.

Plotkin, H. C. (ed.) (1988) *The Role of Behaviour in Evolution*, Cambridge, Mass.: MIT Press.

Plotkin, H. C. and Odling-Smee, F. J. (1979) 'Learning, change and evolution', *Advances in the Study of Behaviour*, 10: 1–41.

—— (1981) 'A multiple level model of evolution and its implications for sociobiology', *Behavioral and Brain Sciences* 4: 225–68.

—— (1982) 'Learning in the context of a hierarchy of knowledge gaining processes', in H. C. Plotkin (ed.) *Learning, Development and Culture*, Chichester: John Wiley.

Popper, K. R. (1972) *Objective Knowledge: an Evolutionary Approach*, Oxford: Oxford University Press.

Potter, J., Ho, M. W., Bolton, H., Furth, A. J., Swallow, D. M. and Griffiths, B. (1985) 'Human lactase and the molecular basis of lactase persistence', *Biochemical Genetics* 23: 423–39.

Pulliam, H. R. and Dunford, C. (1980) *Programmed to Learn*, New York: Columbia University Press.

Reeke, G. N. and Edelman, G. M. (1988) 'Real brains and artificial intelligence', *Daedalus* 117: 143–73.

Richards, G. R. (1987) *Human Evolution*, London: Routledge & Kegan Paul.

Roitt, I. (1980) *Essential Immunology*, 4th edn, Oxford: Blackwell.

Romme, W. H. and Despain, D. G. (1989) 'The Yellowstone fires', *Scientific American* 261 (5): 20–9.

Rose, S., Kamin, L. J. and Lewontin, R. C. (1984) *Not in our genes*, Harmondsworth: Penguin.

Ruckelhaus, W. D. (1989) 'Towards a sustainable world', *Scientific American* 261: 114–20.

Rumelhart, D. E., McClelland, J. R. and the PDP Research Group (1986) *Parallel Distributed Processing: Explorations in the Microstructure of Cognition*, vol. 1, Cambridge, Mass.: MIT Press.

Sahlins, M. (1976) *The Use and Abuse of Biology*, Ann Arbor: University of Michigan Press.

Saunders, P. T. (1988) 'Sociobiology: a house built on sand', in M. W. Ho and S. W. Fox (eds) *Evolutionary Processes and Metaphors*, Chichester: John Wiley.

Schull, J. (1990) 'Are species intelligent?', *Behavioral and Brain Sciences* 13: 63–108.

Sherry, D. F. and Galef, B. G. (1984) 'Cultural transmission without imitation: milk bottle opening by birds', *Animal Behaviour* 32: 937–8.

Simon, H. A. (1982) *The Sciences of the Artificial*, 2nd edn, Cambridge, Mass.: MIT Press.

Slatkin, M. (1979) 'Frequency and density-dependent selection on a quantitative character', *Genetics* 93: 755–71.

Sober, E. (1984) *The Nature of Selection*, Cambridge, Mass.: MIT Press.

Staddon, J. E. R. (1983) *Adaptive Behaviour and Learning*, Cambridge: Cambridge University Press.

Standen, V. and Foley, R. A. (eds) (1989) *Comparative Socioecology*, Oxford: Blackwell.

Tonegawa, S. (1985) 'The molecules of the immune system', *Scientific American* 253: 104–13.

Trivers, R. (1985) *Social Evolution*, Menlo Park, Cal.: Benjamin Cummings.

Vrba, E. S. and Eldredge, N. (1984) 'Individuals, hierarchies and processes: towards a more complete evolutionary theory', *Paleobiology* 10: 146–71.

Waddington, C. H. (1959) 'Evolutionary systems: animal and human', *Nature* 183: 1634–8.

—— (1960) 'Evolutionary adaptation', in S. Tax (ed.) *Evolution After Darwin, I: The Evolution of Life*, Chicago: University of Chicago Press.

—— (1969) 'Paradigm for an evolutionary process', in C. H. Waddington (ed.) *Towards a Theoretical Biology, 2: Sketches*, Edinburgh: Edinburgh University Press.

Walbot, V. and Holder, N. (1987) *Developmental Biology*, New York: Random House.

Weber, B. H., Depew, D. J. and Smith, J. D. (1988) *Entropy, Information and Evolution*, Cambridge, Mass.: MIT Press.

Wilson, E. O. (1975) *Sociobiology: the New Synthesis*, Cambridge, Mass.: Harvard University Press.

Wilson, D. S. and Turelli, M. (1986) 'Stable underdominance and the evolutionary invasion of empty niches', *American Naturalist* 127: 835–50.

FURTHER READING

Axelrod, R. (1984) *The Evolution of Co-operation*, New York: Basic Books.

Bodmer, W. F. and Cavalli-Sforza, L. L. (1976) *Genetics, Evolution and Man*, San Francisco: Freeman.

Boyd, R. and Richerson, P. J. (1985) *Culture and the Evolutionary Process*, Chicago: University of Chicago Press.

Campbell, D. T. (1974) 'Evolutionary epistemology', in P. A. Schlipp (ed.) *The Philosophy of Karl Popper*, Chicago, Ill.: Open Court.

Cavalli-Sforza, L. L. and Feldman, M. W. (1981) *Cultural Transmission and Evolution: a Quantitative Approach*, Princeton, NJ: Princeton University Press.

Dawkins, R. D. (1989) *The Selfish Gene*, new edn, Oxford: Oxford University Press.

Durham, W. H. (1991) *Coevolution: Genes, Culture and Human Diversity*, Stanford, Cal.: Stanford University Press.

Lewontin, R. C. (1983) 'Gene, organism and environment', in D. S. Bendall (ed.) *Evolution from Molecules to Men*, Cambridge: Cambridge University Press.

Lumsden, C. J. and Wilson, E. O. (1981) *Genes, Mind, and Culture: the Coevolutionary Process*, Cambridge, Mass.: Harvard University Press.

Maynard Smith, J. (1986) *The Problems of Biology*, Oxford: Oxford University Press.

—— (1989) *Evolutionary Genetics*, Oxford: Oxford University Press.

Plotkin, H. C. (1988) *The Role of Behaviour in Evolution*, Cambridge, Mass.: MIT Press.

Plotkin, H. C. and Odling-Smee, F. J. (1981) 'A multiple level model of evolution and its implications for sociobiology', *Behavioral and Brain Sciences* 4: 225–68.

Richards, G. R. (1987) *Human Evolution*, London: Routledge & Kegan Paul.

Trivers, R. (1985) *Social Evolution*, Benjamin Cummings, Cal.: Menlo Park.

Waddington, C. H. (1969) 'Paradigm for an evolutionary process', in C. H. Waddington (ed.) *Towards a Theoretical Biology, 2: Sketches*, Edinburgh: Edinburgh University Press.

Wilson, A. C. (1985) 'The molecular basis of evolution', *Scientific American* 253: 148–57.

Wilson, E. O. (1975) *Sociobiology: the New Synthesis*, Cambridge, Mass.: Harvard University Press.

Wyles, J. S., Kunkel, J. G. and Wilson, A. C. (1983) 'Birds, behavior and anatomical evolution', *Proceedings of the National Academy of Science* 80: *USA* 4394–7.

8

MODES OF SUBSISTENCE: HUNTING AND GATHERING TO AGRICULTURE AND PASTORALISM

Roy Ellen

SOME CONCEPTUAL ISSUES

It may be fairly stated that the analysis of modes of subsistence has in the past received insufficient theoretical attention, though this cannot be said of the *relations* between material conditions and social life. Most of those who have sought to understand human culture have been prepared to accept subsistence practices as basically unproblematic, requiring for their analysis no more than simple typologies and a bit of common sense. No doubt this view owes something to the familiarity of such practices, their concreteness and visibility compared with more esoteric aspects of culture; but it is a position now barely tenable.

There are three underlying issues which highlight the problem. The first concerns the critical concepts of *technology* and *environment*, without which any analysis of modes of subsistence is impossible, the second the relationship between *mode of subsistence* and *mode of production*, and the third the classification of types and the use of particular labels.

With regard to the first issue there has been a notable tendency to confuse technology with equipment: the knowledge of how to do something with the physical artefact (often) required to do it (Ingold 1986). The distinction is a crucial one, and its erroneous elision has underscored a view that somehow subsistence is wholly about things, *material* culture, in turn encouraging a conflation between technology and environment, and a resulting bias towards *materialist* explanations of subsistence patterns. Much cultural activity directed towards subsistence, however, does not involve tools so much as know-how, and it is fallacious to infer a 'primitive technology' from a restricted toolkit. The growth of, first, Stewardian cultural ecology and, from the

1960s onwards, systems ecology, has led most anthropologists nowadays to be rather more sophisticated in their conceptualization of what constitutes 'environment' and of the place of culture and social relations in ecological systems (Ellen 1982).

The second issue addresses the question of whether the major means of gaining a livelihood − hunting, agriculture, animal husbandry and so on − are no more than assemblages of technical knowledge and inventories of equipment, which somehow stand apart from social organization, or whether no mode of subsistence can be understood except through its theoretical conceptualization as a *social* form. The position adopted (and defended) here is that a mode of subsistence is an abstraction from any given social reality consisting of *the aggregate of extractive processes characterizing a particular population.* [1] These certainly involve technical practices, but also environmental modification in the broader sense (including intensification of 'natural' patterns of distribution and long-term genotypic changes in plant and animal resources), movement strategies, general cultural information, population control, areal specialization and exchange, all of which combine to ensure an adequate supply of food and other material resources.

All modes of subsistence, no less than separate technical practices or tool-using behaviours, are necessarily embedded in particular webs of social and ecological relations. Every such web may be conceptualized as a specific *mode of production* situated in historical and evolutionary space, and through which humans socially interact in order to produce, circulate and consume things or images accorded with value. Thus, no mode of subsistence can be understood except as part of such a socially constituted structure, nor can it be approached analytically apart from this context, for it is inevitably a consequence of social action which is in part purposive, and has its origins in particular social relations of appropriation. People accordingly *produce* their own subsistence, while social consciousness is integral to production. There is, then, much more to the labour process than a mere sequence of behavioural executions.

The concept of mode of subsistence as an *aggregate* of extractive processes can in itself say nothing of the means by which its particular manifestations are socially integrated. Any designated mode will be composed of a number of more specific techniques or elements, though it is hardly to be expected that these will always be discrete entities. Because the kinds of activities referred to by the conventional labels merge into each other (e.g. hunting → trapping → fishing → collecting...), and because the particular combinations of techniques are so varied, simple typologies are dangerous and best avoided. Nevertheless, there are at least two reasons why a concept of mode of subsistence defined in such terms is inescapable.

The first is that there is no fixed relationship between particular subsistence strategies or practices (or combinations of such) and relations of production and distribution. If social relations can vary while practical activity is held constant, then the latter cannot be characterized in terms of the former. By maintaining the conceptual independence of the mode of subsistence, we are able to distinguish the one from the other and avoid any implication of technicist reduction. The second reason is one of practical academic discipline. If we reject a concept of mode of subsistence defined in this way, we are left with no way of describing variation, or of engaging in effective comparison. The social constructionist approach seems to rule out in principle the legitimate separation of the technical from the social, apparently overriding distinctions which experience has shown to be analytically useful. It seems to me that if we do not distinguish between mode of production and mode of subsistence, as between the social and the 'technical', people will anyway continue to do so implicitly. Mode of subsistence is — if you will — a device which permits some degree of description and comparison without making assumptions regarding the generalizability of particular definitions or invoking typologies of a more abstract and general nature.

All this casuistry may seem interesting, but is arguably far removed from the realities of ethnographic description or archaeological inference. In practical terms the problem is that there is not always agreement on the meanings of labels for individual techniques, or on how best to classify ethnographically identifiable mixtures of techniques. Take for example the definition of hunting. Different writers, with different purposes, have defined this variously as something *humans* do (that is, making it a species characteristic), as a mode of intentional social production (Ingold 1986: 103), as active *searching* (by contrast, say, with trapping or scavenging), or as the acquisition of *animal protein*, whether by humans or animals (Potts 1984a). Each definition could be defended in a particular analytic context, though in general terms I would favour the third as a basal referent for a human cultural technique. It is not intrinsically any better, only more useful in most situations where it is likely to be needed. With Ingold, I would distinguish hunting from *predation*, which must be understood as a strictly ecological relation.

Most variation in modes of subsistence lies in the combination and relative significance of different techniques, rather than in differences between the techniques themselves (Ellen 1982: 128), while the comparative ecological effects of the same technique practised in different ways may be more significant than the effects of using different techniques. Thus, if it is difficult to agree upon definitions of techniques, how much more difficult it becomes to define assemblages of strategies used by particular populations, to establish what criteria we should recognize, and to distinguish them.

The remainder of this article does not aim to answer all these questions, even less provide a systematic coverage of all known human patterns of subsistence in space and time. But it does try to point to critical axes of variation and to discuss the dynamics of transition from one pattern to another. In so doing it begins from the observation that different strategies, and therefore different modes of subsistence, have different ecological profiles: in terms of energy transfer, limiting factors and carrying capacity, the degree of human effort required, their effects on the landscape, the cultural regulation of environmental relations, and so on. Indeed, one of the major advances over the last twenty-five years has been the refinement of our descriptions of subsistence in terms of ecological parameters, and a consequent scepticism towards simple indices such as those linked to carrying capacity (Ellen 1982: 41–46).

We are now able to compare different subsistence systems and their component parts not only in terms of technology (including equipment) or species exploited, but also according to gross physical manipulation of the ecosystem, total and patterned ecological inputs and outputs, overall and patterned human effort, variations over time (such as seasonal fluctuations), spatial distribution and proportions of human population involved; and the various measures of relative and absolute association and productivity which can be computed from such data (see Ellen 1982: 123–76). We are in a position to measure realistically the efficiency of different strategies, and the systems of which they are part, and to show that they vary depending on whether you take a short-term or a longer-term view. The short-term view is that reflected in simple input–output models based on, say, energy budgeting over a period of up to a year, an approach which underlies conventional neoclassical theories of economic maximization, as well as optimal foraging theory (e.g. Winterhalder and Smith 1981, though see Dwyer 1983) and neo-Darwinist concerns with reproductive fitness. Longer-term efficiency, though it may be concerned with the strategies of individuals, is generally less concerned with these than with the cumulative effects of the activities of entire populations on the ability to sustain a particular subsistence base, with the maintenance of reproductive viability on the population level, and with the reproduction of the social systems which make particular modes of subsistence possible, or which are dependent upon them. All of these factors have consequences for social organization, but social organization is never reducible to them. To highlight the difficulties of conventional typologies, when uncritically applied. I pay particular attention to unusual and transitional types, and also to the relationship between analytic descriptions of ethnographically known populations and the reconstruction of evolutionary and historical sequences. The biases evident in the choice of examples reflect my own knowledge and interests.

FOOD-COLLECTING POPULATIONS

It is usual to describe those modern peoples who subsist primarily by gathering undomesticated plants and animals as 'hunter-gatherers'. This usage is now so well established that it may hardly seem possible to eliminate it, although arguments in favour of its elimination are increasingly heard. One simple but obvious objection is that, looking at populations so described on a global level, most rely more on vegetable matter than animal flesh; while the extraction of aquatic resources and those populations which rely upon them have tended to be sidelined in general discussion (Palsson 1988). The term 'hunter-gatherer' deceptively suggests uniformity, although we know that there is variation in terms of subsistence strategies, technology and environmental impact. On current evidence, tropical and subtropical groups rely most on vegetable matter, while arctic and sub-arctic groups tend to include a very high proportion of meat in their diet. It has been suggested that in some temperate areas, large game animals may be selectively hunted for their fat, which serves to offset nutritional stress brought about by seasonal caloric deficiency (Speth and Spielman 1983).

Various authors have argued that hunting and gathering, in the context of the social relations of the 'band', should be distinguished as a distinct mode of production (Ingold 1988, Meillassoux 1969), rather than as a mode of subsistence. The qualification concerning the band is important, since 'hunter-gatherers' are not exclusively organized in band societies in the conventional sense. In this view, hunting and gathering entail a distinctive set of social relations, the practices of hunting and gathering themselves being self-consciously planned, alternating phases of activity, involving predation and extraction (foraging) but not reducible to them. This view is very much a reaction to the position that somehow hunting and gathering, as forms of procurement behaviour, are *external* to social relations (Ingold 1988). In order to avoid further confusion it is at least necessary to distinguish the purely ecological mode of engagement from the social, to distinguish in other words the mode of subsistence from the mode of production. The mode of subsistence we might describe as 'food collecting', a way of life in which populations extract from the environment without sustained efforts to regulate it. And we might distinguish food *extraction* from food *production* as different but often simultaneous processes. Prehistorians, especially, have often taken 'food production' to mean agriculture and animal husbandry, presumably on the grounds that in such regimes human effort is expended on the extracted species *before* harvesting. The meaning is more or less clear, but in attempting to understand major human evolutionary transitions it is problematic, suggesting that no production in the usual sense occurs in pre-agricultural populations. But if we do make such a distinction then we have an obligation to be consistent.

Today, the number of extant food-collecting populations is very small, and their distribution is restricted to just a few peripheral zones: the tundras and forests of the circumpolar North, the tropical forests and the arid savannahs – by and large, places where cultivation can be practised only with difficulty. There are now less than a quarter of a million food collectors, representing 0.003 per cent of humankind. But despite the paucity of their numbers, their significance for understanding human prehistory and social evolution, and for making informed generalizations about human culture and social organization, is immense. I have more to say later (pp. 203–4) about the inappropriateness of projecting back simplistic models of hunter-gatherer society onto earlier hominids; but, more than this, as sedentary agriculture has come to dominate global ecology and regional social organization, many food-collecting groups have become 'encapsulated' (Woodburn 1988) within wider social formations, of which they may sometimes be seen as no more than specialist components. Such populations may be involved in collecting forest products which enter the world system (Dunn 1975, Hoffman 1984), and are often dependent upon inputs from non-food-collecting groups for their biological and social reproduction (Morris 1982, Peterson 1978). In some cases there is historical, ethnographic and linguistic evidence to indicate that food-collecting groups are indeed pioneer offshoots of a previously or otherwise sedentary agricultural population, which have penetrated into afforested areas and ecotones where a purely extractive subsistence was more productive (Hutterer and Mcdonald 1982: 7); but in only a few such cases have the people become completely economically isolated and reproductively autonomous. It does, however, make sense to distinguish *primary* food collectors who have become absorbed into wider economies, from *secondary* collectors who are offshoots from them.

It is the absence of elaborate mechanisms for regulating the environment which is perhaps the most significant characteristic of a food-collecting way of life. As long as population densities remain low, the flexibility derived from not having to maintain environmental regulators is highly adaptive. In some temperate zones, such as along the American Northwest Coast, a food-collecting mode of subsistence has coexisted with highly complex, centralized and stratified sedentary social formations (as for example among the Kwakiutl). Elsewhere, however, the conventional pattern is of small groups undergoing cycles of concentration and dispersal depending on seasonal and other constraints. At the extremes of environmental variation, this may be exemplified by the seasonal migration of the Inuit, geared to the state of sea ice and movements of game animals (Mauss 1979 [1905–6]), and by the seasonal movements of the !Kung San of the Kalahari, whose band composition fluctuates in response to the condition of waterholes (Lee 1972). At both these extremes, and in many situations in between, flexibility in group size and band composition is the key to the ability to manage. Indeed, food collectors have sometimes been attributed with cognized modes of environmental adjustment which can better be explained as a function of low population density. Where seasonal fluctuations are not so marked, as in tropical rain forests and in the East African savannah, groups are equally small, even though movements are not constrained by basic limiting factors. And yet in all these areas, at least where traditional ways of life have not been subverted by national government policy or modernization, a diverse and balanced diet together with regular movement have contributed to good health compared with that of sedentary neighbours, while necessary work inputs are relatively low (Sahlins 1972). In short, in ecological terms such populations appear to be highly efficient.

Small group size, population mobility, dispersal and the general absence of any technical necessity to co-operate in the extraction of food or in the regulation of its supply, have meant that many food-collecting populations neither

202

require, nor have the opportunity to create, much by way of a framework of social institutions. Kinship networks and patterns, at least in Africa and Asia, are minimal; and organized political leadership is rare. Social control is informal, and groups are held together through a characteristic ethic of sharing. Whether this is conceptualized as a type of behaviour, a cultural rule or integration through face-to-face relationships (Ingold 1988: 283), sharing is an intrinsic part of the mode of production. Moreover, the distributive system thus socially realized is characteristically geared to the immediate consumption of harvested resources; individual surpluses are eliminated through redistribution, storage being either unnecessary or problematic for nomadic populations, especially under tropical conditions. However, there is a second group of populations relying on food collecting, where this now classic model either does not apply or requires considerable modification. These are diverse in their social characteristics, but the two best-known variants are Aboriginal Australians and the peoples of the American Northwest Coast. It is misleading to lump these two groups together in any serious comparative exercise: the first have a band organization and patterns of movement which conform in many ways to the classic model, and there are no formal political institutions or corporate kinship groups. They differ, however, in their marked investment in material things, in the existence of complex schemes of kin classification which determine patterns of marriage, in a pronounced male-biased gender inequality and in the scope of exchange systems. It has been suggested that Australian Aborigines and Northwest Coast Amerindians have one crucial feature in common which contrasts them with populations of the first kind, namely delayed as opposed to immediate consumption (Testart 1982, Woodburn 1982).

Turning from the subsistence patterns of recent and contemporary food-collectors to those of early hominid populations, though our knowledge of the latter is rudimentary and speculative, in the terms which I have outlined their mode of subsistence could have been none other than food-collecting. However, the consensus once embodied in the so-called 'Man the Hunter' paradigm (Lee and DeVore 1968), which involved the retrojection of a simple model based on the band organization of contemporary hunter-gatherers, has been questioned (Binford 1978, Foley 1988: 211–12). Although Binford's (1981, 1984) claim that early hominids did not hunt and ate little meat is probably incorrect, they were certainly not like contemporary hunter-gatherers (see Gamble in this volume, Article 4). Their home-ranges were not as large and it is not yet clear whether they foraged from a central place or home base. If home bases did not exist, it is even less certain that they shared food, or that labour was divided by sex. However, although the extent of hunting and of meat-eating (which are not the same thing) and dependence on wild vegetable matter have been difficult to demonstrate archaeologically, the general consensus favours an omnivorous diet, progressively shifting towards a higher proportion of non-vegetable matter as technology improved, and as the scale of social co-operation increased. Since we know from studies of free-ranging higher primates that modes of food extraction and diet can vary considerably from group to group, we must surmise that this was also the case for early hominids, as we now know it has been for modern humans.

What typifies these early modes of subsistence is (a) a relatively low range of variation, (b) restricted equipment or technology, and (c) low levels of collaboration in food-getting activities. By and large, individuals consumed what they themselves procured, and sharing was limited to relations between parents and young offspring. Thus, the formative period of hominid evolution was characterized by (a) an elaboration of cognitive and technical skills related to the procurement of food, well documented in the archaeological record, (b) increasing levels of social co-operation, though primarily between siblings, parents and offspring and between male–female pairs, conceptualized as social *relationships*, and (c) the emergence of a means of communicating about such activities and employing food symbolically to underwrite social relationships. Thus, through these formative processes there emerged what was truly a mode of production in the sense first conceived by Marx (cf. Marx and Engels 1977: 42). Amplification along all three of these axes, and the movement of hominids into different environments, led to greater differentiation of techniques within and between populations, often permitting extraction from a range of different biotopes. We may reasonably assume that the movement of hominids into temperate and arctic zones led to an increasing prevalence of hunting, since in these zones plant foods alone offered a more precarious resource base. Certainly, the Upper Palaeolithic hunters of Europe are the first that we can unambiguously describe as hunters and gatherers, with all the contemporary connotations such description entails.

TRANSITIONS FROM EXTRACTIVE TO REGULATIVE SYSTEMS

Attempts to control sources of food must have been characteristic of even the earliest stage in the evolution of human food-getting, that control having arisen from an ability to register conditions of relative scarcity. After all, if resources are abundant then no kind of control is necessary.

We might distinguish two types of control: pre-emptive and retrospective. Pre-emptive control is the use of techniques to maintain, concentrate or expand the conditions of reproduction or growth of other plant and animal species. Retrospective control is the conservation of extracted resources – i.e. storage. In this sense, cultivation might be viewed as storage in the live form (Gast *et al.* 1979, 1981, 1985). It is a mistake to assume, however, that the regulation of resources is confined to the activities of plant cultivation or animal husbandry, though ecological systems which find their *underlying dynamic* in regulation are indeed either pastoral or agricultural.

The extreme mobility characteristic of certain food-collecting populations appears to represent an adaptation to special conditions, either of high dependence on herd ungulates which are themselves migratory, or of great environmental instability. This may have typified a relatively early stage in human evolution. The evidence for food-sharing and home-bases from East Africa is rather shaky (Binford 1984, Foley 1987: 147, Isaac 1984, Potts 1984b). Foley (1987: 184–5) argues that early hominid evolution was characterized by increasing size of home ranges, selective pressure for cognitive skills, and home-bases as means of shelter which led to food-sharing and increased social activity. Isaac (e.g. 1983) argues that home-bases are an essential component of hominid foraging patterns: with a division of labour consequent upon the incorporation of meat into the diet, the separation of foraging activities puts a premium on food-sharing, which in turn requires central places. However, others have argued that there is no archaeological evidence for home-bases, and that the centrality of meat-eating cannot be assumed (Binford 1981, 1984). Potts (1984a) suggests that hominids would aim to spend as little time as possible in places where carcasses are found, because of threats from carnivores, and argues that home-bases were focused on sites where tools were cached, as has also been observed among chimpanzees (Boesch and Boesch 1983). As the sizes of foraging areas increased, so there would have been more pressure to re-use tools and materials (Foley 1987: 186).

Contemporary food collectors of the tropical forest are not particularly nomadic, and need not be. If suitable food sources are available then a remarkable degree of sedentism is possible, and with it the mobilization of large amounts of food for social purposes. In parts of South-east Asia and Melanesia extensive reserves of palm sago make this possible. For example, the Penan of Sarawak make considerable use of *Eugeissona utilis*, while elsewhere *Metroxylon* is the mainstay of clan-based social organization in permanent locations, although the degree of dependence is often obscured by simultaneous involvement in swidden cultivation (e.g. Ellen 1988). On the other hand, the extent to which forest food collectors can sustain themselves on root tubers has recently been questioned (Headland 1987), with the implication that they must always have had access to other starch staples, perhaps through trade.

Populations dependent on fishing may also achieve a sedentary life-style, ranging from the modest settlements of the Andaman islanders to the substantial villages of certain peoples of the American Northwest Coast. It was this observation which led Carl Sauer to hypothesize that fishing was responsible for the origin of sedentism. What characterizes such maritime hunter-gatherers (Yesner 1980) is a high resource biomass, the high sustainable culling rates which their resources permit, a high degree of territoriality, reduced constraints on population growth (with a wider age range of persons involved in productive activity), a high degree of sedentism, high population density, the reduced impact of seasonality, and a marine diet based on shellfish, fish and crustacea. Ethnographically, these conditions are met in the rich coastal habitats of equatorial north Australia, which supported high population densities. Higham (1989: 84–5) discusses an archaeological example from southern Thailand, dated to between five and six thousand years ago.

Moreover, there is now increasing evidence for the nucleation of settlement in the absence of animal or plant domestication, from the prehistoric Near East. Natufian data from the Levant have revealed permanent settlements supported by the reaping and storage of wild cereal grains (Henry 1983). It has been argued that this permitted more frequent births, and that the consequently increased population pressure amplified trends towards more obvious cultivation practices. What makes this possible, in addition to reliable self-replenishing wild stocks of food species, is exchange. But in other cases sedentism may have arisen through the necessity to store, either to overcome short-term and seasonal shortages or to fulfil increasingly important obligations of social consumption. From this it should be clear that storage need not be an inevitable accompaniment of cultivation, nor need food-collecting be an indication of its absence. As we know from numerous contemporary and historical examples, once sedentism becomes the dominant mode it may provide a temporary or permanent means for food-collectors or pastoralists to tide themselves over periodic or chronic environmental crises (as in the Sahel), while the need to control nomadic populations and perceptions of the moral superiority of sedentism may provide the impulse for states to intervene and forcibly settle mobile groups. At any event, once sedentism is established it sustains a dynamic of its own, of which an important feature is an inclination towards large group formation, complex property relations and elaborate social exchange.

There is now plenty of evidence for minimal regulation of plant resources (incipient or proto-cultivation) in otherwise food collecting populations, such as replanting the heads of wild yams and the protection of fruit-bearing trees. Those peoples engaged in 'wild' palm sago extraction, extract selectively, detach and protect suckers thrown out by mature palms and exercise certain forms of ownership (Ellen 1988). There is widespread evidence from Aboriginal Australia (Bailey 1980: 341) for small-scale husbandry, where cereal seeds and cuttings of rootstocks were occasionally replanted to ensure a crop the following year, and other practices were aimed at increasing the productivity of a range of animal resources, from emus to witchetty grubs. Fire was also used by Tasmanian, Centralian and Arnhem Land people to alter vegetation patterns and improve conditions for game and plant resources. Regular burning creates a mosaic of niches promoting both the variety and the richness of resources, and facilitating their acquisition. All this suggests, along with the preadaptation of knowledge and equipment (for example, grinding stones; see Kraybill 1977), that the cultural preconditions for the emergence of agriculture existed long before its emergence as a major mode of subsistence. It is additionally worth noting at this point that the knowledge base required for effective agriculture is actually smaller than that required for hunting and gathering.

THE ORIGINS OF PLANT CULTIVATION

The archaeological evidence for early plant cultivation is variable. At the time of writing carbon dates for the earliest appearance of obviously domesticated plants, by region, are as follows: Near East 17,000 BP (seasonal harvesting of various large-seeded wild grasses), Thailand 12,000–8,000 BP (rice), India 9,500 BP, Mesoamerica 10,000–4,000 BP (squash, beans, early maize), Peru 8,500–9,000 BP (gourd), South-east Asia 8,000 BP (taro), Japan 5,000–7,500 BP (grain), China 6,000 BP (millet), Ethiopia 6,000 BP (millet, sorghum), New Guinea highlands 5,000 BP, North America 4,000–5,000 BP (squash, sunflower, marsh elder) and Peru 2,000 BP (manioc). The transition to agriculture – which here includes both animal husbandry and plant cultivation – seems to have happened very quickly, within a time band of less than 4,000 years, though we cannot assume that it happened only once. It is now clear that the historic pathways to agriculture have been several, and were often followed independently in geographically separated populations (Harris 1977a).

The literature on the origins of pristine systems of plant cultivation is confusing – conceptually, theoretically and empirically – and it is helpful to distinguish between agricultural systems and the process of domestication (that is, those genetic changes resulting from human interaction with other species).

Agriculture, as practised today, involves various techniques which modify the environment in which a cultivated plant grows, namely tilling, artificial selection (including weeding), harvesting, storage and planting, though the acquisition of technology alone is insufficient to define a mode of subsistence which has had such radical social and cultural consequences. Agricultural systems have simplified ecologies, agricultural plants are – like weeds – colonizers of disturbed habitats, and plots are patches in which the earliest stage in an ecological succession is maintained. The primary effect of agriculture is to induce dependence on plant *domestication* which, by contrast, is a gradual Darwinian process of co-evolution of associated species of plants and animals, including but not only *Homo sapiens* (Rindos 1984: 129). Thus, the occurrence in *Manihot esculenta* (manioc) of sweet as opposed to bitter varieties is to be explained in terms of the increased fitness of those varieties more attractive to humans (Rogers 1965). Rindos has distinguished incidental domestication (the result of human dispersal and protection of plant species without the intention to do so) from specialized domestication which is a result of the environmental impact of humans in local areas culminating in a characteristic ecological setting. Agricultural domestication is the outcome of both of these processes, and this is what is generally meant by domestication in most of the literature on agricultural origins.

Theories of agricultural origin have been concerned with two main problems. The first is to identify the various kinds of subsistence stress presumed to provide the necessary impetus: human population pressure (Cohen 1977), competition between humans and herbivorous ungulates (Orme 1977: 42), climatic and other environmentally induced stress, the reduction of mobility (Harris 1977b), competition between human groups for scarce resources, and social perturbations (e.g. Bronson 1977, Hayden 1981). The second problem concerns the opportunities presented by favourable ecological circumstances for accelerated domestication and human reliance on agriculture. Of course, sometimes the cause of the stress may itself provide part of the mechanism; an example is the greater selective pressure in favour of rice domestication induced by decreasing temperatures in Northern China. But among the main attempts at explaining the mechanism of transition is the so-called 'refuse heap' model, which posits that domestic waste near human habitations allowed seeds to germinate in favourable conditions, that the convenience of this was recognized and that this led to the encouragement of dooryard gardens (Anderson 1969). Such a model favours the primacy of fixed-plot horticulture over swiddening (Harris 1973: 400), about which more will be said later.

The possibility of being able to generalize about causes and mechanisms seems nowadays to have receded. For example, the condition of sedentism can hardly have been pivotal in Mesoamerica, where domesticated crops are known to have preceded permanent settlements by several millennia. But it may well be reasonable to generalize about the dynamics of process – as Rindos (1984) does – and about specific trajectories in particular regions. Thus, prehistoric populations of late glacial Europe were heavily dependent on meat, but the retreat of the ice triggered off new opportunities for obtaining food from vegetable sources which were more cost-effective. Reed, Flannery and others have suggested that in South-west Asia food-collecting must have continued indefinitely in areas of abundance, but that a rising population is likely to have expanded out into less favoured areas. Such 'broad spectrum' (Binford 1968) food-collecting from many life zones must have led to the introduction of plants into new areas, resulting in their domestication. Flannery (1969) has suggested that in South-west Asia edible grains were selected, along with new weeds, from among many wild grains, while fallowing provided pasture for animals and irrigation new environments for palms, vegetables and so on.

In terms of processual dynamics the South-west Asian case seems to reflect a general pattern. Increasing environmental predictability of the agricultural system results in a shift from r- to K-selection for many cultivated plants[2]. Early domestication of both types (incidental and specialized) is characterized as a negative feedback process, whereas agricultural domestication is a positive feedback process, such that settlement amplifies and enhances those feeding behaviours which were eventually to bring about agriculture (Rindos 1984: 175). This explains its chronological rapidity in human prehistory, the broad-spectrum revolution which preceded it towards the end of the

Pleistocene in certain areas of concentration, and its sudden and virtually simultaneous appearance in all the major parts of the then inhabited world. As domestication proceeded through its incidental, specialized and agricultural phases, different species were subject to the most intense selective pressures, since the more highly valued they were as food, the greater was the demand for them.

It has been usual to draw a distinction between the cultivation of root crops and that of grains and forbs, and to suppose that the former appeared before the latter. This would appear to follow from the assumption that root crops required less domestication, and that from the human point of view their transformation into edible food was technologically simpler. But it is not evolutionary history which best differentiates grains from vegecultural plants, but rather their respective ecological settings: whereas root crops are typical of semi-humid areas with a short dry season, grains are typical of semi-arid areas with a long dry season (Harris 1973: 397–8). The relationship between seasonality and dispersibility in this connection is crucial (Rindos 1984: 168–71). Domestication proceeds along different lines in seasonal and non-seasonal environments, and vegecultural and grain-based agricultural systems have differing potentials for dispersibility based on differences in resilience. The high resilience of grain-based systems is in part due to r-selection lessening the number of constraining environmental factors.

This said, however, there is good evidence for non-grains preceding grains in certain parts of the world, such as in South-east Asia and the Pacific, where we find impressive arrays of roots, starch palms and fruit-bearing trees. Tubers provided the food base for the densely populated areas of highland Melanesia, but at least in prehistoric times, systematic arboriculture appears never to have taken off as a dependable resource base for large, complexly organized populations. This is perhaps owing to the long maturation period of trees, and to the difficulties of achieving sufficiently attractive yields per unit of land area and of confining plantations within an acceptably short distance from settlements. Worldwide, cereals have been the major food resource behind sedentary, nucleated lifestyles.

THE DEVELOPMENT OF ANIMAL HUSBANDRY

Both the archaeological and comparative ethnographic evidence suggest strongly that dogs were the first animals to be domesticated, the consequence of a pre-existing symbiosis between packs of wild canids and human populations. The earliest dates presently available are as follows: South-east Asia 12,000 BP, North America 11,000–13,000 BP, East Asia 9,000 BP and South America 8,000 BP. The significant point here is that dog bone from the archaeological record is associated with Upper Palaeolithic hunting peoples, thus indicating its appearance well before systematic plant cultivation. Among present-day food-collectors, *Canis dingo* has long been used by Aboriginal

Australians who moved from mainland Asia before plant cultivation began there (Meggitt 1965). The early North American evidence similarly suggests that dogs may have accompanied humans into the western hemisphere from Asia. As well as being used in hunting and for protection they were almost certainly eaten.

The domestication of most other animals seems to have been a product of agriculture, and to have first appeared in contexts where plants were also being cultivated. Indeed, Flannery (1969) has suggested that the sheep—goat—cow triad emerged as a response to high-risk agriculture in arid regions. We have evidence for the emergent domestication of animals from South-west Asia (sheep at 10,750 BP), Europe (sheep at 8,000 BP), India (sheep, goats and cattle at 7,000 BP), China (pigs at 6,000 BP), and South America (guinea-pigs and camelids by 7,000 BP); in each case this occurs at the boundary between Mesolithic and Neolithic cultural traditions. The evidence is almost entirely confined to changes in bone structure, though reconstructions of possible transitions from wild to domestic stock are now possible using genetic techniques and haemoglobin recombination. Additional early data on taming and herding comes from the deliberate dispersal of animals from their original centres of evolution through human agency. Where there is only more recent information for husbandry outside known focal areas of domestication (such as South-west Asia), there must be a strong presumption of diffusion, as in the appearance of cattle, goats and sheep in the Late Neolithic of mainland Southeast Asia (Higham 1989). The artefacts of human husbandry are less commonly found archaeologically, though there are early representations of animals being used for human traction. Understandably, most of our archaeological knowledge comes from populations which must have been largely sedentary, as material from nomadic societies with temporary camps is much more difficult to come by (Cribb 1991).

At present, most agriculturalists keep some domesticated animals, used for transport and traction, as sensors and drivers, as producers of manure, or as sources of both food and non-edible raw materials. The species involved range from honey-bees, through fish to monkeys, though the main groups have been fowl, dogs and ungulates. In some cases the ritual importance of such animals may match or even eclipse any material uses which they might have, as with pigs on Vanuatu, Tuareg horses, and sacred cows in Hindu India (Cranstone 1969).

The conceptual distinction between domestication, as a Darwinian process of species modification, and cultivation, as an ecological association involving close mutual dependence, holds for animal as well as for plant husbandry, though animal husbandry differs from plant cultivation in the sense that animals are secondary producers. That is, whereas plants can capture energy directly by photosynthesis, animals must rely on plants. Thus, the main limitation on keeping animal stock is the ability to provide adequate feed. The main response to shortage of feed is movement, though to varying degrees sedentary human populations have become involved in the specialist production of fodder. Swidden cultivators tend to have few animals as they do not produce enough to feed them, though in some parts of Melanesia considerable agricultural production may be diverted to the maintenance of pig populations, to the extent that they begin to threaten social and ecological stability (e.g. Rappaport 1967).

In the same way as it is necessary to distinguish food-gathering as a mode of subsistence from the particular forms of techno-social organization in which it occurs, so we must distinguish animal husbandry from the various forms of economic production of which it is a significant part. Failure to do so has caused much confusion in the literature. To do this it is necessary to place animal husbandry within the entire spectrum of possible relations between humans and animals. Broadly, three kinds of human–animal relations can be distinguished: (a) asocial predation, (b) social predation and (c) relations of domestication, taming and herding (Ingold 1980). Asocial predation occurs when solitary animals catch and kill prey, usually for their own consumption. Social predation occurs when the predators act as co-operative groups: such co-operation may be more or less innate, as in the hunting of pack animals, or cultural, as in humans. By contrast, domestication entails control of an animal's reproductive capacity (i.e. breeding); taming is the training of animals to live in close proximity with humans and to perform certain tasks, usually for some reward; and herding refers to the supervision of animals in the terrain. The distinctions between hunting and herding as productive practices, and between predation and symbiosis as ecological relations, are rendered most problematic in cases where it is common for domestic stock to interbreed freely with wild or feral animals, as happens with pigs in parts of New Guinea, or where the systematic reliance of wild animals on feeding in cultivated or fallow areas in turn provides (sometimes deliberate) opportunities for human predation (Linares 1976); or in reindeer economies where otherwise wild animals are owned and periodically rounded up for slaughter (Ingold 1980).

Most discussion of animal husbandry is dominated by the subject of pastoralism, indeed sometimes the two concepts are treated interchangeably. Various classifications are possible, but the main criteria adopted tend to be the degree of dependence on animals and the extent and form of mobility. Khazanov (1984) distinguishes six types, from pastoral nomadism to sedentary animal husbandry, including a focus on the way peoples engage in, say, seasonal altitudinal transhumance as part of a more complex subsistence strategy (e.g. the Gaddis of Himachel Pradesh (Bhasin 1988)). Pastoral nomadism is always characterized by animal husbandry as the predominant form of economic activity, by its extensive character connected with the year-round supervision of herds, by periodic mobility, and by the involvement of the majority of the population. Ingold (1980) offers a more ecological and encompassing definition of pastoralism in general, as that mode of economic production which uses the technique of animal husbandry (involving degrees of taming, herding and breeding), and where animal populations are allowed to increase naturally under human protection, are periodically tapped either parasitically (in milch or blood pastoralism) or by predation (in carnivorous pastoralism), and where social relations involve divided access to animals but common access to land. It is characterized by low human population densities, principally determined by the carrying capacity of the land for the kind of livestock in question. By contrast, ranching is that form of economic production where animals accumulate through unprotected natural increase, are periodically predated upon, and where social access to both land and animals is divided. In other forms of animal husbandry social access to animals is divided, though access to land, and the degrees of protection and regulation of animal breeding, all vary.

The label 'pastoralism' is often used to describe many peoples not wholly dependent on livestock for survival. In most populations so described it is an important source of protein in a broader strategy which includes cultivation, as in the East African cattle-keeping area, or among the Fulani of northern Nigeria. On the other hand, the Amerindian peoples who occupied the North American Plains in the nineteenth century, though often called 'hunter-gatherers', in fact relied on herds of horses and were therefore, strictly speaking, pastoralist-hunters.

In relatively few populations is the raising of animal stock the only significant technique in terms of human effort, nutrition and ecological relations. Among those populations unusual in this respect we may include arctic reindeer herders, some Bedouin groups and certain central Asian nomadic peoples. But, with the possible exception of direct transformations from arctic hunting to reindeer herding (Ingold 1980), pastoralism in that great belt of peoples stretching from Morocco to Mongolia can only be understood as the historic outcome of interaction with agricultural peoples. The emergence of nomadic pastoralism in central Asia was stimulated by an increase in the size of herds beyond the grazing capacity of the land around the settlements in a period of increasingly dry conditions. This resulted in a transition from sedentary foraging and herding to seasonal migrations in search of grazing, and then to mounted nomadic pastoralism, which existed on the steppes between the Dnieper and Ural rivers from about 4,500 BP (Zvelebil 1980: 254). All of these peoples seem to have maintained close contacts with sedentary groups, from whom they obtained cereal grains.

No one social form is common to all pastoral nomadic peoples, though the possibilities are constrained by a specialized system of production on the one hand, and the pattern of nomadic movement on the other. We can say that pastoralist social relations are focused on the family and on a domestic division of labour; that animals are generally husbanded by individual households, though sometimes by groups of households. Above this domestic level, sociopolitical organization is usually agnatic, segmentary and acephalous; it is focused on the lineage and is quintessentially tribal. It is these relations that determine access to pasture. If local corporate descent groups are to be found, they tend to be units of between one hundred and three hundred persons, holding joint rights in water resources.

All pastoralist peoples live close to carrying capacity in marginal environments, and exhibit a range of short-, mid- and long-term strategies to respond to hazard. The immediate response is, of course, movement. Movement is typically seasonal transhumance (as between summer and winter pastures at different altitudes, or between wet, tsetse-infested and drier, tsetse-free areas). Seasonality has marked consequences for patterns of settlement and social organization. Evans-Pritchard (1940) classically contrasted the Nuer in the region west of the upper Nile, which offers only isolated areas of higher ground for wet-season occupation, with the eastern Nuer, whose territory is characterized by more extensive areas of higher ground. Among the former, seasonal movements are confined and tribal units are of around ten thousand persons, while among the latter, though water supplies are more restricted, the area available for settlement is greater, leading to wider population dispersal and political groups of between fifty and sixty thousand persons. Another example of water sensitivity in social organization is found in the Karimojong cluster of Kenya-Uganda. Here, as we move from the Jie to the Karimojong to the Turkana, we find that agnatically related groups split up at an ever earlier stage of development. This is correlated with greater uncertainty and aridity, and increasing marginalization of agriculture.

In the mid-term, as resources continue to decline, intensification of existing practices is the rule, though intensification of stock-raising may be difficult. It is usual to move to a broader strategy and to rely more on hunting, gathering and cultivation. In the arid climate of Karimoja, where poor crop yields are expected every five years and complete failure every ten, large cattle herds are an insurance against famine. The Karimojong also grow a drought resistant sorghum, which, although it does not store longer than a year, has its usefulness extended through social relations: ceremonial redistribution, begging and trading. In effect, people intensify through social storage rather than technical innovation. Other characteristics of pastoralist populations which serve their longer-term adaptive interests are slow population growth, due to a skewed sex distribution in favour of males, post-natal sexual abstinence, and delayed marriage encouraged by high bridewealth payments (e.g. among the Tuareg).

The practice of pastoralism on marginal lands, and the links maintained with agrarian peoples, have always meant that it has been subject to periodic decline, though this need not be wholesale or irreversible. *Sedentarization* is most usually associated with demographic decline following drought, a pattern which is well documented for the Sahel from the 1960s to the 1980s, affecting groups as widespread as the Tuareg, Somali and Fulani. But pastoralists have also been the victims of forced resettlement initiated by governments or resulting from military invasion (for example the Yörük of Turkey, and the Yomut Turkmen of Iran), partly because pastoralists have in places represented a challenge to the stability of sedentary polities, partly because nomadism is administratively inconvenient for national states, and partly because it has been thought to be a morally inferior lifestyle. But, less dramatically, there is always a steady but uncoerced fall-away of individual households which, exposed to particular risks, prefer to invest in land. Many of these changes lead to a shift in subsistence emphasis rather than a radical transformation, which is neither irreversible nor irresistible, though it may have some detrimental consequences for both nomads and settled people. However, at the same time there has been a progressive and accelerating increase in the vulnerability of pastoralists during the last half-century or so as market and political integration have reduced mobility and encouraged intensification, and as desertification has increased. The consequences have been in some cases peripheralization, certainly underdevelopment, and in a few cases the incorporation of a modified traditional pattern into a wider modern economy, such as in highly capitalized ranches or socialist collectives (Humphrey 1983).

AGRICULTURAL POPULATIONS

In one form or another, agriculture has been the dominant mode of human subsistence, in terms of the total amount of energy transformed and the populations supported, for some six thousand years. It established its dominance, and most of its possible forms, with remarkable rapidity. There is evidence of floodwater farming in Syria–Palestine from about 9,500 BP, followed by irrigation both here and in the Zagros by 7,000 BP (Sherrat 1980). During that time it has expanded, diversified and intensified, with dramatic effects on the physical landscape, global chemistry, plant ecology, human demography and social organization.

What is certain is that the socio-ecological dynamics involved in the independent innovation of agriculture differed from those involved in its subsequent spread. For example, once agriculture has been established on a systematic basis, the high live birth rates made possible by sedentism, as compared with nomadic food-collecting, may mean that the proportion of farmers to collectors over successive generations would increase relentlessly (Ammerman and Cavalli-Sforza 1972). Moreover, once farming was established there would be created a frontier between agriculture and food-collecting, initially highly permeable, with farming peoples adopting hunting and gathering techniques in pioneer situations, and increasingly remnant hunter-gatherers maintaining the option of plant cultivation (e.g. Nicolaisson 1976). Depending on the geographical region in which the domesticated plant and animal complex was to be found, and on the expertise of the farmers, this moving frontier could last from a century to several thousand years (Alexander 1977).

Any attempt to understand the relationship between agriculture and other aspects of human culture, social organization and population biology, must make sense of all its variant forms. The usual response is to set up typologies,

214

but all typologies are hazardous. The literature is bedevilled by classifications of putatively comparable forms based on non-comparable criteria. These contrast, say, 'horticulture' (a category based on scale of production) with 'irrigated agriculture' (where the key feature is the control of access to water), or hoe cultivation (defined in terms of a piece of equipment). In particular, there has been much criticism of the distinction between horticulture and agriculture (Sigaut 1982); the former is usually focused on the garden (a unit dedicated to consumption, ecologically diverse, characterized by the attention paid to individual plants, socially closed), whereas the latter is focused on the field (a unit dedicated to production, ecologically simplified, characterized by generalized attention to plants, socially open and collective). In addition, certain terms regularly employed in the analysis of agricultural systems prove problematic when subjected to closer scrutiny. In particular, planting strategies (reflecting *intention* based on one kind of knowledge) are sometimes confused with necessary responses to environmental pressure (reflecting a different kind of short-term knowledge). This is no better illustrated than with respect to rotation and fallow, which are both intentional strategies with deliberate ecological goals, as opposed to crop-sequencing and leaving land vacant as a consequence of there being no other option (Berreman 1978).

Though a few general (and understandably vague) terms are scarcely avoidable, and perhaps even useful, it is far better to avoid single all-embracing classifications, and to examine variation in terms of a series of technical, ecological and botanical criteria, namely: cultigens grown, crop combinations, cultivation practices, size and permanence of plots, equipment used and ecological consequences. Sometimes these cohere around ecologically and technically distinctive agricultural systems about which it may indeed be sensible to generalize. The most widely discussed systems of this kind have been swiddening and wet rice cultivation, though the generalizations made about them have often been contentious (for example, see Geertz 1963 and his critics).

Different cultigens set up different constraints and possibilities. In the first place, the cultigens grown are limited by *external* factors such as ecology, though this can be modified to a certain extent by human technical inputs. Maize was originally a plant of the humid tropics, though through selective breeding its range has been extended into temperate zones; while most tropical fruits can now be grown anywhere under controlled greenhouse conditions. Also, the critical limitations imposed by geography were more or less removed by European colonial expansion from the sixteenth century onwards, which mainly dispersed plants of American origin to the rest of the world. Cultigens also impose restrictions by virtue of their *internal* characteristics, though these too are subject to human manipulation. The restrictions include rate of maturation, resistance to predators, size of edible parts, and difficulties in harvesting, food preparation and propagation.

As I have already mentioned, a general distinction is often drawn between vegecultural and seed-cultural agricultural systems, that is in terms of the

215

method of propagation; and between tubers and grains in terms of significant edible parts. Between them, these two types of cultivation account for most calories consumed by humans (potato, manioc, taro, yams and so on, on the one hand; wheat, rice, maize, sorghum, etc. on the other). However, in contrasting tuber and grain cultivation we run the risk of downplaying the significance of other forms (Sigaut 1982: 356): crops grown for their leaves, nuts, fruits (especially bananas and breadfruit) and for their stalks, including locally very important sources of starch such as palm sago and sugar-palm. The main problems with trees have already been encountered; they require long-term investment because of their slow rate of growth, and at the same time they reduce subsistence flexibility and population mobility. Tubers can be productive (as in parts of the Andes and highland New Guinea), though there are limits on their intensification, and therefore − in the normal way − on the human populations which they can support. While under certain conditions they may require considerable inputs of labour, such as in mounding (e.g. Waddell 1972), in comparison with grains the technical knowledge and effort required for their successful growth is less. Most areas of dense population and political centralization are based on the domestication of a limited number of highly productive grains: wheat, rice and maize, particularly the first two. Rice, especially, can in some parts of the world be intensified to an extraordinary degree, both by selecting suitable varieties, by growing the plants closely together, by minimizing crop failure, and by increasing the number of harvests per year.

The limitations of individual species may be circumvented by judicious *crop combinations*. These may have both ecological advantages (e.g. planting nitrogen–fixing legumes) and economic advantages (where different crops have differing patterns of seasonality). The extent of combination varies from the promiscuous intercropping typical of some small-plot swidden systems in South-east Asia to the monocropping of vast areas typical of the modern North American plains. The crops grown place a restriction on the degree of intercropping possible. Most grains are better monocropped, which reduces the amount of weeding required and facilitates effective harvesting. Other techniques, such as irrigation, place limits on the numbers of different cultigens which can be grown together.

Manipulation of crop combinations constitutes a specific instance of *environmental modification*. There must be few parts of the world where agriculture can be said to exist without causing some modification to the environment. Minimal forms of modification include tuber or tree planting in open patches of forest; or planting tubers or sowing seeds directly adjacent to houses. Vegetation *clearance* is the first major form of modification, and we can also include *banking* and *terracing* to prevent erosion and to create space on otherwise less useful land. *Weeding* is a continuation of initial clearance, but is most typical in intensive grain farming. The physical composition of the substrate is changed through *digging* or *ploughing*, which may also lead to certain chemical changes. The moisture and nutrient level of the soil can be adjusted by fallowing, rotation, drainage, irrigation or by the addition of organic and artificial fertilizers. Of these, fallowing[3] is usually understood to imply something about the *degree of permanence* of plots, though vacancy itself or even the periodic movement of entire settlements does not necessarily imply fallowing. The humid tropics alone exhibit every degree of agricultural permanence, from fixed fields to patches utilized for less than one calendar year and then abandoned. Where fallowing is intentional, periods can be reduced and the nutrient level maintained by crop rotation. In some cases these changes lead to wholesale modification of the landscape, which finds its extremes in Ifugao rice terraces (Conklin 1980) and Dutch polders. Such systems can only be sustained through a very high and constant level of human input.

In terms of *equipment*, it has been conventional to make a three-fold distinction between digging-stick, hoe and plough (Forde 1934). Certainly, in each case productivity can usually be increased by moving from one to the other, though too much significance is probably attached to the distinctions, given for example the sophistication of pre-sixteenth-century Andean agriculture. What separates much agriculture from food-collecting, at least of the broad spectrum variety, is the paucity of equipment actually used. In many vegecultural systems the digging-stick and bushknife are the only tools employed.

Each of the variables reviewed above has important consequences for social organization. Quite apart from the advantages and disadvantages of a sedentary life-style, agriculture involves larger labour inputs than other modes of non-industrial subsistence, though the labour demands vary enormously from land- and labour-extensive swiddening at one extreme, to intensive cultivation at the other, where large inputs are required to maintain a system totally defined by human activity. Moreover, the vegetable component of production needs more investment in preparation (threshing, milling, cooking) and in storage. Both storage (Sigaut 1978) and long-term investment in particular plots of land and in plants radically alter property relations, make the appropriation of surpluses easier, encourage variation in output per owned unit and therefore promote the development of relations of economic inequality. The higher carrying capacities that can be achieved permit greater sedentism and population concentration, which in turn have massive implications for institutions of social control. The degree of political centralization and the formation of effective corporations depend much on the degree of permanence of cultivated plots and of human settlements, as does the size of these settlements. Agricultural settlement patterns vary from the complete dispersal of households (as in the Philippine Subanun) to maximum nucleation, though this latter is feasible only with the more intensive forms of cultivation.

One type of extensive agriculture which is often treated as if it were a well-defined combination of certain of the specific features listed above is swiddening, and because it has been written about so much it merits specific mention. Otherwise known as long-term or forest-fallow agriculture, swidden cultivation is a technique which involves the removal of forest or bush and a short cropping cycle of between one and three years, spaced with longer fallow periods. It may involve fallow periods of as long as twenty-five years under tropical conditions, and support population densities of more than sixty persons per square kilometre. Beyond that, however, swidden cultivation takes highly variable forms. It may be root-crop-based or grain-based. The degree of movement of the human population can vary from the rapid, unidirectional expansionist pattern of the pioneer Iban of Borneo with their preference for virgin forest (Freeman 1970), to that of the Mnong Gar of Vietnam (Condominas 1980) with a pattern where villages are vacated every seven years and where movement is geographically cyclical, permitting eventual reoccupation. By contrast, the Nuaulu of Seram (Ellen 1978) have maintained a swidden system with sedentary villages for many decades at a time. It must be said, however, that given its land requirements, the inner dynamics of swid-dening are expansionist; relocation of settlements can only be avoided if popu-lation densities are low, if settlements are dispersed and relatively unnucleated, or if there are significant food subsidies coming from other sub-sistence strategies. In the Nuaulu case, the system of sedentary settlement is only viable because of the undeveloped character of swiddening and the reli-ance on wild palm sago. Elsewhere the appropriate subsidy may come through trade. The swidden cultivation of cereals is quite demanding in terms of soil nutrients and the quality of land required to support a viable cropping and fallow system (Harris 1972), and it can lead to soil erosion and the spread of uncultivable grasslands if fallows are too short. Swiddening tends, therefore, to expand if it is not constrained by surrounding populations or geographical barriers; and without alternative energy sources it must be considered to impose limits on the growth of social and political superstructures (Harris 1972). Moreover, although as an agricultural form it must have appeared quite early on, it cannot easily serve as a model for the formative phase of plant husbandry. It is more energy-intensive than fixed-plot cultivation and anyway would have provided an improbable nursery for the early evolution of cultigens (Harris 1973: 401–2). It is much more likely to have been a consequence of population expansion and overproduction in fixed fields near settlements, as it still is in certain parts of the world.

AGRICULTURAL INTENSIFICATION

Intensification of agricultural production may be a response to demographic stress: an attempt either to release more food for a growing population, or to maintain levels of food production in a situation where environmental and social pressures are reducing the amount of land available for cultivation or – whether through disease or inadequate growing conditions – the amount of plant food available for consumption. It may also be an attempt to meet social

218

imperatives for the reproduction of particular kinds of groups and relations, or to meet the demands of exchange partners who supply necessary goods in return. As Boserup (1965 [1975]) has shown, people generally choose the techniques which yield a given return with minimum effort rather than the maximum yield for a given outlay of effort, unless they are under great nutritional stress. In some circumstances intensification occurs as a means of doing exactly this. Independently induced technological changes (innovations) may result in greater productivity, which results in population increase, which in turn stimulates more marked intensification. Population growth may therefore be cause or consequence, or both, and can seldom be treated as a wholly independent variable. (For a more extensive treatment of this issue, see Article 10.)

Intensification may be achieved in several ways. The productivity of cultigens may be increased by breeding for better varieties, or by improving growing conditions. The productivity of land may be increased by growing plants closer together or by increasing the number of harvests each year. Whether this is possible depends very much on the cultigen, the climate and local ecology. Grains, in particular rice, respond well to this kind of intensification, but root tubers do not. In both cases improvement in the growing conditions may involve new technological inputs: crop rotation, shortening of fallow, artificial fertilizers, irrigation, and more efficient equipment for the various stages of the agricultural cycle – soil preparation, sowing, weeding and harvesting. Usually, intensification is effectively achieved only through specialization and its assumed economies of scale: reducing the number of cultigens in a single patch, aggregating the patches of single cultigens, concentrating on one, but occasionally several, crops and reducing the total number of crops grown. Sometimes intensification may be avoided by improved technologies of storage and by ensuring that a greater proportion of the seeds or rootstocks planted survive to harvest.

The consequences of intensification may include, as we have seen, further population growth, higher labour (or other energy) costs and new kinds of labour, higher standards of living, and the ecological instability which accompanies specialization. Given such instability, the absence of buffers to cope with uncertainty may make populations more sensitive to crop failure, though the market integration which often accompanies specialization may itself come to serve this function where circumstances permit. The most extreme social and ecological consequence of intensification is *involution*, where the reliability of production is maximized through increasingly intricate agricultural arrangements and social relationships, but where the overall form of society remains basically unchanged (Geertz 1963). Despite its strong inbuilt tendencies to positive feedback, intensification is not an irreversible process, and there are known examples of regression, for example from the history and prehistory of Melanesia (Allen 1977: 175).

219

LOCAL SUBSISTENCE IN MORE ENCOMPASSING SYSTEMS

Nowadays it is difficult to conceive of the evolution of human subsistence systems, and the social formations whose reproduction they permit, in terms of so many bounded entities only occasionally coming into contact with each other for the exchange of material and information. Although global in scale, the trend towards the increasing openness of systems (especially in the last two centuries) is obvious. It is probably inaccurate to model the process as one of progressive incorporation of local closed systems; it should rather be seen as the incorporation of systems of varying degrees of openness. Indeed, it is advisable to begin from the observation that most human subsistence systems are to a degree connected, and that few have ever been isolated for more than a few generations at a time. We are thus presented with the notion of a continuous, spatio-temporal, biophysical and cultural landscape, throughout which all possible subsistence forms are distributed and which are in degrees of transformation from one to another. And there is no reason to doubt that this has always been so ever since the first sentient humans began to colonize the earth.

There is now strong evidence in the archaeological record for contact between early hominid groups, for the rapid diffusion of elements of learned cultural tradition, and for the integration during antiquity of vast areas through trade and exchange. From the ethnographic record, there is evidence of trade among food-collectors, such as the trade throughout Aboriginal Australia in stone and wooden tools, weapons, sandstone grinding slabs and narcotics. There were, moreover, complex networks of ceremonial exchange (Bailey 1980: 340). Such regions can often be appropriately visualized as interlocking ecological systems, redistributing energy and materials, and it is precisely this feature which promoted the positive feedback of historically significant innovations. For instance, the sophistication of Mesolithic trading networks in Europe furthered the rapid spread of plant domestication from the east, once local conditions encouraged it (Sherratt 1980: 111), while local systems of exchange in the Moluccas underpinned the production of certain spices, and their intercontinental trade, long before 1500. What the European creation of a global system did, in effect, was to increase exponentially the degree of interdependence between primary and distant secondary centres, and to leapfrog existing connections between local systems through which all contact had hitherto been mediated.

One implication of this view for our understanding of subsistence is that it subverts simple models of adaptation based on the assumption of homeostasis. There is no particular reason why certain kinds of subsistence system should be regarded as existing in an evolutionary steady state with a high degree of self-regulation. The segmentary system of the pastoral Nuer is clearly self-amplifying and expansionist (Kelly 1985), and many swidden systems are also. Such systems expand until checked by other endogenous stresses and by external barriers, both social and ecological. It is thus far more realistic to treat much adaptation as occurring through links with other populations (see Ellen 1984), and social evolution as the co-evolution of systems of various degrees of connectedness.

NOTES

1 This definition and the greater part of the next three paragraphs follow closely the postscript to an earlier paper (Ellen 1988: 133–4).
2 Where *r*-selection obtains, it works in favour of plants that invest their energy in producing the maximum quantity of seed. Under conditions of *K*-selection, by contrast, plants are favoured that produce only limited quantities of seed but invest their energy in maximizing its viability.
3 As has recently been indicated (Gast *et al.* 1979, 1981, 1985, Sigaut 1978), early historical meanings of the term 'fallow' and its cognates in other European languages referred to the several ploughings in orderly succession during the spring and summer in preparation for sowing winter cereals. The use of the term to refer to a period of rest is more recent. But while caution is obviously necessary in the analysis of historical European farming, the term is too well entrenched in its modern sense to be dispensed with.

REFERENCES

Alexander, J. (1977) 'The "frontier" concept in prehistory: the end of the moving frontier', in J. V. S. Megaw (ed.) *Hunters, Gatherers and First Farmers Beyond Europe: an Archaeological Survey*, Leicester: Leicester University Press.

Allen, J. (1977) 'The hunting neolithic: adaptations to the food quest in prehistoric New Guinea', in J. V. S. Megaw (ed.) *Hunters, Gatherers and First Farmers Beyond Europe: an Archaeological Survey*, Leicester: Leicester University Press.

Ammerman, A. J. and Cavalli-Sforza, L. L. (1972) 'Measuring the rate of spread of early farming in Europe', *Man* (N.S.) 6: 674–88.

Anderson, E. (1969) *Plants, Man and Life*, Berkeley: University of California Press.

Bailey, G. N. (1980) 'Holocene Australia', in A. Sherratt (ed.) *The Cambridge Encyclopaedia of Archaeology*, Cambridge: Cambridge University Press.

Berreman, G. D. (1978) 'Ecology, demography and domestic strategies in the western Himalayas', *Journal of Anthropological Research* 34: 326–68.

Bhasin, V. (1988) *Himalayan Ecology, Transhumance and Social Organisation: Gaddis of Himachal Pradesh*, Delhi: Kamla-Raj.

Binford, L. R. (1968) 'Methodological considerations of the archaeological use of ethnographic data', in R. B. Lee and I. DeVore (eds) *Man the Hunter*, Chicago: Aldine.

—— (1978) *Nunamiut Ethnoarchaeology*, London: Academic Press.

—— (1981) *Bones: Ancient Men and Modern Myths*, New York: Academic Press.

—— (1984) *Faunal Remains from Klasies River Mouth*, New York and London: Academic Press.

Boesch, C. and Boesch, H. (1983) 'Optimization of nut-cracking with natural hammers by wild chimpanzees', *Behaviour* 83: 265–85.

Boserup, E. (1965 [1975]) *The Conditions of Agricultural Growth. The Economics of Agrarian Change Under Population Pressure*, London: Allen & Unwin.

Bronson, B. (1977) 'The earliest farming: demography as cause and consequence', in C. A. Reed (ed.) *Origins of Agriculture*, The Hague and Paris: Mouton.

Cohen, M. N. (1977) *The Food Crisis in Prehistory: Overpopulation and the Origins of Agriculture*, New Haven: Yale University Press.

Condominas, M. (1980) 'The Mnong Gar of Vietnam', in D. R. Harris (ed.) *Human Ecology in Savanna Environments*, London: Academic Press.

Conklin, H. C. (1980) *Ethnographic Atlas of Ifugao: a Study of Environment, Culture and Society in Northern Luzon*, New Haven and London: Yale University Press.

Cranstone, B. A. L. (1969) 'Animal husbandry: the evidence from ethnography', in P. J. Ucko and G. W. Dimbleby (eds) *The Domestication and Exploitation of Plants and Animals*, London: Duckworth.

Cribb, R. (1991) *Nomads in Archaeology*, Cambridge: Cambridge University Press.

Dunn, F. L. (1975) *Rainforest Collectors and Traders: a Study of Resource Utilization in Modern and Ancient Malaya*, Monographs of the Malaysian Branch of the Royal Asiatic Society no. 5.

Dwyer, P. D. (1983) 'Etolo hunting performance and energetics', *Human Ecology* 11, 143–72.

Ellen, R. F. (1978) *Nuaulu Settlement and Ecology: an Approach to the Environmental Relations of an Eastern Indonesian Community* (Verhandelingen van het Koninklijk Instituut voor Taal-, Land- en Volkenkunde 83), The Hague: Martinus Nijhoff.

—— (1982) *Environment, Subsistence and System. The Ecology of Small-Scale Social Formations*, Cambridge: Cambridge University Press.

—— (1984) 'Trade, environment and the reproduction of local systems in the Moluccas', in E. F. Moran (ed.) *The Ecosystem Concept in Anthropology*, AAAS Selected Symposium no. 92, Boulder, Col.: American Association for the Advancement of Science.

—— (1988) 'Foraging, starch extraction and the sedentary lifestyle in the lowland rainforest of central Seram', in T. Ingold, D. Riches and J. Woodburn (eds) *Hunters and Gatherers, 1: History, Evolution and Social Change*, Oxford: Berg.

Evans-Pritchard, E. E. (1940) *The Nuer. A Description of the Modes of Livelihood and Political Institutions of a Nilotic People*, Oxford: Clarendon.

Flannery, K. V. (1969) 'Origins and ecological effects of early domestication in Iran and the Near East', in P. J. Ucko and G. W. Dimbleby (eds) *The Domestication and Exploitation of Plants and Animals*, London: Duckworth.

Foley, R. (1987) *Another Unique Species: Patterns in Human Evolutionary Ecology*, Harlow: Longmans.

—— (1988) 'Hominids, humans and hunter-gatherers: an evolutionary perspective', in T. Ingold, D. Riches and J. Woodburn (eds) *Hunters and Gatherers, 1: History, Evolution and Social Change*, Oxford: Berg.

Forde, D. (1934) *Habitat, Economy and Society. A Geographical Introduction to Ethnology*, London: Methuen.

Freeman, J. D. (1970) *Report on the Iban*, LSE Monographs no. 41, London: Athlone.

Gast, M., Sigaut, F. and Beutler, C. (1979, 1981, 1985) *Les Techniques de conservation des grains à long terme: leur rôle dans la dynamique des systèmes de cultures et des sociétés*, Paris: CNRS.

Geertz, C. (1963) *Agricultural Involution, the Process of Ecological Change in Indonesia*, Berkeley and Los Angeles: University of California Press.

Harris, D. (1972) 'Swidden systems and settlement', in P. J. Ucko, R. Tringham and G. W. Dimbleby (eds) *Man, Settlement and Urbanism*, London: Duckworth.

Harris, D. R. (1973) 'The prehistory of tropical agriculture: an ethnoecological model', in C. Renfrew (ed.) *The Explanation of Culture Change*, London: Duckworth.

—— (1977a) 'Alternative pathways toward agriculture', in C. A. Reed (ed.) *Origins of Agriculture*, The Hague and Paris: Mouton.

—— (1977b) 'Settling down: an evolutionary model for the transformation of mobile bands into sedentary communities', in J. Friedman and M. J. Rowlands (eds) *The Evolution of Social Systems*, London: Duckworth.

Hayden, B. (1981) 'Research and development in the stone age: technological transitions among hunter-gatherers', *Current Anthropology* 22: 519–48.

Headland, T. N. (1987) 'The wild yam question: how well could independent hunter-gatherers live in a tropical rainforest ecosystem?', *Human Ecology* 15 (4): 463–92.

Henry, D. O. (1983) 'Adaptive evolution within the epipalaeolithic of the Near East', in F. Wendorf, and A. E. Close (eds) *Advances in World Archaeology*, New York: Academic Press.

Higham, C. (1989) *The Archaeology of Mainland Southeast Asia: from 10,000 BC to the Fall of Angkor*, Cambridge: Cambridge University Press.

Hoffman, C. (1984) 'Punan foragers in the trading networks of southeast Asia', in C. Schrire (ed.) *Past and Present in Hunter-Gatherer Studies*, London: Academic Press.

Humphrey, C. (1983) *Karl Marx Collective: Economy, Society and Religion in a Siberian Collective Farm*, Cambridge Studies in Social Anthropology no. 40, Cambridge: Cambridge University Press.

Hutterer, K. L. and Mcdonald, W. K. (eds) (1982) *Houses Built on Scattered Poles*, Cebu City: University of San Carlos.

Ingold, T. (1980) *Hunters, Pastoralists and Ranchers*, Cambridge: Cambridge University Press.

—— (1986) *The Appropriation of Nature: Essays on Human Ecology and Social Relations*, Manchester: Manchester University Press.

—— (1988) 'Notes on the foraging mode of production', in T. Ingold, D. Riches and J. Woodburn (eds) *Hunters and Gatherers, 1: History, Evolution and Social Change*, Oxford: Berg.

Isaac, G. (1983) 'Bones in contention: competing explanations for the juxtaposition of artefacts and faunal remains', in J. Clutton-Brock and C. Grigson (eds) *Animals and Archaeology, 1: Hunters and their Prey*, Oxford: BAR International Series.

—— (1984) 'The archaeology of human origins: studies of the lower Pleistocene in East Africa 1971–1981', *Advances in World Archaeology* 3: 1–79.

Kelly, R. C. (1985) *The Nuer Conquest: the Structure and Development of an Expansionist System*, Ann Arbor: University of Michigan Press.

Khazanov, A. M. (1984) *Nomads and the Outside World*, Cambridge: Cambridge University Press.

Kraybill, N. (1977) 'Pre-agricultural tools for the preparation of foods in the old world', in C. A. Reed (ed.) *Origins of Agriculture*, The Hague and Paris: Mouton.

Lee, R. (1972) '!Kung spatial organisation. An ecological and historical perspective', *Human Ecology* 1: 125–47.

Lee, R. and DeVore, I. (eds) (1968) *Man the Hunter*, Chicago: Aldine.

Linares, O. F. (1976) '"Garden hunting" in the American tropics', *Human Ecology* 4(4): 331–49.

Marx, K. and Engels, F. (1977) *The German Ideology*, ed. C. J. Arthur, London: Lawrence & Wishart.

Mauss, M. (1979 [1905–6]) *Seasonal Variations of the Eskimo: a Study in Social Morphology*, trans. J. Fox, London: Routledge & Kegan Paul.

Meggitt, M. J. (1965) 'The association between Australian aborigines and dingoes', in A. Leeds and A. P. Vayda (eds) *Man, Culture and Animals: the Role of Animals in Human Ecological Adjustments*, Washington, DC: American Association for the Advancement of Science.

Meillassoux, C. (1969) 'On the mode of production of the hunting band', in P. Alexandre (ed.) *French Perspectives in African Studies*, London: Oxford University Press.

Morris, B. (1982) *Forest Traders: a Socio-Economic Study of the Hill Pandaram*, London School of Economics Monographs on Social Anthropology no. 55, London: Athlone.

Nicolaisson, L. (1976) 'The Penan of Sarawak', *Folk* 18: 205–36.

Orme, B. (1977) 'The advantages of agriculture', in J. V. S. Megaw (ed.) *Hunters, Gatherers and First Farmers Beyond Europe: An Archaeological Survey*, Leicester: Leicester University Press.

Palsson, G. (1988) 'Hunters and gatherers of the sea', in T. Ingold, D. Riches and J. Woodburn (eds) *Hunters and Gatherers, 1: History, Evolution and Social Change*, Oxford: Berg.

Peterson, J. T. (1978) *The Ecology of Social Boundaries: Agta Foragers of the Philippines*, Illinois Studies in Anthropology no. 11, Urbana, Chicago, London: University of Illinois Press.

Potts, R. (1984a) 'Hominid hunters? Problems of identifying the earliest hunter-gatherers', in R. Foley (ed.) *Hominid Evolution and Community Ecology*, New York and London: Academic Press.

—— (1984b) 'Home bases and early hominids', *American Scientist* 72: 338–47.

Rappaport, R. (1967) *Pigs for the Ancestors: Ritual in the Ecology of a New Guinea People*, New Haven: Yale University Press.

Rindos, D. (1984) *The Origins of Agriculture: an Evolutionary Perspective*, Orlando: Academic Press.

Rogers, D. J. (1965) 'Some botanical and ethnological considerations of *Manihot esculenta*', *Economic Botany* 19 (4): 369–77.

Sahlins, M. (1972) 'The original affluent society', in *Stone Age Economics*, Chicago: Aldine-Atherton.

Sherratt, A. (1980) 'The beginnings of agriculture in the Near East and Europe', in A. Sherratt (ed.) *The Cambridge Encyclopaedia of Archaeology*, Cambridge: Cambridge University Press.

Sigaut, F. (1978) *Les Réserves de grains à long terme: techniques de conservation et fonctions sociales dans l'histoire*, Éditions de la Maison des Sciences de l'Homme, Lille: Presses Universitaires de Lille.

—— (1982) 'Techniques et société chez les cultivateurs de tubercules: quelques réflexions critiques', *Journal d'agriculture traditionelle et de botanique appliquée* 29 (3–4): 355–65.

Speth, J. D. and Spielman, K. A. (1983) 'Energy source, protein metabolism, and hunter-gatherers', *Journal of Anthropological Archaeology* 2: 1–31.

Testart, A. (1982) 'The significance of food storage among hunter-gatherers: residence patterns, population densities, and social inequalities', *Current Anthropology* 23 (5): 523–37.

Waddell, E. (1972) *The Mound Builders: Agricultural Practices, Environment and Society in the Central Highlands of New Guinea*, Seattle: University of Washington Press.

Winterhalder, B. and E. A. Smith (eds) (1981) *Hunter-Gatherer Foraging Strategies: Ethnographic and Archaeological Analyses*, Chicago: University of Chicago Press.

Woodburn, J. (1982) 'Egalitarian societies', *Man* (N.S.) 17: 431–51.

—— (1988) 'African hunter-gatherer social organization: is it best understood as a product of encapsulation?', in T. Ingold, D. Riches and J. Woodburn (eds) *Hunters and Gatherers, 1: History, Evolution and Social Change*, Oxford: Berg.

Yesner, D. R. (1980) 'Maritime hunter-gatherers: ecology and prehistory', *Current Anthropology* 21: 727–50.

Zvelebil, M. (1980) 'The rise of nomads in central Asia', in A. Sherratt (ed.) *The Cambridge Encyclopaedia of Archaeology*, Cambridge: Cambridge University Press.

FURTHER READING

Anderson, E. (1969) *Plants, Man and Life*, Berkeley: University of California Press.

Barnard, A. (1983) 'Contemporary hunter-gatherers: current theoretical issues in ecology and social organisation', *Annual Review of Anthropology* 12: 193–214.

Bennett, J. W. (1976) *The Ecological Transition*, New York: Pergamon.

Bronson, B. (1977) 'The earliest farming: demography as cause and consequence', in C. A. Reed (ed.) *Origins of Agriculture*, The Hague and Paris: Mouton.

Carlstein, T. (1982) *Time, Resources, Society and Ecology*, London: Allen & Unwin.

Clutton-Brock, J. (1987) *A Natural History of Domesticated Mammals*, Cambridge, London: Cambridge University Press, British Museum (Natural History).

Cohen, M. N. (1977) *The Food Crisis in Prehistory: Overpopulation and the Origins of Agriculture*, New Haven: Yale University Press.

Ellen, R. F. (1982) *Environment, Subsistence and System. The Ecology of Small-scale Social Formations*, Cambridge: Cambridge University Press.

Harris, D. R. (1972) 'Swidden systems and settlement', in P. J. Ucko, R. Tringham and G. W. Dimbleby (eds) *Man, Settlement and Urbanism*, London: Duckworth.

—— (1973) 'The prehistory of tropical agriculture: an ethnoecological model', in C. Renfrew (ed.) *The Explanation of Culture Change*, London: Duckworth.

Ingold, T. (1980) *Hunters, Pastoralists and Ranchers*, Cambridge: Cambridge University Press.

—— (1986) *The Appropriation of Nature: Essays on Human Ecology and Social Relations*, Manchester: Manchester University Press.

Khazanov, A. M. (1984) *Nomads and the Outside World*, Cambridge: Cambridge University Press.

Lee, R. and DeVore, I. (eds) (1968) *Man the Hunter*, Chicago: Aldine.

Leeds, A. and Vayda, A. P. (1965) *Man, Culture and Animals: the Role of Animals in Human Ecological Adjustments*, Washington, DC: American Association for the Advancement of Science.

Netting, R. McC. (1974) 'Agrarian ecology', in B. J. Siegal, A. R. Beals and S. A. Tyler (eds) *Annual Review of Anthropology*, Palo Alto: Annual Reviews.

Rindos, D. (1984) *The Origins of Agriculture: an Evolutionary Perspective*, Orlando: Academic Press.

Sahlins, M. D. (1972) *Stone Age Economics*, London: Tavistock.

Ucko, P. J. and Dimbleby, G. W. (1969) *The Domestication and Exploitation of Plants and Animals*, London: Duckworth.

9

THE DIET AND NUTRITION OF HUMAN POPULATIONS

Igor de Garine

INTRODUCTION

As nutrition is one of man's primary needs, the quest for food occupies a large part of his schedule. However, food and nutrition have only recently become a focus of major importance for anthropologists. Richards, in the two books she published in 1932 and 1939 on the Bemba of Northern Rhodesia (Zambia), was one of the first to deal with food systems as a main topic. This was followed by a few scholars such as Firth (1934), Malinowski (1935) and Mead, who, with Guthe in 1945, in the framework of the US National Academy of Science, set up the Committee on Food Habits, and published the first manual on this theme (Guthe and Mead 1945). At that time the neo-Freudian 'culture and personality' movement, under the impulse of Kardiner and Linton, emphasized the importance of attitudes towards food in the shaping of personality (Kardiner et al. 1945). At the end of the Second World War the structuralist school was developed, whose principal advocate, Lévi-Strauss, identified food as a major field of investigation by means of which 'hopefully, one might discover for each particular case the way in which a society's cuisine acts as a language through which it unconsciously expresses its structure' (Lévi-Strauss 1968: 411). More recently, questions of food and nutrition have been dealt with primarily by researchers with interests in human ecology, who are concerned with the flows of energy involved and the estimation of foraging efficiency (Rappaport 1968, Lee 1965, Sahlins 1972, Winterhalder 1977, Thomas et al. 1979), and with finding clues about the food habits of our protohistorical ancestors (Lee and DeVore 1968, Clark 1968).

Nowadays the anthropology of food and nutrition is a fashionable theme. Study groups, such as the International Commission for the Anthropology of Food and Food Problems of the IUAES (International Union of Anthropological and Ethnological Sciences), have been set up, and publications have proliferated in the field of basic and applied research as well as among the well-informed public (Simoons 1961, Arnott 1976, Chang 1977, Bayliss-Smith and Feachem 1977, Farb and Armelagos 1980, Goody 1982, Harris 1985, Mennell 1985, Fieldhouse 1986). Systematic bibliographies have been published (Wilson 1979, Freedman 1981, 1983), but for a long time little advantage was taken of the fact that food is a strategic field in which, as Lévi-Strauss might have put it, 'Nature' and 'Culture' come into contact, and in which biologists and anthropologists can fruitfully collaborate. It is a domain in which non-tangible cultural factors such as food taboos can have a material, measurable effect on individuals' nutritional status and biology through their diet. However, the interdisciplinary work of Richards and Widdowson (1936) remained unparalleled until recently. Today multi-disciplinary research is spreading, allowing for collaboration between social and biological scientists in which quantitative data are given more importance (Jerome *et al.* 1980, Minnis 1985, Harris and Ross 1987, Garine and Harrison 1988), and in which multi-disciplinary approaches are recommended and methodologies discussed (Walcher *et al.* 1976, Yudkin 1978, Sahn *et al.* 1984, Pelto *et al.* 1989, Harrison and Waterlow 1990). In this field, the contribution of anthropologists is being increasingly welcomed by biologists and public-health specialists alike.

The nutritional adaptation of human beings has provided a good opportunity for dialogue and confrontation between those who argue that adaptation has a genetic basis, and those who attribute it to cultural change primarily affecting the phenotype. Sociobiologists and cultural materialists (Alland 1970, Harris 1978, 1980) have argued with proponents of idealist approaches (Bateson 1972, Goodenough 1957), as well as with structuralists (Lévi-Strauss 1964). The field of human feeding behaviour is immensely complex and difficult to study, and our present knowledge hardly allows the motivational and other factors involved to be deciphered. It is certainly too early for general conclusions to be reached. It may, therefore, be wise to adopt an intermediate, eclectic position between materialist and ideational theories of culture. As Keesing (1981: 51) suggests:

> conceiving culture as an ideational subsystem within a vastly complex system, biological, social and symbolic, grinding our abstract models into concrete particularities of human social life should make possible a continuing dialectic that yields deepening understanding [leading] us to ask strategic questions and to see connections that would otherwise have been hidden.

PREHISTORY

The earliest data available about the hominid diet come from the Lake Rudolf Basin and the Omo Valley in Kenya and Ethiopia. The study of the Koobi Fora formation in the east Rudolph area suggests that about 2.5 million years ago (Myr BP) hominids were already involved in the manufacture and use of tools, meat-eating and – presumably – hunting, that they were operating out

227

of a home-base, and carrying food to be shared (Isaac *et al.* 1976: 548). Early butchering sites show a variety of prey: several species of antelopes, pigs, giraffes and porcupines, and the bones of large animals such as the hippopotamus. At the same time, coprolites from the comparable Olduvai site contain remains of mice, squirrels, small birds and lizards, the types of animals which are still collected by contemporary hunter-gatherers. The hominid remains belong both to the genus *Australopithecus* (*A. Africanus* and *A. Boisei*), dated to about 2.5 Myr BP, and to *Homo habilis* and *H. erectus*, from around 1.1 Myr BP (Coppens *et al.* 1976: 530, see also Tobias, Article 3 in this volume). On other sites, such as Zhoukoudian in China, the coexistence of similar genera suggests that cannibalism may have occurred.

The rather unspecialized hominid dentition does not allow us to determine whether the diet was mostly vegetarian or carnivorous. Although leaf casts (probably *Ficus*) are available from the same Koobi Fora sites (Isaac *et al.* 1976: 536), we have no reliable testimony that human diets were vegetarian prior to 10,000 years BP. Fire, probably used for cooking purposes, was known at a much earlier date (from half a million years ago in Vértesszöllös, Hungary) (Vertés 1975). The better conservation of animal remains should not mask the fact that, as among contemporary hunters, the bulk of food intake was probably provided by plants, except during the glacial periods.

NON-HUMAN PRIMATES

Ecologically oriented anthropologists (Lee and DeVore 1968, Vayda 1969) have established a dialogue with primatologists (Washburn and DeVore 1961, Isaac 1971, Teleki 1974, Harding 1975) in which they have compared some of the most 'primitive' foragers, such as the !Kung San and the Hadza, with the most 'human' apes. Most observations are based on the chimpanzee, which offers the most striking similarities with human beings. Behavioural adaptations to hunting, tool-using, meat-eating and food-sharing are the aspects most commonly highlighted, since they suggest the birth of something like culture (Van Lawick-Goodall 1968, Teleki 1973a, 1974, 1975, Suzuki 1965, 1975). Among chimpanzees, hunting often takes place after long periods of feeding on vegetable matter, which suggests that, in addition to its nutritional interest, hunting may have a social function demonstrating collaborative relations. In a similar way, meat-sharing establishes temporary relations focused on consumption (manifested in interactions in which individuals beg or offer food) between the successful hunter and the other members of the group, perhaps a forerunner of 'table manners' in shaping social organization (Teleki 1973a,b, 1975, Hladik 1973, Wrangham 1977). Observations on chimpanzees fall short of demonstrating any circulation of food between groups, which is such a conspicuous feature of human feeding behaviour (Nishida and Kawanaka 1972, Mizuno *et al.* 1976). Unlike non-human primates, human beings do not lead a hand-to-mouth type of life. They do not consume simple foods but rather complex dishes, at different times and in different places from where their ingredients were obtained.

The learning of new food habits, as exemplified by the 'potato-washing behaviour' (Kawai 1965) observed in semi-natural conditions among Japanese macaques, and the differences in food habits between free-ranging groups of apes, both seem remarkably 'human-like'. Not all chimpanzee groups use stones to break *Coula edulis* and *Panda oleosa* nuts (Teleki 1974, Hladik 1976: 487). In Gabon and Gombe (Tanzania) they do not consume the same species of insects, although they are available in both areas. Chimpanzees use a fibrous vegetable food to chew with insects, consisting of peeled bark in Gabon and coarse leaves in Gombe. The combination of tasty insects and bulky vegetable matter is reminiscent of one that is common to human diets as well: a tasty sauce or relish including animal proteins to accompany a starchy carbohydrate staple. Though data on non-human primates can be used to construct models for the evolution of human food consumption and subsistence practices, we must consider such models as very speculative, owing to the lack of supporting data from archaeological sources (Isaac 1971).

SPECIFICITY OF HUMAN FEEDING BEHAVIOUR

More than any other species of animal, human beings are able to adjust their subsistence practices to diverse environmental conditions. Their remarkable biological adaptability as omnivorous animals, and the technology they have invented as social beings endowed with culture, enable them to live in the Arctic as well as in tropical deserts. No other species is confronted with the problem of satisfying its nutritional needs under such diverse environmental conditions. As long as they are able to fulfil a minimum of nutritional needs (and to draw, for instance, 12 to 15 per cent of their caloric intake from protein sources), they can thrive on meat and fat like the Inuit or, to the contrary, consume mostly carbohydrates, like many agriculturalists in Africa or New Guinea.

We have a general idea of human nutritional requirements, but the heated discussions which take place during the periodic revision of these standards, by a joint committee of international experts (FAO/WHO/UNU 1985), suggest that we have not totally come to terms with the range of human nutritional adaptability, so that some populations appear to subsist on diets which seem quite aberrant when compared with official nutritional standards. This is the case for inland New Guinea populations which grow tubers (especially sweet potatoes) as their staple food and consume, apparently with little biological damage, a diet remarkably devoid of animal proteins (Hipsley and Kirk 1965, Oomen and Corden 1970, Ferro-Luzzi *et al.* 1975, Fujita *et al.* 1986). The accepted figures concerning the energy and protein requirements of the 'reference individual' ('adult male weighing 65 k, moderately active in a temperate climate') have been noticeably adjusted over the past decade.

Table 1 Nutritional value of diets in different regions of the world (daily averages)

Populations and places		Kilo-calories	Total proteins (g)	Animal proteins (g)	Carbohydrates (g)	Fat (g)
*Inuit** (a)						
Barter Island	(winter)	3,800	160	160	418	164
	(summer)	3,170	157	157	380	176
Anaktuvuk Pass	(summer)	4,650	199	199	357	257
*New Guinea**						
Waropen (Nubuai) (b) – coast		1,460	9	7	347	?
Chimbu (Pari) (b) – mountain		1,900	20	0	0	?
Kaul (c) – coast		1,944	36.9	9.1	366	39
Lufa (c) – mountain		2,523	47.1	9.5	529	29
*Africa***						
!Kung San (d)		2,140	93.1	32.1	337	?
Evodula, Cameroon (e) – forest		1,634	40.1	11	251	53.7
Batouri, Cameroon (e) – forest		1,611	31	10	336	16
Douala, Cameroon (e) – forest		1,719	54.5	31	245	56.7
Khombole, Senegal (e) – savanna		2,028	62.8	20.2	299	75.6
Cabrais, Togo (e) – savanna		1,797	55.4	3.2	332	36
Golompoui, Cameroon (e) – savanna		2,220	85.1	13.1	408	28
Massa, Cameroon (f) – savanna		2,544	97	37	507	30
Chiga, Uganda (e) – mountain		2,051	102	0.2	398	12.5
Nepal						
Tamang (g) – mountain		1,845	50	3	392	17
Rural France (h)						
N. Brittany – oceanic climate		3,980	111	51	486	133.5
Adour – southern oceanic climate		3,220	108.2	51.2	443	107.5
Gard – mediterranean climate		2,690	88	40	358	73

Notes: *The following figures refer to adult males.
**The following figures refer to general average.

Sources: (a) Rodahl (1964); (b) Oomen (1971); (c) Norgan *et al.* (1974); (d) Lee (1969); (e) Périssé (1966); (f) Garine and Koppert (1988); (g) Koppert (1988); (h) Trémolières *et al.* (1952).

Table 2 Average daily diets of neighbouring populations in savanna and rain forest areas of Cameroon (simplified)

	Savanna		Rain forest		
	Agriculturalists Musey (g)	Agr./herd./fshermen Massa (g)	Agric. Mvae (g)	Sea fishermen Yassa (g)	Hunter-gatherers Bakola Pygmies (g)
Meat	14	11	201	26	288
Fish	51	162	45	220	19
Milk	0	47	0	0	0
Cereals	421	638	0	0	0
Tubers	0	3	713	789	770
Leafy vegetables	40	44	76	7	20
Pulses and seeds	122	23	83	30	10

Sources: Hladik *et al.* (1990); Garine and Koppert (1988); Garine (1980).

Suggested calorie requirements have decreased from 3,200 kcal in 1957 to 2,780 in 1985, and protein requirements from 46.5 g in 1965 to 37.5 g in 1985 (FAO 1957, FAO/WHO 1965, 1973, 1974, FAO/WHO/UNU 1985).

The variety of diets consumed by contemporary populations is so wide that it is hard to believe that the available figures all concern a single species (Tables 1 and 2). Obviously, however, local environmental factors impose particular demands on bodily functioning, and the adequacy of a diet in meeting basic nutritional requirements can only be judged in relation to these demands. For instance, topographical features condition the energy needed to move around, while climate and altitude influence the basal metabolic rate and the number of calories consumed in thermoregulation and breathing.

FOOD, BIOLOGY AND CULTURE

Human food behaviour is rooted in biology. There are universal, innate reactions to flavours in the newborn infant: positive for sugar, negative for bitter tastes (Steiner 1977). The latter may be traced back to the remote genetic adaptation of hominids consuming wild vegetable foods, who would have been warned about toxic alkaloid contents by their bitter taste. Rozin and Fallon (1980, 1987) make a point when they distinguish between 'distaste', corresponding to sensory rejection, and 'disgust', corresponding to refusal on cognitive grounds. Humans are social beings, their food habits are established during the first months of life, and they are taught to eat and enjoy what is normally consumed by other members of the group. Guthe and Mead (1945: 13) emphasized the influence of culture when they defined food habits as 'the ways in which individuals or groups of individuals, in response to social and cultural pressures, select, consume and utilize portions of the available food supply'.

MATERIAL CULTURE

Food-processing activities

A population's food and nutrition obviously depend upon the food resources available in its environment and on the material means available to exploit them. The human niche, however, is significantly broadened by the mobility of individuals and groups, and by the circulation of food in exchange. Nevertheless, the quest for food and its consumption are critical to all human societies, leading some analysts to accord priority to these tangible 'infrastructural processes' in the characterization of societies of different types (Harris and Ross 1987: 5). It has been conventional to distinguish between hunting and gathering societies, herding societies and farming societies, and to place them in an evolutionary sequence: however this typology needs to be refined, since more societies practise a mixed rather than a pure mode of subsistence, and in some cases populations which once practised agriculture, such as the Cheyenne Indians of the Southern Plains (Will and Hyde 1917), have reverted to hunting and gathering.

Hunting and gathering

This is the first type of food-procuring activity, probably going back among hominids some 2.5 Myr. For theoretical reasons, contemporary hunter-gatherers have aroused the interest of many anthropologists. Particulary after the celebrated 1966 symposium on 'Man the Hunter' (Lee and DeVore 1968), a somewhat Rousseauian stereotype was popularized of the altruistic forager, as opposed to the hoarding cultivator, making optimal use of the resources in his or her environment, and enjoying a good diet while spending comparatively little time in securing it (Sahlins 1972). Until recently hunter-gatherers appeared to fit this image fairly well. The !Kung San of the Kalahari desert in Botswana had access to game in abundance and for six months of each year could gather the very nourishing mongongo nut (*Ricinodendron rautanenii*) and other vegetable staples (Lee 1973). The Amerindian tribes of British Columbia, notorious for their extravagant activities of ceremonial exchange, inhabited an area so rich in fish and game that they could live an almost sedentary life. By contrast, peoples of the American Southwest, such as the Shoshone, had a more difficult time, with little animal protein available, and depended on the collection of acorns and pine kernels. In the case of African Pygmies, there is today some controversy (Hart and Hart 1986, Headland 1987) as to whether, because of the seasonal lack of food, they could subsist over a whole annual cycle in their rain forest environment without the help of neighbouring agricultural villagers. Hunter-gatherers usually live a nomadic life, moving according to the availability of food and allowing animal species to recover their numbers after having been depleted by hunting. They practise little storage, yet are often credited with a rather more secure life than cultivators. It is said that they treat the natural environment itself as their food store (Sahlins 1972, Testart 1988). But it is not a store that can always be relied upon. For instance, in 1950, north-western Canadian Inuit almost died of hunger as a result of the alteration of the migration route of the caribou, their main food resource, and were saved only by the prompt intervention of the Canadian government (Scrimshaw and Young 1976: 51).

Data on food consumption among hunter-gatherers are lacking in precision, giving only approximate levels of per capita consumption, and are based on very small samples. They indicate significant differences between populations and, within the same population, between subgroups (e.g. between !Kung and Gwi San, and between Bakola, Aka, Twa and Efe Pygmies). A few general trends, however, stand out. In most cases (except in the Arctic), vegetable foodstuffs provide the bulk of the diet; animal proteins (mostly meat) represent from 20 to 45 per cent of the total food energy intake. Seasonal variations are noticeable everywhere, although they do not seem to have much influence on general nutritional status. Hunters and gatherers cope with the uncertainty of the food supply by instituting a sharing system which allows the unsuccessful individual to receive a portion of the general bounty. For instance, the Aka Pygmies cannot eat the meat of their own quarry but can partake of the game killed by their fellow hunters (Bahuchet 1985).

Obtaining the necessary ingredients to cook a meal implies a division of labour and collaboration between the sexes. Women forage for vegetables and small animals, closer to the living quarters than the men, who generally undertake hunting and more dangerous collecting activities such as honey-gathering. The profound and extensive knowledge that hunters and gatherers have of the plants and animals in their environments has been very well documented − this does not mean, however, that all known species that are potentially edible are actually consumed. Thus, according to Lee (1969: 59), the !Kung San name 200 plants and 220 animals, of which they consider 85 as edible among the first category and 55 among the second. However, the daily energy intake is derived from 9 vegetable species only, among which the mongongo nut is by far the most commonly eaten (Lee 1973). Similar observations have been made among many other populations. Indeed, given the omnivorous capacities of human beings, the degree of selectivity actually exercised in their food choices is remarkable.

The foraging way of life depends on ample availability of land, freedom of movement and low demographic pressure; today hunter-gatherers are either disappearing or being forced to adopt a mixed type of subsistence economy. Hunter-gatherers may be vanishing but their trade is not, for it is carried on among most agricultural populations. Vegetables are picked daily in the bush to enrich cultivated plant relishes, and fruit and berries are consumed outside the home. Resorting to bush food also appears to be a very efficient way of coping with famine. In affluent societies, hunting is a luxury; game, mushrooms and even snails and frogs are prized delicacies (not only in France!).

Fishing

The fisherman's food system is very similar to that of the hunter-gatherer, except that food is collected from the aquatic rather than the terrestrial environment. However, fish are no more basic to the fisherman's diet than is meat to that of the hunter. In both cases, the staple is a carbohydrate. In South-east Asia, for instance, many fishing populations also grow rice and thus benefit from a well-balanced diet. In many cases, fishermen have to obtain a portion if not all of their cereal or tuber staple food from outside sources. Practitioners of a sophisticated fishing technology, these groups are also shrewd traders, basing their economy on exchange (Firth 1966). The marketing of dried and smoked fish or fish concentrates (e.g. *nuoc mam* in Vietnam) is among the most important activities in most traditional fishing societies. The Polynesians may be regarded as having outstripped all other fishing populations in their knowledge of the sea and of the habits of fish, in the array of fishing techniques they have invented, in their many ways of consuming fish (both cooked and raw), and in the central role they accord to fish in myth and ritual. The Polynesian food economy (as well as that of a number of Melanesian populations, e.g. on the islands of Vanuatu) is based on the complementarity between shore-dwelling fishing groups and subordinate, tuber-producing cultivators who live inland.

Herding

In the quest for food, herders are in a paradoxical situation. They raise domestic animals and, in most cases, are reluctant to slaughter them for food, preferring to use them for more prestigious social purposes such as providing bridewealth or creating a 'clientele' through transacting them as gifts or loans. Meat is far from being daily fare and herders have to rely on milk and milk products (but not to an extent that would jeopardize the growth of the young animals) and carbohydrates obtained by trading their cattle. The Turkana and neighbouring African tribes are known to bleed their animals and consume the blood, sometimes mixed with flour (Little *et al.* 1988).

The oldest remains of domestic animals have been found in the Near East. Sheep (*Ovis aries*) and goats (*Capra hircus*) are dated to around 8,000 BC in Europe, in northern Iraq (Zawi Chemi and Shanidar) and in Palestine (Jericho). Cattle (*Bos taurus*) are reported at about the same period in Greek Thessalia. In the same area, domestication appears to be contemporary with the adoption of sedentary agriculture (Flannery 1969). The range of animals domesticated by our ancestors was broader than in our own time. In dynastic Egypt around 3,000 BC, oryx and addax antelopes, gazelles, buffalo, and even hyena were kept for fattening, as demonstrated by an abundant iconography (Smith 1969, Darby *et al.* 1977). In the New World, however, apart from the horse (borrowed from European invaders), the Andean llama, the Guinea pig and the turkey, the range of domestic animals was conspicuously small. The same is true of Melanesia and Polynesia, where in many islands the pig (*Sus scrofa*) is the only edible commensal species which actually competes with humans for garden produce.

'Pure' herders are mostly nomadic and have to move according to the availability of fodder; their diet is subject to seasonal variations in the milk yield of their cattle. In Niger, among the Woodabe (Fulani) consumption varies from 0.5 l per day during the dry season (February to May) to 2.5 l during the 'rainy' season (June to September) (Loutan 1985: 213). Among the Tamasheq Tuareg in the same country, it is about 1.7 l year-round for male nobles, but only 0.5 l for servants. In both groups about 0.5 kg of cereals per person is consumed daily, and around 30 kg of meat per family (of 5 persons) every month (Wagenaar-Brouwer 1985: 232). Most of the time, cereals are obtained from agricultural groups, sometimes from former tributaries.

Herders, like hunter-gatherers, have a detailed knowledge of their natural environments and they often supplement their diet by hunting and gathering. Many societies practise a mixed economy in which relatively sedentary herding complements cultivation. As a rule, smaller animals, such as sheep and goats as well as poultry, are more readily consumed than cattle. Some of the most remarkable pastoral diets are to be found among the peoples of Mongolia. They raise a whole range of animals – sheep, goats, cows, horses, yaks and camels – and use their milk in the most varied ways: cream and butter (some of which is clarified), together with crumbled cheese, enrich the Mongol tea; the 'skin' of the milk, fermented milk (a base for yoghurt or alcohol from mares' milk – *kumiss*), curdled milk, and various kinds of cheese are also used (Accolas *et al.* 1975). The diet is supplemented by home-produced meat, purchased cereals, and berries and roots collected from the steppe (Hamayon 1976). Indeed, the Mongol diet is probably even richer in animal products than that of the Inuit.

Farming

Farming entails the systematic and repetitive activities of tilling the soil, weeding and harvesting. In the Old World, cereal farming appeared at about the same time as herding, around 8,000 BC in the same area of the Near East. Some of the older sites containing domesticated species of seeds are in the Zagros mountains (Jarmo) in Iraq, in Iranian Khuzistan (Alikosh), Anatolia (Çatal Hüyük) and Jericho in Palestine. Early cultivated wheats – einkorn (*Triticum monococcum*), emmer (*T. dicoccum*) and bread wheat (*T. aestivum*) – are present, as well as barley (*Hordeum distichum*) and millet (*Panicum miliaceum*). Pulses were available – peas (*Pisum sativum*) and lentils (*Lens esculenta*) (Renfrew 1969) – and also fig (*Ficus carica*), caper (*Capparis spinosa*), pistachio (*Pistacia vera*), and almond trees (*Prunus amygdalus*) (Flannery 1969). Evidence of cultivated rice, finger millet (*Eleusine coracana*), and pulses is reported from around 1,500 BC in India and Pakistan. In the New World, maize and squash have been dated back to 8,000 BC in the Tehuacan Valley, Mexico. As mentioned by Alexander and Coursey (1969: 422), root cultivation (of cassava) may have been carried out in the third millennium in the same area. The vegetative propagation of tubers is the dominant type of agriculture in the humid tropical lowlands of all continents, and is the only one possible in Oceania. It involves a broad range of species, the best-known being cassava (*Manihot esculenta*), sweet potato (*Ipomoea batatas*), taro (*Colocasia esculenta*), yam (*Dioscorea spp.*), cocoyam (*Xanthosoma sagittifolium*) and arrow root (*Tacca pinnatifida*). To these staples should be added vegetables, pulses, fruit, kernels and berries.

Although the life of cultivators has been less idealized than that of hunter-gatherers, their mode of subsistence nevertheless allows higher food yields to be obtained, permitting demographic increase as well as combating seasonal uncertainty. Agriculture entails a more sedentary life, more cohesive units of production, and in many cases more well-defined property rights, than is found among allegedly altruistic hunter-gatherers. Nowadays the agricultural way of life is central to any food system. Contemporary hunter-gatherers, fishermen and herders all have to rely to varying degrees on agricultural produce in order to secure an adequate, year-round subsistence. Agriculture is still the core of food production in the industrialized world.

FOOD SELECTION

Although humans are omnivorous, they are also selective in their food choices. What, then, are the criteria of choice? A frequently cited experiment, carried out by Davis in 1928, showed that newly weaned children, when given a free choice of foods, tend to make a selection which is not nutritionally aberrant, suggesting some kind of genetic predetermination. In line with Darwinian thinking, evolutionary anthropologists are inclined to suppose that human societies are making the best, most nutritionally sound choices among the potential foodstuffs at their disposal, and that the underlying motivations can be analyzed in cost–benefit terms. Even human sacrifice among the Aztecs has been interpreted as a response to chronic lack of meat due to population increase (Harner 1977, Harris 1978). However, experience shows that people do not always make the best nutritional choices, and that lack of knowledge and technical ability cannot always be blamed for this. Neighbouring groups can make quite different choices. The Massa and Toupouri of Cameroon live in a similar environment, intermarry, and are fully aware of each others' agricultural techniques. However, the southern Massa, who grow only one staple crop of red rain sorghum (*Sorghum caudatum*) and constantly suffer from seasonal food shortage, have, until recently, refused on religious grounds (a ban by 'Mother Earth') to cultivate the dry-season white pricked sorghum (*S. durrah*) used by their Toupouri neighbours, whom they consider dirty and frivolous. In addition, this latter species was borrowed from their common enemy, the Fulani, and they prefer to assert their cultural autonomy on symbolic grounds rather than to solve their material food problem (Garine 1980). Similarly, it is difficult to find any nutritional rationale for the ban on the consumption of animals (and animal proteins) decreed by Hinduism on the grounds of a respect for life (*ahimsa*).

To paraphrase Lévi-Strauss (1962a: 128), foods which are good to think are not necessarily biologically good to eat. Katz *et al.* (1975) have shown how the use of alkaline water to cook maize in Mexico optimizes the vitamin PP value of this food and prevents pellagra. But negative examples can as readily be cited: the Gurage of Ethiopia toil over a very unsatisfactory staple food, the false banana (*Ensete edulis*), which contains mainly starch, whereas they could cultivate a much more nourishing one (Shack 1966). And although traditional societies manage to store foods of vegetable origin, especially cereals, rather successfully, they are not always so good at preserving animal protein foods, which are often consumed in a state of slight decay, with unfortunate gastric consequences. Greens are often dried in the sun or boiled for hours, reducing their vitamin B and C contents.

The weaning diet is an obvious area in which traditional societies display what, in Darwinian terms, would be regarded as maladaptive habits. Infants are usually properly breast-fed, although sometimes for too long. When the time for weaning comes, they are given what is considered culturally or symbolically to be the most secure and nourishing food – 'the daily bread', a carbohydrate staple. If it happens to be a cereal containing protein, the infant is better off than if it is a tuber. Animal proteins are seldom offered; they are frequently unfresh and are empirically known to cause digestive troubles. People lack any engrained knowledge of the specific protein needs of growing children. The children often suffer from malnutrition, one of the main causes of death at this age. This might, of course, be interpreted by some adaptationists as a providentially inbuilt system, which functions to ease demographic pressure.

Nor is there any spontaneous tendency in Western urban populations to adapt their diet to the conditions of sedentary life. Many urban dwellers exercise too little and eat too much. Offered an unlimited choice, they often pick foods which are rich in proteins, fats and sugar, and are conducive to degenerative disease. People can even go one step further, whether for reasons of prestige or psychopathology, and ingest food, alcoholic drinks and drugs which are clearly detrimental to health. One example will suffice: the Japanese Puffer fish, fugu (*Tetrodon ostechtyes*), whose liver and genital organs contain a deadly poison, is served in fashionable restaurants and takes its toll of victims, who are stimulated by the risk involved.

In nutritional terms, there is no more reason to attribute wisdom than folly to humanity. Human societies attain various nutritional states through the diets they have chosen, whether on the basis of empirical experience or for symbolic reasons. Diets are viable, not optimal, and – objectively – some groups enjoy a better nutritional status and physical health than others. Malnutrition and undernutrition, whether seasonal or permanent, have diverse effects on the biology of various categories of individuals, their demography, and their work capacity. Nutrition also affects their personality, their style of social life as well as what Durkheim (1938: 110) called their 'collective consciousness', more or less overtly displayed in the sharing system, valued body image, magico-religious life, myths and many aspects of oral tradition.

STAPLE FOODS

Every society has its daily bread, which Jelliffe (1967: 279) called its 'cultural superfood'. This is always a carbohydrate and usually contributes the greatest proportion of energy to the diet. At the global level the staples are rather few (see Table 3).

A distinctive feature of human food systems is that in many cases staple foods are of foreign origin (Table 4). Cassava and maize are the cultural super-foods of many populations in equatorial Africa, although they are of American origin. Potatoes are the staple of many Himalayan groups, cassava and sweet potatoes are the daily bread of Indonesian and Melanesian populations and can be found in the remotest valleys of central New Guinea. The discovery of the Eastern and Western Indies as well as of America triggered the distribution of many foodstuffs throughout the world. The spread of cassava and rice was linked to the colonial system. The expansion of Western civilization is presently contributing to the distribution of wheat throughout the world. The same applies to secondary foodstuffs and, of course, to spices. Tomatoes, of American origin, are consumed everywhere. Surprisingly, the chilli pepper (*Capsicum annuum*), which is a symbol of good luck and virility around the Mediterranean, originated in the New World.

SEASONALITY

Seasonality is a common dimension of all traditional food systems (Garine and Harrison 1988). It has recently been documented in equatorial climates, where it had not been supposed to occur (Pagezy 1988b, Bahuchet 1985, Hladik *et al*. 1990). Only recently have Western civilizations eradicated seasonal food uncertainty – to replace it by food insecurity linked to income. Seasonality has biological, psychological and social consequences. Of course, these have to be interpreted according to local conditions, both as they objectively occur and as they are culturally perceived. Seasonal fluctuations range from well-accepted, predictable periods of shortage to catastrophic, keenly felt famines (Chambers *et al*. 1981, Garine and Koppert 1990). They elicit material responses (with biological consequences) in relation to priorities regarding food production, money expenditure and the management of stores. At an

Table 3 Main staples (in millions of tons)

Wheat	513			Maize	481
Rice	470			Barley	176
Sorghum	81			Millet	31
Potatoes	226	Sweet Potatoes	170	Cassava	136

Source: FAO 1986.

239

Table 4 Geographical origin of main food plants

Europe	Mediterranean, Near East and Persia	India, Himalaya and Central China	South and East Asia, Oceania	Africa	America
Beet (*Beta vulgaris*)	Emmer (*Triticum dicoccum*)	Foxtail millet (*Setaria italica*)	Rice (*Oryza sativa*)	Finger millet (*Eleusine coracana*)	Maize (*Zea mays*)
Chicory (*Cichorium intibus*)	Einkorn (*Triticum monococcum*)	Buckwheat (*Fagopyrum esculentum*)		Bulrush millet (*Pennisetum* sp.)	
Cabbage (*Brassica oleracea*)	Breadwheat (*Triticum aestivum*)		Soybean (*Glycine max*)	Guinea corn (*Sorghum* sp.)	Common bean (*Phaseolus vulgaris*)
Swede (*Brassica napobrassica*)	Barley (*Hordeum* sp.)	Chickpea (*Cicer arietum*)	Yam bean (*Pueraria lobata*)	African rice (*Oryza glaberrima*)	Ground-nut (*Arachis hypogea*)
	Rye (*Secale cereale*)	Black gram (*Phaseolus mungo*)		Hungry rice (*Digitaria exilis*)	
	Oats (*Avena* sp.)	Hyacinth bean (*Dolichos lablab*)	Arrowroot (*Canna orientalis*)		Irish potato (*Solanum tuberosum*)
	Millet (*Panicum miliaceum*)	Sesame (*Sesamum indicum*)	Taro (*Colocasia esculenta*)	Bambara groundnut (*Voandzeia subterranea*)	Sweet potato (*Ipomoea batatas*)
			Asiatic yams (*Dioscorea alata; D. esculenta; D. opposita; D. bulbifera*)	Pigeon pea (*Cajanus cajan*)	American arrowroot (*Marantha arundinacea*)
	Lentil (*Lens esculenta*)	Ginger (*Zingiber officinale*)		Cow-pea (*Vigna unguiculata*)	American yam (*Dioscorea trifida; D. convulvacea*)

Europe	Mediterranean, Near East and Persia	India, Himalaya and Central China	South and East Asia, Oceania	Africa	America
	Pea (*Pisum sativum*)		Chinese cabbage (*Brassica sinensis*)		American cocoyam (*Xanthosoma sagittifolium*) Ullucu (*Ullucus tuberosus*)
	Broad bean (*Vicia faba*)	Calabash (*Lagenaria vulgaris*)	Sugarcane (*Saccharum officinarum*)	African yams (*Dioscorea cayenensis-rotundata; D. dumetorum*)	
		Cucumber (*Cucumis sativus*) Eggplant (*Solanum melongena*)			Cassava (*Manihot utilissima*)
	Sweet cyperus (*Cyperus esculentus*) Carrot (*Daucus carota*) Parsnip (*Pastinaca sativa*)	Mustard (*Brassica juncea*) Amaranth (*Amaranthus* sp.)	Palmyra palm (*Borassus flabellifer*) Sago (*Metroxylon* sp) Banana (*Musa sapientum*)	Watermelon (*Citrullus vulgaris*) Roselle (*Hibiscus sabdariffa*)	Tomato (*Lycopersicum esculentum*) Peppers (*Capsicum* sp.) Marrow (*Cucurbita pepo*)
	Celery (*Apium graveolens*) Turnip (*Brassica rapa*) Radish (*Raphanus sativus*)	Basil (*Ocimum basilicum*) Mango (*Mangifera indica*)	Coconut (*Cocos nucifera*) Breadfruit (*Artocarpus altilis*) Jackfruit (*Artocarpus orientalis*)	Okra (*Hibiscus esculentus*)	Pumpkin (*Cucurbita maxima*)
	Onion (*Allium cepa*) Garlic (*Allium sativum*) Spinach (*Spinacea oleracea*)	Citrus fruits (*Citrus* sp.)	Grapefruit (*Citrus maxima*) Litchi (*Litchi chinensis*) Longan (*Euphoria longana*)	Date (*Phoenix dactylifera*) Oil palm (*Elaeis guineensis*)	Avocado (*Persea gratissima*) Chayote (*Sechium edule*)

(continued)

Table 4 Continued

Europe	Mediterranean, Near East and Persia	India, Himalaya and Central China	South and East Asia, Oceania	Africa	America
	Asparagus (*Asparagus officinalis*)		Durian (*Durianus zibethinus*)		Pineapple (*Ananas comosus*)
	Artichoke (*Cynara scolymus*)		Rambutan (*Nephelium lappaceum*)		Quinoa (*Chenopodium quinoa*)
	Lettuce (*Lactuca sativa*)		Mangosteen (*Garcinia mangostana*)		
					Cashew (*Anacardium occidentale*)
					Pecan nut (*Carya pecan*)
	Grapes (*Vitis vinifera*)				Guava (*Psidium guajava*)
	Almond (*Prunus amygdalus*)				Papaya (*Carica papaya*)
	Fig (*Ficus carica*)				Guanabanana (*Annona muricata*)
	Olive tree (*Olea europea*)				
	Plums, cherries, peaches, apricots (*Prunus* sp.)				
	Apples (*Malus* sp.)				
	Pears (*Pirus* sp.)				
	Chestnut (*Castanea* sp.)				
	Walnut (*Juglans regia*)				
	Hazel nut (*Corylus* sp.)				

organizational level, they involve the mobilization of social networks. Finally, in the symbolic field, they stimulate ritual responses influencing the psychological well-being of members of society.

It is not possible to ignore the emotional aspects of food shortage. Among the rain forest populations of Africa, such as the Oto and Twa in Zaïre, seasonal hunger – entailing heavy psychological stress and even having deleterious consequences for children's growth – is mainly due to the reduced supply of the most valued items in the diet. Fresh meat and fish, which otherwise accompany all meals, are present on only 70 per cent of occasions, although quantities remain at the acceptable level of 70 g daily (Pagezy 1988a). Hunger and various levels of resulting discomfort are defined culturally, and may well be due to the absence of a valued food, such as prestigious meat or the divinely blessed staple, rather than the actual nutritional value of the food consumed, which can be maintained by substituting less esteemed foods.

As argued many years ago by Kardiner (1939: 219) regarding the Marquesans, food is a constant concern in traditional societies, as displayed by people's overt behaviour, attitudes towards food consumption, body images and mythology. As demonstrated in the monumental work of Lévi-Strauss, food-related themes abound in myths which, at first glance, manifest a more immediate concern with food than with sex. The same applies to tales and other aspects of oral tradition, where themes of hunger flourish and gluttony and greed are constantly stigmatized. Becoming a starving ghost after death is a particular concern to the Mussey of Chad. The privilege of male initiates lies in having learnt where to go after death in order to be fed ritually by their surviving co-initiates.

COOKING

Following the work of Lévi-Strauss (1964, 1965), attention has been focused on cooking, since, beyond simple descriptions of the material phenomena involved, it lends itself to formal structural analysis. Such analysis is said to reveal universal patterns in relation to human thinking, such as the principle of binary opposition drawn from Jakobson's structural linguistics (Jakobson and Halle 1956). The 'culinary triangle' first described by Lévi-Strauss, and thereafter the subject of endless commentary (Lehrer 1969, 1972, Leach 1974, Goody 1982, Mennell 1985), purports to illustrate how 'gustemes' (similar to 'lexemes' in linguistics) such as 'raw', 'cooked' and 'rotten', may be so connected as to signify the transition from Nature to Culture on which the essence of humanity is supposed to rest. Drawing upon first-hand data, and adopting a somewhat different structural–symbolic approach, Douglas (1957, 1972, 1977, 1978) has attempted to 'decipher' the symbolic significance of meals in the framework of specific cultures.

Cooking is a distinctive feature of human feeding behaviour, and it serves to modify the chemical and physical composition of foods, increasing the digestibility of plant materials with high starch and cellulose content and of crude proteins (Stahl 1984: 157). It may also reduce their vitamin B and vitamin C content. The fact that humans have been eating cooked food over a long period has probably influenced the biology of the digestive tract. However, many foods are extensively processed, in order to make them edible, before they even reach the kitchen: an example is the elimination of toxic cyanic principles from cassava tubers. These processing practices contribute towards the establishment of homogeneity of taste and nutritional value in specific food systems. Many groups, like the Hausa in Africa, soak and ferment their cereals before making flour, which has both gustatory and nutritional consequences. The art of cooking depends upon the available technology and the cultural priorities accorded to these activities. North American peoples such as the Huron, some of whom cooked in bark receptacles, or New Caledonians, who lacked earthenware vessels, or modestly equipped housewives from the Sudan, could hardly compete with the sophisticated chefs of French cuisine. Utilitarian constraints count also; for example, Chinese cuisine reconciles the need to cook all kinds of foodstuffs while using as little fuel as possible by chopping the ingredients into small pieces and cooking them rapidly over a brazier, stir-frying them in a wok, or steaming them in vessels comprising several tiers.

Each society also has its own cuisine. In some cases, it is codified as gastronomy (giving rise to an abundant literature) in which conservatism and innovation make the best use of available foodstuffs and technical means in order to provide sensory pleasure – according to cultural standards – based on taste, smell, sight and touch (texture, shape and temperature). African cookery uses a range of mucilaginous products such as okra (*Hibiscus esculentus*), which Europeans may find unpleasant, while the smell of a ripe cheese is distasteful to most Africans. Asiatic cooking has developed a range of raw, crispy, crunchy foods, privileging their physical qualities. In addition, Japanese cooking relies on visual aesthetics, as does French *haute cuisine*. Food habits perpetuate themselves as social markers on both everyday and festive occasions among populations undergoing acculturation, long after the rest of their original cultural features have disappeared.

In traditional societies, cooking is mainly utilitarian, preparing food to be ingested in order to replenish the stomach. It is centred on the preparation of the main staple, for example millet (*Pennisetum* spp.) among the Wolof of Senegal. The pounded grain is sieved to obtain various kinds of flour and semolina, steamed, and then cooked in water or oil to produce a whole range of basic dishes to be combined with a variety of relishes. Traditional diets would appear very monotonous to Western urbanites. The Massa of northern Cameroon consume sorghum porridge with 97 per cent of their meals. Many rural Béarnese, from southern France, have a snack of eggs and home-cured bacon every day of the week and are content with that. However, in most rural groups monotony nevertheless brings satisfaction through the daily renewal of a culturally conditioned sensory experience familiar since childhood.

Dishes have to supply a minimum nutritional need, but at the same time they have a hedonistic function, which is not necessarily attuned to human biological requirements. As White stated some years ago, 'man is the only animal able to distinguish between distilled water and holy water' (White 1949: 24). Human beings play with symbols and comfort themselves psychologically and socially at the same time as they ingest food and fulfil their nutritional needs. For Christians, bread is the body of Christ and wine His blood. In the same way, millet was given to the Sérères of Senegal by their God and came down to earth to save them from starvation. This explains why food is handled with such care in traditional societies. Food is a gift from God, not to be taken for granted; for this reason, during daily meals, people often eat their fill in silence. Playing and fiddling with food is the privilege of the sophisticated and affluent.

Food is emotionally charged and symbolically significant. Hindu Brahmans, obsessed by purity and pollution, differentiate between raw foods and milk products which are pure, *pakka*, and cooked foods, *kachcha*, which are easily polluted, and attune their daily behaviour to this distinction. According to Granet (1968: 309), the Hong Fan, one of the oldest (500 BC) Chinese meditations on the universe, teaches how to handle the various classifications according to which the general order works and the ways of adjusting the human body as a microcosm to the universal macrocosm. To the five elements – wood, fire, earth, metal and water – correspond human activities as well as tastes, smells, vegetable foods, domestic animals, zoological categories and viscera, all of which are linked to cardinal points, seasons, elements and musical notes. For instance, the note *kio* (east, spring, wood) stimulates the liver, and so on. There is a cosmic reading of Chinese culture, of which cookery is a part, which has to fit into the general principles of complementarity between *yin* and *yang*, in the rhythmic organization of the Tao universe. The same type of system operates in India; however, the feelings which accompany the episodes of feeding are distinct. While eating, the Indian Brahman applies the rules as a rather solemn medical code; restraint and fasting are in the background. The Chinese, on the contrary, indulge in food, even when undertaking rituals, as has been demonstrated in a masterly way by Chang (1977). In the various 'summons of the soul', the departing spirit is enticed back with delicious foods such as '...plump orioles, pigeons and geese, flavoured with broth of jackal's meat' (Hawkes 1959: 111).

A similar observation could be made by comparing English and French attitudes towards food (Mennell 1985: 102), apparently invoking Protestant puritanism or Catholic *laissez-faire*, but in reality translating into a familiar field the deep-rooted ethos of each society.

FOOD TABOOS AND PROHIBITIONS

Brillat-Savarin wrote (1885): 'Tell me what you eat, and I will tell you who you are', and a German proverb states: 'Man is what he eats'. The general principle governing food consumption by people in all societies, from hunter-gatherers to Western business executives, is that appropriate foods must be apportioned, symbolically and materially, to each category of consumer according to specific criteria. In this respect food is a counter point to the dynamics of social organization. The concept of taboo, applied to food, defines negative attitudes and behaviour towards food which should not be consumed or manipulated for fear of incurring inescapable damaging consequences. This concept is not to be mistaken with rejection out of mere distaste. According to Morenhout (1959: 529), in Polynesia a taboo was a rule according to which objects were declared sacred or forbidden. Preventing fruit or fish from being touched, it also allowed these items – and some individuals – to share divine essence and be venerated. Such items were considered to be charged with *mana* (a supernatural power, symbolically comparable to radioactivity), and contact with them to result in unavoidable magico-religious punishment. Compared with the notion of taboo, the terms 'food avoidance' and 'food prohibition' may be used more generally. They refer to transgressions which are socially acknowledged but whose effects can be more easily neutralized or remedied. Needless to say, each culture has its own notions concerning such matters.

Food taboos are seldom isolated beliefs. They are often indicative of an underlying structure into which they are inserted. The problem of understanding the association of animals with social groups, whereby each animal was taboo, as food, to the members of the group for which it was a totem, gave rise to a classic anthropological controversy between advocates of utilitarian approaches such as Radcliffe-Brown (1951, 1952) and Harris (1975, 1978), and those, such as Lévi-Strauss (1962a, b) and Douglas (1966), who argued that these prohibitions should first of all be interpreted as symbolic markers by which humans differentiate between kinds of animals in terms of the differences between themselves, and vice versa. Food taboos appear to some anthropologists of a structuralist persuasion as a good field for demonstrating the specific penchant of human beings for classification; nevertheless, as Tambiah (1969: 457) writes, 'cultures and social systems are, after all, not only thought but also lived'. There is no reason why utilitarian and symbolic-structuralist viewpoints should exclude each other, and food may be tabooed or fancied for empirical as well as for symbolic reasons. Besides, the debate bears specifically on permanent taboos on animals. There are temporary ones as well, and avoidances may also be directed towards plants or inanimate objects. Prohibitions are not necessarily totemic, nor do they always have to do with the consumption of the tabooed object, as we recall from Freud's thesis in *Totem and Taboo* (1969 [1913]), where totemism and exogamy are linked to the primordial murder of the father. Taboos may simply bear on touching or handling the forbidden object; for example, in Chad some of the Mussey have to respect a taboo on drinking sorghum beer out of a calabash gourd.

Permanent taboos provide some grounds for an idealist interpretation. It is fairly obvious that permanent prohibitions have a classificatory, emblematic value. They encompass human groups of various sizes, from entire religious civilizations (e.g. Judaic, Islamic, Hindu, Christian), through various kinds of kinship or occupational groupings to specific categories of individuals. An example of a very widely applied taboo is the prohibition on pork respected by the Jewish and Muslim civilizations and founded on very similar sacred texts (Leviticus XI and the fifth Surah of the Koran). This taboo has been interpreted in terms of hygiene, of economic costs and benefits, and also of possible symbolic significance. Leviticus XI (new revised standard translation) states:

> These are the living things you may eat among all the beasts that are on the earth. Whatever parts the hoof and is cloven-footed and chews the cud, among these animals you may eat. Nevertheless, among those that chew the cud or part the hoof, you shall not eat these ... the swine, because it parts the hoof and is cloven-footed but does not chew the cud, is unclean to you.

As Douglas suggests, pigs should not be eaten because they constitute something of a taxonomic anomaly in the order of the world as conceived by the ancient Jews (Douglas 1966: 55).

One of the best-known permanent food taboos is observed in India. In Hinduism, according to the principle of non-violence, it is forbidden to kill and, a fortiori, to consume any living being. There are very many variations in the observance of these prohibitions according to sect, region and individual idiosyncrasy. The ovo-lacto-vegetarians are probably the most numerous and have no difficulty in securing a balanced diet, but members of the Jain creed include micro-organisms among their prohibitions, and go so far as to filter their drinking water for fear of ingesting living germs (Mahias 1985).

Besides kinship groups, among some of which totemism may be practised, food avoidance may also characterize social groups whose membership is defined on the basis of economic and technical criteria. This is illustrated by the many endogamous professional groups encountered, for instance, in Africa (butchers, drummers, heralds, leathersmiths, blacksmiths, dyers, etc.) or in the caste system of India. Food prohibitions may also be linked to what appears in the cultural framework as the intrinsic properties of various categories of individuals. Women, who are sexually desirable, sweet, vulnerable and entrusted with child-bearing, should avoid foods which are considered symbolically and materially 'too strong' or 'too dangerous'. The list may be quite long and is sometimes interpreted by home economists as a product of the selfishness and gluttony of men. Permanent prohibitions may also apply to members of initiation or possession groups, and serve to confer on them a socially recognized status.

Finally, permanent food prohibitions may be the result of an outstanding personal experience, involving supernatural intervention. This is important, as it allows prohibition systems to be considered as dynamic structures open to historical events, as illustrated by individual totemism among North American Indians, where the initiate is forbidden from consuming his own guardian spirit. A permanent avoidance may also be due to a miracle which occurred to a living individual or an ancestor. For instance, a Mussey hunter lost in the bush was dying of thirst. He followed a bush pig and found a pond. From then on he avoided killing this animal and his behaviour was transmitted to his off-spring. Many clan taboos are likely to have originated in this way. Besides having a discriminatory function, they are also commemorative of past events.

Except in India, few permanent taboos have nutritional consequences. They often involve animals which are difficult to obtain, such as lions or leopards, or exceptional individuals within a given species, such as albinos. It may safely be said that permanent taboos act as social markers to display differences between individuals and groups, to influence attitudes and behaviour, and to facilitate the functioning of social systems.

Turning from permanent to temporary avoidances: these accompany important periods in the religious and social cycles of populations. Fasting periods in the framework of Hinduism or Buddhism could be mentioned, as well as Ramadan among Muslims or Lent and meatless Fridays among Catholic Christians. They aim to demonstrate the holiness of the episodes and the purity of those taking part in them.

Most of all, temporary food prohibitions stress the crucial events of individual life-cycles: there are the food avoidances of the pregnant, then nursing, woman; of the baby before and after weaning; of children prior to and after puberty; then the prohibitions associated with menstruation, and so on. We should also mention food prohibitions in relation to affines, where transgression is redolent of incest. Anthropologists such as Lévi-Strauss (1949: 40) have stressed the parallel between rules governing the exchange of foods to be eaten and that of women to be married, both distinctive features of human society. Food prohibitions associated with mourning, bereavement, physical and mental disease, symbolic aggression (for instance, through witchcraft or curses) should be added, as well as those marking crises such as going to court, or recovering from committing a murder, performing dangerous hunting activities, or climbing to collect honey. Finally, food avoidances are frequently linked to complex technical processes, often those involving physico-chemical transformation such as smelting ores, firing earthenware, brewing beer or distilling alcohol.

Food prohibitions all have an emblematic meaning. In this respect, the field of food obviously helps to publicize significant differences between categories of individuals, resulting in their differential treatment. Temporary avoidances, however, are mostly meant to have material therapeutic effects based on symbolic metonymical and metaphorical correspondence, relying on sympathetic magic as well as utilizing sound empirical knowledge. However, in this field, cultural imagination – which sometimes leads the way to scientifically sound nutrition – appears to follow its own course. Among the Douala, in Cameroon, a pregnant woman must not eat over-ripe bananas for fear that the mottled spots on the skin be transmitted to her baby, nor may she eat beef for fear that the child might dribble like the cow (Ekalle 1947: 73). Among Yassa adults, a man should refrain from eating the meat of the ground turtle because of its wrinkled skin and non-erectable tail! For the same reason, he should avoid eating cassava cooked in a soft-stemmed *marantaceae* leaf. Such prohibitions will not have a very serious effect on the diet of the adult male, but in some cultures pregnant women are forbidden access to most protein sources, as among the Abasamia in Kenya, where poultry, eggs, mutton, pork, game, several species of fish, and milk are involved (Ojiambo 1967: 217) – hardly the appropriate way to promote the birth of a healthy baby. It should be acknowledged, however, that the list of prohibitions which are known and described is usually much longer than that of prohibitions which are actually put into practice.

Food prohibitions may also appear as the more obvious corollary of nutritional beliefs which are more difficult to uncover. If women are given a restricted diet during their pregnancy for allegedly symbolic reasons, it is also to avoid giving birth to an oversized baby. Such births are difficult to achieve in traditional societies and failure is perceived as a tragedy. If women have to respect food taboos, they are also prescribed specific foods. Among the Yassa, a pregnant mother should eat meat from a chimpanzee – a sturdy animal – in order to give birth to a strong baby. In all societies galactogenic preparations are recommended to nursing mothers. The link between food and medicine is, most of the time, tenuous.

All populations have a more or less well-defined nutritional ideology. In some cases it takes the form of a structured theory. Humoral medicines can be observed in many contemporary civilizations: in the Arabian world, China, India, South-east Asia and Latin America. Basically they still follow the principles established during classical antiquity by Hippocrates and Galen, according to which food prohibitions and prescriptions are meant to correct humoral imbalances. For instance, food conceived as 'hot' should be consumed to counteract 'cold' ailments. However, one should be careful not to overgeneralize and to imagine that 'hot' and 'cold' are universal categories of foods, as there are also neutral, unmarked foods (Laderman 1981: 474, Mintz and Van Veen 1968: 90). Each culture has its own concepts and strategies in this field. In Malaya, for example, after giving birth mothers are perceived as suffering from a very cold state and must avoid eating squash, a particularly cold food (Laderman 1981: 471). The reverse obtains in Mexico, where newly confined mothers are considered to be in a hot state and are given cooling dishes. It is always important to distinguish the physical (thermic) quality of the food from the humoral quality attributed to it (Laderman 1981: 469). In the Malayan context, a steaming hot dish of squash would nevertheless be considered 'cold' food.

Food prohibitions make up a very complex field in which symbolic and material or utilitarian concerns do not exclude each other. Here, the only way to gain insight is by analysing specific situations from diverse viewpoints, before attempting any kind of generalization.

MEALS AND SHARING – RITUAL AND PROFANE FOODS

By contrast to non-human primates, feeding bouts in human societies occur regularly at fixed hours of the day within the framework of a group. Some are constant and strongly codified – we shall call these *meals*; others are more informal in relation to time, place and the composition of the sharing group – these we can call *snacks*. Both depend upon the artefacts used to contain and manipulate the food to be ingested, the dishes which can be presented simultaneously or sequentially, and the table manners which fix the way the food should be handled and consumed according to the social status of the consumers. There are different kinds of meals and snacks: in and outside the home, and involving central, secondary or peripheral foods in the local system (Figure 1).

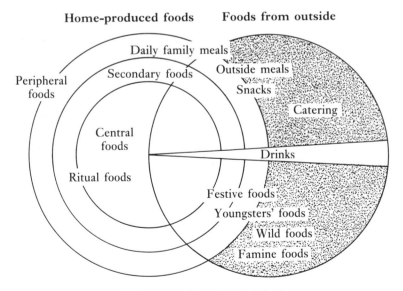

Figure 1 Diagram of a traditional food system

Ordinary meals

These usually number three per day, their time depending on the work schedule. Usually the most important one is taken at the end of the day. It corresponds to a home-cooked type of meal prepared by mature and responsible female members of the household, using everyday food products. Consumption groups vary according to sex and age. In many traditional societies wives eat the food they have cooked with their young children of both sexes and with their older daughters, and provide the men and older male children with specific portions. Except in societies where purity is an important issue, consumers often pick their food out of a common dish according to a strict etiquette. Specific vessels are provided for outsiders and individuals who are considered materially or symbolically dangerous, such as diseased people, menstruating women, elderly people, those suspected of sorcery or simply strangers. In other societies, individual portions are served on separate plates.

Ordinary meals offer the most regular opportunity for members of the household to communicate, and fulfil an important function in the socializing process. They can appear as a repetitive play in which each member of the family acts out his or her role, and demonstrates his or her status.

Festive meals

These entail a more elaborate cuisine and sometimes involve specialized personnel. Male cooks are recorded in China since the Shang dynasty, eighteenth century BC (Chang 1977: 11). In less sophisticated societies, festive meals offer the main opportunity for meat consumption. They involve groups of various sizes ranging from the household (or specific individuals in it) to large groups such as entire communities engaged in public, clan-based or state-sponsored ceremonies. Such ceremonies may be periodic commemorations or occasional celebrations. It is also possible to distinguish between those which put the emphasis on the convivial or profane aspect, like asking neighbours to dinner, and those stressing the ritual or sacred aspect, like partaking of the meat of a sacrificed animal during a communion feast. Social festive meals put the accent on prestige and covert competition − 'fighting with food' (Young 1971). Ritual celebrations demonstrate appropriate communication with the supernatural, as well as affirming participants' sense of belonging to the group. These two aspects do not, of course, exclude each other, but the distinction between ritual and profane foods remains important in conditioning attitudes and behaviour towards food and in affecting the emotional tone of the transaction. It is likely that the most elaborate culinary art arose from ritual celebrations, as demonstrated by ancient Chinese data (Chang 1977: 35). Ritual meals are usually taken in the household or within the territorial framework of the community.

Social celebrations can take place outside the home in more profane sites – 'downtown' or at the market place. They have generated a professional cuisine, ranging from market stands to sophisticated gastronomic restaurants. Although there is a constant, two-way flow between household cookery and professional catering, for technical reasons and owing to time constraints the range of dishes is different in each case. One further type of meal that is taken outside the home, and involves professional catering, is at the workplace or school. Collective feeding in relation to work or educational activities is gaining increasing prominence nowadays in shaping food habits according to time availability, economic constraints and peer influence.

Drinks

Both non-alcoholic beverages and spirits play an important part in the food system and should be mentioned here (Heath 1987). Beer brewing and alcohol distillation are parts of many rituals. Drinks are often consumed outside the home and seldom accompany ordinary meals, as is the case in a number of European cuisines. Similarly, savouries, pastries and fruit are frequently eaten outside the home.

Snacks

These correspond to less-structured feeding bouts that take place outside mealtimes and range from an occasional fruit or nut picked in the orchard or bush to light snacks taken by farmers at mid-morning, or at elevenses or tea-time in areas under British influence. Travel foods and eating-while-you-work should be mentioned here too.

The organization of meals has biological consequences, and results in various categories of consumers having different access to food, both qualitatively and quantitatively. Traditional family meals can be depicted as fixed performances in which the household head (i.e. the dominant male) usually receives the lion's share and where other consumers are offered food in proportion to their status as this is culturally defined. In many cases, men are favoured as compared with women, adults in relation to children, and elders in relation to junior siblings. The resulting differences in nutritional status do not necessarily enhance the biological fitness of the population as a whole. Among the Massa of Cameroon, some adult men have privileged access to milk and consume large quantities of sorghum porridge during fattening sessions (Garine and Koppert 1991), whereas the women and children, on whom the reproductive success of the population as a whole depends, receive a poorer diet and, consequently, pay a higher price in morbidity and mortality. In a similar way, the shorter life expectancy of Indian women (Naik and Bardhan 1974) is partly due to their restraint at meals in favour of the male resource-provider of the family. In highly impoverished populations in Central America

(Scrimshaw 1978: 193) or India (Mitra 1974: 47), sick children who respond decreasingly to their mother's stimulation are progressively allocated less attention and food, resulting in avoidable infant mortality.

In daily life housewives are constantly faced with alternative choices in apportioning food. Brown (1983) shows how, in Chad, the Nar woman in a polygynous compound is confronted every day with delicate decisions. Should she favour her own children, or also give something to her co-spouses. Should she be partial to her husband or to her brothers? The choice she makes will not satisfy everybody, even if objections are not openly voiced. In food-sharing, social practice constantly challenges more or less established collective norms. In this respect, meals could be interpreted as social dramas in which the sociometric composition of the group may interact with the traditional pattern of food distribution. Considerations of kinship, alliance, residence and status are all at work, as well as those of friendship and love. These emotional linkages may cut across the normal network of social ties and highlight the events of each individual's personal history. Food-sharing is obviously related to social bonding, but it may be futile to ask whether sharing creates a link or is the manifestation of an existing one. As Mauss (1950) showed in his classic essay on the gift, the essence of food is to circulate, to establish communication and reciprocal exchange, paralleling and often accompanying the circulation of women in which lies, according to Lévi-Strauss (1949: 40), the essence of human society.

Sociologically speaking, what is the role of meals and food sharing? There is a wealth of ethnographic data showing how food sharing serves to confer as well as to demonstrate the status and role of each individual, not only among the living but also in relation to the supernatural world. Everybody is aware of the many, and sometimes conflicting levels to be considered. Nowadays no-one would attempt to credit different types of societies, globally defined, with dominant types of food-sharing, from pooling in face-to-face groups to precise reciprocation in larger structures, as Cohen (1961: 323), for instance, tried to do. Many authors have described the sharing of hunter–gatherers in Apollonian terms, but things are not that simple. We should not forget Cephu, the Pygmy villain of Turnbull's book (1961: 88), who constantly tried to take advantage of his mates. Conflicts between opposed individual interests and personal cravings creep daily into food-sharing, ruling out any simple application of general principles like Durkheim's 'collective conscience', or the genetic imperative – posited by sociobiological theory – to behave altruistically towards kin who carry copies of one's own genes.

CONTEMPORARY TRENDS

Today, human diet and nutrition are undergoing profound changes. Although it seems that the food resources of the planet are not quite keeping up with demographic increase, the situation varies between countries, regions, populations and social groups. The distribution of food resources between the rich food-producing parts of the world and the undernourished, underdeveloped countries is governed by profit incentives and is therefore uneven. However, the world is coming to resemble a common ecosystem in which communication and transport are generalized and in which any local event is ultimately likely to have repercussions for the rest of the planet. Humanity is, therefore, heading towards a global pattern of life and feeding behaviour, under the influence of dominant industrial civilizations. This does not mean that regional differences have disappeared and that it is no longer possible to encounter hunter-gatherers or nomadic herders, but these life-styles are being progressively marginalized as they come under the influence of the world system.

What are the characteristics of this system in the field of food and nutrition? The production, transformation, storage, and distribution of food have undergone such technological advance that today it is possible to consume in any part of the world any kind of food, in any quantity, at any time of the year – provided the potential consumers have at their disposal the money necessary to obtain it. Monetization of the economy, including the food domain, is a general tendency, but this is seldom sufficient to provide for the harmonious fulfilment of the dietary needs and wants of everybody. Incomes are too low and too irregular, and the priorities accorded to buying food are often inappropriate to ensure the adequate nutrition of all family members. In many parts of the world, the introduction of cash crops has contributed to the elimination of local subsistence production, without providing any satisfactory substitute. Consumers, including those from rural areas, have to use money (which they do not handle as well as their food stores) to buy their food from external sources. This has severed many of the emotional ties linking people to their daily bread and to their environment. Such attachments are brought back to life on special celebrations such as the Sabbath, Thanksgiving Day, etc.; many minorities and migrant groups maintain a range of comforting, emblematic dishes. However, in most cases food has become a profane commodity to be manipulated at will and even stolen in case of dearth, something that used to be unheard of for fear of supernatural sanction. Food is now used not only to fulfil nutritional needs but also for pleasure and to demonstrate status and 'distinction', to use Bourdieu's terminology (1979: 209), according to a whole range of criteria, the first of which is economic affluence and the availability of money. In modern towns, as among traditional populations, food remains an area through which people display and gain status.

Communication allows for comparison not only between neighbouring groups but on a worldwide basis between whole societies, civilizations and modes of life. Until today, the major trendsetter has been the Western urban–industrial Protestant culture; large food companies have spread their food production throughout the world; fast-food catering is present everywhere and so are soft drinks. The hegemony is slightly challenged by the more food-indulgent civilization of a southern European or Mediterranean style, through which knowledge of *haute cuisine* and wine-tasting is becoming a universal social asset. Together with its ideology, the revival and spread of Islam is also conveying distinct attitudes towards eating and food.

In developing countries, changes in food behaviour do not exactly follow Western models, but receive the imprint of local trendsetting groups. For instance, in Senegal food habits are influenced by the urbanized style of Dakar, where the Wolof traditional culture dominates. Food habits change according to general patterns but are shaped by the leading local culture. At the same time, the merging of regional cultures into national entities, as well as access to modern education, professional knowledge and profit, obviously lead to social classes having much in common, including food habits, independently of the traditional origin of their members.

The availability and palatability of modern foods have given rise to a dominant tendency to eat for pleasure, to overeat and to adopt a type of diet in which fats, sugar, and animal proteins dominate, while the fibre content of food is reduced. The *grande cuisine française*, codified by chefs like Carême (1847) or Escoffier (1957 [1903]), which spread worldwide among the affluent classes during the last two centuries as a sign of supreme refinement (Brillat-Savarin 1885, Aron 1973), would dismay a modern professional nutritionist. Today, the avowedly dietetic *nouvelle cuisine* (Bocuse 1976) is constantly challenged by more permissive styles. Modern life, especially in towns, does not allow for enough exercise and expenditure of energy to compensate for a plethoric diet which completely contradicts the generalized ideal of a slim body. The result is widespread overweight and the prevalence of a whole range of physical and psychopathological ailments such as cardiovascular disease, diabetes, anorexia nervosa or bulimia, a pattern which has been exported to acculturating societies such as the Samoans (Baker *et al.* 1986) and to Mexican and Indian minorities in the United States like the Pima (Danforth *et al.* 1981). But at the same time, a certain dietary uniformity is spreading because of limitations of time and money, and the search for safe and easy-to-prepare nutritious foods. New foods and preparations appear daily on the market, and gourmet restaurants open up beside fast-food snack-bars. Wine-tasting clubs proliferate alongside oriental philosophy circles promoting the consumption of brown rice and bamboo shoots; at the same time Green movements are campaigning against agribusiness. There are probably as many people who consider that the Golden Age was when Grandmother had time to simmer stews out of natural home products as there are who have faith in the future and modernity and in pure and rational new foods, and who reject rustic archaism. This contemporary ambivalence has its source in the constant overlap between utilitarian and symbolic concerns in human feeding behaviour. What this behaviour expresses, through its innumerable cultural forms, is the food-related anxiety of a species endowed with self-consciousness, and subjected, as an omnivorous creature, to what Rozin (1976)

– following Bateson – calls a 'double bind', having to balance conservatism against innovation, security against adventure in food choices.

At the same time scheduling constraints, the intensification of work, and the competitiveness and aggressivity of the urban environment create stresses which can be partially soothed through comforting ingestion – indulging in food, drugs, and alcoholic drinks. In a world where migrants and groups undergoing cultural change constitute the bulk of disadvantaged socio-economic strata, anomie, insecurity, and low self-esteem are widespread. Alcohol offers some catharsis and an opportunity for conviviality. It is likely to become, on a worldwide scale (Heath 1987), a much more important problem than malnutrition. During the nineteenth century, in response to the explosion in the urban–industrial way of life and as an inheritance of puritanism (Mennell 1985: 106), the doctrine of 'moral eating' appeared, precisely designed to improve the virtues of the miserable working classes whose hunger was to be satisfied without waste or pleasure.

Today, 'eating for health' has become a campaign issue and a profitable advertising argument in many affluent societies. Modern man is expected to become a rational dietetic consumer. He is supposed to attune his wants to his needs according to both up-to-date standards of scientific health and the food-producing capacity of the world. He should satisfy his true and moderate nutritional needs through a diet which is emotionally rather neutral, but he is prompted to do so by a campaign of advertising that appeals directly to his emotional sensibilities. As food habits are mostly learnt at an early stage in life, nothing is beyond the grasp of a ruthless and worldwide educational programme. Observations of the dominant trendsetting groups of our world show that material changes have occurred which may have biological effects, such as the disappearance of seasonal food rhythms, the influence of time constraints on food preparation and consumption, and the increased pollution of foodstuffs. At a different level, in the social field, daily life may have increased the influence of peers as compared with parents in the acquisition of food habits, and television during meals reduces communication between household members. However, food fads and savour clubs, where 'knowledge' and attitudes towards food determine membership, are flourishing. Since the epoch of hunter-gatherers and possibly carnivorous apes, nurture has lost none of its non-nutritional functions: establishing communication between individuals and groups, contributing to their psychosocial well-being, making available an ever-present counterpoint to the translation of the eternally renewed wealth of human symbolic abilities. To paraphrase Mauss (1950: 147), feeding behaviour in human beings is still a 'total social phenomenon', which cannot be reduced to merely biological considerations.

REFERENCES

Accolas, J. P., Deffontaines, J. P. and Aubin, F. (1975) 'Les activités rurales en République populaire de Mongolie – I. Agriculture et Élevage; II. Produits laitiers', *Études Mongoles* 6: 7–98.

Alland, A. Jr, (1970) *Adaptation in Cultural Evolution – an Approach to Medical Anthropology*, New York: Columbia University Press.

Alexander, J. and Coursey, D. G. (1969) 'The origins of yam cultivation', in P. J. Ucko and G. W. Dimbleby (eds) *The Domestication and Exploitation of Plants and Animals*, London: Duckworth.

Arnott, M. (ed.) (1976) *Gastronomy: the Anthropology of Food Habits*, The Hague: Mouton.

Aron, J. P. (1973) *Le Mangeur du XIX° siècle*, Paris: Robert Laffont.

Bahuchet, S. (1985) *Les Pygmées Aka et la forêt centrafricaine: ethnologie écologique*, Paris: Société d'Études linguistiques et anthropologiques de France (SELAF).

Baker, P. T., Hanna, J. M., and Baker T. (eds) (1986) *The Changing Samoans*, Oxford: Oxford University Press.

Bateson, G. (1972) *Steps to an Ecology of Mind*, New York: Ballantine.

Bayliss-Smith, T. and Feachem, R. (eds) (1977) *Subsistence and Survival. Rural Ecology in the Pacific*, New York: Academic Press.

Bocuse, P. (1976) *La Cuisine du marché*, Paris: Flammarion.

Bourdieu, P. (1979) *La Distinction – critique sociale du jugement*, Paris: Éditions de Minuit.

Brillat-Savarin, A. (1885) *Physiologie du goût*, Paris: Librairie de la Bibliothèque Nationale.

Brown, E. P. (1983) 'Nourrir les gens, nourrir les haines', *Études et documents tchadiens* 8, Société d'Ethnographie, Paris: 108–13.

Burnett, J. (1966) *Plenty and Want: a Social History of Diet in England from 1815 to the Present Day*, Harmondsworth: Pelican.

Carême, M. A. (1847) *L'Art de la cuisine française au dix-neuvième siècle*, 5 vols, Paris: Au Comptoir des Imprimeurs Unis.

Chambers, R., Longhurst, R. and Pacey, A. (eds) (1981) *Seasonal Dimensions to Rural Poverty*, New York: Frances Pinter.

Chang, K. C. (ed.) (1977) *Food in Chinese Culture – Anthropological and Historical Perspectives*, New Haven: Yale University Press.

Clark, J. D. (1968) 'Studies of hunter-gatherers as an aid to interpretations of prehistoric societies', in R. B. Lee and I. DeVore (eds) *Man the Hunter*, Chicago: Aldine.

Cohen, Y. E. (1961) 'Food and its vicissitudes: a cross-cultural study of sharing and non sharing', in Y. E. Cohen (ed.) *Social Structure and Personality*, New York: Holt, Rinehardt & Winston.

Coppens, Y., Howell, F. C., Isaac, G. L. and Leakey, R. E. F. (eds) (1976) *Earliest Man and Environments in the Lake Rudolf Basin. Stratigraphy, Paleoecology and Evolution*, Chicago: University of Chicago Press.

Danforth, E. Jr, Darjel, R. J., Katzeff, H. L., Ravussin, E. and Garrow, J. S. (1981) 'Thermogenic responsiveness in Pima', *Indian Clinical Research* 29 (3): 663.

Darby, W. J., Ghalioungui, P. and Grivetti, L. (1977) *Food, the Gift of Osiris*, 2 vols, London: Academic Press.

Davis, C. M. (1928) 'Self-selection of diets by newly-weaned infants: an experimental study', *American Journal of Disabled Children* 36: 651–89.

Douglas, M. (1957) 'Animals in Lele religious symbolism', *Africa* 27: 46–58.

—— (1963) *The Lele of the Kasai*, London: Oxford University Press.

—— (1966) *Purity and Danger*, London: Routledge & Kegan Paul.

—— (1972) 'Deciphering a meal', *Daedalus* 101: 61–82.

—— (1977) 'Structures of gastronomy', in *Annual Report 1976–77 of the Russell Sage Foundation*, New York.

—— (1978) 'Culture', in *Annual Report 1977–78 of the Russell Sage Foundation*, New York.

Durkheim, E. (1895) *The Rules of Sociological Method*, 2nd edn, trans. S. Solovay and J. Mueller, 1938, New York: Free Press.

Ekalle, S. (1947) 'Croyances et pratiques obstetricales des Douala', *Bulletin de la société d'Études camerounaises* 19: 70–5.

Escoffier, G. A. (1957 [1903]) *A Guide to Modern Cookery*, 2nd edn, London: Hutchinson.

FAO/WHO (1957) *Calorie Requirements*, FAO Nutritional Studies no. 15, Rome: Food and Agriculture Organization of the United Nations.

—— (1965) *Besoins en protéines*, Rapport d'un groupe mixte d'experts FAO/OMS, Réunions de la FAO sur la nutrition, Rapport no. 37, Rome: FAO.

—— (1973) *Besoins énergétiques et besoins en protéines*, Rapport d'un comité spécial mixte FAO/OMS d'experts, Réunions de la FAO sur la nutrition, Rapport no. 52, Rome: FAO.

—— (1974) *Manuel sur les besoins nutritionnels de l'Homme*, Études de nutrition de la FAO no. 28, Rome: FAO.

—— (1986) *Organisation des Nations Unies pour l'alimentation et l'agriculture: rapport et perspectives sur les produits*, Rome: FAO.

FAO/WHO/UNU (1985) *Energy and Protein Requirements*, Report of a joint FAO/WHO/UNU expert consultation, Technical Report Series no. 724, Geneva: WHO.

Farb, P. and Armelagos, G. (1980) *Consuming Passions – The Anthropology of Eating*, New York: Washington Square Press.

Ferro-Luzzi, A., Norgan, N. G. and Durnin, J. V. G. A. (1975) 'Food intake in relationship to body weight and age, and its apparent nutritional adequacy in New Guinean children', *The American Journal of Clinical Nutrition* 28: 443–453.

Fieldhouse, P. (1986) *Food and Nutrition: Custom and Culture*, London: Croom Helm.

Firth, R. (1934) 'The sociological study of native diet', *Africa* 7: 4.

—— (1966) *Malay Fishermen – Their Peasant Economy*, New York: W. W. Norton.

Flannery, K. V. (1969) 'Origin and ecological effects of early domestication in Iran and the Near East', in P. J. Ucko and G. W. Dimbleby (eds) *The Domestication and Exploitation of Plants and Animals*, London: Duckworth.

Freedman, R. L. (1981) *Human Food Uses – a Cross-Cultural Comprehensive Annotated Bibliography*, Westport, Conn.: Greenwood Press.

—— (1983) *Human Food Uses – a Cross-Cultural Comprehensive Annotated Bibliography*, Supplement, Westport, Conn.: Greenwood Press.

Freud, S. (1969 [1913]) *Totem and Taboo*, 2nd edn, London: Hogarth Press.

Fujita, Y., Okuda, T., Rikimaru, T., Ichikawa, M., Miyatani, S., Kasiwara, N., Date, C., Minamide, T., Koishi, H., Alders, M. P. and Heywood, P. F. (1986) 'Studies of nitrogen balance in male highlanders in Papua New Guinea', *Journal of Nutrition* 116: 536–44.

Garine, I. de (1980) 'Approaches to the study of food and prestige in savanna tribes – Massa and Mussey of northern Cameroon and Chad', *Social Science Information* 19 (1): 39–78.

Garine, I. de and Harrison, G. A. (eds) (1988) *Coping with Uncertainty in Food Supply*, Oxford: Clarendon Press.

Garine, I. de and Koppert, G. J. A. (1988) 'Coping with seasonal fluctuations in food supply among savanna populations: the Massa and Mussey of Chad and Cameroon', in I. de Garine and G. A. Harrison (eds) *Coping with Uncertainty in Food Supply*, Oxford: Clarendon Press.

—— (1990) 'Social adaptation to season and uncertainty in food supply', in G. A. Harrison and J. C. Waterlow (eds) *Diet and Disease in Traditional and Developing Societies*, Cambridge: Cambridge University Press.

—— (1991) 'Guru – fattening sessions among the Massa', *Ecology of Food and Nutrition* 25 (1): 1–28.

Goodenough, W. H. (1957) 'Cultural anthropology and linguistics', in P. Garvin (ed.) *Report of the Seventh Annual Round Table meeting on Linguistics and Language Study*, Institute of Languages and Linguistics, Monograph Series on Languages and Linguistics, no. 9, Washington, DC: Georgetown University Press.

Goody, J. (1982) *Cooking, Cuisine and Class. A Study in Comparative Sociology*, Cambridge: Cambridge University Press.

Granet, M. (1968) *La Pensée chinoise*, Paris: Albin Michel.

Guthe, E. and Mead, M. (1945) 'Manual for the study of food habits', *Bulletin of the National Research Council*, 111, National Academy of Sciences.

Hamayon, R. (1976) 'L'os distinctif et la chair indifférente', *Études Mongoles* 6: 99–122.

Harding, R. S. O. (1975) 'Meat-eating and hunting in baboons', in R. H. Tuttle (ed.) *Socioecology and Psychology of Primates*, The Hague: Mouton.

Harner, M. (1977) 'The ecological basis for Aztec sacrifice', *American Ethnologist* 4: 117–35.

Harris, M. (1975) *Cows, Pigs, Wars and Witches – The Riddles of Culture*, New York: Vintage Books, Random House.

—— (1978) *Cannibals and Kings – the Origins of Culture*, New York: Vintage Books, Random House.

—— (1980) *Cultural Materialism – the Struggle for a Science of Culture*, New York: Vintage Books, Random House.

—— (1985) *The Sacred Cow and the Abominable Pig. Riddles of Food and Culture*, New York: Simon & Schuster.

Harris, M. and Ross, E. B. (eds) (1987) 'Theoretical overview', in *Food and Evolution. Towards a Theory of Human Food Habits*, Philadelphia: Temple University Press.

Harrison, G. A. and Waterlow, J. C. (eds) (1990) *Diet and Disease in Traditional Developing Societies*, Society for the Study of Human Biology, Symposium 30, Cambridge: Cambridge University Press.

Hart, T. and Hart, J. (1986) 'The ecological basis of hunter-gatherers subsistence in African rain forests – The Mbuti of Eastern Zaïre', *Human Ecology* 14: 29–55.

Hawkes, D. (1959) *Ch'utz'u – The Songs of the South*, Oxford: Clarendon Press.

Headland, T. N. (1987) 'The wild yam question: how well could independent hunter-gatherers live in a tropical rain forest ecosystem?', *Human Ecology* 15 (4): 463–91.

Heath, D. (1987) 'A decade of development in the anthropological study of alcohol use: 1970–1980', in M. Douglas (ed.) *Constructive Drinking – Perspectives on Drink from Anthropology*, Cambridge and Paris: Cambridge University Press and Éditions de la Maison des Sciences de l'Homme.

Hipsley, E. A. and Kirk, N. E. (1965) *Studies of Dietary Intake and the Expenditure of Energy by New Guineans*, Technical Paper no. 147, South Pacific Commission, Noumea, New Caledonia.

Hladik, C. M. (1973) 'Alimentation et activité d'un groupe de chimpanzés réintroduits en forêt gabonaise', *La Terre et la Vie* 27: 344–413.

—— (1976) 'Chimpanzees of Gabon and chimpanzees of Gombe. Some comparative data on the diet', in T. H. Clutton-Brock (ed.) *Primate Ecology: Studies of Feeding and Ranging Behaviour in Lemurs, Monkeys and Apes*, New York: Academic Press.

Hladik, C. M., Bahuchet, S. and Garine, I. de (eds) (1990) *Food and Nutrition in the African Rain Forest*, Paris: CNRS, Unesco/MAB.

Isaac, G. L. (1971) 'The diet of early man: aspects of archaeological evidence from Lower and Middle Pleistocene sites in Africa', in D. Roe (ed.) *World Archaeology*, London: Routledge & Kegan Paul.

Isaac, G. L., Harris, J. W. K. and Crader, D. (1976) 'Archaeological evidence from the Koobi Fora formation', in Y. Coppens, F. C. Howell, G. L. Isaac and R. E. F. Leakey (eds) *Earliest Man and Environments in the Lake Rudolf Basin. Stratigraphy, Paleoecology and Evolution*, Chicago: University of Chicago Press.

Jakobson, R. and Halle, M. (1956) *Fundamentals of Language*, The Hague: Mouton.

Jelliffe, D. B. (1967) 'Parallel food classifications in developing and industrialized countries', *American Journal of Nutrition* 20 (3): 273–81.

Jerome, N. W., Kandel, R. F. and Pelto, G. (eds) (1980) *Nutritional Anthropology*, Pleasantville, New York: Redgrave.

Kardiner, A. (1939) *The Individual and His Society – The Psychodynamics of Primitive Social Organization*, with a Foreword and two ethnological reports by R. Linton, New York: Columbia University Press.

Kardiner, A., Linton, R., Du Bois, C. and West, J. (1945) *The Psychological Frontiers of Society*, New York: Columbia University Press.

Katz, S. H., Hediger, M. L. and Valleroy, L. S. (1975) 'The anthropological and nutritional significance of traditional maize processing techniques in the New World', in E. Watts, B. Lasker and F. Johnson (eds) *Biosocial Interrelations in Population Adaptation*, The Hague: Mouton.

Kawai, M. (1965) 'Newly-acquired precultural behaviour of the natural troop of Japanese monkeys on Koshima Island', *Primates* 6 (1): 1–30.

Keesing, R. M. (1981) *Theories of Culture. Language, Culture and Cognition – Anthropological Perspectives*, New York: Macmillan.

Koppert, G. J. A. (1988) 'Alimentation et culture chez les Tamang, les Ghalé et les Kami du Népal', thesis presented at the Faculty of Law, Economics and Political Sciences, Aix/Marseille.

Laderman, C. (1981) 'Symbolic and empirical reality. A new approach to the analysis of food avoidances', *American Ethnologist* 8: 468–93.

Leach, E. (1974) *Lévi-Strauss*, London: Fontana/Collins.

Lee, R. B. (1965) 'Subsistence Ecology of !Kung Bushmen', Ph.D. dissertation, Berkeley: University of California.

—— (1969) '!Kung Bushman subsistence', in A. P. Vayda (ed.) *Environment and Cultural Behavior*, New York: The Natural History Press.

—— (1973) 'Mongongo: the ethnography of a major wild food resource', *Ecology of Food and Nutrition* 2 (4): 307–22.

Lee, R. B. and DeVore, I. (eds) (1968) *Man the Hunter*, Chicago: Aldine.

Lehrer, A. (1969) 'Semantic cuisine', *Journal of Linguistics* 5: 39–56.

—— (1972) 'Cooking vocabularies and the culinary triangle of Lévi-Strauss', *Anthropological Linguistics* 14: 155–71.

Lévi-Strauss, C. (1949) *Les Structures élémentaires de la Parenté*, Paris: Presses Universitaires de France.

—— (1962a) *Le Totémisme aujourd'hui*, Paris: Presses Universitaires de France.

—— (1962b) *La Pensée sauvage*, Paris: Plon.

—— (1964) *Mythologiques. I. Le Cru et le cuit*, Paris: Plon.

—— (1965) 'Le triangle culinaire', *L'Arc* 26: 19–29.

—— (1966) *Mythologiques. II. Du miel aux cendres*, Paris: Plon.

—— (1968) *Mythologiques. III. L'Origine des manières de table*, Paris: Plon.

—— (1971) *Mythologiques. IV. L'Homme nu*, Paris: Plon.

Little, M. A., Galvin, K. and Leslie, P. W. (1988) 'Health and energy requirements of nomadic Turkana pastoralists', in I. de Garine and G. A. Harrison (eds) *Coping with Uncertainty in Food Supply*, Oxford: Clarendon Press.

Loutan, L. (1985) 'Nutrition amongst a group of Woodabe (Fulani Bororo) pastoralists in Niger', in A. G. Hill (ed.) *Population, Health and Nutrition in the Sahel*, London: Routledge & Kegan Paul.

Mahias, M. C. (1985) *Délivrance et convivialité: le système culinaire des Jaïna*, Paris: Éditions de la Maison des Sciences de l'Homme.

Malinowski, B. (1935) *Coral Gardens and their Magic. A Study of the Methods of Tilling the Soil and the Agricultural Tribes in the Trobriand Islands*, London: Allen & Unwin.

Mauss, M. (1923) 'Essai sur le don, forme et raison de l'échange dans les sociétés archaïques', *Année Sociologique* 1923–4, 2 (1), 2nd edn (1950) in *Sociologie et Anthropologie*, Paris: Presses Universitaires de France.

Mennell, S. (1985) *All Manners of Food. Eating and Taste in England and France from the Middle Ages to the Present*, Oxford: Blackwell.

Minnis, P. E. (1985) *Social Adaptation to Food Stress – a Prehistoric South-Western Example*, Chicago: University of Chicago Press.

Mintz, A. M. J. and Van Veen, A. G. (1968) 'A sociological approach to a dietary survey and food habits study in an Andean community', *Tropical Geographical Medicine* 20: 88–100.

Mitra, A. (1974) 'Cost and benefit of special nutrition programmes', in *Proceedings of the International Union of Nutritional Sciences, Committee on Economic, Social and Cultural Aspects of Nutrition*, New Delhi.

Mizuno, A., Kawai, M. and Shigeri (A.) (1976) 'Ecological studies of forest-living monkeys in the Kebala forest of Uganda', *African Studies* (Kyoto University) 10: 1–36.

Morenhout, J. A. (1959 [1835]) *Voyage aux Iles du Grand Océan*, 2nd edn, Paris: Maisonneuve.

Naik, J. P. and Bardhan, K. (1974) 'Nutritional problems of women in India – some socio-economic aspects of nutrition', in *Proceedings of the International Union of Nutritional Sciences, Committee on Economic, Social and Cultural Aspects of Nutrition*, New Delhi.

Nishida, T. I. and Kawanaka, K. (1972) 'Inter-unit group relationship among wild chimpanzees of the Mahali mountains', *African Studies* (Kyoto University) 7: 131–69.

Norgan, N. G., Ferro-Luzzi, A. and Durnin, J. V. G. A. (1974), 'The energy and nutrient intake and the energy expenditure of 204 New Guinean adults', *Philosophical Transactions of the Royal Society of London*, ser. B 268: 309–48.

Ojiambo, J. A. (1967) 'A background study of the food habits of the Abasamia of Busia District, Western Province, Kenya – a preliminary study 1965–6', *Nutrition* 21 (4): 216–21.

Oomen, H. A. P. C. (1971) 'Ecology of human nutrition in New Guinea', *Ecology of Food and Nutrition* 1: 1–18.

Oomen, H. A. P. C. and Corden, M. W. (1970) *Metabolic Studies on New Guinean Nitrogen Metabolism in Sweet Potato Eaters*, South Pacific Commission, Technical Paper, no. 163, Noumea.

Pagezy, H. (1988a) 'Contraintes nutritionnelles en milieu forestier équatorial liées à la saisonnalité et à la reproduction: réponses biologiques et stratégies de subsistance chez les Ba-Oto et les Ba-Twa du village de Nzalakenga (Lac Tumba), Zaire', thesis for Doctorat d'État ès Science, University of Aix/Marseille.

—— (1988b) 'Coping with uncertainty in food supply among the Oto and the Twa living in the Equatorial Forest near Lake Tumba (Zaïre)', in I. de Garine and G. A. Harrison (eds) *Coping with Uncertainty in Food Supply*, Oxford: Clarendon Press.

Pelto, G., Pelto, P. J. and Messer, E. (eds) (1989) *Research Methods in Nutritional Anthropology*, Tokyo: United Nations University.

Périssé, J. (1966) 'L'Alimentation en Afrique intertropicale. Étude critique à partir des données des enquêtes de consommation 1950–65', thesis presented at the Faculty of Pharmacy, University of Paris, University Series no. 436.

Radcliffe-Brown, A. R. (1951) 'The comparative method in social anthropology', *Journal of the Royal Anthropological Institute* 81: 15–22.

—— (1952) *Structure and Function in Primitive Society*, London: Cohen & West.

Renfrew, J. M. (1969) 'The archaeological evidence for the domestication of plants: methods and problems', in P. J. Ucko and G. W. Dimbleby (eds) *The Domestication and Exploitation of Plants and Animals*, London: Duckworth.

Rappaport, R. (1968) *Pigs for the Ancestors. Ritual in the Ecology of a New Guinean People*, New Haven: Yale University Press.

Richards, A. I. (1932) *Hunger and Work in a Savage Tribe. A Functional Study of Nutrition Among the Southern Bantu, with an Introduction by B. Malinowski*, London: Routledge.

—— (1939) *Land Labour and Diet in Northern Rhodesia: an Economic Study of the Bemba Tribe*, London: Oxford University Press.

Richards, A. I. and Widdowson, E. M. (1936) 'A dietary study in northeastern Rhodesia', *Africa* 9 (2): 166–96.

Rodahl, K. (1964) 'Les besoins nutritionnels dans la région polaire', in *Médecine et Santé publique dans l'Arctique et l'Antarctique, Cahiers de Santé Publique* 18: 109–29.

Rozin, P. (1976) 'The selection of foods by rats, humans and other animals', in J. S. Rosenblatt, R. A. Hinde, E. Shaw and C. Beer (eds) *Advances in the Study of Behaviour*, New York: Academic Press.

Rozin, P. and Fallon, A. E. (1980) 'The psychological categorization of foods and non-foods. A preliminary taxonomy of food reflections', *Appetite* 1: 193–201.

—— (1987) 'A perspective in disgust', *Psychological Review* 94 (1): 23–41.

Sahlins, M. (1972) *Stone Age Economics*, London: Tavistock.

Sahn, D. E., Lockwood, R. and Scrimshaw, N. S. (eds) (1984) 'Methods for the evaluation of the impact of food and nutrition programmes', *Food and Nutrition Bulletin* 8, Tokyo: United Nations University.

Scrimshaw, N. S. and Young, V. R. (1976) 'The requirements of human nutrition', *Scientific American* 23: 3.

Scrimshaw, S. C. M. (1978) 'Infant mortality and behaviour in the regulation of family size', *Population and Development* 3: 380–7.

Shack, W. (1966) *The Gurage, a People of the Ensete Culture*, London: Oxford University Press.

Simoons, F. J. (1961) *Eat Not This Flesh: Food Avoidance in the Old World*, Madison: University of Wisconsin Press.

Smith, H. S. (1969) 'Animal domestication and animal cult in Dynastic Egypt', in P. J. Ucko and G. W. Dimbleby (eds) *The Domestication and Exploitation of Plants and Animals*, London: Duckworth.

Stahl, A. B. (1984) 'Hominid dietary selection before fire', *Current Anthropology* 25 (2): 151–68.

Steiner, J. E. (1977) 'Facial expressions of the neonate infant indicating the hedonics of food-related chemical stimuli', in J. M. Weiffenbach (ed.) *Taste and Development: the Genesis of Sweet Preference*, Washington, DC: US Government Printing Office.

Suzuki, A. (1965) 'An ecological study of wild Japanese monkeys in snowy areas focusing on their food habits', *Primates* 6: 31–72.

—— (1975) 'The origin of hominid hunting: a primatological perspective', in R. H. Tuttle (ed.) *Socioecology and Psychology of Primates*, The Hague: Mouton.

Tambiah, S. J. (1969) 'Animals are good to think and good to prohibit', *Ethnology* 8: 423–57.

Teleki, G. (1973a) *The Predatory Behavior of Wild Chimpanzees*, Lewisburg, Pennsylvania: Bucknell University Press.

—— (1973b) 'The omnivorous chimpanzee', *Scientific American* 228 (1): 32–42.

—— (1974) 'Chimpanzee subsistence technology: materials and skills', *Journal of Human Evolution* 3: 575–94.

—— (1975) 'Primate subsistence patterns: collector-predators and gatherer-hunters', *Journal of Human Evolution* 4: 125–84.

Testart, A. (1988) 'Food storage among hunter-gatherers: more or less security in the way of life?', in I. de Garine and G. A. Harrison (eds) *Coping with Uncertainty in Food Supply*, Oxford: Clarendon Press.

Thomas, R. B., Winterhalder, B. and McRae, S. D. (1979) 'An anthropological approach to human ecology and adaptive dynamics', *Yearbook of Physical Anthropology* 22: 1–46.

Trémolières, J., Serville, Y., Vinit, F. and Colson, A. (1952), 'Géographie de l'alimentation en France', *Recherche Française, Recueil des Travaux*, Institut National d'Hygiène, Tome 4, vol. 2: 503–6.

Turnbull, C. (1961) *The Forest People*, New York: Simon & Schuster.

Van Lawick-Goodall, J. (1968) 'The behaviour of free-living chimpanzees in the Gombe Stream Reserve', *Animal Behaviour Monographs* 1 (3): 161–311.

Vayda, A. P. (ed.) (1969) *Environment and Cultural Behavior*, New York: Natural History Press.

Vertés, L. (1975) 'The lower Palaeolithic site of Vertesszöllös, Hungary', in R. Bruce-Milford (ed.) *Recent Archaeological Excavations in Europe*, London: Routledge & Kegan Paul.

Wagenaar-Brouwer, M. (1985) 'Preliminary findings on the diet and nutritional status of some Tamasheq and Fulani groups in the Niger Delta of Central Mali', in A. G. Hill (ed.) *Population, Health and Nutrition in the Sahel*, London: Routledge & Kegan Paul.

Walcher, D. N., Kretchmer, N. and Barnett, H. L. (1976) *Food, Man and Society*, New York: Plenum Press.

Washburn, S. L. and DeVore, I. (1961) 'Social behaviour of baboons and early man', in S. L. Washburn (ed.) *Social Life of Early Man*, Chicago: Aldine.

White, L. A. (1949) *The Science of Culture*, New York: Noonday Press.

WHO (1985) *Energy and Protein Requirements*, Technical Report Ser. 724, Geneva: World Health Organization.

Will, G. F. and Hyde, G. E. (1917) *Corn Among the Indians of the Upper Missouri*, Lincoln: University of Nebraska Press.

Wilson, C. S. (1979) 'Food custom and nurture, an annotated bibliography on sociocultural and biocultural aspects of nutrition', *Journal of Nutrition Education* 4 (suppl. 1): 210–63.

Winterhalder, B. (1977) 'Optimal foraging in a patchy environment – foraging strategy adaptations of the boreal forest Crees. An evaluation of theory and models from evolutionary ecology', Ph.D. dissertation, Cornell University.

Wrangham, R. W. (1977) 'Feeding behaviour of chimpanzees in Gombe National Park, Tanzania', in T. H. Clutton-Brock (ed.) *Primate Ecology: Studies of Feeding and Ranging Behaviour in Lemurs, Monkeys and Apes*, London: Academic Press.

Young, M. W. (1971) *Fighting with Food. Leadership, Values and Social Control in a Massim Society*, Cambridge: Cambridge University Press.

Yudkin, J. (1978) *Diet of Man: Needs and Wants*, London: Applied Science Publishers.

FURTHER READING

Bayliss-Smith, T. and Feachem, R. (eds) (1977) *Subsistence and Survival. Rural Ecology in the Pacific*, New York: Academic Press.

Blaxter, Sir K. and Waterlow, J. C. (eds) (1985) *Nutritional Adaptation in Man*, London: John Libbey.

Chang, K. C. (ed.) (1977) *Food in Chinese Culture − Anthropological and Historical Perspectives*, New Haven: Yale University Press.

Clutton-Brock, T. H. (ed) (1977) *Primate Ecology: Studies of Feeding and Ranging Behaviour in Lemurs, Monkeys and Apes*, New York: Academic Press.

Freedman, R. L. (1981) *Human Food Uses − a Cross-Cultural Comprehensive Annotated Bibliography*, Westport, Conn.: Greenwood Press.

—— (1983) *Human Food Uses − a Cross-Cultural Comprehensive Annotated Bibliography*, Supplement, Westport, Conn.: Greenwood Press.

Garine, I. de, and Harrison, G. A. (eds) (1988) *Coping with Uncertainty in Food Supply*, Oxford: Clarendon Press.

Gast, M. (1968) *Alimentation des populations de l'Ahaggar: études ethnographiques*, Paris: Arts et Métiers Graphiques.

Goody, J. (1982) *Cooking, Cuisine and Class. A Study in Comparative Sociology*, Cambridge: Cambridge University Press.

Guthe, E. and Mead, M. (1945) 'Manual for the study of food habits', *Bulletin of the National Research Council*, 111, National Academy of Sciences.

Harris, M. and Ross, E. B. (eds) (1987) 'Theoretical overview', in *Food and Evolution. Towards a Theory of Human Food Habits*, Philadelphia: Temple University Press.

Harrison, G. A. and Waterlow, J. C. (eds) (1990) *Diet and Disease in Traditional Developing Societies*, Society for the Study of Human Biology, Symposium 30, Cambridge: Cambridge University Press.

Jerome, N. W., Kandel, R. F. and Pelto, G. (eds) (1980) *Nutritional Anthropology*, Pleasantville, New York: Redgrave.

Khare, R. S. (1976) *The Hindu Hearth and Home*, New Delhi: Vikas Publishing House.

Lee, R. B. (1979) *The !Kung San. Men, Women and Work in a Foraging Society*, Cambridge: Cambridge University Press.

Mahias, M. C. (1985) *Délivrance et convivialité: le système culinaire des Jaïna*, Paris: Éditions de la Maison des Sciences de l'Homme.

Mennell, S. (1985) *All Manners of Food. Eating and Taste in England and France from the Middle Ages to the Present*, Oxford: Blackwell.

Minnis, P. E. (1985) *Social Adaptation to Food Stress − a Prehistoric South-western Example*, Chicago: University of Chicago Press.

Pelto, G., Pelto, P. J. and Messer, E. (eds) (1989) *Research Methods in Nutritional Anthropology*, Tokyo: United Nations University.

Richards, A. I. (1932) *Hunger and Work in a Savage Tribe*, London: Routledge.

10

DEMOGRAPHIC EXPANSION: CAUSES AND CONSEQUENCES

Mark N. Cohen

Recent research on the origins of modern human beings suggests that *Homo sapiens* may all be descended from a relatively small number of individuals (no more than a few families) who lived as recently as 100,000 to 200,000 years ago (Vigilant *et al.* 1991). The intervening period has seen the expansion of the species to nearly six billion people. The generally increasing size and density of the human population is revealed in the progressively increasing number, size, and permanence of archaeological sites. But it is not only the total size of the human population that has generally increased, but also its average rate of growth. Most reconstructions suggest that there may have been no more than fifteen million people on the earth as recently as fifteen thousand years ago; some scholars suggest there were as few as five million. This indicates that the human population grew at an average rate of less than 0.01 per cent per year through most of the history of the species. The growth rate accelerated to as much as 0.1 per cent per year by around ten thousand years ago, and has reached figures of 1.0 to 2.0 per cent or more per year in recent centuries (Hassan 1981, Cohen 1977, Coale 1974).

During the period of recorded history, the pace of growth has not been even or steady. It is clear that the overall trend of growth is compounded from periods of relative stability interrupted by episodes of very rapid growth and by periods of significant decline or population 'crashes'. The most notable crashes have been the massive destructions of non-Western populations (particularly the American Indians and the inhabitants of Australia from the sixteenth to the nineteenth centuries) associated with the expansion of the West and the spread of new infectious diseases (Ramenofsky 1988, Dobyns 1983, McNeill 1975). These destructions are considered more fully in Article 11.

Population trends of the more remote past are likely to have had a similarly chequered history. For example, the colonization of the New World by Old World hunters, which by most accounts occurred within the last twenty thousand years, appears to have marked a period of comparatively rapid population growth (see, for example, Martin (1973), who estimates that population growth rates during the period of rapid migration may have reached 3 per cent or more per year). The 'collapse' or dispersion of Classic Mayan populations in the ninth century AD, and the apparent collapse or dispersion of large Upper Palaeolithic aggregates in Europe some ten to fifteen thousand years earlier, may also be cases in point. But whether the pattern of acceleration and decline – of 'peaks' and 'crashes' – in prehistory matched or exceeded the jagged patterns of recent history remains an issue of contention.

THE EVOLUTION OF HUMAN SOCIETIES

Concomitant with the overall increase in human population throughout prehistory, there have occurred a number of significant – even revolutionary – shifts in the nature of human adaptation and in the structure of human communities and political units. Populations of *Homo sapiens*, initially committed to open, game-rich environments (savannas and open forests) at moderate latitudes of the Old World, have expanded geographically into almost every physical environment, a testimony to human cultural versatility as well as to our omnivorous and flexible dietary patterns. Human beings penetrated the New World, apparently by crossing a now-submerged land bridge between Siberia and Alaska, and they entered Australia by sea. They proceeded to fill the world's continents, exploiting an increasing array of ecological biomes from hot deserts and tropical rainforests to high mountain peaks and the arctic tundra (Butzer 1971, Cohen 1977). While having initially fed themselves by exploiting a select array of wild foods, including several species of large mammals, human beings gradually broadened the spectrum of wild resources they exploited to place more emphasis on small game animals, birds and rodents, aquatic resources (fish and shellfish), and a wider array of vegetable foods including small nuts and seeds which required extensive processing. Apparently, growing human numbers necessitated a gradual broadening of dietary range as well as an increase in the total percentage of vegetable foods (as opposed to animal foods) in the diet.

This trend culminated around ten to fifteen thousand years ago in what archaeologists call the 'broad spectrum revolution'. Up to a point, the trend may be more apparent than real – an artefact of archaeological preservation. For example, the scarcity of smaller animal bones in earlier sites may reflect their poor preservation. But there are good grounds for regarding much of the trend as having a basis in fact. For example, the increasing frequencies in Mesolithic sites of seed-processing tools such as grinding stones, mortars and pestles can hardly be attributed merely to the changing circumstances of archaeological preservation. Moreover, the fact that the same trends have been replicated over short periods of time by recent colonists in different regions of the world (for example in New Zealand – see Anderson 1983), and the fact that the trends conform with the predictions of so-called 'optimal foraging theory' (see p. 279), suggest that they are no mere artefacts of preservation.

As part of the broad spectrum revolution, human beings in various regions of the world began to manipulate the growth of selected food species (primarily plants). Within the last ten thousand years they began to control their breeding and to alter their hereditary characteristics (to 'domesticate' them), thus initiating what has come to be known as the 'Neolithic' era, in which farming or agriculture replaced hunting and gathering as the prevailing mode of subsistence. Human beings also began increasingly to modify the landscape to permit more frequent harvesting of crops, to grow more of each crop per unit of land area, and to grow crops on more and more marginal lands, a series of processes together referred to as the intensification of agriculture (for a fuller account, see Article 8 in this volume).

Since both broad-spectrum foraging and agriculture tended to entail a greater reliance on stored food, the once highly mobile human species became largely committed to a sedentary life. Where previously people had travelled to find food, food was now moved to people. As a result, the choice and preparation of food have been increasingly governed by the requirements of storage and transport, and the location of human settlements has come to be dictated by access to trade routes rather than to resources *per se*.

It appears that human populations originally formed small, homogeneous groups, loosely defined and largely self-sufficient, without formal political or economic structures, organized primarily along lines of kinship and friendship, with exchange and decision-making determined much as they are among small groups of friends and kin in the modern world. However, in a pattern roughly correlated with the adoption of sedentism, storage, and agriculture, people gradually became committed to larger, more permanent communities. These communities, in turn, were more formally organized: their members were subdivided, categorized and stereotyped to permit easier recognition, to make the behaviour of strangers more predictable, and to establish formal expectations for interactions with hitherto unknown individuals. Relations of exchange, once simply confined to sharing between friends and kin, were organized into larger centralized systems of redistribution in which positions of leadership became ascribed, formally defined and permanent.

In various parts of the world, no more than about five thousand years ago, there began what has been referred to as the 'Urban Revolution' or the rise of 'civilization'. This was marked by the emergence of very large communities supported by intensive agriculture, and utilizing the specialized skills of artisans concentrated in cities. The cities themselves were linked together in complex networks of trade, and the whole structure was organized by systems of codified law which were often, although not always, set down in writing.

These changes in the size and density of the human population, in food production and in social organization appear to run in parallel and to interact causally with one another. There is little question that farming and its intensification have been associated historically with higher population densities, and with larger groups, than hunting and gathering; nor is there much doubt that the adoption of sedentary farming economies is associated, by and large, with accelerated rates of population growth. It is equally clear that the rise of specialists (in crafts, trade, and administration), the elaboration of social classes, and the emergence of the political apparatus of the state are associated with high densities of population (Cohen 1981). What is not clear is precisely how changes in the three spheres – of population, food procurement, and social organization – have affected one another; whether changes in any of the three spheres can be said to be the primary motivators of changes in the other two; or whether a more complex pattern of interaction among all three spheres can be discerned.

CLASSICAL MODELS OF CULTURAL EVOLUTION

Prior to the 1960s, most models of human cultural evolution focused on the role of technological innovation and its effects on food supply as the prime determinants of population growth and changes in social organization (see Article 34 in this volume for a review). According to models then prevailing, the available food supply limited the potential density of human populations (i.e., the number of people who could feed themselves per unit of land area). In a world in which almost all transportation was by foot, limited food supplies also limited the size of local communities. A community could house no more people than could travel daily to hunting or gathering grounds or farmed fields. Hunting groups remained small because relatively small amounts of wild resources could be obtained within the walking radius of a single camp. Groups remained mobile simply because wild resources were easily exhausted within the vicinity of any particular camp. In short, groups remained small and mobile because they lacked the technological sophistication to secure food in such quantity as to sustain large numbers of people for indefinite periods on the same territory. According to these models of human evolution, improvements in the technology of food production, such as farming, increased food supplies, thereby permitting the growth and aggregation of human populations. Increased population density and the greater size of local population aggregates in turn generated changes in social and political organization (Childe 1951).

In a similar vein, the emergence of civilization was viewed as the consequence of a succession of technological advances indicating ever-greater levels of sophistication and accomplishment. The creation of massive storage facilities, and irrigation systems or other land improvement devices, along with the extension of trade networks, further enhanced the capacity of the population to feed itself while at the same time providing a wealth of exotic, 'civilized' luxuries for the élite. Great pyramids and other monuments attested to immense architectural and engineering skill, even if they actually served little economic purpose.

Explicit, or at least implicit, in this argument was the assumption that the pace of technological change was constrained only by the limits of human knowledge and the slow pace of invention. Knowledge and invention themselves were taken to be independent variables. It was assumed that changes in technology were clear 'improvements', not only increasing the total available supply of food but also increasing the efficiency of human labour and improving the welfare of individual human beings. Once it was invented, the adoption of a technological innovation therefore required no further explanation.

Models of explanation in archaeology, prior to the 1960s, generally focused on identifying where and when a new innovation first appeared; what combination of circumstances facilitated innovation; how innovations spread or diffused; and whether certain innovations had been invented repeatedly in different parts of the world or had diffused from one or a few single points of origin. Archaeologists did not, as a rule, concern themselves with the question of why a certain innovation might be accepted or rejected — or if they did, the answer was in terms of the irrational (or at least uneconomic) biases of certain cultural systems which eschewed technological advance in the name of ideology, cultural values or some vaguely defined cultural conservatism.

A corollary of this argument was that human population was a dependent variable limited by Malthusian constraints: the sheer inability, under a particular regime of production, to supply enough food to feed more than a certain number of mouths was seen as the only check on population growth. Primitive human groups were perceived to be operating at or near the demographic limits imposed by their ignorance, enduring a constant struggle to maintain themselves on limited resources. Moreover, they were commonly perceived to have operated at very high levels of fertility, approaching the biological maximum for our species. Only by these means, archaeologists believed, was it possible for these groups to offset the inexorably high mortality of primitive life (Acsádi and Nemeskéri 1970).

MODELS OF THE 1960S: WYNNE-EDWARDS, BOSERUP AND LEE

A somewhat more optimistic assessment of the primitive human condition gained favour during the 1960s through the introduction into anthropology of a model proposed by the animal ecologist V. C. Wynne-Edwards (1962). Wynne-Edwards suggested that many animal populations do not normally face starvation because they are 'self-regulated' by some form of mechanism which restrains reproduction to keep population within the 'carrying capacity' of resources — i.e., below the level at which the survival and reproduction of the resources themselves would be threatened, and below the level at which animal (or human) numbers would come to be limited directly by starvation. The regulation of human fertility (presumed to occur primarily through deliberate infanticide or abortion; see Birdsell 1953, 1968) could account for the apparent stability of population without our having to assume extraordinarily high rates of natural mortality.

But if self-regulation protected populations against starvation, the level around which they were regulated was still dependent on technology. Regulated populations posed no threat to existing resources, but they also generated no stimulus for economic change (Flannery 1969). Populations grew only when fortuitous improvements in technology increased the food supply, thereby temporarily relaxing the need for social constraints on reproduction. Prevailing models suggested that, in the absence of technological advance, prehistoric populations would have maintained a well-tuned, homeostatically regulated equilibrium with their natural environments for many thousands of years (Birdsell 1968). A few dissenters (e.g. Hayden 1972) noted that such self-regulation might be costly to maintain from the perspective of the individual decision-maker, and might function less perfectly than was generally assumed.

In 1965, Ester Boserup, an agricultural economist, suggested an alternative perspective. Her work, although specifically concerned with the development of agricultural techniques, had much wider implications for our understanding of demographic and economic history. Boserup argued that human population growth could be treated, at least in part, as an independent variable and that it could provide the necessary stimulus for innovation and change in agricultural technology. She suggested that agricultural technology, rather than proceeding from fortuitous innovation, developed in a dependent and elastic manner as population density increased.

A key foundation of Boserup's theory was the recognition that techniques which promoted the more efficient use of *space* by increasing the amount of food obtainable from the land (and hence permitting the support of denser human populations) were not necessarily more efficient in terms of the yield of human *labour*, nor did they necessarily imply any improvement in the economic well-being of the individual labourer. Boserup suggested, in fact, that as they intensified their use of agricultural land, people appeared to be trading labour efficiency for efficient use of space, something they would be likely to do only when the increasing demand for food became compelling. She suggested specifically that techniques such as hoeing, ploughing, irrigation, or intensive fertilization (which increase the total food supply by permitting more frequent cropping of the land or the cropping of more marginal land) entailed diminished returns on labour. More generally, her model suggested that what appeared 'primitive' for lack of modern technology was often an efficient adaptation to low population density and small social scale rather than an accommodation to ignorance. The rejection of new technology, she concluded, might be an informed and rational response if the labour costs of the techno-logical innovation were high and the level of demand for increased production were low.

Around the same time, work by Richard Lee and his colleagues (Lee 1969, 1972, 1976, Lee and DeVore 1968) on the !Kung San – a hunter-gatherer population of the Kalahari Desert of southern Africa, and one of the world's smallest and technologically 'least sophisticated' populations – appeared to suggest that Boserup's thesis was more generally applicable to human econo-mies. The San – who became famous as exemplars of the 'primitive' hunting and gathering lifestyle – were described as 'affluent' (Sahlins 1968, 1972) people who hunted and gathered by choice, rather than on account of an ignorance of farming, because it enabled them to obtain a more than adequate diet with relatively little effort.

Lee's observations of the San, many of which have been replicated among other, similar groups, also provided an important new perspective on the evolution of large and complex communities. They suggested that aggrega-tions of large numbers of people for long periods of time, such as occasionally occur among hunter-gatherers, entail high social as well as economic costs. Large groups tended, spontaneously and consistently, to become fragmented as a result of social tensions, even when sufficient food was on hand to feed greater numbers. These observations challenged the assumption that groups would normally grow to be as large as food supplies would permit. Increased group size had to be seen as the result of a careful balance of conflicting needs, rather than as an easy and obvious response to increased food supplies.

POPULATION PRESSURE AND DIMINISHING RETURNS

Combining the perspectives of Boserup and Lee, a number of prehistorians suggested that the initial adoption of farming by hunter-gatherers, as well as the later intensification of agriculture, might have been the result of gradually increasing demand rather than fortuitous technological innovation – the demand in turn being consequent either on the prior growth of the human population, on the decline of wild resources, or on changes in social organiza-tion which required increased productivity for social purposes (Flannery 1969, Binford 1968, see also Bender 1978, Lourandos 1985).

In a book published in 1977, I argued that the 'broad spectrum revolution', and the subsequent adoption of agricultural economies in various parts of the world, appeared to involve diminishing returns in accordance with Boserup's model. Although diminishing returns might result from the growth of the human population, from increased social demand, or from climatic change or other natural phenomena that could reduce the supply of preferred wild resources, it appeared to me that the sequence of events, occurring indepen-dently but in a parallel manner in so many different parts of the world, was largely independent of local climates and specific cultural regimes. The

271

parallelism suggested that some common force was operating on diverse cultural ecological systems. It appeared that only the growth of the human population *per se* could explain the general sequence of events on the scale at which it occurred.

At the same time I argued that local variations in climate, culture, or the biology of particular food resources were crucial to any explanation of what went on in specific locations – for example, why domestication occurred earlier in some parts of the world than in others, or why some crops in some regions (such as wheat in the Middle East) actually became domesticated in the sense of undergoing genetic alteration, whereas other 'crops' which were just as intensively exploited (such as acorns in California) never underwent domestication (see also Harris 1977). Population growth could explain the broad parallels in the cultural evolution of different populations, but it could not explain local variables of culture history.

A major tenet of the 'population pressure' model of the origins of agriculture was that agricultural staples – cereals and tuberous crops – appeared to be valuable primarily because they could be grown in abundance and stored rather than because they were particularly desirable or nutritious foods or could be produced with particular ease. One corollary of the theory was the expectation that the archaeological record of human health associated with the broad-spectrum and Neolithic revolutions would demonstrate diminishing returns on labour and a reduction rather than an improvement in health and nutrition (Smith 1972, Cohen 1977, 1984).

It also appeared that despite prevailing models of the self-regulation of human populations, population growth, rather than being conditional upon technological advance, could well operate as a variable (though not necessarily an 'independent' variable) stimulating cultural evolution. Since human beings can choose from a wide range of potential foods, and almost always appear to be selective in their eating habits (an observation borne out repeatedly by recent work in 'optimal foraging theory' as discussed below), and since, moreover, people are generally aware of ways – beyond those currently in use – to increase the productivity of their selected crops, their numbers need not have been limited by the availability of any one resource. Increasing human population might simply entail changing patterns of diet selectivity and greater investments of labour. Cultural factors might not have limited population numbers around fixed limits or 'carrying capacities' so much as they might have limited the *pace* of population growth, keeping it to a level at which – very much as with slow inflation – the economic compromises involved were not so rapid as to be felt too sharply in the short run (Cohen 1977, Hayden 1972).

Lee's work, as well as that of Binford, Smith, and others (Lee 1969, Binford 1968, Smith 1972), also suggested that sedentism, rather than being an obviously desirable strategy whenever abundant food supplies permitted, might be an adaptive compromise which was adopted when growing human populations were forced to spend increasing periods of time in the vicinity of seasonally plentiful and storable foods, a compromise achieved at the cost of greater accumulations of rubbish and filth, with their attendant risks of parasitic infestation and disease. Moreover, quite apart from the curtailment of freedom of movement, sedentism renders a group less knowledgeable about the surrounding environment, more vulnerable to attack by neighbours, and less secure nutritionally as a result of the loss of variety in the diet.

Increase in the size of local groups also took on a new meaning. It could be seen not merely as fulfilling the potential of enlarged food supplies, but perhaps also as responding to a new need for the protection of improved land or stored resources in the face of increasing inter-group competition. Community size became an essential facet of competition in an arms race among communities no longer protected by their own mobility (Hassan 1981).

The need to adopt sedentary life-styles and the consequent premium on increased group size might in turn have stimulated the acceptance of new principles for maintaining social order — more formal group subdivisions, centralized and permanent positions of leadership, and centralized exchange — in groups for which fission was no longer a viable political option. Building on Lee's work, Johnson (1982) developed the concept of 'scalar stress' and showed how new modes of organization were necessary to facilitate the flow of information as groups became too large for face-to-face interaction. Carneiro (1967) has observed that the complexity of social institutions appears not only to correlate with the number of people in a community, but also to increase and decrease with changes in community size, suggesting that social complexity itself responds in an elastic manner to the 'demand' generated by a growing or aggregating population. Building on the work of Johnson, Carneiro, and others such as Colson (1978), as well as on the work of social psychologists (Epstein 1980, Baron 1980, Karlin 1980, Freedman 1980), I suggested (Cohen 1981) that complex social organization involving formal permanent subdivisions and centralization of trade and leadership were essentially adaptations to the stresses of 'crowding' — the problems stemming from congestion, information overload, and the loss of privacy and of personal control that accompany increasing group size. I also suggested that although temporary crowding such as that discussed by Carneiro might occur as the result of periodic windfalls of choice wild resources, the more important, largely irreversible trend toward increasing community size and social complexity appears to be associated with the more intensive use of secondary resources and is largely a function of need engendered by growing population rather than an opportunity born of plenty.

Similar arguments have been developed with reference to the emergence of even more complex forms of social organization. Civilization, once identified by its visible technological monuments such as pyramids, has more recently been described in terms of the implied changes in social organization and, more specifically, the social stratification, political organization, and coercion

273

entailed in the building of these monuments (Fried 1967, Carneiro 1970). The political power to build a pyramid − rather than the technology to do so − became the defining characteristic of the new social order, the state, in which an élite class monopolized the use of force and controlled direct access to essential resources such as land, or water, while the bulk of the population was forced to exchange its labour for food. Society became an institution of competing interests held together by coercion rather than by homogeneity and positive personal bonds.

Some theories of the origins of the state suggest that stratification might have arisen out of the collective economic advantage of centralized leadership, such as the power to design and build irrigation systems (Wittfogel 1957), or to store and distribute large quantities of food. As such, social stratification could be seen as a function of increasing population density and the growing pressure on resources, which would have demanded heavier and more sophisticated collective investment in land improvement (Cohen 1981).

However, many theories of the origin of the state now stress the role of conquest, or at least the use of force, as a means of exerting control over previously more egalitarian societies. The correlation between high population densities and this social transformation suggests (see, for example, Carneiro 1970) that the origin of the state might be found in a combination of population growth and 'circumscription', the latter referring to those geographical factors (such as mountains or deserts) or social factors (in the form of competing populations) which limit the scope for territorial expansion of a growing population and limit the centrifugal tendencies of individual groups trying to escape the dominance of their would-be rulers.

In short, scholars agree that the state combines two things: large-scale managerial functions which accomplish certain collective tasks beyond the power of individuals or small groups; and the coercive power to maintain and profit from inequalities in basic wealth. But whether the state arises primarily on a voluntaristic basis to regulate and protect large populations, or primarily as a means of exploiting populations rendered captive by their size and by geographical limits to expansion, remains an issue of contention. A further issue is whether the emergence of the state, once considered a great advance in the history of human civilization (and one which undoubtedly conferred considerable competitive advantage on the state societies themselves), might have appeared detrimental rather than advantageous to the individual members of the populations in question. For further discussion of these issues, see Article 34 in this volume.

RECENT REVISIONS AND NEW PERSPECTIVES

To sum up, each of the great transformations in human society appears to be clearly associated with increases in the human population. In each instance the direction of causality − whether population growth is to be seen as cause or consequence — remains an issue for debate; but in contrast to ideas prevailing before the 1960s a good case can be made in each for population growth as a causative factor. Moreover, in each case some question remains as to whether changes that served collective needs and that enhanced the competitive status of the group also served the needs of individuals. These changes may have been perceived to confer clear advantages to everyone and therefore may have been readily adopted; or they may have been perceived by individuals as bringing with them the threat or reality of diminishing returns, and so may have been adopted only under pressure of growing population, increasing competition, or political coercion.

In the period since these arguments were first framed, a number of reservations have surfaced concerning the data from which Lee and Boserup drew their initial conclusions. First, it has been pointed out that, like other contemporary hunter-gatherers, the Kalahari San are less a remnant of the Palaeolithic past than we used to believe, and more a creation of the recent history of contact and colonization; it is therefore debatable whether they can be used as analogues for modelling prehistoric behaviour (Schrire 1980, 1984, Denbow and Wilmsen 1986, Bird 1983). Indeed, it is now clear that neither the Kalahari San nor any other hunting and gathering group of recent history can be considered a pristine remnant of ancient life. All such groups function at least in part as hunting and gathering specialists (and a few even as tourist attractions) in the larger political and economic contexts of the farming or pastoral communities and the states which surround them — a position which provides both advantages and disadvantages and which undoubtedly affects their activities. The conclusions we draw from studies of their behaviour have to be modified accordingly. The primary value of such studies for reconstructing the past may be that they enable us to investigate the systematic interrelationships between certain specific variables which can then be incorporated into models designed to simulate various aspects of ancient lifestyles.

A second criticism of the San material is that the initial descriptions by Lee, DeVore and their colleagues presented an excessively optimistic picture of their lifestyle. In particular, it has been argued that the San diet, although nutritionally well balanced in terms of the intake of protein, vitamins and minerals, may be deficient in calories; and that heat, lack of water, and exhaustion rather than satiety may account for some of their apparent 'leisure' (Hawkes and O'Connell 1985, Blurton-Jones and Sibley 1978, Wilmsen 1978). Simple measures of the productivity of their labour seem to suggest that their work is less efficient, that it produces fewer calories per hour than does the work of most subsistence farmers (Harris 1985).

A review of recent literature on the San and other hunter-gatherers (Cohen 1989) suggests that they are indeed somewhat less 'affluent' than once portrayed. But it also suggests that stereotypes based on the original descriptions are not as misleading as some critics would have us believe. In contrast to the other poor of the modern world, contemporary hunter-gatherers suffer few vitamin and mineral deficiencies, and kwashiorkor caused by protein deficiency is virtually unknown among them. The most commonly reported shortages are indeed of calories, but in marked contrast to the nutrition of most contemporary groups, hunter-gatherers generally appear to enjoy well-balanced diets even when caloric intakes are low. Furthermore, their caloric intakes, though they could hardly be described as 'affluent' by modern standards, do compare favourably with average caloric intakes in much of the Third World. These conclusions concerning the nutritional status of hunter-gatherers are particularly remarkable, given that most such dietary surveys have been carried out in environments which are clearly not habitats of choice. The San, living in a desert environment, enjoy a diet which is probably somewhat below the average in its caloric adequacy compared with that of other hunter-gatherers, and their food procurement strategies are apparently relatively inefficient (Hawkes and O'Connell 1985). Yet compared with modern Third World nations, in which daily caloric intakes commonly lie between 1,800 and 2,200 kcal per person per day or less, the San enjoy a caloric intake which is about average and a protein intake which is well above average (Cohen 1989). Recent descriptions of the Hadza hunter-gatherers of Tanzania, who occupy an environment similar to those preferred by our pre-historic ancestors, suggest a far richer and more reliable diet (O'Connell *et al* 1988, Woodburn 1968).

The general well-being of the San portrayed in early studies is borne out in later studies of disease. The San do appear to enjoy relative freedom from parasitic infections because their desert environment is not conducive to the survival of parasite and vector species. But if other hunter-gatherers in moister climates suffer heavier parasite loads, the data suggest none the less that, in general, small and mobile groups suffer lower rates of parasitic disease than do denser and more sedentary populations living in similar environments (Cohen 1989). Apparently, small group size and mobility confer a real advantage in reducing the frequency of infection. Since parasites tend to inhibit the intake and absorption of nutrients, to destroy tissues which have to be replaced, and to require 'wasteful' diversion of nutrients into building defensive tissues, low rates of parasitic infection also confer a real nutritional advantage.

In short, though the descriptions of the San may have initially provided a slightly misleading picture of affluence, they and other contemporary hunter-gatherers do appear to fare relatively well compared with much of the Third World, albeit not so well as the affluent, industrial West. Lee's conclusions about the well-being of hunting and gathering populations do not seem to have been so misleading as some critics contend. Prehistoric hunter–gatherers living in richer environments are likely to have fared even better.

Boserup's work has been similarly criticized by a number of researchers (Harris 1985, Simon 1983, Bronson 1972), who point out that intensive agriculture need not be less efficient than 'primitive' extensive agriculture.

Much of the diminishing returns she anticipates in association with the inten-sification of farming may be offset in several ways: (1) by the provision of better-quality tools; (2) by economies of scale; and (3) by the introduction of task specialization. With reference to tools, several studies suggest that metal tools add significantly to the efficiency of agricultural labour (see Cohen 1989). Concerning economies of scale, many tasks can be done more efficiently on a larger than on a smaller scale — and some tasks such as irrigation cannot be undertaken at all by small groups. The critics provide figures suggesting, con-trary to Boserup's expectations, that the productivity of the individual agricul-tural labourer is greater in intensive regimes of agriculture than under more extensive systems.

But researchers come to different conclusions concerning the productivity of agricultural labour, depending on the variables they take into account: for example, whether they count the labour of prior investment (e.g. in land improvements) or only the work done in a particular year; whether they take into account the proportion of the product that must be dedicated to specialists performing other essential tasks; whether the efficiency of the indi-vidual farmer increases faster than does the proportion of population devoted to other tasks; and whether improvements in farming efficiency are sufficient to offset the demands of upper classes who, under regimes of intensive farming, control land and other resources but do not contribute labour. Simon (1983), pointing to the successes of agricultural intensification in the past few decades, suggests that growing population can stimulate increasing rewards for all. Geertz (1963), by contrast, has provided a graphic description of the diminishing returns accompanying increasing population density and associated with the failure to reinvest surplus production. Harris (1985), with an eye to expropriation by privileged classes, notes that the farmers themselves may not benefit from increases in productivity. A look at the physical anthro-pology (discussed below) suggests that either Boserup, Geertz, or perhaps Harris is closer to the truth than is Simon.

SOCIOBIOLOGY, OPTIMAL FORAGING THEORY AND PALAEOPATHOLOGY

During the 1970s and 1980s, at least three new avenues of scientific inquiry stimulated further debate on these issues. First, there was a revolution in our understanding of the relationship between the reproductive behaviour of indi-vidual organisms and the adaptive requirements of whole populations. The major premise of the new field of sociobiology — that animals have evolved so that they are predisposed to pursue improvements in their own inclusive fit-ness (i.e the representation of their genes in future generations) rather than in group welfare — has forced us to reconsider arguments about population regulation. The question is no longer one of how or why animal populations regulate their numbers collectively but one of how individual animals achieve optimal reproduction for their genes. Models of demographic homeostasis based on social contracts or the perception of shared ecological need have largely been refuted. The argument that human groups might be prevented from growing by inescapable limitations geared to 'carrying capacity' has been undermined, although it is still possible to argue that human groups have culturally instituted social contracts which modify or override the genetically inherited predispositions. Such voluntary limitation of reproduction as occurs in human groups is now more often seen as serving the long-term interests of particular kin groups, and as being relatively independent of wider group interests or of aggregate measures of the balance between population and resources. Whether human or animal populations are capable of growing and exerting pressure on resources no longer appears to be at issue.

Second, research based on 'optimality' theory has also changed the way we look at the economic behaviour of animal and human populations. Optimal foraging studies predict how an economically 'rational' animal should adjust its foraging behaviour. For the sake of simplicity, most predictions assume that animals will attempt to maximize the number of calories they obtain for each unit of time or labour expended (Winterhalder and Smith 1981). For our present purposes, the most important result is that it has prompted researchers to make very careful measurements of foraging efforts and returns in a number of human populations operating under a variety of conditions.

Third, a major new line of evidence has emerged from the field of palaeopathology, the study of prehistoric health and nutrition through the analysis of human remains (faeces, mummies, but most often skeletons). Although the field has long existed as a branch of medical history, tracing the ancient occurrence of specific diseases and syndromes, it has emerged only recently as an anthropological tool for the analysis of social change (Buikstra and Cook 1980, Cohen and Armelagos 1984, Huss-Ashmore et al. 1982). Palaeopathology should allow us to provide statistical descriptions of patterns of basic health and nutrition in whole populations, and thereby to assess the economic impact (and therefore, indirectly, the motivation) of major economic changes such as those under discussion here. Palaeopathological techniques should enable us to measure changes in work load, in overall nutrition, in the availability of specific nutrients, in the frequency of infection, and in the number of episodes of acute stress experienced by the average individual. (In practice, interpreting palaeopathological data is proving to be harder than some of us thought; see Sattenspiel and Harpending 1983, Wood et al. 1992.)

Neither the studies stimulated by optimal foraging theory nor those in palaeopathology provide complete or conclusive proof about the nature of pre-historic economic transitions; but taken together, I believe, they add substantial weight to an interpretation of the major transitions along the lines originally suggested by Boserup. Two lines of evidence suggest, for example, that the broad-spectrum revolution – the increasing focus during the

278

Mesolithic era on small game, seed crops, and aquatic resources – should best be viewed as entailing diminishing returns on labour.

Studies of the efficiency of hunting and gathering conducted in various parts of the world indicate that when large game animals are encountered, they can generally be harvested with an efficiency equal to or greater than (and often far greater than) the efficiency with which other resources can be obtained. If we simply measure caloric returns for effort expended (and ignore other nutritional advantages of animal foods, the utility of hides, or the cultural values that people commonly seem to place on eating meat), 'harvesting' a large animal that has been encountered is generally a more efficient activity than harvesting available shellfish, small game, seeds or most other vegetable foods. Anadromous or migratory fish can be harvested with similar efficiency, but only after complex weirs have been set up. Some species of nuts can be harvested with an efficiency equal to that of the harvest of large game, but when a large animal has been taken it can be converted into food with relative ease. Nuts, by contrast, are very time-consuming to prepare as food and this greatly reduces their overall value.

Optimal foraging studies also suggest that when they are available, large animals can be harvested with relatively high efficiency irrespective of whether the hunters have only spears or possess the complete complement of 'more sophisticated' Mesolithic equipment – small projectiles, snares, etc. Hunting available large animals with spears appears to be more efficient than hunting smaller prey with more 'modern' weapons. Comparative analysis of the relative contributions of stone and metal tools indicates that metal tools assist hunting relatively little, although they do assist vegetable gathering far more, suggesting that in a Stone Age world, the relative efficiency of harvesting large game would have been even greater than it has been shown to be by modern comparisons conducted among people with metal technology. In short, the presence or absence of large animals was apparently a more important determinant of the overall efficiency of foraging than was the development of sophisticated new hunting and gathering technologies towards the close of the Stone Age (for a review of data and sources see Cohen 1989).

The relative efficiency with which big game can be harvested suggests, moreover, that it is often worth searching for (even when other resources are more readily available), so long as the search can be expected to identify prey within a reasonably short time. For example, if people can obtain 10,000 to 20,000 calories for each hour's work killing and preparing a large animal, but only 1,000 calories per hour from obtaining and processing small seeds, small animals or shellfish (a not unrealistic comparison), they might be expected to hunt so long as, on average, they could expect to find a large animal within two or three days' hunting (10–20 hours).

When large mammals are encountered frequently, big-game hunting can yield an exceptionally rich harvest, averaging more than 10,000 kcal per person-hour of hunting, as contemporary observations in Zambia and Kenya indicate (Marks 1976, Blackburn 1982). The conditions under which these observations were made approximate, better than any others of recent times, those which would have prevailed during the expansion of early human populations through environments rich in megafauna unaccustomed to hunters and the dangers they presented.

In the modern world, in which much of the large fauna has now become extinct and in which most hunting and gathering societies find themselves in marginal, game-poor environments (or subjected to local game laws), the majority of hunter-gatherers have few opportunities to encounter large animals. They are forced, therefore, to adopt mixed strategies in which the efficiency of harvesting each resource is balanced by the probability of finding the resource on any given day. Under these circumstances hunting may be relatively inefficient because search time is so high. Even in a prehistoric world, richer in game, foraging was probably always based on a mixed strategy, balancing various risks and probabilities and providing a heterogeneous and varied diet. Moreover, as Speth (1988) has pointed out, there may be an upper limit to the proportion of the human diet which can come from meat before nutritional deficits associated with the internal processing of excess protein are encountered.

Nevertheless, the harvesting efficiency data do suggest that when large animals were more plentiful (as we know to have been true of the past), resources such as seeds or shellfish would not have become more commonly exploited simply because new technology was invented, for they would still have been less efficient to exploit than large game. Thus they would have come into use only as larger animals became harder to find. The very strong implication is that the broad spectrum revolution was motivated by increasing human numbers, reductions in available foraging territory, and the decline of large game animals. Moreover, although large sedentary aggregates of people are occasionally associated in early prehistory with periodic abundance of choice resources such as large game (Soffer 1985), the more common association, late in prehistory, of increased group size and sedentism with what appear to have been secondary resources (seeds and shellfish) suggests that this trend, too, results from a compromise dictated by necessity rather than opportunity or invention.

The bulk of the available palaeopathological data, although scanty and subject to conflicting interpretations, also suggests that the broad-spectrum revolution involved diminishing economic returns associated either with reduced labour efficiency or with the negative effects of sedentism (and consequently increased parasitism) on health. Data on human stature throughout the Old World fairly consistently suggest that people became smaller during the course of this transition (Angel 1984, Smith et al. 1984, Meiklejohn et al. 1984, Kennedy 1984), and small stature is a frequently used measure of economic deprivation. Other indicators, such as certain nutritionally related skeletal measures, more often than not also suggest declining nutrition.

Moreover, measurements of episodic stress during childhood growth (indicated by linear enamel hypoplasia of teeth) suggest steady or increasing rates of stress (Cohen and Armelagos 1984, cf. Wood *et al.* 1992). These data are generally consistent with the hypothesis that nutrition did not improve but rather declined during the broad spectrum revolution.

Studies of the relative efficiency of farming and hunting and gathering now suggest, despite contentions several of us have previously put forward, that farming is calorically the more efficient strategy, producing higher average returns for a given investment of time than observed foraging strategies (Cohen 1989). My own guess is that although farming is clearly more efficient than broad-spectrum foraging dominated by resources which entail high processing costs, it is probably not, on average, as efficient calorically as the hunting-dominated strategies once followed by our ancestors in game-rich environments. This could explain why broad-spectrum foragers around the world – but not their hunting forebears – were motivated to switch to agricultural economies.

The available palaeopathological data comparing pre- and post-Neolithic populations are somewhat more abundant than for earlier periods. Good comparative sequences are now available for more than twenty regions of the world (Cohen and Armelagos 1984, Cohen 1989). If the data are taken at face value (but cf. Wood *et al.* 1992) a number of patterns emerge:

1   Changes in the prevalence of arthritis and in skeletal robusticity (both indicative of work load) are varied. In some cases, farming seems to have involved a heavier work load, and in some cases a lighter one, so that these data reveal no clear common trend (the trends sometimes seem to be in opposite directions for males and females).

2   Most regional comparisons of the skeletons of hunter-gatherers and farmers suggest that rates of infection increased as groups became larger and more sedentary (a result confirming standard predictions from epidemiology and consistent with observations indicating that the propagation of many parasites is density-dependent). Rates of non-specific infection of bone (osteitis, osteomyelitis) increase, as do rates of specific diseases identifiable in the skeleton, such as yaws and tuberculosis. One study using mummies (Allison 1984) demonstrates an increase in intestinal infections with sedentism. Since infection has a negative impact on the absorption and utilization of nutrients by the body, the result is likely to have been a net loss of available nutrients regardless of the quality of the food produced. Moreover, the clear positive association of sedentism with infection means that there was a perceptible disincentive to aggregation and to the adoption of sedentary life-styles. This strengthens the argument that such life-styles must have been motivated by other compelling reasons such as the increasing need for storage and defence.

3   Most regional comparisons also suggest that the quality of nutrition

declined with the adoption of agriculture. For example, porotic hyperostosis, the skeletal index of anaemia, almost universally appears to increase with the adoption of sedentism or agriculture, either as a consequence of declining dietary quality (for example, high-cereal diets can inhibit the absorption of iron; see El Najjar 1977) or as the result of increasing rates of parasitism and infection (Walker 1986). In addition, although the trends are mixed, people more often than not appear to have become smaller in stature after the adoption of agriculture. Indeed, a downward trend in human stature appears to be more the rule than the exception in human history until the last few centuries, when the trend was reversed in affluent American and European (but not most other) populations. Other skeletal indices of nutrition – reduced diameter of the pelvic outlet, declining development of the base of the skull, reduction in tooth size, increasing rates of premature osteoporosis, and diminishing length of diaphyses (bone-shafts) in children of comparable ages – have all been suggested as signs of deteriorating nutrition among early agricultural populations in different areas of the world (Cohen and Armelagos 1984).

4   Skeletal and dental evidence of childhood stresses (episodes of severe illness, starvation, or malnutrition), such as linear enamel hypoplasia or microscopic Wilson bands on dental enamel, generally appear to become more common after the adoption of agriculture. These data suggest that far from providing better buffering of the population, sedentism and agriculture were commonly associated with increasing frequencies of severe stress from starvation or childhood disease. This would in turn have provided an incentive to return to nomadic life unless compelling factors such as increased population density prevented such a move.

5   Although possibly skewed by poor preservation and subject to contradictory interpretation (cf. Sattenspiel and Harpending 1983, Wood *et al.* 1992), relatively large cemetery samples suggest only modest rates of infant and child death (*c.* 20 per cent infant mortality and 40 to 50 per cent before the age of 15) for pre-agricultural populations. These rates are often lower than those of later prehistoric agricultural populations, and are comparable to those of much of Europe as late as the eighteenth and nineteenth centuries. Average adult ages at death in pre-agricultural populations are very low (as in fact are average adult ages at death in almost all populations studied through skeletons), yet they are commonly no lower, and are often higher, than those of early farming populations in the same region. In North America, adult ages at death in the earliest good samples of hunting and gathering populations (of the Archaic and Woodland periods) commonly match or exceed those in the latest agricultural populations (of the Mississippian period). In the Old World, ages at death appear first to have dropped in the Neolithic period (when the growth rates of populations apparently increased), and then to have increased only later, beginning in the Bronze Age.

Palaeopathological data concerned with the emergence of complex societies and early states are surprisingly mixed, but there is no clear indication that state-level organization commonly improved the overall health and nutrition of the bulk of the people, or that it relieved them of the threat of episodic stress. Rathbun (1984) finds nothing in data on mortality in Iran from the Stone Age through the Bronze Age to suggest an improvement in life expectancy or the buffering of populations. Smith *et al.* (1984), in their Levantine sample, find that the highest levels of several types of pathology occur in the most recent populations. Martin *et al.* (1984) find high rates of stress associated with agricultural populations in Nubia and note an inverse correlation between health and the development of political ties between Nubia and the larger political empires of the region.

In the New World, improvements in health in later periods are associated with some sites in Georgia (Blakeley and Brown 1985) and Alabama (Powell 1988), but decreased life expectancies and very poor health and nutrition are commonly associated with late or 'civilized' populations. Instances of increased stress in later populations are reported from Illinois (Goodman *et al.* 1984), from Tennessee (Storey 1985), from Kentucky (Cassidy 1984) and from metropolitan Teotihuacan, Mexico (Storey 1985).

In short, a substantial body of information from both optimal foraging studies and from palaeopathology supports the contention that the major economic and political advances of prehistory – although they made possible the support of larger human populations and contributed to the success of larger political units – were achieved at the expense of individual health and nutrition. This in turn suggests that growing population and competition, rather than technological progress, played the more significant role in stimulating economic and political change. Much of the observed change seems to have represented a compromise between, on the one hand, the demand for greater quantities of food and for defence in the face of increasing political competition, and on the other, the desire to maintain dietary quality and good health.

FACTORS INFLUENCING POPULATION GROWTH

We are faced with something of a paradox. Why did rates of population growth remain low among prehistoric hunter-gatherers, who, as our data suggest, were relatively healthy? And why did the rate of growth then accelerate after the adoption of agriculture despite what appears to have been a decline in relative health and nutrition?

One possibility which merits further consideration is that we have substantially underestimated the size of the human population at the dawn of the Neolithic revolution, and therefore misrepresented the rates of growth in the pre-Neolithic and Neolithic periods. Most estimates of pre-Neolithic populations are based on measures of population densities among remnant hunter-gatherers, most of whom live in desert environments. Populations like the San or the Australian Aborigines have been considered typical (Birdsell 1968), whereas large and dense populations subsisting on wild resources, such as those living in California at the time of European contact, were assumed to be the exceptions. Recent re-evaluations of material from Europe (Soffer 1985, Price and Brown 1985) and from Australia (Lourandos 1985, Webb 1984), as well as the recognition that many sophisticated Amerindian cultures developed in North America independently of significant maize-based agriculture, may force us to reassess the total size of the human population on the eve of the Neolithic revolution. (We expect, for example, that the hunter-gatherers actually observed by Europeans in America and in Australia may already have been reduced in numbers by as much as 90 per cent from the population which existed as little as a century before.) However, even if we increase the estimate of terminal hunting and gathering populations very substantially, it is still hard to reach a figure which would allow us to calculate an average growth rate for pre-Neolithic populations (over a hundred-thousand-year time span) which would even approach rates observed in more recent history. No matter how we do our calculations, it appears that pre-Neolithic growth rates were relatively low.

It does seem likely that this low average masks marked temporal variation. I would suggest that growth is likely to have been relatively rapid during periods of game-rich hunting, such as characterized the expansion of early North American populations, but to have slowed significantly as the efficiency of resource utilization declined in the Mesolithic (see Hassan 1981).

The average rate of population growth in the pre-Neolithic period could have been low for any of several reasons: (1) because despite the apparent good health of prehistoric hunter-gatherers as revealed in skeletal evidence, these groups actually suffered very high rates of mortality (see Wood *et al.* 1992, who argue that cemetery samples may give a misleading impression of the state of health of living populations); (2) because although normally enjoying reasonable life expectancies and growing quite rapidly, prehistoric populations crashed more frequently than did those of recent history; or (3) because fertility was either naturally low or maintained at artificially low levels. In the following paragraphs I shall review each of these alternatives in turn.

Constantly high mortality

While recognizing the possibility that palaeopathological data may be misleading. I believe that there are reasons to take much of these data at face value. The apparent increase in infection which commonly occurs in archaeologically recorded populations with the adoption of sedentary habits and large population aggregates could be an artefact of skeletal sampling. But such an increase is also predicted by epidemiological theory, and it is observed repeatedly when mobile ethnographically documented populations adopt sedentary habits. Similarly, an increase in anaemia with the adoption of sedentism is predicted as a function of increasing parasitism, and can be observed in the ethnographic record. Hunter-gatherers rarely suffer from anaemia even when their more sedentary neighbours are afflicted. Similarly if, as some studies suggest, enamel hypoplasia is associated with weanling diarrhoea — which is much more common among children in sedentary populations than in mobile ones — it too is likely to have actually increased with the adoption of farming. Ethnographic examples also support the evidence from skeletal samples in suggesting that hunter-gatherer life expectancies are not exceptionally low by historical standards.

In her comprehensive account of San demography, Nancy Howell (1979) suggested that the San enjoyed an average life expectancy at birth of about 30 to 35 years. The figure was surprisingly high, comparing favourably with many recent and historic populations. Moreover, it suggested a level of survivorship more than adequate to permit the maintenance and growth of a human population experiencing average fertility. Her analysis suggested that infants had about a 20 per cent probability of dying in their first year of life, and about a 45 to 50 per cent chance of dying before the age of 15 (the traditional point from which adult survivorship is measured). She further calculated (using modern life tables) that individuals reaching the age of 14 should expect, on average, another 30 to 35 years of life.

Howell's figures for infant and child mortality appear to be about average for the world's known hunting and gathering populations; they are also about the same as rates reported for the best-documented and most complete prehistoric cemeteries (Cohen 1989). The figures are in fact quite moderate by the standards of historical and recent populations and are not high enough to be population-threatening. Indeed, it should not surprise us that rates of infant and child mortality among hunter-gatherers are not conspicuously high by historical standards. Mobility surely does impose stresses and threaten life, but the combination of low population densities and high mobility (which reduces intestinal parasites), as well as the availability of relatively good-quality weaning foods, reduce the risk of synergistic weanling diarrhoea, which is elsewhere a major childhood killer. Moreover, in a world not yet adapted to major epidemics, deaths may not have been concentrated in childhood to the extent that they came to be in historical times (see Lovejoy *et al.* 1977).

Howell's figures for adult life expectancy (from the age of 15) are higher than most others reported for ethnographically recorded groups of hunter-gatherers (which, on average, add only a further 25 years from the age of 15) and are substantially higher than the apparent adult life expectancies of prehistoric cemetery populations. Therefore, prehistoric population growth could have been slow because, despite reasonable rates of infant and child survivorship, adults had very short life-spans. This conclusion would lend support to the high constant mortality model (see Lovejoy *et al.* 1977).

On the other hand, combining the life expectancies for adults and children derived from archaeological and ethnographic observations, using tables such as those provided by Weiss (1973; see Cohen 1989), life expectancy at birth appears to have averaged about 25 years in hunting and gathering groups, a figure adequate to permit the continuation and growth of populations with average human reproduction, and which also matches reported figures for life expectancy at birth for much of Europe as late as the eighteenth century, and for urban Europe into the nineteenth. Moreover, estimates of adult survivorship in both ethnographically and archaeologically recorded populations of hunter-gatherers are probably artificially low. Among modern hunter-gatherers, outside the Arctic where deaths from starvation and accidental exposure are relatively common, the great majority of observed deaths result from infectious diseases, and particularly from newly introduced epidemic diseases which probably did not exist in the prehistoric world, suggesting that prehistoric hunter-gatherers may have enjoyed longer life. A disproportionately high impact on adults rather than children is precisely the effect we would expect from exogenous diseases newly introduced to once-isolated populations, and this would help to explain the poor adult survivorship in contemporary hunter-gatherers.

In addition, almost all archaeologically studied groups, not just of hunter-gatherers, display low average adult ages at death – some observers would claim they are too low to be credible, suggesting that methods of determining age at death in skeletons may systematically underestimate such ages for adults (Howell 1982, Bocquet-Appel and Masset 1982, cf. Van Gerven and Armelagos 1983). And, as noted, the observed ages at death of prehistoric hunter-gatherers, though low, are often higher than those of subsequent and presumably faster growing populations in the same region (Cohen and Armelagos 1984). For reasons discussed in detail by Sattenspiel and Harpending (1983), the rate of population growth will affect the distribution of ages at death in a cemetery, so that faster-growing groups will appear to be dying younger. The comparison, therefore, may not be meaningful; nevertheless there is no evidence, either archaeological or ethnographic, to suggest that prehistoric hunter-gatherers died at ages which were exceptionally low by historical standards. Finally, prehistoric hunting and gathering populations appear to have been capable of very high rates of growth (as in the apparently rapid colonization of the New World), suggesting that growth was not inexorably limited by constant high mortality.

Episodic high mortality

The second possible explanation for the slow growth of pre-agricultural populations is that overall, average growth rates conceal a series of peaks and crashes, analogous to historically observed episodes of depopulation, but with the crashes occurring somewhat more frequently in the pre-Neolithic era than has been the case in more recent history (Ammerman 1975). The best-documented population crashes of recent times, however, seem to be associated with the spread of epidemic diseases. This requires two conditions which are unlikely to have obtained in the prehistoric world: high population densities and relatively rapid transport of people, their domesticates and their parasites from place to place. Models of the transmission of diseases such as measles, influenza, mumps, rubella, cholera, and others suggest that they are not capable of sustaining themselves without very large supplies of new victims (by birth or immigration, or by the transmission of the diseases to new populations), because they 'burn up' potential victims (by death or by conferral of immunity) very rapidly. Measles, for example, has been estimated to require a coherent host population of several hundred thousand people to be self-sustaining. Most medical historians therefore consider the major epidemic diseases to be modern diseases of civilization. If measles had appeared by mutation (as it apparently did from the distemper virus of dogs – see Fiennes 1978) prior to the advent of civilization, it might have proved lethal to a local population (as it does today when newly introduced to a 'virgin' population), but it would have burned itself out without spreading very far. The more important point is that not just measles but *any* disease acting like measles would have met a similar fate. In the historical world, the devastating effects of these epidemics have been associated with the rapid propagation of infection to large but previously isolated populations, a pattern unlikely to have been duplicated in early prehistory.

In addition, other lethal and historically important diseases such as bubonic plague or falciparum malaria, which are less dependent on critical thresholds of human population (because they can be housed and carried by animal or insect vectors), are none the less clearly associated with high population density. Even in the relatively densely populated and cosmopolitan world of eighteenth-century France, the plague seems to have had far more devastating effects in towns and cities – and particularly those situated on major trade routes – than in small, isolated communities, despite the fact that the disease is carried by black rats, a relatively mobile alternative host species. In short, by extrapolating what we know from contemporary observations about the behaviour of disease organisms to the conditions of the past, we would be led to expect that population crashes on a large scale due to infectious disease would, if anything, have been far less common in prehistory.

A second possibility is that prehistoric groups endured high rates of famine-induced mortality. Episodic hunger and occasional starvation are reported among historical and contemporary hunting and gathering groups (e.g. Hayden 1981), but it is hard to make a convincing case that such episodes were significantly more frequent before the onset of the Neolithic than after. For one thing, most of our observations of contemporary hunter-gatherers – and particularly the documentation of starvation – come from very cold or very dry environments, e.g., the Arctic or the Central Desert of Australia, environments in which more powerful groups do not even attempt to support themselves unless specialized resources such as gold or oil make it profitable to undertake the large-scale importation of food. (Of course, during the Pleistocene ice ages, pre-Neolithic hunter-gatherers lived in a world of more arctic conditions and might have sometimes faced starvation; but they also lived in a world exceptionally rich in game.) Though starvation may be a common cause of death among Arctic hunters, it is virtually unknown among hunter-gatherer groups in temperate and tropical regions. Thus, although Howell (1979) documents hunger among the !Kung San in the Kalahari, she found no history of starvation-related mortality. And the Hadza, living in the type of environment once preferred by our prehistoric ancestors, rarely go hungry and have not been observed to face any serious environmental crisis that might have affected the whole spectrum of their diet (Woodburn 1968, O'Connell *et al.* 1988). It seems unlikely, then, that prehistoric hunter-gatherers, inhabiting environments still relatively rich in large game animals, would have faced starvation with a frequency unparalleled in later history.

Nor is it clear from recent experience that mobile populations living off wild resources are necessarily more prone to famine than sedentary agricultural groups. In fact the opposite appears to be the case. Domesticated plants often lack the hardiness of their wild forebears because they have been selected for human needs and human palates. Moreover, they are often grown both at artificially high densities, rendering them susceptible to blight, and outside the geographical environments to which they are genetically adapted. Moreover, the cultivation of domestic crops involves a prior investment of labour, often by several months, so that unpredictable shortages cannot easily be overcome. And of course, farming populations, themselves expanding within a territory circumscribed by the presence of other groups, would be relatively limited in their ability to move to new resources when faced with crop failure. Finally, much of the starvation which occurs in the modern world results from failure not of the crop but of storage and transport technology (Rotberg and Rabb 1983), as well as from political and economic barriers to the movement of food (Sen 1981, Dando 1980).

It is hard to make any direct, empirical comparison of the relative significance of starvation in pre-agricultural and agricultural regimes, but there is no clear evidence that human progress has reduced the risk of famine as it has come to support ever larger populations. One cross-cultural survey of the risk of starvation (Gaulin and Konner 1977) found that ethnographically recorded hunter-gatherers fared about as well as agricultural populations. Records of stress in prehistoric populations as revealed in skeletal material (particularly teeth) may suggest that hunter-gatherers faced fewer such disruptions than more recent populations; however, the skeletal evidence does not enable us to distinguish starvation-induced mortality from that due to other stresses (see Cohen and Armelagos 1984).

Low natural fertility

A third explanation for the slow growth of pre-agricultural populations, which has gained some popularity among anthropologists, is that hunter–gatherers enjoy naturally low fertility. Howell's (1979) careful documentation of !Kung San fertility suggested that a woman who lived to complete her reproductive span would produce, on average, only about 4.7 children, a figure well below Third World averages for child production (6 to 8) and which, combined with average San life expectancy, would yield a population growth rate very near to zero. Whether this helps to explain the low growth rate of prehistoric hunter–gatherer populations depends on whether the San can be regarded as typical of hunter–gatherers in this respect, as well as on whether a mechanism can be found which can explain the low fertility and which can be extrapolated with confidence into the past.

Howell herself suggested that the extreme leanness of San women might explain their low fertility, since it is associated with late menarche, irregular ovulation, long post-partum amenorrhoea, and early menopause. (She concedes, however, that gonorrhoea, presumed to be a recent introduction, may also contribute to low reproductive rates.) Another possibility is that exercise, which stimulates the production of the contraceptive hormone prolactine, may contribute to low fertility among hunter–gatherers, much as it does among modern athletes (Malina 1983).

The data from optimal foraging studies and from palaeopathology, however, make it appear that prehistoric hunter–gatherers would, on the whole, have been better nourished and fatter than the contemporary San. Moreover, a smaller proportion of the work load may have fallen on women prior to the broad-spectrum revolution. These observations suggest that the physiological consequences of leanness or heavy exercise would not have operated in any systematic way during the prehistoric past as mechanisms for reducing fertility. Indeed, they might better fit a model in which populations of hunters in game-rich environments expanded rapidly while the growth of Mesolithic populations was slowed down.

Low fertility can also be explained by prolonged lactation, a mechanism known to have contraceptive effects (Lee 1980, Konner and Worthman 1980, Habicht et al. 1985), and one whose operation may be extrapolated into the past with somewhat more assurance. One major limit of a pre-Neolithic diet appears to have been the scarcity and 'expense' of appropriate weaning foods, no matter how rich the diet available to adults and despite the relatively high dietary quality of what weaning foods were available. Whatever their other shortcomings, diets based on ground cereals provide readily available weaning foods and might have tended, on average, to lower the age of weaning and shorten birth spacing, resulting in higher fertility.

A comparative review of contemporary hunter–gatherer fertility indicates a wide range of variation from low levels like those of the San to higher levels such as those documented among the Aché of Paraguay (Hill *et al.* 1984) and the Agta of the Philippines (Goodman *et al.* 1985), which reach the modern Third World average of more than six live births per woman. (The Agta are particularly notable because the women participate actively in various phases of hunting life.) On the other hand, data on births among other hunter-gatherers (which usually do not distinguish between birth control and natural infertility) indicate that these groups, on average, have a fertility below modern Third World levels (Cohen 1989). And there is evidence from various contexts that the fertility of hunter-gatherers is lower than that of their own more sedentary neighbours, and that fertility does increase when they, too, settle down (Cohen 1989). My own reading of the data on fertility and life expectancy in hunting and gathering groups suggests that although the San may be an extreme case, average rates of child production may have been only slightly higher in prehistoric groups and average life expectancies only slightly lower, producing very low average rates of population growth which could, in turn, have been cancelled out by episodic crashes, even though such crashes were neither particularly common nor severe by the standards of later history. Population growth accelerated after the Neolithic because fertility increased, not because mortality was reduced.

I am not convinced, however, that the low fertility of hunting and gathering groups is entirely the result of natural contraception. None of the natural mechanisms which have been proposed is wholly convincing as an explanation for prehistoric patterns, and critics have argued that much of the low fertility (even among the San) is produced by infanticide and abortion (Dickeman 1975). Hassan (1981) concluded that rates of child production might have increased in the Neolithic as the parameters of birth control choices were altered by the reduced costs and greater marginal utility of children under agricultural regimes of production, and as group size came to confer a competitive political advantage. I, too, am inclined to suspect that conscious economic decision-making has played a larger part in the process than is assumed in some of the naturalistic models.

But this in turn leaves us with a final paradox. Given the sociobiological premise that individuals should be predisposed to maximize their reproductive fitness, and the data I have adduced on probable patterns of prehistoric health and nutrition, why did pre-agricultural populations not grow faster? Two possibilities occur to me, one of which reflects a minor deviation from sociobiological doctrine, the other a more major deviation. First, even if ultimately motivated by the goal of improving reproductive fitness, animals and people may well judge their success by means of proximate indicators (in much the same way that the sensations of pain and pleasure which motivate our activities are fairly reliable, but not perfect, guides to how well those activities are actually conducive to fitness). Rearing a small number of children with a relatively low percentage of loss − and keeping them in good health − may have been the 'strategy' adopted by prehistoric hunter-gatherers, even though, in retrospect, subsequent events proved that having more babies, suffering more illness and losing a higher proportion of infants and children (as post-Neolithic populations did) was the fitter strategy in the long run.

The second possibility is to suggest that pre-Neolithic parents, like their modern counterparts, were more concerned with their own lifetime comfort than with their genetic fitness. In a world relatively free from childhood diseases, they may have reared fewer children, partly in order to increase their own economic returns and partly because of their confidence that enough children would survive to protect them in their old age. Thus the increased rates of reproduction after the Neolithic may have resulted in part from considerations of economic utility, and in part from parents' appreciation of their increased vulnerability to the loss of descendants in childhood.

CONCLUSION

The archaeological record displays a history of continuous and accelerating population growth which interacts causally with changes in the social, economic and political structure of human societies. Population growth seems to play a significant role in stimulating each of the major transformations of prehistory: the broad-spectrum and Neolithic revolutions, the emergence of complex social organization and the origins of the state. The rate of population growth appears, in turn, to have been responsive to economic and social patterns, particularly those associated with sedentism and farming. Whether the acceleration of population growth resulted from reduced mortality or from increased fertility is not clear. However, taken as a whole the data do not support the once-fashionable Hobbesian image of extreme hardship and high mortality among our prehistoric ancestors. They rather suggest that prehistoric hunter-gatherers were reasonably well nourished and relatively free from infectious disease, with rates of childhood death and overall life expectancy that were moderate by historical standards.

REFERENCES

Acsádi, G. and Nemeskéri, J. (1970) *History of Human Lifespan and Mortality*, Budapest: Academei Kiadó.

Allison, M. (1984) 'Paleopathology in Peruvian and Chilean populations', in M. N. Cohen and G. J. Armelagos (eds) *Paleopathology at the Origins of Agriculture*, New York: Academic Press.

Ammerman, A. J. (1975) 'Late Pleistocene population dynamics: an alternate view', *Human Ecology* 3: 310–34.

Anderson, A. (1983) 'Faunal depletion and subsistence change in the early prehistory of southern New Zealand', *Archaeology in Oceania* 18: 1–10.

Angel, J. L. (1984) 'Health as a crucial factor in the changes from hunting to developed agriculture in the Eastern Mediterranean', in M. N. Cohen and G. J. Armelagos (eds) *Paleopathology at the Origins of Agriculture*, New York: Academic Press.

Baron, R. M. (1980) 'The case for differences in the responses of humans and other animals to high density', in M. N. Cohen, R. S. Malpass and H. G. Klein (eds) *Biosocial Mechanisms of Population Regulation*, New Haven: Yale University Press.

Bender, B. (1978) 'Gatherer-hunter to farmer: a social perspective', *World Archaeology* 10: 204–22.

Binford, L. (1968) 'Post-Pleistocene adaptations', in L. Binford and S. R. Binford (eds) *New Perspectives in Archaeology*, Chicago: Aldine.

Bird, N. (1983) 'Wage gathering, socio-economic changes and the case of the food-gathering Naikens of south India', in P. Robb (ed.) *Rural South Asia: Linkages and Development*, London: Curzon.

Birdsell, J. (1953) 'Some environmental and cultural factors influencing the structure of Australian Aboriginal populations', *American Naturalist* 87: 171–207.

—— (1968) 'Some predictions for the Pleistocene based on equilibrium systems among recent hunters', in R. B. Lee and I. DeVore (eds) *Man the Hunter*, Chicago: Aldine.

Blackburn, R. (1982) 'In the land of milk and honey: Okiek adaptations to the forest and neighbors', in E. Leacock and R. B. Lee (eds) *Politics and History in Band Societies*, Cambridge: Cambridge University Press.

Blakeley, R. and Brown, A. (1985) 'Functionally adaptive biocultural diversity in the Coosa Chiefdom of 16th century Georgia', *American Journal of Physical Anthropology* 66: 146.

Blurton-Jones, N. and Sibley, P. M. (1978) 'Testing adaptiveness of culturally determined behavior: do Bushman women maximize their reproductive success?', in *Human Behavior and Adaptation*, Society for the Study of Human Biology, Symposium 18.

Bocquet-Appel, J.-P. and Masset, C. (1982) 'Farewell to paleodemography', *Journal of Human Evolution* 11: 321–33.

Boserup, E. (1965) *The Conditions of Agricultural Growth*, Chicago: Aldine.

Bronson, B. (1972) 'Farm labor and the evolution of food production', in B. Spooner (ed.) *Population Growth: Anthropological Implications*, Cambridge: Mass.: MIT Press.

Buikstra, J. E. and Cook, D. C. (1980) 'Paleopathology: an American account', *Annual Review of Anthropology* 9: 433–70.

Butzer, K. (1971) *Environment and Archaeology*, Chicago: Aldine.

Carneiro, R. (1967) 'On the relationship between size of population and complexity of social organization', *Southwest Journal of Anthropology* 22: 234–43.

—— (1970) 'A theory of the origin of the state', *Science* 169: 733–8.

Cassidy, C. M. (1984) 'Skeletal evidence for prehistoric subsistence adaptation', in M. N. Cohen and G. J. Armelagos (eds) *Paleopathology at the Origins of Agriculture*, New York: Academic Press.

Childe, V. G. (1951) *Social Evolution*, London: Watts.

Coale, A. (1974) 'The history of human population', *Scientific American* 231: 41–5.

Cohen, M. N. (1977) *The Food Crisis in Prehistory*, New Haven: Yale University Press.

—— (1981) 'The ecological basis of New World state Formation', in G. D. Jones and R. Kautz (eds) *The Transition to Statehood in the New World*, Cambridge: Cambridge University Press.

—— (1984) 'Introduction to the symposium', in M. N. Cohen and G. J. Armelagos (eds) *Paleopathology at the Origins of Agriculture*, New York: Academic Press.

—— (1985) 'Prehistoric hunter-gatherers: the meaning of social complexity', in T. D. Price and J. A. Brown (eds) *Prehistoric Hunter-Gatherers: the Emergence of Cultural Complexity*, New York: Academic Press.

—— (1989) *Health and the Rise of Civilization*, New Haven: Yale University Press.

Cohen, M. N. and G. J. Armelagos (eds) (1984) *Paleopathology at the Origins of Agriculture*, New York: Academic Press.

Colson, E. (1978) 'A redundancy of actors', in F. Barth (ed.) *Scale and Social Organization*, Oslo: Universitetsforlaget.

Dando, W. A. (1980) *The Geography of Famine*, London: Edward Arnold.

Denbow, J. R. and Wilmsen, E. M. (1986) 'Advent and course of pastoralism in the Kalahari', *Science* 234: 1509–15.

Dickeman, M. (1975) 'Demographic consequences of infanticide', *Annual Review of Ecology and Systematics* 1: 107–38.

Dobyns, H. (1983) *Their Number Become Thinned*, Knoxville: University of Tennessee Press.

El Najjar, M. (1977) 'Maize, malarias and the anemias in the Precolumbian New World', *Yearbook of Physical Anthropology* 28: 329–37.

Epstein, Y. (1980) 'Physiological effects of crowding on humans', in M. N. Cohen, R. S. Malpass and H. G. Klein (eds) *Biosocial Mechanisms of Population Regulation*, New Haven: Yale University Press.

Fiennes, R. (1978) *Zoonoses and the Origins and Ecology of Human Disease*, New York: Academic Press.

Flannery, K. V. (1969) 'Origins and ecological effects of early domestication in Iran and the Near East', in P. J. Ucko and G. W. Dimbleby (eds) *The Domestication and Exploitation of Plants and Animals*, London: Duckworth.

Freedman J. L. (1980) 'Human reactions to population density', in M. N. Cohen, R. S. Malpass and H. G. Klein (eds) *Biosocial Mechanisms of Population Regulation*, New Haven: Yale University Press.

Fried, M. (1967) *The Evolution of Political Society*, New York: Random House.

Gaulin, S. and Konner, M. (1977) 'On the natural diet of primates including humans', in R. J. Wurtman and J. J. Wurtman (eds) *Nutrition and the Brain*, vol. 1, New York: Raven Press.

Geertz, C. (1963) *Agricultural Involution*, Berkeley: University of California Press.

Goodman, A., Lallo, J., Armelagos, G. J. and Rose, J. C. (1984) 'Health changes at Dickson Mounds AD 950–1300', in M. N. Cohen and G. J. Armelagos (eds) *Paleopathology at the Origins of Agriculture*, New York: Academic Press.

Goodman, M., Estioko-Griffin, A., Griffin, P. B. and Grove, J. S. (1985) 'Menarche, pregnancy, birth spacing and menopause among Agta women foragers of Cagayan Province, Luzon, the Philippines', *Annals of Human Biology* 12: 169–78.

Habicht, J.-P., Davanzo, J., Butz, W. P. and Meyers, L. (1985) 'The contraceptive role of breast feeding', *Population Studies* 39: 213–32.

Harris, D. (1977) 'Alternative pathways toward agriculture', in C. Reed (ed.) *The Origins of Agriculture*, The Hague: Mouton.

Harris, M. (1985) *Culture, People, Nature*, 4th edn, New York: Harper & Row.

Hassan, F. (1981) *Demographic Archaeology*, New York: Academic Press.

Hawkes, K. and O'Connell, J. F. (1985) 'Optimal foraging models and the case of the !Kung', *American Anthropologist* 87: 401–5.

Hayden, B. (1972) 'Population control among hunter-gatherers', *World Archaeology* 4: 205–21.

293

—— (1981) 'Subsistence and ecological adaptation of modern hunter-gatherers', in R. S. O. Harding and G. Teleki (eds) *Omnivorous Primates*, New York: Columbia University Press.

Hill, K., Kaplan, H., Hawkes, K. and Hurtado, A. (1984) 'Seasonal variance in the diet of Aché hunter-gatherers in Eastern Paraguay', *Human Ecology* 12: 145–80.

Howell, N. (1979) *Demography of the Dobe !Kung*, New York: Academic Press.

—— (1982) 'Village organization implied by a paleodemographic lifetable: the Libben Site, Ottawa Country, Ohio', *American Journal of Physical Anthropology* 59: 263–70.

Huss-Ashmore, R., Goodman, A. H. and Armelagos, G. J. (1982). 'Nutritional inference from paleopathology', *Advances in Archaeological Method and Theory* 5: 395–474.

Johnson, G. (1982) 'Organizational structure and scalar stress', in C. Renfrew, M. Rowlands and B. Seagraves (eds) *Theory and Explanation in Archaeology*, New York: Academic Press.

Karlin, R. (1980) 'Social effects of crowding on humans', in M. N. Cohen, R. S. Malpass and H. G. Klein (eds) *Biosocial Mechanisms of Population Regulation*, New Haven: Yale University Press.

Kennedy, K. (1984) 'Growth, nutrition, and pathology in changing paleodemographic settings in South Asia', in M. N. Cohen and G. J. Armelagos (eds) *Paleopathology at the Origins of Agriculture*, New York: Academic Press.

Konner, M. and Worthman, C. (1980) 'Nursing frequency, gonad function, and birth spacing among !Kung hunter-gatherers', *Science* 207: 788–91.

Lee, R. B. (1969) '!Kung Bushman subsistence: an input–output analysis', in A. P. Vayda (ed.) *Environment and Cultural Behavior*, New York: Natural History Press.

—— (1972) 'The intensification of social life among the !Kung Bushmen', in B. Spooner (ed.) *Population Growth: Anthropological Implications*, Cambridge, Mass.: MIT Press.

—— (1976) '!Kung spatial organization', in R. B. Lee and I. DeVore (eds) *Kalahari Hunter-Gatherers*, Cambridge, Mass.: Harvard University Press.

—— (1980) 'Lactation, ovulation, infanticide and women's work; a study of hunter-gatherer population regulation', in M. N. Cohen, R. S. Malpass and H. G. Klein (eds) *Biosocial Mechanisms of Population Regulation*, New Haven: Yale University Press.

Lee, R. B. and DeVore, I. (eds) (1968) *Man the Hunter*, Chicago: Aldine.

Lourandos, H. (1985) 'Intensification and Australian prehistory', in T. D. Price and J. A. Brown (eds) *Prehistoric Hunter-Gatherers: the Emergence of Cultural Complexity*, Orlando: Academic Press.

Lovejoy, C. O., Meindl, R. S., Prysbeck, T. R., Barton, T. S., Heiple, K. G. and Kotting, D. (1977) 'Paleobiology at the Libben Site, Ottawa Co., Ohio', *Science* 198: 291–3.

McNeill, W. (1975) *Plagues and Peoples*, Garden City, NY: Anchor.

Malina, R. M. (1983) 'Menarche in athletes: a synthesis and hypothesis', *Annals of Human Biology* 10: 1–24.

Marks, S. (1976) *Large Mammals and a Brave People*, Seattle: University of Washington Press.

Martin, D., Armelagos, G., Goodman, A. and Van Gerven, D. P. (1984) 'The effects of socioeconomic change in prehistoric Africa: Sudanese Nubia as a case study', in M. N. Cohen and G. J. Armelagos (eds) *Paleopathology at the Origins of Agriculture*, New York: Academic Press.

Martin, P. (1973) 'The Discovery of America', *Science* 179: 969–74.

Meiklejohn, C., Schentag, C., Vanema, A. and Key, P. (1984) 'Socioeconomic change and patterns of pathology and variation in the Mesolithic and Neolithic of Western Europe: some suggestions', in M. N. Cohen and G. J. Armelagos (eds) *Paleopathology at the Origins of Agriculture*, New York: Academic Press.

O'Connell, J. F., Hawkes, K. and Blurton-Jones, N. (1988) 'Hadza scavenging: implications for Plio/Pleistocene Hominid subsistence', *Current Anthropology* 29: 356–63.

Powell, M. L. (1988) *Status and Health in Prehistory*, Washington, DC: Smithsonian Institution Press.

Price, T. D., and Brown, J. A. (eds) (1985) *Prehistoric Hunter-Gatherers: the Emergence of Cultural Complexity*, Orlando: Academic Press.

Ramenofsky, A. F. (1988) *Vectors of Death*, Albuquerque: University of New Mexico Press.

Rathbun, T. (1984) 'Skeletal pathology from the Paleolithic through the metal ages in Iran and Iraq', in M. N. Cohen and G. J. Armelagos (eds) *Paleopathology at the Origins of Agriculture*, New York: Academic Press.

Rotberg, R. I. and Rabb, T. A. (1983) (eds) *Hunger in History*, Cambridge: Cambridge University Press.

Sahlins, M. (1968) 'Notes on the original affluent society', in R. B. Lee and I. DeVore (eds) *Man the Hunter*, Chicago: Aldine.

—— (1972) *Stone Age Economics*, London: Tavistock.

Sattenspiel, L. and Harpending, H. (1983) 'Stable populations and skeletal age', *American Antiquity* 48: 489–98.

Schrire, C. (1980) 'An inquiry into the evolutionary status and apparent identity of the San hunter-gatherers', *Human Ecology* 8: 9–22.

—— (ed.) (1984) *Past and Present in Hunter-Gatherer Studies*, Orlando: Academic Press.

Sen, A. (1981) *Poverty and Famines*, Oxford: Oxford University Press.

Simon, J. (1983) 'The effects of population on nutrition and economic well-being', in R. I. Rotberg and T. A. Rabb (eds) *Hunger in History*, Cambridge: Cambridge University Press.

Smith, P., Bar-Yosef, O. and Sillen, A. (1984) 'Archaeological and skeletal evidence for dietary change during the Late Pleistocene–Early Holocene in the Levant', in M. N. Cohen and G. J. Armelagos (eds) *Paleopathology at the Origins of Agriculture*, New York: Academic Press.

Smith, P. E. L. (1972) *Food Production and its Consequences*, Menlo Park, Cal.: Cummings Publishing Company.

Soffer, O. (1985) 'Patterns of intensification as seen from the Upper Paleolithic of the Central Russian Plain', in T. D. Price and J. A. Brown (eds) *Prehistoric Hunter-Gatherers: the Emergence of Cultural Complexity*, Orlando: Academic Press.

Speth, J. (1988) 'Hunter-gatherer diet, resource stress and the origins of agriculture', *Symposium on Population Growth Disease and the Origins of Agriculture*, Rutgers University, New Brunswick, NJ.

Storey, R. (1985) 'An estimate of mortality in a pre-Columbian urban population', *American Anthropologist* 87: 519–35.

Van Gerven, D. P. and Armelagos, G. J. (1983) 'Farewell to paleodemography: a reply', *Journal of Human Evolution* 12: 352–66.

Vigilant, L., Stoneking, M., Harpending, H., Hawkes, K. and Wilson, A. C. (1991) 'African population and the evolution of human mitochondrial DNA', *Science* 253: 1503–7.

HUMANITY

Walker, P. (1986) 'Porotic hyperostosis in a marine-dependent California Indian population', *American Journal of Physical Anthropology* 69: 345–54.

Webb, S. (1984) 'Prehistoric stress in Australian Aborigines', thesis, Department of Prehistory, Australian National University.

Weiss, K. M. (1973) *Demographic Models for Anthropology*, Memoir of the Society for American Archaeology no. 27.

Wilmsen, E. M. (1978) 'Seasonal effects of dietary intake on the Kalahari San', *Federation Procedings* 37: 65–72.

Winterhalder, B. and Smith, E. A. (eds) (1981) *Hunter-gatherer Foraging Strategies*, Chicago: University of Chicago Press.

Wittfogel, K. (1957) *Oriental Despotism*, New Haven: Yale University Press.

Wood, J., Milner, G., Harpending, H. and Weiss, K. (1992) 'The osteological paradox: problems of inferring prehistoric health from skeletal samples', *Current Anthropology* 33: 343–70.

Woodburn, J. (1968) 'An introduction to Hadza ecology', in R. B. Lee and I. DeVore (eds) *Man the Hunter*, Chicago: Aldine.

Wynne-Edwards, V. C. (1962) *Animal Dispersion in Relation to Social Behaviour*, Edinburgh: Oliver & Boyd.

FURTHER READING

Barth, F. (1978) *Scale and Social Organization*, Oslo: Universitetsforlaget.

Boserup, E. (1965) *The Conditions of Agricultural Growth*, Chicago: Aldine.

Childe, V. G. (1951) *Social Evolution*, London: Watts.

Cohen, M. (1977) *The Food Crisis in Prehistory*, New Haven: Yale University Press.

—— (1989) *Health and the Rise of Civilization*, New Haven: Yale University Press.

Cohen, M. and Armelagos, G. J. (eds) (1984) *Paleopathology at the Origins of Agriculture*, New York: Academic Press.

Dando, W. A. (1980) *The Geography of Famine*, London: Edward Arnold.

Dobyns, H. (1983) *Their Numbers Become Thinned*, Knoxville: University of Tennessee Press.

Fried, M. (1967) *The Evolution of Political Society*, New York: Random House.

Hassan, F. (1981) *Demographic Archaeology*, New York: Academic Press.

Howell, N. (1979) *The Demography of the Dobe !Kung*, New York: Academic Press.

Johnson, A. and Earle, T. (1987) *The Evolution of Human Society*, Stanford: Stanford University Press.

Lee, R. B. and DeVore, I. (eds) (1968) *Man the Hunter*, Chicago: Aldine.

—— (1976) *Kalahari Hunter–Gatherers*, Cambridge, Mass.: Harvard University Press.

McNeill, W. (1975) *Plagues and Peoples*, Garden City, NY: Anchor Press.

Powell, M. L. (1988) *Status and Health in Prehistory*, Washington: Smithsonian Institution Press.

Price, T. D. and Brown, J. A. (eds) (1985) *Prehistoric Hunter-Gatherers*, Orlando: Academic Press.

Ramenofsky, A. F. (1988) *Vectors of Death*, Albuquerque: University of New Mexico Press.

Schrire, C. (ed.) (1984) *Past and Present in Hunter-Gatherer Studies*, New York: Academic Press.

11

DISEASE AND THE DESTRUCTION OF INDIGENOUS POPULATIONS

Stephen J. Kunitz

INTRODUCTION

My focus in this article is on the impact that European contact has had upon non-Europeans. The topic is vast since indigenous populations, by which I mean the native peoples of non-European lands, are enormously diverse — a diversity that is matched by their disease experience. I shall proceed by examining the sources of diversity, on a series of progressively finer levels of analysis. On the broadest and most inclusive level, there is the difference between the Old World of Eurasia and Africa and the New World of the Americas and Oceania. Then there are the differences among colonizing European nations. Third, there are differences between populations subject to the same European power, but inhabiting different ecological settings. Fourth, we can compare alternative cultural adaptations of different indigenous groups to the same ecological setting. And finally, there are differences in the ways in which members of the same indigenous population have experienced European contact. All of these contrasts have important consequences for the health and diseases of indigenous peoples. To exemplify the many different ways in which European contact has influenced the health of indigenous peoples, I shall draw on a number of specific case studies from sub-Saharan Africa, North and South America, and the Pacific.

Before proceeding, it is important to recognize the distinctions between non-infectious and infectious diseases and, among the latter, between chronic and acute infections. Acute infectious diseases are those that have short latency and infectious periods and a short illness followed by either transient or permanent immunity. Chronic infectious diseases are characterized by slow recovery rates and long periods of infectiousness, and do not result in permanent immunity. The differences are crucial, for acute infectious diseases generally require a large population in order to be sustained on a permanent basis (something in the order of at least 500,000 in the case of measles, for instance) whereas chronic infectious diseases may be sustained in much smaller populations.

It seems to be the case that for most of our species's time on earth our ancestors lived in bands of perhaps fifty people and supported themselves by hunting and gathering. Under such conditions the diseases that afflicted them were those that had evolved along with them from their primate ancestors or those (such as malaria) that they picked up from the animals in their environments. The diseases were chronic rather than acute, for it is generally agreed that the acute infectious diseases (such as smallpox and measles) only evolved when populations had reached sufficient size to support them, and this did not occur until the development of agriculture some ten thousand years ago.

Once large populations developed in Eurasia, epidemics of acute infectious diseases evolved which spread across the entire continent. McNeill (1976) argues that it was during the first fifteen hundred years of the present era that the centres of civilization in China, India, the Near East, and Europe were microbially united by epidemics of acute infectious diseases (such as smallpox and measles) and by epizootics (such as bubonic plague). The timing and causes of the subsequent diminution in epidemics are topics beyond the bounds of the present chapter and are currently contentious (McKeown 1976, Flinn 1981, Omran 1971). Suffice it to say that as pandemics and epidemics waned — sometimes as the result of the growth of stable nation states, sometimes owing to public health interventions such as immunizations for smallpox — a residuum was uncovered of endemic infectious diseases. These tended to be chronic in nature (such as tuberculosis, typhoid, typhus, and the pneumonia-diarrhoea complex of childhood) and, unlike the epidemic diseases, seem to be more lethal when the host is malnourished (Kunitz 1986).

The endemic diseases have in their turn responded to improvements in living conditions (increasing income and education, improved sanitary facilities, changing standards of personal hygiene, and preventive and curative medicine) and have been replaced in importance by chronic and presumably non-infectious diseases and man-made afflictions. Whether such afflictions as violence, automobile accidents, and substance abuse are to be considered 'diseases' is itself a matter of debate. Because I am concerned with all causes of mortality and morbidity, I shall include afflictions of this kind within the compass of this article, and ignore the definitional issue entirely.

As for the non-infectious conditions that are widely agreed to be diseases — e.g. ischaemic heart disease, stroke, cancer, and diabetes — there is some debate about how prevalent they were in past times when infectious diseases were more common. The consensus appears to be that while none of them was unknown, virtually all occur at higher rates now than in the past. This is not simply the result of increasing survival to older ages but represents a real increase even when the changing age structure is taken into account. This is an important issue, because indigenous peoples are increasingly experiencing these so-called diseases of civilization.

THE OLD WORLD AND THE NEW

For my purposes the Old World includes Eurasia and Africa. The New World includes the Americas and Oceania. The expansion of Europe had a profound impact on all non-Europeans, but epidemiologically and demographically it took a somewhat different form in each World. To the degree that European contact with non-Europeans in Asia and Africa had health-related consequences, they were the result primarily of political and economic domination. In the Americas and Oceania, by contrast, contact-induced disease was as much a prelude to European domination as its aftermath. Here domination was facilitated, and even made possible, by the devastating pandemics that decimated and demoralized whole populations, and which often spread in advance of the invading Europeans, carried by natives who fled before them (Borah 1964).

These differences are accounted for by the fact that the diseases carried by Europeans, most notably perhaps smallpox, measles, and influenza, were diseases which they themselves had been exposed to, survived, and become immune to. This was also true for large parts of Eurasia and for some areas of Africa.[1] It was not the case in the New World, where the natives had never been exposed to such diseases and where entire populations were afflicted almost simultaneously, leaving no one to carry on with the vital tasks of nursing the sick and the production of subsistence. Whether these people were also immunologically more vulnerable because their ancestors had never been exposed to these conditions is a matter of debate. It is plausible but not necessary to explain what happened. In so-called 'virgin soil' populations exposed for the first time to an acute infectious disease, everyone exposed becomes sick. In severe diseases such as smallpox and measles, the debility may be such as to make it impossible for people to care for themselves. High death rates, demoralization and social collapse ensue. Often the religion of the invaders was thought, by both Europeans and natives, to be more powerful than the religious beliefs and practices of the natives, further increasing the demoralization of the latter and making conquest that much easier.

In addition to sharing many diseases with Europeans, non-European natives of the Old World had some unique diseases of their own to which Europeans had not been exposed. These were the so-called tropical diseases, most of which cannot flourish in temperate climates. Europeans often fared poorly when exposed to such disease environments. Since the native populations of Africa and Asia were not being decimated by European diseases, and since European settlers and soldiers were often weakened if not killed by the tropical diseases, the same kind of European demographic wave that engulfed the natives of the New World did not overwhelm those of the Old (Hartwig and

Patterson 1978: 10). But this is not to say that European contact was without effect on the health of Asians and Africans. I draw my examples now from Africa south of the Sahara because, though part of the Old World, its disease pool was not so thoroughly mixed with that of the Europeans as was the Asians' disease pool or that of North Africans.

Africa south of the Sahara is a land in which a large number of chronic infectious diseases — such as typhoid, leprosy, trypanosomiasis (sleeping sickness) and malaria — have been endemic, presumably for centuries. Though often lethal (especially sleeping sickness), more often than not their effect has been debilitating. It is generally agreed that a rough sort of equilibrium must have developed between the human and microbial populations. The human adaptations were both physiological and socio-cultural, though the distinction is not always a clear one. Among physiological adaptations by far the best known is the sickle-cell trait, which enhances resistance to malaria. Among socio-cultural adaptations was the tendency for trade to be carried on at the borders of territories:

> Before the European arrival in the interior of central Africa, trade was localized and organized in such a way that one ethnic group transported its goods to the limits of its district, and the next group did the same. Under such conditions, numerous diseases could remain endemic indefinitely.
>
> (Azevado 1978: 127)

European colonization, beginning in the sixteenth century but intensifying enormously in the nineteenth, upset what must have been at best an unstable equilibrium. For instance, devastating epidemics of smallpox and measles are recorded from Angola in the sixteenth century (Dias 1981: 358), but whether these were true 'virgin soil' epidemics affecting people never before exposed, or epidemics affecting a population that had been exposed intermittently in the past, is not clear. The proximity of Africa to both Europe (at the Straits of Gibraltar) and the Near East (at the northern and southern ends of the Red Sea) makes the latter more probable.[2]

Beyond the possible introduction of new diseases, however, European colonialism caused major disruption by forcing large groups of people to work on plantations in areas distant from their homes, usually under unhealthy and unsanitary conditions (DeLancy 1978). In addition, long-distance trade and troop movements became increasingly frequent. And the shift from subsistence farming to the monocropping of cash crops for sale in the world market led to landlessness, urban migration, and deteriorating nutritional status. Though adequate registration data are not available, the far from unanimous consensus is that the colonial period beginning in the nineteenth century saw a deterioration of the health situation in southern Africa.

Moreover, during the post-colonial era attempts at economic development have often had the paradoxical and untoward effect of worsening the health situation in ways not unlike those of the colonial era. For example, damming rivers in Ghana has expanded the zone of river blindness (onchocerciasis). Road construction in Liberia, migrant labour from Upper Volta, Mali and Niger to Southern Ghana, and settlement relocation from high plateaus to lowland agricultural areas in northern Nigeria have all been implicated in the dissemination of sleeping sickness (trypanosomiasis) (Hughes and Hunter 1970: 453–4). The construction of irrigation systems has resulted in the spread of schistosomiasis and malaria. Diamond and gold mining in South Africa have caused the spread of venereal disease and tuberculosis, as well as the disruption of families (Kark 1949, Kark and Cassel 1952).

Despite the facts that disease control programmes have had an impact on improving health in some regions, and that one major killer – smallpox – has been eradicated, life expectancy has increased only modestly since the Second World War, and infant and child mortality remain extremely high (UN 1982: 95–6). Indeed, close to half of all deaths occur among children under the age of 5, the vast majority from infectious and parasitic diseases and diseases of the respiratory system, followed by diseases of the digestive system (UN 1984: 114–19). A number of reasons have been proposed including impoverishment, inflation, and international indebtedness, natural disasters, warfare, and declining aid from abroad (UN 1982: 95, Adediji 1985), all of which are causes of infant and child malnutrition. To add to the burden, Africa's complex ecology, combined with changing norms of sexual behaviour, have led to the emergence of yet another epidemic of a chronic infectious disease, acquired immune deficiency syndrome (AIDS), whose costs in terms of human suffering and socio-economic devastation are as yet incalculable.

In summary, the health of Africans has worsened and then improved only slowly since the time of intense colonization by Europeans in the nineteenth century. Much is accounted for by the nature of Africa's disease ecology, but it seems safe to say that the spread of epidemics and the presumed deterioration of life expectancy followed upon the heels of the assertion of social and political control by Europeans.

The situation was reversed in the New World, where social, political, and economic domination by Europeans followed upon the heels of epidemics. Here the epidemiological and demographic consequences of European contact were even more catastrophic for the indigenous populations than they were for indigenous Africans (Borah 1964). Since contact in the Americas occurred earlier than in Oceania, and was something of a model for what was later to occur there, I shall limit my discussion here to the American continent.

The New World encountered by Spanish, Portuguese, English, French and other explorers and colonists was highly diverse both ecologically and culturally. It encompassed arctic, temperate, and tropical climates; small bands of hunter-gatherers and large complex empires based upon irrigation agriculture; low-lying river basins and high mountain ranges. I shall consider some of the consequences of that diversity in subsequent sections. Here I point to the similarities. For no matter where they lived, no matter how sophisticated their cultures, and no matter how complex their social organization and technology, the overwhelming fact is that demographic collapse was the fate of virtually all indigenous groups in the Americas.

The primary causes seem to have been acute infectious diseases introduced by Europeans, most notably smallpox and measles (Dobyns 1963, 1983, Crosby 1972, 1986, Newman 1976, Snow and Lanphear 1988). Indigenous Americans had evidently not been exposed to these diseases previously, presumably because the animal hosts in which they first evolved and from which they spread to humans were not present in the Western Hemisphere. These diseases were followed by others, some transmitted directly by Europeans (such as typhus and diphtheria), others by African slaves (such as malaria, yellow fever, and hookworm).

In addition to the impact of introduced epidemics, other factors were important as well. For example, some authorities argue that tuberculosis had existed in the pre-contact indigenous population but became a major killer only when the hardships and stress of European contact and domination made themselves felt (Buikstra 1981). Other causes of depopulation were famine induced by the destruction or confiscation of crops by the invaders; forced labour in mines and on plantations; warfare; the absence of marriage partners (both a cause and a consequence of depopulation); and epidemic-induced panic, social disorganization, and demoralization.

Though the fact of demographic collapse is universally acknowledged, its magnitude and timing have been sources of disagreement and debate. There are a variety of ways of estimating aboriginal population which I need not describe here (Thornton 1987: 21–2). They result in very different figures for the 1490s, the time of first significant European contact,[3] from a low of 8.4 million to a high of 112 million (Denevan 1976: 3). The higher the initial figure, the greater the magnitude of subsequent loss to the nadir. Indeed, some authorities believe that the decline across the entire Western Hemisphere was over 90 per cent. Other authorities argue that the scale of depopulation was much lower, conceivably even lower than 50 per cent. Since the nineteenth century the disease experience of different American Indian populations has tended to diverge, and it is to some of the distinctions among them that I now turn.

SPANISH AND ENGLISH AMERICA

Numerous observers have commented on the differences between Spanish and English colonization of the new world. According to McAlister (1984: 108) one formulation has it that 'whereas the English came to America to settle and till the soil, the Spaniards came only to plunder'. But, he continues, there was far more to Spanish policy than that, for while plunder was indeed intended and occurred, the concern was also to create a 'Christian republic where men lived in polity and justice *according to their rank and station* and made the land

302

bear fruit' (emphasis added). I have emphasized 'rank and station' because race
– Indianness – became in Spanish America a measure of both, and the lowest
of each.

For the Spanish the availability of Indian labour – first for work in mines,
ultimately for work on haciendas – was crucial. Indians provided a servile
labour force to be exploited, but they were also human beings and members
of the polity. The latter did not protect them from the devastating consequences of the former. Indeed, it meant that those Indians who survived came
to form the lowest stratum of the new societies that developed after the conquest. Because Indians were deemed to be members of the polity, and because
far more Spanish men than women came to the Indies, there was a good deal
of mixing between the races. The result was the emergence in many parts of
Spanish America of a mestizo stratum intermediate between the Spanish and
the Indians. As time wore on, and particularly after the colonies achieved
independence in the early nineteenth century, many mestizos rose higher in
the social hierarchy.

Policy in English America was different: 'The British, unlike their rivals, the
French and the Spaniards, never developed an overall eighteenth-century
colonial policy that gave the Indian a place and a future in the structure of the
empire' (Jacobs 1969: 100; see also Hanke 1959: 99). Indians were widely
viewed as savages to be dominated and eliminated (a similar policy prevailed
in Australia; see Jacobs (1971)). The epidemics which decimated the Indians
were widely considered to be evidence of God's favour. As savages, Indians
were supposed inevitably to give way to a higher civilization (Pearce 1965).

It was only in the late nineteenth century, not coincidentally at the same
time that Anglo-Americans began to worry about the preservation of their
natural environment and to create national parks, that concern about the survival of American Indians began to be expressed, and that expression found
its way very slowly into policy. Indians in the eastern half of the country had
been largely exterminated by then and their remnants were placed on small,
fragmented reservations overseen by state governments. In the west, however,
sizeable Indian populations still survived, and their treaties were made with
the federal government. They were placed on reservations that, as the
twentieth century wore on, and particularly after the 1930s, were increasingly
well protected legally and well-served medically, though their natural
resources were generally extracted by, and in the interests of, others.

What, then, were the consequences for the health of Indians of these
different colonial policies? Of course all of Latin America is far more diverse
than the United States and Canada; demographic responses to contact differed
widely from one place to another within Latin America (Newson 1985); and
data on Indian health status are harder to find there than in North America.
In general, however, the effect of the contrasting policies has been that the
health of North American Indians has improved far more rapidly than has that
of Indians in Latin America. Data from Bolivia, Ecuador, and Guatemala in

the 1970s show that the probability of death at various ages is greater for Indians than non-Indians, even when allowance is made for the factors of urban versus rural residence and the educational attainment of the mother (in the case of infant and child mortality) (UN 1982: 169). Infant and child mortality in a rural Zapotec Indian community in Mexico were substantially higher, though declining, in the period 1945–70 than were infant and child mortality in all of Mexico, and were similar to rates reported from highland Maya Indian communities.[4] Moreover, adult heights showed no increase over the previous century, suggesting no improvement in nutritional status (Malina and Himes 1978). And studies of body composition and growth of Cakchiquel Indian children in Guatemala indicate no improvement in nutritional status over a period of two decades, and reduced nutritional reserves when compared with non-Indian children (Bogin and MacVean 1984). These data reveal a continuing pattern of death in infancy and childhood due to endemic infectious diseases and malnutrition. On the other hand, there is some evidence that Indian mortality is declining in some areas and converging with non-Indian mortality rates (Early 1982: 53).

The situation has evolved somewhat differently in the United States. Compared with all US races, Indians have twice the unemployment rate, half the per capita income, and less than half the proportion of college graduates. On the other hand, life expectancy and causes of death have been changing profoundly. Table 1 shows life expectancy at birth for American Indians and Alaskan Natives and for the white population of the United States. Notice that for both sexes the rate of improvement in life expectancy has been more than twice as rapid for Indians as for whites, but that Indian life expectancy still lags by about three years for each sex.

Table 2 shows the ratios of age-specific death rates of Indians to those for all races. At ages below 44 Indians die at greater rates than the rest of the population. Between 45 and 64 the rates are the same. At 65 and above Indians die at lower rates.

Table 1 Life expectancy at birth

Year	Indian and Alaskan Natives		US white population	
	Male	*Female*	*Male*	*Female*
1940	51.3	51.9	62.1	66.6
1950	58.1	62.2	66.5	72.2
1960	60.0	65.7	67.4	74.1
1970	60.7	71.2	68.0	75.6
1980	67.1	75.1	70.7	78.1
Average annual improvement (%)	0.77	1.1	0.34	0.43

Source: IHS 1989: 41.

Table 2 Ratios of age-specific death rates, Indians: US (all races)

Age group	Ratio of death rates
1–14	1.4
15–24	1.7
25–44	1.8
45–64	1.0
> 65	0.7

Source: IHS 1989.

This pattern is the result of the different causes of death among Indians and non-Indians (see Table 3). Over the past thirty to forty years infectious diseases have declined in significance, cancer and cardiovascular diseases have not become as significant as they are among non-Indians, and violence and substance abuse have remained higher among Indians and account for most of the difference in life expectancy at birth.[5]

The colonial policies of Spain and England have had a profound impact both on the subsequent economic development of Latin America and the United States and on policies regarding the treatment of Indians. Spanish policy, as noted above, was to incorporate Indians as the lowest social stratum of the polity. In combination with the generally low level of economic development characteristic of most Latin American countries, the result has been a persistent pattern of high infant mortality and deaths from endemic infectious diseases. In the United States, on the other hand, the great wealth of the country, the special status which Indians ultimately achieved, and the provision of services on reservations have not resulted in dramatically improved economic conditions but have led to the control of infectious diseases and the emergence of non-infectious diseases and violence as the most important causes of reduced life expectancy (Kunitz 1983, IHS, 1989). The situation for Canadian Indians is much the same as it is for Indians and Alaskan Natives in the United States.

Table 3 Ratios of age-adjusted death rates by cause, Indians: US (all races)

Year	Infant mortality	All accidents	Suicide	Homicide	Alcohol	Cancer	TB	Diabetes	Cardiovascular
1955	2.4	3.4	1.2	5.0	n.a.	0.7	2.4	1.0	n.a.
1965	1.6	3.5	1.1	3.1	n.a.	0.5	2.5	1.1	n.a.
1975	1.2	3.2	1.7	2.1	7.2	0.5	2.2	1.0	n.a.
1985	0.9	2.2	1.3	1.7	4.2	0.5	0.9	1.4	0.8

Source: IHS 1989.

Table 4 Estimates of the size of the indigenous
population of the Americas (millions)

Region	1492[*]	1960s–1970s
North America	4.4	1.5 to 2.0[***]
Central America	21.4	5.0[**]
South America	20.0	10[**]

Sources: [*]Denevan 1976: 291. [**]Salzano 1968: 60–1.
[***]Thornton 1987: 223, 244.

The decline of mortality from epidemic diseases in Latin America and from epidemic and endemic infectious diseases in North America has resulted in the growth of the Indian population. I have already observed that there is much disagreement surrounding estimates of the number of Indians living in the Americas at the time of contact. It is equally difficult to arrive at a figure for the present Indian population, since 'Indian' is as much a social as a biological designation (Thornton 1987: 186ff.). Keeping in mind the difficulties of estimation and enumeration, it is still useful to give some figures for the population of Indians in about 1492 and almost five centuries later (see Table 4).

It is generally agreed that the low point of Latin American Indian population occurred in the seventeenth and eighteenth centuries (e.g. Newson 1986: 330, Lovell 1985: 146). Population began to increase as a result of the decline of epidemics, especially in the nineteenth century. Improvements in medical care and public health seem not to have played much of a role until well into the twentieth century (Kunitz 1986). The low point of North American Indian population occurred around the turn of the present century (Thornton 1987:159). By the late twentieth century there had been substantial recovery all across the Western Hemisphere, though some peoples had become extinct and the cultures of the surviving peoples had been irrevocably changed.

ECOLOGICAL IMPACTS: THE AMAZONIAN EXPERIENCE

The Spanish conquered large Indian empires, and the subjects they acquired were primarily agriculturalists. Indeed, it was the large, settled indigenous populations that attracted the Spanish (Odell and Preston 1978: 126–31). Moreover, the rates of survival of Indians in the Aztec, Maya, and Inca empires tended to be higher than they were among the peoples in lowland coastal areas (Newson 1985). In the preceding section I was primarily concerned with the descendants of the former. But of course Iberian America contained not only sedentary agricultural populations but also more mobile peoples who lived by hunting, gathering, and swidden cultivation. Many did not survive, but some did. It is to the impact of European contact on these groups in Amazonia that I now turn.

In drawing a contrast between the indigenous populations of two quite different kinds of ecological environment, namely the agricultural empires of the highlands and the hunter-gatherer-cultivators of the forest lowlands, I am disregarding differences that might be attributed to the fact that these populations were not, strictly speaking, subject to the same colonial regime. Most of the Amazonian lowlands fall within the territory of Brazil, which came under the control of Portugal rather than Spain. None the less, in all significant respects, Portuguese colonial policy was identical to that of the Spanish (McAlister 1984: 266–9), and I proceed on this assumption.

Like the Spanish, the Portuguese debated the human and civil status of their newly acquired subjects. Unlike the Spanish, however, the Portuguese did not acquire large Indian empires which they could decapitate and then control. The Indians in what became Brazil were more mobile than those in what became Mexico, Central America, and Peru. Many fled the coastal areas where the Portuguese first established themselves, and many died from the new diseases, warfare, and slaving expeditions to which they were exposed. Within a relatively short time there were virtually no Indians in the coastal areas, and the Portuguese were importing African slaves to work their newly established sugar plantations. With the Africans came falciparum malaria, hookworm, onchcerciasis and yellow fever. (The Portuguese had evidently introduced vivax malaria themselves; Kiple, personal communication.)

The newly introduced European and African diseases spread inland to afflict the Indians to varying degrees. Malaria, which seems to have penetrated the Amazon Basin in the eighteenth century, was the most severe affliction by the nineteenth (Hemming 1987: 279–83). The areas along the river banks were at the time of contact densely settled and relatively accessible, but by the end of the eighteenth century they were almost entirely depopulated. Their inhabitants had died out within 150 years of first contact (Meggers 1971: 121), as a result of the new diseases and warfare. Many forest-dwelling peoples remained, only to be afflicted by European diseases and depredations in the nineteenth and early twentieth centuries consequent on the rubber boom (Weinstein 1983, Hemming 1987: 271–315). Over sixty groups became extinct in Brazil in the first half of this century; nevertheless about 120 relatively isolated groups survive in the Amazon and central Brazil (Davis 1977: 9). As their territory has become of interest to outsiders, however, they have experienced decreasing isolation and increasing exposure to disease, and their numbers have diminished, sometimes almost to the point of extinction.

The tropical rain forest is a delicate and complex ecosystem which is not nearly as lush and fertile as is usually imagined. Heavy rains have leeched the minerals out of the soil, and what replenishment it receives comes from the falling leaves of the trees themselves. The dense foliage protects the ground from direct sunlight, captures nutrients, and reduces erosion (Meggers

1971: 17). Plants in the forest have a relatively low protein content. Hence the herbivores tend to be small. Moreover, many of the rivers have few or no fish as a result of the low oxygen content, acidity, and sterility of their waters (Meggers 1971: 12). In the forest (by contrast with the river banks) the human population has adapted to these conditions by living in small units in widely separated areas, by moving every few years, and by practising swidden cultivation. This allows reforestation to occur, preventing irreparable damage to the environment, while the populations themselves remain quite isolated.

Thus although exotic diseases must have entered the region at various times over the past several centuries, the people have remained sufficiently isolated from each other that not everyone was affected, and acute infectious diseases have not become endemic. Indeed, the acute diseases die out in small populations, as Black (1975) has shown in his summary of data from nine isolated Brazilian tribes. Endemic diseases that are common and persistent in these groups are herpes, Epstein–Barr virus, cytomegalovirus, hepatitis B, and Treponema. All cause little morbidity and persist for long periods in the host. Enzootic diseases that occur in animal reservoirs are also very prevalent in these tribes: among them yellow fever and toxoplasmosis. Diseases that are persistent (chronic), and that were introduced into the population, are malaria and tuberculosis.[6] These are not benign diseases and are undoubtedly contributing to the continuing decline of these populations (Davis 1977: 86). Most dramatic in their consequences are the acute infectious diseases which, when they do occur, cause explosive epidemics and affect everyone who has not previously been exposed. In many of these tribes serum surveys indicate that a high proportion of the population has not been exposed to at least some of the following: measles, mumps, rubella, influenza (various strains), para-influenza 2, and polio 1 (Black 1975).

I noted above that there has been some debate about the nature of the impact that epidemics of introduced diseases have in 'virgin soil' populations. Some writers believe that in previously unexposed populations newly introduced diseases such as measles and tuberculosis are especially virulent because the victims have not been selected for resistance by epidemics that affected their ancestors. Others argue that it is demoralization and social collapse that lead to high case-fatality rates.[7]

On at least two occasions medically trained observers have reported on the course of introduced diseases in 'virgin soil' populations of Brazilian Indians. Nutels (1968) observed tuberculosis among previously tuberculosis-free Indians newly relocated to the Xingu Park, and Neel and his colleagues observed an outbreak of measles among the Yanomama living on the border of Brazil and Venezuela (Centerwall 1968, Neel *et al.* 1970). In each instance the observers believed that it was social collapse and the absence of adequate care that accounted for the high mortality rate, rather than a hereditary susceptibility to sicken and die from an exotic infection (see also McDermott 1968).

The pace of contact between Amazonian Indians and outsiders has increased substantially since 1964, when the military assumed control of Brazil. Exploration, road building, mining, and ranching have all been encouraged by the government, multinational corporations, and the World Bank (Maher 1989). The result has been exposure to exotic diseases (some of them allegedly introduced on purpose in order to exterminate native populations); violent confrontations with intruders; continuing shrinkage of the Indians' land base; destruction of the rain forest itself; and, of course, continuing population losses (Davis 1977). Even when a few individuals survive from a particular tribe, the culture itself is destroyed. From an estimated one million Indians in Amazonia in 1500, the number has now declined to between 39 and 57 thousand (Hemming 1978: 492–501).

The impact of Brazilian and World Bank development policy is illustrated graphically by the fate of the Nambiquara. Their population is estimated to have been between 15 and 22 thousand in 1500 (Hemming 1978: 498). As late as the turn of this century they were still estimated to number as many as 20 thousand. By 1938 there were between 2 and 3 thousand Nambiquara; in 1959, 1,500; and in 1969, 600. The census in 1975 counted 534. The death rate between 1969 and 1975 was 60 per 1,000, the birth rate was 45 per 1,000, and life expectancy at birth was 23 years (Price 1989: 37).

Ecology has made a difference to survival, but the isolation that sheltered the forest-dwelling Indians of the Amazon region when more accessible tribes were being conquered is no longer sufficient to protect them. Despite efforts to provide some measure of protection, we see in our own time the same sort of process at work that has already destroyed indigenous peoples and their cultures in the Americas and Oceania for the past five centuries.

DIFFERENT ADAPTATIONS TO THE SAME ENVIRONMENT: THE HOPI AND THE NAVAJO

The point I wish to make in this section is that the way in which different peoples adapt to the same environment has profound demographic and epidemiological implications, even when access to health services and government policy are essentially the same. My examples are the Hopi and Navajo Indians living on reservations in the US Southwest. The two tribes share a similar semi-arid environment on the Colorado Plateau in Northern Arizona (Jorgensen 1983: 686–7).

The Hopis are agriculturalists living on or near three mesas which provide sufficient moisture for growing corn, beans, squash, and – since the entry of the Spanish in the sixteenth century – apricots and peaches. They appear to be descended from early inhabitants of the region, the Anasazi, who lived in small, scattered settlements wherever farming was possible. Some time in the thirteenth century the Anasazi abandoned their scattered settlements and withdrew to the present Pueblo settlements in New Mexico and Arizona, of

309

which the Hopi villages are the westernmost. The reasons for the abandonment are not entirely clear, but were probably related to changes in rainfall patterns which made it necessary to be near permanent sources of water. Increasing incursions by other tribes are also a possible explanation, however.

It is not clear when the Navajos, an Athapaskan people closely related to the Apaches, entered the Southwest, or whether their arrival had anything to do with the abandonment by the Anasazi of their scattered farmsteads (Brugge 1983). They were hunters and gatherers who seem to have learned agriculture and to have acquired certain religious beliefs and practices from the Pueblos they encountered once in the Southwest, particularly after many Pueblos joined them during the Spanish reconquest in 1692. In addition to these acquisitions from other Indians, the Navajos acquired sheep and horses from the Spanish. By 1800 they had made the shift to a largely semi-sedentary pastoral economy, living in dispersed, extended-family units.

During the nineteenth century incursions by whites into Navajo territory increased, as did conflict. The result was the incarceration of most Navajos at Bosque Redondo in eastern New Mexico from 1864 to 1868, followed by their return to a treaty reservation straddling what is now the border between Arizona and New Mexico. They quickly spilled over the boundaries of that first reservation and ultimately returned to areas west to the Colorado and Little Colorado Rivers that they as well as other tribes had previously used. In the process they engulfed the Hopi mesas. This has given rise to a legal dispute over control of the land with which I do not deal here.

Despite far from adequate data, it is clear that the Hopi and Navajo populations have followed very different trajectories. From the eighteenth century to the late nineteenth century Hopi population seems to have been stable, perhaps even declining slightly. In 1874 it was estimated to be 1,950. It was approximately the same in the early 1900s. Estimates vary, but in 1930 the population may have been about 2,700. By 1985 the population was estimated to be 7,600 on the reservation, about 80 per cent of the total population of perhaps 9,500 (Kunitz 1974a, Levy *et al.* 1987). Thus since the beginning of this century the Hopi population has increased no more than five-fold. By contrast, the Navajo population of perhaps 4,000 in 1800 increased to 10,000 to 12,000 in 1868, 20,000 to 24,000 in 1900, and perhaps 200,000 on and off the reservation at present. Thus over the course of the present century Navajo population has increased between eight- and ten-fold.

How may we account for these differences in growth during the reservation period, that is essentially the last 120 years? There are only a few possible factors: fertility, mortality, and net migration. We may dispose of the last by noting that prior to the Second World War, permanent emigration from each of the reservations does not seem to have been of great significance, though some part-time emigration did occur. Since the War, a substantial proportion of each tribe has emigrated more or less permanently, though precise figures are impossible to obtain.

There seems little doubt that until the 1930s Hopi mortality was higher than Navajo mortality. Several epidemics of smallpox in the 1850s, 1860s, and 1870s had devastating consequences for the Hopis. I have found no mention of anything similar among Navajos. Observers at the turn of the century commented on the unsanitary nature of Hopi villages and homes, the comparative cleanliness of Navajo camps, and the better health of Navajos than Hopis (Kunitz 1983: 32). And an analysis of returns from the 1900 census showed that Hopi women aged between 18 and 52 years had given birth to an average of 5.7 children, of whom an average of 2.9 were still alive. Among Navajo women the comparable figures were 4.4 and 3.6 respectively (Johannson and Preston 1978). Thus despite the higher Hopi fertility, as compared with the Navajos, Hopi infant and child survival were lower at the turn of the century and population growth was slower.

The situation changed during the present century. Deteriorating socio-economic conditions resulted in an increase in Navajo infant mortality rates. Even so, in the the late 1930s crude death rates were lower among the Navajos than among the Hopis (16 vs. 25 per 1,000) (Kunitz 1983: 78). The predominant causes of death in each tribe were the chronic endemic infectious diseases, chief among them tuberculosis. Indeed, the death rate from tuberculosis seems to have worsened from 1900 to 1940. After the development of antibiotics that effectively controlled tuberculosis, as well as other infectious diseases, the death rate began to drop precipitously in both tribes.

On the other hand, both fertility rates and deaths from non-infectious causes followed different paths in each tribe. Turning first to fertility, the Hopis reduced their birth rate very dramatically after the Second World War; so much so, indeed, that they may appropriately be compared with the Japanese in this regard. By the 1970s few women bore children beyond their late 20s. In contrast, the Navajos had a much slower rate of fertility decline and in the early 1970s women continued childbearing into their late thirties and forties (Kunitz 1974a, b, Kunitz and Slocumb 1976).

Thus rates of Hopi population growth tended to be lower than Navajo rates in the early years of the century as a result of higher mortality. Sixty years later, Hopi rates of growth were lower as a result of more rapidly declining birth rates. Unlike the Navajos, who were able to expand with their flocks into territory abandoned by the Anasazi, the Hopis have been much more tightly constrained by their environment and have had to be more sensitive than the Navajos to the problem of balancing population against available resources. The changing balance between births and deaths suggests − but does not prove − that fertility control has been one of the ways in which they have coped.

On the other hand, Navajo fertility rates have declined much more slowly than Hopi rates. Indeed, in this respect, Navajos resemble many Third World populations. Living in scattered camps, more inaccessible than Hopi settlements, and with lower educational levels (at least until recently), they did not accept family planning nearly as readily. This suggests − but once again does not prove — rather less sensitivity to the constraints of the environment, perhaps because the environment has not until recently been quite so constraining for the Navajos as it has been for the Hopis.

I turn now to a brief consideration of non-infectious and man-made causes of death. I wish to suggest that the conditions that currently generate most concern — accidents and other violent causes, and alcohol abuse — may best be understood not simply as responses to the disruptive effects of Anglo-American domination but also as manifestations of the culture and social organization of each tribe. Even though life has changed dramatically over the past century, I argue that sufficient stability has been retained on these relatively remote reservations to allow old forms of social organization and socialization to persist and to contribute to shaping people's behaviour and their response to Anglo-American institutions. How long this will continue to be true is, of course, an open question.

The 'Hopi way' has often been said to be a way of harmony, peacefulness, and co-operativeness, all characteristics conducive to community life. This is especially the case where people live, as do the Hopis, in compact villages in a harsh environment. When conformity and co-operation are not forthcoming, individuals may be coerced by a variety of mechanisms of social control: gossip, mocking at public dances, witchcraft accusations, and — if all else fails — expulsion from the community. Active aggression is not easily tolerated.

In partial contrast, the Navajos have not valued peacefulness to nearly the same degree as have the Hopis. While not notorious raiders like other Apacheans, they fought the Mexicans and Americans who attempted to invade their territory in the nineteenth century. They have nevertheless been influenced by their contacts with Pueblo peoples. Thus, according to Kaplan and Johnson,

> Navajo culture comprehends two historically distinct traditions, one based on the Apache hunting and raiding past and a second based on comparatively recent Pueblo contact. Each tradition has its related set of values, which not only are different from each other but are in important respects opposed and conflicting. Our undoubtedly oversimplified formulation is that the central principle of the earlier tradition is concern for personal and magical 'power', while maintenance of social control and harmony is the central principle of the second.
>
> (Kaplan and Johnson 1964: 204)

Whether or not this is an adequate formulation, it is certainly the case that aggression is more readily accepted among Navajos than Hopis.

In a series of studies my colleagues and I have examined the epidemiology of suicide, homicide, and alcoholic liver disease among Hopis and Navajos (Levy *et al.* 1969, Levy and Kunitz 1971, 1974, 1987, Kunitz *et al.* 1971, Levy *et al.* 1987). Space does not permit a lengthy review of the results of this work, and I shall make only a few brief points With regard to alcoholic cirrhosis, a condition that develops after long-term, frequent consumption of alcohol, in the 1960s and early 1970s death rates were higher among Hopis than Navajos. This was a surprise at the time, because it was Navajos who had the reputation as heavy and even flamboyant drinkers, whereas Hopis were known for their sobriety. Our explanation hinged on the distinction between drinking in groups and solitary drinking. Among young Navajo men group drinking was a common occurrence and well documented since the late nineteenth century. While it could lead to accidents and withdrawal symptoms, it was intermittent enough for men to receive adequate nutrition between drinking bouts, keeping the incidence of cirrhosis relatively low. Among Hopis group drinking was not at all common. The pattern was of solitary, even hidden, drinking, and the men who engaged in such behaviour tended to be those who went on to become chronic alcoholics and developed cirrhosis.[8]

Hopi alcoholics were found in all villages, but in those with an intact ceremonial cycle and theocracy the social control mechanism of expulsion of deviants was still operative. Thus chronic alcoholics from these villages tended to be found off the reservation. In villages where these traditional mechanisms no longer functioned, chronic alcoholics tended to remain, because they could not be expelled.

The most significant cause of death among American Indians is accidents, especially those involving motor vehicles. Alcohol is often implicated as a causal factor. Judging by the patterns of alcohol consumption described above, it is no surprise that the rate of death among Navajos is substantially higher than the rate among Hopis. In 1972–8 the average annual rate for Navajos was 106 to 122 per 100,000; for Hopis it was 52 to 77 per 100,000. There is no reason to believe that Navajos on average do more driving than Hopis, and when they do drive they use many of the same roads.

The way people drink and the way they drive reflect what they have learned about appropriate and inappropriate behaviour. Clearly ideas of appropriateness differ among societies. Navajo have tended to be more aggressive than Hopis, who value constraint and self-control. The patterns of death I have reported are consistent with these psycho-social differences. These examples suggest that the different ways Hopis and Navajos have adapted to the same environment have resulted in patterns of social organization and socialization that lead to very different ways of using alcohol and handling motor vehicles. Thus social organization and culture, so inextricably bound up with the ways in which Hopis and Navajos have adapted to their common environment, continue to be an important part of the explanation of non-infectious causes of death, just as they were of the infectious causes.

DIFFERENCES IN THE INCIDENCE OF DISEASES WITHIN THE SAME POPULATION

In the preceding section I have shown that even after the decline of infectious diseases, differences *between* societies in traditional patterns of social organization and culture may be responsible for contrasting of patterns of disease and mortality from man-made and non-infectious causes. I now consider how differences in degrees of 'traditionalism' and 'modernism' *within* the same indigenous population are related to the prevalence and incidence of non-infectious diseases. I draw my examples from studies of Pacific Island societies.

The impact of European contact on the indigenous populations of Oceania was in general similar to its impact in the Americas: epidemics, the slave trade, and demoralization resulted in major population reduction. (New Guinea is an exception, as demographic decline does not seem to have occurred there (Jacobs 1971).) Also like the Americas, there has been population recovery during this century, especially since the Second World War (MacArthur 1968, Carroll 1975, Bayliss-Smith 1975). The decline of the epidemic and endemic infectious diseases (some of which, such as malaria in New Guinea, antedated European contact) has been uneven across the Pacific. In general infant and child mortality is higher, life expectancy is lower, and infectious diseases account for a larger proportion of mortality the further west one goes. This is partially accounted for by the distribution of malaria in several Melanesian countries.

Taylor *et al.* (1989: Table 6) have classified the island nations of the Pacific according to their position in the epidemiological transition. Populations in Papua New Guinea, the Solomon Islands, Vanuatu, Kiribati, and the Federated States of Micronesia in the early 1980s still had life expectancies at birth of less than 60 years and high rates of death from infectious diseases. At the other extreme, Guam, the Cook Islands, American Samoa, Niue, Palau, and the Marianas all had populations with life expectancies of over 65 years and a smaller proportion of deaths from infectious diseases. The remaining island populations lay on a spectrum between these two extremes. There were some notable anomalies, such as the Micronesian island of Nauru with a relatively low life expectancy as a result of high rates of death from accidents. coronary artery disease, and non-insulin dependent (type II) diabetes (Taylor and Thomas 1985, Schooneveldt *et al.* 1988). Indeed, this population has one of the highest prevalence rates of diabetes so far reported.

The waves of migration across the Pacific have created a complicated mix of peoples (Rouse 1986), and there is reason to believe that they differ in their susceptibility to several non-infectious conditions. For example, Zimmet *et al.* (1989) have presented evidence suggesting that low susceptibility to diabetes is found in non-Austronesian Melanesians (Papua New Guineans and Solomon Islanders); an intermediate susceptibility occurs in Austronesian Melanesians (Fijians); and high susceptibility is observed among Micronesians and Polynesians. Friedlaender (1987: 360) has suggested a genetic propensity to obesity among Polynesians. These are important observations for they suggest that the epidemiological transition to non-infectious diseases will not invariably lead to the same disease spectrum occurring in every population.

I shall consider hypertension and diabetes, two of the most significant non-infectious conditions affecting Pacific populations as well as North American Indians. Hypertension is an important risk factor for cardiovascular and cerebrovascular diseases, and it has been the subject of debate between those who seek a biomedical explanation for the 'diseases of modernization' and those who seek a psycho-social explanation. Thus it has been observed that in so-called traditional societies blood pressure is, on average, lower than in modern societies, and does not increase with age. One explanation has to do with changes in diet and exercise as modernization proceeds: especially increasing salt consumption, decreasing activity levels, and increasing obesity. An alternative explanation invokes changes in social organization and value systems: from a coherent, harmonious community life to disjointed, rapidly changing, and stressful patterns of association (Cassel *et al.* 1960, Henry and Cassel 1969).

Of course these explanations are not mutually exclusive, but they are often treated as though they were. Unfortunately, in virtually all studies of the link between social change and hypertension, the necessary data on social interactions and support networks have not been gathered. 'Social' variables are typically treated as characteristics of individuals (education, preferred language, etc.), on a par with characteristics like level of sodium consumption and skin-fold thickness. Thus characteristics of community, and of the person's place in it − precisely the variables of interest − are rarely, if ever, adequately considered, so that a true test of alternative hypotheses has scarcely been carried out.

A number of prevalence studies of hypertension have been made among Micronesians, Melanesians, and Polynesians. Analyses may be specific to either the community level or the individual level. In the first case, attributes of individuals in a community are aggregated and entire communities are ranked by level of 'modernity' or 'traditionality' and mean systolic and diastolic blood pressures are compared from one to another.[9] At this aggregate level the results are inconsistent. A study of the Micronesian island of Palau found blood pressure, obesity, and serum lipids to be higher in the modern community (Labarthe *et al.* 1983). On the Micronesian island of Ponape, by contrast, inter-community differences were not observed (Patrick *et al.* 1983).

At the individual level of analysis, consistent differences are more often observed. But the variables − 'marital status, place of residence, occupation, English proficiency, educational level, source of income, and the segment of the economy from which that income was derived' (Patrick *et al.* 1983: 37), as well as dietary preferences − do not capture the sense of cultural coherence that is said to be so significant. None the less, there does tend to be an association between modernization as measured by these variables and elevation of blood pressure, and among people with higher levels of education and involved in wage work blood pressure tends to increase with age.

Finally, in a small cross-sectional study of the association between catecholamine excretion (as a measure of stress) and blood pressure, four groups of young Samoan men were compared. They ranged from urban students and workers to village agriculturalists. The villagers had lower levels of urinary catecholamine excretion and lower blood pressures, and it was suggested that this was because village life was less stressful than urban life (James *et al.* 1985).

The studies cited above were of prevalence: several communities were surveyed at one point in time and comparisons were made among them. The problem with such studies is that the factors which led people to move from one community to another may also influence the level of blood pressure. Ideally one would like to examine all members of a single community at a baseline and then follow them as they migrate or remain in their home community. This has been done in one Polynesian population, and it is to that study that I now turn.

The Tokelau Islands are a group of three atolls 300 miles north of Western Samoa. First European contact occurred in the late eighteenth century. During the nineteenth century traders, missionaries (including several Samoans) and slavers all had dealings with the Tokelauans. Population losses occurred which kept numbers from increasing throughout the century. Demographic recovery began about the turn of the present century. By that time there had been considerable emigration and immigration as well as intermarriage with Europeans, and by the late twentieth century the islanders represented a genetic mixture but were still overwhelmingly Polynesian (Hooper and Huntsman 1974).

Since 1925 the islands have been a dependency of New Zealand, and since the 1940s the islanders have had the right of entry into that country. Following a hurricane in 1966, the New Zealand government established a resettlement programme 'as a means of dealing with the expanding population and very limited resources and scope for development on the atolls' (Prior *et al.* 1974: 225). Surveys and medical examinations were made of the entire population in 1968 and 1971, before resettlement began. This provided the baseline from which migrants and non-migrants were followed (Prior and Tasman-Jones 1981: 247).

Pre-migrant men tended on average to be slightly taller and heavier than non-migrants. At younger ages systolic and diastolic blood pressures were also slightly higher for pre-migrant than for non-migrant men. There was a tendency among both men and women for blood pressure and serum cholesterol to increase with age. In general, no substantively significant differences between pre-migrants and non-migrants were observed either in physiological measures or in the presence of a number of diseases, including diabetes and hypertension (Stanhope and Prior 1976).

The results of follow-up studies of both adults and children showed that both weight and blood pressure increased more among migrants than among those who remained on the islands (Prior and Tasman-Jones 1981: 250–1). Furthermore, in an attempt to understand the possible etiological role of social interaction, a more intensive study was carried out of Tokelauans living in New Zealand. The variables considered included such factors as: length of time in New Zealand; ethnic affiliation of workmates and friends; club and association memberships; degree of participation in Tokelauan community functions; fluency in Tokelauan and English; and so on. The results suggested that, adjusting for body mass and age, there was a significant positive association between degree of interaction with New Zealand society on the one hand, and both systolic and diastolic blood pressure on the other. In addition, hypertensives and borderline hypertensives tended to have more interaction with New Zealand society than normotensives (controlling for age, body mass, and length of time in New Zealand). In a multiple regression analysis, however, between 1.4 and 2.3 per cent of the variance in blood pressure (depending upon whether it was systolic or diastolic, and whether men or women were being considered) was explained by social interaction, whereas on average about five times as much of the variance was explained by the factors of body mass and length of residence (Beaglehole et al. 1977: 811). Thus the social interactional variables are statistically but not substantively significant contributors to the explanation of increased blood pressure among migrants.

The other disease I consider here is non-insulin-dependent (type II) diabetes. It is important as a cause of disability (retinopathy, gangrene, peripheral neuropathy, renal failure) and death. Among Samoans, for instance, death rates due to diabetes exceed those for most populations (Baker 1986: 11), and the population of Nauru has one of the highest prevalence rates of diabetes ever recorded. I have already mentioned the belief of some observers that Polynesians may have a greater propensity to become obese than other Pacific Island populations, and that Polynesians and Micronesians also seem to be at especially high risk of developing diabetes. The two are evidently related because obesity is one of the risk factors for diabetes in some Pacific populations (King et al. 1984).[10]

A genetic mechanism, the so-called 'thrifty-gene hypothesis', has been suggested as an explanation of the high prevalence of diabetes in this as well as American Indian and Australian Aboriginal populations (Neel 1962, 1982). In essence the explanation is that among hunter-gatherers for whom a constant supply of food is problematic, natural selection favoured those who were efficient in storing fat during times of plenty. But in the present era, with food supplies more assured, the ability to deposit fat efficiently (coupled with diminished physical activity) is maladaptive and leads to obesity, insulin resistance, hyperinsulinemia, exhaustion of the pancreatic cells that produce insulin, and diabetes (Zimmet *et al.* 1989). Though an attractive hypothesis, it has not yet been confirmed or rejected, one of the difficulties being the question of whether food supplies really fluctuated as widely for hunter–gatherers as the hypothesis assumes.

None the less, there is no doubt that diabetes has increased dramatically among Polynesians and Micronesians since the Second World War (Zimmet and Whitehouse 1981: 209); that it occurs at higher rates among those living a more 'modern' life; and that risk factors vary depending upon the population. Among Polynesians obesity seems to be especially important. Among other populations level of activity or an interaction effect between various risk factors may be more significant (King *et al.* 1984).

In Table 5 I list prevalence rates of diabetes among several Pacific Island

Table 5 The prevalence of diabetes in several Pacific populations

Country	Ethnic group	Prevalence of diabetes at ages > 20 years (%)	
		Men	Women
Australia[*]	Europeans	5.1	3.7
	Aborigines – Urban	16.7	14.6
Papua New Guinea[*]	Non-Austronesian Melanesians	0	0
Solomon Islands[*]	Non-Austronesian Melanesians		
	Rural	0	1.4
	Urban	0	1.5
Fiji[*]	Austronesian Melanesians		
	Rural	1.5	1.6
	Urban	4.6	8.6
Wallis Islands[*]	Polynesians – Rural	1.5	3.3
Western Samoa[*]	Polynesians		
	Rural	1.3	4.1
	Urban	7.1	6.8
Kiribati[*]	Micronesians		
	Rural	3.2	3.5
	Urban	9.9	9.4
Nauru[*]	Micronesians – Urban	24.6	23.9
New Zealand[**]	Europeans	1.5	3.1
	Maori – Polynesians	8.7	6.9
Rarotonga[**]	Polynesians	5.5	4.3
Pukapuka[**]	Polynesians – Rural	0.4	1.6
New Zealand[**]	Tokelauans – Polynesians		
	1972–4	5.6	8.0
	1975–7	5.4	13.6
Tokelau	Polynesians		
	1968–71	1.0	3.3
	1976	3.7	8.6

Sources: [*]Zimmet *et al.* 1989: 17. [**]Prior and Tasman-Jones 1981: 252, 254.

populations. Notice that within the same population urban rates are always higher than rural ones. But notice, too, that there is some evidence that the distinction is not permanent. The prevalence rates of diabetes among Tokelauans in Tokelau and in New Zealand, each at two points in time, indicate that diabetes is increasing in both places.

Thus while much about diabetes remains unexplained, there is quite convincing evidence (1) that it is a new disease among indigenous peoples; (2) that some groups are genetically more susceptible than others; (3) that among the susceptible populations increased obesity and diminished physical activity associated with a shift in way of life are the most important risk factors; and (4) that there may be increasing homogeneity within populations as diet and exercise patterns become more nearly similar.

In these examples we have seen that the appearance of non-infectious diseases within indigenous populations does not affect everyone equally but occurs first among those becoming most acculturated to European ways of life (Finau *et al.* 1982). It appears, however, that such distinctions will become less and less predictive of disease as changes in diet, exercise, values, and social organization are adopted by more and more people, even those in hitherto isolated and traditional communities. Indeed, it is even possible that the prevalence of some conditions, for instance obesity and diabetes, may decline as educational levels improve and people become aware of the risks of early disability and death that they are incurring. Declining rates of mortality from ischaemic heart disease in Western Europe and among Europeans overseas indicate that the structure of mortality from non-infectious diseases is not immutable, and that it need not be so for indigenous peoples either.

CONCLUSIONS

The magnitude of the impact of European contact on indigenous peoples depended largely upon whether or not they shared a common microbial environment before contact occurred. Indigenous peoples in the Americas and Oceania had been isolated from Eurasian sources of infection, so that when contact was made the consequences were catastrophic. Something similar seems to have happened to indigenous peoples in Siberia (Crosby 1986), but this was a relatively uncommon occurrence in the old world.

For the survivors of those early epidemics and their descendants the post-contact evolution of disease patterns has taken several different paths depending upon national policy, economic growth, industrial development, ecological setting, local culture and social organization, and individual genetic endowment. Virtually everywhere in Oceania and the Americas the infectious diseases that have long been the most common and lethal afflictions of indigenous peoples are receding or have already receded. In their place have emerged non-infectious and man-made causes of disease, disability, and death. Broadly, then, the problems confronted by indigenous peoples are similar to those facing people of European origin, but patterns are far from homo-geneous because ways of life continue to differ.

It has been suggested that the highly differentiated micro-environments and epidemiological regimes that once characterized indigenous island populations are becoming increasingly homogenized in the rising tide of non-infectious diseases (Friedlaender 1987: 358). Prediction is always difficult, but my belief is that epidemiological patterns will remain highly diverse among indigenous peoples, as they have done among Europeans. Just as the post-contact evolu-tion of disease patterns has been influenced by a wide variety of factors in the past, so it seems likely that the same will be true in the future. The way people sicken and die is an expression of how they have lived. I see no necessary reason to doubt that convergence and homogenization of ways of life will be more than counterbalanced by divergence and heterogeneity. If we live in a global village, it is likely to continue to be a highly diverse one.

ACKNOWLEDGEMENTS

Stanley Engerman, Kenneth Kiple, and Emoke Szathmary provided helpful comments on an early version of this article.

NOTES

1   When Europeans embarked upon trade with Japan in the 1860s, no epidemics ensued because the Japanese, unlike the populations of the New World, had been exposed to the same pool of infectious diseases as the Europeans themselves, and for just as long (Janetta 1987).
2   In addition, it has been suggested that tuberculosis was introduced by Europeans as well (Kimble 1960: 39).
3   Early Norse contacts were insignificant in their effects.
4   The classic studies of the interaction between malnutrition and diarrhoea were carried out in Mayan villages in the Guatemala highlands (Scrimshaw et al. 1967; Early 1970).
5   A broadly similar pattern is observed among Canadian Indians (Young 1988: 48–52).
6   The exotic source of tuberculosis is a matter of disagreement, as I have indicated above.
7   The case-fatality rate is the proportion of people with a disease who die from it.
8   Though the data are patchy, there is some evidence that since the early 1970s death rates from cirrhosis may have declined among the Hopis from more than 40 per 100,000 to 14 to 24 per 100,000 (depending upon the population estimate employed) in 1979–81.
9   I have set 'modernity' and 'traditionality' in quotation marks because it is clear that the communities labelled 'traditional' have been very heavily influenced by contact with Europeans. A more appropriate distinction is between rural and urban.
10 North American Indians and Hispanics with a high degree of Indian ancestry also tend to have increased prevalence rates of type II diabetes (Szathmary 1987).

REFERENCES

Adediji, A. (1985) 'Foreign debt and prospects for growth in Africa during the 1980s', *Journal of Modern African Studies* 23: 53–74.

Azevado, M. J. (1978) 'Epidemic disease among the Sara of southern Chad, 1890–1940', in G. W. Hartwig and K. D. Patterson (eds) *Disease in African History*, Durham, NC: Duke University Press.

Baker, P. T. (1986) 'Modernization, migration and health: a methodological puzzle with examples from Samoans', *Journal of the Indian Anthropological Society* 21: 1–22.

Bayliss-Smith, T. P. (1975) 'The central Polynesian outlier populations since European contact', in V. Carroll (ed.) *Pacific Atoll Populations*, Honolulu: University of Hawaii Press.

Beaglehole, R., Salmond, C. E., Hooper, A., Huntsman, J., Stanhope, J. M., Cassel, J. C. and Prior, I. A. M. (1977) 'Blood pressure and social interaction in Tokelauan migrants to New Zealand', *Journal of Chronic Diseases* 30: 803–12.

Black, F. L. (1975) 'Infectious diseases in primitive societies', *Science* 187: 515–18.

Bogin, B. and MacVean, R. B. (1984) 'Growth status of non-agrarian, semi-urban living Indians in Guatemala', *Human Biology* 56: 527–38.

Borah, W. W. (1964) 'America as a model: the demographic impact of European expansion upon the non-European world', *Actas y Memorias, XXXV Congreso Internacional de Americanistas*, Mexico City, 1962.

Brugge, D. M. (1983) 'Navajo prehistory and history to 1850', in A. Ortiz (ed.) *Handbook of American Indians*, vol. 10, Southwest, Washington, DC: Smithsonian Institution.

Buikstra, J. (ed.) (1981) *Prehistoric Tuberculosis in the Americas*, Evanston, Ill.: Northwestern University Archaeological Program.

Carroll, V. (1975) 'The population of Nukuoro in historical perspective', in V. Carroll (ed.) *Pacific Atoll Populations*, Honolulu: University of Hawaii Press.

Cassell, J., Patrick, R. and Jenkins, D. (1960) 'Epidemiologic analysis of the health implications of culture change: a conceptual model', *Annals of the New York Academy of Sciences* 84: 938–49.

Centerwall, W. R. (1968) 'A recent experience with measles in a "virgin-soil" population', in PAHO, *Biomedical Challenges Presented by the American Indian*, Washington, DC: Pan American Health Organization.

Crosby, A. (1972) *The Columbian Exchange: Biological and Cultural Consequences of 1492*, Westport, Conn.: Greenwood Publishing.

—— (1986) *Ecological Imperialism: The Biological Expansion of Europe, 900–1900*, Cambridge: Cambridge University Press.

Davis, S. H. (1977) *Victims of the Miracle: Development and the Indians of Brazil*, Cambridge: Cambridge University Press.

DeLancy, M. W. (1978) 'Health and disease on the plantations of Cameroon, 1884–1939', in G. W. Hartwig and K. D. Patterson (eds) *Disease in African History*, Durham, NC: Duke University Press.

Denevan, W. M. (ed.) (1976) *The Native Population of the Americas in 1492*, Madison: University of Wisconsin Press.

Dias, J. R. (1981) 'Famine and disease in the history of Angola c. 1830–1930', *Journal of African History* 22: 349–78.

Dobyns, H. (1963) 'An outline of Andean epidemic history to 1720', *Bulletin of the History of Medicine* 37: 493–515.

—— (1983) *Their Number Become Thinned: Native American Population Dynamics in Eastern North America*, Knoxville: University of Tennessee Press.

Early, J. D. (1970) 'The structure and change of mortality in a Maya community', *Milbank Memorial Fund Quarterly* 48: 179–201.

—— (1982) *The Demographic Structure and Evolution of a Peasant System: The Guatemalan Population*, Boca Raton: University Presses of Florida.

Finau, S. A., Prior, I. A. M. and Evan, J. G. (1982) 'Ageing in the South Pacific: physical changes with urbanization', *Social Science and Medicine* 16: 1339–49.

Flinn, M. W. (1981) *The European Demographic System, 1500–1820*, Brighton: Harvester Press.

Friedlaender, J. S. (ed.) (1987) *The Solomon Islands Project: A Long-Term Study of Health, Human Biology, and Culture Change*, New York: Oxford University Press.

Hanke, L. (1959) *Aristotle and the American Indians*, Bloomington: Indiana University Press.

Hartwig, G. W. and Patterson, K. D. (eds) (1978) *Disease in African History: An Introductory Survey and Case Studies*, Durham, NC: Duke University Press.

Hemming, J. (1978) *Red Gold: The Conquest of the Brazilian Indians, 1500–1760*, Cambridge, Mass.: Harvard University Press.

—— (1987) *Amazon Frontier: The Defeat of the Brazilian Indians*, London: Macmillan.

Henry, J. P. and Cassel, J. C. (1969) 'Psychosocial factors in essential hypertension: recent epidemiologic and animal experimental evidence', *American Journal of Epidemiology* 90: 171–200.

Hooper, A. and Huntsman, J. (1974) 'A demographic history of the Tokelau Islands', *Journal of the Polynesian Society* 82: 366–411.

Hughes, C. C. and Hunter, J. M. (1970) 'Disease and "development" in Africa', *Social Science and Medicine*, 3: 443–93.

IHS (1989) *Trends in Indian Health – 1989: Tables*, Rockville, MD: Division of Program Statistics, Office of Planning, Evaluation and Legislation, Public Health Service, Department of Health and Human Services.

Jacobs, W. R. (1969) 'British-colonial attitudes and policies toward the Indian in the American colonies', in H. Peckham and C. Gibson (eds) *Attitudes of Colonial Powers Toward the American Indian*, Salt Lake City: University of Utah Press.

—— (1971) 'The fatal confrontation: early native–white relations on the frontiers of Australia, New Guinea, and America – a comparative study', *Pacific Historical Review* 40: 283–309.

James, G. D., Penner, D. A., Harrison, G. A. and Baker, P. T. (1985) 'Differences in catecholamine excretion rates, blood pressure and lifestyle among young Western Samoan men', *Human Biology* 57: 635–47.

Janetta, A. B. (1987) *Epidemics and Mortality in Early Modern Japan*, Princeton: Princeton University Press.

Johannson, S. R. and Preston, S. H. (1978) 'Tribal demography: the Hopi and Navajo populations as seen through manuscripts from the 1900 US census', *Social Science History* 3: 1–33.

Jorgensen, J. G. (1983) 'Comparative traditional economics and ecological adaptations', in A. Ortiz (ed.) *Handbook of North American Indians*, vol. 10: Southwest, Washington, DC: Smithsonian Institution.

Kaplan, B. and Johnson, D. (1964) 'The social meaning of Navaho psychopathology and psychotherapy', in A. Kiev (ed.) *Magic, Faith, and Healing*, New York: Free Press.

Kark, S. (1949) 'The social pathology of syphilis in Africans', *South African Medical Journal* 23: 77–84.

Kark, S. and Cassel, J. (1952) 'The Pholela health centre: a progress report', *South African Medical Journal* 26: 101–4, 131–6.

Kimble, G. H. T. (1960) *Tropical Africa*, vol II: Society and Polity, New York: The Twentieth Century Fund.

King, H., Zimmet, P., Raper, L. and Balkau, B. (1984) 'Risk factors for diabetes in three Pacific populations', *American Journal of Epidemiology* 119: 396–409.

Kunitz, S. J. (1974a) 'Factors influencing recent Navajo and Hopi population changes', *Human Organization* 33: 7–16.

—— (1974b) 'Navajo and Hopi fertility, 1971–1972', *Human Biology* 46: 435–51.

—— (1983) *Disease Change and the Role of Medicine: The Navajo Experience*, Berkeley: University of California Press.

—— (1986) 'Mortality since Malthus', in D. Coleman and R. Schofield (eds) *The State of Population Theory*, Oxford: Blackwell.

Kunitz, S. J. Levy, J. E., Odoroff, C. L. and Bollinger, J. (1971) 'The epidemiology of alcoholic cirrhosis in two Southwestern Indian tribes', *Quarterly Journal of Studies on Alcohol* 32: 706–20.

Kunitz, S. J., and Slocumb, J. C. (1976) 'The use of surgery to avoid childbearing among Navajo and Hopi Indians', *Human Biology* 48: 9–21.

Labarthe, D., Reed, D., Brody, J. and Stallones, R. (1973) 'Health effects of modernization on Palau', *American Journal of Epidemiology* 98: 161–74.

Levy, J. E. and Kunitz, S. J. (1971) 'Indian reservations, anomie, and social pathologies', *Southwestern Journal of Anthropology* 27: 97–128.

—— (1974) *Indian Drinking: Navajo Practices and Anglo-American Theories*, New York: John Wiley.

—— (1987) 'A suicide prevention program for Hopi youth', *Social Science and Medicine* 25: 931–40.

Levy, J. E., Kunitz, S. J. and Everett, M. (1969) 'Navajo criminal homicide', *Southwestern Journal of Anthropology* 25: 124–52.

Levy, J. E., Kunitz, S. J. and Henderson, E. B. (1987) 'Hopi deviance in historical and epidemiological perspective', in L. Donald (ed.) *Themes in Ethnology and Culture History: Essays in Honor of David F. Aberle*, Berkeley: Folklore Institute.

Lovell, W. G. (1985) *Conquest and Survival in Colonial Guatemala: A Historical Geography of the Cuchumatan Highlands 1500–1821*, Kingston and Montreal: McGill–Queen's University Press.

McAlister, L. N. (1984) *Spain and Portugal in the New World, 1492–1700*, Minneapolis: University of Minnesota Press.

McArthur, N. (1968) *Island Populations of the Pacific*, Canberra: Australian National University Press.

McDermott, W. (1968) 'Comments', in PAHO, *Biomedical Challenges Presented by the American Indian*, Washington, DC: Pan American Health Organization.

McKeown, T. M. (1976) *The Modern Rise of Population*, New York: Academic Press.

McNeill, W. H. (1976) *Plagues and Peoples*, Harmondsworth: Penguin.

Maher, D. J. (1989) *Government Policies and Deforestation in Brazil's Amazon Region*, Washington, DC: The International Bank for Reconstruction and Development/ The World Bank.

Malina, R. M. and Himes, J. H. (1978) 'Patterns of childhood mortality and growth status in a rural Zapotec community', *Annals of Human Biology* 5: 517–31.

Meggers, B. J. (1971) *Amazonia: Man and Culture in a Counterfeit Paradise*, Chicago: Aldine-Atherton.

Neel, J. V. (1962) 'Diabetes mellitus: a "thrifty" genotype rendered detrimental by "progress"', *American Journal of Human Genetics* 14: 353–62.

—— (1982) 'The thrifty genotype revisited', in J. Kobberling and R. Tattersall (eds) *The Genetics of Diabetes Mellitus*, New York: Academic Press.

Neel, J. V., Centerwall, W. R., Chagnon, N. A. and Casey, H. L. (1970) 'Notes on the effect of measles and measles vaccine in a virgin-soil population of South American Indians', *American Journal of Epidemiology* 91: 418–29.

Newman, M. (1976) 'Aboriginal new world epidemiology and medical care, and the impact of Old World disease imports', *American Journal of Physical Anthropology* 45: 667–72.

Newson, L. (1985) 'Indian population patterns in colonial Spanish America', *Latin American Research Review* 20: 41–74.

—— (1986) *The Cost of Conquest: Indian Decline in Honduras Under Spanish Rule*, Boulder, Col.: Westview Press.

Nutels, N. (1968) 'Medical problems of newly contacted Indian groups', in PAHO, *Biomedical Challenges Presented by the American Indian*, Washington, DC: Pan American Health Organization.

Odell, P. R. and Preston, D. A. (1978) *Economies and Societies in Latin America: A Geographical Interpretation*, New York: John Wiley.

Omran, A. R. (1971) 'The epidemiologic transition: a theory of the epidemiology of population change', *Milbank Memorial Fund Quarterly* 49: 509–38.

Patrick, R. C., Prior, I. A. M., Smith, J. C. and Smith, A. H. (1983) 'Relationship between blood pressure and modernity among Ponapeans', *International Journal of Epidemiology* 12: 36–44.

Pearce, R. H. (1965) *Savagism and Civilization*, Baltimore: Johns Hopkins University Press.

Price, D. (1989) *Before the Bulldozer: The Nambiquara Indians and the World Bank*, Cabin John, MD: Seven Locks Press.

Prior, I. A. M., Stanhope, J. M., Evans, J. G. and Salmond, C. E. (1974) 'The Tokelau Island migrant study', *International Journal of Epidemiology* 3: 225–32.

Prior, I. A. M. and Tasman-Jones, C. (1981) 'New Zealand Maori and Pacific Polynesians', in H. C. Trowell and D. P. Burkitt (eds) *Western Diseases: Their Emergence and Prevention*, Cambridge, Mass.: Harvard University Press.

Rouse, I. (1986) *Migrations in Prehistory*, New Haven: Yale University Press.

Salzano, F. M. (1968) 'Survey of the unacculturated Indians of Central and South America', in PAHO, *Biomedical Challenges Presented by the American Indian*, Washington, DC: Pan American Health Organization.

Schooneveldt, M., Songer, T., Zimmet, P. and Thomas, K. (1988) 'Changing mortality patterns in Nauruans: an example of epidemiological transition', *Journal of Epidemiology and Community Health* 42: 89–95.

Scrimshaw, N. S., Guzman, M. A. and Gordon, J. E. (1967) 'Nutrition and infection field study in Guatemalan villages, 1959–1964, I: study plan and experimental design', *Archives of Environmental Health* 14: 657–62.

Snow, D. R. and Lanphear, K. M. (1988) 'European contact and Indian depopulation in the Northeast: the timing of the first epidemics', *Ethnohistory* 35: 15–33.

Stanhope, J. M. and Prior, I. A. M. (1976) 'The Tokelau Island migrant study: prevalence of various conditions before migration', *International Journal of Epidemiology* 5: 259–66.

Szathmary, E. (1987) 'Genetic and environmental risk factors', in T. K. Young (ed.) *Diabetes in the Canadian Native Population: Bio-Cultural Perspectives*, Toronto: Canadian Diabetes Association.

Taylor, R., Lewis, N. D. and Levy, S. (1989) 'Societies in transition: mortality patterns of Pacific Island populations', *International Journal of Epidemiology* 18: 634–46.

Taylor, R. and Thomas, K. (1985) 'Mortality patterns in the modernized Pacific Island nation of Nauru', *American Journal of Public Health* 75: 149–54.

Thornton, R. (1987) *American Indian Holocaust and Survival: A Population History Since 1492*, Norman: University of Oklahoma Press.
UN (1982) *Levels and Trends of Mortality since 1950*, ST/ESA/SER.A/74, New York: Department of International Economic and Social Affairs, United Nations.
—— (1984) *Mortality and Health Policy*, ST/ESA/SER.A/91, Department of International Economic and Social Affairs, United Nations.
Weinstein, B. (1983) *The Amazon Rubber Boom*, Stanford: Stanford University Press.
Young, T. K. (1988) *Health Care and Cultural Change: The Indian Experience in the Central Subarctic*, Toronto: University of Toronto Press.
Zimmet, P. and Whitehouse, S. (1981) 'Pacific islands of Nauru, Tuvalu and Western Samoa', in H. C. Trowell and D. P. Burkitt (eds) *Western Diseases: Their Emergence and Prevention*, Cambridge, Mass.: Harvard University Press.
Zimmet, P., Serjeantson, S., Dowse, G. and Finch, C. (1989) 'Killed by the "good life": the chronic disease epidemic — adverse effects of life-style change in developing Pacific nations', paper presented at the Health Transition Workshop, National Centre for Epidemiology and Population Health, Australian National University, Canberra.

FURTHER READING

Carroll, V. (ed.) (1975) *Pacific Atoll Populations*, Honolulu: University of Hawaii Press.
Crosby, A. (1986) *Ecological Imperialism: The Biological Expansion of Europe, 900–1900*, Cambridge: Cambridge University Press.
Hartwig, G. W. and Patterson, K. D. (eds) (1978) *Disease in African History*, Durham, NC: Duke University Press.
Hemming, J. (1978) *Red Gold: The Conquest of the Brazilian Indians*, Cambridge, Mass.: Harvard University Press.
—— (1987) *Amazon Frontier: The Defeat of the Brazilian Indians*, London: Macmillan.
Kunitz, S. J. (1983) *Disease Change and the Role of Medicine: The Navajo Experience*, Berkeley: University of California Press.
McAlister, L. N. (1984) *Spain and Portugal in the New World. 1492–1700*, Minneapolis: University of Minnesota Press.
McNeill, W. H. (1976) *Plagues and Peoples*, Harmondsworth: Penguin.
Omran, A. R. (1971) 'The epidemiologic transition: a theory of the epidemiology of population change', *Milbank Memorial Fund Quarterly* 49: 509–38.
Trowell, H. C. and Burkitt, D. P. (eds) (1981) *Western Diseases: Their Emergence and Prevention*, Cambridge, Mass.: Harvard University Press.

2 CULTURE

12

INTRODUCTION TO CULTURE

Tim Ingold

WHAT IS CULTURE?

One of the most striking features of human life is the extraordinary diversity of ways of living it. In anthropology, it is customary to register this diversity by means of the concept of culture. Questions about culture, therefore, typically have to do with how and why human beings differ in their forms of life. As such, they may be contrasted with the questions, addressed in Part I of this volume, about humanity as a species, which tend to focus on those respects in which all human beings — at least in their presently evolved form — may be regarded as more or less the same. However, the concept of culture itself has obstinately resisted final definition. In an earlier era of anthropology, when it was assumed that societies differed according to their degree of advancement on a universal scale of progress, culture was held to be synonymous with the process of civilization. Later, as the idea of progress lost ground to the perspective of relativism, according to which the beliefs and practices of any society can only be judged by the values and standards prevalent in that society, anthropologists began to speak of cultures in the plural rather than of culture as the singular career of humanity at large. Each culture was regarded as a traditional way of life, embodied in a particular ensemble of customary behaviour, institutions and artefacts. Later still, as the emphasis shifted from manifest patterns of behaviour to underlying structures of symbolic meaning, culture came to be defined in *opposition* to behaviour, much as language was opposed to speech. Every culture was seen to consist in a shared system of concepts or mental representations, established by convention and reproduced by traditional transmission. But even this view has come under threat from an approach that seeks the generative source of culture in human *practices*, situated in the relational context of people's mutual involvement in a social world, rather than in the structures of signification wherein that world is represented.

It is clear that throughout the history of anthropology, scholars have adapted their notions of culture to suit the dominant concerns of the day, and they will no doubt continue to do so. Little is to be gained, therefore, from attempts to legislate on the proper meaning of the term. It is sufficient to note that whatever the sense in which it may be employed, the concept of culture entails a very high level of abstraction. In other words, culture is not something that we can ever expect to encounter 'on the ground'. What we find are people whose lives take them on a journey through space and time in environments which seem to them to be full of significance, who use both words and material artefacts to get things done and to communicate with others, and who, in their talk, endlessly spin metaphors so as to weave labyrinthine and ever-expanding networks of symbolic equivalence. What we do *not* find are neatly bounded and mutually exclusive bodies of thought and custom, perfectly shared by all who subscribe to them, and in which their lives and works are fully encapsulated. The idea that humanity as a whole can be parcelled up into a multitude of discrete cultural capsules, each the potential object of disinterested anthropological scrutiny, has been laid to rest at the same time as we have come to recognize the fact of the interconnectedness of the world's peoples, not just in the era of modern transport and communications, but throughout history. The isolated culture has been revealed as a figment of the Western anthropological imagination. It might be more realistic, then, to say that people *live culturally* rather than that they *live in cultures*.

Even in an encyclopedic volume of this kind, it is of course impossible to cover every aspect of cultural life; nevertheless, an attempt has been made to achieve a reasonable balance among its principal themes, as these are registered in human experience. This is not, however, matched by their representation in anthropological literature. Indeed it is worthy of comment that whereas on certain themes, such as magic, myth and religious symbolism, the literature is thick with studies, other areas which are equally central to cultural experience are scarcely represented at all. Surely, for example, nothing can be more ubiquitous in everyday cultural life than technics, yet in his attempt to establish an anthropological science of technics, which he calls 'technology', Sigaut (Article 16) has had virtually to start from scratch. Likewise, although all human life takes place in an environment that extends in space, and although people everywhere 'construct' their surroundings – in their heads if not on the ground – Rapoport (Article 17) notes that the study of spatial organization and the built environment has been neglected in anthropology, and no agreed-upon approach or conceptual vocabulary yet exists to tackle it. Turning from space to time, temporality must be an equally universal facet of human experience; however, as Adam observes (Article 18), there are hardly any time specialists in anthropology, and anthropological theorizing about time remains in its infancy. Until very recently, the same was true of the visual arts, as well as of music and dance. For the greater part of the twentieth century, Morphy reports (Article 23), anthropologists paid little attention to those items of material culture that might be classified as 'art', and such attention as they were accorded was not integrated with other aspects of anthropological inquiry. Finally, music and dance, which are found in all human societies and implicated in one way or another in practically every domain of activity, have for the most part been relegated to the periphery of anthropological concern (Seeger, Article 24).

The reasons for this erstwhile neglect of large areas of cultural experience are several. Here I would like to mention just three. The first lay in the tendency of an anthropology once portrayed as the study of 'other cultures' (i.e. non-Western ones) to exoticize the objects of its attention, by characterizing their principal features through an opposition to those of 'Western culture'. Thus our technology was opposed to their magic, our scientific knowledge to their religious beliefs, our architecture and design to their symbolic structures, our performing arts to their ritual, our literature to their myth, and so on. The second reason is that, in many cases, the areas neglected by anthropology were already 'claimed' by other disciplines — architecture, drama, history of art, ethnomusicology — which operated within frameworks of assumptions that could not always be easily reconciled with the relativistic canons of anthropological inquiry. The third reason touches not so much on anthropology's interface with contingent disciplines as on an issue of fundamental contemporary significance within anthropology itself. This concerns the status of language as a repository of cultural meaning. It has long been a basic axiom of anthropological method that in order to gain access to a people's cultural understandings of the world it is necessary to be proficient in their language. As a corollary, it is assumed that in rendering these understandings in a form accessible to an external readership, the ethnographer's task is essentially one of translation. In its application, however, this axiom automatically biases attention towards those areas of cultural knowledge that are amenable to linguistic articulation. Yet we know from our own experience that much of the knowledge that we use to get by in everyday life is downright resistant to such articulation, and moreover that any attempt to 'put it into words' fundamentally transforms its nature. This is true, for example, of the practical skills of craftsmanship; and it is equally true of music and dance. No wonder, then, that these are matters on which anthropology has traditionally tended to remain silent.

Behind this issue an even larger question is at stake, concerning the very nature of the way in which human beings perceive the world. We may agree that two people from different backgrounds, if placed in the same or a similar situation, will differ in what they see there. But why should this be so? Is it because the raw data of bodily sensation, common to both, is processed by their respective intellects in terms of contrasting conceptual schemata, yielding alternative mental constructs of what the world 'out there' is like? Or is it because they have been trained, through previous experience of carrying out different kinds of practical tasks, involving particular bodily movements and sensibilities, to orient themselves in relation to the environment and to attend to its features in different ways? The first account rests on the premise that the perceiving subject apprehends the world from a position outside it, so that the world has first to be be configured, in the mind, prior to taking significant action. Anthropologists who adopt this approach commonly regard such configuration as an exercise in classification, in which the substance of sensory experience — in itself fluid and unstructured — is fitted to a stable system of received conceptual categories. The second account, by contrast, situates the perceiver from the start in an active engagement with his or her surroundings, so that perception is an achievement not of the mind, working on the data of sense, but of the whole body-person — as an undivided centre of action and awareness — in the practical business of dwelling in the world. Form and meaning, in this latter account, are not imposed by the mind on the world, but arise within the situational contexts of human dwelling activities.

It is fair to say that in the opposition between these two accounts, one of which may be called 'cognitivist' in its orientation, the other broadly 'phenomenological', lies the most fundamental division in current approaches to understanding human cultural difference. Three implications of the contrast deserve particular emphasis. The first has to do with the ontological status of the human body. In the cognitivist perspective, the body is understood as a passive instrument in the service of cultural reason, delivering sensations for processing by the mind and, in turn, executing its commands. For the phenomenologist, on the other hand, the body is *active*, intentional rather than instrumental, not something that is used by the cultural subject but rather the very form of the subject's presence as a being in the world. Second, and stemming from this, the stability of cultural form is seen to lie, in the former view, in the intergenerational transmission of linguistically coded, conceptual information (much as the stability of biological form is attributed to the inheritance of genetically coded information). In the latter view, by contrast, cultural form is seen to be held within the current of human relationships: what each generation contributes to the next are not templates or schemata for the organization of experience, but rather the specific conditions of development under which successors, growing up in a social environment, acquire their own embodied skills and dispositions. Third, if we would seek to know what the world means for the people who live in it, the cognitivist approach directs us to attend to their mental representations, whereas the phenomenological approach directs our attention to bodily kinaesthesis. For one the concept, for the other the performance, is the starting point of analysis.

CULTURE AS A HUMAN CAPACITY

But is cultural diversity an exclusively *human* phenomenon? Most anthropologists believe that it is, though the belief is more easily asserted than demonstrated. Many biologists and psychologists, however, have observed that the intergenerational transmission of knowledge and skills by non-genetic means is very common in the animal kingdom, and since this minimally depends on interaction between one individual (the 'model') and another (the 'novice'), such transmission is often called 'social'. In Article 13, David and Ann James Premack show why evidence of social learning is an insufficient basis on which to ground claims for the existence of culture. Adopting an approach that is firmly rooted in the cognitivist tradition, they argue that human beings are indeed uniquely cultural and that, for the same reason, they are the only animals that can be said to have a history. There have, in other words, been significant changes in the patterns of human life in the absence of any corresponding changes in the biological endowment of the species. The possibility of culture and history is underwritten, in the Premacks' view, by two factors: first by a distinctive way of transmitting information across the generations, and second by an innate capacity to recognize certain kinds of categorical distinctions.

To denote the mode of intergenerational transmission specific to culture, the Premacks adopt the term 'pedagogy'. Pedagogy differs from other forms of social learning in that not only does the novice imitate the model, but the model also observes the novice's performance, judges it against a set of normative standards and intervenes in an intentional way in order to help bring the novice's performance into line with these standards. To be able to do this, both the pedagogue and the novice must be able to attribute mental states to one another, and to understand each other's behaviour in terms of these states: in other words, they must have a 'theory of mind'. If any non-human animal kind is capable of this, we would expect it to be our nearest relative, the chimpanzee. On the basis of studies of chimpanzees, both under 'natural' conditions and in captivity, the Premacks conclude that while they have the *cognitive capacity* to engage in pedagogy, and while captive chimpanzees have been observed to come very close to achieving this, the capacity has never been realized in wild populations. In the absence of human companions, chimpanzees evidently have no disposition either to practise their behaviour (in the sense of attempting to perfect it through rehearsal) or to share their experience with others. The disposition to share, the Premacks argue, is a condition not only for pedagogy but also for language, and this is why the two occur together, even though language is not itself necessary for pedagogic instruction. But it is not just because they do not transmit their traditions by pedagogy that non-human animals lack culture. For, in the Premacks' view, cultural knowledge, in the form of beliefs about the world, also builds upon a fundamental and pre-linguistic capacity, with which every human infant is 'primed', to categorize experience into distinct domains. This capacity is the seed from which culture grows, both in the life of each individual, and in history as a whole.

Foster, in Article 14, agrees with the Premacks that the intergenerational transmission of information by behavioural means – as in the social learning of non-human animals – does not suffice as a criterion for culture. In her view, however, the essence of culture lies in a uniquely human capacity to recognize and exploit likeness, or, in other words, to operate analogically. To construct an analogy (or metaphor) is to establish a relation between phenomena drawn from different domains of experience, in terms of a perceived similarity. Any real-world object, as it is caught up in the nexus of analogical relations, can become a symbol. We can discover the meanings of symbols by attending to the multiple social contexts in which they are used: what each symbol does is to bring together these contexts into a single focus, anchored in a concrete form. The more experience is brought together in one focus, the greater the symbolic resonance of the object by which it is represented. In the course of social life, new analogic linkages are forever being forged against the background of existing convention, only to become conventional in their turn: thus over time the meanings of symbols change. The analogic drive, in short, is the very motor of the cultural process.

From an evolutionary perspective, the problem is to understand how this drive came to be established. Foster reviews five possible ways of investigating this problem. We can look for possible antecedents of analogical thinking in the capacities for imitation or mimicry of non-human species; we can examine ancient stone artefacts for indications that they may have been accorded symbolic significance; we can consider the evidence of the earliest prehistoric art for what it reveals about the mental processes of its producers; we can study the way in which the capacity to recognize and exploit likeness develops in the life history of contemporary children, and suggest that human evolution may have proceeded through a similar sequence of stages; and we can attempt to reconstruct early patterns of cultural behaviour using methods similar to those employed by linguists in reconstructing the earliest forms of human language. One conclusion that seems to emerge from all these approaches is that words and other symbols originally referred not to entities and events but rather to movements and processes; another is that the overall tendency in the history of human symbolic representation has not been from realism to abstraction but rather the reverse. This latter conclusion, however, depends on the assumption that the function of symbols has always and everywhere been a representational one. There is, as we shall see in connection with Weiner's discussion of the meaning of myth in Article 21, some doubt about the validity of this assumption. Indeed early symbols, far from being abstract depictions of the world, might better be regarded as signposts that serve to conduct people's attention *into* it.

ARTEFACTS AND SKILLS

The cultural process, driven by analogic thought and practice, builds itself on the one hand into the social forms of persons and groups, and on the other into the material forms of objects and features in the landscape. These latter forms comprise what is generally known as 'material culture', the subject of

Miller's discussion in Article 15. Though the objects of material culture are commonly described as 'artefacts', it is impossible, as Miller shows, to establish a precise boundary separating the domain of 'artificial' from that of 'natural' things. The boundary is more a product of a way of thinking that separates conceptual design from material substance and that envisages the activity of making as an intentional imposition of design on substance to yield manufactured objects. The reality is that both people's designs and the things they make are caught within the historical trajectory of their relations with one another and with their material surroundings.

But artefacts are also ambiguous in another way. Western anthropologists, reacting against the apparently meaningless proliferation of industrially produced commodities in the societies from which they have come, are inclined to dwell upon the extent to which people in small-scale and technologically 'simple' societies invest their limited inventory of artefacts with meaning, treating them as belonging inalienably to persons, or even as though they were persons themselves. By contrast, Western capitalist society is supposed to reduce persons or their parts to alienable things. Yet it is in the nature of artefacts, whatever their social provenance, to confound the orthodox dichotomy between things and persons. By their sheer physicality and inanimacy they are intrinsically thing-like, but in their incorporation into the nexus of social relations they are also personalized. We should not, Miller warns, ignore the sense of alienation that may accompany attitudes to material culture in the societies we study as well as in our own, nor should we underestimate the degree to which people in Western societies succeed in converting mass-produced consumer goods into inalienable personal possessions. The extent and manner in which such personalization occurs will, however, depend upon the temporal longevity of artefacts relative to the human life-cycle. Clearly, where these are of the same order, the potential for incorporating artefacts into personal identities will be greatest.

One further aspect of Miller's argument deserves special mention. It concerns the comparison between artefacts and words. Anthropologists working in the traditions of structuralism and semiotics have often suggested that the artefacts of a society may be regarded, like the words of its language, as the constituent signs of a system of communication, in which each sign takes its meaning from its oppositional relations to each and every other. Suggestions of this kind, however, fail to take account of the crucial difference that whereas spoken words are materially present only in the moment of their utterance, artefacts have an enduring physical presence as components of the environment within which communicative events are framed. Coming across artefacts as objects that are already to hand, we tend to take their existence − and with that the cultural codes they objectify − as part of the natural order of the world. In that way, people not only bring order to things, by incorporating them into their social and cultural arrangements; they are also ordered *by* them, perceiving the world in accordance with the frameworks of meaning embodied in their artefacts. As Miller suggests, it is by composing the taken-for-granted background to our attention, rather than by capturing its focus, that artefacts may exert their greatest influence on perception.

From the properties of artefacts we move, in Article 16, to the procedures – and above all to the knowledge and skills – involved in making and using them. Much has been written about the history and philosophy of human technical accomplishments; a true anthropology of technics, however, must build upon the data of empirical observation, that is on *technography*. Sigaut's article is an attempt to establish a framework of precise concepts for comparative technographic analysis. Defining a technical action as any intentional bodily movement directed towards social goals that are also material, in that they bring about a change of state in some physical system, Sigaut introduces the concepts of 'operation' (the minimal unit into which any such action can be divided), 'path' (the sequence on which an operation is located) and 'network' (an organization of interconnected paths). Where alternative operations can occupy the same position on a path, each establishes a 'technical lineage' – a concept that Sigaut employs here without any progressive or diachronic implications. And in the analysis of any artefact, he points to the need to distinguish between its function (what it does in the context of a specific operation), its workings (the principles whereby this effect is achieved) and its structure (form, materials, and so on).

While these concepts may suffice for the purpose of examining technical action as it were, 'from the outside', for an inside view we have to turn to consider the nature of knowledge and skill. Yet as Sigaut insists, skill is not – or not merely – a form of knowledge; it is also a condition for effective action. Knowledge becomes skill at the point where it is fully incorporated into the bodily *modus operandi* of the expert agent: at this point it is no longer a science to be applied, but exists only as the agent's practical application of his or her own *self* to the task at hand. Moreover no society, either today or in the past, has been able to do without it. Despite continual efforts to construct machines that would substitute for skilled practitioners, building into them an 'algorithmized' version of the latters' embodied knowledge, the reliance on skill has not in the least diminished. For, as fast as machines replace old skills, new skills grow up around the machines. However, it is only thanks to their involvement in various kinds of social grouping that persons acquire their particular skills. It follows that technical action, to be materially effective, must also be embedded in the context of social relations. Yet as Sigaut points out, anthropological theorizing has proceeded, for the most part, as though technics and society constituted domains of activity that are mutually exclusive. And this has led analysts to turn a blind eye to skill and, in consequence, to treat every technical action as if it were a purely mechanical performance.

SPACE, TIME AND WRITING

If anthropology presently lacks adequate concepts for dealing with technical skills, it is equally impoverished when it comes to the environments in which such skills are exercised. These environments have two critical properties in common: they are laid out in space, and are to various degrees 'constructed'. In Article 17, Rapoport seeks to develop a comprehensive conceptual framework for analysing the ways in which people organize space and build their environments. His approach, like that of the Premacks in Article 13, rests upon explicitly cognitivist foundations. Thus variations in the ways in which space is organized, and thereby converted into settings for human activities, are attributed to the different cognitive schemata that people bring with them, in the form of mental maps, into their encounter with the physical landscape. Environments are initially constituted in thought, through the attachment of meanings to a naturally given substrate; this may or may not be followed by a process of building in which the substrate is itself physically transformed to bring it into conformity with the preconceived mental image. For example, a conceptually imposed boundary dividing off one area from another (e.g. private from public space) may be realized physically in the form of a built feature such as a wall. Features of this kind can exert instrumental effects, as in obstructing or facilitating movement, but they can also have semiotic functions as symbolic markers which serve both to express and to communicate cultural meaning. Moreover, since people's movements in space are necessarily in time as well, the organization of space cannot but have a temporal component to it. In short, as Rapoport argues, any analysis of the built environment must relate together the organizations of space, time, meaning and communication.

A particularly noteworthy aspect of Rapoport's discussion, which bears comparison with what Miller has to say, in Article 15, about the differences between artefacts and words, concerns the various levels of meaning attributable to the built environment, from high-level 'cosmological' meanings, through middle-level 'social meanings', to low-level 'instrumental' meanings. In a non-literate society, words are no substitute for built forms as the enduring embodiments of a people's most fundamental cosmological notions. But with the development of literacy, words are inscribed in a solid medium and, collected in volumes, they can 'take over' from the built environment as the principal repository of cultural knowledge and tradition. For the written word *is* an artefact. At the same time, however, as societies increase in scale, complexity and internal heterogeneity, the middle- and lower-level meanings of their built environments are likely to become increasingly prominent. Thus the modern city contains a plethora of social markers which indicate and delimit the spaces available to members of different groups, or to people of different identity or status, as well as instrumental markers which serve as guides to expected behaviour and as aids to wayfinding. People living in large and complex societies might not read their cosmologies in the land-scape, as for example do Australian Aboriginal hunter–gatherers, but they do rely at every turn on artefactual cues in the built environment in order to navigate successfully in a highly differentiated social milieu.

With Article 18 we turn not only from organizations of space to perceptions of time, but also to an approach very different from the one adopted by Rapoport. Adam is openly critical of the conventional portrayal of the Western anthropologist as the disinterested translator of the worldviews of other cul-tures. It has often been suggested, in anthropological writings, that people in 'traditional', non-Western cultures lack our 'modern' sense of time as a linear and unidirectional chronological sequence, and that theirs, by contrast, is a time that is cyclical, reversible, not a container for unique events but contained within the regular repetition of the events of everyday life. Yet this contrast is implicit in the very operation that constitutes the 'traditional culture' as an object of anthropological attention. When we look more closely at the way in which people in Western societies actually perceive time, we find that the rendering of this perception as a linear sequence is as much a caricature as is the contrastive rendering of the time perception of the 'other' as cyclical. Sorting the manifold ways in which Westerners speak about time into the four categories of time frames, timing, temporality and tempo, Adam concludes that someone from a non-Western society, reviewing these categories, would find in them nothing out of the ordinary. It is quite normal, for example, for native speakers of English to affix qualitative values to time (e.g. 'good' and 'bad' times), and to locate the 'when' of social events in terms of the regular round of daily tasks (e.g. 'mealtimes' and 'bedtime').

So where, if anywhere, lies the distinctiveness of the Western sense of time? It cannot lie in the existence of clocks and calendars, for these are of both wide distribution and considerable antiquity. It was the experience of industrializa-tion, Adam argues, that converted what had once been an abstract chronology for the measurement of time into something that people came to perceive, and to which they would relate, as time itself. Thus reified, clock time – mech-anical, impersonal, detached from the relational contexts of social life – figured as a commodity that could be saved or used up, exchanged for money, and made the object of contests of control. Conditioned to this commodification of time in their own society, Western anthropologists are inclined to turn to non-industrial societies to recover the temporality intrinsic to the multiple rhythms of social life. In just the same way, following Miller's point in Article 15, it is the Western experience of the commodification of artefacts that leads observers to be so impressed by the extent of their personalization in 'traditional' societies.

But in reality, as Adam shows, reified clock time has not replaced the intrinsic temporality of lived, social experience; it has only changed its meaning. Behind the specific experience of the industrial West lies a core of temporal awareness common to all humanity, which consists in the capacity of human beings to reflect upon the conditions of their own existence. In this awareness both linearity and repetition are mutually implicated, and which of these aspects is emphasized will depend upon the perspective of the observer. If, as in the classical approach to viewing other cultures, linearity is built into the framework of assumptions that are brought to the project of observation, then attention will naturally gravitate to the component of cyclicity in the temporal experience of the people observed. Yet, in truth, there is no society in which the components of linearity and cyclicity are not combined. The dichotomy between the linear time of the West and the cyclical time of non-Western societies is, in Adam's view, at best a convenient anthropological fiction, at worst a serious source of misunderstanding.

Alongside the linear sense of time, another characteristic commonly attributed to Western societies is literacy: indeed the two are often related on the grounds that the preservation of documentary records contributes to a view of history as a chronologically ordered sequence of events. The impact of literacy on society has already emerged as an issue highlighted in Rapoport's comparison (Article 17) between the inscription of cultural meaning in the built environment and in written texts. Though literacy has often been regarded as a technology of language, the acquisition and use of literacy skills are invariably embedded in particular social contexts. This exemplifies the general point raised by Sigaut (Article 16), that when it comes to skilled practice, the domains of technical and social activity are inseparable, and it forms one of the premisses from which Street and Besnier, in Article 19, launch their discussion of aspects of literacy. Their other premiss is that literacy should not be regarded as a unitary phenomenon, something which people either have or lack, which inevitably confers some determinate intellectual advantage on its possessors, and which has regular impacts on the forms of their social and cultural life. Rather, the notion of literacy covers a multitude of varied situations whose only common denominator is the representation of words in a graphic medium. In this respect, Street and Besnier incline towards the so-called 'ideological model' of literacy, according to which the role that literacy is made to play will depend upon the social, historical and cultural forces that have shaped it, as opposed to the 'autonomous model', which treats literacy as an independent variable having predictable consequences for the individuals and societies exposed to it.

In line with this ideological stance, Street and Besnier view literacy as an assortment of practices rather than a total package, and regard its adoption not as a process of passive acquiescence, but as one wherein people actively select certain practices and reject others, depending upon the communicative possibilities that the chosen practices afford them in their current circumstances. Thus particular forms of literacy may serve as vehicles of either domination or resistance in the relations, for example, between men and women, between people of different social class, or between ethnic groups. They may serve to unite or divide nations, or as instruments of colonial or post-colonial

339

domination. And, of course, the literacies of the school and the home, and the correspondences and discrepancies between them, are crucially significant for everyone concerned with the policies and practice of education. In all these respects, as Street and Besnier show, anthropological studies can contribute to our understanding of literacy not so much as an evolutionary advance in human society and cognition but rather as a set of resources that people can turn to their adaptive advantage under particular social and historical conditions.

BELIEF, MYTH AND RITUAL

Attempts to describe and understand the beliefs of people of other cultures have long been central to the anthropological enterprise. These endeavours, however, have become mired in some of the most intractable philosophical problems of the discipline, problems that Lewis explores in Article 20. How, for example, can we ever know what people really think, when all we have to go on are what they say or do, or what they have to say about the things they do? And how can we pretend to be able to characterize the belief system of an entire culture on the basis of what a handful of key informants have told us? The scope for interpersonal variation in belief has tended to be obscured by an assumption that the small-scale societies which anthropologists often study are marked by a relatively high degree of consensus, and by a greater commitment to the force of tradition as against reasoned argument. And this assumption, in turn, reinforces the tendency to regard the rationality of people in such societies as uncertain, and therefore − unlike our own rationality, which we take to be self-evident − as standing in need of anthropological verification. Indeed this uncertainty is reflected in the very choice of the term 'belief' rather than 'knowledge' to describe the claims that people make about the world: for to speak of belief is at once to insinuate that there is some element of unreliability surrounding the truth of what is asserted.

On the other hand, without some appeal to a core of rationality common to humanity there would seem to be no way of establishing any ground on which to build mutual, cross-cultural understanding. Without such a bridge-head, how can we even begin to tap into the belief system of an alien culture? The very possibility of translation, as Lewis points out, appears to require that people, whatever their beliefs, confront the same external, objective reality, and that what they say is backed by some basic rational conceptual commitment.

The problem lies, to a large measure, in ambiguities inherent in the notion of belief itself. Is a belief an article of faith, one of those unquestioned and unquestionable assumptions within which thinking necessarily proceeds, or is it a product of thought, a rational prognosis that is nevertheless provisional and subject to amendment in the light of new facts? It is all too easy, as Lewis shows, to compare beliefs of the second kind among scientifically informed, 'modern' thinkers with those of the first kind held by people of 'traditional' cultures. Thus failing to compare like with like, we are led not only to the erroneous conclusion that modern thought is 'open' whereas traditional thought is 'closed', but also to ignore both the extent to which supposedly traditional people engage in common-sense reasoning based on observation and inference, and, conversely, the extent to which even Western science is grounded in ontological assumptions that are not themselves open to negotiation. One of these assumptions is that the world exists 'out there' for the rational mind to hold beliefs or propositions about: indeed the separation between mind and world – and its corollary, that the world can only be known in so far as it is represented in the mind – is implicit in the very notion of belief. But this propositional attitude is not generally shared by the peoples among whom anthropologists study, so that verbal utterances that *we* might interpret as statements of belief, sayings which reveal some inner mental conviction, might for *them* be forms of engagement intended to place speakers in a certain *relation* to the world, affording the possibility of knowledge through immediate revelation. Their words, in short, should perhaps be understood not as statements at all, but rather as producing an *effect*, both on the speakers themselves and on those who are moved by their speech.

This latter suggestion forms the point of departure for Weiner's novel recasting, in Article 21, of the classic anthropological themes of myth, totemism and magic. Orthodox theories generally assume an a priori differentiation between, on the one hand, the domain of verbal discourse and, on the other, the world that this discourse describes. Thus it is supposed that the language of myth encodes a comprehensive and logically coherent account of the origins and nature of the world – a cosmology – that also serves as a charter validating existing social institutions. The language of totemism is supposed to establish analogical resemblances across human and animal domains that, in the real world, are naturally segregated. And the recitation of verbal magic is classically distinguished from ordinary speech on the grounds of the magician's belief in the power of his words to produce real, physical effects, a belief that confounds the distinction we draw between language and the world. Weiner sets out from the opposite premiss that these forms of linguistic utterance – whether mythical, totemic or magical – are as much situated in the world as are the phenomena on which they comment. They are real actions which have real effects. Thus a mythical narrative, for example, serves not to represent or reinforce a more significant social reality but to 'open it up', to render the conventional transparent by way of its allegorical impingements on the established order of things – including the semantic conventions of ordinary language itself. For if no absolute line of demarcation separates language from the world, then the effect that myth produces in the world cannot be separated from its effect on language.

A central theme of Weiner's argument concerns the role of metaphor. Here he ingeniously plays two views of metaphor off against one another: the first is characteristic of (though by no means exclusive to) the Western tradition of thought; the second is exemplified, *inter alia*, by the Foi people of Papua New Guinea, among whom Weiner has carried out his own fieldwork. Every metaphor involves the conjunction of a similarity and a difference: in that respect, as Foster also points out in Article 14, it establishes a relation of *likeness* rather than identity. In the Western view the specific task of the human mind is to seek out the similarities between entities that, in the world 'out there', are already naturally differentiated. Foster's discussion of analogical thinking is an exemplary instance of this view which, for the most part, has been carried over unquestioned into anthropological analysis. In Foi thinking, by contrast, what is given from the start is a world that is continuous, undifferentiated and all-encompassing, such that the human task is to *establish difference*, to divide the continuum of being into separate domains. To say that one thing is like another, then, is not to highlight their resemblance or commonality against a background of presumed separateness, as in the work of classification, but rather to highlight their distinction against a background of presumed continuity. Weiner's thesis, in a nutshell, is that the phenomena of myth, totemism and magic can all be understood as workings out of the more fundamental theme of this inversion in figure-ground relations.

If myth is an impingement upon the conventions of ordinary language, what is the relation between ritual and ordinary life? This is one of the key issues addressed by Schechner in Article 22. Schechner adopts a performative approach to ritual, regarding it as a kind of drama; another kind is theatre, and the relation between ritual and theatrical performance is a second issue that is central to his discussion. Here I shall comment only briefly on these two issues. As regards the first, it is clear that ritual is no mere reflection of the institutional conventions of quotidian life, but, like myth, it plays creatively upon them and thereby participates in the continuous process wherein conventions are built up and dissolved. It is clear, too, that even outside the bounds of 'staged' ritual or theatrical performance, people play their parts in acting out the social and political dramas of real life. In the model developed by Schechner, the relation between the 'social drama' and the 'aesthetic drama' is interactive rather than mimetic: the latter does not copy the former, but affects and is affected by it in a spiral of positive feedback. In aesthetic drama, social and political actions that have real consequences in the world provide the underlying context within which the rhetorical devices and principles of judgement of the culture are made manifest. Conversely, in social drama these devices and principles, drawn from the aesthetic domain, provide the implicit framework within which are managed the consequential actions of social life. Ritual, however, refuses to be accommodated within the terms of the distinction between the social and the aesthetic: it draws on both, and derives much of its power from the fact.

Turning to the second issue of the relation between ritual and theatrical performance, it is often argued that theatre has its origins in the rituals of 'archaic' peoples. Schechner, however, disagrees. In his view, theatre is as old as ritual, and the two emerged together as early as the Palaeolithic era. The distinction is not absolute, but one of emphasis: ritual emphasizes the *efficacy* of the performance, theatre emphasizes its value as *entertainment*. No performance is ever purely one or the other – thus even the most ostensibly instrumental ritual, put on for example to heal the sick or to bring rain, contains an element of fun. And even if we visit the theatre for no other reason than our own entertainment, we are never wholly unaffected by the experience. Over time, however, the relative weighting placed on efficacy and entertainment in a society may fluctuate, so that rituals can become increasingly theatrical, and theatre increasingly ritualized. But what lies behind all genres of performance, from the most ritualistic to the most theatrical, is the element of *play*. Play is a creative dissembling of conventional orders, blurring the distinction between the real and the unreal, and in that way opening up a space of pure potential, of the boundless possibilities of being. In their different ways, in different cultural circumstances, these possibilities are open to children, to neurotics and to 'technicians of the sacred' such as shamans and artists. What is common to their experience, Schechner argues, is the degree of its exposure and susceptibility to the disturbing outpourings of the unconscious mind. But how can a view of play as inherently anti-structural be reconciled with neurological accounts which explain ritualistic behaviour by the 'hard wiring' of the human brain? Schechner's solution to this dilemma is to suggest an analytic distinction between ritual as a type of behaviour common to humanity, and the *experiences* of ritual, which are unique to participants and cannot be generalized. Neurology, then, provides the universal armature for playful improvization.

ART, MUSIC AND DANCE

For many people in the West, theatrical performance, along with certain genres of literature, painting, sculpture, music and dance, fall under the rubric of what are generally called 'the arts'. The cultivation of these fields is widely taken to be an index of culture in the progressive sense of civilization. The close coupling of the idea of art with the evaluative criteria of Western civilization has, however, placed particular problems in the way of its adoption as a concept of anthropological analysis. While examples of so-called 'primitive art' are exhibited in galleries and museums around the world, it seems that these works have become art for *us* – and not for the people who produced them – only through having been removed entirely from the contexts of their production, and converted into objects of detached contemplation for our own delight and edification as privileged spectators of the tapestry of human variation. Is there, then, any way in which we can apply the concept of art to the works of people from non-Western cultural backgrounds in a sense that does justice to local frameworks of meaning? How can we distinguish what count as 'art objects' from the artefactual assemblages of material culture in general? Precisely because the idea of art carries such strong evaluative connotations, questions of this kind cannot be avoided, and they form the starting point for Morphy's review, in Article 23, of the newly developing field of the anthropology of art.

In the West, objects can 'count' as art either because they have been admitted to the exclusive institutional settings in which art is exhibited and marketed, or because they are intended by their producers to be regarded as works of art, or because they possess certain attributes with which any such work is supposed to be endowed. None of these criteria readily lend themselves to cross-cultural application. However, it does seem generally to be the case that of works produced in any particular cultural context, certain objects are singled out on iconographic, aesthetic or functional grounds. That is, in relation to the projects and principles of judgement of the producers, these objects may be credited with semantic properties, or the effects they induce on the senses may be accorded aesthetic value, and for these reasons they may be called upon to serve specific presentational or representational purposes. Of course an object may have other properties besides the semantic or aesthetic, and so too it may have other uses: thus it might more appropriately be said to have an 'art aspect', rather than to be an object of art *per se*. With this qualification, it may be possible, as Morphy suggests, to define the anthropology of art as the comparative study, within and between cultural contexts, of the semantic and aesthetic aspects of objects of material culture, and of their corresponding uses.

To establish this field it was necessary to bring together concerns with form and style, traditionally the province of art historians, and concerns with meaning and function which had become central to an anthropology that had adopted fieldwork as its principal method of investigation. The pioneering studies of the 1960s and 1970s, in line with a general trend in the study of material culture at that time, emphasized the semantic properties of objects, treating art as a system of communication. Yet as we have already seen, in connection with Miller's discussion of the meanings of artefacts in Article 15, this emphasis can obscure the direct sensory effects that objects can have by virtue of their sheer presence in an environment. The painted and decorated body of a dancer, for example, may terrify or dazzle the beholder: terror and brilliance, however, are effects that are palpably felt, not abstract meanings that are communicated in the dance. To attend to these sensory effects, and to the ways in which they are culturally valorized, is to focus on the aesthetic rather than the semantic properties of art, and correspondingly on its presentational rather than representational significance.

The example of body painting serves to illustrate a further point of crucial importance: that objects and designs are very often perceived *in motion*, kinematically tied to the movements of the human body, and achieve their effects only for that reason. In other words, they are perceived in performance. If

344

anthropologists have been slow to recognize this point, it is largely due to the lingering influence of a deep-seated inclination in the Western intellectual tradition to prioritize form over process, and thus to regard movement as nothing more than the revelation of pre-existing design and meaning. Even in the case of the so-called 'performing arts' – theatre, music, dance – we tend to imagine that every work has an existence of its own, quite independent of its several instantiations in performance. Yet while music and dance are found in all human societies, in most cases there exists nothing like a score. Rather, it is within the contexts of performance itself that musical and choreographic form is generated. And, likewise, it is by attending to and seeking to emulate the movements of the performers that each new generation of novices becomes adept in the musical and dance traditions of its predecessors, incorporating them into its own patterns of bodily awareness and response. As Seeger points out in Article 24, this recognition of the primacy of performance in the generation and transmission of form is not limited to the study of music and dance, but has come about through a more fundamental and wide-ranging reorientation of anthropological inquiry, from structural, concept-led approaches to those that accord a central place to process and practice in the constitution of culture and society. The effect of this reorientation, however, is to move music and dance from the periphery to the heart of anthropological concern: no longer are they seen to be merely expressive of a given, structural-symbolic order; rather they are viewed as intrinsic to the very processes wherein that order is constituted.

There are of course problems with applying the concepts of music and dance cross-culturally, just as there are with the concept of art. How are we to distinguish music from all the other sound-patterns that people produce as they go about their tasks? And how can dance be distinguished from other patterns of bodily movement? Both sounds and movements may, as Seeger suggests, be arrayed in a continuum whose dimensions of variation are from unintentional to intentional, from unstructured to structured, and from utilitarian to expressive. We might place music and dance at the latter extreme on each of these dimensions, but other societies may divide the continuum quite differently, lumping together what we distinguish and distinguishing what we might group under a single term. Even the distinction between sound and movement, on the basis of which we separate music from dance, is somewhat arbitrary and is not universally recognized: thus the Suyá Indians of Brazil, among whom Seeger has carried out fieldwork, do not make any separation of this kind. Equally problematic are the distinctions between vocal music (i.e. song) and speech, and between dance movement and gestural signs, both of which rest on the assumption that words and gestures possess the property of semantic reference, conveying conceptual meanings that are detachable from the signs themselves. This assumption, in turn, raises profound issues in linguistic theory concerning the ways in which signs acquire meaning. If, as more pragmatically oriented approaches to language suggest, signs derive their meanings from the situational contexts of use rather than from their external attachment to concepts, then it is no longer possible to draw an absolute dividing line between speech and song, or for that matter between gesture and dance.

CULTURE, POLITICS AND ETHNICITY

We are used to thinking of music and dance, indeed of 'the arts' in general, as falling within a sphere of expressive culture quite separate from the more utilitarian spheres of political and economic life. In anthropology this separation is reflected in a tendency to treat political economy on the one hand, and symbolic meaning on the other, as occupying distinct 'levels' of social experience, calling for different concepts and methods of analysis. However, with the repositioning of music, dance and other performative genres from the margins to the centre of the constitutive processes of culture and society, this difference is effectively dissolved. As Seeger shows, musical and dance performances are directly implicated in economic life, on the sides of both production and consumption. Moreover their capacity to tap the most basic sources of human feeling makes them powerful vehicles of political mobilization and solidarity. Because of the playful, anti-structural nature that they share with many genres of theatrical performance, they most often figure in political struggles on the side of the oppressed, as part of a challenge to the injustices of the established order and to the straitjacket it imposes on action and thought. That is why they are so often perceived as a potent threat by those in authority.

However, it is in the formation of ethnic identities, and the various kinds of solidarity based on them, that expressive culture enters most directly and powerfully into the political process. This is a theme taken up by Smith in Article 25. His major concern is with the ways in which communities based on shared ethnic affiliation, which he calls *ethnie*, convert themselves into nations. Why, despite increasingly intensive pressures towards global interdependence and regional fragmentation, does the world continue to be divided into autonomous nation states? And why, in the face of persistent opposition and bitter experience, do nationalisms continue to flourish? In addressing these questions, Smith seeks a middle road between the alternatives, most frequently mooted in the literature, of 'primordialism' and 'instrumentalism'. Primordialists argue that ethnic ties are founded in people's sense of harbouring within themselves, sedimented in their consciousness, ways of thinking and feeling of timeless antiquity; instrumentalists, by contrast, maintain that ethnicity figures as a resource to be mobilized in competitive struggles for political power. Advocates of the former view imagine that nations have always existed; advocates of the latter generally insist that the nation is a phenomenon of modernity. Where the one exaggerates the 'prehistory' of the nation, the other disregards it.

To reach a more satisfactory account, Smith argues, we should attend more closely to the pre-modern social and cultural backgrounds of modern-day nations. This approach leads him to distinguish between two opposed processes in the formation of ethnic communities (allowing that, in practice, they may combine in various, often contradictory ways). In the first, the community extends itself widely in space, while socially it recruits from a narrow band of élite status. In the second, the community remains territorially compact, bound to a 'homeland', but recruits from all sectors of the population by appealing to the 'folk' and to their vernacular language and culture. To this dichotomy, between 'lateral' and 'vertical' *ethnie*, there corresponds a further distinction between two routes to nation formation, one preceding the rise of nationalism, the other following as a consequence of it. The first route leads from the lateral *ethnie* to the 'civic–territorial' national state, exemplified by the nations of the West; the second leads from the vertical *ethnie* to the 'ethnic–genealogical' nation typical of Central and Eastern Europe and of many parts of Asia. To each kind of nation there corresponds its distinctive brand of nationalism. Civic–territorial nationalisms emphasize the rights of every citizen within the territorial framework of the state, defining the identity of the nation in terms of its external opposition to other nations of similar order. Ethnic–genealogical nationalisms, by contrast, are inward-looking, emphasizing the unique values, historical memories and myths of origin of folk culture. Yet neither variety of nationalism can entirely dispense with the other. The former needs to draw on ethnic–genealogical imagery to lend substance to the identity of the civic–territorial state; the latter, seeking such benefits of modernity as wealth, education and literacy, needs to appeal to the civic–territorial values that underwrite them.

With the study of nationalism, the anthropology of history catches up with the history of anthropology. We have thus come full circle, from a review of anthropological studies of culture to the cultural foundations of anthropological study itself. For anthropology did not, of course, invent the concept of culture; rather the concept was fashioned within the same movement of European thought that gave rise to the discipline of anthropology. And the context of this movement was one of emergent nationalisms, of both civic–territorial and ethnic–genealogical varieties. In the framework of civic–territorial ideology, 'culture' (in the sense of civilization) was harnessed to a rationalistic anthropology conceived as an inquiry into the advance of global humanity. In the framework of ethnic–genealogical ideology, 'culture' (in the sense of tradition) was harnessed to a relativistic anthropology conceived as an inquiry into the diversity of local forms of life. Nowadays, with the development of modern transport, communications and mass-media, this contrast between global and local perspectives has taken a new turn. Predictions that local diversity would be swamped by a homogeneous 'mass culture' of worldwide distribution show no signs of being borne out. On the contrary, new forms of local distinctiveness are forever being constructed and asserted:

however, the materials from which such identities are composed, far from being of exclusively local provenance, can come from almost anywhere. In the study of these processes of identity formation in the contemporary world, the concept of culture will surely have further work to do, and its meaning will no doubt continue to change in consequence.

FURTHER READING

Anderson, B. (1983) *Imagined Communities: Reflections on the Origin and Spread of Nationalism*, London: Verso.

Appadurai, A. (ed.) (1986) *The Social Life of Things: Commodities in Cultural Perspective*, Cambridge: Cambridge University Press.

Basso, K. and Selby, H. (eds) (1976) *Meaning in Anthropology*, Albuquerque: University of New Mexico Press.

Bonner, J. T. (1980) *The Evolution of Culture in Animals*, Princeton, NJ: Princeton University Press.

Bourdieu, P. (1990) *The Logic of Practice*, Stanford: Stanford University Press.

Carrithers, M. (1992) *Why Humans Have Cultures*, Oxford: Oxford University Press.

Clifford, J. (1988) *The Predicament of Culture: Twentieth Century Ethnography, Literature and Art*, Cambridge, Mass.: Harvard University Press.

Coote, J. and Shelton, A. (eds) (1992) *Art, Anthropology and Aesthetics*, Oxford: Oxford University Press.

Fabian, J. (1983) *Time and the Other: How Anthropology Makes its Object*, New York: Columbia University Press.

Finnegan, R. (1988) *Literacy and Orality: Studies in the Technology of Communication*, Oxford: Blackwell.

Foster, M. L. and Brandes, S. H. (eds) (1980) *Symbol as Sense: New Approaches to the Analysis of Meaning*, New York: Academic Press.

Geertz, C. (1973) *The Interpretation of Cultures*, New York: Basic Books.

Gell, A. (1992) *The Anthropology of Time: Cultural Constructions of Temporal Maps and Images*, Oxford: Berg.

Hobsbawm, E. and Ranger, T. (eds) (1983) *The Invention of Tradition*, Cambridge: Cambridge University Press.

Howes, D. (ed.) (1991) *The Varieties of Sensory Experience: a Sourcebook in the Anthropology of the Senses*, Toronto: University of Toronto Press.

Jackson, M. (1989) *Paths Toward a Clearing: Radical Empiricism and Ethnographic Inquiry*, Bloomington: Indiana University Press.

Kertzer, D. I. (1988) *Ritual, Politics and Power*, New Haven: Yale University Press.

Layton, R. (1991) *The Anthropology of Art*, 2nd edn, Cambridge: Cambridge University Press.

Leach E. R. (1976) *Culture and Communication: the Logic by which Symbols are Connected*, Cambridge: Cambridge University Press.

Lévi-Strauss, C. (1978) *Myth and Meaning*, London: Routledge & Kegan Paul.

Miller, D. (1987) *Material Culture and Mass Consumption*, Oxford: Blackwell.

Oliver, P. (1987) *Dwellings: the House Across the World*, London: Phaidon.

Rapoport, A. (1990) *The Meaning of the Built Environment*, revised edn, Tucson: University of Arizona Press.

Sahlins, M. D. (1976) *Culture and Practical Reason*, Chicago: University of Chicago Press.

Schechner, R. (1988) *Performance Theory*, London: Routledge.

Shweder, R. A. and LeVine, R. A. (1984) *Culture Theory: Essays on Mind, Self and Emotion*, Cambridge: Cambridge University Press.

Smith, A. D. (1986) *The Ethnic Origins of Nations*, Oxford: Blackwell.

Spencer, P. (ed.) (1985) *Society and the Dance*, Cambridge: Cambridge University Press.

Sperber, D. (1982) *On Anthropological Knowledge*, Cambridge: Cambridge University Press.

Street, B. V. (ed.) (1993) *Cross-cultural Approaches to Literacy*, Cambridge: Cambridge University Press.

Tambiah, S. J. (1990) *Magic, Science, Religion and the Scope of Rationality*, Cambridge: Cambridge University Press.

Turner, V. (1974) *Dramas, Fields and Metaphors*, Ithaca, NY: Cornell University Press.

Tyler, S. (1978) *The Said and the Unsaid: Mind, Meaning and Culture*, New York: Academic Press.

Wagner, R. (1981) *The Invention of Culture*, revised and expanded edn, Chicago: University of Chicago Press.

13

WHY ANIMALS HAVE NEITHER
CULTURE NOR HISTORY

David Premack and Ann James Premack

All species are unique, but the human is uniquest.

(Dobzhansky 1955: 12)

INTRODUCTION

History is a sequence of changes through which a species passes while remaining biologically stable. The historical changes undergone by human populations during ancient times were, by contemporary standards, very slow, allowing archaeologists to identify the principal, successive epochs with corresponding changes in the technological and material bases of cultural life. In modern times, changes are too complex to be identified in this manner; they involve not only technology and material culture, but also major transformations in social, political and economic organization. Moreover, the rate at which these changes now occur has increased profoundly since ancient times and is still rising.

While a vast number of histories have been written about human beings, one could not write a history of the chimpanzee, nor of any other animal. One could perhaps write a history of how humans have *treated* the chimpanzee, beaver, pigeon, or whatever, but not one of the animal itself, for animals have not undergone significant change while remaining biologically stable. For example, basic social practices in the chimpanzee have remained the same: the female leaves the natal group today, as she did, so far as we know, five million years ago. The 'technology' has remained essentially unaltered, the chimpanzee's nest being – again so far as we know – the same as it was in the distant past.

Of course, we do not really know what kind of nest the chimpanzee made in the past, what it ate, or if the female left the natal group. However, at least two factors argue strongly for the view that practices among chimpanzees have

350

remained unchanged. First, in the hundred years or so during which humans have observed chimpanzees, no changes of historical significance have been noted. Second, the observed differences among contemporary chimpanzee groups are equally insignificant. They include: one group eating nut A, another nut B; one group cracking nut A by striking it with a rock, another by slamming it against a tree; one group peeling the bark from twigs which it uses in fishing for insects, another group not doing so.

History is not, however, an automatic by-product of the human brain; nor is it an inevitable concomitant of culture. A group whose members are equipped with a human brain, as well as with the culture that such a brain essentially guarantees, may yet have no history. To have history, a group must act on the world so as to change it — in so doing, changing itself. For example, the construction of permanent shelters, a major forerunner of other environmental changes to come, had a radical impact on the family and other spheres of social relations (P. J. Wilson 1988; see also Rapoport, Article 17 in this volume).

Many writers outside anthropology, including biologists and psychologists, find the concept of culture vague, but none the less ask, 'Do animals have culture?' Sidestepping the question 'What is culture?', they ask instead 'How is animal behaviour transmitted?' If a 'tradition' is transmitted across generations by 'appropriate social mechanisms', then the behaviour is deemed to be cultural (e.g. Galef 1992). This is not a view peculiar to one or two writers, but is very commonly adopted by non-anthropologists interested in the question of 'animal culture'. Using this inadequate definition of culture, most conclude, as E. O. Wilson does (1975: 168), that 'culture, aside from its involvement with language, which is truly unique, differs from animal tradition only in degree.'

But animals have neither culture nor history. Furthermore, language is not the only difference between, say, chimpanzees and humans: a human is not a chimpanzee to which language has been added. That one of the world's leading zoologists, who knows every hair on an ant's body and could tell a right-handed from a left-handed ant at twenty paces, cannot differentiate an ape from a human is startling. Turning to the work of Goodall (1986), we read that the chimpanzee, being unable to talk, cannot sit down with its peers, as humans do, and decide what to do tomorrow. Wilson is an expert on ants, Goodall is an expert on chimpanzees. Neither knows humans. Would it not be wiser for them to confine their comparisons to ants and chimpanzees?

SOCIAL TRANSMISSION OF INFORMATION

The transmission of information and skills across generations — 'turning the young into adults' — is a problem confronted by all species. The primary unit for the transmission of social information is a dyad: parent—offspring, older sibling—younger sibling, model—novice. One can distinguish three grades of socially transmitted information, depending on the degree of *intention* in the dyad. In the lowest grade of transmission, information is exchanged without intention by either party. For instance, a rat often eats as its first solid food one whose odour it encountered in its mother's milk. The information exchanged was not transmitted intentionally: the neonate did not seek the information, nor did the mother seek to impart it.

In the intermediate grade, the novice behaves intentionally, though the model remains unintentional. This is what has traditionally been known as imitation or observational learning. For instance, a monkey, ape or child observes a model, and acquires thereby a new technology, but the model's behaviour is indifferent to the presence or absence of the novice.

In the highest grade, both novice and model act intentionally. Not only does the novice seek information, the model also seeks to impart it. The novice, as in the case of imitation, observes the model; but now the model returns the observation, not just observing, but judging and correcting the novice when he or she fails to conform to a standard. This, the most efficient form of social transmission of information, is *pedagogy*. A biological novelty, it is found only in humans.

The mechanism underlying the simplest form of social transmission of information is conditioning or associative learning. This is a primitive mechanism found even in the rat. The rat's social learning does not end with weaning; as an adult, when it develops a map of the food sources in its area, it uses the map in conjunction with the odours it detects on the bodies of its peers in finding particular foods (Galef 1982).

However, the rat's system is more effective in imparting positive information than negative. If a familiar food is made toxic or even fatal, so as to become a source of negative information, a rat encountering the odour of the food on its conspecific will nevertheless seek the food. Indeed, it will pursue and eat the food, even if it encounters the odour of the food on the body of a dead conspecific!

The second level of social transmission of information is seen in observational learning. Two monkeys − one a model, the other an observer − are seated across from one another, each provided with two buttons, one button delivering food, the other an electric shock (Miller 1967). The model learns to avoid a shock by directly experiencing the association between the use of one button and shock. The observer avoids a shock simply by observing the experience of the monkey being shocked.

Observational learning of this kind, though typically discussed in connection with monkeys, is primitive enough to have recently been reported even in the octopus. But such learning can be more complex and may require an animal to learn how to *use* an object, and not merely how to *select* it. An infant chimpanzee, watching its mother (for example) fish for termites by inserting twigs into the holes of a termite mound, might: (1) develop an interest in twigs, selecting them over other objects; (2) understand the purpose of the mother's action, and, being fond of termites, follow her whenever she picked up twigs, or even press twigs into her hands to induce her to carry out the act; (3) copy the mother's action, thus obtaining termites itself; or (4) do all of the above. A child, given the same opportunity, would of course copy the mother's action, obtaining termites for itself. There is little evidence that this is true of the chimpanzee.

The word 'imitation' has been largely reserved for the novice's copying the action of the model. Despite widespread belief to the contrary, as epitomized in the phrase 'monkey see, monkey do', evidence for imitation in monkeys or even in apes is scarce (for recent thoughtful reviews in support of this conclusion, see Visalberghi and Fragaszy 1990, Galef 1992). Indeed, the best evidence for imitation in animals lies, not in the behaviour of primates, but in the mimicry of birds.

The human infant, by contrast, imitates from within minutes of birth − 42 minutes to be exact (Meltzoff and Moore 1983). The infant sticks out its tongue or turns its head, copying the model. Because these are not necessarily novel acts, one can question whether this is true imitation. However, by 16 weeks, the infant copies not one act but novel *sequences* of acts, and not only immediately but even after appreciable delay (Meltzoff 1988). Furthermore, by as early as 11 months, the infant goes a step beyond imitation; it recognizes when it is being imitated by the adult, and repeats those acts that will lead the adult to copy its own behaviour. Thus, the infant not only imitates, but is already well on its way towards recognizing that there is such a thing as imitation.

The extraordinary spontaneity of imitation further distinguishes humans from other primates: the infant monkey spontaneously clings to its mother; the slightly older chimpanzee spontaneously rides on her back; the human infant spontaneously imitates its mother. The magnitude of the role played by imitation in the transmission of tradition in these species is consistent with these differences in spontaneous behaviour. In non-human primates, imitation plays no role (or none that has yet been demonstrated) in the transmission of information, whereas in humans it plays a major role.

If we were to test for imitation with the chimpanzee as we do with the infant, offering a model who sticks out her tongue, the chimpanzee would fail. Even if disposed to imitate, the animal could not, because it lacks full voluntary control of its tongue. To evaluate imitation in the chimpanzee, we would have to restrict tests to tasks involving placement of limbs or general body posture. These may be the only major motor systems over which the chimpanzee has full voluntary control; it evidently lacks such control for facial expression and vocalization (Chevalier-Skolnikoff 1976). Human beings may be the only species capable of implementing their intentions with all parts of their bodies. Human uniqueness is not confined to cognition, but is embedded in the motor system itself (Premack 1993).

Although there is no convincing evidence for imitation in chimpanzees reared in the wild, such is not the case for those raised by humans. Sarah, an African-born chimpanzee reared from infancy in the laboratory, demonstrated an especially interesting kind of spontaneous imitation in the reassembly of a puzzle (the photographed parts of a face). After placing the eyes, nose and mouth in appropriate topographical positions on the face outline, she then transformed the assembly, placing certain parts in a hat-like position. Sarah constructed these transformations after having observed the trainer wearing hats or after she herself had worn them. In fact, twenty-four hours after having observed herself or her trainer in hats, she removed the 'nose' from its usual position, reversed it, and placed it on the head; furthermore, she 'dressed' the head with discarded banana peel that lay in her cage (Premack 1975). Transformations of this kind represent a rather complex and unusual form of imitation.

In an example of classic imitation, Sarah would simply have copied her trainer, placing a hat on her own head. But a hat was not available to Sarah, and so instead she created an appropriate image by placing various items in a hat-like position on the photograph. This unique solution, however, was not her only use of an indirect form of imitation.

In a subsequent test, she was given to wear (or observed her trainers to wear) either glasses or a necklace as well as hats. She again transformed the photograph of the face, now placing bits of clay in appropriate positions. She placed the clay on top of the head, in the area of the eyes, or on the neck, twenty-four hours after having viewed herself or her trainers in hats, glasses or necklaces. When Sarah was not exposed to any apparel, she did not use the wad of clay in appropriate positions, but tore the clay into pieces, and placed them in face-like positions on the photograph (Premack 1986).

Imitation as indirect and complex as this has not been reported in other human-reared chimpanzees, but many instances of classical imitation have been noted in such animals (e.g. by Hayes and Nissen 1971, Kohts 1935). The disparity between behaviours observed in human-reared, as against wild, chimpanzees is not confined to imitation alone; another example will be provided in a later section, in which we discuss the possibility of pedagogy in chimpanzees. Field observations are poor forecasters of the potential behavioural complexity of the chimpanzee. And although some of this complexity is brought about by explicit training, much of it, as in the examples presented above, is completely spontaneous.

PEDAGOGY: CONFINED TO HUMANS

In imitation, the novice observes the model, copying his or her behaviour – the model does not return the observation. Pedagogy is immediately distinguishable from imitation because in pedagogy the model *does* observe the novice. In addition, the model judges the novice, and intervenes actively to modify the novice's performance. Pedagogy thus consists in a combination of *observation*, *judgement*, and *intervention* (Premack 1984).

In deciding whether pedagogy is confined to humans we must take into account *parental investment*, which may involve behaviours that appear to resemble pedagogy. Most examples of parental investment in animals (e.g. those provided by Caro and Houser 1992) can be divided into two kinds: social control, and provisioning. In social control, a parent is said either to encourage or discourage certain of its offspring's acts. But this is no more than a case of the parent's response being either a reward/punishment for the offspring's action, or a stimulus for its action. Provisioning, in which the parent provides its offspring with stimuli critical for the acquisition of certain skills, more closely resembles pedagogy.

A commonly cited example is that of the cat bringing mice to its kittens – mice which the growing kittens then come to stalk with increasing efficiency. Provisioning of this kind is found in many carnivores (Ewer 1969, Leyhausen 1979). Is this pedagogy?

It is not, for the cat's investment shows no apparent sensitivity to feedback from her progeny. If a kitten were inept, falling behind her littermates, would the parents give her additional training – bringing her extra mice and delaying her departure until she caught up with her siblings?

We lack evidence that animal parents judge the quality of infant perfor- mance and modulate their 'training' accordingly. But this is not the result of a failure to make appropriate observations, for there are cases in which animals have been closely observed, for instance in Ewer's (1969) acute description of parental training in the domestic cat. What follows is the closest approxima- tion to 'parental judgement' she observed: a mouse that escaped was recap- tured by the parent and returned to the kittens. But note: this is a parental reaction to the mouse, not to the kittens – in pedagogy it is the kitten that the cat is supposed to 'train', not the mouse.

The parental investment of non-primates further departs from pedagogy in that it is largely confined to one domain of activity (food acquisition). Human pedagogy has no such restriction, but applies to every conceivable domain.

Closer approximations to human pedagogy can be found in non-human pri- mates. Both monkey and ape mothers have been observed to remove from the mouths of their infants leaves of plants not eaten by the species. Gorilla and chimpanzee mothers hold their infants away from them, encouraging them to walk towards them (Yerkes 1916). Unlike our earlier examples, these are not species-specific, do not apply only to food acquisition, and, while exceedingly simple, have about them something of the flavour of pedagogy. Nevertheless, these examples could still be disregarded on account of their sheer infrequency. Wrangham and Nishida report only two instances of removal of leaves from infants' mouths after approximately 150 hours of field observation (personal communication 1986). Human pedagogy could be ignored, too, were it equally infrequent.

355

'Toilet training' in the monkey is more common. When an infant voids while being carried by its mother, she is likely to pull the infant away from her and hold it away until it stops. The infant screams when first torn from its comfortable perch, though in time both animals improve their reading of each other's signals, so that the mother is eventually able to anticipate the infant and release it before it voids. This is not pedagogy, however, because no matter how subtly mother and infant may communicate, the mother's response is little more than a simple reaction to an aversive stimulus.

The macaque weans her infant in much the same manner, pushing it from her breast, denying it further access and even, if the infant persists, striking it. The macaque's style of weaning is a good example of the punishment animals frequently use in modifying one another's behaviour; bitches use similar methods in weaning their pups.

One can find appreciably more complex cases which, nonetheless, remain responses to aversive stimuli. For example, the male Hamadryas baboon bites the nape of the female's neck when she wanders too far afield (Kummer 1971); here again, the male's reaction is an innate response to a negative state of affairs. It is basically the same when the chimpanzee mother intervenes to terminate the excessively rough play that caused her infant to shriek (Goodall 1986). Finding the infant's shrieking aversive, she acts to terminate it. The infant may benefit from its mother's intervention, but protection is not pedagogy. One can help or protect another without training it in any way.

Chimpanzees that have been trained by humans to form linguistic signs with their hands are inclined, it is said, to mould the hands of other chimpanzees in the same manner. Though this may resemble pedagogy, it is more likely to be delayed social imitation. Suppose a chimpanzee, tickled under the chin by a human, then tickled another chimpanzee in the same manner. Would we call this pedagogy, or recognize it for what it is: delayed social imitation, one animal doing to another what was done to it earlier?

Is there, then, any way to tell imitation from pedagogy? Certainly there is. The act that the chimpanzee applies to others must *differ* from the act that was applied to it. For example, if a chimpanzee taught to form signs with its hands went on to correct the eating manners, walking style, tricycle riding, etc. of another, this could be pedagogy (in any case, it could not be imitation). When, however, the act the animal applies to others is the same as the act applied to it, there are no grounds for regarding it as anything other than imitation.

Chimpanzees, according to Boesch (1991), teach nut-cracking, a practice in which the animal holds a nut against a root and strikes it with a rock. But why should they teach this practice when, as even Boesch agrees, they do not teach anything else? The answer he gives is that nut-cracking is especially difficult and takes some ten years to master. This answer leads to a paradox. If the chimpanzee is 'taught' nut-cracking, why should it take so long to learn? Either the chimpanzee's alleged pedagogy is grossly ineffective, or what is called pedagogy in the chimpanzee bears little resemblance to human pedagogy. Indeed, the would-be teaching of nut-cracking has the character of other activities cited as examples of animal pedagogy. A mother is observed to 'adjust' the position of the nut or the 'hammer' her offspring is holding, to do this once, perhaps twice, in the course of, say, one hundred hours of nut-cracking. She does *not* observe, judge, and correct hundreds of times, if necessary, until the child reaches a desired form. If the chimpanzee mother did so, her infant would learn to crack nuts in far less than ten years!

PEDAGOGY IN CAPTIVE CHIMPANZEES?

Chimpanzees in captivity, however, engage in training that more closely approximates human pedagogy. It is important to note that this disparity between behaviour in the wild and in captivity is not confined to pedagogy; as we have already shown in the case of imitation, appropriate captivity brings out more complex behaviour of all kinds. Let us describe an example of one of several cases of such complex training that have been observed in the laboratory.

Among captive chimpanzees, one of the prerogatives claimed by the dominant animal is that of being accompanied when changing locations. Submissive animals may move to new locations by themselves, but dominant ones demand company. The dominant animal will not move unless the submissive one attaches itself to it, either by grasping the dominant one around the waist from behind or by lining up beside it and putting an arm around its shoulder. Once this is done, the two set off to a location chosen by the dominant animal. What happens when the submissive animal fails to comply?

Sadie and Jessie were a dominant–submissive pair among four juvenile animals that had lived in a group in the laboratory for over three years, but they were not a natural pair. When they were first placed together, Jessie ran off whenever the dominant Sadie approached. Sadie's first task was thus to calm a skittish Jessie. She approached Jessie repeatedly, until finally Jessie remained still. She then patted Jessie's head and shoulders. Stationing herself beside Jessie, she took Jessie's arm, lifted it, ducked her head, and dropped Jessie's arm around her shoulder. Why did Sadie not simply place her own arm around Jessie? Because, in this social exchange, it is the submissive animal that places its arm around the dominant one, and it was this canonical form that Sadie taught Jessie.

The animals then set off. But Jessie was too short for Sadie. Her arm slipped from Sadie's shoulder, down Sadie's spine, until her full weight lay across Sadie's back. Sadie stopped; whereupon Jessie ran off. Sadie did not pursue Jessie, but instead reinstated the training cycle, beginning with the slow, patient approach. At the end of about two hours, Jessie was trained. She carried out perfectly the services of the submissive animal. When Sadie approached, Jessie abandoned her current enterprise, lined up beside Sadie, placed her own arm around Sadie, and the two set off together. The problem caused by Jessie's stature had not been solved, of course, and after a short distance Jessie slumped across Sadie's back again. The two stopped. But now, rather than running off, Jessie adjusted herself, and the two took off once again.

We have described this case in detail to show that one can occasionally find in the chimpanzee training that has the cognitive complexity of the human case. Sadie's behaviour had everything we could wish for to enable us to argue that the trainer has in mind a representation of a desired state of affairs consisting of the behaviour of the other, and carries out a highly deliberate set of planned acts to realize that representation. Sadie's acts were not simple reactions to an aversive stimulus. On the contrary, she successfully inhibited the disposition to strike or attack the originally uncooperative Jessie, substituting calmness and even a few pats for the inhibited aggression. And putting Jessie's body into the desired position, a beautiful act of passive guidance, also differs from chasing a fleeing female or pulling a voiding infant from one's body. Lifting the other one's arm and placing it around her own shoulder probably had no precedent; that is, it probably occurred in no other setting than this one. It was an act designed for the occasion.

In every respect save one, Sadie's training of Jessie was a perfect example of pedagogy. What was the exception? The training was carried out not for the benefit of the student but for that of the trainer. One could prove this quite easily in principle. The distinction could be drawn in this manner: allow Sadie to train two animals, Jessie and her twin sister Leslie. In the case of Leslie, allow Sadie the opportunity not only to train but also to benefit from the training, whereas in the case of Jessie allow the training but not the benefits. Does Sadie train both of them or rather concentrate her efforts on Leslie, ignoring Jessie from then on? If, in the long run, Sadie trains only Leslie, we can be reasonably confident that the point of the training was to benefit the trainer. By contrast, a pedagogue, tested in the same way, would not differentiate between the two sisters, but would seek to bring the performance of *both* into conformity with his or her standards. This, as we noted earlier, is the goal of pedagogy.

Suppose that we changed the goal of the training, however, requiring that it benefit the trainer. Such a change need affect neither the efficiency of the training nor any of its internal properties, but it would have a profoundly adverse effect on the distribution of the training and the occasions on which it occurred. No longer would a pedagogue's eye roam over the young, surveying their performance in the light of her standards; no longer would she intervene wherever she found a deficiency. On the contrary, she would train only those whose improved performance was of benefit to her. This change in the motivational basis of pedagogy would leave numerous individuals untrained.

Some human pedagogy has this character, as when, under special circumstances, a parent teaches her child to carry out acts of economic value.

358

Under adverse conditions in India, for example, parents teach children to make matches, in other cases to pick fruit and plant tobacco. However, self-interest is not the only motivational source in human teaching, for children are taught a wide range of cultural practices, not only acts of economic benefit to the parent, and thus pedagogy has served throughout history to transmit culture across generations.

THEORIES OF MIND AND THE SHARING OF EXPERIENCE

The behaviour of the captive chimpanzee shows that it has the cognitive capacity to carry out pedagogy. In addition, the captive chimpanzee has been shown to have a 'theory of mind' (Premack and Woodruff 1978, Premack 1988), which may be regarded as a major prerequisite for pedagogy. Individuals with a theory of mind attribute mental states to others and understand their behaviour in terms of these states (Leslie 1987, Wimmer and Perner 1983, Perner 1991, Wellman 1990). For example, if shown an individual reaching for inaccessible food, they understand that the individual *wants* food and is *trying* to get it. Furthermore, if shown an individual whose view of food is obstructed, they understand that the individual cannot *see* the food. This knowledge would enable one individual to alleviate the problems faced by another − to obtain food for the one, to remove the obstruction for the other.

To teach effectively, one must understand what the other *sees*, *knows*, *wants* and is *trying* to achieve. Recent laboratory evidence demonstrates, surprisingly, that the chimpanzee has such knowledge in some degree, though not to the degree that it is present in humans (Premack 1988, in press). It is not found at all in the monkey (see, e.g., Povinelli *et al.* 1991).

In spite of the captive chimpanzee's demonstrable capacity for pedagogy, and its unexpected theory of mind, the wild chimpanzee demonstrates no evidence for pedagogy. Why? There are two principal reasons. One has to do with an aesthetic factor which is extremely strong in humans but either weak or absent in animals. For instance, humans not only train others, they also train themselves (Premack 1984, 1991). They spend hours honing their skills, that is in *practising*, not primarily for extrinsic reward but for the intrinsic satisfaction of mastering the skill. The sense of standards or excellence implicit in practising also operates in pedagogy, and is responsible for the *imperative* of human pedagogy, for the fact that the intervention is not desultory (as in the chimpanzee) but pursued until the child attains a standard. Practising − the training of self − and pedagogy − the training of others − go hand in hand. The one is never found without the other.

Second, chimpanzees have no discernible disposition to 'share experience'. In humans, this is a major disposition, detectable from early infancy. For instance, a 6-month-old infant, clinging to a teddy bear, makes eye contact with an observer, then glances at its teddy bear, inviting the observer to share with it the presence of the bear and of the child's possession of it. In the child of 11 or 12 months, who is likely to have a few words, the evidence takes a more overt form. The child points excitedly at an object, almost always a moving one — a bus, truck, fish swimming in a bowl, even an ant crawling on the ground — calling out its name repeatedly, at the same time avidly seeking eye contact with the observer (Bates 1979, Premack 1990b). The child is not requesting the object, as tests have shown (Premack 1990b), but is inviting the recipient to share the excitement of the object that the child has encountered. No comparable behaviour has been reported in chimpanzees, neither visual behaviour analogous to that of the preverbal child, nor combined visual–verbal behaviour (in the language-trained animal) analogous to that of the older child. The disposition to share experience is, to our knowledge, unique to humans.

This disposition is likely to have played a key role in the evolution of the human species. Since language and pedagogy are independent — as demonstrated by Sadie's elaborate non-verbal training of Jessie — the combination of these two separate competences could, in principle, have resulted in four kinds of species: those with both language and pedagogy, those without either, and those with either one or the other. But, in fact, we do not find 'mixed' cases, of species having language without pedagogy, or pedagogy without language; rather, we find species with either both competences or neither.

This restriction on the range of logical possibilities can be explained by the disposition to share experience. Given this factor, both language and pedagogy are likely to evolve; without it, neither is. The common code or sharing of symbols that language presupposes is unthinkable without a disposition to share experience. Such a disposition seems equally essential for the evolution of pedagogy, for pedagogy involves bringing others into conformity with the standards one applies to oneself. The absence of this disposition might well explain the absence of both language and pedagogy in the chimpanzee. It is a high price to pay for the lack of what, on the surface, would appear to be an entirely secondary factor!

Adult chimpanzees do not engage in activities that young chimpanzees cannot acquire for themselves by a combination of maturation and learning. Moreover, the offspring's learning largely repeats that of the parent because, as we have seen, chimpanzees do not significantly change their environments: parent and offspring grow up in virtually the same world. By contrast, adult humans engage in numerous activities that children cannot acquire without assistance. They could not, in ancient times, have acquired advanced lithic tool-making skills by themselves, nor can they, today, acquire reading, writing, or arithmetic in this way. Moreover, children's learning does not repeat that of parents, for, as we have seen, parents and children do not grow up in the same world.

Two features of human intelligence — its modular character and the presence of large individual differences — put an additional premium on pedagogy. These features make for more specialized competence than is found in other species — resulting in 'gifted' tool-makers, hunters, cooks, shamans, and the like. The innovations introduced by these gifted individuals are unlikely simply to diffuse through the group, but must be taught to others. Pedagogy plays two roles in human culture: not only that of transmitting existing skills, but also that of preserving the innovations of gifted members.

CULTURE AND BELIEF

Earlier we observed that non-anthropologists tend to deal with the issue of 'animal culture' by focusing on how culture is transmitted, not on the question of the *content* of culture. This is regrettable, for the content of culture illuminates certain distinguishing facets of human beings, while the mode of transmission does not. In particular, a focus on content requires that we attend to the nature and sources of *belief* (see Lewis in this volume, Article 20).

Belief comes in two varieties, weak and strong. Weak belief arises when an individual simply questions the veracity of his or her own perception: Did I really see a snake? Was that a red dot, or only a reflection from the sun? And so on. Perception normally leads directly to action, but in this case action is suspended while one questions the veracity of the perception. If one verifies the perception and therefore *believes* it, one acts. This form of belief is weak because it still depends heavily on evidence and is only removed by a small step from perception.

The strong form of belief is far removed from perception; its relation to evidence is no longer simple but now quite complex. The complexity is well demonstrated by religious beliefs. Consider, for instance, the relation between the evidence and the belief that Jesus is the son of God, that the consumption of pork is evil, that the devil is a fallen angel. Let it not be assumed that the relation between belief and evidence is complex only in these cases. Take such beliefs as: germs cause disease, or that the universe began with a big bang. Though these beliefs are widely accepted, most of us do not hold them because of the evidence on which they stand. What proportion of those who believe unswervingly in the germ theory of disease have ever seen a germ, or even requested to see one as a condition for their belief?

A theory of disease is one of the standard components of human culture. The germ theory is a replacement for an earlier theory that distinguished between the body and the soul, holding that illness was caused by the soul leaving the body, so that the healer's task was to recover and return it. The big-bang theory is a version of yet another universal component of human culture, an origin myth, an account of how the world began. No human culture lacks such an account.

One hardly needs a comprehensive list to observe that beliefs of this kind are not found in non-human animals. Although the weak form of belief might possibly be found in them, there is no evidence for the strong form. A strong belief is essentially an informal theory, concerned, for example, with how the world began, the elements of which it is made, what holds these elements together, what causes disease, and so on. It therefore raises all the questions concerning evidence that are raised by more formal theories.

On what do these cultural beliefs or informal theories depend? Ultimately, of course, on language, for they could not be propagated without it. But language is, both ontogenetically and phylogenetically, a late prerequisite, applicable only to a developed stage of belief. There are earlier prerequisites, such as the existence of a set of categorical domains into which the infant is primed to divide the world – physical object, mind, biological kind, and number being presently recognized examples. There is increasing evidence that the infant divides the world into such domains, entertaining hypotheses concerning not only what constitutes a member of the domain, but also the privileged changes to which the members of a domain are subject (Hirschfeld and Gelman 1993).

For instance, inanimate are distinguished from animate objects by the character of their movement. The former move only when acted upon by other objects, whereas the latter start and stop their own motion – that is, they are self-propelled. The infant assigns different interpretations to the two kinds of movement. Induced motion – for example, one object launching another – is interpreted as caused (Leslie and Keeble 1987), whereas self-propelled motion is interpreted not as caused but as intentional (Dasser et al. 1989, Premack 1990a). In addition, children consider biological kinds to have special properties, which include growth and reproduction as well as disease. Strong beliefs (or informal theories) as to what causes disease are, as we have already seen, an invariant component of culture. The kinds of theories of which cultures are composed are likely to bear a close relation to the different domains recognized by the infant. In every case, cultural theory may represent an attempt to explain the changes that are specific to a domain – or that an infant considers to be specific to it.

Non-human animals lack culture not only because they do not propagate their traditions by imitation or pedagogy, but also because they are without the foundations on which cultural belief depends. In other words, it is not just the lack of language that prevents them from holding theories about the world, but, more fundamentally, the fact that they lack the categorical distinctions that are the principal prerequisites for theory-building. Perhaps they are not primed, as is the infant, to divide the world into categories whose members undergo distinctive kinds of changes.

What conception does the chimpanzee have of biological kind? Does it understand – as young children do (Keil 1989) – that members of such a kind grow (as inanimate objects do not), undergoing appreciable physical transformation while at the same time preserving their identity? Although highly testable, by means of the same non-verbal procedures that are applied to infants, these questions have not been answered. Animals, we can speculate, will either prove to recognize no domains, or their domain-recognition will be less well formulated than that of human infants. This could itself explain the animal's lack of culture, for the seeds of culture lie in the human infant's domain-recognition.

In holding theories about the world, humans are beset by the questions to which these theories lead. Disposed to share experience, they pursue these questions together. The initial environmental changes that humans made, and which set history in motion, were all changes arising from practical matters – a shift to agriculture, large settlements, permanent shelters. Practical interventions continue to give rise to environmental changes, but more recent changes have come from another source. What are the basic particles of which the world is made? What forces hold them together? How did it begin? Concerted attempts to answer these profoundly theoretical questions brought about the nuclear revolution, a more momentous change than any brought about by practical concerns. Indeed, the rate of historical change linked directly to practical concerns is meagre compared with that resulting from attempts to answer theoretical questions. All the questions for which special sciences have been developed are adumbrated in informal theories of culture. In addressing these questions, human beings have quickened the pulse of history and widened their gulf from the animals.

REFERENCES

Bates, E. (1979) *The Emergence of Symbols: Cognition and Communication in Infancy*, New York: Academic Press.

Boesch, C. (1991) 'Teaching among wild chimpanzees', *Animal Behavior* 41: 530–2.

Caro, T. M. and Hauser, M. D. (1992) 'Is there evidence of teaching in animals?', *Quarterly Review of Biology* 67: 151–74.

Chevalier-Skolnikoff, S. (1976) 'The ontogeny of primate intelligence and its implications for communicative potential: a preliminary report', in S. R. Harnad, H. D. Steklis and J. Lancaster (eds) *Origins and Evolution of Language and Speech*, Annals of the New York Academy of Sciences, vol. 280.

Dasser, V., Ulbaek, I. and Premack, D. (1989) 'The perception of intention', *Science* 243: 365–7.

Dobzhansky, T. (1955) *Evolution, Genetics and Man*, New York: John Wiley.

Ewer, R. F. (1969) 'The "instinct to teach"', *Nature* 222: 698.

Galef, B. G. (1982) 'Studies of social learning in Norway rats: a brief review', *Developmental Psychobiology* 15: 279–95.

—— (1992) 'The question of animal culture', *Human Nature* 3: 157–78.

Goodall, J. (1986) *The Chimpanzees of Gombe*, Cambridge, Mass.: Harvard University Press.

Hayes, K. and Nissen, C. H. (1971) 'Higher mental functions of a home-raised chimpanzee', in A. M. Schrier and F. Stollnitz (eds) *Behavior of Nonhuman Primates*, New York: Academic Press.

Hirschfeld, L. and Gelman, S. (eds) (1993) *Domain Specificity in Cognition and Culture*, Cambridge: Cambridge University Press.

Keil, F. (1989) *Concepts, Kinds, and Cognitive Development*, Cambridge, Mass.: MIT Press.

Kohts, N. (1935) *Infant Ape and Human Child*, Moscow: Scientific Memoirs of the Museum Darwinianum.

Kummer, H. (1971) *Primate Societies*, Chicago: Aldine.

Leslie, A. (1987) 'Pretense and representation: the origins of "theory of mind"', *Psychological Review* 94: 412–26.

Leslie, A. and Keeble, S. (1987) 'Do six-month-old infants perceive causality?', *Cognition* 25: 265–87.

Leyhausen, P. (1979) *Cat Behaviour: the Predatory and Social Behaviour of Domestic and Wild Cats*, London: Garland.

Meltzoff, A. N. (1988) 'Infant imitation after a 1-week delay: long-term memory for novel acts and multiple stimuli', *Developmental Psychology* 24: 470–6.

Meltzoff, A. N. and Moore, M. K. (1983) 'Newborn infants imitate adult facial gestures', *Child Development* 54: 702–9.

Miller, R. E. (1967) 'Experimental approaches to the physiological and behavioral concomitants of affective communication in rhesus monkeys', in S. A. Altman (ed.) *Social Communication Among Primates*, Chicago: University of Chicago Press.

Perner, J. (1991) *Understanding the Representational Mind*, Cambridge, Mass.: MIT Press.

Povinelli, D. J., Parks, K. A. and Novak, M. A. (1991) 'Do rhesus monkeys (*Macaca mulatta*) attribute knowledge and ignorance to others?', *Journal of Comparative Psychology* 105: 318–25.

Premack, D. (1975) 'Putting a face together', *Science* 188: 228–36.

—— (1984) 'Pedagogy and aesthetics as sources of culture', in M. Gazzaniga (ed.) *Cognitive Neuroscience*, New York: Plenum Press.

—— (1986) *Gavagai! Or the Future History of the Animal Language Controversy*, Cambridge, Mass.: MIT Press.

—— (1988) '"Does the chimpanzee have a theory of mind?" revisited', in R. W. Byrne and A. Whiten (eds) *Machiavellian Intelligence*, Oxford: Oxford University Press.

—— (1990a) 'The infant's theory of self-propelled objects', *Cognition* 36: 1–16.

—— (1990b) 'Words: what are they, and do animals have them?', *Cognition* 37: 197–212.

—— (1991) 'The aesthetic basis of pedagogy', in R. R. Hoffman and D. S. Palermo (eds) *Cognition and Symbolic Processes*, Hillsdale, NJ: Erlbaum Press.

—— (1993) 'Prolegomenon to the evolution of cognition', in T. A. Poggio and D. A. Glaser (eds) *Exploring Brain Functions: Models in Neuroscience*, New York: John Wiley.

Premack, D. and Woodruff, G. (1978) 'Does the chimpanzee have a theory of mind?', *Behavioral and Brain Sciences* 1: 515–26.

Visalberghi, E. and Fragaszy, D. M. (1990) 'Do monkeys ape?', in S. T. Parker and K. R. Gibson (eds) *'Language' and Intelligence in Monkeys and Apes*, Cambridge: Cambridge University Press.

Wellman, H. (1990) *Children's Theories of Mind*, Cambridge, Mass.: MIT Press.

Wilson, E. O. (1975) *Sociobiology: The New Synthesis*, Cambridge, Mass.: Harvard University Press.

Wilson, P. J. (1988) *The Domestication of the Human Species*, New Haven: Yale University Press.

Wimmer, H. and Perner, J. (1983) 'Beliefs about beliefs: representation and constraining function of wrong beliefs in young children's understanding of deception', *Cognition* 13: 103–28.

Yerkes, R. (1916) *The Mental Life of Monkeys and Apes*, New York: Holt.

FURTHER READING

Bates, E. (1979) *The Emergence of Symbols: Cognition and Communication in Infancy*, New York: Academic Press.

Bock, K. E. (1980) *Human Nature and Human History: a Response to Sociobiology*, New York: Columbia University Press.

Bonner, J. T. (1980) *The Evolution of Culture in Animals*, Princeton, NJ: Princeton University Press.

Byrne, R. W. and Whiten, A. (eds) (1988) *Machiavellian Intelligence: Social Expertise and the Evolution of Intellect in Monkeys, Apes and Humans*, Oxford: Clarendon Press.

Carrithers, M. (1990) 'Why humans have cultures', *Man* (N.S.) 25: 189–206.

Galef, B. G. J. (1976) 'Social transmission of acquired behaviour: a discussion of tradition and social learning in vertebrates', *Advances in the Study of Behavior* 6: 77–100.

Geertz, C. (1964) 'The transition to humanity', in S. Tax (ed.) *Horizons of Anthropology*, Chicago: Aldine.

Goodall, J. (1986) *The Chimpanzees of Gombe*, Cambridge, Mass.: Harvard University Press.

Hirschfeld, L. and Gelman, S. (eds) (1993) *Domain Specificity in Cognition and Culture*, Cambridge: Cambridge University Press.

Holloway, R. L. (1969) 'Culture, a *human* domain', *Current Anthropology* 10: 395–412.

Ingold, T. (1988) 'The animal in the study of humanity', in T. Ingold (ed.) *What is an Animal?* London: Unwin Hyman.

McGrew, W. C. and Tutin, C. E. G. (1978) 'Evidence for a social custom in wild chimpanzees', *Man* (N.S.) 13: 234–51.

Parker, S. T. and Gibson, K. R. (eds) (1990) *'Language' and Intelligence in Monkeys and Apes*, Cambridge: Cambridge University Press.

Premack, D. (1984) 'Pedagogy and aesthetics as sources of culture', in M. Gazzaniga (ed.) *Cognitive Neuroscience*, New York: Plenum.

—— (1986) *Gavagai! Or the Future History of the Animal Language Controversy*, Cambridge, Mass.: MIT Press.

Premack, D. and Premack, A. J. (1983) *The Mind of an Ape*, New York: Norton.

Premack, D. and Woodruff, G. (1978) 'Does the chimpanzee have a theory of mind?', *Behavioral and Brain Sciences* 1: 515–26.

Pulliam, H. R. and Dunford, C. (1980) *Programmed to Learn: an Essay on the Evolution of Culture*, New York: Columbia University Press.

Zentall, T. R. and Galef, B. G. J. (eds) (1988) *Social Learning: Psychological and Biological Perspectives*, Hillsdale, NJ: Lawrence Erlbaum.

14

SYMBOLISM: THE FOUNDATION
OF CULTURE

Mary LeCron Foster

CULTURE AS SYMBOLISM

Without symbolism there could be no culture. A symbol is an artefact: a 'thing' that exists out there somewhere in space and time. As a 'thing', a symbol has material reality and is experienced through the senses. It is a 'thing' that represents: that is culturally involved in such a way that it can be used in a multiplicity of contexts to convey meaning, not just about itself, but about cultural processes and relationships. Every symbol participates in a web of significances that we call culture. In other words, any symbol *resonates* with meaning. The meaning of a symbol is *not* a 'thing', and it can only be grasped inductively by observation of many instances of the social uses of that symbol, or similar symbols. It is only by observing praxis that ethnologists can discover cultural symbolic constructs, hence culture itself. Culture is not itself formed of symbols, but of the meaning that lies behind and unites symbols. This meaning only exists in the minds of participants in culture, but it is acted out through the manipulation of symbols, which objectify meaning.

A single symbol is any entity that has socially participative meaning. Each symbol shares parts of its meaning with other symbols. It is this semantic resonance that underlies institutionalization, the preservation of socially constituted and conventionally manipulated networks of symbols. Culture is thus an elaborate system of classification whose units are symbols. It is a generalization from symbolic meanings shared within a society and realized during social interaction.

The abstract system that is culture is founded on, and held together by, the human capacity to operate analogically. Networks of meaning constrain change in any part. This constraint contributes to cultural stability, but because the ability and drive to construct new analogies are omnipresent in the individual human biological heritage, change is also inevitable. Change is principally due to the creative human drive to readjust symbols — which means, in essence, to reorganize culturally transmitted analogical structures. Change was both slow and modest until the Upper Palaeolithic, which suggests that, until that time, symbolic organization was rudimentary.

The hallmark of culture, then, is *institutionalization*, founded upon *classification*, the symbolic organization of meaning. Each culture has evolved, and continues to evolve, through social experimentation in understanding, controlling, and utilizing, to its perceived advantage, sentient and insentient natural forces. The artefacts of culture, constituting the web that holds its institutions together, are *symbols* which are defined as the socially objectified loci of meaning.

Because symbols form a web of meaning for members of any given culture, no symbol has a meaning apart from the context of its relations with other symbols. To study symbolism it is necessary to examine and compare cultural contexts. This is the function of cultural anthropology. To understand symbolism as the foundation of culture it is also necessary to unravel the symbolic past.

SYMBOLIC CATEGORIZATION

Symbols fall into classes because of shared likenesses, and are manipulated and reacted to in ways defined by those likenesses. Generalizations are based upon class likeness. It is the possibility for generalization that underwrites institutionalization. Human thought (by contrast to the thought of other species) depends upon the capacity to generalize beyond the obvious or immediate. This generalization is facilitated by language, which of all symbolic systems is the most important. It was words that created culture; and, before words, either there were no symbols or symbols were so rudimentary in their resonance as to have little effect on behaviour or its organization. In animal communities without language, the few meanings that are shared are effectively used only in relation to the here and now — the momentarily shared situation. Language, like other symbolic systems, is expressed in material form. The primary material form of language is movements within the mouth and throat. A secondary material form — writing — is less evanescent, as are modern electronic sound-tracks of various kinds. Preservation of the materiality of language preserves the cultural past and promotes the power of symbolic generalization.

While non-human animals are able to classify experience to the extent that they can distinguish items that serve as food from those that do not, or, in some cases, kin from non-kin, or ally from foe, etc., distinctions within the range of their experience are more or less instinctive responses. It is the ability to perceive and manipulate an extraordinary range of symbolic affinities that distinguishes human beings from other animals. Only humans manipulate symbols, and this is so because at some point in the Pleistocene a group of primates began purposefully to exploit likeness.

Exploitation of likeness began with an instinctive mammalian tendency towards mimicry as an ontogenetic learning strategy for food procurement. Later, primates extended this ability to intentional mimicry. Hominids put this ability to new uses, which ultimately, after many millennia of experimentation, resulted in human culture. This evolutionary sequence will be explored later in this article. First, it is necessary to discuss some anthropological hypotheses about the role of symbolism in culture.

SYMBOLISM IN CULTURE

In addressing a subject as complex as how symbolism constitutes the basis of culture, one must obviously stand on many shoulders. In selecting one particular theme as my major focus, I have had to be selective, citing only those sources that either explicate points I wish to make, or have added insights which uniquely further my thesis: that symbolism arose and evolved into human culture because of a growing appreciation and social utilization of abstract likenesses between objects and events separated in space and time.

The idea of symbolism *as* culture has been growing in anthropology and is now widely accepted by theorists of social meaning. One representative statement defines culture as a body of premises carried by a system of symbols that specify the nature of the universe and man's place in it (Schneider 1976: 202–3). Another defines culture as a web of man-made significance, and the analysis of culture as a matter of interpretation rather than explanation, a quest after symbolic meaning (Geertz 1973: 5). A third definition asserts that the whole of culture is organized by a single, coherent, semiotic principle – that of the 'trope' – which reveals meaning within cultural reference points (Wagner 1986: 126).

While most anthropologists interested in symbolism speak frequently of the use of metaphor, Wagner's definition of culture as tropological or figurative, although it would be disputed by some, is the position that emerges most clearly from recent symbolic anthropology. It is generally agreed that culture is systematic – based on categorization and classification. Classification, like metaphor, is based on the perception and utilization of *likeness* as an operational principle. This is central to human cognition and behaviour.

DEFINING MEANING

Anthropologists use the terms 'semiotic' and 'semiological' loosely when discussing meanings in culture. These terms have their respective origins in the work of the American philosopher Charles Sanders Peirce (1931–5), and of the Swiss linguist Ferdinand de Saussure (1959). For Peirce, semiotics was the study of meaning-bearing elements he called 'signs'. The three types of sign were: 'index', having a causal or associational connection to its meaning, 'icon', bearing a sensory likeness to its meaning, and 'symbol', whose meaning is wholly arbitrary. Saussure, who was concerned to place the study of language within a semiological domain, distinguished between signs, with arbitrary meanings, and symbols, whose meanings are dependent upon sensory likeness. In general, anthropologists have tended to ignore these inconsistently labelled distinctions, speaking generally of symbolic anthropology as the investigation of meaning in culture.

Firth (1973: 75) has tried to apply Peirce's terminology to symbolic anthropology, but with some awkwardness, as the following quotation suggests:

> *Symbol* − where a sign has a complex series of associations, often of an emotional kind, and difficult (some would say, impossible) to describe in terms other than partial representation. The aspect of personal or social construction in meaning may be marked, so no sensory likeness of symbol to object may be apparent to an observer, and imputation of relationship may seem arbitrary.

This hedging − i.e. 'often', 'difficult to describe', 'may' rather than 'is' − indicates the difficulty of applying this terminology to culture.

In his discussion of symbol and meaning, Firth focuses more on function than on Peirce's kind of 'logic'. This seems more pertinent to the anthropological enterprise. Social manipulation of meaning-bearing elements (symbols) allows any of them to function at different times as any one of Peirce's sign-types. Cultural meaning is always dependent upon context. Thus, 'arbitrariness', or the lack of it, is itself a thoroughly arbitrary designation, depending completely upon the frame of reference of the participant or the observer.

A certain confusion about the properties of symbols seems to stem from structural linguistic theory, in which words are said to *refer*. This can all too easily create the illusion that words refer to *things* rather than to concepts. This, in turn, leads to the additional fallacy that language is essentially a system of 'naming'. In fact, words only refer to things if such specificity is part of the context, such as when a noun is accompanied by a definite article or a demonstrative, e.g. 'this', or 'the', or when an utterance is accompanied by a pointing gesture. Otherwise, reference is not to a 'thing' but to a generic *conceptualization* of specific thing-ness, such as chair, ball, jumping, or a more abstract non-thing-ness, such as 'love', or 'religion'. Such abstraction is based on classification, or conceiving and acting towards things as *like* one another, thus substitutable for one another in certain contexts. Without language, classificational abstraction from the particular to the general is impossible.

Dolgin *et al.* (1977: 22) reject the view that a symbol is an object. In their view, 'to hold that meaning and symbol are in themselves objects is to commit the fallacy of misplaced concreteness ... they are relations, not objects.' This formulation, however, leaves no room for the objectivity of the symbolic interaction. While a symbol is experienced sensually (i.e. objectively), meaning is

369

organized neuronally. *Meaning* derives from temporal and spatial relationships formed between symbols that are objectively experienced during social interaction. Meanings adhere to symbols, or constitute things as symbols, by way of human agency. Moreover, meaning is not constant, but changes because of human activity in relation to the symbol in the context of other symbols. Meanings are not really 'out there', but only seem so when they are expressed in words that are sensorily formed and apprehended – spoken or written, heard or seen. Given such expression, they become objectified as symbols which have oral–auditory substance and which can be manipulated in their relationships (and in consequence in their meanings) through human agency. Because the meanings of every symbol constitute a *class*, it would seem that without language there could be no symbolism – except perhaps a very rudimentary sense of cognized interrelationships – and certainly no culture. Words are themselves a class of symbols, concretely realized by means of oral or written manipulations. Wagner (1986) provides an insightful discussion of the nature of figuration characteristic of symbolization, and with it of human thought.

ANTHROPOLOGICAL APPROACHES TO SYMBOLISM

Within anthropology there have been a number of major ways of thinking about symbolism, exemplified in the writings of Lévi-Strauss, Schneider, Geertz, Sperber, and Wagner. These positions both define the goal of anthropology differently and recommend divergent ways by which anthropologists should deal with symbolic behaviour.

At one extreme is a formalist approach whose most influential exponent, Lévi-Strauss, argues that as anthropologists, 'our ultimate purpose is not so much to discover the unique characteristics of the societies that we study, as it is to discover in what way these societies differ from one another. As in linguistics, it is the *discontinuities* which constitute the true subject matter of anthropology' (1963: 328). In effect, he divorces culture from society in presenting symbolic systems as variations of a universal formal code.

Schneider (1976: 197) rejects this extreme formalism, insisting that 'it is the anthropologist's special task to deal with the cultural aspects of social action, although he necessarily deals with norms as well.' Anthropologists of this persuasion (e.g. Dolgin *et al.* 1977: 34) recognize that while forms impart regularity to human social interactions, 'our task is not to study forms, but to study *praxis* (which makes use of, creates, and relates to forms) – self-consciousness and conscious action' (emphasis in original).

Geertz (1973: 5), in contrast with both the above approaches, views anthropology not as 'an experimental science in search of law but [as] an interpretive one in search of meaning'. Thus, while cultures are systems of symbolic meaning, the meaning cannot be separated out from the process of social interaction. He focuses on ethnography, or 'thick description', as a way of 'cutting ... the culture concept down to size' and, through a semiotic approach, of searching for the webs of meaning by which culture is constituted (1973: 4–6). For Geertz, 'the aim of anthropology is the enlargement of the universe of human discourse' (1973: 14), although he admits other aims, such as 'the discovery of natural order in human behaviour' – which, presumably, is also the aim of Lévi-Strauss. In pursuit of his aim, Geertz focuses on the orientation of actors in particular events and attempts to clarify what each event and the actors' behaviour in it mean. Where Geertz differs from formalists such as Lévi-Strauss is in his insistence that the web of meaning that constitutes culture cannot be divorced from the human actor and his or her intentions. In a critique of formal analysis, he writes that 'Cultural analysis is (or should be) guessing at meanings, assessing the guesses, and drawing explanatory conclusions from the better guesses, not discovering the Continent of Meaning and mapping out its bodiless landscape' (1973: 20).

Another critic of Lévi-Straussian formalism is Sperber (1974). However, he follows a quite different line of argument in positing two diametrically opposed ways of thinking, one rational and the other symbolic. He argues that to study symbolism it is necessary to postulate that it is a system of relationships, and to elucidate the principles that govern it (Sperber 1974: 2). But, in his view, symbolism is characterized by a mysterious quality of non-rationality, a quality that is, indeed, its defining feature. Thus,

> a representation is symbolic precisely to the extent that it is not entirely explicable, that is to say, expressible by semantic means. Semiological views are therefore not merely inadequate: they hide, from the outset, the defining features of symbolism.

In his view, symbolism arises from the human effort required to handle information of a kind that 'defies direct conceptual treatment' (1974: 148). For Sperber, human individuals are endowed with two ways of processing information, a learning strategy and a symbolic mechanism. The learning strategy looks for the most systematic and coherent way of handling environmental input. Whatever cannot be explained thus is processed symbolically; 'the symbolic mechanism has as its input the defective output of the conceptual mechanism' (1974: 141). It operates by modifying the focal structure of this defective output:

> it shifts the attention from the statements describing the new information to the unfulfilled conditions that have made the representation defective ... it explores the passive memory in search of information capable of re-establishing the unfulfilled conditions. At the end of this process of evocation, information thus found is submitted to the conceptual mechanism which uses it together with the previously unfulfilled condition to reconstruct a new conceptual representation. The latter is the interpretation of the initial symbolic representation. The output of the symbolic mechanism thus serves as the input to the conceptual mechanism. In other words, the symbolic mechanism is a feedback device coupled to the conceptual mechanism.
> (1974: 142)

This seems to be a needlessly complex way of distinguishing between learning from observation of cause and effect and learning through observation of the structural similarities between objects or events. Symbolism operates primarily in the latter mode. It organizes new material in terms of its congruence with already assimilated modes of structuring. New rituals are adapted to the patterns of the old. Both are rational manoeuvres, if rationality is defined as using the mind adaptively. The extraordinary adaptive success of the human species is due to the fact that human beings are unique in their capacity to operate in an elaborated inductive (i.e. symbolic, or cultural) manner.

There is no need for the kind of mental dichotomy postulated by Sperber. Illustrating his argument with ethnographic material from the Dorze of Ethiopia, he describes the 'errors' in Dorze classification of their world as their symbolism (1974: 3). He fails to see that the human world, his as well as that of the Dorze, can *only* be symbolic. Perceptions of cause and effect are dealt with in accordance with established symbolic templates. Classifications are arbitrary because they are never more than partial, based on an arbitrary selection of qualities. Science, which almost everyone would accept as 'rational', is also based on arbitrary classification. The symbolic mechanism is endlessly creative because it is individually worked; hence, symbol systems and cultures are both coherent and changeable.

If symbolism dealt only with the leftovers of defective conceptualization there would be no culture. Culture arose because one primate species developed the ability to see and to utilize analogic possibilities. In other words, ancestral hominids (perhaps already *Homo habilis*) began to appreciate likeness and deal with it conceptually rather than only as mimicry. Within the animal kingdom, this abstraction of likenesses from manifold particulars arose as a totally new, and crucially human, mode of conceptualization. The end result was an elaboration of systems and hierarchies of classification, and the ability to abstract qualities to be classified. This enables human beings to deal not only with the here and now but also with the abstractions of past, potential, and imaginary events, as well as to deal with eventualities in terms of such abstractions. The symbolic mechanism *is* the conceptual system for humankind.

Some of the problem in defining the task of anthropology seems to lie in a confusion between recognition of the symbol itself as an object, capable of separation from its meaning, and its subjective interpretation, in part particular to the individual and in part common to his or her society. Lévi-Strauss and other structuralists are concerned with the formal relationships between symbols as objects, which may be drawn differently into the life of different societies while, at the same time, retaining certain universal relational aspects. Others, such as Schneider and Geertz, tend to lose sight of the formal aspects of symbolism in their efforts to understand the flow of social-symbolic manipulation. Successful integration of the formal or structural aspects of symbolism with aspects of its social manipulation is a task for future anthropological study. Some interesting arguments, largely drawn from fields peripheral to anthropology, indicate the direction that such a task might take.

Linguistic theory has had an impact on theoretical anthropology in setting the stage for formalism. But, as I shall now show, it also holds the potential to resolve the anthropological problem outlined above.

SYMBOL IN LINGUISTIC THEORY

In linguistics a paradigm is a set of items constituting a 'class' such that any item in the class can be substituted for another in a particular position or positions within a sequence. This contrasts with a 'syntagma', which is a sequence into which any member of a paradigm can be inserted at a specifiable point. Any event, whether linguistic or not, is a syntagma, in that it is characterized by spatio-temporal sequencing. Every argument, explanation, statement, or question is a linguistic syntagma. 'Norms' for ordering are paradigmatic: they constitute substitution classes. Analogies lie in the paradigmatic domain. If one action within an event is performed rather than another possible one, both actions together form a paradigm. Unlike a syntagma, a paradigm is never realized as such; when any member of the paradigm actually occurs it is already a part of the syntagma. Surface structure lies in the syntagma, deep structure in its paradigmatic generalization. Thus, if two or more syntagmata are compared in such a way that generalizations are formed about them as members of a class, they, in turn, form paradigms.

In discussing the relevance of extending structural linguistic theory to cultural analysis, both Sperber (1974) and Silverstein (1976) point to a methodological problem. Unlike language, culture does not *refer*, it only *implies*, because it is essentially pragmatic (Silverstein), or evocative (Sperber). In my view this is a pseudo-problem. Since culture is an abstraction from reality, it can hardly be either pragmatic or evocative. However, social events, as syntagmata, are both, as indeed are speech events, which use reference as argument.

In general, those anthropological approaches to symbolism that have drawn on linguistic theory have focused on its paradigmatic qualities. This was particularly so in the work of anthropological linguists situated in the structural tradition of the first half of this century. This linguistic tradition was disrupted by the decidedly non-anthropological, Chomskyan 'revolution' (e.g. Chomsky 1957), which led to questions of meaning being ignored in favour of an exclusive focus on establishing rules for formal syntagmatic distributions. In contrast to post-Chomskyan linguists, anthropologists have continued in their attempt to use structural approaches to understand paradigms.

FORMAL METHODOLOGY

Metaphoric equations between symbols adduced in a variety of events serve to distinguish paradigmatic categories. For example, Needham (1973),

following Hertz, explored the formal semantic dimensions of dual, or oppositional, symbolic classifications. Analysis of syntagmata showing opposition
between male and female, for example, showed that they are equated paradigmatically (i.e. in structurally similar syntagmata) with such other oppositions
as good versus bad, and right versus left. These alternative realizations
are surface transformations (syntagmata) that reflect a deep symbolic
(paradigmatic) structure.

Needham's approach, like that of Lévi-Strauss, is formal and structural,
although it is only to the Lévi-Straussian approach that the designation 'structural anthropology' has generally been applied. While Lévi-Strauss has used
it primarily in the study of the domains of kinship (1949) and mythology
(1964–5), other anthropologists have applied it to the analysis of other
cultural systems, in particular religious ritual (e.g. Reichel-Dolmatoff 1971,
Hugh-Jones 1979). Leach (1976) gives examples of the use of structural
methodology in understanding various domains of everyday life.

A rather different structural approach was, at its inception, characterized as
'the new anthropology'. It was derived from the linguistic field of phonology,
which set out to specify the various underlying properties, such as voicing or
aspiration, of a sound unit called a 'phoneme'. In anthropology, 'componential
analysis' has similarly involved formal specification of the properties shared by
members of a paradigmatic class. These, then, were found to be arranged in
a hierarchical order from specific to general with respect to the possession or
lack of some particular semantic component. Hierarchical paradigms
abstracted from cultural systems are often called 'folk taxonomies'. Berlin
(1981, Berlin et al. 1974), for example, has studied the hierarchical properties
of plant taxonomies to discover prototypical levels of focus.

Prototype theory (Lakoff 1987) largely developed within the fields of psychology and linguistics, shares with componential analysis the goal of
specifying principles of human categorization that are central to human cognition (e.g. Berlin and Kay 1969, Rosch 1983, Lakoff 1987). Lévi-Strauss similarly aims to discover 'the constraining structures of the mind', believing that
'the final aim of anthropology is to contribute to a better knowledge of
objectified thought and its mechanisms' (1964–85, I: 10).

The goal of formal methodology, then, is to reveal the meanings that lie
behind the articulation of any event as an instance of the paradigm that
includes similar events, and to situate those meanings in a hierarchy that leads
from the concrete social event to the culturally general, and ultimately to the
universal. Yet this procedure excludes any understanding of the meaning of
the event in its particular social context and in relation to other experienced
or anticipated contexts. This is the area in which syntagmatically oriented
anthropologists search for more cogent meaning.

A paradox arises here from the fact that without ethnographic detail it is
impossible to factor out any meaningful structure on which to build a paradigmatic hierarchy that might ultimately lead to the formulation of universal

principles. This makes it necessary to invent an anthropology able to effect a synthesis of paradigmatic and syntagmatic approaches, which would guide us from the particular event into the the complex web of symbolic acts that characterize a culture, and would eventually suggest methods for linking the specific to the universal in culture.

ETHNOLOGY AND SYMBOLISM

If we accept that culture is a system of symbolic meanings, and that symbols themselves are behavioural artefacts by which people manipulate and continuously transform the total web of meanings within the system, then cultural anthropology should be concerned both with abstracting deep symbolic meanings from the surface structure of observed events, and with exploring these meanings both synchronically and diachronically in behavioural contexts. Synchronic exploration would involve close examination of behaviour, looking at the ways in which participants in the behaviour (including the anthropologist him- or herself) influence its outcome. For the only way to *study* culture is to observe the flux of social interaction, but to *understand* culture it is necessary to understand forms and the relationships between forms. And these, of course, are precisely what we mean by 'structure'. But to do this is also to practise anthropology in both the Geertzian and the Lévi-Straussian senses.

Geertz's 'cutting culture down to size' argues for a reduction of culture to its lowest common denominator, the particular ethnographic event. Paul's (1982: 5) cogent response is to point out that

> in themselves, lowest common denominators are, by their nature, quite uninformative. But, as one pole of a dynamic system, they are essential to a powerful and elegant comprehension of the multiplicity of phenomena. If in Geertz' formulation the study of anthropology investigates man's generic potentialities focused into his specific performances, then it is essential that we do not shrink from making statements about just what those generic potentialities might be.

With regard to the structuralist approach, which is essentially paradigmatic in nature, it is also worth recalling Reichel-Dolmatoff's (1971: 252) conclusion to his structural-paradigmatic analysis of Tukano symbolism:

> And here our inquiry ends. In the course of it we have travelled through the Universe; an immense world of signs and symbols, of images and colours, has opened before us; in this world we have, at times, recognized forms of thought that are not foreign to us, because they are universal.
>
> That such a world could have been created in a corner of the Amazon, that such an effort has been exerted to construct this great scheme of being and becoming in the rain forests of the Vaupés, cannot but arouse our admiration and confirm our conviction that the world we label 'primitive' contains values we can ill-afford to deprecate.

SYMBOLIC MEANING

Due to symbolic interaction, no cultural artefact has meaning only by itself. It derives meaning from its total spatio-temporal context. The visual qualities and spatial characteristics of a given symbol are not unique to itself but conjure up characteristics of other symbols with interconnected cultural meanings. One part of a symbol's meaning can be said to be referential, or denotative. A word, a photograph, or a statue represents something other than itself. A national flag represents a country, but not necessarily iconically. Partial, or metaphoric iconicity of representation is found in the United States flag's fifty stars and thirteen stripes.

Wagner's (1986) view of trope as the coherent organizing principle of culture sums up and defines the complex conceptual paths that lie behind the human capacity for symbolization. Other writers recognize symbolic metaphor, but usually discuss it only as reflected in myth and religious ritual. Wagner, however, has grasped that culture – in all its complexity – *is* metaphor. Like Geertz and many other recent writers, Wagner rejects structure as the major determinant of symbolization. Instead, he subordinates structure to what he calls 'obviation' – a process of metaphoric expansion of successive tropes such that each builds upon the last. In this process, structure is '*subsumed* as orienting features of a landscape might be, within the co-ordinating binocular perspective that organizes detail into significance' (1986: 131). Obviation defines a force that 'makes the referential categories of convention peripheral to its ultimate realization of an encompassing image.' Linguistically speaking, this image might be called the deep structure underlying successive metaphors that are realized in the particulars of any communicative act.

The concrete features of structure are the necessary counters in communication and learning. While functioning as points of reference, they convey meaning only obliquely, serving at best as its elicitors. Since metaphor operates through the medium of analogy, this is the basic human faculty that makes culture and symbolizing, its structural medium, possible. According to Wagner:

> meaning is a perception *within* what we would call the 'value space' set up by symbolic points of reference, a 'stereoscopic' view, if you will, of different symbolic points of reference brought to focus at a single cyclopean 'retina'. It is thus the perception of analogy, and its expansion into larger forms, or frames, of culture takes the form of a 'flow' of analogy.
>
> The identification of the sign as a mediator between percept and symbolic concept establishes *abstraction* – the birth of order as accomplished fact – as the single constitutive act in the emergence of meaning.
>
> (Wagner 1986: 18–19)

The symbol, as a 'microcosm', abstracted from the 'macrocosm' that is perception, restricts, or focuses, the meaning and allows it to enter into a code in which it recurs. This recurrent sensual coding conveys a sense of referential invariance (Wagner 1986:19).

The existence of such concretized foci makes it possible to study structure in either language or other forms of culture. Structure is always a structure of reference. In order to move beyond reference, which is a minimal component of meaning, it is necessary to compare temporal or spatial congeries of recurrent symbols, establishing samenesses and searching out differences – for it is in such differences that the clues to meaning lie.

Because symbols are metaphoric, they represent themselves (Wagner 1986: 4). Conventional reference, in the sense that words *refer* or *denote*, is probably only applicable to language. Culturally crucial symbols are not referential or denotative but connotative or figurative. Words not only *denote*, but like all other symbols, *connote* as well. According to Wagner:

> Figurative usage, ... because it makes a kind of prism of conventional reference, cannot provide a literal field of reference. It is not formed by 'indicating' things, or by referencing them, but by setting pointers or reference points into a relation with one another, by making them into a relation that is innovative upon the original order of reference. It 'conveys' a renegotiated relation, but, not being 'literal' in any sense, cannot 'point' to it. Thus we may say that it 'embodies' or 'images' its object, figuring sympathetically by becoming itself that which it expresses. When we speak of things that do not have conventional referents, then our manner of speaking must itself become the referent. The effect of the construction is embodied in its impingement upon conventional reference; this impingement is simultaneously what it *is* and what it is *about*.
>
> (1986: 6)

The connotative resonance of symbols differs greatly; one might almost construct a graduated scale of symbolic resonance. Compare, for example, the differing resonance, in Western countries, of a triangle, a star, and a cross, or, in the United States, of an orange, a hot dog, and a roast turkey. Extremely resonant symbols have been called by a variety of terms – e.g. key, master, elaborating, core. The degree of resonance of a symbol is determined by its use-potential: the different contexts in which it can be brought into play and the emotion that is generated in members of a given society by such deployment.

THE DERIVATION OF MEANINGS

Anthropologists studying symbolism in depth often arrive at the conclusion expressed here by Wilson (1971: 5):

> Symbols are rooted in the common biological nature of man – male and female, birth, death, mating, menstruation, pregnancy, suckling, sickness, elimination, and so forth; in the physical structure of the universe – the seasons, the waxing and waning of the moon, drought and flood, and in the local environment. The same social conflicts within men and between men, such as ambivalent attitudes towards

incest, parental authority, and birth and death, are repeatedly represented; and the conception of pollution, which constantly recurs, as constantly has a physiological reference.

And according to Douglas (1970: vii–viii) the human body, common to all of humanity, is the basis of symbols used to express different social experiences:

> there is a strong tendency to replicate the social situation in symbolic form by drawing richly on bodily symbols in every possible dimension ... the most fundamental assumptions about the cosmos and man's place in nature are coloured by the socially appropriate image of the human body.

Freud, of course, saw mental imagery and mental disturbance as rooted in the bodily experiences of infancy, and problems in social relationships as rooted in ontogenetic familial experiences of powerlessness. Paul (1982) construes Tibetan religious and social symbolism as a metaphoric re-enactment and resolution of the Oedipus complex. This is supported by a meticulous structural analysis of ritual forms. Thus, the Oedipal complex serves as a template for social interaction. Indeed the notion of a deep structure of patterns or templates informing symbolic action has gained considerable currency in anthropology, although most anthropologists would not give it as Freudian an interpretation as does Paul.

STRUCTURAL CONCORDANCE

The entire opus of Lévi-Strauss (1964–85) is devoted to the process of cultural transformation of mythic templates across time and space. Because such symbolic patterns restrict the possibilities for new formulations, culture can be studied as if it were unchanging. These patterns have been called 'p-structures' by Ardener (1980), and 'structures of significance' by Sahlins (1981). Ardener (1980) demonstrates that mental templates of this kind are brought to bear on the unexpected events of everyday life, in order to 'explain' them. 'P-structures' are the underlying paradigmatic patterns abstracted from similar actualized 's-structures' – i.e. syntagmatic structures, or events. Sahlins (1981) has developed the comparable notion of cultural pattern which, in the historical context, serves both as a constraint on change, and as a way of interpreting it. He provides detailed examples of the way in which events in early European contacts with Hawaii were interpreted and mentally reconstructed by Hawaiians as exemplars of a familiar mytho–historical template. Because some aspects of contemporary events fitted roughly with the structure of earlier, or mythologically represented events, they were interpreted or enacted in accordance with the template structure. History thus becomes the re-enactment of the underlying semantic requirements of the template. In order to endure, changes must be attributed with some degree of congruence with the template.

In order to deal with such structural transformations as can be isolated ethnographically, I have coined the term 'concordant structure'. Concordant structures encompass both nesting sets of symbolic structures that are informed by some over-arching structure of meaning, and the symbols that bridge, or co-ordinate, such sets (Foster 1983a). The symbolic network that constitutes a particular culture provides a template for metaphoric interplay between, as well as within, encompassed concordant structures (i.e. lower-level templates). 'Concordance' can be extracted on many deeper semantic levels, but is only realized in the particular social event. The notion of concordance is thus comparable to Ardener's notion of p-structure, but is more comprehensive. Structural concordance can be demonstrated for any cultural domain. For example, over-arching templates for marriage ritual in Tzintzuntzan (a village in south-western Mexico) provide the structure for other kinds of ritual events. The original metaphoric impetus (the deepest paradigmatic template) lies in the physiological and social conditions of procreation, prefigured by the ritualized marriage alliance.

The abstraction of templates as guides to the acceptability of people's enactment or understanding of events can also indicate what is considered disruptive or unacceptable. While the manipulation of symbols is not in itself culture, *ways* of manipulation reflect cultural forms. Manipulative distortions can also be culturally determined – in other words, templates imply patterns of both use and misuse. For example, in Tzintzuntzan, symbolic codification specifies that the parents of the groom put on the ceremonial feast that takes place after the wedding, to honour the god-parents and parents of the bride. The parents of the bride, according to the code, put on a less elaborate supper on the evening before the wedding, to honour the god-parents and parents of the groom. If the young couple have eloped without receiving parental permission for a formal union, then the bride's parents are expected to be angered and must be ritually placated by the groom's parents through god-parental mediation. The bride's parents can manipulate the event by refusing to be placated, either by refusing to offer the evening meal, thus blocking the opportunity for the ritual god-parental embrace confirming ritual kinship between the parents and god-parents, or by refusing to attend the post-wedding feast. With such manipulation the outcome is unsure, protocol is disrupted and consternation among participants ensues. The template of appropriate behaviour is countered by a template of inappropriate behaviour, both of them culturally specified. This is a case of 'horizontal' rather than 'vertical' concordance.

Similarly, concordant structures often operate *across* mutually discordant templates to effect change, transforming one template by introducing elements of the other. Lévi-Strauss's (1963: 228) formula for mythic transformation exemplifies this. The more deeply embedded the level of the template, the less it is subject to change. Surface changes rarely disrupt more than the concordant structures at one or two levels higher than that of the event, leaving higher levels intact.

EVOLUTIONARY PERSPECTIVE

In order to comprehend human cultural evolution, it is necessary to understand the profundity of the difference between the cognitive systems that inform human social life and those that inform the social life of other animals. In the attempt to bring culture within the scope of an evolutionary account stressing the continuity between human beings and non-human, ancestral forms, it has sometimes been suggested that culture is widespread in the animal kingdom. Bonner (1980: 10) maintains this position by defining culture as 'the transfer of information by behavioural means, most particularly by the process of teaching and learning'. If this were all that culture entails, the development of an evolutionary sequence from non-human to human would not have given rise to the serious problems that it has. For Hallowell (1960: 316) these problems stem from the preoccupation of anthropologists with culture as the unique possession of *Homo sapiens*. This, he argues, 'led to a *re*creation of the old gap between man and the other primates which, it was once thought, the adoption of an evolutionary frame of reference would serve to bridge'.

As may be seen from the foregoing discussion, culture is far more than teaching and learning, as Bonner would have it. (On how teaching exceeds learning, see the Premacks' discussion in Article 13.) Anthropologists are right to stress that only human beings have culture, in the sense that culture is constituted by a complex classificatory network of shared understanding of the meanings that inform behaviour. These meanings are symbolic, and symbols, in their complexity, are unique to humanity. That the sharing of meaning involves teaching and learning is one aspect of culture but in no sense can define it.

It is here that the puzzle of the human difference must be attacked if the symbolic foundations of culture are to be discovered: how did hominids move from the physically motivated signal or sign to the physically arbitrary symbol as a means of representing one thing by something very different in kind?

FROM SIGNAL AND INDEX TO SYMBOL

A symbol is an artefact that has metaphoric meaning beyond itself and is used in the production of a system of interrelated meanings. If the meaning of an artefact lies only in its direct appropriation as a material substance for use, involving a cause–effect relationship between substance and user, that artefact is not symbolic because it is not used representationally. Sharing of signs provides the basis for social life. Shared signs are instinctively or automatically responded to by many species, for example in courtship displays of various kinds. When shared signs become conventionalized, institutionalized, and semantically interrelated through shared metaphoric understanding, culture is born.

While humans are the major manipulators of their environments, other creatures change their environments on a lesser scale; e.g. ants build anthills, bees build hives with a more complex structure, birds build nests. If these artefacts have any meanings for their users beyond that of their functions in use, this is certainly not revealed in their behaviour. By contrast, the behaviour of human beings with respect to any artefact, whether or not it is found in nature, is quite different. We speak of nesting behaviour, or 'love nests', by *analogy* to — as metaphoric of — their use by birds. We talk about a human 'hive of activity', by analogic reference to bee behaviour. Whatever we can use analogically in another context constitutes the symbolic value of any artefact. Nature is the source of meaning but not its end.

Physical similarity between sign and referent is not peculiar to icons but may also apply to indices. For example, experiments with infant monkeys have shown that they cling to cloth surrogate mothers for reassurance — the softness of cloth substitutes here for the softness of the mother's fur. This is an icon, but also a synechdoche (i.e. the taking of a part for a whole), serving for the monkey child as an index. For either an index or an icon to become a symbol, it must be not only denotative, or directly representational of something beyond itself, but also connotative, or indirectly (i.e. figuratively, or 'arbitrarily') representational.

In speech, a word has representational meaning. As an oral production it is a physical event that *refers to*, or *represents*, not a *particular* object or event, but an unrealized, mentally evoked, *category* (i.e. paradigm) of objects or events. Beyond this, it implies whatever is intended by the speaker or called to mind in the hearer. These will, at least to some extent, be similar if speaker and hearer are members of the same society, with an understanding of their shared culture. An act of speech is thus a secondary reality, projecting listener and speaker beyond the event in which it occurs, and providing a springboard to individual mental metaphoric gymnastics of a kind that the speechless activity of non-human animals cannot attain. The latter can *intend*, just as we can. They can make some rational (logical) choices and decisions. These choices are rational in terms of their learned experience of cause and effect, but are influenced by habit rather than by metaphoric templates. Ours, whether rational or not, are always affected by cultural templates.

THE SYMBOLIC PAST

To suggest a path that hominids may have followed in order to move meaning from index and signal to symbol, it is necessary to look for incipient tendencies to recognize and exploit likenesses. For it is here, as we have seen, that the foundation of symbolic behaviour lies.

There are five major ways in which we might go about this: (1) by contrasting the behaviour of humans and other mammals; (2) by studying the structure of prehistoric artefacts; (3) by examining prehistoric art; (4) by extrapolating from the stages of human ontogeny; and (5) through the comparative reconstruction of behavioural sequences. Some advances have been made in all these directions, but further work must be informed by as complete an understanding as possible of the cognitive skills that characterize the symbolic process.

The behaviour of humans and other mammals

In the preceding discussion I have developed the theory that analogical processing is crucial to culture. If culture is limited to human beings, it is important to ascertain to what extent non-human creatures also behave analogically. A limited capacity for analogical processing would seem to be available to all sentient creatures in their ability to distinguish food from non-food, or, on a somewhat more advanced scale, threat from non-threat. Creatures that have adopted social bonding as their adaptive strategy have raised analogical processing to the level of conspecific emulation. Social bonding requires the ability to recognize oneself as similar to others of the group, and different from those outside the group. Because of their evolutionary development as primates, humans share this adaptive pattern. Archaeology reveals that human behaviour changed very slowly until the symbolizing faculty was well developed. It can be assumed that change in ape behaviour was similarly slow, and that present-day apes are not so very different from their ancestors of the period before hominids learned to make stone tools – the first archaeological indicators of a dawning symbolic capacity.

Play in youth is a testing of the imitative capacity. It decreases with age for most species, but is especially prolonged during the lifetime of the human primate. This prolongation can be seen as the continuation of a trend towards neoteny (Gould 1977). Bonner (1980) makes a case for teaching and learning as an evolutionary road to human culture, but fails to carry it through to an examination of the development of mimicry from iconism to symbolic culture. For human primates are able to mimic not only the movements of other species but any movement or spatial relationship observable in insentient nature. These relationships are *generalized* – i.e. abstracted from nature. This broadening of mimicry moves analogy from the concrete to the abstract.

We have already seen one example of a tendency toward analogical processing in baby monkeys, which find reassurance in a softness that is *like* that of the mother's fur. It may be significant that the likeness is only partial. Monkeys and apes have long been assumed to be more capable of mimicry than are other non-human mammals, though the degree to which this leads to actual imitation of novel behaviour has recently been questioned (Visalberghi and Fragaszy 1990). Limited experimental evidence seems to indicate that neither monkeys nor apes are capable of imitation in the field of tool-use. Anecdotal information suggests that juvenile apes do imitate the gestures of other juveniles in play, and, perhaps, to some extent imitate their mothers in the acquisition of foraging techniques, but not without a great deal of personal manipulative experimentation. While imitation of novel behaviours may be in question, emulation does seem to play a greater part in the behaviour of apes than in that of other non-human species.

Studies of ape communication have been dominated by the Saussurian (1959) view of language as a system of arbitrary signs. Thus, apes have been studied more for their possible use of arbitrary signs as meaningful units than for their capacity to manipulate analogy. Consequently, we have learned very little from these studies that is germane to an investigation of symbolic potential.

Prehistoric artefacts

Archaeology unearths material traces of the activities of early humans as well as of their bodily structure. Through interpretation of these enduring fragments from past lives it is possible to reconstruct sequences in the evolution of humankind. For many millennia the only enduring traces were stones that had been fractured for use as tools. The evolution of conceptualization can be inferred from the changes in tool-making over time. Since human conceptualization is a symbolic process, we need to ascertain to what degree stone tools can be said to be symbolic.

Although during the Middle Palaeolithic era change in tool manufacture was very slow, it is my belief that more symbolism can be discovered from early tools than is usually supposed. It is clear that planning for the future was involved, and this indicates that the tool-makers were thinking beyond the present moment. This thinking also meant *sequential*, or ordered, planning, operating from a learned template, generating a paradigmatic class of actions appropriate to each position in the sequence. As tool-making became more elaborated, hafting − the fitting together of parts to make a whole − showed that the value of unification of differentiated parts was recognized.

In a pioneering article, Wynn (1979) compared operations in Acheulean tool-making, 300,000 years ago, to the stages posited in Piagetian genetic epistemology. He came to the conclusion that these Acheulean hominids employed the infra-logical operations of whole-part relations, qualitative displacement, spatio-temporal substitution, and symmetry, from which it seemed to follow that in terms of organizational ability their thinking was equivalent to that of modern humans (p. 383).

Prehistoric art

As early as the Acheulean, deliberate abstract markings were made on stone (Marshack 1976: 278−9), precursors of the frequent abstract markings made on cave walls and elsewhere during the Upper Palaeolithic. This suggests that the ability to abstract salient visual characteristics may have preceded the ability to represent iconically. If that is true, it suggests, in turn, that the symbolic template arose very early in human prehistory.

Art of any kind is essentially a form of illusion that uses arbitrary spatial organization and deliberate choice of whatever is considered most salient to represent an idea in the mind of the artist or common to the minds of the members of his or her social group. While artistic skill is an individual talent, art style depends upon cultural convention, and the choice of saliencies in depiction depends upon culturally determined themes. The aspects of Upper Palaeolithic art that are least 'realistic' in modern terms have been given little attention. It is on these that I intend to focus.

When the splendid paintings and engravings of animals on cave walls in southern France and the Spanish Pyrenees were first recognized and accepted as the productions of early *Homo sapiens*, the world of art and archaeology was stunned that men of many thousands of years ago (then, as today, the assumption was that the artists were males) possessed a manual and visual skill that would allow them to depict nature so realistically and dramatically. The assumption was then, and still is to a considerable extent, that skill in art depends upon the ability to reproduce, either two- or three-dimensionally, the contours and spatial relationships of natural objects.

However, the earliest art — even that seemingly most 'real' — is thoroughly abstract in the sense that its iconism is selective of those features that most clearly symbolize the cultural reality of the artist and his or her public. What is too often overlooked is that art is a form of symbolization, and what underlies every symbol is a desire to represent something that *is* by means of something which it *is not*. In order for a representation to convey meaning, it must *highlight* some aspect of the something-which-it-is-not that bears at least a tenuous similarity to the something-that-is.

In Palaeolithic graphic representation, abstract signs pre-date outlines of recognizable objects, while the earliest recognizable objects are animals, or rather truncated animals, presumably depicting only such body parts as had symbolic significance for social reasons as yet poorly understood. Even in late Palaeolithic art, such as the paintings in the Lascaux cave, no objects other than animals, or the occasional unrealistic human figure, are depicted. The animals are typically in movement and interaction with one another. Alongside the animals, or superimposed on animal bodies, are abstract signs, the meaning of which is obscure. However, since shapes are repeated and found in similar or different contexts, it is apparent that they were referential, and might even be decipherable, like the Rosetta stone, if only the code could be discovered.

If the ability to represent abstractly arose as early as the Mousterian, as the Pech de l'Azé engraved bone (Marshack 1976) seems to show, this suggests that early hominid thinking was not thing- or noun-oriented but process- or verb-oriented. What this would mean is that early iconicity, whether of graphic design or language, conveyed an idea of motion or spatial relationship (ground) rather than concrete object (figure): 'becoming' rather than 'having become'. This 'becoming' could be all-inclusive, in the sense that metaphor as ground can include any member (figure) that fits the 'likeness' requirements. Thus, iconicity of representation is not necessarily iconicity of figure, as we tend to assume.

A finger, the lips, or a stick could all be used for the action of pointing. By the same token, a finger, the arm, the tongue, the breast, the penis, a stick, a stone, a stone tool could be, and were, each inserted *into* or *between*. The open mouth, a cupped hand, a vagina, or a hole in the rock or earth could accept such an insertion. Thus, any one of these things, or any other of similar shape, had the potential to become an icon to represent the process itself. This is the mode of concordant structure.

A visit to Upper Palaeolithic caves is a lesson in the economy of abstraction. Why represent the whole animal in detail if only a part is intended to receive iconic emphasis? Thus, what seems to be a depiction of a concrete entity is instead a depiction of an abstract processual concept, or symbolic template, transcending the object which serves as the communicative vehicle.

The earliest graphic art was largely schematic: divided triangle for vulva, linear strokes or branching lines for phallus. Where animal outlines were depicted, details were lacking, distortions were standardized, and only certain parts represented the whole. There were conventions for doing this which changed over time. In the beginning, animal legs were usually only rudimentarily represented, horns were depicted frontally, body lines were represented in profile, while many details were either omitted or barely suggested. Frontal human faces had only eyes and no mouths. Where animal shapes were extremely conventionalized – bison horns shown only frontally, hoofs and genitalia omitted in the beginning, and later sometimes exaggerated – they were easily recognizable because the contoural lines differentiated each species from the others. Despite the obvious facility in the production of a realistic line to depict a particular animal, such realism was absent from the earliest portrayals of human beings. Women were conventionalized, with grossly distorted buttocks and pendulous breasts. Men were generally stick-like figures, often with exaggerated penises. Figurative, rather than referential, meaning was surely intended by these distortions. Some figures were part animal, with horns, fur, and tails, but upright, and ichthyphallic.

We are so accustomed to representation that it hardly occurs to us that some degree of iconicity is a necessary component. It is easy to find this iconicity in a photograph or a realistic portrait, despite the loss of the third dimension. Iconicity is even more obvious when represented in sculpture. Much iconicity is discoverable in use, and can just as well be expressed by the iconicity of representative objects as by that of representative nouns in speech. Not for nothing are weapons referred to as 'arms', and weaponry competitiveness as 'arms control', for arms and weapons are both obvious extensions of the human body that can be used for striking. Nails and teeth are both sharp and can be used to cut and tear. The earliest stone tools were fashioned after iconicity of function. But the tool was related metonymically to the action, and paradigmatically to other items that might serve the same function — perhaps teeth, or fingernails. The function, such as cutting, scraping, or pounding, was the ground, or symbolic template, or p-structure — thus more important symbolically than the figure, whether the latter was tooth, nail, or fist. If early representation used a concrete object to represent process, the process was metaphorically halted by apprehension of the meaning, much as written language halts the action it describes.

Just as a graphic representation can be interpreted as a symbolic template, mimicry can also be interpreted as the bodily enactment of iconicity. By the Upper Palaeolithic, the bodily enactment that was characteristic of primates until that time was being supplemented by graphic and sculptural iconic depiction, using non-bodily materials. The representational capability of human beings had finally become highly selective of the details reproduced, of the aspects of nature that were selected for re-creation as symbols for a new and numinous reality — that is as nouns representative of verbal (i.e. processual) meanings.

For early hominids, as for other mammals, satisfactions were based on biological imperatives. The reflexivity born of an expanded capacity for perceiving analogies opened many new avenues. Language made possible communication of what was past, potential, fancied or desired, as well as what was present. The development of the analogical potential made it possible to give metaphoric reality, both linguistically and artistically, to the formerly ineffable. Evidence for this mythologizing is found in Upper Palaeolithic art. If an individual could halt time, and re-create it by means of the production or apprehension of templates, then death itself became a moment in a process rather than a point of termination.

Ontogenesis

While ontogeny does not generally recapitulate phylogeny in any direct sense (Gould 1977), both biological evolution and the stages in the child's cognitive development follow much the same progression of evolutionary stages as that suggested in the archaeological record (Borchert and Zihlman 1990, Bates 1979, Wynn 1979). Unfortunately, studies such as that of Bates and her colleagues do not look to the capacity to discover and exploit likenesses as the crucial evolutionary key to learning culture. Instead, the capacity to 'name' at about 13 months is taken as the essential Rubicon in becoming fully symbolic. Imitative play is considered important only in learning surface structure, rather than as a first step in mastering symbolic analogies. However, at about 9 months children begin to use objects symbolically, 'as if' they were something other than themselves, e.g. pretending to drink from a block as if it were a cup.

Another crucial key to the ontogenetic expansion of the capacity to symbolize is that early words, such as 'up', 'down', and 'dada', are used globally rather than specifically. 'Up' and 'down' are, for children, not locations but announcements of movement from one kind of space to another. 'Dada' announces the appearance, or emergence on the scene, of another kind of person rather than a specific individual. When objects are named, it is the shape or function rather than the particular object that is the crucial aspect of meaning. Thus, one child, having been shown the moon, applied the word 'moon' to a variety of objects with similar shapes as well as to the moon itself (Bowerman 1980). This spatial globality of reference is consistent with the archaeological appearance of graphic abstraction before graphic realism.

A major evolutionary advance lies in the child's receipt of symbolic modelling from caregivers of a kind that was unavailable to Palaeolithic children. This is especially true of language. Western parents are so accustomed to the stasis of object reference that object naming is a principal pedagogical device. This obscures the changing nature of experience, and, for children of Western upbringing, it provides at a very early stage a cultural template by which to interpret the world. It would seem that the template provided for a Navaho child is very different, for Navaho is primarily an action-oriented language, with words that describe objects of a particular shape in a state of flux.

Comparative reconstruction of behavioural sequences

A fifth avenue to the investigation of prehistoric symbolism has been largely neglected. Studies of culture change, although still in their infancy, could use much the same methodology to shed light on cultural beginnings as has been pioneered by linguistics in the reconstruction of early forms of language. Because most of the insights that I have gained into prehistory have come from linguistic theory, whether synchronic or diachronic, I start with language structure and linguistic symbolism as a first key to the reconstruction of the symbolic past.

Language reconstruction is an inductive procedure developed during the nineteenth century. Observation of similarities between the classical languages, Latin, Greek and Sanskrit, stimulated the effort to find a sure means of reconstructing proto-forms that could account for these similarities. It was observed that between these languages there was regularity of sound correspondences within words with the same or similar meanings, and of similar but not identical phonological shape. From this the 'comparative method' was born.

Even without a specific modelling of the process, we can assume that the growing appreciation of the power of iconic representation, as revealed in the archaeological record, was also responsible for the invention of language. Although early language, unlike early art, has not been materially preserved, it is possible to demonstrate the iconic process lying behind it by means of careful comparison of historical languages. While movements of the face, and especially those of the most flexible part of the face − the lips and oral tract − had long been used for signalling, at some point in human history these movements began to be used symbolically, as representations of movement and spatial relationships observed in nature.

Exploration of repeated meanings for a given articulatory segment found in a series of root morphemes in any language can demonstrate the lingering effects of this phenomenon. Using English as an example, and starting with the sound [1] as the segment to be explored, we find it in many roots and words, e.g. loose, lose, lazy, lax, limp, linger, or in a non-initial position, as in slip, slide, sloppy, flow, flex, floppy. In each of these words we can recognize a correlation between a general lack of firmness of the tongue in the pronunciation of [1] and an idea of lack of firmness, or weak spatial connectedness, which forms the common component of semantic meaning in the words in question. If we contrast this with the movement of the tongue in pronunciation of the sound [t] we find a similar correlation between the firmness of the tongue and the common component of meaning in such English words as tap, touch, tense, stop, stay, step, strike, and the like. Through cross-linguistic comparison it is possible to discover the cognate forms and abstract space-relational meanings of fifteen such phonological meaning-bearers (e.g. Foster 1978, 1983b, 1990, in press). Careful comparison of any of the world's languages reveals the language-specific cognate realization of primordial *1 and *t, with the respective meanings of laxity or firmness in words in which they occur.

Language, like all of human culture, is a method of classifying experience, and classes are only established on the basis of likeness of some kind. In language, or, better, in languages, phonemes fall into classes on the basis of both articulator likeness and distributional likeness. Thus, in English, [p], [t] and [k] are alike in that they are all stopped consonants − when they are articulated, the passage of air through the mouth is temporarily halted. They are also alike in that all three are voiceless − there is no simultaneous vibration of the vocal cords as there is for their voiced counterparts, [b], [d] and [g]. Distributionally, they have in common their uniqueness in occurrence after [s] and before a vowel or a liquid. Thus, we find spit and split but not *sbit and *sblit, stick and stricken but not *sdick and *sdricken. The class of words called nouns is minimally classified by phonetic structure in the singular, but in the plural by the addition of a morpheme (minimal meaningful segment), which is usually −s (or so written). Nouns typically occur syntactically after articles or adjectives, and before verbs. Thus, distribution now establishes their likeness, as previously did the common semantic ground of articulatory form.

Comparative analysis across the boundaries of established families or stocks, with reconstruction of original sounds and meanings of word roots (the minimal segments which provide the basic meaning of a word, and to which other morphemic segments can be attached to modify the meaning in some way, as does the noun plural -s), shows that in its beginnings language must have been phonetically iconic. As it grew and developed, so that more and more semantic subtleties could be expressed, the phonetic iconism gradually became obscured as no longer necessary to the communication of meaning, which since became dependent upon distribution.

Interestingly, the earliest meanings were somewhat different from those with which we are now familiar. They were not nominal or verbal, but expressed spatial relationships. They were iconic with their articulatory characteristics, as are [1] and [t] in the examples provided above. Since the sounds themselves were meaning-bearers, words as we know them must have come into being only later, probably first as two-consonant segments, separated by a vowel, which became roots as other modifying (grammatical) segments were added to make meanings more precise. Often later, in many languages, modifying segments became frozen to shorter roots, so that the original root is no longer segmentable. This is the case in Semitic languages, where three-consonant roots became conventionalized. In Indo-European – both as a reconstructed proto-language (PIE) and in its daughter-languages – most roots contain two consonants, although both shorter and longer roots are found.

As groups of speakers became isolated from one another through migration, languages grew and developed in differing ways from the common prototype, known as 'primordial language' (PL). Successive splits over time left greater or lesser resemblances. Thus, for example, Semitic languages resemble one another because their divergences from one another came later in time than the divergence of the Semitic prototype from the Indo-European prototype. It is therefore much more difficult to discover a common, older prototype that gave rise to these two (or more) language stocks than it is to reconstruct the prototypes on the more recent level. In fact, the received linguistic wisdom is that ancient prototypes are unrecoverable, and many linguists still believe that this is true. However, received wisdom often (and perhaps usually) blocks the advance of knowledge. This is an example of the constraining power of a well-entrenched symbolic template in inhibiting rapid culture change.

COGNITIVE EVOLUTION

There are many intellectual advantages to be gained from the exploration of linguistic prototypes (which of course will not take place so long as linguists persist in the firm belief that it cannot be done). The major advantage is the light that reconstruction sheds on cognitive processes, and particularly on cognitive evolution. The reconstruction of early stages of language evolution shows that spatial relationships and movements were of paramount interest to early humans, and that these were abstracted and cognitively unbounded in the beginning, corresponding to the flux of nature. Thus, there were not identifiable *things* (denoted by nouns) but only relationships in space and time. Some extant languages still preserve this feature, even though they have also changed a great deal from the prototype. Among these, and perhaps most strikingly, are languages of the Athabascan family, such as Navajo of the American South-west (Carroll 1956). For example, an irreducible stem may have the meaning 'loose materials (e.g. sand or gravel) drop or fall'. By adding other meaningful segments in rule-governed sequence, the word can become, for example, 'loose stuff pours over the brim of a container', or 'loose stuff (e.g. skin) peels off', etc. Our verbs 'peel' or 'pour' share something of this nature, since both imply the nature of the shape relationships of the material that moves. The Navajo stem is still more abstract than these, however, since it includes the possibility of either peeling or pouring.

Understanding of language as symbolism has been hampered by the failure of linguists to see it as consisting of iconically motivated, rather than arbitrary, signs. Although the original iconicity of phonemes has become obscured, the whole structure of language is held together by analogy, and analogy is iconic where it is representative, as language surely is.

As a theory of the emergence of language, the evolving exploitation of iconicity accounts more satisfactorily for the 'why', 'what' and 'how' of early human communication than any other explanation proposed to date, because it ties the emergent speaker most firmly to his or her biological history as a mimicking primate, using the body as the original icon. By means of comparative reconstruction it is possible to develop an idea of the iconic structure of prehistoric language through various stages of development.

Turning now from language to other aspects of culture, attempts to reconstruct early forms by global comparison of cultural sequences have scarcely begun. Lévi-Strauss's (1964–85) reconstructions of the baseline structures of native American myth through comparison of mythic templates points the way, but has met with considerable resistance. Paradigmatic research of whatever kind tends to be resisted within our positivistic scientific tradition, as shown, for example, in the criticisms launched by action-oriented symbolic anthropologists against componential analysis and structuralism, as reviewed above.

Other examples of template comparison in a historical framework are found in Ardener (1980) and Sahlins (1981). Berlin and Kay's (1969) global comparison of the semantics of colour, and Needham's (1973) interesting attempt at the global comparison of right/left paradigmatic metaphors, are both based on unit paradigms rather than on syntagmatically sequenced sets of paradigms. The pioneering work of global template analysis by Santillana and Dechend (1969) has, unfortunately, been largely ignored within anthropology. Hall (1990) makes similar cross-cultural comparisons. The justification for comparative template analysis over other paradigmatic approaches lies in the sheer complexity of these organized sequences of meaning. It is difficult to believe that they could have had multiple origins. To the contrary, their global distribution suggests a single, probably Palaeolithic, source.

390

CONCLUSIONS

By using the development of an iconic capacity as the clue to symbolic evolution and to the formation of the symbolic classificational complex that is human culture, a plausible hypothesis of the direction and stages of cultural evolution can be postulated. This hypothesis accounts for continuity between the biologically determined behaviour of lower species and the increasingly complex symbolic behaviour of human beings as reflected both in the archaeological record and in child development.

This is not a causal hypothesis: it tells us 'how' rather than 'why'. Causation seems to lie in the possibilities that life forms have of expanding already existing capacities in interaction with their environments. As Lock (1982: 112) has pointed out, when any ecological change takes place, new niches are opened up. In this way evolution provides itself with the conditions for its own occurrence. The new form reflects what the niche implies. This evolutionary mode seems to be just as applicable to cultural as to biological events (see Article 7 for a full theoretical exposition of this point).

A plausible scenario for the evolutionary exploitation of likeness may be constructed as follows. Mammalian mimicry arose in the context of subsistence procurement. Offspring began to watch parents and match their feeding techniques. Such mimicry was necessary to survival in new niches where food was not easily obtained. Selection favoured individuals who were best able to learn to find and extract food. Infant play rehearsed the techniques that emerged in their developed form in adulthood. Early hominids, like chimpanzees, discovered that a twig was *like* a finger in facilitating extraction of food from a hole. Expanding on the perception of *likeness*, the metaphor was extended to copulation as penetration and extraction, but this time for sexual pleasure. A sharp stone was *like* fingernails or teeth in separating food from non-food. A heavy stone was *like*, but more effective than, a fist in self-protection. As more things were discovered that could be conceived and used in similar ways, paradigms of likeness expanded. New possibilities for the exploitation of likenesses continually arose, so that categories and choices of ways of doing things slowly but steadily increased.

At the end of this long process came symbolism, symbolic templates as guides to action, and 'culture as we know it'. Because of their capacity to exploit iconicity in hierarchically organized, abstract ways, human beings from the Upper Palaeolithic onwards have become conscious of themselves and of their fate. This reflexive capacity was born of their ever-increasing experimental curiosity and drive to manipulate one another and the external environment.

Symbolism has proved extraordinarily adaptive for the human species. The drive to exploit likeness has become a human instinct. This drive led to the discovery of ever more ways to manipulate the environment, radically modifying it for all living creatures, and destroying it for many. It is impossible to predict where the symbolic drive will lead us in the future. It may have to be turned from external to internal uses if the human species is to continue to adapt and survive. How this is to be done is not clear. Given the rapidity of environmental destruction and the tenacity and resistance to change of symbolic templates, it may not be possible. The tenacity of the positivist template in science is a case in point. However, the human mind has the potential to resolve the template problem and may yet be able to move the symbolic condition – and through it the environmental conditions – towards new adaptive possibilities.

REFERENCES

Ardener, E. (1980) 'Some outstanding problems in the analysis of events', in M. L. Foster and S. H. Brandes (eds) *Symbol as Sense: New Approaches to the Analysis of Meaning*, New York: Academic Press.

Bates, E. (1979) *The Emergence of Symbols: Cognition and Communication in Infancy* (in collaboration with L. Benigni, I. Bretherton, L. Camaioni, and V. Volterra), New York: Academic Press.

Berlin, B. (1981) 'The concept of rank in ethnobiological classification: some evidence from Aguaruna folk botany', in R. Casson (ed.) *Language, Culture, and Cognition: Anthroplogical Perspectives*, New York: Macmillan.

Berlin, B. and Kay, P. (1969) *Basic Color Terms: Their Universality and Evolution*, Berkeley and Los Angeles: University of California Press.

Berlin, B., Breedlove, D. E. and Raven, P. H. (1974) *Principles of Tzeltal Plant Classification*, New York: Academic Press.

Bonner, J. T. (1980) *The Evolution of Culture in Animals*, Princeton, NJ: Princeton University Press.

Borchert, C. M. and Zihlman, A. (1990) 'The ontogeny and phylogeny of symbolizing', in M. L. Foster and L. J. Botscharow (eds) *The Life of Symbols*, Boulder, Col.: Westview Press.

Bowerman, M. (1980) 'The structure and origin of semantic categories in the language-learning child', in M. L. Foster and S. H. Brandes (eds) *Symbol as Sense*, New York: Academic Press.

Carroll, J. B. (ed.) (1956) *Language, Thought and Reality: Selected Writings of Benjamin Lee Whorf*, New York: John Wiley.

Chomsky, N. (1957) *Syntactic Structures*, The Hague: Mouton.

Dolgin, J. L., Kemnitzer, D. S. and Schneider, D. M. (eds) (1977) *Symbolic Anthropology: A Reader in the Study of Symbols and Meanings*, New York: Columbia University Press.

Douglas, M. (1970) *Natural Symbols: Explorations in Cosmology*, New York: Pantheon Press.

Firth, R. (1973) *Symbols: Public and Private*, Ithaca, NY: Cornell University Press.

Foster, M. L. (1978) 'The symbolic structure of primordial language', in S. L. Washburn and E. R. McCown (eds) *Human Evolution: Bio-social Perspectives*, Menlo Park, Cal.: Benjamin/Cummings.

—— (1983a) 'Tzintzuntzan marriage: an analysis of concordant structure', in J. Oosten and A. de Ruijter (eds) *The Future of Structuralism*, Göttingen: Herodot.

—— (1983b) 'Solving the insoluble: language genetics today', in E. de Grolier (ed.) *Glossogenetics: The Origin and Evolution of Language*, Paris: Harwood Academic.

—— (1990) 'The birth and life of signs', in M. L. Foster and L. J. Botscharow (eds) *The Life of Symbols*, Boulder, Col.: Westview Press.

—— (in press) 'Reconstruction of the evolution of language', in A. Lock and C. Peters (eds) *Handbook of Symbolic Evolution*, Oxford: Oxford University Press.

Geertz, C. (1973) *The Interpretation of Cultures*, New York: Basic Books.

Gould, S. J. (1977) *Ontogeny and Phylogeny*, Cambridge, Mass., and London: Harvard University (Belknap) Press.

Hall, R. L. (1990). 'Cognitive cores and flint flakes', in M. L. Foster and L. J. Botscharow (eds) *The Life of Symbols*, Boulder, Col.: Westview Press.

Hallowell, A. I. (1960) 'Self, society, and culture in phylogenetic perspective', in S. Tax (ed.) *Evolution after Darwin*, vol. II: *The Evolution of Man*, Chicago: University of Chicago Press.

Hawkes, T. (1977) *Structuralism and Semiotics*, Berkeley and Los Angeles: University of California Press.

Hugh-Jones, S. (1979) *The Palm and the Pleiades: Initiation and Cosmology in Northwest Amazonia*, Cambridge: Cambridge University Press.

Lakoff, G. (1987) *Women, Fire, and Dangerous Things: What Categories Reveal about the Human Mind*, Chicago and London: University of Chicago Press.

Leach, E. (1976) *Culture and Communication: the Logic by which Symbols are Connected. An Introduction to the Use of Structuralist Analysis in Social Anthropology*, Cambridge: Cambridge University Press.

Lévi-Strauss, C. (1949) *The Elementary Structures of Kinship*, Boston: Beacon Press.

—— (1963) 'The structural study of myth', in *Structural Anthropology*, New York and London: Basic Books.

—— (1964–85) *Mythologiques*, I–V, Paris: Plon.

Lock, A. J. (1982) 'A note on the ecology of meaning', *Quaderni di Semantica* 3(1): 112–17.

Marshack, A. (1976) 'Some implications of the Paleolithic symbolic evidence for the origin of language', *Current Anthropology* 17(2): 274–82.

Needham, R. (ed.) (1973) *Right and Left: Essays on Dual Symbolic Classification*, Chicago and London: University of Chicago Press.

Paul, R. A. (1982) *The Tibetan Symbolic World: Psychoanalytic Explorations*, Chicago: University of Chicago Press.

Peirce, C. S. (1931–5) *The Collected Papers of Charles Sanders Peirce*, vols 1–4, Cambridge, Mass.: Harvard University Press.

Reichel-Dolmatoff, G. (1971) *Amazon Cosmos: The Sexual and Religious Symbolism of the Tukano Indians*, Chicago and London: University of Chicago Press.

Rosch, E. (1983) 'Prototype classification and logical classification: the two systems', in E. Scholnick (ed.) *New Trends in Cognitive Representation: Challenges to Piaget's Theory*, Hillsdale, NJ: Lawrence Erlbaum.

Sahlins, M. (1981) *Historical Metaphors and Mythical Realities: Structure in the Early History of the Sandwich Islands Kingdom*, Ann Arbor: University of Michigan Press.

Santillana, G. de and Dechend, H. von (1969) *Hamlet's Mill: An Essay on Myth and the Frame of Time*, Boston: Gambit.

Saussure, F. de (1959) *Course in General Linguistics*, New York: Philosophical Library.

Schneider, D. M. (1976) 'Notes toward a theory of culture', in K. H. Basso and H. A. Selby (eds) *Meaning in Anthropology*, Albuquerque: University of New Mexico Press.

Silverstein, M. (1976) 'Shifters, linguistic categories, and cultural description', in K. H. Basso and H. A. Selby (eds) *Meaning in Anthropology*, Albuquerque: University of New Mexico Press.

Sperber, D. (1974) *Rethinking Symbolism*, Cambridge: Cambridge University Press.

Visalberghi, E. and Fragaszy, D. M. (1990) 'Do monkeys ape?', in S. T. Parker and K. R. Gibson (eds) *'Language' and Intelligence in Monkeys and Apes: Comparative Developmental Perspectives*, Cambridge: Cambridge University Press.

Wagner, R. (1986) *Symbols that Stand for Themselves*, Chicago: University of Chicago Press.

Wilson, M. (1971) *Religion and the Transformation of Society: a Study in Social Change in Africa*, Cambridge: Cambridge University Press.

Wynn, T. (1979) 'The intelligence of later Acheulean hominids', *Man* (N.S.) 14(3): 371–91.

FURTHER READING

Basso, K. H. and Selby, H. A. (eds) (1976) *Meaning in Anthropology*, Albuquerque: University of New Mexico Press.

Dolgin, J. L., Kemnitzer, D. S. and Schneider, D. M. (eds) (1977) *Symbolic Anthropology: A Reader in the Study of Symbols and Meanings*, New York: Columbia University Press.

Douglas, M. (1970) *Natural Symbols: Explorations in Cosmology*, New York: Pantheon Press.

Fernandez, J. W. (ed.) (1991) *Beyond Metaphor: The Theory of Tropes in Anthropology*, Stanford, Cal.: Stanford University Press.

Firth, R. (1973) *Symbols: Public and Private*, Ithaca, NY: Cornell University Press.

Foster, M. L. (1983) 'Tzintzuntzan marriage: an analysis of concordant structures', in J. Oosten and A. de Ruijter (eds) *The Future of Structuralism*, Göttingen: Herodot.

Foster, M. L. and Botscharow, L. J. (eds) (1990) *The Life of Symbols*, Boulder, Col.: Westview Press.

Foster, M. L. and Brandes, S. H. (eds) (1980) *Symbol as Sense: New Approaches to the Analysis of Meaning*, New York: Academic Press.

Geertz, C. (1973) *The Interpretation of Cultures*, New York: Basic Books.

Lakoff, G. (1987) *Women, Fire, and Dangerous Things: What Categories Reveal About the Human Mind*, Chicago and London: University of Chicago Press.

Laughlin, C. D. Jr, McManus, J. and d'Aquili, E. G. (1990) *Brain, Symbols and Experience: Toward a Neurophenomenology of Human Consciousness*, Boston and Shaftesbury: New Science Library.

Leach, E. (1976) *Culture and Communication: the Logic by which Symbols are Connected. An Introduction to the Use of Structuralist Analysis in Social Anthropology*, Cambridge: Cambridge University Press.

Lévi-Strauss, C. (1963) *Structural Anthropology*, New York and London: Basic Books.

Needham, R. (ed.) (1973) *Right and Left: Essays on Dual Symbolic Classification*, Chicago and London: University of Chicago Press.

Sahlins, M. (1981) *Historical Metaphors and Mythical Realities: Structure in the Early History of the Sandwich Islands Kingdom*, Ann Arbor: University of Michigan Press.

Santillana, G. de and Dechend, H. von (1969) *Hamlet's Mill: An Essay on Myth and the Frame of Time*, Boston: Gambit.

Wagner, R. (1986) *Symbols that Stand for Themselves*, Chicago: University of Chicago Press.

Wynn, T. (1979) 'The intelligence of later Acheulean hominids', *Man* (N.S.) 14(3): 371–91.

15

ARTEFACTS AND THE MEANING OF THINGS

Daniel Miller

INTRODUCTION

Imagine we decide to establish a museum of contemporary material culture in order to preserve for posterity the artefacts of today. A comprehensive collecting policy is intended. It will not be very long before the farcical nature of this scheme becomes apparent. Some things, such as houses and ships, are too big, some things, such as candy floss and daisy chains, too ephemeral. Is a softwood plantation a natural or an artefactual form? Do we start with industrially produced goods and, if so, do we include every brand of car door mirrors and shampoo, and if a company proclaims a change in the product is this a new artefact or not? What about self-made artefacts, those that children have made at school, or that individuals have knitted on the bus? Clearly we cannot create such a museum, although we may observe the extraordinary variety of exhibitions that might be put on, featuring collections of anything from matchboxes to garden gnomes.

To acknowledge the problems faced by such a proposal, however, is liable to produce a rather uneasy feeling that we live in a world that has gone beyond our capacities of ordering. As Simmel (1968: 43–4) argued at the turn of the century, to be continually faced with objects which we cannot assimilate is one of the key problems of the modern age. We constantly strive for such assimilation. That is, artefacts appear as given concrete forms, but human societies have always striven – through their construction, alteration, consumption and application of meaning – to make them internal to, and in part definitional of, themselves. In many ways it is the very physical nature of artefacts, at once the product of human desires, yet in themselves inanimate, which will always render them ambiguous as regards the dualism between persons and non-persons. It is intrinsic to their nature as social things.

This problem has constituted a kind of meta-context for the study of anthropology. Anthropologists have generally come from societies which are experiencing a massive increase in the quantity of material culture, whether these societies are industrial nations or developing countries with rapidly increasing importation of consumer goods in exchange for primary products. The general sense of an infinitude of new varieties of things and the new flux of fashion and transience may itself be the prime source of this feeling that artefacts are threatening to us. There is a continual unease about being what is colloquially termed 'materialistic'. An underlying question has therefore been to understand the manner by which persons come to identify with objects or even to become undifferentiated from them.

When the phrase the 'meaning of things' is used in anthropology it tends to implicate something beyond the narrow questions of semanticity by which artefacts, like words, might have sense and reference. Rather, the notion of meaning tends to incorporate a sense of 'meaningful' closer to the term 'significance'. When we think of buildings, foods, clothes and other artefacts we automatically concern ourselves with meaning in the sense of asking what does this building or drink mean to us and for us? Is this an artefact I identify with as conforming to my 'taste' or 'style', or do I think of it as relating primarily to some other person or group? Is it a suitable present for ..., is it a suitable environment to be inhabited by ..., is it an appropriate symbol of ...? And so forth. Artefacts are very different from words, and when we talk about the meaning of things we are primarily concerned with questions of 'being' rather than questions of 'reference'. Artefacts are a means by which we give form to, and come to an understanding of, ourselves, others, or abstractions such as the nation or the modern. It is in this broad sense that their very materiality becomes problematic, and it is this problematic which I shall take as the central theme of this article.

This point is not always acknowledged in anthropology, since the primary concern has tended to be with the meaning of artefacts for others, in particular for those living in relatively small-scale communities with a relatively limited and clearly defined array of artefacts. But here, as in so much of anthropology, the very interest in what have tended to be presented as small, closed systems can be fully understood only in relation to, and often in contrast with, the preoccupations of the societies from which the anthropologists have come and for whom they write, societies in which simplicity in the relation to objects is consigned to remote places or far-off times. Therefore, to understand the meaning of things for anthropology, both ends of this polarity have to be considered. On the one hand anthropologists can call on their experience of living and participating in small communities, where to study the meaning of things is almost always to assume that such artefacts are 'full' of meaning, often integrating various otherwise disparate elements of cultural life. On the other hand all contemporary anthropologists, as members of their own societies, also relate to objects, for example by going shopping. Whether selecting car seat covers, ice cream flavours or a new novel to read, we are constantly aware that the choice threatens to be problematic, that we might find ourselves delaying others as we strive internally torn between choices on a menu. The problem lies less in the time expended than in the awareness that it is very hard to justify, to find criteria which would lend importance to such decisions and therefore make sense of this activity as a substantial element in our lives. We feel that to be unable to choose the appropriate birthday card in a shop is symptomatic of a new banality. Modern mass material culture has made us all feel silly at different times, and it is this which makes the study of material culture such a serious pursuit.

The concept of the artefact is best defined in the broadest terms. There is little point in attempting to distinguish systematically between a natural world and an artefactual one, except when we are concerned with the ways in which terms such as 'natural' may have particular consequences or entailments, as when a commodity in the shops is labelled 'natural' simply because a single ingredient, such as a chemical dye, has been deleted, or when something as apparently natural as radiation is taken to be antithetical to true 'nature'. It is not only in industrial societies that virtually all objects encountered are artefactual. If we remove ourselves to the South Pacific, for example to a Polynesian outlier within the Solomon Islands, then at first glance we might seem to encounter a dense natural forest environment within which villages represent clearings. This, however, would be to ignore the highly developed arboriculture which over several centuries has removed virtually all trees which are not of direct economic value to the inhabitants, to leave an environment which is in fact entirely the product of cultivation. Plants and animals are natural species, but is not a lap-dog produced by selective breeding over generations an animated artefact – still more a bonsai tree? Even when it comes to those objects such as the sea or snow which we do not control, we still interact with them as classified and therefore structured sets of forms, which are experienced through such human ordering. Snow for the Inuit out hunting is only in the most trivial sense the same thing as snow experienced by a London youth at Christmas.

It would be similarly pointless to attempt to define material culture as the outcome of specific desires or to differentiate the products of intention from those of history – artefacts which are made deliberately as opposed to those which come down to us as given forms. Since intentions themselves have their source in subjects who are inevitably situated historically, the argument would always tend to circularity, because we would find that the artefacts we have received in turn influence the artefacts we choose to make. Few contemporary inhabitants of Sweden wear the clothes fashionable in the eighteenth century, but this is not the result of some calculative decision. The micro-element of conscious decision between perceived possibilities can be attributed to intentionality, but the alternatives from which we choose, and the strategies which inform our taste in objects, are usually derived from larger historical forces.

If material culture is not defined in relation to its artificiality or intention-ality, what alternative basis can be found? It seems most reasonable to take it as a subset of culture, so that a theory of artefacts as material culture would be derived from a more general theory of culture. If culture is understood not in the narrow sense of some particular element of the human environment, but in the more general sense of the process through which human groups con-struct themselves and are socialized, then material culture becomes an aspect of objectification, consisting in the material forms taken by this cultural process. Hence to study material culture is to consider the implications of the materiality of form for the cultural process.

This sense of material culture as a form of being-in-the-world becomes clearer when we consider the process of socialization. From quite early on, the infant born in one cultural context becomes recognizably distinct in manners and outlook from an infant socialized in another setting. Much of this results from the micro-routines of daily life, in which we become oriented to and by the spaces, the objects and the small but significant distinctions in object forms through which we form our classifications and habits. In turn these create our expectations, which allow much of the world to become quickly absorbed as a 'taken-for-granted' context for our lives. In this sense our cultural identity is not merely embodied but literally 'objectified' (Bourdieu 1977).

This suggests a starting point for examining the cultural process, which lies in the manner by which we order things and are ordered by things. Subse-quently two further problems arise: first, the implications of the very materi-ality of things, and second, the dualism by which we tend to think of things as being opposed to persons.

THE ORDER OF THINGS (1): ORDERING THINGS

In this section my central concern is both with elucidating dominant principles by which arrays of artefacts are ordered and with showing how these are der-ived by means of different methodologies developed for the study of material culture. Both historians and anthropologists have argued that particular socie-ties or particular historical periods have tended to emphasize particular prin-ciples of classification. Foucault, for example, divides European history into separate 'epistemes' based on the dominant principle of classification employed in each. He argues that with the rise of natural history, sight became dominant over smell and touch (1970: 132–3), while forms of resemblance and affinity were similarly demoted as against other principles of order. With the rise of the sciences it was not enough to assume that a root which happened to have a shape reminiscent of the human body was therefore likely, when eaten, to have an effect upon the body. Rather, from systematic collections of natural objects, such as butterflies or rock forms, patterns of affinity were sought which could then be analysed in conjunction with consistent theories of their connectivity.

399

The order of things is also culturally constructed. Strathern (1988: 268–305) has argued that in traditional Melanesian societies transformative principles are stressed, rather than those of either affinity or theory. An object is always perceived in terms of its ability to transform into or elicit another object: a tool is the potential creator of garden crops, a boy is a potential man, a shell necklace may attract another form of valuable. Objects are thus viewed less in themselves than for their place in an exchange or ritual which will have an effect. In some cases it is forbidden to eat or consume that which you have yourself produced, because to do so prevents the object from becoming part of an exchange (e.g. Munn 1986: 49–60) or some other process through which it may act on the world in a transformative capacity. Hence one's sense of any given thing is one in which other things are always implicated.

When we set out to represent a set of objects, the dimensions by which an order is constructed either explicitly or implicitly give meaning to the array of forms. In nineteenth-century museums, for example, objects such as musical instruments or arrows were often organized into a sequence from the most simple to the most sophisticated. What was illustrated, but equally taken as 'demonstrated', was the sense in which material culture has 'evolved' from primitive forms to the refinements of advanced civilization by direct analogy with what were assumed to be the principles of biological science. Ethnographers might then search for the 'missing link' in the guise of some tribal form which would show how one stage in this process gave way to the next (Steadman 1979: 74–102). This principle, by which museums tend to reflect wider changes in attitudes towards classification, continues to operate today. In the 1980s, when the desire for the holistic emerged with new force in areas as diverse as alternative medicine and 'whole' foods sold in the supermarket, an ethnographic exhibition of, for example, South Asian peasant life would have attempted to provide an image of the village as it was lived in, allowing the visitor almost to breathe the dust and smell the odours which belonged to the original context of the artefacts displayed (though it was the smell of spices rather than that of urine or garbage which seemed to survive this change of setting). Often, virtually all the detailed labelling characteristic of earlier exhibition forms was removed, so as to leave no barrier to the sense of entering into a whole and natural social environment.

If the meaning of objects derives from the orders into which they are incorporated, then the same artefact may change its implications simply by being introduced into some new order. Gilsenan (1982: 192–214) writes about the construction of old towns or the old quarters of towns in the Middle East which are often visited today by tourists who view them as picturesque remains. Clearly at one time such areas were themselves new, and for a long period they were merely the ordinary form of urban environment, but once the point is reached at which much of the rest of the town has been rebuilt in a new style, the remaining areas may be redesignated as the 'old' city and gain thereby an aura of being quaint or traditional, the ideal haunt for tourists: a dark, obscure and fossilized form. This is not, as some have assumed, a new type of change. A very similar process occurred two millennia earlier when the same areas with which Gilsensan is concerned were Hellenized or Romanized. As with modern colonialism, the Greek sector of the city may well have appeared modern and as the inevitable outcome of historical change which rendered the original, non-Hellenized sector of, for example, Jerusalem quaint, barbaric or merely scruffy.

At least one major paradigm in anthropology, that of structuralism, has made the ordering of things central to its understanding of human culture. Although the 'things' in question were often non-material, such as myths or kinship rules, structuralist studies of the internal logic of symbolic systems — linked as they were to semiotic studies of the relations between symbols and their external referents — led to many refinements in the study of cultures as cosmologies whose sense of order and integrity emerged in large part through the logical ordering of concrete objects. Two examples may serve as illustrations. The first is Lévi-Strauss's own study (1982: 93) of the masks used by the Indians of the American Northwest Coast, in which these figure as material equivalents of myths. Like myths, they would undergo inversion, either in their physical attributes or in the symbolic interpretation of their material form, at the boundaries between different tribal groups. Thus the Xwexwe mask of the Kwakiutl, with its bulging eyes, protruding jaws and tongue, is the inverse transformation of their Dzonkwa mask, which has sunken eyes, hollow cheeks, and no tongue, but is the same as the mask called Swaihwe of the neighbouring Salish. Here the objects of one society are seen to derive their meanings not only from their relations of opposition one with another, but from the ways in which this system of relations undergoes partial inversion as it crosses the boundaries with neighbouring societies. It is as though the meanings of British foods only become clear when they are seen as systematic inversions of French culinary symbolism.

While anthropological structuralism was much influenced by the linguistic theory of de Saussure, many other studies of the order embodied in artefacts were inspired by the subsequent and equally influential linguistics of Chomsky (e.g. Faris 1972). In Chomsky's 'generative grammars' we were able to see how systems of rules which are never explicit are applied through language to determine what combinations of sounds form meaningful sequences rather than unintelligible juxtapositions. Each grammar is specific to a particular group of speakers.

For my second illustrative example I draw on the work of Glassie (1975), who has applied similar ideas to a study of historical folk housing in Middle Virginia. Noting the repetition in geometric form and combinations of elements, Glassie argues that rules are being systematically applied. As with language, these are not conscious, and there are no professional architects. Rather, these 'rules' determined the normative order which generated buildings with which the people of the time felt comfortable, and which were acceptable in their general aesthetics. Overall, he argues that nine subdivided rule-sets can account for the generation of all the culturally acceptable vernacular buildings that are found. These include such micro-elements as 'fenestration of the façade' or 'the fireplace must be central to the wall on which it is located' (Glassie 1975: 29). The analysis is a dynamic one which reveals how, around the middle of the eighteenth century, a major change occurred by which chimneys and central halls became incorporated into the main building, and a new concern with symmetry appeared along with a homogenization of the exterior around a more conspicuously ordered façade associated with the Georgian style. (For another perspective on Glassie's work, see Wynn's discussion in this volume, Article 6.)

This historical study may be brought up to date by ethnographic work being carried out in the nearby area of coastal North Carolina (Forrest 1988, especially 192–203). As in other recent studies, the tendency has been to move away from the tight and rather formal methods of strict structural analysis and to allow a more flexible, contextual and interpretive dimension, while still examining patterns which link different sets of artefacts. In this case the aesthetics of house outlines are linked to interior decoration, including items such as quilts or the recipes used for home cooking. The aesthetics of the home interior are compared with the decoration of the church and contrasted to objects used outside the home and associated with men, such as the duck decoys used in sports. The ethnography allows the physical and spatial forms to be presented in the context of the aesthetics of smell and taste, and of more general sensual appreciation. An overall 'message' is seen to emerge consistent with the more explicit messages of the church. This is directed particularly to men, who, after spending much of their life outside the home milieu, often working at some distance from the community and associated with a more material–transactional ethos, are then encouraged to return to the fold of religion and domestic life as reflected in a more incorporative aesthetic and practice. At this stage, however, we have moved from a focus on the ordering of things to the manner by which we might be said to be ordered by things.

THE ORDER OF THINGS (2): ORDERED BY THINGS

In the above studies the patterning found in material culture is essentially a reflection of a dominant mode of classification imposed either by the anthropologist as analyst or by the group being studied (in practice, usually some amalgamation of the two). The other side of the coin, however, lies in the impact the taxonomic order of things has upon those who are socialized into that environment. The original Portuguese title of Gilberto Freyre's classic work on the early development of Brazilian society is *Casa-Grande e Senzala* – that is, *The Big House and the Slave Quarters*. Within this work the author constantly attempts to evoke the manner by which social relations are established by reference to this spatial context, the setting for a sensual and languid life in the hammock, where to have to use one's legs was to risk a degrading comparison with slaves and plebeians (Freyre 1986: 429). The development of particular behaviours in relation to sexuality and sadism is closely tied to the way their normality is enshrined in a spatial nexus defined by the architectural forms and the institutions they represented and literally channelled into particular relations.

There has recently been a return to this kind of more impressionistic anthropology in which such material paraphernalia as clothing forms or baroque façades are understood as core elements in evoking a sense of 'atmosphere' in which certain social relations and activities develop and become normative. In industrial societies commercial classifications often clarify such relations. Objects made by the London-based firm Heal's in the late nineteenth century clearly constructed systematic stylistic distinctions contrasting the furnishing appropriate for servants against that appropriate for the mistress (Forty 1986: 85). This distinction was given symbolic form in every decorative detail and may be set alongside that ubiquitous Victorian phrase of people 'knowing their place'. Forty (1986: 156–81) examines the development of concepts of hygiene and cleanliness, and activities such as constant dusting, promoted on the grounds of their being based on important discoveries in medical science but then elevated to something rather more in the formation of the modern role of the housewife. 'Disorder and lack of cleanliness should cause a sort of suffering in the mistress of the house. Put in these terms the condition of total cleanliness was comparable to a religious state of grace, and just as unattainable' (1986: 169). The decline in this obsession with dusting has not led to a perceptible rise in poor health, but the point made by Forty is not just that the concept of cleanliness was central to changes in gender relations but that it was literally enshrined in a wide array of new furnishing forms, colours, textures and designs which constituted the acceptable standard of interior decoration. Cleanliness was transformed into beauty.

In some societies such ordering principles appear to be all-encompassing. South Asian caste society is usually described not only as hierarchically ordered by caste but also as deriving all forms of classification from hierarchy, so that even different woods or metals are seen as high or low. All object and material classifications evoke social distinctions, such that aluminium vessels are seen as more suitable for lower-caste use than brass vessels, one wood is more appropriate to high-caste ritual use than another, and so forth. It is commonly argued that to be brought up in such an environment, in which all things declare the ubiquity of a particular ordering principle, will result in a perception of the world which takes this principle as second nature, close to the concept of habit, an order accepted without any conscious thought or consideration as to the way things might otherwise be. Many of those authors who have concentrated on the place of material culture in socialization have tended to emphasize the way in which ordinary objects can have this effect without appearing to do so (e.g. Bourdieu 1977). However, recent work (see the example from Trinidad on p. 414) suggests that we have tended to exaggerate the homogeneity of such meaning, and to ignore the degree of contradiction and ambivalence.

The effect of artefacts in creating a taken-for-granted meaning which is thereby less likely to be challenged than a more explicit set of principles has come under recent scrutiny with the impact of feminism. A vast number of ordinary commercial objects are 'gendered' according to what appear to be consistent patterns. For example, where objects are destined for males it is more likely that the machine parts will be exposed to view. When typewriters switched from being mainly associated with male clerks to being used largely by female secretaries the keys were enclosed; likewise when the motor scooter was developed as a female equivalent to the male motorbike it not only enclosed the engine but took its lines from the familiar children's scooter (Hebdige 1988: 84). Although individual instances of such practices are easy to locate, as in the dichotomy between playing with dolls and trains, it is the overwhelming ubiquity of this trend and the realization that there are many other more subtle manifestations of distinction which frustrate those who desire to end what is regarded as an asymmetrical division. The debate is complicated by the sense of deliberate commercial involvement in creating meanings as images for artefacts in a world of commodities, and by the existence of professionals such as advertisers whose job it is to give meaning to artefacts. It gives rise to the question, however, as to how this situation may be compared with instances from non-industrial societies where similar symbolic schemes operate to 'gender' village material culture without deliberate recourse to any such mechanisms.

From here it is a small step to the study of ideology using material culture (Larrain 1979, Miller and Tilley 1984). This tends to be based upon two assumptions. The first is that certain interest groups in a society have more influence to create the world of artefacts in such a manner that they embody the ordering principles established by those same interests. The second is that people who are brought up surrounded by artefacts which embody such ordering principles will tend to understand the world in accordance with this order, with the result that dominated groups will tend to have some difficulty in understanding the nature of their own interests, since these are not given concrete form in the world they inhabit. Since higher-caste Indians dominate the spatial order of villages and the forms of village goods, these spatial orders and material forms will embody a caste view of the world which reproduces the interests of these same higher castes. This view of ideology as misrecognition or false consciousness has certainly been challenged, but central to its credibility is the notion that ordinary artefacts have a considerable impact in ordering people. It may be noted that this approach does not presuppose deliberate manipulation by dominant groups, merely that those with power will anyway tend to construct the world according to the perspectives from which they view it.

What are the implications for groups of people who are living within a world which largely manifests the ideals and values of others? For anthropologists this question presents itself most acutely in terms of a fragmentation of what had previously appeared as a relatively simple opposition between *our* kinds of material culture and *theirs*, which I introduced at the beginning of this article. In the contemporary world, the ethnographer who travels to highland New Guinea or goes to study shamans in Brazil is likely to have the uncomfortable experience of finding people who will ask questions about the latest shifts in popular music styles or the characters of a soap opera on national television. The study of material culture today takes place under conditions in which multinational firms have a presence in virtually every country, and where the same chocolate milk drink, brand of blue jeans, paperback books, gift perfumes and videos are readily available. Once again people who did not initially see material culture as of primary importance are faced with such overwhelming visible changes that certain questions simply force themselves into the foreground. If these are the material forms being employed today, at the very least the problem arises of whether it makes any difference to *this* kinship system if the dowry has to include a fridge, or to *that* ritual if a plastic doll figures in it prominently. More importantly for the study of the significance of image construction, what are the implications of photography or film, which as a medium allows ordinary villagers access to visual images which had previously been reserved for deities? Finally, does a quantitative increase in material culture bring about a qualitative change for the society concerned?

The initial reaction to these changes has tended to be to see them as the harbinger of the end of anthropology as we have known it, since they spell the end of the simple or isolated society, and the end of the authentic 'unspoiled' humanity which for so long has provided a foil for the industrial world. Homogenization of material culture is thus taken as symptomatic of the homogenization of culture itself. This process is often called Americanization, since the United States is viewed as a symbol for mass consumption in general. Similarly the quantitative increase in goods is taken to represent an immediate fall into alienation, and the ensuing problems are generalized as those of 'modernity'. Furthermore, since these goods are made in metropolitan societies by multinational corporations, their spread is assumed to be tantamount to a form of actual control over the peoples who now become subject to the goods and thus subservient to the values and authorities from which they emanate. Yet, in recent years, anthropologists have increasingly realized that the societies represented in their ethnographies were never so isolated, ahistorical, functional or in some sense authentic as they had often been portrayed to be. If New Guinea societies could adopt such radical innovations as the sweet potato prior to colonial contact, was it reasonable to argue that a Melanesian group which had proved to be entrepreneurially adept at harnessing the possibilities of high coffee prices was necessarily less traditional or authentic than the group which was better known as reacting to new possibilities through cargo cults? Given this broad context, however, it is becoming clear that questions about the meaning of artefacts are increasingly tied up with larger issues about whether the world is literally becoming more or less meaningful, and about how far artefacts marketed with a homogenizing global meaning are given specific local meanings in the contexts in which they are consumed (e.g. Miller 1992).

THE MATERIALITY OF ARTEFACTS

The importance of considering the materiality and specificity of the world of artefacts should now be clear. A discussion of the way in which we order things and are in turn ordered by things certainly makes 'things' sound very orderly. In practice, however, artefacts may relate more to a multiplicity of meanings and identities, and the relations between form and meaning may be complex and ambiguous. The ingenuity displayed by human societies in investing the world with meaning is one of the abiding lessons of anthropology, and it is very difficult therefore to insist that artefacts always *do* this or *are* that. It is, however, possible to argue that objects, by their nature, tend to lend themselves to certain kinds of cultural appropriation. In constructing such an argument around the intrinsic potential of artefacts, their very physicality must play a major part.

The specificity of artefacts is considered here first by way of a critical account of that approach which centres on the meaning of artefacts in the narrower sense based on an analogy with language. From this there follows a concern with the differences between the artefactual and linguistic domains. While in linguistics the study of semantics (reference) and syntax (grammar) has tended to predominate over the study of pragmatics (context), we may expect an anthropological approach which is sensitive to the relativity of context to emphasize pragmatics.

We have already seen that approaches to material culture have often been profoundly influenced by ideas derived from the study of language. Both structuralist techniques for examining the internal relations and oppositions between objects, understood as parts of relatively closed systems, and the complementary techniques of semiotics which examine the reference of objects as signs, have been applied to artefacts. To make the analogy with language work, however, artefacts have tended to be detached from their physical nature and functional context and to be treated as relatively arbitrary signs formed through the application of contrast, making them potential meaningful units which could then be combined to produce something resembling a text. The influence of linguistics continues in the framework of trends in post-structuralist analysis, which has tended to focus upon the hidden agenda of messages, the dominant myths which are promulgated through language. Influential writers in this tradition, from Barthes (1973) to Baudrillard (1981), have emphasized the use of mundane artefacts as carriers of these myths, which they have seen it as their task to expose to scrutiny.

The linguistic analogy has proved very fruitful in demonstrating the symbolic malleability and power of artefacts, but it also has its limitations. Artefacts are not words, and the differences between them may provide further clues as to what artefacts really are. Langer long ago pointed out (1942: 90–3) that language always works through sequences of sounds, and that as examples of what she called 'discursive' forms, linguistic utterances *unfold* as meaning. By contrast, objects are typically what she termed 'presentational' forms − that is, they present themselves with all their aspects at one time. Compared with words, artefacts much less often have clear propositional content, and the patterns and distinctions found may not necessarily correspond to units of meaning. Although certain anthropologists have claimed to be able to reveal grammar-like structures in objects, these are generally much looser and do not have the same necessity as grammar in language. Clearly objects relate to wider perceptual functions than do words. Remarkably subtle distinctions can be evoked through smell, taste, touch and most especially sight; by comparison, language may appear as a clumsy vehicle for the conveyance of difference. Try to describe in words the difference in smell between two kinds of fish, or the shape of two different shirts! This subtlety can also be seen in the extremes of personal identification. The problem of choosing between hundreds of pairs of shoes is most often caused less because we are spoilt for choice, and more because of the extraordinary feeling that despite the diversity not one of these pairs is quite right for us. To recall such a familiar experience helps us to acknowledge the subtleties in the way we differentiate between objects as meaningful forms and so to resolve the anthropological puzzle of why, say, one particular representation of a crocodile was an acceptable totemic representation while another, apparently almost identical to the first, had to be discarded.

The central difference lies, in the physicality of objects, however. Earlier (p. 398) it was suggested there is little to be gained through attempting to impose a rigorous distinction between the artefactual world and the natural world; later on (p. 403) it was suggested that objects operate with particular effectiveness as ideology, making the taxonomic orders of a particular culture appear to the individual as second nature. These two observations are clearly connected. Objects often appear as more 'natural' than words, in that we come across them in the main as already existing things, unlike at least spoken language, which is produced in front of us. This quality of artefacts helps, as it were, to entrance us, to cause us to forget that they are indeed artefacts, embodiments of cultural codes, rather than simply the natural environment within which we live. Artefacts and their physicality tend to become implicated in a wide variety of similar ambiguities. In English there is a strong sense of instrumental function, and it is commonly by their functions that artefacts are semantically labelled − e.g. 'frying pan' or 'hammer'. Nevertheless, for most ordinary artefacts it is extremely difficult to determine any clear boundary between functionally based and purely decorative aspects of form (see Wynn's discussion of this problem in Article 6). Most pots have as their functional role the act of containing some substance, but the diversity of shape is only relatively loosely related to the range of needs for particular kinds of containment (Miller 1985: 51–74). If decoration communicates symbolically, can this be said to be its function? This ambiguity reinforces that between the natural and the artefactual, because the relation between form and function is generally taken to be 'natural', while other elements of form are more evidently expressive of a deliberate ordering. In all such cases, objects appear to orient us in the world, but in a way that remains largely implicit.

In a sense artefacts have a certain 'humility' in that they are reticent about revealing their power to determine what is socially conceivable. Curiously, it is precisely their physicality which makes them at once so concrete and evident, but at the same time causes them to be assimilated into unconscious and unquestioned knowledge. When viewing a work of art, it is often the frame which determines our perception of the quality of the content (that is, it cues us in to the fact that we are about to have an aesthetic experience), when the contained item, left to itself, might well have failed to evoke the 'proper' response. In a similar fashion, 'subtle' cosmetics are intended to enhance the attractiveness of the face without drawing attention to themselves. Thus artefacts may be most effective in determining our perception when they express a sense of humility in which they avoid becoming the direct focus of our attention. Many artefacts, whether house decorations or daily clothing, incline to this position on the borders of our perception rather than, as with the picture itself, capturing the focus of our gaze. They most often attract our attention when we feel there is either something new or something wrong about them.

Ethnographic findings seem to have an almost perverse tendency to refute any generalization produced by anthropological theory. Clearly words are capable of having any of the effects and properties which have here been associated with objects. As Derrida's (1977) work has shown, the difference in relative physicality between written and oral language may be of enormous significance. Equally, objects may occupy almost any of the propositional niches utilized by words. Thus the argument presented above has to be seen as one of tendencies rather than absolutes. However, although a particular society may refuse to exploit a given potential, the physical properties of artefacts nevertheless lend themselves to their being used to construct this sense of a frame,which does not have to pass through consciousness in order constantly to reconstruct the context of our experience of the world.

THE SPECIFICITY OF ARTEFACTS

Apart from these general qualities of artefacts, which arise from their physical materiality, they also have many qualities which are important for understanding their specific place in particular social contexts. Each of these qualities may become a focus within material culture studies, but for purposes of illustration only one, that of temporality, is discussed in any detail here. Artefacts are manufactured objects which may reveal in their form the technology used, but may equally seek to hide it. Items such as craft products may be conspicuously hand-made to highlight the contrast with industrial goods; alternatively, the stoneworker may seek to emulate the prestige of the blacksmith by using techniques which are inefficient when applied to stone but create a similar style, which in that particular context underwrites status. Again the instrumental function of an object may be exploited symbolically, or buried under decorative ornament. Artefacts may establish an individualistic relation, as with the emblem of a ruler or the prized blue jeans of a teenager, or they may stand for a wider social group such as a nation state. An object may confer added prestige through its having been imported from a considerable distance, through being rare or made from a rare raw material. An object may derive its specific meaning as part of an emergent style or order, such as a particular ceramic style in ancient China or a style of cathedral building seen as quintessentially Gothic.

The point to bear in mind is that all of these potential symbolic elements are exploitations of the specific nature of artefacts, is, that they are manufactured, come from a particular place and are used in particular ways. Size itself can be expressive, as in monumentality or, at the other extreme, in the concept of the 'petite', where small is also feminine. The vast symbolic potential to be drawn from exploiting the attributes of things is limited only by the ingenuity of a particular social group. In order to provide more substantial illustration of this symbolic potential and the resourcefulness of cultures in exploiting it, I now turn, in what follows, to consider the temporality of artefacts. Temporality is intrinsic to objects in the sense that there is always a period of time between their creation and the moment they are being considered, but this temporal quality may be either entirely inconsequential or, as with an heirloom, the element which endows the object with meaning.

THINGS, PERSONS AND TIME

To examine the relationship between the meaning of artefacts and temporality, three situations will be explored. In the first, the artefact, or at least that which the artefact represents, outlasts persons and thus becomes the vehicle by which persons attempt to transcend their own temporal limits. In the second situation there is some temporal equivalence between persons and artefacts which tends to give rise to issues of representation. In the third, artefacts are regarded as relatively ephemeral compared with persons, and the focus is then on the manner in which identity is carried along by the flood of transforming things. By drawing examples from various cultural contexts I do not mean to suggest their likeness; on the contrary, what is revealed is the very diverse manner in which the same relation between time and artefact is constructed and used in the manifold contexts of different human groups.

Longevity

All people initially experience the world as something given by history rather than something they create. The child struggles to control, often vicariously through play, at least some elements of the encountered world, but this desire is constantly frustrated by ever-expanding vistas of the massiveness of this already created world. Among the items encountered are those which children may be taught to treat with special respect because they are icons of identity, commonly tokens of the longevity of their culture and of cross-generational continuity − a heritage which must never be lost because it has always existed. For example, in many Australian Aboriginal groups the male youth is presented at puberty with the sacred objects which have come down from the ancestors of the Dreamtime (the period in which the world was first created). The identity of an Indian peasant may be focused upon a piece of land that has been owned by the family for generations. The Jew may be constantly reminded of ritual knowledge enshrined in books which only exist because each generation has maintained them in the face of persecution. In all such cases the mere fact of the previous existence of things confers responsibility at the same moment that it bestows identity. Just as persons know themselves through identification with their clan totem or with the boundary stones of their land, so it is now their duty to ensure preservation through to the next generation.

Monuments are, in general, very large material forms built specifically to embody such a notion of transcending the generations − for example to symbolize the enduring nature of a 'thousand-year Reich'. But the same notion may equally be embodied in a simple ancestral shrine. Such objects may also fix the corporate entity on which identity and responsibility should fall. In the case of a national monument such as the Eiffel Tower, it is the nation state; in the case of the burial place of a deceased relative established through geomancy, future connections are determined by specific genealogical rules. With monuments it is the quality of size which is exploited, with burials it is spatial fixity. It need not be the case that these are ideological notions foisted by small élites on the population at large; the enormous heritage industry which has developed in most industrial societies includes countless small local museums or historical shrines to industrialization, as well as engaging many groups from all classes of society in archaeological excavations amounting to a collective act of self-consecration. This does presuppose, however, that a historical identity has already been established and rendered conventional.

An irony of this process is that whereas the material objects may actually transcend the generations, the corporate groups with which they are associated are themselves likely to change. Stonehenge is now a symbol of Britain, but was probably established initially by some tribal grouping in the Wessex region, and in the intervening period has undergone many changes in its symbolic appeal. Different groups may struggle over who built Great Zimbabwe, or who should retain the Elgin marbles from the Parthenon, aware that there is much more at stake than simple historical veracity or quality of conservation. Both Constantinople and Rome have been fought over at different historical periods for their ability to confer imperial legitimacy, and the Saudi authorities who possess Mecca spatially may nevertheless find themselves confronted by conflicting spiritual claims from, for example, the Iranian *haj*. On a smaller scale, disputes may arise over access by different castes to a village temple in India. Such conflict becomes particularly poignant in the conflicting claims to rights over cemeteries lodged by archaeologists and the descendants of those buried therein. The former try to incorporate the dead in the collective heritage, the latter treat them as their specific ancestral legacy.

Weiner (1985) has noted that for Polynesian peoples such as the Maori there may develop a special category of objects termed *taonga*, which are rendered inalienable precisely because they come to evoke the ancestral past. For example, items made of nephrite may come to have individual names and 'biographies' which are held to bear witness to events at which they were present, or to owners who are now deceased (1985: 217–18). She refers to the case of a nephrite adze which was lost for seven generations but recognized on its rediscovery in 1877 when the stories associated with it were retold. Such valuables are often imbued with special meaning by virtue of the rich symbolic nexus which ties in their semantic or decorative properties with cosmological ideas relating to such events as birth, death and renewal.

Temporal identity

The second form of relationship between artefacts and persons is derived from a temporal equivalence in which objects stand for the particular states of persons at that time, so that a change in the material attributes of the person is indicative of a change in the person him- or herself. This is the relationship which commonly most concerns anthropologists, because their technique of participant observation tends to freeze the relationship between persons and artefacts in one frame of time, within which the logic of the relationship may be studied. For example, the project of Mass Observation led by the anthropologist Tom Harrison attempted to study and characterize Britain in the years before the Second World War. In one of the best-known studies the team attempted to deal with that key British institution, the pub, in Worktown. The interest was not directly in material culture but in understanding class, and the social implications of the pub as an institution. However, in order to accomplish this task a further element of material culture, clothing, became a key index. Considerable effort went into the differentiation of caps, bowler hats, ties, and so forth, and many statements fix the sociological variables in sartorial form; for example: 'caps are a working class badge, scarves around the neck instead of collar and tie usually indicate middle and lower (unskilled and semi-skilled) working class – but they are not necessarily invariable indications' (Mass Observation 1987: 144). So we are informed that for their clientele of beerhouse vaults between week-night and Saturday, the proportion of caps goes down from 92 to 80 per cent while that of bowlers goes up from 0 to 6 per cent. This is set against the observation that, contrary to expectations, Sundays show less of a move to respectable clothing than Saturdays. This, in turn, starts a chain of analysis leading to an important discussion of the relationship between the place of religion and of drinking for the inhabitants of the town (1987: 140–67), according to which a change in an individual's dress sense becomes the instrument for signifying a desire to change his or her social position.

Similarly, in the anthropology of South Asia the focus of most ethnographic attention has been the institution of caste, and initially the study of food preparation, transaction and ingestion was developed simply because it seemed to provide the best set of indicators for an 'objective' study of caste hierarchy that would complement verbal accounts. It was argued that if you examined who actually accepted particular kinds of food from whom, then this would provide a picture of caste hierarchy in practice. Increasingly, however, it was appreciated that – partly because Hinduism has a much more sustained philosophy of the direct relationship between that which is ingested and the resultant qualities of the person ingesting – the study of food has to become integral to the understanding of caste as much more than a simple system of sociological categorization. A classification is not just made manifest through its correlation with material forms, but the experience of a particular identity and sense of being is created through the very sensual qualities involved in preparing and ingesting foodstuffs (compare Marriot 1968 with Marriot 1976). In moving from meaning to the meaningful, from cognitive to sensual expression, what is involved is not only the anthropological task of 'translating' another culture through widening the power of evocation, but a more profound appreciation of the manner by which culture reveals itself as a constitutive process.

Since my concern in this section is neither with the longevity nor with the transience of artefacts, but rather with their ability to relate to the larger cultural project of the moment, it is appropriate to consider the possibility of using changes in the materials as a means of investigating cultural change. Shanks and Tilley (1986: 172–240), for example, have investigated the different approaches taken to alcoholism by the Swedish and British states, as indicated in the designs of beer cans. Their work exemplifies an emphasis on the precise forms of the material artefacts themselves, which are then related to the wider contexts of their production. One hundred and twenty beer cans, half from each country, were subjected to a formidable analysis including 45 variables such as forms of lettering or whether or not there was a design band around the top of the can. Detailed accounts were then provided of representational designs, names and other features on the can, and these in turn were related to a systematic analysis of advertisements, articles in newspapers about alcoholism, and so forth. Overall the differences in design and the manner in which alcohol is marketed were related to the distinction traced by the authors over the last century according to which the Swedish state has tended to take a more interventionist stance influenced by earlier prohibitionist tendencies, which, as Shanks and Tilley put it (following Foucault), were linked to a desire to discipline its population (1986: 191–8). In Britain, by contrast, the state took a more *laissez-faire* but also more fiscally minded approach, emphasizing the possibilities for raising income through taxation.

Shanks and Tilley's work is directed to archaeologists, who are as much concerned as are anthropologists with questions of the meaning of artefacts. The task of the archaeologist is to reconstruct past societies on the basis of their material remains, and this in turn must depend a good deal on how the relationship between persons and artefacts is understood. In the past the tendency has been to invert the social — anthropological bias by making persons merely representations of the movements of things. Thus prehistorians documented such movements as 'the invasion of the black burnished pottery folk', or the rise of the 'jade axe peoples'. This was eventually opened out to encompass a more general concern with reconstructing the internal structure of ancient societies. Often the key sources of information for this were burials. If the grave goods buried with the deceased were highly differentiated, the society was supposed to be hierarchical; if less differentiated, it was supposed to be egalitarian. If one brooch signalled a commoner and two brooches a chief, then three brooches indicated a regional lord.

The problem with this approach may be clarified by means of a contemporary analogy. British society today includes vast differences in wealth and social status, but this would certainly not be evident from a visit to the cemeteries, where gravestones are used to express a belief about equality in death and where the most common concern of mourners is to avoid ostentation. Archaeologists are thus increasingly coming to realize that their interpretations of the nature of ancient societies are dependent upon developing a more sophisticated and less mechanical approach to the meaning of the artefacts which they uncover (e.g. Hodder 1986).

Transience

Transience, as also longevity, is a potential property of the relationship between persons and things, but its cultural significance may vary considerably. It is usually assumed that a concern with the ephemeral nature of artefacts is a peculiar condition of modernity, but, as with most other characteristics of being modern, there is no a priori reason to suppose that there are not, or have not been, other societies which have focused upon this quality of objects as having profound implications for the nature of their world. Kuechler (1988) has pointed out, with respect to the Malangan wooden funerary carvings of New Ireland, that although these are now incorporated as art objects in museums around the world, the major consideration in their original use in rituals associated with death was that they would rot away, and in this context even the smells associated with this process of deterioration were of central importance in the cosmology of the people concerned.

On the island of Trinidad certain sections of the community are generally regarded as having a particular penchant for style (Miller, in press). Considerable effort and expense may be directed towards originality in constructing effective displays. Here it is the very transient quality of industrial goods which is the focus of concern. Although international fashions are exploited, the mere following of fashion is left to the more conservative elements in the community, since style demands a more creative appropriation and juxtaposition of items. Individuals involved in this pursuit of style are often also characterized as reacting against those institutional and structural mechanisms which would otherwise place them in more stable and more hierarchical frameworks. There may be an unwillingness to associate closely with any occupation or social role. Many of the familiar structural forms of kinship may be denied, for example through recognizing little sense of obligation towards persons simply on the basis of some genealogical connection, preferring pragmatic and dyadic forms of social association.

The use of material culture in transitory modes in which no lasting or affective relationship is built up with any particular objects is clearly related to the search for autonomy and independence in these other arenas. The particular mode may well be related to a strongly expressed concern for freedom whose historical roots may go back to the experience of slavery and indentured labour of the ancestors of many of those concerned. It has certainly been affected by the rise of industrialization and mass consumption, in this case paid for largely by profits from an oil-based economy. Indeed, mass consumption may be taking over from kinship as the main vehicle by which this historical project of freedom may be objectified.

In such circumstances there are considerable advantages to be gained from moving away from a medium such as kinship where transience is generally condemned by those whose models of proper family relations are developed elsewhere. By concentrating instead on the medium of fashion, the sense of style which is created may be positively expressed and blessed by international canons which favour creativity in this expressive field. Thus what locally may be the same cultural project, that is of creating an experience of transience as freedom, is either condemned or envied, depending upon whether a social or a material medium is used to express it. Style, far from being superficial, has here become the central instrument by which identity is constructed without its being made subservient to social institutional structures. Within the same society there is an opposing tendency associated with highly structured kinship and emphasis on intergenerational continuity. In this case the accumulation of property and goods, and the control over resources which goes with it, is seen to provide an alternative route to freedom from control by others, and thereby to emancipation.

An analysis such as that presented above assumes that people are able to appropriate and transform the products of international manufacture, in this case largely because tendencies in economic development happen to have been pre-empted by tendencies in the development of local culture. In many other contexts it seems that the capacity of transience to demolish received structures is not matched by the possibilities of appropriation, and the result is closer to the experience of alienation so often observed in the rise and spread of mass and transient material culture. Unfortunately, anthropologists have so far paid very little attention to the analysis of industrial material culture and mass consumption, and the articulation between macro-economic shifts and the local elaboration of cultural projects is little understood. Such issues are of considerable importance today, particularly because it is becoming increasingly evident that in much of the developing world, expenditure patterns have moved swiftly towards prioritizing objects such as televisions and new forms of clothing, often at the expense of those priorities proposed by international agencies, such as achieving adequate levels of nutrition and shelter. We are nowadays confronted with images of decaying slums festooned with cars and television aerials.

EMBODIMENT AND OBJECTIFICATION: AGAINST A DUALISM OF ARTEFACTS AND PERSONS

So far in this article we have considered the idea that the meaning of artefacts goes beyond the narrow cognitive questions of sense and reference, we have examined the dialectical interplay between ordering objects and being ordered by them, we have explored the implications of their physicality and their differences from the words of language, and we have discussed their symbolic qualities in regard to the factor of time. To conclude, I now lift the argument onto a slightly more abstract level to challenge the most basic of the assumptions underwriting consideration of these questions: that we are dealing with the relations between two quite separate kinds of entities, namely persons and things.

For a long time anthropologists have assumed that a pristine level of 'social relations' furnishes the authentic foundation for what they are supposed to be studying. The theoretical rationale for this approach was provided by Durkheim, and the study of kinship provided its ethnographic substance. Thus whatever cultural domain was being investigated was ultimately treated as symbolic of underlying social relations. The meanings of artefacts were always seen to lie in their positioning within such symbolic systems. When the term 'constituting' became fashionable in the literature, it seemed to grant a more active role to these cultural forms than the more passive-sounding notion of 'symbolizing', and this reflected a move from a simple 'social' anthropology towards a sense of 'cultural' anthropology in which social forms are created by the same media that express them. An example of this approach was presented in the previous section, where the use of fashion was seen to be in some sense equivalent to kinship in expressing and constructing a historically situated cultural project. Recently, further attempts have been made to erode the asymmetry in the relationship between social relations and cultural forms.

In theoretical writings which have come to be known as 'post-modernist' or 'post-structuralist' (e.g. Foucault 1970) the demise of this act of reference to social relations was in one sense welcomed, since it was suggested that the idea of a pure humanity or individual person was a fiction of relatively recent times which virtually deified the human in order to fill the void left by a secular rejection of the divine (e.g. Barthes 1977: 142–8, Foucault 1977: 113–18). However, the trend was also seen as a negative one in that it was said to reflect a new era of mass commodities in which objects refer mainly to lifestyles comprising the association with other sets of objects, and have lost the ability to relate 'authentically' to any cultural project (e.g. Baudrillard 1981).

One area in which anthropologists have been most effective in establishing an image of culture which is not based on a dualistic opposition of persons and artefacts is in the literature on gifts and gift exchange, as established originally by Mauss and subsequently developed mainly in writings on Melanesia and the Pacific (see Article 33). In his essay of 1925 on *The Gift*, Mauss (1954) argued that the gift had to be returned because it carried with it a sense of the inalienable – that is, something which could never really be given away. This something involved, among other elements, the sense that the object retained attributes of the person by whom it was given, and, furthermore, the object was seen to embody a relationship which exists between persons by virtue of their mutual obligation to give and return gifts. This also helped to account for the observation that persons might be exchanged as gifts in a manner which did not diminish their sense of humanity or value, since to be so exchanged (as, for example, with the 'gift' of a bride in marriage) is not to be reduced to some less exalted, thing-like status. In recent anthropological literature, especially on Melanesian societies, the subtleties of such processes have been much further elaborated (e.g. Strathern 1988).

Unfortunately, Mauss also established a means by which this new understanding could be incorporated into a romantic primitivism, according to which small-scale societies could be seen as having a totalizing vision which repudiates any simple distinction between persons and things. These societies were then contrasted with those which were based on commodity exchange and which, following Marx, were seen to have gone to the other extreme in not only creating this fundamental dualism but also establishing institutions in which persons achieve a sense of humanity only to lose it through being reduced to thing-like status.

As I noted at the beginning of this article (pp. 396–7), these concerns have been paramount in establishing the framework within which scholars have considered the question of the meaning of artefacts. For example, Durkheim's writings on – and concern with – mass consumption (Williams 1982: 322–42) help us to understand why he developed a 'social' rather than a 'cultural' approach. This may also explain why anthropologists, who have successfully elucidated how objects like canoes or spears may be caught up in complex networks of symbolic meaning connecting diverse domains within small-scale societies, nevertheless tend to join the post-modernists in dismissing the possibility of a similarly complex exegesis of industrial artefacts.

There have, however, been some recent attempts to soften this dualism between persons and objects, or between gifts and commodities. Appadurai (1986: 3–63), for example, has attempted to do this by examining the literature on exchange, while Miller (1987) explores the manner in which the notion of objectification might be used to overcome a dualistic or reductionist approach to material culture. Ironically, while writers on post-modernism discover that artefacts no longer seem to make reference to 'people', this may in part be because commodities as well as gifts have the capacity to construct cultural projects wherein there is no simple dichotomy between things and persons. Indeed, anthropologists have exaggerated the totalizing holism of small-scale social groups, often ignoring contradictions and feelings of alienation, while on the other hand failing to see the strategies by which people in industrial societies attempt to appropriate their own material culture.

It may be preferable in all cases to resist the assumption, which is given in the experience of ethnography, that we are dealing with an already established set of objects whose social meaning has to be (retrospectively) determined. For, in reality, such objects only come into being through prior acts of construction, and in the process of their manufacture they manifest a particular system of categorization. Likewise, persons only come into being, with the particular cultural identities that they have, through a process of socialization involving these same material taxonomies. The process does not stop with socialization, however, for material forms remain as one of the key media through which people conduct their constant struggles over identity and confront the contradictions and ambiguities that face them in their daily lives. To go beyond a dualistic approach means recognizing that the continual process by which meaning is given to things is the same process by which meaning is given to lives.

REFERENCES

Appadurai, A. (1986) 'Introduction', in A. Appadurai (ed.) *The Social Life of Things*, Cambridge: Cambridge University Press.
Barthes, R. (1973) *Mythologies*, London: Paladin.
—— (1977) *Image–Music–Text*, London: Fontana.

Baudrillard, J. (1981) *For a Critique of the Political Economy of the Sign*, St Louis: Telos Press.

Bourdieu, P. (1977) *Outline of a Theory of Practice*, Cambridge: Cambridge University Press.

Derrida, J. (1977) *Of Grammatology*, Baltimore: Johns Hopkins University Press.

Faris, J. (1972) *Nuba Personal Art*, London: Duckworth.

Forrest, J. (1988) *Lord I'm Coming Home*, Ithaca, NY: Cornell University Press.

Forty, A. (1986) *Objects of Desire*, London: Thames & Hudson.

Foucault, M. (1970) *The Order of Things*, London: Tavistock.

—— (1977) *Language, Counter-Memory, Practice*, Ithaca, NY: Cornell University Press.

Freyre, G. (1986). *The Masters and the Slaves*, Berkeley: University of California Press.

Gilsenan, M. (1982) *Recognizing Islam*, London: Croom Helm.

Glassie, H. (1975) *Folk Housing in Middle Virginia*, Knoxville: University of Tennessee Press.

Hebdige, D. (1988) *Hiding in the Light*, London: Routledge.

Hodder, I. (1986) *Reading the Past*, Cambridge: Cambridge University Press.

Kuechler, S. (1988) 'Malangan: objects, sacrifice and the production of memory', *American Ethnologist* 15(4): 625–37.

Langer, S. (1942) *Philosophy in a New Key*, Cambridge, Mass.: Harvard University Press.

Larrain, J. (1979) *The Concept of Ideology*, London: Hutchinson.

Lévi-Strauss, C. (1982) *The Way of the Masks*, Seattle: University of Washington Press.

Marriot, M. (1968) 'Caste ranking and food transactions: a matrix analysis', in M. Singer and B. Cohn (eds) *Structure and Change in Indian Society*, Chicago: Aldine.

—— (1976) 'Hindu transactions: diversity without dualism', in B. Kapferer (ed.) *Transactions and Meaning: Directions in the Analysis of Exchange and Symbolic Behaviour*, Philadelphia: Institute for the Study of Human Issues.

Mass Observation (1987) *The Pub and the People*, London: Century Hutchinson.

Mauss, M. (1954) *The Gift*, London: Cohen & West.

Miller, D. (1985) *Artefacts as Categories*, Cambridge: Cambridge University Press.

—— (1987) *Material Culture and Mass Consumption*, Oxford: Blackwell.

—— (in press) *Modernity: An Ethnographic Approach*, Oxford: Berg.

Miller, D. and Tilley, C. (eds) (1984) *Ideology, Power and Prehistory*, Cambridge: Cambridge University Press.

Munn, N. (1986) *The Fame of Gawa*, Cambridge: Cambridge University Press.

Shanks, M. and Tilley, C. (1986) *Re-constructing Archaeology*, Cambridge: Cambridge University Press.

Simmel, G. (1968) *The Conflict in Modern Culture and Other Essays*, New York: New York Teachers College Press.

Steadman, P. (1979) *The Evolution of Designs*, Cambridge: Cambridge University Press.

Strathern, M. (1988) *The Gender of the Gift*, Berkeley: University of California Press.

Weiner, A. (1985) 'Inalienable wealth', *American Ethnologist* 12(2): 210–27.

Williams, R. (1982) *Dream Worlds*, Berkeley: University of California Press.

FURTHER READING

Appadurai, A. (ed.) (1986) *The Social Life of Things: Commodities in Cultural Perspective*, Cambridge: Cambridge University Press.

Bourdieu, P. (1977) *Outline of a Theory of Practice*, Cambridge: Cambridge University Press.
—— (1984) *Distinction: A Social Critique of the Judgement of Taste*, London: Routledge & Kegan Paul.
Douglas, M. (ed.) (1987) *Constructive Drinking: Perspectives on Drink from Anthropology*, Cambridge: Cambridge University Press.
Forty, A. (1986) *Objects of Desire*, London: Thames & Hudson.
Glassie, H. (1975) *Folk Housing in Middle Virginia*, Knoxville: University of Tennessee Press.
Gombrich, E. (1979) *The Sense of Order*, London: Phaidon Press.
Guss, D. (1989) *To Weave and Sing*, Berkeley: University of California Press.
Hebdige, D. (1988) *Hiding in the Light*, London: Routledge.
MacKenzie, M. (1992) *Androgynous Objects: String Bags and Gender in Central New Guinea*, New York: Harwood Press.
Miller, D. (1987) *Material Culture and Mass Consumption*, Oxford: Blackwell.
Mintz, S. (1985) *Sweetness and Power*, New York: Viking Penguin.
Price, S. (1984) *Co-Wives and Calabashes*, Cambridge: Cambridge University Press.
Schama, S. (1987) *The Embarrassment of Riches*, London: Fontana.
Shanks, M. and Tilley, C. (1987) *Re-constructing Archaeology*, Cambridge: Cambridge University Press.
Stocking, G. (ed.) (1985) *Objects and Others: Essays on Museums and Material Culture*, Madison: University of Wisconsin Press.
Strathern, M. (1988) *The Gender of the Gift*, Berkeley: University of California Press.
Thomas, N. (1991) *Entangled Objects*, Cambridge, Mass.: Harvard University Press.
Walens, S. (1981) *Feasting with Cannibals*, Princeton: Princeton University Press.
Weiner, A. and Schneider, J. (eds) (1989) *Cloth and Human Experience*, Washington: Smithsonian Institution Press.

16

TECHNOLOGY

François Sigaut

In order properly to speak about techniques, one has first of all to know something about them. Now there is a science that deals with techniques, called technology, which, in France, has not received the recognition it deserves.

(Marcel Mauss 1948: 71)

Broadly speaking, technology is the way people do things.

(Lynn White, Jr 1940: 141)

INTRODUCTION TO A SCIENCE OF TECHNICS

Of all aspects of social life, contemporary anthropologists are perhaps most reticent about technics. This was not the case in the nineteenth century; but since the first half of the twentieth, the anthropology of technics has been undeniably neglected. In English-speaking countries, interest began to decline around the turn of the century and reached its low point about 1960 (Oswalt 1976: 8–9, 213–18, Sturtevant 1969). The story has been somewhat different on the Continent. In Central Europe, the folklorists (*Volkskunde*), the so-called *Kulturkreise* school and the linguistic *Wörter und Sachen* school retained a more favourable attitude for a time, but at the price of cutting themselves off from other anthropological currents. In France, beginning in 1935, André Leroi-Gourhan and A. G. Haudricourt inspired a number of studies, but researchers of their bent remained in the minority and relatively isolated in their own country (Digard 1979). On the whole, it was as though technics were not an ordinary object of anthropology: either one ignored them or one cut oneself off from one's colleagues. It was a rare anthropologist indeed who was honest enough to set down in black and white his reservations or uneasiness on the subject (Malinowski 1935, 1: 240, Pouillon 1976: 64).

But it is not only anthropologists who feel ill at ease with technics. The same has been true of intellectual milieux at least since the appearance of writing, and true perhaps of all societies whose hierarchical structure was sufficiently developed to include an élite exempt from at least some manual tasks.

420

On the other hand, the role of technics in the history of humankind and in the differentiation of societies is so obvious that no mythology, ideology or philosophy has managed to ignore it altogether. Some arts separate human beings from other animals: fire, cooking, ornamentation. Others — farming, ceramics, weaving, metallurgy, etc. — separate some human groups from others and, according to many mythologies, civilized peoples from savages. Sometimes the arts have been regarded as the gift of a benevolent god or goddess (e.g. Triptolemus, inventor of the plough and patron of agriculture). But more often they are said to have been stolen, bringing down all manner of misfortune onto the heads of either the thief (Prometheus) or mankind in general (Genesis). Invention is double-edged, benign or malignant, as ambiguous as the civilizing hero of mythology, who is often depicted as ambitious, shifty, cunning: in short a trickster. Perhaps no other mythic figure is more widespread. He is found among peoples whose level of material culture is often considered to be the lowest, like the Australian Aborigines. But he is also alive and well today, for example in our science-fiction figure of the 'mad scientist'. The mad scientist has the same character traits as the trickster, the same adventures befall him, and he often suffers the same fate, as the victim of his own inventions. Our century has given birth to a host of mad scientists: Wells's Doctor Moreau or Čapek's Professor Rossum, the inventor of the robot ... The line is long, going back through Frankenstein and Faust to our classical Antiquity, where Daedalus was probably the prototype.

There is reason to believe therefore that, ever since their emergence as a species, human beings have puzzled over that strange thing called technics, something they acquire without knowing how, that they possess but which possesses them even more, that is not a part of them but without which they would not be what they are. I have just mentioned science fiction as a modern form of this questioning. Philosophy is another, and here again our century has been ambitious and long-winded in its pursuit of a tradition that goes back to pre-Socratic thinkers. The authors are innumerable (see for example Mitcham and Mackey 1973); I need mention only a few well-known names of the period between 1900 and 1960, such as Berdiaeff, Ellul, Heidegger, Mumford, Ortega y Gasset, Sombart and Spengler. The philosophy of technics, and the ideologies for which that philosophy furnishes one of the favourite media of expression, have a long history on which we have either only very general views (Auzias 1971, Moser 1973, Schuhl 1938) or, on the contrary, highly detailed but specialized studies (Adas 1989, Espinas 1897, Herf 1985). Although we may still be ignorant of most of this philosophical tradition, we must be aware that it exists, because it gave rise to the anthropology and history of technics proper. Two works seem to me to be perfectly paradigmatic in this respect. They are Lewis Mumford's *Technics and Civilization* (1934) and André Leroi-Gourhan's *Le Geste et la parole* (1964–5). Both are particularly clear illustrations of how history, in the first case, and anthropology, in the second, may be used to serve explicitly philosophical ends.

Philosophizing is neither an illegitimate nor a useless pursuit. But sooner or later there comes a point where reflection can go no further, and that is when the need for another type of thinking makes itself felt, one more closely tied to knowledge of its object. If its object is well chosen, this reflection will gradually become what we call a scientific discipline. The transition, which is the beginning of all science, has never been easy. It is what Durkheim had in mind when he appealed for 'social facts to be regarded as things' (1960 [1895]). And Marcel Mauss is saying the same thing in the passage cited at the head of this article. Like all other social facts, technical facts, too, must be regarded as things. We can no longer be content to approach them with our common-sense ideas or doctrines for their application. We must observe and describe them as they are, for there is no science beyond that which can be observed. Or, in other words, it is only by beginning with the task of any science – that is, by constructing its object – that the anthropology of technics can itself become a science.

It is exclusively to this science that, following in Mauss's footsteps and faithful to an ancient European ethnological custom, I apply the name *technology*. Of course this immediately raises a problem of nomenclature. For this sense of 'technology' conflicts with the originally Anglo-American usage, which in the last thirty years has become widespread, and according to which the term 'technology' applies to 'a kind of refined technique, a sophisticated technique' (Daumas 1965: xvii), to 'highly sophisticated techniques of modern engineering' (Rapp 1974: vii) or, in short, to those technics that are informed by a relatively scientific content and methods.

It is clear that this line of reasoning can only lead us astray. For how are we to distinguish in practice between a scientific technique and an unscientific one? Once we go beyond commonly accepted appearances, we soon see that not only is the problem insoluble, it also leads us away from our goal. For instead of constructing our object, we find ourselves discussing one of the criteria which enables us to break it down; a criterion whose real import is impossible to gauge for lack of comparison. The notion of technology, in today's common parlance, is one of those prenotions of which Durkheim warned, 'It is not by developing [these prenotions], however you may go about it, that you will ever discover the laws of reality' (1960 [1895]: 16). This judgement is confirmed by the fact that attempts to define technology in this perspective usually turn out to be contradictory (Ingold 1988) and, in the end, as useless as they are numerous (Sigaut 1985).

Let there be no ambiguity. Technology is a science; and because technical facts are facts of human activity, it is a human science, a branch of anthropology. Technology is to technics what every science is or would be to its object, what linguistics is to language, for instance, or ethology to behaviour. The two analogies are all the more relevant as techniques are one aspect of behaviour, or, better, they are at the same time a product, a part and a prerequisite of culture, just as Lévi-Strauss said of language (1958: 78).

422

These features do not constitute a definition, and far be it from me to propose one. For while it was necessary to eliminate any ambiguity concerning technology as a scientific approach, it would be premature at this stage to attempt a definition of technics which might lock us into common-sense categories. A few definitions do exist, but only a few: White's, 'the way people do things' (1940: 142), is no doubt the broadest; and Mauss's is probably the most elaborate: 'A technique is any set of movements or acts, usually and mostly manual, organized and traditional, combined to achieve a known physical, chemical or organic goal' (1948: 73). But for our purposes such definitions are only so many declarations of intent. While they are useful for directing our gaze, they cannot tell us what we will see. And, above all, they are no substitute for constructing our own object through observation and description, that is through the work of *technography*.

It is not for the pleasure of introducing yet another neologism that I use this term; nor is it all that new, since it can be found in the writings of such nineteenth-century authors as Reuleaux (1884: 76) and Mason (1888: 515). I have a specific reason. It has long been accepted that it is fieldwork, ethnographic investigation, that makes the difference between scientific anthropology and anecdote or speculation. Our area is no different: without technography, there can be no truly scientific technology. And there is the rub. 'To describe the facts of a culture with anything like the necessary detail would result in an unreadable catalogue', writes Heider (1970: 241), who confesses his own inability to solve the problem. But how could he have found a solution in the absence, for the last three-quarters of a century, of any established tradition of research on the subject?

The obstacle is so formidable that anthropologists are not the only ones to have balked at it. Beginning in the seventeenth century, a number of philosophers and engineers have voiced the need for a true science of technics based on description and analysis. The most memorable names are Leibniz (1646–1716), Polhem (1661–1751), Diderot (1713–84), Beckmann (1739–1811), Reuleaux (1829–1905) and Simondon (1924–89), and the potential list is much longer. But these men were scattered and isolated, so that their efforts ended in failure or at least fell into oblivion (Guillerme and Sebestik 1966, Sebestik 1983, Sigaut 1987a, Simondon 1969, *Techniques et culture* 1987). But not forever, for there will always be non-conformists who refuse to allow that the 'mechanical kingdom' – or 'technonature', as some call the world that we have made for ourselves – should continue to be that part of our surroundings about which we know the least. This refusal runs like a thread through the work of the scholars listed above. But it was perhaps Lafitte (1884–1966) who expressed it best. 'Every day', he wrote, 'the natural phenomena produced within machines give rise to many remarkable works adding daily to our knowledge in mechanics, physics and chemistry. But the machines are never considered as phenomena themselves. So the study of machinery proper, as an independent science, does not exist' (Lafitte 1972 [1932]: 16–17).

At the end of his essay, Lafitte came to the conclusion that the science of machines, which he called 'mechanology', is a social science, a branch of sociology (1972 [1932]: 109). Here engineer and anthropologist meet, for Lafitte's mechanology is manifestly the same as the ethnologists' technology. Both have the same purpose: to understand technical facts for what they are, namely social facts.

DESCRIBING TECHNICAL FACTS: OPERATIONS, PATHS AND NETWORKS

Our starting point, then, must be the observation of facts. But which facts? We cannot simply go out and observe techniques, since we do not yet know what they look like. What we see, to paraphrase White (1940), is 'people doing things': a neighour painting his shutters, the plumber fixing a bathroom leak, the barber cutting a customer's hair, a mechanical shovel digging a trench in the street, and so on. However dissimilar these activities may be, they all have points in common. First of all, they are actions; this is obvious but must be borne in mind. Next, they are material actions, in the sense that they all make a material change in something. Finally, they are intentional, and are so on several levels. For instance, the shovel driver deliberately digs a trench of a certain gauge: he is following instructions from his foreman. But he also knows – or someone else knows – that this trench will hold pipes, that the pipes will carry natural gas, that the natural gas will be used for cooking and for heating the houses in the area, and so on. In some ways all human activities are responses to such successive goals, which, step by step, affect every aspect of life in society; so this cannot be the feature that distinguishes technical activities from all others. What does distinguish them, perhaps, is that, as in the above examples, the social goals have taken the form of material needs, and these have become the agent's true goals. The activities we are concerned with are not simply material, they are *intentionally* material. That is perhaps their most characteristic trait.

In a sense, this remark is implicit in Mauss's definition – indeed it was already present in the system of Aristotle's causes (Mason 1895: 15). Moreover, technical action looks like a special case of what, in cybernetics, is called a goal-directed system or mechanism (Couffignal 1978: 26). Interesting though they may be, however, I will not go into these cybernetic theories here, as it would further distract us from our purpose, which is to indicate how directly to observe facts. If it is important to note that the material changes are intentional, this is because it enables us to identify these changes as the main factor that gives technical actions their meaning. In no society are ultimate social and material goals separable. But there are some activities in which the social goals have become material imperatives for their agents; and these are what we customarily call 'technical'.

In practice, this means that the goal of every action is to bring a physical system from some state to another. This can be represented as follows:

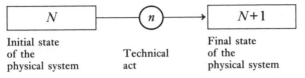

Let us further assume that the change is an elementary one, that it is either impossible or meaningless to identify any intermediate steps between (N) and ($N+1$): we will call the corresponding technical act an 'operation'. The operation is 'someone doing something' when that something is the smallest material change that can be usefully observed. The operation so defined is the first kind of technical fact that can be observed directly.

Our task is taking shape. It consists of identifying and describing the operations performed within the human group with which we are concerned. But before proceeding, it should be pointed out that no hypothesis has yet been made as to the nature of the physical systems or the changes made in them. The physical system can be the human body, as in many of Mauss's (1936) *techniques du corps* ('techniques of the body'). The changes may be as simple as moving something from one place to another; they may even be non-changes, to the extent that the goal is to retard or arrest certain undesirable natural processes, for instance in canning or freezing food. The concept of 'operation' applies to all these cases; it does not depend on the nature of either the system or the changes introduced by human actions. All that is required is that the changes must be observable by the methods of the natural sciences.

The last point is crucial, for our ability to analyse action into operations depends ultimately on the accuracy of the methods of scientific observation that are used. In the eighteenth century, for example, grinding wheat '*à la grosse*', as they called it in rural areas of France, involved a grand total of two operations: crushing the grain between the millstones and then sifting it. Today the working of a modern mill involves dozens of operations. Both the number and the precision of the operations have clearly increased with the increasing accuracy of the material means of analysing the product.

This raises another, more general, problem. What should be used as the basis for identifying operations: 'our' sciences or 'native' knowledge? The answer to this question depends on how well the one translates into the other. In the Far East, the making of 'beer' from rice or other grains has been described by many ethnographers (e.g. Toffin 1987), and the practices involved are very different from those used in making European beers. In most cases the grains are ground and cooked, and a starter that has been prepared beforehand is then added. I was personally never able to make sense of these practices, despite good, detailed descriptions, until I learned from a Japanese colleague that the starter was in fact a culture of micro-organisms that saccharified the cereal starch (Ankei 1986). In Europe, saccharification, induced by the germination of the grain (malting), is entirely separate from fermentation, and so the two operations are readily identifiable in the descriptions. In Asia, they are much harder to distinguish because the starter plays a part in both.

Of course this is only our own personal interpretation of indigenous practices, and it would be a mistake to attribute it to the people we observe, if only as empirical foreknowledge or unconscious intuition. Nevertheless, experience shows that, without such interpretation, it is indeed difficult to carry out ethnographic observation, and the results are often unusable. The problem of access to indigenous knowledge stands, then, but unless we use the methods of observation afforded us by the natural sciences, we must renounce all hope of solving it.

As a rule, operations do not occur in isolation but as parts of a sequence that can be called a 'path' [*Translator's note*: the author uses the French technical term '*filière*', which designates a die for the threading of screws or through which metal is extruded to make wire; the idea is that of an obligatory passage-way] (Gille 1978: 16). 'Path' is an almost intuitive notion, and most technical works contain a wide variety of examples (Figure 1a–c). In the example of beer making, the path is composed of two specific operations, saccharification and fermentation, along with a number of other, secondary, ones. Each path is part of a larger process. In Europe, the brewing of beer is preceded by growing barley and hops and culturing yeast; it demands a variety of devices that have had to be made by the corresponding craftsmen; it burns fuel, and so on. Step by step we realize that all the paths present in any one society are interwoven, in some way or other, into a sort of *network*, which is in fact the economic organization of that society.

It would clearly make no sense to try to describe in detail the overall economic network of a society, however simple. It would be a never-ending task, and the result would be unusable, which was exactly the difficulty raised by Heider in the passage to which I referred above. The notion of network is a limit-notion, whose sole purpose is to remind us that paths cannot be regarded as isolated units any more than can operations. What we must do is to locate the technical facts within the social space: such concepts as 'operation', 'path' and 'network' are only instruments with which to do so.

It is easy to understand that the identification of technical facts requires a consideration not only of their physical and chemical entailments but also of their positioning on a path. It was biochemistry and biology that enabled us to identify a particular stage in beer-making as 'starch saccharification'. But it is the goal of producing beer that gives meaning to 'saccharifying starch', for this operation is indispensable to the fermentation that follows. Saccharification does not appear in other food-preparation paths; or, if it does, we

(a)

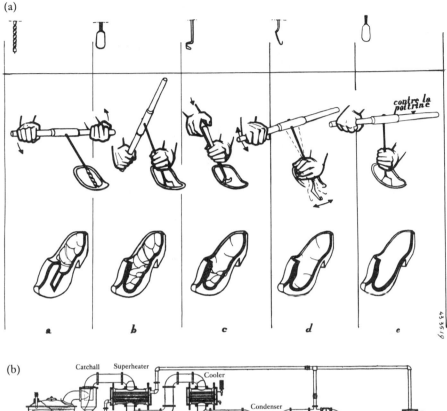

(b)

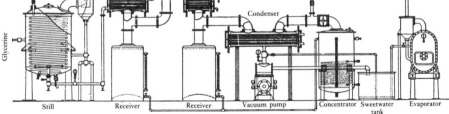

Figure 1 Some examples of how technical paths (sequences of operations) are currently represented.

(a) The making of a wooden shoe, France, 1940s. The sequence represented shows the final operations in hollowing out the shoe. It includes realistic depictions of the tools, the movements and the product. (From Enquiry no. 1810 with Auguste Becoulet, clog-maker at Cuze (Doubs), 1943, investigators Barré and Perreau, Archives of the National Museum of Popular Arts and Traditions, Paris)

(b) Production and distillation of crude glycerine, United States, 1900s. The diagram portrays realistically the machinery employed. (After Lamborn 1918: 605)

(c) Traditional processing of cereals, South India, 1980s. This is an abstract representation (a flow-chart). Materials, products and operations are identified by name only. Implements are not represented. (After Kimata 1987: 44)

427

(c)

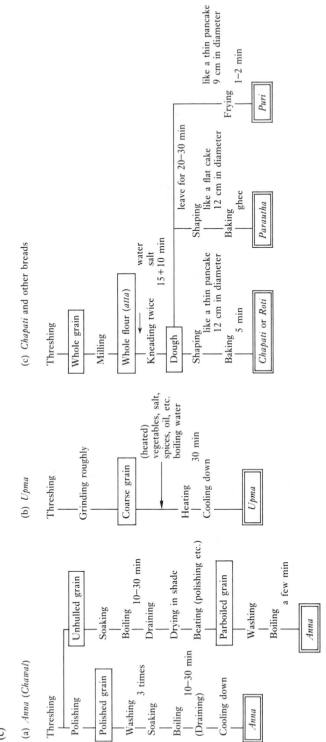

(a) *Anna (Chawal)*

Threshing
Polishing — Unhulled grain

Polished grain

Soaking
Boiling — 10–30 min
Draining
Drying in shade
Beating (polishing etc.) — Parboiled grain

Washing — 3 times
Soaking
Boiling — 10–30 min
(Draining)
Cooling down

Washing
Boiling — a few min

Anna

Anna

(b) *Upma*

Threshing
Grinding roughly — Coarse grain

(heated)
vegetables, salt, spices, oil, etc.
boiling water
Heating — 30 min
Cooling down

Upma

(c) *Chapati* and other breads

Threshing — Whole grain
Milling
Whole flour (*atta*)

Kneading twice

water
salt
15 + 10 min

Dough

Shaping — like a thin pancake 12 cm in diameter
Baking — 5 min

Chapati or *Roti*

leave for 20–30 min

Shaping — like a flat cake 12 cm in diameter
Baking — ghee

Paratha

Frying — like a thin pancake 9 cm in diameter 1–2 min

Puri

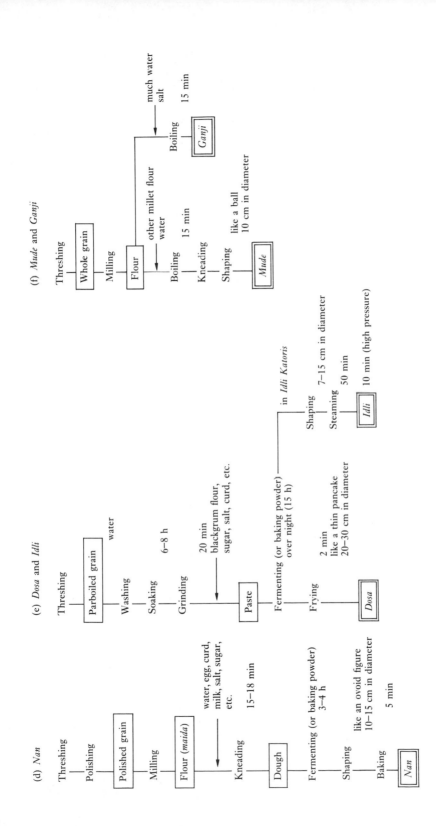

(f) *Mude* and *Ganji*

Threshing
Whole grain
Milling
Flour — other millet flour
          water
Boiling   15 min
Kneading
Shaping   like a ball
               10 cm in diameter
Mude

Boiling — much water
          salt
          15 min
Ganji

(e) *Dosa* and *Idli*

Threshing
Parboiled grain
Washing — water
Soaking   6–8 h
Grinding   20 min
               blackgrum flour,
               sugar, salt, curd, etc.
Paste
Fermenting (or baking powder) over night (15 h)
Frying   2 min
               like a thin pancake
               20–30 cm in diameter
Dosa

Shaping   in *Idli Katoris*
               7–15 cm in diameter
Steaming   50 min
               10 min (high pressure)
Idli

(d) *Nan*

Threshing
Polishing
Polished grain
Milling
Flour (*maida*)
Kneading — water, egg, curd,
           milk, salt, sugar,
           etc.
           15–18 min
Dough
Fermenting (or baking powder)
           3–4 h
Shaping   like an ovoid figure
               10–15 cm in diameter
Baking   5 min
Nan

must expect it to be in some completely different way that makes a different operation of it.

The preparation of cereals for cooking is full of such cases. In India, the parboiling of rice is a type of pre-cooking that is separate from the cooking proper, basically because it takes place before, rather than after, the grain is milled (Gariboldi 1974). The parboiled rice is then dried, which makes it possible to store it and to treat it more or less like ordinary rice. In Central America maize is treated to an operation much like parboiling, *nixtamalization* (Muchnik 1981: 28, Katz *et al.* 1974). The difference is that the kernels are not left to dry but are crushed while still moist between two stones (*mano/metate*) to produce a kind of dough, which is made into tortillas. That is why nixtamalization and parboiling are not the same, but different operations. And it is also why Mesoamerican grindstones, however much they may resemble Old World prehistoric stones, must be regarded as different tools with a different functional significance.

All of this points to one conclusion: defining an operation by its physico-chemical properties is not enough to identify it properly. Its location on the path must also be defined. 'Crushing', 'cutting', 'washing', 'drying', 'sifting' and 'kneading' are not operations but empirical or indigenous categories of action. They have some meaning on a physico-chemical level, and that is why they are handy tags – all too handy, perhaps. For the purposes of technological analysis, however, unless they are redefined in terms of rigorously observed operations, such tags are insufficient, or worse, a source of error. We must know exactly not only what is crushed, cut up or washed, but also why – that is, where along the path the action of crushing, cutting, etc. occurs. In eighteenth-century Europe, fallow land was ploughed several times, at set times of the year; each ploughing had its particular characteristics and name ('fallowing', 'stirring', 'laying up', and so on): each of these ploughings was an observable reality, while 'ploughing' in general is only an abstraction (Sigaut 1977). Because operations can be observed, they must be our starting point if we are not to find ourselves prisoners of purely common-sense categories.

This rule is especially important for archaeology and museology, that is for all areas of study that start from the physical object, the tool. It is obviously necessary to study artefacts because they are often all we have. But given our ignorance of the true nature of the operations in which they were used, there is a serious danger of grouping them arbitrarily. Our own notion of 'knife', for example, is so familiar to us that we have a hard time seeing beyond it. Thus Leroi-Gourhan (1965, 2: 125) felt confident enough to write that 'the palaeontology of the knife can be traced back without a break to the first tools' (Figure 2). This statement assumes that there is only one type of knife (our own), of which others are simply more or less incidental variations. Surprisingly, the author seems unaware of the fact, reported as early as 1867 by

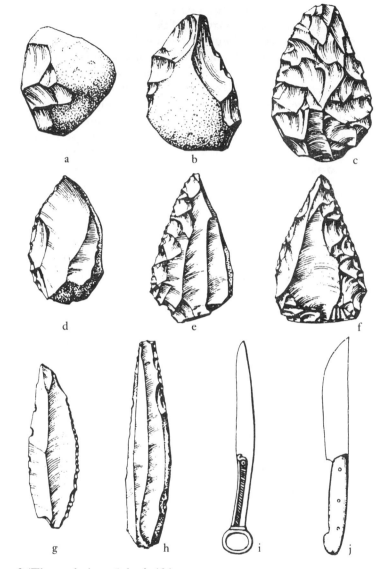

Figure 2 'The evolution of the knife'.
Lower Palaeolithic: a, chopper; b, rudimentary handaxe; c, Acheulean handaxe.
Middle Palaeolithic: d–e, scrapers; f, Levalloisian point.
Upper Palaeolithic: g, Châtelperronian point; h, Magdalenian scraper.
Bronze Age: i, knife from Siberia.
Iron Age: j, knife from contemporary Greece.
This chart was intended to illustrate, in the author's own words, that 'the palaeontology of the knife can be traced back without a break to the very first tools.' (After Leroi-Gourhan 1965, 2: 127)

Pitt-Rivers (1906: 74), that our everyday hafted knife appears only with metal, and is altogether different from cutting implements made from stone. Leroi-Gourhan seems especially unaware of the extraordinary diversity among present-day 'knives', of which Figure 3 gives only some idea, as it does not show an Inuit woman's knife (Mason 1892), an Indonesian or African reaping knife (Fischer 1937, 1939), a North American hooked knife, or the odd-looking (to our eyes) Indian stand-knife – which is held upright with the foot, the object to be cut being brought down on the knife (Figure 4) – not to mention the whole range of knives that can be bought in our modern hardware stores. Clearly nothing useful can be gained from lumping all these together as 'knives', because neither the notion of knife nor the corresponding idea of cutting really makes sense. Both belong to those prenotions that Durkheim warned us about and which are certainly largely to blame for the near-paralysis that has long gripped the anthropology of technics.

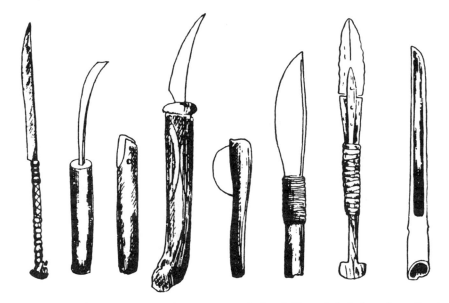

Figure 3 A textbook selection of some recent 'knives'. From left: knives from Persia and West Africa; a woodcarving knife, Eskimo; a knife for cutting the umbilical cord, Gilyak; a razor from Turkey; hunting knives, Orotche and Eskimo; a tool for scaling fish from Japan. This selection shows quite clearly that tools put together on the basis of their form ('knives') and of their mode of working ('cutting by pression'), but with their functions either unknown or ignored, cannot constitute a unit of any analytical value. (After Hirschberg and Janata 1980: 163)

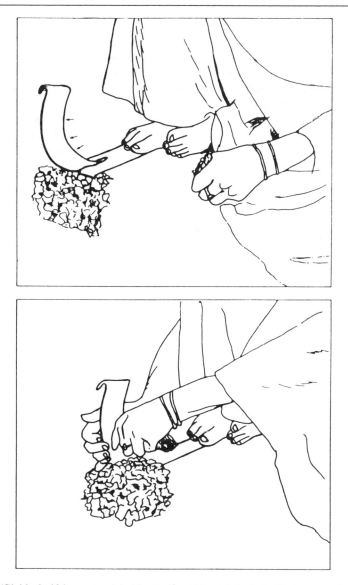

Figure 4 'Sickle-knife' or stand-knife, India. The blade is held in a vertical plane, cutting edge upward and backward, with the help of the right foot. The vegetables to be cut are pressed against the edge with both hands. In many Indian languages, this tool is given the same name as the sickle. Moreover, true sickles are sometimes used in the same way, the handle being held down by the foot instead of using the small plate shown here. Any concept of the 'knife' that does not include examples like this one is incomplete, and therefore invalid as an analytical tool. (After Mahias 1985: 180)

TECHNICAL LINEAGES AND WORKINGS

It is because I believe that the concept of 'operation' can help us go beyond this kind of prenotion that I thought it useful to stress the term. In technology, as in all empirically based sciences, analysis assumes comparison, and comparison is valid only if the elements concerned are comparable or homologous – that is, if they occupy the same place in their respective systems (Gould 1986). The example of the knife shows us that, generally speaking, common-sense categories do not embrace truly comparable items. This is not the case if we use the notion of 'operation'. As we have seen, an operation is identified both (1) by the nature of the changes it produces in a physical system and (2) by its location on a production path or network. Identifying an operation means locating it in both its physical and social spaces. When two operations have been found to occupy the same places in both, they are 'homologous'. Then it is possible to compare the various ways in which these operations are performed by different (or sometimes the same) human groups. On the whole, the ways will be different, and it is to these different ways of carrying out homologous operations that we apply the term 'techniques'. Having reached this point, we have come full circle to White's definition, 'the way people do things', having simply added a few clarifications.

To return to the example of beer: saccharification is a biochemical transformation which we know must take place in all paths of beer making and in the same place – the saccharification operations are therefore homologous. Now saccharification may be obtained in three ways: by insalivation, by the use of a starter, and by malting. These three ways constitute three *technical lineages*, which produce three families of products:

Technical lineage	*Product family*
insalivation	chicha
starter	sake
germination (malting)	beer (*sensu stricto*)

Obviously this list, which is not original (see Ankei 1986 for sources), does not exhaust the topic. Making beer is always a long process involving many operations made up of numerous variable elements. Each of these elements must in turn be analysed in this manner. But the method remains the same: it consists of plotting the analysis along two axes: a vertical y-axis, which charts the successive transformations by means of which a human group appropriates certain natural objects, and a horizontal x-axis, along which are placed the various alternatives for carrying out each transformation. The operation is the point at which the two axes intersect.

The scope of this article makes it difficult to go much beyond a general presentation of a few basic concepts. And perhaps it is not even desirable to go further, in as much as anthropologists are still in the first stages of their thinking on this subject, and have not yet achieved consensus on their conceptual vocabulary. In such circumstances, any moderately serious discussion runs the risk of turning into a semantic battle. Nevertheless, I would like to clarify two important points: first, the notion of technical lineage that has just been proposed, and second, with respect to artefacts, the ill-recognized but indispensable notion of their workings, which falls between structure and function.

The actual expression 'technical lineage' goes back some thirty years (Simondon 1969 [1958]: 40–9), but the idea is older still. It is implicit in two virtually inescapable common-sense observations: that techniques progress; and that this comes about by successive, orderly accretions, which creates an impression of linear progression (the internal-combustion engine was invented after the steam engine, the alternator after the direct-current dynamo, and so on). Perhaps no one has expressed these two concepts as vigorously as Pitt-Rivers, who took them as guidelines for his museum displays, and in particular his tool collections (Pitt-Rivers 1906, Sigaut 1990).

Technological evolutionism of this kind seems so simplistic today that it is almost too easy to criticize. But if as a theory it is indefensible, as a problem it is not, for it is not possible simply to brush away the appearances it was supposed to explain. It may seem preferable to compare the process of innovation to a game of Scrabble (Callon and Latour 1985) rather than to one of dominoes (Pitt-Rivers 1906: 19), but the two analogies point to the same process of recombining pre-existing elements with a view to achieving goals that remain basically the same: to do something better, cheaper and faster. From a diachronic perspective, then, the evolution of techniques inevitably gives the impression of a veritable orthogenesis. It has even been argued that this apparent predictability is one of the distinctive features of technical as opposed to scientific evolution, the latter being fundamentally unpredictable (Cazenobe 1987).

Clearly this traditional idea of the technical lineage lies at the heart of an extensive debate. But the concept of lineage, as presented here, falls outside this debate because it is purely descriptive. It is designed for analysing techniques as they are defined above: as alternative ways of carrying out a given operation. Techniques are first of all actions, movements of the body and limbs. But these movements are mechanical in nature and produce all sorts of results, mechanical and otherwise. It is because human movements bring into play something other than themselves that they are effective. This other thing can be called an 'effect', a term borrowed from physics, as in 'Joule effect', 'Doppler effect', etc. To come back to our example of beer-making, we have seen that there was always one indispensable operation, starch saccharification. If we compare the technographic descriptions of this operation, we obtain a host of different techniques. But, at a first level of analysis, all these techniques use one of three effects – insalivation, starter, or malting – which can be distinguished by biochemical means. Every starch saccharification technique belongs to one of the three corresponding technical lineages. Or, to put it another way, it is the use of a given effect in a given operation that identifies a technical lineage.

Contrary to the old idea of technical lineage discussed above, the concept as it has just been defined is an analytical and descriptive tool entirely free of diachronic connotations. It groups techniques in terms of their nature, not their history. This is approximately equivalent to Deforge's meaning (1985: 95–125), although he uses 'principle' where I would have used 'effect'. Other terms are possible as well (method, process, and so forth). But whichever finally prevails, it is important to understand that an effect is not a technique: it is only one of the components of a technique. Centrifuging, for example, is an effect involved in operations as dissimilar as separating uranium isotopes, testing blood, separating milk, spinning the wash, certain circus acts and fair rides, and so on. It is clear that the only thing they have in common is centrifugal motion, and that the 'centrifuge effect' can be used to identify a technique only once the operation concerned has itself been unambiguously identified.

And yet effect and technique are frequently confused. This can be explained by the important role of effects in technicians' discourse – engineering is essentially a science of effects – and by the spectacular, not to say miraculous, nature of the innovations that make use of hitherto unknown effects, like the electromagnet in the nineteenth century or today's microwave oven. The popular history of technics has always been fascinated with innovations of this kind. But it is precisely the confusion between effect and technique that has spelled the failure of all attempts to classify techniques, however necessary it was to try. It was the same confusion that led someone like Lucien Febvre (1935) to think that a distinction could be made between a technical history and a social history of technics. There is no such thing as a non-social or an asocial history of technics. What Febvre meant by a 'technical history of technics' was no doubt a history of effects; if such a history is possible, it is probably a branch of the history of science.

The current inability to distinguish, in artefacts, between workings and function is a consequence of the common confusion of effect and technique. Workings and function are classic cybernetic concepts (Couffignal 1978 [1963]: 28); we also run across them in neurobiology (Paillard 1976: 37, 1986: 1385) – indeed they are necessary for describing any goal-directed system. In technology, they correspond to two questions that spring to everyone's mind when confronted with an unfamiliar object: 'What is it for?' (function) and 'How does it work?' (workings). To these must be added the concept of structure, answering the question 'What is it?' or 'What is it made of?' It is therefore all the more startling to find technological literature commonly confusing the two (Cazenobe 1985, 1987, Sigaut 1987b). The shortcomings in the notion of 'knife' were just a case in point. We think we are talking about function when we say that a knife is used for cutting. But 'cutting alone' (Leroi-Gourhan 1965, 2: 125) is not a function, it is at most a category of working modes, and a heterogeneous and arbitrary one at that. The butcher who cuts the steak I have just ordered does not go about it in the same way or with the same kind of knife as will I, an hour later, when I cut up the steak on my plate. For 'cutting' to be a function, we must know exactly what is cut, in what context and to what precise purpose; in other words, we must know what operation we are talking about.

It is the location within a specific operation, with all the finalities this implies, that defines the function of an artefact. Its workings – how it actually works – lie in the way it intervenes in the effect that is to be produced. And its structure is the set of geometric and physical properties that result from the artefact's manufacture and use: shape, size, materials, assembly, solidity, elasticity, resistance to heat, and so on. Any study of an artefact must therefore include three levels of analysis: the structure of the artefact, the way it works and its function. On the structural level the analytic procedure is obvious: it means using all available means of investigation – geometric, physical, etc. – to describe the object itself. This is the natural starting point for the study of any object, the results of which are limited only by the capacity of the physical apparatus used. The difficulty begins with the next level. Some aspects of an object's workings are dictated by its shape (as with baskets, files, flutes): these can be discovered by the same methods of investigation as before. The archaeological study of artefacts is an example. But stone tools, the prehistorian's staple, are a very special case. If, for example, it were possible to reproduce an ancient musical scale on a lithophone (Condominas 1965: 333–53), the same experiment would make no sense with a violin. On the whole, the unknown object does not 'speak'; you have only to think of a collection of knitting needles. Museum store rooms and old hardware catalogues are full of such objects, perfectly ordinary for those familiar with them, but perfectly puzzling for the layman; and in the latter case, the interpretations can be hilarious. A humorous book presenting just such interpretations was written by Macaulay (1979), but he was making a serious point. Given an unidentified object, the means of investigation available allow us to describe its structure and to figure out something about its workings, but they do not allow us to discover much more, least of all its function. The only way to accomplish this is to proceed by analogy, that is to compare the object under study with similar objects whose function is already known. The danger comes when the analogy is implicit and therefore unreasoned. For instance, for a long time any object that resembled a sickle was considered to *be* a 'sickle' – that is, a tool used to reap cereals (function). In the case of stone-bladed sickles, this interpretation seemed to be corroborated by an examination of wear marks (silica gloss). But the available ethno-historical information on reaping techniques tells us that the sickle is anything but a primitive tool. There are at least seven lineages of reaping techniques that use tools more simple than the sickle, which is never found among peoples unacquainted with metal, nor even among most peoples who, although possessing iron tools, do not use animal power – such as those in sub-Saharan Africa and Indonesia (Sigaut 1978, 1991). Moreover, new methods of examining wear marks have shown that those observed on stone 'sickles' matched those made by the cutting of grasses, reeds, rushes, etc., as well as by the cutting of cereals proper (Anderson-Gerfaud 1983). And so today flint blades with silica gloss are no longer regarded, as they once were, as providing unequivocal evidence of agricultural activity. Their interpretation has become more complex and, at the same time, more interesting. But in order to arrive at this stage, researchers had to stop confusing workings with function.

The foregoing presentation of technographic analytical concepts may have tried the patience of some readers, and perhaps all the more sorely because it is still a very sketchy outline. Are these concepts really valid and useful, or might better ones not be found? The question must remain open until a real discussion of the subject is undertaken by contemporary anthropologists. The only conviction that I would like to share is that, without adequate concepts – those proposed above, or others – we may continue to see a more or less interesting philosophy of technics; but there can be no scientific technography, and therefore no real *anthropology* of technics.

TECHNICAL INTELLIGENCE: KNOWLEDGE AND SKILLS

So far we have been looking at technics from the outside, and have not concerned ourselves with the knowledge and skills they require. And yet the importance of these is unquestionable, as is obvious in the case of the machines and sophisticated devices that surround us. It becomes even more obvious when we consider that, aside from a bare dozen innate reflexes, the child must learn step by step, one movement at a time, every way of doing things that will make him or her a normal person. We rediscover some of these along with the child, for we adults had internalized and, in a sense, forgotten them long ago. The fading of knowledge in the process of assimilating it, or, better, literally embodying or incorporating it, is an essential feature of effective action, and thus of technics. The same holds both for machines and for the nervous system. Learning is not complete until the transmitted patterns of action have become automatic; a machine cannot be considered to be perfected until it no longer needs constant repairs or adjustments. The perfect machine has often been compared to a black box, which means not only that you can no longer see how it works, but also that you no longer need to know. An expert's nervous system is an even more impenetrable black box. 'After a century of study, it is still something of a mystery how typists can type as fast as they do' (Salthouse 1984). The knowledge built into a machine can always be retrieved, at least in theory. But we still seem ill-equipped to identify the skills embodied in our own nervous systems.

Skills should not be confused with knowledge, however; the condition for effective action is not knowledge but skills — it is not sufficient to know how a car is driven or a piano played if one is actually to be able to drive a car or play the piano. Turning knowledge into skills takes a learning period of anything from a few minutes to many years, but the learning is always necessary. Similarly, turning the idea for a machine into the real thing necessitates a whole process, which Simondon has called 'concretization' (1969 [1958]: 19–49), at the end of which the initial abstract combination of elements has disappeared, leaving in its place a new material object. It is for this reason that technics cannot simply be reduced to applied science. As early as the last century, Reuleaux (1865: viii) vigorously denounced this misconception. More recently, the example of Marconi's invention of the radio demonstrated that scientific knowledge takes on a different function, meaning and content even when it passes into the technical realm (Cazenobe 1983, 1986). In short, it stops being scientific, and that is why it is artificial and futile to search for a distinction between so-called scientific techniques and what we call crafts or traditional techniques. The 'savage mind' does not exist; the 'Neolithic paradox' even less (Lévi-Strauss 1962: 22–4). There are just two kinds of practice: in one, knowledge is subservient to material action; in the other, action is subservient to knowledge. In daily life, the two are usually so intimately bound up that they are often claimed to be indistinguishable. If we were to follow this argument, however, we would have to abandon any attempt at making distinctions with regard to human behaviour, and with it the task of analysis. In reality, the rare cases for which we have sufficiently detailed studies would seem to indicate that technical innovation does not result directly and necessarily from the progress of knowledge alone. It even happens that stating a problem in overly scientific terms leads away from the solution: a good example might be the graphiola epidemic, the epiphytic disease that, since 1970, has destroyed nearly all French and English elms. In over ten years of assiduous research, biologists have not found a cure; indeed they have not even been able to rediscover the remedy already developed in the 1850s, at the time of an earlier outbreak of the same disease (Fleury 1988)! The accumulation of knowledge follows its own logic, and this logic alone does not necessarily produce effective solutions.

In other words, knowledge is necessary for action, but the fact that it is embodied in the very process of action means that this is no longer the kind of 'knowledge' we are used to talking about — that is, knowledge as the goal of action. And this has led to a certain reticence on the subject among researchers, even when they have not preferred to ignore it altogether. Technical intelligence, if we may use this expression to designate the knowledge and skills used in the course of technical action, is nearly virgin research territory. There are few overviews of the subject (Gille 1978: 1416–77, Leplat and Pailhous 1981), especially by anthropologists (Chamoux 1978). Field studies are hardly less scarce (Chamoux 1986, Chick and Roberts 1987, Sagant 1987), and, on a point as essential as the analysis of basic body movements and postures, research has only recently begun to make a comeback (Bril 1984, Devine 1985, Kawada 1988) after a blackout that has lasted since the late 1930s (Boas 1938: 119). This blackout was part of a total eclipse which affected not only technology in general, but also neighbouring disciplines such as psychology and ethology (Ardrey 1969, Griffin 1984). It was due to a veritable censorship exercised by doctrines such as functionalism and structuralism in anthropology, and behaviourism in psychology. In the last twenty years, ethological field studies, mainly of primates, have exploded the traditional frameworks. This work has gone hand in hand with the development of what we may call experimental psycho-archaeology, with the slightly paradoxical result that the repertoire of technical gestures of chimpanzees or *Homo habilis* is, if not actually better known, at least better studied than that of contemporary men and women. We know everything, or nearly everything, about chimpanzees' techniques for cracking nuts or fishing out termites. About human body movements used in pounding and grinding grains, shredding roots or peeling fruit, we know just enough to be able to say that they vary from one cultural area to another, and that the difference is often striking. But since Mason's articles (1892, 1899), no work has been carried out on the ways of using a knife. And on such a fundamental subject as manual grasping, it is significant that we owe the only information we have (Marzke and Shackley 1986, Napier 1980) to a triple detour through primatology, psychoarchaeology and robotics.

In fact the study of technical intelligence and its component elements (knowledge, skills, gestural habits, etc.) is no more advanced than it is because, in ordinary research situations, the difficulties and misunderstandings overwhelm the student. This is why specific research situations that reduce the difficulties are of particular interest. Marzke and Shackley's work provides us with three such situations: in primatology and in experimental archaeology, because body movements that appear too ordinary to be worth observing in today's human beings suddenly become fascinating in apes or in relation to prehistoric artefacts; and in robotics, because in order to transfer human skills to a machine, they must first be made explicit, at least partially or by analogy. A fourth propitious situation is in sports, because this is an area in which detailed analysis of skills is of obvious concern (Simonet 1986), especially in top-level competition, where the financial stakes are huge and the race to stay at the top unrelenting. Moreover, sports have something in common with experimental archaeology, in that, be it the boomerang or the crossbow, equitation or sailing, these are areas in which experimenters have a ready audience and willing sponsors (e.g. Spruytte 1977).

Sports can also be compared to various organizations that, for purposes of pedagogy or social criticism, encourage their followers to turn to techniques other than those prevailing at a given time. These movements go back to the beginning of the century, and can perhaps be traced directly to the writings of H. D. Thoreau (*Walden*, 1854). As 'alternative technologies' and the like, they were fashionable in the 1970s. Subsequently having come under attack (Schnaiberg 1982), these movements have today turned to criticizing development models ill-adapted to Third-World realities (Chambers *et al.* 1989, De Walt 1988, Oasa 1985). But, interestingly, all these movements have contributed, willy-nilly, to a clearer explanation of certain types of technical knowledge (e.g. Tresemer 1981).

One last area that has of late given rise to situations favouring the clarification of types of technical knowledge is industry. From 1870 to around 1970, the predominant ideology in its various forms (e.g. scientism, Taylorism, economism) had almost emptied the notion of technics of its content. Technics had become nothing more than the practical application of knowledge (Le Châtelier), the execution of orders (Taylor) or the result of economic forces, points on which Marxist and classical economic thinking scarcely differed. Such thinking led to the then widespread idea that innovation was a commodity available on demand, so to speak. As Landes wrote (1969: 538), 'Man can now order technological and scientific advance as one orders a commodity'; and in the same year man's first steps on the moon seemed to prove him right. Three years later, the Club of Rome attacked this illusion in its now famous report (Meadows *et al.* 1972) whose conclusions, almost unanimously rejected at the time, have since been widely confirmed, first by the economic crisis (Mensch 1975, Baily 1986, Presutti 1987) and then by the headline-making problem of waste (O'Leary 1988). But this is not the place to trace the history of these events and the accompanying ideological about-face. One important consequence does emerge, however, and that is the current change in the image of technology in the industrialized world. Taylorism has not completely disappeared, of course. But it is no longer regarded as the most efficient model of organization, or even a credible model of reality. Engineers and industrialists have begun to understand that, if the workers do not think about what they are doing, as Taylor wanted, production becomes impossible, even – and especially – in the most highly automated plants. The traditional separation between thinking and doing has been thrown into question, as has that between schooling and work: the reputation of apprenticeship has improved, decentralized decision-making and initiative are encouraged at the expense of the traditional values of hierarchy and discipline (Riboud 1987). At the same time, the use of an ethnological vocabulary to describe industry has become widespread. Like its forerunners, this new ideology has its myths and misunderstandings. But what is important is that it recognizes the existence of intelligence in technical action, something that was practically unthinkable in the days of applied science and Taylorism.

Of course it is not certain that what we have designated by the term 'technical intelligence' corresponds to any reality and is not simply an artificial notion. Is it really possible to distinguish several types of human intelligence? Put in this way, the question probably cannot be answered. On the other hand, it seems certain that human intelligence must be studied in all its shapes and forms, including the technical, if our theories are not to run the risk of being biased. As we have seen, though, observation in the technical realm encounters its own difficulties. Technical intelligence is hidden behind the results of the technique by a whole variety of mechanisms: the deceptive ease of the acrobat or the magician presents us with the classic stage image. In a sense, the ideology of applied science succumbed to this mystification. Anthropology must not fall into the same trap.

When all is said and done, we know next to nothing of what goes on behind the scenes (Reuleaux 1877: 3). We only know that we must go and see, and that in order to do this we must find situations and methods that permit observation. That is what I have been saying here.

ADAPTATION AND INNOVATION

In the last two centuries, technical development has been so spectacular that the European mind has, in certain respects, been almost captivated (Adas 1989). The notion of the industrial revolution was perhaps the first indication of this fascination. The expression had appeared in the writings of Marx and Engels by the middle of the nineteenth century (Rioux 1971: 8), and with Toynbee (1884) and Mantoux (1973 [1906]) it became a veritable historical paradigm, which was to provide the inspiration for the notion of the agricultural revolution (Gras 1925: 208–32) and for Childe's (1936) notions of the Neolithic and urban revolutions. Concurrently, evolutionists relied heavily on techniques and artefacts to distinguish successive prehistoric periods (Thomsen 1836, Lubbock 1865), or stages of civilization (Morgan 1877, Mumford 1934), or modes of production (Marx) and economic forms (Hahn 1896, Forde 1934).

Today no one still takes evolutionists seriously. And yet we have inherited some of their deeply rooted mental habits. Some are simply handy, like the Thomsen–Lubbock typology (Palaeolithic, Neolithic, etc.) which, with a few adjustments, remains the frame of reference for prehistorians today. Others are more debatable, like the categories hunter-gatherer, agriculturalist, pastoralist, etc. that anthropologists have commonly used following the precedent of Forde (1934). This vocabulary implies that, on a certain level, societies are defined by their techniques, a hypothesis that has only to be stated to reveal how risky it is. Moreover, in the case of a category like hunter-gatherer, the hypothesis is all the more indefensible in that the real criterion of classification is not positive but negative, not the presence of hunting and gathering techniques but the absence of farming. On this basis, it has been claimed that man has spent 99 per cent of his existence as a hunter-gatherer (Lee and DeVore 1968: 3), but this claim is not based on any tangible evidence, any more than are the countless theories implying the uniqueness of the industrial, post-industrial or technological society compared with all other forms of society that have gone before. Of course techniques play a role in the way societies function. But if this role is assumed to be self-evident from the outset (as in the ideology of progress), there is no chance that it will ever be elucidated. This fundamental error may well be part of the reason for the demise of evolutionism, despite the real and little-known richness of other aspects of the evolutionists' thought (Sigaut 1990). The same error has proved all the more fatal, since it seems to have elicited, as a counter-reaction, the equally erroneous idea that techniques are entirely determined by social relationships. While the steam engine certainly does not explain industrial capitalism, capitalism does not explain the steam engine either. This type of alternative merely proves that the problem was badly defined in the first place.

And perhaps it was badly defined simply because it was defined too hastily. Using techniques as a criterion assumes that they are already known, which locks the researcher into false common-sense assumptions from the start. For example, we continue to characterize the Neolithic by the presence of agriculture. But since we know so little about Neolithic agriculture, that is about the techniques it used, this is a purely verbal exercise. Moreover, some of the things we do know are strangely ignored. For example, agriculture and animal husbandry are usually considered to be essentially food-producing activities; most recent research in cultural ecology is conducted on this premiss. But this ignores the importance of clothing. As far as we know, the value of skins and fleeces, in the Near East, was immeasurably greater than that of meat, which would explain the domestication of sheep and goats much more cogently than do the strictly food-producing hypotheses (Sigaut 1980). But the simple fact of taking clothing into consideration breaks up the classic categories of hunter-gatherers and farmers. For where do you put peoples like the eighteenth-century Iroquois, Pawnees, and others, who farmed for their food but hunted for their clothing?

Pre-Columbian America turns out to be a particularly rich field for analysis. Because of the absence of metal tools and work animals, and because of the few basic plants cultivated (maize, manioc, potato), its agrarian systems were much less varied than those of the Old World. And if the zones in which there was no agriculture, for mainly ecological reasons, are set aside, it would seem that clothing habits, resources and techniques were what made the difference. Clothing is important throughout the Pacific region, from Peru to New Mexico; garments are usually woven from fibres obtained from either cultivated plants or domestic animals, and most agricultural tasks are performed by men. In the eastern regions, on the other hand, from Argentina to the Saint Lawrence, clothing is either absent (in the tropical zones) or made of the skins and furs of hunted animals, and most agricultural tasks are performed by women. It is no doubt not a matter of chance that societies with the strongest hierarchies or a state organization developed in the Pacific zone. And it is evident that only by studying and comparing the functions of clothing and weaving techniques (e.g. Murra 1962, Driver 1969 [1961]: maps 8, 21, 26) will we perhaps come to understand this development.

This example raises a set of problems that are important for many, though no doubt not all, techniques: those of their geographical distribution. The problems are old ones (Mason 1894) but, despite the efforts of a few diehards (e.g. the articles of D. S. Davidson cited in Brace 1980; Driver and Massey 1957), they attract little attention today. It is obvious that a certain type of ethnological mapping is a sterile exercise at best (Bromberger 1984). But cartography as a tool is less to blame than the way in which it has been used. In the case of techniques, at any rate, their geographical distribution is a sort of synthesis of several types of very basic social processes: processes of adaptation to surroundings or, better, management of resources and physical constraints, on the one hand; and processes of producing and transmitting innovations, on the other.

Adaptive processes were the first to come to mind. Human geography and, long before that, climate theory attempted to explain societies in terms of adaptation; today cultural ecology has taken up the same challenge. The trouble with the notion of adaptation is that it assumes, a priori, an identifiable environment to which societies then proceed to adapt. But environment in this sense has no observable existence. The only truly observable environment is the one a group perceives and uses, and, in particular, the set of resources and constraints that it recognizes as such in speech and practice. Each social group, then, has its 'own' environment, which can be and often is different from that of another group sharing the same territory. The only way to identify this environment is by technological analysis, to which all ecological analyses should be subordinated.

In the case of non-Mediterranean Europe, for instance, technological (and dialectological) analysis immediately shows sod or turf to be one of the decisive factors in the development of farming techniques specific to this region (Sigaut 1975). Now, with a few rare exceptions (Evans 1970: 5–6), the abundant literature on European agricultural history ignores sod as an environmental factor, which means that an essential piece is missing from all theories which have, up to the present, tried to explain this history. Another example, which we have already used here, is that of fermented beverages: chichas, beers and sakés. Technological analysis teaches us to differentiate them. It also teaches us that the level of amylase in sprouted grains is a decisive environmental factor. Barley has an exceptionally high level, and Europe makes beer. Rice, on the other hand, has a very low level, and all the rice-growing regions of Asia make saké. Now the industrial destiny of beers and sakés has clearly been quite different, as has the evolution of the modes and rituals of consumption associated with each. The point is obviously not to explain all differences between European and Far Eastern societies by the greater or lesser suitability of soils for growing sod, or by the higher or lower level of amylase in barley and rice. The points are simply (1) that these factors belong fully to the environments specific to these societies, and (2) that only by technological analysis is it possible to identify them. It must be understood that the notions of environment and adaptation have no scientific content outside this analytic context. And that is probably why, since the beginning of human geography, most research on the theme of adaptation has yielded such disappointing results.

Compared with adaptation, the themes of the production and the circulation of innovations have stimulated much less research, even though they are just as important for human geography. Edmonson's (1961) model of the circulation of innovations, according to which innovations springing up at random in a uniformly inhabited space and spreading at a constant rate tend to collect at the centre of the space, has oddly enough received no attention at all. 'Rather than starting in Iraq and diffusing outward, the "Neolithic" appears to a considerable extent to have converged on it', Edmonson concluded (1961: 72), and this view has, on the whole, been confirmed by subsequent research. The model needs to be adjusted to take into account the physical and social differences within real inhabited spaces. But, with this one reservation, it appears to be of considerable heuristic value. For Europe, in any case, the concentration of the most highly developed forms of agriculture and industry in the region extending from the Po River plain to the Low Countries, which has been observed since the late Middle Ages and which has once more become apparent after having been masked for two centuries by the coal and steam episode, must no doubt be explained in this way. However uniform the geographical environment is assumed to be, innovation inevitably introduces differences that increase with time: this is perhaps the essential lesson to be learned from Edmonson's model.

Geography is no less important to the production of innovations than to their circulation, though obviously for different reasons. The tendency for all workshops or crafts to gather in one area or village is probably quite universal, since it has been observed in so-called primitive societies (Malinowski 1935, 1: 12–23) as well as in our modern industrial societies, and most notably in California's Silicon Valley. The location of resources or infrastructures is only part of the explanation of this phenomenon. An interpretation in terms of exchanges (Lowie 1934: 108–9, 146, Lemonnier 1981) is broader in scope, but leads to a chicken-and-egg alternative: was it the need to exchange that led to specialization, or specialization that made it necessary to exchange? The only solution, it seems to me, is to bring into consideration a too often neglected element: the production and reproduction of technical skills.

THE SOCIAL PRODUCTION OF TECHNICAL SKILLS

As I have already argued, skills are not – or not simply – forms of knowledge. They cannot exist apart from permanent practice. They cannot be written

445

down – at least not all of them – nor transmitted by speech, as in classroom teaching. They owe their existence to constant renewal in the course of practical action, a renewal of which innovation and apprenticeship are only particular aspects (on the necessity for apprenticeship, see Wynn, in this volume, Article 6). The French say '*c'est en forgeant qu'on devient forgeron*', the English, 'practice makes perfect'; both proverbs are more apposite than ever, whether they are applied to high-level sporting competition, heavily automated industry, or computer science – which is all the more outstanding an illustration as it was unexpected. We were expecting Big Brother, that is, the victory of completely algorithmized, centralized expertise. What we have, at least for the time being, are practical jokers, pirates, bugs and viruses – in short, 'computerized anarchy' – because neither the machines nor their users are behaving as expected (Gonin and Joffrin 1983, Denning 1988, Marshall 1988). This is nothing new; it could be called 'the law of the irreducibility of skills'. It has been observed throughout the history of 'communicating machines' (Perriault 1989). Indeed it runs through the entire history of technics, which from this point of view might be interpreted as a constantly renewed attempt to build skills into machines by means of algorithms, an attempt constantly foiled because other skills always tend to develop around the new machines. Mason already saw this nearly a century ago: 'It is sometimes said that the substitution of unerring machinery has taken away the cunning of the human hand. The case is not nearly as bad as that, however. No change of apparatus can deprive the human race of geniuses, for the man of knack will be found excelling in the handling of the new machines' (Mason 1895: 26).

What concerns us here, however, is that the production (including the reproduction) of skills is inseparable from the production of material goods, and, consequently, the way societies organize themselves to produce – the Marxists' 'mode of production' – depends as much on the skills as on the goods to be produced. It seems that this point has never really been made. After having recognized the failure of purely economic explanations, for example, industrial historians turned to cultural explanations ('Why isn't the whole world developed?', Easterlin 1981). This was real, but only partial, progress, in that the notion of culture invoked seemed too broad to be an effective guide to research (Dellheim 1987). To precisely what cultural differences can variations in productivity be attributed (Clark 1987)? My hypothesis is that the mode of production and reproduction of skills, as only ethnography can reveal it, plays an essential role.

It is probably no coincidence that more and more students, ethnologists or not, are turning to ethnography in their attempt to understand what really goes on in factories, stores, offices, etc. In the last ten years, vocabulary borrowed from ethnology has come to be routinely used in the sociology of the sciences, as for example in a recent book entitled *Academic Tribes and Territories* (Becher 1989). And journalists have not been far behind; after the October 1987 stock market crash, the media virtually swamped us with articles on that exotic people, the Golden Boys, their various tribes, dialects, rituals, identity tags, customs — including clothing and sexual practices — etc. (Camé and Filloux 1987a). Clearly these elements are not pieces of folklore, in the derogatory sense of the term, but external manifestations of the culture within which are produced the skills needed for stock markets to work. Of course, to work they also need machines (telephones, computers, and so on) and theoretical knowledge (the Golden Boys are university trained). But these would be useless without the skills developed on the spot, of which one of the most striking to the outsider is the sign language used on the floor of the Paris Futures Exchange (Camé and Filloux 1987b; a similar language was used in the Chicago Grain Exchange at the beginning of the century: Perrignon de Troyes 1926). We may note in parentheses that the example of the Golden Boys points up a dimension needed by economics if it is to become a true science: economists must take into account the way markets work in reality and not only in theory. But the main interest of this example is its visibility. The Golden Boys are only a special case of a universal phenomenon, the constitution of identifiable social units around certain skills, which in this case happened to make the front pages.

The problem, then, is to elucidate the relationship between the social units and the skills produced in them, which is only a more general way of putting the problem raised earlier with regard to geographical examples like Silicon Valley. It is still rare to find research conducted from this perspective. The work I have come across (e.g. Darré 1985, Kuhn 1985) suggests the following series of hypotheses:

1 Normal social life requires that each person acquire a minimum number of materially and socially effective practices.
2 The skills underpinning these practices can be produced and transmitted only in groups of a certain size, not too small and not too large.
3 In order to last any length of time, these groups must have a recognizable and recognized identity, a minimum of internal cohesion, procedures for recruiting and initiating new members, for settling conflicts, and so on.
4 Furthermore, each group must balance its exchanges with the outside, which depends on the efficacy of the skills it produces. An effective group will see its social status rise. One that is not effective will decline until it falls under the domination of other groups or disappears altogether.

These hypotheses call for further development, which would exceed the scope of the present article; but just to give some idea, I will comment briefly on two points: the skill-producing group itself and the notion of efficacy.

Why does an individual need to belong to a group, and not just any group, to acquire the skills he needs to live? On one level the answers are so obvious that I need not go into them — for example, there is no innovation without tradition, and no tradition without a social unit to carry it on. But there is also something more than these self-evident truths. There is the fact, long ago recognized by Espinas (1897: 537–8), that reality is real only if there is some social consensus to recognize it as such – that is, if others allow the person to interpret his or her feelings and perceptions as evidence of reality. Of course, these 'others' are not just anyone. They must be individuals whom the person knows and with whom he or she shares the same general experience. Which is to say that 'others' are a group whose identity is defined by common abilities, and whose numbers are restricted by the condition that everyone must know everyone else to several persons or at the most several dozens.

A California research laboratory (Latour and Woolgar 1979) or the farmers of a small area of the Artois region, in northern France (Darré 1985), are examples of such groups. There are big differences between the two. The farmers form a group of peers with no visible hierarchy, carrying out similar tasks in the same environment but working independently; a stable group, slow to change, culturally and economically dominated rather than dominant, which reacts to this domination by drawing inward. By contrast, the California laboratory is characterized chiefly by a very strong but rather mobile hierarchy, since it depends on each member's scientific credit, which can be gained or lost by producing (or not) the innovations that are the mainstay of the laboratory's status in the outside world. The way in which new members are recruited also shows obvious differences. Artois farmers are all native to the area. The members of the California lab come from China, Finland, France, Germany, Israel, Mexico – there are even a few Americans – and most are there for only a few years. But, beyond the differences, there is one basic similarity. Both groups have a well-defined and visible identity, which stems as much from their being concentrated in a specific space (which is not always the case; non-localized groups also exist) as from a special use of language and specific material practices, usually incomprehensible to the uninitiated. In both areas (that is, language and practices), the line between members and non-members is clearly marked.

From a technological point of view, the skill-producing group is a basic social unit present in all societies because a society without techniques is inconceivable. This unit can take a wide variety of forms and enter into extremely diverse combinations with other units such as the family, the residence group, the age-group, etc. All of this is a function of such factors as the kinds of skills concerned, the social values placed on them, indigenous ideas on learning, the distribution of activities by rank and gender, and so on. Ideally, the morphology of all societies ought to be reconstructed from scratch, taking into account this necessary but, until now, unnoticed unit. We are obviously far off the mark.

From this perspective, the notion of efficacy is essential because it regulates a group's relative position. But efficacy is a hazy notion at best: its meaning is physical as well as social; the difficulties arise when we try to relate the two. Competitive sport in contemporay societies is an extreme example inasmuch as pure material efficacy is the avowed aim of the competition. But how is this measured? Simply by designating winners and losers, usually, without a qualm about the statistical significance of the few fractions of a second that separate the two. Questioning the validity of this process would be *de rigueur* in any scientific experiment, but is unthinkable, and would even appear sacrilegious, in the world of sports. Moreover, this ill-measured efficacy has no reality outside the highly artificial conditions of the competition, as anyone can see by taking a look at a Formula One racing car. The curious result is that the more purely material the efficacy (and the skills it entails) is considered to be, the more stringent the social determinations that make it possible.

But is this result really so odd? Is it not rather our habit of separating the material and social spheres that should be questioned? Material efficacy is effective only if it is also social — that is what the example of today's sports tells us — but it can be effective in a number of ways. Efficacy is always a generator of identity; and in sports it produces little else, which is their main peculiarity. In this sense sports reveal, as it were, some of the most deeply ingrained tendencies of our society in their pure state (Bromberger *et al.* 1987). Efficacy is an indispensable notion in technology, and it enters into the very definition given by Mauss; the problem lies in knowing what it represents in each case. What conception of efficacy, for example, underpins India's caste system? Within our own contemporary European conception, the caste system remains ill understood, despite several generations of research. But if, contrary to our custom, we were to include in our conception of efficacy such notions as purity and pollution, merit and blame, etc., the caste system might begin to seem less strange. In particular, the obsession of its members with hierarchical rank is perhaps not without analogies to the obsession with rank characteristic of our own sportsmen and sportswomen.

EXCLUDING TECHNICS FROM THE IDEA OF SOCIETY: THE CASE OF SLAVERY

The main problem in technology consists in the inadequacy of the concepts at our disposal to account for the facts. Extant concepts are often inadequate for the purposes of straight technographic description; and when we try to broaden the analysis, the gap only widens, as we have just seen with the notion of efficacy. The present situation is the product of a long history of 'building in' or embodying technical facts and relationships, which effectively removes them from the realm of conscious awareness even as they are produced. Or, to quote Akrich (1989: 53), 'the construction of a technical system ... can be considered complete only when its effects are denied.' Traditional anthropology and history have perpetuated the denial by developing their impossible, atechnical conception of society. Perhaps an example in which this conception is shown clearly to be inadequate will demonstrate the need for a change of approach.

Let us take ancient slavery as that example. This is an old problem, older even than that of India's castes, since, according to Finley (1980: 35), the first modern view on the subject was published by Reitemeier in 1789. Two centuries and several thousand titles later (Miller 1985), the solution seems as far away as ever. The accumulated corpus of knowledge is impressive, but no meaningful pattern seems to be emerging: that is the implicit conclusion to which Finley himself has come at the end of a long life of research devoted in large part to the problem (1980: 66). What, then, is still needed for this corpus, and our vision of it, to make sense?

The answer, probably, is a good technologist's assessment of the situation. Indeed, until very recently, all historians of Greek economics were divided among three beliefs. The first, to which Finley himself (1965) contributed liberally, was that technical development in Greece was weak, or at any rate had prematurely ground to a halt. The second was that slavery was one of the main causes of this weakness. The third, made famous by Engels, was a sort of mirror image of the second: slavery tempered technical inadequacy, it was the consequence rather than the cause of the insufficiency.

But 'insufficient' compared with what? There is no need to be a deep thinker to realize the paucity of supporting evidence for these beliefs. They are even in blatant contradiction with the facts. Greece was one of the first regions to develop the use of iron, not only for ornamentation and weaponry, but also for tools, including everyday tools such as those used in agriculture. It was in the Greek and Greek-speaking world that the first rotary-motion machines appeared: olive crushers, mills, water-lifting devices such as the saqiya, noria, Archimedes' screw, etc., to which must be added new lever and screw presses. If we go on to count architecture, animal-drawn vehicles, shipbuilding, war machines, glass-making, etc., the evidence becomes overwhelming. Classical Antiquity was the theatre of a veritable technical revolution the likes of which can be found only in the Near East during the fourth millennium BC and in our present-day technical revolution. That a scholar of Finley's calibre failed to see this can be explained only by what could be called a cultural blindness that besets otherwise literate Western intellectuals when it comes to things technical.

What about slavery, then? It cannot, of course, have been either the cause or the consequence of a technical stagnation that did not exist. On the contrary, we are led to ask whether it did not play a positive role in Antiquity's remarkable technical development, since the two were associated. But what role? When one looks into a question like the milling of grain, for example, one notes that, over a period of four centuries, ancient society went from the simple saddle-quern to the water mill, and at the same time it went from a situation in which grinding grain was women's work to one in which it was men's work. Could there then be some relation between the three simultaneous changes: the technical innovation, the new sexual distribution of labour, and slavery?

Such, at least, is the hypothesis suggested by the facts. For in most societies the sexual division of labour is one of the components of sexual identity, which makes any change especially difficult. In particular, a freeman cannot normally perform women's tasks without ceasing to be a man – as was the case of the famous North American transvestites, *berdaches* (Callender and Kochems 1983) – or without ceasing to be free – which would have been the outcome in Ancient Greece. Following this line of thinking, slavery in Antiquity would have been a systematic means of making men do women's work, which would explain its vital importance for the economy. Slavery made it possible to take a number of tasks out of the family or home, to which they had until then been confined, and to turn them into commercial trades. Moreover, slaves were bought. Therefore the financial capital they represented had to be made to bear fruit: technical innovation was the means. In this respect, the same holds true whether the capital comprises humans or animals. The effort to increase the returns of animal labour was, for thousands of years, one of the principal sources of technical innovation; why then should human labour be any different? And could not grinders, mills, presses and other machines of Antiquity have been to the 'domestication' of men more or less what the *tribulum*, the ard and wheeled vehicles had been to the domestication of animals three thousand years earlier?

Stated in such succinct terms, the hypothesis can only be incomplete; and perhaps false as well. But this is not the place to elaborate on it. For our present purposes the hypothesis is more interesting for its exemplary value than for its content. It is most remarkable for its total dismissal of the vast historiographic corpus on slavery in Antiquity mentioned above. In two centuries of assiduous research on slavery, it would seem that the authors scrupulously examined every possibility except the one to which all the facts point: that there might be some relation between slavery, technical innovation and the sexual division of labour (for a partial exception, see Pryor 1977: 4, 234). How can such an extraordinary blind spot be explained if not by a prevailing vision of society from which technics are systematically excluded?

THE FUTURE OF TECHNOLOGY

We will make this last remark our conclusion. The anthropology of technics is just now coming into existence. Of all the branches of anthropology, it is probably the one that has the most work to do and the fewest workers. Following a promising start in the nineteenth century, it was nearly abandoned for three generations. In such circumstances, it is not surprising that unresolved difficulties and unanswered questions outweigh positive results. But we must not let this discourage us. For the very gains made by anthropology in other areas tend to highlight the continuing obscurity of this branch. In fact, if anthropologists do not want to see their whole discipline doomed to stagnation, they will have to make an effort to reintegrate technics into their vision of culture and society. New voices have been heard recently in support of this view (Reynolds 1983, Beckerman 1985, Pfaffenberger 1988). What will this new, balanced vision of the future look like? It is too early to say; we can only suppose that it will be very different from the present one, mainly perhaps in regard to today's so-called advanced societies, in which an excess of information and commentary on technological innovation is just as great an obstacle to understanding as are ignorance and lack of information for ancient and exotic societies.

Never has there been so much talk about technics, but perhaps never has the abundance of words had a greater effect of masking reality. One of the perverse effects of informatics is that users are obliged to expend considerable effort simply in protecting themselves from irrelevant information (Dennett 1986, Bennett 1988), and this would explain the disappointing growth rate in productivity (Baily 1986). Those who attempt to think seriously about technics today find themselves the victims of this effect, which is why we have left it largely to one side in the foregoing discussion. If we refuse to follow popular wisdom, which contrasts present-day high technology with, shall we say, the low technology of a mythical former age, we suddenly realize that there is little left to say. We do indeed have computers, satellites and some other items that our ancestors did not, and it is unquestionable that our society has changed since their time. But so what? Our great-grandparents boasted in approximately the same terms about their own *Wonders of Science* (Figuier 1867–70), and two centuries before them Charles Perrault (1688, I: 72) was already entranced with the 'prodigious progress of Science and the Arts over the last fifty or sixty years'. In the thirteenth century, Roger Bacon voiced similar sentiments, which there is no reason to deny to the Romans, Greeks, Sumerians, and so on. What makes *our* modernity different from these earlier versions? We have no answer.

It is no accident that, in this situation, we have almost no alternative but to turn to history. For perhaps the most direct means of demystifying the image of modernity that stands between us and the reality of our societies is to look back at history. That being said, and despite a development out of all proportion to that of anthropology, the history of technics still falls far short of providing us with the means of interpreting our present and future with any greater clarity. Until now, it has managed more to corrode traditional ideas than to develop new ways of thinking. This is not surprising, since the whole edifice of the social sciences was built as if technics did not exist or were of only minor importance. How could technics be made to fit in smoothly? Technology cannot hope to develop without engendering conflict. The future of technology, as a social science, is as unpredictable as the future of technics and society today.

REFERENCES

Adas, M. (1989) *Machines as the Measure of Men*, Ithaca and London: Cornell University Press.

Akrich, M. (1989) 'La construction d'un système socio-technique. Esquisse pour une anthropologie des techniques', *Anthropologie et Sociétés* 13 (2): 31–54.

Anderson-Gerfaud, P. (1983) 'A consideration of the uses of certain backed and "lustred" stone tools from late Mesolithic and Natufian levels of Abu Hureyra and Mureybet (Syria)', in M.-C. Cauvin (ed.) *Traces d'utilisation sur les outils néolithiques du Proche Orient*, Lyon: Maison de l'Orient.

Ankei, T. (1986) 'Discovery of Saké in Central Africa: mold-fermented liquor of the Songola', *Journal d'Agriculture traditionnelle et de Botanique appliquée* 33: 29–47.

Ardrey, R. (1969) Preface to E. Marais, *The Soul of the Ape*, Cape Town and London: Rousseau and Blond.

Auzias, J.-M. (1971) *La Philosophie et les techniques*, Paris: P.U.F.

Baily, M. N. (1986) 'What has happened to productivity growth?', *Science* 234: 443–51.

Becher, T. (1989) *Academic Tribes and Territories: Intellectual Enquiry and the Cultures of Disciplines*, Milton Keynes: Open University Press.

Beckerman, S. (1985) 'Pour une anthropologie expérimentale: l'étude des techniques', *Techniques et Culture* 5: 139–48.

Bennett, C. (1988) 'Démons, machines et thermodynamique', *Pour la Science* 123: 91–7.

Boas, F. (1938) *The Mind of Primitive Man*, New York: Macmillan.

Brace, C. L. (1980) 'Australian tooth-size clines and the death of a stereotype', *Current Anthropology* 21 (2): 141–64.

Bril, B. (1984) 'Description du geste technique: quelles méthodes?', *Techniques et Culture* 3: 81–96.

Bromberger, C. (ed.) (1984) 'L'ethnocartographie en Europe', *Technologies, Idéologies, Pratiques* 4, 1–4, Actes de la Table ronde internationale organisée par le Centre d'Ethnologie Méditerranéenne, Aix-en-Provence, 25–27 November 1982.

Bromberger, C., Hayot, A. and Mariottini, J.-M. (1987) 'Allez l'O.M.! Forza Juve!', *Terrain* 8: 8–41.

Callender, C. and Kochems, L. M. (1983) 'The North American Berdache', *Current Anthropology* 24 (4): 443–70.

Callon, M. and Latour, B. (1985) 'Les paradoxes de la modernité', *Prospective et Santé* 36: 13–25.

Camé, F. and Filloux, F. (1987a) 'Do you speak golden boys?', *Libération* 23 October: 5.

—— (1987b) 'La planète des signes', *Libération* 31 October–1 November: 11.

Cazenobe, J. (1983) *La Visée et l'obstacle, étude et documents sur la 'préhistoire' de l'onde hertzienne*, Cahiers d'histoire et de philosophie des sciences, 5, Paris: Belin.

—— (1985) 'Essence et naissance de l'électro-aimant', *History and Technology* 2(2): 177–201.

—— (1986) *Limailles, lampes et cristaux, essai sur les origines de l'électronique*, Cahiers d'histoire et de philosophie des sciences, 15, Paris: Belin.

—— (1987) 'Esquisse d'une conception opératoire de l'objet technique', *Techniques et Culture* 10: 61–80.

Chambers, R., Pacey, A. and Thrupp, L. A. (1989) *Farmer First*, Southampton: Intermediate Technology.

Chamoux, M.-N. (1978) 'La transmission des savoir-faire: un objet pour l'ethnologie des techniques?', *Techniques et Culture* 3 (1st ser.): 46–83.

—— (1986) 'Apprendre autrement', in P. Rossel (ed.) *Demain l'artisanat*, Paris and Geneva: P.U.F. and Cahiers de l'IUED.

Chick, G. E. and Roberts, J. M. (1987) 'Lathe craft: a study in "part" appreciation', *Human Organization* 46 (4): 305–17.

Childe, V. G. (1936) *Man Makes Himself*, London: Watts.

Clark, G. (1987) 'Why isn't the whole world developed? Lessons from the cotton mills', *Journal of Economic History* 47 (1): 141–73.

Condominas, G. (1965) *L'Exotique est quotidien*, Paris: Plon.

Couffignal, L. (1978 [1963]) *La Cybernétique*, Paris: P.U.F.

Darré, J.-P. (1985) *La Parole et la technique, l'univers de pensée des éleveurs du Ternois*, Paris: L'Harmattan.

Daumas, M. (1965) 'Introduction', in M. Daumas (ed.) *Histoire générale des techniques, II: Les premières étapes du machinisme*, Paris: P.U.F.

Deforge, Y. (1985) *Technologie et génétique de l'objet industriel*, Paris: Maloine.

Dellheim, C. (1987) 'The creation of a company culture: Cadburys, 1861–1931', *The American Historical Review* 92 (1): 13–44.

Dennett, D. C. (1986) 'Information, technology, and the virtues of ignorance', *Daedalus* 115 (3): 135–53.

Denning, P. J. (1988) 'Computer viruses', *American Scientist* 76: 236–8.

Devine, J. (1985) 'The versatility of human locomotion', *American Anthropologist* 87 (3): 550–70.

De Walt, B. R. (1988) 'Halfway there: social science *in* agricultural development and the social science *of* agricultural development', *Human Organization* 47 (4): 343–53.

Digard, J.-P. (1979) 'La technologie en anthropologie: fin de parcours ou nouveau souffle?', *L'Homme* 19 (1): 73–104.

Driver, H. E. (1969 [1961]) *Indians of North America*, Chicago and London: University of Chicago Press.

Driver, H. E. and Massey, W. C. (1957) 'Comparative studies of North American Indians', *Transactions of the American Philosophical Society* 47: 165–456.

Durkheim, E. (1960 [1895]) *Les Règles de la méthode sociologique*, Paris: P.U.F.

Easterlin, R. A. (1981) 'Why isn't the whole world developed?', *Journal of Economic History* 41 (1): 1–19.

Edmonson, M. E. (1961) 'Neolithic diffusion rates', *Current Anthropology* 2: 71–102.

Espinas, A. (1897) *Les Origines de la technologie*, Paris: Félix Alcan.

Evans, E. E. (1970) 'Introduction', in A. Gailey and A. Fenton (eds) *The Spade in Northern and Atlantic Europe*, Belfast: Ulster Folk Museum and Institute of Irish Studies.

Febvre, L. (1935) 'Réflexions sur l'histoire des techniques', *Annales d'histoire économique et sociale* 6: 532–5.

Figuier, L. (1867–70) *Les Merveilles de la science*, Paris: Furne, Jouvet.

Finley, M. I. (1965) 'Technical innovation and economic progress in the ancient world', *The Economic History Review* 18 (1–2–3): 29–45.

—— (1980) *Ancient Slavery and Modern Ideology*, London: Chatto & Windus.

Fischer, H. T. (1937) 'Reispflücken und Reisschneiden in Indonesien', *Internationales Archiv für Ethnographie* 34: 83–105.

—— (1939) 'Das indonesische Reismesser ausserhalb Indonesiens', *Paideuma* 1 (3): 147–52.

Fleury, D. (1988) 'La science a-t-elle une mémoire? Le cas de la maladie de l'orme', *La Recherche* 197: 406–10.

Forde, C. D. (1934) *Habitat, Economy, and Society, A Geographical Introduction to Ethnology*, London: Methuen.

Gariboldi, F. (1974) *L'Étuvage du riz*, Rome: F.A.O.

Gille, B. (1978) *Histoire des techniques*, Paris: Gallimard.

Gonin, J-M. and Joffrin, L. (1983) 'L'anarchie informatique', *Libération* 20 September: 19–30.

Gould, S. J. (1986) 'Evolution and the triumph of homology, or why history matters', *American Scientist* 74 (1): 60–9.

Gras, N. S. B. (1925) *A History of Agriculture in Europe and America*, New York: F. S. Crofts.

Griffin, D. R. (1984) *Animal Thinking*, Cambridge, Mass.: Harvard University Press.

Guillerme, J. and Sebestik, J. (1966) 'Les commencements de la technologie', *Thalès* 12: 1–72.

Hahn, E. (1896) *Demeter und Baubo, Versuch einer Theorie der Entstehung unsres Ackerbaues*, Lübeck: Max Schmidt.

Haudricourt, A.-G. (1987) *La Technologie science humaine. Recherches d'histoire et d'ethnologie des techniques*, Paris: Editions de la Maison des Sciences de l'Homme.

Heider, K. G. (1970) *The Dugum Dani, A Papuan Culture in the Highlands of West New Guinea*, New York: Wenner-Gren Foundation.

Herf, J. (1985) *Reactionary Modernism: Technology, Culture and Politics in Weimar and the Third Reich*, Cambridge: Cambridge University Press.

Hirschberg, W. and Janata, A. (1980) *Technologie und Ergologie in der Völkerkunde*, vol. 1, Berlin: Dietrich Reimer.

Ingold, T. (1988) 'Tools, minds and machines: an excursion in the philosophy of technology', *Techniques et Culture* 12: 151–76.

Katz, S. H., Hediger, M. L. and Valleroy, L. A. (1974) 'Traditional maize processing techniques in the New World', *Science* 184: 765–73.

Kawada, J. (1988) 'Les techniques du corps et la technologie traditionnelle', in J. Kawada (ed.) *Boucle du Niger – approches multidisciplinaires*, Tokyo: Institut de Recherches sur les langues et les cultures d'Asie et d'Afrique.

Kimata, K. (1987) 'Grain crop cookery in South India', in S. Sakamoto (ed.) *A Preliminary Report of the Studies on Millet Cultivation and its Agro-Pastoral Culture Complex in the Indian Subcontinent*, Kyoto: Kyoto University.

Kuhn, T. S. (1985) 'Scientific development and lexical change', unpublished Ms, Thalheimer Lectures, The Johns Hopkins University, 12–19 November 1984.

Lafitte, J. (1972 [1932]) *Réflexions sur la science des machines*, Paris: Vrin.

Lamborn, L. L. (1918) *Modern Soaps, Candles and Glycerin*, New York: Van Nostrand.

Landes, D. S. (1969) *The Unbound Prometheus, Technological Change and Industrial Development in Western Europe from 1750 to the Present*, Cambridge: Cambridge University Press.

Latour, B. and Woolgar, S. (1979) *Laboratory Life, The Construction of Scientific Facts*, Beverly Hills and London: Sage.

Le Châtelier, H.-L. (1925) *Science et industrie*, Paris: E. Flammarion.

Lee, R. B. and De Vore, I. (eds) (1968) *Man the Hunter*, Chicago: Aldine.

Lemonnier, P. (1981) 'Le commerce intertribal des Anga de Nouvelle-Guinée', *Journal de la Société des Océanistes* 27: 70–1.

Leplat, J. and Pailhous, J. (1981) 'L'acquisition des habiletés mentales: la place des techniques', *Le Travail humain* 44 (2): 275–82.

Leroi-Gourhan, A. (1964–5) *Le Geste et la parole*, 2 vols, Paris: Albin Michel.

Lévi-Strauss, C. (1958) *Anthropologie structurale*, Paris: Plon.

—— (1962) *La Pensée sauvage*, Paris: Plon.

Lowie, R. H. (1934) *An Introduction to Cultural Anthropology*, New York: Farrar & Rinehart.

Lubbock, J. (1865) *Pre-Historic Times, As Illustrated by Ancient Remains and the Manners and Customs of Modern Savages*, London: Williams & Norgate.

Macaulay, D. (1979) *Motel of the Mysteries*, Boston: Houghton Mifflin.

Mahias, M.-C. (1985) *Délivrance et convivialité*, Paris: Éditions de la Maison des Sciences de l'Homme.

Malinowski, B. (1935) *Coral Gardens and their Magic*, 2 vols, New York, Chicago, Cincinnati: American Book Co.

Mantoux, P. (1973 [1906]) *La Révolution industrielle au XVIIIe siècle*, Paris: Éditions Génin.

Marshall, E. (1988) 'The scourge of computer viruses', *Science* 240: 133–4.

Marzke, M. W. and Shackley, S. (1986) 'Hominid hand use in the Pliocene and Pleistocene: evidence from experimental archaeology and comparative morphology', *Journal of Human Evolution* 15 (6): 439–60.

Mason, O. T. (1888) 'An account of the progress in anthropology in the years 1887–1888', in *Smithsonian Report* for 1888, Washington, DC: G.P.O.

—— (1892) 'The ulu, or woman's knife, of the Eskimo', in *Report of the US National Museum* for 1890, Washington, DC: G.P.O.

—— (1894) 'Technogeography, or the relation of the earth to the industries of mankind', *American Anthropologist* 7: 137–52.

—— (1895) *The Origins of Invention, A Study of Industry among Primitive Peoples*, London: Walter Scott.

—— (1899) 'The man's knife among the North American Indians', in *Report of the US National Museum* for 1897, Washington, DC: G.P.O.

Mauss, M. (1936) 'Les techniques du corps', *Journal de Psychologie* 32: 271–93.

—— (1948) 'Les techniques et la technologie', in I. Meyerson *et al.* (eds) *Le Travail et les techniques*, Paris: P.U.F.

Meadows, D. H., Meadows, D. L., Randers, J. and Behrens, W. W. (1972) *The Limits to Growth*, New York: Universe Books.

Mensch, G. (1975) *Das technologische Patt*, Frankfurt: Umschau.

Miller, J. C. (1985) *Slavery, A Worldwide Bibliography, 1900–1982*, New York: Kraus International Publications.

Mitcham, C. and Mackey, R. (1973) *Bibliography of the Philosophy of Technology*, Chicago and London: University of Chicago Press.

Morgan, L. H. (1877) *Ancient Society*, London: Macmillan.

Moser, S. (1973) 'Kritik der traditionnellen Technikphilosophie', in H. Lenk and S. Moser (eds) *Techne, Technik, Technologie*, Pullach bei München: Verlag Dokumentation.

Muchnik, J. (1981) *Technologies autochtones et alimentation en Amérique latine*, Massy: ENSIA and Paris: GRET.

Mumford, L. (1934) *Technics and Civilization*, London: G. Routledge.

Murra, J. (1962) 'Cloth and its functions in the Inca state', *American Anthropologist* 64 (4): 710–28.

Napier, J. R. (1980) *Hands*, New York: Pantheon Books.

Oasa, E. A. (1985) 'Farming systems research: a change in form but not in content', *Human Organization* 44 (3): 219–27.

O'Leary, P. (1988) 'Managing solid waste', *Scientific American* 259 (6): 18–24.

Oswalt, W. H. (1976) *An Anthropological Analysis of Food-Getting Technology*, New York: John Wiley.

Paillard, J. (1976) 'Réflexions sur l'usage du concept de plasticité en neurobiologie', *Journal de Psychologie* 1: 33–47.

—— (1986) 'Système nerveux et fonction d'organisation', in J. Piaget, L. Mounoud and J.-P. Bronckart (eds) *Psychologie*, Paris: Gallimard.

Perrault, C. (1688) *Parallèle des anciens et des modernes, en ce qui regarde les arts et les sciences*, Paris: J.-B. Coignard.

Perriault, J. (1989) *La Logique de l'usage, essai sur les machines à communiquer*, Paris: Flammarion.

Perrignon de Troyes (1926) 'Le commerce des grains aux États-Unis d'Amérique', *Revue du Service de l'Intendance Militaire* 33: 930–44.

Pfaffenberger, B. (1988) 'Fetishized objects and humanized nature: towards an anthropology of technology', *Man* (N.S.) 23 (2): 236–52.

Pitt-Rivers, A. H. Lane Fox (1906) *The Evolution of Culture and Other Essays*, Oxford: Clarendon Press.

Pouillon, F. (1976) 'La détermination d'un mode de production: les forces productives et leur appropriation', in F. Pouillon (ed.) *L'Anthropologie économique*, Paris: Maspéro.

Presutti, W. D. Jr (1987) 'Productivity: questioning the assumptions for improvement – a role for applied history', *History and Technology* 3 (4): 349–64.

Pryor, F. L. (1977) *The Origins of the Economy*, New York: Academic Press.

Rapp, F. (1974) 'Introduction', in F. Rapp (ed.) *Contributions to a Philosophy of Technology*, Dordrecht: D. Reidel.

Reuleaux, F. (1865) *Der Constructeur*, Braunschweig: F. Viehweg.

—— (1877) *Cinématique, principes fondamentaux d'une théorie générale des machines*, trans. A. Debize, Paris: F. Savy.

—— (1884) *Eine Reise quer durch India im Jahre 1881*, Berlin: Allgemeiner Verein für deutsche Literatur.

Reynolds, B. (1983) 'The relevance of material culture to anthropology', *Journal of the Anthropological Society of Oxford* 14 (2): 181–226.

Riboud, A. (1987) *Modernisation, mode d'emploi*, Paris: Union Générale d'Éditions.

Rioux, J.-P. (1971) *La Révolution industrielle, 1780–1880*, Paris: Seuil.

Sagant, P. (1987) 'Traditions enfantines. L'apprentissage des techniques au Népal oriental', in B. Koechlin, F. Sigaut, J. M. C. Thomas and G. Toffin (eds) *De la voûte céleste au terroir, du jardin au foyer*, Textes offerts à Lucien Bernot, Paris: Éditions de l'EHESS.

Salthouse, T. A. (1984) 'The skill of typing', *Scientific American* 250 (2): 94–9.

Schnaiberg, A. (1982) 'Did you ever meet a payroll? Contradictions in the structure of the appropriate technology movement', *The Humboldt Journal of Social Relations* 9 (2): 38–62 special issue, 'Socially Appropriate Technology'.

Schuhl, P.-M. (1938) *Machinisme et philosophie*, Paris: P.U.F.

Sebestik, J. (1983) 'The rise of the technological science', *History and Technology* 1 (1): 25–44.

Sigaut, F. (1975) *L'Agriculture et le feu*, Paris/La Haye: Mouton.

—— (1977) 'Quelques notions de base en matière de travail du sol dans les anciennes agricultures curopéennes', *Journal d'Agriculture traditionnelle et de Botanique appliquée* 24 (2–3): 139–69; special issue, 'Les Hommes et leurs sols'.

—— (1978) 'Identification des techniques de récolte des graines alimentaires', *Journal d'Agriculture traditionnelle de la Botanique appliquée* 25 (3): 145–61.

—— (1980) 'Un tableau des produits animaux et deux hypothèses qui en découlent', *Production pastorale et société* 7: 20–36.

—— (1985) 'More (and enough) on technology!', *History and Technology* 2 (2): 115–32.

—— (1987a) 'Préface', in A.-G. Haudricourt, *La Technologie: science humaine*, Paris: Éditions de la Maison des Sciences de l'Homme.

—— (1987b) 'Des idées pour observer', *Techniques et Culture* 10: 1–12.
—— (1990) 'De la technologie à l'évolutionnisme, l'oeuvre de Pitt Rivers (1827–1900)', *Gradhiva* 8: 20–37.
—— (1991) 'Les techniques de récolte des grains: identification, localisation, problèmes d'interprétation', in M.-C. Cauvin (ed.) *Rites et rythmes agraires*, Lyon: Maison de l'Orient and Paris: De Boccard.
Simondon, G. (1969 [1958]) *Du mode d'existence des objets techniques*, Paris: Aubier.
Simonet, P. (1986) *Apprentissages moteurs, processus et procédés d'acquisition*, Paris: Vigot.
Spruytte, J. (1977) *Études expérimentales sur l'attelage*, Paris: Crépin-Leblond.
—— (1982) *Early Harness Systems* (trans. of above), London: J. Allen.
Sturtevant, W. C. (1969) 'Does anthropology need museums?', *Proceedings of the Biological Society of Washington* 82: 619–50.
Techniques et Culture (1987) nos. 9 and 10, 'Des idées pour observer'.
Thomsen, C. J. (1836) *Ledetraad til nordiske Oldkyndighed*, Copenhagen: det Kongelige Nordiske Oldskrift-Selskab.
Toffin, G. (1987) 'La fabrication de la bière chez deux ethnies tibéto-birmanes du Népal: les Tamang et les Néwar', in B . Koechlin *et al.* (eds) *De la voûte céleste au terroir, du jardin au foyer*, Textes offerts à Lucien Bernot, Paris: Éditions de l'EHESS.
Toynbee, A. (1884) *Lectures on the Industrial Revolution in England*, London: Rivington.
Tresemer, D. (1981) *The Scythe Book: Mowing Hay, Cutting Weeds, and Harvesting Small Grains with Hand Tools*, Brattleboro: By Hand & Foot.
White, L. Jr (1940) 'Technology and invention in the Middle Ages', *Speculum* 15 (2): 141–59.

FURTHER READING

Journals

There are a number of journals devoted to the history of technics, the most widely known being *Technology and Culture*. By contrast, there is only one journal specifically dealing with technology from an anthropological perspective, *Techniques et Culture* (since 1983). Other journals are more concerned with objects from a museological point of view, like *Objets et Mondes*, published by the Musée de l'Homme, Paris.

Recently, however, several journals have published special numbers on technology where the main issues being discussed in this chapter are considered:

'Des systèmes techniques', *Anthropologie et Sociétés* (Quebec) (1989) 13 (2).
'Technology in the humanities', *Archaeological Review from Cambridge* (1990) 9 (1).
'Savoir-Faire', *Terrain* (1991) 16.

Handbooks and classics

Forde, C. D. (1934) *Habitat, Economy and Society*, London: Methuen.
Giedion, S. (1948) *Mechanization Takes Command*, New York: Oxford University Press.
Haudricourt, A.-G. (1987) *La Technologie: science humaine*, Paris: Éditions de la Maison des Sciences de l'Homme.
Hirschberg, W. and Janata, A. (1980) *Technologie und Ergologie in der Völkerkunde*, Berlin: Dietrich Reimer.

Hume, I. N. (1974) *All the Best Rubbish*, London: Victor Gollancz.
Lustig-Arecco, V. (1975) *Technology, Strategies for Survival*, New York: Holt, Rinehart & Winston.

Mechanics, physics, chemistry, etc. for the technologist

Cardon, D. and du Chatenet, G. (1990) *Guide des teintures naturelles*, Neuchâtel and Paris: Delachaux & Niestlé.
Cotterell, B. and Kamminga, J. (1990) *Mechanics of Pre-industrial Technology*, Cambridge: Cambridge University Press.
Steinkraus, K. H. (ed.) (1983) *Handbook of Indigenous Fermented Foods*, New York and Basel: Marcel Dekker.

Recent thematic works and monographs

Atzeni, P. (1988) *Il corpo, i gesti, lo stile, Lavori delle donne in Sardegna*, Cagliari: CUEC editrice.
Chevallier, D. (ed.) (1990) *Savoir faire et pouvoir transmettre*, Paris: Éditions de la Maison des Sciences de l'Homme.
Collins, H. (1990) *Artificial Experts, Social Knowledge and Intelligent Machines*, Cambridge, Mass.: MIT Press.
Coy, M. W. (ed.) (1989) *Apprenticeship*, Albany: State University of New York Press.
Darré, J.-P. (1985) *La Parole et la technique*, Paris: L'Harmattan.
Lave, J. and Wenger, E. (1991) *Situated Learning*, Cambridge: Cambridge Univerity Press.
Roux, V. and Corbetta, D. (1990) *Le Tour du potier, spécialisation artisanale et compétences techniques*, Paris: CNRS.
Sillitoe, P. (1988) *Made in Niugini, Technology in the Highlands of Papua New Guinea*, London: British Museum.

17

SPATIAL ORGANIZATION AND THE BUILT ENVIRONMENT

Amos Rapoport

INTRODUCTION

The organization of this article reflects the lack of any generally agreed approach, taxonomy or conceptualization of the topic, which is a highly inter-disciplinary one. The particular approach adopted is based on a synthesis of ideas that I have developed in a number of previous publications. These are listed in the references, and the reader is referred to them for more extended discussion and examples. In some cases, however, specific references are given to provide guidance.

The article is divided into two major parts. The first introduces the approach and the relevant concepts; the second deals with some more substantive aspects of spatial organization and the built environment.

I – CONTEXT

Conceptualization of the built environment

A striking feature of built environments is their extraordinary variety, when they are considered cross-culturally or historically, starting with the suggested hominid sites at Olduvai Gorge of approximately two million years ago. As a result, many environments from other cultures and periods seem not merely strange and unfamiliar, but even chaotic. However, since built environments are a product of purposeful human (and, earlier, hominid) activity, and of cul-ture, they can never be chaotic, in the sense of being random; there is always an order present. What are regarded as chaotic environments are those that are not understood, not liked or felt to be inappropriate for a given observer or group. It then becomes necessary to understand the particular order and its underlying spatial and conceptual organization. For example, whereas in the West built environments tend to be characterized by geometrical design, the principles that structure the environment of non-Western societies may be social, ritual or symbolic in nature (e.g. Littlejohn 1967, Tambiah 1973, Bourdieu 1973, Rykwert 1980, Wheatley 1971 among many others). Although these principles may be expressed through overt geometrical patterning, this is not always or necessarily so. To Western observers, accustomed to seeking a geometric order, such environments may appear incomprehensible. The same applies when observers used to one kind of geometric order attempt to understand the built environment of a culture ordered by a different geometry. Thus American observers find it hard to comprehend the Islamic city, and French observers are dismayed by the American city (for further examples, see Rapoport 1977, 1984, 1990a, Hull 1976: 122).

Any consideration of built environments must take into account not only the 'hardware' but also people, their activities, wants, needs, values, life-styles and other aspects of culture. Three broad sets of questions underlie the study of any human environment:

1 Which characteristics of people as members of a species and of various social groups, or as individuals, affect how built environments are shaped?
2 What effects do what aspects of the environment have on individuals and groups, under what sets of conditions and under what circumstances, and why?
3 Given this mutual interaction between people and environments there must be mechanisms that link them. What are these mechanisms?

Although all three questions need to be considered, studied and understood, for any given enquiry some become more important and relevant than others, with consequent shifts of emphasis. In the different sections of this article, one or other of these questions may be uppermost; all three, however, need always to be borne in mind.

Although animals build environments, and although all living things in some sense both 'organize' space and are organized in space, our concern at this point is with human environments. There are human groups, such as Australian Aborigines or the Indians of Tierra del Fuego, who organize space conceptually while building very little. In other words, conceptual organization precedes building, and in that sense built environments are a subset of all human environments. There have been, and are, different ways of conceptualizing these (e.g. Ittelson 1960, Lawton 1970, Moos 1974: 6), not all of which are equally pertinent to the present topic. Many conceptualizations are complementary rather than conflicting, and some are synthesized and used in this article.

Before discussing the conceptualization which is employed in this article, I need to introduce and discuss briefly the notion of the 'setting'. As I use it here, it is a combination of the idea of a 'behaviour setting' (e.g. Barker 1968, Wicker 1979, 1981) and that of a 'role setting' (e.g. Goffman 1957, 1963). A setting comprises a milieu with an ongoing system of activities, where the milieu and the activities are linked by rules as to what is appropriate and expected in the setting. These rules, while always specific to setting and situation, also vary with culture. The physical attributes of the setting are cues that act as mnemonics, reminding people about the situation and hence about appropriate behaviour, making effective co-action possible (Rapoport 1990a).

Settings cannot be considered singly but are organized into systems within which activities, which are likewise systematically organized, take place. Settings are connected in varying and complex ways not only in space, in terms of their proximities, linkages, and separations, but also in time — in terms of their sequential ordering. They are also organized in terms of their centrality, the rules that apply, who is included or excluded, and so on. All of these are culturally variable. It follows that the extent of any system, and the settings of which it is composed in any given case, cannot be assumed a priori but need to be discovered. This does not apply just to the dwelling in its larger setting, or what can be called the house-settlement system (Rapoport 1977). For the dwelling itself can also be shown to be a system of settings within which given systems of activities occur. Unless this is taken into account, cross-cultural comparisons of dwellings are likely to be highly misleading (Rapoport 1980, 1986a, 1990c, cf. Vayda 1983). It also follows that what happens in one part of the system greatly influences what happens, or does not happen, elsewhere. This is because activities occur not only in buildings, but also in outdoor areas, settlements and beyond — in the whole cultural landscape.

It is important to emphasize that settings are *not* the same as neighbourhoods, streets, buildings or even rooms. Any one of these may contain a number of settings, at larger scales often hundreds or even thousands. Thus, in terms of settings, spatial organization is at least partially independent of the hardware, the plans of settlements, buildings or rooms as defined by walls and the like. A single-plan unit can comprise different settings at one time. Moreover, the same space can become different settings, or systems of settings, at different times. For example, a vacant piece of land may become a market, a political rally or a theatrical performance (each of which, respectively, comprises multiple settings), a soccer field, a playground, and so on. In such cases people and objects (respectively non-fixed and semi-fixed feature elements) are used to establish the setting boundaries, and to provide cues within the larger space defined by fixed-feature elements (see Figure 1).

Settings like these, therefore, do not persist and cannot be studied, or even identified, when the people or objects are no longer there (and have not been recorded). They are *temporary* (like temporary territories or jurisdictions), although they can be periodic and even regular. Such temporary organizations in space, like permanent ones, can be formed on the basis of shared values or community of interests (as with recreational groups in natural environments, or participants in a rally); these, then, are a specific manifestation of *perceived*

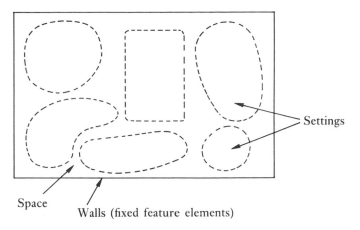

Figure 1 Settings within a space: either at one time or over time

homogeneity on the basis of which people, like other animals, congregate and cluster.

Several points follow that are critical for cross-cultural studies. One is that, as cultural rules change, so do the activities appropriate to various settings, which themselves can exist in the same space. For example, a temporary change of rules turns a street from a setting for traffic into one for a street party. More permanent differences in rules account for the major contrasts among street activities as between, say, the United States and India (Rapoport 1987, 1990d). It follows that what happens (or does not happen) in some settings greatly influences what happens in others. Unless the extent and nature of the relevant system of settings have been discovered, specific spaces or parts of built environments cannot be understood or studied. It further follows that the very definition of units of comparison depends on this. As already pointed out, a dwelling itself can be shown to be a particular system of settings within which given sets of activities take place. Thus one cannot, as is so often done, compare buildings as dwellings merely because — in form and structure — they appear to us as such. In the study of dwellings the proper units of comparison are the systems of settings, which have first to be discovered before they can be compared (see Figure 2). This discovery helps to avoid the problems that can arise from the discrepancy between our own analytic concepts and those of the peoples whom we study, that is between 'etic' and 'emic' models.

The cues that communicate the appropriate situation and behaviour, and the elements defining settings, are not only architectural, or what can be called 'fixed feature elements'. More important are semi-fixed feature elements — the furnishings of environments, whether outdoor or indoor: signs, plants, elements of personalization, furniture, bric-à-brac, and so forth. Their

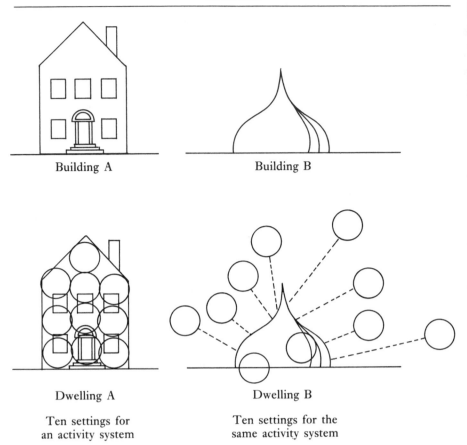

Figure 2 Comparing buildings and dwellings. Above: The two buildings cannot be compared as dwellings, but only as buildings, in terms of size, shape, structure, materials, etc. Below: The two systems of ten settings each define the dwelling and are the units suitable for cross-cultural comparison. (Based on Rapoport 1990c: 16, Figure 5.)

importance is due partly to the fact that they are easily moved or changed, hence more easily and directly used to define and communicate various settings. They also respond more easily and quickly to social and cultural changes. In addition, settings include, and can be defined by, 'non-fixed feature elements' – people and their behaviour and activities. Settings and systems of settings – the cultural landscape – therefore include fixed, semi-fixed and non-fixed feature elements (these terms are based on Hall 1966). Thus the cultural landscape not only comprises the built environment but also includes much of material culture: signs, furniture, furnishings, landscaping and plants, decorations, art objects, and so on.

At the very least, any environment – whether built or unbuilt – that expresses spatial organization involves relationships among people (or, if non-human environments are considered, among animals), between people (or other animals) and inanimate components of the environment, and among these inanimate components themselves — the 'hardware' of settlements, buildings, and the like. Thus one can think of the members of a group organized in space without taking account of physical enclosures or markings, one can consider a group in relation to the enclosures and cues in its environment, or one can envisage the enclosures and cues without taking into account the people. This leads to the conceptualization of the built environment that, together with the idea of settings and of fixed, semi-fixed and non-fixed feature elements, is used to structure the rest of this article. According to this conceptualization, the built environment, broadly defined as a human creation, involves *the organization of four elements: space, time, meaning and communication.* It will be apparent, moreover, that the environments of non-human animals can also be conceptualized in this way. These four elements can be studied separately to an extent, but the interactions and relationships among them must also be considered. Although the emphasis is on the organization of *space*, we have already seen that the same space can become different settings — that is, it can be used differently and mean different things — at different *times*, which is tantamount to the organization of time.

For example, the spatial distribution of certain kinds of groups (such as tribes, clans, or ethnic groups) is uneven and may be relatively 'permanent', change being slow and extending over long time-periods. In the case of cities this allows us to speak of the social geography or ecology of the city. Group distribution can also change more rapidly, so that different groups may occupy the same area of the city at different times. At small scales one finds single street corners or intersections being taken over by different groups at various times (see Duncan's study of Hyderabad, India (1976: 397)). At a somewhat larger scale, beaches, parks, etc. may be occupied by different groups at different times. For example, Uhuru Park, Nairobi, was occupied by various ethnic groups according to unwritten but apparently precise rules (Kamau, n.d.), as were parts of a small Chicago neighbourhood (Suttles 1968). Subjective perceptions of relative safety can lead to large areas of cities being used or avoided at certain times (Rapoport 1977: 153–4). Such notions of safety are encoded in urban images, cognitive schemata or mental maps for given towns or cities. These have been shown to be specific to particular time-periods, so that daytime and night-time images are very different (e.g. Tranter and Parkes 1977).

These images or schemata impose constraints on people's movements which are as much temporal as spatial. Temporal organization, therefore, needs to be studied as much as spatial organization, although it has tended to be neglected. Recently, however, with the development of *chronogeography*, attempts have been made to link the organizations of space and time at the scale of regions and cities (e.g. Parkes and Thrift 1980, Carlstein *et al.*

1978a, b, c, Pred 1981). These show that it is impossible to study the organization of space without also considering the organization of time.

Constraints on movement such as those just discussed (and these are not the only ones) are based on *meaning* and, in turn, affect *communication*; that is, they involve the organization of both meaning and communication. Clearly, then, the environment of human beings (and of many, if not all, non-human animals) involves the organization of time, meaning and communication as well as that of space. The organization of space cannot really be understood without considering the others. Thus in the discussion of spatial organization in this article we must always take the others into account, even if they are not emphasized or addressed explicitly. The joint effect of all four can be captured by bearing in mind, asking and attempting to answer the question: 'Who does what, where, when, including/excluding whom, and why?'

The organizations of space and time can act together to reinforce one another, achieving greater redundancy. Thus not only can the spatial organization and the relevant cues indicate expected uses, but such spaces may only be used at certain times, not being used at all at others. Examples might be pilgrimage sites, Maya 'empty villages' used only on Sundays and festivals, or sports stadia. The patterns of use and non-use reinforce the spatial organization intended for certain uses. The walls, doors and furnishings of classrooms that indicate and facilitate use are also reinforced by scheduling, so that classes are separated in time as well as space.

Spatial and temporal organization can also be separate, or one may substitute for the other. For example, the organization of time may, in some cases, replace the organization of space as a way of avoiding unwanted interaction, that is as a privacy mechanism – as in the example of Uhuru Park mentioned above. The organization of space responds to, is partly for the purpose of, and influences the organization of, communication. Patterns of communication and interaction are affected by clustering in space, by means of social networks, acquaintanceship, neighbouring, travel and visiting. The organization of meaning influences not only space and time but also communication. For example, urban cues that are interpreted as representing dangerous areas discourage communication and travel and lead to the spatial localization of groups. These groups, in turn, often organize time very differently, further isolating each other. In that way the organization of space and meaning influences behaviour, for example movement, access and the like, hence information flows and knowledge, and consequently also the organization of communication. These, in turn, reinforce the organization of meaning. Through their working together, redundancy is increased so that effects are magnified.

Such redundancy is needed to provide clear cues for behaviour and also to facilitate it. As an example, consider privacy in the sense of control of unwanted interaction. This can be achieved by organizing time, by avoidance or by scheduling. Avoidance can also be achieved by the rigid regulation of behaviour or by separation in space, for example moving to a remote setting or localizing in widely dispersed areas. One can achieve separation by putting up markers, which can be very subtle; for example, a change in ground surface in an Australian Aboriginal camp can indicate private space and an ash heap in a Bedouin camp can indicate the public area, while a larger roof beam within a Norwegian farmhouse distinguishes semi-public from private space (Rapoport 1979a, 1990a). Making markers stronger increases clarity and the strength of cues, and hence reinforces the organization of meaning. The whole process of erecting walls, doors, shutters, and the like, and of providing signs, blinds or curtains, locks, chests, drawers, cupboards and closets, and so forth, is the clearest and strongest physical expression of expected norms of privacy. Moreover, by using multiple mechanisms (time, rules, distance, and so on), redundancy can be further increased. The complex system of interactions among the organizations of space, time, communication and meaning add up to a complete ecological system.

The origins of the built environment

The topic of this chapter is the *human* use and organization of space as expressed in cultural landscapes and built environments. However, in some sense, all living things organize space. Even plants do not occupy space uniformly — they are distributed spatially in very diverse and complex ways, forming mosaics and landscapes that are studied by ecologists, botanists, biogeographers, landscape ecologists, and so on. They are evidently organized in space, but although they colonize space they do not organize space actively. It is clear that animals, even lower animals, occupy space in a very non-uniform manner and effectively organize it, often quite actively; this is most obvious in the case of higher animals. It is a fundamental evolutionary fact that all living organisms both are organized in space and organize it. This is often seen ecologically in terms of resource availability for both non-human animals and human beings: there is a link between the nature, abundance and predictability of resources and the form of spatial organization (e.g. Dyson-Hudson and Smith 1978; see Taylor 1988, pt I, for a review). However, these resources can also be symbolic and social — the latter aspect becoming important among higher animals (Wynne-Edwards 1962, Wilson 1975), and dominant in the case of humans.

There is a continuity between human built environments and those of other animals. One can consider a three-step evolutionary sequence from animals (Bonner 1980, Wilson 1975, von Frisch 1974, Taylor 1988), through hominids (Tobias 1981 and this volume, Article 3, Isaac 1972, 1983, Taylor 1988) to humans (Rapoport 1979a, b, 1990b, Taylor 1988 and references therein). It appears that as one moves through this sequence, resources increasingly include latent (symbolic), as opposed to manifest (instrumental), ones. It is also possible that as human societies become larger, more differentiated and more complex, the role of latent aspects of resources continues to increase (e.g. McGuire and Schiffer 1983), *although not necessarily in the built environment*. Thus whereas the spatial organization of non-human animals may respond primarily to the distribution of ecological resources and other environmental factors (e.g. nutrients, climate, predators, etc.), first in hominids and even more in humans, latent (or symbolic) factors exert an ever-increasing influence. Such latent aspects can then lead to variations in man-made environments, as exemplified in the very different cultural landscapes to be found on either side of political borders. These variations, in turn, attract people differentially, so that cultural habitat selection takes place, further reinforcing the spatial organization that can be perceived in the diverse cultural landscapes of regions of various kinds and scales.

Returning to the sequence from non-human animals, through hominids to humans, it is clear that animals, including insects and other invertebrates, organize space, learn about their environments, use regular routes over their home ranges, and occupy territories, sleeping roosts, feeding sites and leks (areas for male display during breeding) (Emmel 1987, Kaneshiro and Ohta 1987). All of these activities have, of course, long been known among reptiles, birds and mammals (e.g. Topoff 1987). Many of the spatial concepts to which I refer later are derived from ethological studies (territory, core area, home range, personal space); others, derived from studies of human beings (jurisdiction, setting), can be applied equally to non-human animals. As with humans, the animal habitat involves the organization of space, time, meaning and communication. It involves relationships between organisms and inanimate components of the environment, which thus become invested with meaning, as well as relationships among these inanimate components themselves, together comprising the organization of space. Like humans, animals possess cognitive schemata or 'maps' of their lifespace, with territories, barriers and paths organized in relation to considerations of hierarchy and status, as well as to the distributions of resources and predators. In other words, animals live not only in a spatial environment but also in a social environment with its various settings. As long ago as 1909, von Uexküll pointed out how complex animals' schemata of their environment can be, and how these schemata relate to the perceived environment and action space of animals in ways very similar in principle to what has since been found in humans (von Uexküll 1957). In that sense human schemata have evolved just as has culture itself (e.g. Bonner 1980). Animals also build fairly complex settings (von Frisch 1974, Collins 1987, cf. Prigogine and Stengers 1984 on termite nests). Animals select habitats and thus occupy very different locations; they mark boundaries and paths using various methods, such as sound (song, howls), scent (urine, faeces, glandular secretions) and visual markers (scratches, body elements, genital displays); they even seem occasionally to decorate their settings, as in the object assemblages ('furnishings') and painting of bower-birds, and in less striking examples among other organisms (including fish). In every case the maintenance of spatial organization, territories, boundaries, and so on, demands communication among groups and individuals, whether human or non-human. Once again we find a link between the organization of space, communication and meaning.

The construction of what appear to be stone circles almost two million years ago among Upper Pliocene Australopithecines at Olduvai Gorge, following the invention of stone tools but preceding the use of red ochre, fire, art and burials (Tobias 1981: 48), apparently relates to what might be an important behavioural development among hominids, namely the establishment of 'home-bases' (Isaac 1972, 1983). This is still a highly contentious issue (see Gamble in this volume, Article 4); if such bases were established at this stage, however, it implies two important things: a central site for the family group, and food sharing. Some trace this to an even earlier point in evolution, to protohominids (Taylor 1988, ch. 3). The supposed buildings at Olduvai, inferred from semicircular stone arrays that may have been either windbreaks or bases for huts two metres across, are believed by some scholars to be related to the *marking* of this home-base. Thus the non-shelter functions of such constructions were probably as important as their function as shelters, possibly more so. By 300,000 years ago, one finds fairly sizeable buildings arranged in camps housing groups of families, implying complex social organization (Rapoport 1979a, b). This early evolutionary development suggests, or rather implies, that such socio-territorial arrangements were adaptive for proto-hominids, early hominids and humans.

Among humans, all groups mark specific locales and organize space by using it differentially, establishing certain rights over portions of it, whether these are areas, sites or paths. As a result, humans form a mosaic of groups in space, by congregating in particular spots on the earth's surface. Once permanent, such congregations eventually become cities or other components in the spatial hierarchy of settlement (Connah 1987). There is some argument about whether ownership or control is always involved in the appropriation of space, and, if so, whether it is always of resources. It may well be that even if resource use and control underlie the initial establishment of groups in space, once in place such organization may *persist* even after ecological conditions have changed. Such spatial organization can then be studied in terms of status, power, group membership and social networks, as well as in terms of cultural meaning as expressed in myth, ritual and symbolism. These later factors have, in fact, been suggested as among the principal reasons for the origins of cities (e.g. Wheatley 1971, Rykwert 1980). This view becomes even more likely if one accepts the argument that the sacred served initially to legitimate forms of spatial organization that are themselves based on ecological and resource criteria (e.g. Rappaport 1979).

Once again we find a link between the organization of space and meaning. Resource use may, as in hunting and gathering, pastoralism and swidden cultivation, also involve the organization of time, which, in turn, reflects and influences patterns of communication. Since individuals and groups exist and interact in space, human space is anisotropic. The *systematic* use of space generates, and is indeed equivalent to, spatial organization, based on rules, life–styles and meanings, and hence ultimately on culture. Space is culturally classified and socially regulated. This, then, results in shifting boundaries. If made permanent, for example by marking, such boundaries eventually come to constitute the built environment. *The built environment is the physical expression of the organization of space – spatial organization made visible.*

Reasons for, and purposes of, built environments

In the previous section I began to consider possible reasons both for organizing spaces and for building environments. Different assumptions and approaches (e.g. materialist, ecological, symbolic, cognitive) may lead to an emphasis on different reasons. However, the reasons involved are also open to empirical investigation. Moreover, it is doubtful whether there is any *single* reason for the built environment (Rapoport 1969). I have suggested that in human evolution latent (i.e. symbolic) aspects gain in importance *vis-à-vis* manifest, instrumental functions, even if the latter were the original determinants of spatial organization. Thus different aspects may come to the fore, depending on the point in its development at which a system is studied, and on what questions are being posed – for example whether they concern proximate or ultimate causation.

Latent functions tend to emphasize *meaning*. This makes them important, because as one moves from the instrumental to the latent functions of activities, *variability increases.* Variability is one of the most important of the attributes of built environments that need to be explained. I am suggesting that a consideration of latent aspects offers a potential explanation, particularly since there are approaches from three different disciplines that make much the same point (see Table 1).

Although these three sequences are not fully comparable, they do all suggest that as one moves from instrumental function, concrete object or technomic function to latent function, symbolic object or ideo-technic function, variability increases. The relatively few types of activities typical of most built environments would imply little variability. Thus the transition from the instrumental to the symbolic has potential explanatory value. Some brief examples may help make the point.

All human groups cook. How one cooks varies significantly, the way cooking is systematically associated with other activities varies even more, and the meanings of cooking, its latent aspects, are the most variable, because they may involve status (Zeisel 1973), ritual (Esber 1972), patterns of enculturation, and so on. These lead to a need for very different and culture-specific settings, and this variability is reinforced by the different ways of working and by the variable activity systems. The same applies to other activities. Binford's

Table 1

Rapoport (1977: 19, 1990a, b) (Environment–behaviour studies)	Gibson (1950, 1968) (Psychology)	Binford (1962) (Archaeology)	
Function of activity itself (instrumental function)	Concrete object	Technomic function	
How done	Use object	Socio-technic function	
How associated into systems	Value object		
Meaning of the activity (latent function)	Symbolic object	Ideo-technic function	

(The left and right margins are labelled "Variability increases" with downward arrows.)

(1962) analysis of function is very similar in principle. He divides artefacts into those whose primary function lies in coping directly with the physical environment ('technomic' artefacts), those used principally in the conduct of social relations ('socio-technic' artefacts) and those serving to symbolize key cultural ideas ('ideo-technic' artefacts). While socio-technic functions vary more than technomic ones, ideo-technic functions vary most of all, and this leads to a corresponding variability among artefacts. Gibson's (1950, 1968) point is that most humans perceive trees (the concrete objects) in the same way. Whether one uses trees for firewood, shade or ornament will greatly change the cultural landscape; how trees are valued has an even bigger impact and ultimately depends on the meaning trees have – that is as symbolic objects. An (unpublished) analysis of advertisements for housing land in Australia over a twenty-year period showed that negative meanings attached to native trees (with land being 'cleared of native bush') were replaced by highly positive meanings, with an emphasis on the preservation of native vegetation. The two resulting cultural landscapes were obviously very different.

By responding to these latent aspects of activities, functions and objects, built environments become not only more variable but also increasingly culture-specific. Cultural differences may be conveyed (and thus reinforced and perpetuated) by differences in language, costume, food habits, and so on, but they may also be conveyed by ways of carrying out the limited range of activities and by the systems of settings in which they are carried out. Among various other consequences, this makes it easier for groups, cultures and languages to retain their cultural distinctiveness, by upholding critical cultural settings and institutions which facilitate non-verbal and verbal communication. This is why, throughout history and cross-culturally, clustering by perceived homogeneity has tended to occur especially in groups with lowered competence and under greater stress, such as ethnic or linguistic minorities and recent migrants.

Variability can exist, and can increase as cultural variables play a greater role, because of the *low criticality* of built environments. Physical constraints, as well as those of resources, knowledge, mobility, and so on, although not insignificant, tend to be relatively permissive, and many possible ways of satisfying needs usually exist. This is why latent aspects of activities can find such prominent expression in the built environment. Moreover, even specific constraints can have different meanings for different subgroups. For example, in saying that 'traditional' and 'modern' societies differ because of 'resource constraints', one could mean that these constraints are:

1 'Absolute', in terms of the amount of available goods, technology or knowledge.
2 'Relative', in terms of the differential access of groups to goods, technology or knowledge due to affordability, information, prejudice or status.
3 Culturally imposed − by tradition, custom or sumptuary laws.

Although, as we see below (pp. 484−7), spatial organization and territoriality are *not* synonymous, there are links between them, as there are between both and privacy, regarded as the control of unwanted interaction (and information flows). That is, they are linked to the organization of communication. Moreover, what is 'unwanted', what counts as 'interaction', between whom, and using what mechanisms, are all culturally variable (Rapoport 1977: 289−90). This leads to differences in domains of privacy, patterns of access and degrees of penetration. All involve forms of control and *boundary regulation* (e.g. Altman 1975). These may be exercised by individuals or groups, and can be manipulated to regulate information flows or interaction. They also frequently involve systems or sequences of boundaries which can become fairly complex, and which structure and articulate the cultural landscape. They may be merely known, or marked more or less clearly, or defined physically by walls, fences, hedges, doors, gates, etc. Such physical features and associated semi-fixed elements, which constitute the built environment, both reflect and influence behaviour and social interaction. Note, however, that the physical elements, although important, are nevertheless secondary − boundaries, like spatial organization and built environments, are thought before they are built or given physical expression.

The analysis of boundaries, and of what they contain and separate, involves many of the concepts already discussed, and those still to come, and runs as a dominant theme through much of the literature. Boundaries separate different areas of space, and enclose social, cognitive, symbolic or other domains. One can analyse boundaries in terms of their formation and dissolution, their function, their regulation and/or defence, their permeability, the ways they are marked, the rules associated with them, and so on.

Built environment, meaning and writing

In emphasizing the importance of latent aspects in the human organization of space and built environments, the role of meaning was emphasized. The notion of meaning, however, is excessively broad, and in considering the meanings communicated by built environments it is helpful to distinguish at least three different levels:

1 'High-level' meanings related to cosmologies, cultural schemata, world views, philosophical systems, the sacred, and so on.
2 'Middle-level' meanings: those communicating identity, status, wealth, power, and so on – that is, the latent rather than the instrumental aspects of activities, behaviour and settings.
3 'Lower-level' instrumental meanings: material cues for identifying the uses for which settings are intended, and hence the social situations, expected behaviour and the like; privacy; accessibility; penetration gradients; seating arrangements; movement and way-finding, and so on. These enable users to behave appropriately and predictably, making co-action possible (Rapoport 1988, 1990a: Epilogue).

The meanings encountered on these different levels vary cross-culturally and over time. There are also suggestive links between the three levels and the hierarchies shown in Table 1. One particularly important change occurs with the invention of writing (e.g Goody 1977) and the subsequent elaboration of other symbolic systems, which together comprise what Popper (1972) called 'World Three'. With this, high-level meanings *in the built environment* become less important, and many of the meanings of built environments emphasized in the anthropological literature on non-literate societies will tend to disappear (e.g. Bourdieu 1973, Littlejohn 1967, Tambiah 1973, Wheatley 1971, Rykwert 1980, Paul-Lévy and Segaud 1983). It is most unlikely that a literate culture could be destroyed by destroying its built environment, as was apparently the case with the Amazonian Bororo (Lévi-Strauss 1957). Moreover, as the scale, heterogeneity and internal specialization of both activities and settings in society increase, changes occur in the other levels of meaning. For example, middle-level meanings tend to become relatively (and often absolutely) more important, as does the need for much stronger expression of lower-level meanings – resulting in greater redundancy. This makes it possible to compare the role of built environments, differences in spatial organization, the use of space and the marking of boundaries in developed and developing countries, in more or less traditional groups in the latter, in different subcultures in developed countries, in rural as against urban settlements, in large as against small urban settlements, in neighbourhoods (or peripheral areas) as against centres, in homogeneous as against heterogeneous neighbourhoods, in special-use areas, and so on. It also provides many ways of analysing, classifying and comparing groups as one moves from nomadic to semi-nomadic groups, and from unspecialized groups in developing countries to the usually more specialized groups in developed countries.

Nomads typically use movement as a mechanism of conflict resolution and, in camps, subtly shift door directions or the relative locations of dwellings, erect 'spite fences' and so on, all as reflections of shifting social relationships (Woodburn 1972, Rapoport 1978, Ingold 1986, ch. 7). In semi-nomadic groups changes and shifts still occur. Thus in Oceania both residential patterns and the locations of houses themselves are impermanent. This is because the houses represent kinship and other social links, and their spatial organization and relationships represent meanings that articulate land and people (Rodman 1985). Hence house locations are sensitive to changes in social relations above the household level. These relations do not, of course, change when the whole settlement (whether camp or village) moves. Hence spatial mobility and residential flux are different and need to be distinguished.

Since in contemporary settled societies it is much more difficult to move, people tend to cluster with others like themselves. Some may also have more extensive social networks, interacting with selected others on bases other than that of propinquity. Interaction and involvement may also be avoided altogether (e.g. Baumgartner 1988). Moreover, when people do move, they usually do so to very similar communities (Feldman 1990). The result is a more or less permanent distribution of different groups in space, yielding a social geography of neighbourhoods, settlements, regions and countries. In societies with a simple division of labour and few specialized activities, single spaces are typically used for many different activities; in other words they contain many settings (e.g. Rapoport 1969, Kent 1984). But whereas spatial organization is simple, activities are organized and co-ordinated in time in very complex ways according to elaborate rules. In societies with a complex division of labour and many specialized activities, on the other hand, there are also many specialized spaces, each often comprising a single setting for a particular activity. This calls for highly redundant meaning cues, strong boundary control, and hence expressions in the form of physical barriers, signs, semi-fixed objects, and so on. Space is organized in ever more complex ways and marked ever more clearly and strongly.

Relationships between the built environment and culture

The concept of culture is clearly central to our topic. The definition of culture is contentious and complex, and is discussed elsewhere in this volume (see Article 14). However, in order to be able to make this concept more operational in relation to built environments, it needs to be briefly considered.

The many traditional definitions of culture can be seen to fall into three broad classes. These are: culture as a way of life typical of a group; culture as a system of symbols, meanings and schemata transmitted through enculturation; and culture as a set of adaptive strategies for survival in relation to resources and ecology. One can also ask what culture does, or is *for*, rather than what it *is*. Again, three types of answers can be found: the role of culture is to distinguish among groups and to maintain their identities; culture carries information, i.e. it is a set of instructions for assembling components (what one could call a 'design for living'); culture provides a structure or framework which gives meaning to particulars (see Rapoport 1986b).

These definitions of what culture is and does are not conflicting but complementary. Moreover, each class of definitions is relevant to an understanding of the built environment as a material expression of spatial organization. However, as it stands, the concept of culture is still both too general and too abstract. It is virtually impossible even to begin to discuss or analyse the relationship between 'culture' and 'built environment' at that level of generality and abstraction (and at least as difficult to think of 'designing for culture'). As with the concept of 'built environment', the concept of culture needs to be made less general and less abstract by 'dismantling' it.

Dismantling the concept of 'culture'

There are clearly different ways of dismantling the concept of culture to make it more useful in considering spatial organization and the built environment (e.g. Low and Chambers 1989: 6–8.) In the approach I adopt, the dismantling can be visualized along two axes – one addressing the view that 'culture' is too abstract, the other that it is too global or general (see Figure 3).

The vertical axis takes the position that culture is an ideational concept, and that it is manifested in more concrete social expressions, the actual social structures – groups, family structures, institutions, social networks, roles, status relations (e.g. by age or gender), and so on. These social structures often have settings associated with them or are reflected in (and influenced by) spatial organization and built form; they can thus be much more easily identified, studied and analysed. The horizontal axis takes the position that culture is a general concept, which can be broken down into more specific expressions, such as world views, values, life-style and activities. World views are still difficult to relate to built environments, but values, life-style and activities can relatively easily and directly be related to components of built environments (Rapoport 1990c). The point is that whereas spatial organization and built environments (as conceptualized above) can be related to activity systems, life-styles and even values, on the one hand, and to status, roles, institutions, social groups and networks on the other, they *cannot* be related to 'culture' as such.

Specifics of important components of culture

I cannot discuss here all the components of culture in any detail, or establish or develop the linkages between them and the more general definitions of culture and aspects of built environments; some of the latter become clearer in

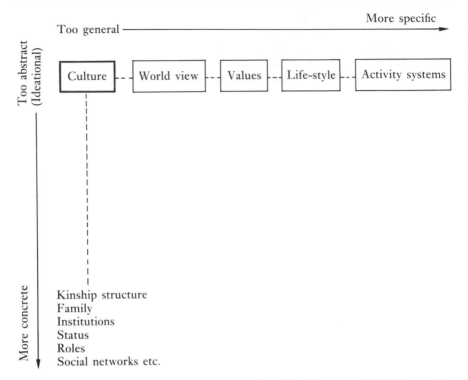

Figure 3 'Dismantling' the concept of culture. (Based on Rapoport 1977: Figure 1.9, 1990c: Figure 1)

the second part of this article. Some, however, which seem particularly pertinent to our topic, need to be emphasized. Activities, particularly if their latent aspects are included, are very important to understanding spatial organization and built environments, and have already been introduced (see Table 1). Lifestyle has proved to be a particularly crucial component of culture; both in analysing environments and in designing them, it is best conceptualized as the result of choices made on the basis of values about the allocation of resources of all sorts.

Institutions, such as those of recreation, commerce, government, and so on, and the ways in which they operate, are intimately linked with systems of settings, are fairly easily analysed and have profound consequences for spatial organization and built form; a good example is King's (1976) comparison of institutions in the indigenous and colonial city in India. Roles are often associated with particular activities and settings; again they can readily be related to the built environment. Social groups of various sorts can be easily connected to spatial organization, which is, in effect, the uneven distribution of such groups in space. Social networks have been much studied, but their spatial aspects have been neglected. Yet they often organize space, and 'natural' breaks or discontinuities in networks often correspond with spatial boundaries. Given that tight networks are typical in homogeneous (and more traditional) groups, marking through personalization or other means becomes more clearly expressed, because markers 'add up' instead of cancelling, in the sense that an area (region, settlement or neighbourhood) takes on a singular character rather than generating many discordant or conflicting expressions (see Figure 4). These then become an important aspect of built environments — the visible expression of the social mosaic. In that sense social structure and spatial structure are closely related (e.g. Gregory and Urry 1985).

I conclude, therefore, that these two sets of expressions of culture offer a useful and practical way of exploring the cultural dimensions of systems of settings, the organization of space, time, meaning and communication, and the fixed and semi-fixed feature elements — all of which comprise the built environment.

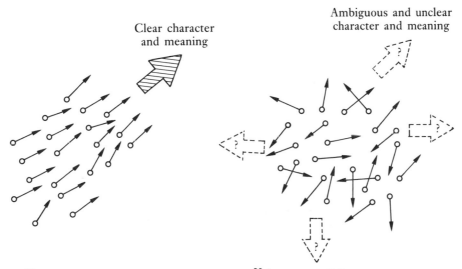

Clear character
and meaning

Ambiguous and unclear
character and meaning

Homogeneous area
Individual personalizations
reinforce each other and
produce a clear, strong
message.

Heterogeneous area
Individual personalizations cancel
each other and do not produce
any clear message.

Figure 4 The aggregation of individual personalizations in homogeneous and heterogeneous areas. (Based on Rapoport 1990a: 138, Figure 21)

477

II – SPATIAL ORGANIZATION AND THE BUILT ENVIRONMENT

We are now ready to turn to the substantive question of this article: how is the human organization of space and its expression in built environments to be approached and understood?

Analysis of the concept of space

'Space' is not a self-evident concept. It is far more than the relatively simple notion of *physical* space that is implicit in many discussions, i.e. the three-dimensional extension of the world; the intervals, separations and distances among people, between people and things, and among things. In fact there are many kinds of space that need to be distinguished before one can turn to the cultural classification of space and its expression in built environments, ranging from cultural landscapes, through settlements, neighbourhoods, urban spaces, buildings and rooms to furniture groupings. The listing that follows does not represent a complete or exhaustive catalogue of possible meanings or types of space; nevertheless, it serves to indicate some of the more significant distinctions. Note that these are all 'etic', that is they are based on the analyst's criteria rather than those of the people studied.

The first and most basic distinction is between *human* and *non-human space* (a subset of which has been called *machine space*). Space can be *designed* (in the sense of being organized) or *non-designed*, although all human space is designed (and contrasts in this respect with natural space). Designed space incorporates various forms of ordering, and cultures differ greatly in the types of order used (Rapoport 1984). Some ways of ordering will be discussed later, but one can contrast the *abstract geometric space* of, say, modern Western settlements with the space of many traditional cultures that is organized, and made safe and habitable, in terms of an essentially religious opposition between the sacred and the profane: the order imposed is sacred rather than geometric (Duncan 1990, Rykwert 1980, Wheatley 1971). The order may also be social, which leads to *social space*, reflecting the patterns and regularities of social relations, networks, hierarchies, roles, and so on. Space can be *symbolic*, although, except to those who understand the symbolism, such space may be indistinguishable from other forms of space and may not even appear organized at all (as symbolic space contrasts not only with geometric space but also with *economic space* – defined in terms of monetary and other economic values). One can also speak of *behavioural space* – that available as a possible setting or system of settings to a given individual or group. This availability, which may differ on the basis of age, gender, religion, race, mobility, and so on, means that such behavioural space, for example in a city, can be very different from the kind of space shown on a map.

Behavioural space, in turn, influences what is known (*informational space*), and also what is perceived (*perceived space*). The latter, in turn, varies with the alternative sensory modalities, so that one can speak of different sorts of *experiential* or *sensory space*. These are all subsets of *psychological space*, another type of which is *cognized space*, the mental schema or map which, again, can be different from physical space, distorted in various ways, hence non-veridical. Cognized space includes *subjective space*, involving subjectively perceived distances, areas and directions, i.e. a subjective morphology which, in the case of distances, also involves subjective time. More generally one can speak of cognitive space in another sense − as *cultural space*, consisting of the domains related to cognitive categories. One specific type of cognitive space is *imaginary space*, which may be 'imaginary' only from the point of view of an observer from another culture or period, but is quite real to the participants. Behaviour is influenced by just this imaginary space, which may be completely non-empirical, as is the case with heaven, hell, the underworld, paradise, Shangri-La or Eldorado. Such spaces often merge with sacred or with symbolic space. Recently the concept of *electronic space* has been proposed in order to study the impact of new communications technologies on spatial organization (e.g. Mitropoulos 1986). In the past it has also been the case that as transportation has become faster and cheaper, space has 'shrunk', and the way in which it is used and organized has consequently changed. This applies to the world as a whole, to regions, cities, and so on. One result has been the creation of the new spatial order of the North American city, a poly-nucleated 'urban-land', which has been well documented in the US, but is so difficult to understand for European observers as to require special interpretation (e.g. Holzner 1985).

My intention, as noted above, is not to provide a complete catalogue (even if that were possible), but to demonstrate that the 'space' that is being organized is rather complex. Moreover, each of the types listed could be greatly elaborated, and, in many cases, voluminous bodies of literature could be cited. But enough has been said to make the point. Depending on the problems or questions posed, various types of space may be more relevant, significant or important than others. The emphasis will depend on the topic of analysis.

The study of spatial organization

A variety of disciplines study spatial organization, its characteristics and attributes, and the reasons for it. Each discipline deals with different aspects of the domain and uses different concepts. Once again, my intention is not to provide a complete listing but rather to discuss briefly the principal disciplines and their specific concerns and emphases, inasmuch as they concern spatial organization only; clearly, much could be written about each.

Ecology studies the spatial organization of living things in general, including plants. *Behavioural ecology* is concerned with the interaction of spatial organization, cognition, territoriality, population density, resources and behaviour among non-human animals and human beings. *Ethology* also considers animal spatial organization, but emphasizes the behavioural and social aspects; its approach and methodology can also be applied to humans. *Evolutionary biology* and *sociobiology* address more specifically the principles of organization among animals, hominids and humans, seeking their ultimate causes in the operation of natural selection.

Human ecology concentrates on human beings from a variety of points of view and at a variety of scales. At large scales *social ecology* (and its subfield *urban ecology*) consider how various groups are distributed in space – e.g. clustered, segregated, dispersed. At small scales *small-group ecology* studies human spatial organization at the level of group actions and interactions, proxemics, personal space, and so on. *Landscape ecology*, a relatively new field, considers the visible landscape as a result of the interplay of ecological processes and human activities and actions (e.g. Forman and Godron 1986, Vink 1983).

Human geography in general plots human cultural phenomena in space (most, if not all, such phenomena can be so plotted and mapped, including food habits, costume, songs and music, housing styles, burial customs, and so on). Its concern is with the cultural landscape. The various subfields of geography study specific aspects of the above. Thus *behavioural geography* studies how human behaviour (seen broadly) is expressed spatially. *Regional geography* studies the interaction of a variety of physical, biotic and human phenomena to create identifiable regions. *Social geography* studies the distribution of groups in space – it thus overlaps with social ecology and, at the relevant scale, with urban ecology and *urban geography*, which is also concerned with the spatial aspects of urban phenomena. *Historical geography* studies all these phenomena diachronically, *political geography* is concerned with the spatial expression of political processes, forces and decisions (i.e. with *political space*). *Economic geography* studies and tries to explain the spatial patterns resulting from economic decisions and forces, thus its concern is with the economic landscape and with location (and central place) theory. At that level it partly overlaps with *regional and urban planning* and *ekistics* (a relatively new field defined as 'the science of human settlements'). At smaller scales, and more concerned with the built environment, are the related design fields – *landscape architecture, urban design* and *architecture*, all of which are normatively concerned with spatial organization, although they lack an empirical research base and a concern with explanation. This gap is filled by *environment–behaviour studies*, the perspective of the present chapter – which is, by nature, a highly interdisciplinary one.

Also concerned with the diachronic study of human spatial organization and its explanation is *archaeology*, which deals with the spatial distribution of artefacts of all kinds – buildings, tools, bones, refuse, and so on. This is based on the notion that all such materials are spatially patterned, and that this patterning contains information, which can be decoded, about social organization, hierarchy and status, ethnicity, ritual and religion, cognition and meaning. In order to extract this information, analogies with known human behaviour have to be drawn, and archaeology has consequently expanded to include experimental archaeology and ethnoarchaeology. The latter, of course, overlap with *anthropology* (e.g. Kent 1984, 1987; cf. Rapoport 1990b) and its various subfields – *social*, *cultural* and *ecological* (e.g. Vayda 1969, Rappaport 1979), *symbolic* (e.g. Basso and Selby 1976, Paul-Lévy and Segaud 1983), and others. All of these are concerned with understanding humans as cultural animals and, in the present context, their spatial organization and built environments.

Note that many of these disciplines study spatial organization etically. The anisotropy of space means that organisms (plants, animals, humans), settlements, buildings, roads and semi-fixed feature elements, processes, behaviours, activity systems, settings, territories, and so on can all be mapped because they are systematically distributed in space. If such studies are diachronic, they combine the organizations of space and time. Some of these disciplines are also concerned with emic aspects of spatial organization, that is with the meanings assigned to space by the people studied. Both emics and etics are required for an understanding of the topic, and the use of derived etic categories is critical for any comparative work.

It is also important not to view these disciplines and their concerns as conflicting or competing, but rather as complementary. Each studies a few aspects of a particular subdomain. If one is careful to consider the questions asked, and the conceptual and methodological positions adopted, it is possible, at least in principle, to identify commonalities and to achieve some synthesis and integration which, as a first step, requires at least a knowledge of the range of disciplines involved. Indeed, an adequate understanding of spatial organization and its expression in the built environment requires that these varied approaches and findings be integrated and synthesized. This becomes possible because, at the most basic level, all these fields study the anisotropic nature of the world, the non-homogeneous spatial distribution of 'something' on the face of the earth. This, in turn, involves the segmentation of space whereby locales are differentiated and, as a result, divided by boundaries.

These boundaries are, in the first place, cognitive, and in some cases these may be all there is, although some physical marking is usually present which, by making such boundaries clearer, leads to wider consensus about their locations. Australian Aboriginal spatial organization provides a good example. The very complex system of areas, sites and paths that dissect the Aboriginal landscape implies a very high degree of differentiation, and any differentiation inevitably implies boundaries. These may, of course, be permeable rather than rigid, but in the Aboriginal case they generally coincide, in the first instance, with natural features such as rocks, waterholes, large trees, and so on, which may be more clearly marked by rituals or by changes in ground texture (Rapoport 1975, Sutton 1988). In other cases a large range of cues may be used, including fences, walls and other structures. In general, the clearer the cues and the more redundant – and hence stronger – the message, the clearer the boundaries, as in the case of the subjective definition of urban neighbourhoods (Rapoport 1977, 1980–1).

In the human organization of space the process of differentiation is active, and in some sense purposeful (even if not always explicitly intended). Space is segmented and locations are differentiated, and then organized into systems at various scales from furniture groupings, through rooms, buildings and urban spaces, neighbourhoods, settlements and settlement systems, regions and cultural landscapes, to countries. Locales are linked by various forms of transportation and communication which are expressions of, and means for, the most important form of linkage – human activities. Locations are labelled and belong to, or are used by, particular individuals and groups; thus spatial organization and identity are frequently linked (Duncan 1981). Locations, and the settings that constitute them, have rules associated with them about appropriate behaviour, who belongs there and has (how much) access, who controls or uses resources (and which), and so on, in other words cultural rules about who does what, where, when, including or excluding whom (and why). Thus behaviour and activity systems are organized relative to spatial organization and built environments, as these are expressed in systems of settings. One result of this process is that boundaries are created, and then maintained and controlled. Boundaries are selectively permeable: various people are admitted to, or excluded from, various spatial domains or settings and may penetrate deeply or just minimally, may become central or controlling or remain peripheral, depending on who they are, and what rules apply. This is likely to vary over time; people typically excluded may be allowed to cross boundaries and enter spatial domains at certain times (e.g. Kamau n.d., Suttles 1968).

Boundaries may be marked or unmarked, clear or fuzzy, agreed or disputed, acknowledged by others or ignored, constant and consistent or variable. They may also have different rules associated with them. When this is the case, they represent different domains, for example: *personal occupancy* (e.g. the dwelling), which imposes the strongest restrictions on admission and behaviour; *community occupancy* (e.g. a private club), where restrictions within defined limits apply; *society occupancy* (e.g. a street), where access is available to all members of society, although this varies cross-culturally in terms of the specifics, the cues used, and the context (and even in Western culture there may be unwritten rules that modify this); and *free occupancy* (e.g. a deserted beach), where there are, effectively, no controls (Brower 1965). (Other comparable classifications are offered by Chermayeff and Alexander 1965, and by Lyman and Scott 1970.) Some of these categories may themselves be culturally variable and may or may not apply, depending on the context.

The elements of space, types of systems, boundaries, rules and so on are all culturally variable. Understanding these is essential for understanding regional and settlement patterns and built environments. Since spatial organization and built environments not only reflect and contain culture but are also actively used in cultural processes, their study is essential for a full understanding of culture.

How space is organized – specifics and concepts

The many and very different ways in which space is organized at all scales can be understood as physical expressions of cognitive schemata. This applies as much to temporary and to non-territorial organizations as to others; all reflect, express and embody schemata, although they need not be expressed physically in the sense of being built, or marked permanently. For example, Australian Aborigines have clear cognitive maps of the environment, expressed in their art, which represents and reinforces a particular order of relationships among people and between people and land. Aboriginal paintings depict social and mythic maps that structure the landscape cognitively and socially. Landscapes (especially in Central Australia) are criss-crossed by mythic tracks which represent the travels of many different ancestral beings. The sites associated with them and with their activities are not usually marked, although, as noted above, they often coincide with relatively prominent features of the landscape. In effect, social space, mythic space and geographic space coincide, and where they overlap is marked through periodic actions such as rituals (Rapoport 1975, Sutton 1988: 80, 86, 93, 121–2). There are other examples of such boundaries that are *known* but not marked except by human activity. When marking develops, spatial organization and various social and cultural phenomena still tend to 'condense' at special sites (e.g. Kuper 1972). These are then appropriately marked, and knowing and understanding them is crucial to any attempt to know and understand the social life of the group. Moreover, because these structures and organizations reflect cognitive schemata, the latter can, in turn, be identified – as, for example in the case of Southern Africa (Kuper 1972, 1980).

In short, the world is divided into cognitive domains, the domains are named (labels are attached), and rules apply about who does what, where, when, and including or excluding whom. The boundaries around such domains, although they may only be known, are usually marked or indicated in some way to remind people within a specific cultural context of the situation and hence of how to act appropriately; the marking is thus a mnemonic. In that sense behaviour and spatial organization are always related. Spatial organization and the underlying cognitive schemata represent a balance between repulsion and attraction, between dispersive and cohesive forces, avoidance and interaction, competition and co-operation.

Cognized spatial domains are also related to various cognitive codes, of which they are a specific expression (e.g. Bernstein 1971, Douglas 1973). They are important in enculturation and are themselves learned: one learns the spatial classification or principles of ordering, the rules, the meanings of cues, the relevant behaviour, and so on. Thus, at the most basic level, at least three things are involved in spatial organization:

1 Some form of *classification* of space into domains, settings, etc. that reflects cognitive schemata and codes, and includes associated rules.
2 The rules involve some form of *control*, strong or weak, formal or informal, by individuals or groups of various sizes. These rules control access, penetration and behaviour.
3 In general, some form of *communication* of the type of domain and setting, boundaries and rules is involved, using various cues, such as walls, markers, signs, semi-fixed elements, and so on (cf. Sack 1987: 21–2).

Cognitive schemata are culture-specific and are fundamental to spatial organization. They underwrite the areal classification into cognitive domains, the boundaries that surround them and the rules that apply therein. All else follows. Once cognitive domains are known or expressed through the natural or built environments, they may then be decoded, so that the underlying schemata are reproduced in the form of cognitive 'maps' (or 'mental maps') in observers and users. These can be highly accurate (or veridical) if the cues in the environment communicate effectively, or non-veridical, with distortions of various sorts regarding area, distance, proximity, direction, and so on, all subjectively defined and different from the actual. These distortions can be studied and measured. Although this is not our topic, the existence of subjective morphology is important. This is because it is usually cognized rather than actual spatial organization that influences behaviour. For example, if an area is regarded as being dangerous because of crime, it will be avoided even if in reality the crime rate is not unusually high. Similarly a route perceived as longer than another will be avoided, even if it is really shorter. Note that cognitive schemata are found not only in human beings but also in non–human animals.

Settings with their cues defining the situation, with rules for penetration and appropriate behaviours, are specific kinds of cognitive domains. Examples might include: a sleeping area (or bedroom in some cultures); a baseball or cricket game; a church or temple; a family room, tavern or pub, sweat lodge, menstruating hut, men's house, senior common room, dance ground, yam house, living room, toilet, and so on. The ongoing patterns of behaviour, and how specialized or overlapping they are, depend on cultural codes and are, in fact, elicited by the cues marking the setting. Settings, in effect, have associated with them repertoires of appropriate behaviours. A given setting, by defining a situation, suggests a sequence of behaviours that are frequently highly routinized (Rapoport 1990a). Settings, as already shown, never occur alone, nor are they used in isolation, so that systems of settings must be considered.

It is also very important to distinguish clearly between *spatial organization* and *territoriality*, which is not only a concept of a different order but also much more specific, i.e. it refers to a type of spatial organization. The two terms are not synonymous. In principle, the former can exist without the latter. Spatial organization is fundamental and inescapable, because one's very presence in space differentiates it, makes it anisotropic and hence organized; a territory, on the other hand, is a specific type or category of space. In other words, not all organized space is territory, and territories can be seen as a particular kind of cognitively defined domain, with particular rules leading to certain behaviours and thus having social, psychological and ecological entailments (e.g. regarding resource use). Definitions of territoriality in the literature differ greatly (e.g. Altman 1975, Malmberg 1980, Sack 1987, Taylor 1988). There is a common core , however. This includes some form of 'ownership' and control by individuals or groups of a particular delimited site or location, hence control of its boundaries and of access to its resources. Control, which implies the possibility of exclusion, operates through various displays, ways of marking, forms of defence, and so on. The definition of territorial boundaries is *not* the same as the definition of spatial boundaries.

Much has been written on human territoriality, about which three views are possible:

1 That it is entirely genetic or 'hard-wired', that it is an 'instinct' similar to what is found in many non-human animals.
2 That it is purely social, that it developed late in the evolution of human society, that is after the development of agriculture and hence of property. In that sense it is seen as derived, related to social inequality and hierarchy, power, ownership and control and perhaps, in addition, to social co-operation and orderly social interaction.
3 That it *is* a product of biological evolution, but nevertheless is *not* hard-wired (e.g. Taylor 1988 and references therein; for an alternative view and classification see Ingold 1986, chs 6 and 7, especially pp. 134–7). This is an intermediate position which is based on the notion of gene–culture co-evolution (Boyd and Richerson 1985).

The third view can be understood as reconciling the other two. It allows for a genetically based, instinctual component, but in a weaker form.

Assuming that territoriality evolved as a strategy for maximizing fitness, it follows that where resources are such that 'ownership' is adaptively inappropriate, it will not be expected to develop (e.g. Dyson-Hudson and Smith 1978, Taylor 1988). Neither will it develop where hierarchy is weak, or where control is not needed or not possible. In other words, even when there is a predisposition for territorial behaviour, its expression may depend on the presence of eliciting conditions. Among such conditions is the salience, primacy or centrality of the situation, so that territorial behaviour is more likely to develop, and to be stronger, in highly salient, primary and central locales than in peripheral, secondary ones.

There is also disagreement about scale. In some views the concept of territoriality can be extended to include large-scale units such as countries or nations (e.g. Soja 1971, Malmberg 1980, Sack 1987, Merelman 1988). In other views, particularly those that regard territoriality as an evolutionary adaptation, it cannot be extended to such large scales and should be limited to fairly central or primary settings of limited size and to face-to-face groups (e.g. Taylor 1988). In this latter view, neighbourhoods, settlements, regions, countries or empires, although all forms of spatial organization, owned in some sense, and controlled in terms of access, use of resources and the regulation of behaviour, are nevertheless *not* territories.

In this connection it is essential to consider territories (as owned and defended areas) as part of a larger system. The concept of territory can be related to several other concepts (see Figure 5):

1 *Home-range* The usual extent of regular movement and activities definable as a set of behavioural settings and linking paths.
2 *Core-area* These are those areas within the home-range that are most commonly used, and best known.
3 *Jurisdiction* An area 'owned' or controlled for a limited time only and by some agreed rules.
4 *Personal space* The movable 'bubble' of space surrounding an individual.

Spatial organization can vary, depending on the specific conjunction of territories, core-areas, personal space, home-ranges, and jurisdictions, as well as the other factors discussed here. For example, one can have a home-range without territories, and a jurisdiction both at the group and at the individual level (as in my earlier examples of Chicago or the Nairobi park). Various combinations are possible but, as for other forms of systems of settings, the organization has an important temporal component and involves *movement*. Thus, once again, the organizations of space and time are linked. This means that spatial organization involves not only *areas* but also lines and nodes (Sutton 1988, Ingold 1986). There is a connection here with the idea, suggested by Lynch (1960), that edges, paths, nodes, districts and landmarks may play an important role in the way people construct cognitive maps of urban areas. Despite some problems with these categories (Rapoport 1977, ch. 3), they have proved influential, and it does seem that cities are construed in terms of paths along which one moves; certain nodal points such as squares, major road intersections, and so on; landmarks such as statues or prominent buildings; edges − for example where built-up areas meet land or greenery, or where there are clear changes in character; and districts − areas of special character, often named and clearly defined, which become units or elements in the city.

There is also a connection with the notion of patches, corridors and matrices used in landscape ecology (e.g. Forman and Godron 1986). In this view, landscapes are understood as consisting of patches of vegetation, buildings, and so on, of different sizes, shapes and configurations. These are linked by corridors which are linear elements which vary in their widths, connecting patterns, the nature of the nodes where they intersect, and the presence or absence of

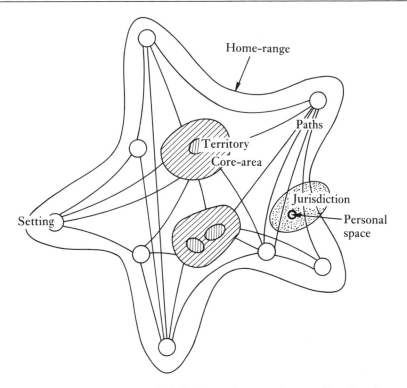

Figure 5 Home-range, core-area, jurisdiction and personal space. (Based on Rapoport 1973: 32, 1977: Figure 5.6)

breaks. There are also matrices which may vary in their nature, relative area, connectivity, and so on.

The idea of movement is most important because it entails that space, as a system of settings, can be organized without its having to be divided into mutually exclusive, 'owned' territories. Movement may have both practical and ritual dimensions, as among Australian Aborigines, Maya, and in many other ethnographic instances (Rapoport 1975, 1977, 1990a, Sutton 1988, Vogt 1969). Thus Aborigines 'belong to country' rather than owning country, although in some sense they do 'own' it by exercising ritual rights. In such cases there may, but need not, be a link through ritual between a group and an area, site or node. Not only can ritual movement be a *form* of spatial organization; it can also be the rationale for spatial organization − as in the various urban forms emphasizing movement and related to the processional element. Bechhoefer (1989), for example, has shown how, in the case of a Sri Lankan village processions and movement are the principal activity system that gives meaning to the settlement form, organizes time and also organizes the settlement form itself by linking settings into a specific system. In this case the

487

elements comprise the temple with its various components; the houses with their subdivisions, linked by the street; the village, fields, and so on – again involving a range of scales.

My discussion suggests that there are different cultural ways of structuring space, which can vary along manifold dimensions, for example those of ownership or control, accessibility to outsiders, purposes or use, degree of enclosure, etc. (e.g. Goodsell 1988: 10). Different cultures also use various underlying rationales to organize space – ecological, economic, social, political, ethnic, religious (e.g. Hakim 1986), ritual (e.g. Feng Shuei in China), and so on. Space can also be organized or ordered in terms of being open or closed, public or private, specialized or unspecialized. In any given case, emic, culture-specific categories or dimensions are used by particular groups to classify and order domains and settings, thereby to structure space and hence to organize it. These orderings and organizations can then be expressed through physical means, resulting in built environments. In effect, the organization of space cognitively precedes its material expression; settings and built environments are thought before they are built – as is shown by those cases where they are never built, as for example among Australian Aborigines (Rapoport 1975). In such cases, however, they are still used and activities occur in them. These must be appropriate to the settings involved, however; the cognitive definition of a domain entails appropriate rules and the resultant activities. While such unbuilt environments can be studied among contemporary groups, for the prehistoric past all that we have are material traces from which spatial organization has to be inferred, and from which inferences may, in turn, be made about social, cognitive, symbolic and other aspects of behaviour (e.g. Rapoport 1990b).

Cross-cultural comparison of emic categorizations does often reveal regularities. These have frequently been expressed in the form of binary oppositions. I adopt here the same procedure because it is easy and clear, although this should not be taken to imply any commitment to structuralist ideas. Among such binary oppositions one finds:

inside/outside	initiated/uninitiated
closed/open	good/bad
female/male	clean/unclean
left/right	sacred/profane
back/front	safe/dangerous
hidden/exposed	domestic/wild
specialized/unspecialized	culture/nature
central/peripheral	primary/secondary

These can vary over time (as do settings) and they typically vary with culture. They may vary with both, as cultures evolve and change. Thus the respective locations of what is safe and what is dangerous can change between day and night (e.g. Tranter and Parkes 1977), and the dangerous can change from being due to evil spirits to being due to fear of crime (Rapoport 1977: 153–4). Some distinctions may disappear or weaken (e.g. initiated/uninitiated or men/women) and new ones may develop (e.g. human/machine). Thus some are lost, some are changed or modified in terms either of dimensions or of rules and boundaries, some remain unchanged, and new ones emerge. The number of specialized settings can increase along with an increase in the number of dimensions used to classify and organize space and settings.

Middle terms or even multiple terms are frequently found, such as personal, community, society and free occupancy; or private, semi-private, semi-public, public, and even more complex sequences. These all reflect culturally variable cognitive schemata and domains and the boundaries within them; their locations and the permitted, accepted or customary behaviour associated with them all vary. These variations have psychological, ecological and other outcomes regarding resource use, knowledge of places and of people (or lack of it), and so on, which, in turn, influence behaviour through a feedback effect. One result is that unknown areas, for example in cities, tend not to be used.

This latter effect is due to the fact that spatial organization often restricts access of the 'wrong' people on the basis of various dimensions of perceived homogeneity or heterogeneity. Among these, looked at historically and cross-culturally, have been ethnicity, class, income, religion, language, race, caste, occupation, place of origin, ideology, and so on. Without supposing that 'ownership' of space or resources is necessarily central, it is nevertheless the case that all spatial organization is an attempt, by individuals or groups, to control, affect or influence people, phenomena and relationships by controlling access to some delimited area or setting. In some cases, this serves to prevent or reduce stress partly through facilitating 'backstage' behaviour and through enhancement of the ability to understand the subtle cues of non-verbal behaviour, unwritten rules, and so on.

Spatial organization, social complexity and societal scale

As societies become larger and more complex, a number of developments take place that have significant consequences for spatial organization. These effects seem quite clear, whatever the current status of social evolutionary models. As the number of groups and their heterogeneity increases, these groups develop highly diverse cognitive codes. As a result, relationships between groups and the spaces or settings they occupy tend to become more complex. This is not simply a matter of an increase in the number and diversity of settings, in their specialization, or in their linkages and separations. In many cases the 'natural' course of development is distorted by various policies based on ideology or politics, as well as by codes, regulations, insurance requirements, and the like. Moreover, most individuals and groups no longer organize for themselves the fixed feature elements defining space, or shape their own built environments, but rather occupy already existing buildings. By changing the rules governing the use of these buildings and by altering their semi-fixed feature elements, they can, of course, employ these spaces differently — that is, they can create new systems of settings within them.

Another consequence is that the number and specialization of settings, both cognitive and actual, rises very markedly because the underlying cognitive codes are more elaborated (Bernstein 1971, Douglas 1973). This leads to more complex spatial organization with more articulation among elements, more and more varied rules, more complex linkages and separations. This, in turn, particularly given more numerous and heterogeneous groups, requires that the cues, markers and indicators of both boundaries and expected behaviour within settings achieve greater force and clarity. The *redundancy* of the cues communicating meaning therefore needs to be increased. Thus modern regions, cities and buildings require complex systems of iconic and verbal signs; these are superimposed upon the spatial organization, which, in itself, no longer communicates adequately. Similarly the known, or very subtle, cues in the built environment also become inadequate, and their redundancy increases. For example, in a traditional Australian Aboriginal camp an area surrounding the windbreak is swept several times a day. This change of ground texture indicates more private areas (the extent of which is, in any case, also well known). In contemporary urban and other settings, walls, fences, doors, gates, signs and other cues are necessary to achieve the same objectives. It is possible that in some subdomains, such as the sacred and the mythical, traditional spatial organization may be as complex, or more complex, than in modern counterparts, but the redundancy of cues is always less.

Traditionality is, however, not purely temporal (Rapoport 1989). There are traditional groups in developing countries that change both the use and the form of built environments according to the degree of their adoption of modern Western models. There are also various forms of syncretism between the two (Rapoport 1983). Even within a single country like the United States or Britain there are various groups that use space, particularly domestic space, in 'traditional' ways, in the sense that the same room may be many settings both simultaneously and sequentially (Kent 1984, Borchert 1979, Hanson and Hillier 1982–3). These cases also allow different spatial codes to be identified and compared, and changes in them to be observed.

Spatial organization at different scales

Space is usually organized hierarchically, being congruent with, and expressive and supportive of, social institutions, activity systems, groups and their cognitive schemata. As a result, space is also organized, and built environments likewise occur on various physical scales. Again, one must bear in mind that spatial organization is related to, and accompanied by, organizations of time, meaning and communication. Airports, highways, railroads, telephone lines, radio and TV towers, mail systems, streets, pipelines and other services are forms of the organization of communication that also play an important role in structuring contemporary cultural landscapes. Meaning systems involve not only the built environment itself, but also the complex informational systems superimposed upon it, as well as political and administrative boundaries. The latter, in turn, affect how communication is organized.

The last example suggests that human spatial organization at the largest scale involves empires, political blocs and alliances. Continents as such can be considered to be natural units, although there is, of course, a cognitive component in their classification. At the level of countries spatial organization is clearly strong, although, as already mentioned, there is disagreement as to whether they are, or can be, territories (despite the fact that the term originally meant a domain of political sovereignty or jurisdiction) (Malmberg 1980, Soja 1971, Merelman 1988, Taylor 1988). Within countries are spatial units of varying hierarchical scale: provinces, states and regions. Then follow systems of settlements (as studied by central place theory): settlements — megalopolises, cities, towns and villages; parts of settlements, such as sectors, wards, neighbourhoods and ethnic enclaves; group areas and specialized districts; groups of buildings; buildings; parts of buildings, such as rooms, corridors, attics or the areas in traditional dwellings (Bourdieu 1973, Littlejohn 1967, Kamau 1978–9, Tambiah 1973, Vogt 1969, Rapoport 1977, 1979a, 1990a); parts of rooms (e.g. furniture groupings), and shifting groups of people and their spatial and social relations. There is thus a continuum of units of spatial organization from very large to very small.

Various classifications of such scales exist, one example being the logarithmic Ekistic scale developed by C. A. Doxiadis, with fifteen units ranging from the person through the room, dwelling, house group and neighbourhood to the ecumenopolis — the whole earth. Other forms of classification have already been discussed, such as the model presented in Figure 5 (incorporating personal space, territory, jurisdiction, core area and home range), and the concept of system of settings. It has also been suggested that a single unit may be used, repeated and built up to form environments at ever-larger scales, the hierarchical arrangement being in terms of the number of such units assembled into larger units (Scheflen 1976, Scheflen and Ashcraft 1976). There can also be a single cognitive organizational schema underlying spatial organization at a variety of scales from the house to the neighbourhood to the city and realm, as a number of studies in Mexico have shown (e.g. Wood 1969, Ingham 1971, Marcus 1976, Flannery 1976, Broda et al. 1987) or as was the case in southern Africa (e.g. Kuper 1980).

Recall that settings occur within the spatial framework of fixed feature elements and are often defined by semi-fixed elements (objects, furnishings and the like) in that space which communicate appropriate meanings. Recall also that in systems of settings, through their systemic linkages, different parts of the system are influenced at various scales, as is what happens in which parts. Through an examination of context it is possible to understand how different parts of the built environment are designed and laid out. To give a very simple example, the same domains, units or elements can be constituted by being aggregated in various ways (an additive process) or by being subdivided within an established envelope (a subtractive process) (Rapoport 1969). Taken together, settings at all these different scales, and the systems they form, reflect cognitive schemata about divisions, hierarchy, names, boundaries, use and behaviour, penetration and privacy, and all the many different ways of organizing space already discussed. Figure 6 suggests how some of these models may be combined.

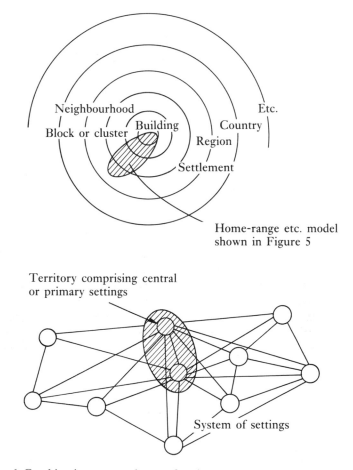

Figure 6 Combinations or syntheses of various concepts of spatial organization

Material expressions of spatial organization – the built environment

I have argued that although boundaries and settings may be known, they are usually marked in some way, and that this marking makes routinized behaviour and co-action much easier, more likely and more *predictable*. The marking of both boundaries and the contents of settings and domains, what was called the 'mnemonic function' of cues, reduces the need for information processing; it takes the remembering away from people and puts reminders regarding the situation, rules and behaviour into the settings (Rapport 1990a). Markers are also found among non-human animals, but are further developed in the course of hominid and human evolution. Thus, although environments are thought before they are built, the importance of the built environment is considerable. I have already shown that settings can vary from just being known to being very minimally marked to being strongly defined, with high levels of redundancy and using multiple means. Marking can thus vary from minimal semi-fixed feature cues, through a range of fixed cues to extremely strong, highly redundant systems. Built environments, of course, also include semi-fixed elements which are used to communicate aspects of spatial organization and setting. The presence of people (non-fixed features) reinforces this communication. All of these marking functions change with increases in scale, heterogeneity, complexity, specialization of settings, and so on.

It is possible to consider and develop inventories of ways in which spatial organization and its underlying cognitive schemata can be expressed or communicated. These are in addition to, and reinforce, location. Such lists, lexicons or repertoires can become very lengthy, but would include posts, singly or in lines, rocks or stones, graven images (which often parallel postural displays and other forms of bodily expression in non-human primates and other animals) and various forms of personalization which in homogeneous areas communicate similar meanings, thus reinforcing each other (as shown in Figure 4). Materials, colour, textures, grains, plants and landscaping, fences, walls and other enclosures, signs and signposts, and even urban graffiti, can all play this role.

These repertoires, which can be decoded and understood not only on the ground but (by researchers) from the air and even from satellites (see references in Rapoport 1990a, Hublin 1989), can communicate different kinds and levels of meaning inherent in the desired spatial organization, and can be employed differently in various cultures or periods, and at various scales of settlement. They can also be used in conjunction to increase redundancy. Available elements from the repertoire can moreover be employed to demarcate territories (as a special type of domain or setting), and to help define boundaries. The importance of boundaries has already been discussed; for one thing, they often serve to establish, define and maintain group identity. To do this, both internal and external agreement are necessary (e.g. Barth 1969).

Much marking has to do with identity, particularly in traditional situations where *group* identity predominates as compared with the greater individualism of modern society. Marking for 'external consumption' needs to be stronger, with higher redundancy. Again, it is important to reiterate the qualification that cases exist where such group domains, particularly if temporary or periodic (i.e. organized in time), although known, nevertheless remain unmarked, and can even exist in public space (e.g. Kamau n.d., Suttles 1968, Lofland 1973, Duncan 1976). Thus, spatial organization may be defined by knowledge, behaviour or physical boundaries, but typically all three are involved – behaviour and knowledge (or lack of it) define boundaries, and physical boundaries influence knowledge and behaviour.

Typically, by communicating cultural meaning, marking defines areas of various sorts – including territories, the level of control, and rules of access, penetration and behaviour. Boundaries also imply an included content or a centre, and these, too, can be hierarchically disposed, as in D. W. Meinig's identification of core, domain and sphere for the Mormon culture region in the US Southwest, a classification that has also proved applicable to other places and situations (Rapoport 1977: 256).

In order to be effective, any cues need, first, to be noticed; that is where redundancy comes in. Second, they need to be understood – that is, they must be culture-specific. Third, those who do decode and understand them must then be prepared to 'obey' and act accordingly and appropriately, so that they can co-act. Although such agreement tends to be higher in traditional than in modern situations, in most cases people still conform. Although behaviour is not strictly determined, the probability of conformity is generally quite high, so that these mechanisms work quite effectively, as they must do if conflict is to be avoided and co-action and the co-ordination of activities facilitated. If the cognitive schemata of users match actual spatial organization, and if the markers or cues are noticeable and comprehensible, then way-finding and orientation work smoothly. If, however, these conditions do not obtain, then orientation and way-finding can become very difficult, which can be a serious matter. Forms of organization related to orientation and way-finding, such as in urban environments, vary considerably with culture, as do principles of 'navigation'. Way-finding and orientation as processes are also culturally variable, and even vary among groups within a culture, depending on education, age, gender, and other factors. Such cultural subgroups may use very different orientational and navigational systems.

In many cases differences in people's objectives and ways of cognitively structuring space result in different forms of spatial organization on the ground. For example, divergent views about levels of mobility and levels of access, and for whom, lead to forms as contrastive as Moslem and North American cities, as shown in Figure 7 (cf. Wheatley 1976). However, terms such as 'Islamic' or 'Moslem' are too broad, and need to be qualified by region, country and other criteria (e.g. for Iran see Bonine 1979, 1980).

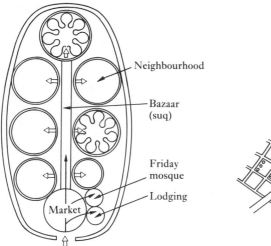
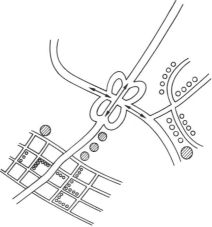

Traditional Moslem city: controlled access, limited mobility.
Accessible areas: market, bazaar (suq), lodging, Friday Mosque.

North American city: general access, maximum possible mobility.
Accessible areas: almost everywhere.

Figure 7 Accessibility and mobility in the Moslem and North American city: a schematic comparison. (Based on Rapoport 1977: 21, Figure 1.10)

In other cases, different means of marking and physical expression, and the diverse forms of spatial organization associated with them, may provide alternative ways of achieving the same form of social organization (that is, organization of communication). An example is the establishment of privacy as the control of unwanted interaction. Thus, a neighbourhood composed of courtyard houses (what could be called the 'inside-out city'), a homogeneous neighbourhood with a strongly ethnic character, and an extremely low-density area of widely separated houses may appear very different, as indeed they are. At the same time, however, they all achieve similar ends − to keep unwanted and hence stressful information and interaction to a minimum, to reduce overload, or in other words to increase privacy. They just use different means: respectively, physical barriers, social barriers inhibiting verbal and non-verbal communication with strangers, and distance. Similar ends are achieved in nomadic societies by moving.

This observation reinforces three points made earlier. First, to understand the built environment and its underlying spatial organization one needs to consider and understand the relevant cognitive schemata. Second, it is not enough to look merely at the physical manifestations of spatial organization; it is essential also to consider the relationship between these physical expressions and social, behavioural, sacred, mythical and other types or aspects of space. Very often in the contemporary world one encounters major incongruencies as environments (such as housing) are designed in ways that ignore behavioural, ritual and other considerations. While situations of this kind have been mainly documented, and are possibly most acute, in developing countries (e.g. Chua 1988, Grimaud 1986, Rapoport 1983), the phenomenon is rather more general. Third, to look at spatial organization alone is not enough – the organization of time, meaning and communication must also be considered. So, indeed, must all the other factors introduced in this article.

CONCLUSION

Spatial organization and its partial expression in built environments, cultural landscapes and material culture is an inescapable aspect of life – which of course is a process that takes place in space. Yet, by and large, it has been somewhat neglected by the social and behavioural sciences, including anthropology. Understanding spatial organization and built environments is an inherently interdisciplinary endeavour. Built environments play an important role in enculturation. They are not merely containers for culture but are used actively by people in the contexts of cultural processes. Moreover, since the effects of ill-conceived planning and design decisions can be devastating to groups and cultures, and since anthropology has some expertise in the area of cultural understanding, it should use that expertise in helping to change and to improve spatial organization and built environments for the benefit of the people who dwell therein. Unfortunately, even applied anthropology has neglected planning and design.

There is no single, agreed upon way of conceptualizing or discussing the organization of space, or of classifying it. Such agreement is badly needed. We need a shared taxonomy, vocabulary, and set of concepts. Without these, progress in the field remains seriously inhibited. The many isolated studies, descriptions and findings (and there are many) cannot be compared or synthesized. In effect, they are 'lost'.

It thus seems most important to get rid of conceptual fuzziness, and to sharpen our definitions and taxonomies. Research is needed, but in order to do it and to ask appropriate questions, one needs an adequate foundation from which to begin. The approach discussed in this article, which seeks above all to place spatial organization in the context of the organizations of time, meaning and communication, aims to provide just this. The interactions outlined here are complex, but they can be analysed and studied. Spatial organization reflects, reinforces and then guides the organization of communication. The physical expression of spatial organization is an aspect of the organization of meaning. Spatial organization itself – the location of objects, individuals and groups in space – also communicates meaning at all scales, concerning such matters as wealth, status, power, life-style, values, social organization, privacy, and so on, especially when reinforced by semi-fixed (and fixed) feature elements. Temporal organization is also reflected in the organizations of space, meaning and communication, and can sometimes substitute for them. Like space, time is inescapable − everyone lives in time as well as space. Built environments as systems of settings are organized not only in space but also in time. Within such systems of settings, patterns of activities occur − and these are also organized in time, which sometimes substitutes for spatial organization, at other times reinforces it, and at yet others is in conflict with it. Since activity systems include their latent aspects we can begin to explain the variability of built environments and cultural landscapes.

Underlying all these are cognitive schemata. Though culturally specific, they have, like culture itself, evolved, and show continuities not only with those of our hominid and pongid ancestors but also with those of other animals. I hope that this brief summary has made clear the rather fundamental nature of the topic, and its fascination. It deserves much more attention than it often receives.

REFERENCES

Altman, I. (1975) *The Environment and Social Behavior*, Monterey, Calif.: Brooks/Cole.

Barker, R. G. (1968) *Ecological Psychology*, Stanford: Stanford University Press.

Barth, F. (1969) *Ethnic Groups and Boundaries*, Boston: Little, Brown.

Basso, K. H. and Selby, H. A. (eds) (1976) *Meaning in Anthropology*, Albuquerque: University of New Mexico Press.

Baumgartner, M. P. (1988) *The Moral Order of the Suburb*, New York: Oxford University Press.

Bechhoefer, W. (1989) 'Procession and urban form in a Sri Lankan village', *Traditional Dwellings and Settlements Review* 1(1): 39−48.

Bernstein, B. (1971) *Class, Codes and Control*, vol. 1: *Theoretical Studies Towards a Sociology of Language*, London: Routledge & Kegan Paul.

Binford, L. R. (1962) 'Archaeology as anthropology', *American Antiquity* 28(2): 217−26.

Bonine, M. E. (1979) 'The morphogenesis of Iranian cities', *Annals, Association of American Geographers* 69(2): 208−24.

—— (1980) 'Aridity and structure: adaptations of indigenous housing in Iran', in K. H. Clark and P. Paylore (eds) *Desert Housing*, Tucson: University of Arizona Press.

Bonner, J. T. (1980) *The Evolution of Culture in Animals*, Princeton, NJ: Princeton University Press.

Borchert, J. (1979) 'Alley landscapes of Washington', *Landscape* 23(3): 3−10.

Bourdieu, P. (1973) 'The Berber house', in M. Douglas (ed.) *Rules and Meanings*, New York: Penguin.

Boyd, R. and Richerson, P. J. (1985) *Culture and the Evolutionary Process*, Chicago: University of Chicago Press.

Broda, J., Carrasco, D. and Matos, E. (1987) *The Great Temple of Tenochtitlán: Center and Periphery in the Aztec World*, Berkeley: University of California Press.

Brower, S. M. (1965) 'The signs we learn to read', *Landscape* 15(1): 9−12.

Carlstein, T., Parkes, D. and Thrift, N. (eds) (1978a) *Making Sense of Time*, New York: John Wiley.

—— (1978b) *Human Activity and Time Geography*, New York: John Wiley.

—— (1978c) *Time and Regional Dynamics*, New York: John Wiley.

Chermayeff, S. and Alexander, C. (1965) *Community and Privacy*, Garden City, NY: Anchor Books.

Chua, B. H. (1988) 'Adjusting religious practices to different house forms in Singapore', *Architecture and Behavior* 4(1): 3–25.

Collins, N. E. (1987) 'Evolution of nestbuilding', in N. Eldredge (ed.) *The Natural History Reader in Evolution*, New York: Columbia University Press.

Connah, G. (1987) *African Civilizations: Precolonial Cities and States in Tropical Africa: An Archaeological Perspective*, Cambridge: Cambridge University Press.

Douglas, M. (1973) *Natural Symbols*, New York: Vintage.

Duncan, J. S. (1976) 'Landscape and the communication of social identity', in A. Rapoport (ed.) *The Mutual Interaction of People and Their Built Environment*, The Hague: Mouton.

—— (ed.) (1981) *Housing and Identity: Cross-Cultural Perspectives*, London: Croom Helm.

—— (1990) *The City as Text: The Politics of Landscape Interpretation in the Kandyan Kingdom*, Cambridge: Cambridge University Press.

Dyson-Hudson, R. and Smith, E. A. (1978) 'Human territoriality: an ecological reassessment', *American Anthropologist* (80): 21–41.

Emmel, T. C. (1987) 'Adaptation on the wing', in N. Eldredge (ed.) *The Natural History Reader in Evolution*, New York: Columbia University Press.

Esber, G. S. (1972) 'Indian housing for Indians', *The Kiva* 37: 141–7.

Feldman, R. M. (1990) 'Settlement-identity: psychological bonds with home places in a mobile society', *Environment and Behavior* 22(2): 183–229.

Flannery, K. V. (ed.) (1976) *The Early Mesoamerican Village*, New York: Academic Press.

Forman, R. T. T. and Godron, M. (1986) *Landscape Ecology*, New York: John Wiley.

Frisch, K. von (1974) *Animal Architecture*, New York: Harcourt Brace Jovanovich.

Gibson, J. J. (1950) *The Perception of the Visual World*, Boston: Houghton Mifflin.

—— (1968) *The Senses Considered as Perceptual Systems*, London: George Allen & Unwin.

Goffman, E. (1957) *The Presentation of Self in Everyday Life*, Garden City, NY: Doubleday.

—— (1963) *Behavior in Public Places*, New York: Free Press.

Goodsell, C. T. (1988) *The Social Meaning of Civic Space: Studying Political Authority through Architecture*, Lawrence: University Press of Kansas.

Goody, J. (1977) *The Domestication of the Savage Mind*, Cambridge: Cambridge University Press.

Gregory, D. and Urry, J. (eds) (1985) *Social Relations and Spatial Structures*, London: Macmillan.

Grimaud, V. (1986) 'Société hiérarchique et habitat en Inde', *Architecture and Behaviour* 2(3–4): 207–27.

Hakim, B . (1986) *Arabic-Islamic Cities*, London: Kegan Paul International.

Hall, E. T. (1966) *The Hidden Dimension*, Garden City, NY: Doubleday.

Hanson, J. and Hillier, B. (1982–3) 'Domestic space organization', *Architecture and Behavior* 2(1): 5–25.

Holzner, L. (1985) 'Stadtland USA – zur Auflösing und Neuordnung der U.S.–Amerikanischen Stadt', *Geographische Zeitschrift* 73(4): 191–205.

Hublin, A. (1989) 'Analyzing aerial photographs of traditional Maroon settlements', *Traditional Dwellings and Settlements Review* 1(1): 83–102.

Hull, R. W. (1976) *African Cities and Towns Before the European Conquest*, New York: W. W. Norton.

Ingham, J. M. (1971) 'Time and space in ancient Mexico: the symbolic dimensions of clanship', *Man* (N.S.) 6(4): 615–29.

Ingold, T. (1986) *The Appropriation of Nature: Essays on Human Ecology and Social Relations*, Manchester: Manchester University Press.

Isaac, G. L. (1972) 'Comparative studies in Pleistocene site locations in East Africa', in P. J. Ucko, R. Tringham and G. W. Dimbleby (eds) *Man, Settlement and Urbanism*, London: Duckworth.

—— (1983) 'Human evolution', in D. S. Bendall (ed.) *Evolution from Molecules to Men*, Cambridge: Cambridge University Press.

Ittelson, W. H. (1960) 'Some factors influencing the design and function of psychiatric facilities', Brooklyn College, Dept of Psychology (Nov.) (mimeo).

Kamau, L. J. (n.d.) 'Social boundaries and public space', Chicago: Northeastern Illinois University, Department of Anthropology (mimeo).

—— (1978–9) 'Semipublic, private and hidden rooms: symbolic aspects of domestic space in urban Kenya', *African Urban Studies* 3: 105–15.

Kaneshiro, K. Y. and Ohta, A. T. (1987) 'The flies fan out', in N. Eldredge (ed.) *The Natural History Reader in Evolution*, New York: Columbia University Press.

Kent, S. (1984) *Analyzing Activity Areas: An Ethnoarchaeological Study of The Use of Space*, Albuquerque: University of New Mexico Press.

—— (1987) 'Understanding the use of space: an ethnoarchaeological perspective', in S. Kent (ed.) *Method and Theory for Activity Area Research: An Ethnoarchaeological Approach*, New York: Columbia University Press.

—— (cd.) (1990) *Domestic Architecture and the Use of Space: An Interdisciplinary and Cross-Cultural Study*. Cambridge: Cambridge University Press.

King, A. D. (1976) *Colonial Urban Development: Culture, Social Power and Environment*, London: Routledge & Kegan Paul.

Kuper, A. (1980) 'Symbolic dimensions of the Southern Bantu homestead', *Africa* 50(1): 8–23.

Kuper, H. (1972) 'The language of sites in the politics of space', *American Anthropologist* 74(3): 411–25.

Lawton, M. P. (1970) 'Ecology and aging', in L. A. Pastalan and D. H. Carson (eds) *Spatial Behavior of Older People*, Ann Arbor: University of Michigan Press.

Lévi-Strauss, C. (1957) *Tristes Tropiques*, Paris: Plon.

Littlejohn, J. (1967) 'The Temne house', in J. Middleton (ed.) *Myth and Cosmos*, Garden City, NY: Natural History Press.

Lofland, L. H. (1973) *A World of Strangers: Order and Action in Urban Public Space*, New York: Basic Books.

Low, S. M. and Chambers, E. (eds) (1989) *Housing, Culture and Design*, Philadelphia: University of Pennsylvania Press.

Lyman, S. M. and Scott, M. B. (1970) *A Sociology of the Absurd*, New York: Appleton–Century–Crofts.

Lynch, K. (1960) *The Image of the City*, Cambridge, Mass.: MIT Press.

McGuire, R. H. and Schiffer, M. B. (1983) 'A theory of architectural design', *Journal of Anthropological Archaeology* 2: 277–303.

Malmberg, T. (1980) *Human Territoriality*, The Hague: Mouton.

Marcus, J. (1976) *Emblem and State in the Classic Maya Lowlands*, Washington, D.C.: Dumbarton Oaks.

Merelman, R. M. (1988) 'The political uses of territoriality', *Environment and Behavior* 20(5): 576–600.

Mitropoulos, M. (1986) 'Communications technology and the organization of space', *Ekistics* 53(320/321): 330–3.

Moos, R. H. (1974) 'Systems for the assessment and classification of human environments: an overview', in R. H. Moos and P. M. Insel (eds) *Issues in Social Ecology: Human Milieus*, Palo Alto, Calif.: National Press Books.

Parkes, D. and Thrift, N. (1980) *Times, Spaces and Places: A Chronogeographic Perspective*, Chichester: John Wiley.

Paul-Lévy, F. and Segaud, M. (1983) *Anthropologie de l'espace*, Paris: Centre Georges Pompidou.

Popper, K. R. (1972) *Objective Knowledge: An Evolutionary Approach*, Oxford: Clarendon Press.

Pred, A. R. (ed.) (1981) *Space and Time in Geography*, Lund: Gleerup.

Prigogine, I. and Stengers, I. (1984) *Order Out of Chaos: Man's New Dialogue with Nature*, New York: Bantam Books.

Rapoport, A. (1969) *House Form and Culture*, Englewood Cliffs, NJ: Prentice-Hall.

—— (1970) 'The study of spatial quality', *Journal of Aesthetic Education* 4 (Oct.): 81–95.

—— (1973) 'Some perspectives on the human use and organization of space', *Architectural Association Quarterly* 5(3): 27–37.

—— (1975) 'Australian Aborigines and the definition of place', in P. Oliver (ed.) *Shelter, Sign and Symbol*, London: Barrie & Jenkins.

—— (1976) 'Environmental cognition in cross-cultural perspective', in G. Moore and R. Golledge (eds) *Environmental Knowing*, Stroudsburg, PA: Dowden, Hutchinson and Ross.

—— (1977) *Human Aspects of Urban Form*, Oxford: Pergamon Press.

—— (1978) 'Nomadism as a man–environment system', *Environment and Behavior* 10(2): 215–46.

—— (1979a) 'On the cultural origins of architecture', in J. C. Snyder and A. J. Catanese (eds) *Introduction to Architecture*, New York: McGraw-Hill.

—— (1979b) 'On the cultural origins of settlements', in A. J. Catanese and J. C. Snyder (eds) *Introduction to Urban Planning*, New York: McGraw-Hill.

—— (1980) 'Towards a cross-culturally valid definition of housing', in R. R. Stough and A. Wandersman (eds) *Optimizing Environments: Research, Practice and Policy* (EDRA 11), Washington, DC: EDRA.

—— (1980–1) 'Neighborhood heterogeneity or homogeneity', *Architecture and Behavior* 1(1): 65–77.

—— (1981) 'Identity and environment: a cross-cultural perspective', in J. S. Duncan (ed.) *Housing and Identity: Cross-Cultural Perspectives*, London: Croom Helm.

—— (1983) 'Development, culture change and supportive design', *Habitat International* 7(5/6): 249–68.

—— (1984) 'Culture and the urban order', in J. Agnew, J. Mercer and D. Sopher (eds) *The City in Cultural Context*, Boston: Allen & Unwin.

—— (1986a) 'The use and design of open spaces in urban neighborhoods', in D. Frick (ed.) *The Quality of Urban Life: Social, Psychological and Physical Conditions*, Berlin: de Gruyter.

—— (1986b) 'Culture and built form – a reconsideration', in D. G. Saile (ed.) *Architecture in Cultural Change: Essays in Built Form and Culture Research*, Tucson: University of Arizona Press.

—— (1987) 'Pedestrian street use: culture and perception', in A. Vernez-Moudon (ed.) *Public Streets for Public Use*, New York: Van Nostrand Reinhold.

—— (1988) 'Levels of meaning in the built environment', in F. Poyatos (ed.) *Cross-Cultural Perspectives in Nonverbal Communication*, Toronto: C. J. Hogrefe.

—— (1989) 'On the attributes of tradition', in J-P. Bourdier and N. Al Sayyad (eds) *Dwellings, Settlements and Tradition: Cross-Cultural Perspectives*, Lanham, Md: University Press of America.

—— (1990a) *The Meaning of the Built Environment*, revised edn, Tucson: University of Arizona Press.

—— (1990b) *History and Precedent in Environmental Design*, New York: Plenum Press.

—— (1990c) 'Systems of activities and systems of settings', in S. Kent (ed.) *Domestic Architecture and the Use of Space*, Cambridge: Cambridge University Press.

—— (1990d) 'Indirect approaches to environment-behaviour research', *National Geographical Journal of India* 36(1–2): 30–46.

Rappaport, R. A. (1979) *Ecology, Meaning and Religion*, Richmond, Calif.: North Atlantic Books.

Rodman, M. C. (1985) 'Moving houses: residential mobility and the mobility of residences in Longana, Vanuatu', *American Anthropologist* 87: 56–72.

Rykwert, J. (1980) *The Idea of a Town*, Princeton, NJ: Princeton University Press.

Sack, D. (1987) *Human Territoriality*, Cambridge: Cambridge University Press.

Scheflen, A. E. (1976) 'Some territorial layouts in the United States', in A. Rapoport (ed.) *The Mutual Interaction of People and Their Built Environment*, The Hague: Mouton.

Scheflen, A. E. and Ashcraft, N. (1976) *Human Territories: How We Behave in Space-Time*, Englewood Cliffs, NJ: Prentice-Hall.

Soja, E. W. (1971) *The Political Organization of Space*, Commission on College Geography, Resource Paper no. 8, Washington DC: Association of American Geographers.

Suttles, G. D. (1968) *The Social Order of the Slum: Ethnicity and Territory in the Inner City*, Chicago: University of Chicago Press.

Sutton, P. (ed.) (1988) *Dreamings: The Art of Aboriginal Australia*, New York: George Braziller/Asia Society Galleries.

Tambiah, S. J. (1973) 'Classification of animals in Thailand', in M. Douglas (ed.) *Rules and Meanings*, New York: Penguin.

Taylor, R. B. (1988) *Human Territorial Functioning*, Cambridge: Cambridge University Press.

Tobias, P. V. (1981) 'The emergence of man in Africa and beyond', *Philosophical Transactions of the Royal Society of London*, Series B 292: 43–56.

Topoff, H. (1987) (ed.) *The Natural History Reader in Animal Behavior*, New York: Columbia University Press.

Tranter, P. and Parkes, D. (1977) 'Images of timed spaces in the inner city: Newcastle, N.S.W.', University of Newcastle (Australia) Research Papers in Geography no. 13.

Ucko, P. J., Tringham, R. and Dimbleby, G. W. (eds) (1972) *Man, Settlement and Urbanism*, London: Duckworth.

Uexküll, J. J. von (1957) 'A stroll through the world of animals and men' (A translation of *Umwelt und Innenwelt der Tiere* (Berlin 1909)), in C. H. Scholler (ed.) *Instinctive Behavior*, New York: International Universities Press.

Vayda, A. P. (ed.) (1969) *Environment and Cultural Behavior: Ecological Studies in Cultural Anthropology*, Garden City, NY: Natural History Press.

—— (1983) 'Progressive Contextualization: methods for research in human ecology', *Human Ecology* 11(3): 265–82.

Vink, A. P. A. (1983) *Landscape Ecology and Land Use*, London: Longmans.

Vogt, E. Z. (1969) *Zinacantan: A Maya Community in the Highlands of Chiapas*, Cambridge, Mass.: Harvard University (Belknap) Press.

Wheatley, P. (1971) *The Pivot of the Four Quarters*, Chicago: Aldine.

—— (1976) 'Levels of space awareness in the traditional Islamic city', *Ekistics* 42(253): 354–66.

Wicker, A. W. (1979) *An Introduction to Ecological Psychology*, Monterey, Calif.: Brooks/Cole.

—— (1981) 'Nature and assessment of behavior settings: recent contributions from the ecological perspective', in P. McReynolds (ed.) *Advances in Psychological Assessment*, San Francisco: Jossey Bass.

Wilson, E. O. (1975) *Sociobiology: The New Synthesis*, Cambridge, Mass.: Harvard University Press.

Wood, D. (1969) 'The image of San Cristobal', *Monadnock* 43: 29–45.

Woodburn, J. (1972) 'Ecology, nomadic movement and the composition of the local group among hunters and gatherers: an East African example and its implications', in P. J. Ucko, R. Tringham and G. W. Dimbleby (eds) *Man, Settlement and Urbanism*, London: Duckworth.

Wynne-Edwards, V. C. (1962) *Animal Dispersion in Relation to Social Behaviour*, Edinburgh: Oliver & Boyd.

Zeisel, J. (1973) 'Symbolic meanings of space and the physical dimension of social relations', in J. Walton and D. E. Carns (eds) *Cities in Change – Studies on the Urban Condition*, Boston: Allyn & Bacon.

FURTHER READING

Broda, J., Carrasco, D. and Matos, E. (1987) *The Great Temple of Tenochtitlán: Centre and Periphery in the Aztec World*, Berkeley: University of California Press.

Duncan, J. D. (1990) *The City as Text: the Politics of Landscape Interpretation in the Kandyan Kingdom*, Cambridge: Cambridge University Press.

Flannery, K. V. (ed.) (1976) *The Early Mesoamerican Village*, New York: Academic Press.

Forman, R. T. T. and Godron, M. (1986) *Landscape Ecology*, New York: John Wiley.

Goodsell, C. T. (1988) *The Social Meaning of Civic Space: Studying Political Authority Through Architecture*, Lawrence: University Press of Kansas.

Ingold, T. (1986) *The Appropriation of Nature: Essays on Human Ecology and Social Relations*, Manchester: Manchester University Press.

Kent, S. (ed.) (1990) *Domestic Architecture and the Use of Space: an Interdisciplinary and Cross-cultural Study*, Cambridge: Cambridge University Press.

King, A. D. (1976) *Colonial Urban Development: Culture, Social Power and Environment*, London: Routledge & Kegan Paul.

Lynch, K. (1960) *The Image of the City*, Cambridge, Mass.: MIT Press.

Oliver, P. (1987) *Dwellings: the House Across the World*, London: Phaidon.

Paul-Lévy, F. and Segaud, M. (1983) *Anthropologie de l'espace*, Paris: Centre Georges Pompidou.

Rapoport, A. (1969) *House Form and Culture*, Englewood Cliffs, NJ: Prentice-Hall.

—— (1977) *Human Aspects of Urban Form*, Oxford: Pergamon.

—— (1990) *The Meaning of the Built Environment*, revised edn, Tucson: University of Arizona Press.

—— (1990) *History and Precedent in Environmental Design*, New York: Plenum Press.

Sack, D. (1987) *Human Territoriality*, Cambridge: Cambridge University Press.

Taylor, R. B. (1988) *Human Territorial Functioning*, Cambridge: Cambridge University Press.

Waterson, R. (1991) *The Living House: An Anthropology of Architecture in South-East Asia*, Singapore: Oxford University Press.

Wheatley, P. (1971) *The Pivot of the Four Quarters*, Chicago: Aldine.

Wilson, P. J. (1988) *The Domestication of the Human Species*, New Haven: Yale University Press.

18

PERCEPTIONS OF TIME

Barbara Adam

INTRODUCTION

The experience of time permeates everyday life. It is both immediate and mediated, all-pervasive and multi-faceted. It is indeed integral to human existence. However, the way we perceive and conceptualize that experience varies with cultures, historical periods and contexts, with members of societies and with a person's age, gender, and position in the social structure. The meanings and values attributed to time, in other words, are fundamentally context-dependent. Despite this ubiquity of time, however, there are virtually no time specialists in anthropology. 'Anthropological theorizing about time perspectives and time reckoning schemes is still in the formative stage,' wrote Maxwell in 1972. 'The cross-cultural study of time has not yet been given a name, nor have " schools" of thought about the subject emerged within the discipline' (1972: 47–8). This statement is still applicable today. Numerous studies have been conducted, but these have remained isolated, and little by way of theoretical integration has been achieved so far. These studies, which have tended to concentrate on systems of time-reckoning in different societies and on how time is perceived, organized and structured, are complicated by two factors. First, time is implicated not only in the subject matter of anthropology but also in the lives, understandings, and methods of those who conduct the studies. Second, in spite of its omnipresence, time is curiously invisible and constitutes one of the most taken-for-granted features of our lives. As such it forms the largely implicit base from which our studies are conducted. For these reasons I want to suggest that when anthropologists write about the times, for example, of Amerindians, South Asians, Africans and Australian Aborigines, they are not – as has been suggested in the past – merely confronting the difficulties of translation between cultures. The problem, I propose, extends far deeper, to the unquestioned understanding of Western time; it reaches the very base from which researchers explicate the time of 'the other'.

Anthropologists have conventionally emphasized the differences between 'modern' and 'traditional' societies. This has led to a proliferation of dichotomies in which the time perception of 'traditional' cultures has been constructed through its opposition to the dominant images of 'our Western time'. Thus it is proposed that 'their' time is cyclical rather than linear, qualitative rather than quantitative, reversible rather than irreversible, encapsulated in tradition rather than constituting the motor of history, organized by routine and practical tasks rather than by the clock, oriented to stability rather than change, geared to natural rather than calendrical rhythms, and reckoned ecologically rather than by an abstract scale. This dichotomization of 'traditional' and 'modern' time has been extensively criticized, most notably — with reference to Lévi-Strauss's work — by Barnes (1971). He argues that in order to

> escape from an amusing but ultimately sterile ballet of symbols in which history and anthropology, synchrony and diachrony, consciousness and unconsciousness, continuity and discontinuity, reversible and irreversible time dance endlessly round each other until the audience decides to go home, we have to break down dichotomies, establish continua and feed in more facts.
>
> (Barnes 1971: 545)

More recently a number of additional problems have been identified with this classical approach. There has been criticism of the portrayal of a 'uniformity across the population and of cultural forms unchanged for decades and centuries' (Cottle and Klineberg 1974: 164) as well as condemnation of the tendency to lock our interlocutors into the frozen present of anthropological discourse. 'Functionalism, in its fervour to explore the mechanisms of living societies,' Fabian (1983: 20) further contends, 'simply put on ice the problem of time.' With Fabian's seminal work on *Time and the Other*, the pendulum has swung from an emphasis on difference to a recognition of coevalness (McElwain 1988), and with the writings of Adam (1987, 1988, 1990) and Ingold (1986, ch. 4), the Newtonian and Cartesian premises of our Western theories have been exposed.

Closely associated with these critiques is a rising awareness of both the constitutive nature of knowledge (Harries-Jones 1985) and the need for reflexivity (Cohen 1990a, b, Ortner 1984). Harries-Jones (1985: 238) proposes a necessary shift from an archaeology of knowledge to an activist approach to culture, and Cohen (1990a) states boldly that 'selfless anthropology is out of date'. The self, Cohen continues, needs to be accommodated 'as a matter of scholarly principle and practice'. The positivist belief in an uncontaminated, objective reality is, however, so deeply engrained in anthropological practice that researchers tend to view their own assumptions as *immaterial* and resist treating them as matters for reflection. Few go further than paying lip-service to Habermas's (1973: 161) insistence that

> the terms that we bring from within ourselves to the process of inquiry — in any and every domain, including science — are amenable to a reflection that is *rational* for

504

the very reason that it carries the potential for a more inclusive conceptualization that is better attuned to the common interest of the human condition.

An emphasis on reflexivity is not new, of course. In *The Critique of Pure Reason*, Kant (1966 [1781]: 16) pointed out that we are like judges who compel their witnesses to answer questions that they themselves have posed. Over two hundred years ago Kant was arguing that observers bring their own faculties of reason to the constitution of the objects of their observation and thus to the formative moment of knowledge. With respect to our topic, this implies that we cannot understand the approaches to time of people of other cultures without drawing on our own understanding. Reflexivity is thus necessary not only because knowledge is constitutive but also because we construct others to the templates of our own theoretical models. In view of the longstanding acceptance of Kant's insights and the recent anthropological emphasis on reflexivity, it seems surprising that the backcloth upon which our descriptions are drawn remains unattended to, that the nature of our own time is left unexamined, and that we fail to acknowledge that *any* analysis of 'other time' is a simultaneous commentary on 'our own time'. An explicitly reflexive approach to time becomes imperative, however, once we recognize, first, that the 'alien' time is commonly explicated in terms of what it is *not*, and, second, that the existing dualistic models of 'our own time' and 'other time' are fundamentally flawed.

For this reason I highlight here the backcloth upon which anthropological descriptions are drawn, and aim to make visible the assumptions that inform the Western understanding of time. Not the explicated 'other time' but the implicit time of the 'invisible observer' is therefore the primary focus of my attention. To make explicit what we know intimately at the non-discursive level requires a phenomenological anthropological attitude. It demands that we extricate ourselves from the natural attitude and take the position of the stranger; that we look at our own time through the eyes of those who are conventionally the objects of anthropological attention. First, however, we shall take a brief look at some classical studies of 'other time'. These will serve to exemplify the role played by our unquestioned assumptions in analyses of times that differ from contemporary Western conceptualizations.

'OTHER TIMES' AND IMPLICIT TEMPLATES

The studies of Evans-Pritchard (1940) and Whorf (1956) furnish us with classical analyses of time perceptions that deviate from Western ones. I am not, however, interested in the nature of those differences or in the many critiques that have been offered in response to these studies. For the reasons outlined above, I am concerned with the unquestioned stereotypical backdrop of 'Western time' against which the respective time perceptions of the 'traditional' cultures are delineated.

From Whorf's (1956) linguistic study of Hopi Amerindian cosmology the experience of Western time emerges as a unidirectional, continuous flow, with sequences of events 'strung up' on a line that extends from the past into the future. The Western concept of time is portrayed as being abstract, linear, and associated with motion. It is invoked when Whorf attempts to describe the Hopi view of time in terms of what it is *not*. He writes of a world in which experiences are *not* sequentially stretched out on a line but are simultaneous, cumulative, and amalgamated in an organic complex. He depicts a time that is *not* an objectified spatialized quantity, a time that is *not* made up of discrete instants that follow each other but is characterized by a cumulative getting later. 'For the Hopi, for whom time is not a motion but a "getting later" of everything that has ever been done,' Whorf (1956: 151) writes, 'unvarying repetition is not wasted but accumulated'. The Hopi's linguistic thought background, he suggests further (1956: 57), is without our abstract, linear, sequential concept of time and lacks a notion of time as a 'smooth flowing continuum in which everything in the universe proceeds at an equal rate, out of a future, through a present, into a past'.

The same approach to the analysis of 'other time' can be detected in Evans-Pritchard's (1940) study of the Nuer, a Nilotic tribe of the southern Sudan. Evans-Pritchard constructs the tribal time of ecological cycles and structural relations against a backcloth of calendrical and clock time. With respect to the ecological cycles, he argues that 'a twelve-month system does not incommode Nuer', that they 'do not to any great extent use the names of months to indicate the time of an event', that there are 'no units of time between the month and day and night', that 'time has not the same value throughout the year', that their time words are 'not pure units of time reckoning', and finally, that they 'have no expression equivalent to "time" in our language, and they cannot, therefore, as we can, speak of time as though it were something actual, which passes, can be wasted, can be saved, and so forth' (1940: 99–103). With respect to Nuer structural time he proposes that, unlike our time, which passes and progresses, the movement of their time must be recognized as an illusion, because the tribal time structure stays constant. This means that their 'perception of time is no more than the movement of persons, often as groups, through the structure'. He then contrasts this time with our historical one, in which each event is accorded a unique position in the time grid of dates and clock-time units. He proposes that our time stretches over far greater distances than does their tradition, and that in their myth, unlike our history, one event does not precede another, 'for myths explain customs of general social significance rather than the interrelations of particular segments and are, therefore, not structurally stratified' (1940: 107–8).

Western time emerges from these two studies in association with a number of clustered characteristics: as an abstract, spatialized quantity that is divisible into single units; as a two-dimensional, linear, directional flow or succession of constant rate that extends from the past to the future (or vice versa); and as something that passes or can be saved, sold, or wasted. All these aspects appear in the analyses in isolation from one another, untheorized in relation to each other, and for the sole purpose of providing the contrast to the alien time, which is portrayed as simultaneous, qualitative, cumulative, amalgamated and complex in the case of Whorf's analysis, and as cyclical, structural time *in* events, processes and social relations in Evans-Pritchard's account.

These classical studies can serve to exemplify the traditional kind of anthropological research on time, in which detailed observation and interviews with informants would provide the raw data from which researchers would seek to uncover the implicit assumptions and worldviews of their interlocutors, and upon which they would build models and construct interpretations. In such traditional research the assumptions upon which the questions, observations, and models were based invariably remained unquestioned. Before comparing those implicit theories of Western time with the way time is expressed in everyday communication among English speakers, however, I want to look briefly at an analysis of 'other time' that deviates from the classical tradition.

As an African who has been subject to missionary influence, Mbiti (1969) learnt to see his familiar world through the eyes of a stranger. Furthermore, in order to become part of another world he had to make the strange familiar: he had to get to know the Western time of the missionaries before he could participate in their life. It is not surprising, therefore, that Mbiti's account of the backdrop of Western time, against which he explains African time, far surpasses in its sophistication that of his Western colleagues. In Mbiti's (1969) work on African religions and philosophy the image of Western time emerges once more as both linear and subject to the threefold division into past, present, and future. But, unlike the Western time of the analyses described above, Mbiti's backdrop time is complex and theorized in relation to abstraction, objectification, spatialization, context-independence and commodification. Mbiti contrasts the 'produced time' of African peoples with the commodified time of the West, which is exchanged on the labour market as an objective quantity. Similarly, he distinguishes between the need of members of traditional African societies to experience and constitute time and the need of Western and Westernized societies to measure out time in units of days, hours and minutes. Unlike Evans-Pritchard and Whorf with their shadowy image of linearity, succession, and motion, Mbiti identifies the characteristics of linearity and of equal past and future extension, attributed to Western time, *in relation to* numerical, context-independent calendars. Furthermore, he implies a connection between the mathematical abstracted time of calendars and time as a commodity; between days, months, and years and a time that can be used, sold, exchanged, and controlled.

From the differences between the two approaches we can see that it *matters* whether the backdrop time is merely assumed or given equivalent status in the analysis. For Western anthropologists to treat their taken-for-granted time as an object of reflection requires that they bring the everyday into high relief and focus on that which remains unattended to in studies of 'other time'. I propose therefore to investigate the way time is used in daily communication, as a starting point from which to assess the antinomies that lock the objects of anthropological discourse and their implicated counterparts into a timeless 'ethnographic present'. The illustrations that follow, however banal, will help to highlight the immense variability and complexity of social time and to expose the poverty and inadequacy of models that force us to choose between time and temporality, clocks and natural rhythms, linearity and cyclicality, change and order, history and myth, quantity and quality, events in time and time in events. Life in Western societies, as we shall see, takes place not only on the two-dimensional plane of linear, chronological time.

THE INVISIBLE TIMES OF EVERYDAY LIFE

'Time' has been established as the most widely used noun in the English language. It is not surprising therefore that our everyday communication is full of references to time. The same word, however, is used to convey a multitude of very different meanings that are grounded in a variety of implicit theories of time. We speak of clock time and winter time, of opening times and bad times, of the right time for action and the timing of an interaction. We refer to the time of things and processes, to a time that flies and a time that takes its toll. We move freely between all these senses of time and know them intimately without giving much thought to their differences. Yet it is quite clear that they entail diverse qualities and the attribution of different meanings to the common term. Time for us is not exhausted by the clock-time measure. It is multi-faceted: it is involved in physical processes and social conventions, in the abstract relations of mathematics and in the concrete relations between people. We measure it in units of clock time, by celestial motion, with the aid of recurrent events, and through changes in our bodies. We utilize it as a medium of exchange for goods and services, or as a means of payment. We use it as a resource of nature, of society, of people, and of institutions, each in turn constituting a boundary within which choices and selections for action have to be made. The minute, the hour, the week, the day, the phase of the moon, the year, Christmas and Easter, cycles of production and growth, generations and the lifetime of a person all form time frames within which we plan and regulate our daily lives. The parameters of birth and death, the rhythms of nature, and the recurrent patterns of socially structured events together constitute the temporal matrix by virtue of which we can live *in* time.

Looking at these different times more closely, we can identify a 'time when': when the banks are open, when the children are expected to go to bed, when we were young, when we had social unrest, when the storm demolished the sea defences and the roof of our house. In Western societies this 'when' is likely to be based on a time grid provided by the calendar, the clock, or both, but clocks and calendars are unlikely to be the only sources for the timing and temporal location of these social activities and natural phenomena. While bank opening times, for example, are unimaginable without the aid of clocks and calendars, the latter are not the sole regulators of this particular banking convention. Not only are bank opening times co-ordinated with the daytime working activities of those likely to use the bank's services, they are also guided by the law of the land, which regulates other opening times, and by considerations relating to internal work schedules and tradition. Likewise, children may be told that it is bedtime because it is getting dark outside or because a specific television programme has finished. For children these are far more persuasive arguments than the fact that it is eight o'clock in the evening.

Furthermore, the existence of clock and calendar time does not prevent us from locating the past, present, and future with reference to events, processes and social relations. Dates and clock time may not feature at all when we remember our childhood, a period of social unrest, or a particular storm. This means that, quite contrary to Evans-Pritchard's portrayal of fundamental difference, the Nuer would have found much common ground with our Western selves in terms of the 'when' of social activities, events and traditions. Notwithstanding conventional analyses that polarize 'traditional' and 'modern' societies, clock and calendar time are not our only sources of reference and cannot therefore be contrasted with natural, social, and religious times. We need to recognize that considerations relating to social interaction and to the physical environment have not been replaced by the rationalization of time. They still play an important part in deciding when it is time for certain events to take place. Our social actions can, if necessary, be internationally organized and co-ordinated through a standardized network of time that spans the globe, and this time is deeply embedded in the fabric of our society. But its existence does not obliterate the rich sources of local, idiosyncratic and context-dependent time-awareness that are rooted in the social and organic rhythms of everyday life. The abstract, quantified, spatialized time of clocks and calendars forms *only one aspect* of the complex of meanings associated with Western time.

This becomes even more obvious when we are dealing with 'good' and 'bad' times for action. If Western time really was linear and quantative, as with clock and calendar time, then any reference to 'good' and 'bad times' would be meaningless. As Gioscia (1974: 83) points out, 'in assuming that time is two-dimensional (i.e. linear), we make it impossible for phrases like "a hard time", "an easy time", a "high time", and/or "a low time" to be anything other than euphemism'. Clock and calendar time, which could indeed be dominant with regard to the specification of time 'when', recede into the background in decisions about the 'right' time to ask about a pay rise, to end a friendship, or to apply for a job. Questions about 'good' or 'bad' times for action are primarily about *timing*, and this in turn may be dependent on a wide variety of factors. The day of the week or the hour of the day might be one consideration, but other things will play an equal if not more important role in such decisions.

Issues relating to the past and future of that particular relation or event become pertinent. The participants' well-being and strengths, their skills, anxieties, and weaknesses, as well as the state of their relationships, must be allowed for. Furthermore, the socio-historical, economic, and political context may play a crucial role in decisions as to what constitutes the 'right' time, as will the norms, practices and values of those involved. Even the weather and the seasons may make an important difference and might therefore be taken into consideration.

All types of 'when time' could entail considerations relating to clock and calendar time, but these are never the only ones. The rhythms of nature and the seasons, social norms, traditions and habits, physiological changes, knowledge of the past and anticipations of its consequences, all are brought to bear on calculations about the future. They all come together and become inextricably interwoven in judgements about what constitutes the 'right' time to engage in certain activities. While the existence of clock time facilitates context independence and global standardization, decisions about the timing of even the most habitual of actions are made on a one-off basis and with reference to a particular context. 'When time', we can conclude, exists in all societies. In its particular expressions, however, we find that some clusters of sources are shared, while others are culturally unique. Neither quantity nor quality, neither society nor nature, neither the clock nor the routine of tasks seems to furnish the single source for any specific cultural expression. It therefore makes little sense to contrast the time of traditional cultures with Western industrial time along these lines.

In addition to timing and location *in* time, *temporality* forms a central component of time in everyday English communication. Time taking its toll, spring time and the coming alive of nature, growing old and feeling old, these times could also be about a time 'when' – when the apple tree blossoms, when I am old, when I was born, when my time comes to die – but contained in these ideas is also the fundamental knowledge of irreversible change fused with cycles of return. Whereas timing and time frames are dominant aspects of 'when time', temporality comes to the fore when we focus on processes. Plants grow, produce seeds and wither. People and animals are born, live and die. Though we speak of the cycle of life and death, within each cycle the changes are unidirectional. There can be no un-ageing, no un-dying, no un-birth. We can relive past moments in our minds but we cannot reverse the processes of the living and material world. We know the unidirectionality of time from geological and historical records, from physical processes involving energy exchange, from the irreversible accumulation of knowledge, and from the fact that people and things get older and never younger and newer. We know that the sequence of the diurnal cycle goes from dawn to midday to dusk and night, and not backwards from dusk to midday to morning. These examples demonstrate that cyclicality and irreversible linearity are not the dominant time perceptions, respectively, of traditional and modern societies, but are integral to all rhythmically structured phenomena (Adam 1990: 70–6, 87–90).

Yet, when we say that time takes its toll and that people, animals, and things get older, we attribute to time aspects additional to those of cycles of return and of linear directionality. Each directional cycle constitutes a time frame within which we organize, plan and regulate our daily existence. To use Heidegger's (1967, 1972) terminology, our lives are lived unto death, and during each present the past we have already lived and the future we still expect to live play a central role in the way we experience, plan and act. Not only that, we also have a relationship to our past, present and future; we take an attitude to our origin and destiny. Collectively these aspects of time affect the way we see ourselves, our families, our society, and our fellow human beings. They influence the timing of our interactions, the way we relate to others, and how we interpret daily and extraordinary events. The 'timing' and 'time-frame' aspects of time are thus implicated in temporality, just as temporality is implicated in timing and time frames. This triple implication, however, does not yet exhaust the complexity of the concept as it is used in everyday communication: *tempo* is a further aspect of the meaning complex of Western time.

Within the boundaries set by the many and various physical, biological and cultural time frames, the timing and temporality of processes assume different speeds. We speak of time passing slowly or going by too quickly. Time flies when we are having fun. It tends to drag when we are waiting. There never seems to be enough of it when we are busy, and there is too much of it during periods of idleness. Tempo and intensity are thus integral components of the meaning complex of time. They surround us at every level. We know that waiting for a birthday tomorrow can feel like an eternity to a little child, while a birthday one year ago can seem like only yesterday to an old person. The dormant period of winter is followed by a burst of growth in spring. One job needs to be rushed to completion, while another has to be slowed down to stay in phase with other production processes. Rates of action and reaction, be they metabolic or social, are fundamentally implicated in how much can be achieved within any given time frame, in the timing of actions, and in the temporality of existence. All, in turn, are involved in our experience of the speed of time passing.

Once we come to focus on the backcloth against which anthropologists explicate their ethnographic data we are forced to abandon cherished dualisms and to conceptualize together what traditional analyses insisted on separating. We then realize that cyclicality is neither the opposite of linearity nor separable from moments passing and recurring; that it is not the opposite of the unidirectional temporality of physical and living things or of social processes of Western societies, but rather is fundamentally entailed therein. We become aware of the mutual implication of time (frames), timing, temporality and tempo whenever the concept of time is used in everyday communication, and, by the same token, we begin to question whether members of traditional societies would regard much of what we have outlined so far, in characterizing 'our own time', as in any way alien or 'other'. It makes a difference, however, whether the time frames within which we organize our lives are based on natural rhythms or on machine time. It is this difference to which we next need to turn in our exploration of the conventionally unquestioned background to anthropological studies of 'other time'.

THE REAL FACE OF CLOCK TIME

The time frames afforded by seconds, minutes, hours and days, unlike those of the lifetime, the seasons, and the diurnal cycle, are characterized by invariance, context-independence, and precision. The 24-hour clock measures the 'same' 24 hours in Iceland during the winter as in Britain during the summer.[1] Today one hour of clock time is one hour wherever we are. We no longer use variable 'hours' that change with the seasons, or the plethora of 'local times' that preceded world time. Time is standardized across the globe, which since the late eighteenth century has been divided into zones separated by differences of one hour, ahead as we move east and behind as we move west, with the strange result that we can gain or lose a day by crossing the international date-line. Moving amongst the Aleutian Islands in the Pacific, for example, we can celebrate a birthday twice or miss it altogether (Alwyn Jones, personal communication). This rationalization of time and its association with the clock exerts a key influence on social life in industrial societies and permeates even those aspects of time that we share with other societies across the world. Moreover, it is deeply implicated in the taken-for-granted understanding of time that forms the basis from which Western anthropologists construct their images of 'traditional' societies. It is therefore worthy of more detailed attention.

Both calendars and clocks incorporate time as a measure and they both measure time (*pace* Ingold 1986: 165–6). We need to appreciate this double role, because it results in a fundamental paradox: the measure is designed to the principle of invariance, while the natural time it measures is characterized by fundamental variance. In other words, the hours of daylight change slightly every day, the constellations of the stars do not recur in exactly the same positions, not every year has 365 days. This makes the measure qualitatively different from that which it measures.[2] Unlike the variable rhythms of nature, the invariant, precise measurement is a human invention, and in our society it is this *created time* which has become dominant to the extent that we often relate to it as time *per se*, as if there were no other times.

Furthermore, the clock is a machine designed to the laws of classical mechanics. Like all other machines, it is a material artefact that embodies the principles of idealized invariance, simplification, motion without change, and reversibility (Adam 1990: 50–5, Shallis 1983, especially chs 2 and 4). As a mechanical model of the universe the clock expresses time as distance travelled in space. But it also creates a time that is no longer dependent on its source. The development of the pendulum played a central role in the creation of this first artificial, independent time standard. The pendulum's regular oscillations are counted and translated into a directional succession, yet, as I indicate elsewhere (Adam 1988: 209), the direction is an artefact of the numbering system. It is not an integral aspect of machine time, because the counting of the oscillations is irrelevant to the working of the machine, and their directional succession is given only by the mathematical convention by which, say, the number three follows the number two, and not vice versa. The meaning of time, on the other hand, is encapsulated neither in the oscillations nor in the number system. We cannot tell by looking at a clock whether it is 8 o'clock in the morning or the evening, summer or winter, in the northern or southern hemisphere, since this knowledge fundamentally depends on the rhythms of nature. Context-independence and rationalization have been traded off against meaning, qualitative difference, and harmony with natural and social rhythms. Yet clock time has not *replaced* the multiple social, biological, and physical sources of time; it has rather *changed* the meanings of the variable times, temporalities, timings, and tempos of bio-cultural origin.

So central is the clock to our taken-for-granted notion of what time is, and so pervasive its influence, that we find it difficult to raise this influence to an explicit level of understanding. The distinctiveness of clock time does, however, become visible in the realm of industrial work, where employers buy the time of their workers. In this context, time is the medium through which labour is translated into an abstract exchange value: it is fundamental to the exchange of work for money (Giddens 1981: 130–4). Furthermore, time is contested in industrial disputes. Conflicts over time control can be observed throughout the history of strikes where the duration of the working day, week, year and working life, the pace of work and break times, overtime and time off, holidays and paid leisure time are at the centre of the disagreements (Rinderspacher 1985: 217–27, Starkey 1988, Thompson 1967). Labour time as a quantitative and abstract exchange value is no longer merely used, passed or filled. It has become a commodity. With this commodification, the control of time has become an ineradicable, integral aspect of industrial life and as such it affects the timing, the tempo and even the temporality of that life. Both the commodification and the control of time thus need to be recognized as specific phenomena of industrial and industrializing societies. This dual characteristic is conventionally associated with clocks and the measurement of time. The relation, however, is a complex one. Chronological and calendrical time, related to as an independent, objectively given reality – tantamount to time *per se* – is pivotal to the time-awareness of industrial society. But neither the existence of calendars nor the invention of clocks should be understood as the *cause* of this reification and subsequent commodification and control of time, because all societies reckon time in some way.

To reckon time entails that we know the times proper to things, events and processes and that we can recognize the time of each as consistent in relation to others that are shorter and longer, or faster and slower. It is therefore not necessarily their regular, rhythmic occurrence, but rather our knowledge of their consistency in relation to other events and processes, that matters. Cooking rice or burning a particular stick, for example, are processes that are consistent with reference to other processes, and as such they can be used as measures for short time spans, just as are innumerable other similarly consistent processes that have been employed for time-reckoning purposes all over the world and from the dawn of human history. Like the estimation of short periods by such methods, the capacity to reckon long time spans is by no means limited to modern civilizations. Many ancient societies arrived at complicated calendrical systems without relating to the time measured as a resource or a commodity. Archaeological evidence for the notation of lunar cycles shows that lunar time-reckoning goes back some 30,000 years (Marshack 1972, cited in Fraser 1987: 46). Stonehenge, which is widely believed to have served a calendrical function, is dated to between 1800 and 1400 BC, and the earliest waterclocks, discovered in Egypt, were in existence since the fifteenth century BC. Early civilizations such as that of the Maya had established complex calendars, and the Chinese had invented a mechanical clock that predated that of the Western world by many centuries. Therefore, neither the reckoning of time nor its measurement with the aid of a clock constitutes the specific essence of industrial time. Rather, the latter is a time that is *abstracted* from its natural source; an independent, de-contextualized, rationalized time, almost infinitely divisible into equal spatialized units, used as such in daily interaction, and related to as time *per se*.

The measurement of time, we can thus conclude, is not the prime source of what is distinctive about the time-awareness of modern Western society. Rather, machine time has been reified to a point at which we have lost touch with other rhythms and with the multiple times of our existence. Most importantly, with the dominance of this reified time we seem to have forgotten that the entirety of our existence needs constantly to be reactivated and re-created in the present; that all of our past needs to be gathered up in the present and reconstructed in the light of new knowledge. It appears that we can recognize such time-constituting processes only when we encounter them in societies whose perceptions of time differ markedly from our own. Such societies, we consequently argue, *construct* time in the present through traditional practices, myths, and rituals, whereas we supposedly live *in* a time that is a 'smooth flowing continuum in which everything in the universe proceeds at an equal rate' (Whorf 1956: 7). In our world of years, days, hours, and seconds, of time budgeting, deadlines, and time pressure, time seems no longer to be primarily associated with the creation of reality.[3] Science, philosophy and history have replaced myth and sacred traditions. Yet the process has remained the same; through it we preserve and transmit not only our knowledge but also our existence. Like the members of 'traditional' societies we construct and constitute time in the present. We have merely lost our awareness of it: our reification of artefactual time as time *per se* has crowded out that knowledge from our conscious perception. This created time of de-contextualized, abstract intervals is implicated wherever *time* is controlled and wherever it is used as a medium for the translation of labour power into a monetary value. Unlike the time-transcendence which is characteristic of human culture generally, this homogenized, quantitative time which we use, allocate, control, and sell on the labour market is not a human universal. It belongs firmly with the history of industrialization (Adam 1987: 327–63, Giddens 1981, Hohn 1984, Thompson 1967).

The aim and the capacity to transcend our species-specific time, on the other hand, seems to be common to all humanity. It is evident in the existence of religions, myths and theories, art and architecture, agriculture and technology: asking metaphysical questions, having a relationship to our own finitude, accommodating a temporal world to the principles of permanence, all contribute to the process of time-transcendence. This means that such 'traditional' societies as the Nuer and the Hopi do not lack this capacity simply because they have not objectified and abstracted time; they merely differ in the way they practise this time-transcendence. Humanity shares an effort to control the environment, the timing and synchronization of collective action, the entropic processes of decay and the deterioration of our bodies. Imposing their control over the time embedded in their living conditions, humans have consistently transcended the times of their existence. Hägerstrand further accentuates this point when he argues that 'culture can be viewed as a system of major modifications of naturally embedded time in the material world' (1985: 10). It is this embedded time, common to humanity, which needs to be differentiated from the created, artefactual time associated with industrialization and the rationalization of social life. The differentiation cannot, however, be achieved in dualistic terms.

Only the created time can be used as a resource, related to as if it were real, controlled in its own right, and exchanged for money. Due to the prominence of commodification and control, industrial time seems best conceptualized by reference to power. Furthermore, we need to recognize that those relations of power are not restricted to situations in which time is exchanged for money: they permeate the moments 'when', the right time to act, the timing of interaction, the tempo embedded in natural and social processes, and the time frames within which we organize social life. The multiple rhythms of living and social organization are nested inside one another, and new rhythms are not merely grafted onto existing ones, but change their nature in the process. Once created, the artefactual time has become an integral, ineradicable aspect of industrial social life, and as such it affects the control, the timing, the tempo and even the temporality of that life. Clearly, then, 'Western time' cannot be distinguished from 'other times' in terms of an either–or opposition. Time frames, timing, temporality and tempo are integral to all human time, even though particular cultural expressions may differ with respect to any or all of these aspects. Clock time, which alters both the meaning of time in practice, and the constitution of its complexity, pervades humanity to varying degrees: few societies are nowadays completely untouched by it – many live out a compromise between that artefactual time and their local times, but no society has completely replaced the multiplicity of social time with the singularity of clock time. In other words, there exists no society for which machine time constitutes the only source of social time. This effectively disqualifies dichotomous constructions from anthropological analyses of culturally specific times.

Having now revealed something of the complexity of the 'taken-for-granted' time of the anthropological observer, we can now turn to consider some of the dominant conceptualizations and models of time to be found in anthropological analyses of non-Western societies, and assess their adequacy.

DUALISMS TESTED AND REJECTED

We build models in order to render our subject matter intelligible. We construct representations so that Nuer time-reckoning and Hopi cosmology, for example, become meaningful in the context of our own understanding. It is inevitable that descriptions and explanations simplify that which they represent. It could not be otherwise, for even the most minute aspect of social reality is almost infinite in its complexity. It is not the practice of model-building, then, but the nature of the models and of the assumptions underpinning them, that is at issue here. For the assumptions are rarely questioned or held up for scrutiny, and the models seem invariably to be built on dichotomies that construct the time of other cultures in contradistinction to our own. Cyclical time and an emphasis on repetition are contrasted with linear time and historical being, and, as we have seen earlier, a 'smooth flowing continuum in which everything proceeds at an equal rate' is contrasted with a 'shallow' past-and-future extension (Whorf 1956: 57, Evans-Pritchard 1940: 108). Lévi-Strauss, the 'most notable model architect' (Barnes 1971: 538), has provided anthropology with an additional host of time-based dichotomies that are all too readily adopted as templates for models with which to contrast 'traditional' and 'modern' societies.[4]

Lévi-Strauss distinguishes Western time, dominated by history, irreversibility, and succession, from the times of societies in which simultaneity and non-cumulative, cyclical and even reversible processes prevail. Accordingly, Lévi-Strauss argues, the social sciences have to deal with two different categories of time:

> Anthropology uses a 'mechanical' time, reversible and non-cumulative ... [while in contrast] historical time is 'statistical'; it always appears as an oriented and non-reversible process. An evolution which would take contemporary Italian society back

516

to that of the Roman Republic is as impossible to conceive of as the reversibility of the processes belonging to the second law of thermodynamics.

(Lévi-Strauss 1972: 286)

This passage epitomizes the extraordinary claims that Lévi-Strauss makes with reference to time and the nature of anthropological theory. An 'evolution' that would take a small-scale agricultural society 'back' to its hunter–gatherer past is surely no more conceivable than one that would return contemporary Italian society to the Roman Republic. We may of course speak of societies 'reverting back' to historically earlier forms of socio-economic organization, but this can never be more than a figure of speech, since social reversibility is no more possible than growing younger, ashes turning back into logs, or a day progressing from evening to midday to morning. What possible basis could there be for characterizing traditional peoples' time as reversible, non-cumulative, non-directional, simultaneous, and cyclical, rather than irreversible, cumulative, directional, successive, and linear? And how could we possibly justify the use of a mechanical model of 'reversible time', given Lévi-Strauss's own requirement that the model has to be adequate to its subject matter, and his insistence that the 'the best model will always be that which is *true*' (1972: 281)? These questions take on a further significance when we recognize that, as even Lévi-Strauss admits, the terms of such dichotomies cannot be regarded as mutually exclusive, since 'even the most elementary kinship structure exists both synchronically and diachronically' (1972: 47).

If the concern of anthropology as an academic discipline is to be with the construction of mechanical, non-cumulative models based on the idea of 'reversible time', then, according to the above analysis of artefactual time, the anthropological approach would be most suitable to the study not of traditional, but of contemporary Western, societies! For only the latter are geared to a mechanical time based on the Newtonian principle of reversibility. Yet, as I have shown, even for industrial societies machine time is but one aspect of social time in all its complexity. However, because the dichotomies between cyclical and linear (or reversible and irreversible) time, between repetition and orientation to change, between 'cold' and 'hot' societies, and between synchronic and diachronic analysis, hold such a powerful sway both in anthropology and in the social sciences more generally, they call for closer examination. My purpose, I should stress, is neither to trace the many mutations and adaptations that these dichotomies have undergone in the history of anthropological theory, nor to provide new and better interpretations of the ways in which particular authors have employed them. Rather, I want to show their potential, or lack of it, for explaining social time in its culturally specific complexity, and, in so doing, to make explicit the assumptions underpinning the structuralist model – assumptions directly derived from classical mechanics (Lévi-Strauss 1972: 314).

Cyclical time is the time mode conventionally attributed to traditional, small-scale societies, in contradistinction to an assumed linear time of contemporary industrial societies. It entails the idea of an impoverished or 'shallow' past extension and a barely existent future orientation, even of life in a 'timeless present' (Kluckhohn and Strodbeck 1961). It conjures up a world of 'eternal return', a world in which the difference between past and future can be dispensed with, because what has been recurs and what is to come has already been, a world in which destiny is synonymous with origin. Some historians and social scientists, however, have presented evidence to the contrary and have argued that no real human society could be said to live in such a cyclical time (Adam 1990: 127–48, Aguessy 1977, Bergmann 1992, Bourdieu 1979, Dunne 1973, Eliade 1989, Fabian 1983, Kinget 1975, McElwain 1988: 267–78, Nowotny 1985). This is neither to deny that for some societies the heading towards the future is simultaneously a regaining of the past, nor to argue against anthropological findings that some societies put greater efforts than others into the active creation of permanence. Rather, it is to suggest that these are variable features of all human cultures in the same way that time frames, temporality, timing and tempo, relations to the past, present, and future, and, to a limited extent, even clock and calendar time, form integral parts of contemporary human existence. It is to insist that this complexity of times cannot be expressed through dualisms such as that of cyclicity versus linearity. In other words, the antimonies become meaningless with respect to the direction, form and process of time once we recognize that the times of even the most archaic societies are constituted on the basis of *general* cultural characteristics that defy classification in these terms. The presence of myths and religious beliefs, the relationship to birth and death, and the creation of tools, artefacts, art, and architecture suggest a past-and-future extension and a time-transcendence that vastly exceed the cycle of the seasons or even a person's lifetime. This applies irrespective of whether time has been developed as a separate concept, of whether the language is tensed like ours, and of whether time has been objectified in some way. To ask metaphysical questions, to have a relationship to one's existence, and to reconstruct a temporal world to the principles of permanence are marks of culture and attest to a time extension that cannot be encompassed by any concept of cyclical time.

To have a relationship to death, for example, extends human beings beyond the cycles of nature, even when their daily lives are dominated by concerns that do not extend beyond the growth cycle of the seasons. Furthermore, to take an attitude towards the realm of the caused, the actual, and the potential transforms the problem of existence into a conscious act of living unto the future, into an achievement of pre-emptiveness, anticipation and creativity. 'The human thing is not merely to live, to act, to love,' writes Dunne (1973: 20). 'It is to have a relationship to one's life, one's action, one's love, even if the relationship is simply one of consent, simply a "Yes".' To relate to birth and death, origin and destiny is an existential condition of human cultural life.

What makes our lives worthy of being preserved in memory and story, of being kept alive after our death, Dunne argues (1973: 23), is the transcendence of the division between life and death. This transcendence is always an immortality of the spirit which is constituted by our relationship to the temporality of life. To conceptualize archaic or traditional societies with reference to cyclical time thus constitutes not only a denial of the spiritual dimension of their lives but also a denial of culture. It even denies them a symbolic capacity, because knowledge of a past and a future entails representational, symbolically based imagination. Endowed with such imagination, human beings do not merely undergo their presents and pasts; they also shape and reshape them. With the capacity to objectify meaning, they are able not only to look back, reflect and contemplate but also to reinterpret, represent, restructure, and modify the past. They can plan alternative futures, imagine past futures, and dread future pasts. Thus, the idea of *any* society living in a cyclical time of endlessly recurring sameness is as untenable as the contrastive idea that people in our own society have a sense of time that is exclusively linear.

It is essential to appreciate that all social processes display aspects of both linearity and cyclicity, and that we recognize a cyclical structure when we focus on events that repeat themselves and unidirectional linearity when our attention is on the process of the repeating action. Whether we 'see' linearity or cyclicity depends upon the framework of observation and interpretation. Indeed, to conceptualize traditional societies as cyclical and therefore 'timeless' is in itself to identify time with historical, chronological dating. While there is no doubt that the time-creating, time-eliminating and time-transcending practices of traditional societies, expressed through ritual, myth and worship, are qualitatively different from their equivalents in our own society, it is inappropriate to call them 'cyclical', 'timeless' or 'out of time', because such notions are fundamentally tied to a sense of time that is chronologically based. It is not the concept of cyclicity itself that is at issue here, because cyclical processes *by definition* involve the combination of repetition with variation, linearity and progression. The problem lies in the meaning associated with cyclical time in anthropological studies, and with the fictitious contrast to a 'Western linear time'. We can thus obviate the unsatisfactory dichotomy between cyclical and linear time by demonstrating both their fundamental mutual implication and their relativity to the perspective of the observer. No such resolution, however, is available in the case of the opposition between reversible and irreversible time.

The contemporary idea of reversibility, promulgated by Lévi-Strauss and more recently employed by Giddens (1981), is derived from Newtonian physics, in which abstract motion is postulated as symmetrical with respect to the past and the future. It is applied in classical physics to such phenomena as the swinging of the pendulum, or the elastic collision of billiard balls, where, if a film were taken of the events, we could not tell whether it was running forwards or backwards. As I have shown, the Newtonian concept of reversibility is based on the assumption that everything is given, so that, irrespective of the number of transformations a system undergoes, it could, in principle, retrace all the changes and return to its original state. It is a general mathematical property of dynamic equations, explain Prigogine and Stengers (1984: 61), 'that if the velocities of all points of a system are reversed, the system will go "backward in time" .... What one dynamic change has achieved, another change, defined by velocity inversion, can undo, and in this way exactly restore the original condition.' Reversibility signifies the possibility of un-acting, un-relating and un-associating, un-knowing and un-structuring. It means that ashes igniting themselves and turning back into logs, leaves picking themselves off the ground and attaching themselves to the branches of trees, and old rusty cars turning back into gleaming limousines all have to be considered as being just as possible, in principle, as what actually occurs in the world of our experiences. Applied to social life, this idea is clearly absurd. Moreover, it even poses major problems within the natural sciences. It contradicts not only common-sense knowledge but also some of the most recent theories in theoretical physics (Hawking 1988, Prigogine 1980), by which temporality has been established as a law of nature.

With respect to human social life, we can state that events may recur at regular intervals, and in a seemingly unchanging way, without being reversible. Rather, cultural life engenders time, entails time and is enacted in time: it creates a new past and a new future and involves time as sequence, duration, intensity, passage and irreversible direction. In other words, time is fundamentally implicated in even the most repetitive of social phenomena. Furthermore, it is not time itself but events and tasks that are endlessly repeated. Consciousness, experience, knowledge, and the implementation of the tasks, in contrast, are irreversible: they constitute time. Going to work every morning, tending the animals, organizing the food for the family and washing the dishes could be classified as recurrent, repetitive, habitual activities, but this makes neither them, nor the time in which they occur, reversible, because there can be no un-going to work, no un-tending the animals, no un-washing up. Nothing can be undone and restored to its 'original condition': time neither stands still nor goes backwards.

Having shown reversibility to be an abstraction, a Newtonian idealization inapplicable to human social life, we need now to look briefly at the idea of sameness; to examine the proposition that we can dispense with the distinction between past and future because that which has been recurs, and that which is to come has already been. 'Repetition of the same' is often considered particularly apt as a description of the tenor of life in apparently traditional or very slow-changing societies, or those that in Lévi-Strauss's terminology would be categorized as 'cold'. People in such societies are supposed to be concerned to annul, as far as they can, the effects of the temporality of social life. Yet, even for physicists, the assumption of sameness is highly problematic. It has been estimated that one cubic centimetre of air would be likely to recur in exactly the same composition only once in 10 to the power of 10 million million million years (Eigen 1983: 37–41) – which is a mathematical expression for 'as good as never'. If 'repetition of the same' is that unlikely for a mere cubic centimetre of air, we can safely consider it beyond the bounds of the possible for any human social event to repeat itself so exactly that we might classify it to be 'the same'. The effort to fix the transient world into knowable stability and permanence is a general human endeavour, not merely a characteristic of traditional and archaic societies. Writing music, or making films and compact discs, are contemporary efforts to reproduce originals in unchanging form. But neither a myth being told nor a record being played can be considered to be 'the same' in their repetition. For the storytellers and their stories, the listeners, their records and their equipment, all have grown older. They constitute a different past and present and anticipate an altered future, regardless of the explicit efforts to produce an unaltered re-enactment of some original state or event. As Stegmüller (1969: 175) explains with reference to Heidegger's work on time,

> Repetition is no empty bringing back of the past; not a mere binding of the present to that which has irrevocably gone, but a deep response to that which has been, while simultaneously being a decisive revocation of the effects of the past in the present (my translation).

Repetition can be the 'same' only in abstraction, by artificially excluding contexts and effects.

Emphasizing the repetitive aspects of habit, tradition and structuration at the expense of 'presencing' and the reality-creating aspect of recurrent activities misses a vital dimension of repetition in all human societies. We need to recognize that repetition and irreversibility are not separate or even separable concepts. They are both linked to the becoming of the possible. By conflating repetition, cyclicity, and sameness with reversibility, the opportunities to theorize the creation of reality and the relation between cycles of return and directional change have been missed (Adam 1990: 28–31). Furthermore, what is generally conceptualized as 'timeless' refers mostly to rates of change that are very much slower than those to which observers are accustomed: traditional societies are only extremely slow-changing by contemporary Western standards, but are not so, for example, in relation to evolutionary change. Once more we find that the implicit frame of reference of the observer is centrally implicated in the definition and classification of the objects of anthropological observation. We thus need to allow for the constitutive nature of our frameworks and to free ourselves from the positivist belief in the existence of an objective reality untouched by our observations.

We also need to apply this awareness to the concern to define the subject matter of anthropology as distinct from, and in relation to, history. It has been argued that anthropology and history attempt, respectively, synchronic and diachronic analyses of social and cultural phenomena. This identification of anthropology with synchronic study should be recognized as part of the discipline's quest for scientific status, in that the synchronic method is considered to meet the requirement that analyses be 'uncontaminated by time'.

This, of course, is an illusion because, as Fabian (1983: 24) correctly points out, 'no matter whether one chooses to stress "diachronic" or "synchronic", historical or systematic approaches, [both] are *chronic*, unthinkable without reference to time.' Both are based on the abstract time of clocks and calendars. Both offer a description of their subject matter either as it exists at one moment, or 'over time'. Moreover, as synchronic and diachronic analyses are exclusively tied to clock and calendar time, both may be inappropriate for analyses of societies that do not share our abstract, objectified time frame. Furthermore, neither is sufficient on its own to grasp social life. As Giddens (1981: 17) notes, 'a stable order is one in which there is close similarity between how things are, and how they used to be.' It is therefore misleading to suppose, he continues,

> that one can take a 'timeless snapshot' of a social system as one can, say, take a real snapshot of the architecture of a building. For social systems exist *as* systems only in and through their 'functioning' (reproduction) over time.

It is not only the identification of time with change, in analyses couched in terms of the synchrony–diachrony distinction, that is erroneous; equally mistaken is the way such analyses tie the nature of change to the reversible time of Newtonian physics. This, as I have shown above, excludes the embedded time of things and processes, life and knowledge; and it leaves us with no foundation from which to conceptualize creativity, novelty or the constitution of time in the present. The effect of contrasting routine and sameness with progressive change and creativity is to confine our understanding within a straitjacket of either–or alternatives, leading us to dichotomize what are integral aspects of *all* human life. In our own society the emphasis on the linear seems, to many of us, to crowd out the recognition of the cyclical, and we lose sight of the vital part that repetition plays in the constitution of our own social structure. Having lost touch with our own cyclicity, we project it onto the objects of our investigation. We construct it as 'other time'. If we are to correct the resulting distortions, then it is imperative that we should get to know our own time and to recognize its fundamental role in the constitution of the time of those whom, and among whom, we study.

REFLECTION

The study of 'other time' demands reflection. It necessitates an explicit understanding of the complexity of 'our own time' and a rigorous examination of the assumptions that underpin our traditional models. It requires, as Honneth and Joas (1988: 8) point out, 'the identification and the making explicit of the natural bases and the normative implications that are always assumed in the substantive work of the social sciences'. This involves investigations that anthropologists have traditionally regarded as lying outside their domain: concern with disconcerting matters of epistemology and with issues of ontology. Time is necessarily central to these investigations, since it is fundamentally implicated in the constitution of 'reality' for both observers and observed, and in their respective theories. Without a better understanding of the complexity of time in its general and particular expressions, anthropological studies of time will stay locked in a kind of science that leading contemporary natural scientists have already left behind. These scientists have taken on the challenge of time and have recognized that 'timeless' statements and de-temporalized models belong to Newtonian science rather than to science *per se*. They have established temporality as a principle of nature, elevating it to the status of a natural law, and in so doing they have changed the very meaning of 'law' (Adam 1988: 211–14, 1990: 61–9). To be a scientist today no longer entails translating the temporal world into models based on de-temporalized and reversible time. Rather, it involves the transcendence of disciplinary boundaries, since time permeates all levels of our contemporary reality. Moreover, there is no one path that is better or more appropriate than others. There is no short cut to analyses that take us beyond Cartesian dualisms and Newtonian science. To suggest that time, temporality, timing, tempo and the relation to the past, present and future all have to be *implicated* whenever any one aspect is *explicated* is merely a first step in that direction.

ACKNOWLEDGEMENT

I would like to thank Jan Adam and Tom Keenoy for their perceptive comments on an earlier draft of this article.

NOTES

1 For physicists there is a fundamental dilemma here, because it is in fact impossible to compare two times simultaneously. At the level of accuracy with which we normally have to deal, however, it is sufficient to say that clocks measure the 'same' hour irrespective of context.

2 Clocks may be designed to the principle of invariance, but the measure of the hour, the minute and the second is in fact variable. It is subject to environmental influences such as gravity, but we tend to disregard that variability and focus on the invariable abstraction: the *idea* of the second, the minute and the hour. The invariability of the measure is an artefact of universal scaling.

3 Ingold (1986: 202) suggests that we can recognize the time-constituting process only after we have transcended dualistic thinking in which we oppose persistence and change, synchrony and diachrony.

4 Barnes (1971), Fabian (1983) and Ingold (1986) are notable exceptions.

REFERENCES

Adam, B. E. (1987) 'Time and Social Theory', PhD thesis, University of Wales.

—— (1988) 'Social versus natural time: a traditional distinction re-examined', in M. Young and T. Schuller (eds) *The Rhythms of Society*, London and New York: Routledge.

—— (1990) *Time and Social Theory*, Cambridge: Polity Press.

Aguessy, H. (1977) 'Sociological interpretations of time and pathology of time in developing countries', in *Time and the Philosophies. At the Crossroads of Cultures*, London: UNESCO.

Barnes, J. A. (1971) 'Time flies like an arrow', *Man* (N.S.) 6: 537–52.

Bergmann, W. (1992) 'The problem of time in sociology: an overview of the literature on the state of theory and research on the "sociology of time", 1900–1982', *Time and Society* 1: 81–134.

Bourdieu, P. (1979) *Algeria 1960*, Cambridge: Cambridge University Press.

Cohen, A. P. (1990a) 'The Future of The Self', paper presented at the Annual Conference of the Association of Social Anthropologists, University of Edinburgh, 2–5 April 1990.

—— (1990b) 'Self-conscious anthropology', in J. Okley and H. Callaway (eds) *Anthropology and Autobiography*, London: Routledge.

Cottle, T. J. and Klineberg, S. L. (1974) *The Present of Things Future. Explorations of Time in Human Experience*, New York: Free Press, Macmillan.

Dunne, J. S. (1973) *Time and Myth. A Meditation on Storytelling as an Exploration of Life and Death*, London: SCM Press.

Eigen, M. (1983) 'Evolution und Zeitlichkeit', in A. Peisl and A. Mohler (eds) *Die Zeit*, Munich: Oldenburg Verlag.

Eliade, M. (1989 [1954]) *Cosmos and History. The Myth of Eternal Return*, trans. W. R. Trask, London: Arkana.

Evans-Pritchard, E. E. (1940) *The Nuer*, Oxford: Oxford University Press.

Fabian, J. (1983) *Time and the Other*, New York: Columbia University Press.

Fraser, J. T.(1987) *Time the Familiar Stranger*, Amherst: University of Massachusetts Press.

Giddens, A. (1981) *A Contemporary Critique of Historical Materialism*, vol. 1: *Power, Property and the State*, London: Macmillan.

Gioscia, V. (1974) *Timeforms: Beyond Yesterday and Tomorrow*, New York: Interface.

Habermas, J. (1973) 'A Postscript to Knowledge and Human Interests', *Philosophy of the Social Sciences* 3: 157–89.

Hägerstrand, T. (1985) 'Time and culture', in G. Kirsch, P. Nijkamp and K. Zimmermann (eds) *Time Preferences: An Interdisciplinary Theoretical and Empirical Approach*, Berlin: Wissenschaftszentrum.

Harries-Jones, P. (1985) 'From cultural translator to advocate: changing circles of interpretation', in R. Paine (ed.) *Advocacy and Anthropology*, St Johns: ISER, Memorial University of Newfoundland.

Hawking, S. W. (1988) *A Brief History of Time. From the Big Bang to Black Holes*, London and New York: Bantam Press.

Heidegger, M. (1967) *Being and Time*, trans. J. Macquarrie and E. Robinson, Oxford: Blackwell.

—— (1972) *On Time and Being*, trans. J. Stambaugh, New York: Harper & Row.

Hohn, H.-W. (1984) *Die Zerstörung der Zeit. Wie aus einem göttlichen Gut seine Handelsware wurde*, Frankfurt-am-Main: Fischer Alternativ.

Honneth, A. and Joas, H. (1988) *Social Action and Human Nature*, trans. R. Meyer, Cambridge: Cambridge University Press.

Ingold, T. (1986) *Evolution and Social Life*, Cambridge: Cambridge University Press.
Kant, I. (1966 [1781]) *The Critique of Pure Reason*, trans. F. M. Müller, New York: Doubleday Anchor.
Kinget, G. M. (1975) *On Being Human. A Systematic View*, New York: Harcourt Brace Jovanovich.
Kluckhohn, F. R. and Strodbeck, F. L. (1961) *Variations in Value Orientations*, New York: Harper & Row.
Lévi-Strauss, C. (1972 [1963]) *Structural Anthropology*, Harmondsworth: Penguin.
Marshack, A. (1972) *The Roots of Civilization*, New York: McGraw-Hill.
Maxwell, R. J. (1972) 'Anthropological perspectives', in H. Yaker, H. Osmond and F. Cheeck (eds) *The Future of Time*, London: Hogarth Press.
Mbiti, J. S. (1969) *African Religions and Philosophy*, London: Heinemann.
McElwain, T. (1988) 'Seneca Iroquois concepts of time', *Cosmos 4. Amerindian Cosmology*, Edinburgh: Traditional Cosmology Society.
Nowotny, H. (1985) 'From the future to the extended present − time in social systems', in G. Kirsch, P. Nijkamp, and K. Zimmermann (eds) *Time Preference: An Interdisciplinary Theoretical and Empirical Approach*, Berlin: Wissenschaftszentrum.
Ortner, S. B. (1984) 'Theory in anthropology since the sixties', *Comparative Studies in Society and History* 1: 126−66.
Prigogine, I. (1980) *From Being to Becoming. Time and Complexity in the Physical Sciences*, San Francisco: W. H. Freeman.
Prigogine, I. and Stengers, I. (1984) *Order out of Chaos: Man's New Dialogue with Nature*, London: Heinemann.
Rinderspacher, J. P. (1985) *Gesellschaft ohne Zeit. Individuelle Zeitverwendung und soziale Organisation der Arbeit*. Frankfurt-am-Main: Campus.
Shallis, M. (1983) *On Time. An Investigation into Scientific Knowledge and Human Experience*, Harmondsworth: Penguin.
Starkey, K. (1988) 'Time and work organization: a theoretical and empirical analysis', in M. Young and T. Schuller (eds) *The Rhythms of Society*, London and New York: Routledge.
Stegmüller, W. (1969) *Hauptströmungen der Gegenwart*, Stuttgart: Alfred Körner.
Thompson, E. P. (1967) 'Time, work-discipline, and industrial capitalism', *Past and Present*, 36: 52−97.
Whorf, B. L (1956) *Language, Thought and Reality*, Cambridge, Mass.: MIT Press.

FURTHER READING

Adam, B. E. (1990) *Time and Social Theory*, Cambridge: Polity Press.
Barnes, J. A. (1971) 'Time flies like an arrow', *Man* (N.S.) 6: 537−52.
Bourdieu, P. (1979) *Algeria 1960*, Cambridge: Cambridge University Press.
Dunne, J. S. (1973) *Time and Myth. A Meditation on Storytelling as an Exploration of Life and Death*, London: SCM Press.
Eliade, M. (1989 [1954]) *Cosmos and History. The Myth of Eternal Return*, trans. W. R. Trask, London: Arkana.
Evans-Pritchard, E. E. (1969 [1940]) *The Nuer*, Oxford: Oxford University Press.
Fabian, J. (1983) *Time and the Other*, New York: Columbia University Press.
Forman, F. J. and Sowton, C. (eds) (1989) *Taking Our Time. Feminist Perspectives on Temporality*, Oxford: Pergamon Press.
Fraser, J. T. (1987) *Time the Familiar Stranger*, Amherst: University of Massachusetts Press.

Geertz, C. (1973) 'Person, time and conduct in Bali: an essay in cultural analysis', in C. Geertz, *The Interpretation of Cultures*, New York: Basic Books.

Gell, A. (1992) *The Anthropology of Time: Cultural Construction of Temporal Maps and Images*, Oxford: Berg.

Giddens, A. (1981) *A Contemporary Critique of Historical Materialism*, vol. 1: *Power, Property and the State*, London: Macmillan.

Ingold, T. (1986) *Evolution and Social Life*, Cambridge: Cambridge University Press.

Kern, S. (1983) *The Culture of Time and Space 1880–1918*, London: Weidenfeld & Nicolson.

Luce, G. G. (1977 [1973]) *Body Time. The Natural Rhythms of the Body*, St Albans: Paladin.

Maxwell, R. J. (1972) 'Anthropological perspectives', in H. Yaker, H. Osmond and F. Cheek (eds) *The Future of Time*, London: Hogarth Press.

Mbiti, J. S. (1985 [1969]) *African Religions and Philosophy*, London: Heinemann.

Rutz, H. (ed.) (1991) *The Politics of Time*, Washington: American Ethnological Society.

Time and Society, an International Interdisciplinary Journal, London: Merlin Press.

Young, M. (1988) *The Metronomic Society*, London: Thames & Hudson.

Young, M. and Schuller, T. (eds) (1988) *The Rhythms of Society*, London: Routledge.

19

ASPECTS OF LITERACY

Brian V. Street and Niko Besnier

Until the early part of the twentieth century, the ability to read and write was commonly thought to be the crucial factor distinguishing 'civilized' from 'primitive' peoples, history from prehistory. While contemporary anthropology has for the most part eschewed such overarching determinism, traces of it remain in much anthropological work on literacy and its consequences for society and the individual. What follows is a critical examination of current thought about literacy, its role in society, and its place in sociopolitical life.

Literacy has been viewed alternatively as a technology and as a social phenomenon. First, it is a system of secondary signs, in that written signs refer to another semiotic system consisting of the signs of spoken language. The encoding and decoding of this secondary semiotic system require certain cognitive skills akin to the skills associated with various technologies. Second, using literacy in normative ways presupposes certain kinds of sociocultural knowledge: constructing written texts; knowing when, where, and how to consume them; and understanding the associations of literacy with other aspects of the life of the group are all essential for a person to function as a literate member of society. In exploring these various aspects of literacy, we here opt for a strategy that differs from more traditional accounts in at least two ways. Rather than seeking broad generalizations regarding the impact of literacy on society, culture, and the human mind, we demonstrate that literacy is a varied phenomenon, and that an investigation of this variety must take priority over the search for a priori, universalist generalizations. Further, we argue that technological and social aspects of literacy are so intricately interwoven that it may be counterproductive to address them through separate analytic approaches. In particular, both aspects are heavily constrained, even probably determined, by culturally constructed ideologies.

LITERACY AS TECHNOLOGY

In this section we present a brief overview of the historical development of writing systems, and of their diversity as technologies. For more detailed discussion of both topics, the reader is referred to Diringer (1968), Gaur (1984) and Gelb (1963); works more specifically concerned with the origin of writing are Harris (1986) and Senner (1989); on writing systems, see Coulmas (1989), DeFrancis (1989) and Sampson (1985).

The origin of writing

It is generally agreed that writing is semiotically different from pictographic representation, or 'pre-writing', and this difference is commonly used to define writing operationally in opposition to other semiotic systems. Graphic representations of objects, ideas, and notions (e.g. road signs, maps, drawings) differ from writing in that they are iconic signs with non–linguistic (notional) referents, while written signs are symbols, which refer to (spoken) linguistic units.

Little is known for sure about the antiquity and purposes of the earliest literacies, and of the processes which led up to their invention. Commonly thought to have been first invented in the third or fourth millennium BC in Sumerian Mesopotamia, writing appeared in various parts of the world shortly after that date: in Egypt around 3000 BC, in the Indus Valley around 2500 BC, and in China around 2000 BC. Everywhere, there seems at first to have been a strong connection between early literacy and religious practices; the uses of reading and writing diversified only slowly over the course of their history. In Sumeria, this connection was probably mediated by economic needs, like record keeping in economic transactions, but these clearly fell under the jurisdiction of religious officialdom. In Mesoamerica, more than a dozen literacy traditions flourished between the third century AD and the Spanish Conquest. There again, writing arose as a religious practice, particularly in connection with extremely complex calendrical systems, and remained an élite art until its disappearance (Lounsbury 1989). While some archaic writing systems may have been the result of diffusion, particularly in the Middle East, writing was invented independently in at least Sumeria, the Far East, and Mesoamerica. (However, the later spread of literacy in the Mediterranean region, throughout south and south-east Asia, in the Far East, and elsewhere was certainly due to diffusional processes.) In each case, writing was developed from pictograms through a shift from iconicity to symbolization, and from non–linguistic to linguistic reference, accompanied by a trend toward greater stylization of the signs. All evidence underscores the gradual and complex nature of this process. For many centuries, graphic representations consisted of an amalgam of pictographs and different writing systems.

Types of writing systems

Three major types of writing systems are commonly recognized. The type usually taken to be the earliest is *logographic* (or ideographic) writing, a system in which each symbol represents a word. In *syllabic* writing, by contrast, individual symbols refer to syllables, and in *alphabetic* writing they refer to contrastive sound units, or phonemes. A *consonantal* alphabet provides symbols exclusively for consonants, a *phonemic* alphabet includes symbols for both consonants and vowels, while the symbols of a *featural* alphabet are made up of graphic elements that refer to the phonological characteristics of sounds. Commonly invoked as illustrations of each of these types are Chinese characters, early Egyptian hieroglyphics, and Mayan hieroglyphics for logographic writing; Japanese *katakana* and late Assyrian cuneiform for syllabic writing; the systems used for Hebrew and Arabic for consonantal alphabets; the Greek, Roman, and Cyrillic systems for phonemic alphabetic writing; and the Korean writing system for featural alphabets.

The three systems, according to the orthodox view (e.g. Goody 1977, 1986, 1987, Goody and Watt 1963, Ong 1982), follow an evolutionary order. According to this view, logographic systems were the first to arise in history, are the closest in nature to pictographic representations, and constitute the most 'primitive', cumbersome, and inefficient technology of literacy, in that knowledge of many symbols is required to represent even simple utterances. Gradually, logographic symbols became more stylized and came to represent syllables (i.e. sequences of sounds) rather than whole words. At the same time, the inventory of symbols needed to represent a comprehensive range of linguistic meanings decreased radically. Eventually, syllabic symbols came to represent single sounds, their inventory again decreased radically, and the system reached maximal technological efficiency.

But a closer look at the writing systems that are attested today or reconstructed from historical records demonstrates that none fits these prototypes. For example, the system used for writing Chinese does not exhibit the sort of one-to-one correspondence between written symbol and word (or even morpheme) associated with prototypical logography. Most words in spoken Mandarin Chinese are compounds of two or three morpheme-like monosyllabic elements, the meanings of which frequently do not add up straightforwardly to the meaning of the whole, and each of these elements is written with a separate character:

語
yŭ 'discourse'

語 法
yŭfă 'grammar'

法
fă 'rule'

語 言
yŭyén 'language'

言
yén 'utterance'

言 語
yényŭ 'speech'

Thus many lexical units can be written by combining a small number of characters in various configurations. In contrast, the many homophones in spoken Chinese are represented with different characters, all of which are read in the same manner:

斤 *jīn* 'catty'   金 *jīn* 'gold'   津 *jīn* 'ford'   筋 *jīn* 'tendon'   襟 *jīn* 'lapel'

Furthermore, many Chinese characters contain elements which provide visual cues to the phonological shape of the words they represent. For example, the characters in the following series share a common visual element, which indexes the homophony or near-homophony of the words they represent (which are semantically unrelated):

詩 *shī* 'poetry'   時 *shí* 'time'   侍 *shì* 'wait on'   恃 *shì* 'rely upon'

Thus the Chinese writing system is neither the vast, complex, and unsystematic inventory that it is often depicted to be (e.g. Goody and Watt 1963), nor is it devoid of references to the sound system of the language it represents. Rather, Chinese writing is adapted to the structure of the language, as well as to the sociolinguistic context of its use. The Chinese-speaking area is fragmented into regions in which are spoken numerous mutually unintelligible varieties, but all dialects that are commonly written share a basic stock of characters. While in practice literate speakers of one dialect cannot easily read a text written in a more distant dialect, the system still provides homogeneity in a highly fragmented linguistic situation. (The structural and sociolinguistic features of Chinese writing are treated at length in Coulmas 1989, Norman 1988, and Sampson 1985.)

The trichotomy between logographic, syllabic and alphabetic writing, which may be of some use as a theoretical model based on largely unattested prototypicality, is inadequate as a descriptive device. Furthermore, evolutionary models of writing systems, which are frequently based more on enduring stereotypes than on empirical observations, often fail to recognize that writing systems are used in particular contexts. It is particularly sobering to note that these evolutionary accounts identify the historical 'perfectioning' of writing with the rise of Western civilization in the Mediterranean region. But even in Middle Eastern and Greek antiquity, the development of writing from logographs to the alphabet via syllabic systems was by no means a straight road: in the course of the history of many writing systems, logographic elements were discarded and then reintroduced, because they were viewed as more efficient representations of linguistic units in written texts (Davies 1986). Rather than ranking all writing systems in a single order from the most unwieldy and cumbersome to the most efficient and learnable, a comparative perspective should approach the question as a problem of *adaptation* (Barton 1988). For example, the very complex character of a writing system may serve specific social functions, as Crump (1988) argues for Japanese writing, and 'complexity' itself is very difficult to define precisely. Writing systems are adapted to the structural characteristics of the linguistic code and the macrosociolinguistic context. Situations in which different writing systems compete or coexist, and situations of transition from one writing system to another (e.g. the change from a Sinitic-derived syllabary to the Roman alphabet in Vietnam between the seventeenth and nineteenth centuries) offer fruitful grounds for investigating the different adaptive dimensions of writing systems. The physical characteristics of writing systems also bear the imprint of the technological and social practices surrounding literacy. For example, incisions made with a stylus in clay, as practised in ancient Sumeria, necessarily have a very different shape from handbrushed classical Chinese characters on paper and from Mayan hieroglyphics carved on stone monuments.

A particularly rich illustration of the way in which a writing system refracts broader technological and social dynamics is provided by the Hanunóo of Mindoro island (Philippines). The Hanunóo Sanskritic-derived syllabary is most commonly carved on green bamboo stalks (but also tattooed on human arms), and both the shape of the characters and their usual bottom-to-top directionality are a direct consequence of the position of the carver with respect to the bamboo stalk and of the nature of the tools involved. But the patterns go further. Norms governing Hanunóo writing are remarkably flexible: for example, the symbols can be written in mirror-image fashion and in any direction besides the standard one (thus easing the task for left-handed individuals); certain phonemic contrasts in the language are indicated in writing by some individuals, but not by others. The systemic laxness of the writing system can only be understood in its broader social context, as a token of the non-directive and egalitarian ethos which the Hanunóo value. The

Hanunóo case illustrates that many aspects of writing systems can only be understood in relation to their technological and social contexts.

LITERACY AS A SOCIO-CULTURAL CONSTRUCT

Much has been written on the relationship, on the one hand, between literacy and its converse, orality, and on the other hand, between social and cultural institutions and the intellectual makeup of individuals. In this section, two broad schools of thought are first contrasted critically; two case studies are then presented; and the question of the impact of literacy on language is broached.

Literacy and its consequences

Anthropological interest in literacy is deeply embedded in the history of anthropological thought and that of related disciplines. Early in the development of social-scientific thinking, literacy was implicated, more or less explicitly, as a determinant of differences between 'primitive' and 'civilized' thought and action (Tylor), collective and individualistic consciousness (Durkheim, Mauss), prelogical and logical mentalities (Lévy-Bruhl, Luria), closed and open systems (Popper), *pensée sauvage* and *pensée domestiquée* (Lévi-Strauss), mythopoeic and scientific thinking (Lévi-Strauss, Cassirer), and context-bound and context-free cognitive processes (Vygotsky). The view that literacy plays a pivotal role in bringing about fundamental changes in the individual and society has been most clearly articulated by Goody (in increasingly mitigated terms, in Goody and Watt 1963, Goody 1977, 1986, 1987; also Havelock 1976, Illich and Sanders 1988, Innis 1972, McLuhan 1962, Parsons 1966). This work, represented in what has come to be referred to as the 'autonomous' or 'Great Divide' model of literacy, takes to task earlier dichotomies for their lack of an explanatory dimension, and proposes that 'many of the valid aspects of these somewhat vague dichotomies can be related to changes in the mode of communication, especially the introduction of various forms of writing' (Goody 1977: 16).

According to the autonomous model, literacy, particularly alphabetic literacy, causes (or, in more recent versions, facilitates) basic changes in the makeup of both society and the individual because of its inherent properties. For example, writing leads to permanent records which can be subjected to critical scrutiny, and as a result it gives rise to historical and scientific verifiability and concomitant social designs. Similarly, bureaucratic institutions and complex state structures depend crucially on the types of long-distance communication that literacy makes possible. The individual's psychological functions are also altered by literacy: a written text, particularly if written in an alphabetic script, is in some sense more abstract and less context-dependent than a comparable spoken text, and the ability to produce and process written texts presupposes and brings about context-free thinking (Olson 1977). Further, literacy affects memory in significant ways, making possible rigorous recall of lengthy texts, compared with the imprecise, pattern-driven memory of preliterate individuals (Hunter 1985).

The premises and claims of the autonomous model have been subjected to severe critical scrutiny by researchers in a variety of fields, including social anthropology (Street 1984), sociolinguistics (Heath 1983), psychology (Scribner and Cole 1981), rhetoric (Pattison 1982), folklore (Finnegan 1988) and history (Clanchy 1979, Graff 1979, Harris 1989). For most critics, literacy should be viewed not as a monolithic phenomenon but as a multi-faceted one, whose meaning, including any consequences it may have for the individual and society, depends crucially on the social practices surrounding it and on the ideological system in which it is embedded. Proponents of an 'ideological model' view literacy as a socio-cultural construct, and propose that literacy cannot be studied independently of the social, political, and historical forces which shape it (Street 1984). They point out, for example, that literacy is found in many societies of the world without the social and cognitive characteristics which the autonomous model predicts should accompany it.

To meet these objections, advocates of the autonomous model have proposed that there exist various situations of so-called *restricted literacy* (Goody 1977), in which constraints on the scope of literacy have inhibited the full realization of its expected social and cognitive potentials. Thus literacy is said to be *socially* restricted when it is available only to a political or intellectual (usually male) élite, which uses it as a tool for control; it is said to be *functionally* restricted when it is used by many people, but for a narrow range of purposes; and it is said to be *intellectually* restricted when, for some reason, it has failed to trigger the intellectual changes that are engendered in 'fully' literate individuals and groups. Advocates of the ideological perspective view with suspicion the assumptions underlying these qualifications, which more or less explicitly equate non-restricted literacy with Western middle-class standards, and they ask whether any society is in fact 'fully' literate in this sense. For example, the use of literacy and associated institutions by the political and intellectual élites of Western societies, in order to control access to symbolic capital (Bourdieu 1984), fits the description of a socially restricted literacy. By contrast, in sixteenth-century insular South-east Asia, literacy was deeply ingrained in the everyday life of every social stratum, particularly among women (Reid 1988). Even though this situation clearly does not fit the definition of restricted literacy, it did not give rise to Western-style history, science, political structures, or even schooling.

The ideological reaction to autonomous approaches to literacy represents a retreat from generalization, a call back to the ethnographic drawing board, which some have criticized for its sociological reductionism (Cole and Nicolopoulou 1992). Underlying the ideological view is the belief that generalizations are much more likely to be discovered in the relationship between literacy and its socio-cultural, political, and ideological context than in the inherent properties of literacy itself (Besnier 1991). In fact, these very properties are frequently the subject of contention. Compare, for example, the premise that 'speech is transient, writing is permanent' (Crystal and Davy 1969: 69) with the contradictory premise that 'speech, once uttered, can rarely be revised, no matter how much we might struggle to unsay something we wish we had not said. But writing can be reflected upon, and even erased at will' (Smith 1983: 82). Clearly, what is represented in these two statements is the articulation of two different ideologies, or perhaps two facets of the same ideology.

Literacy and literacies

The diversity of literacy experiences, which the ideological model takes as the object of its inquiry, is illustrated here with two case studies: Scribner and Cole's (1981) work on literacy among the Vai of Liberia, and Heath's (1983) analysis of literacy in three rural Appalachian communities in the United States. These now classic studies complement one another in several ways: while Scribner and Cole examine the cognitive consequences that the autonomous model ascribes to literacy, Heath is concerned with the social and cultural correlates of literacy; the former demonstrates the intrinsic variety of literacy experiences within a single group, whereas the latter illustrates variety across social groups in a complex society; both studies demonstrate how ethnographically informed work in two different disciplines, psychology and sociolinguistics respectively, leads to congruent conclusions on the meaning of literacy; and they illustrate how an ideological approach can inform work on the role of literacy in both 'traditional' and Western societies. In both works, a common theme will emerge, which will be taken up later in this article: the complex intertwining of literacy and schooling.

Among the Vai of Liberia, three different types of literacies are attested, each being associated with different languages, institutions, and social activities: Vai literacy, which exploits a locally devised syllabary and is used to write letters and keep records of economic transactions; Koranic literacy, which is learnt in religious schools and used to read Muslim scriptures; and English literacy, learnt in school and used in transactions with the outside world. In this ideal comparative laboratory, Scribner and Cole (1981) set out to test two claims put forward in 'autonomous' approaches: that significant cognitive consequences can be ascribed to literacy; and that alphabetic writing in particular fosters analytic thought. They administered a battery of psychological tests adapted to the Vai situation, such as syllogistic problems, memory tasks, and rebus games. The results demonstrated that literacy itself is not a good predictor of cognitive skills. Rather, the cognitive performance of different Vai subpopulations is best explained in terms of the psychological and social accompaniments of each literacy tradition, particularly those that are given

salience during apprenticeship in literacy. For example, Koranic literates perform well on incremental recall tests, a reflection of the importance of memory
work in Koranic schools. Subjects literate in the Vai syllabary perform well
in rebus-solving tests, because using the Vai syllabary involves rebus-like
problems. Vai subjects literate in English, who all attend Western-style
schools, do well on tests that resemble school activities, like syllogisms. Thus
the pedagogical practices that characterize each literacy experience, rather
than literacy itself, shape the individual's cognitive makeup: 'particular
practices promote particular skills' (Scribner and Cole 1981: 258).

Learning how to read and write is not simply a process of developing cognitive skills associated with these activities, but also of learning how these skills
are to be used in their social context. Heath (1983) investigates the implications of this proposition in three communities of the rural American South:
Maintown, a white middle-class community; Roadville, a white working-class
town; and Trackton, a black working-class community. She found strikingly
divergent patterns in how children are socialized in these three groups with
respect to such language-related activities as story-telling and reading books.
In Maintown, pre-school children are taught to pay attention to books from
an early age. Bedtime stories are accompanied by pedagogical practices like
question—answer and 'initiation—reply—evaluation' sequences. In particular,
questions like 'What did you like about the story?' resemble the sort of analytic
questions that children are expected to answer early on in school contexts.
Similarly, Maintown children learn turn-taking mechanisms (i.e. when to be
silent, when to speak) and fictionalization skills that are valued in schools. In
contrast, Roadville children learn to find connections between literacy and
'truth'. Christian Roadville parents use literacy for instruction and moral
improvement, and explicitly value the 'real' over the 'fictional'. Reading to
children in Roadville is an uncommon performance in which children are passive participants, and written materials are not connected to everyday life.
Finally, Trackton children learn early in life how to defend themselves orally
and to engage in verbal play. Young children receive attention from adults if
they can offer a good verbal performance. Adult Trackton residents are not
literacy-oriented, and do not read to children. Children are not asked pedagogical questions about their surroundings; Trackton adults assume that they will
learn through their own efforts and observations of adults. In these three communities, children are thus exposed to different pedagogical practices, and
learn very different associations with literacy in pre-school years, which will
accompany them to school and in large part determine their performance in
such middle-class-dominated institutions.

The two case studies summarized here demonstrate the pronounced heterogeneity of literacy experiences both within and across social groups. Literacy
is deeply embedded in, and derives its meaning from, the social practices
which are most clearly articulated in pedagogical contexts. Both case studies

535

demonstrate that it is futile to try to arrive at a decontextualized characterization of the cognitive and social consequences of literacy, and they provide an alternative route: a focus on the *activities* and *events* in which literacy plays a central role (Basso 1974, Szwed 1981).

Spoken and written language

The important question of the impact of literacy on language is one which has received little attention until recently. Here again, one finds in the evolution of the problem a history of a priori overgeneralizations followed by a return to 'thicker' descriptive approaches.

Ever since de Saussure, Bloomfield, and Sapir, arguably the founders of modern linguistics, emphasized that the primary goal of linguistics was the study of spoken language, few scholars in that field had paid much attention to literacy. In the late 1970s and early 1980s, two subfields of linguistics, sociolinguistics and discourse analysis, witnessed a surge of interest in the study of written language. Primarily motivated by questions of structural comparison between spoken and written language, studies of this sort would typically take particular linguistic structures (e.g. complex-sentence structures) and analyse their distribution across various types of spoken and written texts (for a comprehensive overview of this research, see Chafe and Tannen 1987). The resulting correlations would then be explained in terms of what the researcher perceives as the 'natural' adaptation of language users to various communicative environments. This leads on to discussion of various oral and literate 'strategies', viewed as the overall patterns of language users' structural and stylistic 'choices' in adapting to such factors as the presence or absence of an immediate audience, and the degree of personal 'involvement' or 'detachment' that the language producer experiences *vis-à-vis* the text (Tannen 1985).

Work in this vein recognizes that spoken and written communication are neither structurally nor functionally opposed, but lie on a continuum from most literate-like (e.g. academic writing) to most oral-like (e.g. informal conversation); most registers, or situational varieties of language use, fall between these two extremes. Thus the pitfalls of the 'Great Divide' approach are to a certain extent overcome. But problems remain. For example, in order for there to be a continuum, there must be well-defined extremes, the most literate-like of which is pretheoretically associated with such features as the effacement of the authorial voice, structural complexity, and informational 'repleteness' (for the text to be amenable to processing with little knowledge of the extratextual context). Furthermore, the responses of communicators to different communicative contexts along this continuum, which are evident in the structural characteristics of the texts they produce, are explained in cognitive terms; in this respect, this tradition of work does not differ from other areas of mainstream linguistics, which defines its task as a search for universal cognitive explanations for language (of course, there are many different accounts of what 'cognition' consists of). In addition, there is evidence that a uni-dimensional continuum is inadequate to accommodate the variations in linguistic behaviour across contexts of oral and written communication (Biber 1988).

Sociolinguistic investigations of literacy can be better contextualized in the perspective of broader socio-cultural issues. Most work to date suffers from the virtual lack of a cross-cultural and cross-social perspective, being largely based on the speaking and writing activities of the Western middle-class academic élite. This has led researchers to confuse cognitive behaviour and socio-cultural norms which have become, in the process of a long socio-historical evolution, 'naturalized', i.e. made to appear as if they were the only valid way to communicate through the medium of literacy. As we go on to show, this naturalization is a powerful device in controlling access to such institutions as schooling, and is thus pivotal in the maintenance of socio-cultural hegemony.

THE SPREAD OF LITERACY

Goody (1968) has stressed the importance of writing as a means of communication in a society formerly without it, or where writing has been confined to particular groups. Yet the processes which lead up to, accompany, and follow the introduction of literacy to preliterate groups remain largely undocumented. From what is known of such situations, a variety of patterns emerges. These patterns can be characterized in terms of tensions between preliteracy and literacy, between introduced and locally devised literacies, and between different literacy practices.

Tensions between preliteracy and literacy

Literacy is commonly introduced to preliterate groups in conjunction with many other technologies, institutions, and practices, among which religion figures prominently. While historically, literacy had accompanied the spread of Islam, Buddhism, and Hinduism, since the nineteenth century Christian missionization has provided the most common vehicle and rationale for the spread of literacy, and this has frequently been underscored by a First-World–Third-World dichotomy. Since the middle of the twentieth century, many agents of proselytization have legitimized their existence by invoking their literacy-promoting campaigns, in tune with Western middle-class ideology which views literacy, and in particular essayist literacy, as an essential tool for 'progress', 'happiness', and integration into the post-modern world. The explicitness with which literacy, religious conversion, and political economy are intermeshed in missionizing discourse clearly calls for an analytic stance that recognizes the complexity of these relationships.

The reactions of target groups to the introduction of literacy depend on many different factors, among which figure the relationship between the group and the introducing agents, attitudes toward socio-cultural elements concurrently being introduced to the group, and the social and political associations of literacy (Spolsky *et al.* 1983). Frequently, where literacy is initially viewed as a means of gaining access to the economic or symbolic capital associated with the agents of introduction, it is readily incorporated into the communicative repertoire of the target group. Witness, for example, nineteenth-century missionary reports of the enthusiastic acceptance of literacy in various parts of the insular Pacific (cf. Parsonson 1967, Jackson 1975). However, the reconstruction of a group's ideological reaction to literacy is primarily an exercise in historical critique; the texts on which it relies must be read as much for the ideology in which they are embedded (e.g. the belief that 'low culture' can only be attracted to and awed by 'high culture' and its tokens) as for what they say about the people observed (MacKenzie 1987).

A group's reaction to literacy can also function as an idiom of resistance: among many post-contact Native American groups, one witnesses a basic suspicion towards literacy, which is viewed as yet another element of socio-cultural hegemony and an encroachment from the outside, associated with the American government's Bureau of Indian Affairs, Christian proselytizers, and other institutions of the dominant culture (Leap 1991, Philips 1975, Spolsky and Irvine 1982; but see McLaughlin 1989). Comparable disinterest is encountered in contemporary Papua New Guinea, the theatre of many missionizing and literacizing onslaughts (Schieffelin and Cochran-Smith 1984). The acceptance or rejection of literacy technologies and practices can thus play a symbolic role in defining a group's stance towards powerful outsiders, and the nature of its involvement in socio-political and ideological dynamics imposed from without the group. In all cases, it is important to view the group to which literacy is being introduced as actively 'taking hold' of literacy, rather than remaining a passive participant in the process (Kulick and Stroud 1990).

The spread of literacy can be accompanied by various types of engineering efforts on the part either of the group introducing literacy or of those on the receiving end. Outside agents may devise orthographies for the language of the newly literate group, translate texts, and set up pedagogical institutions, as many contemporary missionizing agencies do. There are even cases where the party introducing literacy has devised new writing systems; such systems were invented for Cree, Kutchin Athapaskan, and Inuit in Northern and Western Canada, where they are still in use (Scollon and Scollon 1981, Walker 1981). On the other hand, agents of introduction may provide no more than training in literacy consumption, in an attempt to restrict their trainees' access to writing; such is the case of nineteenth-century missionaries in much of Polynesia, who brought printing presses with them, printed catechisms and other religious literature, but left the islanders to fend for themselves when it came to writing. The spread of literacy from literate to preliterate groups often accompanies the introduction (sometimes the imposition) of a new language, be it a 'major' language like English or Arabic or a locally based lingua franca, often a creole (e.g. Tok Pisin in Papua New Guinea). Even when it is the policy of the introducing agent to base literacy on local languages, a lingua franca generally looms not far behind. In contemporary Mexico, education policy-makers advocate the use of Mesoamerican languages as a medium for instruction in literacy for Native American minorities, but view it only as a bridge to literacy in Spanish (King 1994). Thus arise compartmentalized situations, whereby a 'local' or 'vernacular' literacy is used in some contexts, and a more 'global' literacy (commonly equated with print and 'national' literacies) in another set of contexts. The spread of literacy must thus be placed in the context of histories of contact between intrusive languages and local languages.

At the 'receiving' end, many aspects of literacy undergo redefinition, in that the literacy practices developed by newly literate groups frequently differ from those of introducing agents. For example, in the later half of the nineteenth century, the Diyari of central Australia were taught to read and write by Lutheran missionaries for the purpose of reading the Scriptures. They co-operated in the process because schooling gave them access to food and other economic resources. But soon, empowering the technology, they began to write letters and keep records, neither of which were encouraged by the missionaries. Thus literacy acquired a very different cultural meaning from the one it had had for the agents of introduction (Ferguson 1987). Similarly, on Nukulaelae Atoll in the Central Pacific, letter writing developed very soon after the introduction of literacy in the 1860s, even though literacy was first brought there, again, to turn Nukulaelae Islanders into consumers of Christian Scriptures. Letter writing quickly became well integrated into the secular life of the community, in which it fulfilled specific functions, such as the expression of certain types of affect (Besnier 1989). Literacy can also become a new vessel for communicative practices already extant in the oral mode. Among the Gapun of Papua New Guinea, face-to-face interaction frequently involves tension between two conflicting aspects of the Gapun self, individualism and other-centredness, and the very same conflict can be witnessed in the Gapun's literate activities (Kulick and Stroud 1990).

The diversity of initial literacy experiences illustrated here leads one to hypothesize that newly literate groups do not necessarily perceive literacy as a homogeneous, monolithic phenomenon, but rather as a set of diverse communicative possibilities, defined in part with the contextual background to the introduction of literacy technologies and ideologies, and in part by the communicative dynamics already in place (Street 1993). Situations where preliteracy and literacy come into contact are often extremely complex, and commonly occur together with great social and cultural upheavals, which are usually brought about by the very same agents introducing literacy.

'Invented' literacies

One of the most remarkable feats of literacy engineering since the invention of the technology itself was the creation of new writing systems, usually syllabaries, by preliterate individuals. Several cases are known to have occurred in the course of the nineteenth and twentieth centuries, in various parts of West Africa (among the Mende and the Vai, for example), in Native North America, among the Apache and the Cherokee, and in South-east Asia (Smalley, Vang and Yang 1990). The best-known case is that of Sequoyah, a preliterate Cherokee who spent several years in the 1810s and 1820s devising a functional 85-symbol syllabary for his native language, using symbols from the Roman alphabet and probably the Greek and Cyrillic alphabets, supplemented by symbols of Sequoyah's invention (Walker 1981). The system was first viewed with much suspicion (its inventor was even tried for witchcraft), but within a few years literacy was widespread, and an active tradition of print literacy was established, principally in the form of newspapers. The currency of the writing system subsequently declined owing to the forced relocation of the Cherokee from the Southeastern United States to Oklahoma in 1839 along the infamous Trail of Tears, and to subsequent efforts by the American government to 'integrate' the Cherokee, which culminated in their confiscation of the Cherokee newspaper press in 1909. Today, Sequoyah's syllabary is used for a limited range of purposes: for reading the Christian Bible, and for recording and reading curing formulae for traditional medical practices.

Most invented literacies were developed to answer the needs of an economically and politically disadvantaged group, dominated by a literate society in which literacy was associated with power. This association was evident to Sequoyah, who was reputedly obsessed with the idea that the Cherokee should learn to communicate in the written mode if they were to ensure their survival in the face of Anglo-American encroachment. Thus the very invention of the syllabary was motivated by aspects of the dominant group's ideology regarding literacy. The extent to which Cherokee literacy practices were influenced by Anglo-American literacy practices is unclear. But invented literacies obviously arose from more or less extensive contact with the pre-existing literacy of the dominant group (Harbsmeier 1988). However, they differed from other contexts in which the technology spread from a dominant to a subordinate group in that they arose with no encouragement from the former. In fact, in the Cherokee case, literacy existed against the wishes of the dominant group.

Tensions between literacy practices

The basic diversity in literacy experiences around the world leads to literacy practices with differing historical and socio-cultural associations coming into contact with one another. First, different literacy practices may be associated with different social groups. Heath's (1983) work on three Appalachian communities, reviewed above, demonstrates how tensions between the literacy practices of middle-class, white working-class, and black working-class groups both reflect and reinforce inequality, oppression, and hegemony.

Second, distinct literacy practices may be associated with different contexts of use, and may thus play divergent roles in the lives of members of a society. In a rural community in pre-revolutionary Iran, three sets of literacy practices have been described, which Street (1984) calls '*maktab*' literacy, 'commercial' literacy, and 'school' literacy. Before state schools were introduced into the rural areas, villagers learnt reading and writing in Koranic schools, or *maktabs*. While these have been denigrated by many Western commentators and educationalists as involving only rote learning and repetition, in this case the literacy learnt in that context was transferred to other contexts. During the boom years of the early 1970s, there was a growing demand from urban areas for village produce, and villagers developed entrepreneurial skills in marketing and distributing their fruit that required an ability to write, make out bills, mark boxes, use cheque-books, etc. These literate skills were particularly evident among those who had been to the *maktab* and had continued their Koranic learning in their homes; they were able to transfer literacy skills from one context to another, at the same time extending both their content and their function. School literacy remained relatively one-dimensional from this point of view, and did not provide an entry into commercial literacy. It did however provide a novel social and economic route to urban professional employment, notably through entry to urban schools. The three literacies belonged to different social domains, although a single individual might learn more than one of them.

Third, situations abound in which different literacy practices compete for the same or for closely related intellectual and social spaces in the lives of members of a group. In Scal Bay, an Aleut village in Alaska, one finds two sets of literacy practices, having different historical antecedents, and conflicting social and symbolic associations: a 'village' literacy, associated with the Russian Orthodox church and conducted in Aleut (written in Cyrillic); and 'outside' literacy, which is associated with English, schooling, economic transactions, and Baptist missionaries (Reder and Green 1983). These two literacies, which until recently remained functionally separate, have begun to compete in certain contexts. Characteristically, the competition between literacies is both a reflection and an enactment of conflicts between 'tradition' and 'intrusion', between different economic systems, and between competing religious ideologies.

The ways in which literacy can symbolize processes of conflict in society are thus varied. Different literacy traditions and practices may be associated with various social groups, social contexts, and historical antecedents. The resulting tensions between literacies frequently become a focus of struggle between groups, contexts, and individuals. Literacy practices are thus part and parcel of broader social and cultural processes.

LITERACY AND SOCIO-POLITICAL PROCESSES

The emphasis on social rather than cognitive processes in the study of literacy practices has opened up new and fruitful areas of inquiry for social anthropology. We now examine four connected themes in the light of the concepts and approaches outlined in the earlier sections: the relationship between literacy and nationalism; literacy and gender relations; literacy and education; and literacy and development.

Literacy and nationalism

A number of recent studies of the emergence and persistence of nationalism have attributed a significant role in these processes to literacy. Those who argue that nationalism is a relatively modern phenomenon ground a great deal of their case on the supposed nature of literacy. Gellner (1983), for instance, sees the homogeneity required by the modern state as being made possible only through a common national literacy, unavailable in previous 'agro-literate' stages of social development. The literacy of these agro-literate societies was of what Goody (1977) calls the 'restricted' kind. In the modern state, on the other hand, literacy has to be available to the mass of the population and not simply to an élite: indeed, in Gellner's view, it is the development of such mass literacy that explains the rise of the modern nation state itself. Modern industry requires a mobile, literate, technologically equipped population and the nation state, Gellner claims, is the only agency capable of providing such a work force, through its support for a mass, public, compulsory and standardized education system.

The literacy being referred to here is that of the 'autonomous' model. A single, nationally sanctioned literacy supposedly rises above the claims of the different ethnic communities that may constitute the state. The education system, according to Gellner, genuinely provides a neutral means of authenticating knowledge through reasonably impartial centres of learning, which issue certificates 'on the basis of honest, impartially administered examination'. Scholars who have focused upon the concept of a plurality of literacies, rather than a single autonomous literacy, are less inclined to take these claims at face value: while they are evidently part of the rhetoric of nationalism, they do not necessarily correspond to the social reality, in which it is much more usual to find a variety of different literacy practices. Accounts of the uses of literacy to express identity among youth groups in urban situations (Shuman 1986, Weinstein 1993, Camitta 1993), of mode-switching as well as code-switching in the Moroccan community in London (Baynham 1993), of mother-tongue literacy among Latin American migrants in Toronto (Klassen

1991), and of 'community' literacy in Lancaster, England (Barton and Ivanič 1991), challenge the view of the modern world as consisting of homogeneous nations each with a single, homogenizing literacy.

Likewise, scholars who stress the symbolic and cultural dimensions of ethnic ties and nations focus upon the variety of routes to nationalism and put less weight on the claims made for literacy in its emergence (Smith 1986, and this volume, Article 25). The account of the growth and persistence of modern nationalism requires analysis not only of the exigencies of modern technology and economy but also of the ideological and cultural aspects of literacy practices in nationalism's 'prehistory'. Recent studies of medieval and early modern Europe have thrown into question the extent to which literacy was the preserve simply of an élite, and describe a range of different literacies there too (Houston 1988, Graff 1987). McKitterick (1990) argues that literacy in eighth- and ninth-century Carolingian France and Germany was not confined to a clerical élite, but was dispersed in lay society and used for government and administration as well as for ordinary legal transactions among the people of the Frankish kingdom. Clanchy (1979) describes the shift to a 'literate mentality' in the centuries following the Norman Conquest in England, where the growth of a bureaucratic centralized system was associated with the colonizers' claims for legitimacy and was resisted over a long period through counter-claims for orality and for indigenous language and literacy. Thomas (1986) describes the association of literacy with religious beliefs and teaching, such that terms like 'primer' referred not so much to an aid in the process of learning to read and write as to one in the process of learning to pray.

A similar story of variation in the uses and meanings of literacy in the pre-modern period and subsequently is emerging with regard to other parts of the world. In South-east Asia, literacy was widespread in the era preceding Western impact. This was a matter neither of élite nor of commercial interests but of a variety of local customs and practices. Writing in the Philippines in the sixteenth century, for instance, served no religious, judicial or historical purposes, but was used only for notes and letters. Elsewhere women actively used writing for exchanging notes and recording debts, while in southern Sumatra as late as 1930 a large proportion of the population employed literacy for poetic courting contests (Reid 1988). The arrival of Islam and Christianity had the effect of *reducing* literacy rates, particularly among women, by restricting writing to the male, sacral, and monastic domains. In the Philippines knowledge of the traditional scripts disappeared within a century of Christianization and a similar fate befell pre-Islamic scripts in Malaya and parts of Sumatra. The Indic-based script used by the Hanunóo, as described above, represents perhaps one of the few modern survivals of these local literacies. The variety and complexity of social and ideological uses of literacies in the pre-modern era suggest that simple accounts of 'agro-literate' society, as divided between a literate élite and an illiterate peasantry, may have to be revised. Theories of the rise of nationalism founded on such assumptions are consequently being subjected to serious critique.

Some scholars have attempted to engage with this complexity by describing how the social and linguistic hierarchies that Gellner attributes to agro-literate society have persisted into modern society. Adapting Ferguson's (1964) concept of 'diglossia' – the distinction between 'high' and 'low' language uses within a speech community – Fishman (1986) attempts to predict the course of modern nationalism with respect to language conflict. He constructs a typology of modern nation states that differs slightly from that offered by Smith, coining the term 'nationism' where the emphasis is on politico-geographic boundaries and retaining 'nationalism' for cases where the emphasis is on socio-cultural and ideological identities. Many of the 'old' nations, he suggests, may have begun as forms of nationalism, in which socio-cultural identity emerged first and only later became attached to the geographically bounded 'nation'. For these nations language was a prior criterion of national identity, in the sense of 'nationalism', and only later became an issue at the level of 'nation', once these societies had made the transition from nationalism to nationism. For the 'new' nations, however, Fishman identifies a different development. They have begun in many cases as geographical-political entities and are not yet 'ethnic nations'. In these cases, he suggests, the trend in language and politics is more likely to be towards 'diglossian compromises' (Fishman 1986: 47): local languages may continue to be used for local purposes, while a different, often international language such as English will be employed for educational and technological purposes. The spread of new literacies plays a major part in these processes. The effect of campaigns to introduce all members of the nation to a single literacy, for instance, may be to counter the trend towards 'diglossian compromise' and to underscore the process of 'nationalism' rather than 'nationism'. Once the dominant literacy has become enshrined, there is pressure for the language associated with it to acquire similar dominance, thus marginalizing other languages that might have survived with oral diglossia. The 'English only' movement in some parts of the United States, which has lobbied to exclude Spanish from schools, may stem from the dominant role and significance attributed to English literacy there (Rockhill 1987a, Woodward 1989).

These questions have yet to be investigated in any depth with regard to the role of literacy, although recent studies on literacy campaigns in Mexico (King 1994), on the persistence of oral speech conventions in Somalia despite a mass literacy campaign there in the 1970s (Lewis 1986), and on the significance of 'politicized ethnicity' in the Nicaraguan Literacy Crusade (Bourgois 1986) suggest that a more complex pattern is emerging than that suggested either by Fishman, in terms of the concept of diglossia, or by Gellner, in his proposed linkage of modern nationalism with autonomous literacy.

Literacy practices and the construction of gender

The example of widespread literacy in South-east Asia, prior to western expansion there, raises novel questions about the relative participation of men and women in literacy, and about the uses made of it. Since literacy was not taught in any formal institution and had no vocational or religious value, its transmission tended to be mainly a domestic matter, largely the responsibility of mothers and older siblings. The social context in which literacy practices were learned probably facilitated their uses by women, who employed them not only in the poetic courting contests mentioned above but also for exchanging notes, recording debts and other commercial matters which were in the female domain (Reid 1988). As a result, literacy rates for women were at least as high as those for men, and some travellers found them even higher (Reid 1988: 219). The advent of Westerners, with their male-oriented religious institutions, shifted the balance towards male literacy and formal schooling. Such imbalance characterizes many accounts of gendered literacy practices in the contemporary world.

Until recently, statistical and quantitative surveys of the gender imbalance in schooling have dominated the agenda in studies of literacy, gender and development (Kelly 1987, Stromquist 1989). Bown, for instance, writes: 'In the Third World countries of Africa, Asia and Latin America, women's enrolment in schools lags behind that of men ... fewer girls go to schools than boys, and they remain in schools for a shorter time than boys' (Bown 1990). Where researchers have attended to literacy, statistics invariably demonstrate that rural women are the least likely to be literate, while urban men have retained the command of the secular and bureaucratic literacy of the state that they had previously held in religions of the book (Kaneko 1987).

Recently, researchers have begun to ask the subjects themselves for their opinions, studying for instance adult women's motivations in coming forward for literacy programmes (Opiyo 1981, Saraswathi and Ravindram 1982). The balance between economic and 'personal' motives is frequently cited, government agencies tending to focus on the former while women themselves, when given the opportunity, frequently express the latter (MacCaffery 1988, Mac-Keracher 1989), although Saraswathi and Ravindram (1982) put women's interest in 'economic and gender justice' above their concern for literacy. A project undertaken by the Council for Social Development of India (1972, 1975) highlights the extent to which groups may differentiate between male and female models of literacy. Local women assumed that literacy was associated with male, white-collar, urban labour and saw no reason for attending classes. The project team's model was likewise male-oriented, but focused on the role of women as wives and mothers, directing literacy to them as a means of improving their health management. It thus ignored the significance of the major economic role played by women in family and village life, and the role of structural poverty in explaining their children's poor health. It assumed that literacy was associated with cognitive advance, whereas oral skills were presumed to be 'weak' when it came to acquiring new knowledge. Literacy itself would improve 'general skills for efficient functioning'. These classic assumptions of the autonomous model of literacy were undermined by the outcome of the project: those classes that involved practical health-care support and oral instruction, but no literacy, were successful by the project's criteria, while classes that involved only functional literacy, but lacked practical backup, registered the highest drop-out rates. The message was that it is not women's lack of literacy that leads to poor nutrition and high infant mortality, but the structural problems of poverty, employment and gender relations.

Some writers are beginning to address these social dimensions of gender and literacy, to shift the focus away from 'women' as a given category and from the problems associated with their access to 'literacy', and to focus on questions of definition rather than of access: which literacies are which women and men gaining access to and who has the power to define and name them? Other work has emphasized the association between specific literacy practices and the formation of particular gender identities. Horsman (1989), for instance, complains that the complexity of literacy and illiteracy in women's lives has been lost in traditional frameworks, which concentrate on motivation and which see literacy as a simple set of skills that a woman needs to acquire in order to function adequately in society. For the women she interviewed in Eastern Canada, literacy was bound up with identity and the relationships in their lives: when they attended classes, they were seeking to find meaning in their lives and often to pursue a dream for their children. A number of other studies have focused on meaning rather than function and have introduced an anthropological perspective into the complex relations of women and men to writing processes. In counter-balancing the dominant accounts of male literacy, they have provided evidence of what women in different places and times actually do with literacy and what it means to them. For instance, Ko (1989) describes how, in seventeenth-century China, educated middle-class women wrote poetry as a means of constructing a private female culture, against the homogenizing male character of late Imperial Chinese culture; and Mikulecky (1985) records the uses by fifteenth-century English women of the literacy skills being developed by the rising gentry to write letters concerning the 'business affairs of the family, personal intrigues, duty and death' (Mikulecky 1985: 2).

Rockhill (1987a, b) attempts to provide a theoretical framework for the study of how literacy is gendered. She points out how literacy practices are significant in constructing different identities for women and men. For Hispanic women in Los Angeles, among whom she conducted life history interviews, literacy practices are defined and ruled by the men in their lives, and resistance involves considerable personal and political strain. Women do the literacy work of the household, purchasing goods, paying bills, transacting with social services, and dealing with children's schooling. These forms of literacy remain invisible, as do many of women's contributions to the household. The women are labelled by men as 'illiterate' while the men, who acquire and use more spoken English to obtain jobs in the 'public' domain, consider themselves 'literate'.

Women sometimes attempt to break the cycle of dependency and to undertake the schooling necessary to acquire the kind of literacy skills required in public jobs. Their husbands, however, frequently try to prevent them, often through the use of violence. Rockhill characterizes the women's approach to public literacy in terms of 'threat/desire'. They expressed their wish for schooling in terms of a desire, initially for self-defence or survival, but subsequently they often shifted towards espousing an ideal of advancement, of 'getting ahead'. The first, limited sense of literacy learning fitted with the functional domestic chores the women already performed, and represented little change in their situation. But literacy in the second sense, associated with the weight placed upon education for citizenship and self-fulfilment in American society, carries the symbolic connotation of a movement into a better, more powerful class and culture, another world, and another life, which is both desired and feared. The men fear this movement because it represents a threat to their control over women and to their assumed superiority; women themselves fear it because it appears to require a move out of the known and secure, albeit violent and impoverished, world towards that alien but desired culture apparent in media representations of the smart secretary and the woman of the world: to become literate in this sense is to change identity, to become a 'lady' (Rockhill 1987b).

'Literacy practices', then, help to position women and men in relation to authority and submission, to the public and private domains and to personal identity (Cameron 1985, Moore 1988). Models of literacy are differentiated by gender as well as by class and ethnicity. Research has only begun in this field, but it is evident that it will have to be informed by insights from the 'New Literacy Studies' (Street 1993) of multiple and socially varied literacies, on the one hand, and by feminist writing on multiple and socially varied constructions of gender, on the other.

Literacy and development

The shifts in approaches to literacy practices evident in many of the publications of the 1980s have considerable implications for policy on literacy and development. The theory and findings of the new literacy studies should have made it harder for development and literacy agencies to persist with a single, dominant, and frequently ethnocentric view of literacy. But in many cases the assumptions of earlier times have persisted. Wagner asserts that while 'specialists have been developing a much more complete understanding of literacy and the kinds of skills required in the coming millennium ... the transfers of information between researchers and policymakers are fragile at best' (1989). In the post-war era it was assumed that 'development' for Third World countries meant following in the footsteps of the 'West' (Rogers 1992). With regard to education and literacy, this meant providing institutions and procedures that would enable Western literacy to be disseminated throughout a population. Literacy was seen as a causal factor in development.

Anderson, for instance, links a 40 per cent 'literacy threshold' to the attainment of 'economic take off', a principle to be found in many agency accounts (Anderson and Bowman 1965). Development workers interested in education also tended to associate cognitive change with the acquisition of literacy (Oxenham 1980). For Lerner (1958), literacy would effect the change from a 'traditional' to a 'modern' mentality, the latter characterized by 'empathy', flexibility, adaptability, willingness to accept change, and an entrepreneurial and confidently outgoing spirit. Traditional societies were seen to embody the negation of all of these qualities: they were perceived to be ignorant, narrow-minded, and, from the evidence of early development campaigns, to be intransigent to 'modern' ideas. As a catalyst of the transition to modernity, literacy was supposed to be 'functional', a term that, being sufficiently ambiguous to embrace the political interests of the many different governments and agencies involved in literacy work, came to dominate the field. Unesco, for instance, adopted in 1965 a programme of 'Work-Oriented Functional Literacy Campaigns' that targeted social groups which, once literate, would be expected to contribute to the functioning of the modern economy in their country (Furter 1973, Unesco 1973). The programme failed, among other reasons, because of the lack of attention to local uses and meanings of literacy, and because of the narrow, Western interpretation of 'functionality' it employed (Unesco 1976, Berggren and Berggren 1975, Lankshear and Lawler 1987).

Alternative approaches to the spread of literacy have favoured 'mass' campaigns, such as that used in early Soviet Russia (Unesco 1965a), Cuba (Unesco 1965b, Kozol 1978) and Nicaragua (Black and Bevan 1980). Bhola (1984) has advocated this model for non-revolutionary situations too. However, many of these approaches have also been criticized for being ethnocentric and for their lack of attention to local meanings and uses of literacy and orality. Much development literature is still characterized by programmatic and moral pronouncements that assume that literacy is monolithic, autonomous, and Western (Amove and Graff 1987, Hamdache and Martin 1986).

The work of Freire, a Brazilian educator whose ideas have underpinned many literacy campaigns, is frequently cited as representing a challenge to this view (Berggren and Berggren 1975). Freire (1972, 1978, 1985) places greater emphasis on the political aspect of literacy education, believing that programmes should be about 'conscientization', helping the oppressed to understand the reasons for their disadvantage. 'Functional' approaches, he believes, disguise the true power relations beneath a spurious optimism about the enhanced life prospects that will follow from the acquisition of literacy.

Educators who follow Freire's approach see themselves as animators or facilitators rather than top-down teachers. They start from local knowledge and concerns, beginning a literacy class, for instance, by writing a key local word on a board and using it to generate a discussion that raises student consciousness. The term *favela* ('slum'), for example, would generate discussion about the social conditions that lead to such poverty and inequality. The educational process, including the decoding of letters for their sounds and the building of words out of syllables, is not simply one of filling previously empty minds, as envisaged in the 'banking' theory of education, but a process of collective consciousness-raising.

From an anthropological perspective, however, there are a number of problems with this apparently more culturally sensitive approach. The identification of local 'key words', for instance, raises problems regarding interpretation and authority as well as of methodology. In Nicaragua, the Sandanistas, despite their use of Freirean perspectives in the Nicaraguan Literacy Crusade, did not at first understand the cultural differences evident on the Atlantic coast (Freeland 1988, Bourgois 1986). Their imposition of Spanish culture, language and literacy was seen there as differing little from that of the Samoza regime before them. In this case, accounts of cultural variation, as well as the growing political disaffection of ethnic groups on the Atlantic coast, led to changes in the literacy programme. These problems may not arise simply from the implementation of Freire's approach but may be endemic to it: how well it is really capable of taking account of local meanings and of cultural and ethnic variation within a nation state, and how far teachers are able and prepared to give up their positions of authority and adopt a facilitating role on a level of equality with students, need further research. Despite evident problems, until recently very few commentators have dared to criticize Freire's work in any depth (but see Mackie 1980, Freire and Macedo 1987, Verhelst 1990).

With regard to the role of literacy in formal schooling and development, some research has begun to take account of the kinds of questions regarding knowledge and meaning familiar to anthropological inquiry. Schooling, like literacy, has been seen as far more uniform than it really is. We need to ask what actually is being communicated in processes of instruction, if we want to know what carries over from school experience into social and economic 'effects'. Drawing on experimental and ethnographic data from the Mswambeni region of coastal Kenya, Eisomon (1988) examines ways in which the school experience is transformed into school effects. It was not literacy itself, he concludes, nor simply the experience of school, that enabled students to interpret written material, but rather 'prior knowledge' and 'procedural skills': schools, however, often fail to make this kind of knowledge explicit or to help students organize it. How to make inferences from particular written texts, and how to apply the scientific principles that the texts assume, need as much attention as the technical skills of reading and writing and the mere attendance at school that appear to remain the aims of many development programmes.

Studies such as Eisomon's highlight the possibility both of linking theory and practice, and of extending anthropological perspectives in the field of education and development (Roberts and Akinsaya 1976, Vulliamy *et al.* 1990, Fetterman and Pitman 1986). The many ethnographies of literacy produced in the last decade and summarized above have suggested the kinds of questions that need to be asked in the context of development programmes, whether formal or informal: what literacy actually means, why it is being imparted, for whom and by whom; which literacies are developed in which contexts, how they relate to the literacies that were there before the campaign; and what complex relations are set up between oral and written language uses in these situations (Wagner 1987, Street 1984, 1987, Schieffelin and Gilmore 1986, Bledsoe and Robey 1986, Finnegan 1988, Fingeret 1983). There is also considerable scope for ethnographies of the literacy campaigns themselves. Who engages in the campaign as organizers, animateurs and teachers, and why? How do ethnic variations within a country affect the content and form of a literacy campaign? (King 1994, Sjostrom and Sjostrom 1983.) These questions have not traditionally been on the agendas of either development workers or anthropologists, but shifts in approaches to literacy of the kind outlined in this chapter, and recent shifts in anthropological approaches to development (Grillo and Rew 1985), suggest that they may become considerably more prominent in future research.

Literacy and education

Since the time of Boas and Mead, social and cultural anthropologists in the United States have been concerned with issues of education and society (Erikson and Bekker 1986), whereas in Britain the level of interest in this field has remained fairly low. However, with the development of new directions in literacy studies, particular aspects of the education process are being opened up to anthropological analysis in both American and British traditions.

From a sociological and educational perspective, the major questions have focused on the underperformance in school of children from specific, 'disadvantaged' backgrounds, whether defined in class or in ethnic terms. Anthropological insights have suggested both a broadening and a narrowing of this focus. They are broadening in the sense that they lead to the study of educational institutions and processes themselves as social phenomena rather than allowing the institutions and processes of education to remain as the sole arbiters of what is to be regarded as problematic. Anthropologists have been interested in questions of socialization (Spindler 1974, Hanson 1979), social reproduction (Bourdieu and Passeron 1977, Collins 1986, 1988) and the ritual and symbolic aspects of schooling (McLaren 1986, Turner 1982). Anthropological perspectives have also narrowed the focus in the sense that they suggest ethnographies of the school (Willis 1977, Everhardt 1983, Schieffelin and Gilmore 1986), of the classroom (Cazden 1978, Michaels and Cazden 1986) and of the home (McDermott and Varenne 1982, Taylor 1985). Thus the minutiae of daily literacy and education-related behaviours such as 'homework' are analysed as social and cultural processes and not simply in terms of their educational objectives and success. Bloome (1989), for instance, has criticized the emphasis, in studies of schooling, on efficiency and access and has called for analysis of the nature of classroom communities as social groups, while micro-studies of the language of the classroom (Erikson 1982, 1984, Collins 1986) have linked local ethnography, including family literacy, to wider political and economic currents in the culture.

The continuities and discontinuities between home and school culture have remained an axis of attention, with anthropologists demonstrating how in many non-Western societies schooling tends to be more closely integrated with everyday social life, at least until Western forms of schooling develop (Fishman 1991, Bloch 1993, King 1994). Literacy practices provide a rich ethnographic focus for such inquiry and the development of ethnographies of literacy in the community and the home (Philips 1975, Varenne and McDermott 1986, Barton and Ivanič 1991) is beginning to undermine still further assumptions regarding the natural dominance of schooled literacy.

In much of the educational literature, the increasingly recognized divergence between home and community literacies was, for a long time, defined as a 'problem': home literacies were seen as 'deficient', requiring to be overcome by the intervention of educational institutions bearing proper, schooled literacy. Thus Heath's (1983) account of the varieties of literacy in three communities in the American South reviewed earlier in this article (p. 535), far from being taken as evidence of rich learning outside of school on which educational institutions might build – as Heath herself intended and worked to implement practically – has been interpreted as providing evidence of the failure of home culture. Where Heath recognized that children were learning complex oral and literacy skills that tended to be ignored when they arrived at school, many educationalists pointed to what they saw as the inadequacies of mothers who did not read bedtime stories or 'scaffold' their children's 'emergent literacy' towards school achievement (Teale and Sulzby 1986). Nevertheless, even in middle-class America there are variations in the uses and meanings of literacy that suggest discontinuity between home and school, as well as intra-class and intra-ethnic variation, so much so that heterogeneity rather than homogeneity now appears to be the norm. This raises the question of how it is that the model of a single literacy is sustained: how, amidst this variation, does the model of 'schooled' literacy (Cook-Gumperz 1986) come to be taken as the standard and indeed as the 'natural' form of literacy, thus marginalizing other literacy practices?

Ethnographies of literacy that may begin to answer some of these questions are becoming part of the educational agenda in parts of Britain and the United

States, although Bloome (1989) has warned that 'what passes for ethnographic research in education may or may not be based on theoretical constructs from cultural anthropology, it may have only the trappings of anthropological method'. Nevertheless, the teacher–researcher movement in particular has looked to ethnography as a means whereby teachers may investigate their own practice, combining their considerable knowledge and experience of classrooms with skills traditionally in the domain of the university researcher (Lytle and Cochrane-Smith 1990). One area in which this aspect of ethnographic inquiry has developed is in relation to the teaching of reading and writing in schools. The Writing Process movement, in Britain and the United States, has led to the introduction into the classroom of features of everyday literacy practices such as collaborative literacy, interactive literacy using dialogue journals, the extension of whole-language approaches to reading and writing in school, and the notion of 'real' reading and writing (Dombey 1988, Meek 1991, Lytle and Botel 1988, Bruffee 1986, Erikson 1985, Rudy 1990). Both the process approach to writing and the product approach that it replaced have been exhaustively researched, often employing some aspects of the ethnographic method (Freedman *et al.* 1987).

Many of these changes stemmed from the work of educationalists such as James Britton, whose classic accounts of how children learn, and notably of the importance of speech in classroom interaction, led to greater attention being paid to the processes of language and literacy acquisition and their implications for pedagogy. Willinsky's summary of the 'new literacy' in the United States, and the focus of Meek and fellow educationalists in Britain on children's own uses of reading and writing from an early age, shifted attention from product to process and from teacher to student (Meek 1991, Willinsky 1990, Kimberley *et al.* 1992). Czerniewska, for instance, documents the National Writing Project in Britain that attempted to build the writing curriculum on the insight that children brought into the classroom from their homes' and communities' rich knowledge of literacy practices (Czerniewska 1992). The apparent scribbles and badly spelled texts that children passed among themselves were evidence of early understanding of the uses and meanings of literacy, to be built upon rather than rejected and denigrated as in traditional schooling. 'Correct' spelling and grammar could be taught once children had a motivation for writing in the first place. They were to be encouraged, for instance, to write reflectively in journals about their experience, and teachers would respond in the same journals, thus making the writing process genuine communicative interaction rather than a dry classroom exercise. Or children would be given the opportunity to read 'real books' in 'book covers' in the classroom, designed as supportive and comfortable environments for enjoying reading, so that reading would no longer seem like a chore, or be undertaken solely in order to pass administered tests.

In the field of adult literacy a similar qualitative movement is under way, both in research and in teaching. The traditional view of adults with literacy needs in modern industrial society has shifted from the confident post-war assumption that the whole society was literate, to the discovery of 'illiteracy', a concept associated on the one hand with metaphors of 'disease' as something to be eradicated as a danger to public health, and on the other with courageous but disadvantaged individuals bravely managing but basically inadequate. More recently, the focus of research, particularly with an ethnographic aspect, has turned attention to more complex analyses of the social and cultural corre-lates of the many different literacies to be found in different communities and cultural contexts (Levine 1986, Mace 1979, 1992, Hunter and Harman 1979, Barton and Hamilton 1990). Fingeret (1983), for example, investigates the reciprocity associated with literacy and other skills in urban American commu-nities: a person may exchange his or her skills as a mechanic for the literacy skills of a fellow community member, who will help fill in forms and transact with the institutions of the state that lean heavily on writing. Immigrants may get by in similar ways, one member of the community learning standard literacy and acting as a 'cultural broker' for others (Weinstein 1992, Klassen 1991, Grillo 1990).

The design of standard evaluations and tests given to 'screen' people with literacy difficulties has also been subjected to anthropological analysis. Levine shows how these tests may be the product of an employer's own cultural preconceptions about literacy, perhaps stemming from his own experience of schooling rather than being functionally associated with the employment being applied for (Levine 1986). Lytle and Wolfe (1987) show how prospective stu-dents' notions of their own 'illiteracy' may not relate to functional skills or incapacities but rather to self-images constructed through popular cultural stereotypes of literacy. Hill and Parry (1988) have examined the tests given to adults in the United States and other parts of the world for evidence of cul-tural bias, and have noted the common trend in many countries for local cul-tural features of the 'real' communicative repertoire to be downgraded at the expense of artificially constructed models of communication whose only social reality resides in the test situation itself (Holland and Street, in press).

While the relationship between literacy and education remains a focus for much of this research, the introduction of anthropological perspectives has provided a recognition, not always apparent in the educational literature, of the extent to which literacy exists in social contexts independent of educational institutions. Where literacy *is* associated with education, anthropological research has drawn attention to the social and cultural nature of schooling, of the classroom environment and of the conceptualizations of knowledge and learning on which they are based. But historical and cross-cultural evidence shows that literacy practices are to be found in many contexts other than those of education, formal learning and essayist conceptions of reading and writing. This has implications both for the model of literacy purveyed in educational settings and for the relationship of school literacy to the literacies of the home and the community. The heterogeneity and complexity of literacy practices, evident in studies of the relations between literacy and nationalism, gender, and development, are coming to be recognized as equally central to our understanding of the relationship between literacy and education.

ACKNOWLEDGEMENTS

We are indebted to David Barton for his comments on this chapter, to Harold Conklin for providing us with details on Hanunóo literacy, and to Helen Siu for her help with the Chinese data presented here. The characters on p. 530 were drawn by Ye Ding.

REFERENCES

Anderson, C. A. and Bowman, M. (eds) (1965) *Education and Economic Development*, London: Frank Cass.

Arnove, R. and Graff, H. (eds) (1987) *National Literacy Campaigns: Historical and Comparative Aspects*, New York: Plenum Press.

Barton, D. (1988) *Problems with an Evolutionary Account of Literacy*, Lancaster Papers in Linguistics no. 49, Department of Linguistics, University of Lancaster.

Barton, D. and Hamilton, M. (1990) *Researching Literacy in Industrialized Countries: Trends and Prospects*, Hamburg: Unesco Institute for Education.

Barton, D. and Ivanič, R. (1991) *Writing in the Community*, London: Sage.

Basso, K. H. (1974) 'The ethnography of writing', in R. Bauman and J. Sherzer (eds) *Explorations in the Ethnography of Speaking*, Cambridge: Cambridge University Press.

Basso, K. H. and Anderson, N. (1977) 'A Western Apache writing system: the symbols of Silas John', in B. G. Blount and M. Sanches (eds) *Sociocultural Dimensions of Language Change*, New York: Academic Press.

Baynham, M. (1993) 'Code switching and mode switching: community interpreters and mediators of literacy', in B. Street (ed.) *Cross-Cultural Approaches to Literacy*, Cambridge: Cambridge University Press.

Berggren, C. and Berggren, L. (1975) *The Literacy Process: Domestication or Liberation?* London: Writers and Readers Publishers' Cooperative.

Besnier, N. (1989) 'Literacy and feelings: the encoding of affect in Nukulaelae letters', *Text* 9: 69–92.

—— (1991) 'Literacy and the notion of person on Nukulaelae atoll', *American Anthropologist* 93: 570–87.

Bhola, H. (1984) *Campaigning for Literacy*, Paris: Unesco.

Biber, D. (1988) *Variation across Speech and Writing*, Cambridge: Cambridge University Press.

Black, G. and Bevan, J. (1980) *The Loss of Fear: Education in Nicaragua before and after the Revolution*, London: World University Service.

Bledsoe, C. and Robey, K. (1986) 'Arabic literacy and secrecy among the Mende of Sierra Leone', *Man* (NS) 21: 202–26.

Bloch, M. (1993) 'The uses of schooling and literacy in a Zafimaniry village', in B. Street (ed.) *Cross-Cultural Approaches to Literacy*, Cambridge: Cambridge University Press.

Bloome, D. (ed.) (1989) *Classrooms and Literacy*, Norwood, NJ: Ablex.

Bourdieu, P. (1984) *Homo Academicus*, Paris: Éditions de Minuit.

Bourdieu, P. and Passeron, J-C. (1977) *Reproduction in Education, Society and Culture*, London: Sage.

Bourgois, P. (1986) 'The Miskitu of Nicaragua: politicized ethnicity', *Anthropology Today* 2(2): 4–9.

Bown, L. (1990) 'Women, literacy and development', Action Aid Development Report, No. 4., London.

Bruffee, K. (1986) 'Social construction, language and the authority of knowledge: a bibliographic essay', *College English* 48(8): 773–90.

Cameron, D. (1985) *Feminism and Linguistic Theory*, London: Macmillan.

Camitta, M. (1993) 'Vernacular writing: varieties of literacy among Philadelphia high school students', in B. Street (ed.) *Cross-Cultural Approaches to Literacy*, Cambridge: Cambridge University Press.

Cazden, C. (1978) 'Learning to read in classroom interaction', in L. Resnick and P. Weaver (eds) *Theory and Practice in Early Reading*, Hillsdale, NJ: Laurence Erlbaum.

Chafe, W. L. and Tannen, D. (1987) 'The relation between written and spoken language', *Annual Review of Anthropology* 16: 383–407.

Clanchy, M. T. (1979) *From Memory to Written Record: England 1066–1307*, London: Edward Arnold.

Cole, M. and Nicolopoulou, A. (1992) 'Literacy: intellectual consequences', in W. Bright (ed.) *International Encyclopaedia of Linguistics*, vol. 2, New York and Oxford: Oxford University Press.

Collins, J. (1986) 'Differential treatment and reading instruction', in J. Cook-Gumperz (ed.) *The Social Construction of Literacy*, Cambridge: Cambridge University Press.

—— (1988) 'Language and class in minority education', *Anthropology and Education Quarterly* 19(4): 299–326.

Cook-Gumperz, J. (ed.) (1986) *The Social Construction of Literacy*, Cambridge: Cambridge University Press.

Coulmas, F. (1989) *The Writing Systems of the World*, Oxford: Blackwell.

Council for Social Development (1972) *An Experimental Non-formal Education Project for Rural Women to Promote the Development of the Young Child: Project Design*, New Delhi: Council for Social Development.

—— (1975) *An Experimental Non-formal Education Project for Rural Women to Promote the Development of the Young Child: Final Report*, New Delhi: Council for Social Development.

Crump, T. (1988) 'Alternative meanings of literacy in Japan and the West', *Human Organization* 47: 138–45.

Crystal, D. and Davy, D. (1969) *Investigating English Style*, London: Longmans.

Czerniewska, P. (1992) *Learning about Writing*, Oxford: Blackwell.

Davies, A. M. (1986) 'Forms of writing in the ancient Mediterranean world', in G. Baumann (ed.) *The Written word: Literacy in Transition*, Oxford: Clarendon Press.

DeFrancis, J. (1989) *Visible Speech: The Diverse Oneness of Writing Systems*, Honolulu: University of Hawaii Press.

Diringer, D. (1968) *The Alphabet: A Key to the History of Mankind*, 3rd edn, London: Hutchinson.

Dombey, H. (1988) 'Moving into literacy in the early years of school', in J. McCaffery and B. Street (eds) *Literacy Research in the UK: Adult and School Perspectives*, Lancaster: Research and Practice in Adult Literacy.

Eisomon, T. (1988) *Benefitting from Basic Education, School Quality and Functional Literacy in Kenya*, Oxford: Pergamon.

Erikson, F. (1982) 'Classroom discourse as improvisation: relationships between academic task structure and social participation structure in lessons', in L. C. Wilkinson (ed.) *Communication in the Classroom*, New York: Academic Press.
—— (1984) 'School literacy, reasoning and civility: an anthropologist's perspective', *Review of Educational Research* 54(4): 525–46.
—— (1985) 'Qualitative methods in research on teaching', in W. Hrock (ed.) *Handbook of Research on Teaching*, New York: Macmillan.
Erikson, F. and Bekker, G. (1986) 'On anthropology', in J. Hannaway and M. Lockheed (eds) *The Contributions of the Social Sciences to Educational Policy and Practice: 1965–1985*, Berkeley: McCutchan.
Everhardt, R. (1983) *Reading, Writing and Resistance: Adolescence and Labour in a Junior High School*, London: Routledge & Kegan Paul.
Ferguson, C. A. (1964) 'Diglossia', in D. Hymes (ed.) *Language in Culture and Society*, New York: Harper & Row.
—— (1987) 'Literacy in a hunting-gathering society: the case of the Diyari', *Journal of Anthropological Research* 43: 223–37.
Fetterman, D. and Pitman, M. (eds) (1986) *Educational Evaluation: Ethnography in Theory, Practice and Politics*, Beverly Hills: Sage.
Fingeret, A. (1983) 'Social network: a new perspective on independence and illiterate adults', *Adult Education Quarterly* 33(3): 133–46.
Finnegan, R. (1988) *Literacy and Orality: Studies in the Technology of Communication*, Oxford: Blackwell.
Fishman, A. (1991) '"Because this is who we are": writing in the Amish community', in D. Barton and R. Ivanič (eds) *Writing in the Community*, London: Sage.
Fishman, J. (1986) 'Nationality-nationalism and nation-nationism', in J. Fishman, C. Ferguson and J. Das Gupta (eds) *Language Problems of Developing Nations*, New York: John Wiley.
Freedman, S., Dyson, A., Flower, I. and Chafe, W. (1987) *Research in Writing: Past, Present and Future*, technical report no. 1, Center for the Study of Writing. Pittsburgh, PA: Carnegie Mellon University.
Freeland, J. (1988) *The Atlantic Coast in the Nicaraguan Revolution*, London: World University Service.
Freire, P. (1972) *The Pedagogy of Process*, London: Penguin.
—— (1978) *Pedagogy in Process*, New York: Seabury Press.
—— (1985) *The Politics of Education: Culture, Power and Liberation*, London: Macmillan.
Freire, P. and Macedo, D. (1987) *Literacy: Reading the Word and the World*, Granby, Mass.: Bergin & Garvey.
Furter, P. (1973) *Possibilities and Limitations of Functional Literacy: the Iranian experiment*, Paris: Unesco.
Gaur, A. (1984) *A History of Writing*, London: British Library.
Gelb, I. J. (1963) *A Study of Writing*, 2nd edn, Chicago: University of Chicago Press.
Gellner, E. (1983) *Nations and Nationalism*, Oxford: Blackwell.
Goody, J. (ed.) (1968) *Literacy in Traditional Societies*, Cambridge: Cambridge University Press.
—— (1977) *The Domestication of the Savage Mind*, Cambridge: Cambridge University Press.
—— (1986) *The Logic of Writing and the Organization of Society*, Cambridge: Cambridge University Press.
—— (1987) *The Interface between the Written and the Oral*, Cambridge: Cambridge University Press.

Goody, J. and Watt, I. (1963) 'The consequences of literacy', *Comparative Studies in Society and History* 5: 304–45.

Graff, H. J. (1979) *The Literacy Myth: Literacy and Social Structure in the Nineteenth Century*, New York: Academic Press.

—— (1987) *The Legacies of Literacy: Continuities and Contradictions in Western Culture and Society*, Bloomington: Indiana University Press.

Grillo, R. (1990) *Social Anthropology and the Politics of Language*, London: Routledge.

Grillo, R. and Rew, A. (eds) (1985) *Social Anthropology and Development Policy*, ASA Monograph 23, London: Tavistock.

Hamdache, A. and Martin, D. (eds) (1986) *Theory and Practice of Literacy Work: Policies, Strategies and Examples*, Paris: Unesco.

Hanson, J. (1979) *Sociocultural Perspectives on Human Learning: An Introduction to Educational Anthropology*, Englewood Cliffs, NJ: Prentice-Hall.

Harbsmeier, M. (1988) 'Inventions of writing', in J. Gledhill, B. Bender and M. T. Larsen (eds) *The Emergence and Development of Social Hierarchy and Political Centralization*, One World Archaeology 4, London: Unwin Hyman.

Harris, R. (1986) *The Origin of Writing*, London: Duckworth.

Harris, W. V. (1989) *Ancient Literacy*, Cambridge, Mass.: Harvard University Press.

Havelock, E. (1976) *Origins of Western Literacy*, Toronto: Ontario Institute of Education.

Heath, S. B. (1983) *Ways with Words: Language, Life, and Work in Communities and Classrooms*, Cambridge: Cambridge University Press.

Hill, C. and Parry, K. (1988) *Reading Assessment: Autonomous and Pragmatic Models*, Teachers' College Occasional Papers, Columbia University, New York.

Holland, D. and Street, B. (in press) 'Assessing Adult Literacy in the UK: the Progress Profile', in C. Hill and K. Parry (eds) *From Testing to Assessment*, London: Longman.

Horsman, J. (1989) 'From the learner's voice: women's experience of illiteracy', in M. Taylor and J. Draper (eds) *Adult Literacy Perspectives*, Toronto: Culture Concepts.

Houston, R. (1988) *Literacy in Early Modern Europe: Culture and Education 1500–1800*, London: Longman.

Hunter, C. and Harman, D. (1979) *Adult Illiteracy in the United States*, New York: McGraw-Hill.

Hunter, I. M. L. (1985) 'Lengthy verbal recall: the role of text', in A. Ellis (ed.) *Progress in the Psychology of Language*, vol. 1, London: Lawrence Erlbaum.

Illich, I. and Sanders, B. (1988) *ABC: The Alphabetization of the Popular Mind*, San Francisco: North Point Press.

Innis, H. A. (1972) *Empire and Communications*, 2nd edn, Toronto: University of Toronto Press.

Jackson, M. (1975) 'Literacy, communications, and social change: a study of the meaning and effect of literacy in early nineteenth century Maori society', in I. H. Kawheru (ed.) *Conflict and Compromise: Essays on the Maori since Colonization*, Wellington: A. H. & A. W. Reed.

Kaneko, M. (1987) *The Educational Composition of the World's Population: A Data Base*, Washington, D.C.: World Bank.

Kay, P. (1977) 'Language evolution and speech style', in B. G. Blount and M. Sanches (eds) *Sociocultural Dimensions of Language Change*, New York: Academic Press.

Kelly, G. (1987) 'Setting state policy on women's education in the Third World: perspectives from comparative research', *Comparative Education* 23(1): 95–102.

Kimberley, K., Meek, M. and Miller, J. (1992) *New Readings: Contributions to an Understanding of Literacy*, London: A. & C. Black.

King, L. (1994) *Roots of Identity: Language and Literacy in Mexico*, Stanford, Calif.: Stanford University Press.

Klassen, C. (1991) 'Bilingual literacy: the adult immigrant's account', in D. Barton and R. Ivanič (eds) *Writing in the Community*, London: Sage.

Ko, Y.-Y. D. (1989) 'Toward a social history of women in seventeenth century China', PhD thesis, Stanford University.

Kozol, J. (1978) 'A new look at the literacy campaign in Cuba', *Harvard Educational Review* 48(3): 341–77.

Kulick, D. and Stroud, C. (1990) 'Christianity, cargo and ideas of self: patterns of literacy in a Papua New Guinea village', *Man* (N.S.) 25: 286–304.

Lankshear, C. and Lawler, M. (1987) *Literacy, Schooling and Revolution*, Brighton: Falmer Press.

Leap, W. L. (1991) 'Pathways and barriers to Indian language literacy-building on the Northern Ute reservation', *Anthropology and Education Quarterly* 22: 21–41.

Lerner, D. (1958) *The Passing of Traditional Society*, Edinburgh: Glencoe Free Press.

Levine, K. (1986) *The Social Context of Literacy*, London: Routledge & Kegan Paul.

Lewis, I. M. (1986) 'Literacy and cultural identity in the Horn of Africa: the Somali case', in G. Baumann (ed.) *The Written Word: Literacy in Transition*, Oxford: Clarendon Press.

Lounsbury, F. G. (1989) 'The ancient writing of Middle America', in W. Senner (ed.) *The Origins of Writing*, Lincoln, Nebraska: University of Nebraska Press.

Lytle, S. and Botel, M. (1988) *Reading, Writing and Talking across the Curriculum*, University of Pennsylvania, Dept of Education, Philadelphia.

Lytle, S. and Cochrane-Smith, M. (1990) 'Learning from teacher research: a working typology', *Teachers College Record* 92(1): 83–103.

Lytle, S. and Wolfe, M. (1987) 'Alternative Assessment Project', unpublished report, submitted to Literacy Assistance Center, New York.

McCaffery, J. (1988) 'Combining research and practice', in J. MacCaffery and B. Street (eds) *Literacy Research in the UK: Adult and School Perspectives*, Lancaster: Research and Practice in Adult Literacy.

McDermott, R., Varenne, H. and H. Buglione, V. (1982) *'I teach him everything he learns in school': The Acquisition of Literacy for Learning in Working Class Families*, New York: Teachers' College, Columbia University.

Mace, J. (1979) *Working with Words*: London, Chameleon.

—— (1992) *Talking about Literacy*. London: Routledge.

MacKenzie, D. F. (1987) 'The sociology of a text: oral culture, literacy and print in early New Zealand', in P. Burke and R. Porter (eds) *The Social Life of Language*, Cambridge: Cambridge University Press.

MacKeracher, D. (1989) 'Women and literacy', in M. Taylor and J. Draper (eds) *Adult Literacy Perspectives*, Toronto: Culture Concepts.

Mackie, R. (ed.) (1980) *Literacy and Revolution: The Pedagogy of Paulo Freire*, London: Pluto Press.

McKitterick, R. (1990) *The Carolingians and the Written Word*, Cambridge: Cambridge University Press.

McLaren, P. (1986) *Schooling as a Ritual Performance*, London: Routledge & Kegan Paul.

—— (1988) 'Culture or canon? Critical pedagogy and the politics of literacy', *Harvard Educational Review* 58(2): 213–34.

McLaughlin, D. (1989) 'The sociolinguistics of Navajo literacy', *Anthropology and Education Quarterly* 20: 275–90.

McLuhan, M. (1962) *The Gutenberg Galaxy*, Toronto: University of Toronto Press.

Meek, M. (1991) *On Being Literate*, London: Bodley Head.

Michaels, S. and Cazden, C. (1986) 'Teacher/child collaboration as oral preparation for literacy', in B. Schieffelin and P. Gilmore (eds) *The Acquisition of Literacy: Ethnographic Perspectives*, Norwood, NJ: Ablex.

Mikulecky, B. (1985) 'The Paston letters: an example of literacy in the fifteenth century', unpublished MS.

Moore, H. (1988) *Feminism and Anthropology*, Oxford: Polity.

Norman, J. (1988) *Chinese* (Cambridge Language Surveys), Cambridge: Cambridge University Press.

Olson, D. R. (1977) 'From utterance to text: the bias of language in speech and writing', *Harvard Educational Review* 47: 257–81.

Ong, W. J. (1982) *Orality and Literacy: The Technologizing of the Word*, London and New York: Methuen.

Opiyo, M. (1981) 'Kenya case study on women's literacy and development projects', *Adult Education and Development* 16: 73–82, Bonn: German Adult Education Association.

Oxenham, J. (1980) *Literacy: Writing, Reading and Social Organization*, London: Routledge & Kegan Paul.

Parsons, T. (1966) *Societies: Evolutionary and Comparative Perspectives*, Englewood Cliffs, NJ: Prentice-Hall.

Parsonson, G. S. (1967) 'The literate revolution in Polynesia', *Journal of Pacific History* 2: 169-90.

Pattison, R. (1982) *On Literacy: The Politics of the Word from Homer to the Age of Rock*, New York and Oxford: Oxford University Press.

Philips, S. U. (1975) 'Literacy as a mode of communication on the Warm Springs Indian reservation', in E. H. Lenneberg and E. Lenneberg (eds) *Foundations of Language Development: A Multidisciplinary Approach*, vol. 2, New York: Academic Press.

Reder, S. and Green, K. R. (1983) 'Contrasting patterns of literacy in an Alaskan fishing village', *International Journal of the Sociology of Language* 42: 9–39.

Reid, A. (1988) *Southeast Asia in the Age of Commerce: 1450–1680*, New Haven, Conn.: Yale University Press.

Roberts, J. and Akinsaya, S. (eds) (1976) *Schooling in the Cultural Context: Anthropological Studies of Education*, New York: David McKay.

Rockhill, K. (1987a) 'Gender, language and the politics of literacy', *British Journal of the Sociology of Education* 8(2): 153–67.

—— (1987b) 'Literacy as Threat/Desire: longing to be SOMEBODY', in J. S. Gaskell and A. McLaren (eds) *Women and Education: A Canadian Perspective*, Calgary: Detselig.

Rogers, A. (1992) *Adults Learning for Development*, London: Cassel.

Rudy, M. (1990) 'The dynamics of Collaborative Learning of Writing (CLW) in secondary classrooms: control or cooperation?', PhD thesis, University of Pennsylvania.

Sampson, G. (1985) *Writing Systems: A Linguistic Introduction*, Stanford, Cal.: Stanford University Press.

Saraswathi, L. S. and Ravindram, D. J. (1982) 'The hidden dreams: the new literates speak', *Adult Education and Development*, 19: 183–88, Bonn: German Adult Education Association.

Schieffelin, B. and Cochran-Smith, M. (1984) 'Learning to read culturally: literacy before schooling', in H. Goelman, A. Oberg and F. Smith (eds) *Awakening to Literacy*, Exeter, N.H.: Heinemann.

Schieffelin, B. and Gilmore, P. (eds) (1986) *The Acquisition of Literacy: Ethnographic Perspectives*, Norwood, NJ: Ablex.

Scollon, R. and Scollon, S. B. K. (1981) *Narrative, Literacy, and Face in Interethnic Communication* (Advances in Discourse Processes series, 7), Norwood, NJ: Ablex.

Scribner, S. and Cole, M. (1981) *The Psychology of Literacy*, Cambridge, Mass.: Harvard University Press.

Senner, W. (ed.) (1989) *The Origins of Writing*, Lincoln: University of Nebraska Press.

Shuman, A. (1986) *Storytelling Rights: The Uses of Oral and Written Texts by Urban Adolescents*, Cambridge: Cambridge University Press.

Sjostrom, M. and Sjostrom, R. (1983) *How Do You Spell Development?*, Uppsala: Scandavian Institute of African Studies.

Smalley, W. A., Vang, C. K. and Yang, G. Y. (1990) *Mother of Writing: The Origin and Development of a Hmong Messianic Script*, Chicago: University of Chicago Press.

Smith, A. (1986) *The Ethnic Origins of Nations*, Oxford: Blackwell.

Smith, F. (1983) *Essays into Literacy*, Exeter, NH: Heinemann.

Spindler, G. (1974) *Educational and Cultural Process: Toward an Anthropology of Education*, New York: Holt, Rinehart & Winston.

Spolsky, B., Engelbrecht, G. and Ortiz, L. (1983) 'Religious, political, and educational factors in the development of biliteracy in the Kingdom of Tonga', *Journal of Multilingual and Multicultural Development* 4: 459–69.

Spolsky, B. and Irvine, P. (1982) 'Sociolinguistic aspects of the acceptance of literacy in the vernacular', in F. Barkin, E. A. Brandt and J. Ornstein-Galicia (eds) *Bilingualism and Language Contact: Spanish, English, and Native American Languages*, New York: Teachers' College Press.

Street, B. V. (1984) *Literacy in Theory and Practice*, Cambridge: Cambridge University Press.

—— (1987) 'Literacy and social change: the significance of social context in the development of literacy programmes', in D. Wagner (ed.) *The Future of Literacy in a Changing World*, Oxford: Pergamon Press.

—— (ed.) (1993) *Cross-Cultural Approaches to Literacy*, Cambridge: Cambridge University Press.

Stromquist, N. (1989) 'Recent developments in women's education: closer to a better social order?', in R. Gallin *et al.* (eds) *The Women and International Development Annual*, vol. 1, Boulder, Colo.: Westview Press.

Szwed, J. F. (1981) 'The ethnography of literacy', in M. F. Whiteman (ed.) *Writing: The Nature, Development, and Teaching of Written Communication*, vol. 1, Hillsdale, NJ: Lawrence Erlbaum.

Tannen, D. (1985) 'Relative focus on involvement in oral and written discourse', in D. R. Olson, N. Torrance and A. Hildyard (eds) *Literacy, Language. and Learning: The Nature and Consequences of Reading and Writing*, Cambridge: Cambridge University Press.

Taylor, D. (1985) *Family Literacy*, London: Heinemann.

Teale, W. H. and Sulzby, E. (eds) (1986) *Emergent Literacy: Writing and Reading*, Norwood, NJ: Ablex.

Turner, V. (ed.) (1982) *From Ritual to Theatre: the Human Seriousness of Play*, New York: Performing Arts Journal Publications.

Thomas, K. (1986) 'The meaning of literacy in early modern England', in G. Baumann (ed.), *The Written Word: Literacy in Transition*, Oxford: Clarendon Press.

UNESCO (1965a) *Report on the Elimination of Illiteracy in the USSR*, Tashkent: Unesco.

—— (1965b) *Means and Methods Utilized in Cuba to Eliminate Illiteracy*, Havana: Unesco.

—— (1973) *Experimental World Literacy Programme: Practical Guide to Functional Literacy*, Paris: Unesco.

—— (1976) *The Experimental World Literacy Programme: A Critical Assesment*, Paris: Unesco.

Varenne, H. and McDermott, R. (1986) '"Why" Sheila can read: structure and indeterminacy in the reproduction of familial literacy', in B. Schieffelin and P. Gilmore (eds) *The Acquisition of Literacy: Ethnographic Perspectives*, Norwood, NJ, Ablex.

Verhelst, T. (1990) *No Life Without Roots*, London: Zed Press.

Vulliamy, G., Lewin, K. and Stephens, D. (eds) (1990) *Doing Educational Research in Developing Countries*, Brighton: Falmer Press.

Wagner, D. (ed.) (1987) *The Future of Literacy in a Changing World*, Oxford: Pergamon Press.

—— (1989) 'Literacy campaigns: past, present, and future', *Comparative Educational Review* 33(2): 256–60.

Walker, W. (1981) 'Native American writing systems', in C. A. Ferguson and S. B. Heath (eds) *Language in the USA*, Cambridge: Cambridge University Press.

Weinstein, G. (1993) 'Literacy and social process: a community in transition', in B. Street (ed.) *Cross-Cultural Approaches to Literacy*, Cambridge: Cambridge University Press.

Willinsky, J. (1990) *The New Literacy: Redefining Reading and Writing in the Schools*, London: Routledge.

Willis, P. (1977) *Learning to Labour*, Farnborough: Saxon House.

Woolard, K. A. (1989) 'Sentences in the language prison: the rhetorical structuring of an American language policy debate', *American Ethnologist* 16: 268–78.

FURTHER READING

Barton, D. and Ivanič, R. (eds) (1991) *Writing in the Community*, Newbury Park, Cal.: Sage.

Coulmas, F. (1989) *The Writing Systems of the World*, Oxford: Blackwell.

Finnegan, R. (1988) *Literacy and Orality: Studies in the Technology of Communication*, Oxford: Blackwell.

Goody, J. (1977) *The Domestication of the Savage Mind*, Cambridge: Cambridge University Press.

—— (ed.)(1968) *Literacy in Traditional Societies*, Cambridge: Cambridge University Press.

Graff, H. J. (1987) *The Legacies of Literacy*, Bloomington, Ind.: Indiana University Press.

Harris, R. (1986) *The Origin of Writing*, London: Duckworth.

Heath, S. B. (1983) *Ways with Words: Language, Life, and Work in Communities and Classrooms*, Cambridge: Cambridge University Press.

Kimberly, K., Meek, M. and Miller, J. (1992) *New Readings: Contributions to an Understanding of Literacy*, London: A. & C. Black.

Kintgen, E. R., Kroll, B. M. and Rose, M. (eds.) (1988) *Perspectives on Literacy*, Carbondale, Ill.: Southern Illinois University Press.

Mace, J. (1992) *Talking about Literacy*, London: Routledge.

Meek, M. (1991) *On Being Literate*, London: Bodley Head.

Mercer, N. (ed.) (1988) *Language and Literacy from an Educational Perspective: A Reader*, 2 vols, Milton Keynes: Open University Press.

Säljö, R. (ed.) (1988) *The Written World: Studies in Literate Thought and Action*, Springer Series in Language and Communication no. 23, Berlin & New York: Springer.

Schieffelin, B. and Gilmore, P. (eds) (1986) *The Acquisition of Literacy: Ethnographic Perspectives*, Advances in Discourse Processes no. 21, Norwood, NJ: Ablex.

Scribner, S. and Cole, M. (1981) *The Psychology of Literacy*, Cambridge, Mass.: Harvard University Press.

Street, B. V. (1984) *Literacy in Theory and Practice*, Cambridge Studies in Oral and Literate Cultures no. 9, Cambridge: Cambridge University Press.

—— (ed.) (1993) *Cross-Cultural Approaches to Literacy*, Cambridge Studies in Oral and Literate Cultures, Cambridge: Cambridge University Press.

Stubbs, M. (1980) *Language and Literacy: The Sociolinguistics of Reading and Writing*, London and Boston: Routledge & Kegan Paul.

Wagner, D. A. (ed.) (1983) 'Literacy and Ethnicity' (*International Journal of the Sociology of Language* 42), Berlin: Mouton.

Wagner, D. A. and Puchner, L. D. (1992) *World Literacy in the Year 2000*, Annals of the American Academy of Political and Social Science 520, Newbury Park, Cal.: Sage.

Willinsky, J. (1990) *The New Literacy: Redefining Reading and Writing in the Schools*, New York: Routledge.

20

MAGIC, RELIGION AND THE RATIONALITY OF BELIEF

Gilbert Lewis

INTRODUCTION

The questions of belief to be considered in this article necessarily bring religion and rationality together. On the one hand, reason was taken to be the defining characteristic of humanity. The Latin dictionary gives 'wise, sensible, prudent, judicious' for the meaning of '*sapiens*'. Linnaeus chose it as the adjective with which to identify the human species (see Ingold and Tobias in this volume, Articles 2 and 3). There were ancient precedents for doing so. Aquinas, following Aristotle, held that man had the power of reasoning and an immortal soul, whereas animals had neither. Human behaviour was rationally determined after reflection, animal behaviour was governed by instinct. Without that fundamental difference, as Descartes put it, man would have no greater right to eternal life than gnats or ants (Williams 1978: 287). After Darwin, the view came to prevail that human reason must have evolved by natural selection. People, it was thought, used reason to correlate experience and behaviour; they tried to satisfy their needs and achieve various purposes. Social evolution was said to reveal the emergence and development of a more articulate, deliberate and effective use of mind (Hobhouse 1913). But religion and magic, on the other hand, and especially the beliefs of others, often provoked incredulity or at least sceptical dissent; faith seemed to challenge reason. And so discussion of rationality has come to be linked in anthropology above all with the questions of religion and of belief in magic.

It is still odd, however, that religion and magic rather than economics or politics, for example, should be the usual field in anthropology for comparisons of rationality. In economic and political activities, arguments, decisions and plans are made with explicit purposes in view and entail conscious calculation: these are not necessarily so evident in religion and magic, where motives may be complex and elusive (Freedman 1976: 49). Surely it is tendentious to compare religious practice in one society with science or technology in another as a way of assessing the relative place each gives to reason in its affairs; but something like that has often been done when the religious or magical beliefs of people in non-literate societies are contrasted, implicitly or explicitly, with some general idea of scientific reasoning in industrial societies. Like should be compared with like: religion in one society with religion in the other. People exercise reason on many problems; the selective forces which may act to show up reasoning as right or wrong are not of one strength, kind or clarity. The contexts in which people make statements and act must always be taken into account.

Ideas, reasoning and ways of thought have been attributed both to individuals and to collectivities (whether whole societies, cultures or historical periods): different interpretations imply varied assumptions about the nature of evidence for thought, individual psychology and cultural conceptions. Whatever the interpretation, however, it is important to bear in mind that it is actually people, and not abstract entities like cultures or historical periods, who do the thinking and reasoning. There have, in addition, been many attempts to contrast the ways of thought of 'primitive' or 'traditional' and 'modern' societies, though some have stated the contrast more confidently than others. Thus of the Andaman Islanders, Radcliffe-Brown asserted that 'the Andamanese like other savages have not acquired the power of thinking abstractly. All their thought necessarily deals with concrete things' (Radcliffe-Brown 1922: 390). A more recent elaboration of the same idea is offered by Hallpike (1979).

Hallpike advances various reasons for why, in his words

the primitive milieu should foster thinking that is context-bound, concrete, non-specialized, affective, ethnocentric, and dogmatic, as opposed to the generalizable, specialized, abstract, impersonal, objective, and relativist. But one of the most important factors in maintaining these broad characteristics of primitive thought is the absence of schooling and literacy.

(Hallpike 1979: 126)

He argues that in societies where experience is roughly the same for everyone, where behaviour is largely dominated by custom and where institutions are part of a social structure which is not the subject of debate, the verbal analysis of experience and behaviour will be given low priority. There is no call to compare, analyse and generalize for the benefit of strangers, and scant need to justify ways of doing things if everyone else accepts them. A fixed and familiar environment offers little challenge to curiosity and explanation; machines which might provide models for mechanistic causal explanations are lacking; the natural world is examined only when it is of direct concern to people; technologically, the range of problems is narrow, and they can be solved by traditional means; education is largely provided by participation in activities and by experience rather than by decontextualized verbal instruction;

non-conformity is suppressed, and there is no detailed experience of alternative belief systems or of other modes of social organization (Hallpike 1979: 126–34). In Hallpike's view, these are the characteristics of small-scale, non-literate societies, and were also supposedly characteristic of early stages in the evolution of human society.

Stasis, traditionalism and relative isolation were also taken to be typical of the 'closed' condition in Horton's influential comparison of African traditional thought and Western science (Horton 1967, 1982), while the 'open' condition was characterized by the readiness to consider alternatives stemming from exposure to the ideas of other societies. Goody, however, argues against setting up such radical dichotomies – for example primitive–advanced, simple –complex, traditional–modern and closed–open. Rather than opting instead for a diffuse relativism (see below, p. 566) he favours a third course, which is to specify particular mechanisms of change and differentiation (Goody 1977). Modes of thought, he contends, depend on processes of communication; thus the experiences of literacy and formal teaching make possible certain developments as regards the growth of knowledge and critical reasoning.

Questions about prehistory, primitive man and the early stages of human society often lay behind the selective interest taken by Western scholars in observations of the religion, magic and science of contemporary non-literate societies. Certain themes, in particular, caught the attention of these scholars because they could be interpreted as holding the essence of 'primitive' religious ideas or of 'rudimentary' science. Many of these themes remain prominent in discussions of exotic religion and rationality, for example: totemism, taboo, belief in spirits, *mana*, witchcraft, 'virgin birth' and comparable ideas about conception, magic and divination. Such topics have an established place in speculation about the origins of religion and the history of ideas. The choice of these topics has also helped to make it seem as if anthropological contributions to the study of religion are especially focused on the role of the irrational in the life of other cultures. This focus served to throw into contrastive relief the idea of progress or social evolution associated with technology and the rise of science in Europe.

Whether phrased as progress, development or evolution in culture and intellectual outlook, the question of change – in knowledge and ideas, in attitudes to nature and morality, in modes of reasoning and in the legitimation of belief (Gellner 1974) – has been an important and recurring issue for discussion. Behind much of this discussion there has lurked a taken-for-granted distinction between belief and knowledge, with the implicit connotation that whereas knowledge is in some sense true, belief is – by the same token – false (Needham 1972). The very word 'belief' often implies, in its use, a judgement about the uncertain truth or reliability of that which has been asserted; 'knowledge' does not convey the same doubt. 'Knowledge' is legitimate; 'belief' only questionably so. Both terms may refer to an attitude or state of mind on the part of the subject (that of believing, knowing); both may refer to the content or proposition (that which is believed, known). Concern with propositions and the content of ideas is one major aspect of comparison and inquiry; concern with the logic and process of reasoning is the other. Behind both loom basic philosophical questions about truth, relativity and facts.

It is obvious that societies or cultures differ in the substance of the knowledge they maintain and transmit, in their interests, in the scope of their accumulated ideas – these are issues of the content of their knowledge. It is not obvious that an individual's processes of reasoning differ in fundamental psychological respects according to the society from which he or she comes; brain, senses, basic psychological endowments are the same for all members of the species. But cultures differ in the stimuli and training they provide, the values set on different achievements and capacities, the techniques used to preserve and transmit knowledge and experience, methods of argument and criteria of valid experience. The processes of thought and feeling depend on a bio-psychological endowment that is universal; the uses to which that endowment is put and the values assigned to different kinds of activity and experience vary according to culture. Types of thought may also depend upon whether the task at hand is boring, habitual, urgent, critical or performed to a deadline: these all affect attention and the quality of thought. Likewise, differences in modes of thinking may be related to the experience of time, whether as duration, succession, simultaneity or process, or whether linear, alternating or cyclical. Methods of reckoning time may also affect the possibilities of social planning and communication, altering attitudes to time and changing its value according to circumstance and task (Barnes 1974: ch. 7; Goody 1968; for a critical review see Adam in this volume, Article 18).

The degree to which people's ranges of experience, and their judgements about truth and facts, may differ is at the heart of questions on cultural relativity and the legitimation of belief. Relativism is a doctrine in the theory of knowledge which asserts that there is no unique truth, no unique objective reality. What may naïvely be taken as such is the product of the cognitive apparatus of the particular individual, community or historical period whose view is under consideration.

There are two fundamental issues at stake in arguments about relativism and universals in human thought. First, is there one world, or are there many? Can it be shown that there is one and only one objective reality, of whose diverse aspects people have different visions? Second, is there one kind of man, or are there many? Are all people alike in their basic internal nature and cognitive equipment, and, if so, how are we to account for the divergences in their views of reality (Gellner 1981)? Human beings, of course, are of one species among many, and species differ in their capacities of vision, voice, locomotion, etc. Human faculties are not the same as those of cats or magpies; we cannot experience the world as a cat or a magpie does. Indeed, even the strongest cultural relativist would not impute to different categories of people such radical differences in experience and view as those that exist between species – although some racist theories have gone some way towards implying such differences. But the problem posed by relativists is the extent to which different cultural visions of reality can be compared or translated into other terms (or each other's terms) and judged by a common standard as to their truth or falsity (MacIntyre 1970, Winch 1970).

Other disciplines are also concerned with many of these issues and with related matters: for example, history and sociology with the place of religion and science in society, and with culture, ideology and mentalités; psychology with cognition, learning and reasoning, and with affect, attention and perception; philosophy with rationality, logic and epistemology, and with questions of belief and science, truth and relativity; theology with religious belief and practice. Traffic in ideas between anthropology and these other disciplines has been sporadic but fruitful. It would be rash for anthropologists, for instance, to offer a theory about rationality or the human mind or the nature of belief which was blind to objections from psychology or philosophy. There is a lot more to the human mind than binary oppositions and logic, a lot more to cognition than science and ethnoscience, or Enlightenment views on correct reasoning (Shweder 1984).

RELIGION AND BELIEF

In anthropology, as in many of the disciplines just mentioned, beliefs are often ascribed to people taken as a group or collectivity. Belief is meant in a collective sense. The content of belief is at issue, rather than distributional questions about precisely who holds which beliefs, under what conditions, and with what degree of sincerity or commitment. But this can lead to confusion if a statement about the content of collective beliefs is supposed to entail the same attitudes and commitment on the part of all individuals in the group. The distribution of attitudes to some belief is not necessarily uniform. Indeed it is unlikely to be so in religion and magic, where secrecy, sacredness, prestige or access to power and authority may be associated with knowledge. It is common and notorious that people may be excluded from information or experience by age, gender or prejudice against them. If knowledge is thought to bring power or wealth, competition and controls are likely. The views of the religious expert or the specialist do not necessarily convey collective representations in the sense of those beliefs which are shared generally by everyone, even though the expert's statement and explanations may be more complete, perspicacious and coherent. It is understandable that anthropologists should be tempted to rely on those who appear most articulate and expert, people like the Ndembu expert Muchona, with whom Turner worked (1967: 131–50), or Ogotemmeli, the blind old Dogon who instructed Griaule (1972). But the order and illumination they bring to explanations of religious ideas and symbolism may give them a misleading coherence (Brunton 1980). The problem of discrepancy between expert and layman is similar, and perhaps greater, in the case of those world religions with bodies of sacred written texts and specialist priests; the élite can read the texts, and they have authority, but they do not speak for the average man or woman, or the folk tradition.

Another risk of confusion lies in assuming that someone's statement of religious doctrine, or participation in ritual, necessarily shows personal conviction and commitment. The motives for conforming may be mixed and complex, statements can leave room for either literal or metaphorical interpretations. 'Belief', in the dispositional sense, designates a relation between a believer and a proposition. It does not refer only to absolute faith and unalterable conviction. The things someone says, what he feels, what he does, do not have to stand in any simple relation of consistency to each other. Take, for example, sorcery as an example of magical belief. If we assume a man's true and literal belief in his sorcery, then either violence or the sorcery will seem to be ways to harm his enemy. The sorcery might substitute for the violence. But if we slacken the certainty of his belief, impute less of the literal to his statement, allow him some measure of recognized and voluntary illusion, a half-belief, then his sorcery action may become that much more of an act which stands for something violent he would like to do but which he does not wholly dare, and perhaps does not really desire, to carry out. It is a substitute, but a partial one. And it becomes in part symbolic to the man himself. It does not bear quite the same relation to fulfilling his desire to cause harm as does setting out to shoot his enemy with an arrow.

The way that symbolic action is recognized differs, depending on whether one looks from the outside at the beliefs of others, knowing that one's own beliefs are not involved, or instead seeks to grasp and understand the experience of someone for whom these things are part of the real business of his life and involve him in decision and commitment. People must differ individually in how they view the truth of what they assert in common with others in their community, and must differ too in their inward reflections as circumstance, impulse, and motive wax or wane to allow them a degree of detachment which is inconstant. Emotion and feeling as well as reason enter into the link between assertion and conviction; emotion and interest can alter that detachment which might enable someone to see certain objects or actions as symbolic, or instead mistake them for reality (Lewis 1980: 186–99).

Religious belief is not one thing, but a complex of ideas, attitudes and feelings. Much in religion is learnt from others and shared. If the ideas are empirically indeterminate (e.g. doctrines of rebirth, life after death, the virgin birth of a particular person in the past), knowledge of them must depend on learning about them from others. The ideas gain credibility if many people seem to believe them. Numbers persuade and reinforce belief. The truth of the empirically indeterminate ideas depends upon affirmation, on social and subjective rather than empirical factors. Belief becomes representative of a group, a community, or a church. The collective belief is emblematic of membership. A Nuer may take the existence of God as a basic premiss; he takes it for granted as axiomatically true, and the focus of his concern is with the religious significance of this datum. A modern Christian may take the significance for granted but consider the truth of God's existence to be at issue. Those who can sincerely consider or discuss the truth of their basic religious tenets may be thought to have already ceased to be believers in the sense of fully participating in the religious life (Southwold 1979). But belief, considered from the point of view of the individual, is not all-or-none, an issue either of commitment or disbelief; it may be a matter of degree, qualified or changing according to circumstance, dependent on who is asked, how and when. Most Javanese, for example (Geertz 1960), consider themselves to be Muslim, but even in the context of one town, peasants, traders and the gentry give quite different interpretations to this in worship, outlook and behaviour, and they criticize each other's religious interpretations and behaviour accordingly.

The distribution of knowledge and opinion on religious matters may be a worthwhile topic for investigation, but there are valid senses in which religious and magical ideas and practices can be treated as characteristics of collectivities. In *The Elementary Forms of the Religious Life*, Durkheim (1961 [1915]) argued that religion was essential to society to preserve its distinctive order and values. The sacred was serious, obligatory, and set apart from question. The work of Robertson Smith (1889) was particularly influential in leading Durkheim to this view of the obligatory quality of the sacred. Robertson Smith had focused his discussion on sacrifice in the Old Testament. He wrote in the spirit of what was then a new radical critical approach to the dating and interpretation of the Biblical text. The ancient Semites were originally a nomadic tribal people, born into their religion; the rules of the community were binding on all its members; the rules distinguished them from surrounding tribes and served in a period of intertribal warfare to weld the people together into a unity. They created a distinctive sense of identity, a religious identity as a people set apart from other, neighbouring tribes similar to them. Jehovah was their God, other tribes had other gods. The religious rules were public and not private matters. The individual who broke them endangered the community. Actions counted more than conscience or private feeling.

Robertson Smith considered the religion of the Semites in the contexts of the people's political history and changing circumstances. The functions of taboos and sacrifices altered over time; and ideas of wrong-doing and sin changed too. People, Robertson Smith thought, are likely to draw on their own experiences for analogies and images to help them form ideas of their relationship to God. So a nomadic tribal people will draw on the imagery of shepherd and flock, the ties of kinship and communal fellowship, the relation of father to son. Religious ideas and imagery can also be linked to other social facts. With settlement and the establishment of a victorious kingdom, the reigning images become those of king and servant, tribute and homage, the supreme and single judge whose decrees are laws. When the large, once powerful kingdom is divided and begins to fall, the prophets cry out against the back-sliding of the people; the sense of celebration, joy and prosperity disappears from worship, to be replaced increasingly by a sense of guilt, offence against God, and the need to pacify his just anger by expiation and propitiation. After the destruction of the kingdom and the experience of exile, the themes of sin and punishment, of the need to atone, come to dominate the whole sacrificial system. An ethical framework develops which is increasingly concerned with the moral behaviour of the individual. After the fall of the kingship, the priests gain leadership of the people in exile. The systematic shaping of the sacrificial cult, Robertson Smith concluded, was the work of priests in the time of their authority and in accord with their views on guilt and sin. Most of the texts on sacrifice bear the priestly stamp; the priests compiled different traditions, arranged them and gave them a coherent shape.

Robertson Smith's account of sacrifice can be read as a direct inspiration – or as the forerunner – for much subsequent discussion of the relationship between religion and society. He thought of sacrifice as the typical act of worship in Semitic religion. He stressed the continuity of the rite. Worship was given specific forms. Religion cannot wholly remain a matter of inward ideas and feelings; people need to express them visibly and audibly in acts of worship. People are born into a particular society and learn the beliefs accepted in it. Robertson Smith associated sacrifice with changing political and social circumstances; he noted how the imagery used to identify and interpret the relationship between God and worshipper reflected social experience – that of the pastoralist or the tribesman, the citizen, the supplicant; the experience of a people's success, or of their exile. Political change affected religious forms. The growth of the state, the central locus of the temple, and priestly speciali-zation, led to changes in the sacrificial cult, in concepts of distance from God and of his demands; changes came with the control of the cult by temple priests, issues of sin and salvation became important with priestly rationaliza-tion of the cult, leading to a more coherent formal system and the emergence of new ethical frameworks. With hindsight, many of these issues might be seen to point the way towards themes which are now more generally associated with the work of Weber (1965) on the sociology of religion: the affinity between religious ideas and social forms, the socio-political dynamics of change, the development of specialization in religious organization, the growth of rationalization and the increasing prevalence of ethical concerns. Bellah (1964) has written a synopsis of religious evolution along these lines.

Durkheim directly acknowledged Robertson Smith's influence on his own theories of religion. It led him to view the concepts of the sacred, cleanliness and taboo as ways of defining social identity and social boundaries; to recog-nize the importance of the religious community and the heightened sense of fellowship created in communal worship and celebration; and to stress the way that collective values are reinforced by participation in ritual. And he endorsed

Robertson Smith's conclusion from his study of sacrifice, that rites (the actions) were more durable than the ideas and beliefs that people at particular times offered to explain them. Rites showed the greater stability.

However, to speculate on the relative priority of ritual and belief is likely to be a vain enterprise. Robertson Smith, of course, was able to draw on textual sources, as well as the weight of Biblical scholarship and theological history. But such materials are rarely available to the anthropologist who works on the religion of a non-literate society. One exception is Bloch's (1986) study of the circumcision ritual of the Merina of Madagascar. Bloch found records on the ritual dating back two centuries, and was able to use this material to provide an analysis of the way it changed over that time. Great political changes took place during the period – political expansion of the Merina kingdom, conversion to Christianity, colonization, rebellion, then independence. The fortunes of the ritual rose and fell, but Bloch also stresses, following Robertson Smith, that there was a basic stability in core features of the rite. He argues that the persistence of such rituals may help to explain long-term cultural continuities. Rituals influence people's perceptions of changing politico-economic circumstances and their reactions to them. But they may, in turn, play a part in moulding events. The ambiguity of ritual – half statement and half action – leaves room for adaptation to varying circumstances and allows it to survive perhaps little changed in the long run. The nature of ritual may be revealed only slowly through its interaction with practical aspects of culture and historical events. If the significance of ritual can best be seen through a long-term perspective, then the study of such historically well-documented examples as Old Testament sacrifice or the Christian mass should have clear advantages for demonstrating its properties.

One cannot assume anything about the private convictions of a given individual from knowledge of the collective beliefs and practices customary in his or her community. But a public act of prayer, for example, or a grace spoken before a meal, must imply the presence in the community of some idea of a god or spirit to whom, at least in theory, words can be addressed. We may still consider the public facts, what they entail, whether they fit into a pattern, and how they might be related to other social facts. This argument was vigorously put by Leach (1966a) in his discussion of the beliefs about conception held by certain groups of Australian Aborigines, by Trobriand Islanders and by various other peoples, who were said to deny that a woman's insemination by a man was necessary for her to conceive a child. Leach considered these beliefs alongside the Christian doctrine of the virgin birth of Jesus. The beliefs, he argued, were not necessarily expressions of ignorance. On the contrary, they might be sophisticated ways of conveying a religious message, the idea of supernatural or mystical power, something going beyond or against ordinary experience. They were, in other words, religious dogmas. Other aspects of explanation might lie in the way they fit within a pattern of values and social structure. For example, the Trobriand idea that the father makes no contribution (through semen) to his child might tie in with the lack of contribution from the father according to Trobriand rules of descent and inheritance, which are matrilineal. Likewise, perhaps the role of the Father in the doctrine of virgin birth could fit a social pattern in which the authority of the father is paramount (Delaney 1986). Religious dogmas may put demands, sometimes, on faith rather than reason; and by the same token they may contradict reason. Tertullian's famous sentence on faith is anti-rational in force: *Certum est quia impossibile est* – 'It is certain because it is impossible'. Contradiction can serve positively to convey a religious message: mystical forces, influences and actions are held to be imperceptible to the senses, but none the less real. They defy common-sense explanation. The supernatural transcends ordinary experience and reasoning.

MODES OF THOUGHT

Many efforts have been made by anthropologists (and other foreign observers) to explain strange ideas. They have focused on things which stood out to them as false or nonsensical. Lévy-Bruhl (1910, 1922, 1927) characterized 'primitive mentality' by its indifference to logical inconsistency and by ideas of what he called 'mystical participation'. The people referred to (mystical) forces linking them to things such as their names, totems, shadows, discarded clothes, objects they had made or used, or trees they had planted. He regarded this mystical participation as a form of identification, entailing the notion of an invisible tie to things that could influence the person or be acted upon. He stressed, moreover, that these beliefs were shared by all members of the community, and were not just individual aberrations. Their lines of reasoning, he argued, followed from underlying assumptions which differ from our own.

But if these assumptions are accepted, the explanations of phenomena offered by the people themselves may be recognized as both logical and consistent. This was the burden of Evans-Pritchard's (1965: 82–106) influential critique of Lévy-Bruhl's arguments, exemplified by his own celebrated study of witchcraft among an African people, the Azande (Evans-Pritchard 1937). In this study, Evans-Pritchard analysed Zande assumptions about witchcraft, the ways they are applied in explaining experiences of misfortune, and the elliptical phrasing of the explanations. His questions revealed how the scope of Zande explanations could include both the observable level of physical events and the invisible level of mystical forces. He showed how the social context as well as the nature of the misfortune or wrong-doing might determine the focus and relevant level of inquiry and explanation. Secondary elaboration of explanatory details enabled people to account for apparent discrepancies or errors; these blocks to the falsifiability of their basic assumptions could be introduced *ad hoc*.

Lévy-Bruhl had erred, according to Evans-Pritchard, in failing to see how he was misled by his own choice and isolation of examples. He failed to consider adequately how types of explanation might vary within one society according to the issues and circumstances. A hunting accident, an illness, adultery or a theft pose very different problems of interpretation with respect to psychological or moral understanding and factual explanation. As the facts deemed relevant change, so people look for different things. The way a theft was done, who did it, the motives of the thief, the morality of the action, whether it was a sin – the event may be the same, but the questions asked about it are not. The framing of the questions influences the relevance of the facts. This is part of the logic of question and answer. It is also what makes it difficult to compare explanations when they seek to answer different questions; they draw on different explanatory frameworks or 'paradigms'.

Customary beliefs affect perception; attention is selective. We look out for what we expect, what we think is relevant. A certain view of witchcraft and of the powers of the person may characterize the interpretation of nature and experience in a certain society. It moulds the interpretation of particular events and provides an explanation of them. People follow the logic of these key ideas in explaining illness, for example, and in seeking its causes. We may ask what hold these ideas really have over experience. How can people maintain such beliefs? The same event may call forth diverse interpretations: one set of people calls it witchcraft, another calls it illness. The facts people would look for to explain it would depend on the significance they think the event has.

In the lagoon area of the Côte d'Ivoire, Augé (1975) found that belief in witchcraft was bound into an understanding of human capacities that generally informed their interpretation of events. They had an attitude to experience that was, he thought, surrealist. Witchcraft fitted into an elaborate metaphor they used to construe the occult significance of events. They looked on things that happened as signs, as indicators of powers at work beneath the surface of appearances. Ideas of witchcraft and sorcery permitted more profound interpretations of ordinary experience. The surrealist takes account of real happenings and their apparent contradictions, but he discerns deeper meanings in them, more profound relationships in the contradictions. Events of daily life 'speak' to the person who can 'understand': they may indicate things about himself and his relations with the world and other people. The clairvoyant, the diviner, the ordeal pierce through the surface of human affairs. Wealth, health, poverty and sickness do not explain things; they are rather signs of something else. Wealth and health may attract witchcraft, but lasting wealth and health are proof of a person's resistance. A violent man shows weakness because he uses physical force when real strength would be something hidden: the power of witchcraft. Someone who has survived an ordeal of inquiry has proved his strength, not his innocence.

People use their theories of witchcraft to express what they feel about their relationships to events and to the situations of their lives. Beliefs in witchcraft and sorcery are more fundamental to their thought than we should suppose were we to think of such beliefs only as ways of expressing and interpreting social tensions between people, or as ways of reinforcing rules of conduct by presenting repellent or horrifying images of what would happen if the rules were overturned (Douglas 1970, Marwick 1965). The Ivoirian people had a certain 'logic of representations' – an *idéo-logique* (Augé 1975: 120). This outlook or approach was, Augé argued, coherent, even though people did not discuss the principles of reasoning and evidence behind it. They did not try to systematize these principles. They were not specialists concerned with the principles and methods of their own thought.

People do not draw up their own *idéo-logique* for themselves. A worldview, like an *idéo-logique*, is formulated for a descriptive or analytic purpose by someone else, not by the people who are supposed to have that view. Apart from observers with professional interests and occasional individuals within a society, such as a prophet or an idealistic revolutionary, why should anyone try to spell out a concise synoptic view or a synthesis and summary of their outlook on the world? Yet there may be special contexts in which this, or something like it, is done (for example, in the recitation of the Bagre myth by LoDagaa in northern Ghana; see Goody 1972). But usually the observer, historian or sociologist tries to pick out for him- or herself the characteristic ideas and attitudes shared by people of a particular group. There are problems of focus and of the mix of light and shade in such a representation. Augé, in formulating his notion of *idéo-logique*, aims to capture the heart of an outlook. He confines himself to the master-interests or core principles. This approach is narrow in perspective when set beside other ways in which a worldview might be described. It is a matter of analytic judgement whether to search for twenty themes or just two principles to catch the 'spirit of an age' or of a people.

In any epitome, selection is the problem. Bias towards the exotic makes us more likely to examine such notions as those of witchcraft and magic. We neglect everyday reasoning. The classification of foods into 'hot' and 'cold' (Anderson 1987) provides an example of a folk system of ideas which is coherent, practical and effective, an explanatory framework which might justifiably be likened to a paradigm in the sense proposed by Kuhn (1962) – a set of theoretical assumptions, rules, and methods for applying them, shared by a particular (scientific) community. Though not scientific, the hot–cold classification encodes much useful information, it is easily learnt and provides practical guidance in daily life as well as in critical cases of illness. Ideas about hot and cold foods fit into a more comprehensive system of ideas about balance, the humours and health (see also De Garine in this volume, Article 9). They rest on a universal tendency to simplify and generalize, to see things in terms of polar or binary oppositions. Once established, the system is highly resistant to change; its simplicity and clarity protect it. The ideas rest on various observations: that excess of either heat or cold causes damage; that fever, inflammation and chills are signs of illness; that hot and cold seasons bring different diseases; that certain kinds of food stimulate the body, give the feeling of heat or irritation or cooling. The principles are clear and simple, but capable of great extension and elaboration. Balance and harmony are thought basic to health in Chinese folk medicine, which is the subject of Anderson's (1987) discussion: the idea of balance in the diet fits into a wider pattern of Chinese ideas about balance in the humours of the body, about harmony in social relations and in relationships to the environment, to the landscape and to nature, and about the need for balance and harmony in relations with the supernatural. It is part of a consistent peasant view, a general cognitive set.

Although we rarely bother to pay as much attention to the evidence of common-sense − of careful observation and logical deduction in daily life − as we do to such matters as witchcraft and sorcery, the evidence is there to see in the conduct of practical affairs and subsistence. Kalahari Bushmen make detailed observations of the habitats and behaviour of animals; Nigerian farmers exercise effective pest control of grasshoppers through their knowledge of the insect's breeding habits; the Mende of Sierra Leone select varieties of rice on the basis of trial-and-error tests of crop yields: these and other examples provide unequivocal testimony to the use of experiment and deductive reasoning by African subsistence producers (Chambers 1985: ch. 6; Richards 1985: chs 5 and 6). They reveal African thought in a different light, drawing attention away from the stereotypes that have resulted from an all too exclusive attention to magic, witchcraft and religion as the grounds on which to characterize it.

PROBLEMS OF OBSERVATION AND TRANSLATION

The literature on religion and magic in other cultures is marked by some disproportion between theory and observation. This is always a risk, particularly when the observations of others are reanalysed at second or third hand. Observations may be abbreviated by summary, sometimes almost to the barest sentence (e.g., 'The Nuer say that twins are birds'), and then that summary or sentence is given an interpretation which is both ingenious and laden with philosophical sophistication. Theory blots out the original observations. Explanations may be offered for something (a problem, a supposed belief) for which there is inadequate evidence, or which was set in a special context. The first job of the field anthropologist is to describe and represent as accurately as possible the views of other people, their ideas and behaviour. There is no point in building theories and explanations on the grounds of false reports or imaginative fabrications.

Theories concerning the Polynesian concept of *mana* illustrate the point. Firth's (1940) article on the concept is an excellent example of the empirical approach. By the time he wrote, *mana* had already been the subject of sixty years of controversy and discussion. In 1902 Mauss and Hubert (1972) had used the concept in elaborating a general theory of magic. They thought the idea of *mana* was composed of a series of unstable ideas that were confused one with another. It could be, alternately or simultaneously, a quality, a substance and an activity. Firth observed that the confusion and instability noted by Mauss and Hubert seemed to have its source in anthropologists' analyses rather than in native ideas. The difficulty in rendering the term is that of bringing under one rubric a number of considerations that we ordinarily separate: the inherent uncertainty in natural phenomena; differences in human ability; dependence on spiritual entities, and success as gauged by tangible results. In his essay Firth sought to show that the concept of *mana*, at least on the island of Tikopia where he conducted his fieldwork, is non-mystical, always has a concrete referent, and is quite capable of being handled in a non-intellectual way. The complexity of the concept only begins to arise when anthropologists insist that *mana* is a sort of ether: imponderable, incommunicable and capable of spreading by itself. Firth's own approach was to try to find in translation precise verbal equivalents to Tikopian ideas by obtaining linguistic explanations from the people themselves, by studying the ways in which the word was actually used in the course of normal behaviour and in diverse contexts of application, and by eliciting local comments on such usages.

Similarly, a great deal of theoretical weight has been placed on the mysterious concept of '*hau*', a term of New Zealand Maori provenance which was supposed to denote that force in the gift given which impels the recipient to make a return (Mauss 1954). The term has prompted dispute partly because the evidence is elusive and partly because the Maori text on which much of the discussion has focused needs careful interpretation (Firth 1967: 8–17; Sahlins 1972: 149–68). As the examples of *mana* and *hau* show, to grasp the significance of a strange concept, the linguistic data – consisting of words and statements of belief – are not usually enough. The ideas only come to life when they are placed in their total behavioural context. This central point was strongly urged by Malinowski in his article on '*Baloma*, the spirits of the dead in the Trobriand Islands' (1972 [1916]), in which he first presented an account of Trobriand beliefs about conception. He reports what people said, their answers – whether vacillating, contradictory or confident – when he challenged them with questions, his impressions of their readiness to speculate or to extemporise an answer, the way they spoke to spirits in prayers, the offerings which showed ideas of their presence, the behaviour of mature unmarried girls while bathing and their precautions to avoid sea scum and dead leaves floating on the surface of the water because of the risk of becoming pregnant with a spirit embryo (*waiwaia*) sent by the *baloma* or brought by the action of the sea. Rather than presenting one-dimensional facts, or the opinions of one or two selected informants, he provides a picture of the variety of contexts, and of the diversity and multiplicity of ideas and behaviours.

Clearly, if we are to understand ideas expressed in other languages, translation is critical. But in the field of religion and rationality this presents many formidable problems, for example concerning content, logic, rhetoric, and the situations to which particular ideas are relevant. There is an obvious difficulty in finding counterparts for words whose conceptual meaning is unfamiliar: to achieve precise fidelity is never possible. Moreover, direct translation may give no hint of the cultural connotations of even familiar objects: we may know, for example, that a particular word translates as 'dog', but this does not tell us whether the dog is perceived as an animal to be sacrificed or an urban nuisance, a hunting companion or a pet.

To reveal the logic of propositions and causal reasoning may require skilled linguistic analysis of those little words technically known as 'connectives', such as (in English) 'as', 'and', 'either', 'but', 'if', etc., as well as of the grammatical forms which indicate reference, negation, quantity, tense, mood and timing. These are essential to argument and to expressing ideas about cause and effect. We translate what is said, but sometimes without noticing what we have assumed or inserted. Firth (1966) has re-examined the now notorious assertion of the Nuer that 'twins are birds'. He pointed out that the word 'are' (or 'is'), which has to be inserted to make an acceptable English sentence, carries many possibilities of interpretation, indeed too many. It could refer to a state of being, identity, analogy, metaphor or resemblance. Whether the phrase is eccentric or not depends on the meaning given to 'are'. By taking a metaphor in a literal sense we can enter a strange world in which, for example, a person can 'cry her heart out', or 'be an ass'. We must recognize the presuppositions of different contexts in order to be able to distinguish between ellipsis, irrationality, paradox, poetry and so on (Levinson 1983: 97–225).

Frame and context enable the listener to gauge rhetoric, the assumptions implicit in metaphor, elliptical expression, irony, etc. Paralinguistic features and actions also contribute to meaning. Situations may add to or alter the sense of what is said. Hutchins (1980) has analysed the language of Trobriand disputes in detail to show the assumptions and the elliptical devices which are used in argument and reasoning. A particular setting may give relevance to certain remarks whose significance will escape a stranger to the culture. A seemingly plain description of recent events may contain some focus for attention as the possible explanation for a person's illness because of local ideas about the risks from spirits or mystical attack. To the insider the description is heavy with implications and may even amount to an implicit accusation; but to the outsider it sounds like a simple account of recent events (Lewis 1975: 247–67).

The point about distinguishing literal statement from metaphor can be extended to the interpretation of ritual action. Such action is marked particularly by its expressive and symbolic aspects (Leach 1966b: 403–4; Firth 1951: 222). Some argue that ritual has an essentially expressive aspect, regardless of whether it is thought to be effective instrumentally as well (Beattie 1966: 202–3). To assume that people who perform magic, for example in gardening or for treating illness, intend their actions to be empirically effective just as does a scientist or an engineer is, according to Tambiah (1973), an ethnocentric blunder. By imputing scientific or pseudo-scientific instrumental aims to others, we can make them seem irrational. But the expressive aim might make performance an end in itself. To have said well whatever it expressed would be worth while, whether or not it was also instrumentally effective. The action might bring emotional satisfactions to the people involved, even if it had no immediate practical effect. Tambiah thus distinguishes between the aims of magic and of science. Magic is not empirically tested, ritual action is not justified by material results (Leach 1964, 1968).

But do these views represent the opinions of the actors? If someone said that he intended his treatment, for example, to take away the sufferer's pain and fever, how could we still maintain that his essential aim was really expressive or symbolic rather than instrumental? In many cases where rituals have been observed, the actors in fact provide few or no explicit statements of the reasons for what they are doing. Much depends on inference by the observer. We see someone kick a chair on which he has barked his shin: shall we call this an expressive, a symbolic, a punitive, or a vengeful act? People differ in the attention they give to their actions. They vary in their attitudes to what they say they believe. They vary, too, in candour and in self-knowledge. We might consider the relation of someone to what he or she says in terms of sincerity, conviction, honesty, intention, care, forethought, calculation, experience, certainty. The psychological issues are complicated and entwined with the situation, the events and the questioning.

The aims of ritual action or magic may be intelligible to an observer on the basis of certain assumptions about collective or shared beliefs (e.g. that the words of a blessing or a prayer are addressed to some sort of being – an invisible spirit or agency). The actions are institutionalized, the pattern of behaviour is expected and generally known. But what one particular person may really think or believe cannot necessarily be guessed from what they do. It is not possible to judge with certainty from outside whether someone is being rational or irrational, whether they aim at natural or supernatural effects, whether they mean to express a feeling or a symbolic meaning, or to achieve some instrumental purpose. Motives and intentions do not have to be single or exclusive. People may aim to produce an effect by skill and effort, but fail because of mistakes or ignorance. There are, for instance, many examples of Western medical treatments which were once recommended by the experts of the time and are now discarded as erroneous and useless (medical belief in the benefits of chaulmoogra or hydnocarpus oil to treat leprosy is a striking example; see Iliffe 1987: 214–30). The fact of errors now revealed does not, by itself, justify a retrospective judgement of the action as irrational or magical. For any such judgement would depend on our also knowing the beliefs of the actors.

IDEAS OF NATURE AND MAGIC

Nadel (1954: 1–8) noted how anthropologists must veer between judging the transcendentality of things by their own way of thinking and through the eyes of the people they are studying (by imputing to them the thought of transcending the given reality). People may aim at empirical effects achievable by ordinary human skill, effort and knowledge of natural processes; they may aim at supernatural or magical effects which go beyond normal processes. But views about nature and about what is possible are culturally variable. Our own views are entangled in the complex meanings of the word 'nature' (Williams 1976: 184–9). First of all, the word carries its original sense of an essential quality in things – the inborn element of its Latin origin, 'natus', 'natura' – such that the nature of spirits differs from the nature of people. Second, there is nature viewed as the existing system of things in space and time – natural phenomena – such that we speak of 'this worldly' and of 'other worldly' or 'supernatural' things. Third, there is nature viewed as a universe acting according to inherent forces, rules or laws – this view of regularity in nature is enshrined in the concept of 'natural laws'. 'Supernatural' may convey the idea of something happening outside the ordinary operation of cause and effect.

> But it may not at all times have that sense for primitive man. For instance, many peoples are convinced that deaths are caused by witchcraft. To speak of witchcraft being for these peoples a supernatural agency hardly reflects their own view of the matter, since from their point of view nothing could be more natural.
>
> (Evans-Pritchard 1965: 109)

And if nature is thought to be animate, interested and responsive to human action, the field of possibilities is changed. Nature may be considered to judge human action in a more active, moral sense. The distinction between nature and convention, between 'is' and 'ought', is blurred.

In magical action, people may address objects in their environments as if they could understand and respond to prayers or appeals, or be bound by them. Many of the actions seem to be modelled on intelligible human behaviour; thus the object is given a reason to act, or is commanded. Conventional links, invoked in the magic, are treated as though they could have the effective force of natural links of cause and effect. Skorupski (1976: 125–59) examines why people might believe in the causal efficacy of purely symbolic enactment. He suggests that people in small-scale and traditional societies may be relatively insensitive to the distinction between conventionally constituted rules and naturally given regularities of process. Speech and command are effective in everyday social life. They provide a model. People respond to speech, so should not nature likewise respond? The crucial difference between prescriptive and descriptive rules is here neglected; the laws of nature and the conventions of society (i.e. human laws) can be confused. After a fine analysis of the logic implicit in various kinds of magical action and ritual, Skorupski concludes that magic is a heterogeneous category:

> What is for *us* in the end most striking about magical practices is that they require assumptions which in one way or another run counter to the categorical framework

579

within which we (at least officially) interpret the world: as with the notion of a real identity between symbol and thing symbolized, or of the cosmological power of language, or the treating of objects around one as agencies; or beliefs that future events can productively affect the present which are implicit in most forms of divination. In this lies their interest, and the strangeness which are from our point of view their common characteristic. But – clearly – this is a characteristic which they can only have from a standpoint *outside* that of the socially shared consciousness in which they play an accepted role.

(Skorupski 1976: 159)

If magic is so heterogeneous a category, embracing diverse practices whose only common characteristic is that they rest on interpretive premises contrary to our own, it is unreasonable to expect that a single theory will fit all cases.

RATIONALITY AND BELIEF

In judging rationality we must also consider a number of criteria: the intrinsic relationship between means and end in the achievement of a goal, coherence and consistency, the knowledge of the actor and what he or she aimed to do. These provide various grounds for calling an action irrational: because the action is based partly or wholly on false information or error; because it is inconsistent or illogical given the aims and ideas of the actor; because the actor's aims and ideas are nonsensical, unintelligible or mad (Lukes 1970). But actions may seem irrational because the context or aims have been misunderstood. The actor might have been concerned primarily to conform to certain values or some custom, to express an emotion, or to save someone else; thus he or she might have had quite other aims from the ones the observer supposed.

Judgements about the rationality of someone's action cannot therefore be made without regard to the ideas held by the actor him- or herself. Ritual actions and magic may involve collective beliefs or symbols, but it is either a mistake or a form of shorthand to speak of institutions, actions or rites as being rational or not. It is not the institution or the rite that can be in error, have a purpose, seek to display or convey a meaning, or deceive, but rather the people who use the institution or perform the rite. Rationality is a property of processes of reasoning. It may be rational for someone who believes in ghosts and ancestors to placate them, but not for someone who is a materialist and an atheist. The action carried out might be identical in both cases, but the first differs from the second in its rationality (Gardner 1983). In approaching the seemingly irrational we usually assume that other people are rational, even if they are sometimes imperfectly so (Watkins 1970). We cannot begin to understand the meaning of utterances in an unknown language without making the assumptions, first, that the other speaker perceives the world more or less as we do (so that we can then try to relate his utterance both to some equivalent of ours and to the world); and second, that the speaker is a rational being whose beliefs are on the whole logically connected, and whose utterances express those beliefs. Some overlap in concepts and percepts is a necessary condition for successful translation (Hollis 1970: 214–20). These assumptions, that there exists an independent and external objective reality, and that some fundamental rational conceptual commitments are common to all of us, provide the only basis from which we can begin the attempt to understand the language and beliefs of people from another culture. We impute rationality wherever possible, allowing irrationality when it is necessary to do so but with the proviso that irrational beliefs will always need some additional special explanation (e.g., the actor had inadequate or misleading information, was blind or drunk, or acted under coercion). We may impute some belief to the actor or cite some other fact in order to find a warrant for his action or assertion. But Gellner (1970) warns against the charity that goes too far in always trying to devise something to explain and rationalize whatever strange action confronts one. Winch (1970), at the other extreme, argues that we go too far in trying to explain other people's beliefs by our own assumptions about reality and reason.

Cultures differ in their views about reality and reasonable behaviour; their criteria of evidence, proof and truth may not be the same as ours. Strong versions of cultural relativity, like Winch's, may appeal to us for a number of reasons. One is the romantic appeal of the mysterious and exotic that tends to accompany the idea of the social construction of a different reality: the popularity of Castaneda's writings (e.g. 1972) demonstrates this. Castaneda (1972: 167–72) reports an experience of growing bird's legs, feeling wings come out of his cheekbones, and then flying in company with three crows. He asks the shaman Don Juan, 'Did I really become a crow?' Don Juan, in reply, orders him to stop trying to think like that about the things he 'sees' in order to 'understand' them; one either 'knows' or does not. In effect he forbids the anthropologist to analyse his experience on the basis of Western cultural assumptions (Heelas 1972).

Referring to Evans-Pritchard's study of the witchcraft beliefs and practices of the Azande, Winch (1970) has argued that Zande criteria of truth and reality are rooted in Zande language and society, and that Evans-Pritchard was wrong to conclude that scientific conceptions correspond with reality whereas Zande views do not. Winch's position here is not unlike a fideist one that forbids or denies the analysis of some experience by logic and scientific reasoning because such analysis is inappropriate and will misrepresent and distort it. The argument for the validity of the experience is this: you cannot understand what a certain kind of pain is except by feeling it; you cannot know what 'scarlet' means except by seeing it; you cannot grasp what belief in God means except by the grace of faith. For the fideist, to know God is to love him; there is no theoretical understanding of the reality of God; no way of grasping it by analysis and reasoning. The strong relativist would likewise oppose the idea of trying to understand another religious system or another belief system in terms of one's own (ethnocentric) system of beliefs and assumptions. And this leads to a second reason why strong relativism holds a special appeal for anthropologists: it carries an implicit justification for participant observation. Experience is necessary for understanding. Evans-Pritchard, in his essay on 'Religion and the anthropologists' (1962), and Firth, in his 'Religious belief and personal adjustment' (1948), present cases for and against the necessity of personal religious experience for understanding religion in other societies.

The position which denies the possibility of understanding other belief systems by analysis and reason is distinctly anti-rational and somewhat authoritarian. It appears to say, 'I have been there and you have not, therefore you must accept what I say'; it blocks further discussion and analysis. The strong relativist position would indeed be repugnant if it were taken to imply that people who seem to accept a different logic or who seem to perceive reality differently from ourselves must be inferior or less fully human than we are – that Australian Aborigines or Africans or Indians are more like children or animals or the insane. We cannot follow the thought processes of the insane; we cannot enter the cognitive world of the spider or the cretin. Hollis (1977: 107–64) rejects the strong relativist position. Someone's beliefs may provide reasons for his or her actions. But good reasons differ from bad ones. The poorer the reasons given for an action, the more we are left only with an explanation for the action, but not for the actor's belief. A man thinks he is a poached egg, so he goes to find a piece of buttered toast to sit on. Although we have found a reason for the action we have not found one for the belief. Purely subjective criteria may make us think that all actions are equally rational; they may also make us think we are sick. But we can have delusions about ourselves, and doctors may make mistakes in diagnosis. And the assertions of people in other cultures may be false too. Hollis warns us (1977: 126–7) not to be tempted by our habit of accepting objectively bad reasons as good-from-the-agent's-point-of-view into collapsing the distance between the ideally rational and the ideally irrational.

INDOCTRINATION, EXPERIENCE AND CHANGE

The content and accumulation of knowledge in any society depends on the experience of its members, their learning, and their methods for preserving and transmitting information (Goody 1977, Barth 1990). The division of labour, forms of specialization and the political control of knowledge all contribute to the relativity of ideas in different societies. Differences in teaching methods, in the kinds of stimulus and incentive given to people at successive stages of their development, provide grounds for understanding how cultural variations in attitudes to knowledge and values are established. Boas (1955: ch. 9) reviewed the results of studies undertaken by his collaborators in several North American Indian societies, of the explanations provided by the Indians for the meanings of specific design motifs found in beadwork, painting and carving. In some of the societies consistent and uniform answers were obtained, but in others the answers were highly varied and differed according to the age and sex or the personal identity of the respondent, or the context in which the motif was set. The societies were by no means identical in the control exercised over symbolic interpretation, or in the uniformity or consistency they seemed to achieve in transmitting bodies of cultural ideas.

Various authors have stressed the serious and obligatory quality of religious belief. Durkheim connected it with the functions he ascribed to religion: to reflect, maintain and reinforce the social rules and values on which the society depended. Marxist views of religion have stressed the ideological element — that religion fosters the political and economic interests of a dominant class or section of society and stifles dissent. It inspires devotion to beliefs and attitudes that secure the continuing dominance of that class or section of society at the expense of others whose members are misled or mystified by the illusory promises and persuasions of religion (Morris 1987: 5–50). In the search for correlations between social structure and cosmology, Richards (1967: 289) recommended that it might be most fruitful to investigate the differences in social mechanisms for preserving knowledge of religious symbols, myths and categories of experience, and for passing it on to the next generation. These views suggest that we should consider the importance of indoctrination in establishing belief, the techniques of persuasion and the stimuli involved.

Religious rituals offer many examples of strong emotional stimulation. The techniques used are diverse — physical ordeals, crowding, noise, rhythm, dance, exhaustion, starvation, gratification, shock, reversals of normal rules, and so on. They may combine instruction with aesthetic and persuasive suggestion. The initiation procedures of the Abelam (Forge 1970) and Arapesh (Tuzin 1980) of New Guinea expose boys and young men to a whole series of ceremonies in which they are shown paintings, masks and carved objects under conditions of great tension and associated with rituals of which they understand little but which have the recurrent theme of pain. The ceremonies are terrifying and aesthetically magnificent. They are accompanied by deceptions, revelations, demands and instruction. It would clearly be foolish to limit appreciation of Abelam or Arapesh religion to its intellectual or cognitive dimensions and to neglect the emotional and aesthetic contexts in which religion is practised. To understand the hold of particular ideas, we have to look at the methods by which people are socialized into their religious vision, the timing of exposure to different forms of instruction and experience (whether in childhood or adolescence, whether abrupt or staged) and the art and imagery used (Munn 1986, Griaule and Dieterlen 1965, Morphy 1989 and this volume, article 23). The experience of men and women may differ greatly; other categories of persons may be differentiated within a society on grounds of age-set membership, vision quests, schooling, spirit possession, illness, etc. These aspects of the organization and development of religious experience also provide reasons for the diversity to be found in beliefs and convictions (Barth 1987).

Experience is bound to influence people's explanations and interpretations of the world. It comes from everyday life, as well as from especially contrived ceremonial. Many examples of the influence of everyday experience are to be found in the use of models which draw on some ordinary craft or technique to provide explanations for processes that cannot be seen or for novel phenomena. Examples of such explanatory analogies from European culture might include the body as machine or mechanism, and the mind as a play of forces — hydraulic, electric or magnetic. Technological changes have influenced views of the natural world, notably the change from conceptions of a world that is animate, moralized and organized in terms of sympathies and correspondences, to one seen as mechanical and regular, working as a machine does. More subtle reasons for change may lie in social experience. The word 'law' has, in its use to denote the idea of scientific law, slipped adrift from its primary sense, so that now we hardly think of its original juridical associations. The metaphor has, so to speak, 'dried up', but it was a lively stimulus to thought in the past. It called into question the relation of God to creation, his powers (the miracles, monsters and prodigies of nature which showed his power to intervene), the notions of design, purpose, fitness and function; it extended ideas of conformity, duty and obedience to nature, and it found regularity, pattern and mechanism — necessity in nature. The Chinese did not use this metaphor of law. A different understanding of social duty and conformity stressed harmony, co-operation and respect for a given order. The composition and motions of all particular things were fixed in regard to other things in the woven pattern of nature's relationships. Some Taoists used this language and imagery of silk and textile weaving to explain order in nature (Needham 1969: 299–327).

In Durkheim's epistemology, logical thought and science, as well as religion, had social origins:

> It is not surprising, therefore, that social time, social space, social classes and causality should be the basis of the corresponding categories since it is under their social forms that these different relations were first grasped with a certain clarity by the human intellect.
>
> (Durkheim 1961 [1915]: 492)

The relationships expressed in logical thought could not have been learned except in and through society, for it was in society that they had immediacy and their force was felt. Intuitions of relationships between facts grew from the perception of forces evident in social life: love and hate, attraction and repulsion, opposition, association, unity, intention, purpose, cause, aim, negation, the action of agent on object, resistance.

Such sociological explanations of knowledge associate ideas with the type of society and social structure. They look for consistency, continuity and integration; they imply mostly conservative effects. If the social structure persists, then so will the functions and values which produced and maintained the key ideas. Society and social structure are bound to influence ideas by mass effect. The people share a language, concepts, upbringing and outlook. The shared experiences orient and motivate many of their interests and attitudes. The general theme of this sociological account is the power of social experience to mould people's attitudes. But if laws and rules only imply the idea of order and conformity, they can tell us little about the causes of change.

A more historical perspective may provide some clues. In Europe, early Greek thought was distinguished from that of the neighbouring contemporary civilizations of the Near East by a strong spirit of critical inquiry. Lloyd (1979) ascribes this particularity to the social and political causes which stimulated it. The Greeks developed an interest in notions of proof, rigorous demonstration and formal analysis; they showed a new readiness to bring into the open questions of logic and argument, fundamental second-order questions concerning the nature of reasoning and inquiry itself. In many centralized states, the law was sanctioned by divine or regal authority: the ordinary person had to accept in the law an authority that was established and arbitrary. But in the Greek city states between the sixth and the fourth centuries BC, the free citizen came to expect to participate in discussions of the laws and of the constitution. They questioned how they should govern themselves. People sought to convince each other by argument and proof; skills in reasoning were valued in competitive debate. All free men had a duty to participate in the decisions that would affect them; it was not left to experts or those in authority to decide. Lloyd's argument is that the development of critical inquiry and logic, the readiness to challenge deep-seated assumptions, owed something to Greek political experience, even to the instability of the political situation. The beginnings of literacy were already there; as also were the technology, the wealth, and the institution of slavery which allowed some citizens leisure for reflection and debate; foreign contacts and trade exposed them to other societies, alternative ways of thought and the curious relativity of custom. These factors undoubtedly contributed to Greek originality, but they are insufficient to account for it, since the Greeks shared these other attributes with their ancient Near Eastern neighbours.

Many causes must come together to propel change. Active involvement in political debate, open to all men, as well as the questioning of rules, may occur in many small-scale, non-centralized societies, and obviously do not on their own suffice to produce sceptical attitudes and critical interests in formal analysis and logic. The historical particularity of events at different times and in different places throws up different combinations in each case. A particular experience of politics and debate may change the style of rhetoric, methods of argument and proof, as Lloyd has argued; or bureaucratic transactions and petitioning may influence the understanding of ritual action and its efficacy, as well as the treatment of illness (Ahern 1979, 1981); or legal experience may

585

prompt ideas of regularity and exception, of conformity with law (Needham 1956: 518–83).

Doubts that arise from unsatisfactory explanations of experience may motivate changes in ideas, but the changes will still reflect the inherent possibilities and limitations of the pre-existing system. Indeed, continuity is implied in the very notion of development. But events, people, ideas and objects which come from outside the system, and which induce change in it, need fit in no way with pre-existing ideas or organization. There is no necessary coherence or continuity in the impact of outside things. No society, of course, remains wholly isolated from foreign ideas, new technologies, or other external forces. Beliefs depend on being shared by many, however, if they are to have much effect. Thus events which strike many people can move them to doubt. The Great Lisbon Earthquake of 1755 wrecked some beliefs and had intellectual repercussions far beyond the time and place of its material destructions (Glacken 1967: 522–3). Periods of radical change in ideas often seem to arise from a more general ferment of the times, promoting a readiness to criticize established tenets. We cannot ignore the upsetting effects of exploration, conquest and colonialism, the diffusion of material goods, changes in technology, improvements in travel and communication, and so on, in favour of subtler considerations of intellectual philosophy. The introduction of a simple tool, like a steel axe (Sharp 1962), can have far-reaching effects. These are not necessarily confined to the obvious material ones. They may shake up social experience in quite unexpected ways and break continuity with past practice, religious ideas and moral rules. The changes are not developed from something intrinsic and already given or potential in the original system, but are quite contingent and extrinsic to what went before. It is too much to expect that everything can be made to fit together smoothly.

It is also too much to expect of anyone's consistency that a single set of assumptions – or an ideology – should colour all his decisions, all his understandings and actions. You cannot reduce a whole people's outlook to a core or essence without cutting out a great deal of ordinary life. It cannot be true except in an indirect and dilute sense that ideas about witchcraft and powers of the person, for example, guide the understanding of every event among the people of the Côte d'Ivoire. Rather, the ideas are there, sometimes to be called on when events prompt that kind of reflection. Individuals will vary in their disposition to do this, just as some events will be more likely to stir them than others. There is indeed a contrast between everyday thinking and theoretical thinking, as Horton (1967: 53–8; 1982: 228–31) has stressed. The desire for uniformity and consistency with theory cannot be taken for granted. The scholastic bias, which favours intellectual neatness and closure, may lead us to detect more system and more theory than is in fact there. The point was made by Durkheim in his discussion of religious cult and faith. People do not celebrate ceremonies for which they see no reason:

586

For faith is before all else an impetus to action, while science, no matter how far it may be pushed, always remains at a distance from this. Science is fragmentary and incomplete, it advances but slowly and is never finished; but life cannot wait. The theories which are destined to make men live and act are therefore obliged to pass science and complete it prematurely. They are possible only when the practical exigencies and the vital necessities which we feel without distinctly conceiving them push thought in advance, beyond that which science permits us to affirm.

(Durkheim 1961 [1915]: 479)

REFERENCES

Ahern, E. (1979) 'The problem of efficacy', *Man* (N.S.) 14: 1–17.
—— (1981) *Chinese Ritual and Politics*, Cambridge: Cambridge University Press.
Anderson, E. N. (1987) 'Why is humoral medicine so popular?', *Social Science and Medicine* 25: 331–9.
Augé, M. (1975) *Théorie des pouvoirs et idéologie: étude de cas en Côte d'Ivoire*, Paris: Hermann.
Barnes, R. H. (1974) *Kédang*, Oxford: Oxford University Press.
Barth, F. (1987) *Cosmologies in the Making: a Generative Approach to Cultural Variation in Inner New Guinea*, Cambridge: Cambridge University Press.
—— (1990) 'The guru and the conjurer', *Man* (NS) 25: 640–53.
Bellah, R. (1964) 'Religious evolution', *American Sociological Review* 29: 358–74.
Beattie, J. (1966) *Other Cultures*, London: Routledge & Kegan Paul.
Bloch, M. (1986) *From Blessing to Violence*, Cambridge: Cambridge University Press.
Boas, F. (1955) *Primitive Art*, New York: Dover.
Brunton, R. (1980) 'Misconstrued order in Melanesian religions', *Man* (N.S.) 15: 112–29, 734–5.
Castaneda, C. (1972) *The Teachings of Don Juan*, Harmondsworth: Penguin.
Chambers, R. (1985) *Rural Development*, London: Longmans.
Delaney, C. (1986) 'The meaning of paternity and the virgin birth debate', *Man* (NS) 21: 494–513.
Douglas, M. (ed.) (1970) *Witchcraft Accusations and Confessions*, London: Tavistock.
Durkheim, E. (1961 [1915]) *The Elementary Forms of the Religious Life*, New York: Collier.
Evans-Pritchard, E. E. (1937) *Witchcraft, Oracles and Magic among the Azande*, Oxford: Clarendon Press.
—— (1962) *Essays in Social Anthropology*, London: Faber & Faber.
—— (1965) *Theories of Primitive Religion*, Oxford: Clarendon Press.
Firth, R. (1940) 'The analysis of mana', *Journal of the Polynesian Society* 49: 183–510.
—— (1948) 'Religious belief and personal adjustment', *Journal of the Royal Anthropological Institute* 128: 25–43.
—— (1951) *Elements of Social Organization*, London: Watts.
—— (1966) 'Twins, birds and vegetables', *Man* (N.S.) 1: 1–17.
—— (ed.) (1967) *Themes in Economic Anthropology*, London: Tavistock.
Forge, A. (1970) 'Learning to see in New Guinea', in P. Mayer (ed.) *Socialization: the Approach from Social Anthropology*, London: Tavistock.
Freedman, M. (1976) 'Social and cultural anthropology', in J. Havet (ed.) *Main Trends of Research in the Social and Human Sciences* 2, vol. 1, The Hague: Mouton/Unesco.
Gardner, D. (1983) 'Performativity in ritual', *Man* (N.S.) 18: 346–60.
Geertz, C. (1960) *Religion in Java*, Chicago: University of Chicago Press.
Gellner, E. (1970) 'Concepts and society', in B. Wilson (ed.) *Rationality*, Oxford: Blackwell.

—— (1974) *The Legitimation of Belief*, Cambridge: Cambridge University Press.

—— (1981) 'Relativism and universals', in B. Lloyd and J. Gay (eds) *Universals of Human Thought: Some African Evidence*, Cambridge: Cambridge University Press.

Glacken, C. J. (1967) *Traces on the Rhodian Shore*, Berkeley: University of California Press.

Goody, J. R. (1968) 'The social organization of time', in D. Sills (ed.) *International Encyclopedia of the Social Sciences*, vol. 16, New York: Macmillan, Free Press.

—— (1972) *The Myth of the Bagre*, Oxford: Oxford University Press.

—— (1977) *The Domestication of the Savage Mind*, Cambridge: Cambridge University Press.

Griaule, M. (1972 [1965]) *Conversations with Ogotemmeli*, Oxford: Oxford University Press.

Griaule, M. and Dieterlen, G. (1965) *Le Renard Pâle*, Paris: Institut d'Ethnologie.

Hallpike, C. R. (1979) *The Foundations of Primitive Thought*, Oxford: Clarendon Press.

Heelas, P. (1972) 'Expressing the inexpressible: Don Juan and the limits of formal analysis', *Journal of the Anthropological Society of Oxford* 3: 133–48.

Hobhouse, L. T. (1913) *Development and Purpose*, London: Macmillan.

Hollis, M. (1970) 'The limits of irrationality', in B. Wilson (ed.) *Rationality*, Oxford: Blackwell.

—— (1977) *Models of Man*, Cambridge: Cambridge University Press.

Horton, R. (1967) 'African traditional thought and Western science', *Africa* 37: 50–71, 155–87.

—— (1982) 'Tradition and modernity revisited', in M. Hollis and S. Lukes (eds) *Rationality and Relativism*, Oxford: Blackwell.

Hutchins, E. (1980) *Culture and Inference: a Trobriand Case Study*, Cambridge: Harvard University Press.

Iliffe, J. (1987) *The African Poor*, Cambridge: Cambridge University Press.

Kuhn, T. S. (1962) *The Structure of Scientific Revolutions*, Chicago: Chicago University Press.

Leach, E. R. (1964) 'Magic', in J. Gould and W. Kolb (eds) *A Dictionary of the Social Sciences*, London: Tavistock.

—— (1966a) 'Virgin birth', *Proceedings of the Royal Anthropological Institute of Great Britain and Ireland for 1965*: 39–50.

—— (1966b) 'Ritualization in man in relation to conceptual and social development', in J. Huxley (ed.) *Ritualization of Behaviour in Man and Animals*, Philosophical Transactions of the Royal Society of London, ser. B: 403–8.

—— (1968) 'Ritual', in D. Sills (ed.) *International Encyclopaedia of the Social Sciences*, vol. 13, New York: Macmillan, Free Press.

Levinson, S. (1983) *Pragmatics*, Cambridge: Cambridge University Press.

Lévy-Bruhl, L. (1910) *Les Fonctions mentales dans les sociétés inférieures*, Paris: Alcan.

—— (1922) *La Mentalité primitive*, Paris: Alcan.

—— (1927) *L'Ame primitive*, Paris: Alcan.

Lewis, G. (1975) *Knowledge of Illness in a Sepik Society*, London: Athlone Press.

—— (1980) *Day of Shining Red*, Cambridge: Cambridge University Press.

Lloyd, G. (1979) *Magic, Reason and Experience*, Cambridge: Cambridge University Press.

Lukes, S. (1970) 'Some problems about rationality', in B. Wilson (ed.) *Rationality*, Oxford: Blackwell.

MacIntyre, A. (1970) 'Is understanding religion compatible with believing?', in B. Wilson (ed.) *Rationality*, Oxford: Blackwell.

Malinowski, B. (1972 [1916]) 'Baloma: the spirits of the dead in the Trobriand Islands', reprinted in *Magic, Science and Religion and Other Essays*, London: Souvenir Press.

Marwick, M. (1965) *Sorcery in its Social Setting*, Manchester: Manchester University Press.

Mauss, M. (1954) *Essay on the Gift*, New York: Free Press.

Mauss, M. and Hubert, H. (1972 [1902]) *A General Theory of Magic*, London: Routledge & Kegan Paul.

Morphy, H. (1989) 'From dull to brilliant: the aesthetics of power among the Yolngu', *Man* (N.S.) 24: 21–40.

Morris, B. (1987) *Anthropological Studies of Religion*, Cambridge: Cambridge University Press.

Munn, N. (1986) *Walbiri Iconography*, Chicago: University of Chicago Press.

Nadel, S. (1954) *Nupe Religion*, London: Routledge & Kegan Paul.

Needham, J. (1956) *Science and Civilization in China*, vol. 2: *The History of Scientific Thought*, Cambridge: Cambridge University Press.

—— (1969) *The Grand Titration*, London: Allen & Unwin.

—— (1972) *Belief, Language and Experience*, Oxford: Blackwell.

Radcliffe-Brown, A. R. (1922) *The Andaman Islanders*, Cambridge: Cambridge University Press.

Richards, A. (1967) 'African systems of thought: an Anglo-French dialogue', *Man* (N.S.) 2: 286–98.

Richards, P. (1985) *Indigenous Agricultural Revolution*, London: Hutchinson.

Robertson Smith, W. (1889) *Lectures on the Religion of the Semites*, Edinburgh: A. C. Black.

Sahlins, M. D. (1972) *Stone Age Economics*, London: Tavistock.

Sharp, L. (1962) 'Steel axes for Stone Age Australians', in E. Spicer (ed.) *Human Problems in Technological Change*, New York: Russell Sage Foundation.

Shweder, R. A. (1984) 'Anthropology's romantic rebellion against the Enlightenment, or there's more to thinking than reason and evidence', in R. Shweder and R. LeVine (eds) *Culture Theory*, Cambridge: Cambridge University Press.

Skorupski, J. (1976) *Symbol and Theory*, Cambridge: Cambridge University Press.

Southwold, M. (1979) 'Religious belief', *Man* (N.S.) 14: 628–44.

Tambiah, S. (1973) 'The form and meaning of magical acts', in R. Finnegan and R. Horton (eds) *Modes of Thought*, London: Faber & Faber.

Turner, V. (1967) *The Forest of Symbols*, Ithaca, NY: Cornell University Press.

Tuzin, D. (1980) *The Voice of the Tambaran*, Berkeley: University of California Press.

Watkins, J. (1970) 'Imperfect rationality', in R. Borger and F. Cioffi (eds) *Explanation in the Social Sciences*, Cambridge: Cambridge University Press.

Weber, M. (1965) *The Sociology of Religion*, London: Methuen.

Williams, B. (1978) *Descartes: the Project of Pure Inquiry*, Harmondsworth: Penguin.

Williams, R. (1976) *Keywords*, London: Fontana.

Winch, P. (1970) 'Is understanding religion compatible with believing?', in B. Wilson (ed.) *Rationality*, Oxford: Blackwell.

FURTHER READING

Bloch, M. (1986) *From Blessing to Violence*, Cambridge: Cambridge University Press.

Bloch, M. and Parry, J. (1982) *Death and the Regeneration of Life*, Cambridge: Cambridge University Press.

Durkheim, E. (1964) *The Elementary Forms of the Religious Life*, London: George Allen & Unwin.

Evans-Pritchard, E. E. (1937) *Witchcraft, Oracles and Magic among the Azande*, Oxford: Clarendon Press.

Fortes, M. (1983) *Oedipus and Job in West African Religion*, Cambridge: Cambridge University Press.

Geertz, C. (1960) *The Religion of Java*, Chicago: University of Chicago Press.

Gilsenan, M. (1973) *Saint and Sufi in Modern Egypt*, Oxford: Oxford University Press.

Herdt, G. (ed.) (1982) *Rituals of Manhood: Male Initiation in Papua New Guinea*, Berkeley: University of California Press.

Lessa, W. and Vogt, E. (eds) (1972) *Reader in Comparative Religion*, New York: Harper & Row.

Lewis, G. (1980) *Day of Shining Red*, Cambridge: Cambridge University Press.

Lewis, I. M. (1971) *Ecstatic Religion*, Harmondsworth: Penguin.

Lienhardt, G. (1961) *Divinity and Experience: the Religion of the Dinka*, Oxford: Oxford University Press.

Lukes, S. and Hollis, M. (eds) (1982) *Rationality and Relativism*, Oxford: Blackwell.

Marwick, M. (1965) *Sorcery in its Social Setting*, Manchester: Manchester University Press.

Morris, B. (1987) *Anthropological Studies of Religion*, Cambridge: Cambridge University Press.

Skorupski, J. (1976) *Symbol and Theory*, Cambridge: Cambridge University Press.

Tambiah, S. (1970) *Buddhism and Spirit Cults in North-East Thailand*, Cambridge: Cambridge University Press.

Turner, V. (1969) *The Ritual Process*, Harmondsworth: Penguin.

Weber, M. (1965) *The Sociology of Religion*, London: Methuen.

Wilson, B. (1973) *Magic and the Millennium*, London: Heinemann.

21

MYTH AND METAPHOR

James F. Weiner

INTRODUCTION

One of the cornerstones of anthropological approaches to the study of human societies for much of this century has been the assumption that different human endeavours are partitioned into discrete institutional sectors. Anthropologists have characteristically divided the content of their monographs among such entries as kinship, politics, religion and economics. However, the so-called small-scale societies on which anthropologists traditionally focused often lacked any manifest institutional divisions of this kind. The apparent separation of the economic, political and symbolic activities of the people in these societies was more a product of the differentiations inherent in anthropological discourse, which served to delineate and establish a thoroughgoing division of theoretical labour.

Even when it is admitted that religious, political and economic functions are inseparable in small-scale social worlds, a broader contrast is often retained between activities or action itself and thought. Assigned to the latter category is cosmology, the so-called worldview of a particular community, a theory of how the different parts fit together into a unified totality. Commonly, myths are thought to contain much cosmological information: they explain how the world, its particular features and categorical demarcations, originated. However, the problem of institutional differentiation and integration is not disposed of in this way, it is only shifted from the behavioural and normative to the epistemic.

Because myth is seen to serve a theoretical and institutional function of its own in small-scale societies, it mirrors our own concerns with characterizing the theoretical orientations of our study of it. I therefore want to talk not strictly about myth and cosmology but about the broader relationships between myth and language, and between language and the world (which includes human action). For it is a particular theory of representation that

591

leads us to regard myth as a cosmological construction, framed in thought, of the conditions of human perception and action in the world.

MYTH, CHARTER AND CONVENTION

Let me start by suggesting that two alternatives are available to us. One is to see myth as an expression or crystallization of centrally important cultural tenets or principles, as the authorization of some conventional state of affairs, frequently bolstered by reference to the activities of mythic creator beings. Myth in this view becomes a charter for social reality, an origin story of how the world and the humans in it came to be in their present form. Such a view assumes that there is a self-evident distinction between social reality and the ways people have of discursively depicting it to themselves; in short, a distinction between the world and ways of talking about it.

Characteristically, from Malinowski's time to the present day, mythology has been viewed as a repository of central cosmological formulae and explanations of origin. But from the outset this charter view of myth concealed a paradox, never quite clearly articulated: if social institutions function in the real, historical world, why are they often depicted as having atemporal, other-worldly, non-human origins? Why are statements of origins most commonly phrased in allegorical terms?

Writers such as Malinowski (1954) felt that myth and social reality were functionally interrelated. Myth confirmed, supported and maintained the social state of affairs. It provided an account of origins − of the world, of people and of their conventions. The structuralists, who succeeded Malinowski, while discarding such overt functionalism, nevertheless retained a somewhat more abstract version of it: they maintained that myth provided the *conceptual* rather than the normative supports for a social world. If, for the proponents of both functionalism and structuralism, the members of a society were seen to be in possession of something as coherent as a cosmology, this was largely an effect of these anthropologists' search for a stable or ordered cultural world in which to place them. Accordingly, myth and ritual came to stand to semantic structures much as avoidance relations and 'rituals of rebellion' (for the last three generations of British social anthropologists) stood to social convention, and both were said to function in the same paradoxical manner: to preserve the integrity of society by subverting, allegorizing, or inverting its conventional premises in other-worldly, supernatural terms, and thereby focusing people's attention on them.

But there is an alternative way in which we can view myth that avoids this paradox, or at the very least, allows the articulation of the paradox to be part of its methodology. We can assume that nothing so substantial as culture or language or convention exists except as it is tacitly revealed by the continuously innovative, extemporized, and experimental behaviour of people in interaction with each other (see Weiner 1992). We can view culture, convention, the utterances that defer to it and invoke it, and the body of rules by which we codify it, as things that emerge *post facto*, varieties of retrospective judgement on the part of actors, singly and collectively, as to the appropriateness, creativeness, felicity, infelicity, etc. of particular actions (including speech actions – that is, the utterances themselves).

This view would discourage us from drawing a sharp divide between language and the world, or between myth and language. It would see all actions and utterances as potentially subversive, introducing distinctions (temporarily, for the most part) in an otherwise undifferentiated world, drawing boundaries between words, people, and objects so as to release a flow of meaningful relations between them. Myth in such a world does not concern itself with origins as such. An origin story asks the listener to consider the kinds of things that cannot possibly have origins – language, gender, clan organization, humanity – and the myths that tell these stories produce an allegorical effect on language itself, a recognition of its contingency and the contingency of the conventional representations established through it. Each story provides an insight, an oblique and novel perspective that disabuses us from the normal, everyday habit of taking our world, our descriptions of it, our way of acting in it, and our beliefs as true, natural and self-evident.

The possibility of such an anti-charterist view of myth was first recognized by Lévi-Strauss in his classic article, 'The story of Asdiwal', where he began by commenting on the mythographic work of Franz Boas. In the early years of this century, Boas, together with his Native American assistant George Hunt, undertook to record, as fully as possible, the myths of the Tshimshian, a people of the Pacific coast of the American North-west. His goal, in analysing this corpus of material, was to arrive at 'a description of the life, social organization and religious ideas and practices of a people ... as they appear in their mythology' (Boas and Hunt 1916: 320). Yet Lévi-Strauss, in his reinterpretation of one of the myths that Boas collected – the story of Asdiwal – argues that in the formulation of his programme, Boas failed to stipulate a *relationship* between myth and other social phenomena:

> The myth is certainly related to given facts, but not as a *representation* of them. The relationship is of a dialectic kind, and the institutions described in the myths can be the very opposite of the real institutions. ... This conception of the relation of the myth to reality no doubt limits the use of the former as a documentary source. But it opens the way for other possibilities; for in abandoning the search for a constantly accurate picture of ethnographic reality in the myth, we gain, on occasions, a means of reaching unconscious categories.
>
> (1976: 172, 173)

With this aim in mind, Lévi-Strauss goes on to analyse myths only in relation to other myths – his intent in the four volumes of *Mythologiques*, his comprehensive survey of Native American mythology. Since their relationship to social organization is at best problematic, myths afford no more than a partial window on ethnographic reality. Myths provide a guide or template, sure enough, but only to other myths, only to other forms of classification.

Lévi-Strauss approached the question of the relationship between language and world correctly: by rephrasing it as a problem of the relationship between one kind of language and another. He therefore forced us to consider the broader analytic problem of representation itself, and of how anthropologists construe the relationship between myth and the rest of social discourse, and, more generally, between vehicles of representation and that which is represented. Lévi-Strauss sees myth as similar to music: it shares superficial syntactic and contrapuntal similarities with language but is essentially non-linguistic in form and effect. It could accordingly be said that a myth must stand outside language if it is to represent something other than itself. We would then have to agree, as did Lévi-Strauss, with Richard Wagner, who thought that music and myth have the power to convey messages that ordinary language cannot. But both Wagner and Lévi-Strauss felt that these extra-linguistic forms ultimately functioned to unify and co-ordinate the worldview and morality of a community. In other words, though the forms of myth and music are not conventional, their effects *are*. And this is just another version of the functionalist paradox.

We could say, on the other hand, that myth must stand outside convention by proposing meanings that are interstitial or tangential to it. We would then be taking the position of Roy Wagner, who holds that myth does not express conventional significances, but rather makes the latter visible by way of its innovative impingements upon them. Thus he argues, 'A myth, a metaphor, or any sort of tropic usage is ... an *event* − a dislocation, if you will − within a realm of conventional orientations' (1978: 255), a formulation that shares much in common with Geertz's (1973) notion of the dialectical relationship between the 'is' and the 'ought', and with Bateson's (1972) theories of rules and communication. A similar view has been propounded by Burridge (1969) in his landmark study of the narrative of the Tangu people of Papua New Guinea. Myth 'juxtaposes [images], it does not classify', according to Leen-hardt (Clifford 1982: 181); it interprets rather than squarely represents, and from this point of view, its role in *maintaining* some represented social order is more ambiguous and complex than a functionalist or charterist theory would have us believe. Lévi-Strauss himself says, at the end of the last volume of *Mythologiques*, that '*conter* (to tell a story) is always *conte redire* (to retell a story) which can also be written *contredire* (to contradict) ...' (1981: 644).

The perception that there are two conflicting theories of myth − as cosmo-logical and epistemological charter on the one hand, and as what Max Müller called a 'disease of language' on the other − emerges as such largely because of anthropology's assumption of the conventionality of language and of social action more generally. In this article I want to play this contrast in theories of myth off against the contrast that Lévi-Strauss himself sets up between myth and totemism. Lévi-Strauss felt that totemism was a language or code that readily lent itself to expressing or creating social divisions, whereas the language of myth, on the other hand, was a world unto itself. I want to show first how the most important form of totemic differentiation – detotalization – may have as aesthetic and interpretive an effect on conventional discursive usages as does myth. The conventional status of any form of discourse is not therefore a function of its role in underpinning or expressing a conceptual system, but is situationally determined only in relation to all other forms of discourse.

Secondly, I suggest that totemic and mythic language differ in terms of what we can call the form of their linguistic embodiment. Linguistic embodiment begins with the premiss that semantic equivalence is not open-ended and indefinitely expansive, but always comes up against limits that originate outside the domain of conventional linguistic signification. The human body often literally provides these limits, but other forms of discourse do so just as often. I will exemplify this by referring to the relationship between myth and magic, particularly with respect to what language both reveals and conceals in any given speech event.

TOTEMISM AND NAMING SYSTEMS

In his classic study *The Elementary Forms of the Religious Life* (1976 [1915]), Durkheim, referring to material on the Aranda of Central Australia, claimed that the clan is identified by the totem, and that the totem itself becomes the most obvious focal point of ritual attention. In effect, when the clan makes its totem sacred through the performance of ritual, it is in fact worshipping itself. Thus religion, for Durkheim, was the act of society imbuing its functions with sacred values.

Fifty years later, in his influential study, Lévi-Strauss (1963) suggested that totemism is not necessarily a religious phenomenon, but rather a classificatory one. He regarded totemism as a label for a certain kind of logic by which people employ the distinctions found in nature for the purpose of imposing distinctions between categories of people. Totemic designations do more than merely label persons and groups; they also establish a certain structure of relationships between them.

Both of these features are intrinsic to the Foi naming system. The Foi of Papua New Guinea, with whom I conducted fieldwork between 1979 and 1988, used to refer to any of the totemic species of their clans as individual namesakes. For example, a man of the Momahu'u clan, upon hearing the cry of the *Raggianna* bird of paradise, remarked 'that's my namesake'. The Foi recognize a special relationship between people who bear the same name. They call each other *ya'o*, as if it were a kinship term, which indeed it is, and exhibit the same sharing behaviour as do close consanguines. In many cases, the *ya'o* or namesake relationship supersedes genealogical designations. If a small child, related to one as, say, classificatory brother, has bestowed upon him the name of one's deceased true mother's brother, one addresses that child as 'mother's brother' rather than by the term that designates the nominal genealogical relationship between the child and oneself.

Lévi-Strauss notes that ethnographers' accounts, from the earliest times to the present, attest to the remarkably detailed knowledge of the animate and inanimate environment possessed by non-literate peoples. Moreover, such peoples recognize many different species of each natural plant and animal category, each one distinguished through a peculiarity of form, colour, habit, habitat, and so forth. For Lévi-Strauss, such classifying 'has a value of its own; it meets intellectual requirements' − those of ordering the universe − 'rather than or instead of satisfying needs' (1966: 9). Thus, 'the thought we call primitive is founded on a demand for order' (1966: 10).[1]

But in what does this order consist? To answer this question I now return to the Foi, to consider their metaphor of clan identity. Associated with each Foi clan is a collection of bird, animal, and vegetable species which 'stand for it'. A member of the Momahu'u clan is thus represented, for example, by the *Raggianna* bird of paradise, the *sena'a* species of sugarcane, the black palm tree, and others. In fact, each Foi clan has 'standing for it' an element or species in the garden vegetable, tree, fish, bird, marsupial and wild vegetable domains, and perhaps others that I am unaware of − that is, in every domain which the Foi see as comprising their cosmos. A human differentiation − that between clans − always overarches those of species within any generic category.

The fact that the *sena'a* sugarcane and the *Raggianna* bird of paradise stand for the same clan is more important than the fact that they are technically different kinds of things. The shared clan designation covers over this technical distinction. We can say that the distinction between the domains themselves is ignored or concealed or *backgrounded*. The difference between items in different domains (the *Raggianna* bird of paradise and the *sena'a* sugarcane, both of which stand for the Momahu'u clan) is not as significant as the difference between elements *within* a domain (such as between the *Raggianna* bird of paradise and the sulphur crested cockatoo, the latter of which stands for the So'onedobo clan).

Within the domains themselves, therefore, is replicated the differentiation between Foi clans. They are all internally speciated in a homologous way. In fact, every generic domain the Foi recognize functions in this way to distinguish clans from each other, and correspondingly, because different items such as the black palm, the *Raggianna* bird of paradise, and the *sena'a* sugarcane all stand for the same clan, they stand in an analogic relationship to each other, which cuts across generic distinctions. Taking the system to its logical conclusion, every Foi clan could have an unlimited number of totems, and every generic domain the Foi recognize could serve as a field of totemic *differentiation*.

As Lévi-Strauss notes:

> the operative value of the systems of naming and classifying commonly called totemic derives from their formal character: they are codes suitable for conveying messages which can be transposed into other codes, and for expressing messages received by means of different codes in terms of their own system.
>
> (1966: 75–6)

Yet nowhere, not even in Foi, does this process achieve such an indefinite expansion. There are always limits which define the scope within which homologic expansion is allowed free play. As Schrempp (1992) has convincingly illustrated in his recent analysis of Lévi-Strauss's approach to myth and totemism, Lévi-Strauss envisioned the transition from nature to culture as involving the movement, cognitively speaking, from the complete continuity of nature to the structured discontinuity required by the human mind. He suggested that the Tikopian, Ojibwa and Bororo creation myths (1969: 50–5) illustrate different attempts to introduce discontinuity and limit into a primordially infinite or continuous series so as to produce the categorical oppositions necessary for ordered social life. For example, in the Tikopia myth, the gods were originally no different from men; they were the direct representatives of the clans. At this time, all the foods in the world were owned by the Tikopian gods. A visiting god managed to steal all the food items and run off with them, dropping only four items in making his escape: a coconut, a taro, a breadfruit, and a yam. These foods remained the property of Tikopians and became the totemic emblems of the four Tikopian clans. In such cases, Lévi-Strauss observes:

> totemism as a system is introduced as *what remains* of a diminished totality, a fact which may be a way of expressing that the terms of the system are significant only if they are *separated* from each other, since they alone remain to equip a semantic field which was previously better supplied and into which a discontinuity has been introduced.
>
> (1963: 26)

In this example, myth itself provides the limits to the social expansion of classificatory analogy. Such a view cannot be easily reconciled with a simple charterist theory of myth.

Seen from this perspective, myth and totemism provide different avenues for the expansion of metaphor. A metaphor, we can say, is a comparison that depends on both a relationship of similarity and one of difference between the things compared. The metaphor establishes not the *identity* of two entities, x and y, connected by the phrase 'x is a y', but their *likeness*. The phrase 'I am a parakeet', uttered by a Bororo individual, would be recast by Lévi-Strauss in the following way: 'As a man, I am to other men what a parakeet is to other birds'. Depending on one's point of view, however, the two statements in quotation marks, which we assume are synonymous, have very different epistemological implications. The first, attributed to a Bororo speaker, does not deliberately focus on the differentiation of clans, but rather on the identification between man and animal – leaving the clan differentiation to emerge as a result of human effort (through, for example, exchange, behavioural proscriptions among certain categories of kinsmen, and the like). The second statement, attributed to Lévi-Strauss, which is the one that analytically minded Westerners would judge as more accurate, focuses attention instead on the differentiation that is the product of such identification. Our Western tendency is to see the work of resemblance as a specifically human task, that of finding similarities between entities that are already naturally differentiated.

This contrast is a theme to which I will return in this article, and it can be summed up by the following statements: (1) There is an element of similarity and difference in any symbolic representation. (2) Similarity and difference cannot, however, be simultaneously revealed in any one symbolic statement, because they undermine each other. (3) Each, however, serves as the background against which the limits of the other are defined. (4) Certain forms of discourse, like music, myth and poetry, deliberately play similarity and difference off against each other, such that each is alternately figure and ground, or reverse the terms by which the contrast is normally presented, thereby revealing its conventional foundation. In sum, in uttering the first statement above, the Bororo man is speaking and living a myth (cf. Leenhardt 1979), while in uttering the second statement we make of this living myth a cosmology more in line with our Western requirements for conceptual order.

THE FORM AND BODY OF MYTH

Because he considered the most important properties of what he called the 'totemic operator' to be semiotic, metaphoric and analogical, rather than botanical or zoological in the strict sense, Lévi-Strauss emphasized that it is not the existence of any *particular* species of plants or animals that is important for totemic differentiation, but rather the fact that plants and animals exist *as species*. Any field, domain or series can be speciated, that is 'detotalized', as Lévi-Strauss put it, and consequently used to introduce social distinctions in human communities. The topography of a community's territory, for example, can be divided up into places, a possibility that may once again be illustrated with reference to the Foi system of naming.

All Foi infants are named after relatives. Usually, they are given the name of a close elder relative of either the father or the mother – in over 80 per cent of the cases, the elder sibling or parent of one of the parents. That infant is henceforth seen as the future replacement of his or her namesake, and for this reason, the Foi told me, it is not good to name an infant after a person who is still relatively young, lest it be thought that the namesake's death is being hastened. The infant inherits not only the secret name, the one true name, which only his parents and his namesake ordinarily know, but all the nicknames and public names that the namesake acquired during his or her

lifetime. While the namesake is alive, the infant is publicly addressed by a distinguishing nickname — which is not one of the namesake's appellations: the
Foi believe that there should be only one bearer of each name (though
common names recur in distant villages among Foi communities that have
little contact with each other).

The Foi periodically hold pig-killing festivals called *sorohabora*, which can
be translated as 'song-making'. These are held on such occasions as the completion of a new men's longhouse, or the construction of an especially large
canoe. The festival is named after the mourning songs, *sorohabora*, that are
performed on the night of the slaughter of the pigs and the exchange of pork
for shell valuables (see Weiner 1991). The songs are sung to commemorate
those men who have died in the recent past. In addition, past songs of earlier
deaths that are well-remembered because of the pathos and beauty of their
poetry may be repeated again. For the songs are the Foi's own poetic medium,
and like our own poetry, the composition of *sorohabora* is subject to constraints
of metre and rhythm (though not of rhyme) as well as restrictions on the range
of topics and metaphorical allusions that may or may not be used in everyday
speech.

Although many different themes emerge in *sorohabora* the most common
are those which link the life of the deceased to the geographical areas which
he inhabited when alive. The following song, recorded in December 1985, is
fairly typical:

The Mountain Masiba
Has been covered with bush
The Mountain Masiba
Reclaimed by the bush

Boy, your secret sleeping place in the cave
Has been covered up with bush
Boy, your Kubarihimu path
Has been covered over with bush

The path at Damekebo
The gap has been covered over
The path leading up to Masiba
It is now covered over

The Egadobo clan man, his father, Humane
His son, Hagiabe
The Ononodobo woman Horaro
Her son, Sera

[*4th stanza repeated*]

The life of the deceased is depicted as a series of places that belonged to
him, or that he inhabited. In an important sense, the names of these places
become the names of the deceased too, and are passed on to his namesake.

The song also evokes the sadness that is felt because, since the person is dead, the gardens and sago stands that the deceased made at those places have been reclaimed by the forest, covered over with weeds. The last two stanzas are called the *dawa* in Foi poetical terminology and reveal, first, the public name of the deceased (Hagiabe), secondly, the names and clan names of his parents, and finally his secret name, Sera, which is revealed publicly for the first time. It should also be emphasized that every single spot in Foi territory is named – there are no unnamed patches of ground. Like people, places can receive new names if significant or memorable activities happened on those spots, so that the naming process in Foi involves a constant dialectic between person and place, ever changing, yet always serving to anchor each Foi individual within the same fabric of social relations.

Now let us return for a moment to Lévi-Strauss's discussion in *The Savage Mind*, drawing upon the example of the Osage Indians of North America. Each Osage clan possesses a totemic 'symbol of life' – puma (a large wild cat), golden eagle, young deer, etc. 'The clans are thus defined, in relation to each other, by means of differentiating features' (1966: 149). Yet in certain ritual texts, the totem animal is presented as a 'charcoal animal', parts of whose body are blackened to symbolize what for the Osage is the protective role of fire and its product, charcoal, which Osage warriors use to blacken their faces before going into battle. In a ritual text related to this practice, each totem issues a declaration of the following kind:

> Behold the soles of my feet, that are black in colour.
> I have made the skin of the soles of my feet to be as my charcoal.
> When the little ones [men] also make the skin of the soles of my feet to be as their charcoal.
> They shall always have charcoal that will easily sink into their skin as they travel the path of life.
> Behold the tip of my nose, that is black in colour, etc.
> Behold the tips of my ears, that are black in colour, etc.
> Behold the tip of my tail, that is black in colour, etc.
>
> (LaFlesche 1917–18: 106–7)

As this example indicates, totemism need not be, and generally is not, the bare linking of species with clans or other groups – each species can also be *detotalized*, as Lévi-Strauss puts it, into parts such as feet, nose, ears, tail, etc., which together add up to a complete totemic series in miniature. Note that these series, too, stand in homologous relation one to another, such that the nose of the puma is analogous to the beak of the eagle or the snout of the deer, and so forth. In just the same way, the name of the deceased Foi is 'detotalized' into a series of place names that, taken in their entirety, stand for the totality of a person's life history.

This dialectic between detotalization and (re-)embodiment may be taken to epitomize the way that any discursive field simultaneously defines the possibilities of semantic extension or innovation, and the limits of such extension.

Differentiation and identification do not proceed in a void. There are always limits on how far a similarity can be perceived, always limits as to how many distinctions can be drawn between entities (as the Tikopia, Bororo and Osage myths cited earlier show). Our common Western theory of language sees it as a collection of lexical items and the rules of their combination. In this view, language is built up by the endless stringing together of elements in novel combinations, producing discrete 'bodies' of discourse – conversations, monologues, books, theories, academic disciplines, histories, each of which has its own internal organic differentiation.

Other people, like the Foi, are more likely to see language as something which is already laid out in its entirety in the world – they would say that the name of an item is a part of it in the most unremarkable way possible. When Foi people speak, they don't so much see themselves as stringing words together; rather, they strive to create an effective verbal environment for these different names so as more effectively to invoke the object to which the names belong. This also includes, as we have seen above, placing words and names in their appropriate spatial, geographic and temporal contexts.

Learning about the world and learning about language are not distinct endeavours, in this view. The Foi are less concerned with what words mean in the abstract than with what kinds of effect they have on others when they are used. The Foi often used the word *ga* ('base', 'origin', 'source', 'meaning', 'significance') in response to my queries about the meanings of utterances. But it was clear that they were not referring by this to what we would call the lexical or dictionary meaning, but to the history, the mythic and supernatural context of the word itself, the story which accounts for how the designated item came to be and how it acquired all its names (including its secret names, which are the ones needed to make use of the item magically).

These contexts, too, can be thought of as the bodies of words or utterances. But as the Osage and Foi examples show, it is very often the literal animal or human body which provides the contours for the detotalizing of various semantic fields. For the Fali of Northern Cameroon (Guidoni 1975) and the Dogon of Mali (Griaule 1965), the human body always provides the outlines for this laying-out of language, architecture, and myth (Guidoni 1975: 124–34). 'All of reality is involved in a series of correspondences that have the human body as reference' (Guidoni 1975: 130). As is the case in Tikopia, there are four Fali groups, each of which identifies with a different cardinal direction. The earth itself is divided into four parts, the head, trunk, upper limbs and lower limbs, with the sexual organs representing the geometric centre of this scheme. The disposition of the buildings in a Fali compound is likened to a prone human form: the sleeping quarters are the head and knees, the auxiliary granaries the shoulders and hips, the central granary the groin. Not only is the all-important Fali granary of the same height as a person but also the parts of the human body are used as labels for its own components: the top is the head, continuing down to the neck, body and lower members, which are the stones upon which the edifice rests.

My purpose in presenting this example is not merely to illustrate a form of 'body symbolism' but rather to show how the world is lived and thought through the body (see Jackson 1989). For the Dogon, there is a distinctive 'mode of speech' corresponding to each productive technique, plant (and the detotalized parts of the plant), animal (and the detotalized organs of the animal) and the human body and its component detotalized parts. Each one has a specific moral and affective value and each has a correspondingly specific mode of graphic representation which is produced on various ritual occasions (Calame-Griaule 1986: 109–10). This differentiation of speech forms was revealed by various creator beings, who perceived that the human body was incomplete without speech: 'None of [the body's] organs could attain their full proportions until man's speech training was complete' (Calame-Griaule 1986: 98). In living their life and in rendering this life iconically in its various graphic representations, the Dogon simultaneously make speech a function of the embodiment and detotalization of their total world.

MYTH AND STRUCTURAL ANALYSIS

As I noted earlier, Lévi-Strauss was careful to point out that a myth could only be compared with another myth. Between myth and other forms of language and activity there is only a relationship of aesthetic impingement or impressionistic rendering. Some practitioners of structural analysis, however, have sought to establish this relationship in more normative, Durkheimian terms. Of the myths of the Kwakiutl, for example, Walens argues that the story of the creator being _Q!aneqelaku_ (the Transformer) 'expresses the charter of Kwakiutl society' (1981: 137). This charter enjoins the control of hunger in the interests of maintaining an orderly sociality. 'Kwakiutl rituals enact the ideas embodied in this myth' (1981: 137).

Walens sees language only in semantic terms, that is, only in terms of sign relations. And in the same manner that a sign can only signify in one direction – the signifier can only represent the signified and not the other way around – so, for many anthropologists, myth and ritual can only depict a more significant social reality. From this initial assumption of the gap between language and everything it describes, the assumption of discrete levels of all social discourse necessarily follows. What Lévi-Strauss (1976) once described as a multiplicity of explanatory levels came to be seen as reflecting a multiplicity of institutional perspectives. That is, where myth, ritual and politics are assumed to be separate phenomena, the relationship between them always appears to be problematic. And in the elucidation of this relationship is seen to lie the 'function' of structural analysis.

Stephen Hugh-Jones elaborates upon this function in his study of the myth and ritual of the Barasana Indians of north-west Amazonia (1979). Ritual for

Hugh-Jones mediates between myth and social praxis, but in contrast to the assumed *dis*continuities between these modes of social discourse lies the Barasana's encompassing notion of *He*:

> The word *He* is ... used in a more general sense as a concept which covers such things as the sacred, the other world, the spirit world, and the world of myth. Used in this latter sense, the word is often added as a prefix to other words. ... *He* pertains to the world of myths ...
>
> Barasana myths describe the establishment of a differentiated cosmos from an undifferentiated life-principle, and describe the establishment of order from chaos. This ordered cosmos, implied by the concept of *He*, and established as changeless in the mythic past, is seen by the Barasana as being the 'really real' (Geertz 1973) of which the human social order is but a part.
>
> (1979: 139, 248)

It seems that the Barasana, like the Foi, accord to humans the task of *differentiating* themselves and their society from a more encompassing and immanent cosmos. As is the case with Aboriginal Australians (see, for example, Myers 1986), their myth and ritual is the ongoing attempt to reconcile these social differentiations with what they perceive to be a natural continuity between humans and their surrounding world. A Barasana myth may not be a repository of semantic equations so much as a form through which to elicit an insight into the nature of *He*.

Let us next examine a tribal society in which such differentiation is *not* the overt focus of human attention. In Michael Jackson's book, *Allegories of the Wilderness* (1982), we are confronted with a distinction between the conventional and non-conventional that is apparently identical to that of our own Western culture. For the Kuranko of Sierra Leone, among whom Jackson conducted his research, 'behaviour and temperament reflect an interaction between acquired moral knowledge and innate dispositions' (p. 21). Hence, the enactment of socially and morally approved roles must always be negotiated through the subverting influence of individual variation and idiosyncrasy. 'Ethical judgements have to be revised according to the particularities of the situation at hand', Jackson thus notes (p. 26). 'In a society with fixed rules and roles, a crucial moral problem is the indeterminate relationship between birth and worth, position and disposition, the man-made and the God-given' (p. 27).

The fictional narratives that Jackson analyses represent ways in which conflicts between the expectations of conventional morality and individual action are explored and resolved. The narratives achieve this through the device of 'contrived ambiguity', as Jackson calls it (p. 2), in which the distinction between conventionally contrasted realms is initially dissolved, and then re-established, thereby emphasizing the moral quality of their distinctiveness. 'By overthrowing the normal order of things and suspending disbelief, Kuranko narratives create an ecstatic situation in which each person must redefine the world for himself' (p. 40). What facilitates the moral function of these narratives is the allegorical quality of the tales themselves: locating the relevant action in liminal settings, focusing on characters that are themselves peripheral or ambiguous such as the *nyenne*, 'bush spirits', or a set of three brothers who were born at identical times — making differentiation by birth order impossible — and so forth. Such liminal characters serve a *mediatory* function, according to Jackson. Because they have ambiguous characteristics, they act as foci around which categories that have become blurred can be redefined and their moral foundation affirmed.

But the Kuranko storyteller is himself a mediatory figure, 'like a diviner', Jackson notes (p. 59). In the Kuranko language, the diviner is 'one who lays out pebbles', bringing to mind a word used by another African people, the Ndembu of Zambia: '*chinjikijulu*, from *ku-jikijila* "to blaze a trail", by cutting marks on a tree with one's axe or breaking and bending branches to serve as guides back from the unknown bush to known paths' (Turner 1967: 48). Turner translated this term as 'symbol'.

The assumptions underlying the function of these folktales in making visible certain aspects of Kuranko sociality are not unlike those made by certain followers of Lévi-Strauss. According to Jackson, 'Crucial transformations in the narratives are usually associated with liminal situations' (p. 46). In exactly the same manner, Hugh-Jones states that:

> One of the main points of significance that I see emerging from my work ... is that rites of initiation, which combine 'birth' and 'death' and which are conceptually half-way between these two uncontrollable natural processes, *recreate them, through the use of symbols, in a controlled and ordered fashion.*
>
> (1979: 256; my emphasis)

Turner and Hugh-Jones feel that language always serves to order and disambiguate, and hence the forms or products of language — among them, myth and ritual — are devices for maintaining and affirming conventional orders. In such a view, the symbol-making and using capacity of humans does not compete with the world, but makes it more comprehendable. This view encourages us to consider a myth or a ritual as a fixed text or recipe, and to divorce the structure of a myth from the context of its utterance as an act of speech. It tacitly assumes that if the myth stays alive by being told and retold, it is retold in the same form. But what, one might ask, does a community achieve through the continual repetition of a story its members already know?

In contrast to the approach that leads to this dilemma, Jackson calls Kuranko folktales 'allegories' in that they 'say one thing and mean another', or in other words, they are metaphors in the *marked* sense that I have distinguished. It is in keeping with my theme in this article, that the impact of myth on convention is destructive and displacing rather than supportive, that Jackson invokes Fletcher's definition of allegory: 'It destroys the normal expectation we have about language, that our words "mean what they say"' (1964: 2). Allegory and metaphor have this pathological effect on language, rendering permeable the ordinarily opaque boundaries of convention, and exposing them as subject to performative and particularizing influences rather than immutable superorganic constraints. Myth, then, is as much like literature in its imaginative innovation upon conventional moral significances, as it is the science of semantic analogy that structuralism would make of it.

To put it another way, anthropologists have characteristically appropriated to themselves the responsibility for articulating the 'secrets' of any given culture, in the form of symbolic equivalences to which their analyses give them special access – structural analysis is our form of 'magic'. But for people like the Foi and Barasana, their magical equations are not open-ended; they are bounded by the myths and rituals that frame them. Let us then compare in several cases the contextualization of mythical and magical utterances.

MYTH AND MAGIC

I have been arguing that language always has an enframing skin around it. This boundary can be the contours of the human body, or the geography of an inhabited region, but it can also be another discursive shape – myths provide the limits to other myths as well as to other forms of speech. My suggestion is that a metaphor seals symbolic representation off from unlimited semantic expansion.

I can illustrate what I mean by reference to the relationship between myths and their associated magic spells among the Foi. It was only after I had listened to and translated many myths that my hosts were able to explain to me the relationship between myth and the corpus of magical formulae called *kusa*. The basic format of all Foi magic spells is as follows:

I am not doing *x*.
I am doing *y*.

Or, to rephrase it in another common form:

This is not an *x*.
This is a *y*.

For example, in a spell uttered while planting a new sago sucker, a man might say:

I am not planting this sago sucker.
I am planting the skull of the boy Tononawi.

Tononawi is the name of a character in a myth which accounts for the origin of one of the first and most common varieties of sago that the Foi possess (see Weiner 1988: ch. 10). If one inspects the overt content of the myth, it has little to do with the origin of sago. In analysing the myth I suggested that its theme centres on the kind of reciprocity that surrounds revenge killing and the way in which this kind of reciprocity is reserved for men of high status.

605

Only men who know the spell would be aware of the magical power of Tononawi's name, while for others the myth would be just another story.

F. E. Williams, who was the first anthropologist to work among Foi speakers of Lake Kutubu shortly after they were contacted in 1935, reported that they made a distinction between myths of fundamental importance, which were hedged with secrecy (called *hetagho*), and those which were narrated chiefly for purposes of entertainment (called *tuni*). During my fieldwork between 1979 and 1988, I never heard the Foi people of Hegeso village (which is not part of the Lake Kutubu region), where I worked, use the term *hetagho*. They called all their myths *tuni*, even the ones I later found out had associated, secretly known, magic spells. I heard very few stories that belonged in the first category Williams described − or so I thought at first. At least in theory, so the Foi men of Hegeso told me, every magic spell has a myth associated with it. A magic spell, on the other hand, is individual property and spoken to no other person, except in the act of its transfer for payment, like any other valuable. But *tuni* are above all for public narration; the longhouse is the most common and perhaps the only socially approved setting for their telling. Because the spells themselves were jealously guarded personal property, their relationship to mythology was not known by all Foi men. *Tuni* might be a term for a myth that has become severed from the spell which is its kernel, the Foi key to its significance.

The myth provides the (unknown) ground of the analogy articulated in the magic spell; likewise, the 'story' of the magic spell is the detached myth. The Foi hide the relationship between the two from each other, so as to allow the discovery of the connection between them to exert a more pronounced effect on their world of meaning.

The magic spell, in the detotalizing series of analogies it repetitively articulates, depicts analogy and resemblance as unbounded. The power of the spell lies in the opening up of the power of resemblance generally and in the capacity for repetition and replication made possible by resemblance. In a magic spell, a Foi man is asserting that an analogy exists, and that the recognition of this analogy encompasses a source of power. The discursive force of the myth, on the other hand, lies in the way it closes off a series of images, shows the arbitrary limits of conventional analogy itself, and works to efface the difference between convention and innovative impingement.

Like the Foi, the Kalauna of Goodenough Island, Papua New Guinea, possess a class of myths, *neineya*, which contain their most important magical formulae. '*Neineya* give title to and provide narrative vehicles for systems of magic concerned with weather control, crop fertility, gardening prowess, and the suppression of hunger' (Young 1983: 12). But unlike the Foi myths, these Kalauna stories are *not* for public narration; a *neineya* story can be narrated publicly *as* a story only if the speaker omits the secret names, spells and other information that would indicate its magical significance.

These myths are the property of individual men, the pre-eminent magicians of the different Kalauna clans, who pass them on to their heirs along with other heritable wealth. But in taking responsibility for the magic of fertility which the myths contain, these men, the *toitavealata* (those 'who look after the village', Young 1983: 53), take on the personalities of the mythical characters themselves – Kalauna biography thus becomes the unravelling of the life of a magician and of the myth whose collective significance he personally embodies in his actions. But far from using them solely to promote the collective welfare of the community, these umbrageous magicians use the magic to avenge themselves upon their competitors. They seek to demonstrate their own supremacy, that of their clans and of their magic by withholding fertility spells or, conversely, by invoking the dark magic of gluttony (*tufo'a*) and famine (*loka*). The myths thus become not charters for group cohesion, but images of individual assertiveness. 'Through their myths,' Young writes, 'not only did [the magicians] legitimize their roles and personal identities, they also attempted to enforce a consensus of their qualities and powers' (p. 261). As each Foi myth differentiates itself by presenting a particular and pre-emptive interpretation of sociality, so do the magicians of Kalauna seek to obviate their competitors' mythical claims to the magical basis of Kalauna social prosperity. The myth-teller in *any* culture is a magician, because he or she discursively recreates the lineaments of convention in the act of narration itself.

But the relationship between myth and magic also invokes the problem of discrete contexts – their utterance is demarcated by pragmatically ordained rules, revealing 'secrecy' as both a discursive and a symbolic phenomenon. In all cases, the myth-telling event is rigidly separated from the domain of quotidian activity. Kuranko storytellers said that they were prohibited from relating their tales during the day, lest one of their parents should die. The Foi told me that it was traditionally believed that if one told myths during the day, one's anus would close up and one would be unable to defecate. And of course, the circumspection surrounding the telling of Kalauna myths is obvious, since they are personal property and the formulae entailed within them have magical power. 'So consequential are such myths that even truncated narrations are believed to evoke a cosmic response (*towava*) of thunder, lightning and rain' (Young 1983: 12). It seems that not only do myths exist outside language, they also exist outside a certain domain of *parole*, of 'speech' itself.

But because myth is part of the linguistic condition itself, although it stands outside of *parole*, it is constrained by performative considerations that embody the very social significance on which it comments. Like its message, the telling of a myth encompasses its own social context: it 'sets down' its narrator and audience even as the storyteller 'sets down' the pebbles of significance that intersubjectively fuse speaker and hearer.

In his concluding chapter to *Allegories of the Wilderness*, Jackson says that:

For me, one of the most arresting aspects of everyday life in a Kuranko village is

607

the great amount of time people devote to the intense discussion of matters which to a stranger often seem trivial, time-consuming, and even pointless....

The delight with which people initiated argument and the volubility of their discourse seemed quite baffling to me, until I realized that speech was one of the keys to understanding the tenor and purpose of Kuranko social life.

(1982: 261)

This situation can be contrasted with that of the Foi, among whom public knowledge is *not* articulated communally through *dialogue*, but individually, through *rhetoric*: the set of special insights and veiled allusions which are the prerogatives of men of high status. Like magical formulae, the figures of speech that Foi men of prestige employ contain metaphorical equations that afford an insight into the relationship between putatively separate domains of power and efficacy. Their deployment in any given political confrontation lends these equations particular significance, especially if, when used successfully, they can convey messages at two different levels at once. Speech therefore does more than communicate messages; it forms the integument of social and individual identities and is the raw material for their constitution and presentation. The volubility of the Kuranko community and the reticence of the Kalauna *toitavealata* are rendered intelligible in this light, for they are each placed within cultural settings that define the limits and power of conventional discourse in radically different ways. To what is speech opposed if not secrecy? Secrecy is not merely the absence of information, but a message in its own right, conveying the idea that the power to perceive and establish analogy has social consequences and should be restricted.

For the Foi, the notion of secrecy itself reveals the manner in which their culture is articulated. For Foi men, the metaphoric equations that underlie the power of magic, cult, sorcery and oratory are not consciously *created*, they are *discovered*. The equations exist by virtue of an undifferentiated cosmos that admits of the free transfer of qualities between domains. These equations only assume a role in maintaining personal power when they are hoarded or guarded by individual men; when their transcendent reality is channelled into maintaining individual power and identity.

Like the restricted flow of wealth objects and the procreative potential that is an aspect of it, secrecy is the result of restricting the flow of analogy or metaphor itself − indeed, the constraint and secrecy that accompany Foi betrothal and marriage arrangements may be understood in this light. They are part and parcel of a cultural tradition that takes differentiation and restriction to be the domain of human intention and action.

Myth, then, becomes public because its insights and equations are elusive, not baldly and syntagmatically stated as in a magic spell. Whereas a magic spell is hidden because of what it reveals, myths are revealed precisely because of what they hide: the creation of morality and human convention out of the particular actions and dilemmas of archetypal characters.

Malinowski (1954) asserted that myths were charters for the permanence and stability of a society; that they elucidated immutable truths and premisses which provided the guidelines for community morality. I would prefer to see each storyteller and native mythopoet as providing his or her own charter, his or her own theory of sociality. Just as the Ndembu ritual expert blazes his own exegetical trail by breaking the branches along the paths of conventional wisdom, so is the Kuranko storyteller the *til'sale*, the 'one who sets down stories' (Jackson 1982: 50).

The characters of myth 'live' a certain parody of Foi or Kuranko or Barasana culture. By the same token, Young maintains that Kalauna magicians are 'living myths' (perhaps in the same sense that Aboriginal Australians live in particular Dreamings that bear some determinate relationship to each other). The founding ancestors of the Kalauna 'anchored' each clan to its territory through the magic of stasis and permanence, *bakibaki* (Young 1983: 44). The leading magicians must promote this permanence through their deployment of garden magic. When they do so, the magicians are spoken of as '"sitting still" in order to anchor the community in prosperity' (Young 1983: 4). Whereas the Kuranko and Ndembu storytellers lay down or break their own trails, Kalauna myths set down the myth-tellers themselves.

The characters of Foi myth 'live' through the magic spells to which their names give power; Kalauna magicians, in their outbursts of self-destructive vengeance (called *unuwewe*), their scrupulous adherence to productive protocols, and their recognition of the social impetus behind their competitive exchanges, publicly 'live' the collective significances of myth. By demonstrating their personal efficacy, they maintain the viability and fertility of the village; it is the very competition among themselves that ensures their zeal in demonstrating the success of their fertility magic. The other side of the coin of *manumanua*, garden fertility, is the destructive sorcery of famine which destabilizes a village so that its members are forced to wander in search of food.

If Kuranko narratives 'express the conventional wisdom of the collectivity through ... individual perspectives' (Jackson 1982: 262), then Foi myths do precisely the reverse: they dislocate convention, as Wagner puts it (1978: 255), by their particularizing effect upon it. For the Kalauna, this particularization becomes the very point at which social and political efficacy and identity are articulated, for the secret of Kalauna myth is that its significances are *not* shared, but are hoarded in the interests of personal ritual ascendancy.

Myth in these societies 'works' not by upholding conventional orders but by impinging upon them; by particularizing what is at any given time contrastively identified as some collective image of sociality. I say 'at any given time' deliberately, to stress that the effect of such collective representations is only possible in so far as they assume the force of reality for those individuals seeking to discover their lineaments. Myth is a discovery procedure *par excellence* (like the tools of structural analysis we bring to make it visible as such). The secrets of myth are not self-evidently political in function in all societies, nor are they necessarily concerned with social control. What they do control is something rather more personal – as Wagner describes it, 'a point of power formed by discourse ... that welds individual and social into a living, moving destiny' (1985: 205).

NOTE

1 By way of an aside, we can note the similarity between such statements and the view advocated by Radcliffe-Brown and a subsequent generation of British social anthropologists, that institutionalized beliefs and practices are founded on a need to preserve the social order. One might say, as did Lévi-Strauss, that things become sacred when they are ordered: 'Sacred objects therefore contribute to the maintenance of order in the universe by occupying the places allocated to them' (1966: 10). From this point it is a small step indeed to the ideas of Mary Douglas (1966) concerning the ritual potency of the boundaries separating one category from another.

REFERENCES

Bateson, G. (1972) *Steps to an Ecology of Mind*, New York: Ballantine Books.

Boas, F. and Hunt, G. (1916) *Tshimshian Mythology*, Bureau of American Ethnology, 31st Annual Report, 1909–10, Washington, DC: Smithsonian Institute.

Burridge, K. (1969) *Tangu Traditions*, Oxford: Clarendon Press.

Calame-Griaule, G. (1986) *Words and the Dogon World*, trans. D. LaPin, Philadelphia: Institute for the Study of Human Issues.

Clifford, J. (1982) *Person and Myth: Maurice Leenhardt in the Melanesian World*, Berkeley: University of California Press.

Douglas, M. (1966) *Purity and Danger*, London: Routledge & Kegan Paul.

Durkheim, E. (1976 [1915]) *The Elementary Forms of the Religious Life*, trans. J. W. Swain, London: George Allen & Unwin.

Fletcher, A. (1964) *Allegory: The Theory of a Symbolic Mode*, Ithaca: Cornell University Press.

Geertz, C. (1973) *The Interpretation of Cultures*, New York: Basic Books.

Griaule, M. (1965) *Conversations with Ogotommeli*, London: Oxford University Press.

Guidoni, E. (1975) *Primitive Architecture*, London: Faber & Faber.

Hugh-Jones, S. (1979) *The Palm and the Pleiades*, Cambridge: Cambridge University Press.

Jackson, M. (1982) *Allegories of the Wilderness*, Bloomington: Indiana University Press.

—— (1989) *Paths Toward a Clearing*, Bloomington: Indiana University Press.

LaFlesche, F. (1917–18) *The Osage Tribe: Rite of Vigil*, 39th Annual Report, 1917–18, Washington DC: Smithsonian Institute.

Leenhardt, M. (1979) *Do Kamo: Person and Myth in a Melanesian World*, Chicago: University of Chicago Press.

Lévi-Strauss (1963) *Totemism*, Boston: Beacon Press.

—— (1966) *The Savage Mind*, New York: Basic Books.

—— (1969) *The Raw and the Cooked* (*Mythologiques*, vol. 2), New York: Harper & Row.

—— (1976) 'The story of Asdiwal', in *Structural Anthropology*, vol. 2, New York: Basic Books.

—— (1981) *The Naked Man*, New York: Harper & Row.

Malinowski, B. (1954) *Magic, Science and Religion*, Garden City, NY: Doubleday Anchor Books.

Myers, F. (1986) *Pintupi Country, Pintupi Self*, Washington: Smithsonian Institute.

Schrempp, G. (1992) *Magical Arrows: The Maori, the Greeks, and the Folklore of the Universe*, Madison: University of Wisconsin Press.

Turner, V. (1967) *The Forest of Symbols*, Ithaca, NY: Cornell University Press.

Wagner, R. (1978) *Lethal Speech: Daribi Myth as Symbolic Obviation*, Ithaca, NY: Cornell University Press.

—— (1985) Review of M. Young, *Magicians of Manumanua*, *American Anthropologist* 87: 204–5.

Walens, S. (1981) *Feasting with Cannibals*, Princeton, NJ: Princeton University Press.

Weiner, J. (1988) *The Heart of the Pearl Shell: The Mythological Dimension of Foi Sociality*, Berkeley: University of California Press.

—— (1991) *The Empty Place: Poetry, Space and Being among the Foi of Papua New Guinea*, Bloomington: Indiana University Press.

—— (1992) 'Against the motion II', in T. Ingold (ed.) *Language is the Essence of Culture*, Group for Debates in Anthropological Theory no. 4, Department of Social Anthropology, University of Manchester.

Young, M. (1983) *Magicians of Manumanua: Living Myth in Kalauna*, Berkeley: University of California Press.

FURTHER READING

Baal, J. van (1966) *Dema: Description and Analysis of Marind-anim Culture (South New Guinea)*, The Hague: Martinus Nijhoff.

Berndt, R. (1952) *Djanggawul*, Melbourne: F. W. Cheshire.

Douglas, M. (1966) *Purity and Danger*, London: Routledge & Kegan Paul.

Fernandez, J. (1982) *Bwiti: An Ethnography of the Religious Imagination in Africa*, Princeton, NJ: Princeton University Press.

Gus, D. (1989) *To Weave and Sing*, Berkeley: University of California Press.

Heusch, L. de (1982) *The Drunken King: or, The Origin of the State*, Bloomington: Indiana University Press.

Hugh-Jones, C. (1979) *From the Milk River*, Cambridge: Cambridge University Press.

Lawrence, P. (1956) *Road Belong Cargo*, Manchester: Manchester University Press.

Leach, E. (1976) *Culture and Communication*, Cambridge: Cambridge University Press.

Leenhardt, M. (1979) *Do Kamo: Person and Myth in the Melanesian World*, Chicago: University of Chicago Press.

LeRoy, J. (1985) *Kewa Tales*, Vancouver: University of British Columbia Press.

—— (1985) *Fragmented World: An Analysis of Kewa Tales*, Vancouver: University of British Columbia Press.

Lévi-Strauss, C. (1963) 'The effectiveness of symbols', in *Structural Anthropology*, vol. 1, New York: Basic Books.

—— (1979) *Myth and Meaning*, New York: Schocken Books.

Mimica, J. (1988) *Intimations of Infinity: The Cultural Meanings of the Iqwaye Counting System and Number*, Oxford: Berg.

Morphy, H. (1991) *Ancestral Connections*, Chicago: University of Chicago Press.

Munn, N. (1969) 'The effectiveness of symbols in Murngin rite and myth', in R. Spencer (ed.) *Forms of Symbolic Action*, Seattle and London: University of Washington Press.

—— (1973) *Walbiri Iconography*, Ithaca, NY: Cornell University Press.

Reichel-Dolmatoff, G. (1971) *Amazonian Cosmos*, Chicago: University of Chicago Press.

Sahlins, M. (1976) *Historical Metaphors and Mythical Realities*, Ann Arbor: University of Michigan Press.

Wagner, R. (1972) *Habu: The Innovation of Meaning in Daribi Religion*, Chicago: University of Chicago Press.

—— (1981) *The Invention of Culture*, Chicago: University of Chicago Press.

22

RITUAL AND PERFORMANCE

Richard Schechner

Rituals are performative: they are acts done; and performances are ritualized: they are codified, repeatable actions. The functions of theatre identified by Aristotle and Horace – entertainment, celebration, enhancement of social solidarity, education (including political education), and healing – are also functions of ritual. The difference lies in context and emphasis. Rituals emphasize efficacy: healing the sick, initiating neophytes, burying the dead, teaching the ignorant, forming and cementing social relations, maintaining (or overthrowing) the status quo, remembering the past, propitiating the gods, exorcising the demonic, maintaining cosmic order. Theatre emphasizes entertainment; it is opportunistic, occurring wherever and whenever a crowd can be gathered and money collected, or goods or services bartered. Rituals are performed on schedule, at specific locations, regardless of weather or attendance. They mark days and places of importance (Lent to Easter in Christendom, the half-month leading up to *dasahara* among Hindus, New Year's Day in Japan, Ramadan and the hadj in Islam, and so on); or are hung on life's hinges where individual experience connects to society: rites of passage send people through birth, puberty, marriage, induction, resignation, and death. Ritual texts – verbal, musical and theatrical – are fixed and often sacred. When improvisation is encouraged, as in the ritual clowning of native American or African shamans, strict rules govern who the clowns are, whom they aim their laughter at, and what kinds of obscene or other farcical acts they perform.

But this list of differences (not oppositions) does not support the tendency in Western scholarship to suppose that ritual performance precedes or is at the origin of theatre. The Sanskrit text on performance, *Natyasastra* (second century BC to second century AD), is correct on this point. 'In drama there is no exclusive representation of humans or the gods; for the drama is a representation of the states of the three worlds' (i.e. of gods, humans and demons) (Bharata-muni 1967: 14). In other words, far from being limited to the divine, the human or the demonic, the field represented by drama covers *all there is*, all that is possibly conceivable. The inclusiveness posited by the

Natyasastra is confirmed by anthropological evidence. Phenomena that rightly ought to be called 'theatre' or 'dance' occur among all the world's peoples and date back at least to Palaeolithic times. Dancing, singing, wearing masks and costumes; impersonating other people, animals, gods, and demons (and being possessed by these others); acting out narratives; rehearsing or in other ways preparing actions; and making ready places where people can gather to perform and witness performances, are all integral to being human. Theatre and ritual are as night and day, chicken and egg – neither has priority over the other.

PERFORMANCE IN PALAEOLITHIC EUROPE

The earliest known performance spaces are the caves of south-west Europe where, for example at Tuc d'Audoubert, one must 'crawl through claustrophobic low passages to reach the startling footprints of ancient dancers in bare feet and the models of copulating bisons, in clay on the floor beyond' (La Barre 1972: 397). What was going on in this barely accessible theatre (or temple or shrine)? The size and shape of the footprints indicate that the dancers, not yet fully grown, moved crouching in a circle; surviving bone and ivory artefacts indicate that they danced accompanied by percussive sounds and perhaps the roar of bullroarers (Pfeiffer 1982: 180–4). Although it is probable that a ritual was being performed, it is wrong to dismiss the possibility that it also involved self-conscious theatrical display. Recent evidence – chemical analysis of the paints used in the caves – indicates that perhaps 'each prehistoric artist or group of artists had its own hallmark paint recipes just as did the studios of Renaissance Italy' (Wilford 1990: C1).

The caves also show traces of masking and impersonation – of acting in the theatrical sense. The famous 'sorcerer' of Les Trois Frères (Figure 1) is a composite. He has human feet and legs, a lion's or bear's claws, a lion's torso and testicles, a dangling penis that could be human or animal, and a long horse's or wolf's tail. His face, topped by tufted ears and deer's antlers, is twisted sharply to the left, staring directly out through wide owl's eyes. He is in a half-human, half-animal crouching pose, his right foot raised as if dancing. This figure is a masked performer costumed in animal skins. The sorcerer's expression and pose resemble those of a Yaqui deer dancer (Figure 2). Indeed, the function of the Yaqui dance may be close to what was going on deep in Tuc d'Audoubert: a fertility rite. The Yaquis sing to the deer they hunt, asking its permission to make the kill; this is common among hunting peoples, who know that what is taken must be replenished.

By using a self-conscious theatrical display to assure themselves of replenishment, people express a double desire: first, to be in a positive relationship to natural forces, and second, to be able to invent symbolic, representational techniques – theatre, if you will – that successfully put them into such a relationship. In other words, the representations – the rituals, paintings and dances – become the focus of attention preceding and following any number of direct encounters with 'nature'. Nature is thus mediated by means of performative representation. This invention of consciously symbolic action – the mastery of the artist – is experienced not only as functional ritual but also as entertainment. Entertainment is meant here in its fullest sense: actions enjoyed not only for what they can achieve beyond the setting of the performance itself, but also for the sheer pleasure that they bring in the here and now. Thus probably in the Palaeolithic epoch, as in today's world, fun was an intrinsic part of ritual performance. The tendency to deny this has more to do with the anti-theatrical bias of Judaeo-Christian and Islamic traditions (see Barish 1981) than with anything else. Indeed, having a good time is integral to many ritual performances, including Christian ones influenced by

Figure 1 The 'sorcerer' of Les Trois Frères. Drawing by the Abbé Breuil (1952: 166)

Figure 2 Young deer dancer from the Yaqui Pacua pueblo near Tucson, Arizona. (Photo: Richard Schechner)

non-Christian attitudes and practices. In African-American churches the singing, dancing, trancing, and sharing of food is a braid of entertainment and ritual. Many black entertainers began their careers in the church. African religions as well as Hinduism and Shinto integrate ritual and theatre.

GATHERING AND HUNTING CIRCUITS, CEREMONIAL CENTRES, THEATRES

The earliest human societies were gathering and hunting bands. These were neither primitive nor poor. The best evidence suggests an abundance of food, small families (birth control was practised), and an established range. Humans did not live in one spot, nor did they wander aimlessly. Each band had its own circuit, a more or less fixed route through a known time–space. I call it 'time–space' because the hunting routine was not haphazard; it took into account the movements of game, weather patterns, and geographic features. The cultural level of people by 25,000 BC – as evidenced by their painting and sculpting – was very high: the cave art of south-west Europe and the mobile art of Eurasia are testimony enough. In brief, humans occupied an eco-logical niche that kept bands on the move in regular, repetitious patterns, fol-lowing game, adjusting to the seasons, creating art and ritual.

Indeed the pattern was repetitious beyond modern imagination. Certain decorated caves were in continuous use for more than ten thousand years. What kinds of use? Human bands numbered from forty to seventy individuals, occupying adjacent or overlapping ranges. For most of the year bands prob-ably met only occasionally, by chance, or to exchange information and goods. Maybe relations between some bands were hostile. But arguing by analogy from the few gathering and hunting peoples that survive today – the celebra-tions of the !Kung San of the Kalahari, the ceremonies of Aboriginal Australians – we may infer that at special times when game was plentiful in an area, when edible roots, fruits, and nuts were ripe, a concentration of bands took place. Today as well, the farming and hunting peoples of highland Papua New Guinea stage elaborate 'payback' or exchange ceremonies on a regular basis (Rappaport 1968, Schechner 1988). Pilgrimages, potlatches, and family reunions marked by feasting and the exchange of gifts all play out the same basic pattern.

Even non-human primates engage in similar activities. Ethologists V. and F. Reynolds report that six times in the Bundongo Forest of Uganda they wit-nessed what the locals call a *kanjo*, or carnival, of chimpanzees:

> The 'carnivals' consisted of prolonged noise for periods of hours, whereas ordinary outbursts of calling and drumming lasted a few minutes only. Although it was not possible to know the reason for this unusual behaviour, twice it seemed to be associated with the meeting at a common food source of bands that may have been relatively unfamiliar to each other. ... Calls were coming from all directions at once and all groups concerned seemed to be moving about rapidly. As we oriented the source of one outburst, another came from another direction. Stamping and fast running feet were heard sometimes behind, sometimes in front and howling out-bursts and prolonged rolls of drums (as many as 13 rapid beats) shaking the ground surprised us every few yards.
>
> (1965: 408–9)

The Reynolds are not sure what the 'carnivals' are for. They think they may signal a move from one food source to another – *kanjo*s occur when edible fruits are ripe. Might these *kanjo*s be prototypes of celebratory, theatrical events? Their qualities are worth noting: (1) a meeting of bands whose members are neither totally familiar nor total strangers; (2) sharing food or, at least, a food source; (3) rhythmic movement and sound making – if not yet singing, dancing and drumming at least something akin to entertainment or celebration; (4) using a place that is not 'home' for any group.

Where two or more groups assemble on schedule, where there is abundant food available, and where there is a landmark – a cave, hill, waterhole, or whatever – there a ceremonial centre is likely to develop (Figure 3). A key difference separating human from ape ceremonial centres is that only humans permanently transform a space by 'writing' on it or attaching a spoken lore to it. The painting and sculpting preserved in the cave art of Palaeolithic Europe (as well as of Australia, and in the more recent cave and rock art from Africa and the Americas) was a way of transforming natural spaces into cultural places, a way of making theatres. The 'writing' need not be visual; it can be oral, as with so much Aboriginal Australian lore, which transforms rocks, waterholes, and barely visible paths into repositories of narrative and performative knowledge (see Gould 1969). Or similarly, but in an environment as different as can be imagined from the Australian desert, the Mbuti of Zaire move confidently through the rainforest singing and dancing their Molimo (Turnbull 1962, 1985, 1990). The Molimo is characterized by the sound of

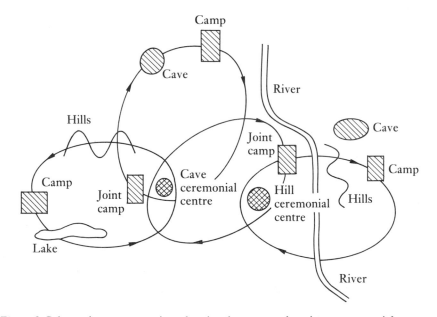

Figure 3 Schematic representation showing how camp locations, ceremonial centres and landscape features might have related to each other in the annual cycles of movement of hunter–gatherer bands during the Palaeolithic epoch. It is my contention that ceremonial centres emerge where bands regularly come close to each other at geographically significant sites such as hills, caves, river crossings, and so on. (After Schechner 1988: 156)

a wooden trumpet. The trumpet-Molimo, hidden

> vertically in a tree near the sacred centre of the forest, moves towards the camp, relocating the sacred centre as it breathes air, drinks water, is rubbed with earth, and finally manifests itself over fire. At this point the sanctity of the forest centre envelops the camp.
>
> (Turnbull 1985: 16)

The Australian and Mbuti cases teach us to be cautious about assuming that an area that contains little visual evidence of high art is necessarily artistically bereft. Music, singing, acting, storytelling, and dancing leave few traces.

Sometimes what appears to the uninitiated to be an ordinary landscape is a world fully marked and populated to those who understand it. Bruce Chatwin (1988) writes of the 'songlines' that cross Aboriginal Australia, marking the journeys of the Dreamtime Ancestors who, at the start of time and history, transformed themselves into the hills, rocks, riverbeds, trails, and other landmarks which are still visible today. Aboriginal people who are ritually educated and fully initiated can read the living geography in very precise ways both practically and mythically. The Ancestral Beings not only formed the world, they also sang and devised the first rituals:

> The Ancients sang ... the rivers and ranges, salt-pans and sand dunes. They hunted, ate, made love, danced, killed: wherever their tracks led they left a trail of music. They wrapped the whole world in a web of song.
>
> (Chatwin 1988: 81–2)

From a traditional Aboriginal view, today's people ought not to disrupt the landscape, but should live in close harmony with it. As Gould has put it:

> The desert Aborigines do not seek to control the environment in either their daily or their sacred lives. Rituals of the sacred life may be seen as the efforts of man [sic] to combine with his environment, to become 'at one' with it.
>
> (Gould 1969: 128)

We might go so far as to say that the entire landscape of Aboriginal Australia is itself a 'total work of art', a world constructed and infused with particular meanings. But this is to understand 'art' in a sense very different from that enshrined in the Western tradition, according to which it entails the conscious human transformation of 'raw' or 'natural' material in the production of 'artefacts'. From the traditional Aboriginal perspective, however, the distinction between what is natural and what is artificial does not apply; rather, the whole natural world is a reminder of the power of transformation exercised by the Dreamtime Ancestors. Aboriginal art, in so far as it is produced by living people, is thus not so much 'creative' as evocative of what is always in danger of being forgotten if it is not insistently reperformed. Lamentably, this traditional approach to the land and to performance is no longer widespread in Australia, or for that matter elsewhere. It has been overwhelmed by

Western economies and power relations, and by Christian or Islamic religious ideologies.

A theatre is a place to enact not only modern artworks, but also these kinds of evocative performances. This kind of place did not arrive late in human culture, say with the Greeks, but was there at least from Palaeolithic times. The first theatres were ceremonial centres; they were not 'natural spaces' (such as Bundongo Forest where the chimpanzees carnivalled) but 'cultural places', a synthesis of humanly modified landmarks, calendrically marked time, and predictable social interactions. It is impossible to ascertain the details concerning *mise-en-scène*, dancing and acting styles, costumes, masks, music, and so on, nor can we know exactly what the functions of the performances were. More often than not theories of what went on and why suit the tastes of the reconstructor: suggestions include initiation, healing, burial rites, fertility rites, and so on. In addition to the above ideas, there is much to be said for the view of Rappaport (1968) and Kertzer (1988): that performances of ritual regulate or even create economic, political and religious relations among peoples who are ambivalent about each other. As Rappaport puts it, 'ritual, particularly in the context of a ritual cycle, operates as a regulating mechanism in a system, or set of interlocking systems' (1968: 4).

Extrapolating from the evidence and opinions at hand, the performances at ceremonial centres functioned in at least the following ways: (1) to create or maintain friendly relations; (2) to exchange goods, food, mates, techniques; (3) to show, enjoy, and exchange dances, songs, stories. These meetings followed an obvious but important overall pattern beginning with the gathering of the groups, followed by specific performances, exchanges of goods and information and the sharing of food, and ending with the dispersal of the participants. People came to a special place, did something that could only be done at that place, something that could be called 'theatre' (and/or 'dance and music') and went on their separate ways. Simple and obvious as this constellation of events may seem to be, they are not inevitable when two or more groups approach each other. The groups could avoid each other, meet in combat, or give greeting and pass by as travellers do on a road. The pattern of gathering, performing, and dispersing is a specifically theatrical one.

HUNTING, RITUAL, PLAYING, AND PERFORMANCE

The 'dramatic' behaviour of groups assembled at ceremonial centres is based more on hunting than on gathering. Hunting is inherently dramatic. A script, not written but well known, sketches out what is supposed to happen: hunters follow agreed strategies designed to culminate in a successful confrontation; the slaughter of an animal is followed by the distribution of meat, cooking, and feasting. The behaviours involved are both agonistic (towards the prey) and co-operative (among the hunters). Signals during the hunt often include deceptive animal-like sounds; sometimes costumes are worn as camouflage or as a magical imitation of the prey. After a successful kill, there is much dancing and feasting as the meat is shared according to particular rules. The feast is followed by total relaxation.

Often, as among the deer-hunting Yaquis of Mexico and Arizona, the prey is thought to give itself willingly to the hunters. The meal following a successful hunt is a communion; sharing the flesh of the kill is a way of acquiring the slaughtered animal's particular powers and genius, as well as of affirming the solidarity of the group eating the meat. Yet we should be wary in our interpretations of such practices. It is all too easy for the interpreter to fall into the trap of attributing some meaning to an event that, in fact, belongs to the interpreter's own deeply held prior narratives. Thus both the view that the confrontation between hunters and prey is violent and agonistic (the dramatic model), and the alternative view which claims a mutuality in the relationship between hunters and prey (the willing sacrifice model), are versions of two strong founding myths of the Western tradition. The violent story is a retelling of humankind's supposedly bloodthirsty carnivorous past ('red in tooth and claw'), while the story of willing surrender leading to a communion of flesh and blood is, of course, the Christ tale.

Hunting demands not only co-operation but also sudden bursts of energy, climaxes balanced against extended periods of stealth and waiting. Besides, it needs a great deal of practice, of learning from more experienced hunters. This is where play comes in – especially creative or 'free play'. One of the qualities of play in higher primates, as observed in the wild, is its balance between improvisation and rule-governed behaviour. In fact, playing is the improvisational imposition of order on events. And where play is not autistic it involves playmates. Although play prepares young novices for more than hunting, hunting is a particularly full use of what play teaches. The most difficult hunts are those where the prey is intelligent and strong. To be successful on such hunts, plans have to be made; the present moment is conditioned by what is presumed to be coming next on the basis both of a knowledge of what happened on previous hunts and of the wisdom of lore. What develops is a game involving the hunters, the prey, and the environment; a game based on past experience told, retold, and learned. Thus not only is hunting itself dramatic: the way young hunters learn is also by not-for-real practice (rehearsal), apprenticeship, and listening to more skilled hunters tell stories (narrative).

Playing is a way not only to learn but also to manage energy. Energy is spent on fighting, mating, determining and keeping hierarchy, defining and defending turf, and hunting. Crises arise sporadically, but when they do, the animal that cannot swiftly mobilize high energy is doomed. Decisively, play allows kinetic potential to be maintained not by being stored but by being spent; and when such energy is spent in playing, the experience is fun. When a crisis arises, an animal is able to meet it by switching play energy into fight energy or hunting energy, for example, and to enjoy doing so. Hunting is a kind of playing-for-real that is strategic, future-and-crisis-oriented, violent and agonistic. It has winners and losers, leaders and followers; it uses costumes and disguises; it has a beginning, middle, and end. Its underlying themes are fertility–replenishment, strength, prowess and leadership. Hunting emphasizes individual or small-group action and teamwork. Transforming hunting or playing-at-hunting into theatre may be a function of what ethologists call 'displacement activity': when two or more conflicting impulses prevent each other from being activated, a different, seemingly unrelated action is performed. So, for example, when members of certain species dare not fight a stronger adversary and cannot flee, they begin intense self-preening. In humans, the conflicting impulses may be the wish to 'hunt' people as against bonds to members of one's own community. The displacement activity is a ritual performance in which humans kill humans, but only in play, 'for fun', or as a sacrifice (see below, pp. 634–5). Or instead of being hunted, loved ones are circumcised, painted, tattooed, scarred, or otherwise marked with signs written upon the body. Through the ordeal of being temporary prey-in-play, the initiated, the sacrificed, or the performer gains the status of the hunter-hunted.

EFFICACY AND ENTERTAINMENT

The relationship between ritual and theatre takes the form of an interplay between efficacy and entertainment. This relationship is both thematic and historical. Efficacy and entertainment are not opposed to each other; rather they form the poles of a continuum:

Entertainment ------------------------ *Efficacy*	
Theatre	**Ritual**
fun	results
for those here now	for a divine Other
performer displays learned skills	performer possessed, in trance
individual creativity	collective creativity
audience watches	audience participates
audience appreciates	audience believes
criticism flourishes	criticism discouraged

Whether a specific performance is 'ritual' or 'theatre' depends mostly on context and function. A performance is called theatre or ritual because of where it is performed, by whom, and under what circumstances. If the performance's purpose is to effect transformations, to heal, or to appease or appeal to transcendent Others (gods, ancestors, divine royalty, etc.) – to get 'results' – then the qualities listed under the heading 'efficacy' will most probably prevail and the performance may be regarded as a ritual. Conversely, if the qualities listed under 'entertainment' prevail, it may be regarded as theatre. No performance, however, is pure efficacy or pure entertainment.

The matter is complex because one can look at specific performances from several vantage points, and to change perspectives is also to change one's characterization of the event. For example, a Broadway musical is entertainment if one concentrates on what happens on stage and in the house. But if the point of view is extended to include rehearsals, backstage activities before, during, and after the show, the function of the roles in the lives of each performer, the money invested by the backers, how the audience arrives and settles in, the reasons spectators are attending (as critics, fun-seekers, or companions), how they obtained their tickets (given by management, purchased as individuals, on expense accounts, as members of a theatre party) and how all this information indicates the use each is making of the performance (as entertainment, as a means to advance careers, as a profit-making enterprise, as a donation), then even a Broadway musical is more than entertainment, it is also ritual, economics, and a microcosm of social structure and process.

In the 1960s and 1970s in the West, artists began to open the theatre-making process to the public. At first this was as simple as showing lighting instruments or doing away with the front curtain (as Brecht urged). But from about 1965 experimenters began to show workshops, rehearsals, and other previously hidden or unconscious procedures. Environmental theatre staging and audience participation became more common (see Schechner 1973). These processual elements of theatre were made problematic, subject to active inquiry. The procedures concerned have to do with the theatre-in-itself; they are, as regards the theatre, efficacious: that is, they are what makes theatre 'theatre', regardless of story, characterization or other 'elements of drama'. Theatre makers discovered reflexivity even as they discarded (temporarily) narrativity. The story of 'how this performance is being made' replaced the story the play would ordinarily have told. This self-referencing, reflexive mode of performing is an example of what Gregory Bateson called 'metacommunication' – signals whose 'subject of discourse is the relationship between the speakers' (Bateson 1972: 178). Theatre's reflexive phase signalled loudly that spectators were to be included as 'speakers' in the theatrical event. Thus it was natural that reflexivity in theatre went hand in hand with audience participation.

Along with the attention paid to the theatrical process, the role of the actor – redefined and expanded as 'performer' – underwent a similarly deep examination. Led by Jerzy Grotowski, Peter Brook, Joseph Chaikin, Eugenio Barba and others, the actor was no longer seen as the mouthpiece of the author working under the guidance (if not complete control) of the director, but as a quasi-shaman, a person of power who could express his or her own feelings, interrogate the author's text and the audience, and serve as a conduit for energies liberated by the theatrical event. These energies do not emanate from written texts but are what Robert Plant Armstrong (writing about Africa) called the 'powers of presence' (1981): alive only in the immediacy of performance. Previously impervious walls separating the genres of music, theatre and dance began to crack. Dancers found their voices, actors mastered difficult movements and vocal techniques, musicians – especially pop musicians – displayed extraordinary *mise-en-scènic* virtuosity.

All this attention paid to the process of theatre-making and to the powers of the performer was a way of ritualizing performance, of making theatre efficacious. In a period when authenticity was, and is, difficult to define, when public life has been theatricalized, the performer was asked to doff his or her traditional masks – to be not an agent of 'playing' or 'fooling' or 'lying' (public masquerades) but one who 'tells the truth'. If not this, then at least she or he should show how the masks are put on and taken off – perhaps in that way educating the public to the theatricalized deceptions practised on them by political leaders and media dons. Instead of mirroring the age, performers were asked to remedy it. The professions taken as models (and frequently enough cited by Grotowski and others) included the priesthood and medicine. No wonder shamanism became so popular: it is that branch of doctoring that is religious, and at the same time the kind of religion that is theatrical.

In the 1960s and 1970s (in the West and in Western-influenced theatre) efficacy usurped the once dominant position of entertainment. Although the 1980s and 1990s have seen an apparent return to the dominance of entertainment, this is not so in reality. First, certain procedures advanced in the 1960s have become commonplace: performance events are routinely staged in 'untheatres', the preparation and 'process' phases of performance are displayed, very personal material is integrated into – or shown side by side with – public and fictional materials, and so forth. Second, many performance artists, as well as practitioners of 'third' or 'alternative' or 'new age' theatre, draw directly on shamanic techniques while involving themselves in creating community celebrations or other ritually efficacious events. Paratheatrical events dissolve the audience–performer dichotomy, while a whole branch of performance aims at eliminating the dichotomy between 'art' and 'life' (Kaprow 1983). Finally, there has been a sea-change in the perception of what is 'theatrical' so that political action, conflictual or disharmonic behaviour on both the personal and the 'social drama' levels, role-playing in everyday life, job training using acting exercises and theatrical simulations all attest to the increasingly complicated interactions between, and continuing convergence of, theatre and ritual.

Figure 4 shows how the history of Western theatre can be given overall shape as a fluctuating relation between efficacy–ritual and entertainment–theatre. This model can be applied to any culture. During each historical period in every culture either entertainment or efficacy is dominant; but the situation is never static: one rises while the other declines. The changes in the relationship between entertainment and efficacy are part of the overall pattern of social change. Performance is more than a mirror of social change, however; it participates in the complex process that *creates* change. For Western theatre, at least, in periods when efficacy and entertainment were both present in

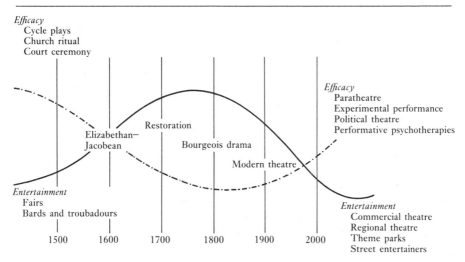

Figure 4 The fluctuating relationship between efficacy and entertainment over time, as exemplified in Western theatre and drama. (After Schechner 1988: 122)

nearly equal degrees, theatre flourished. During these relatively brief historical moments the theatre answers needs that are ritualistic as well as pleasure-giving. Both the Athenian theatre of the fifth century BC and that of Elizabethan England show this kind of convergence.

In the twelfth century, Honorius of Autun wrote:

> It is known that those who recited tragedies in theatres presented the actions of opponents by gestures before the people. In the same way our tragic author [i.e. the celebrant] represents by his gestures in the theatre of the Church before the Christian people the struggle of Christ and teaches to them the victory of his redemption. [Honorius then compares each movement of the Mass to an equivalent movement of tragic drama.] When the sacrifice has been completed, peace and Communion are given by the celebrant to the people.... Then by the *Ite, missa est*, they are ordered to return to their homes with rejoicing. They shout *Deo gratias* and return home rejoicing.
>
> (Quoted in Hardison 1965: 39–40)

What is extraordinary about Honorius's description is that it is a medieval view, not a backward glance by a modern. Yet Honorius's Mass is familiar to those who have attended avant-garde performances. The medieval Mass used many avant-garde techniques – or, more to the point, experimental theatre uses many techniques drawn from ritual. The medieval Mass was allegorical and stylized rather than naturalistic; it encouraged, even forced, audience participation; it treated time teleologically; it integrated drama, dance, and music; it extended the spatial field of the performance from the church to the roadways to the homes of the congregants. Yet for all this, the Mass was more of a ritual than an entertainment. Why? Because its whole point was efficacy.

As Hardison comments, 'the service ... has a very important aesthetic dimension, but it is essentially not a matter of appreciation but of passionate affirmation' (1965: 77). The Mass was a closed circle embracing the congregation and those officiating, leaving no room for appreciators. Because of its hold on the congregation, and its guarantee of efficacy, the Mass was not theatre in either the classical or the modern sense.

Theatre comes into existence when attendance is voluntary, allowing enough distance to open between spectators and the performers for the former to pass judgement on the latter. The paradigmatic theatrical situation is a group of performers soliciting an audience who may or may not attend. If they dislike what they see, spectators may express their dissatisfaction. And if they stay away, or boo, it is the theatre that suffers, not its audience. In ritual, staying away means rejecting the congregation or being rejected by it (or excommunicated). If only a few are absent, it is they who suffer, but if many stay away the congregation – and the community it represents – is faced with dissolution or schism. Or, to put it another way, the participants in ritual depend on it, while theatre depends on its participants. But the differences are not cut-and-dried. The relationship between performers, spectators, and performance, like that between entertainment and efficacy, is dynamic, moulded by specific social, cultural, and historical developments.

SOCIAL DRAMA/AESTHETIC DRAMA

Victor Turner (1974: 23–59) located 'four main phases of public action', which constitute 'the diachronic profile of social drama': (1) breach, (2) crisis, (3) redressive action, and (4) reintegration or schism. A breach is a violation of 'norm-governed social relations' within a family, work group, village, nation, or set of nations. A crisis is a widening of the breach until 'it becomes coextensive with some dominant cleavage in the widest set of relevant social relations to which the conflicting or antagonistic parties belong. It is now fashionable to speak of this sort of thing as the "escalation" of crisis'. A crisis is a situation that cannot be overlooked, that must be dealt with here and now. Redressive action is what is done to resolve the crisis, to end the conflict. This 'may range from personal advice and informal mediation or arbitration to formal juridical and legal machinery, and, to resolve certain kinds of crises or legitimate other modes of resolution, to the performance of public ritual'. Reintegration is the elimination of the breach that engendered the crisis. If, however, reintegration is not possible, either the problem will fester or there will be a schism. This schism can be creative, as when dissident groups or individuals set out for themselves – whether physically or conceptually – to found new settlements, religions, art movements, or whatever. Turner's model can be applied just as well to two classes of event sequences: social happenings and aesthetic dramas. This comes as no surprise, for Turner derived his processual or dramaturgical model from what he knew about aesthetic drama (as well as drawing on the thought of Max Gluckman, Kenneth Burke, Erving Goffman, and Milton Singer).

Social dramas are always happening. They occur in humdrum ordinary life – divorces, tensions between parents and children, and dozens of other quotidian crises – and they occur as highly publicized 'historical moments', splashed all over the media to be relished by reader–spectators. An historical moment that also figured as social drama was the firing in November 1975 of several cabinet members by U.S. President Gerald Ford in the aftermath of the Watergate scandal. The breach was the fact that Ford was not an elected president – he was appointed by Richard Nixon after Vice-President Spiro Agnew resigned; later Nixon himself resigned. Ford inherited a number of Nixon–Agnew cabinet people. Thus Ford was forced to defend policies he did not originate as well as to bear the stigma of a disgraced administration. At the same time Ford wished to seek the presidency on his own account in 1976. The crisis was the disclosure that American agents planned to assassinate foreign heads of state, and that they had been tapping the phones of many Americans as part of a widespread secret-police apparatus whose operations mushroomed under Nixon. Moreover there was a growing feeling in the nation that Ford was stupid and indecisive (it was commonly joked that he could not walk and chew gum at the same time). The redressive action, as described in the *New York Times* of Monday, 3 November 1975, was typically dramatic (as well as introducing into the White House a person still prominent on the national stage):

> President Ford has dismissed Secretary of Defence James R. Schlesinger and William E. Colby, Director of Central Intelligence, in a major shuffling of his top national security posts. Administration officials said that the President had also asked Secretary of State Henry A. Kissinger to relinquish his post as national security adviser in the White House, but to stay on as head of the State Department. White House officials said that Mr Schlesinger would probably be replaced by the White House chief of staff, Donald H. Rumsfeld, and that Mr Colby's likely successor would be George Bush, the present head of the American liaison office in China.

This redressive action did not end the crisis, but generated further developments ('one thing leads to another'). Vice-Pesident Nelson Rockefcllcr told Ford he would not stand for the vice-presidency in 1976 – meaning he was fired by Ford or preparing to challenge the President for the Republican nomination. Finally, the Secretary of Commerce resigned and was replaced by Elliott Richardson, the one person from the Nixon administration whose reputation was not only untarnished but enhanced. The reintegration phase of this social drama took some time as Ford established 'his own' government in preparation for the 1976 elections (which he lost to Jimmy Carter).

In Turner's four-phase scheme, while the breach may fester for a long time, the critical action can erupt suddenly, unpredictably, because a precipitating event is often the 'straw that broke the camel's back'. Once entrained, redressive actions may continue for a long time and reintegration is not certain. But

627

once a social drama is over, analysts can look back and see what happened, detecting an orderly development of events congruent with Turner's scheme – for, as Sartre once noted, death transforms every life into a destiny. But in the midst of events, things appear to happen suddenly, even haphazardly.

Let us now apply Turner's model to an aesthetic drama, Shakespeare's *Romeo and Juliet*. The breach is the long-standing feud between Montagues and Capulets. The crisis is Romeo and Juliet falling in love with each other at first sight. Romeo recognizes the crisis at once – having kissed Juliet and finding out who she is, he exclaims, 'Is she a Capulet?/O dear account! my life is my foe's debt' (I, v, 22–23). Juliet is equally aware, 'My only love sprung from my only hate!' (I, v, 142). Most of the rest of the play is taken up by the burgeoning crisis met by increasingly dangerous redressive actions. Shakespeare brilliantly counterpoints each note of love against the increasing pressure of discovery and catastrophe. The danger becomes critical when Romeo kills Tybalt, a prominent Capulet. Friar Laurence's plan to get the young lovers out of Verona is classic schismogenesis: the founding of a new social unit in a new place in order to avoid or end conflict. Laurence knows that when Juliet is presumed dead her suit with Paris is ended; after she is buried with the other Capulets, Romeo can carry her to Mantua where there is nothing keeping a Montague from marrying a Capulet. But this is not to be. Throughout the redressive action phase the tension heightens between the lovers' passion for each other and their families' hatred. The action of the play is strung like a tightrope connecting two opposite but identical poles: love and hate. Everyone in the play passionately loves or hates and everyone must take sides, as Laurence does with the lovers, the Nurse with the parents. The play ends in tragedy – but a tragedy teetering on farce as Juliet's false death provokes Romeo to his real one, which precipitates Juliet's.

In all tragedy and many farces (the genre closest to tragedy) redressive action fails to offer the heroes a way out: they end up dead, maimed, and/or exiled – separated from the community but also sacrificed on behalf of the community. Sacrifice is the ritual foundation of tragedy, the necessary prelude to reintegration. At the tomb of their children, Capulet and Montague end their feud; Oedipus's exile heals the Theban plague. It is a depressing drama that does not knit up the unravelled social order. That kind of theatre we know from Samuel Beckett (he was not the first, remember Euripides and Büchner). *Waiting for Godot* is all redressive action; Gogo and Didi have forgotten what (if any) breach and crisis brought them to the appointed place to wait. Painfully yet ludicrously there is no crisis, though one is desired. Reintegration or schism (Godot arriving, their leaving) are out of the question.

What comparisons can be made between President Ford's cabinet shakeup and *Romeo and Juliet*? The hidden structure of the one is the visible structure of the other – not in terms of a plot, but in terms of the underlying rhythm and flow of causation. Figure 5 models the relation of dynamic positive feedback whereby social dramas affect aesthetic dramas, and vice versa. What

Ford and his advisers wished to keep quiet until the 'right' moment, Shakespeare divulges for the delectation of his audience. The world of drama reveals intimate talk and interactions; the world of politics conceals and manipulates events. In *Richard III*, Shakespeare depicts this very duplicity. The visible actions of a given social drama are informed, shaped, conditioned, and guided by the aesthetic principles and specific theatrical-cum-rhetorical devices of the culture depicted. Reciprocally, a culture's visible aesthetic theatre is informed, shaped, conditioned, and guided by that culture's processes of social interaction. This is an interactive theory, not a mimetic one. Aesthetics and social life interact, as depicted in Figure 5. Politicians, lobbyists, militants, terrorists, doctors, lawyers, teachers, whether acting individually or in a group, use theatrical techniques (staging, characterization, scenography, manipulation of reception) to create and manage social events — actions that are consequential, 'real', designed to change the social order or maintain the status quo, to change a person's life or maintain it. The theatre artist uses the consequential actions of social life as the underlying themes, frames, and rhythms of his or her art. Ritual performance, occupying as it does the middle ground between aesthetic drama and social drama, is especially powerful because it equivocates, refusing to be solely aesthetic (for looking only) or social (wholly committed to action now); rituals participate both in the aesthetic and the social, drawing their power from both and operating within both.

Turner very much liked the 'infinity loop' model shown in Figure 5. He used the loop in two essays elaborating his theories of social drama (1982: 61–88; 1990: 8–18):

Notice that the *manifest* social drama feeds into the latent realm of stage drama; its characteristic form in a given culture, at a given time and place, unconsciously, or perhaps preconsciously, influences not only the form but also the content of the stage drama of which it is the active or 'magic' mirror. The stage drama, when it is meant to do more than entertain — though entertainment is always one of its vital aims — is a metacommentary, explicit or implicit, witting or unwitting, on the major social dramas of its social context (wars, revolutions, scandals, institutional changes). Not only that, but its message and its rhetoric feed back into the *latent* processual structure of the social drama and partly account for its ready ritualization. Life itself now becomes a mirror held up to art, and the living now *perform* their lives, for the protagonists of a social drama, a 'drama of living', have been equipped by aesthetic drama with some of their most salient opinions, imageries, tropes, and ideological perspectives. Neither mutual mirroring, life by art, art by life, is exact, for each is not a planar mirror but a matricial mirror; at each exchange something new is added and something old is lost or discarded. Human beings learn through experience, though all too often they repress painful experience, and perhaps the deepest experience is through drama; not through social drama, or stage drama (or its equivalent) alone but in the circulatory or oscillatory process of their mutual and incessant modification.

(Turner 1990: 16–17)

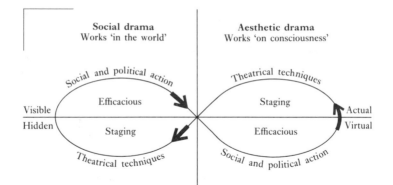

Figure 5 Infinity loop model of the relation between social drama and aesthetic drama. (After Schechner 1988: 190)

To return now to President Ford and *Romeo and Juliet*. Ford's actions were guided by a well-worked-out scenario. At both the conscious and non-conscious level, the President's stage directors planned a phased release of information designed to dramatize Ford as a man of determination, will, strength, purpose, and independence: all qualities expected of a president by Americans. But bumbling Gerry Ford blundered in his social drama (and lost himself the election). This failure was clearly expressed in theatrical terms by the *New York Times* of 4 November 1975:

> The strategy behind Vice President Rockefeller's withdrawal, the dismissal of Defence Secretary James R. Schlesinger and other possible moves yet to come is to put a distinct Ford imprimatur on his Administration's domestic and foreign policies, Administration sources said today.... But this carefully planned scenario went awry yesterday when the dismissals and switches were leaked prematurely to the press.... The leaks gave off highly undesirable and conflicting signals.

Thus what was supposed to show a deft handling of state affairs did the opposite, and the President's 'image' − his theatrical character − suffered.

If aesthetics underlies the script Ford's scenarists composed (but were unable to carry off), politics underlies *Romeo and Juliet*. By making Romeo a Montague and Juliet a Capulet, i.e. members of Verona's leading families, Shakespeare ensures that the young lovers' fate is entwined with the city's core social life. If the lovers were commoners, as in *West Side Story* (the musical based on *Romeo and Juliet*), their plight would be as moving but the effect on the *polis* less strong. Shakespeare's story is richer for being played out against and within the war of their parents − a war that affects everyone in Verona. Shakespeare, like the Greek tragedians and the masters of Japanese *kabuki* theatre, knows how to deploy his dramas of persons in fields of state events. Like a spider's web, what touches one spot vibrates the whole. *West Side Story* similarly embodies its social milieu with its democratizing myths. The field of

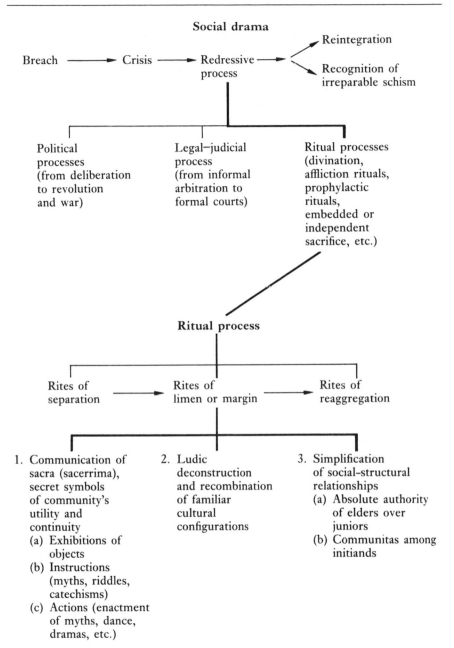

Figure 6 The relationship between social drama and ritual process. (From Turner 1986: 293; reprinted by permission of the University of Arizona Press)

play for both President Ford and Shakespeare is not some abstract legendary community but this or that particular *polis*, tense with contending classes and castes, conflicting interests and rivalries. The Ford drama relates to Shakespeare's at another level, too. The President's handlers used theatrical techniques ranging from how to stage the release of news to how Ford should make up his face, wear his costume, speak his script. Their failure was not of intent but of their abilities as theatre directors. Ford's failure, however, was as a performer.

Turner, on whose ideas I am building, did not believe that aesthetic drama derived from — or was a model of — the whole social drama scheme:

> The world of theatre, as we know it both in Asia and in America, and the immense variety of theatrical sub-genres, derive not from imitation, conscious or unconscious, of the processual form of the complete or 'satiated' social drama — breach, crisis, redress, reintegration, or schisms — but specifically from its third phase, the one I call redress, especially from redress as *ritual* process [see Figure 6].... The third, redressive phase, the reflexive phase, [is] the phase where society pulls meaning from that tangle of action, and, therefore, these performances are infinitely varied, like the result of passing light through a prism. The alternative versions of meaning that complex societies produce are innumerable. Within societies there are different classes, ethnicities, regions, neighbourhoods, and people of different ages and sexes, and they each produce versions which try painfully to assign meaning to the particular crisis pattern of their own society. Each performance becomes a record, a means of explanation. Finally, it should be noted that the interrelation of social drama to stage drama is not in an endless, cyclical, repetitive pattern; it is a spiralling one. The spiralling process is responsive to inventions and the changes in the mode of production in the given society. Individuals can make an enormous impact on the sensibility and understanding of members of society.
>
> (1990: 9–11, 17)

Turner is proposing an evolutionary scheme; I am using the social-drama–aesthetic-drama model structurally.

SACRIFICE AND VIOLENCE

Rituals integrate music, dance and theatre. They use colourful and evocative masks and costumes. The processions, circumambulations, singing, dancing, storytelling, food-sharing, fire-burning, incensing, drumming, and bell-ringing along with the body heat and active participation of the crowd create an overwhelming synaesthetic environment and experience. At the same time, rituals embody values that instruct and mobilize participants. These embodied values are rhythmic and cognitive, spatial and conceptual, sensuous and ideological. In terms of brain function, ritual excites both the right and left hemispheres of the cerebral cortex, releasing pleasure-giving endorphins into the blood. Marx's aphorism, 'religion is the opium of the people', may be literally true. People are more than 'susceptible' to rituals of all kinds — religious, political, sportive, aesthetic; they need the kind of satisfaction only ritual performances can provide, a powerful kind of total theatre.

But why violence? Dramatic narratives, theatrical actions, and religious myths and enactments are so often, and in so many diverse cultures, explicitly violent. At the start of the Western 'great tradition' Queen Clytemnestra murders King Agamemnon (after he has sacrificed their daughter Iphigenia), Agave dismembers her son, Pentheus, and Oedipus kills his father in a rage and then, decades later, when he discovers whom he has murdered, and who his wife is, he rips out his own eyes. Christianity is founded on the torture of crucifixion and propagated by the stories of many martyred saints. Hindu mythology is full of wars and bloodthirsty demons. Even Buddhism – in its Tibetan and Sri Lankan versions – includes the most horrific demons and violent exorcisms. The core drama of shamanism in Asia and the Americas is a perilous journey climaxing in a life-and-death struggle of the shaman against powerful adversaries. Shia Muslims re-enact and mourn with extreme and bloody self-wounding the martyrdom of Imam Hussein, grandson of the Prophet Muhammad. Examples of the conjunction of belief and violence can be multiplied endlessly from every corner of the earth. The English Renaissance's most celebrated dramas feature slaughters such as the one that ends *Hamlet*, gratuitous horrors such as the blinding of Gloucester in *King Lear*, or the multiple atrocities characteristic of Jacobean theatre. The modern repertory is also full of murders, suicides, torture, and 'psychological violence', as even a cursory reading of Ibsen, Strindberg, Pirandello, Brecht, O'Neill, Genet, Shepard, and Churchill shows. The avant-garde, too, seems to delight in assaults on the body, from Chris Burden's famous shootings to Stellarc's suspensions by means of hooks inserted into his flesh. Rituals around the world abound with cutting, scarring, and other painful markings. Farce and popular entertainments, too, from pornography to Grand Guignol, from demolition Derbies to wrestling and horror movies, indulge in chaotic, erotic violence. Violence is endemic to both ritual and aesthetic theatre.

René Girard, in his *Violence and the Sacred* (1977), offers one possible explanation. Girard argues that real violence always threatens the social life of a group:

> Inevitably the moment comes when violence can only be countered by more violence. Whether we fail or succeed in our effort to subdue it, the real victor is always violence itself. The mimetic attributes of violence are extraordinary – sometimes direct and positive, at other times indirect and negative. The more men strive to curb their violent impulses, the more these impulses seem to prosper.
>
> (1977: 31)

Girard goes on to link violence to sexuality:

> Like violence, sexual desire tends to fasten upon surrogate objects if the object to which it was originally attracted remains inaccessible; it willingly accepts substitutes. And again, like violence, repressed sexual desire accumulates energy that sooner or

later bursts forth, causing tremendous havoc. It is also worth noting that the shift from violence to sexuality and from sexuality to violence is easily affected, even by the most 'normal' of individuals, totally lacking in perversion. Thwarted sexuality leads naturally to violence, just as lovers' quarrels often end in an amorous embrace.

(1977: 35)

Girard believes (and I agree) that ritual sublimates violence: 'The function of ritual is to "purify" violence; that is to "trick" violence into spending itself on victims whose death will provoke no reprisals' (1977: 36). All this sounds very much like theatre – especially a theatre whose function is cathartic, a theatre that 'redirects' violent and erotic energies. Cathartic or not, theatre always manufactures substitutes, specializing in multiplying alternatives. Is it accidental that so many of these alternatives combine the violent with the erotic?

The 'sacrificial crisis', as Girard sees it, lies in the dissolution of distinctions within a society – from the erasure of the reciprocal rights and responsibilities of parents towards their children, to the elision of hierarchy. Incest and regicide are radical attacks on differentiation. Girard asserts: 'Wherever differences are lacking, violence threatens' (1977: 57). The enactment of ritual death – whether the victim is actually or theatrically killed – restores distinctions by emphasizing the difference between the victim and the rest of society:

> The surrogate victim plays the same role on the collective level as the objects the shamans claim to extract from their patients play on the individual level – objects that are then identified as the cause of the illness.
>
> (1977: 83)

In theatre the substitutions are more complex than in shamanism, for here the actor is a substitute for a surrogate. The actor who plays Pentheus, Oedipus, Lear, or Willie Loman is not that 'character', which itself is not a 'real person'. There may be no 'real person' at all behind the scenes, but only the play of embodied representations, thus:

[victim] – character – actor :: audience – society

At the place where the actor meets the audience – that is, in the theatre – society faces the sacrificial victim thrice-removed. The audience itself is once-removed from the society which it is part of and represents. Individuals 'leave' society and 'go to' the theatre where they respond to the performance more as a group than as discrete individuals. The social role that spectators play is analogous to the character roles that actors play. At least one of the characters stands in for the sacrificial victim. Thus an actor playing such a character is performing a representation of a representation. In ritual performances two representations are stripped away: there is neither character nor audience. In ritual the encounter is:

[victim] – actor :: society

Or, if a real sacrifice is performed:

victim :: society

A priest performing the Eucharist 'stands for' or 'elevates' Christ while the congregants are Christendom itself. The 'actor :: audience' interface is looser, more given to playfulness, change, and individual creativity than the 'actor :: society' interface. When the victim faces society directly, the actual sacrifice that takes place is usually not of a life. It may be a cutting or scarring or tattooing; or an immersion, the exchange of rings, the giving of a thread or some other painless but irrevocable act. Can an initiate or a bride and groom be regarded as 'victims'? Surely they can, for the shadow of a sacrificial victim lies behind even the most celebratory of ritual actions.

There are ways other than Girard's to explain the apparently universal association of violence, sexuality, ritual and theatre. In *Totem and Taboo* (1962 [1913]) Freud proposed an analogy between the thought of animists, neurotics, children, and artists:

> It is easy to perceive the motives which lead men to practise magic: they are human wishes. All we need to suppose is that primitive man had an immense belief in the power of his wishes.
> Children are in an analogous psychical situation.... They satisfy their wishes in an hallucinatory manner, that is, they create a satisfying situation by means of centrifugal excitation of their sense organs. An adult primitive man has an alternative method open to him. His wishes are accompanied by a motor impulse, the will, which is later destined to alter the whole face of the earth in order to satisfy his wishes. This motor impulse is at first employed to give a representation of the satisfying situation in such a way that it becomes possible to experience the satisfaction by means of what might be described as motor hallucinations. This kind of representation of a satisfied wish is quite comparable to children's play, which succeeds their earlier purely sensory technique of satisfaction.
>
> (1962: 83–4)

This 'omnipotence of thoughts', as Freud called it, makes a world where 'things become less important than ideas of things' (p. 85). Freud believed that neurotics also live in this 'world apart', where 'they are only affected by what is thought with intensity and pictured with emotion, whereas agreement with external reality is a matter of no importance' (p. 86). Freud noted that neurotics undergoing psychoanalysis are 'unable to believe that thoughts are free and will constantly be afraid of expressing evil wishes, as though their expression would lead inevitably to their fulfilment'. In this way, neurotics reveal their 'resemblance to the savages who believe they can alter the external world by mere thinking' (p. 87). Freud, like many of his contemporaries, thought that artists were more like children, neurotics or 'savages' than they were like 'responsible' (male) adults.

Freud was also a cultural evolutionist. He argued for a progression from an animist view of the world to a religious view, and thence to a scientific view:

> At the animistic stage men ascribe omnipotence to themselves. At the religious stage they transfer it to the gods but do not seriously abandon it themselves, for they reserve the power of influencing the gods in a variety of ways according to their wishes. The scientific view of the universe no longer affords any room for human omnipotence; men have acknowledged their smallness and submitted resignedly to death and to the other necessities of nature. None the less some of the primitive belief in omnipotence still survives in men's faith in the power of the human mind, taking account, as it does, of the laws of reality.
>
> (1962: 88)

Each successive stage credits 'external reality' with more autonomy. Yet even as Freud was proposing his evolutionary schema, Niels Bohr and Werner Heisenberg were developing their ideas of indeterminacy – ideas that categorically deny to 'external reality' its independent existence while also denying to the human mind any claims to omniscience.

Freud drew attention to one mode of 'civilized thought' that remains unreconstructed:

> In only a single field of our civilization has the omnipotence of thoughts been retained, and that is in the field of art. Only in art does it still happen that a man who is consumed by desires performs something resembling the accomplishment of those desires and that what he does in play produces emotional effects – thanks to artistic illusion – just as though it were something real. People speak with justice of the 'magic of art' and compare artists to magicians. But the comparison is perhaps more significant than it claims to be. There can be no doubt that art did not begin as art for art's sake. It worked originally in the service of impulses which are for the most part extinct today. And among them we may suspect the presence of many magical purposes.
>
> (1962: 90)

Extinct impulses? Looking at Freud through a contemporary lens means rejecting the notion that some humans are more 'primitive' or 'aboriginal' than others. Biologically and culturally, all individuals of the species *Homo sapiens* share a history of equal duration. Although, as Freud believed, the child might be the father to the man, the so-called primitive is not the child of the so-called civilized. Nor is the neurotic an unreconstructed child–primitive–artist – or vice versa. What we have is a diversity of cultures, none of which is closer to the beginning of human history than any other; and a set of human actions whose similarities with each other are discomforting to those who believe cognitive thinking is the crown of human achievement.

Each culture embodies its own system of organizing experience. Freud can surely be credited with extraordinary insight (even granting the sexist and cultural-imperialist outlook that stains many of his ideas): how, then, can his views be recomposed to harmonize with today's view of things? Perhaps we should say that certain systems are more porous in relation to the subconscious than other systems. But the ways in which this porosity is encouraged or repressed, guarded, regulated, and used differ vastly not only from culture to culture but also within every culture. Children, neurotics, and 'technicians of the sacred' (Rothenberg 1985) each encounter and filter differently what Ehrenzweig (1970) calls 'primary process'. Children are porous to the unconscious because they have not yet learned how to repress material streaming into their emerging consciousness: their selves are in the process of formation. Neurotics are by definition people whose defences are weak or wrongly positioned – but behaviour that might be 'neurotic' in one culture, or in one setting within a given culture, might prove very effective in other contexts. Extremely neurotic people have been not only great artists, but also royals, presidents, tycoons, and war chiefs. Shamans, artists, and others who perform the 'omnipotence of thoughts' seek out teachers and techniques to help them master the powerful impulses streaming into consciousness.

Account after account tells the same story: a future shaman is 'called' but resists the call. But he or she cannot control the experiences 'coming' in the form of dreams, visions, uncontrollable impulses, and sickness. After a period of doubt and terror, the neophyte submits, and finds someone to teach him or her the tricks of the trade. Becoming an artist, even in the West, is not unlike learning to be a shaman; the techniques and the ambivalent social status of artist and shaman approximate each other. In modern Western cultures it might be said that the impulses from which art is made out of the experiences of the artist (the shaman's 'call', the artist's 'raw material') originate in difficult confrontations between daily life and the unconscious. In many cultures such impulses are said to originate with gods, ancestors, demons, ghosts, and the like. I believe these represent material streaming into consciousness as unmediated primary process. The materials of primary process manifest themselves in dreams, visions, obsessive thoughts, trance possession, speaking in tongues, and feared yet violent and erotic wishes. Sometimes these impulses or desires and their manifestations lift the recipient to ecstasy, happy beyond the power of description; and sometimes the recipient is terrified.

Ehrenzweig's theories fit nicely with those of Girard, who believes that lack of differentiation brings about the 'sacrificial crisis' which is remedied by the mimetic violence of ritual. Ehrenzweig celebrates what he calls the 'global vision' of the child – systematically sought after by the adult artist – which

> remains undifferentiated as to its component details. This gives the younger child artist the freedom to distort colour and shapes in the most imaginative and, to us, unrealistic manner. But to him – owing to his global, unanalytical view – his work is realistic.
>
> (1970: 22)

Ehrenzweig sounds like Girard when he says that 'the truly unconscious and potentially disruptive quality of undifferentiation' threatens to introduce 'the catastrophic chaos which we are wont to associate with the primary process' (1970: 37–8). But that which terrifies the neurotic is what the artist plays out publicly. Or, as is frequently the case, the artist–neurotic (or shaman—neurotic) is compelled to explore the very process that terrifies him or her. It is fashionable today to say that artists are healthy whereas neurotics are sick − that ten years of art are worth a psychoanalytic cure (Sartre on Genet). Perhaps. But from an operational perspective art and neurosis are closely linked because both are generated by a porous and shifting boundary between the unconscious and the conscious. And what art manipulates on an individual basis, ritual does collectively. Ritual gives violence its place at the table of human needs. As Kafka noted,

> Leopards break into the temple and drink to the dregs what is in the sacrificial pitchers; this is repeated over and over again; finally it can be calculated in advance, and it becomes part of the ceremony.

> (1954: 40)

NEUROLOGY, RITUAL, PERFORMANCE, AND PLAY

> One may trace the evolutionary progression of ritual behaviour from the emergence of formulation through the co-ordination of formalized communicative behaviour and sequences of ritual behaviour to the conceptualization of such sequences and the assignment of symbols to them by man.
>
> (d'Aquili *et al.* 1979: 37)

D'Aquili and his colleagues propose what they call a 'cognitive imperative': a human being 'automatically, almost reflexively, confronts an unknown stimulus by the question "What is it?" Affective responses such as fear, happiness, or sadness and motor responses are clearly secondary to the immediate cognitive response' (1979: 168). If their thesis is true, then humans work from the top down, from the cerebral cortex (cognition) to the old mammalian brain (feelings) and thence down to the brain stem (movement). The human need to make narratives, to tell plausible stories, is, according to d'Aquili, not only 'hard-wired' into the brain but also dominant. But if the brain works from 'top down' it also works from 'side to side'. The cognitive imperative is dialectically linked to the often very powerful, oceanic, and ecstatic experience of ritual that can be understood as a function of brain lateralization. Barbara Lex, another of d'Aquili's associates, proposes that trance − and other supremely affective states of flow (Csikszentmihalyi 1975) − results from the extreme stimulation of both the ergotropic (left) and trophotropic (right) hemispheres of the brain.

> Exposure to manifold, intense, repetitive, emotion-evoking stimuli ensures uniformity of behaviour in ritual participants.... Rituals properly executed promote a feeling of well-being and relief, not only because prolonged or intense stresses are alleviated, but also because the driving techniques employed in rituals are designed to sensitize or 'tune' the nervous system and thereby lessen inhibition of the right hemisphere and permit temporary right-hemisphere dominance, as well as mixed trophotropic—ergotropic excitation, to achieve synchronization of cortical rhythms in both hemispheres and evoke trophotropic rebound.
>
> (Lex 1979: 120, 144−5)

People seek experiences that provide a 'rebound' or 'spillover', simultaneously exciting both left and right hemispheres of the forebrain (Fischer 1971, Goodman 1986, 1990). Thus the narrativity of the cognitive imperative responds dialectically to the ecstasy of the spill over experience.

These ethological and neurological theories answer some of the questions about ritual performance, but they fail to explain the creative, anti-structural, playful aspects of ritual. Ritual is more than a conserver of evolutionary and cultural behaviour. It is, as Turner (1969) showed, a generator of new images, ideas, and practices. Reviewing the theories of d'Aquili, Turner was troubled by their failure to deal with play:

> As I see it play does not fit in anywhere particular; it is transient and is recalcitrant to localization, to placement, to fixation − a joker in the neuro-anthropological act. ... Playfulness is a volatile, sometimes dangerously explosive essence, which cultural institutions seek to bottle or contain in the vials of games of competition, chance, and strength, in modes of simulation such as theater, and in controlled disorientation, from roller coasters to dervish dancing.... Play could be termed dangerous because it may subvert the left−right hemispheric switching involved in maintaining the social order.... The neuronic energies of play, as it were, lightly skim over the cerebral cortices, sampling rather than partaking of the capacities and functions of the various areas of the brain. As Don Handelman (1977) and Gregory Bateson (1972) have written, that is possibly why play can provide a metalanguage (since to be 'meta' is to be both beyond and between) and emit metamessages about so many and varied human propensities and thus provide, as Handelman has said, 'a very wide range of commentary on the social order' (p. 189). Play can be everywhere and nowhere, imitate anything, yet be identified with nothing.... You may have guessed that play is, for me, a liminal or liminoid mode, essentially interstitial, betwixt-and-between all standard taxonomic nodes, essentially 'elusive'.
>
> (1983: 233−4)

For Turner, play cannot be 'located' because it is quintessentially relational. It is not to be found 'in' the brain (or 'in' culture), but is everywhere 'in between'.

Turner celebrated the anti-structural dimensions of ritual − the playful, the creative, the artistic. But there is a contradiction between his theories and those of the ethologists and neurologists. To them ritual develops as part of evolution, it is 'wired' into the brain. But Turner casts adrift the creative aspects of ritual, placing these 'betwixt and between'. Perhaps this contradiction can be resolved if ritual, the genre, is considered separately from ritualizing, the experience. Ritual can be understood as a performed behavioural artefact, a structure, an armature, while ritualizing can be conceived of as the in-body experience of performing rituals and − as such − anti-structural, destabilizing, and liminal. Ritual organizes, conserves, and narrates, while ritualizing brings on hemispheric spillover, oceanic feelings, and radical, playful volatility.

Turner went far beyond Van Gennep in theorizing that the artworks and leisure activities of industrial and post-industrial societies, which he called

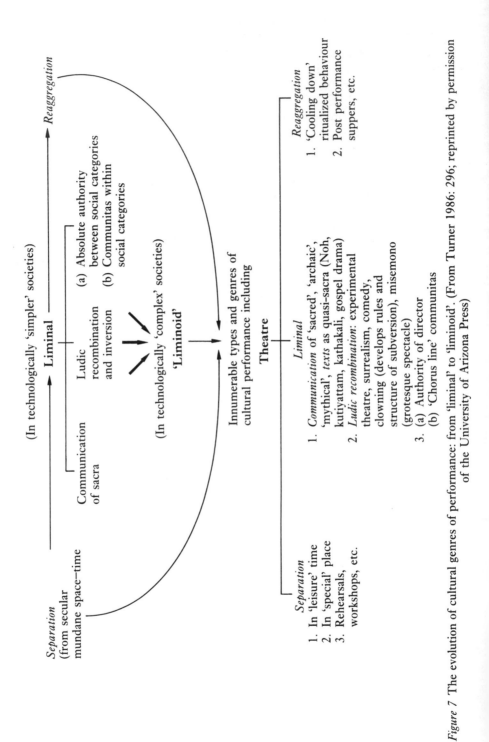

Figure 7 The evolution of cultural genres of performance: from 'liminal' to 'liminoid'. (From Turner 1986: 296; reprinted by permission of the University of Arizona Press)

'liminoid', were like the rituals of tribal, agrarian, and traditional societies (Figure 7).

> Liminality can perhaps be described as a fructile chaos, a fertile nothingness, a storehouse of possibilities, not by any means a random assemblage but a striving after new forms and structure, a gestation process, a fetation of modes appropriate to and anticipating postliminal existence. It is what goes on in nature in the fertilized egg, in the chrysalis, and even more richly and complexly in their cultural homologues.
> Theatre is one of the many inheritors of that great multifaceted system of pre-industrial ritual which embraces ideas and images of cosmos and chaos, interdigitates clowns and their foolery with gods and their solemnity, and uses all the sensory codes to produce symphonies in more than music: the intertwining of dance, body languages of many kinds, song, chant, architectural forms (temples, amphitheatres), incense, burnt offerings, ritualized feasting and drinking, painting, body painting, body marking of many kinds including circumcision and scarification, the application of lotions and drinking of potions, the enacting of mythic and heroic plots drawn from oral traditions. And so much more. Rapid advances in the scale and complexity of society, particularly after industrialization, have passed this unified liminal configuration through the analytical prism of the division of labour, with its specialization and professionalization, reducing each of these sensory domains to a set of entertainment genres flourishing in the leisure time of society, no longer in a central, driving place.... Nevertheless, there are today signs that the amputated specialized genres are seeking to rejoin and to recover something of the numinosity lost in their *sparagmos*, their dismemberment.
>
> (1990: 12)

The workshops in experimental theatre and dance as well as the gropings toward sacred experiences of 'new age shamans' exemplify this effort to rejoin and recover. 'Parashamans' of experimental theatre and dance – Jerzy Grotowski, Eugenio Barba, Peter Brook, and Anna Halprin (to name four of many) – practise aesthetics not simply or even primarily to entertain, but to research, recall, re-enact, and experience sacred knowledge, ritual ecstasy, and initiatory permanence (see Grimes 1982: 255–66, Halprin 1989, Grotowski 1991, Osinski 1991, Winterbottom 1991, Lendra 1991). It is this explicit intention to transform people that has led these and other performance artists to investigate in a most rigorous way the techniques of traditional performers and ritual specialists both within and beyond Western cultures. The practice of the parashamans turns orthodox ritual on its head. Ethological procedures are mimicked, neurological responses are elicited – but in the service of ideas and visions of society that are anything but conservative. Thus has the avant-garde enlisted ritual in art's permanent revolution.

RITUAL PROCESS AND TRAINING, WORKSHOP, REHEARSAL PROCESS

Ritual, aesthetic, and social performances are linked at the fundamental processual level of where performances are made. To 'make believe' and to 'make belief' are closely related. Although the rehearsal process and the ritual process are connected, the terms used to describe them do not fit together neatly. This is because scholars have often treated play, art and religion separately. Preparing to do theatre (or music or dance) often includes memorizing gestures, words, sounds and movements, and achieving a mood

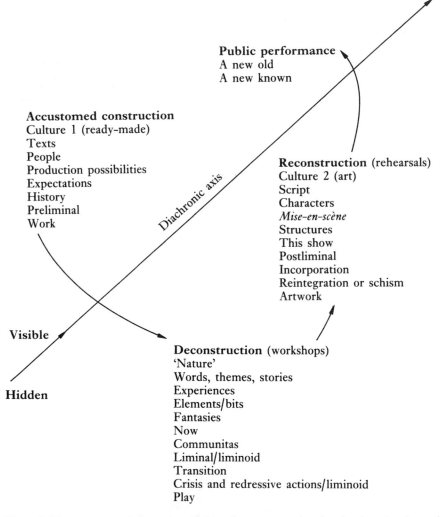

Figure 8 The process of deconstruction and reconstruction in ritual and rehearsal (after Schechner 1985: 288). Once a performance is 'made' it tends to 'slow up' in relation to the diachronic axis. That is, it changes little as time goes on. While in the phases of deconstruction and reconstruction, however, it changes relatively rapidly. Absolutely 'traditional' performances would be 'vertical' relative to the diachronic axis — that is, frozen in time.

where apparently 'external' behaviours 'take over' the performer. Behaviour that is 'other' is transformed into the performer's own behaviour. In some genres — ballet in the West, *kathakali* or noh in Asia — years of rigorous training reshape the performer's body and muscle memories so that she or he is able to enact properly the very particular codes of the art. A similar process of deconstruction and reconstruction trains the spirit, the emotions, and the intellect.

The prepared performer, reformed by training, is further reshaped by workshops and rehearsals leading up to specific performances. Like the neophyte undergoing initiation who is made to fit the society into which he or she is being initiated, the performer is remade first to fit the genre and then for the specific performance at hand. To achieve such a radical change, the performer, like the initiand, is separated from ordinary existence — trained for years by a master or at school, then isolated for weeks or months of intense rehearsals. The period of training and rehearsal is liminal: betwixt and between, belonging neither to ordinary life nor to the finished performance. Old habits, the old body, old ways of thinking and doing are fiercely attacked, deconstructed, and eliminated even as new ways of doing, thinking, and feeling are being built. In many contemporary performing arts not only the performers but also literary or traditional texts — often the most 'honoured' texts of a culture (e.g. Shakespeare, Kalidasa) — are deconstructed and reconstructed. Figure 8 depicts this process.

CONCLUSIONS

Ritual performances, aesthetic performances and social performances are closely related to each other. Ritual is part of the warp and woof of every kind of performance, sacred and secular, aesthetic and social. But, conversely, aesthetic considerations inform ritual performances. For example, the Yaquis of Mexico and Arizona celebrate a Lenten cycle telling the story of Jesus's pursuit, crucifixion, and resurrection, which they call Waehma (Spicer 1980, Schechner 1993). Waehma begins on the first Friday after Ash Wednesday and culminates with the redemption of the whole Yaqui community on Holy Saturday. It combines native American ritual clowns and deer dancers with sixteenth-century Spanish religious theatre, and with the narrative of the Passion introduced to the Yaqui by Jesuit missionaries in the seventeenth century. Waehma employs both outdoor processions around the Way of the Cross and more private ceremonies occurring inside individual homes. Strictly Catholic ritual imported from Europe is balanced against the drama of pre-Columbian native American masked characters called *chapayekas*, who are enlisted in the pursuit and crucifixion of Jesus.

After a series of highly dramatic scenes performed from Palm Sunday to Good Friday, the *chapayekas*, on Good Friday night, led by Judas their saint, celebrate the crucifixion by dancing drunkenly around a crèche or bier containing a small figure of Jesus on the Cross. But sometime during this 'mock Fiesta' Jesus is taken away (soon to be resurrected) and a teddy bear is substituted. By the time the *chapayekas* discover the trick their anger is rendered helpless by drunkenness. But both the anger and the inebriation are played, for during the holy weeks of Lent no Yaqui, least of all those dedicated to the sacred role of *chapayeka*, tastes alcohol. Defeated, the *chapayekas* slink away. But on Saturday morning, joining with their allies the Soldiers of Rome, they storm the church three times in an attempt to recapture Christ. This time the forces of evil are transformed by being drenched with the blood of Jesus – represented by leaves and flowers – showered on them by Pascolas, deer dancers, *matachini* dancers, and a great crowd of spectators. The *chapayekas* discard their masks, which are burned, and rush into the church, not as enemies of Christ, but as Yaqui men desirous of redemption. Kneeling, they receive blessings. Then begins the year's biggest fiesta, featuring deer dancers, Pascolas, and the life-giving *matachini* dancers. The deer and Pascolas are pre-Columbian, the *matachinis* derive from Europe. The Yaqui manifestly enjoy all this mixing of popular entertainment, church ritual, mournful procession, tragic narrative, deer and *matachini* dancing, parody, tomfoolery and feasting.

Categories slip. Underneath all the performative genres – or, better, permeating all performative behaviour – is play. Play is in the subjunctive mood, the 'what if' or 'as if', the provisional, the open, the anti-structural. Playing confers an ontological status to lying. In such a state of fecund deception humans invent 'unreal' (as yet untreated) worlds. Performance is the way these worlds are given concrete shape in time and space, expressed as gestures, dances, words, masks, music and narratives. Moreover, in the Western theatrical tradition, characters and stories – Oedipus, Hamlet, Willie Loman, Godot – achieve a kind of archetypal, mythic status. These narratives and characters persist over time; they are 'recreated' by generations of actors, each of whom stamps them with a particular meaning. Socially, too, certain roles – the Mother, the President, the Soldier, the Artist, the Judge, the Priest, the Wife, the Farmer, plus many others – achieve immanence in concrete shapes and rhythms.

Of course, different cultures handle their own stories, characters and archetypes in different ways. Specifying those differences is a way of comprehending divergent cultural processes. For example, artists, critics and spectators of modern Western theatre demand 'new' and individuated versions of characters and narratives, whereas Japanese *kabuki* actors readily give up their born names for the names of great actors of past generations. Among the Kwakiutl of the North-west Coast of North America, masks, dances, and stories are valuable and heritable properties. The owner of a mask or dance can perform it himself or invite someone else to perform it for him – in which case the main honour of the performance goes not to the dancer but to the owner (much as the producer of a play or film in Western capitalist societies earns the lion's share of the profits).

Despite the similarities, there are no universal themes, narratives, or archetypes of performance. But there are universal ethological and neurological processes shaping the formal qualities of performances; these processes yield unique experiences to those making performances and to those participating in them. The similarity of the ritual process to the training–workshop–rehearsal process is evidence of the close and indeed indissoluble links between ritual, aesthetic, and social performances.

REFERENCES

Armstrong, R. P. (1981) *The Powers of Presence*, Philadelphia: University of Pennsylvania Press.

Barish, J. (1981) *The Anti-Theatrical Prejudice*, Berkeley: University of California Press.

Bateson, G. (1972) *Steps to an Ecology of Mind*, New York: Ballantine Books.

Bharata-muni (1967) *The Natyasastra*, ed. and transl. Manomohan Ghosh, Calcutta: Granthalaya.

Breuil, H. (1952) *Four Hundred Centuries of Cave Art*, transl. M. E. Boyle, Montignac, Dordogne (France): Centre d'Études et de Documentation Préhistoriques.

Chatwin, B. (1988) *The Songlines*, London: Picador.

Csikszentmihalyi, M. (1975) *Beyond Boredom and Anxiety*, San Francisco: Josey-Bass.

d'Aquili, E., Laughlin, C. D. and McManus, J. (eds) (1979) *The Spectrum of Ritual*, New York: Columbia University Press.

Ehrenzweig, A. (1970) *The Hidden Order of Art*, St Albans: Paladin.

Fischer, R. (1971) 'A cartography of the ecstatic and meditative states', *Science* 174: 897–904.

Freud, S. (1962 [1913]) *Totem and Taboo*, New York: W. W. Norton.

Girard, R. (1977) *Violence and the Sacred*, Baltimore: Johns Hopkins University Press.

Goodman, F. (1986) 'Body postures and the religious altered state of consciousness: an experimental investigation', *Journal of Humanistic Psychology* 26: 81–118.

—— (1990) 'Trance dance with masks: research and performance at the Cuyamungue Institute', *TDR: A Journal of Performance Studies* 34(1): 102–14.

Gould, R. A. (1969) *Yiwara: Foragers of the Australian Desert*, New York: Charles Scribner's Sons.

Grimes, R. (1982) *Beginnings in Ritual Studies*, Washington: University Press of America.

Grotowski, J. (1990) 'Performer', in *Workcenter of Jerzy Grotowski*, Pontedera, Italy.

Halprin, A. (1989) 'Planetary dance', *TDR: A Journal of Performance Studies* 33(2): 51–66.

Handelman, D. (1977) 'Play and ritual: complimentary frames of metacommunication', in A. J. Chapman and H. Fort (eds) *It's a Funny Thing, Humour*, London: Pergamon Press.

Hardison, O. B. Jr (1965) *Christian Rite and Christian Drama in the Middle Ages*, Baltimore: Johns Hopkins University Press.

Kafka, F. (1954) *The Notebooks of Franz Kafka*, London: Secker & Warburg.

Kaprow, A. (1983) 'The real experiment', *Artforum* 22(4): 36–43.

Kertzer, D. I. (1988) *Ritual, Politics, and Power*, New Haven: Yale University Press.

La Barre, W. (1972) *The Ghost Dance*, New York: Dell.

Lendra, I. W. (1991) 'Bali and Grotowski: some parallel aspects of training process', *TDR: A Journal of Performance Studies* 35(1).

Lex, B. (1979) 'The neurobiology of ritual trance', in E. G. d'Aquili, C. D. Laughlin and J. McManus (eds) *The Spectrum of Ritual*, New York: Columbia University Press.

Osinski, Z. (1991) 'Grotowski blazes the trails: from objective drama (1983–1985) to "ritual arts" (since 1985)', *TDR: A Journal of Performance Studies* 35(1): 95–112.

Pfeiffer, J. (1982) *The Creative Explosion*, New York: Harper & Row.

Rappaport, R. A. (1968) *Pigs for the Ancestors*, New Haven: Yale University Press.

Reynolds, V. and Reynolds, F. (1965) 'Chimpanzees of the Budongo Forest', in I. DeVore (ed.) *Primate Behavior: Field Studies of Monkeys and Apes*, New York: Holt, Rinehart & Winston.

Rothenberg, J. (1985) *Technicians of the Sacred*, Berkeley: University of California Press.

Schechner, R. (1973) *Environmental Theatre*, New York: Hawthorn.

—— (1985) *Between Theatre and Anthropology*, Philadelphia: University of Pennsylvania Press.

—— (1988) *Performance Theory*, London & New York: Routledge.

—— (1993) 'Waehma: space, time, identity, and theatre at New Pascua, Arizona', in R. Schechner, *The Future of Ritual*, London: Routledge.

Spicer, E. H. (1980) *The Yaquis: A Cultural History*, Tucson: University of Arizona Press.

Turnbull, C. (1962) *The Forest People*, Garden City, NY: Doubleday.

—— (1985) 'Processional ritual among the Mbuti Pygmies', *TDR: A Journal of Performance Studies* 29(3): 6–17.

—— (1990) 'Liminality: a synthesis of subjective and objective experience', in R. Schechner and W. Appel (eds) *By Means of Performance*, Cambridge: Cambridge University Press.

Turner, V. (1969) *The Ritual Process*, Chicago: Aldine.

—— (1974) *Dramas, Fields, and Metaphors*, Ithaca: Cornell University Press.

—— (1982) *From Ritual to Theatre*, New York: PAJ Publications.

—— (1983) 'Body, brain, and culture', *Zygon* 18(3): 221–46.

—— (1986) *On the Edge of the Bush*, Tucson: University of Arizona Press.

—— (1990) 'Are there universals of performance in myth, ritual, and drama?', in R. Schechner and W. Appel (eds) *By Means of Performance*, Cambridge: Cambridge University Press.

Wilford, J. N. (1990) 'Scholars say first atelier was in a cave', *New York Times*, 15 May 1990: C1, C9.

Winterbottom, P. J. (1991) 'Two years before the master', *TDR: A Journal of Performance Studies* 35(1): 140–54.

FURTHER READING

d'Aquili, E. G., Laughlin, C. D. and McManus, J. (1979) *The Spectrum of Ritual*, New York: Columbia University Press.

Drewal, H. J. and Drewal, M. T. (1983) *Gelede: Art and Female Power among the Yoruba*, Bloomington: Indiana University Press.

Driver, T. F. (1991) *The Magic of Ritual*, San Francisco: Harper.

Goffman, E. (1959) *The Presentation of Self in Everyday Life*, Garden City, NY: Doubleday.

Grimes, R. (1982) *Beginnings in Ritual Studies*, Washington: University Press of America.

—— (1990) *Ritual Criticism*, Columbia: University of South Carolina Press.

Grotowski, J. (1968) *Towards a Poor Theatre*, Holstebro, Denmark: Odin Teatret.

Handelman, D. (1977) 'Play and ritual: complementary frames of metacommunication', in A. J. Chapman and H. Fort (eds) *It's a Funny Thing, Humour*, London: Pergamon Press.

Kapferer, B. (1983) *A Celebration of Demons*, Bloomington: Indiana University Press.

Kertzer, D. I. (1988) *Ritual, Politics, and Power*, New Haven: Yale University Press.

MacAloon, J. (ed.) (1984) *Rite, Drama, Festival, Spectacle*, Philadelphia: Institute for the Study of Human Issues.

Moore, S. F. and Myerhoff, B. G. (1977) *Secular Ritual*, Amsterdam: Van Gorcum.

Pfeiffer, J. (1982) *The Creative Explosion*, New York: Harper & Row.

Rothenberg, J. (1985) *Technicians of the Sacred*, Berkeley: University of California Press.

Rothenberg, J. and Rothenberg, D. (eds) (1983) *Symposium of the Whole*, Berkeley: University of California Press.

Schechner, R. (1988) *Performance Theory*, London: Routledge.

—— (1993) *The Future of Ritual*, London: Routledge.

Schechner, R. and Appel, W. (eds) (1990) *By Means of Performance*, Cambridge: Cambridge University Press.

Thompson, R. F. (1974) *African Art in Motion*, Berkeley: University of California Press.

Turner, V. (1969) *The Ritual Process*, Chicago: Aldine.

—— (1974) *Dramas, Fields, and Metaphors*, Ithaca: Cornell University Press.

—— (1982) *From Ritual to Theatre*, New York: PAJ Publications.

—— (1985) *On the Edge of the Bush*, Tucson: University of Arizona Press.

23

THE ANTHROPOLOGY OF ART

Howard Morphy

A DEFINITIONAL PROBLEM

Anyone writing about the anthropology of art is eventually forced to confront the problem of how art is to be defined. In the recent past they may also have felt obliged to deal with the question of the label 'primitive' (see Gerbrands 1957, Anderson 1979, Layton 1991). In the case of this latter term, however, I am content to assume that the battle has been won in anthropology, if not in art history (cf. Rubin 1984: 6ff.) The addition of the label 'primitive' adds nothing but confusion to the literature on the art of non-Western societies (see Layton 1991 for an informed discussion, but Gell 1992: 62 fn. 1 for a qualified defence of the use of the term). However, the fact that the word 'primitive' was applied to these arts for so long tells us something about the European concept of art and the role it has played in the positioning of 'other cultures' in European thought, and highlights why it is so necessary that any review of the anthropology of art should begin with the definitional problem.[1]

In the nineteenth century, art, like religion, was one of those concepts used to exclude people from civilization and to distance them from European culture. Art was something that made its appearance on the higher rungs of the evolutionary ladder (Morphy 1988), especially in its most pure form of 'fine art' − art freed from any functional context (Goehr 1992). One of the reasons why the notion of 'primitive art' has been so unsatisfactory is that it is almost by definition a contradiction in terms. However, just as art could be used in the nineteenth century to distance 'other' people from the civilized Europeans, it can also be used today as a rhetorical device to include them within a world culture of people who are equally civilized. 'Art' can be, *par excellence*, a tool of cultural relativism (Clifford 1991: 241).[2] The demise of the adjective 'primitive' can be seen as part of this process. Its removal gets rid of any connotations that the art of other cultures is either, in any simple sense, evolutionarily prior to Western European art, or that it belongs to an inferior civilization. The term 'art' remains, however, an instrument of value, and it is important that we should get the definitional issues clear before embarking on questions of analysis.

In her analysis of the concept of a 'musical work' Goehr has argued that the Western concept of fine art has a relatively recent origin, and that it was associated with the development of the Romantic Movement during the late eighteenth and early nineteenth centuries. Many people, she writes,

> have believed that the closer any music embodies the conditions determined by the romantic work-aesthetic, the more civilized it is. For them, classical music is not only regarded as quintessentially civilized, but as the only kind of music that is. The same is believed of fine art more generally, so that it often serves as a standard when one wants to attribute positive value to something.... 'work of art' is used with evaluative as well as classificatory sense. What we see under imperialistic influence is a conflation or contamination of the two senses.
>
> (1992: 249)

Thus in order for something to gain recognition as an object of high value it has to be made into a work of art. This may, in turn, seriously affect the way in which it is interpreted and understood, and eventually it will affect the conditions of its production. Goehr argues that the emergence of the concept 'work of art' represented a major shift from the concept that was current before the emergence of 'fine art' in the eighteenth century, in which 'the class art included all utilitarian works of skilled manual labour' (1992: 155).

As anthropologists we do not wish to be bound by one particular definition of art, but it is equally unhelpful if instead we choose to step aside from processes in our own culture and proceed to use some earlier definition of art that is not part of its current core meaning, or even choose to invent an entirely unique anthropological definition of the term. In the latter case we would do better not to use the word 'art' at all, and in the former case we could be accused of not engaging with the debates of the present and of disconnecting the debate from our own history. Anderson provides a definition of art that comes very close to this:

> Those things are considered to be art which are made by human beings in any visual medium, where production requires a relatively high level of skill on the part of their maker, skill being measured when possible according to the standards traditionally used in the maker's society.
>
> (1979: 11)

Such a perspective has a long history, and provides a definition that accords with the etymology of the word 'art' (derived from the Old French 'ars', meaning skill). But it corresponds more closely to an eighteenth-century definition of art (in Goehr's terms) than it does to more recent definitions. Yet Anderson's book contains an analysis of precisely those kinds of objects that one would expect to appear in a twentieth-century book on art. Consequently Anderson includes in his analysis a far more restricted set of objects than his definition would imply. His book is not about pottery, or fishtraps, or harpoons, nor – in practice – is skill in manufacture the criterion he uses for the selection of the objects he discusses. Rather, the objects belong to the contemporary category of 'art object', and are chosen on the basis of a complex set of criteria, of which skill is only one.

Any narrow definition of art based on a single criterion tends either to exclude most of the objects conventionally included within the category (e.g., art objects are 'non-functional'), or to include many objects that are not (e.g., art objects are 'skilful works'). Layton and Anderson, who have written the most recent introductory textbooks on the anthropology of art, have very different definitions (Layton's (1991: 4) is much more broadly based, having two components: aesthetic factors and communication), yet both include many of the same sets of objects. I would expect that most people who buy a book on the anthropology of art know what kinds of objects will be illustrated, irrespective of the particular definition of art that is proposed. The category 'art' is differentiated from most other classes of material culture objects in that there is no minimal functional or material criterion that allows for the unequivocal exclusion of objects from the category. With a functional category, for example 'boat', there may be no simple agreed definition but it is easy to exclude the majority of objects from the category – the paradigm case of exclusion being perhaps the sieve. Likewise, in the case of a technological category such as 'pottery', it is easy to exclude the majority of other objects, even if there are some ambiguous cases on the margins. 'Art', however, is a much more accepting category. While acknowledging the fuzziness around the edges of all semantic categories, even those that are primarily functionally defined, I feel that in the case of the Jumblies and Winnie-the-Pooh, it is art that extends the category 'boat' to include, respectively, 'sieve' and 'umbrella'.

Yet, just as with any other category, the majority of objects in existence at any one time are excluded from 'art'. If art was just a rag-bag into which everything could be equally easily fitted, then there would not be a problem. Nor would there be, in any meaningful sense, an anthropology of art. Art is a category into which some works fit more easily than others: the average painting by Picasso fits while the average sieve does not. Rather than attempting a simple definition of art we need to consider the broad range of attributes associated with works of art and the conditions under which objects gain acceptance into the category. I do not expect to come up with a definition that unites all objects included within the category: the Western category of art is always open to new members because criteria for inclusion are always changing.

My justification for beginning this discussion of the definition of art from the perspective of contemporary Europe is that 'art' is one of those words that exists in anthropological discourse through extension of its conventional usage in the West to other cultures. There is no generally agreed definition of 'art' in some metalanguage of anthropology, and it is almost a cliché (perhaps a little too unexamined) to remark that there is no word for art in the language of this or that people. It is possible to identify three different aspects of the European definition of art, or to distinguish three kinds of definition: an institutional definition, a definition in terms of attributes of the objects and definition by intent.

As far as the institutional definition is concerned, art objects are like members of an exclusive club, membership of which allows entry into certain rooms and allows the attachment of certain labels to the object. Artworks are exhibited in art galleries as opposed to museums, and are labelled 'fine art' in auction catalogues as opposed to 'craft', 'folk art' or 'ethnographic artefact'. As Vogel writes (1988: 11): 'Because today the forms and materials of art are frequently the same as those of non-art objects, the setting or context in which art is displayed may be its most evident defining characteristic. A pile of tyres in a museum is to be viewed as art whereas the same pile in a gas station is clearly not.' The institutional definition of works of art is part of a process that is linked closely to the marketing of objects and to abstract processes of value creation (see Graburn 1978: 66 for an amusing example). Its significance as far as the anthropology of art is concerned, apart from as a subject of analysis in its own right (see for example Bourdieu 1984), is that the process of definition of works as institutional fine art is linked both to their market value and to the evaluation of the cultures that produce them. The institutional definition of art is challenged by artists from Europe and elsewhere and by the works of art that are excluded from it, yet at the same time tempts those who challenge it with the rewards that follow on from inclusion within it. Things that are labelled as art objects by institutions can fulfil many other functions, or can have had very different functions at earlier stages of their life history (see Appadurai 1986), but it is not their function that makes them works of art. Only one function unites institutionally defined works of art, and that is their function as repositories of value on the international art market. Once accepted as an institutional art object, an item gains a value that may increase exponentially according to factors of supply and demand.

The second way to define art is to identify certain attributes of the objects in question that, from the way people write about art objects, appear to be relevant to their inclusion within the category. These attributes tend to be concerned with visual or interpretative properties of the objects rather than with any specific function that they fulfil. Function may be relevant to their interpretation, but it is not the primary reason for including them within the category of artwork. Thus, although the majority of early European works of art were produced for religious purposes, the religious context appears to be irrelevant to their contemporary definition as art objects. Today, art appropriates their function. Whereas at the time of their production their function in religious performance or practice may have been central to the kind of objects that they were, today that function is auxiliary to their place in art history and to the interpretation of their iconography. The kinds of attributes associated with art objects include skill in manufacture, aesthetic features and semantic or interpretative properties.

The third kind of definition concerns intention and is complementary to the institutional definition: art objects are ones that are *intended* to be works of art by their makers. With most types of object, intention is subordinate to functional or institutional specification – the intention to make a boat is insufficient if the object is incapable of floating. In the case of art objects the individual has a little more freedom, since the category is always open to persuasion, always open to include something else within it, and open to many different kinds of criteria and routes of inclusion – the European category of art is, in Sutton's (1987) terms, 'additive'. In contemporary European art acceptance as an artist licenses the person concerned to designate his or her products as works of art. The freedom is not absolute, and acceptance is by no means a guarantee that the work will be valued and appreciated widely, but the definition of a work of art as 'a work intended as an artwork produced by a recognized artist' has some validity. It is one of the ways in which works of art are created in contemporary Europe. The artist is of course only one category of person who has the possibility of persuading markets and audience that a work should enter those institutions that designate it as art. Art historians, dealers, agents and many other opinion-formers, singly or in conjunction (or collusion), operate to change the designation of objects.

There is a complex interrelationship between individual intention, the interpretative context of works of art and their institutional definition, that results in similar objects being included in different categories. Works gain their meaning through their incorporation into 'art worlds' (see Danto 1973, Becker 1982) and through their historical position. An artist's power to designate something as a work of art is constrained by the interpretative context in which he or she is working. Duchamp's 'ready mades', which consisted of everyday objects presented as works of art, were possible artworks at the time he designated them as such, but may well not have been at any previous point in the history of art. Paintings in the style of Titian, so long as they were produced at the time of the Renaissance, have a value that they would not be accorded, were they produced in the 1990s: in the latter case they would be pushed to the very margins of acceptability as 'fine art'. But once a work is given a particular historical position as an artwork, that position tends to be relatively immune from subsequent developments, though the possibility of re-evaluation is always open. Duchamp's urinal, one of his major 'found' works, retains its value even though subsequent, albeit identical objects are no longer included in the category. It became an artwork in a sense different from all other urinals of the same type which, although incorporated by his action within the same discourse, were rejected from membership of the category. Duchamp's urinal was included by autographic process: it was signed 'R. Mutt'. Although its significance lay in the concept behind it – the reflexive statement made about the category 'art' – the art market ironically required that it have the work in material form (see Davis 1990 for a relevant discussion).

APPLYING THE CONCEPT OF ART CROSS-CULTURALLY

Having examined, albeit briefly, the ways in which objects gain inclusion in the Western category of art, we are now in a position to see if this category, or any of the ways of defining things as art objects, is useful for the analysis of things across cultures. If we assume for the moment that the purpose of an anthropological analysis of objects is to understand them and explain aspects of their form in relation to the cultures that produce or use them, then the first and third definitions of art objects appear on the surface to be of limited utility. The institutional definition of art, as I have outlined it, depends on the concept of 'fine art' developed in post-Renaissance Europe in association with the growth of such institutions as museums, art galleries, and the art-historical tradition. Neither the institutional definition nor the set of objects that it designates as art is relevant to the anthropological analysis of objects in their cultural contexts, except in so far as those European institutions are themselves a part of these contexts. An anthropology of art should not be limited by the objects that are included in the Western category of art: on a priori grounds that category is likely to be entirely arbitrary from the viewpoint of the producing culture.

Similar considerations apply to a definition that appeals to intention, since this is inextricably linked to the European institutional category of art. Artists working outside the European tradition have not as a rule been motivated to produce objects that Europeans will define as 'art', and have therefore not been party to that definitional process. If their work has entered the European fine art category then it has done so irrespective of the producers' intentions. Tikopian headrests become art in the European sense because anthropologists, or art historians, or art dealers, have used one or more of the criteria of fine art successfully to persuade the institutions to move them from the ethnographic museum into the art gallery (cf. Firth 1973).

At this stage it is necessary to add two qualifications to my apparent dismissal of the applicability of the institutional definition of art to other cultures. First, although an anthropology of art cannot be concerned primarily with objects that Europeans define as art, there may be analogous institutional contexts in other cultures, and other societies may include individuals who play a role in defining the works that can be included in such contexts. The institutions I have in mind are ones in which objects are collected and curated partly for the purposes of display. Such institutions are extremely widespread and vary from the courts of West African kingdoms (Dark *et al.* 1960, Fagg 1970), through the mortuary displays of New Ireland (Lewis 1969, Küchler 1992) and the Tiwi (Mountford 1958), to the 'cabinets of curiosity' of New Guinea cult groups (see Craig 1990) and the galleries of Sepik men's houses (Forge

1966, Bowden 1983, 1992). While these institutions have no necessary relationship to one another, the possibility of there being some similarities in particular cases is at least worth exploring. Certainly the overlap between the kinds of objects that are included in those contexts, and the works that Europeans eventually include or appropriate for their category, is considerable.

The second qualification is that the production of objects in most 'other' cultures is today inextricably linked within a world system in which the values of objects in many different contexts are relevant to their meaning and to how they are understood. The European institutional definition of art is often relevant to the production of objects by indigenous peoples who may intend to produce work that will be accepted as art by a European market (see Graburn 1976, Morphy 1991). And it is important to note that this is a two-way process. Just as European artists have played an active role in changing the content of the institutional category, so too, to an increasing extent, have producers of works from outside Europe and America, either directly or indirectly through the mediation of their anthropological and art-world interpreters.

So far I have not considered the cross-cultural applicability of the attributes associated with the European concept of fine art. Here again there is no reason to suppose a priori that they should be useful in defining particular categories of object cross-culturally, even though they may be applied as concepts to all kinds of objects. Thus the concept of skill in manufacture can be applied usefully in other cultures to see how differential skill is recognized and evaluated, how general the concept is across objects of different types, and so on. The attributes associated with 'artworks' (Goehr 1992) in Europe have changed over time, moving from a period in which skill, function, and religious meaning were all integral to works labelled as art to a period when aesthetic and expressive factors were emphasized. This suggests, in turn, that no set of definitive attributes can be simply transferred across cultures. Just as the attributes associated with the European concept of art have changed over time, so too are we likely to find variations in space.

TOWARDS A DEFINITION OF ART FOR ANTHROPOLOGY

From the discussion thus far we might conclude with some justification that the whole enterprise of trying to apply the concept of art cross-culturally is misguided and that we should instead look for some less value-laden and less culture-bound term. Perhaps we should only have an anthropology of material culture to which we could apply, where appropriate, concepts of aesthetics or skill or symbolism. However, this would be to miss the point of what we have learned about the category of art – culture-bound it may be, imprecise it may be, but it does refer to a set of objects that cannot be included together in more narrowly defined functional categories, and on the whole people appear to be able to allocate objects as members of the set. Moreover the various qualities that are focal to discussions about the definition of art do seem relatively discrete. But the caution against ethnocentrism must be heeded: the anthropology of art is not the study of objects of other cultures that Europeans have accepted as belonging to their category 'art'. If the anthropology of art is to make a useful contribution, then it must be by virtue of a concept of art that is sufficiently open to allow the analysis of objects from other cultures on their own terms, while at the same time, perhaps, helping to identify categories of objects in other cultures that, though not identical with the European category of art objects, overlap with it to a certain extent. Just as we have found it possible to make connections over time between sets of objects designated as art in different periods, despite changes in the definition of the category, so too it might be possible to discover meaningful connections in space.

As might be expected from the discussion up to now, the study of non-European art as a subject has been established on two foundations: the existence of sets of objects from other cultures that Europeans classify as art, and the idea that other cultures may have categories of objects that are analogous to the Western category 'art object'. Many exhibition catalogues and books of non-Western art history are based on the former foundation alone, and are almost by definition non-anthropological. They are concerned with sets of objects that are arbitrary or lacking in coherence from the perspectives of the producing cultures. Although the initial stimulus for looking at a set of objects may be that they are classified as art objects by Europeans, when it comes to anthropological analysis that set must be adjusted to relate to ethnographic circumstances. The analysis of the objects must be framed in terms of their place and meaning within the producing culture. If an object has aesthetic properties, then the relevant considerations are not those that contributed to its being labelled art for a Western audience, but rather the aesthetic considerations and interpretations of the producers.

Recent analyses of objects that have been labelled 'art objects' suggest that many of the same attributes are relevant cross-culturally. Certain themes or foci or analytic perspectives recur time and again. In relation to form, 'art objects' are analysed from three main perspectives: iconographic, aesthetic and functional. From the first perspective they are viewed as objects that encode meaning, or represent something, or that create a particular meaning. From the second they are analysed for their aesthetic effect or their expressive qualities. From the third, functional perspective, putting aside for the moment the function of art as a commodity, three considerations tend to predominate in discussion: the uses of objects in ritual and religion, in the marking of value, and in making something pleasing. Many other possible functions could be listed for objects that can be classed as art objects, but the ones mentioned above figure most frequently in analyses of art.

For heuristic purposes, an anthropologically useful definition of art that overlaps with the European concept might be 'objects having semantic and/or aesthetic properties that are used for presentational or representational purposes'. Art in this sense embraces a series of polythetic sets in which the objects included in the European set are liable to share some but not all of their attributes with objects included in other sets. Indeed there may be some members of particular sets that, although they share attributes in common with other members of their own set, have nothing in common with members of another. And I must stress again that the relevant set of objects for anthropological analysis must be developed independently of the European classification of objects as art. An analysis of religious objects used in an ancestor cult may include consideration not only of carved wooden images that would easily gain a place in many Western galleries, but also collected toenail clippings that would seem out of place in that context, unless the persuasiveness of Western art praxis had already opened the road for their inclusion. As Sillitoe writes of the Wola, a people of New Guinea,

> an outsider's appreciation of another culture's 'art' may be a subjective and ethnocentric distortion of the indigenous view. The paintings which the Wola put on their shields we would label as art, but not the wooden crosses. So the category we gloss as art is presumably something different from that held by the Wola because for them the cross is a design of some sort which relates to their paintings.
>
> (1980: 498)

ART AND ANTHROPOLOGY

Historically the relationship between art and anthropology has been an uncomfortable one, partly because of problems over the definition of art and the question of its cross-cultural applicability, partly because of the more general neglect of material culture by anthropologists (see Ucko 1969, Miller 1983). It was not that 'art' objects were studied as something else, for example, as masks, as aesthetic artefacts, as court regalia or as clubs or shields; for much of the twentieth century at least, the objects have hardly been studied at all. Particularly rare have been studies concerned with their form. There was therefore no way in which the study of objects, whether or not they were included under the general rubric of art, could contribute to the analysis of more general anthropological problems, such as the effectiveness of ritual, where an understanding of the way in which objects were used and understood might well have proved invaluable.

In British anthropology the source of this neglect of art and material culture can be traced to the end of the nineteenth century and the beginning of the twentieth, and is associated with the rejection of the evolutionary paradigm. Material culture had become too closely associated with the more extreme aspects of social evolutionary approaches in which cultures were defined by clusters of traits that could be positioned within evolutionary sequences. As interest in anthropology shifted away from evolution towards an understanding of presently existing societies, material evidence appeared for a while to be less crucial to the enterprise. The change in theoretical emphasis was associated with the development of systematic and extended fieldwork. The study of art and material culture should have benefited just as much as any other area of anthropology from the fieldwork revolution, and indeed was well covered in a few of the pioneering ethnographies (in particular, in the works produced around the turn of the century by Spencer and Gillen (1899) and by Haddon and other members of the Torres Straits expedition (Haddon 1912)). But increasingly it was neglected.

In America the tradition of cultural anthropology founded by Boas and his students might have been expected to take a different course, especially when Boas's own lifelong interest in art and material culture is borne in mind. However, developments in art and material culture studies in American anthropology paralleled those in Britain, and were likewise characterized, for much of the twentieth century, by the neglect and marginalization of the topic (see Sturtevant 1969, Stocking 1985).

Ironically, the neglect of art by anthropologists had the result that the main studies that were undertaken were precisely of the type that were the most culture-bound. The study of non-European art became constrained by the terminology and interests of the European and Euro-American art history of the time. Concepts of style, tradition, and form had a prominent place in art history, being customarily applied in contexts in which much could be taken for granted about the cultural background and significance of the objects, and in which there were independent ways of dating objects and associating them with particular places or schools of art. Applied to non-European art these concepts and methods tended to result in sterile, descriptive and typological studies charting the formal relationships between objects, with a view to constructing hypotheses about regional developments in style over time and their possible historical correlates. Such studies offered no independent means of assessing the validity of the analyses, and had much in common with the speculative history against which functionalist anthropology was reacting.

Other studies used such concepts as 'schools' (of artists) and 'master–apprentice' relationships, borrowed from the history of the European art of a particular time period, often without establishing their relevance to a different context. The art history of West Africa was for a time constructed on the basis of analogy with that of Western Europe (see Goldwater 1973: 3ff. for an explicit justification of such an approach). Where they went beyond description and the definition of culture-areas or some other kind of spatial unit on the basis of formal analysis alone, these studies tended to continue the discourse of a previous generation of anthropologists. The debates over evolution, diffusion, and independent invention remained on the agenda of the anthropology of art long after they had ceased to be the focal points of attention in other areas of the subject.

I do not of course mean to imply that the problems that were addressed were not valid topics for research. It was merely that the study of art and material culture came to be set apart from the rest of anthropology. Indeed, there was a positive side to such survivals of theoretical interest from the past: it meant that in one area at least, anthropology continued to address what, in principle, are perfectly relevant and proper problems of cultural history. It meant that on the periphery, anthropology continued to enter into a discourse with art history that has proved ultimately beneficial. The identification of the works of individual artists (e.g. by Fagg 1948, Bascom 1973, Vogel 1980), and concerns with the relative autonomy of form (Holm 1965, Kubler 1962) and with the developments of traditions over time (Willett 1972), were all useful enterprises that ran counter to the tendency of much social anthropology to be overly synchronic, ahistorical and normative in its approach (see Thomas 1989). In recent years the potential of art and material culture to provide a basis for increasing the time depth of the anthropological database has been used in the case of rock art to analyse the trajectories of regional systems over time (e.g. Chaloupka 1985, Taçon 1989), and in the case of museum collections as a means of analysing colonial interactions and systems of trade and exchange (see Thomas 1991).

Nevertheless, any branch of a subject that remains apart from the changing interests of the remainder of the discipline is liable to stagnation, and is unlikely to contribute to the discipline's more general theoretical development. It is good for the anthropology of art that anthropology has now moved away from narrow functionalism. However, it was not so good that, at the time when functionalism was at its height, art remained apart from the movement, since today we are missing those rich ethnographies of art that could have been produced as part of the fieldwork revolution. Anthropologists of art, with their nineteenth-century problematic, remained behind with their museum collections, or, when they did go into the field, did not number among their objectives the production of detailed ethnographies. However, it would be wrong to neglect the rich resources for the study of art and material culture that do exist from the period when functionalism was triumphant, in particular some of the more unfashionable ethnographies that were often written by ex-government officials (e.g. Rattray's (1927) work on the Ashanti, and Mills's (1937) and Hutton's (1921) on the hill tribes of Assam).

A HISTORY OF APPROACHES TO THE ANTHROPOLOGY OF ART

One consequence of the separation of the study of art from fieldwork during the first half of the twentieth century was the detachment of the study of form from the study of meaning and function. Anthropologists who studied religion and social organization, trade or ceremonial exchange, may have referred to the function of things such as masks, sacred objects or exchange valuables in their analyses, but they paid no attention to their form. On the other hand those anthropologists who were concerned with form paid little attention to function and context. In neither case was meaning or iconography a central concern. A few exceptional fieldwork-oriented studies were produced, notably by Griaule (1938) and his co-workers in France, by Firth (1973) in Britain and by Boas (1955 [1927]) and his students — followed by Herskovits (1938) — in the United States, but these were very much the exceptions.

Three main types of analysis of art dominated until the 1960s. One method, developed in the nineteenth century, was to construct typological sequences and link them to evolutionary or diffusionist hypotheses (e.g. Haddon 1895, and Balfour 1893). Interest in diffusion has remained strong, but in more recent studies it is combined with a concern for meaning (e.g. Fraser 1962). A second method of analysis, also linked with long-established interests in art history, concentrated on the formal properties of the art. The method sought to explain form in relation to aesthetic effect and to demonstrate the formal principles that underlay artistic expression. The *locus classicus* for this approach is the work of Franz Boas (1955 [1927]). His work was set in opposition to the naïvety of simplistic evolutionary theory, though he drew on certain theoretical perspectives on the origin of designs which, in the hands of others, were accorded evolutionary significance. Boas's perspective on art was a broad one, and he covered many areas that had been neglected by others, above all in his studies of the iconography of the art of the native peoples of the American North-west Coast. Nevertheless, in his writings meaning was subordinate to form, and the contextual aspect of meaning was largely neglected. For all of the richness of his ethnography of the Kwakiutl, it made little of the connections between art, social organization and ritual. The third method of analysis in the anthropology of art, like the first, involved the creation of types, but in this case they were stylistic types associated with culture-areas, tribes or schools. Such stylistic analysis was, in America, linked with culture-area and diffusionist schools of anthropology, and in Britain it was most strongly associated with art-historically influenced studies of African art (e.g., the one-tribe, one-style approach of Fagg 1965; for a critique see Kasfir 1984).

Art re-entered the anthropological mainstream under two main influences. One was the renewed interest in material culture studies stimulated in part by a growth in culturally oriented archaeology (see for example Ucko 1969, 1977, and later Hodder 1982, Miller 1985, Morphy 1989, Tilley 1991). The other was the developing emphasis on the anthropology of meaning and symbolism (in particular, see Bateson 1937, 1973, Fernandez 1972, Leach 1954, 1973, Turner 1967). Interest in how symbols were organized and how they encoded meaning, rather than in the meanings themselves, closed the gap between the anthropology of art and the anthropology of religion, joined content with form, and projected a new set of issues into centre stage. The need for fieldwork and for the establishment of new frameworks for studying non-European art had been discussed in a few theoretical publications (notably by Gerbrands 1957), and in the late 1950s anthropologists again began to choose art as a topic for fieldwork. Through the work of, among others, Munn (1962, 1973), Forge (1962, 1973a, b), and Biebuyk (1973), art began to be reintegrated within the mainstream concerns of anthropology.

Munn and Forge both put meaning at the centre of the ethnographic study of art. Their perspectives were developed independently and involved the reuniting of form with function and meaning in the context of the analysis of the society as a whole. In both Munn's study of the art of the Walbiri, an Aboriginal people from central Australia, and Forge's study of the art of the Abelam of New Guinea, art is treated as an independent system of communication in which meanings are created. Forge (1970: 269) wrote that 'Abelam flat painting acts directly on the fully adult initiated male as a system of communication and not as a representation of any other communication system such as myth'. Munn (1973: 5), following Lévi-Strauss, saw Walbiri art as an ordering system that creates meaning by ordering relationships between different dimensions of reality. Her theoretical perspective owes something to Durkheim in that art was shown to be part of a system of collective representations that is integral to the way in which society reproduces itself. However she was also influenced by semiotics and phenomenology. Both Munn and Forge emphasized the importance of a formal analysis of the properties of the respective systems, to show the ways in which they encode meanings.

In the Walbiri case specific interpretations are given for elements of the designs, even though the designs are multivalent and meaning is productive within certain constraints. Walbiri art consists of a series of geometric elements, each of which is associated with a range of possible meanings which refer to features of the landscape or to human activities and mythological events (Figure 1). The particular meanings of the elements depend on context, and a key is often required to interpret them. The multivalency of the art enables the paintings to be interpreted further on an individual basis, creating additional connections between the meanings encoded in the elements of a particular object or composition. In Abelam art, perhaps as a consequence of the absence of mythological referents, the meanings are more elusive. Forge was nevertheless able to demonstrate convincingly the structural properties of the system and the kinds of meanings that were created in a ritual context. If these analyses are to be criticized it is because they too easily abstracted art as communication from the functional contexts in which it was produced and used, neglecting to consider in detail the dynamics of interpretative processes and the political contexts of meaning.

During the 1960s and 1970s anthropologists began increasingly to see art again as data, and even though relatively few monographs were published (exceptions include Biebuyk 1973, Brain and Pollock 1971, Gerbrands 1967, Faris 1972, Strathern and Strathern 1971), the number of major edited volumes and collections increased significantly (e.g. Biebuyk 1969, d'Azevedo 1973, Forge 1973b, Greenhalgh and Megaw 1978, Jopling 1971, Mead 1979, Otten 1971, Ucko 1977). Indeed, perhaps the most significant thing was that art had ended its period of neglect, and re-entered the discourse of anthropology. However, anthropologists will only gain real benefit from its reincorporation if they develop methods that take advantage of its particular properties,

Element		Range of meanings

Element   **Range of meanings**

1 | Spear
Fighting stick, when not upright in ground
Digging-stick
Human actor lying down
Animal, that is, dog or kangaroo lying stretched out
Fires when flanking each side of shade

2   Actor in motion − walking, running, dancing
Spearing

3   Actor(s) dancing

4   Actor walking
Actor dancing (one instance only)

5   Actor lying down on side, as in sleep

6   Boomerangs

7   Bough shade or shelter
Line or grove of trees (see also 8)

8   Grove of trees

9   Hut

10   Actor sitting

11   Creek bed
Blanket or 'bed'

12   Food or water scoop
Baby carrier
Shield
Spear-thrower
Oval 'bed' (*ngura*), hollow in ground for sleeping

13   Nest
Hole
Waterhole
Fruits and yams
Tree
Hill
Prepared food
Fire
Upright fighting stick
Painting material
Billycan
Egg
Dog, when curled up in camp
Circling (as, for example, dancing around), or any encircling object

Figure 1 Walbiri graphic signs and their meanings. The elements, drawn from Munn (1973, Figure 1), show the multivalence of signs used in Walbiri women's sand drawings. Arrows represent direction of movement.

661

which are shared with other material artefacts (see Ucko 1969, and Miller in this volume, Article 15). For art to be analysed to greatest advantage it is necessary to focus on its material aspect and to reconnect the anthropologist's interest in meaning with the art historian's concern with form.

FORM AND FUNCTION: A METHODOLOGICAL PERSPECTIVE ON THE ANALYSIS OF ART

The achievement of these objectives requires that a central focus in the anthropology of art must be on the explanation of form. The focus on form provides a 'point of entry' into understanding other aspects of art, and of cultural processes more generally. I define form broadly to refer to both shape and details of composition and construction that might otherwise be included under technique and substance (i.e. how, and of what, an object is formed). By seeking the explanation of form I mean little more than asking why the object has the shape, componental structure and material composition that it has, and analysing how these attributes relate to its use in particular contexts. There is no necessary expectation that its formal and material attributes will bear a relationship to its use in all contexts, but at least the question must be asked, and if answered in the negative, then other reasons must be found for its use in that particular context. The search for the explanation of form enables a work of art to be used as an independent key to unlocking particular socio-cultural processes, disclosing structures and connections of which the anthropologist might otherwise be unaware. For example, an analysis of art may be an excellent way to approach the question of individual and group identity, revealing how people compete with one another at one level and express common identity at another (see O'Hanlon 1989, Hodder 1982). The material object also provides a vehicle for engaging in dialogue with members of a culture to see how different people at different times and places, and of different age, status, and gender, respond to, or interpret, or use, or make, the same object or the same type of object. For example it has proved useful in the Australian Aboriginal context in revealing the structure of systems of knowledge and meaning (see Munn 1973, Morphy 1991).

The most productive initial approach to the explanation of form is through function: what the object is used for, what it does, what its effects are, always in relation to the wider context in which it is embedded. In many cases it is necessary to separate out the question of what the art aspect of an object does from other aspects of the object. Many objects can be considered not only as art objects but also in many other ways as well. A Marquesan club (Figure 2), for example, possesses many of the attributes of art – fine craftsmanship, aesthetic appeal, signs of status and religious symbolism – but it could also be used to crack someone's skull. Its functional attributes as a weapon have no necessary connection with its attributes as art. Certainly it could function as a weapon without the latter attributes. However, not all cases are as clear-cut as this.

Figure 2 A Marquesan double-headed club (*u'u*) from the original Pitt-Rivers collection, probably dating from the early nineteenth century. The clubs were a principal weapon in warfare but also functioned as ceremonial staffs. They were carved from ironwood by specialist craftsmen. The burnished black effect was achieved by soaking the club in the mud of a taro patch and subsequently polishing it in coconut oil. Unfortunately, little is known of the meaning of Marquesan designs. (Pitt-Rivers Museum. 1184. 12. 283)

A mask may function simultaneously to obscure a person's face and to create a new identity. A block of wood could function to obscure the face equally well, just as a lump of wood could crack a person's skull, but in the case of the mask its form is simultaneously integral to both its function in concealing the person's identity and its function in creating a new identity. However nothing can be assumed, for, after analysing a particular masking tradition, it may become clear that identity is not concealed but rather transformed or even emphasized. And in the case of the club its capacity to destroy may interact with aesthetic aspects of its form to give it particular connotations as an art object that it may not otherwise have had. Conversely, at least from the viewpoint of the people themselves, the designs on a club or its aesthetic power may interact with its destructive capacity to make it more effective as a weapon (Sillitoe (1980) provides a discussion of the significance of designs on Wola shields which is relevant to this point).

In analysing an art object that is simultaneously a member of another category, such as 'club' or 'boat', it is important to pay attention to those aspects of the form of the object that set it apart from other members of the functional set to which it belongs, as well as those that it shares with them. The 'art aspect' of an object – i.e. its semantic/aesthetic dimensions – may provide a way of establishing connections across objects in different functional sets, for example by defining ceremonial sets or sets of objects associated with social groups or classes, or it may be a way of linking classes of objects with ideology or cosmology (see the analyses of *kula* canoes from the Trobriand Islands, by Campbell 1984, summarized in Gell 1992, Munn 1977 and Scoditti 1989). In the case of many objects it seems that their art aspect is a set of attributes that either complement or exist independently of other functionally determined attributes, and that embellish the objects aesthetically and semantically. Across different cultures we would expect, however, to come up with certain functional categories that are especially likely to include, and perhaps even produce, art objects or objects possessing attributes of art, because their function is linked with communication or aesthetic expression: sacred objects, masks, personal ornaments and so on. But there is really no limit to the kinds of objects that can also be members of the category 'art'.

Ideas are often conveyed not by words but by things. And there are an increasing number of rich analyses of art and architecture that show the ways that objects are linked to concepts of the world through cultural praxis: Munn's (1977) analysis of Gawan canoes, Guss's (1989) analysis of Yekuana baskets, MacKenzie's (1991) analysis of Telefolmin string bags, Blier's (1987) analysis of house form, and Witherspoon's (1977) analyses of Navaho sand-paintings. The analysis of form does not imply, as some critics of semiological approaches to the study of art have supposed (e.g. Sperber 1976), that meanings are assumed by the analyst to be fixed and located outside of systems of representation and interpretation. As objectifications of cultural processes and expressions of individual understanding (see Csikszentmihalyi and Roshberg-Halton 1981, Miller 1987, Appadurai 1986), as objects of exchange (Munn 1986) and as instruments of action (Tippett 1968), artefacts enter into people's relationships with the world and reflect changes that occur in both concept and practice (see Article 15). Analysis of the details of form is indeed one of the ways in which anthropologists are able to discover how people are socialized into meanings, and how those meanings change over time.

REPRESENTATIONAL SYSTEMS

The main recent focus of studies in the anthropology of art has undoubtedly been on art as a system of meaning and communication. For this reason the study of representational systems, or of how art encodes meaning, are of crucial importance. The concept of a representational system is central because there is an interrelation between meaning and the way it is encoded or represented, in other words how something is encoded may influence its meaning as well as affect how that meaning can be communicated to others. Morse code has a very different communicative potential from sign language, the feel of an apple has very different connotations from its smell, a line drawing of an apple conveys very different information from that conveyed by a colour photograph.

There are of course innumerable ways in which art encodes meaning, and many distinctions can be made to differentiate one system from another. One of the most useful distinctions has been that between iconic and non-iconic systems. Overlapping but not identical to this distinction are the series of oppositions between motivated and arbitrary signification, between continuous and discontinuous systems of meaning, and, more associated with Western art history, between figurative and abstract art. These terms are all semiological in the sense that they are concerned with the relationship within a system between signifier and signified, with whether meaning is encoded on the basis of similarity – of shape, of colour, of material and so on – between signifier and signified, or whether in some other way. The dividing line between these contrasting types of encoding is not always clear-cut, moreover different codes may operate in conjunction to produce meaning in any particular case (see Morphy 1991, Taylor 1989).

All of the concepts discussed so far in this section imply that the art concerned is representational, in the sense that it can be interpreted to mean something that is, or becomes, external to itself: it may represent an object of the external world such as an animal species, or an idea such as kingship, or a social group. Representation in the sense that I use it here is a broad concept, set in opposition to such concepts as decoration, which refers to a quality with no referential meaning. The presence or absence of decoration, and the kind of decoration, can of course be analysed from the perspective of representation, since 'decoration' can form part of the way in which particular contexts or statuses are defined, e.g. as domestic rather than public, as hierarchical rather than egalitarian, as female rather than male, and so on.

Many of the theoretical controversies in the analysis of art (and of cultural forms in general) have resulted from a failure to recognize the multidimensional nature of objects and the immense variety of ways in which meanings can be represented. To assert that art is representational says very little about the kind of system it is and the particular way in which form relates to function in context. The perspective is one that directs the analysis rather than determines the outcome.

Different systems of representation have different properties, different potentials for encoding meaning, different conditions of interpretation and communication and so on. Munn (1973) and Forge (1973a) have drawn attention to the language-like properties of, respectively, Walbiri and Abelam art, and I have done the same in analysing the art of the Yolngu, an Australian Aboriginal people from north-eastern Arnhem Land (Morphy 1991). In all three cases art is associated with creating images of ancestral power and is itself a manifestation of the sacred, but the differences between the two Australian systems (Walbiri and Yolngu) and the New Guinea system

(Abelam) are in many ways greater than the similarities. In Walbiri and Yolngu art, referential meaning is integral to the system, art is part of the process of encoding myth, paintings are interpreted consistently by the initiated and can be associated precisely with places, social groups and ancestral tracks. By contrast, in the Abelam case, Forge argues that meaning is internal to the system, and although paintings are part of men's secret knowledge they are not part of a systematic process of releasing meaning over time.

Despite their differences as representational systems, some of the paintings produced by Yolngu and Abelam artists can look formally very similar. Of itself this requires no explanation; the paintings belong to different 'art worlds', or in Kubler's (1962) terms, they have different positional values as parts of separate cultural trajectories. Similarity of form across cultures may have no significance. On the other hand it may be worth pursuing formal similarities to see if they reflect similar structural properties of the system, or similarities in functional context or expressive value. The frequent association of geometric art with secret contexts may reflect general properties of such systems as against those of figurative art, or it may be the case that certain aesthetic effects may trigger similar emotional responses cross-culturally.

The body decoration system prevalent in societies of the New Guinea Highlands (Strathern and Strathern 1971) can also usefully be analysed as a representational system, even though it differs markedly in its properties from both Yolngu and Abelam art. Wahgi Valley body decoration (O'Hanlon 1989, 1992), in addition to being an expression of 'well-being', is a symbol of male values, in particular of group identity, as well as a means of generating and condensing power. In contrast to Walbiri and Yolngu art, not every element of the Wahgi body decoration necessarily 'means' something; what is most important is the overall effect of the design and the value of the components – opossum fur, cassowary feathers and so on – even if they are invisible. Though some aspects of the art can be analysed from a semiological perspective (see Layton 1978), the linguistic analogy should not be pushed too far. The painted and decorated artist is not making a statement 'I am fierce', rather he is creating an image of fierceness, power, and group identity that is integral to the presentation itself. The body painting works not only as communication to others but on the person's self, creating an image of power that is palpably *felt*.

The art of the Mende of Sierra Leone is, like Wahgi body decoration, concerned with processes of transformation and the creation of self (Boone 1986). In the Sande society, for example, masks are worn by senior members of the society to construct a concept of female beauty which provides both a model for the female person and a way of interpreting the female self. In contrast to the Wahgi, the system employed is a figurative one in which formal resemblance plays an important role – though, as always, representation is part of a dual process in which the representation in part constitutes the object it represents. In the masquerade the dancer creates a figure of transcendent female authority, that makes female beauty central to the health of the society.

Boone's (1986) analysis of the *sowo-wui* mask involves isolating components of the mask and explaining their form in relation to Mende concepts of beauty and the meaning of facial features and facial decoration. Although Boone can be criticized for, among other things, overemphasizing the concept of female beauty and adopting a somewhat essentialist aesthetic (e.g. Phillips 1993), she has contributed significantly to the understanding of the *sowo-wui* mask.

Determining the potential of a system for encoding meaning is only part of the analysis, since it is at the same time necessary to connect structure to the process of encoding, to show how particular meanings are relevant to the use of art in particular contexts. Meaning neither resides in the formal properties of the particular system, nor does it exist entirely independently of the means by which it is communicated (Morphy 1991: 143–5). There is a relative autonomy in the relationship between form and function in material culture in general, that is perhaps most apparent in art systems (though in Article 6 of this volume, Wynn makes the same point about tools). In analysing art it is therefore important to rid oneself of any preconceptions as to how a particular system operates or why a particular object is produced, in order to concentrate, in the specific case, on form, function and context, in relation to the pragmatics of interpretation and the processes of encoding and value creation.

Figurative art can operate in the same functional context as can nonfigurative art; it can serve similar purposes and even encode related meanings. *Toas*, direction signs of the Lake Eyre region of Central Australia, are a case in point, in which the same message may be encoded in an iconic figurative sign or in an arbitrary geometric one (Figures 3 and 4) – though the conditions of interpretation in the two cases are different (H. Morphy 1977, Jones and Sutton 1986). On the other hand, two figurative systems in the same culture may have almost nothing in common: one may operate as pictographic writing whereas another may be a way of representing the landscape. The art of the North-west Coast of America provides an excellent example of the structured relationship between the properties of different representational systems and the respective functional contexts in which they occur (see F. Morphy 1977, Rosman and Rubel 1990).

As well as acknowledging cross-cultural variation it is important to recognize that interpretation and value will vary within a culture according to innumerable contextual factors. Context and the themes associated with context are liable to influence the way a design or object is interpreted or understood. The same sculpture will have a different impact according to whether it is on a tomb, in a public square or in an art museum. Likewise, art varies in meaning according to the status, position and even the mood of the observer: the Wahgi body design has a different effect on the observer, depending on age, gender and group affiliation; the meaning of the eye shape in a Mende mask may vary according to the viewer's own self-image. Although such variation in interpretation is inevitable, it would be wrong to conclude that everything depends on interpretation and context. Just because something

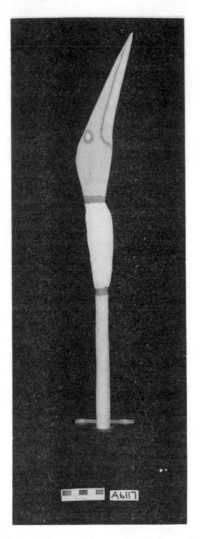

Figure 3 Toa of Pelican Lake. The *toa* directs the finder to Tampangaraterkana, 'the lake where the pelicans were'. Tampangaraterkana is in Tirari country near Lake Eyre in Central Australia. The *toa* represents a pelican's head with the lake as the white clay band underneath. The place was named by the ancestral being Mandramankana, who saw many pelicans on the lake. In order to interpret the message the person finding the *toa* has to identify the representation and then associate it with the attributes of a particular locality. In virtually all cases where the *toa* has a figurative element the figure represents a component of the place name. The *toa* could be interpreted by people who have never seen the object before, so long as they possess the relevant knowledge of indigenous geography and are familiar with the schema for a pelican's head (for a detailed analysis see Morphy 1977). This example was collected by the Reverend R. G. Reuther at Killalpaninna probably between 1903 and 1906. (Photograph courtesy the South Australian Museum)

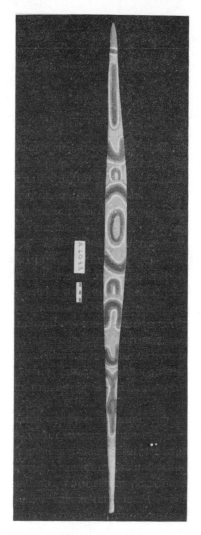

Figure 4 Toa of Pingalpiri, Central Australia. This *toa* represents a place on Cooper's Creek in Dieri country named Pingalpiri, after a kind of grass that grows there in profusion. The overall shape of the *toa* is said to represent a length of Cooper's Creek. The black vertical stripe near the top of the *toa* and the crescent below represent washed-out waterholes. The horse-shoe shape below them represents a camp site beside Pingalpiri waterhole (the next crescent). The oval in the centre represents the creek bed expanding with raised ground in the centre, the white outer ring representing water. The lower black figures represent further washed-out waterholes and the oval within the bottom figure represents a heap of stones. Pingalpiri grass is nowhere represented on the *toa* and the *toa* cannot be interpreted on the same basis as the one shown in Figure 3. Other *toa*s for Pingalpiri have bunches of the grass attached and can be interpreted by associating an iconic or indexical sign with the place. This particular *toa* is similar in form to Central Australian sacred objects. The geometric signs have different meanings in different contexts (see Figure 1) and do not accurately represent topographic reality. The message can only be interpreted by someone who is already familiar with the object and, in this case, knows that it is associated with Pingalpiri waterhole. (Photograph courtesy the South Australian Museum)

669

is multivalent we should not infer that it can mean anything. The analyst must examine the formal properties of representational systems, look for consistencies of interpretation and for constraints on what something can mean. In short, it is necessary to analyse the relationship between code and context.

THE PLACE OF STYLE

Not all aspects of the form of a work of art can be explained in terms of encoding meaning and indeed, in some cases, the concepts of code and representation may be of little relevance. Much of the form of art calls for explanation in terms of historical tradition and techniques, as well as its instrumental function and overall aesthetic effect. A concept that has frequently been used in the study of art is style. Style is an elusive concept, and 'classic' papers on it often appear as compendia of competing definitions (cf. Shapiro 1953). According to Conkey and Hastorf (1990: 2, citing Davis 1986: 124), 'most would agree that at its most delimited and fundamental level, style is some sort of a "formal statement of the particular ways in which different artefacts are similar to each other"'. Notwithstanding such agreement, opinions differ greatly as to which similarities to define as stylistic and how these similarities should be explained. Often style has a connotation that reflects the analyst's general theoretical focus, and some concepts of style are almost diametrically opposed to others. Forge (1973a), for example, sees style in Abelam art as integral to the functioning of the system – style is the way in which the object communicates meaning, or as Goodman (1978: 35) puts it, style concerns 'properties of the functioning of the work as symbol'. Dunnell (1978), on the other hand, opposes stylistic elements to functional ones and virtually defines them as embellishments without adaptive significance. While it is possible to see the logic behind Dunnell's position, in that he is trying to provide a definition of style that is less general than that of formal similarity and less specific than some of the more narrow functional definitions, the opposition between functional and stylistic elements which he sets up is unsustainable. As Sackett (1990: 43) has argued, style and function are conceptually separable but interrelated aspects of the same attribute; hence an attribute can be multiply determined by the simultaneous operation of both 'stylistic' and functional factors.

Part of the problem with the concept of style lies in the failure to recognize that it is used in two quite different senses: to refer to formal resemblances between objects as these are adduced by the anthropological observer or art historian, and to refer to such resemblances as they arise as part of what the producer *intends* – in other words where part of the producer's intention is that an object should have the formal properties it does in addition to functioning in the way intended. It is not always easy to separate out style that is consciously maintained from formal resemblances that are the product of people working within a particular tradition to reproduce objects that are in

670

continuity with past forms. The problem is to distinguish formal resemblances that stem from deliberate efforts on the part of producers to maintain and reproduce the 'style', from formal resemblances that stem from the unself-conscious replication of acquired practices and routines. In the former case the formal resemblance is intended by the producer, in the latter case it arises more or less automatically as a by-product of the transmission of technical skills, and may be apparent only to the outside observer. The difference between 'style' consciously maintained and 'style' unselfconsciously replicated may only become apparent in the context of change, where in the former case 'style' acts as more of a constraint on what can be produced than it does in the latter. However, as consciousness of style is not a given but something that is in turn produced, it is quite possible for it to develop or fade as part of the very process of change.

Style can itself be incorporated within a semiotic system, rather than, as Forge argues in the Abelam case, be the product of one. The presence of deco-ration of a particular style may mark a time, a place, a status or a category. Style may be part of a set of distinctions that reflect structural aspects of a socio-cultural system, and it may be a component in the process of their reproduction. It is this potential of style to reflect structured processes that has tempted some to use it as a means of approaching wider historical or social transformations, though such analyses seldom address the problem of linking abstract general characterizations with the details of social life and of indi-vidual action (for some interesting attempts see Fischer 1961, Berndt 1971, Faris 1978).

The analyst's explanation of a particular style, as defined within the observer's frame of reference, will include consideration of whether or not it is consciously maintained by the producers, but it will also involve the more general consideration of why the elements are present and what produces their organization. It may be because of the properties of a particular encoding system, or a technique of manufacture, or to mark group identity. It is most likely to be a combination of such factors. As Boas (1955 [1927]) showed long ago, in his analysis of Chilkat blankets, style can be both the product of the application of principles of representation and an independent determinant of form (Figure 5). He showed how some elements in the blankets are there pri-marily for semantic reasons and some are there as decorative motifs – to create a particular sense of balance, a spacing out of the design, or an overall visual effect. This does not mean, of course, that the separation of decorative and semantic motifs is an absolute one. The components of the blanket are better conceived as parts of an interrelated whole in which both aesthetic factors and semantic principles operate, some components being determined more by one factor than the other.

Style is a concept that mediates between form and function, between past practice and present production, and which is used to reflect on how form is organized as part of cultural process. As such it has been defined and applied

671

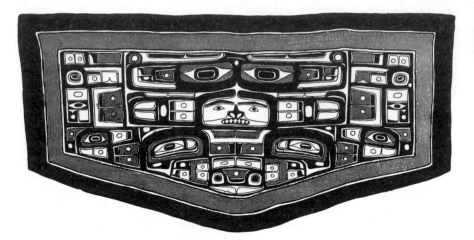

Figure 5 A Chilkat blanket from the American North-west Coast. The design represents a killer whale. As is conventional in Chilkat blankets, the central design represents the face. In the lateral panels to either side the dorsal fins are represented and elsewhere are other attributes of the form of the animal, including repeated eye designs. Boas (1927: 262) wrote that 'the intervening spaces which are not filled by large eye designs, the body, the tail, and extremities, are filled with a variety of patterns which depend only in part on the animal to be represented, but are very largely determined by aesthetic considerations'. This drawing by Emmons was originally used by Boas in his *Primitive Art*, Figure 273a. (Reproduced by permission of the American Museum of Natural History)

in an immense variety of different ways. It is a useful concept in that it gives some autonomy to form and suggests that a level of motivation exists in relation to the appearance of an object as a whole, and not simply in the process of combining the parts. Style may be the product of a particular combination of parts, or of the use of particular principles of representation, but it is also the product of reflections on the whole that can modify it and give it coherence at a different level.

AESTHETICS: BEYOND FORM AND MEANING

Part of the definition of art that I proposed earlier (p. 655) was that art objects should include those possessing aesthetic properties. What is of primary concern to the anthropologist is the aesthetics of the object in the context of the producing culture. As Coote (1989: 237) has argued, 'the explication of the differences between different cultures' ways of seeing should...be the primary task of the anthropology of aesthetics'. Although it may be perfectly reasonable to see other people's works through the eyes of one's own culture, the anthropologist's job is to reconnect aesthetics with the culture that produced the object. I can no longer postpone the task of defining a little more precisely what I include under the rubric of aesthetics. I have discussed the issue of cross-cultural aesthetics in detail elsewhere (Morphy 1992a, b), and only summarize the arguments here.

In the case of material culture, 'aesthetics' refers to the effects of properties of objects on the senses, to the qualitative dimension of the perception of objects. Salient properties include such physical ones as an object's form, texture, feel, and smell. They may also include non-material attributes of the object that are signified by it or associated with it, such as the attribute of age or distant place or magical substance. In relation to physical properties these latter attributes stand as connotation to denotation. Many of the physical properties are apprehended cross-culturally. Attributes such as weight, shininess, softness, perhaps even symmetry and balance, are analogous to electricity in that they can have an impact on the nervous system irrespective of the cultural background of the person experiencing them. Recognition of the non-material attributes, by contrast, presupposes cultural knowledge.

The properties of the object are not in themselves aesthetic properties, any more than is an electric shock. They become aesthetic properties through their incorporation within systems of value and meaning that integrate them within cultural processes. Shininess and symmetry, as aesthetic properties, are interpreted or appreciated on the basis of certain evaluative criteria that in simple terms cause them to be viewed positively or negatively, either in themselves or in relation to other properties or combinations of properties. This valorization converts an abstract or almost physical property into an aesthetic quality, and this quality cannot be assumed to be invariant across cultural boundaries. The aesthetic quality may in turn be linked to particular cultural meanings. As Forge (1967) wrote of the Abelam artist, 'I think that the skilful artist who satisfies his aesthetic sense and produces beauty is rewarded not for the beauty itself, but because the beauty, although recognized as such, is regarded by the rest as power' (Gell's (1992) idea of art as a technology of enchantment is relevant here).

One of the classic examples of the incorporation of aesthetic properties of objects within an overall system of value comes from the Massim region of Papua New Guinea, where the property of heaviness is associated with land, agricultural production and femaleness, and the property of lightness with voyaging, the exchange of goods and male careers (see Munn 1986: 80ff.). Thus aesthetics involves not simply how something looks and is appreciated, but also how it is felt and understood. This insight illustrates both the difficulties and the potentialities of communicating aesthetic values cross-culturally. Understanding the aesthetic response of a member of another culture to an object requires suspending one's own response to it, and learning how that object and its attributes are incorporated into systems of value and meaning. If one can teach people to interpret and value the properties of the objects of another culture according to the aesthetics of that culture, then one may provide a powerful insight into that world, and into what it feels like to be a member of it.

Similar aesthetic effects can have very different meanings cross-culturally, and one of the tasks of an anthropology of art is to demonstrate these differences: to show the ways in which different values are created and associated with particular qualities. This again renews the link between anthropology and

Figure 6 Mithinari painting at Yirrkala, Northern Australia. The Yolngu artist Mithinari of the Galpu clan, who died in 1975, is at work on a bark painting of the lake Garimala. The final stage of the painting process is to cover the surface with cross-hatched lines in white, red and yellow, to create an effect of shimmering brilliance. (Photograph H. Morphy, 1974)

art history, with its concern with expressive form. A comparison of the art of the Yolngu, the Wahgi Valley people and the Mende provides us with an example of the way in which a similar aesthetic effect is incorporated in different ways within different systems, and how it becomes associated with different though related values. In all three cases the aesthetic effect is that of shimmering or shining brilliance.

In the Yolngu case the effect of *bir'yun* ('shimmering brilliance') is produced by covering the surface of a painting with fine cross-hatched lines (Morphy 1992b; see Figure 6). Painting is seen as a process whereby a rough, dull state is transformed into a shimmering, brilliant state. The paintings themselves are believed to be manifestations of the ancestral past and the shimmering effect is interpreted as the power of the ancestral beings shining out from the painting. The image is reinforced by song and by an emphasis in myth on similar images of transformation between dark and light.

Wahgi body paintings, like the Yolngu paintings, are evaluated by the extent to which they shine. In his analysis O'Hanlon (1989) argues that shininess is associated with images of health and fertility, but also with power and strength, because people decorate themselves for war. Shininess condenses in a positive form most aspects of Wahgi existence. The body decoration has a natural analogue in the form of pig fat, which is also a key element in Wahgi ritual, economy, and social reproduction (see Figure 7).

Figure 7 Wahgi dancers: a phalanx of painted and decorated dancers at a pig festival in the Wahgi Valley, Papua New Guinea. (Photograph M. O'Hanlon)

In the case of a major [pig] payment the line of overlapping pork sides, displayed fat outermost, stretches away in a gleaming stream for eighty yards or even further. ... It is perhaps possible to see pork fat as the material embodiment or condensation of the fertility/growth sought during the Pig Festival, and of the ancestral favour on which these are said to depend... [the public consumption of pork fat would be the] literal internalization or reabsorption of the qualities men claim to have engendered during the festival.

(O'Hanlon 1989: 120)

In the case of the Mende, in contrast to the Yolngu and the Wahgi, the brilliance comes not out of light colours, but out of the burnished blackness of the *sowo-wui* mask (see Figure 8). According to Boone (1986: 238), the blackness of the mask reflects the 'extraordinary beauty and shining blackness' of the paradise towns in the depths of the water, from where the Sande Sowo, the dancing masked figure, is supposed to come. In this case the shiny blackness of the mask reflects itself onto female initiates, creating positive images of self.

In all three cases we can see how the creation of a particular aesthetic effect is integral to the art, not simply because the effect excites admiration but also because it is part of the semantics of the art and of the way in which art is

Figure 8 Sowei (*sowo-wui*) dancing. A Sowei dancer is in full flight at Gofor, Makpele chiefdom, Pujehun District, Sierra Leone. (Photograph Ruth Phillips)

integrated within the cultural system as a whole. In each case it provides a means whereby values are associated with qualities which cross-cut contexts. Brilliance, wherever it is found, can become respectively a manifestation of ancestral power, a sign of fertility or well-being,[3] or a reflection of female health. In this respect aesthetics involves the cultural control over, and production of, certain selected and culturally conceived properties or qualities of the natural world, or in Munn's (1986) expression, 'qualisigns' of value. The differences in interpretation do not reflect simply the existence of different meanings that could be learnt or experienced independently of the cultural processes and structures which give rise to them – to grasp them is not merely a matter of translating the words of one language into another. The particular interpretations are related to the cultural context of their production and to the ways in which they are encountered and experienced – to how they are *presented* to the individual. In the Yolngu case brilliance is integrated within a system of restricted knowledge, associated with concepts of underlying transcendent powers. In the Wahgi case brilliance is produced in the context of rituals of competitive display, and is regarded as partial testimony to the true state of the wearers' relationships with fellow clanspeople and extra-clan sources (O'Hanlon 1992: 606). And in the Mende case brilliance emerges in the arena of public masquerade, but in a society in which gender, peer-group and authority relations are structured by secret societies. Aesthetic effects such as brilliance are among the means whereby the felt values and emotional states associated with the contexts of their production are transmitted across the generations, and are involved in the reproduction of the very cultural processes and structures of which they are a part.

CONCLUSION

The anthropology of art has in recent years gained a new impetus through its interaction with other disciplines, in particular archaeology and art history, and through the increasing symbolic and economic importance of art and other cultural forms in political and cultural relations between the developed world and the Third and Fourth Worlds. From being an esoteric, museum-based branch of the discipline it has moved, almost unawares, into the front line. Through tourism, films, exhibitions, cultural festivals and the sale of craft products, art has increasingly been inserted into the space between indigenous peoples and the developed world. It provides an area of interaction and of value exchange, a means of asserting cultural identity, and, increasingly, a context for political action through copyright and cultural heritage legislation.

Thus the anthropology of art provides a way of understanding global processes that links the traditional practices of small-scale communities with world institutions such as the United Nations. And these processes are ones that not only involve conceptual changes on the part of indigenous peoples, but are also linked to consequent or parallel changes in Western categorizations of things. The sale of art to outsiders has consequences for the use of art in indigenous contexts, as well as providing a means for integration within a wider world economic system. In the West the way in which these products are categorized has begun to change as the objects have begun to move out of the ethnographic museum and into the art gallery, and as the distinction between the 'authentic' pre-European products of 'primitive art' and the 'contemporary' products of indigenous peoples has broken down. Because of the high status accorded to art in the recent history of Western culture, this change has altered the Western perception of the non-Western 'other', an alteration that is part and parcel of a more general process of value change.

Anthropology has, in the past, neglected the topics of art and aesthetics because they have been tainted by ethnocentricism and difficulties of definition. One of the positive developments to have come out of contemporary post-modernism and reflexive anthropology has been the challenge to those categories with which anthropologists traditionally felt themselves to be most secure: social institutions, kinship behaviour, exchange relations, gender. The recognition that concepts, as well as being prerequisites for thought, are at the same time the products of thinking about things in the world and therefore themselves liable to change, has enabled the concept of art to re-enter anthropology in a new guise, as the foundation for an approach that looks in two directions. It looks towards the objects of other cultures that it seeks to analyse as art, and it looks towards an understanding of art as a category that has an important place in Western culture and politics. The perspective on the comparative method developed by Marilyn Strathern is very relevant to the cross-cultural study of art:

> Comparative procedure, investigating variables across societies, normally decontextualizes local constructs in order to work with context-bound analytic ones.... The study of symbolic systems presents a different problematic.... The task is not to imagine one can replace exogenous concepts by indigenous counterparts, rather the task is to convey the complexity of indigenous concepts in reference to the particular context in which they are produced. Hence I choose to show the contextualized nature of indigenous constructs by exposing the contextualized nature of analytical ones.
>
> (1988: 8)

Indeed, I would argue that one of the main achievements or even consequences of the anthropology of art has been to pose questions about the Western category and concept of art and to expose its contextualized nature.

NOTES

1   The category 'primitive art' was for a time an extremely broad one. Indeed, the narrowing down of its definition to include mainly the works of small-scale indigenous societies, often referred to as 'tribal art', took place in the twentieth century (see Rubin 1984: 2). In this century Clive Bell, in his book *Art*, includes Indian,

Japanese, Chinese, Mesoamerican, Sumerian and Egyptian art within the category 'primitive' (1987 [1914]: 22).

2   It could be argued that cultural relativism in this context is a distancing mechanism that places the relativist on a plain of absolute superiority, standing above any particular culture: art is thus a tool used by relativists themselves in the reproduction of their own superiority over everyone else (Ingold, personal communication). From a different perspective others have argued that the way Europeans have presented non-European art has involved an appropriation of that art in the interests of academics and the capitalist economy (see for example Fry and Willis's (1989) critique of Peter Sutton's (1988) exhibition of Australian Aboriginal art, and replies from Sutton (1992) and Benjamin (1990)). Certainly the way some art historians write about the discovery of the 'art' in primitive art can convey an impression of the existence of a superior cultural arbiter. Rubin (1984: 7), for example, writes, 'We owe to the voyagers, colonials and ethnologists the arrival of these objects in the West. But we owe primarily to the pioneer modern artists their promotion from the rank of curiosities and artefacts to that of major art, indeed to the status of art at all.' There is always a danger that anthropologists, when promoting cultural equality to a Western audience, will adopt too strongly the values and categories of that audience; that they will accept uncritically the Western concept of art and its institutional underpinnings and simply allocate to it selected objects from other cultures. Against this I would argue that cultural relativism arises out of the development of anthropology as a metalanguage for analysing cultural variation and difference, which has the objective of being as value-free as possible. In practice anthropologists will often develop concepts and discourses which challenge the assumptions of their own cultures. Rather than asserting that the products of other cultures have been wrongly classified as non-art, I would challenge the development of a concept of art that has separated Westerners from others and which has become associated with a hierarchy of cultural value.

3   See also Coote (1992: 252–3) on the appreciation of sheen among Nilotic-speaking cattle herders, where it is also considered an indicator of health.

REFERENCES

Anderson, R. L. (1979) *Art in Primitive Societies*, Englewood Cliffs, NJ: Prentice-Hall.
Appadurai, A. (ed.) (1986) *The Social Life of Things: Commodities in Cultural Perspective*, Cambridge: Cambridge University Press.
Balfour, H. (1893) *The Evolution of Decorative Art*, London: Percival.
Bascom, W. (1973) 'A Yoruba master carver, Duga of Meko', in W. L. d'Azevedo (ed) *The Traditional Artist in African Societies*, Bloomington: Indiana University Press.
Bateson, G. (1937) *Naven*, Cambridge: Cambridge University Press.
—— (1973) 'Style, grace and information in primitive art', in J. A. W. Forge (ed.) *Primitive Art and Society*, London: Oxford University Press.
Becker, H. (1982) *Art Worlds*, Berkeley: University of California Press.
Bell, C. (1987 [1914]) *Art*, London: Chatto & Windus.
Benjamin, R. (1990) 'Aboriginal art: exploitation or empowerment', *Art in America*, July: 73–80.
Berndt, R. M. (1971) 'Some methodological considerations in the study of Australian Aboriginal art', *Oceania* 29: 26–43.
Biebuyk, D. (ed.) (1969) *Tradition and Creativity in Tribal Art*, Berkeley: University of California Press.

Biebuyk, D. (1973) *Lega Culture: Art, Initiation and Moral Philosophy among a Central African People*, Berkeley: University of California Press.

Blier, S. P. (1987) *The Anatomy of Architecture*, Cambridge: Cambridge University Press.

Boas, F. (1955 [1927]) *Primitive Art*, New York: Dover.

Boone, S. A. (1986) *The Radiance from the Waters*, New Haven: Yale University Publications in the History of Art.

Bourdieu, P. (1984) *Distinction: a Social Critique of the Judgement of Taste*, trans. R. Nice, London: Routledge & Kegan Paul.

Bowden, R. (1983) *Yena: Art and Ceremony in a Sepik Society*, Pitt-Rivers Museum Monograph 3, Oxford: Pitt Rivers Museum.

—— (1992) 'Art, architecture and collective representations in a New Guinea Society', in J. Coote and A. Shelton (eds) *Anthropology, Art and Aesthetics*, Oxford Studies in the Anthropology of Cultural Forms, Oxford: Clarendon Press.

Brain, R. and Pollock, A. (1971) *Bangwa Sculpture*, London: Duckworth.

Campbell, S. (1984) 'The art of the Kula', PhD thesis, Canberra: Australian National University.

Chaloupka, G. (1985) 'Chronological sequence of Arnhem Land Plateaux rock art', in R. Jones (ed.) *Archaeological Research in Kakadu National Park*, Canberra: Australian National Parks and Wildlife Service.

Clifford, J. (1991) 'Four Northwest Coast museums', in I. Karp and S. D. Levine (eds) *Exhibiting Cultures: the Poetics and Politics of Museum Display*, Washington, DC: Smithsonian Institution Press.

Conkey, M. and Hastorf, C. (1990) 'Introduction', in M. Conkey and C. Hastorf (eds) *The Uses of Style in Archaeology*, New Directions in Archaeology, Cambridge: Cambridge University Press.

Coote, J. (1989) 'The anthropology of aesthetics and the dangers of "Maquetcentricism"', *Journal of the Anthropological Society of Oxford* 20(3): 229–43.

—— (1992) 'Marvels of everyday vision', in J. Coote and A. Shelton (eds) *Anthropology, Art and Aesthetics*, Oxford Studies in the Anthropology of Cultural Forms, Oxford: Clarendon Press.

Csikszentmihalyi, M. and Roshberg-Halton, E. (1981) *The Meaning of Things*, Cambridge: Cambridge University Press.

Craig, B. (1990) 'Relic and trophy displays as art among the Mountain-Ok, Central New Guinea', in A. and H. Hanson (eds) *Art and Identity in Oceania*, Honolulu: University of Hawaii Press.

Danto, A. C. (1973) 'Artworks and real things', *Theoria* 34: 1–17.

Dark P., Forman, W. and Forman, B. (1960) *Benin Art*, London: Hamlyn.

Davis, W. (1986) 'Comments on Natalie Franklin, "Stochastic vs. emblematic: an archaeologically useful method for the analysis of style in Australian rock art"', *Rock Art Research* 3(2): 124–5.

—— (1990) 'Style and history in art history', in M. Conkey and C. Hastorf (eds) *The Uses of Style in Archaeology*, New Directions in Archaeology, Cambridge: Cambridge University Press.

d'Azevedo, W. L. (ed.) (1973) *The Traditional Artist in African Society*, Bloomington: Indiana University Press.

Dunnell, R. (1978) 'Style and function: a fundamental dichotomy', *American Antiquity* 43: 192–202.

Fagg, W. (1948) 'A master sculptor of the Eastern Congo', *Man* 48: 37–8.

—— (1965) *Tribes and Forms in African Art*, New York: Tudor.

—— (1970) *Divine Kingship in Africa*, London: British Museum.

Faris, J. C. (1972) *Nuba Personal Art*, London: Duckworth.

—— (1978) 'The productive basis of aesthetic traditions: some African examples', in M. Greenhalgh and J. V. S. Megaw (eds) *Art in Society: Studies in Style, Culture and Aesthetics*, London: Duckworth.

Fernandez, J. W. (1972) 'Persuasions and performances: of the beast in every body ... and the metaphors of everyman,' *Daedalus*, winter 1972: 39–60.

Firth, R. (1973) 'Tikopia art and society', in J. A. W. Forge (ed.) *Primitive Art and Society*, London: Oxford University Press.

Fischer, J. L. (1961) 'Art styles as cultural cognitive maps', *American Anthropologist* 63(1): 79–93.

Forge, J. A. W. (1962) 'Paint – a magical substance', *Palette* 9.

—— (1966) 'Art and environment in the Sepik', *Proceedings of the Royal Anthropological Institute for 1965*: 23–31.

—— (1967) 'The Abelam artist', in M. Freedman (ed.) *Social Organization: Essays presented to Raymond Firth*, London: Frank Cass.

—— (1970) 'Learning to see in New Guinea', in P. Mayer (ed.) *Socialization: the Approach from Social Anthropology* (A.S.A. Monograph, 8), London: Tavistock.

—— (1973a) 'Style and meaning in Sepik art', in J. A. W. Forge (ed.) *Primitive Art and Society*, London: Oxford University Press.

—— (ed.) (1973b) *Primitive Art and Society*, London: Oxford University Press.

Fraser, D. (1962) *Primitive Art*, New York: Doubleday.

Fry, T. and Willis, A. M. (1989) 'Aboriginal art: symptom or success?', *Art in America*, July: 108–17.

Gell, A. (1992) 'The technology of enchantment and the enchantment of technology', in J. Coote and A. Shelton (eds) *Anthropology, Art and Aesthetics*, Oxford Studies in the Anthropology of Cultural Forms, Oxford: Clarendon Press.

Gerbrands, A. A. (1957) *Art as an Element of Culture: Especially in Negro Africa*, Medelingen van het Rijksmuseum voor Volkekunde no. 12, Leiden: E. J. Brill.

—— (1967) *Wow-Ipits: Eight Asmat Carvers of New Guinea*, The Hague: Mouton.

Goehr, L. (1992) *The Imaginary Museum of Musical Works: an Essay in the Philosophy of Music*, Oxford: Clarendon Press.

Goldwater, R. (1973) 'Art history and anthropology: some comparisons of methodology', in J. A. W. Forge (ed.) *Primitive Art and Society*, London: Oxford University Press.

Goodman, N. (1978) 'The status of style', in N. Goodman (ed.) *Ways of Worldmaking*, Indianapolis: Bobbs-Merrill.

Graburn, N. H. H. (1976) *Ethnic and Tourist Arts: Cultural Expressions of the Fourth World*, Berkeley: University of California Press.

—— (1978) 'I like the things to look more different than that stuff did', in M. Greenhalgh and J. V. S. Megaw (eds) *Art in Society: Studies in Style, Culture and Aesthetics*, London: Duckworth.

Greenhalgh, M. and Megaw, J. V. S. (eds) (1978) *Art in Society: Studies in Style, Culture and Aesthetics*, London: Duckworth.

Griaule, M. (1938) *Masques Dogons*, Travaux et mémoires de l'Institut d'Ethnonologie de l'Université de Paris, Paris.

Guss, D. G. (1989) *To Weave and Sing: Art, Symbol and Narrative in the South American Rain Forest*, Berkeley: University of California Press.

Haddon. A. C. (1895) *Evolution in Art*, London: Walter Scott.

—— (ed.) (1912) *Reports on the Cambridge Anthropological Expedition to the Torres Straits*, vol. 4: *Arts and Crafts*, Cambridge: Cambridge University Press.

Herskovits, M. J. (1938) *Dahomey: An Ancient African Kingdom*, 2 vols, New York: J. J. Augustin.

Hodder, I. (1982) *Symbols in Action*, Cambridge: Cambridge University Press.

Holm, B. (1965) *North West Coast Indian Art: an Analysis of Form*, Seattle: University of Washington Press.

Hutton, J. H. (1921) *The Angami Nagas*, London: Macmillan.

Jones, P. and Sutton, P. (1986) *Art and Land: Aboriginal Sculptures of the Lake Eyre Region*, Adelaide: South Australian Museum.

Jopling, C. F. (ed.) (1971) *Art and Aesthetics in Primitive Societies: a Critical Anthology*, New York: Dutton.

Kasfir, S. L. (1984) 'One tribe one style? Paradigms in the historiography of African art', *History in Africa* 9: 163–93.

Kubler, G. (1962) *The Shape of Time*, New Haven: Yale University Press.

Küchler, S. (1992) 'Making skins: *Malangan* and the idiom of kinship in northern New Ireland', in J. Coote and A. Shelton (eds) *Anthropology, Art and Aesthetics*, Oxford Studies in the Anthropology of Cultural Forms, Oxford: Clarendon Press.

Layton, R. (1978) 'Art and visual communication', in M. Greenhalgh and J. V. S. Megaw (eds) *Art in Society: Studies in Style, Culture and Aesthetics*, London: Duckworth.

—— (1991) *The Anthropology of Art*, Cambridge: Cambridge University Press.

Leach, E. R. (1954) 'A Trobriand Medusa?', *Man* 54: 103–5.

—— (1973) 'Levels of communication and problems of taboo in the appreciation of primitive art', in J. A. W. Forge (ed.) *Primitive Art and Society*, London: Oxford University Press.

Lewis, P. (1969) *The Social Context of Art in New Ireland* (Fieldiana Anthropology, 58), Chicago: Field Museum of Natural History.

MacKenzie, M. A. (1991) *Androgynous Objects: String Bags and Gender in Central New Guinea*, New York: Harwood.

Mead, S. M. (ed.) (1979) *Exploring the Visual Art of Oceania*, Hawaii: University of Hawaii Press.

Miller, D. (1983) 'Things ain't what they used to be', *Royal Anthropological Institute Newsletter* 59: 5–17.

—— (1985) *Artefacts as Categories: a Study of Ceramic Variability in Central India*, Cambridge: Cambridge University Press.

—— (1987) *Material Culture and Mass Consumption*, Oxford: Blackwell.

Mills, J. P. (1977) *The Rengma Nagas*, London: Macmillan.

Morphy, F. (1977) 'The social significance of schematisation in North-west Coast American Indian art', in P. J. Ucko (ed.) *Form in Indigenous Art: Schematisation in the Art of Aboriginal Australia and Prehistoric Europe*, Canberra: Australian Institute of Aboriginal Studies.

Morphy, H. (1977) 'Schematisation, communication and meaning in *toas*', in P. J. Ucko (ed.) *Form in Indigenous Art: Schematisation in the Art of Aboriginal Australia and Prehistoric Europe*, Canberra: Australian Institute of Aboriginal Studies.

—— (1988) 'The original Australians and the evolution of anthropology', in H. Morphy and E. Edwards (eds) *Australia in Oxford*, Pitt Rivers Museum Monographs 4, Oxford: Pitt Rivers Museum.

—— (1989) 'Introduction', in H. Morphy (ed.) *Animals into Art*, London: Unwin-Hyman.

—— (1991) *Ancestral Connections: Art and an Aboriginal System of Knowledge*, Chicago: University of Chicago Press.

—— (1992a) 'Aesthetics in a cross-cultural perspective: some reflections on native American basketry', *Journal of the Anthropological Society of Oxford* 23(1): 1–16.

—— (1992b) 'From dull to brilliant: the aesthetics of spiritual power amongst the Yolngu', in J. Coote and A. Shelton (eds) *Anthropology, Art and Aesthetics*, Oxford Studies in the Anthropology of Cultural Forms, Oxford: Clarendon Press.

Mountford, C. (1958) *The Tiwi: Their Art, Myth and Ceremony*, London: Phoenix House.

Munn, N. D. (1962) 'Walbiri graphic signs: an analysis', *American Anthropologist* 64(5): 972–94.

—— (1973) *Walbiri Iconography*, Ithaca: Cornell University Press.

—— (1977) 'The spatiotemporal transformation of Gawan canoes', *Journal de la Société des Océanistes* 33 (54–5): 39–53.

—— 1986. *The Fame of Gawa*, Cambridge: Cambridge University Press.

O'Hanlon, M. D. P. (1989) *Reading the Skin: Adornment Display and Society among the Wahgi*, London: British Museum.

—— (1992) 'Unstable images and second skins: artefacts, exegesis and assessments in the New Guinea Highlands', *Man* (N.S.) 27(3): 587–608.

Otten, C. M. (ed.) (1971) *Anthropology and Art: Readings in Cross-cultural Aesthetics*, Garden City, N.Y.: Natural History Press.

Phillips, R. B. (1993) *Representing Woman: the Sande Society Masquerades of the Mende*, Los Angeles: Fowler Museum of Cultural History.

Rattray, R. S. (1927) *Religion and Art among the Ashanti*, Oxford: Clarendon Press.

Rosman, A. and Rubel, P. G. (1990) 'Structural patterning in Kwakiutl art and ritual', *Man* (N.S.) 25(40): 620-39.

Rubin, W. (1984) 'Modernist primitivism, an introduction', in W. Rubin (ed.) *Primitivism in Twentieth Century Art*, vol. 1, New York: Museum of Modern Art.

Sackett, J. (1990) 'Style and ethnicity in archaeology: the case for isochretism', in M. Conkey and C. Hastorf (eds) *The Uses of Style in Archaeology*, New Directions in Archaeology, Cambridge: Cambridge University Press.

Scoditti, M. G. (1989) *Kitawa: a Linguistic and Aesthetic Analysis of Visual Art in Melanesia*, Berlin: Mouton de Gruyter.

Shapiro, M. (1953) 'Style', in A. L. Kroeber (ed.) *Anthropology Today*, Chicago: Aldine.

Sillitoe, P. (1980) 'The art of war: Wola shield designs', *Man* (N.S.) 15(3): 483–501.

Spencer, W. B. S. and Gillen, F. J. (1899) *Native Tribes of Central Australia*, London: Macmillan.

Sperber, D. (1976) *Rethinking Symbolism*, Cambridge: Cambridge University Press.

Stocking, G. W. (1985) 'Essays on museums and material culture', in G. W. Stocking (ed.) *Objects and Others: Essays on Museums and Material Culture* (History of Anthropology 3), Madison: University of Wisconsin Press.

Strathern, A. J. and Strathern, M. (1971) *Self-decoration in Mount Hagen*, London: Duckworth.

Strathern, M. (1988) *The Gender of the Gift: Problems with Women and Problems with Society in Melanesia*, Berkeley: University of California Press.

Sturtevant, W. (1969) 'Does anthropology need museums?', *Proceedings of the Biological Society of Washington* 2: 619–50.

Sutton P. (1987) '"The really interesting suggestion . . .", yet another reply to Donald Brook on *toas*', *Adelaide Review* 35: 5.

—— (1988) *Dreamings: the Art of Aboriginal Australia*, London: Viking/Penguin.

—— (1992) 'Reading Aboriginal Art', in D. Walker, J. Horne and M. Lyons (eds) *Books, Readers, Reading* (*Australian Cultural History* (special issue) 11: 28–38).

Taçon, P. (1989) Art and the essence of being: symbolic and economic aspects of fish among the peoples of Western Arnhem Land', in H. Morphy (ed.) *Animals into Art*, London: Unwin Hyman.

Taylor, L. (1989) 'Seeing the inside: Kunwinjku painting and the symbol of the divided body', in H. Morphy (ed.) *Animals into Art*, London: Unwin Hyman.

Thomas, N. (1989) *Out of Time: History and Evolution in Anthropological Discourse*, Cambridge: Cambridge University Press.

—— (1991) *Entangled Objects: Exchange, Material Culture and Colonialism in the Pacific*, Cambridge, Mass.: Harvard University Press.

Tilley, C. (1991) *Material Culture and Text: the Art of Ambiguity*, London: Routledge.

Tippett, A. R. (1968) *Fijian Material Culture*, Honolulu: Bishop Museum.

Turner, V. W. (1967) *The Forest of Symbols: Aspects of Ndembu Ritual*, Ithaca: Cornell University Press.

Ucko, P. J. (1969) 'Penis sheaths: a comparative study', *Proceedings of the Royal Anthropological Institute for 1968*: 27–67.

—— (ed.) (1977) *Form in Indigenous Art: Schematisation in the Art of Aboriginal Australia and Prehistoric Europe*, Canberra: Australian Institute of Aboriginal Studies.

Vogel, S. (1980) 'The Buli master and other hands', *Art in America* 68(5): 32–42.

—— (1988) 'Introduction', in S. Vogel (ed.) *Art/Artifact*, New York: Center for African Art and Prestel Verlag.

Willett, F. (1972) 'The art of an ancient Nigerian aristocracy', in D. Fraser and H. M. Cole (eds) *African Art and Leadership*, Madison: University of Wisconsin Press.

Witherspoon, G. (1977) *Language and Art in the Navaho Universe*, Ann Arbor: University of Michigan Press.

FURTHER READING

Blier, S. P. (1987) *The Anatomy of Architecture*, Cambridge: Cambridge University Press.

Conkey, M. and Hastorf, C. (1990) *The Uses of Style in Archaeology*, New Directions in Archaeology, Cambridge: Cambridge University Press.

Coote, J. and Shelton, A. (eds) (1992) *Art, Anthropology and Aesthetics*, Oxford Studies in the Anthropology of Cultural Forms, Oxford: Clarendon Press.

d'Azevedo, W. L. (ed.) (1973) *The Traditional Artist in African Societies*, Bloomington: Indiana University Press.

Forge, J. A. W. (ed.) (1973) *Primitive Art and Society*, London: Oxford University Press.

Gell, A. (1975) *Metamorphosis of the Cassowaries: Umeda Society, Language and Ritual*, LSE Monographs in Social Anthropology, no. 51, London: Athlone.

Graburn, N. H. H. (ed.) (1976) *Ethnic and Tourist Arts: Cultural Expressions of the Fourth World*, Berkeley: University of California Press.

Greenhalgh, M. and Megaw, J. V. S. (eds) (1978) *Art in Society: Studies in Style, Culture and Aesthetics*, London: Duckworth.

Guss, D. G. (1989) *To Weave and Sing: Art, Symbol and Narrative in the South American Rain Forest*, Berkeley: University of California Press.

Hanson, A. and Hanson, L. (eds) (1990) *Art and Identity in Oceania*, Hawaii: University of Hawaii Press.

Kubler, G. (1962) *The Shape of Time*, New Haven: Yale University Press.

Layton, R. (1991) *The Anthropology of Art*, Cambridge: Cambridge University Press.

Lévi-Strauss, C. (1983) *The Way of the Masks*, transl. S. Modelski, London: Jonathan Cape.

McNaughton, P. (1988) *The Mande Blacksmiths: Knowledge, Power and Art in West Africa*, Bloomington: University of Indiana Press.

Morphy, H. (ed.) (1989) *Animals into Art*, London: Unwin Hyman.

—— (1991) *Ancestral Connections: Art and an Aboriginal System of Knowledge*, Chicago: University of Chicago Press.

Munn, N. D. (1973) *Walbiri Iconography*, Ithaca: Cornell University Press.
O'Hanlon, M. D. P. (1989) *Reading the Skin: Adornment, Display and Society among the Wahgi*, London: British Museum Publications.
Price, S. (1989) *Primitive Art in Civilized Places*, Chicago: University of Chicago Press.
Ucko, P. J. (ed.) (1977) *Form in Indigenous Art: Schematisation in the Art of Aboriginal Australia and Prehistoric Europe*, Canberra: Australian Institute of Aboriginal Studies.

24

MUSIC AND DANCE

Anthony Seeger

Stop. Do not read the next paragraph of text until you have read this one and stopped to think about the last time you took part in a performance of music and/or dance. I, the author, cannot imagine what you will recall. Perhaps you were in the audience at a rock concert or dance club, perhaps you were in church, or have recently performed modern dance, or attended a political rally. Maybe you have just returned from a powwow and, after storing your special dress and showering, you are sitting down to learn about anthropology. Think back. Recall the time of day or night, the dress of the participants, the feel of the locale, the sensation of the sounds on the ear, the movement of your body and its contact with other bodies, the smells (or lack of them), the actions of the performers, the audiences, and your reactions to all of these. Imagine yourself in several places during that performance – and what you might be feeling and thinking about. Take your time; then read on.

*   *   *

The written word, linear and referential, is singularly unsuited to capture the complexity of events such as the one you just recalled – with its intense combination of individual and shared experiences and emotions. Social-scientific writing is even less able to deal with these events than is fiction or poetry. Anthropologists constantly struggle with language in an attempt to understand and represent the complexity of social life in human societies. It is words, not experience, that have divided up our field of study and have led us to treat music and dance in isolation from the rest of social life.

In fact, music and dance are inextricably involved in human social processes. They take their meaning from, and give meaning to, time, space, the body and its parts, human artefacts, personal experience, social identity, relations of production and social status. Indeed, in virtually every one of the topics covered by the various articles in this Encyclopaedia, music and dance are implicated in one way or another. Found in all societies, where they are often invested with considerable emotional force, economic value, and cultural significance, music and dance are worthy objects of anthropological attention. They can also provide a perspective on human societies that is often absent from conventional analyses of social organization and systems of belief, which tend to emphasize their conceptual bases and to neglect the unique features of performance.

The production of purposive, structured sounds and movements is not unique to human beings. Bird calls have pitch, many animal species perform elaborate movements during courtship and to establish territories. Some writers have even argued that music can be used as a cross-species form of communication (Nollman 1990). Yet so far as we know human beings are unique in the variety of meanings they ascribe to patterned sounds and movements, and in the variety of styles that even one community may perform.

Music and dance differ from much of what anthropologists study in that they are neither verbal nor material. A cursory glance at the anthropological literature of the past century reveals a concentration on language over other forms of communication, on vision over other forms of perception, on kinship and descent over other forms of relationship, and on production-related activities over other forms of action. There are a variety of reasons for this, not the least of them being the heritage of Greek philosophy, Christian theology, and the issues confronting nineteenth-century social philosophers. Aristotle's metaphysics still influence much of anthropology; an emphasis on the text rather than on its performance is characteristic of much of Christian teaching; and concerns about the nature of community, authority, status, the sacred, and alienation, upon which much of nineteenth-century social philosophy focused, probably derived their force from the dramatic changes in society resulting from industrialization and from transformations in the political basis of authority that were apparent to all members of European society (Nisbet 1966).

Music, dance, and the arts were never central to the concerns of European or British social anthropology, and were generally ignored in favour of material and verbal forms of cultural expression, or confined within concept-led analyses of religious ritual. In spite of a brilliantly suggestive article by Marcel Mauss (1936), most anthropologically oriented research on music and dance has been carried out by American scholars in a tradition stretching from Franz Boas, through Melville Herskovitz and George Herzog, to Alan Merriam, David McAllester, Bruno Nettl and their students.

Ethnomusicology, as the comparative study of music came to be called in the United States, is a field strongly influenced by historical musicology and only occasionally touches on the central concerns of anthropological debate. There have always been exceptions. Alan Merriam's *The Anthropology of Music* (1964) was a systematic introduction to music through topics of anthropology, and its author had a profound influence on the field through his own extensive writings and those of some of his students, among them Feld (1982), Stone

(1982) and Kingsbury (1988), to name but a few. He also influenced Keil (1979), Seeger (1987) and many others through his writings and discussions. George Herzog, who had studied in Berlin and joined Boas at Columbia University, founded an ethnomusicology archive (subsequently it became the Indiana University Archives of Traditional Music), and his student David McAllester wrote one of the most important studies of musical values (1954). Bruno Nettl has written influential textbooks (1964, 1983), addressed central issues in the field – such as musical change (1985) – and has trained many students. John Blacking was a major figure not only because of his prolific writings (among them 1967, 1974, 1977, 1985), which reached a wide readership, but also because of the powerfully provocative nature of many of his more general pronouncements. He was, moreover, responsible for the establishment of a strong programme in the study of both music *and* dance within an anthropology department, at Queen's University Belfast.

The systematic study of dance (variously referred to as 'choreology', 'ethnochoreology' and 'dance ethnology') has also developed somewhat apart from anthropological concerns. It has stronger ties to folklore studies, with their emphasis on description and classification (Torp 1990, Giurchescu and Torp 1991, Kaeppler 1978, 1991). Alan Merriam was, however, an important influence on the work of Keali'inohomoku (1976) and Royce (1977).

One researcher in particular stands out for his unswerving interest in demonstrating the integration of music, dance, and speech forms with economic, social, and cultural aspects of societies, namely Alan Lomax. Lomax developed a statistical method for analysing sounds (cantometrics), movement (choreometrics), and speech (Lomax 1968). His approach, based on data from a sample of cultures around the world tabulated in the Human Relations Area Files, together with whatever audio and visual recordings he managed to acquire, has not been adopted by other scholars. It has been strongly criticized for its mode of statistical sampling, for its questionable and outdated anthropological methodology, and on other grounds. Lomax's work remains interesting, nevertheless, for he addresses some very important issues, and with unusual feeling.

First, Lomax made a strong case for the *social* nature of song, and for the significance of its redundancy. 'Singing', he wrote, 'is a specialized act of communication, akin to speech, but far more formally organized and redundant. . . . It is to be expected then that the content of the sung communication should be social rather than individual, normative rather than particular' (1968: 3). Secondly, he addressed the musical features of song, and not just the texts. In so doing, he developed a coding system with 37 parameters that goes far beyond the number of variables represented by most notation systems. Thirdly, Lomax made a passionate case for the documentation, preservation, and encouragement of the diverse musical traditions around the world:

The work is filled with a sense of urgency. . . . The loss in communicative potential for the whole human race is very grave, for these threatened communication systems represent much of what the human race has created in its thousands of years of wandering across the earth. In them lies a treasure, a human resource, whose worth is incalculable and which can never be replaced when it has been wasted and lost.... A verse can recall a whole epoch; a turn in a tune can hearten a people through a generation of struggle; for, if the written word preserves and expands knowledge, the multileveled symbolic structure of music and art can preserve and expand a life style.

(1968: 4–6)

Methodologically controversial though it is, Alan Lomax's work on music and dance stands out for his effort to combine analysis with advocacy, and social science with passion. Lomax is at present working on a multi-media system that will permit the general public to explore the world's music using his stylistic parameters, and give many more people the chance to evaluate cantometrics for themselves.

Although for decades, anthropologists showed little interest in music and dance as part of social process, this has changed somewhat in recent years, in line with more general changes within the discipline of anthropology itself (Ortner 1984). Performance and process have been accorded a central place in the constitution of society. For the past thirty years or so a generation of anthropologists has been pointing to the importance of non-linguistic forms of communication (gesture, music and dance among them), non-visual modes of perception (aural, olfactory, tactile) (Howes 1991), non-structural modes of experience (such as *communitas* (Turner 1968) and hallucination), and non-productive activities (play and theatre; ritual had been studied for a much longer time). These authors have argued for an anthropology that pays more attention to the ongoing construction of meaning, to the relationship of the individual to the group, to emotion, and to performance (see Schechner in this volume, Article 22).

Anthropologists, sociologists, and even folklorists nowadays tend to emphasize performance in their writings. Indeed, anthropologists' descriptions of society have increasingly come to resemble descriptions of music and dance – like music and dance, social life is shown to be replete with structures and repetitions, but ones whose enactment is both dependent on their significance to the actors and audiences, and subject to variation. This suggests the possibility of a musical and kinetic approach to anthropology – one in which we are obliged to seek to understand the sense of repetition, the implications of innovation, and the emotional satisfaction of participation. Perhaps all the world *is* a stage, as Shakespeare famously suggested, but if so, it is not one on which actors must play their expected roles, but rather one such as that on which jazz musicians and hip-hop dancers improvise against and with each other. The end is not pre-established and the way of getting there is always unpredictable.

If, as I have suggested, performance processes lie at the heart of the constitution of society, then music and dance must move from the periphery to the very centre of anthropological concern. Indeed, more than any other specialists in the human sciences, students of music and dance are equipped to deal with structures and their variations.

TECHNOLOGY AND THE STUDY OF MUSIC AND DANCE

Technology has repeatedly influenced the study of sound and movement. In an anthropology much devoted to describing customs and collecting objects, the marginality of music and dance to anthropological interest was heightened by their ephemeral nature. Imagine what it must have been like to study unfamiliar sounds and movements before the days of recording devices and motion picture film. The wax cylinder recorder was invented by Thomas Edison in 1877, and the first ethnographic recordings date from the 1880s. Silent film followed at the turn of the century, and sound film after that. Before then, reports depended either on the ears and eyes of non-specialists, or on specialists who had learned the traditions with their bodies. In subsequent analyses, no one could judge whether those eyes, ears, and bodies were accurate or not. The situation was very different in studies of material culture, where the objects could be stored in museum vaults for further investigation.

Only when travellers and scientists could collect music and speech (recording them on crank-up wax cylinder machines), and bring them back to the laboratory for analysis and preservation, could the comparative study of sound begin. And once people could make and store silent film, the study of dance, gesture, and movement became more systematic.

Yet technology not only made possible the establishment of disciplines such as ethnomusicology and dance ethnology; it also sorely limited them. The development of the audio recorder in 1877 meant that the *sounds* of music were preserved to the exclusion of all else – the performance practice, the context in which it was performed, the heat and sensory richness. Since only the sound could be preserved, the rich context which I invited you to recall at the outset of this article usually receded into the background of concern, research and writing. In dance a similar situation occurred, with silent film and photographs removing music from the movements. Sound film came much earlier to Hollywood studios than it did to field research, and videotape has only recently begun to make its impact on contemporary research and publication.

What would these fields be like today if Thomas Edison had invented a video recorder in 1877, rather than an audio recorder? We certainly would not have divorced the study of music from the study of movement; we might not have forgotten that music and dance are performed by members of a society and witnessed and interpreted by other members; and our principal questions might have been very different.

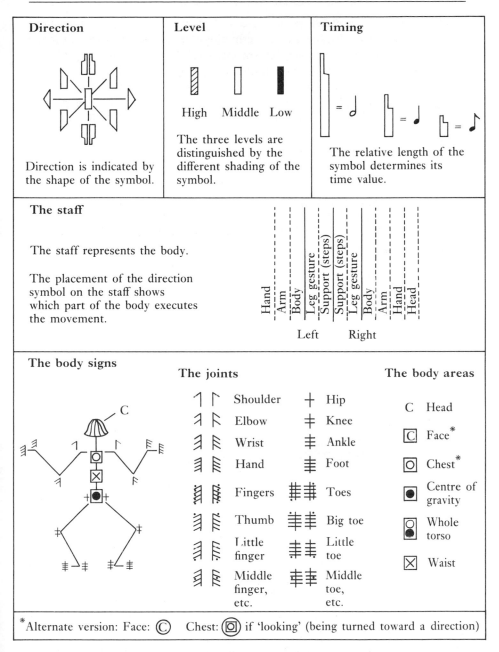

Figure 1 Labanotation symbols for the direction, level, and timing of movements, and symbols for the parts of the body. This kind of notation can be used very precisely.
(From Royce 1977: 46)

After they were invented, recording devices further influenced the development of ethnomusicology and dance ethnology because recordings, although accurate, can provide *too much* information. We have to figure out how to analyse what we have captured on our audio and video recorders. Imagine two videotape recordings of your dancing and singing the same song on two different occasions. The recorded performances will probably be slightly different in pitch, tempo, and tone quality; your movements will rarely be

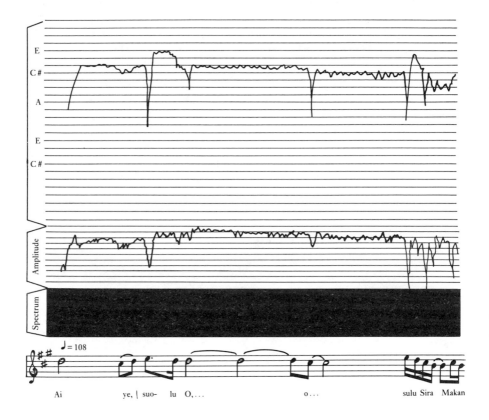

Figure 2 A very short excerpt from a 'melogram' or machine-produced graph of a Mandinka song ('Suolu kili', sung by Nyulo Jebateh), showing pitch, amplitude (loudness) and spectrum, as well as a standard musical transcription below (from Knight 1984: 38ff.):

Mandinka singing is generally forceful and spirited. . . . Some of the stylistic details that contribute to this mood are revealed, or our perception of them is reinforced, by the melogram. . . . Vibrato on sustained notes is apparent throughout the performance . . . A short ascending slide is apparent at the beginning of some phrases, and this feature is used in a highly distinctive way on each *note* in a descending passage. . .

exactly the same. The degree of similarity or difference between the two recordings can only be established through some kind of analysis.

A great deal of time, effort, and writing has been devoted to debate on graphing sound and movement (List 1974, Herndon 1974, C. Seeger 1958 on music, Royce 1977 on dance). Charles Seeger made the important observation that there is a difference between descriptive and prescriptive transcriptions – presenting the sounds as performed as against preparing a score for a performance. The concern in both fields – of music and dance – has been that without good description there can be no taxonomy, and therefore no science of the performance of sound or movement. Extensive debates have been carried on concerning the best method by which to graph sounds – some people argue for the use of the European five-line music stave with modified notation, others for different graphics altogether, while in dance competing notation systems also have their advocates. Figure 1 illustrates one prominent form of dance notation – so-called 'Labanotation' – while Figure 2 shows how a recording of song in the form of a 'melogram' can convey significant information beyond that provided by a standard musical score. Recent efforts at computer analysis are leading to new directions in this area (see Fügedi 1991 and Dunin 1991 for dance), but they will probably raise as many issues as they resolve. In my opinion, no single style of transcription is ideal for all types of analysis. Different theoretical questions and different approaches benefit from different types of transcription, since the purpose of an analytic transcription is to demonstrate the issues to the reader in an easily intelligible way.

The study of music and dance will surely continue to be affected by changes in the technology for recording, playing back, and analysing performances. It is to be hoped that some of the complexity lost using the earlier technologies will be returned in the newer ones, and that they will make it easier for non-specialists to understand and use the data analysed and published by specialists.

LEARNING FROM LOCAL KNOWLEDGE: THE SUYÁ INDIANS SPEAK OF SONG AND DANCE

Anthropologists often seek their answers to general questions in the specifics of investigations in small communities. We do this in order to avoid vapid generalizations, and because we truly believe that other people have important clues to *our* own, as well as *their* own, actions and intentions. As Geertz has argued, anthropologists do not study small communities, but rather study *in* small communities, and 'small facts speak to large issues' (1973: 22–3).

The 120 members of the Suyá community, a single circular village on the banks of the Suiá-missu river in Mato Grosso, Brazil, have lived for centuries by hunting, fishing, horticulture, gathering, and some trading with neighbours. Periodically they have devoted large amounts of time to singing and dancing. Vocal style is central to their musical aesthetics; ceremonies are central to a person's movement through the stages of the life cycle; and they continually introduce new songs and new ceremonies into their repertory (Seeger 1987). Patiently responding to the sympathetic but odd questions of the anthropologist they referred to as 'our Whiteman' during the 1970s, they said the following:

1 The word for 'to dance' is *ngere*; the word for 'to sing' is *ngere*. 'They are one.'
2 'When we sing/dance we are euphoric.'
3 'When we sing/dance we eat a lot of food.'
4 'When we sing/dance we are beautiful/good.'
5 'When we stop singing/dancing, we will be finished.'
6 'It is boring to sing/dance the same thing all the time.'

Of course they said many other things, which I described on paper or captured on tape. But the statements reproduced above are central to an anthropological approach to music and dance.

Definition: 'They are one'

The definition of music and dance varies from community to community. Some, like the Suyá, do not usually distinguish movement from sound – they are both involved in correct performances and there is a single word that covers both, so that only with difficulty can they be distinguished for discussion. Elsewhere, sounds and movements may be precisely distinguished, but in very different ways from standard European usage. In some communities there are no general terms for music or dance, but rather specific terms for what an analyst might call 'different kinds' of music or dance. Japanese scholars, when they began to analyse dance movement apart from its specific forms, had to invent a word for 'dance', which they created from two words for specific dance movements (Ohtani 1991). It would be as if the English language included forms called 'classical', 'pop', and 'religious' but no general term 'music' that united them. An outside analyst could speak of 'music', but would have to note that for the English-speakers there was no such general term nor, perhaps, any recognition of what the forms had in common.

Can we call a performance 'music' when there is no such concept in the community? We can, so long as we are clear that the terms 'music' and 'dance' are *our own* ways of generalizing about types of human action that do not have the same meanings for different groups of people. Thus, while some forms of Islamic prayer might be described as 'singing' by outside observers because of their structure, they are rigidly distinguished from song by most practitioners because of the difference between sacred texts and the profane associations of song. Here, as in other areas of inquiry, anthropologists must constantly work back and forth between the language and concepts of their own society and those of the communities they study.

Rather than trying to arrive at a universally suitable definition, it is more important to recognize that all human societies have various forms of speaking, various styles of movement, and various ways of creating and structuring non-vocal sounds. The specific ways in which they divide their speaking, movement, and sound-making into meaningful units vary widely from place to place. The details of their performance vary, as does their significance. It is the anthropologist's task to elucidate the form and meaning of these variations.

The distinctions between gesture and movement on the one hand, and between speech and song on the other, are not absolute – although they have sometimes been thought to be. In Figure 3, I suggest a continuum from unintentional and unstructured sounds and movements to carefully planned and highly structured performances. Societies vary in their definitions of the specific genres of vocalization (from burp to song), movement (from stumble to dance) and instrumental music (from an accidental thump to a drum solo or from the twang of a rope to the vibrations of an instrument string). I have arbitrarily placed music and dance towards the more heavily structured and purposefully performed end of the spectrum, but a given society may, of course, define some other form as more highly structured.

Figure 3 may be read horizontally or vertically. Reading horizontally, the field of vocalization runs from involuntary sounds through to sounds that are highly structured both tonally and temporally. How a society defines these sounds, however, varies from community to community. Thus some people may classify as 'speech' what other people classify as 'song'. The Suyá, for example, performed a type of 'speech' that was in fact more melodic than some of their 'music'. But they consistently corrected me when I referred to that genre by the term for song/music/dance – because although the form may have been structured like music, the text was made up by humans, rather than revealed by a natural species. And the same kinds of interpretative variations are found for the continua of movement and (non-vocal) sound: an outsider may interpret a dance as a gesture, or music as noise, or exactly the opposite. Reading the diagram vertically also reveals variations in interpretation: thus some communities associate dance with song while others do not. Some

involuntary vocalization	everyday speech	oratory	fixed recitation ... song .....
involuntary movement	everyday movements ... gesture		fixed series patterns .... dance ....
incidental noise	regular noise	structured sound .... music	
unintentional ...	not considered important	intentional and important	status determining

Figure 3 Continua of vocalization, movement, and (non-vocal) sound.

associate movement with structured sound, while others may consider the sounds that accompany movement to be merely incidental noise.

The term 'music', then, is a word taken from English and applied to those forms that more or less conform to our own definitions of intentionally structured, often non-utilitarian, sounds that are performed; likewise the term 'dance' is applied to intentionally structured, often non-utilitarian, movements that are performed. In this way a work song performed before an audience by dancers who neither carry axes nor chop trees may be distinguished from the sound of the axes wielded by silent woodsmen – even though the meter and movements may be identical in both cases.

Physiology and affect: 'When we sing/dance we are euphoric'

However defined, musical and dance performances have important physiological aspects and engender strong emotions. They both entail manipulation of the body itself and affect the performers' perception of themselves and of their environment. Performers in many societies report experiencing 'altered states of being' in successful performances. These changes are probably widely found to be satisfying, since in most societies people repeat them. Sometimes music and dance accompany the ingestion of stimulants, depressants, or hallucinogens, and here the structures of the movements and sounds may define the altered experience, or be created by it, or both (Fuks 1989).

Some of the most careful research on the physiological effects of music and movement has been used in very deliberate ways. Companies that provide 'environmental music' to workplaces find that they can raise the efficiency of workers by increasing the tempo of the music in the mid-afternoon; the music we shop to is not for our entertainment but for our 'success' as consumers (success, that is, as judged from the point of view of the retailer who plays the music). Modern commercial farmers pipe music into cowsheds, where it is said to relax the cows and so to increase milk yield (Ingold, personal communication). Less carefully researched, but no less systematically employed to create emotional responses, some political leaders employ bands playing certain types of music to enhance national or civic feelings; many possession-based religions use rhythms and movements to induce spirit-possession among their adepts; in Brazil, soccer fans armed with percussive instruments spur the players to greater efforts by pounding out rhythms as their teams take the offensive; and rhythms are often used to co-ordinate and focus the activities of work teams – whether in Texas prisons where songs would co-ordinate axe blows and hoeing, or in Oman where they accompany the hauling in of fishnets.[1]

Writings about music and dance come back again and again to a physical feeling of emotional elevation that is apparently important in many societies around the world. Where the Suyá speak of 'euphoria', the Waiapi Indians of Brazil speak of a special sensation of 'feeling good' (Fuks 1989: 315–55).

Durkheim, in his classic study of Australian Aboriginal religious ceremonies, characterized the emotional condition inspired by these ceremonies as a 'collective effervescence' (Durkheim 1933 [1912]). And Schieffelin's study (1976) of the *Gisalo* dance among the Kaluli of New Guinea shows how dancing and singing performers can move the audience to tears and eventually to cathartic anger. Feld's book on the music of the same people supplements Schieffelin's study with a superb examination of emotion and metaphor in the music of a single group (Feld 1982; see Lutz and White 1988 for a bibliographic essay on emotions).

Emotions are not induced by sounds alone, but by their cognitive and experiential associations. Rousseau, in the eighteenth century, already argued that the reasons for Swiss troops being so affected by cattle calls that they cried or deserted were not to be found in the sounds themselves, but in their associations for the troops. This has been further demonstrated by Schieffelin (1976), and by Rouget (1985). Rousseau's words remain appropriate today:

> We shall seek in vain to find in this air any energetic accents capable of producing such astonishing effects. These effects, which are void in regard to strangers, come alone from custom, reflections, and a thousand circumstances, which retraced by those who hear them, and recalling the idea of their country, their former pleasures, their youth, and all their joys of life, excite in them a bitter sorrow for the loss of them. The music does not in this case precisely act as music, but as a memorative sign ...
>
> (1975 [1779]: 267)

Through music and dance, participants endow certain events with powerful affect. Such emotions can mobilize a group to action or keep them from acting, can create solidarity or dissension (Spencer 1985), can forge a collection of individuals into a community or dissolve one. Most of the reported effects of music and dance have been on the side of forging a sense of solidarity and identity, much as Durkheim claimed for Australian Aboriginal ceremonies, but that need not be the case.

If music and dance were not powerful cultural resources in social and political struggles against authority, they would not be so widely censored, controlled, and surrounded with restrictions. All around the world they create loyalties and galvanize opposition so effectively that they sometimes become objects of struggle in themselves, rather than expressions of broader issues. To mobilize people towards a goal, a group needs to make the issues fairly simple and clear, to create a consensus, and to incite its members to act with conviction and emotional commitment. Music and dance have been effectively used in political struggles because they can focus attention on injustices, create feelings of solidarity, and frighten opponents (Berman 1990).

In many parts of the world people create and perform music and dance that is an essential expression of their aspirations and an active part of their struggle against discrimination, poor working conditions, political oppression, or social injustice. The performances are often powerful and moving to outsiders as well as to members of the communities involved. An example familiar to many is the music of the U.S. Civil Rights Movement of the 1960s. Songs from African American churches were slightly altered and used to mobilize hundreds of thousands of members of various ethnic groups, a mobilization that not only changed public attitudes but also led to significant legislative reforms. The music itself became an object of admiration, as the style was adapted by other ethnic groups. The song 'We Shall Overcome', which for a few years became a kind of unofficial anthem of the Civil Rights Movement, was originally sung 'I Shall Overcome'. It has been translated and sung in many different languages by peoples who all identify themselves with the Civil Rights struggle despite the great diversity of their particular circumstances.

Music and production: 'When we sing we eat a lot'

The reason the Suyá eat a lot when they sing is that all music is part of ceremonies, and almost all ceremonies involve not only song and dance but also the mobilization of ceremonial groups and exchanges of large quantities of food. Ceremonies (also called *ngere* – the same word as song/dance) mobilize groups of people in subsistence tasks, in the manufacture of artefacts, in warfare and in collective action outside the community. As in many societies, performance is not incidental to production, but is instead an integral part of it.

The association of music and food is not unique to the Amazon. Ceremonies and feasts are found around the world – the Euro-American Christmas, with its carolling and its family feasting, comes to mind immediately. On a different scale, the entertainment industry in the United States is one of the country's largest exporters, generating a tremendous income for (some of) those involved. The amount of money, human resources, and time spent on the Brazilian *Carnaval* at the start of Lent makes it an economic event of major significance (Da Matta 1991). Music and dance are thus directly implicated in economic life, on the sides of both production and consumption.

Whether we speak of the tiny Suyá community or the huge economy of the United States, music and dance not only consume calories and resources; they also mobilize people to produce them, and they create new forms of interaction or reinforce existing exchange networks. They may also add emotional commitment and physiological energy to economic processes.

Performance and value: 'When we sing/dance we are beautiful and good'

Music and dance, like literature and the visual arts, are often associated with the expression of the fundamental values, or *ethos* (after the ancient Greek term), of a society. Clifford Geertz (1973, 1980, 1983) has probably devoted

698

more attention than any other recent anthropologist to the issues of aesthetics, ethos, and their expression in art and performance.

The full and correct performance of a ritual, and its accompanying movements and sounds, is usually considered to be intrinsically good or rewarding. What the Suyá mean by 'beautiful and good' is that all the members of the society have participated actively according to their age and gender, and have together experienced a collective euphoria.

Music and dance are often associated with the attainment or validation of certain age, status, and gender identifications. Among the Suyá, men sing/dance some songs, women sing/dance others, and in one genre each age-grade sings/dances them differently. In fact, a Suyá man performs in a style defined by who he is: his age, his ceremonial moiety, his name set. A ceremony in which everyone participates is one in which every person has been vocally-cum-kinesically defined or redefined. Often, of course, the status of some participants is transformed. Rites of passage, in which participants move from one status to another (Van Gennep 1960, Turner 1968), are often accompanied by music, dance or noise. Whether one is at a debutante ball or a Suyá Mouse Ceremony, wearing a new ornamentation or making music or dancing in a new, adult way is a concrete expression (and experience) of the new identity.

Music and community identity: 'When we stop singing/dancing we will be finished'

Communities define themselves in many ways – through cuisine, dress, adornment, religion, and through music, dance, gesture, and movement. Any of these can suddenly become an emblem of community identity by figuring as a site of contestation with another group – conflict may be over diet, clothing permitted in public places, or permitted forms of dance or music. Music and dance, like the others, can be used as a means to announce membership in a certain group.

Of course, the Suyá will not literally be finished if they stop singing their songs; nor will singing their songs alone ensure their survival. The issue is not of fact, but of their attitude towards performance as a manifestation of their continuity with the past and their aspirations for the future. In another sense, however, the Suyá are right. If a community stops performing for a generation, it will have lost many of its traditions. Until recently few societies had ways of accurately recording their performance traditions. Music and dance are usually passed on through an oral tradition that requires repetition and continuity for its transmission. If one generation decides to ignore the traditions of its elders, the elders' grandchildren may be unable to recover the lost knowledge and performances. Indeed, in many cases, grandchildren (or great-grandchildren) do become interested in the older traditions, and want to use them to establish an identity or to spearhead a social movement. If they have disappeared, they either borrow them from elsewhere or invent 'new traditions' that may quickly become legitimated through repeated successful performances (Hobsbawm and Ranger 1983).

The fragility of the oral/aural tradition suggests a new use for audio and video archives. Many nations and some research centres and universities have created archives of audio and video recordings, in some cases dating back to the 1880s. Once the equivalent of museums for storing the audio artefacts of colonialism, archives can now begin to serve the populations whose traditions they have preserved by returning them to the communities concerned. Communities and nations around the world are establishing archives whose mission is to repatriate recordings taken out of the country in the colonial era and to make them available to the descendants of those recorded in order to serve their interests (whether these be to research or to perform them).

Music and dance recordings preserved in archives are different from other products of individual research. They may have a new usefulness, which arises after the theoretical work based on them has lost its impact and is no longer much consulted. This potential is realized when the children or grandchildren of the original performers come to recover lost traditions from the vaults. Archives take the results of research and turn them into resources for scholars and future communities. Today, when researchers must justify their projects to local communities, the offer of making archival recordings for long-term preservation and return to the community may improve the chances of local acceptance. Members of many communities are often glad to record their traditions for preservation and future dissemination. However, the promise of artistic renewal from the past as well as innovation in the present can only be realized if the expensive and difficult work of preservation and cataloguing is successfully achieved. Here, digital technology may come to our aid as millions of tapes and films slowly deteriorate around the globe, the traditions on them vanishing with the emulsion or crumbling into dust. Once again technology follows like a shadow on the development of these disciplines.

Innovation and change: 'It is boring to sing the same thing all the time'

The Suyá said this in response to a question about why they kept composing new songs/dances, learning songs/dances from other Indian communities, and making such an effort to learn the songs my wife and I sang in the field. While they valued their 'old songs', they said it added to the euphoria if they could add new sections to their extended ritual sequences.

International popular music, after decades of working from African American musical forms from the early part of the twentieth century, appears to be in one of its innovative phases. Sounds and (to a lesser extent) dances from all over the world have become commonplace in our mass media. Whether it is called 'world beat', 'Afro-pop', 'ethnic', or 'exotic', more and more consumers are accompanying the sonic explorations and discoveries of

Paul Simon, David Byrne, and Mickey Hart, or joining dance groups specializing in the traditions of other communities. Some are following up their interests by listening to the less 'accessible' recordings, reading, and learning to perform the traditions.

Popular music is itself a phenomenon worthy of intensive and thoughtful study – and is indeed receiving it (see Coplan 1985, Frith 1981, Shepherd 1982, Waterman 1990, and the journal *Popular Music*). Juridical anthropologists would do well to spend some time on the values and social hierarchies expressed in the extremely complex and elaborate legal systems that have evolved in the popular music industry to cover rights in intangible property. These speak eloquently to the protection of certain interests over others, and to the influence of Euro-American lobbyists and special interest groups on government (Wallis and Malm 1984, Dannen 1988).

One fairly regular feature of multi-national popular music is the inequitable distribution of benefits – specially to communities whose music is adapted to feed the search for new forms of expression by the popular culture industry (Wallis and Malm 1984, Feld 1988). Researchers of all kinds will have to begin to protect the rights of the peoples they study if we are going to be allowed to continue to record in any communities. In an era in which global communications make everyone aware of the possible fortunes to be gained in popular music, it is increasingly difficult to avoid being seen as part of an exploitative music industry (Seeger 1992).

CONCLUSION

The anthropological study of music and dance was shaped by a technological revolution, and continues to be influenced by it as we move into computerized synthesizers and satellite communication. As elsewhere in anthropology, we have to reflect more on our own attitudes and actions with respect to other peoples' performances. Researchers today must assume greater responsibility for protecting community rights and preserving performances for the future than they have ever done before – at least until communities can do it for themselves.

Music and dance performance, as foci of attention, are relative newcomers to anthropology. Researchers are just beginning to reap the benefits of the shift in anthropological interest towards more processual approaches to social and cultural life. We have a long way to go before we reach an adequate understanding of the physiology of performances and of the emotions engendered by them. We have just begun to establish ways of correlating sounds and movements with social processes and cosmological ideas. We need to focus more on the relationships between music, power, and dissent. And we need to recognize ourselves as actors in the processes we study. These are among the challenges for the turn of the twenty-first century. Armed with videotape recorders and computers, backed by a better understanding of social processes as creative and interpretative, anthropologists can make better use than ever before of the insights offered through the study of music and dance. And students of music and dance will have much more to learn from the resulting anthropology.

ACKNOWLEDGEMENTS

The late John Blacking originally agreed to write this article, but died before he could do much work on it. I wish we could all have read what he would have written. I am very grateful to Adrienne Kaeppler for her careful reading and valuable suggestions on earlier versions of this article.

NOTE

1   This example is taken from a videotape of fishing in Oman, made by Dieter Christensen, and shown at a recent ethnomusicology colloquium.

REFERENCES

Berman, P. (1990) 'The orchestra that overthrew communism', *Village Voice* 35(25): 37–50.

Blacking, J. (1967) *Venda Children's Songs, A Study in Ethnomusicological Analysis*, Johannesburg: Witwatersrand University Press.

—— (1974) *How Musical is Man?*, Seattle: University of Washington Press.

—— (ed.) (1977) *The Anthropology of the Body*, London: Academic Press.

—— (1985) 'Movement, dance, music and the Venda girls' initiation cycle', in P. Spencer (ed.) *Society and the Dance*, Cambridge: Cambridge University Press.

Coplan, D. (1985) *In Township Tonight! South Africa's Black City Music and Theatre*, New York: Longmans.

Da Matta, R. (1991) *Carnivals, Rogues and Heroes*, South Bend, Ind.: Notre Dame University Press.

Dannen, F. (1988) *Hit Men: Power Brokers and Fast Money inside the Music Business*, New York: Times Books (Random House).

Dunin, E. I. (1991) 'Personal computers and dance ethnology research', *Yearbook for Traditional Music* 23: 113–25.

Durkheim, E. (1933 [1912]) *The Elementary Forms of the Religious Life*, transl. G. Simpson, New York: Free Press.

Feld, S. (1982) *Sound and Sentiment: Birds, Weeping, Poetics and Song in Kaluli Expression*, Philadelphia: University of Pennsylvania Press.

—— (1988) 'Notes on world beat', *Public Culture Bulletin* 1: 31–7.

Frith, S. (1981) *Sound Effects*, New York: Pantheon.

Fügedi, J. (1991) 'Dance notation and computers', *Yearbook for Traditional Music* 23: 101–13.

Fuks, V. (1989) 'Demonstration of multiple relationships between music and culture of the Waiapi Indians of Brazil', PhD dissertation, Indiana University, Department of Anthropology.

Geertz, C. (1973) *The Interpretation of Cultures*, New York: Basic Books.

—— (1980) *Negara, the Theatre State in Nineteenth Century Bali*, Princeton: Princeton University Press.

—— (1983) *Local Knowledge, Further Essays in Social Anthropology*, New York: Basic Books.

Giurchescu, A. and Torp, L. (1991) 'Theory and methods in dance research: a European approach to the holistic study of dance', *Yearbook for Traditional Music* 23: 1–10.

Herndon, M. (1974) 'Analysis, the herding of sacred cows?', *Ethnomusicology* 18: 219–62.

Hobsbawm, E. and Ranger, T. O. (1983) *The Invention of Tradition*, Cambridge: Cambridge University Press.

Howes, D. (ed.) (1991) *The Varieties of Sensory Experience, A Source Book in the Anthropology of Experience*, Toronto: University of Toronto Press.

Kaeppler, A. (1978) 'Dance in an anthropological perspective', *Annual Review of Anthropology* 7: 31–49.

—— (1991) 'American approaches to the study of dance', *Yearbook for Traditional Music* 23: 1–10.

Keali'inohomoku, J. (1976) 'Theory and methods for an anthropological study of dance', PhD dissertation, Department of Anthropology, Indiana University.

Keil, C. (1979) *Tiv Song*, Chicago: University of Chicago Press.

Kingsbury, H. (1988) *Music, Talent, and Performance*, Philadelphia: Temple University Press.

Knight, R. (1984) 'The style of Mandinka music: a study in extracting theory from practice', in K. Nketia and J. C. DjeDje (eds) *Selected Reports in Ethnomusicology*, vol. 5: *Studies in African Music*, Los Angeles: Program in Ethnomusicology, Department of Music, University of California, Los Angeles.

List, G. (1974) 'The reliability of transcription', *Ethnomusicology* 18: 353–77.

Lomax, A. (1968) *Folk Song Style and Culture*, Washington D.C.: American Association for the Advancement of Science.

Lutz, C. and White, G. M. (1988) 'The anthropology of the emotions', *Annual Review of Anthropology* 15: 405–36.

McAllester, D. (1954) 'Enemy way music', *Peabody Museum Papers* 41(3).

Mauss, M. (1936) 'Les techniques du corps', *Journal de Psychologie* 32: 271–93.

Merriam, A. P. (1964) *The Anthropology of Music*, Evanston, Ill.: Northwestern University Press.

Nettl, B. (1964) *Theory and Method in Ethnomusicology*, New York: Free Press.

—— (1983) *Ethnomusicology: Twenty-Nine Issues and Concepts*, Urbana: University of Illinois Press.

—— (1985) *The Western Impact on World Music, Change, Adaptation and Survival*, New York: Schirmer Books.

Nisbet, R. A. (1966) *The Sociological Tradition*, New York: Basic Books.

Nollman, J. (1990) *Dolphin Dreamtime: The Art and Science of Interspecies Communication*, New York: Bantam Books.

Ohtani, K. (1991) 'Japanese approaches to the study of dance', *Yearbook for Traditional Music* 23: 23–33.

Ortner, S. (1984) 'Theory in anthropology since the sixties', *Comparative Studies in Society and History* 26: 126–66.

Rouget, G. (1985) *Music and Trance: A Theory of the Relations between Music and Possession*, Chicago: University of Chicago Press.

Rousseau, J-J. (1975 [1779]) *A Complete Dictionary of Music*, New York: AMS Press.

Royce, A. P. (1977) *The Anthropology of Dance*, Bloomington: Indiana University Press.

Schieffelin, E. L. (1976) *The Sorrow of the Lonely and the Burning of the Dancers*, New York: St Martin's Press.

Seeger, A. (1987) *Why Suyá Sing: A Musical Anthropology of an Amazonian People*, Cambridge: Cambridge University Press.

—— (1992) 'Ethnomusicology and music law', *Ethnomusicology* 36(3): 345–59.

Seeger, C. L. (1958) 'Prescriptive and descriptive music writing', *Musical Quarterly* 44: 184–95.

Shepherd, J. (1982) 'A theoretical model for the sociomusicological analysis of popular musics', *Popular Music* 2: 145–78.

Spencer, P. (1985) 'Introduction', in P. Spencer (ed.) *Society and the Dance*, Cambridge: Cambridge University Press.

Stone, R. (1982) *Let the Inside Be Sweet*, Bloomington: Indiana University Press.

Torp, L. (1990) *Chain and Round Dance Patterns: A Method for Structural Analysis and its Application to European Material*, 3 vols, Copenhagen: Museum Tusculanum Press.

Turner, V. W. (1968) *The Ritual Process, Structure and Anti-Structure*, Chicago: Aldine.

Van Gennep, A. (1960) *The Rites of Passage*, transl. M. B. Vizedom and G. L. Caffee, Chicago: University of Chicago Press.

Wallis, R. and Malm, K. (1984) *Big Sounds from Small People: The Music Industry in Small Countries*, New York: Pendragon Press.

Waterman, C. (1990) *Jujú, A Social History and Ethnography of an African Popular Music*, Chicago: University of Chicago Press.

FURTHER READING

Good introductory textbooks

Blacking, J. (1974) *How Musical is Man?*, Seattle: University of Washington Press.

Merriam, A. (1964) *The Anthropology of Music*, Evanston, Ill.: Northwestern University Press.

Royce, A. P. (1977) *The Anthropology of Dance*, Bloomington: Indiana University Press.

Titon, J. T. (1992) *Worlds of Music, An Introduction to Music of the World's Peoples*, 2nd edn, with accompanying CDs and cassette tapes, New York: Schirmer Books.

Some principal English-language journals

Dance Research Journal (formerly *CORD News*), published twice yearly by the Congress on Research in Dance (CORD), New York, first year of publication 1968, continuing.

Ethnomusicology, published three times a year by the Society for Ethnomusicology, Ann Arbor, Michigan, first year of publication 1953, continuing.

Yearbook for Traditional Music (International Council for Traditional Music; this body also has an Ethnochoreology Study Group with its own publications), first year of publication 1982, continuing. Replaced the *Yearbook of the International Folk Music Council* (1969–81).

World of Music (International Institute for Comparative Music Studies, Berlin), first year of publication 1957, continuing.

Popular Music, Cambridge: Cambridge University Press, first year of publication 1981, continuing.

Collections of essays

Yearbook for Traditional Music, vol. 23 (1991).

Shelemay, K. K. (ed.) (1990) *The Garland Library of Readings in Ethnomusicology*, 7 vols, New York: Garland.

Spencer, P. (ed.) (1985) *Society and the Dance*, Cambridge: Cambridge University Press.

Book-length studies

Berliner, P. (1981) *Soul of the Mbira*, Berkeley: University of California Press.

Cowan, J. (1990) *Dance and the Body Politic in Northern Greece*, Princeton: Princeton University Press.

Feld, S. (1982) *Sound and Sentiment: Birds, Weeping, Poetics, and Song in Kaluli Expression*, Philadelphia: University of Pennsylvania Press.

Schieffelin, E. L. (1976) *The Sorrow of the Lonely and the Burning of the Dancers*, New York: St Martin's Press.

Seeger, A. (1987) *Why Suyá Sing: A Musical Anthropology of an Amazonian People*, Cambridge: Cambridge University Press.

Torp, L. (1990) *Chain and Round Dance Patterns: A Method for Structural Analysis and its Application to European Material*, 3 vols, Copenhagen: Museum Tusculanum Press.

Waterman, C. (1990) *Jujú, A Social History and Ethnography of an African Popular Music*, Chicago: University of Chicago Press. (For a music and dance analysis of the same phenomenon, see A. Kaeppler and E. Tatar (in press) 'Hula Pahu: Hawaiian Drum Dances' (2 vols and CD recording), *Bishop Museum Bulletin in Anthropology* 3, Honolulu: Bishop Museum Press.)

25

THE POLITICS OF CULTURE: ETHNICITY AND NATIONALISM

Anthony D. Smith

We are witnessing today a remarkable resurgence of ethnic ties and sentiments in a world of increasingly interdependent power blocks, transnational corporations and computerized information networks. Yet despite growing global pressures, the nation state remains the sole acceptable form of political organization. Regardless of the opposition that the doctrine of nationalism has attracted for over a century, nationalisms of every hue continue to flourish and proliferate as the main inspiration for, and legitimation of, political association.

In the present article I address this paradox by distinguishing between different concepts of the nation and corresponding routes of nation-formation. This requires a consideration of pre-existing ethnic ties and identities that have survived from pre-modern eras in various parts of the world, and of the reasons for their persistence. It will also be necessary to outline the different kinds of pre-modern ethnic community, since they have furnished the points of departure for the two main routes that have been followed in the formation of nations.

My basic purpose is to outline a macro-sociology and history of ethnic and national phenomena, one which emphasizes the symbolic and cultural dimensions of ethnic communities and nations, and their accompanying ideologies of nationalism. Such a broad socio-historical perspective does not pretend to be comprehensive, but is on the contrary necessarily selective, omitting for example any reference to the many micro-sociological and psychological studies of 'situational ethnicity' (see Okamura 1981 among others).

'PRIMORDIALISM' AND 'INSTRUMENTALISM'

We do however need to refer to certain fundamental differences of theoretical approach to ethnic and national phenomena, in order to provide a conceptual framework for the ensuing account of ethnic identity and the rise of nations.

One basic issue concerns the nature of ethnic ties and sentiments. For some theorists, such ties and sentiments are felt to be 'primordial' and even 'natural'. They exist, as it were, almost outside time. Here we need to distinguish a 'strong' from a 'weak' primordialism. The strong version holds that the ties themselves are universal, natural and given in all human association, as much as are speech or kinship. This position, to which many nationalists subscribe even today, commands little support among scholars, though it has been reasserted in another form by certain sociobiologists who regard ethnicity as a kind of behaviour that enhances inclusive fitness (van den Berghe 1979). The weak version of primordialism claims that ethnic ties and sentiments are deepseated and non-rational so far as the participants are concerned; members of ethnic communities feel that their community has existed 'from time immemorial', and that its symbols and traditions possess a 'deep antiquity', which gives them a unique power. 'Participant primordialism', the approach which emphasizes the felt longevity of ethnic ties for the people bound by them (and perhaps for their neighbours as well), commands a somewhat larger following among scholars who, taking their cue from Shils and Geertz, have studied the role of religion, language and expressive symbolism (Shils 1957, Geertz 1963, Fishman 1980).

Opposed to the primordialists are theorists who tend to view ethnicity as a resource to be mobilized, or an instrument to be employed, by particular groups in pursuit of further ends, usually of a political or economic nature. There are several varieties of such 'instrumentalism', from Marxian theories to 'rational choice' and élite competition models. For all these theorists, cultural and symbolic aspects of ethnicity are accessory to fundamental struggles for scarce resources and political power, struggles in which the ethnic constituency represents a 'site of mobilization'. This view is held even where, as with Bell's analysis, due weight is accorded to the affective aspects of ethnic ties (Bell 1975; see Enloe 1973, Brass 1974).

Parallel to this debate about the nature of ethnic ties is an apparently more historical one about the antiquity, or modernity, of nations and nationalism. On the one side are those who argue that nations and even nationalism have always existed, at least since written records began in the early third millennium BC. Again, there is a weaker and a stronger form of the argument. The strong form claims that nations and nationalism are 'perennial'; they are to be found wherever human beings have associated. The weaker form suggests that, although nations are not the normal mode of human association in antiquity or the Middle Ages, they nevertheless appear from time to time in the historical record prior to the advent of the modern age, albeit unaccompanied by 'nationalism'. This argument is often coupled with a sense of the frequent presence of ethnic groups before the modern era in many parts of the world (see A. D. Smith 1984b, Levi 1965).

By contrast, the majority of contemporary scholars consider both the nation and nationalism to be wholly modern phenomena and products of purely modern conditions. The term 'modern' here refers to such novel conditions and processes as the rise of 'rational', bureaucratic states, the spread of capitalism, the secularization of culture and education, and the introduction of machine technology and its application in various institutions. 'Modernity' in this sense refers less to a period than to processes and conditions defined by their opposition to 'tradition' and 'traditionalism'. As I hope to show, this opposition is reflected in the very idea of the 'nation', suggesting alternative models of how it is constituted. The modernists go on to claim that, if nationalism is a doctrine that emerged in Western Europe in the late eighteenth century, the 'nation' is a form of socio-cultural organization that arose only slightly earlier, and certainly not before the late sixteenth century in England, France and Holland (Kohn 1967, Breuilly 1982, Anderson 1983). Against the 'perennialists', the 'modernist' standpoint holds that neither nations nor nationalism could be accommodated within the pre-modern world. In Gellner's formulation, pre-modern 'agro-literate' societies were too divided in terms of both culture and stratification to permit or require the homogeneity characteristic of modern nations. Their élites and their specialist clients generally possessed a high culture which the mass of peasants, themselves divided into separate local cultures, did not and could not share; and nothing in pre-modern social and political organization encouraged cross-class cultural homogenization. Only in the modern era did the requirements of economic growth and industrial mobility erode most cultural divisions and fuse the many local cultures into a single high culture able to unify homogeneous nations of literate citizens (Gellner 1973, 1983: chs 2–3).

From the perspective adopted here, however, both perennialist and modernist views possess a strongly mythical quality, in the sense that they present tales about the past told for dramatic purposes to serve contemporary needs, and which are widely believed (see Kirk 1970, Tudor 1972, Thompson 1985: ch. 1). Both accounts dramatize and exaggerate observable phenomena and trends. Both serve present interests, whether nationalist or anti-nationalist. Neither view offers a neutral, detached or adequate account. 'Perennialism' tends to read features of modern nations into pre-modern ethnic communities, or even to envisage a 'retrospective nationalism', which would treat ancient Greeks or Jews as fully-fledged nations with 'nationalist' movements and programmes. Such a reading can hardly be sustained by the evidence: there is, for example, no doctrine of nationalism to be found in either case. But such views served the interests of nationalistic academics and writers, especially in Central and Eastern Europe before the Second World War. The 'modernist' perspective equally serves the interests of internationalist intellectuals, notably in the social sciences in Anglo-Saxon countries, many of whom are upwardly and geographically mobile, and for whom nations constitute unwelcome barriers. 'Modernism' exaggerates the 'break' between traditional and modern societies and the novelty of 'modern' conditions. The myth of the 'modern nation', in particular, neglects or underplays the 'prehistory' of the nation, its foundations in an 'ethnic substratum' of myths of ancestry, historical memories, common values and traditions, and expressive symbolism and ritual, much of which goes far back, long before the age of nationalism (A. D. Smith 1988).

ETHNIE AND ETHNICISM

This is why a historical and symbolic perspective on the rise of the nation and nationalism is so necessary. This approach places particular emphasis on the role of symbols, myths, values and memories in the formation and persistence of collective cultural identities, and on the way in which such identities can be preserved by often gradual changes in these elements of shared culture. Such a view accepts the importance of cultural boundaries and symbolic 'border guards', as stressed by Barth (1969) and Armstrong (1982); but adds a focus on the changing components of culture that distinguish one bounded collectivity from another and that endow each with its unique historical 'complexion' or 'style'. The ever-present sense of the 'unintelligible' stranger is complemented by, and in part dependent upon, the collective attachments to shared myths, symbols and memories, and the tacit assumptions about common life-styles, traditions and values which, as often as they are challenged by internal cleavages and crises, are also periodically reaffirmed (see A. D. Smith 1984a, Stack 1986: Introduction).

Human beings have always felt themselves bounded by multiple identities. Even in prehistoric societies, the family, clan and settlement vied for their allegiances. By the time we meet historical societies with written records, to the familial and residential circles of identity must be added those of the city state, social stratum and what I shall call the 'ethnic community' or *ethnie*. The *ethnie* can be defined as a human group whose members share common myths of origin and descent, historical memories, cultural patterns and values, association with a particular territory, and a sense of solidarity, at least among the élites. At certain times, as in ancient Egypt, China and Mesopotamia, the *ethnie* is included within a single polity, and territorial allegiances are gradually superimposed upon, or even replace, ethnic ones (Mann 1986: chs 5–9). But more loosely bounded yet nevertheless long-lasting *ethnie* are frequently encountered in the historical record from the ancient Sumerians and Egyptians up to the medieval Mongols and Normans (see Kramer 1963: ch. 9, Moscati 1962, Reynolds 1984: ch. 8).

Some features of *ethnie* are also to be found among 'ethnic categories', that is, populations deemed to constitute potential *ethnie* by outsiders, as the Ewe were by German missionaries or the Slovak-speakers by eighteenth-century observers (see Welch 1966, Paul 1985). In these cases, there is no sense of solidarity among the population, and only shadowy historical memories or myths of origin; but these are nevertheless available for revival in appropriate circumstances.

Perhaps the crucial feature of *ethnie* is the myth of common origin and descent. This most obviously marks off *ethnie* from other cultural collective identities, and forms the point of departure not only for the sense of separate ethnicity but also for those sentiments of group centrality and superiority by which it is so often accompanied. Such feelings may be heightened by various historical memories, as well as by the elaboration of myths of a heroic or 'golden' age. Examples are the classical Greek nostalgia for the Homeric era, Jewish ideals of the Mosaic or Davidic eras, and Arab yearnings for the Age of the Companions. In each of these cases, as well as others, a typical ethnocentrism is reinforced by a myth of ethnic election, in which the ethnic community is promised redemption and salvation on condition that religious or cultural obligations are properly fulfilled (Carmichael 1967, Zeitlin 1984, O'Brien 1988, A. D. Smith 1992).

The myth of ethnic election may also play an important role in ethnic movements of resistance and renewal, or ethnicism. Such movements aim to defend the community from alien threat, whether territorial or cultural. While the historical record reveals that many *ethnie* are ready to submit to foreign invasion and rule, and may even be happy to exchange an oppressive ruler for what may appear a more lenient regime, other *ethnie* may resist or rebel against alien conquerors, as did the Ionians against Persian rule in 499 BC, the Gallic tribes against Caesar in 52 BC, or the Swiss cantons against the Habsburgs from 1291 AD (on which see Thürer 1970: ch. 2). But over and above simple territorial resistance, we also encounter ethnicist movements of cultural restoration and renewal. The best-known cases are the Jewish restoration from Babylonia after Cyrus's decree of 538 BC, and the traditionalist movement of the Hasidim under the Maccebees in 167 BC against Antiochus Epiphanes' hellenizing drives in Jerusalem (Bright 1978: chs 9, 11). Here a sense of being a 'chosen people' in its 'sacred land', the core of a myth of ethnic election not only among Jews, but also among Armenians, Ethiopians, Byzantine Greeks, Orthodox Russians, Catholic Irish, Puritan New Englanders and many others, provided the vital impetus behind the ethnicist movement of cultural restoration and renewal (see also Tcherikover 1970; Armstrong 1982: ch. 7).

My discussion so far points to the significance of shared symbols, myths and memories for the self-definition and political mobilization of ethnic communities. Not only in modern times, but also in past eras, the collation – and collators – of such ethnic memories, myths and symbols have played a crucial role in giving form and meaning to collective experiences. Though we are often hampered by the paucity of records, further research may well reveal just how elaborate and potent such pre-modern mythologies and symbolisms were for forming identities, and equally how much they were the sites of rival interpretations.

ETHNIC SURVIVAL AND DISSOLUTION

An examination of the role of mythologies and symbolisms may also throw new light on the vexed question of ethnic origins or 'ethnogenesis'. For the time being, our theories of ethnic origins are necessarily speculative, though a good case can be advanced for the importance of political factors, as Max Weber argued (Weber 1968: I: 5). But while such factors can be invoked to explain the crystallization of ethnic solidarities (*ethnie* in my terminology), they invariably presume the presence and significance of ethnic differentiation (i.e. 'ethnic categories'). Why 'cultural markers', 'historical memories' and 'myths of descent' should be so widespread and become so socially significant, remain unsolved problems (see Horowitz 1985: ch. 2, Gellner 1983: ch. 5). We are on less speculative ground when the focus of inquiry is shifted from the origins to the maintenance of ethnic identities. Here we can posit a number of factors that have facilitated ethnic persistence. These include the following:

Territorialization

The growth of folk cultures based upon common patterns of work and residence, and the peculiar nostalgia for a past era often associated with agrarian society, help to stabilize and demarcate ethnic communities. Such cultures become repositories of customs, rituals, myths and symbols which ethnic élites may utilize for political purposes. Language and religious rituals (albeit often demotic and hence different from urban élite culture) may provide an overall index of a distinctive and shared identity in contrast to the languages and rituals of outsiders, and these indices are often loosely associated with particular territorial domains. It must be admitted, however, that folk cultures and memories may be territorially fragmented and unable to provide the felt unity typical of pre-modern *ethnie*.

Inter-state warfare

Prolonged warfare between states may well promote the unity that agrarian folk cultures are unable to furnish by themselves. This unity is generated not only by the immediate impact of mobilization against a common danger from outside, but even more by the myths and memories of heroic exploits and turning-points that, once woven into the fabric of communal life, come to influence later generations. Such episodes include the Battle of Agincourt as dramatized by Shakespeare, the fall of Jerusalem in the lamentations of Jeremiah, or a relatively minor episode in early Russian warfare with the Polovstsii in the *Lay of Igor's Host* (Paskiewicz 1954: 336–53).

To the impact of propaganda and myth-making, we must add the influence of the geopolitical location of each *ethnie*, in relation both to its natural environment and to neighbouring *ethnie*, one or more of which may become 'paired' with it as historic enemies or allies. In these cases, inter-state warfare, while in no way creating the original cultural differences, may promote the crystallization of ethnic solidarities and maintain a heightened sense of cultural distinctiveness in neighbouring populations (Simmel 1964: esp. 88–93, Marwick 1974, A. D. Smith 1981b).

Organized religion

Though religious affiliations may divide *ethnie* (as in Germany and Holland) or transcend them (as in Catholicism, Islam and Buddhism), they may also reinforce and even define the sense of common ethnicity. This was particularly true of the ancient, pre-Christian world; even after the expansion of Christianity, we find a tendency for Eastern Christianity to accommodate itself to well-developed ethnic communities in the Near East and Africa (examples include Greek Orthodox Christians, Egyptian Copts, Amharic Monophysites, Gregorian Armenians and Syrian Jacobites; see Atiya 1968). In Persia, too, the Shiah branch of Islam came to reinforce a sense of specific Persian identity that had existed from the time of the Safavids (Keddie 1981: chs 1–3). And in Sri Lanka and Burma, Buddhism was adjusted to the ways and beliefs of dominant Sinhalese and Burmese ethnic communities (Sarkisyanz 1964).

The close links between organized religion and ethnicity can be seen in the overlap between their respective myths of origin and creation, in the role of sectarian communities, and above all in the personnel and channels of communication in each case. In fact, priests and scribes, their sacred scriptures, rituals and liturgies have often emerged as the primary guardians and conduits of ethnic distinctiveness. It is they who organize communal feasts and ceremonies, and who codify and transmit sacred texts and legal codes. Often, they act as chroniclers, poets and missionaries – as much of a communal culture as of a faith; one has only to think of the profound effect of the activities of Cyril and Methodius in Eastern Europe (see Koht 1947, Singleton 1985: 16–20). In South-east Asia, too, priests and *ulema* have often served as guardians and ethnic leaders, as they still do today (von der Mehden 1963).

Myths of ethnic election

I have already drawn attention to the significance of special myths of chosenness. Their role is not only a mobilizing one; they are also important in legitimating the community's 'title-deeds' or land charter. The reward for fulfilment of cultural or religious duties is communal possession and enjoyment of a sacred land as belonging to the community 'by grace' (and, much later, 'by right'). There is a sense that salvation and redemption, by hallowing the community, also sanctify the land which members of the community inhabit

712

as a chosen people. Hence we find the growth of 'sacred centres' in religio-ethnic communities like those of the Sikhs, Sinhalese, Persians, Druse, Amhara, Armenians and Irish, which focus and rekindle an often exclusive sense of election and thereby renew the life of the *ethnie* in each generation (A. D. Smith 1989).

Further research is required to show how far such myths of ethnic election can ensure the viability of *ethnie*, and how far they depend for their effects on other circumstances. The failure or absence of these factors is, however, likely to undermine that viability; a sudden and catastrophic defeat, as inflicted upon the Assyrians, may deliver the *coup de grâce* for an ossified or culturally attenuated *ethnie* (Roux 1964: esp. ch. 22, Saggs 1984: 117–30, 147–51).

'LATERAL' AND 'VERTICAL' *ETHNIE*

At this stage, it may be objected that my account, while allowing for ethnic formation and dissolution, presents a view of *ethnie* as primary historical actors, each of which is a tightly bounded, internally homogeneous, self-aware and durable entity. It is necessary to correct such an impression by qualifying the picture so far presented of the complete 'social penetration', within any community, of a unitary ethnic culture.

Once again, it is necessary to exercise caution; our literary records are often sparse and largely of 'élite' provenance, literacy being confined to sections of the ruling classes. We can, however, make use of artistic and architectural sources to indicate the degree of regional diffusion and social penetration of ethnic culture originating, in many cases, from the élites and transmitted by the priests, scribes, poets and seers among them.

As a first step, it is useful to distinguish between two processes in ethnic life: on the one hand, towards an extension of the *ethnie* in space at the cost of any social depth, and on the other hand, a social 'deepening' of ethnic culture at the cost of its tight circumscription in space. The former process leads to what may be termed 'lateral' *ethnie*, the latter to 'vertical' *ethnie*. These are pure types; in practice, ethnic communities often embody contradictory trends. Yet, at given stages in the history of particular *ethnie*, one or other of these processes may predominate, presenting a close approximation to either the 'lateral' or the 'vertical' type. An example of a 'lateral' *ethnie* in antiquity would be the Hittites. Theirs was a community of largely feudal nobles, priests and warriors, who 'sat on top' of the various Anatolian peasant *ethnie* communities and 'categories' which they had conquered in establishing first their kingdom (*c.* 1800 BC) and later their empire (*c.* 1400–1200 BC). With their tributary peoples they generally established a form of unequal federalism, preserved in distinctive 'treaties', and this was paralleled in religious affairs by what has been termed a 'spiritual federalism', which incorporated Hurrian and other deities into the pantheon of their mountain religion with its central shrine at Yazilikaya (see Moscati 1962: ch. 5, Lloyd 1956: 138–43, Burney and Lang 1971: ch. 4). Other well-known 'lateral' *ethnie* include the Medes and Persians, the Normans and the later Ottomans after they had lost their fanatical *Ghazi* faith (see Cook 1983, Davis 1976, Lewis 1968: ch. 1).

In such 'lateral' *ethnie*, ethnic persistence is bound up with superior status; at the same time, they lack a compact territorial base and their boundaries are diffuse. There is also frequent exchange of upper-class personnel between neighbouring *ethnie*, especially through marriage and warfare, at least within the boundaries of common faith. By contrast, the 'vertical' or demotic type of *ethnie* is much more compact and bounded, and its persistence is associated with the tendency for popular mobilization against outsiders. At these times we find a crusading and missionary quality not confined to aristocratic knights, but embracing the lower classes who may be engaged in battle and in ritual or cultural renewal of the community. City-state amphictyonies, tribal confederations, frontier communities and sects and diasporas often display these demotic tendencies and become in consequence ethnically unified from top to bottom, their 'verticality' often presenting problems for the 'lateral' *ethnie* that dominate polyethnic states or empires, as the Habsburgs found with the Swiss pikemen whom they tried to absorb, or the English aristocracy with the medieval Scots, the Persians with the ancient Greek city states, and various states with Armenians and Jews within their borders (see Steinberg 1976, Duncan 1970, Burn 1960, A. D. Smith 1986a: chs 4–5).

The latent conflict between dominant aristocratic ('lateral') and subordinate demotic ('vertical') *ethnie* is one source of the frequent massacres and expulsions of population – from the Assyrian deportations and destruction of Carthage to the Crusader and Mongol massacres, which presaged modern attempts at wholesale deportations and genocide (Kuper 1981). Recognition of this inherent situation of conflict is also a useful corrective to the 'majoritarian' view of history, which downgrades or neglects the role of the many small demotic *ethnie* in history and politics. The fact is that several of these smaller *ethnie* (Greeks, Jews, Armenians, Irish, Scots, Dutch, Catalans, Czechs, Basques, Amhara and Sinhalese among others) have persisted, albeit often much changed in form and cultural character, for centuries, even millennia, as recognized 'communities of history and destiny', and several of them have made disproportionate contributions to science, literature, religion and the arts (see A. D. Smith 1986a, chs 5–6).

Both kinds of *ethnie*, the lateral and the vertical, display a remarkable capacity for survival. The Hittites, for example, appear in the historical record as major political actors for over six centuries, and much of their culture survived in the 'neo-Hittite' city states of northern Syria for another four centuries. The Philistines display a similar longevity, while in Iran a succession of aristocratic lateral *ethnie* – Achaemenid Persian, Parthian, Sassanid Persian – ruled that country for several centuries each (Wiseman 1975, Frye 1966). Vertical or demotic *ethnie* can be even more durable. Greeks, Jews, Armenians and Copts can boast millennial identities, often much transformed in character and demography; one has only to recall the vast influx of Slavs, Avars and Albanians into the Greek peninsula in the seventh and eighth centuries AD, though even here Greek-speaking populations and culture were driven to the coast lands and islands (Woodhouse 1984: 36–8, Ostrogorski 1968: 93–4, 192–4).

The reasons for differential ethnic survival (many *ethnie* disappeared, usually by absorption, including the Phoenicians, Philistines, Assyrians and Etruscans) have not received the attention that the importance of the topic merits. A number of factors, or sets of factors, suggest themselves. They include the following:

Autonomy

Nationalists have long contended that the survival of the ethnic community, in its 'authentic' form, requires self-rule. But in fact many *ethnie*, usually of the demotic variety, have survived for long periods under foreign rule, notably as 'pariah castes' like the Jews in medieval Europe or the Senmin in medieval Japan, or as *millets* in the Ottoman empire. The same is true of contemporary *ethnie*: Kurds, Ewe, Tibetans, Basques, Bretons and many others maintain their identities even when included within, or divided between, alien states. On the other hand, memories of independent statehood in an earlier epoch may inspire ethnic renewal in a later era, especially if associated with a golden age of heroes. However such memories may, as in many Eastern European nationalisms, be better regarded as furnishing a model than as representing a fundamental cause of ethnic survival (see Sugar and Lederer 1969, Esman 1977).

Territorial rootedness

This too is essential to nationalist visions, which hold that distinct nations must not only occupy 'their own' homelands, but also 'feed off' a unique landscape and a particular soil. Once again, such a romantic conception is not borne out by the facts. A given *ethnie* may 'wither away' or be absorbed by newcomers in its homeland, while an uprooted *ethnie* may renew itself in 'exile': the Normans in France and the Phoenicians are instances of absorption in one's 'own' land, while the Jews and the Armenians are examples of survival as uprooted diasporas (Armstrong 1982: ch. 7). Nevertheless, homelands are important as bases for ethnic survival, not only because they delimit communal boundaries, but also because of the 'poetic landscapes' they offer to members of even exiled *ethnie*. Here again, memories and images of sacred places – rivers, mountains, tombs, sites, monuments – help to keep alive the common sense of ethnicity and provide shared 'maps' for collective regeneration (A. D. Smith 1986a: ch. 8, 1981c).

Cultural isolation

Again, nationalists have argued that only 'pure' nations could survive in the modern world. The idea of isolating ethnie from foreign sources of contamination is not a new one; it already appeared in antiquity, in the Bible, and in the Middle Ages, for example the Spanish *limpieza de sangre*. But in fact many peoples (and quite a few nationalisms) have enhanced their chances of ethnic survival by modifying traditional beliefs and mores and borrowing from other cultures, as the Persians did by adopting Islamic religion and culture, and the Greeks by exchanging paganism for Orthodoxy (see Frye 1966: ch. 8; Carras 1983).

Religion and the mythomoteur

Religious conservatism is often assumed to provide an effective barrier to ethnic dissolution, and conversely a change of religion is assumed to imply ethnogenesis. Neither assumption can be sustained. Religious conservatism may slow down the rate of ethnic assimilation for long periods, but, as both the Assyrian and Phoenician examples demonstrate, it cannot be proof against ethnic extinction (Moscati 1973, Roux 1964: ch. 22). Conversely, as we have seen, pre-existing *ethnie* may adopt a new religion and culture, as with the Persians, and thereby renew themselves and their culture. In pre-modern eras, a distinctive religion or vision of a world religion appears to be the most potent source of ethnic persistence; but it is the social rather than the doctrinal aspects of a religion – its community-forming propensities such as rites, ceremonies, liturgy, script-and-language, sacred texts and clergy, and the value systems they transmit – that are crucial for ethnic survival in the long term. In this light, the act of conversion, of embracing a new religion and way of life, may be seen as a necessary means of crystallizing or enhancing a collective identity. The conversion of the Rus' under Vladimir of Kiev in 988 AD was an event of as great, if not greater, significance in the formation of a Kievan Russian identity as was the conquest of the neighbouring Khazar empire; and so perhaps was Clovis's conversion to Catholic Christianity for the Franks after 498 AD (Pipes 1977: 223–34; James 1988: 121–9).

An important part in the religious underpinning of ethnic survival is played by the various kinds of *mythomoteur*, the constitutive political myth of the *ethnie*. Both dynastic and communal mythomoteurs evoke profound religious sentiments. In the former case, the dynasty and monarch are invested with redemptive and sacred characteristics, as in Byzantium or medieval France; in the communal mythomoteurs found among such *ethnie* as the Arabs, Armenians and Jews, the community itself is endowed with sacred qualities which may generate an almost messianic fervour in times of crisis, particularly when allied to a heightened sense of superiority and a myth of ethnic election (Armstrong 1982: chs 3–6, A. D. Smith 1986a, chs 3, 5).

Many other factors – demographic, social and political – might be included in an examination of ethnic viability, and much work remains to be done on ethnic formation, dissolution, survival and alteration. Such studies need to be integrated with an analysis of the preconditions for nation formation in the early modern and modern eras, since it is only through a deeper understanding of the ethnic foundations and pre-modern social and cultural backgrounds of nations that a more balanced and historically convincing account than those provided by current primordialist or instrumentalist theories can be achieved.

TWO ROUTES TO NATION FORMATION

The concept of the 'nation' and its relation with nationalism, the ideological movement, have been objects of scholarly contention for many decades; and there is no sign of any resolution of these debates. It is not my purpose here to review the different kinds of definition ('objective' versus 'subjective', 'statist' versus 'ethnicist', 'voluntarist' versus 'organicist', etc.) of the concepts 'nation' and 'nationalism', but rather to show how particular concepts and ideologies emerged in the context of social and ethnic processes in particular areas and periods (see, *inter alia*, Rustow 1967: ch. 1, Deutsch 1966: ch. 1, A. D. Smith 1973: s. 1; Connor 1978).

A good starting point for analysing the nature and formation of nations is the historians' distinction between two kinds of nation: the 'old, continuous' nations of Western Europe (France, England, Holland, Spain, Sweden) and the new 'nations of design' in Central and Eastern Europe and Asia (Tilly 1975: Introduction and Conclusion, Seton-Watson 1977: chs 2–3). The first type of nation preceded the rise of nationalism in the eighteenth century, and was the product of unplanned processes. The second type followed the rise of nationalism and was largely the result of political movements and nationalist programmes, often in the wake of wars and treaties. This distinction is closely related to Kohn's well-known typology of 'Eastern' and 'Western' nationalisms: the nationalisms west of the Rhine can be characterized as 'rational' and 'voluntaristic', whereas those to the east have had a more 'organic' and mystical character, in tune with the outlook of their leaders, the romantic intelligentsia (Kohn 1967 [1944]: chs 5, 7–8).

In this vein, we can relate two concepts of the 'nation' to two respective routes of nation formation. The 'Western' concept (found only in certain Western states and sometimes transplanted overseas) is fundamentally civic and territorial. In this conception, the nation is a territorially bound entity, compact and unitary. It is also an association based on common laws and institutions. Although individuals may opt out of particular nations, they must belong to a nation. Moreover, members are in principle equals before the law: they have common rights and duties as 'citizens'. Finally, their citizenship of the nation (as opposed to the state) is conferred by their participation in a common 'civic' culture or 'civil religion' inculcated by a public, standardized mass education system (Gellner 1973, E. Weber 1979).

By contrast to this civic conception, we frequently encounter a more ethnic and genealogical model of the nation, particularly in Eastern Europe and Asia (much less in Africa). Here the emphasis falls upon presumed ties of common descent and the associated myths of genealogical origin. Such a conception gives more weight to vernacular culture, mainly native languages, rituals and customs. There is a correspondingly greater appeal to 'the people', the mobilized folk; and with it a more missionary historical nativism, which singles out the unique traits of the community's historical experience in its homeland or – in the case of diaspora nationalisms – outside (see Fishman 1980, Brock 1976).

Now these two conceptions correspond to, and emerge out of, distinct routes of nation formation. (There are, one should add, other routes, including the 'immigrant' route found for example in America, Argentina and Australia, and the 'colonial' route found in Latin America and sub-Saharan Africa, where the metropolitan-created states attempted to forge new national units out of often heterogeneous populations, producing a 'developmental' nationalism; see Martins 1967, A. D. Smith 1986b). The 'civic–territorial' model emerged in the context of 'national states' created by a long process of ethnic bureaucratic incorporation; whereas the 'ethnic–genealogical' model was the product of the politicization and mass mobilization of 'vernacularized' demotic *ethnie* through a returning intelligentsia.

Let me elaborate briefly. For this purpose it is necessary to return to my earlier distinction between 'lateral' aristocratic *ethnie* and 'vertical' demotic *ethnie*. 'Lateral' *ethnie* provide the starting-point for the rise of national states and hence of the 'civic–territorial' model of the nation, mainly but not exclusively in the West. There have, of course, been several 'ethnic states' in history, if by this term is meant no more than a state dominated by a ruling class drawn from a particular *ethnie* which forms the majority of the state's population: one thinks of ancient Egypt, Persia at certain points in its history, Assyria before it became an empire and Russia before it acquired its empire. But only some of these ethnic states were 'lateral', and only a few managed to build administrative apparatuses which were able to incorporate outlying regions and broader social strata of the dominant ethnic population, and weld them into a culturally cohesive unit. Neither the Hittites, nor the Sassanid (or Safavid) Persians, nor the French Normans, nor the Burgundians managed to incorporate outlying regions and broader social strata and infuse them with their own aristocratic ethnic culture, and thereby create truly 'national' states. These and other 'lateral' *ethnie* either did not desire, or failed, to incorporate other religions and strata, either because they could not evolve the necessary bureaucratic instruments or because, even when they did, they did not or could not use them for 'cultural regulation', in the sense of diffusing their fund of ethnic culture, of myth and symbolism, to other strata and regions. Only in certain cases, notably in England, France and – to a lesser extent – Spain, Sweden and Russia, did attempts at ethnic bureaucratic incorporation meet with a measure of success (one might also add the Solomonic dynasty of Amharic Ethiopia, on which see Ullendorff 1973, ch. 4) (see Corrigan and Sayer 1985, L. Smith 1985, Reynolds 1984: ch. 8, Seton-Watson 1977: ch. 2, A. Lewis 1974: 57–70, Atkinson 1960).

Why was the breakthrough to the modern nation achieved in the West by 'lateral' aristocratic *ethnie*? Why were they able to succeed where the lateral *ethnie* of other 'ethnic states' failed? The answer can only be surmised, but it must lie in a combination of three sets of factors: first, the existence of an underlying 'ethnic core' on which the state was, and could be, built, a core which gave it cohesion and stability *vis-à-vis* outside forces; second, the determination and ability of strong rulers to create bureaucratic states with the necessary administrative, fiscal and military organs; and third, the economic and cultural revolutions of capitalism and secularization, which provided the wealth and the 'rational' techniques and discourse for such unifying ethnic incorporation into the aristocracy's myths, memories, symbols, values and traditions (see A. D. Smith 1986a: ch. 6).

Whatever the reasons, it was in certain 'Western' states that what we may term the 'national state' emerged, a state that was roughly coextensive and congruent with the 'nation', and that emerged with it *pari passu*. It is often assumed that the Western 'rational' state *created* the nation and formed its matrix. But I think it is more accurate to see the first modern nations as products of a complex interplay between the new kind of state and older 'ethnic cores' which gave the population, mainly its upper strata, a sense of community based on myths of shared ancestry and common historical memories, as well as on components of a common culture like language, customs and religion. The new forces of capitalism and secular rationality galvanized this interplay and directed it towards a more politically conscious legal–territorial and civic community or 'nation'.

The second major route of nation formation set out from the base of demotic 'vertical' *ethnie*. Many of these communities can be regarded as 'religion-shaped peoples', ethno-religious groups whose persistence was, more than most, ensured by the hold of a distinctive organized religion throughout its homeland or dispersion, and down its social scale. Among Orthodox Greeks under Ottoman rule, Gregorian Armenians, Monophysite Copts and Amhara, Catholic Irish, Druse, Sikhs and Maronites, and to some extent Orthodox Russians, this pattern of salvation religion with its sacred texts, liturgies and priesthoods, transmitting the values, memories and traditions of the *ethnie* down the generations, has been the chief mechanism of ethnic survival.

At the same time, the conservatism often generated by this hold of organized religion posed grave problems for the emergence of nations from 'vertical' *ethnie*. Usually, there was no ethnic state that could be invoked to break the hold of ecclesiastical authority and its monopoly over traditional ways of thought. In these circumstances, the secular intellectuals and professional intelligentsia had an uphill struggle convincing their ethnic kinsmen that they were not, but should become, a 'nation'. It was, after all, easy to confuse the *ethnie*, with its myths of common ancestry, its memories, culture and homeland, with a full-blown nation; and this no doubt accounts for the emergence of a very different concept of the nation among 'vertical' and demotic *ethnie*. This concept provided a bridge between the pre-existing ethnic realities and the goal of a territorial nation with its civic nationalism, and it was one which found especial favour among the smaller demotic *ethnie* of Eastern Europe and the Middle East (see the essays in Sugar 1980, Atiya 1968, Stavrianos 1961, Kohn 1960).

Of course, the state played an initiating role in these cases, too. Only now, the state in question was an alien, oppressive and interventionist instrument of dominant *ethnie* and their ruling classes. The reforms set in motion within the Habsburg domains by Joseph II, or in the Tsarist empire by Alexander II, introduced new cultural classifications and goals, and had the effect of intensifying pressures on subordinate demotic *ethnie*, especially when the rulers began to appropriate the norms and discourse of the new nationalist ideals that spread throughout Europe in the wake of Napoleon's armies and reforms. It was partly in response to these pressures that a small emergent intelligentsia in each subordinate 'vertical' *ethnie*, led by coteries of educator-intellectuals, began to formulate new definitions and goals for their communities, in tune with the ethnic and social realities of each people. Such redefinitions were not simply the 'inventions' of intellectuals, nor were they straightforward applications of Western models. They were, rather, vernacular adaptations of the new ideals of 'civic' nationalism to their own communities through a process of rediscovering a heroic 'ethnic past'. In this process, the old religious worldview was reversed: the 'people' were no longer seen as a passive, if chosen, vessel of salvation, recipients of divine commands, but rather as the authors of that message within the framework of communal history. Instead of being the *raison d'être* of the *ethnie*, salvation religion now became its supreme expression and the glorious manifestation of the people's genius (A. D. Smith 1983a: ch. 10, Kedourie 1971: Introduction).

It was through a selective return to the ethnic past, or ethnic historicism, that the aspirant intelligentsia effected their moral and political revolution. Their task was to construct a vernacular historical map and a public morality for the demotic *ethnie* which would transform it from a passive, subordinate 'object' of history into a mobilized, politically aware and active 'subject' of history. This was to be achieved by placing the 'masses' at the centre of political concern and by celebrating the role of the 'people' and their collective values, myths and memories. This could only be done when the community controlled its own destiny in its own homeland — a compact, clearly demarcated territory, in which it was united and autonomous. That in turn meant control by the community of its own resources and a concomitant elevation of the people into legal 'citizens', possessed of common rights and duties in their homeland, and socialized into a vernacular culture that restored their dignity by revealing their unique virtues and character. Hence the return to the ethnic past. For only in the history of the community, in its heroes and 'golden age', could its true destiny be read. That is why the *Bhagavadgita* has meant so much to modern Indian intellectuals, why the *Kalevala* has such resonance for modern Finns, the Ulster cycle for many modern Irish and the Bible for even socialist Jews (see Adenwalla 1961, Honko 1985, Hutchinson 1987, Hertzberg 1960).

The upshot of these processes has been the reconstruction of modern nations on the bases of pre-modern *ethnie*, whether lateral or vertical. In the one case, the rational, modernizing state created by aristocratic *ethnie* has, over a long period, incorporated outlying regions and lower social strata to form a 'national state' upon the foundation of a pre-existing 'ethnic core'. In the other case, a returning intelligentsia has responded to the intrusion of modernizing states (as well as the pressures of urbanization and commerce) to redefine the traditional vertical *ethnie* as a modern political nation, by rediscovering a heroic ethnic past to serve as a model and inspiration for a mobilized, autonomous, vernacular citizenry. Herein lie the origins of the majority of the world's nations (A. D. Smith 1986a: chs 6–8).

ETHNIE AND NATIONS IN THE MODERN WORLD

Such a view of the rise of modern nations is at variance with several of the currently fashionable 'modernist' accounts of nations and nationalism. By emphasizing the ethnic bases of both kinds of nation, the territorial and the genealogical, modern nations are seen as more than 'inventions' or 'constructs' of intelligentsias or other élites. This is not to deny the element of 'reconstruction', in some cases even of fabrication, in the formation of nations; nations are also 'imagined', in the sense that a community is conjured up in people's minds by images conveyed by the printed word; and some of their traditions may be 'invented', in the sense that repetitive practices governed by rules and rituals are designed to inculcate values and norms that automatically imply continuity with the past (see Anderson 1983: esp. chs 1, 2, Hobsbawm and Ranger 1983: Introduction and ch. 7). But 'invention' is only sometimes fabrication (as it clearly was with Iolo Morganwg's incorporation of the Druidic Gorsedd into the revived *eisteddfodau* after 1819), and the 'imagined' should not be allowed to fade into the 'imaginary'. The 'modern nation' may be a construct of intellectuals, including scholars; but it is also a deeply felt reality for its members (and outsiders), and like ethnicity, a fundamental feature of the contemporary world (on the Welsh revival, see Morgan 1983).

The twentieth century, and more specifically its latter half, has seen an unexpected revitalization of ethnic ties, and an unforeseen resilience of nations and 'nation-states': unexpected, because statesmen, social scientists and many educated people were convinced that nationalism was a spent force after the horrors of two world wars, and that humanity had outstripped ethnic (or 'tribal') ties in an era of regionalism and increasing global interdependence (see Popper 1961: II 49–58, 60–4, Deutsch 1969); unforeseen, because that same global interdependence appeared to be eroding the bases of the nation-state and leading humanity towards a genuine cosmopolitanism (see Schlesinger 1987).

In fact we have witnessed a proliferation of movements for ethnic autonomy and secession all over the world. In Europe and North America they have taken the form of an 'ethnic revival'. In the older-established industrial–democratic states, this revival has been fuelled by inequality of opportunity in the competition for resources, growing state intervention in peripheral areas, and the demise of colonial empires. Generally, these have been 'middle sector' movements led by an expanding humanistic and technocratic intelligentsia (see Pinard and Hamilton 1984, A. D. Smith 1981a: chs 1, 8, 9, Stone 1979). In the Third World, these movements take the form of wars of secession – in Eritrea, Tigre, Angola, Kurdistan, Punjab, the Philippines and Sri Lanka – or ethnic riots and commotions which challenge the distribution of power and wealth in the new 'plural' states of Africa, Asia and the Caribbean. Here the 'ethnic' concept of the nation comes into conflict with the 'territorial' model espoused by the leaderships of post-colonial states, and many demotic *ethnie* have become mobilized and politically activated in reaction to the power and privilege of the 'over-developed state' and its dominant *ethnie* (see Alavi 1972; Brass 1985; Horowitz 1985: esp. chs 4–6).

While the economic aspects of movements for ethnic secession are important, and in particular the response of élites in developing countries to the massive inequalities generated by imperialism and capitalism, we cannot understand their frequency and intensity without taking political and cultural-symbolic factors into account. The intensity displayed by many Third World movements of ethnic separatism is, in part, a function of the dominance of the post-colonial state and the territorial links which it has forged between previously separated *ethnie*, as well as the rewards (in jobs, housing, education and the like) it is able to allocate to the included ethnic communities and ethnic categories, all of which help to foster a spirit of group cohesion and competition. But equally important are the symbolic and cultural components of ethnicity, and the modern uses of old but reconstructed myths, memories, values and symbols that define and inspire each ethnic community. Here lies a fertile field for the elaborations of intellectuals, but also for the historical resonance of mass sentiments. Élite manipulation of such sentiments can only succeed where the appropriate 'collective chords' are struck (see Nairn 1977: chs 2 and 9, Brass 1979, Robinson 1979).

These collective responses are fuelled by the waves of ethnic migration to the rapidly expanding cities of Africa and Asia. Whether uprooted by the intrusion of the cash nexus and uneven penetration of capitalist exchange relations, or drawn to the city by hopes of employment, housing and education, migrants often settle with their kinsmen in ethnic quarters, whose voluntary associations and competitive support often evoke strong urban ethnic antagonisms and a higher cultural profile than was usually possible in isolated rural milieux. In some cases, traditional ethnic rivalries have been transposed into urban settings by residential proximity and competition for jobs; in other cases, the setting itself has induced rivalries out of initial cultural differentiae (Gellner 1964). Urban ethnicity becomes instrumental for the assurance of collective benefits in exchange and trade (see Epstein 1978, Cohen 1969, Markovitz 1977: ch. 3).

Such urban ethnic competition is not confined to the Third World. It figures significantly in more recent accounts of the 'ethnic revival' in North America. Ethnicity here, having survived the 'melting pot', has become both instrumental and symbolic. Both 'group competition' and 'rational choice' theorists see in American ethnic communities a more powerful site for mass mobilization, and in ethnicity a more useful tool for group manipulation in the competition of élites for wealth and power, than other fields and categories like class. *Ethnie*, as Bell (1975) put it, combine material interests with affective ties. This is what makes them so important symbolically and lends their activities a vibrancy missing from other forms of association (see Greeley 1974, Glazer and Moynihan 1975, Gans 1979, Stack 1986).

The American example, like that of the former Soviet Union, raises in acute form the question of the contemporary relationship between *ethnie* and nations. Can there indeed be 'polyethnic', or even 'multi-national', nations? Theoretically, it is argued, nations must be culturally homogeneous, though in practice, few of them are (Gellner 1983). Empirically, it would appear that the chances of survival of polyethnic nations are poor; the few cases that have succeeded to date, such as Belgium and Switzerland, are unusual in their good fortune (see Petersen 1975, Steinberg 1976).

In the Soviet case, central Party control and a centralizing Communist ideology held these tensions in check for several decades, while territorial federalism permitted the major *ethnie* sufficient cultural space to keep their collective ties and sentiments intact. Until recently, it was possible to argue that the two models of the nation, the ethnic–genealogical and the civic–territorial, reinforced each other, because each was operative at different levels, the former at the cultural and private level, the latter at the political and public level (see G. E. Smith 1985).

But the advent of *perestroika* upset this balance. The calls for greater competence, irrespective of ethnic origins, and for economic efficiency increased the interventionism of the central state into the social affairs of every ethnic community and nationality. *Glasnost'* brought into the open long-suppressed disputes, as in Nagorno-Karabakh and between Uzbeks and Meskhetians, and long-standing aspirations, such as those of the Balts, Georgians and Moldavians. Some of this tension derives from territorial and economic disputes between different ethnic communities and nations; but much of it revolves around the conflict with the dominant Russian nation both at the centre and in each republic and area; at each level, a civic–territorial concept of the nation and its attendant nationalism comes into conflict with the different *ethnie* and their genealogical conceptions and nationalisms (see G. E. Smith 1989).

Once again, we are faced with the conflicting claims of two concepts of the nation and two kinds of nationalism, the civic–territorial and the ethnic–genealogical. The image of the latter, diffused by adherents of German Romanticism, and so attractive to the many smaller demotic *ethnie*, faces inwards to the unique cultural values of the community, while simultaneously seeking the benefits of Western modernity. The resulting tension produces typical responses: traditionalistic, rejecting that modernity while accepting some of its methods; assimilationist, embracing that modernity with cosmopolitan fervour, but often disillusioned in practice by its selectiveness; and the attempt to combine the best of 'tradition' and 'modernity' in either reformist or revivalist positions, so renewing the ethnic heritage by adapting it to modern conditions (see A. D. Smith 1979: ch. 2, Hutchinson 1987: ch. 5).

Civic–territorial nationalisms, on the other hand, face outwards to other territorially defined communities. But they, too, face a dilemma: how far can mere 'territory' and 'citizenship' produce social cohesion and a sense of distinctive identity? If residence is the chief criterion of nationality, if the state is ethnically 'plural', can a sense of 'nationhood' be sustained? Must territorial nations always oscillate between cultural integration and ethnic pluralism? Can they evolve a 'civil religion' over and above the different, constituent ethnic cultures?

One has to admit that the evidence to date does not lend support to the proposition that ethnically plural states can evolve into cohesive and unique 'nations'. This may be a consequence of the hold of ethnic definitions of the nation. But that is only part of the answer. We must remember that even the Western 'territorial' concept of the nation included the component of a binding civic culture, and that, historically, Western 'territorial' nations were formed upon a strong 'ethnic core'. Modern nations, I have argued, are founded upon pre-modern ethnic ties, if not always directly, then through the example and model originally furnished by Western nations and by other ethnic nations since. The idea of fraternity and unity, if not of cultural homogeneity, has been a guiding influence on all nationalists, even when they respected the traditions of different *ethnie* within the nations they were bent on constructing. This construction may take the form of elaborating a new political culture and mythology that will include the various *ethnie* or even nations within the state's borders. Whether the constitution is unitary, as in Britain, or federal as in what was Yugoslavia or the former Soviet Union, the possibility of successfully evolving 'multi-national nations' cannot be ruled out, despite the tensions that such attempts evoke. In these as in other cases, however, the attempt is based on the viability of a long-established 'ethnic core' which anchors the 'territorial nation' (see G. E. Smith 1985, A. D. Smith 1985).

THE ROLE OF NATIONALISM

Attempts to create both ethnic–genealogical and civic–territorial nations are predicated on the culture and ideology of 'nationalism'. It is important to grasp the dual character of nationalism, if we are to understand its continuing wide appeal and its ability to survive, and often to 'annex', other ideologies. 'Nationalism' signifies both an ideological doctrine and a wider symbolic universe and fund of sentiments. The ideology holds that the world consists of separate, identifiable nations, each with its peculiar character; that the nation is the sole legitimate source of political power; that every individual must belong and owe supreme loyalty to one and only one nation; and that nations must be autonomous, preferably in states of their own, for only then can global freedom and peace be assured. To this 'core doctrine', nationalists add their own secondary elaborations, themes and motifs that express the peculiar history and character of each nation, be they German Romantic notions of linguistic purity, or Russian theories of a national-religious mission in Pan-Slavism, or African ideas of Negritude (see Kedourie 1960, A. D. Smith 1973: s. 1, 1983a: esp. chs 1, 7).

But there is also a wider 'culture of nationalism' which underpins the political doctrine and its variations. I have in mind, first, the recurrent central motifs or ideals of autonomy, unity and identity; and second, the panoply of symbols and rituals associated with the drama of the nation. The key motifs continually reappear in the writings and actions of nationalists everywhere, though in varying degrees. The nation, we are told, must have its own character, it must be distinctive; we must 'think our own thoughts', as Herder put it, be 'authentic' and 'individual' in a national sense. The nation must, for that reason, be 'free', in the special sense of being autonomous, of operating according to the 'inward laws' of an abstract community, without any external constraint. These 'inward laws' or 'rhythms' express the seamless unity of a community of citizens who share a common pattern of values and beliefs and are animated by a single will. Fraternity, the familial equality and integration of the nation's members, is as much a social ideal as a territorial and legal expression; as in David's great painting of the single, dynamic compact of the three brothers in *The Oath of the Horatii* (see Figure 1), the union of citizens in a political community is founded upon a myth of fictive descent and heroic destiny (Berlin 1976, Barnard 1965, Rosenblum 1967: ch. 2).

From these key motifs spring the whole gamut of symbols that express the culture and evoke the salvation drama of the nation. In the nation's flags and anthems, its memorials and monuments, its parades and ceremonies, its coins and insignia, its capitals and assemblies, its arts and crafts, and its music and

Figure 1 Jacques-Louis David, *The Oath of the Horatii*, reproduced by kind permission of the Louvre, Paris. © Réunion des Musées Nationaux.

dance are distilled the pride and hope of a 'community of history and destiny' which seeks to shape events and mould itself in the image of its ideals. To this end, the modern nation of fraternal citizens must always return to the idealizations of its past, to its myths of ethnic origin, descent and development, and above all, to the 'golden ages' that guide its path and endow it with a confidence to face the unknown, and to the heroes whose virtues inspire public emulation and exalted faith. For as Durkheim reminded us,

> There can be no society which does not feel the need of upholding and reaffirming at regular intervals the collective sentiments and the collective ideas which make its unity and its personality.
>
> (Durkheim 1915: 387, see A. D. Smith 1986a: ch. 8)

In one sense, then, it is the nationalists who create the 'nation'; but they do so only within circumscribed boundaries and with the ethnic materials bestowed upon them by previous generations of their community. In this sense, for all its abstraction and 'reconstruction', there is nothing imaginary about the nation or about its consequences for the millions of human beings whose lives are shaped by it. If nationalists create nations, *ethnie* and the models of cultural association they embody form the seedbed of nationalisms. If it is the intellectuals who have proposed and elaborated the concept of the nation, its popularity with every class and stratum is nevertheless the consequence of its ethnic lineage. In nationalism we have not only a political ideology of popular government, but also a quasi-religion (or better, a 'surrogate religion') of mobilized ethnic uniqueness. Professionals, bourgeoisie, artisans, workers and peasants, even the lower clergy, have all felt the pull of this surrogate religion, which can combine with practically every ideology and faith, and contrive not just to survive, but to emerge triumphant in the modern world.

There is no corner of the contemporary globe that has not felt the power and attraction of nations and nationalism. The world's most bitter and intractable conflicts are rooted in ethnic diversity and the clash of rival nationalisms. In Indo-China, the Indian subcontinent, the Middle East, the Horn of Africa, southern Africa, Central and Eastern Europe, as well as in a host of more limited but just as long-lasting wars, the power of revitalized ethnic ties and of myths and symbols of ethnic descent are never far below the surface. Even where these conflicts are exacerbated by gross inequalities and struggles for limited resources, even where the humiliations of colonialism and imperialism are recent memories, the drive to create unified and distinct nations on the basis of ethnic and territorial communities is rarely absent. No ideology and no religion can disguise the secular movement of ethnic politicization and national reconstruction. It is this movement that, for the last three centuries and more, the European – and subsequently world-wide – system of states has had to accommodate or risk dissolution. There is no way of knowing whether this accommodation has been largely successful, or whether we shall be engulfed in another wave of ethnic mobilization and national reconstruction requiring a redrawing of political boundaries and new ways of organizing 'nation states' and their interrelations. The signs are that the dual quest for ethnic origins and political emancipation, for collective identity and communal liberty, will continue to disturb the 'iron grid' of state systems in different parts of the globe, and that the lack of congruence between 'ethno-history' and territory, between *ethnie* and statehood, will prove a fertile source of explosive conflicts and unsatisfied nationalisms. A world order that fails in so many instances to satisfy, and that even excites, such deep-seated longings, is always liable to destabilization as it seeks to contain within the confines of hybrid 'nation-states' the social and cultural forces that threaten to dissolve them (Seton-Watson 1971, A. D. Smith 1983b, Connor 1972).

Nationalism, then, has universalized and given political coherence to a general movement from often quiescent ethnic communities to active political nations, and has thereby transformed both the social relations and the political map in every area of the modern world. By harnessing the power of ethnic ties and their attendant myths and symbols, nationalism has created the social and political conditions for its own propagation and for the continuous proliferation of nations. The process seems endless. There is no practical limit to the multiplication of cultural differentiae, or to the rediscovery of ethno-histories and myths of ethnic descent, which can be used to mobilize populations and to inspire them to political action. Whether entry into a 'post-industrial' era will slow the process down, or give it new life, as cultural networks of computerized information penetrate every corner of the globe, remains to be seen (Richmond 1984). For the foreseeable future, political and social life must continue to function within the framework of the 'nation state' and the nationalisms that both uphold and challenge that order.

REFERENCES

Adenwalla, M. (1961) 'Hindu concepts and the Gita in Early Indian national thought', in R. A. Sakai (ed.) *Studies on Asia*, Lincoln: University of Nebraska Press.

Alavi, H. (1972) 'The state in post-colonial societies – Pakistan and Bangladesh', *New Left Review* 74: 59–81.

Anderson, B. (1983) *Imagined Communities: Reflections on the Origin and Spread of Nationalism*, London: Verso Editions and New Left Books.

Armstrong, J. (1982) *Nations before Nationalism*, Chapel Hill: University of North Carolina Press.

Atiya, A. S. (1968) *A History of Eastern Christianity*, London: Methuen.

Atkinson, W. C. (1960) *A History of Spain and Portugal*, Harmondsworth: Penguin.

Barnard, F. M. (1965) *Herder's Social and Political Thought*, Oxford: Clarendon Press.

Barth, F. (ed.) (1969) *Ethnic Groups and Boundaries*, Boston: Little, Brown.

Bell, D. (1975) 'Ethnicity and social change', in N. Glazer and D. Moynihan (eds) *Ethnicity: Theory and Experience*, Cambridge, Mass.: Harvard University Press.

Berlin, I. (1976) *Vico and Herder*, London: Hogarth Press.

Brass, P. R. (1974) *Religion, Language and Politics in North India*, Cambridge: Cambridge University Press.

—— (1979) 'Élite groups, symbol manipulation and ethnic identity among the Muslims of South Asia', in D. Taylor and M. Yapp (eds) *Political Identity in South Asia*, London and Dublin: Centre of South Asian Studies, School of Oriental and African Studies, Curzon Press.

—— (ed.) (1985) *Ethnic Groups and the State*, London: Croom Helm.

Breuilly, J. (1982) *Nationalism and the State*, Manchester: Manchester University Press.

Bright, J. (1978) *A History of Israel*, London: SCM Press.

Brock, P. (1976) *The Slovak National Awakening*, Eastern European Monographs, Toronto: University of Toronto Press.

Burn, A. R. (1960) *The Lyric Age of Greece*, London: Edward Arnold.

Burney, C. and Lang, D. (1971) *The Peoples of the Hills: Ancient Ararat and Caucasus*, London: Weidenfeld & Nicolson.

Carmichael, J. (1967) *The Shaping of the Arabs*, New York: Macmillan.

Carras, C. (1983) *3000 Years of Greek Identity – Myth or Reality?*, Athens: Domus Books.

Cohen, A. (1969) *Custom and Politics in Urban Africa*, Berkeley & Los Angeles: University of California Press.

Connor, W. (1972) 'Nation-building or nation-destroying?', *World Politics* 24: 319–55.

—— (1978) 'A nation is a nation, is a state, is an ethnic group, is a ...', *Ethnic and Racial Studies* 1: 377–400.

Cook, J. M. (1983) *The Persian Empire*, London: J. M. Dent.

Corrigan, P. and Sayer, D. (1985) *The Great Arch: English State Formation as Cultural Revolution*, Oxford: Blackwell.

Davis, R. (1976) *The Normans and their Myth*, London: Thames & Hudson.

Deutsch, K. W. (1966) *Nationalism and Social Communication*, 2nd edn, New York: MIT Press.

—— (1969) *Nationalism and its Alternatives*, New York: Alfred A. Knopf.

Duncan, A. A. M. (1970) *The Nation of Scots and the Declaration of Arbroath (1320)*, London: Historical Association.

Durkheim, E. (1915) *The Elementary Forms of the Religious Life*, transl. J. Swain, London: George Allen & Unwin.

Enloe, C. (1973) *Ethnic Conflict and Political Development*, Boston: Little, Brown.

Epstein, A. L. (1978) *Ethos and Identity*, London: Tavistock.

Esman, M. (ed.) (1977) *Ethnic Conflict in the Western World*, Ithaca, N.Y.: Cornell University Press.

Fishman, J. (1980) 'Social theory and ethnography: neglected perspectives on language and ethnicity in Eastern Europe', in P. Sugar (ed.) *Ethnic Diversity and Conflict in Eastern Europe*, Santa Barbara: ABC-Clio.

Frye, R. N. (1966) *The Heritage of Persia*, New York: Mentor.

Gans, H. (1979) 'Symbolic ethnicity', *Ethnic and Racial Studies* 2: 1–20.

Geertz, C. (1963) 'The integrative revolution', in C. Geertz (ed.) *Old Societies and New States*, New York: Free Press.

Gellner, E. (1964) *Thought and Change*, London: Weidenfeld & Nicolson.

—— (1973) 'Scale and nation', *Philosophy of the Social Sciences* 3: 1–17.

—— (1983) *Nations and Nationalism*, Oxford: Blackwell.

Glazer, N. and Moynihan, D. (eds) (1975) *Ethnicity: Theory and Experience*, Cambridge, Mass.: Harvard University Press.

Greeley, A. (1974) *Ethnicity in the United States*, New York: John Wiley.

Hertzberg, A. (ed.) (1960) *The Zionist Idea, A Reader*, New York: Meridian Books.

Hobsbawm, E. and Ranger, T. (eds) (1983) *The Invention of Tradition*, Cambridge: Cambridge University Press.

Honko, L. (1985) 'The *Kalevala* process', *Books from Finland* 19(1): 16–23.

Horowitz, D. (1985) *Ethnic Groups in Conflict*, Berkeley, Los Angeles and London: University of California Press.

Hutchinson, J. (1987) *The Dynamics of Cultural Nationalism: The Gaelic Revival and the Creation of the Irish Nation State*, London: George Allen & Unwin.

James, E. (1988) *The Franks*, Oxford: Blackwell.

Keddie, N. (1981) *Roots of Revolution: an Interpretive History of Modern Iran*, New Haven and London: Yale University Press.

Kedourie, E. (1960) *Nationalism*, London: Hutchinson.

—— (ed.) (1971) *Nationalism in Asia and Africa*, London: Weidenfeld & Nicolson.

Kirk, G. S. (1970) *Myth, Its Meaning and Functions in Ancient and Other Cultures*, Cambridge: Cambridge University Press.

Kohn, Hans (1960) *Pan-Slavism*, 2nd edn, New York: Vintage Books.

—— (1967 [1944]) *The Idea of Nationalism*, 2nd edn, New York: Collier-Macmillan.

Koht, H. (1947) 'The dawn of nationalism in Europe', *American Historical Review* 52: 265–80.

Kramer, S. N. (1963) *The Sumerians*, Chicago: Chicago University Press.

Kuper, L. (1981) *Genocide*, Harmondsworth: Penguin.

Levi, M. A. (1965) *Political Power in the Ancient World*, transl. J. Costello, London: Weidenfeld & Nicolson.

Lewis, A. (1974) *Knights and Samurai*, London: Temple Smith.

Lewis, B. (1968) *The Emergence of Modern Turkey*, London: Oxford University Press.

Lloyd, S. (1956) *Early Anatolia*, Harmondsworth: Penguin.

Mann, M. (1986) *The Sources of Social Power*, vol. 1: *Power in Agrarian Societies*, Cambridge: Cambridge University Press.

Markovitz, I. L. (1977) *Power and Class in Africa*, Englewood Cliffs, NJ: Prentice-Hall.

Martins, H. (1967) 'Ideology and development: "developmental nationalism" in Brazil', *Sociological Review Monographs* 11: 153–72.

Marwick, A. (1974) *War and Social Change in the Twentieth Century*, London: Methuen.

Mehden, F. von der (1963) *Religion and Nationalism in Southeast Asia*, Madison, Milwaukee and London: University of Wisconsin Press.

Morgan, P. (1983) 'From a death to a view: the hunt for the Welsh past in the Romantic period', in E. Hobsbawm and T. Ranger (eds) *The Invention of Tradition*, Cambridge: Cambridge University Press.

Moscati, S. (1962) *The Face of the Ancient Orient*, New York: Anchor Books.

—— (1973) *The World of the Phoenicians*, London: Cardinal, Sphere Books.

Nairn, T. (1977) *The Break-up of Britain: Crisis and Neo-nationalism*, London: New Left Books.

O'Brien, C. C. (1988) *God Land: Reflections on Religion and Nationalism*, Cambridge, Mass., and London: Harvard University Press.

Okamura, J. Y. (1981) 'Situational ethnicity', *Ethnic and Racial Studies* 4: 452–65.

Ostrogorski, G. (1968) *History of the Byzantine State*, 2nd English edn, Oxford: Blackwell.

Paskiewicz, H. (1954) *The Origin of Russia*, London: George Allen & Unwin.

Paul, D. W. (1985) 'Slovak nationalism and the Hungarian state, 1870–1910', in P. R. Brass (ed.) *Ethnic Groups and the State*, London: Croom Helm.

Petersen, W. (1975) 'On the subnations of Western Europe', in N. Glazer and D. Moynihan (eds) *Ethnicity: Theory and Experience*, Cambridge, Mass.: Harvard University Press.

Pinard, M. and Hamilton, R. (1984) 'The class bases of the Quebec independence movement: conjectures and evidence', *Ethnic and Racial Studies* 7, 19–54.

Pipes, R. (1977) *Russia under the Old Regime*, London: Peregrine.

Popper, K. (1961) *The Open Society and its Enemies*, London: Routledge & Kegan Paul.

Reynolds, S. (1984) *Kingdoms and Communities in Western Europe, 900–1300*, Oxford: Clarendon Press.

Richmond, A. H. (1984) 'Ethnic nationalism and post-industrialism', *Ethnic and Racial Studies* 7, 4–18.

Robinson, F. (1979) 'Islam and Muslim separatism', in D. Taylor and M. Yapp (eds) *Political Identity in South Asia*, London and Dublin: Centre of South Asian Studies, School of Oriental and African Studies, Curzon Press.

Rosenblum, R. (1967) *Transformations in Late Eighteenth Century Art*, Princeton: Princeton University Press.

Roux, G. (1964) *Ancient Iraq*, Harmondsworth: Penguin.

Rustow, D. (1967) *A World of Nations*, Washington DC: Brookings Institution.

Saggs, H. W. F. (1984) *The Might that was Assyria*, London: Sidgwick & Jackson.

Sarkisyanz, E. (1964) *Buddhist Backgrounds of the Burmese Revolution*, The Hague: Martinus Nijhoff.

Schlesinger, P. (1987) 'On national identity: some conceptions and misconceptions criticised', *Social Science Information* 26(2): 219–64.

Seton-Watson, H. (1971) 'Unsatisfied nationalisms', *Journal of Contemporary History* 6: 3–14.

—— (1977) *Nations and States*, London: Methuen.

Shils, E. (1957) 'Primordial, personal, sacred and civil ties', *British Journal of Sociology* 7: 113–45.

Simmel, G. (1964) *Conflict, and the Web of Group Affiliations*, New York: Free Press.

Singleton, F. (1985) *A Short History of the Yugoslav Peoples*, Cambridge: Cambridge University Press.

Smith, A. D. (1973) '*Nationalism*, a trend report and annotated bibliography', *Current Sociology* 21(3), special issue.

—— (1979) *Nationalism in the Twentieth Century*, Oxford and New York: Martin Robertson and New York University Press.

—— (1981a) *The Ethnic Revival in the Modern World*, Cambridge: Cambridge University Press.

—— (1981b) 'War and ethnicity: the role of warfare in the formation, self-images and cohesion of ethnic communities', *Ethnic and Racial Studies* 4(4): 375–97.

—— (1981c) 'States and homelands: the social and geopolitical implications of national territory', *Millennium* 10, 187–202.

—— (1983a) *Theories of Nationalism*, 2nd edn, London: Duckworth.

—— (1983b) 'Ethnic identity and world order', *Millennium* 12: 149–61.

—— (1984a) 'National identity and myths of ethnic descent', *Research in Social Movements, Conflict and Change* 7: 95–130.

—— (1984b) 'Ethnic persistence and national transformation', *British Journal of Sociology* 35: 452–61.

—— (1985) 'Ethnie and nation in the modern world', *Millennium* 14: 127–42.

—— (1986a) *The Ethnic Origins of Nations*, Oxford: Blackwell.

—— (1986b) 'State-making and nation-building', in J. Hall (ed.) *States in History*, Oxford: Blackwell.

—— (1988) 'The myth of the "modern nation" and the myths of nations', *Ethnic and Racial Studies* 11(1): 1–26.

—— (1989) 'The origins of nations', *Ethnic and Racial Studies* 12(3): 340–67.

—— (1992) 'Chosen peoples: why ethnic groups survive', *Ethnic and Racial Studies* 15(3): 436–56.

Smith, G. E. (1985) 'Ethnic nationalism in the Soviet Union: territory, cleavage and control', *Environment and Planning C: Government and Policy* 3: 49–73.

—— (1989) 'Gorbachev's greatest challenge: perestroika and the national question', *Political Geography Quarterly* 8: 7–20.

Smith, L. (ed.) (1984) *The Making of Britain: The Dark Ages*, London: Macmillan.

Stack, J. (ed.) (1986) *The Primordial Challenge: Ethnicity in the Contemporary World*, New York: Greenwood Press.

Stavrianos, L. S. (1961) *The Balkans since 1453*, New York: Holt.

Steinberg, J. (1976) *Why Switzerland?*, Cambridge: Cambridge University Press.

Stone, J. (ed.) (1979) 'Internal colonialism', *Ethnic and Racial Studies* 2(3): special issue.

Sugar, P. (ed.) (1980) *Ethnic Diversity and Conflict in Eastern Europe*, Santa Barbara: ABC-Clio.

Sugar, P. and Lederer, I. J. (eds) (1969) *Nationalism in Eastern Europe*, Far Eastern and Russian Institute, Publications on Russia and Eastern Europe no. 1, Seattle and London: University of Washington Press.

Tcherikover, V. (1970) *Hellenistic Civilization and the Jews*, New York: Athenaeum.

Thompson, L. (1985) *The Political Mythology of Apartheid*, New Haven and London: Yale University Press.

Thürer, G. (1970) *Free and Swiss*, London: Oswald Wolff.

731

Tilly, C. (ed.) (1975) *The Formation of National States in Western Europe*, Princeton: Princeton University Press.
Tipton, L. (ed.) (1972) *Nationalism in the Middle Ages*, New York: Holt, Rinehart & Winston.
Tudor, H. (1972) *Political Myth*, London: Pall Mall Press/Macmillan.
Ullendorff, E. (1973) *The Ethiopians, An Introduction to Country and People*, 3rd edn, London: Oxford University Press.
Van den Berghe, P. (1979) *The Ethnic Phenomenon*, New York: Elsevier.
Weber, E. (1979) *Peasants into Frenchmen: The Modernisation of Rural France, 1870–1914*, London: Chatto & Windus.
Weber, M. (1968) *Economy and Society*, eds G. Roth and C. Wittich, New York: Bedminster Press.
Welch, C. (1966) *Dream of Unity: Pan-Africanism and Political Unification in West Africa*, Ithaca: Cornell University Press.
Wiseman, D. J. (ed.) (1975) *Peoples of Old Testament Times*, Oxford: Clarendon Press.
Woodhouse, C. (1984) *Modern Greece: A Short History*, London and Boston: Faber & Faber.
Zeitlin, I. (1984) *Ancient Judaism*, Cambridge: Polity Press.

FURTHER READING

Anderson, B. (1983) *Imagined Communities: Reflections on the Origin and Spread of Nationalism*, London: Verso Editions and New Left Books.
Armstrong, J. (1982) *Nations before Nationalism*, Chapel Hill: University of North Carolina Press.
Atiya, A. S. (1968) *A History of Eastern Christianity*, London: Methuen.
Barth, F. (ed.) (1969) *Ethnic Groups and Boundaries*, Boston: Little, Brown.
Baron, S. W. (1960) *Modern Nationalism and Religion*, New York: Meridian Books.
Connor, W. (1972) 'Nation-building or nation-destroying?', *World Politics* 24: 319–55.
Deutsch, K. W. (1966) *Nationalism and Social Communication*, 2nd edn, New York: MIT Press.
Esman, M. (ed.) (1977) *Ethnic Conflict in the Western World*, Ithaca, NY: Cornell University Press.
Gellner, E. (1983) *Nations and Nationalism*, Oxford: Blackwell.
Glazer, N. and Moynihan, D. (eds) (1975) *Ethnicity: Theory and Experience*, Cambridge, Mass.: Harvard University Press.
Horowitz, D. (1985) *Ethnic Groups in Conflict*, Berkeley, Los Angeles and London: University of California Press.
Kautsky, J. H. (ed.) (1962) *Political Change in Underdeveloped Countries*, New York: John Wiley.
Kedourie, E. (1960) *Nationalism*, London: Hutchinson.
—— (ed.) (1971) *Nationalism in Asia and Africa*, London: Weidenfeld & Nicolson.
Kohn, H. (1967 [1944]) *The Idea of Nationalism*, 2nd edn, New York: Collier-Macmillan.
Seton-Watson, H. (1977) *Nations and States*, London: Methuen.
Smith, A. D. (1981) *The Ethnic Revival in the Modern World*, Cambridge: Cambridge University Press.
—— (1986) *The Ethnic Origins of Nations*, Oxford: Blackwell.
—— (1991) *National Identity*, Harmondsworth: Penguin.

Sugar, P. and Lederer, I. J. (eds) (1969) *Nationalism in Eastern Europe*, Far Eastern and Russian Institute, Publications on Russia and Eastern Europe no. 1, Seattle and London: University of Washington Press.

Tilly, C. (ed.) (1975) *The Formation of National States in Western Europe*, Princeton: Princeton University Press.

Tipton, L. (ed.) (1972) *Nationalism in the Middle Ages*, New York: Holt, Rinehart & Winston.

3 SOCIAL LIFE

26

INTRODUCTION TO SOCIAL LIFE

Tim Ingold

QUESTIONS OF SOCIALITY

Wherever people live, as they generally do, in the company of others, and act with those others in mind, their mode of life may be called *social*. Questions about social life have therefore to do with elucidating the dynamic properties of human relationships, properties conveyed by such stock-in-trade anthropological notions as kinship, exchange, power and domination. We may ask how these features of human sociality are generated, maintained and managed; how they are implicated in the life-history of the individual from childhood to old age; how they are represented and communicated in discourse; how they structure – and are in turn structured by – the production and consumption of material goods, and how they underwrite (or subvert) diverse forms of moral or political order. These are the kinds of questions addressed in the chapters making up the third part of this volume. They can, of course, be posed on any number of different levels, from the minutiae of everyday life in familiar contexts of face-to-face interaction to the trials and endeavours of whole populations on a world-historical stage. Likewise the temporal scale on which social processes are viewed may range from within a lifetime to the entire span of human history. It is important to remember, however, that it is the perspective of the observer that 'selects' the scale of the social phenomena observed. When anthropologists claim that they generally study small-scale societies rather than large-scale ones, this is not because the world of humanity is objectively partitioned into social units of diverse size, of which the smaller lend themselves more readily to anthropological investigation, but because from a locally centred perspective, the horizons of the social field appear relatively circumscribed.

The concept of society, moreover, is by no means neutral, but trails in its wake a long history of controversy among Western philosophers, reformers and statesmen about the proper exercise of human rights and responsibilities. In this controversy, the meaning of 'society' has varied according to the

737

contexts of its opposition, alternately, to such notions as individual, community and state. Unlike the 'individual', society connotes a domain of external regulation — identified either with the state itself or, in polities lacking centralized administration, with comparable regulative institutions — serving to curb the spontaneous expression of individual interests on behalf of higher ideals of collective justice and harmony. In other contexts, however, society comes to represent the power of the people — as a real or imagined community bound by shared history, language and sentiment — *against* the impersonal and bureaucratic forces of the state. And in yet other contexts, society stands *opposed* to 'community', connoting the mode of association of rational beings bound by contracts of mutual self-interest, as epitomized by the market, rather than by particularistic ties of the kind epitomized by kinship relations. What is clear from this diversity of usage is that the term 'society', far from forming part of a value-free language of description, in fact belongs to a language of argument. To use it is, inevitably, to make a *claim* about the world.

One further opposition, which has proved especially troublesome for anthropology, is between society and 'culture'. So long as society could be regarded as an association of individuals, and culture as the sum of their knowledge, acquired by traditional transmission and imported into contexts of interaction, this distinction seemed straightforward enough. Indeed it served for much of the twentieth century as the rationale for a division between two largely autonomous branches of anthropological inquiry, 'social' and 'cultural', whose intellectual homes lay respectively in Britain and North America. In recent years, however, this division has come to be seen as increasingly artificial. The reasons are various, but at the most fundamental level, they are bound up with a general rejection of what is known as an essentialist viewpoint — that is, one that would treat societies and cultures as real entities 'out there', presenting themselves to anthropological observation as objects to be described, compared and classified. Contemporary anthropology veers more to a process-oriented view, according to which cultural form does not come ready-made, like a suit of clothing to cover the nakedness of the 'biological' individual, but is perpetually under construction within the contexts of people's practical engagements with one another. All culture, then, is social, in that its constituent meanings are drawn from the relational contexts of such mutual involvement; conversely all social life is cultural, since people's relationships with one another are informed by meaning. In short, culture and social life appear to be caught in an ongoing dialectic in which each, in a sense, 'constitutes' the other, through the mediation of human agency.

As the emphasis has shifted from the study of societies as things to the study of social life as process, anthropologists have begun to pose their questions in a rather different way. Instead of asking 'Why do different societies take the forms they do?', they are presently more inclined to ask 'What is it about a form of life that makes it social?'. They have moved, in other words, from questions about society to questions about sociality. What, they ask, is necessary for there to be social life at all? Recent discussions have thrown up three kinds of answers. The first seeks the roots of sociality in some innate biological endowment, an evolved predisposition to associate that will naturally be expressed in varying manner and degree, depending upon the prevailing conditions of the environment. For proponents of this view, sociality is by no means confined to human beings, or even to the order of primates, but extends right across the animal kingdom. The second answer is to identify sociality with moral accountability; that is with the explicit recognition of rules and standards by which people judge their own and others' actions. Insofar as the articulation of these rules and standards depends upon a capacity for language, sociality in this sense is generally attributed uniquely to human beings. The third kind of answer locates the essence of sociality neither in individually held dispositions nor in collective rules, but in the *relationships* that bind people together as fellow participants in a life-process. To grasp the significance of this answer, however, it is necessary to examine the notion of 'relationship' a little more closely. In particular, we need to reconsider the dichotomy, which keeps cropping up especially in discussions of kinship and gender, between *social* and *biological* domains of relationship. This emerges as a central theme of Articles 27, 28 and 29.

SOCIAL AND BIOLOGICAL RELATIONSHIPS

Dunbar, in Article 27, writes as a student of animal behaviour with an intimate knowledge of the elaborate social intrigues typical of everyday life in populations of non-human primates. He leaves us in no doubt that monkeys and apes, like human beings, are caught up in complex networks of relationship with others of their kind. Any one individual may indeed be simultaneously involved in several different networks. Yet such networks, for all their complexity, and for all the intensity of their constituent relationships, do not imply the existence of large or stable groupings. The company an animal keeps may be highly selective, and may vary from one moment to the next according to a host of situationally specific factors. Thus to be bound by relationships is not at all the same thing as to live in a group. In many animal species, including the so-called 'social' insects, birds and mammals, individuals cluster into aggregates of a size and permanence without parallel in the primate order, prior to a relatively late phase in the evolution of human society, yet within these aggregates there may be no relationships to speak of at all. Thus, explanations of why animals live in groups, for example in terms of the facilitation of co-operative foraging, defence of food resources or protection against predators, do not in themselves account for the presence and quality of relationships among their members. How then, are they to be explained? What is the source from which relationships spring?

To these questions, as Dunbar remarks, biological and social anthropologists are inclined to come up with rather different answers. One reason for this lies in a certain disparity between their respective views of what a relationship *is*, and of how it is to be recognized. Social anthropologists discover relationships in the commitments and promises that people make towards one another, in their agreements and obligations, which they do not always live up to in actual practice. For biological anthropologists, on the other hand, the existence of a relationship is a matter of empirical observation, whenever it is found that the same individuals interact on numerous successive occasions, evidently with a knowledge, based on past experience, of each other's identity and character. Consequently, whereas the generative source of relationships lies, from a social anthropological point of view, in the dynamics of total social systems, from the viewpoint of biological anthropology it lies in the behavioural predispositions of individuals. Though these viewpoints need not be mutually exclusive, the former looks from the 'top down', the latter from the 'bottom up'. And this difference in perspective may be linked directly to the fact that each is situated within a different framework of interpretation. In the first, the challenge is to 'make sense' of people's behaviour by placing it in its social context of shared cultural understandings. The second, by contrast, seeks an underlying rationale for social behaviour in terms of its consequences for the survival and reproduction of the individuals concerned, regardless of what construction — if any — they may place on it.

This difference of approach is well illustrated by what Barnard, in Article 28, and Dunbar, in Article 27, have to say about the nature and significance of relations of kinship. Barnard's position is in close accord with that of mainstream social anthropology. Kinship, he argues, is not a fact of nature but is rather constituted within a specifically human discourse on social relationships. This discourse typically includes ideas about the sharing of bodily substance, as conceived within the indigenous theory of procreation. In Western societies, the substance of kinship has commonly been identified with blood (as in the notion of consanguinity), though nowadays this is giving way to a pseudo-scientific conception of genetic material. When people in these societies say that they are of one blood, or that they have inherited the same genes, their statements should be understood not literally, as having reference to a given, 'biological' reality, but rather metaphorically, as ways of talking about an experienced, social reality. In other words, kinship is 'biological' only insofar as 'biology' enters into the vernacular discourse on social relations. And it is in this light, too, that a social anthropologist would interpret the kinds of comments that people make, probably in all societies, about the appearance of children. A child may be said to resemble this parent or that, or to possess features that it has 'received' from certain more distant relatives. The purpose of such commentary, however, is not to discover evidence of actual genetic connection but to *place* the child, and confer upon it a specific identity, within a nexus of social relationships.

Yet Dunbar, resting his argument on the premisses of evolutionary biology, reaches precisely the opposite conclusion! His objective is to show how

740

particular patterns and modes of relationship may have evolved through a process of variation under natural selection. To achieve this it is necessary to suppose, first, that manifest social behaviour is the output of a programme that every individual brings into its encounters with conspecifics, and second, that the constituent elements of this programme – commonly identified with genes – are replicable across generations. The mechanism of genetic replication is assumed to be sexual reproduction, though as Dunbar recognizes, the relation between 'genes', as units of heredity conceived in the abstract, and the actual genetic material in the chromosomes, is far from clear. According to the logic of natural selection, any behaviour that has the effect of increasing the representation, in future generations, of those genes of which it is the outward expression, will tend to become established. To demonstrate that a behaviour has this effect, by conferring a reproductive advantage on those who engage in it, is sufficient to account for its evolution. But granted that an animal may derive some benefit from its association with conspecifics, why should it choose to establish relationships only with *some* particular individuals, while others are avoided?

Sociobiological theory explains this selectivity, in part, on the grounds that, depending on their genealogical proximity, individuals will have a greater or lesser proportion of their genes in common. Hence the consequences of associating with a close relative, in terms of genetic replication, will differ from those of associating with a distant relative or a non-relative. However, if an individual is to associate preferentially with relatives, then it must have some mechanism for their identification. The perception of physical resemblances, according to Dunbar, furnishes just such a mechanism, and in the comments that people habitually make about children's likenesses to their elders ('Doesn't he have grandma's nose!'), we see it in operation. If this argument is correct, then comments of this kind, quite contrary to the social anthropological interpretation offered by Barnard, *do* have a forensic purpose: they are meant to draw attention to actual genetic connections. Such connections, virtually by definition, exist independently of, and prior to, any relationships at all. Thus whatever the people themselves may claim, they are predisposed to attend to physical resemblances not for what they reveal about the relationships within which children come into being as members of society, but for guidance on where to place their investments in succeeding generations. In other words, the configuration of social relations follows from – rather than provides a context for – the recognition of physical affinity.

What, then, makes a relationship a *kinship* relationship? Is it merely a matter of the choice of idiom in which people talk about it, or does kinship have an independent foundation in genetic relatedness? For the biological anthropologist, actual genetic connections are critical, since the evolutionary rationale for kin-based altruism rests on the presumption that individuals identified as potential beneficiaries do in fact share a substantial proportion of the altruist's genes. To the objection, commonly levelled by social anthropologists, that cultural designations of kinship are arbitrarily superimposed upon genetic realities, the biologists' response is that their theory requires no more than a statistical correlation. So long as there is sufficient overlap between culturally perceived kinship and true genetic kinship, the theory should work. Social anthropologists, for their part, while not denying the facts of genetic connection, exclude them from their field of inquiry. Their concern, they say, is with the ways in which certain relationships come to be 'culturally constructed' as relations of kinship by virtue of their grounding in an indigenous biology of shared substance. If genetics figures at all in their discussions, it is as one particular instance of such a biology, namely that of the Western biomedical establishment. To what extent this biology is scientifically more 'correct' than others is not for them to judge.

Ask a social anthropologist to describe a relation of kinship, for some particular society, and the answer — as Barnard shows in Article 28 — is likely to come in two parts. Consider, for example, the relationship between a father and his son. First, there is a set of expectations surrounding the proper performance of fatherhood, as there is attached to being a good son; in this sense 'father' and 'son' are roles to be enacted, and the relationship between them is inscribed within the framework of normative orientations of the society in question. This relationship is said (by the anthropological analyst) to be one of 'social' kinship. Second, members of the society claim that father and son are linked by a bond of substance, by virtue of the father's material contribution to the formation of the body of his child. This sharing of substance is said (again by the analyst) to be constitutive of a relation of 'biological' kinship. Armed with this distinction between the social and biological components of paternity, social anthropologists have gone on to draw attention to cases where one component can occur without the other: where a man extends fatherhood towards children who are not thought to share in his bodily substance; or denies it to children who are. None of this, however, has anything to do with actual genetic connection. Whether the individual who is socially identified as the donor of paternal substance is or is not the same as the true genetic father is irrelevant for social anthropological analysis. For the aim of such analysis is to understand the concordance between social and biological kinship as *culturally perceived.*

There is a remarkable parallel between the history of the biological/social distinction in the study of kinship relations, and that of the sex/gender distinction in the study of relations between men and women. In both cases, the distinction was drawn initially in order to emphasize the independence of socially defined role relationships from underlying biogenetic constraint. Just as the roles of 'father' and 'son' were held to have nothing to do with the genetic connection — if any — between their incumbents, so the expectations defining what it is to be a 'man' or a 'woman' were shown to vary widely from one society to another, lending support to the view that they are independent of innate predisposition. For any society, the distinction of gender — between men and women — was said to belong to a normative order, superimposed upon a given biological substrate of male/female sex differences. While sex as biological fact was thus eliminated from the field of gender relations, it reappeared as a focus of social anthropological attention in quite another guise, as part of a discourse for talking about them. The need therefore arose to introduce a further analytic distinction, between sex as a fact of nature – a prerequisite for physiological reproduction – and 'Sex' as constituted within the cultural discourse on gender relations. The result, as Moore shows in Article 29, is the separation of sex, 'Sex' and gender; a trichotomy that has its precise counterpart in the field of kinship studies in the separation of biology as actual genetic connection, 'biology' as indigenous cultural discourse, and the structure of role relations on which this discourse comments.

This solution, though neat, is not entirely satisfactory. The problem lies in the very notion that the orders of gender and kinship are socially or culturally constructed upon the foundation of biological reality. Critics have pointed out that the recognition of sex differences as pre-existing in nature, independently of the constructions placed on them, belongs to a specifically Western ontology. In other words the distinction between sex and gender, as constituted respectively within the domains of nature and society, is itself the product of a particular set of discursive practices. By incorporating the distinction into its own theoretical apparatus, social anthropology has taken for granted what it should be seeking to explain. By and large, people in non-Western societies do not make this kind of distinction. Far from regarding sexual identities as ready-made, as though every new-born child came into the world completely and unalterably male or female, they hold that these identities are fashioned within life-cycle processes through the exchange and ingestion of male and female substances. Likewise, they would not accept the distinction, built into the framework of the anthropological analysis of kinship, between its biological and social components. Contrary to Western genetics, they would argue that the contributions of paternal and maternal substance that go to make up the body of a child are themselves delivered within the context of an ongoing set of nurturing relationships. In short, as they proceed through life, human beings are thought to incorporate into their very biological constitution the matrix of relationships that, at the same time, furnishes their identities as social persons.

It is tempting, as many anthropologists have done, to accommodate these non-Western views by regarding them as so many cultural constructions of reality, alternative to the Western one. This, however, will not do, for the simple reason that the Western ontology – which yields the distinctions both between sex and gender and between biological and social kinship – also underwrites the logic of cultural construction itself. Applying this logic, what are constituted within social processes are 'meanings' and 'understandings', that are added on to bodies that have been biogenetically pre-programmed in advance of their entry into the social arena. Through the reduction of 'biology' to genetics, human relationships are withdrawn from the real world in which people dwell, as a preliminary to their reinscription on the level of its cultural representation. Thus individuals are perceived to exist in hermetic isolation, while relationships exist in the discourse. In this division between the discursive worlds of culture and naturally given, biogenetic reality, no conceptual space remains for the domain in which human beings live their lives through an active engagement with those around them. The relationships constitutive of this domain are indeed social, but they are no less 'real' or 'biological' for that. For in truth, no more than other animals do human beings come biologically ready-made, to be 'topped up' by culture. They rather emerge with their peculiar capacities, dispositions and intentions in the course of a process which, in the literature of biology and psychology, goes by the name of *development*. In this process, the contributions of other persons in the social environment are critical. And as Poole shows in Article 30, the rather belated recognition that human development is invariably embedded in contexts of social relations requires us to take a fresh look at the time-worn concepts of socialization and enculturation.

BECOMING A PERSON

Traditionally, the project of social anthropology has been distinguished from that of psychology in terms of a distinction between the *individual* and the *person*. In this division of intellectual labour, the nature of individual self-awareness, posited as a human universal, was to be studied by psychologists, while anthropologists focused on the person as a social being, formed within the normative framework of society and its relationships. Having thereby excluded the self as an aspect of human nature from their field of inquiry, anthropologists were able to turn their attention instead to issues of indigenous psychology. In a move strikingly similar to the developments reviewed above in the study of kinship and gender, they could claim that their concern was with the diverse ways in which notions of the self can be brought to bear in the cultural construction of personhood, rather than with the 'actual' psychological foundations of the self as a centre of individual experience. This move, however, leads to precisely the same impasse, in that the opposition between the individual (the psychological self) and the person (the social being), on which the logic of cultural construction depends, is itself constituted within a specifically Western discourse on nature and society. And again, people in non-Western societies seem to be telling us something quite different: namely that as agentive centres of awareness and experience, selves *become*, and that they do so within a matrix of evolving relationships with others. Personhood, in other words, is seen not as the imprint of society upon the pre-social self, but as the emergent form of the self as it develops within a context of social relations.

In Article 30, Poole advocates an approach to understanding the development of personal identity that would take this view as its starting point. To characterize it as 'non-Western' is perhaps misleading, since several prominent social theorists, writing in the Western tradition of scholarship, have gone out of their way to stress the relational aspects of selfhood. Nevertheless, they have written against the grain of the doctrine of individualism which, for many, is the hallmark of the political philosophy with which 'the West' is popularly identified. Conscious of the dangers of importing assumptions based in this doctrine into their studies of non-Western societies, anthropologists have been inclined to portray these societies as holistic or socio-centric in orientation, and to deny the applicability of such notions as 'the individual' and 'individuality' for fear that they may be tainted by their association with individualism. This fear, as Poole points out, is misplaced. It is indeed essential to distinguish between an analytic notion of *individuality* and the various and shifting ideologies of *individualism* to be found in the history of Western discourse. For the former has to do with the ways in which people, in all societies, build unique identities for themselves and for one another out of their own particular experiences and life histories, and the histories of their mutual relationships. The individual of real life, equipped with such an identity, bears only a distant and problematic relation to the abstract, atomic individual as posited within the doctrine of individualism.

The recognition that individual selves *are* social in their very constitution not only dissolves the conventional dichotomy between social anthropology and psychology, but also has radical implications for our understanding of the process of socialization. It has been usual, in the past, to regard this process as one in which the child, initially without a social identity or presence of any kind, is gradually provided with the lineaments of personhood, in the shape of schemata for categorizing and positioning others in the social environment, and guidelines for appropriate action towards them. The acquisition of these schemata and guidelines has been taken to be a precondition for meaningful engagement with other persons, and hence for full participation in social life. This implies, however, that the process of learning that prepares the child for personhood can form no part of that life, and that to study this process is to investigate not the dynamics of social life itself but rather the psychodynamics of acquisition, by the immature individual, of the schemata that enable him or her to enter into it. Herein lies the principal explanation for the unfortunate separation between the psychological study of child development and the anthropological study of culture and social life. The failure, until recently, of developmental psychology to take account of the social context of learning has been matched, by and large, by an equal failure on the part of social anthropology to pay any attention to children and how they learn. Indeed it would be fair to say that in the majority of anthropological accounts, children are conspicuous by their absence.

Poole offers an approach to the rectification of this deficiency, though given the dearth of anthropological studies of child development, it is necessarily somewhat programmatic. Children, he argues, are not to be regarded as passive recipients of social knowledge which 'descends' upon them from an authoritative source in society. On the contrary, they participate actively and creatively in the learning process. They do so by playing their own part in shaping the contexts in which learning occurs and knowledge is generated. Such interaction begins in earliest infancy, growing in complexity and sensitivity as the child's communicative competence increases, above all with the mastery of language. Learning, then, is not preliminary to involvement in the social world, for it is above all through such involvement − in the 'hands-on' experience of engaging with others in practical situations of everyday life − that the child learns. Far from providing a prelude, in the career of each individual, for his or her entry upon the social stage, these situations of interactive learning are the very sites from which social life unfolds. In clear contrast to the scenario of classical socialization theory, according to which children start from a position outside or on the margins of society, whence they must progressively work their way in, the view advanced here holds that children are launched at birth into the very centre of a social world. They learn, not in order to gain entry to this world, but to be able to make their way in it.

Nor does learning end with childhood. To be sure, childhood experience may have a formative quality, underwriting all that occurs in later life. But adult experience too, especially the experience of tutoring children, can be transformative. Indeed as Poole stresses, socialization is a process that carries on over an individual's entire lifetime. There is no point in the life-cycle at which socialization could be said to be 'complete', marking off the period of preparation from the attainment of full personhood. In a sense, then, socialization and social life are two sides of the same coin: on the one side, the enfolding of social relations in the experience and sensibility of the self; on the other, the unfolding of the self in social action.

Perhaps no aspect of socialization is more crucial than the acquisition of language, and in Article 31 DeBernardi presents a comprehensive review of the large literature concerning the social dimensions of language acquisition and use. Here a rather similar shift in perspective is evident to that described above, from a view of language as an abstract structure or code that is 'taken on', more or less unconsciously, by each new generation, to a view that gives a much greater weight to the processual and performative aspects of language use. In this latter view, language is regarded not as a pre-formed totality but rather as perpetually under construction within the dialogic contexts of everyday interaction, including interactions involving infants and young children. Though the effectiveness of linguistic communication depends on the existence of community-wide verbal conventions, such conventions do not come ready made but have continually to be worked at. Current conventions are the sedimented outcomes of the struggles of past generations to make themselves understood: thus words, as DeBernardi observes, condense a community's recollections of its past. This kind of approach requires that much greater attention be paid to the diversity of individual voices. Variations in usage which, from a structuralist perspective, would be dismissed as merely idiosyncratic or as defects of performance, reappear as instances of language in the making. It is the tension between individual circumstance and common code, DeBernardi argues, that provides language with its historical dynamic, keeping it forever 'in play'. For language changes, even as we speak.

POLITICAL ECONOMY

Besides learning to speak, people in all societies must also learn to work, and this generally entails the acquisition of a specific set of practical skills, along with an understanding of the appropriate contexts for their deployment. Learning to work is thus one aspect of socialization, which Ortiz describes in Article 32. Her principal thesis is summed up in the statement that work is as much a social as it is a technological process. This point needs to be argued only because people in Western industrial societies – including many economists and social theorists – are inclined to believe that work is somehow excluded from the domain of social life. The reasons for this, as Ortiz shows, lie partly in the experience of industrialization itself, and partly in the way in which the meaning of work has been framed within the modern science of economics, whose concern is exclusively with the dynamics of commodity production. We may note the following points: first, that under conditions of industrial capitalism, workers labour not for themselves or their families but for employers who command both their capacities to labour and the instruments and raw materials needed for these capacities to be realized; second, that with the automation of production, manual skills tend to be replaced (albeit never completely) by the operation of machines; third, that in the mass production of commodities, the objects produced cease to be identified in any way with their producers; and finally, that with the separation of the 'workplace' from the 'home', the latter comes to be seen as a place of consumption rather than production. This, in turn, leads to the perception of 'housework' as an anomalous category.

Clearly in non-industrial societies, where these conditions do not obtain, the significance of work will be very different. For one thing, people retain control over their own capacity to work and over other productive means, and their activities are carried on in the context of their relationships with kin and community. Indeed their work may have the strengthening or regeneration of these relationships as its principal objective. For another thing, work calls for the exercise of specific skills which identify their possessors as belonging to the communities in which they were acquired. But it is not only by their skills that persons in non-industrial societies are identified; they are also known for what they produce. Through making things, people define themselves. Moreover there is no obvious criterion for distinguishing work from non-work. Many non-industrial societies lack any general term whose meaning would overlap with that of 'work' in the Western industrial context (and even in that context, the term has manifold, often contradictory meanings). Instead, a host of more specific terms are used to denote the various life-sustaining tasks that people are called upon to perform. Thus work, in these societies, is embedded in social life to the extent of being virtually indistinguishable from it. Our modern tendency to see work as opposed to life, or to regard it as technological *rather than* social, is the product of a particular history in the Western world.

This history has also given rise to the notion of the 'economy' as a domain of activity separate from that of 'society', and operating exclusively on the basis of market or market-like principles. The sub-discipline of economic anthropology has emerged largely out of the attempt to show that where these principles do *not* operate, the activities not only of production and consumption but also of exchange, far from being external to society, are embedded in a social relational matrix. However as Gregory shows in Article 33, neither of the two major paradigms of Western economic thought – the 'commodity' paradigm of nineteenth century political economy and the 'goods' paradigm of twentieth century marginalism – was capable of addressing the questions raised by anthropological work in societies where wealth is evaluated and transacted according to principles other than those of the market. Classical political economy distinguished between values in use and in exchange: the former consist in the capacities of objects to fulfil human needs, the latter in the amounts of labour that went into their production. But the distinction was made simply in order to clear the way for an exclusive concern with exchange value, as it is revealed in contexts wherein objects are exchanged as marketable commodities. The neoclassical economists, for their part, did away with both these notions of value, replacing them with a single notion of *utility*, based not in the objective properties of the wealth items themselves but in the subjective preferences of individuals. This approach, apparently applicable to virtually any kind of exchange, offered the prospects of building a deductive theory of great generality and predictive power. Given a knowledge of individual preferences, and of the means available for fulfilling them, one could predict rational courses of action and their aggregate effects.

This theory, however, is quite indifferent to the particulars of social and historical circumstance, and seemed to offer little to anthropologists more interested in developing generalizations by induction, from a comparative analysis of the ways in which wealth is evaluated and distributed in different societies and periods. For them the commodity paradigm has always been more attractive, and the gradual accumulation of ethnographic data from fieldwork-based studies put them in the position of being able to address the questions that it had left unanswered, particularly about the nature of *non-*commodity exchange – ironically at a time when mainstream economists were abandoning the commodity paradigm in favour of the abstract formalism of the theory of goods. What made this possible, Gregory argues, was the development of a positive theory of non-commoditized wealth as consisting in gifts. Gifts have two crucial properties by which they may be distinguished from commodities: first, they are evaluated in terms of a qualitative rather than a quantitative standard (in other words, the principle of their ranking is ordinal rather than cardinal); second, their exchange does not entail any severance of the bond of identification with the persons exchanging them. Thus whereas the exchange of commodities establishes a quantitative relation between the things exchanged, that of gifts establishes a qualitative relation between the exchange partners. Indeed, every exchange of this latter kind is a moment in the constitution of a social relationship. Equipped with a theory of the gift, anthropologists were able to show how the character and significance of transactions, and the evaluation of the materials transacted therein, depend upon the kinds of relationships in which they are embedded.

A further feature of the classical approach to political economy that commended it to anthropological attention lay in its recognition of the ways in which exchange is underwritten by relations of power. The imbalances in exchange set up by these relations enable dominant élites to cream off the surpluses needed to finance their activities and legitimating institutions. In Article 34, Earle reviews the different sources of political power – social, military, ideological and economic – and considers their respective strengths and weaknesses. Social power, based on the ability to draw support from close kin, is necessarily limited in scope, since the strength of support naturally wanes with increasing genealogical distance. Military power, based on threat and intimidation, or on the direct use of physical force, is perhaps more effective but also more difficult to control, since a military cadre can all too easily turn against a leader who has grown too dependent on it. Ideological power is established through the promulgation of belief in the natural right to rule of an élite, backed by religious sanction. But this, too, has its limitations, for power of this kind can be used as much to resist domination as to support it. The final source of power, namely economic, lies in controlling access to the means of production and distribution of necessary goods, whether staple foodstuffs or prestige-conferring valuables.

In different societies, or among competing factions within the same society, élites have based their dominance on different sources of power. However these sources, Earle argues, are neither independent of one another nor equivalent in the control they afford. Of all the four sources, the economic is most fundamental, since it alone can provide a stable basis for the construction and expansion of complex, politically centralized societies. This is not only because of the ease with which economic processes can be controlled (especially with the intensification of the regime of subsistence production), but also because the products of the economy can be reinvested in order to secure control over other sources of power. Social power can be extended by financing strategic marriages, military power by supporting and arming the cadre, and ideological power by financing religious institutions and ceremonies which uphold the legitimacy of élite authority. It is by examining the historical interconnections between the sources of power, Earle contends, that we can best understand the evolution of complexity in human society, from the small, intimate bands of hunter-gatherers, through tribal polities and chiefdoms, to large and highly stratified urban states.

DISPUTE, NEGOTIATION AND SOCIAL ORDER

Political anthropology has its roots in the problem of order. Western philosophers have looked to the institutions of the state as providing a regulative framework within which individuals could peaceably pursue their own legitimate interests. It was assumed that in the absence of such a framework, social life would dissolve into chaos, a war of all against all. Such, indeed, was supposed by many to have been the lot of humankind in its primordial condition of savagery. Anthropological studies among peoples without a state organization, or anything equivalent to it, revealed however that they did not lead disordered lives. Nor did they experience levels of conflict significantly greater than those encountered in state-organized societies. The problem was thus to explain how order in these societies is established and maintained. If behaviour is guided by rules or norms, in what authority are they vested and how are they enforced? And how are disputes handled when they do arise? In Western societies, the answers to these questions come under a single rubric, that of 'law'. The term is used to refer both to a set of codified rules and regulations − backed by the authority of the judiciary − for people to live by, to an institutional apparatus through which government can exercise its role in steering human affairs, and to a set of procedures for the adjudication of disputes. Is there, then, anything equivalent to 'law' in non-Western, and especially in stateless, societies? In Article 35, Roberts reviews the history of attempts by both anthropologists and legal specialists to address this question.

He divides this history into five phases. The first is characterized by the attempts of late nineteenth century scholars to discover the primitive antecedents of what they perceived as an evolved state of modernity. In the second phase, evolutionary questions were replaced by functional ones, as the first generation of anthropologists to have conducted intensive fieldwork asked how the institutions of the societies they studied worked to maintain order and stability. The third phase was marked by a shift of focus from the maintenance of order to processes of dispute, and led to a number of advances in the understanding, for example, of how settlements may be reached without involving third-party adjudication, of the role of litigation in struggles for political power, of the relations between rules and outcomes, and of the differences between legal disputation and physical fighting as mechanisms of conflict resolution. In the fourth phase, anthropologists and historians embarked on a highly critical reappraisal of earlier ethnographic depictions of the so-called 'customary law' of native peoples. This law, it was argued, bore only a tenuous relation to precolonial arrangements, and was largely invented by the colonial authorities, with some assistance from their anthropological advisers, as an instrument of domination by indirect rule. In the fifth and final phase, this radical critique has given way to a more measured view which recognizes the co-existence of a plurality of loosely bounded normative orders, situated at a number of 'legal levels' from metropolitan centres to local communities. The problem, in this 'legal pluralist' approach, is to understand the linkages between what goes on at these different levels. Yet the applicability of the concept of 'law' to normative orders which lack the attributes of state law, that is where the order is not tied to a command structure, remains problematic. In the last analysis, Roberts suggests, what is 'legal' about the anthropology of law may have less to do with its subject matter than with the fact that the majority of its practitioners are now lawyers rather than anthropologists!

While people may sort out their individual differences by verbal contestation or by actually fighting, the same applies at the collective level as well. Collective violence – whatever its causes, which are clearly multiple – typically takes the form of warfare; and the threat or reality of war brings its own countermeasures by way of attempts to promote common security through negotiated settlement. In Article 36, Rubinstein considers the relevance of anthropological understanding in tackling the many large-scale conflicts, affecting the lives of millions of people, that are endemic in the contemporary world. This entails a significant change of perspective, in that diplomats, analysts and politicians who are professionally charged with negotiation at this level are not so much the subjects as the consumers of social scientific research. Rubinstein shows that the approach adopted by these professionals, above all in the Western defence establishment, rests on a set of highly artificial assumptions about how people behave. Ironically known as 'political realism', this approach envisages a world in which the actors are nation states, and in which actions follow the predictions of formal econometric or game-theoretic models, calculated on the basis of a knowledge of objective social scientific facts to maximize economic or military pay-offs. Thus no account is taken of local or indigenous interests below the level of the state, or of the influences of social and cultural experience on people's perceptions and actions, or of sources of power other than the military and economic (for example what Rubinstein calls 'normative power' – roughly equivalent to Earle's concept of 'ideological power' – which can furnish a significant means of resistance against economic and military might). Where political realism *does* take cultural considerations into account, these are typically based in crude stereotypes of how other people behave, insensitive to both history and context. In their application, such stereotypes generate chronic misunderstanding. Good negotiating practice, Rubinstein argues, should be informed by a proper appreciation of the cognitive and emotional force of symbolic forms. This is no minor plea: the future security of entire populations depends on it.

Béteille's discussion, in Article 37, of the premises of inequality in human societies takes us back to the problem of order. A central question in the anthropology of law, as we have seen, is whether any framework of norms and standards can be maintained without a system of imposed regulation: that is, whether there can be 'order' without 'command'. Another way of posing the same question is to ask whether there can be 'society' without 'inequality'. Is an egalitarian society possible, even in theory? The answer, of course, depends on what is meant by society, and by equality. On the face of it the trajectory of social evolution, as laid out by Earle in Article 34, from hunter-gatherer bands through agrarian civilizations to modern nation states, seems to involve a steady increase in inequality until a relatively recent point was reached, marked by the transition to modernity (politically speaking, from aristocracy to democracy), whereupon the trend went into reverse, and orders that were rigidly hierarchical in both ideal and fact gave way to societies premissed upon a formal commitment to equality. Yet it would be absurd to suggest that the equality of the hunter-gatherer band remotely resembles that of the modern industrial state.

Indeed these inequalities rest on entirely different principles: the first on the lack of enduring commitments and dependencies among persons who are nevertheless well-known to one another; the second on an individualistic conception of the person as the singular yet anonymous embodiment of a universal humanity. Those who hold that egalitarian society is an impossibility are inclined to dismiss the evidence from hunter-gatherer societies on the grounds that in the absence of any framework of normative obligation, or of anything that might be recognized as 'social structure', they can scarcely be recognized as societies at all. The very existence of society, they argue, depends on the presence of *rules*, and since it is in the nature of rules that they are sometimes violated, giving rise to disputes that require adjudication, situations are bound to arise which call for the exercise of power by some individuals over others. By this argument, inequality is a necessary condition for ordered social life. The argument, however, can also be turned on its head, such that systems of rules, far from calling for the exercise of power, function as part of an apparatus of domination through which power achieves its effects. The more, then, that power is concentrated in the hands of a dominant élite, the more elaborate the framework of rules and regulations imposed upon the subject population.

When it comes to modern nation states, it is invariably the case that ideological commitments to equality are combined with stark practical inequalities. Citizens may, according to the democratic ideal, be equal *before* the law, but they are very far from equal *after* it. However as Béteille shows, the manner of their inequality will depend upon whether the public commitment is to an ideal of *competitive* equality (judged by the balance of opportunity) or *distributive* equality (judged by the balance of income or result). In the first case, everyone is supposed to have the same chances to compete in the 'market place' of civil society, but due to inherent variations of individual ability, some are said to do better for themselves than others. The successful rise to the top, the unsuccessful sink to the bottom, whilst the majority settle somewhere in between, leading in aggregate to the observed pattern of social stratification. In the second case, the state intervenes to ensure equality of results through an enforced redistribution from the 'haves' to the 'have-nots'. Yet it can do so only because of a concentration of power at the centre. Thus the very promotion of distributive equality sets up further inequalities, experienced as constraints on civil liberties.

Two further aspects of Béteille's argument warrant special emphasis. The first is that while people in society may differ in all kinds of ways — such as in gender, physical appearance, occupation and lifestyle — not all differences count as inequalities. What converts difference into inequality is a *scale of evaluation*, and such scales may vary within as well as between societies. In stressing the possible existence of multiple and partially contradictory scales within the same society, Béteille echoes a point also made by Moore (Article 29) with regard to the evaluation of gender differences, and by Roberts (Article 35) with regard to different fields of law. Second, whether or not a society appears egalitarian will depend to a certain extent on the scale at which it is defined. Large, highly stratified societies may encompass communities that are, internally, markedly egalitarian; conversely small-scale, egalitarian societies may be encompassed within wider social systems structured by relations of pronounced inequality.

This point applies with equal force at a global level. To the extent that Western societies have achieved a basic level of affluence for all, they have done so at the cost of the other societies around the world that they have subjugated and exploited. How they did so is the subject of Worsley's account, in Article 38, of the history of colonial expansion, an expansion that laid the foundations for the contemporary world order. This account effectively demolishes any naïve, evolutionist model of development that would portray the history of non-European peoples as one which began with first European contact, and which has gradually raised them from an original, primitive or traditional condition to a position where they can take their fair share of the benefits of modernity. For one thing, the societies first encountered by Europeans varied from small stateless polities to great empires of a scale, wealth and sophistication far exceeding anything that had been achieved in Europe itself. In many parts of the world, European supremacy was by no means a foregone conclusion, and was achieved only after long and bloody conflicts which often set native peoples at war with one another. For another thing, far from encouraging the development of local industries in the territories they controlled, the colonial powers blocked such development, in order to guarantee for Western industry its supply of raw materials and markets for its goods. Today, in a post-colonial world, key resources remain concentrated in the 'developed' nations of Europe, North America and of course the Far East, while war and starvation stalk the continent of Africa, and indigenous people are being wiped out in the name of progress in parts of South America and

South-east Asia. At the same time, the West is becoming painfully aware of the disastrous environmental consequences of its own expansion. Notwithstanding rumours of a new world order, humankind has still a long way to go before it reaches the far side of history, if indeed it ever will.

FURTHER READING

Barnard, A. and Good, A. (1984) *Research Practices in the Study of Kinship*, London: Academic Press.

Béteille, A. (1987) *The Idea of Natural Inequality and Other Essays*, Delhi: Oxford University Press.

Carrithers, M., Collins, S. and Lukes, S. (eds) (1985) *The Category of the Person: Anthropology, Philosophy, History*, Cambridge: Cambridge University Press.

Collier, J. and Yanagisako, S. (eds) (1987) *Gender and Kinship: Essays towards a Unified Analysis*, Stanford: Stanford University Press.

Comaroff, J. L. and Roberts, S. A. (1981) *Rules and Processes: the Cultural Logic of Dispute in an African Context*, Chicago: University of Chicago Press.

Dumont, L. (1986) *Essays on Individualism: Modern Ideology in Anthropological Perspective*, Chicago: University of Chicago Press.

Earle, T. (ed.) (1991) *Chiefdoms: Power, Economy, and Ideology*, Cambridge: Cambridge University Press.

Fortes, M. (1983) *Rules and the Emergence of Society* (RAI Occasional Paper, No. 39), London: Royal Anthropological Institute.

Foster, M. L. and Rubinstein, R. (eds) (1986) *Peace and War: Cross-Cultural Perspectives*, New Brunswick: Transaction Books.

Gregory, C. A. (1982) *Gifts and Commodities*, London: Academic Press.

Hinde, R. A. (1987) *Individuals, Relationships and Culture*, Cambridge: Cambridge University Press.

Humphrey, C. and Hugh-Jones, S. (eds) (1992) *Barter, Exchange and Value: an Anthropological Approach*, Cambridge: Cambridge University Press.

Ingold, T. (1986) *Evolution and Social Life*, Cambridge: Cambridge University Press.

Johnson, A. and Earle, T. (1987) *The Evolution of Human Societies: from Foraging Group to Agrarian State*, Stanford: Stanford University Press.

Joyce, P. (ed.) (1987) *The Historical Meanings of Work*, Cambridge: Cambridge University Press.

Mann, M. (1986) *The Sources of Social Power*, vol. 1, Cambridge: Cambridge University Press.

Mauss, M. (1990) *The Gift: the Form and Reason for Exchange in Archaic Societies* (trans. W. D. Halls), London: Routledge.

Moore, H. L. (1988) *Feminism and Anthropology*, Cambridge: Polity Press.

Moore, S. F. (1978) *Law as Process*, London: Routledge & Kegan Paul.

Morris, B. (1991) *Western Conceptions of the Individual*, Oxford: Berg.

Riches, D. (ed.) (1986) *The Anthropology of Violence*, Oxford: Blackwell.

Roberts, S. (1979) *Order and Dispute*, Harmondsworth: Penguin.

Rubinstein, R. A. and Foster, M. L. (eds) (1988) *The Social Dynamics of Peace and Conflict: Culture in International Security*, Boulder: Westview Press.

Sahlins, M. D. (1972) *Stone Age Economics*, London: Tavistock.

Schieffelin, B. B. and Ochs, E. (eds) (1986) *Language Socialization across Cultures*, Cambridge: Cambridge University Press.

Schneider, D. M. (1984) *A Critique of the Study of Kinship*, Ann Arbor: University of Michigan Press.

Strathern, A. M. (1988) *The Gender of the Gift*, Berkeley: University of California Press.

Taylor, C. (1989) *Sources of the Self*, Cambridge, Mass.: Harvard University Press.

Wallman, S. (ed.) (1979) *Social Anthropology of Work*, London: Academic Press.

Whiting, B. B. and Edwards, C. P. (1988) *Children of Different Worlds*, Cambridge, Mass.: Harvard University Press.

Wilson, E. O. (1980) *Sociobiology* (abridged edition), Cambridge, Mass.: Harvard University (Belknap) Press.

Wolf, E. R. (1982) *Europe and the People without History*, Berkeley: University of California Press.

Worsley, P. (1984) *The Three Worlds: Culture and World Development*, London: Weidenfeld & Nicolson.

27

SOCIALITY AMONG HUMANS AND NON-HUMAN ANIMALS

R. I. M. Dunbar

The tendency to impute human motivations and forms of social organization to animals has a long and distinguished history. As long ago as the fourth century BC, Aristotle noted that animals differ from each other in disposition, some being stubborn, others mean and scheming, yet others mischievous and wicked, bashful or jealous. On the other hand, his description of bee society is extraordinarily accurate (it was not correctly described again until the mid-eighteenth century), though he persistently refers to the queen in each hive as the (male) 'leader'.

During the three decades since 1960, there has been an unparalleled growth in our knowledge and understanding of animal societies. In part, this has been a consequence of the amount of detailed descriptive fieldwork that has been undertaken. In addition, however, the second half of this period has coincided with major new developments in theory that have revolutionized our understanding of how and why animals behave in the ways they do. This theoretical advance (known variously as 'sociobiology', 'behavioural ecology' or 'evolutionary ecology') has both revealed animal societies in a new light and stimulated a vast amount of empirical research aimed at testing specific hypotheses.

Attempts to interpret human social behaviour in the light of animal behaviour are, of course, a far from recent feature in the history of modern science. Undoubtedly the two most controversial attempts to do so during this century were those associated with the behaviourists in the 1920s and 1930s (e.g. Watson 1919, Skinner 1938) and the ethologists in the 1960s (e.g. Lorenz 1960, Morris 1967). By and large, these proceeded by analogy: if greylag geese behave in a certain way, then human beings will do so too. With the benefit of hindsight from three decades of fieldwork, such reasoning can now be seen as naïve: primates, for example, are so flexible in their behaviour that we cannot always infer the behaviour of one population from that of another population even when they belong to the same species (see Smuts *et al.* 1987, Dunbar 1988). If we cannot do this reliably within a species, then the possibility that we can do it between species (and the more so between those as distantly related as geese and ourselves) becomes even more remote. One of sociobiology's beneficial influences in this respect has been to shift the emphasis away from analogical reasoning of this kind to give greater prominence to the specific contexts in which particular animals or groups of animals find themselves. This is not to say that there are no general principles that apply universally, but rather to emphasize the fact that these principles are at a deep level: the same universal principle may express itself in quite contrary ways in different ecological or demographic contexts.

In this article, I summarize our current understanding of animal sociality and ask what this can tell us about human sociality. I begin with the more general problem of defining sociality, and then elaborate the theoretical perspective that underlies all contemporary studies of animal behaviour. I go on to consider the reasons why animals are social and conclude by attempting to reassess the differences and similarities between animal and human societies.

THE PROBLEM OF SOCIALITY

Animals vary in their social arrangements from the wholly asocial solitary life of some insects and lower organisms (as well as of primates like galagos and the orang-utan) to the highly complex societies of many birds and mammals (particularly the higher primates including, most conspicuously, ourselves). Defining a scale of social complexity that would enable us to make quantitative comparisons between species has always been a major difficulty. Biologists have tended to simplify the situation by drawing a qualitative distinction between the essentially asocial existence of many solitary and semi-solitary species and the obviously social groups of many other species. This has led to a tendency for sociality to be equated with group-living, and for social complexity to be judged in terms of group size (see, for example, Wilson 1975). Thus, gorillas would appear to be social because they live in permanent groups, whereas orang-utans would appear to be asocial because they live solitarily. Such a criterion creates anomalies that beg questions about what we mean by sociality. Chimpanzees, for example, might seem asocial because they tend to forage in 'groups' that average somewhat less than two individuals in size, at least in some populations. Yet, as the detailed studies of de Waal (1982) and Goodall (1986) clearly show, chimpanzee social life is in fact extraordinarily rich.

Likewise, were we to judge complexity by group size alone, we would be obliged to consider antelope that are found in herds of several hundred thousand animals (e.g. wildebeest) as socially more complex than, say, baboons that typically live in groups of 40–50 animals. Yet we know that relationships among primates are of a very different social order from those of antelope, whose groups are often passive aggregations of individuals brought together by particularly good feeding conditions.

This tendency to view sociality in terms of the disposition of animals in groups was in part a consequence of the fact that, until the 1960s, most field studies were of short duration (often no more than censuses): one of the few things that can easily be quantified during a short field trip is the way the animals are distributed around the habitat at any given moment. In addition, the bulk of the fieldwork conducted up to 1960 was carried out on birds, and this fostered a tendency to focus on a small number of functionally relevant social units (notably those involved in mating and rearing) that have special prominence in bird biology.

How, then, should we view animal sociality? The past two decades of field research on primate behaviour have revealed that the complexity of primate societies lies in the relationships among individuals that bind the group of animals together. A shift in emphasis towards a focus on relationships began as early as the 1970s, when Hinde (1976) suggested that a social system could profitably be interpreted in terms of the patterning and quality of relationships among a set of individuals, each of these relationships, in turn, being interpretable in terms of the patterning and quality of the interactions between the two individuals involved. In other words, what we, as observers, describe as a relationship between two individuals is something we abstract from the set of interactions that we observe between them, with the social system as a whole being similarly derived from the set of such relationships between all the individuals in a given region.

One implication of this view is that animals might have relationships (and hence a form of social life), even though they do not spend all of their time together in the same group. This has important implications in the case of chimpanzees, for example. The earliest field studies suggested that chimpanzees did not have social groups of any kind, the only form of stable relationships in evidence being the associations of mothers and their offspring (Goodall 1965). However, subsequent fieldwork at Gombe and in the Mahale Mountains of Tanzania during the 1970s revealed that the loose parties in which chimpanzees were most often found did not form at random. Rather, their members are drawn from a pool of individuals (later known as the 'community') that share a common ranging area (see Wrangham and Smuts 1980). These individuals readily form foraging parties with each other and are antagonistic towards members of other, neighbouring communities.

Subsequently, data from a number of primate species began to suggest that multi-layered societies in which individuals were members of ever more inclusive, hierarchically organized, social groupings might in fact be typical of most, if not all, species (Dunbar 1988, 1989a). African vervet monkeys, for example, live in archetypal primate groups of some ten to twenty individuals. But far from being the socially amorphous entities presupposed in most of the earlier literature, these groups turn out on closer inspection to be highly structured:

individuals living within the same group do not interact with one another at random. Similarly, while neighbouring groups often do have mutually antagonistic relationships and do defend their territories against incursions, this is not necessarily true of all groups. Some groups turn out to have positive relationships with each other, in that they regularly exchange members (Cheney and Seyfarth 1983). From this observation emerged the concept of a local community in which certain groups within the population are bound together by historical and genetic ties.

The gelada baboon provides a more complex example. Gelada live in reproductive units that consist of a single breeding male and up to ten reproductive females and their dependent offspring. These units are themselves organized into highly discrete coalitionary subgroupings, mostly based on close female kin relationships (mother–daughter–sister). These reproductive units, in turn, are grouped into higher-order clusters (bands) based on their occupancy of a common core ranging area, while the bands themselves are organized into still higher-level groupings (communities) which more readily form combined foraging parties (Kawai *et al.* 1983).

Because the relationships between the reproductive units of a band are relatively loose, these units may all be together in one large group on one day, but then dispersed over a wide area on the next; on yet other occasions, some units of one band may join up with units from another band in areas of range overlap. The resulting groupings (termed *herds*) are temporary aggregations that undergo continuous flux as units come and go, but they are none the less an important feature of the gelada social system: they provide the animals with their primary protection from predators (see Kawai *et al.* 1983). In addition, the relationships they entail cut horizontally across the vertically structured groupings that characterize the species's social system. This example serves to remind us that animals may be simultaneously involved in several different networks of social relationships.

Multi-tiered social systems of similar complexity have also been noted in other Old World monkeys (e.g. hamadryas baboons: Kummer 1968, 1984; pigtailed macaques: Robertson 1986). Hierarchically organized groupings have, in addition, been documented in birds (e.g. bee-eaters: Hcgner *et al.* 1982), rodents (e.g. prairie dogs: King 1955) and elephants (Moss and Poole 1983), suggesting, perhaps, that social complexity of this kind may be typical of most higher vertebrates (birds and mammals).

What is important here is not so much the particular form of social organization as the facts that an animal has relationships with a variety of individuals, and that these relationships reflect differing degrees of familiarity and intensity. They may also be expressed behaviourally in quite different ways. Thus, when two individuals of the same elephant family meet after a temporary separation, they commonly engage in an intense, excited, often noisy greeting ceremony, whereas when members of different families (but the same clan) meet they simply place the tips of their trunks in each other's mouths (Moss and Poole 1983).

In many respects, these groupings resemble the social networks discussed by sociologists (see for example Milardo 1988), and they do in fact function in rather similar ways. An individual animal may belong to a number of different networks in just the same way as a man or woman may belong to a set of partially overlapping networks (e.g. networks of relations among work colleagues, friends, kin, members of a political party or church, etc.).

Despite this emphasis on relationships, the grouping patterns of animals remain none the less a central concern for biologists. It is not just the *nature* of the relationships that one animal has with another that is interesting, but also their *number*. Why should an animal have intense relationships with a dozen other individuals and not just with one? Why do some animals prefer to live alone, even though they have relationships with those living nearby? Groups themselves are, after all, simply a reflection of the way certain kinds of relationships cluster in space–time. Understanding why some groups are manifested in this sense, but others not, is an important endeavour. In addition, the size of the group in which an animal lives inevitably places constraints on the number and frequency of other kinds of relationships that it can have. For example, if ecological conditions limit groups to a maximum of two individuals, then the animals concerned will not be able to form coalitionary relationships with third parties *vis-à-vis* one another when disputes arise. Nor will it be possible for one individual to play another off against a third. Thus, understanding the factors that foster the development of groups of a certain size and type remains fundamental.

This raises an important issue of definition. When biologists refer to relationships, it is clear that they mean something rather informal and low-level, little more than a consistent patterning in the interactions of a pair of animals. When social anthropologists refer to relationships, they often mean something closer to a rule-bound contractual arrangement between consenting parties. A similar difference exists in the use of the term 'group'. To a biologist, a group is simply a set of animals bound together in some way and occupying a discrete segment of space–time: groups may be dispersed (when their members do not physically live together) or they may be spatially concentrated. Moreover, a single individual on its own may, for some purposes, be said to constitute a 'group' of size one. There is nothing particularly odd about this usage, but it will probably strike social anthropologists as perplexing because, in general, they tend to regard groups as being the product of contractual arrangements among a set of individuals: by definition, then, it takes two or more to make a group.

These contrasting usages arise from the different explanatory interests of biologists and social anthropologists. That humans organize their relationships on the basis of verbally negotiated contractual arrangements is neither here nor there for the biologist (even though it may be recognized as an intrinsically interesting property of human behaviour). The evolutionary biologist's concern is with the functional consequences of those contractual arrangements, not with their immediate causes. At this level, the mechanisms involved in their creation are immaterial. I draw attention to this point now because it is important to appreciate that the same term may be used to mean quite different things in the two disciplines of social anthropology and biology. I have more to say about the implications of this in the following section.

SOME BACKGROUND THEORY

However we define societies, merely to describe them is not enough. The very fact of their existence, and *a fortiori* the existence of differences between species in their forms of social life, beg questions about why a given society takes the form it does. Biologists have long recognized that even such an apparently innocuous question as asking why something is the case can (and indeed should) be answered at a number of logically different levels (Huxley 1942, Tinbergen 1963). Thus, in asking why a given society takes the form it does, answers might be given in terms of (1) the mechanisms (or processes) that bind it together (explanations of *proximate causation*), (2) the function (or purpose) that a particular form of society serves for its members (*functional* explanations), (3) the developmental processes (specified by some combination of genetic, environmental and cultural factors) that give rise to the particular forms of behaviour that underwrite it (*ontogenetic* explanations) and (4) the historical sequence by which that particular form of society arose from some ancestral form (explanations of phylogeny or *evolutionary history*).

Known nowadays as 'Tinbergen's Four Why's', these questions are logically distinct. Our answer to any one of them in no way predisposes us to a particular form of answer to any of the other three. This distinction between different levels of explanation is fundamental; most disputes over the nature of biological explanations have arisen as a result of a failure to distinguish either between proximate causation and function or between ontogenetic and functional explanations.

Despite the equal importance attached to all four types of explanation by biologists, functional explanations have a particularly important role to play in biology: for it is only by taking function into account that we can understand how evolutionary change can be other than random and chaotic. As has been repeatedly noted, there has been insufficient time since the first appearance of life on earth for the enormous diversity of life-forms that have ever lived to have evolved simply by random mutation, even when assisted by genetic drift. Only Darwinian natural selection is a powerful enough process to direct evolution sufficiently to account for what we observe. The logic of natural selection is, in essence, as follows: in any self-replicating system, operating in a finite environment, in which there is reasonable fidelity of copying between successive generations, any character that serves to enhance the rate of replication of the heritable component will inevitably be selected for. Differential rates of replication will tend to establish characters that are relatively more effective in facilitating future replication.

In a conventional biological context, the material that is passed on from one generation to the next is, of course, genetic, consisting of molecules of DNA. Since only genetic material is transmitted from parent to offspring, evolutionary change can occur only through the inheritance of genes (see, however, Odling-Smee in this volume, Article 7). The rate with which these elements are replicated will be a simple function of the impact they exert on the carrier's ability to reproduce. The gene's rate of replication over time (relative to that of alternative forms) is defined as its *fitness*, and it is this that provides the criterion whereby functional explanations are judged. The structure of Darwinian arguments has been shown to be logically self-contained and to follow from a few simple axioms (see Williams 1970, Dunbar 1982a).

This insistence on the primacy of genes has sometimes been expressed metaphorically by characterizing the gene as 'selfish' (Dawkins 1976). This, of course, has nothing to do with either behaviour or morality; rather, it is intended as a reminder that, since in a Darwinian world it is genes that are passed on from one generation to the next, we must always adopt a 'gene's eye view' when asking questions about the evolutionary function of a given phenomenon. To take any other perspective (for instance, to claim that evolution occurs for the benefit of the individual or the species) is to invite error, because neither individuals nor species have any temporal stability on an evolutionary timescale. This will have important implications when we come to consider the evolution of altruism in a later section.

It is important to be aware that the term 'gene' as used in this context is the Mendelian gene, not the more familiar segment of DNA that lies at the heart of molecular biology. Strictly speaking, the Mendelian gene is a trait or character, not a segment of DNA, even though there must be some definable relationship between these two components of the system. More importantly, they refer to quite different constituencies in the nexus of biological explanation. DNA is relevant to ontogenetic explanations, whereas Mendelian genes are appropriate to functional explanations; as such, Mendelian genes are emergent properties of the underlying DNA and not necessarily identical with it in any simple sense. Indeed, Dawkins (1982) has correctly pointed out that the heritable elements that make the theory of natural selection work need not even be segments of DNA; only fidelity of copying between parent and offspring generations is required. It just so happens that, in many of the contexts with which we are most familiar in biology, the replicating entity is DNA. But it need not be: anything that copies itself with reasonable fidelity is a replicating entity and therefore subject to processes of natural selection. Conventional trial-and-error learning is one example; cultural inheritance of behaviour is another. For this reason it has been possible to develop models of cultural transmission based on Darwinian principles that in no way invoke genetic determinism (see for example Cavalli-Sforza and Feldman 1980, Boyd and Richerson 1986).

Despite persistent claims to the contrary, sociobiological explanations are wholly and only about evolutionary function. They are concerned with the question: Why does a given trait persist in a population? As such, they do not necessarily presuppose any genetic basis for a given behaviour. Indeed, explanations about evolutionary function can, of themselves, tell us nothing at all about the ontogenetic foundations of the trait in question: the mode of inheritance might involve 'memes' (Dawkins's term for cultural replicators), but it equally might involve genes.

This leads naturally to the consideration of a key feature of the social behaviour of higher organisms (especially primates), namely its extraordinary flexibility. The variety of social forms exhibited by different populations of baboons, for example, makes nonsense of the assumptions about species-specific behaviour patterns that characterized the classical ethology of the 1940s and 1950s. Even within a given social group, we may find individuals pursuing radically different social strategies (see, for example, Dunbar 1982b, Caro and Bateson 1986). These kinds of alternative strategies are inherent in any biological system (see, for example, Maynard Smith and Price 1973, Maynard Smith 1982). Indeed, evolution cannot occur within a biological system unless there is variation in a character among the constituent organisms that make up the population. This is not to suggest that species-typical behaviour patterns do not exist: far from it — the smile, after all, is a human universal. But such behaviours are, in themselves, rather uninteresting from an evolutionary point of view: what is of interest is how these behaviours are used in a strategic sense to achieve functionally-related goals.

Given this perspective, one obvious interpretation of social systems is that they function as reproductive strategies. In other words, animals evolve the social systems they do because these enable them to survive and reproduce more effectively in the particular environments in which they live. In effect, a group is a co-operative solution to one or more problems of mutual concern. We can pursue this argument a little further by suggesting that the multi-level societies discussed in the preceding section represent a series of such solutions, each concerned with a different functional problem (Dunbar 1988, 1989a).

Finally, two caveats are in order.

First, it is important in this context to appreciate that evolutionary functionalism has little in common with the functionalism that dominated sociology and anthropology during the 1930s and 1940s. Structural-functionalism in the social sciences concerned itself with the self-regulating properties of whole societies and viewed the individual's place in the social system as subservient to the perpetuation of the monolithic structures of the system itself. In contrast to this top-down view, evolutionary biology adopts a strictly bottom-up view: society as we perceive it is simply the outcome of the series of decisions made by a set of individuals to associate with each other. Even though the structural components of the system may impose constraints on just what those individuals can do (they can, after all, only live in social groups if they are prepared to compromise on their ideal strategies), the system as a whole is intrinsically dynamic and can be expected to change continuously through time as the individual and collective interests of its members change.

Second, care needs to be taken to avoid misinterpreting the anthropomorphisms commonly used by evolutionary biologists. Genes, as well as individuals, are commonly spoken of as though they had goals and made decisions about how to behave for the best, all couched in the language of strategy and gamesmanship. It is, of course, easy to interpret these terms literally. In evolutionary biology, however, they function as shorthand for what otherwise would become impossibly convoluted expressions. This use of metaphor works because evolutionary processes are teleonomic (goal-directed, without being intentionally so). Indeed, in this context 'Tinbergen's Four Why's' are clearly applicable: questions about intentionality or consciousness are concerned with proximate mechanisms, and not with function. The same functional requirements can be met by any number of different proximate mechanisms, one of which entails fully conscious decision-making, another the operation of a pre-programmed automaton.

WHY LIVE IN GROUPS?

Having, I hope, cleared the debris of past misunderstandings out of the way, I can now concentrate on the functional significance of sociality in animals. For purely logistic reasons, it is convenient to partition any discussion of sociality into a number of separate questions. Doing so allows us to concentrate in turn on each of the key problems that arise without confounding issues that are logically distinct. I have already raised the general question of why animals might be social (in the sense of maintaining affiliative or friendly relationships with each other). Once an animal has 'decided' to form relationships of a particular kind, two logically quite separate questions arise. One of these concerns the size of the group it should live in. It might decide to live in a group of size 1 (i.e solitarily) or it might decide to live in a group of size 101. The issue here is the simple question of what determines group size. The second question concerns whom it should form these groups with. I shall deal with the first question in this section; the second question will be the subject of the penultimate section.

One of the central tenets of sociobiology is that whichever sex has the most at stake with respect to reproduction will always be able to exert more influence over the form of the species's mating system. Two points are worthy of comment here. First, it is a matter of accident as to which (genetic) sex incurs the greater cost in reproduction, although we then habitually refer to this sex as 'female' and its gametes as 'eggs' or 'ova'. (In birds, for example, it is the XY sex that lays the eggs, whereas in mammals it is, of course, the XX sex.) Secondly, the imbalances between the sexes in the initial investment in reproduction are very much greater in mammals than in any other taxonomic group (in part because of internal gestation but, more importantly, because of lactation), and they are proportionately more acute in primates than in other mammalian taxa because of the prolonged periods of infant dependency that characterize this group.

In primates, then, females may be expected to exert the most influence and will thus distribute themselves around the habitat in the ways that are most conducive to their successful reproduction, forming groups only when and if these are advantageous. Males will then map themselves onto the distribution pattern of the females in such a way as to maximize their own reproductive success. In primates, at least, there is direct evidence to support this claim (e.g. from releases of animals into new habitats: Charles-Dominique 1977).

Given that the animals in a population distribute themselves around the habitat in groups of a particular size, what factors influence this size? In biological systems, most questions of this kind turn out to have rather complex answers that rest on a balance between the costs and benefits of a given strategy. In principle, the benefits that would accrue to the individual from living in a group, taken on their own, would be expected to result in 'runaway' selection in favour of ever larger groups. However, the fact that organisms are systemic entities means that evolutionary change along one dimension inevitably creates costs along one or more of the system's other dimensions and these act to counter-balance the evolutionary forces driving the system towards any one extreme. Increased group size may have advantages in terms of territorial defence, for example, but large groups impose greater costs on their members because the size of territory that has to be defended to provide the group with the resources it needs increases faster than the area the group can patrol effectively. In most cases, the solutions that animals adopt turn out to be compromises between the conflicting demands stemming from a number of different considerations.

Biologists have suggested four main selective advantages to explain why animals live in groups (see Wrangham 1983, 1987, Dunbar 1988). These are: (1) improved care of young; (2) co-operative hunting; (3) defence of food resources, and (4) protection against predators. Table 1 lists a selection of species for which each of these explanations can plausibly be invoked.

In general, the advantages that accrue in terms of parental care are likely to be restricted to species that are monogamous (i.e. those in which mating occurs only between one male and one female who normally live alone as a pair). Sharing of parental duties between both the male and the female is common only in such species. Indeed, monogamy is exclusive to those species in which male parental care is possible (Kleiman 1977). Of all bird species, for example, 90 per cent are monogamous, whereas monogamy is found in

Table 1 Main benefits gained from group-living, with some examples that seem to constitute instances of these

Hypothesis	Examples
1 Parental care	Jackals, foxes, most birds
2 Co-operative hunting	Lions, wolves, hyaenas
3 Defence of food resources	Primates
4 Protection from predators	Antelope, buffalo, primates

only about 5 per cent of mammalian species. Male birds are just as competent at incubating eggs and feeding the young as are female birds, but internal gestation and lactation make it difficult for male mammals to contribute directly to the business of rearing young.

However, even within the mammals there are marked differences between taxonomic groups. Monogamy is ubiquitous, for example, among the canids (the dog–wolf–jackal family), and in most of these species biparental care is the norm. Lactation in these species is relatively brief and the male is able to feed the female in the den by bringing meat back to her; once the pups are weaned, both male and female are able to bring food back to the den for the pups to eat. Monogamy is also typical of about 15 per cent of all primate species, though here the distribution is very uneven. Most small New World monkeys (e.g. marmosets, tamarins, titis) and all gibbons are monogamous, with monogamy associated with male parental care in the marmosets and tamarins but not in the titis or gibbons. By contrast, monogamy is extremely rare in all other groups of primates. However, it seems unlikely that parental care can be a factor promoting the evolution of monogamy in primates. Instead, it seems more likely that the opportunity for paternal care is a by-product of monogamy rather than its cause, with the evolution of monogamous mating systems having more to do with the risk that females run of infanticide by other males (see van Schaik and Dunbar 1990).

Carnivores may often gain considerable advantages from hunting in groups: there is ample evidence to show, for example, that the size of prey caught increases with group size in species that hunt co-operatively (e.g. lion: Schaller 1972; hyaena: Kruuk 1982). While the advantages of co-operative hunting might be seen as relevant to the later hominids, they are unlikely to be relevant to any non-human primates or to have been so to our early hominid ancestors (e.g. the australopithecines) whose hunting skills appear to have been minimal.

There seems to be general agreement that primates live in groups either as a defence against predators or in order to defend food sources against other members of their own species (van Schaik 1983, Wrangham 1987, Dunbar 1988). It should be noted that defence against predators does not necessarily imply that they are actively driven away, either by members of the group as a whole or by one class of individuals from the group (e.g. adult males).

Although examples of male baboons driving leopards away have been documented, the only unequivocal evidence for active deterrence of predators is that provided by Busse (1977) for red colobus (where the presence of adult males does seem to deter chimpanzees from preying on the smaller members of the group). There is, however, an extensive literature, both theoretical and experimental, on the advantages that prey species gain from living in groups: clumping of prey may make it harder for predators to locate a group, more likely that a neighbour will be taken rather than yourself, more likely that a predator will be detected before it can approach close enough to the group to launch an attack and more likely that a predator may become confused by prey fleeing in all directions (for a general review, see Bertram 1978).

The hypothesis that primates group to defend food resources in the face of intra-specific competition rests largely on the evidence that primate populations, like those of many other organisms, are ultimately food-limited: the amount of food available in the habitat sets the upper limit on a population's capacity to increase its size. Whether this hypothesis specifies an important determinant of group-living thus ultimately turns on the issue of whether or not animals like primates are ever at such high densities that their populations are close to the maximum that their habitats can sustain.

The primate literature is more or less evenly divided on the question of which of these last two hypotheses — reduction of predation risk or defence of food resources — is correct as a general explanation for group-living in primates. Wrangham (1980, 1987), Dittus (1986) and Cheney and Seyfarth (1987) favour the latter; van Schaik (1983), de Ruiter (1986) and Dunbar (1988) favour the former. Where direct tests between the two hypotheses have been possible, however, these have tended to come down in favour of the reduction of predation risk (van Schaik 1983, Dunbar 1988).

In Darwinian terms, no benefit can be viewed in isolation from the corresponding costs. These costs increase with increasing group size and come in two main forms: (1) direct costs in terms of increased competition over specific items of food and other social stresses that ultimately influence an individual's survival and/or reproduction directly, and (2) indirect costs in the form of disrupted time budgets and longer day journeys (because the group needs to search an area each day that is proportional to its size). These effects are well documented for primates (see, for example, Wrangham 1977, van Schaik et al. 1983, Watts 1985, Stacey 1986), and in some cases the physiological mechanisms that mediate them are well understood (e.g. Abbott 1984, French et al. 1984).

The sizes of the social groups in which animals live in a given habitat will thus depend on a balance between the benefits and the costs. If there are few predators in the habitat, little advantage will be gained from living in large groups; the costs of doing so will therefore push group size towards a minimum value. In habitats with many predators, the benefits of large groups will outweigh the costs, and group size will tend to increase despite the disadvantages incurred by the animals.

THE STRUCTURE OF SOCIAL GROUPS

Primate groups differ from those of other animals in two important respects. One is the intensity of their social bonding; the other is in the extent to which alliances are used to minimize the costs of group-living.

Grooming is the main way of cementing social relationships in primates, and monkeys and apes may devote up to 20 per cent of their total waking time to grooming with each other. The actual amount of time spent on social activities seems to be directly related to the size of the group: even within species, animals that live in larger groups devote a higher proportion of their day to social interaction than those that live in smaller groups. Although grooming has an obvious hygienic function, individuals of the more social species groom one another far more than is required to keep the fur clean and free of parasites.

Quite how grooming serves to maintain relationships is far from clear, though it is now known that grooming increases the production of endogenous opiates (the brain's own painkillers) (Keverne *et al.* 1989). Grooming may also provide an excuse for animals to spend time in close proximity and thus to get to know each other better. Familiarity is an important requirement for coalition partners because the value of an ally in a conflict depends on his or her reliability, and knowledge of another individual's reliability can only come through repeated interaction.

Although coalitions are known to occur in other animals besides primates (e.g. lions: Packer and Pusey 1982; swans: Scott 1980), most of these are straightforward relationships based on immediate mutual advantage (for a review, see Harcourt 1989). The coalitions of higher primates (monkeys and apes) seem to differ from these in three key respects.

First, coalitionary relationships are established long before they are needed. Whether grooming partners are more likely to become allies because they spend so much of their time together or whether monkeys and apes deliberately groom with those who might be the most profitable allies at some future time remains uncertain. However, there is at least some evidence to suggest that even juvenile baboons are aware of who the best allies are in that they actively seek to establish grooming relationships with just those individuals (Cheney 1977).

Second, coalitionary relationships among primates are often directed towards minimizing the costs of group-living rather than − as is usual among other mammals − simply enabling animals to gain immediate access to a resource. Among gelada baboons, for example, females form coalitions whose primary function is to reduce the levels of harassment that they inevitably suffer while living in groups (Dunbar 1980, 1989b). Coalitions make it possible for the females to minimize these costs and thereby to remain together and gain the primary advantage that groups are intended to serve (probably the reduction of predation risk: Dunbar 1986).

Third, the coalitions of primates often involve the exploitation of third-party power relationships, whereas those of non-primates tend to be based on mutual interest in a common resource (Harcourt 1989). In other words, monkeys and apes compete for *allies*, not just for resources (see for example Seyfarth 1977, 1983). Moreover, these allies are recruited to provide assistance not just in the heat of the moment (as is the case in other mammals and birds), but for use at some uncertain and unspecified future time: primates *anticipate* the need for coalitionary support (Dunbar 1988). Higher primates exhibit many other behavioural strategies that suggest that they can evaluate the power differentials between other individuals (see Kummer 1982, Byrne and Whiten 1988) as well as recognize higher-order aspects of relationships of a more general nature (e.g. recognizing that A's relationship to B is similar to C's relationship to me: see Cheney and Seyfarth 1986, 1990).

Given the relative sophistication of the coalitionary relationships characteristic of primates, it should not be too surprising to find that the more social primates (i.e. baboons, macaques and chimpanzees) also have mechanisms that allow them to keep alliance relationships going even after they have been destabilized. Many studies have demonstrated that an animal's willingness to go to an ally's aid depends critically on its perception of the risks involved. Macaques and baboons, for example, will not support their allies in a fight if the opponent can call on more powerful allies or if the likelihood of losing the fight anyway is high (Datta 1983, Chapais 1983, Netto and van Hooff 1986). De Waal (1989, de Waal and van Roosmalen 1979) has pointed out that reneging on an alliance in this way weakens a coalition and makes it less likely that the deserted ally will support its partner when that individual finds itself in a similar situation on some future occasion. De Waal has suggested two behavioural processes (termed 'reconciliation' and 'consolation') which macaques and chimpanzees use to restore the equilibrium in a destabilized relationship. Both processes involve behaviours such as approaching and putting an arm around the deserted ally. Reconciliation occurs when the two members of an alliance have themselves been involved in a fight; consolation occurs when one member has failed to support its ally when the latter was involved in a fight with a third party (and especially if the ally lost the encounter).

Such observations have led to the suggestion that primates owe their unusually large brains (and thus greater intellectual abilities) to the need to manage complex social relationships (see Jolly 1966, Humphrey 1976). This, the so-called 'social intellect' or 'Machiavellian intelligence' hypothesis, has gained considerable ground in recent years at the expense of its main rival, the more traditional view that primates' high intelligence is mainly ecological in function. Indeed, comparisons across species reveal a simple linear relationship between relative neocortex size and group size in primates as a whole (Sawaguchi and Kudo 1990, Dunbar 1992).

One interpretation of these results is that there is a cognitive limitation on primates' abilities to hold social groups together that is directly dependent on aspects of brain size (and in particular on neocortex volume). The constraint appears to lie in the brain's ability to process information (in this case, specifically information about social phenomena). This in turn suggests that, among primates, the evolution of larger group sizes under environmental or other selection pressures was dependent on the evolution of the larger brains necessary to service the relationships involved. (Note that the nature of the relationships is crucial in this respect: antelope can form very much larger groups, but these are unstable *aggregations* that are very different from the highly structured *congregations* of the higher primates.)

If we use the regression equation derived from monkeys and apes to predict group sizes in anatomically modern humans, we obtain a figure of around 150. Evidence from hunter–gatherer societies does in fact suggest a level of grouping of about this size, corresponding among sedentary peoples to the typical village and among nomadic peoples to the regional band (Dunbar 1993). In addition, there is considerable sociological evidence to suggest that, even in modern Western societies, the number of people with whom an individual interacts on a regular basis is such as to give rise to groups (or extended networks) of about this size.

These observations have interesting implications for the evolution of language. As we have seen, relationships in primate groups are cemented by social grooming, and the larger the group, the greater the amount of time that is spent grooming (Dunbar 1990). It is not entirely clear why this should be so, and several different mechanisms have been suggested. What is clear, however, is that the effort that has to be invested in social grooming increases with group size. If we use this relationship to determine the grooming time that would be required for modern humans to service relationships within groups of the size expected on the grounds of their neocortex volume we find that they would have to spend more than a third of their waking hours in social grooming. For organisms that also have to make a living in the world, this is not a feasible proposition. Language is an ideal solution to the resulting problem of time-budgeting as it allows an individual to engage in extensive time-sharing in ways that are not possible with grooming. One cannot walk and groom at the same time, nor can one groom more than one individual at a time, but it is possible to walk and talk and to hold several interlocutors in conversation simultaneously. Thus it looks as though the capacity for language might have evolved to solve a problem of social bonding in the large groups in which our ancestors were obliged to live by some (as yet undetermined) aspect of their ecology.

The question of why our ancestors should have been obliged to live in such large groups remains unclear. Our current understanding is that primates live in groups either to defend food resources or for protection against predators, with the latter certainly being the more significant factor in the case of terrestrial species inhabiting relatively open environments. However, no primate species has a mean group size of more than about a hundred individuals (much lower than that predicted for anatomically modern humans). Since many of these live in habitats where the risk of predation is high, it is difficult to see how primates as large as the later hominids could conceivably have been so much more at risk from predators as to require groups that are more than twice the size of most other open-country primates.

Whatever factor lay behind the evolution of very large groups in our ancestors, it must clearly have been some feature of their ecology that is not shared by other primates. Defence against other human groups under conditions of rapidly rising population density has been suggested as one possibility (e.g. Alexander 1989); another lies in the evolution of large-scale co-operative hunting; a third possibility might have been the need to share access to key resources (such as waterholes or dry-season foraging areas) when individual foraging parties were otherwise obliged to disperse over very wide areas. Of these, the hunting hypothesis can almost certainly be ruled out because large-scale hunting is not observed in the archaeological record until well after the evolution of large brain size (see also Wynn 1988).

What is certain, however, is that this increase in group size must have been a relatively late development. Brain size for the australopithecines lies well within the range for extant great apes, suggesting that australopithecines probably did not have group sizes significantly larger than those observed in modern chimpanzees (i.e. 50 to 100 individuals). Although there is an increase in relative brain size with the appearance of the first members of the genus *Homo* (i.e. *Homo habilis* and *H. erectus*), the real jump in brain size does not come about until the appearance of our own species (*Homo sapiens*) approximately 1.5 million years later (Aiello and Dunbar 1993).

SOME SPECIAL ORGANIZING PRINCIPLES

Sociobiology may be said to owe its origins to the attempt to solve the problem of altruism. In this context, altruism is defined in a rather specific way as behaviour that increases another individual's fitness (i.e. its relative contribution to the species' future gene pool) at the expense of the altruist's fitness. If the altruist does not incur such a genetic cost, the behaviour does not count as biological altruism. Paradoxically, perhaps, giving the price of a meal to a beggar is unlikely to count as altruism (unless the altruist is another beggar), but committing suicide would do if it resulted in an improvement in the beneficiary's ability to reproduce (e.g. by reducing the competition for scarce resources or realizing a large insurance claim). That altruistic behaviour clearly exists (and thus must have evolved) is puzzling from a Darwinian point of view: on the face of it, any gene (or meme) for altruism would be heavily selected against and would inevitably be eradicated from the population each time it appeared as a new mutation.

The solution arrived at by Hamilton (1964) depended on the recognition that an individual can contribute copies of its genes to the next generation either by reproducing itself or by enhancing the reproduction of its relatives. Because relatives share a proportion of their genes (by virtue of their descent from a common ancestor), any copy of a shared gene that is passed on by a relative is just as good (from the gene's point of view) as any copy passed on by the altruist. The number of copies of a given gene contributed to the next generation by both routes is referred to as the gene's 'inclusive fitness' and acts as the accounting basis for assessing the evolutionary value of alternative strategies. (Note that individuals are also commonly said to have an inclusive fitness; though strictly speaking incorrect, this is a convenient shorthand used by most biologists.) A gene for altruism can survive and prosper in a Darwinian world even if the altruistic action results in the death of the altruist, providing the act of altruism results in more copies of that gene reaching the next generation via the assisted relative than the altruist would have been able to contribute by its own reproduction had it lived. The mathematical conditions under which this can occur (known as 'Hamilton's rule' for the spread of altruism) are rather precise; together with the associated definition of inclusive fitness and related concepts, they constitute the theory of 'kin selection'.

Kin selection has come to be seen in some quarters as the central tenet of sociobiology. One common assumption, for example, is that kin selection obliges animals (including humans) to behave altruistically towards, or choose to live in groups only with, their kin. Unfortunately, given the definitions of inclusive fitness and Hamilton's rule, this cannot be the case. An organism always has at least two options on how to behave, and it is the balance in their net pay-offs that determines which option is best. The catch is that the net pay-off itself depends on the balance between the direct benefits conferred via the actor's own reproduction and the indirect ones conferred via its relatives. With the exception of a few cases that have odd genetics (e.g. bees), an individual is always more closely related to its own offspring than to a relative's offspring; hence, there will always be a predisposition towards personal reproduction at the expense of that of relatives (see Dunbar 1983). For this reason, mutualism (i.e. cases in which all parties benefit from co-operating: see Wrangham 1982) is probably more important as a driving force behind the evolution of social groups in animals (and certainly in primates) than is kin selection.

In point of fact, kin selection is not the only Darwinian explanation for the evolution of altruistic behaviour: there are at least two others, namely reciprocal altruism (Trivers 1971) and mutualism. Reciprocal altruism allows altruistic behaviour to evolve even when the parties concerned are unrelated to each other genetically (indeed, they may even belong to different species) because the (genetic) 'debt' that the altruist incurs by its behaviour is recouped within its lifetime. In fact, reciprocal altruism and kin selection differ only in the length of time over which the 'debt' is recouped: under kin selection, the debt can be reclaimed in the next generation. Mutualism shortens the time-scale still further to the point where the return to the altruist is immediate (because both parties are simultaneously altruist and beneficiary).

What kin selection may do, however, is bias the choice of fellow group-members in favour of relatives, given that an animal has 'decided' to live in a group in the first place. Even so, kin selection is just one of several evolutionary forces that contribute to an individual's inclusive fitness. An individual will often benefit more in terms of inclusive fitness by forming a coalition or living in a group with an unrelated individual than by doing so with a relative. Thus, male lions will sometimes form coalitions with non-relatives in order to gain control over a pride of females (Packer and Pusey 1982).

In fact, the evidence suggests that, rather than responding automatically to the call of kinship, higher primates (at least) weigh up the relative advantages of kin and non-kin in a given social context. Cheney (1983), for example, has shown that high-ranking vervet monkeys tend to form alliances with close relatives; but low-ranking monkeys tend to prefer alliances with unrelated dominant individuals to alliances with relatives. For an animal that is already high-ranking, additional support from other high-ranking allies may be of marginal benefit, and more may be gained through kin selection by supporting relatives. For a low-ranking animal, by contrast, little is gained by an alliance with a relative, since relatives are also likely to be low-ranking; much more is to be gained by forming an alliance with a high-ranking individual who is likely to have a significant impact on the ally's dominance rank within the group (and hence directly on its own ability to reproduce).

The fact that animals do discriminate between relatives and non-relatives naturally raises important questions about the mechanisms of kin recognition. Even though animals may be unable to recognize relatives in any direct genetic sense, indirect cues like familiarity will usually suffice to allow kin selection to work: evolutionary processes are statistical rather than deterministic and simply require the balance of probabilities to work in favour of a particular effect. Given that mammals have to spend time with their mothers and, perhaps, siblings, it is not hard to see that a simple rule of thumb such as 'Be altruistic towards more familiar individuals' will often have the same genetic effect (and therefore be selected for) as the more direct rule 'Be altruistic towards genetically more closely related individuals'.

There is, however, growing evidence that animals *can* sometimes recognize genetic relatives independently of their familiarity with them. Species as different as Japanese quail and rhesus monkeys have been shown to be able to discriminate relatives from non-relatives, even though they were separated from them at birth (Bateson 1983, Wu *et al.* 1980). Much of the interest in this context has focused on smell and on the genes of the major histo-compatibility (MHC) complex that provide the basis for our immune system (Yamazaki *et al.* 1976, 1978). Even in humans, emphasis may be placed on identifying features that might suggest genetic relatedness. In some cultures, relatives' comments about newborn babies often emphasize inherited features ('Doesn't he have Grandma's nose!' (Daly and Wilson 1982)). That newborn babies are, of course, all but indistinguishable as far as most such features are concerned makes the fact that such references invariably favour paternal relatives rather than maternal ones all the more significant: among mammals, only the female knows for sure that she is related to the infant. In cases where the father normally makes a significant contribution to parental care, the need to convince the father of his genetic relatedness to the offspring becomes important (and becomes proportionately all the more important when there is a possibility of doubt). Obviously, if the male does not invest heavily in his wife's offspring, then the problem does not arise and we would not expect to find comments of this kind that stress paternity. This, of course, is just what we see in those societies where promiscuity is high, paternity certainty (the male's knowledge of his biological fatherhood) low and the avunculate a common practice.

The question of whether, in humans, biological kinship is related to the ways in which kin are culturally classified has long been a bone of contention. Evolutionary biologists have been inclined to insist that such a relationship does exist, mainly on the grounds that cultural kinship classifications are never entirely arbitrary with respect to biological kinship. Given the statistical nature of all biological effects, the fact that humans sometimes make some kinship assignations that have no basis in biological kinship does not, in itself, invalidate this claim. The question at issue is whether there is so *much* misidentification of biological relatives that the evolutionary process would be undermined.

By contrast, social and cultural anthropologists have usually insisted that kinship terminology bears little or no relationship to any underlying biological 'reality' (e.g. Sahlins 1976, Bryant 1981; see also Barnard's discussion in the following article). However, where specific cases have been put forward in support of this claim, detailed investigation has invariably revealed that bio-logical kinship does, in fact, underwrite people's behaviour (e.g. Silk 1980, Hughes 1988).

Hughes's (1988) analyses of many examples of human kinship-naming patterns are particularly important in this context because he draws attention to a misconception underlying many interpretations of sociobiological arguments about kinship and kin selection — one of which even biologists have been guilty. The key issue from an evolutionary viewpoint is not whom you are most closely related to, but rather who is most likely to produce offspring that are most closely related to you. Hence, we need to look at how coefficients of relationship within a group of individuals map onto those individuals' own future reproductive prospects. Hughes's mathematical analyses demonstrate that genetic fitness is maximized not by allying with relatives in proportion to their degree of relatedness, but by allying with those relatives who will produce the largest number of most closely related descendants. These will not always be the individuals who are most closely related to you in absolute terms; indeed, they will seldom be the adults in the population. Rather, they will tend most often to be the older members of the offspring generation (i.e. those approaching or just past puberty). In an analysis of Bryant's (1981) own data for a rural Tennessee community, for example, Hughes was able to show that declared family allegiances (which genuinely bear little relationship to direct genetic relatedness, as Bryant rightly noted) in fact fit rather closely to a pattern of relatedness concentrating on twelve focal groups of siblings in the current offspring generation.

Even though kinship classifications may be underpinned by genetic relatedness in this way, focusing one's kinship allegiances on the offspring generation creates a serious problem: the offspring generation is never the same in two consecutive time periods, because offspring continuously age and join the adult cohort. How, then, is one to establish kin group stability over time? Hughes points out that the obvious solution is, in fact, to refer the kinship group backwards to some ancestor, since the ancestor's status will always remain constant through time, thereby providing a firm point on which to anchor the pedigree. What is particularly interesting in this context is that it makes very little difference whether the members of the kinship group are themselves directly related to that 'ancestor' or not, since beyond about four generations removed in time the coefficients of relationship between two individuals are so low that they are, to all intents and purposes, unrelated. Indeed, it makes little difference whether that ancestor actually existed or not: the sun, the moon and Mother Earth are as functional in this context as one's great-great-great-grandfather.

ANIMAL VERSUS HUMAN SOCIETIES

Several important lessons have been learned by biologists over the past two decades. One is that animal societies are not all of a piece. Species that belong to different groups of organisms may differ radically both in the way their societies are organized and in the biological bases that underlie them. While invertebrates, for example, may reasonably be considered to be genetically determined automata, mammals (and *a fortiori* primates) cannot. None the less, it may still be the case that the general evolutionary principles that underlie the one also underlie the other. Sociobiologists are willing to switch from bees to humans within the same sentence, not because they believe that the behaviour of both bees and humans is determined by the same set of genetic molecules, but because the same *functional* considerations apply universally.

At the same time, biologists have learned to be very cautious of attempts to argue analogically from one species to another. That geese, for example, should behave in a particular way does not mean to say that humans should do so too. Indeed, there is little justification for supposing that generalizations of this kind can be made even across closely related species. This is most clearly the case in the primates where behavioural flexibility is so great that adjacent groups within the same population may be organized on quite different principles. This highlights an important distinction between 'deep structure' and 'surface structure' in the context of social organization. The particular pattern of relationships that the observer notes in any given group is a consequence of the patterning of interaction among the animals, and this in turn is founded on sets of rules that the animals use in order to identify the most profitable social partners. It is these deep structural rules that turn out to be universally true for all species, but the particular social pattern that a given deep structural rule produces depends crucially on the context in which the animals have to apply it. In different contexts, the application of the same rule may yield completely contradictory expectations about the optimal behavioural strategy. Thus, vervet monkeys appear to operate with the rule 'Form those alliances that will allow you to maximize your chances of contributing to the species' gene pool'. Which particular alliance partners best allow one to achieve that goal is, however, very different for high-ranking and low-ranking individuals (Cheney 1983). Similarly, gelada baboon females appear to operate with a similar rule, but the choice of preferred alliance partner depends upon who is available (Dunbar 1984). In part, this is a consequence of the fact that what animals actually do is almost always a compromise between what they would really like to do (in an ideal world) and what the demographic and ecological context allows them to do.

Studies of animals *can* tell us a great deal about the underlying processes in human societies. But, as biologists have long been aware, we cannot learn anything useful by analogical reasoning: studies of non-human animals can tell us little about the fine details of human social behaviour. Much of that may well be culturally determined and owe its origins as much to cultural drift (analogous to genetic drift, itself a perfectly respectable concept in evolutionary biology) as to selection and adaptation. However, behaviour becomes sociobiologically interesting as soon as it has some influence on the rate at which the units of selection (either genes or their cultural analogues, 'memes', in most real world contexts) replicate themselves. From an evolutionary point of view selection on memes in the memetic universe is no less interesting than selection at the genetic level. Indeed, it is quite likely that many cultural institutions actually comprise a number of facets that are subject to quite different evolutionary processes. An example might be the need for a religious system with an omnipotent deity. Belief in a deity of this kind may well help individuals to survive and reproduce more effectively because it gives coherence to an apparently chaotic world. Such a belief might be selected for at the genetic level. But the particular choice of deity to fill this role may have little or no genetic import: Allah, God, Zeus and the Great Spirit in the Sky might all be equally good candidates. If they genuinely do not differ in their consequences for the genetic fitnesses of those who hold them, choice of deity will then be influenced at the memetic level by a process analogous to genetic drift. Alternatively, they may be under memetic (but not genetic) selection for their 'fit' in relation to other aspects of the cultural system: the meme 'Allah' may not mesh well with key elements of the set of cultural institutions of which it tries to become a part, and thus be selected against in favour of a more compatible alternative.

The crucial lesson here is that we have to approach evolutionary issues in a very different (and very much more sophisticated) way from that which has often been the case hitherto. This is especially so with respect to the kinds of evolutionary explanations that have been prevalent in the social sciences. As Ingold (1986) points out, most of these owe their origins to Spencerian and not to Darwinian views of evolution. What makes human sociobiology particularly interesting is the sheer complexity of the biological system once cultural processes are introduced. Its analysis requires a much deeper understanding of the many intrinsic and extrinsic factors that influence an organism's ability to reproduce successfully.

Equally, it is important to remember that questions of the kind that commonly interest social and cultural anthropologists are very different from those that interest evolutionary biologists. As 'Tinbergen's Four Why's' should remind us, this does not mean that one set of interests must be right and the other wrong. Questions about origins or function, for example, cannot be brushed under the carpet merely because they are inconvenient or difficult to answer. In most cases, it is clear that issues that interest one group of scholars are simply not relevant to the interests of the other group. Nevertheless, we will not be said to have achieved a satisfactory understanding of our world until both sets of questions have been answered.

REFERENCES

Abbott, D. H. (1984) 'Behavioural and physiological suppression of fertility in subordinate marmoset monkeys', *American Journal of Primatology* 6: 169–86.

Aiello, L. C. and Dunbar, R. I. M. (1993) 'Neocortex size, group size and the evolution of language', *Current Anthropology* 34: 184–93.

Alexander, R. D. (1989) 'Evolution of the human psyche', in P. Mellars and C. Stringer (eds) *The Human Revolution*, Edinburgh: Edinburgh University Press.

Bateson, P. P. G. (1983) 'Optimal outbreeding', in P. Bateson (ed.) *Mate Choice*, Cambridge: Cambridge University Press.

Bertram, B. C. R. (1978) 'Living in groups: predators and prey', in J. Krebs and N. Davies (eds) *Behavioural Ecology*, Oxford: Blackwell.

Boyd, R. and Richerson, P. (1986) *Culture and the Evolutionary Process*, Chicago: Chicago University Press.

Bryant, F. C. (1981) *We're All Kin: A Cultural Study of a Mountain Neighbourhood*, Knoxville: University of Tennessee Press.

Busse, C. (1977) 'Chimpanzee predation as a possible factor in the evolution of red colobus monkey social organisation', *Evolution* 31: 907–11.

Byrne, R. and Whiten, A. (eds) (1988) *Machiavellian Intelligence*, Oxford: Oxford University Press.

Caro, T. and Bateson, P. (1986) 'Organisation and ontogeny of alternative tactics', *Animal Behaviour* 34: 1483–99.

Cavalli-Sforza, L. and Feldman, M. (1980) *Cultural Transmission and Evolution*, Princeton: Princeton University Press.

Chapais, B. (1983) 'Dominance, relatedness and the structure of female relationships in rhesus monkeys', in R. Hinde (ed.) *Primate Social Relationships*, Oxford: Blackwell.

Charles-Dominique, P. (1977). *Ecology and Behaviour of Nocturnal Primates*, New York: Columbia University Press.

Cheney, D. L. (1977) 'The acquisition of rank and the development of reciprocal alliances among free-ranging immature baboons', *Behavioural Ecology and Sociobiology* 2: 303–18.

—— (1983) 'Extrafamilial alliances among vervet monkeys', in R. Hinde (ed.) *Primate Social Relationships*, Oxford: Blackwell.

Cheney, D. L. and Seyfarth, R. M. (1983) 'Nonrandom dispersal in free-ranging vervet monkeys: social and genetic consequences', *American Naturalist* 122: 392–412.

——, —— (1986) 'The recognition of social alliances by vervet monkeys', *Animal Behaviour* 34: 1722–31.

——, —— (1987) 'Influence of intergroup competition on survival and reproduction of female vervet monkeys', *Behavioural Ecology and Sociobiology* 21: 375–86.

——, —— (1990) *How Monkeys See the World*, Chicago: Chicago University Press.

Daly, M. and Wilson, M. (1982) 'Whom are newborn babies said to resemble?' *Ethology and Sociobiology* 1: 301–9.

Datta, S. (1983) 'Relative power and the maintenance of rank', in R. Hinde (ed.) *Primate Social Relationships*, Oxford: Blackwell.

Dawkins, R. (1976) *The Selfish Gene*, Oxford: Oxford University Press.

—— (1982) 'Universal Darwinism', in D. Bendall (ed.) *Evolution from Molecules to Men*, Cambridge: Cambridge University Press.

Dittus, W. P. J. (1986) 'Sex differences in fitness following a group take-over among toque macaques: testing models of social evolution', *Behavioural Ecology and Sociobiology* 19: 257–66.

Dunbar, R. I. M. (1980) 'Determinants and evolutionary consequences of dominance among female gelada baboons', *Behavioural Ecology and Sociobiology* 7: 253–65.

—— (1982a) 'Adaptation, fitness and the evolutionary tautology', in King's College Sociobiology Group (eds) *Current Problems in Sociobiology*, Cambridge: Cambridge University Press.

—— (1982b) 'Intraspecific variations in mating strategy', in P. Klopfer and P. Bateson (eds) *Perspectives in Ethology* vol. 5, New York: Plenum Press.

—— (1983) 'Lifehistory tactics and alternative strategies of reproduction', in P. Bateson (ed.) *Mate Choice*, Cambridge: Cambridge University Press.

—— (1984) *Reproductive Decisions*, Princeton: Princeton University Press.

—— (1986) 'The social ecology of gelada baboons', in D. Rubenstein and R. Wrangham (eds) *Ecological Aspects of Social Evolution*, Princeton: Princeton University Press.

—— (1988) *Primate Social Systems*, London: Chapman & Hall.

—— (1989a) 'Social systems as optimal strategy sets: the costs and benefits of sociality', in V. Standen and R. Foley (eds) *Comparative Socioecology*, Oxford: Blackwell.

—— (1989b) 'Reproductive strategies of female gelada baboons', in A. Rasa, C. Vogel and E. Voland (eds) *The Sociobiology of Sexual and Reproductive Strategies*, London: Chapman & Hall.

—— (1990) 'The functional significance of social grooming in primates', *Folia Primatologica* 57: 121–31.

—— (1992) 'Neocortex size as a constraint on group size in primates', *Journal of Human Evolution* 20: 469–93.

—— (1993) 'Co-evolution of neocortex size, group size and language in the human lineage', *Behavioral and Brain Sciences* (in press).

French, J. A., Abbott, D. H. and Snowdon, C. T. (1984) 'The effects of social environment on oestrogen excretion, scent marking and sociosexual behaviour in tamarins (*Saguinus oedipus*)', *American Journal of Primatology* 6, 155–67.

Goodall, J. (1965) 'Chimpanzees of the Gombe Stream Reserve', in I. DeVore (ed.) *Primate Behavior*, New York: Holt Rinehart and Winston.

—— (1986) *The Chimpanzees of Gombe*, Cambridge: Mass.: Harvard University Press.

Hamilton, W. D. (1964) 'The genetical evolution of social behaviour, I, II', *Journal of Theoretical Biology* 7: 1–52.

Harcourt, A. H. (1989) 'Social influences on competitive ability: alliances and their consequences', in V. Standen and R. Foley (eds) *Comparative Socioecology*, Oxford: Blackwell.

Hegner, R. E., Emlen, S. T. and Demong, N. J. (1982) 'Spatial organisation of white-fronted bee-eaters', *Nature, London* 298: 264–6.

Hinde, R. A. (1976) 'Interactions, relationships and social structure', *Man* (N.S.) 11: 1–17.

Hughes, A. (1988) *Evolution and Human Kinship*, Oxford: Oxford University Press.

Humphrey, N. K. (1976) 'The social function of intellect', in P. Bateson and R. Hinde (eds) *Growing Points in Ethology*, Cambridge: Cambridge University Press.

Huxley, J. S. (1942) *Evolution: The Modern Synthesis*, London: Allen & Unwin.

Ingold, T. (1986) *Evolution and Social Life*, Cambridge: Cambridge University Press.

Jolly, A. (1966) 'Lemur social behaviour and intelligence', *Science* 153: 501–6.

Kawai, M., Dunbar, R., Ohsawa, H. and Mori, U. (1983) 'Social organisation of gelada baboons: social units and definitions', *Primates* 24: 1–13.

Keverne, E. B., Martenz, N. D. and Tuite, B. (1989) 'Beta-endorphin concentrations in cerebrospinal fluid of monkeys are influenced by grooming relationships', *Psychoneuroendocrinology* 14: 155–61.

Kleiman, D. (1977) 'Monogamy in mammals', *Quarterly Review of Biology* 52: 39–69.

King, J. A. (1955) 'Social behaviour, social organisation and population dynamics in a blacktailed prairiedog town in the Black Hills of South Dakota', *Contributions of the Laboratory of Vertebrate Biology, University of Michigan, Ann Arbor* 67: 1–123.

Kruuk, H. (1982) *The Spotted Hyaena*, Chicago: Chicago University Press.

Kummer, H. (1968) *Social Organisation of Hamadryas Baboons*, Basel: Karger.

—— (1982) 'Social knowledge in free-ranging primates', in D. R. Griffin (ed.) *Animal Mind – Human Mind*, Berlin: Springer.

—— (1984) 'From laboratory to desert and back: a social system of hamadryas baboons', *Animal Behaviour* 32: 965–71.

Lorenz, K. (1960) *On Aggression*, New York: Harcourt Brace and World.

Maynard Smith, J. (1982) *Evolution and the Theory of Games*, Cambridge: Cambridge University Press.

779

Maynard Smith, J. and Price, G. R. (1973) 'The logic of animal conflict', *Nature, London* 246: 15–18.

Milardo, R. M. (1988). 'Families and social networks: an overview of theory and methodology', in R. Milardo (ed.) *Families and Social Networks*, Newbury Park, Calif.: Sage.

Morris, D. (1967) *The Naked Ape*, London: Constable.

Moss, C. and Poole, J. H. (1983) 'Relationships and social structure of African elephants', in R. Hinde (ed.) *Primate Social Relationships*, Oxford: Blackwell.

Netto, W. J. and van Hooff, J. (1986) 'Conflict interference and the development of dominance relationships in immature *Macaca fascicularis*', in J. Else and P. C. Lee (eds) *Primate Ontogeny, Cognition and Social Behaviour*, Cambridge: Cambridge University Press.

Packer, C. and Pusey, A. (1982) 'Co-operation and competition within coalitions of male lions: kin selection or game theory?', *Nature, London* 296: 740–2.

Robertson, J. M. Y. (1986) 'On the evolution of pigtail macaque societies', PhD. thesis, University of Cambridge.

de Ruiter, J. (1986) 'The influence of group size on predator scanning and foraging behaviour of wedgecapped capuchin monkeys (*Cebus olivaceus*)', *Behaviour* 98: 240–58.

Sahlins, M. (1976) *The Use and Abuse of Biology*, Ann Arbor: University of Michigan Press.

Sawaguchi, T. and Kudo, H. (1990) 'Neocortical development and social structure in primates', *Primates* 31: 283–90.

van Schaik, C. P. (1983) 'Why are diurnal primates living in groups?', *Behaviour* 87: 120–44.

van Schaik, C. P. and Dunbar, R. I. M. (1990) 'The evolution of monogamy in large primates: a new hypothesis and some crucial tests', *Behaviour* 119: 30–62.

van Schaik, C. P., van Noordwijk, M. A., Wasone, M. A. and Sitriono, E. (1983) 'Party size and early detection in Sumatran forest primates', *Primates* 24: 211–21.

Schaller, G. (1972) *The Serengeti Lion*, Chicago: Chicago University Press.

Scott, D. K. (1980) 'Functional aspects of prolonged parental care in Bewick's swans', *Animal Behaviour* 28: 938–52.

Seyfarth, R. M. (1977) 'A model of social grooming among adult female monkeys', *Journal of Theoretical Biology* 65: 671–98.

—— (1983) 'Grooming and social competition in primates', in R. Hinde (ed.) *Primate Social Relationships*, Oxford: Blackwell.

Silk, J. B. (1980) 'Adoption and kinship in Oceania', *American Anthropologist* 82: 799–820.

Skinner, B. F. (1938) *The Behaviour of Organisms: An Experimental Analysis*, New York: Appleton-Century-Crofts.

Smuts, B. B., Cheney, D. L., Seyfarth, R. M., Wrangham, R. W. and Struhsaker, T. T. (eds) (1987) *Primate Societies*, Chicago: Chicago University Press.

Stacey, P. B. (1986) 'Group size and foraging efficiency in yellow baboons', *Behavioural Ecology and Sociobiology* 18: 175–87.

Tinbergen, N. (1963) 'On the aims and methods of ethology', *Zeitschrift für Tierpsychologie* 20: 410–33.

Trivers, R. L. (1971) 'The evolution of reciprocal altruism', *Quarterly Review of Biology* 46: 35–57.

de Waal, F. (1982) *Chimpanzee Politics*, London: Jonathan Cape.

—— (1989) *Peacemaking Among Primates*, Cambridge, Mass.: Harvard University Press.

de Waal, F. and van Roosmalen, A. (1979) 'Reconciliation and consolation among chimpanzees', *Behavioural Ecology and Sociobiology* 5: 55–66.

Watson, J. B. (1919) *Psychology from the Standpoint of a Behaviourist*, Philadelphia: Lippincott.

Watts, D. (1985) 'Relations between group size and composition and feeding competition in mountain gorilla groups', *Animal Behaviour* 32: 72–85.

Williams, M. B. (1970) 'Deducing the consequences of evolution: a mathematical model', *Journal of Theoretical Biology* 29: 343–85.

Wilson, E. O. (1975) *Sociobiology: The New Synthesis*, Cambridge, Mass.: Harvard University Press.

Wrangham, R. W. (1977) 'Behaviour of feeding chimpanzees in the Gombe National Park, Tanzania', in T. Clutton-Brock (ed.) *Primate Ecology*, London: Academic Press.

—— (1980) 'An ecological model of female-bonded primate groups', *Behaviour* 75: 262–300.

—— (1982) 'Mutualism, kinship and social evolution', in King's College Sociobiology Group (eds) *Current Problems in Sociobiology*, Cambridge: Cambridge University Press.

—— (1983) 'Ultimate factors determining social structure', in R. Hinde (ed.) *Primate Social Relationships*, Oxford: Blackwell.

—— (1987) 'Evolution of social structure', in B. B. Smuts, D. L. Cheney, R. M. Seyfarth, R. W. Wrangham and T. T. Struhsaker (eds) *Primate Societies*, Chicago: Chicago University Press.

Wrangham, R. W. and Smuts, B. B. (1980) 'Sex differences in the behavioural ecology of chimpanzees in the Gombe National Park, Tanzania', *Journal of Reproduction and Fertility, Supplement* 28: 13–31.

Wu, H., Holmes, W. G., Medina, S. R. and Sackett, G. P. (1980) 'Kin preference in infant *Macaca nemestrina*', *Nature, London* 285: 225–7.

Wynn, T. (1988) 'Tools and the evolution of human intelligence', in R. Byrne and A. Whiten (eds) *Machiavellian Intelligence*, Oxford: Oxford University Press.

Yamazaki, K., Boyse, A. E., Mike, V., Thaler, H. T., Mathieson, B. J., Abbott, J., Boyse, J., Zayas, Z. A. and Thomas, L. (1976) 'Control of mating preferences in mice by genes in the major histocompatibility complex', *Journal of Experimental Medicine* 144: 1324–35.

Yamazaki, K., Yamaguchi, M., Andrews, P., Peake, B. and Boyse, E. (1978) 'Mating preference of F_2 segregants of crosses between MHC-congenic mouse strains', *Immunogenetics* 6: 253–9.

FURTHER READING

Alexander, R. (1979) *Darwinism and Human Affairs*, Seattle, University of Washington Press.

Chagnon, N. A. and Irons, W. (eds) (1979) *Evolutionary Biology and Human Social Behavior*, North Scituate, Mass.: Duxbury Press.

Daly, M. and Wilson, M. (1982) *Sex, Evolution and Behavior*, North Scituate, Mass.: Duxbury Press.

Dunbar, R. I. M. (1988) *Primate Social Systems*, London: Chapman & Hall.

Dawkins, R. (1976) *The Selfish Gene*, Oxford: Oxford University Press.

Hinde, R. A. (1987) *Individuals, Relationships and Culture*, Cambridge: Cambridge University Press.

Quiatt, D. and Reynolds, V. (1993) *Primate Behaviour: Information, Social Knowledge and the Evolution of Culture*, Cambridge: Cambridge University Press.

Rasa, A., Vogel, C. and Voland, E. (eds) (1989) *The Sociobiology of Sexual and Reproductive Strategies*, London: Chapman & Hall.

Rubenstein, D. I. and Wrangham, R. (1986) *Ecological Aspects of Social Evolution*, Princeton: Princeton University Press.

Smuts, B. B., Cheney, D., Seyfarth, R., Wrangham, R. and Struhsaker, T. (eds) (1987) *Primate Societies*, Chicago: University of Chicago Press.

Standen, V. and Foley, R. (eds) (1989) *Comparative Socioecology* Oxford: Blackwell.

Wilson, E. O. (1980). *Sociobiology*, abridged edn, Cambridge, Mass.: Harvard University (Belknap) Press.

28

RULES AND PROHIBITIONS: THE FORM AND CONTENT OF HUMAN KINSHIP

Alan Barnard

There was a time not long ago when kinship firmly commanded the highest position among the theoretical realms of anthropology. This is probably no longer true, but nor is it true that kinship is an idea with a past and no future. Kinship remains as important as ever as an element of human society, and new perspectives within the social and biological sciences offer opportunities to reconsider some old arguments in a new light and to look forward to new debates and new ideas.

The anthropological study of kinship has traditionally been divided into three broad areas: group structure (including descent and residence), alliance (relations through marriage), and the classification of relatives. Rules and prohibitions are marked out within each of these areas, and the very existence of such rules engenders an overlap between them, an overlap which is itself, arguably, the very essence of 'social structure'. The purposes of this article are first to highlight the significance of such rules and prohibitions in the foundation of human society, and second to look at recent developments and reconsider some common preconceptions about kinship, of which some but certainly not all were inherent in the old debates. My focus is on topics which I think have the greatest relevance for the future study of humankind, and not necessarily on those most significant in the history of kinship studies. Thus, for example, the transformational analysis of relationship terminologies is not treated at all (for a review, see Borland 1979), 'prescription' and 'elementary structures' will be treated only in passing, while the debate concerning the meaning and applicability of biological notions of 'kinship' receives greater emphasis.

WHAT'S SO SPECIAL ABOUT KINSHIP ANYWAY?

Although the significance of kinship in anthropological discourse has been on the wane during the last twenty years, there is little doubt that it has been treated as the single most important aspect of society, as far as anthropological theory is concerned, throughout the history of the discipline. There are several reasons for this.

First, whether in respect of the incest taboo or in respect of nurturing and socializing children and thereby establishing social groupings, kinship simultaneously marks a boundary and a bridge between non-human and human social orders. The incest taboo is pre-eminently human, although selective mating is found among non-human primates too. Extensive socialization and the formation of social groups through ties of relationship is an attribute of most primate societies, but the ideological recognition of such ties is commonly thought to define the essence of human social organization.

Second, kinship has long been conceived as somehow logically distinct from other aspects of society. Beattie (1964: 102), for example, describes kinship as 'the idiom through which certain kinds of political, jural, economic, etc., relations are talked about and thought about'. He portrays kinship almost as a contentless form which humans employ to create social relations. Although politics, economics, etc. may function in a similar way (and in my estimation, frequently do), kinship has come to be perceived as different, or at least as of prime significance, in this regard.

Third, in the history of anthropology, it was through kinship that the variety of human conceptual systems and the internal logic of diverse social structures came to be recognized. This was as true of evolutionists such as Morgan (1871) as it was of functionalists such as Radcliffe-Brown (1941). There has indeed been a loosely relativistic streak in most brands of social anthropology ever since the acceptance of monogenism in the late nineteenth century. By definition, monogenism entails an acceptance of humankind's common origin, and one consequence was that anthropologists had to learn to explain differences in kinship structure as variations on a common theme. In the nineteenth century it was supposed that the differences represented stages in a single sequence of evolutionary development, through which all humankind was destined to pass; but in the twentieth century different systems came to be seen more as alternative cultural imprints on a 'blank slate' of universal human biology, or as variants of a limited set of logically possible arrangements for organizing human relationships. I vividly remember my own, somewhat naïve, conversion to relativistic anthropology, which was stimulated more than anything else by the revelation that the Iroquois have an 'Iroquois' relationship terminology structure just as logical as, but profoundly different from, my own English-language one, which in turn is formally of the 'Eskimo' type. Whether the logic of such systems is best understood within evolutionist, interpretivist, or structuralist paradigms is one of the great questions of anthropology.

Fourth, on a not unrelated point, the reason why anthropologists have been especially prone to 'discovering' structural parallels and contrasts within the realm of kinship is that kinship is the most transparently structured of all realms of human life. It is not merely that kinship experts have devised complex notation systems and other technical devices beyond the ken of, say, specialists in religion or politics. The logical primacy of the genealogical grid in kinship studies gives specialists a tool for cross-cultural comparison of a kind that is not available in other fields. Not since the Romans first recognized the equivalence of their gods and goddesses to those in the Greek pantheon have Western minds come up with such a clear-cut datum point for structural comparison – or, if one prefers, cultural 'translation' – as the notion of 'genealogical relationship'.

Fifth, and to turn full circle, kinship studies have promoted a quasi-fallacy that kinship is built on models that are more 'real' than those of religion, of economics, of politics, or of law. In truth, kinship is no more real than these other notions; it is rather that kinship structures are more apparent cross-culturally than the structures identified and studied by specialists in religion, economics and politics. The apparent cross-cultural 'reality' of kinship stems from an erroneous equation of 'kinship' with 'biology'. Kinship, for virtually all human societies, is built upon a putative biological foundation. Nevertheless, this is a cultural phenomenon and not *per se* a biological one. The incest taboo, the family, and the genealogical grid are substantive universals of human culture; but they are not indicators of identical ideological notions in all cultures, or of any specific 'facts' of procreation.

KINSHIP AND BIOLOGY

Humans and animals

Is kinship a distinctively *human* attribute? Dunbar, in the previous article, stressed the scope of comparison between human and non-human sociality, including what biologists often refer to as (non-human) 'kinship'. In another key paper, Fox (1975) considered the specific relationship between human and non-human primate 'kinship'. Fox's argument is in essence one of continuity: human kinship is not, in his biologically oriented view, merely a cultural construct, but is rooted in primate behaviour. Thus, according to Fox non-human primates possess all the important rudiments of human kinship. What makes them different is that some non-human primate societies have 'alliance' without 'descent' (namely those which live in single-male groups), while others have 'descent' without 'alliance' (namely those which live in multi-male groups). Human kinship systems invariably have both alliance and descent.

Such arguments may seem cogent, but they hold only if we accede to the premiss that human society is to be comprehended primarily in behavioural rather than cultural terms. Many social or cultural anthropologists would regard this premiss with some anathema, as a capitulation to 'biological determinism'. The emphasis on culture as *sui generis*, pure and untainted by nature (or 'biology'), marks a common spirit within traditions as diverse as late-nineteenth-century monogenic evolutionism, early-twentieth-century Boasian relativism, and late-twentieth-century structuralism and symbolic interpretivism. On this score, I must declare my sympathies with the mainstream and against Fox, not because he is wrong and they are right, but because, to me, kinship concerns 'biology' in quite a different sense. Fox glosses over those aspects of kinship which are founded in the capacity for language and symbolic thought, of which the notion of 'biology' is itself a product. It is this capacity that both distinguishes human kinship from the so-called 'kinship systems' of non-human animals, and underwrites the diversity of forms of kinship to be found in human societies. This diversity, in turn, provides the point of departure – in most if not all anthropological traditions – for structural and evolutionary comparisons between societies.

While it is reasonable to speak of other animals as having 'kinship', at least in a metaphorical sense, human kinship is fundamentally different from that of other species in that it is characterized by culturally articulated sets of rules which may operate to a great extent independently of observable behaviour. Studies of non-human sociality, among primates for example, are based on the data of observation and, as such, are unavoidably behaviourist in perspective. Studies of human sociality, on the other hand, depend on an understanding of the relation between behaviour and rules. Most studies of human sociality in the sphere of kinship have emphasized the pre-eminence of such rules (see, for example, Sahlins 1976, Fortes 1983). 'Kinship', as defined in the human context, depends on the existence of these rules, which in turn are understood by ordinary human beings in relation to culturally specific sets of linguistic and extralinguistic categories. The notion that kinship has a biological foundation is really dependent on the cultural definition of 'biology'. Even in Western societies, 'biological' kinship is often as much a metaphor for social relations as a statement of relevant biological fact. To me as a social anthropologist, this is exemplified in expressions like 'She has her mother's eyes', or 'He's my own flesh and blood', though sociobiologists may disagree. (Dunbar, in the preceding article, uses a similar example as evidence for precisely the opposite point of view!)

The great debate

Among humans, then, kinship is everywhere a cultural and social construction, whatever facts of reproduction may lie behind the variety of kinship systems to be found. This seemingly simple observation masks an intractable problem of definition, one which was first brought to light in the late 1950s but still casts its shadow on present-day thinking: the problem of 'the concept of kinship'.

The key protagonists in the great debate on this problem have included Gellner, Needham and Barnes. The debate was played out in a series of five articles, originally published in the journal *Philosophy of Science* between the years 1957 and 1963. I shall cite here from the reprints of Gellner's three articles, which appeared, along with other relevant essays, in his book *The Concept of Kinship* (1973: 154–203), as well as from Needham's (1960) reply to the first of Gellner's articles and Barnes's (1961) reply to the second. The minutiae of attack and counter-attack need not concern us. Much more important are the implications of the arguments, which hinge on the relation between 'biological' and 'social' kinship.

Gellner's position is that social kinship is axiomatically bound to a 'biological' foundation (1973 [1957]: 154–62). For Gellner, and indeed for the other protagonists, the terms 'biological' and 'physical' were taken as essentially synonymous and applied to the facts of reproduction. However, his purpose in his original paper was less to explain kinship *per se* than to use 'kinship structure' as a device with which to illustrate the operation of an 'ideal language', as conceived by Wittgenstein and other early-twentieth-century philosophers. The specific aspect of kinship structure which Gellner employed was the relation between generations as constructed in a hypothetical 'naming' system, in which children would bear the 'names' of their ancestors in a certain logical order. For example, 'if Joan has three sons and Joan's name is J, their names would be J1X, J2X, and J3X where X conveys the necessary information about their respective fathers or father and in turn their ancestry' (Gellner 1973: 158). Gellner was apparently assuming that members of his hypothetical society had much the same theory of procreation as members of his own society, for a *biological* physical relationship is assumed to be recognized as a preliminary to the naming of children.

Needham's attack centred on Gellner's apparent confusion of biological and social relationships. For Needham, only the latter are of any significance at all for the anthropologist, although he admits a degree of 'concordance' between 'biology' (here being defined as actual genetic parentage) and 'descent' (the socially defined rules for stipulating the relations between members of different generations). Gellner retorted that this latter admission on Needham's part rules out any attempt to separate biology from descent. They are inextricably bound together. What is important is that 'physical relationships' are used 'for social purposes' (Gellner 1973: 170), to be enunciated or ignored by social actors according to social customs and perhaps individual aspirations.

Barnes's position – which Gellner regarded as a 'refinement' of Needham's – is that the social anthropologist *should* be concerned with 'physical relationships' but only in the form in which these are defined by members of the society under consideration: the Trobriand Islanders, the Nuer, the English, etc. Thus there are three possible levels of analysis: of true genetic relationships between individuals, of 'biological' relationships (as defined by people of the society in question), and of social relationships. For Barnes, the first is irrelevant for social anthropology, while the latter two, and the relation between them, fall firmly within the subdiscipline's rightful domain of enquiry. Gellner (1973: 198–200) counters this suggestion by pointing out that social anthropologists themselves, in their ethnographies, do indeed take for granted 'physical reality' as defined within their own anthropological culture.

It seems to me that despite the apparent plausibility of Gellner's counter-attacks, Needham and more particularly Barnes have got it more or less right. Needham re-articulates the view, generally accepted both before and after Gellner, that anthropology should not concern itself with the truth or lack of truth in other people's belief systems (on this point, see Lewis in this volume, article 20). Thanks to his recognition of a flaw in Gellner's argument – the failure to distinguish between (1) true biological knowledge, or more specifically the knowledge of genetic relationships and the facts of reproduction, and (2) socially constructed 'biological' knowledge – Barnes has given us a useful analytical insight. He has defined precisely what had earlier lain implicit in anthropological understanding: the existence of three rather than two levels of analysis. The interplay between the biological and the social has a middle ground (socially constructed 'biological' knowledge), and the terms of this middle ground are not universal but culturally specific. Nevertheless, none of the contributors to the original debate tackled the final problem alluded to by Gellner: the fact that there is something, which we call 'kinship', that *is* understood cross-culturally and *is* described by anthropologists in a way which presupposes certain universals.

Needham (1971) and Barnard and Good (1984: 187–9) have commented on the need for a polythetic definition of 'kinship'. Kinship is understood cross culturally not because it has a single defining feature in all societies, but because similar sets of features are found in every society, without any single feature being necessary as *the* defining one. There are universals in kinship, but these universals are the constructs of anthropologists rather than of informants. Gellner's initial premiss was that human kinship systems are based on biology, and his conclusion, seven years on in the debate, was that this must be true because anthropologists themselves share a knowledge of certain biological facts and use this biological idiom in their ethnographic descriptions. But does the same biological idiom form part of the knowledge of all human societies? I think not. There is no reason to suppose that Australian Aborigines, Bedouin nomads, or Chinese peasants have the same notions of procreation that we have in the West. Even Western scientists have only relatively recently – in the nineteenth and twentieth centuries – come to understand anything of the mechanisms of ovulation and fertilization which educated Europeans now take for granted (see Barnes 1973: 65–6). The fact that scientific knowledge is itself defined, not in nature, but according to the culture of science, is a further complication.

Gellner's 'cultural universal' is neither true biological knowledge nor a shared cultural knowledge of biology. It is the genealogical grid, a device defined within anthropological culture, but one which is presumed by anthropologists to be of utility for the explanation of any kinship system, no matter what the indigenous theory of biology or of social relationship might be. The genealogical grid is an extremely useful methodological tool, but beyond that its existential status is difficult to establish.

'Fatherhood'

The problems of defining biological fatherhood have been couched in terms of the theoretical issues outlined above. True biology being irrelevant, the notion of 'father' is supposed to encompass two basic elements which, in relation to any particular child, may or may not specify the same individual. These elements are (1) the indigenous recognition of having contributed something by way of material substance to the child, and (2) the recognized conferral on the child of a specific social identity with its attendant rights and obligations. Drawing on a pair of Latin terms, the first element is said in conventional anthropological accounts to specify the child's *genitor*, whereas the second is said to specify its *pater*, or 'social father'.

However, the ethnographic situation is often more complicated than this simple distinction implies. Consider the beliefs of the Trobriand Islanders. Malinowski (1932 [1929]: 140–78) reports that, when a person dies, that person's spirit is believed first to go to the Island of the Dead and later to return to earth to impregnate a woman of its own subclan. Impregnation is said to be either through the head or through the vagina, but there is no suggestion in Malinowski's account that the woman's husband is believed to be involved in the contribution of genetic substance to the child. He simply 'opens up' the woman for childbirth. Children are supposed to resemble their mothers' husbands because of the close physical relationship between husband and wife, not because of the implantation of semen.

In his account, Malinowski took these beliefs at face value, as a reflection of the Trobrianders' alleged ignorance of the male role in conception. In their rather different ways, Spiro (1968) and Leach (1968) argued against this position, by appealing to the contrast between a public doctrine of the denial of physiological paternity and a more matter-of-fact (according to Leach) or repressed (according to Spiro) knowledge of the 'true' process of procreation (see Barnard and Good 1984: 170–4). Yet whatever the Trobriand equivalent of 'genitor' might be, there is little doubt that the Trobrianders have a concept of 'pater' as both genealogical (mother's husband) and social father, at least comparable to the Latin or English notion, though different in some respects. The Trobriand word is *tama*, which is applied rather more widely than its Latin or English equivalents (it denotes not only the father but also the father's brother, father's sister's son, etc.). Some evidence that *tama* really is genealogically, if not biologically, similar in definition to the notion of 'father' in other languages, may be found in the fact that its reciprocal is also the reciprocal of *ina* (mother): both 'parents' apply the word *latu* (child) to their 'children'. Further evidence is that the wife of any (classificatory) *tama* is called one's *ina*, and the husband of any *ina* is called one's *tama*. Socially, we can speak of those called *tama* as 'fathers' because of these genealogical equivalences, but it is always worth remembering that the notion of 'fatherly' attitudes and behaviour in one society may be quite different from that in another. For the Trobrianders, the father is an indulgent figure more akin to a favourite uncle in Western societies, whereas the Trobriand mother's brother is just the opposite, a Freudian father-figure *par excellence*.

'Motherhood'

The concept of 'motherhood' is even more interesting. It actually entails three distinct elements, each of which has potential for social recognition. We can distinguish: (1) the culturally defined genetic mother, (2) the bearing or carrying mother, and (3) the social mother. Following ancient Roman (Latin) usage, modern anthropologists have generally conflated the first two, often under the term *genetrix*, and distinguished the last by the term *mater*. Yet the conflation of the former cannot be sustained, either on logical or on biological grounds. Indeed the distinction, which ancient Romans and anthropologists alike have failed to make, is not new within Western thought.

The culturally defined genetic mother is the female recognized by society as having given material substance to the child. This substance, of course, need not correspond to that which modern biological science deems to be definitive of 'true' genetic motherhood. For example, the common belief, found in many parts of the world, that the child's 'flesh' comes from its mother's 'blood', while its 'bone' comes from its father's 'semen', reflects a notion of genetic motherhood (and fatherhood) which differs from that of Western science. As noted above, the true facts of genetics discovered by nineteenth- and twentieth-century scientists are, as such, largely irrelevant for the anthropological study of kinship; what are important are the indigenous theories. The peculiarity in the study of Western kinship is that Western science itself, or aspects of it, form part of our own folk knowledge.

The bearing or carrying mother is the person who gives birth to the child. Of course, in the *overwhelming* majority of cases, this is the same person as the culturally defined genetic mother, but the concept is nevertheless distinct. Consider three cases: the Orthodox Christian doctrine of the Virgin Mary as *Theotokos*, the Aranda belief in 'conception clans', and the modern medical notion of 'test-tube babies'. In each of these cases, the definition of the 'mother' is closely bound up with the relationship between this 'mother' and a culturally designated 'father'.

Greek-speaking Christians recognized the distinction between the genetic mother and the bearing mother as early as AD 431, when the Council of Ephesus formally proclaimed the doctrine of the Virgin Mary as *Theotokos* (literally 'God-bearer', though generally translated as 'Mother of God'). Nestorius, Bishop of Constantinople, had precipitated a debate on the matter when he denied that such a term should be used, since (he argued) Mary could only be the 'mother' of the human, not the divine, aspect of Christ's person. St Cyril of Alexandria, supported by the Council, disagreed, and it was his view that was accepted. Cyril argued from scriptural evidence that Mary did indeed *bear* the simultaneously fully divine and fully human Christ, and that to assume otherwise would be tantamount to splitting Christ into two separate persons. Similarly today, when modern Orthodox Christians (or indeed Roman Catholics) use the term 'Mother of God', they are not asserting anything about genes or chromosomes. On the contrary, to the Orthodox the doctrine of the *Theotokos* 'safeguards the unity of Christ's person' (Ware 1984: 33).

The idea of the 'conception clan' among the Aranda, an Aboriginal people of central Australia, may be rather different, but a similar distinction between aspects of 'motherhood' is implied in their belief system. The Aranda possess three types of clan: matrilineal, patrilineal and 'conception'. The matrilineal and patrilineal clans are clear enough; a person belongs to the matriclan of his or her mother and to the patriclan of his or her father. The conception clans are of a different order. Unlike the matrilineal and patrilineal clans, the conception clans are not exogamous. A man, his wife, and one or more of their children, may all belong to the same or to different conception clans. Membership in a conception clan is acquired through the belief that part of the 'genetic' substance of a child is contributed by a spirit, representing a totemic being, whose power is vested in a sacred site. If a woman should happen to pass by such a site, she may be fertilized by the totemic spirit. While virtually all Australian Aboriginal peoples recognize some form of spiritual fertilization (often by a spirit of the father's clan), those such as the Aranda who recognize conception filiation are unusual in that they posit a special relationship between the mother and the spirit itself, without reference to the father (see, for example, Maddock 1972: 30–2, Strehlow 1947: 86–96).

Our third example is the idea of the 'test-tube baby'. As an idea, this is hardly new. It was heralded several decades ago by prophetic if little known science-fiction writers like Sam Fuller (1936). Nor is it new to anthropologists. Nearly all existing high-tech procedures of procreation have their equivalents, albeit mystical rather than technical, envisaged in the indigenous ideologies of non-Western peoples (Héritier-Augé 1985). What is different about this notion is that the idea was eventually realized in technical practice. *In vitro* fertilization is now practised in several technologically advanced countries. Modern medicine has also made it possible to implant an ovum (either fertilized or unfertilized) from one woman into another. While 'test-tube babies' may be genetically related to both their prospective social parents, surrogate motherhood is a very real possibility.

All this has important and interesting implications for kinship theory. The distinctions between the various forms of biological and social parenthood and the potential kinship ideologies and social relationships that may emerge from putting them into practice are intricate and enigmatic. While some artificial methods are both possible and realized (artificial insemination *in utero*, fertilization *in vitro*, and ovum transfer), others are theoretically possible if not yet practical or practised. Consider, for example, the possibility of a person other than the genetic mother receiving a fertilized ovum or embryo, and where neither this surrogate mother nor the genetic mother becomes the social mother of the child, and where the sperm donor, too, is a different person from the child's intended social father. This would give the child no less than two 'fathers' and three 'mothers'! This is only one, if the most complex, of a great number of vexing possibilities (see Laborie *et al.* 1985: 14–16). The existence of customs such as wet-nursing among the European upper classes of historical times raises a further consideration, as in such cases the *nurturing* mother is yet another category, and one with a biological as well as a social role.

Of course, knowledge flows both ways. Just as 'test-tube babies' have important implications for kinship theory, so indigenous ideologies (such as those of the Australian Aborigines) have much to add to Western understandings of such medical practices and their social consequences. Yet, as Rivière (1985) has pointed out, little note has been taken of the contribution that anthropology can make in unravelling the cultural perceptions behind biological 'facts'. Politicians, lawyers, doctors and moral philosophers, all new to the problem, have had at least as much trouble explaining the relationship between genetics and parentage as have the Church Fathers, the Aranda, or the anthropologists who have considered such issues. Peculiarly, the Committee of Inquiry into Human Fertilization and Embryology, which reported to the British government in 1984 (Warnock 1985), included no anthropologists. For the time being at least, the philosophers have been left holding the baby.

Social parenthood

Social parenthood is best defined as a culturally recognized relationship which involves one or more of the following roles: nurturing and socialization (these, of course, are not necessarily exclusive of biological input), obligations of guardianship, and equivalent rights as a guardian (either *in rem* or *in personam*). In particular cases, social parenthood may or may not coincide with any specific kind of biological parenthood, but within a given society as a whole it is generally expected that those designated as 'parents' will normally have biological (in the sense of 'shared substance') or pseudo-biological ties, as well as jural ties, to their 'children'.

This definition is clearly imprecise, but it is exactly this imprecision which makes it more or less universally applicable to the great diversity of human societies (cf. Barnard and Good 1984: 187–9). The nature of 'parenting', of course, is extremely variable. As Malinowski (1966 [1927]: 14–19) found, the free and indulgent father–son relationship among the Trobriand Islanders manifested a very different notion of fatherhood from that of his native Central European experience.

Social parenthood is an outgrowth of the nuclear family, another commonly cited human universal. The simple two-parent nuclear family is the statistical norm in many Western and industrialized societies and serves as a basis for family organization elsewhere. Yet two qualifying factors (among other possibilities) deserve special mention: (1) the existence of alternative and more complex domestic arrangements, and (2) the practice of acquiring children from outside the nuclear family. The former is represented by such practices as co-residence of parents and adult children or of siblings, or polygamy and concubinage, and the latter is exemplified by fostering and adoption. Let us examine each in turn.

The classical formulation of the idea of the nuclear family as a universal may be attributed to Murdock (1949: 1–40), who argued that other human family types can be identified as variations on the nuclear family theme, like atoms 'aggregated, as it were, into molecules' (1949: 23). In such societies as have them, these alternative forms often entail 'parental' obligations on the part of other senior members of the domestic unit. Such family types include the compound family (defined as a polygamous household, e.g. a man, his wives and children), the joint family (involving a formalized collectivity of relatives, e.g. a group of brothers, their wives and children), and the extended family when defined as a domestic unit (usually understood as a less formalized collectivity of relatives sharing the same dwelling place). Even the one-parent family is, arguably, a form of nuclear family – simply one that involves one rather than the typical two parents.

The practice of acquiring children from outside the nuclear family is not uncommon. Two ways in which children are brought into the family for nurturing and socialization are 'fostering' and 'adoption'. The distinction between them is commonplace in modern legal systems, especially in the West. Fostering, or fosterage, involves nurturing and socialization without full social parenthood (often as an initial step towards adoption), while adoption does involve full social parenthood. However, this distinction is not always as clear-cut in other societies as it may seem in ours, and finer distinctions are sometimes called for. In West Africa, for example, there exists a complex of fostering practices based upon notions of legal obligation within and between kin groups, as well as upon the economic and political considerations of particular families. Domestic help on the part of fostered girls, apprenticeship and inherited clientship on the part of boys, even the 'pawning' of children between creditors, have all formed part of West African fosterage in recent times (E. N. Goody 1984).

A further word of caution: while in modern Western societies, 'adoption' is most commonly thought of as a method of incorporating and legitimating parentless children into a nuclear family, this is far from its original significance. Nor does the term convey much information about the culturally varied practices which it is called upon to designate. The ancient Roman notion of *adoptio* ('adoption' of a legal dependent), like the related concept of *adrogatio* ('adoption' of an independent), had much more in common with establishing political alliance through marriage than it did with the upbringing of hapless waifs. It had to do with the potential inheritance of wealth by one's chosen 'son'. The adopted 'son', more often than not an adult, would maintain filial affection towards his original parents, while acquiring the legal status of 'son' to someone else (E. N. Goody 1971: 340–2; cf. Rawson 1986: 173–86.)

GROUP STRUCTURE: DESCENT AND RESIDENCE

No one would deny the importance to human groups of close family ties, but 'kinship' in anthropological discourse generally connotes ties beyond even the extended family, and group structures beyond the domestic unit. Fortes (1969: 63–6, 100) distinguished close kin ties (in what he called the 'domestic' or 'familial domain') from more distant ones (representing the 'politico-jural domain'). Although these terms may seem to modern anthropologists both unwieldy and overly functionalist, the distinction drawn is nevertheless useful. The politico-jural domain is our concern in this section.

In describing the elements of that domain, it is also worthwhile to distinguish what may be termed the *formal* properties of rules of descent and residence, or even of descent systems, from those which might be called *substantive*. The formal properties of a rule are those which are derived directly, with mathematical or logical precision, from the rule itself. By contrast, the substantive implications of descent and residence rules will differ according to culture and social context.

Rules of descent

In formal terms, there are six logical possibilities for the transmission of group membership (or of other rights, as with the inheritance of property or succession to office) from one generation to the next (Needham 1971: 10). These correspond to the traditional notions of patrilineal, matrilineal, double, bilateral, parallel, and cross-descent. Patrilineal and matrilineal descent are virtually self-explanatory, whereas the distinction between double and bilateral descent tends to be more troublesome. The final two forms are in fact opposites.

Double (or duolineal) descent comprises simultaneous patrilineal and matrilineal descent: a child belongs to the patrilineal group of its father and the matrilineal group of its mother, and patrilineal and matrilineal groups belong to different sets. To take an imaginary example, the patrilineal groups may be localized clans, say 'Alsace', 'Burgundy' and 'Bourdeau', while the matrilineal groups are non-localized moieties, say the 'Whites' and the 'Reds'. If the groups are exogamous, as ethnographically they often are, then a 'White Alsace' must marry a 'Red Burgundy' or a 'Red Bourdeau' (not, say, a 'White Bourdeau'). Bilateral (or cognatic) descent, by contrast, comprises a recognition of descent from both *sides* of the family in the absence of any specified *lines* of descent. In a system based on cognatic descent there are no unilineal descent groups: no localized clans, no 'White' or 'Red' moieties. Whereas double descent is fairly rare, being found in a few societies in West and Southern Africa and in Australia, bilateral descent is very common, especially at the two ends of the evolutionary scale: in small-scale societies of hunter-gatherers and in modern industrialized societies.

Parallel and cross-descent are very rare forms. Parallel descent involves the transmission of sex-specific group or category membership from father to son and from mother to daughter. Cross (or alternating) descent involves transmission from father to daughter and mother to son (or mother's father to daughter's son and father's mother to son's daughter). These are typically found as secondary modes in conjunction with simultaneous patrilineal or matrilineal descent. For example, the Nama of Namibia formerly possessed both patrilineal clans, which were localized, and exogamous cross-descent name lines, which were not (Hoernlé 1925: 9, 16, Barnard 1975: 9–11).

Rules of residence

There are some seven possible rules of postmarital residence, several of which, when coupled with rules of descent, have formal implications for group structure. These possible rules include virilocal (in the natal locale of the husband), uxorilocal (in the natal locale of the wife), avunculocal (with the husband's mother's brother), amitalocal (with the wife's father's sister), duolocal (the separate residence of husband and wife), ambilocal (in either the natal locale of the husband or that of the wife), and neolocal (in a new locale) residence. Amitalocal residence – formally the inverse of avunculocal residence – is ethnographically unattested, though it might be anticipated in a strongly patrilineal, strongly female-dominated society, if such were ever found.

Virilocal and amitalocal residence, when coupled with patrilineal descent, have the logical propensity to foster the recruitment of *de facto* patrilineal groups. Virilocal residence would keep the men of the group together, while amitalocal residence would keep the women together. Uxorilocal residence and avunculocal residence, when coupled with matrilineal descent, would similarly foster the recruitment to matrilineal groups. Uxorilocal residence would keep the women of the group together, while avunculocal residence would keep the men together. Duolocal residence preserves the stability of existing residential groupings but is generally unstable and, where it is found (as among the Ashanti of West Africa), usually occurs only as an initial stage in married life (see Fortes 1949). In contrast to all of these, ambilocal residence and neolocal residence bear no formal relationship to potential unilineal groups. A composite type, uxori-virilocal residence, is common in societies in which bride-service is practised, since it permits the husband to engage in activities, such as hunting, on behalf of his affines in the early phases of marriage.

Residence and descent: cause and effect?

Over the years, many anthropologists have speculated on the relationship between residence and descent, on the general supposition that rules of post-marital residence are prerequisite to the formation of certain types of descent grouping. Most notable among those who have looked into the problem are Lowie, Murdock, and Ember and Ember.

Lowie (1947 [1920]: 157–62) was among the first to suggest a causative relationship between residence and descent. Drawing on a small number of geographically scattered cases, he argued that unilineal descent is derived from a combination of rules of residence and rules for the transmission of property. Murdock (1949: 201–18) took Lowie's hypothesis a bit further. He suggested that residence and descent are simply the middle part of a chain of causation from environment to social structure. In Murdock's view, environmental conditions and changes in subsistence practices affect patterns of residence. As in Lowie's model, residence rules affect descent group organization. The type of descent group organization, in turn, affects other aspects of social structure, such as relationship terminologies. For example, a system of production in which women perform the most important agricultural tasks might favour the development of uxorilocal residence, perhaps *de facto* at first and *de jure* later on. The recognition of such a rule of residence might result in the formation of matrilineal descent groups. The development of strong matrilineal groups, in turn, could favour the use of relationship terms that give recognition of this fact. Individuals might develop the habit of applying a single term to all relatives of a particular lineage, thus creating a so-called 'Crow' relationship terminology. Murdock set out to test such hypotheses statistically by using a carefully chosen sample of the world's societies to see what broad patterns emerged. Causation was inferred largely through intuition.

A more sophisticated attempt along the same lines was made by Ember and Ember. Using an updated version of Murdock's method of cross-cultural comparison, the Embers (1983) demonstrated a number of interesting correlations and cast doubt on some common assumptions. For example, they virtually disproved the traditional notion that the division of labour is a major determinant of the rule of residence. Instead, their findings indicate that virilocal residence is favoured by societies engaged in internal warfare, while uxorilocal residence is favoured by societies engaged in external warfare where women are involved in subsistence work (1983: 151–97). Avunculocal residence is seen to be a result of the conjunction of uxorilocal residence, matrilineal descent, a high male mortality rate, and a change towards internal (as opposed to external) conflict (1983: 249–59). With regard to descent, Ember and Ember noted (1983: 359–97) that warfare, in the presence of unilocal residence patterns, may act as a catalyst for the formation of unilineal descent groups. They argued that 'putative descent groups' (that is, groups commonly defined as 'clans') develop earlier than what they term 'demonstrated descent groups' (that is, 'lineages', where the genealogy is claimed to be known).

Kinship and property

A significant effect of descent group formation is the establishment of a mechanism for the transmission of property from one generation to the next. This fact was crucial to nineteenth-century evolutionists such as Maine (1861) and Morgan (1877), who regarded changes in the rules which govern the transmission of property as fundamental to the development of 'higher' forms of human society (see Kuper 1988). The theme has continued to inform more recent work, especially that of Goody (e.g. 1969, 1976, 1983), who has paid particular attention to the significance of bridewealth and dowry.

Dowry, which is often found in settled agricultural societies, is a payment by the family of the bride to the bride herself or to her husband. In many societies it is conceived of as payment in lieu of inheritance, in recognition of the fact that a woman has, upon marriage, left her natal kin group, whereas a man remains a member of his. *Bridewealth*, found commonly in patrilineal societies, and especially in pastoral ones, is a payment by a man or his kin to the kinsmen of the bride. Its usual function is the legitimation of children. If it is not paid, children may belong to their mother's rather than their father's patrilineal group (see also Goody and Tambiah 1973). *Bride-service*, found commonly in hunting and gathering and small-scale horticultural societies, is similar but involves the exchange of labour rather than of wealth. Bride-service may however have different implications for relations between men and women, in that it can give male labour (hunting) pre-eminence over female activities (Collier and Rosaldo 1982). Ultimately, all these exchanges are as crucial to alliance as they are to descent, for they help to determine relations between as well as within kin groups.

MARRIAGE AND MARITAL ALLIANCE

Problems in the definition of marriage

There has been much debate concerning the definition of 'marriage'. Rivière (1971: 57) has suggested that 'marriage as an isolable phenomenon of study is a misleading illusion'. Needham (1971: 7–8) concluded that the concept is 'worse than misleading in comparison and of no real use at all in analysis'. Both these authors, in their negative approaches to the problem, were essentially following the more positive, but nevertheless polythetic usage of Leach. Leach (1955: 183) explicitly defined the institution as 'a bundle of rights'. In any specific society these rights may include: legal fatherhood, legal motherhood, a monopoly of sexual access between married partners, rights to domestic services and other forms of labour, rights over property accruing to one's spouse, rights to a joint fund of property for the benefit of the children of the marriage, and recognized relations of affinity such as that between brothers-in-law. According to Leach, there is no single right which defines the institution of marriage, because in each society different sets of these rights will apply.

The most famous 'problem-case' for the universal definition of marriage is that of the Nayar, a high-status South Indian caste group. According to Fuller (1976: 99–122), the problem lies in the fact that traditional Nayar marriage entails two separate male roles which elsewhere in India are combined. Earlier ethnographers sought to define Nayar marriage only according to one or other of these two roles: the *sambandham* partner and the *tāli*-tier. In ordinary, non-Nayar Hindu marriage, the bridegroom ties a *tāli* (the gold emblem that symbolizes the union) around the neck of the bride. In Nayar marriage, a high-caste person, often a Brahman, ties the *tāli*. In an Indian context, the ceremony clearly indicates the first stage of a Hindu marriage. Yet in a world-wide context, the ceremony would seem to resemble more a puberty rite than a marriage, in that it grants the girl full womanhood and enables her to take lovers. The Nayar girl does not sleep with her *tāli*-tier; instead, she takes a series of lovers, called '*sambandham* partners', and they become the genitors of her children. The *sambandham* partners have little to do with the children they father. Children owe allegiance neither to the man who tied their mother's *tāli* nor to their genitors. Rather, since descent is reckoned matrilineally, they owe allegiance to their mother's brothers (cf. Gough 1959).

In an overwhelming majority of human societies, marriage is the mechanism which provides for the legitimation of children and defines their status in relation to the conjugal family and the wider kin group. Thus marriage is often distinguished from concubinage, which may serve similar social functions to marriage but denies full legitimacy to the union. However, in some societies marriage is considered as a *process* rather than an event, and is not easily distinguished from concubinage. This is the case among the Nharo Bushmen of Botswana (Barnard 1980: 120–2). Those Nharo who form liaisons with members of the neighbouring Kgalagari communities are regarded by the Nharo as married to them. Yet the Kgalagari, although they also recognize a processual aspect to marriage, *do* distinguish concubinage as a separate institution. Accordingly, they frequently regard their Nharo mates simply as concubines (cf. Kuper 1970).

In most societies, marriage may be ended by either divorce or death, though death need not always be the end of the union. Sometimes a spouse is claimed (with or without that person's right of refusal) by another member of the family of the deceased. Thus the custom of the *sororate* involves the marriage of a man to the sister of his deceased wife (a woman to the husband of her deceased sister), and the custom of the *levirate* involves the marriage of a man to the wife of his deceased brother (a woman to the brother of her deceased husband). The latter term may also include cases, as among the Nuer of southern Sudan, where the woman is taken in by the brother of her husband, but remains legally married to her dead husband and may bear children in his name.

The Nuer are also anthropologically famous as exemplars of other, more unusual forms of marriage (Evans-Pritchard 1951: 29–123). Apart from leviratic marriage and 'normal marriage', in which bridewealth of cattle is paid from the bridegroom to the family of the bride, there are two intriguing varieties known as 'ghost marriage' and 'woman marriage'. Ghost marriage is somewhat similar to leviratic marriage, except that it occurs when a man dies childless, especially if the death is a result of fighting. The ghost of the man is married to a woman and bridewealth is paid in his name. Children are fathered on his behalf by one of his close kinsmen. Woman marriage occurs usually when a woman is thought to be barren. She becomes socially 'male' and the 'husband' of another woman. The male kin of this female 'husband', or other males, beget children on her behalf. The males are recognized as genitors of her children, while she is defined as the pater.

Woman marriage is in fact found in other parts of Africa as well, perhaps most notably among the Lovedu of South Africa, where historically it has had a powerful impact on the political system. Since around 1800 the Lovedu have been ruled by a line of biologically female, but socially male women, the remote and mysterious 'Rain-Queens'. Ideally, each queen since that time has been polygamously married to other females in a pattern in which an actual (not classificatory) brother's daughter of each of the wives follows her father's sister to the queen's harem. They may remain there to be impregnated by male members of the royal house, or they may be redistributed to the queen's relatives or other subjects elsewhere. This pattern maintains alliances between the royal house and the people of scattered localities, each distant group proudly assenting to the power of the queen, their kinsman (Krige 1975: 249–52).

Incest and exogamy

'Incest' is defined technically as a sexual act between individuals prohibited from engaging in such acts because of their relationship. The relationship may be specified according to affinity or fictive kinship, as well as consanguinity. It may be one of close kinship or, as often as not, of distant relationship of a particular, culture-specific kind. Whereas proximity of relationship is important in Western society, other societies more frequently define as incestuous sexual acts between individuals of the same moiety, phratry or clan, between those defined as members of the mutual classificatory 'sibling' category or of the same household, or even between people related in a ritual or fictive way, such as those who share the same godparents.

The origin of the universal prohibition of incest has been the subject of debate since the late nineteenth century. Some early theorists concentrated on the incest taboo proper. Among these, Westermarck (1891) contended that humans have a natural abhorrence of mating with close kin, while Freud (1960 [1913]) suggested just the opposite. Other writers emphasized the relation between incest regulation and marriage prohibitions. Chief among these was McLennan who, in his famous *Primitive Marriage* (1970 [1865]), argued that the basis of human society was *exogamy*, or 'marrying out', a term which he invented. In McLennan's view, the prohibition of sex and consequently marriage within the tribe was directly related to the development of the capture of women, first as concubines, and later as wives. Indeed the symbols of capture, of yielding, or of giving away the bride are still common throughout the world in societies at all levels of social evolution. Problems like the relative importance of nature and nurture, the relation between descent and alliance, and the genesis of human society itself are also fundamentally related to the origin of this supreme taboo (see Fox 1980, Arens 1986). While the precise definition of an incestuous relationship is specific to each culture, the prohibition of incest is virtually universal. For this reason, Lévi-Strauss, in his most profound book *The Elementary Structures of Kinship* (1969 [1949]: 12–25), equated the incest taboo with the origin of culture itself.

More recently, exogamy has returned as a focus of serious interest. Knight, a contemporary anthropologist in the nineteenth-century mould, has been developing a theory of the origin of culture which hinges on the exchange of sex (from dominant women) for meat (from male hunters). The intricacies of this complex theory are well beyond the scope of this article, but the interesting point about it is that Knight has placed incest in the context of food exchange. Central to the theory is the so-called 'own kill rule', according to which individual hunters will not eat the animals they kill but will instead exchange them (Knight 1986, see also Knight 1991). Among many hunting and gathering and small-scale cultivating peoples, eating one's own kill is likened to incest, and the exchange of food is likened to the exchange of women.

800

Of course, exogamy is only one side of the marital coin. Endogamy also needs to be explained. 'Societies', 'tribes', and 'traditional communities' the world over are largely endogamous, almost by definition, but frequently marriage takes place within smaller units than these. While major reasons for societal, tribal or community endogamy may be geographical proximity and familiarity, the principal reasons for marriage to close kin may be more subtle. One reason is the preservation of the kin group or kin line itself, perhaps expressed symbolically by the notion of the 'purity of the blood'. A classic case of this is brother–sister marriage in Ancient Egypt (Hopkins 1980). Another explanation often encountered is that close kin marriage keeps property in the family or acts to preserve its unity. The best-known case here is preferential marriage to the father's brother's daughter, common in North Africa and the Near and Middle East. In this latter case, the explanation may be made explicit by informants, or, perhaps more commonly, may lie deep in the indigenous kinship consciousness – in what Bourdieu (1977: 30–71) calls the *habitus*, an environment of *dispositions* available to given individuals, which may be simultaneously strategic and unpremeditated. Indeed Bourdieu exemplifies this notion in a discussion of the reasons for father's brother's daughter marriage among the Kabyle of Algeria.

Finally in this connection, it is worth remembering that the rules of incest and those of exogamy need not coincide. As Fox (1967: 54) has put it, 'this is really only the difference between sex and marriage, and while every teenager knows these are different, many anthropologists get them confused.' Nor is it only anthropologists who sometimes make this confusion. The term 'incest' as used in the popular press more often than not refers to the incestuous rape of minors, a very specific form of incest indeed. In common language the term generally has a much wider meaning, though one which is often equated with sex between 'blood' relatives, and this does cause confusion when one considers incest as a legal category, which of course it is in both Western and non-Western societies. It is interesting to note that in Scotland, for example, the laws affecting incest and marriage coincide, and these cover both consanguines and affines. Yet in England and Wales it is perfectly legal to engage in sexual intercourse with certain classes of relatives who are forbidden in marriage. This is because English civil law forbids marriage to close affines and step-relatives while the criminal law of incest applies only to consanguines (Seear *et al.* 1984: 12–13).

Marital exchange

It would offend many in the field of kinship studies if I were to pass on without a word about alliance theory and prescriptive marriage. As Maybury-Lewis (1965: 228) has written: 'To paraphrase Dr Johnson, a man who is tired of issues such as these is tired of social anthropology'. Be that as it may, the theories and debates surrounding this subject are too numerous and too complex for me to review them in detail here (but see Barnard and Good 1984: 95–118). Instead I shall draw attention to just a few of the ideas which have sprung from the copious writings on the subject.

Alliance theory is usually traced to Lévi-Strauss's *The Elementary Structures of Kinship*, published in French in 1949, though not translated into English until 1969 from the French second edition (see also Lévi-Strauss 1963 [1945]: 46–9). In contrast to descent theory, alliance theory concentrates not on the formation of groups, but on the relations established between them through marriage. Lévi-Strauss distinguished 'elementary' from 'complex' structures, the former characterizing societies which have a positive marriage rule (e.g. one must marry someone of the category cross-cousin), the latter characterizing societies which have a negative marriage rule (e.g. as in Western society, one may marry anyone who is not close kin). Elementary structures are further divided into those where there is direct or restricted exchange (normally, marriage to the category of the first or second cross-cousin), those where there is generalized exchange (normally, marriage of men to the category of their matrilateral cross-cousins), and those which practise delayed direct exchange. The last would be a product of the repeated marriage of men to their patrilateral cross-cousins. For formal reasons, matrilateral marriage creates a pattern in which men take women in marriage from the same group as did their fathers, while patrilateral marriage creates a delayed pattern, with women going in one direction in one generation and back again in the next. For this and other reasons, true patrilateral cross-cousin marriage with delayed direct exchange is unworkable and found nowhere as a stable form. By contrast, generalized exchange is common, especially in Asia, and direct exchange is common in Amazonia and Australia (for further discussion of elementary structures in relation to the properties of exchange, see Gregory in this volume, Article 33).

French writers such as Lévi-Strauss, Dumont (e.g. 1975) and Héritier (e.g. 1981) have developed a high degree of sophistication in the comparative and theoretical analysis of structures of kinship alliance, but their approaches differ in subtle ways from their British counterparts, notably Leach (e.g. 1951) and Needham (e.g. 1962). To put it crudely, French theorists have long been expanding the applicability of alliance theory to cover a wider variety of societies, while British theorists (and to some extent also Dumont) have tended to narrow their concerns to the so-called 'prescriptive' systems, originally conceived as those with a precise rule of marriage to members of one particular class of kin. Yet, as Needham (1973) later revealed (if not in so many words), all sides had mistakenly assumed that they were dealing with two sets of phenomena when really there were three. The choice was not between 'prescription' and 'preference', however defined, but between 'prescription', 'preference', and 'practice'. In his new formulation, 'prescription' was equated with formal relations between categories in an idealized terminology structure, 'preference' was applied to the jural rules which are recognized in any given society, and 'practice' described the actual social behaviour of individuals, who may or may not follow such rules, regardless of the type of kinship system they possess. Contrary to earlier usage, these sets of rules and categories may be applied to the study of any kind of society, not just those elusive dwellers of isolated islands and impenetrable jungles who may or may not possess the perfect prescriptive system (cf. Schneider 1965). (For a summary of the current debate on this issue, see Barnard and Good 1984: 95–106.)

THE CLASSIFICATION OF RELATIVES

Morgan's discovery

Morgan's discovery of the 'classificatory system of relationship' is, in my view, the single most significant ethnographic breakthrough of all time. The idea that different societies classified relatives differently had been noted before Morgan, notably by the eighteenth-century missionary among the Iroquois, Joseph Lafitau (1724). Moreover, there is no reason to doubt that North American Indians were aware of the differences between the various indigenous systems of classification before Europeans were. What makes Morgan the pioneer is that he was the first to posit historical and sociological *reasons* for such differences in kinship classification, and to express these within a context of anthropological theory (cf. Rivers 1968 [1914]: 41–45, Service 1985: 13–34, Trautmann 1987).

Morgan had lectured and published on Iroquois kinship from the early 1850s, but his truly definitive statement on the subject was *Systems of Consanguinity and Affinity of the Human Family* (Morgan 1871). In the final chapter of this great work, Morgan advances a theory of the evolution of human society, a theory which hinges on the notion that relationship terminologies are slow to change and thus retain clues to ancient customs no longer practised. For example, if one calls father and father's brother by a single term, this might suggest an earlier rule or practice of marriage of a group of brothers all to the same woman. If one also calls one's mother and mother's sister by a single term, this might further suggest a rule or practice of 'group marriage', where a group of brothers would collectively be married to a group of sisters.

Very few anthropologists today subscribe to Morgan's specific evolutionary theory. Yet ever since Morgan, kinship studies have attempted to tease from relationship terminologies a multiplicity of sociological ideas, both grand and small. The exceptions are few. The most prominent exception in Morgan's own time was McLennan (1876: 329–407), arguably the founder of alliance theory. Although his own, earlier formulation of the stages of human social evolution was largely in agreement with Morgan's, he considered Morgan's classificatory system 'a system of mutual salutations merely' (1876: 366). Even some of those who have denied altogether the sociological importance of relationship terminologies, notably Kroeber (1909), have nevertheless recognized in them a deep psycho-structural significance. Lévi-Strauss, the doyen of both psycho-structuralism and alliance theory, dedicated his *Elementary Structures of Kinship* (1969 [1949]) neither to Kroeber nor to McLennan, but to Morgan.

Relationship terminologies

Morgan's own taxonomy of relationship terminologies included only two types: 'descriptive' and 'classificatory'. Descriptive terminologies were defined as those which distinguish direct relatives (direct ancestors and descendants of ego, plus ego's siblings) from collaterals (all other consanguineal relatives). Classificatory terminologies were defined as those which, at least from some genealogical points of reference, fail to make such a distinction. For example, the relationship terminology of the !Kung Bushmen would be regarded as descriptive, because, as in English, father and father's brother are terminologically distinguished (respectively, *ba* and *tsu* in !Kung; 'father' and 'uncle' in English). The relationship terminology of the Nharo Bushmen would be regarded as classificatory, because, as in Iroquois, father and father's brother are called by the same term (*auba, sauba* or *g//oba* in Nharo, depending on linguistic context; *ha-naih* in Seneca Iroquois). In both Nharo and Iroquois, the mother's brother is called by a different term (*tsxõba* or *mamaba* in Nharo; *hoc-no-sih* in Seneca Iroquois).

After Morgan, typologists came to realize the inadequacy of such a simple, dual classification. It is not merely the presence or absence of one particular distinction (direct versus collateral) which is important. Other distinctions are made in the relationship terminologies of the world, and these, too, require anthropological understanding and explanation. Kroeber (1909), perhaps over-ambitiously, posited eight such distinctions, and of these one emerged as being of special ethnographic and theoretical importance. This is the distinction between parallel relatives (direct relatives and those collaterals who are related through a same-sex sibling link, e.g. mother's sister, mother's sister's son, mother's sister's daughter) and cross-relatives (those who are related through an opposite-sex sibling link, e.g. mother's brother, mother's brother's son, mother's brother's daughter).

On the basis of these two distinctions, applied in the generation of ego's parents, Lowie (1928, 1929) and Kirchhof (1931) recognized four ideal types. Take males of this generation, for example (the structure for female relatives is the mirror image of that for males). (1) One might call father, father's brother, and mother's brother all by a single term (as in the Hawaiian language). Alternatively, (2) one might classify father and father's brother by one term and mother's brother by a different one (as in Iroquois or Nharo). Another possibility (3) is to classify father by one term and father's brother and mother's brother by another (as in English or !Kung). Finally, (4) one might classify each genealogical position by a distinct term (as, say, in Nuer,

Armenian or Gaelic). Lowie called these four ideal types, respectively, 'generational', 'bifurcate merging', 'lineal', and 'bifurcate collateral'; the fifth logical possibility, which would be to equate the father and mother's brother while distinguishing the father's brother, is unattested. Generational terminologies make neither direct–collateral nor parallel–cross distinctions. Bifurcate merging terminologies make parallel–cross distinctions only. Lineal terminologies make direct–collateral distinctions only. Bifurcate collateral terminologies make both kinds of distinction.

While Kirchhof and Lowie emphasized the classification of relatives in the first ascending generation, Murdock (1949) emphasized their classification in ego's own generation. His typology consists of six classes. 'Hawaiian' terminologies are those which make no distinction between siblings and cousins, except of sex. 'Iroquois' terminologies distinguish cross-cousins from parallel cousins (and often classify siblings by the same term as that for parallel cousins). 'Eskimo' terminologies do not make parallel–cross distinctions, but instead distinguish cousins (collaterals) from siblings (direct relatives). 'Sudanese' terminologies, like Lowie's 'bifurcate collateral' ones, make both kinds of distinction. Typically, they lack any general word equivalent to English 'cousin' and call all cousins by strings of possessives. For example, *mac bràthair màthar* (literally 'son of the brother of the mother') is the traditional Scots Gaelic term for a person in that relationship, though it is nowadays also possible to employ a generic, namely *co-ogha* 'co-grandchild'. (It is of course only since the Norman Conquest that English has been transformed from a Sudanese into an Eskimo terminology, thanks to its acquisition of the French word *cousin*.)

Murdock's other two types, 'Crow' and 'Omaha', like Iroquois, distinguish parallel from cross-relatives. The difference is that they treat generational differences in a peculiar way, that is, peculiar for those who do not grow up in such a culture. The defining feature of Murdock's Crow type (also known as 'Choctaw') is that it classifies father's sister and father's sister's daughter by the same term. The defining feature for Omaha is that it classifies mother's brother and mother's brother's son by the same term. Very often, such terminologies make further equations across generational lines. For example, Crow terminologies generally classify father and father's sister's son by the same term, and Omaha terminologies generally classify mother and mother's brother's daughter by the same term. The logic here is simple. In societies which possess Crow terminologies, more often than not matrilineal groups are present, and ego simply assimilates all members of his or her father's matrilineal group and calls them by two terms, one for males and one for females. The Trobriand Islanders are a well-known example. Likewise, Omaha terminologies are frequently found in strongly patrilineal societies, where similar equations are made in reference to ego's mother's patrilineal group. This type is common among North American Indians and throughout much of Africa and South-east Asia. Further equations following the same logic may occur. For example, in many Omaha systems one's mother's mother's brother, mother's mother's brother's son, and other male members of one's mother's mother's patrilineage are all called by the same term.

Crow–Omaha terminology and alliance structures

Over the years, the notions of Crow and Omaha systems have taken on a new significance in the light of Lévi-Strauss's theory of elementary and complex structures. Lévi-Strauss himself (1966: 18–20, 1969: xxxv–xlii) stressed the importance of 'Crow–Omaha' structures, not simply as terminology types, but as mechanisms which make possible the extension of marriage prohibitions to such a degree that the resulting complex structures come to resemble elementary ones.

Take, for example, the Samo of Burkina Faso, described by Héritier (1981: 81–7, 105–26). They trace descent patrilineally, and have a terminology structure of the Omaha type. They prohibit marriage to anyone born into ego's father's, ego's mother's, ego's father's mother's, or ego's mother's mother's patrilineal groups. Members of each of these are classified by terms which indicate their status as 'kin' forbidden in marriage, while the system is further complicated by the practice of polygyny and consequent restrictions on the choice of second and subsequent spouses. The prohibitions are so numerous that specific alliances come to be made between groups by direct exchange.

Crow–Omaha structures are, in effect, *ideologically complex*, because they rely upon negative marriage rules, but *empirically elementary*, because they narrow the range of choice of spouse to specified descent groups (Barnard 1978: 73–4). Although in the Samo case direct exchange is reported, other cases more closely resemble generalized exchange, which Crow-Omaha structures simultaneously mimic and reverse as if through a distorted mirror. Unlike the classic idea of generalized exchange in which sons or daughters repeat the marriages of their parents, the patterns of exchange in Crow–Omaha structures can only be egocentric. In 'true', sociocentric generalized exchange (including classic cases such as the Purum of north-eastern India or the Kachin of Burma) the bonds and the hierarchical relations between groups are strengthened with each marriage. In Crow–Omaha structures, by contrast, the constellation of permitted and prohibited potential spouses changes with each marriage contracted, and repetition is not allowed. In Lévi-Strauss's terms (1966: 19), the one turns 'kinsmen into affines', while the other turns 'affines into kinsmen'. In other words, while to the individual seeking a spouse there may be no logical difference between the two structures, from the standpoint of social groups there is all the difference in the world.

THE FUTURE OF KINSHIP STUDIES

Lévi-Strauss's classic essay on 'The future of kinship studies' (1966) picked out the Crow–Omaha or 'semi-complex' systems as the loci of interest for the coming generation of scholarship. With Héritier's work, as well as that of a host of others in diverse traditions, this prediction has, to some degree, been borne out (see Welter 1988). Nevertheless, there is little doubt that systems of prescriptive alliance have captured more attention than have Crow–Omaha ones. A recent attempt to put Needham's (1973) three-level distinction (between categories, rules, and practices) into effect is Good's (1981) insightful study of the Kondaiyankottai Maravar of South India. But can we go any further in the study of 'prescription'? The major contributors to the theory of prescriptive systems have all gone on to other things. There seems to be little if any room for further refinements in that sphere of interest.

One area which has long been increasing in popularity is mathematical modelling, though this is nothing new. Malinowski (1930: 19), for whom kinship was 'a matter of flesh and blood, the result of sexual passion and maternal affection, of long intimate daily life, and a host of personal intimate interests', berated Rivers and others for their exclusive attention to the formal properties of kinship systems. Indeed Rivers looked forward to the day when 'many parts of the description of the social systems of savage tribes will resemble a work on mathematics in which the results will be expressed by symbols, in some cases even in the form of equations' (1914, I: 10). There is a sense in which Rivers's prediction has come true. The form, if not the content, of human kinship may share properties of algebraic systems, just as algebraic systems in turn share properties with geometric ones. To some, alliance structures are but patterns which can be created through actual or imagined marriages between people belonging to actual or imagined groups or categories. In recent years Australian Aboriginal kinship has been likened to the double helix (Denham *et al.* 1979); twisted cylinders (Tjon Sie Fat 1983); kaleidoscopic reflections, frieze patterns and wallpaper designs (Lucich 1987: 1–150); and barn dances (Allen 1982). But building mathematical models for the sake of it cannot be the answer.

On firmer ground, Lévi-Strauss (1968: 351) once suggested that in presenting Aboriginal kinship in formal terms we might, unknowingly, be 'trying to get back to the older [indigenous] theory at the origin of the facts we are trying to explain'. He had in mind the idea of a primeval 'Plato' or 'Einstein', who used kinship as a means of abstract expression. This idea was ridiculed by Hiatt (1968), and most anthropologists today would probably prefer Hiatt's sceptical empiricism to Lévi-Strauss's conjectures. Von Brandenstein (1970: 49), in turn, has likened Aboriginal thought to medieval alchemy and the four-humour system of Galen, while Turner (1985) offers a brilliant reanalysis of the Book of Genesis through Aboriginal spectacles. The truth is that while wild ideas and grudging squabbles like these give anthropology its purchase on the broader issues of Western philosophy and social theory, at the same time they do as much to obscure as to reveal the cultural systems whose properties and workings we set out to understand.

I believe that the future of kinship studies lies in two directions: first, in the greater awareness of the importance of such studies in understanding our own preconceptions, as they touch on such issues as *in vitro* fertilization, surrogacy, and the law of incest; and second, in the continuing rediscovery that kinship is good to think with. Travel in these two directions can be simultaneous, and by doing so we shall not necessarily end up in two separate places.

REFERENCES

Allen, N. J. (1982) 'A dance of relatives', *Journal of the Anthropological Society of Oxford* 13: 139–46.

Arens, W. (1986) *The Original Sin: Incest and its Meaning*, New York: Oxford University Press.

Barnard, A. (1975) 'Australian models in the South West African highlands', *African Studies* 34: 9–18.

—— (1978) 'Universal systems of kin categorization', *African Studies* 37: 69–81.

—— (1980) 'Sex roles among the Nharo Bushmen of Botswana', *Africa* 50: 115–24.

Barnard, A. and Good, A. (1984) *Research Practices in the Study of Kinship*, London: Academic Press.

Barnes, J. A. (1961) 'Physical and social kinship', *Philosophy of Science* 28: 296–99.

—— (1973) 'Genetrix : genitor :: nature : culture?', in J. Goody (ed.) *The Character of Kinship*, Cambridge: Cambridge University Press.

Beattie, J. H. M. (1964) 'Kinship and social anthropology', *Man* 64: 101–3.

Borland, C. H. (1979) 'Kinship term grammar: a review', *Anthropos* 74: 326–52.

Bourdieu, P. (1977) *Outline of a Theory of Practice*, Cambridge: Cambridge University Press.

Brandenstein, C. G. von (1970) 'The meaning of section and section names', *Oceania* 41: 39–49.

Collier, J. F. and Rosaldo, M. Z. (1982) 'Politics and gender in simple societies', in S. B. Ortner and H. Whitehead (eds) *Sexual Meanings: the Cultural Construction of Gender and Sexuality*, Cambridge: Cambridge University Press.

Denham, W. W., McDaniel, C. K. and Atkins, J. R. (1979) 'Aranda and Alyawara kinship: a quantitative argument for a double helix model', *American Ethnologist* 6: 1–24.

Dumont, L. (1975) *Dravidien et Kariera: l'alliance de marriage dans l'inde du sud et en australie*, Paris/The Hague: Mouton.

Ember, M. and Ember, C. (1983) *Marriage, Family, and Kinship: Comparative Studies of Social Organization*, New Haven: Human Relations Area Files Press.

Evans-Pritchard, E. E. (1951) *Kinship and Marriage Among the Nuer*, Oxford: Clarendon Press.

Fortes, M. (1949) 'Time and social structure: an Ashanti case study', in M. Fortes (ed.) *Social Structure: Studies Presented to A. R. Radcliffe-Brown*, London: Oxford University Press.

—— (1969) *Kinship and the Social Order: the Legacy of Lewis Henry Morgan*, London: Routledge & Kegan Paul.

—— (1983) *Rules and the Emergence of Society*, London: Royal Anthropological Institute Occasional Paper no. 39.

Fox, R. (1967) *Kinship and Marriage: an Anthropological Perspective*, Harmondsworth: Penguin.

—— (1975) 'Primate kin and human kinship', in R. Fox (ed.) *Biosocial Anthropology*, A.S.A. Studies no. 1, London: Malaby Press.

—— (1980) *The Red Lamp of Incest: an Inquiry into the Origins of Mind and Society*, Notre Dame, Ind.: University of Notre Dame Press.

Freud, S. (1960[1913]) *Totem and Taboo*, London: Routledge & Kegan Paul.

Fuller, C. J. (1976) *The Nayars Today*, Cambridge: Cambridge University Press.

Fuller, S. (1936) *Test Tube Baby*, New York: Godwin.

Gellner, E. (1973) *The Concept of Kinship and Other Essays*, Oxford: Blackwell.

Good, A. (1981) 'Prescription, preference and practice: marriage patterns among the Kondaiyankottai Maravar of South India', *Man* (N.S.) 16: 108–29.

Goody, E. N. (1971) 'Forms of pro-parenthood: the sharing and substitution of parental roles', in J. Goody (ed.) *Kinship: Selected Readings*, Harmondsworth: Penguin.

—— (1984) 'Parental strategies: calculation or sentiment? Fostering practices among West Africans', in H. Medick and D. W. Sabean (eds) *Interest and Emotion: Essays on the Study of Family and Kinship*, Cambridge and Paris: Cambridge University Press and Éditions de la Maison des Sciences de L'Homme.

Goody, J. R. (1969) *Comparative Studies in Kinship*, London: Routledge & Kegan Paul.

—— (1976) *Production and Reproduction: a Comparative Study of the Domestic Domain*, Cambridge: Cambridge University Press.

—— (1983) *The Development of the Family and Marriage in Europe*, Cambridge: Cambridge University Press.

Goody, J. R. and Tambiah, S. J. (1973) *Bridewealth and Dowry*, Cambridge: Cambridge University Press.

Gough, E. K. (1959) 'The Nayars and the definition of marriage', *Journal of the Royal Anthropological Institute* 89: 23–34.

Héritier, F. (1981) *L'Exercice de la parenté*, Paris: Gallimard.

Héritier-Augé, F. (1985) 'La cuisse de Jupiter. Réflexions sur les nouveaux modes de procreation', *L'Homme* 94 (xxv [2]): 5–22.

Hiatt, L. R. (1968) 'Gidjingali marriage arrangements', in R. B. Lee and I. DeVore (eds) *Man the Hunter*, Chicago: Aldine.

Hoernlé, A. W. (1925) 'The social organization of the Nama Hottentots of Southwest Africa', *American Anthropologist* 27: 1–24.

Hopkins, K. (1980) 'Brother–sister marriage in Roman Egypt', *Comparative Studies in Society and History* 22: 303–54.

Kirchhof, P. (1931) 'Die Verwandtschaftsorganisation der Urwaldstämme Südamerikas', *Zeitschrift für Ethnologie* 63: 85–193.

Knight, C. D. (1986) 'The hunter's own kill rule', paper presented at the Fourth International Conference on Hunting and Gathering Societies, London, 8–13 September 1986.

—— (1991) *Blood Relations: Menstruation and the Origins of Culture*, New Haven and London: Yale University Press.

Krige, E. J. (1975) 'Asymmetric matrilateral cross-cousin marriage: the Lovedu case', *African Studies* 34: 231–57.

Kroeber, A. L. (1909) 'Classificatory systems of relationship', *Journal of the Royal Anthropological Institute* 39: 77–84.

Kuper, A. (1970) 'The Kgalagari and the jural consequences of marriage', *Man* (N.S.) 5: 355–81.

—— (1988) *The Invention of Primitive Society: Transformations of an Illusion*, London: Routledge.

Laborie, F., Marcus-Steiff, J. and Moutet, J. (1985) 'Procréations et filiations. Logiques des conceptions et des nominations', *L'Homme* 95 (xxv [3]): 5–38.

Lafitau, J. (1724) *Moeurs des sauvages amériquaines, comparée aux moeurs des premiers temps*, 2 vols, Paris: Saugrain L'aîné.

Leach, E. R. (1951) 'The structural implications of matrilateral cross-cousin marriage', *Journal of the Royal Anthropological Institute* 81: 54–104.

—— (1955) 'Polyandry, inheritance and the definition of marriage', *Man* 55: 105–13.

—— (1968) 'Virgin birth' [letter]. *Man* (N.S.) 3: 655–66.

Lévi-Strauss, C. (1963) *Structural Anthropology*, New York: Basic Books.

—— (1966) 'The future of kinship studies', *Proceedings of the Royal Anthropological Institute for 1965*: 13–22.

—— (1968) 'The concept of primitiveness', in R. B. Lee and I. DeVore (eds) *Man the Hunter*, Chicago: Aldine.

—— (1969 [1949]) *The Elementary Structures of Kinship* (second edition), London: Eyre & Spottiswoode.

Lowie, R. H. (1928) 'A note on relationship terminologies', *American Anthropologist* 30: 263–68.

—— (1929) 'Relationship terms', *Encyclopaedia Britannica*, 14th edn, 19: 84–6.

—— (1947 [1920]) *Primitive Society*, 2nd edn, New York: Liveright.

Lucich, P. (1987) *Genealogical Symmetry: Rational Foundations of Australian Kinship*, Armidale: Light Stone Publications.

McLennan, J. F. (1970 [1865]) *Primitive Marriage*. Chicago: University of Chicago Press.

—— (1876) *Studies in Ancient History, Comprising a Reprint of Primitive Marriage*, London: Bernard Quaritch.

Maddock, K. (1972) *The Australian Aborigines: a Portrait of Their Society*, London: Allen Lane.

Maine, H. (1861) *Ancient Law*, London: John Murray.

Malinowski, B. (1930) 'Kinship', *Man* 30: 19–29.

—— (1966 [1927]) *The Father in Primitive Psychology*, New York: W. W. Norton.

—— (1932 [1929]) *The Sexual Life of Savages in North-Western Melanesia*, London: Routledge & Sons.

Maybury-Lewis, D. H. P. (1965) 'Prescriptive marriage systems', *Southwestern Journal of Anthropology* 21: 207–30.

Morgan, L. H. (1871) *Systems of Consanguinity and Affinity of the Human Family*, Washington: Smithsonian Institution.

—— (1877) *Ancient Society: Researches in the Lines of Human Progress from Savagery through Barbarism to Civilization*, New York: Holt.

Murdock, G. P. (1949) *Social Structure*, New York: Macmillan.

Needham, R. (1960) 'Descent systems and ideal language', *Philosophy of Science* 27: 96–101.

—— (1962) *Structure and Sentiment*, Chicago: University of Chicago Press.

—— (1971) 'Remarks on the analysis of kinship and marriage', in R. Needham (ed.) *Rethinking Kinship and Marriage*, A.S.A. Monographs no. 11, London: Tavistock.

—— (1973) 'Prescription', *Oceania* 42: 166–81.

Radcliffe-Brown, A. R. (1941) 'The study of kinship systems', *Journal of the Royal Anthropological Institute* 71: 49–89.

Rawson, B. (1986) 'Children in the Roman *familia*', in B. Rawson (ed.) *The Family in Ancient Rome: New Perspectives*, London: Croom Helm.

Rivers, W. H. R. (1914) *The History of Melanesian Society*, 2 vols, Cambridge: Cambridge University Press.

—— (1968 [1914]) *Kinship and Social Organization*, London: Athlone Press.

Rivière, P. G. (1971) 'Marriage: a reassessment', in R. Needham (ed.), *Rethinking Kinship and Marriage*, A.S.A. Monographs no. 11, London: Tavistock.
—— (1985) 'Unscrambling parenthood: the Warnock Report, *Anthropology Today* 1(4): 2–7.
Sahlins, M. (1976) *The Use and Abuse of Biology: an Anthropological Critique of Sociobiology*, London: Tavistock Publications.
Schneider, D. M. (1965) 'Some muddles in the models: or, how the system really works', in M. Banton (ed.) *The Relevance of Models for Social Anthropology*, A.S.A. Monographs no. 1, London: Tavistock.
Seear, Baroness *et al.* (1984) *No Just Cause. The Law of Affinity in England and Wales: Some Suggestions for Change*, London: CIO Publishing.
Service, E. R. (1985) *A Century of Controversy: Ethnological Issues from 1860 to 1960*, Orlando: Academic Press.
Spiro, M. E. (1968) 'Virgin birth, parthenogenesis and physiological paternity: an essay in cultural interpretation', *Man* (N.S.) 3: 242–61.
Strehlow, T. G. H. (1947) *Aranda Traditions*, Melbourne: Melbourne University Press.
Tjon Sie Fat, F. E. (1983) 'Age metrics and twisted cylinders: predictions from a structural model', *American Ethnologist* 10: 585–604.
Trautmann, T. R. (1987) *Lewis Henry Morgan and the Invention of Kinship*, Berkeley: University of California Press.
Turner, D. H. (1985) *Life Before Genesis: a Conclusion*, New York: Peter Lang.
Ware, T. (1984) *The Orthodox Church*, 2nd edn, Harmondsworth: Penguin.
Warnock, M. (1985) *A Question of Life*, Oxford: Blackwell.
Welter, V. (1988) *Verwandtschaftsterminologie und Sozialorganisation: Einige ethnosoziologische Interpretationen der Crow/Omaha-Systeme*, Emsdetten: Andreas Gehling.
Westermarck, E. (1891) *The History of Human Marriage* (3 volumes), London: Macmillan.

FURTHER READING

Barnard, A. and Good, A. (1984) *Research Practices in the Study of Kinship*, London: Academic Press.
Bohannan, P. and Middleton, J. (eds) (1968) *Kinship and Social Organization*, Garden City: Natural History Press.
Dumont, L. (1971) *Introduction à deux theories d'anthropologie sociale*, Paris and The Hague: Mouton.
Fox, R. (1967) *Kinship and Marriage: an Anthropological Perspective*, Harmondsworth: Penguin.
Goody, J. R. (1969) *Comparative Studies in Kinship*, London: Routledge & Kegan Paul.
—— (ed.) (1971) *Kinship*, Harmondsworth: Penguin.
—— (ed.) (1973) *The Character of Kinship*, Cambridge: Cambridge University Press.
Graburn, N. (ed.) (1971) *Readings in Kinship and Social Structure*, New York: Harper & Row.
Héritier, F. (1981) *L'Exercice de la parenté*, Paris: Gallimard.
Leach, E. R. (1961) *Rethinking Anthropology*, London: Athlone Press.
Lévi-Strauss, C. (1966) 'The future of kinship studies', *Proceedings of the Royal Anthropological Institute for 1965*: 13–22.
—— (1969 [1949]) *The Elementary Structures of Kinship*, 2nd edn, London: Eyre & Spottiswoode.

Morgan, L. H. (1871) *Systems of Consanguinity and Affinity of the Human Family*, Washington: Smithsonian Institution.

Needham, R. (ed.) (1971) *Rethinking Kinship and Marriage*, A.S.A. Monographs no. 11, London: Tavistock.

—— (1973) 'Prescription', *Oceania* 42: 166–81.

—— (1986) 'Alliance', *Oceania* 56: 165–80.

Schneider, D. M. (1980 [1968]) *American Kinship: a Cultural Account*, 2nd edn, Englewood Cliffs, NJ: Prentice-Hall.

—— (1984) *A Critique of the Study of Kinship*, Ann Arbor: University of Michigan Press.

Trautmann, T. R. (1987) *Lewis Henry Morgan and the Invention of Kinship*, Berkeley: University of California Press.

Wolfram, S. (1987) *In-laws and Outlaws: Kinship and Marriage in England*, London: Croom Helm.

29

UNDERSTANDING SEX AND GENDER

Henrietta L. Moore

BIOLOGY AND CULTURE

In the discussion of sex and gender in human social life, one term emerges as particularly problematic, and that term is 'natural'. In public debates concerning the origins of so-called sex differences and the nature of relations between women and men — debates which are conducted in the media, in day-to-day interactions and in academic discourses — a series of assertions are made which utilize the word 'natural' in ways which are fundamentally misleading. These assertions are of several kinds, but a common feature of many is that they describe the differences established in social life between women and men as originating in biology. This apparently quite straightforward proposition has been strongly contested by work in the social sciences over the last two decades. The labour of contestation and refutation has been complicated by a particular view of biology itself: a view which has been shared by many commentators both academic and non-academic.

It is often, as Fausto-Sterling (1985) points out, extremely difficult to unravel arguments about the way in which biology is supposed to determine human behaviour, because of the large number of unconnected or very tenuously associated phenomena which are thrown together under that rubric. One prominent example is the relationship which is supposed to exist between male hormones and aggression. Under a variety of stimuli, these hormones are claimed to provide the biological basis for warfare (understood as organized group aggression), for the political and economic dominance of men, for juvenile delinquency rates in young males, for violent crime in general and for reckless driving (Fausto-Sterling 1985: 125). Fausto-Sterling examines these arguments, and other familiar ones about the biological basis of sex differences, and shows them to be unfounded for a variety of reasons. However, she emphasizes a particular difficulty with arguments of this kind, which is that they imply that the relationship between biology and social behaviour can be understood as a straightforward one of cause and effect. Contemporary research in biology explicitly rejects this view, arguing instead that biology is a dynamic component of our existence and not a one-way determinant. As Fausto-Sterling observes, it is now possible to argue for a more complex analysis, in which

> an individual's capacities emerge from a web of interactions between the biological being and the social environment. . . . Biology may in some manner condition behaviour, but behaviour in turn can alter one's physiology. Furthermore, any particular behaviour can have many different causes. This new vision challenges the hunt for fundamental biological causes at its very heart, stating unequivocally that the search itself is based on a false understanding of biology.

(1985: 8)

This 'new vision' of the relationship between biology and behaviour, and the revised view of biology on which it is based, have been relatively slow to influence thinking in the social sciences because of the way in which social scientists have been, and continue to be, haunted by the shadow of biological determinism, especially in its most recent guise as sociobiology. It was, in part, to try and combat biologically deterministic arguments that feminist anthropologists in the 1970s emphasized the importance of distinguishing biological sex from gender. The idea that the terms 'woman' and 'man' denote cultural constructs rather than natural kinds had been mooted much earlier by Margaret Mead who, in *Sex and Temperament* (1935), had argued that considerable cultural variability exists in definitions of femaleness and maleness. This approach was extended and developed in the 1970s, and much new ethnographic evidence for variability in what the categories 'woman' and 'man' mean in different cultural contexts demonstrates clearly that biological differences between the sexes cannot provide a universal basis for social definitions. In other words, biological differences cannot be said to determine gender constructs, and, as a result, there can be no unitary or essential meaning attributable to the category 'woman' or to the category 'man' (Moore 1988: 7). The distinction between biological sex and gender has proved absolutely crucial for the development of feminist analysis in the social sciences, because it has enabled scholars to demonstrate that the relations between women and men, and the symbolic meanings associated with the categories 'woman' and 'man', are socially constructed and cannot be assumed to be natural, fixed or predetermined. Cross-cultural data have been particularly useful in this regard, providing the empirical evidence to show that gender differences and gender relations are culturally and historically variable.

In spite of this work, however, the actual relationship between biological sex and the cultural construction of gender has remained largely unexamined, since this relationship has been assumed to be relatively unproblematic. Thus, while it is acknowledged that gender constructs are not determined by biological sex differences, there has been a tendency, in much social science writing, to assume that gender categories and gender meanings are cultural devices designed to comprehend and manage the obvious fact of binary sex differences. These sex differences, in turn, are taken to be clearly visible in the physical attributes of the human body, and are recognized as crucial for the biological reproduction of human populations. In short, there has been an implicit assumption that binary biological sex differences underlie, even if they do not determine, gender categories and gender relations (Yanagisako and Collier 1987: 15).

However, this point needs further clarification in the light of the arguments of a number of anthropologists to the effect that some cultures do not emphasize the biological — by which they appear to mean 'physiological' — differences between women and men. In other words, differences between women and men are said to exist in certain domains of social life, for example with regard to spiritual potency, ritual efficacy or moral worth, but are not thought to be derived from biological differences. In such instances, women and men are often conceived to be essentially similar in their physical makeup. This has led some writers to argue that biology does not, in fact, even underlie gender constructs, let alone determine them:

> Natural features of gender, and natural processes of sex and reproduction, furnish only a suggestive and ambiguous backdrop to the cultural organization of gender and sexuality. What gender is, what men and women are, what sorts of relations do or should obtain between them — all of these notions do not simply reflect or elaborate upon biological 'givens', but are largely products of social and cultural processes. The very emphasis on the biological factor within different cultural traditions is variable; some cultures claim that male—female differences are almost entirely biologically grounded, whereas others give biological differences, or supposed biological differences, very little emphasis.
>
> (Ortner and Whitehead 1981: 1)

There are two important points to be made about arguments of this kind. First, they do still posit a radical distinction between (biological) sex and (culturally constructed) gender. In fact, the distinction they suggest is even more radical than in those arguments which assume that gender systems are cultural mechanisms for managing sex differences and the problems of social and biological reproduction. It is clear that such a radical distinction effectively rules out altogether any possibility for the social sciences to address the relationship between biology and culture. The primary difficulty here, as Errington (1990) has pointed out, lies in how to understand human bodies. The meanings given to bodies, and the practices in which they are engaged, are culturally and historically highly variable. However, the experience of embodiment — whereby these meanings and practices are incorporated as the enduring dispositions and competences of real human agents (Bourdieu 1977: 87—95) — is something which could be said to be universal. Although the exact nature of that experience differs, unless social scientists are prepared to consider the relationship between biological sex and gender — that is, between biological entities and social categories – they will make no progress in understanding the manifold ways in which culture interacts with biology to produce that most distinctive of human artefacts: the human body (Errington 1990: 11–15).

It seems very probable that in coming years much new work will be done on the question of embodiment and on the relationship between biology and culture, but this depends not only on the willingness of social scientists to rethink the radical distinction between sex and gender, but also on the willingness of certain biologists to give up their outmoded ideas about biological determinism.

'SEX', SEX AND GENDER

The second issue raised by arguments about whether or not biological differences underlie gender constructs has been that addressed by Yanagisako and Collier (1987) in their recent discussion of the relationship between gender and kinship.

Yanagisako and Collier argue that both gender studies and kinship studies in anthropology are premised on a Western folk model of human reproduction. This folk model assumes that the difference between women and men is natural, given in biology and thus pre-social, and although social constructions are built upon this difference, the difference itself is not viewed as a social construction (1987: 29). The fact that this Western folk model assumes that gender is everywhere rooted in a binary, biologically based sex difference means that anthropological analysis effectively takes for granted a dichotomy which it should in fact be aiming to explain (1987: 15). Thus, the overall argument advanced by Yanagisako and Collier is that gender and kinship studies have failed to free themselves from a set of assumptions about natural differences between people, in spite of a commitment to a social constructionist perspective.

Their critique is a very powerful one, and is of particular interest since they anticipate that the questioning of conventional assumptions that it enjoins 'will eventually lead to the rejection of any dichotomy between sex and gender as biological and cultural facts' (1987: 42). This expectation rests on their view that *both* sex *and* gender (rather than gender alone) are socially constructed, each in relation to the other. Bodies, physiological processes and body parts have no meaning outside of socially constructed understandings of them. Sexual intercourse and human reproduction are not just physiological processes, they are also social activities. The notion of sex, like the concept of gender, is constructed within a set of social meanings and practices: it therefore cannot be a pre-social fact (1987: 31). The conclusion to which Yanagisako and Collier move is that if we recognize that the Western concept of sex is socially constructed, then we cannot argue that this particular model of 'biological' sex everywhere provides the 'raw material' for gender constructs, nor can we argue that it everywhere supplies the basis for people's understanding of the processes of human reproduction. In making this argument Yanagisako and Collier seek to draw attention to the Western cultural assumptions embedded in our analytic categories (1987: 34).

The socially constructed nature of sex and of biological differences is further elaborated by Errington (1990), who develops a notion of the body as a system of signs. She demonstrates that within the Western model, genitals are signs of other differences which are interior to the body and which are themselves indexical signs of an individual's sexual identity. Errington is here referring to 'internal' features of sexual difference such as those based on chromosomes and hormones. As she points out, the contradictions in this model were all too apparent in the cases of the Olympic athletes who classified themselves as women, but were reclassified as men when they turned out not to have perfect chromosomes (1990: 19–20). This example serves to emphasize the point that even the supposed natural or biological facts of sex are subject to interpretation and reinterpretation in the context of a specific discourse of sex and sexual identity.

The arguments advanced by Yanagisako and Collier, and by Errington, are clearly Foucauldian in nature, if not necessarily in inspiration. In the first volume of his *History of Sexuality*, Foucault argues that 'sex' is an effect rather than an origin, and that far from being a given and essential unity, it is, as a category, the product of specific discursive practices.

> The notion of 'sex' made it possible to group together, in an artificial unity, anatomical elements, biological functions, conducts, sensations, and pleasures, and it enabled one to make use of this fictitious entity as a causal principle, an omnipresent meaning, a secret to be discovered everywhere: sex was thus able to function as a unique signifier and as a universal signified. Further, by presenting itself in a unitary fashion, as anatomy and lack, as function and latency, as instinct and meaning, it was able to mark the line of contact between a knowledge of human sexuality and the biological sciences of reproduction; thus, without really borrowing anything from these sciences, excepting a few doubtful analogies, the knowledge of sexuality gained through proximity a guarantee of quasi-scientificity; but by virtue of this same proximity, some of the contents of biology and physiology were able to serve as a principle of normality for human sexuality.
>
> (Foucault 1984: 154–5)

Foucault's point about the mutually constitutive nature of Western discourses of sexuality and biology underscores the argument, made by Yanagisako and Collier, about the mutually constitutive nature of the concepts of sex, gender and kinship in the discourse of anthropology. The realization that sex as a unitary category is established in and through Western discursive practices clearly entails that the Western concept of sex cannot be said to underlie gender constructs around the world. Yanagisako and Collier are therefore correct to argue that as a concept of analysis, gender should be freed from assumptions about the biological 'given-ness' of sex, as a foundation from which to deconstruct the Western model of sex and gender relations on which anthropological work in these areas has rested for far too long. Such an aim is, in any case, firmly in line with feminist theorizing in anthropology which, from the earliest days of its inception, has sought to deliver an internal critique by unpacking the Western assumptions underlying many of the analytical constructs most central to the discipline.

Errington's more radical critique of the Western concept of sex mirrors other aspects of Foucault's argument in *The History of Sexuality*, namely those about the constructed nature of binary and exclusive sex categories.

> Genitals...along with invisible body fluids and substances of which they are believed to be signs, are classed in this [Western] culture as part of the 'natural', 'objective' realm, and humans are assumed to be 'naturally' divided into two categories without the help of cultural ideas or social institutions – and the main *raison d'être* of those two categories is generally believed, whether by religious persons or by secular evolutionary biologists, to be reproduction. I will call this the taxonomy of Sex, with a capital 'S'... By 'Sex' I mean to include the whole complex of beliefs about genitals as signs of deeper substances and fluids and about the functions and appropriate uses of genitals; the assignment of the body into the category of the 'natural' (itself a culturally constructed category); and the cultural division of all human bodies into two mutually exclusive and exhaustive Sex categories.
>
> (Errington 1990: 21)

While recognizing that 'Sex' is socially constructed, Errington nevertheless attempts to distinguish between (in her terms) 'Sex', sex and gender. By 'Sex', she means a particular construct of human bodies prevalent in Euro-America, while sex means the physical nature of human bodies, and gender refers to what it is that different cultures make of sex. She criticizes Yanagisako and Collier for collapsing the distinction between 'Sex' and sex, on the grounds that while we can recognize that the Western understanding of 'Sex' is socially constructed, it is also important to recognize that humans have bodies with distinguishing genitals and that there is therefore a material reality – i.e. sex – which must be taken into account when discussing the meanings which cultures give to bodies and embodied practices – i.e. gender (Errington 1990: 27–8).

The point Errington makes is an important one, but there are still further confusions to be sorted out in this discussion about the relationship between 'Sex', sex and gender. While both Errington and Yanagisako and Collier acknowledge that 'Sex' is an effect of a particular Western discourse for comprehending and categorizing the apparent differences between women and men – a discourse which underlies the analytic categories of anthropological theorizing – they do not seem to acknowledge the point that sex is everywhere 'Sex'; in other words, that although the particular constitution, configuration and effects of 'Sex' clearly vary between cultures, there is, in each case, no way of knowing sex except through 'Sex'. The specific Western discourse of 'Sex' may have influenced anthropological theorizing, but there are many other discourses of 'Sex', and these discourses need to be specified through anthropological analysis.

The fact that all cultures have ways of making sense of, or giving meaning to, bodies and embodied practices, including physiological processes and bodily fluids and substances, means that all cultures have a discourse of 'Sex'. In each case, this discourse stands in a relationship of partial dependency and partial autonomy with other discourses, including, very often, what anthropologists have referred to as the discourse of gender. Gender discourses themselves are refracted in many other discursive domains of culture, giving rise in some instances to discourses of power, potency, cosmology, fertility and death which also appear highly gendered. One example from Western societies of such a gendered discourse is that of nature and culture. Conversely, and by virtue of that relation of mutual constitution so well described by Foucault, the discourse of gender is itself shot through with ideas about what is natural and what is cultural.

There is, in short, no way in any culture to approach sex except through the discourse of 'Sex', and this must surely be particularly true of cultures which have lacked, either now or in the past, the technological means for revealing the true nature of the underlying physiological processes and substances, and thus for distinguishing between sex and 'Sex'. What Errington and Yanagisako and Collier do not seem to realize is that the notion of sex, of a biological property or set of biological processes, existing independently of any social matrix, is itself the product of the biomedical discourse of Western culture. There is a fundamental sense in which, outside the parameters and spheres of influence of this biomedical discourse, sex does not exist. In other words, in most cultures in the world, where indigenous or local knowledge reigns supreme, there is no sex, only 'Sex'.

Anthropology has been very slow to grasp this point, partly because the question is obscured, paradoxically, by an approach which posits a radical separation of sex from gender, and, by extension, of biology from culture. The question we have to ask ourselves for the future is whether it makes sense, except where spurious biological arguments are being used to justify discriminatory social practices, to insist upon separating sex from gender, when the real issue is not sex, but 'Sex'. A further question, however, needs to be posed: is it appropriate to separate 'Sex' from gender, when 'Sex' is understood as the culturally specific discursive practices which make sense of body parts and their relation, indexical or otherwise, to physiological processes and substances, including those associated with human reproduction? This question is the more difficult one, and involves a consideration of the problem of binary sex categorization.

The determination, as I have already pointed out, of two mutually exclusive and fixed categories of sex, the female and the male, is an effect of the Western cultural discourse of 'Sex'. This discourse stands in a mutually constitutive relation with biomedical discourse, such that the former becomes scientized, while the latter is constructed according to a set of understandings about the meaning of sex differences and about the relations to be established between what is cultural and what is natural (Hubbard 1990). The difficulty with the Western discourse on 'Sex', as Yanagisako and Collier point out, is that the 'naturalness' of binary sex categorization is apparently reinforced by the fact that biological females and biological males are required for human sexual reproduction. However, we do not have to suppose that there are peoples around the world who are unable to recognize the differences between female and male genitalia, or who are unaware of the different roles which women and men play in sexual reproduction, in order to question the assumption that biological differences between women and men provide a universal basis for cultural categorizations that assign every individual to one or other of two, discrete and fixed categories, 'female' and 'male', in the manner of Western discourse. There is ample ethnographic evidence to show that this kind of binary categorization is culturally specific, and that it does not arise automatically from the recognition of differences in roles and in physical appearance.

This point is most apparent when we turn to consider theories about the physical constitution of persons. In many societies it is believed that persons are made up of female and male parts or substances. Lévi-Strauss (1969) identified what he called the flesh–bone complex for South Asian societies, in which bones are inherited from the father and flesh from the mother. Marilyn Strathern (1988) has recently discussed the multiply gendered and partible nature of bodies as they are conceived by the people of the Mount Hagen region in the New Guinea Highlands. Hageners see gender as a process rather than as a category: how one becomes rather than what one is. Likewise, according to Meigs (1990), the Hua – another Highlands people – incorporate in their view of gender the idea that persons can become more female or more male depending on how much they have been in contact with and have ingested certain bodily substances thought to be female (e.g. menstrual blood, parturitional fluids and vaginal secretions). Hua men take in these substances as a result of eating food prepared by reproductively active women, as a consequence of sex, and through daily casual contact (Meigs 1990: 109). This means of conceptualizing gender is a processual and multiple one, and it exists in parallel with a mode of categorization based on external genitalia. It is evident from recent ethnographies that many societies have more than one way of conceptualizing and classifying gender, and that this fact has been obscured by the reliance of the social sciences on a model of gender which stresses the fixed and binary nature of sexual difference.

One difficulty which ethnographic data of this kind raise is how to establish, and indeed whether it is possible to establish, the distinction between sex and gender at all. If sexual difference is thought to exist within bodies as well as between them, should we view this as a matter of sex or of gender (Moore 1993)? This question becomes particularly crucial in the light of the previous argument that sex as well as gender must be understood as socially constructed. The result is that the analytic distinction between sex and gender seems very blurred. At least in the context of cross-cultural analysis, it seems that the attempt to uphold a radical distinction between sex and gender will not necessarily help us to gain an improved theoretical perspective.

INEQUALITY AND SUBORDINATION

However, one area in which a distinction between sex and gender has proved very useful to the social sciences is the analysis of gender inequalities. The immediate question raised by cross-cultural analysis has been how to account for the enormous variability in local understandings of gender and gender relations, in the context of what appears to be the universal subordination of women to men (Moore 1988: ch. 2; see also Bétcille in this volume, Article 37). It seemed that there must be some cultural or sociological regularities which would account for male dominance (Rosaldo 1974, Reiter 1975). The value of enquiry into this question was that it drew the social sciences away from a debate about the biological basis for gender inequality towards a discussion of its cultural and sociological determinants. However, there are a number of difficulties with the theoretical solutions which have been proposed to the question of universal female subordination.

Sherry Ortner (1974) proposed that the universal devaluation of women is connected to their symbolic association with the realm of nature, which is itself viewed as subordinate to the realm of culture associated with men (Ortner 1974). At the same time, Michelle Rosaldo (1974) suggested that it is women's association with the domestic sphere, in contrast to men's dominance in the encompassing public sphere of social life, which accounts for the universal tendency for women to be subordinated to men. Ortner's account thus stressed cultural and symbolic factors, while Rosaldo's emphasized sociological considerations. Both these explanations have been widely criticized (Moore 1988: ch. 2). A number of scholars have pointed out that the distinction between women and men is not necessarily associated with the division between nature and culture, and that concepts or notions of nature and culture vary greatly from one society to another, if indeed they exist at all (MacCormack and Strathern 1980). The problem once again lies in the imposition of an analytic dichotomy derived from Western thought in situations where it is not always appropriate. In the case of the domestic–public distinction, Rosaldo made it clear that women's identification with the domestic domain is a consequence of their role as mothers (Rosaldo 1974: 24). This view was strongly criticized by a number of writers, who argued that a search for the universal causes of gender inequality inevitably ends up implying some form of biological determination, even if the theory proposed appears to offer a social or cultural explanation (e.g. Leacock 1978, Sacks 1979). Rosaldo later modified her view and argued that the domestic–public distinction could not provide a universal explanation for women's subordination because, both analytically and sociologically, it is the product of historical developments in Western society (Rosaldo 1980).

A variant of the domestic–public dichotomy emerged in Marxist feminist writing on the position of women and the sexual division of labour. The starting point for much of this debate was the distinction, first made by Engels, between production and reproduction. Engels regarded the subordination of women as being linked to their exclusion from the sphere of production (Moore 1988: 46–49). This debate was initially very ethnocentric in formulation and tended to draw much of its theoretical inspiration from arguments about the role of women's reproductive labour under conditions of capitalist production, where such labour is situated inside the household – as opposed to productive labour which is situated outside it. This is obviously an inappropriate model for understanding production systems in which women are engaged in both productive and reproductive labour within the household (Moore 1988: ch. 3). There was also a tendency to assume that the nature of women's reproductive labour does not change over time. Some writers conflated reproduction with biological reproduction (Meillassoux, 1981), while yet others equated it with women's domestic labour (Boserup, 1970). In spite of attempts to clarify the notion of 'reproduction', and to include not only biological reproduction and domestic work, but also social reproduction in the wider sense (Harris and Young 1981), there has been a persistent tendency to link women's subordination to their role in reproduction, and thus to their position in the sexual division of labour.

However, gender relations cannot be understood as a simple reflection of the sexual division of labour. Cultural representations of gender rarely mirror accurately women's and men's activities, their contributions to society, or their relations with each other (Ortner and Whitehead 1981: 10). A number of feminist scholars have suggested that women's position in society is determined by the extent to which they control their own labour and the products of their labour. But ethnographic analysis has revealed that even this proposition is too straightforward. The difficulty with investigating gender inequality is that one has to analyse not only the political and economic contexts in which gender relations are operative, but also the cultural and symbolic meanings accorded to gender differences.

Ortner and Whitehead have suggested a method for combining the symbolic and the sociological approaches by focusing on what they call 'prestige structures'. Prestige structures are understood as those lines of social evaluation, positions and roles through which a given set of social statuses and cultural values are reproduced (Ortner and Whitehead 1981: 13). As Yanagisako and Collier point out (1987: 27), it is not easy to grasp exactly what is meant by this. Ortner and Whitehead, however, suggest that gender systems – that is gender meanings and gender relations – are themselves prestige structures and that they are correlated in many societies with other axes of social evaluation, such as rational versus emotional or strong versus weak (Ortner and Whitehead 1981: 16–17). This argument is compelling, in one sense, because it does help us to understand why evaluative statements are so often rendered in gendered terms, when what is actually being referred to are relations between people of the same sex or between people of different classes, rather than relations between women and men. Nonetheless, Ortner and Whitehead assume, rather than demonstrate, that prestige structures are rooted in the male-dominated, public sphere of social activity, and that they encompass or dominate the domestic sphere of social life (Ortner and Whitehead 1981: 19). As Yanagisako and Collier note, this means that the notion of prestige structures does little more than replicate the problems inherent in the domestic–public distinction, and that as such it simply assumes a priori what it should be seeking to investigate (Yanagisako and Collier 1987: 28).

The notion of a prestige structure is nevertheless useful because it directs attention to the social evaluations of women's and men's behaviour, and to the meanings given to the differences in their activities and roles. Marilyn Strathern (1981) has used the idea of social evaluation to demonstrate that in Hagen, pursuing socially valued goals ('acting like a man') and pursuing individual interests ('acting like a woman') are types of behaviour open to both women and men, and that although gender idioms are used to describe moral qualities and socially valued behaviour, this does not determine how the actual behaviour of individual women and men would be evaluated in any particular context. The disparity between the cultural representations of gender and the activities of individual women and men raises once more the questions of how the status of women is to be evaluated in any given context, and of what kind of information is necessary to be able to determine the nature and extent of women's subordination to men.

For example, Keeler has pointed out for Java that although gender differences can be used to make distinctions among individuals, differences based on style and status can also be used to do the same thing (Keeler 1990: 128–9). Keeler notes that while gender distinctions are relevant in domestic and public life, they do not prevent women from exercizing control within the household, and from managing their own money as well as their husband's income. Women apparently participate fully in discussions about children's education, business plans and marriage arrangements. Men do some child care, and both women and men farm, and take part in business activities. Many Javanese women enjoy positions of prestige and respect in public life, as government officials and heads of schools, although the numbers holding high office are not great (Keeler 1990: 129–30). Nonetheless, despite women's activities and achievements, they tend to be described as lacking socially and morally valued characteristics such as self-control, patience, spiritual potency, sensibility and insight. Keeler links this overtly negative discourse to the fact that women are believed to lack potency, which is related in Javanese thinking to both prestige and status. However, as he points out, it would be a mistake to assume that because women lack culturally defined prestige they are automatically considered to be inferior in social life.

MULTIPLE MODELS AND MULTIPLE DISCOURSES

What the example from Java demonstrates is the difficulty of combining cultural representations of gender relations and local views of women and men as persons, together with the actual activities and roles of women and men, to produce a single model of gender relations. It is similarly difficult to combine these different types of data to arrive at some formulation of a single position which women could be said to hold in society (Strathern 1987). For one thing, gender is not the only axis of social differentiation within a society, and there may be manifest differences between women due to class, race, religion or ethnicity. This gives rise to a situation in which not all women are subordinate to all men. For example, in the Javanese case, high-ranking women have low-ranking men as subordinates, and in many contemporary societies, class and race are significant axes of social differentiation which organize access to resources, including education, employment and public office, in ways which often cross-cut gender distinctions. However, recent work in anthropology has emphasized that it is a mistake to imagine that societies have only one model, or only one discourse, of gender and gender relations. The recognition of the existence of multiple models and discourses, and the investigation of how those models and discourses intersect in any given context, is providing a new direction for the analysis of gender in anthropology.

Anna Meigs points out that until recently, anthropological work on gender has been based on three assumptions: first, that there are two clear-cut and monolithic categories, female and male; second, that female status is singular and unitary, and third, that each society has a single gender model (Meigs 1990: 102). The cross-cultural variability of the categories female and male, and the manifold nature of female status, have already been discussed. However, with reference again to the Hua people of Highland New Guinea, Meigs details three gender models or discourses which exist simultaneously in their society. The first of these emphasizes that female bodies are disgusting and dangerous to men, and that women lack knowledge and insight. This model is enshrined in many rituals and social institutions, especially male initiation. The second is quite contrary to the first and concerns the Hua belief that the female body is superior to the male. Hua men imitate menstruation and believe that they can become pregnant. This second model is embodied in myth, local belief and ritual practices, including the bloodletting which is an imitation of menstruation. The third model is egalitarian and emphasizes that although female and male bodies are different, neither one is more desirable than the other. This model emphasizes interdependency and complementarity, and is connected to the respect which women and men show each other in daily life (Meigs 1990: 102–3).

Meigs's work is useful because she emphasizes not only that societies will probably have more than one gender discourse or model, but also that many of these different ideas about gender, and about the nature of women and men, will likely conflict with and contradict each other. She also points out that from among these multiple models or discourses of gender, certain of them are more appropriate to particular contexts, or to particular stages in the life-cycles of individuals, than others. Thus, young Hua males at initiation are taught that female bodies are dangerous, and they are forbidden to look at women or eat food from women's gardens or consume any of the foods which resemble the female reproductive system. However, as they get older, these rules fall away, and the ideal of sexual avoidance is replaced by one of relative egalitarianism and co-operation (Meigs 1990: 103–4).

The recognition of the existence of multiple gender models in anthropology has been stimulated by a transformation, over the last fifteen years or so, in the anthropological understanding and definition of culture. Whereas culture was once defined as an overarching set of beliefs and customs that were equally shared by all members of a society, recent work in the social sciences has emphasized the contested and contingent nature of culture. One result of this has been a shift away from imagining culture and social life as based on rules and rule-following to a view which emphasizes that they are constituted through performance and practice (Ortner 1984). The current emphasis in the cross-cultural study of gender on the way in which women's and men's activities are informed by a multiplicity of discourses of gender and gender relations, which are themselves produced and reproduced through those same activities, is a consequence of this shift in the understanding of culture.

CHANGING DISCOURSES OF GENDER AND GENDER RELATIONS

The sexual division of labour is constantly being transformed as social and economic change takes place. In the process, local ideas about women and men, and about the nature of gender relations, change too. The analysis of what determines these changes and of how they take place is complex, and factors which have to be taken into account include the nature of kinship systems, existing political and state structures and the level of development of the economy (Moore 1988: ch. 4). Many writers have noted that colonialism and missionary activity, in their attempts to extract male labour and to construct a public domain in contrast to a domestic life, have often had deleterious effects on local systems of gender and gender relations. Here, economic, political and socio-ideological forces have worked together to transform both concepts of gender and the sexual division of labour. However, it is a mistake to oversimplify this picture. The forces of change have been uneven in their spread and impact, and have not had a uniform effect on gender and gender relations. Until recently, work in this area tended to imply that local systems were simply passive and unable to resist the imposition of exogenous socio-economic and political structures (Moore 1988: 74). In the following paragraphs I briefly review some new studies which challenge this assumption.

Cristina Blanc-Szanton (1990) has described the effect of Spanish colonization and Catholicism, and the later impact of North Americans and the
modern state, on concepts of gender among the Ilonggo of the Philippines.
She notes that despite three centuries of pressure on aspects of sexual morality
and gender symbolism, including attempts to impose a particular view of sexuality and to restructure the nature of gender relations, the result has not been
capitulation to external gender models. Even in the context of unequal and
coercive power relations, the Ilonggo have selectively absorbed and adapted
new notions of gender and, in the process, have creatively reworked many of
these new ideas. For example, Blanc-Szanton argues that in the 1970s, the
Ilonggo manifested a 'remarkable mixture of symbolic references to machismo
and virginity of both Spanish and Judeo-Christian origin, an awareness of the
new sexuality, but also an emphasis on the sameness and comparability of
the sexes' (Blanc-Szanton 1990: 378). In her conclusion, she suggests that the
reason for the syncretic vitality of the Ilonggo gender system lies in the fact
that while the Spanish, the Americans and the modern state have each sought
to transform this system, they have never been able to undermine the reproductive basis of the system itself. Ilonggo gender is based on a notion of non-
hierarchical comparability and equivalence which is enshrined in features of
social organization, including bilateral kinship, and, unless this principle is
undermined, the system will continue to respond syncretically and adaptively
(Blanc-Szanton 1990: 381–2).

Aihwa Ong (1987, 1990) has examined young women's participation in
industrial production in Malaysia, and has investigated the ways in which
sexual symbolism and gender constructs are reinterpreted and transformed in
situations of rapid social change and power conflict. She argues that conflicts
over class and national identity are often constructed as conflicts over gender
and gender meanings, thus transformations in gender relations are the key to
understanding processes of social change. Ong also emphasizes the way in
which contradictory and competing discourses on gender can be produced as
a result of the different interests and struggles of social groups.

Old concepts of gender and gender relations can acquire new meanings and
serve new purposes under changed circumstances (Ong 1990: 387). One
notable example of this last point is the way in which factory managers
guarantee the safety of young women workers, maintain control over their
movements between home and factory, and impress upon parents their concern for the moral reputations of the young women. This system of surveillance accords well with parental values and wishes, and while it has the added
advantage of ensuring an adequate supply of labour to the factory, it also provides the management with a socially legitimate method for controlling
women within the factory, thereby contributing to the formation of a dis-
ciplined and docile workforce. As Ong points out, the traditional moral
authority of men in domestic affairs has been transformed into a system for
the industrial exploitation of Malay women (Ong 1990: 402–3).

On the factory floor, the regime is paternalistic, with male foremen subjecting female workers to control, questioning and surveillance. This situation is made worse by the public image of factory workers as morally loose women who pay insufficient attention to family values and Muslim standards of behaviour. Women workers daily try to resist the factory regime through such methods as making excuses to leave the factory floor for religious reasons or 'female problems' (Ong 1990: 417). A new phenomenon, however, has been the increase in episodes of spirit possession, which often result in women shouting at and resisting male supervisors. The resistance to male control on the factory floor is paralleled by a resistance to male control in the domestic sphere. Working daughters often demonstrate their resistance to their fathers and to the ethic of communal consumption by protesting against undesired marriages, using their savings to plan an alternative career, engaging in premarital sex and refusing money to parents who remarry. These forms of resistance, in the home and the workplace, have to be understood in the context of the increased control over young women's lives exercised through the discipline and surveillance of the factory regime and through the increased vigilance of Islamic state institutions. The result is a situation in which young women actively resist, while simultaneously maintaining family loyalty, Islamic asceticism and male authority as central values (Ong 1990: 420). The struggle over gender and gender relations is also the struggle over family, religious and national identity in the context of political and economic domination.

The confusing nature of resistance and its ambivalent relation to emancipation are well demonstrated by Abu-Lughod's (1986, 1990) work on Bedouin women. Bedouin women have traditionally evaded male control through the institution of the sexually segregated women's world, in which they are able to avoid male surveillance and enjoy a degree of self-determination. They have also exercised power and a certain amount of control through their resistance to undesirable marriages. Lyric poetry and other subversive discourses provide a further medium through which dominant discourses on gender and gender relations can be reinterpreted and resisted (Abu-Lughod 1986). However, Abu-Lughod notes that these traditional forms of resistance are being eroded. The poetry is becoming increasingly associated with young men, who sing the songs, make money out of locally produced cassettes, and use these poems to resist the power of older kinsmen (Abu-Lughod 1990: 325).

Sedentarization has led to a situation in which women's movements are more closely controlled, and in which women spend more time veiled and less time in the relative freedom of the desert camps. However, this has been paralleled by the increasing consumer orientation of young women, as shown in their purchase of items like face creams and lingerie, which has put them at odds with their mothers and female kin. Young women are now less interested in resisting marriage than in trying to secure the kind of marriage which will provide them with access to consumer goods and fulfil their fantasies of a romantic match with an educated and progressive man. Young women aspire to be housewives in a way which their mothers would never have done, because their own security and standard of living is dependent on the favour of husbands in a situation in which everything costs money, but in which women have no independent access to cash (Abu-Lughod 1990: 326–7). Men's power over women now includes the power to buy things and to give or withhold these things. Along with the desire for consumer goods goes a desire for Egyptian music and soap opera, within which many of the new ideas about gender and gender relations are encoded. Older Bedouin women and men try to resist these forms of Egyptianization. As Abu-Lughod points out, although young women are resisting their elders in taking up new patterns of consumption, they are simultaneously becoming caught up in the new forms of subjection which these patterns entail (Abu-Lughod 1990, 328).

All forms of social change involve the reworking of gender relations to greater or lesser degrees. This is because changes in production systems involve changes in the sexual division of labour; political conflicts involve the reconfiguration of power relations within the domestic domain and beyond; and gender as a powerful form of cultural representation is caught up in emerging struggles over meaning and in attempts to redefine who and what people are. This has nowhere been clearer than in the transformations in gender relations which have been sought in many (formerly) socialist and communist countries (Moore 1988: 136–49). That the policies pursued by these countries have enjoyed only partial success demonstrates that politicians, like social scientists, have yet to comprehend how and why gender relations might be transformed in present-day societies and in those of the future.

REFERENCES

Abu-Lughod, L. (1986) *Veiled Sentiments: Honor and Poetry in a Bedouin Society*, Berkeley: University of California Press.

—— (1990) 'The romance of resistance: tracing transformations of power through Bedouin women', in P. Sanday and R. Goodenough (eds) *Beyond the Second Sex: New Directions in the Anthropology of Gender*, Philadelphia: University of Pennsylvania Press.

Blanc-Szanton, C. (1990) 'Collision of cultures: historical reformulations of gender in the lowland Visayas, Philippines', in J. Atkinson and S. Errington (eds) *Power and Difference: Gender in Island Southeast Asia*, Stanford, Cal.: Stanford University Press.

Boserup, E. (1970) *Women's Role in Economic Development*, London: George Allen & Unwin.

Bourdieu, P. (1977) *Outline of a Theory of Practice*, trans. R. Nice, Cambridge: Cambridge University Press.

Errington, S. (1990) 'Recasting sex, gender and power: a theoretical and regional overview', in J. Atkinson and S. Errington (eds) *Power and Difference: Gender in Island Southeast Asia*, Stanford, Cal.: Stanford University Press.

Fausto-Sterling, A. (1985) *Myths about Gender: Biological Theories about Women and Men*, New York: Basic Books.

Foucault, M. (1984) *The History of Sexuality*, vol I, Harmondsworth: Penguin.

Harris, O. and Young K. (1981) 'Engendered structures: some problems in the analysis of reproduction', in J. Kahn and J. Llobera (eds) *The Anthropology of Pre-Capitalist Societies*, London: Macmillan.

Hubbard, R. (1990) *The Politics of Women's Biology*, New Brunswick, NJ: Rutgers University Press.

Keeler, W. (1990) 'Speaking of gender in Java', in J. Atkinson and S. Errington (eds) *Power and Difference: Gender in Island Southeast Asia*, Stanford, Cal.: Stanford University Press.

Leacock, E. (1978) 'Women's status in egalitarian society: implications for social evolution', *Current Anthropology* 19(2): 247–5.

Lévi-Strauss, C. (1969) *The Elementary Structures of Kinship*, Boston: Beacon Press.

MacCormack, C. and Strathern, M. (eds) (1980) *Nature, Culture and Gender*, Cambridge: Cambridge University Press.

Mead, M. (1935) *Sex and Temperament in Three Primitive Societies*, New York: William Morrow & Co.

Meigs, A. (1990) 'Multiple gender ideologies and statuses', in P. Sanday and R. Goodenough (eds) *Beyond the Second Sex: New Directions in the Anthropology of Gender*, Philadelphia: University of Pennsylvania Press.

Meillassoux, C. (1981) *Maidens, Meal and Money*, Cambridge: Cambridge University Press.

Moore, H. L. (1988) *Feminism and Anthropology*, Cambridge: Polity Press.

—— (1993) 'The differences within and the differences between', in T. del Valle (ed.) *Gender and Social Life*, London: Routledge.

Ong, A. (1987) *Spirits of Resistance and Capitalist Discipline: Factory Women in Malaysia*, Albany: State University of New York Press.

—— (1990) 'Japanese factories, Malay workers: class and sexual metaphors in West Malaysia', in J. Atkinson and S. Errington (eds) *Power and Difference: Gender in Island Southeast Asia*, Stanford, Calif.: Stanford University Press.

Ortner, S. (1984) 'Theory in anthropology since the sixties', *Comparative Studies in Society and History* 26(1): 126–66.

—— (1974) 'Is female to male as nature is to culture?', in M. Rosaldo and L. Lamphere (eds) *Woman, Culture and Society*, Stanford, Calif.: Stanford University Press.

Ortner, S. and Whitehead, H. (1981) 'Introduction: accounting for sexual meanings', in S. Ortner and H. Whitehead (eds) *Sexual Meanings: The Cultural Construction of Gender and Sexuality*, Cambridge: Cambridge University Press.

Reiter, R. (1975) *Toward an Anthropology of Women*, New York: Monthly Review Press.

Rosaldo, M. (1974) 'Woman, culture and society: a theoretical overview', in M. Rosaldo and L. Lamphere (eds) *Woman, Culture, and Society*, Stanford, Cal.: Stanford University Press.

—— (1980) 'The use and abuse of anthropology: reflections on feminism and cross-cultural understanding', *Signs* 5(3): 389–417.

Sacks, K. (1979) *Sisters and Wives: The Past and Future of Sexual Equality*, Westport, Conn.: Greenwood Press.

Strathern, M. (1981) 'Self-interest and the social good: some implications of Hagen gender imagery', in S. Ortner and H. Whitehead (eds) *Sexual Meanings: The Cultural Construction of Gender and Sexuality*, Cambridge: Cambridge University Press.

—— (1987) 'Introduction', in M. Strathern (ed.) *Dealing with Inequality: Analysing Gender Relations in Melanesia and Beyond*, Cambridge: Cambridge University Press.

—— (1988) *The Gender of the Gift*, Berkeley: University of California Press.

Yanagisako, S. and Collier, J. (1987) 'Toward a unified analysis of gender and kinship', in J. Collier and S. Yanagisako (eds) *Gender and Kinship: Essays Toward a Unified Analysis*, Stanford, Cal.: Stanford University Press.

FURTHER READING

Atkinson, J. and Errington, S. (eds) (1990) *Gender and Power in Island Southeast Asia*, Stanford, Calif.: Stanford University Press.

Bledsoe, C. (1980) *Women and Marriage in Kpelle Society*. Stanford, Cal.: Stanford University Press.

Caplan, P. (1985) *Class and Gender in India: Women and their Organisations in a South Indian City*, London: Tavistock.

Collier, J. and Yanagisako, S. (1987) *Gender and Kinship: Essays Towards a Unified Analysis*, Stanford, Calif.: Stanford University Press.

Herdt, G. (1987) *Guardians of the Flutes: Idioms of Masculinity*, New York: Columbia University Press.

Kendall, L. (1985) *Shamans, Housewives and Other Restless Spirits: Women in Korean Ritual Life*, Honolulu: University of Hawaii Press.

Kondo, D. (1990) *Crafting Selves: Power, Gender and Discourses of Identity in a Japanese Workplace*, Chicago: University of Chicago Press.

Lamphere, L. (1987) *From Working Daughters to Working Mothers*, Ithaca: Cornell University Press.

di Leonardo, M. (ed.) (1991) *Gender at the Crossroads of Knowledge*, Berkeley: University of California Press.

Meigs, A. (1984) *Food, Sex and Pollution*, New Brunswick, NJ: Rutgers University Press.

Moore, H. L. (1986) *Space, Text and Gender: An Anthropological Study of the Marakwet of Kenya*, Cambridge: Cambridge University Press.

—— (1988) *Feminism and Anthropology*, Cambridge: Polity Press.

Ong, A. (1987) *Spirits of Resistance and Capitalist Discipline*, Albany: State University of New York Press.

Ortner, S. and Whitehead, H. (eds) (1981) *Sexual Meanings*, Cambridge: Cambridge University Press.

Redclift, N. and Sinclair, T. (eds) (1990) *Working Women: International Perspectives on Labour and Gender Ideology*, London: Routledge.

Standing, H. (1990) *Dependence and Autonomy: Women's Employment and the Family in Calcutta*, London: Routledge.

Strathern, M. (1988) *The Gender of the Gift*, Berkeley: University of California Press.

30

SOCIALIZATION, ENCULTURATION AND THE DEVELOPMENT OF PERSONAL IDENTITY

Fitz John Porter Poole

This article explores a particular view of the anthropological study of processes of socialization and enculturation focused on the acquisition of inter-woven social, cultural, and personal dimensions of identity, and of their meanings in the context of socio-cultural understanding and action. The article proceeds from presenting a general portrait of the character of socialization and enculturation, to mapping analytically the mosaic of personhood, selfhood, and individuality as variable and variably interconnected aspects of identity, to considering the ways in which these aspects of identity emerge and are elaborated in the course of early and middle childhood. The exercise is more a sketch of an agenda than a comparative assessment of ethnographic studies. It is suggested that this focus on the confluence of processes of socialization and enculturation, on the one hand, and of schemata of person, self, and individuality, on the other, nevertheless holds some promise for making sense developmentally of Sapir's (1949: 515) prescient claim that the 'true locus of culture is in the interactions of specific individuals and, on the subjective side, in the world of meaning which each one of these individuals may ... abstract for himself from his participation in these interactions'.

SOCIALIZATION AND ENCULTURATION

The processes of socialization and enculturation, though interconnected, are analytically distinguishable in emphasis (cf. Herskovits 1948: 38, Mead 1963, Schwartz 1976). Mead (1963: 185) suggests that socialization has to do with 'the set of species-wide requirements and exactions made on human beings by human societies', whereas enculturation refers to 'the process of learning a culture in all its uniqueness and particularity'. From the perspective of this article, however, my focus is on how, when, where, why, with whom, under what circumstances, and with what individual significance and psychological force, personal configurations of learning of the social and of the cultural occur, and on how social and cultural forms and forces are intertwined in the process of such learning. Thus, the distinction between socialization and enculturation is predicated, in part, upon a further analytic distinction, between society as consisting in pragmatically constituted, negotiated, co-ordinated, and replicated patterns of interaction, and culture as consisting in socially distributed and more or less shared knowledge (including knowledge of social interaction) manifested in those perceptions, understandings, feelings, evaluations, intentions, and other orientations that inform and shape the imagination and pragmatics of social life from the imperfectly shared perspectives of social actors. Somewhat controversially, this perspective instals the individual as the focal locus of culture and as the significant agent in social interaction, and thus calls for a 'person-centred enthnography' (LeVine 1982).

Socialization

Socialization implicates those interactive processes − their structures, contents, contexts, and actors − in and through which one learns to be an actor, to engage in interaction, to occupy statuses, to enact roles, and to forge social relationships in community life, as well as acquiring the competence, skills, sensitivities, and dispositions appropriate to such social participation. It is concerned with the character and condition of learning processes, entailed in the learner's participation in social practices appropriate to particular relationships, by which he or she becomes adapted to, integrated in, and competent at those interactions involved in becoming or being an actor in society. It is bound up with the social apparatuses, institutional arrangements, or socio-ecological contexts, and with significant categories of persons, that together define and exemplify the ranges of socially appropriate behaviours for people having certain social identities and occupying particular statuses in the varied situations of community life (Bronfenbrenner 1979, LeVine 1969, 1977). If, as Giddens (1979: 251) maintains, some negotiation of mutual knowledge is a necessary precondition for social interaction, then socialization is tied in with the interactive processes that promote and facilitate such negotiation through particular forms of 'interactional display of the socio-cultural environment' (Wentworth 1980: 68).

Studies of socialization not only focus on the character of the situations and events in which learning occurs, but also attend to the organization of the interactive processes that promote and facilitate learning of different kinds and significance. It is generally agreed that social interaction both enfolds and shapes the ways in which socio-cultural phenomena are encountered and learned (Bruner and Bornstein 1989), although the manner and circumstances in which this occurs, and its consequences, are highly variable. One of the most important contexts of interactive learning has been identified by Vygotsky (1978) as the 'zone of proximal development'. Learning in this zone involves interactions in which less and more knowledgeable and skilled actors actively contribute to an intersubjective collaboration through engaging in joint activities whose form, focus and direction is intricately and sensitively adjusted to the demands of 'scaffolding' or 'guided participation' (Rogoff 1990). By subtly setting goals and shaping activities, the more competent participant in the interaction attends to the less adept partner's kinds and degrees of knowledge, skill, involvement, reaction, and elicitation, as the learner is given the opportunity to experiment with and discover new understandings. It is also in such contexts of interaction, however, that often tacit messages about personhood, selfhood, and individuality are communicated, apprehended, interpreted, negotiated, and sometimes internalized (Cooley 1902, Lee and Hickman 1983, Lee et al. 1983, Mead 1934).

Within anthropology, probably the most influential model of socialization derives from the studies of Whiting and Whiting (1975), which focused on the social processes of transmission of cultural knowledge to children, who were nevertheless portrayed as more or less passive recipients of such knowledge in the context of 'learning environments'. In the service of comparison, generalization, and explanation, this model attends to supposedly objective features of the milieu of child-rearing and of children's behaviour, but it explores little of how children construct their *own* experiences of the socio-cultural world in which they live and of how they put those experiential understandings to varied personal and social use. In the most recent formulation of Whiting and Edwards (1988: 2), the effort is directed toward 'observations collected in naturally occurring settings of children', with particular attention to children's routine activities in space and time and to the significant social others with whom they interact in these 'learning environments'. Despite the importance of understanding the salient characteristics of the social settings, partners, and interactions that influence children's behaviour, this approach is insufficient on its own, and needs to be complemented by an exploration of how the child – actively and creatively – apprehends, experiments with, represents, communicates, and internalizes aspects of cultural knowledge, and brings them to bear in making sense of and in navigating through the social world of the community. From the perspective of this article, an understanding of the salience of 'learning environments' must take into account the nuances of children's own understandings of them.

Enculturation

Turning from socialization to enculturation, the focus is on those processes by which one acquires understanding, orientation, and competence in the ideational realm that constitutes a culture – schemata, scripts, models, frames, and other images of the organization and contextualization of knowledge that are culturally constituted, socially distributed, and personally construed. Enculturation concerns the acquisition of those rules, understandings and orientations that provide, among other things, contoured maps of the landscape of community life and heuristic guides for effective participation. Through the lens of a 'person-centred ethnography', the study of enculturation attends to how individuals come to develop more or less adaptive (or maladaptive) interpretations, representations, expectations, evaluations, feelings, intentions, and so on, concerning their socio-cultural milieu and their positions within it from perspectives that are both socio-centric and personal.

Research on enculturation holds much promise for enhancing our understanding of the acquisition of cultural schemata (D'Andrade 1981, 1984, Schwartz 1981). More or less widely shared, such schemata (variously conceived as frames, maps, models and scripts) are fundamentally involved in perception, recognition, interpretation, assessment, and other modes of processing information that enable actors to represent the contexts in which they find themselves and to guide their action within them. A schema generally consists of a number of conceptual elements connected to one another within a semantic network. The conceptual elements of a schema exhibit a range of values and connective potentials, can be variously interlinked within a focal schema or among other schemata, and can be variably bound to different aspects of the environment in different instantiations of the schema.

As D'Andrade (1992: 29) suggests, 'a schema is an interpretation which is frequent, well organized, memorable, which can be made from minimal cues, contains one or more prototypic instantiations, is resistant to change, etc.' Cultural schemata facilitate the construction of hypotheses about the identity or conceptual properties of objects, events, situations, actions, or persons, and allow interpretation to proceed beyond the information given in guiding inferences about unobserved, tacit, or ambiguous aspects of such phenomena. Yet each conceptual element of a given schema may itself be a complex schema, for more general, overarching schemata encompass more specific, context-bound subschemata in a hierarchical arrangement. Such subschemata may be activated in various ways and at various hierarchical levels, on the basis of minimal information, as the construction of an interpretation proceeds.

As D'Andrade (1981, 1984) further implies, a distinctive characteristic of most cultural schemata, as marked simplifications of reality, is that they are not entirely explicit or well specified in ordinary discourse. Indeed, certain aspects of such schemata remain tacit, ambiguous, or even opaque, yet are often 'transparent' (Hutchins, 1980: 14) in the sense that they are taken for reality rather than recognized as interpretations *of* reality. In consequence, any particular schema may imply other schemata through often tacit criteria of relevance and inference, criteria that appear so obvious and natural as not to require explicit notation, thus permitting the formation of multiple and various linkages. Indeed, the interwoven networks of concepts that constitute schemata may exhibit strong or weak, complex or simple, dense or diffuse, bounded or unbounded (in Strauss's (1992) sense), and other variable qualities of connectivity, or even gaps in articulation. That is, cultural schemata may vary in the kind and degree of their schematicity, although they ordinarily involve distinct, well-integrated conceptual structures which can be activated rapidly on the basis of a minimal set of learned cues.

Certain cultural schemata, or congeries of schemata, may have a particular centrality, being positioned at the highest hierarchical levels of organization or generality, potentially interconnecting a wide range of other schemata. Such schemata are implicated and instantiated in a large array of objects, events, situations, actions, or perceptions, and come to be bound up with the ways such phenomena are personally construed and evaluated. Indeed, as Strauss (1992: 211–21) suggests, any individual's repertoire of schemata implicates a mosaic of bounded and unbounded semantic networks, both cultural and personal, which are interconnected in complex ways through individual interaction and experience in a socio-cultural milieu. Thus, an appreciation of how schemata provide personally compelling interpretations for any particular individual requires an exploration of the life-history of that individual with respect to his or her self-understandings, marked memories of salient and self-defining experiences, prototypical instantiations of schemata having personal significance, and the kinds of schemata that the individual has experienced and reconstituted for himself or herself in the processes of socialization and enculturation.

Why is it that certain learned cultural schemata, beyond providing intellectual interpretations that may be put to occasional and superficial – albeit appropriate – social use, come to be invested with cognitive, emotional, evaluative or motivational force for the individual, and even to instigate personal action? Not all cultural schemata are found to be so compelling in this sense: that a schema should be implicated in the processes of socialization and enculturation does not in itself tell us whether or why it should carry such personal significance or psychological force. In other words, it does not account for the schema's internalization. Concerning the acquisition of cultural knowledge or belief, Spiro (1982) distinguishes situations where such knowledge is both familiar and well understood but does not command assent, situations where it is seen to make defensible claims but nevertheless does not carry sufficient personal significance to instigate behaviour, situations where it amounts to a personal belief system serving to guide and shape action, and situations where it exerts a compelling force over the entire range of a person's perception, understanding, affectivity, evaluation, and motivation. Only in the last two situations, in which cultural schemata may be said to have been personally appropriated, can we claim that they have been *internalized*.

Following D'Andrade's (1992: 30) hypothesis that 'a person's most important interpretations of what is going on will function as important goals for that person', it may be suggested that among the most pervasive and compelling interpretations are likely to be those having to do with personhood, selfhood, and individuality, and that these will furnish a significant connection between cultural and personal semantic networks (D'Andrade 1990, Quinn 1992). It is probable, then, that those schemata will be internalized that are most closely bound up with schemata of personhood, selfhood, and individuality. They may, too, be associated with identifications of significant other persons who are involved with the learner in the acquisition, through interaction, of these latter schemata.

Rethinking socialization and enculturation

As Schwartz (1976: ix) notes, processes of socialization and enculturation enable one to embody in one's own experiences, to inscribe in one's sense of identity, and to enact in one's learned behaviour, a part of the culture of the community in which one lives one's life (Schwartz 1981). Yet, since different individuals encounter, learn, and internalize different aspects of their socio-cultural environment, their knowledge of, perspectives on, and investments in varying aspects of community life will differ. Even in relatively simple, small-scale, and homogeneous communities, bound by face-to-face relationships, no individual could conceivably take on the entire body of cultural knowledge. This raises the considerable problems of the ways in which, and of the degree to which, cultural knowledge is shared (Roberts 1951, Wallace 1970, Schwartz 1978, Swartz 1991). The acquisition of more or less shared understanding is developmentally complex (Nelson 1985). Commonalities and differences in status–role configurations, socio–cultural experiences, family milieux, circumstances of socialization and enculturation, and so on, result in what Schwartz (1978: 428–30) calls 'idioverses' as the distributive loci and personal organizations of culture. An important aspect of what a child must learn to negotiate, therefore, are the recognized entailments, consequences, and adjustments of its known and intuited idioverse for becoming an effective participant in socio-cultural life. It may be suggested that a child's idioverse is significantly structured, in part, with respect to its senses of personhood, selfhood, and individuality as organizing schemata of great generality. Beyond these considerations, and in view of traditionally prevailing images of the nature of socialization and enculturation, several caveats, some overlapping in concern, are however in order.

First, the phylogenetic heritage underwriting the process of neurobiological maturation undoubtedly provides fundamental developmental resources and constraints encompassing how development can be effected and take shape in any socio-cultural milieu. This evolutionary legacy presumably also sets certain parameters on the ways in which cultures and societies can be designed, realized, rendered adaptively viable, and, thus, shape processes of socialization and enculturation. From a developmental perspective, however, it is essential to recognize that these neurobiological constraints afford not only wide yet ultimately limited variation in the character of the socio-cultural milieu in which socialization and enculturation occur, but also considerable if constrained plasticity in developmental potential, especially during the earlier years of the life-cycle (Brauth *et al.* 1991, Gollin 1981, Lerner 1984, Toulmin 1981).

Second, at the confluence of neurobiological maturation and the shaping of development through socialization and enculturation, there may well be certain sensitive or critical periods during which the nexus between the capacities for gaining significant experience and the incidence of certain structured, marked, elaborated, valued, repeated, and sanctioned experiential opportunities is particularly close (Bornstein 1987). What those formative developmental periods and their conditions are, however, remains problematic and may vary for different abilities, individuals, and socio-cultural environments, although childhood does appear to have at least certain broad, stage-setting functions in shaping some dimensions of the course of development. Yet studies of socialization and enculturation, which are processes that unfold over a lifetime, cannot simply assume that early to middle childhood establishes the essential grounds and configurations of all that emerges thereafter. We must, therefore, direct serious attention to the various ways in which certain periods of development may be formative, and to the socio-cultural conditions under which such periods and their formative potentials arise.

Third, even the youngest children are active, creative participants and also agents in the processes of socialization and enculturation that embed their interactive learning experiences in community life. Further examination is needed of how children variously shape the course of their own development by eliciting, instigating, and otherwise affecting the character of the interactions in which they are engaged. Indeed, more theoretical and ethnographic attention to the entailments and consequences of various genres of interaction in socialization and enculturation is essential (Bruner and Bornstein 1989, Whiting and Edwards 1988). Above all, to grasp the complexities of socialization and enculturation from a person-centred perspective, we need detailed case studies of individual children in diverse cultures and societies, however much such studies may hamper our attempts to reach even local generalizations (Briggs 1991, Poole 1987).

Fourth, processes of socialization and enculturation are both intentional and unintentional, explicit and implicit, marked and unmarked. More ethnographic attention should be paid to the ranges of socio-cultural contexts that function as 'learning environments' for children, and to which they have variable kinds and degrees of access, both direct and indirect. Little is to be gained from supposing that 'learning environments' are either limited to those situations explicitly designed to be so or, at the other extreme, that they embrace the whole of social life. Ethnographic maps of greater subtlety are required to understand how significant 'learning environments' are socio-culturally constituted, without narrowing them down to the intentional, explicit, and marked designs inscribed in local ethnopsychology, or expanding them to embrace the totality of socio-cultural experience. What constitutes an effective 'learning environment' must be understood in terms of a complex interaction of cultural and social factors as these are subjectively and intersubjectively construed and negotiated.

Fifth, socialization and enculturation have potentially transformative significance throughout the life-cycle; for humans retain a capacity for change from early infancy through to old age. Altered circumstances wrought by the individual's movement through the life-cycle and by historical changes in the community may necessitate or provoke various kinds and degrees of personal accommodation. Further understanding of the character and conditions of developmental stability, mutability, and change in the course of the life-cycle requires not only a greater appreciation of the enduring effects of childhood experiences, but also an exploration of the potentially distinctive and transformative nature of adult socialization, enculturation, and development.

Sixth, socialization and enculturation involve not only various kinds of learning, but also varied ways of 'learning to learn' (in Bateson's (1972b) sense). Of deutero-learning, Bateson (1972b: 170) suggests that 'individuals who have complex emotional patterns of relationships with other individuals ... will be led to acquire or reject apperceptive habits by the very complex phenomena of personal example, tone of voice, hostility, love, etc....The event stream is mediated to them through...cultural media which are structured at every point by tramlines of apperceptive habit.' Up to now, anthropological studies of socialization and enculturation have made little headway in grasping how children apprehend the cues, signs, or other features that mark and frame what is important and to be learned, what is a 'learning environment', who are the persons with and from whom one should learn, and how is effective learning to proceed. Children do not simply learn what there is to be learned; they also learn how variously to go about the processes of learning and what they must attend to and take into account to do so. Significant dimensions of the strategies and tactics of learning are themselves learned through socialization and enculturation.

Seventh, learning through socialization and enculturation is geared not only to understanding the cultural concepts, categories, schemata, frames, and scripts governing engagements in social interaction, but also to comprehending the character of the contexts and their focal events, the relevant background knowledge, and the situational cues in which social interaction is embedded (Goodwin and Duranti 1992). Understanding any social activity requires often tacit background knowledge implicated by tacit frames of relevance. Various senses of context must be learned with some subtlety, nevertheless, if individuals are to be able to apprehend and utilize schemata as context-dependent interpretive devices, and thereby to make sense of and deal with the complexities of the social life surrounding them. A child must learn to recognize, attend to, construct, and manipulate myriad aspects of the interactive contexts of those activities in which he or she participates.

Eighth, studies of socialization and enculturation must take account of the interwoven effects of several kinds of change – in the individual's circumstances, positions, and experiences in the life-cycle, in the social forms enveloping the individual (as regards social relationships within family, household, domestic group and beyond), and in the historical character of a particular culture and society. As the individual moves through the life-cycle, his or her positions in and, in part, perspectives on the social world are altered by virtue not only of social maturation and its entailments in terms of generational position, but also of varying kinds and degrees of historical transformation of the society or culture itself. Perhaps in microcosm, such changes are reflected in transformations in the experiences, circumstances, identities, and social relationships of the developing child, for, as Giddens (1979: 130) suggests, the 'unfolding of childhood is not . . . just for the child'. As a child is born and socially matures, its presence and development take place in a qualitatively ever-changing network of persons and social relationships centred on the family, and gradually extending to wider and more complex domains of community life.

Ninth, the socially interactive transmission of cultural knowledge, however it may be personally received, interpreted, and reorganized, is not only transgenerational, but also intra-generational (Tuzin 1990: 82–5, Weisner and Gallimore 1977). In early childhood, the rudiments of a child's self-constructed or interactively constituted understandings of the socio-cultural realm are richly portrayed in pretend play or other fantasy images, which may be solitary or collaborative in their production. Beginning usually in middle childhood, however, children actively, energetically, and creatively construct elaborate socio-cultural worlds of their own that are by no means simply impoverished replicas of adult worlds (Poole 1987, Tuzin 1990). Thus, any exploration of socialization and enculturation must attend to the two-fold milieux of childhood – the child-centred and the adult-centred – and to how each informs the other. The part played in socialization and enculturation by peers – friends and kin of varying ages and different genders – and by the 'societies' and 'cultures' of children are only beginning to be understood (Asher and Gottman 1981, Hartup 1983, Rogoff 1981, Youniss 1980).

A theoretical approach to human development

Any study of socialization and enculturation is predicated on some theoretical perspective on human development, which usually privileges childhood. As Schwartz (1981: 4) observes, however, anthropology has tended to ignore children in culture and society, whereas developmental psychology has tended to ignore the socio-cultural in children. Whatever theoretical approach is adopted, it must rest on some set of foundational assumptions about the unfolding of certain aspects of human nature, the causes or influences governing or shaping their emergence and their stability or change, and the pathways of their enhancement, diminution, stabilization or transformation (Bruner 1986, Feldman and Bruner 1987, Kagan 1986, Shweder 1991, White 1983). The key questions of contemporary developmental theory may be phrased in the following terms: What characteristics are common to all children everywhere at particular moments of development, and what characteristics are peculiar to particular socio-cultural milieux? How does development unfold, and why does it take the course or courses that it does? Which developmentally constituted capacities are preserved and elaborated, which are not, and what conditions determine or shape the stability or mutability of acquired abilities? These questions are founded upon certain basic oppositions: between the developmental roles of biology and experience (Kagan 1981b, Konner 1981, LeVine 1969), between continuity and discontinuity (Emde and Harmon 1984, Kagan 1980, 1983, 1984), between qualitative and quantitative change, between subjective and objective frames of reference, between constructs of a general and of a specific nature, between constancy and mutability across domains or contexts, between stages or transitions and continua, and between the individual and society. It is now generally recognized, however, that developmental trajectories are best understood not in terms of hard-and-fast dichotomies, but as the result of a complex interplay of mutual influences over time.

Theoretical models of socialization and enculturation have as their objective to explain the significance of the cultural and the social in development — and especially those aspects of development that make possible, facilitate, promote, channel, focus, and constrain the orientations, sensitivities, understandings, competences, and agential powers necessary to participate as an actor in society. Central to the development of the potential to become an actor and to its pragmatic realization, however, is the emergence of a sense of identity — a sense of having a place in the community as a more or less complete, normal human being capable of apprehending socio-cultural forms and forces, of communicating and otherwise acting, of authoring, monitoring, and representing one's actions, and of being a recognized person, a reflexive self, both distinguished through one's own actions and 'reflected back' in and through the actions of others (Cooley 1902, Mead 1934).

In consequence, it is essential to explore the unfolding of three intertwined aspects of identity — those of personhood, selfhood, and individuality — through processes of socialization and enculturation in contexts of participation as an actor in a community. Although, as I have already remarked, identity is forever subject to change in at least some respects throughout the life-cycle, my emphasis here will be primarily on early through middle childhood (from about two to twelve years) — a presumably formative segment of the life-cycle with which most anthropological studies of socialization and enculturation have been primarily concerned. The sense in which any aspect of early or later childhood is formative in kind, degree, or force is, nevertheless, theoretically and empirically problematic (Clarke and Clarke 1976,

Shweder 1991). Various aspects of identity may always be subject to transformation under certain circumstances. Thus, the rationale for the emphasis on early to middle childhood in this article is the assumption that cultural understanding and social competence, and the relevant senses of personal identity, however they may be subsequently transformed, first begin to be acquired, organized, made personally significant, and put to social use in the early interactions in which children engage and in the 'societies' and 'cultures' that they construct for themselves both seriously and playfully – and always imaginatively. Although some aspects of what is acquired in childhood socialization and enculturation affect, *mutatis mutandis*, the shape of certain dimensions of subsequent development, these early (re)constructions of socio-cultural experience provide a privileged base for perceiving how an individual comes into being in a 'culturally constituted behavioural environment' (Hallowell 1955: 57).

PERSONHOOD, SELFHOOD AND INDIVIDUALITY

As Fogelson (1982), La Fontaine (1985), Poole (1991), and Whittaker (1992) variously maintain, ethnographic explorations of person, self, and individuality are still at an early and theoretically confused stage of mapping a complex terrain. Analytically, notions of person and self are often conflated, confounded, or seen as synonymous (Geertz 1973, 1984), and ideas about the individual are commonly consigned to a realm of peculiarly Western cultural and intellectual biases. My present perspective, however, proposes a tentative set of analytic distinctions – not prematurely formal definitions, but orientations of emphasis – among personhood, selfhood, and individuality as different dimensions of identity. These distinctions may help us to show how, in diverse socio-cultural contexts, various discriminations and linkages may be made among 'human beings as . . . living entities among many such entities in the universe, . . . [as] centres of being or experience, or . . . [as] members of society' (Harris 1989: 599).

However such aspects of identity may or may not be recognized, constituted, discriminated, interconnected, emphasized, or valued, in whole or in part, in any socio-cultural milieu, there is some heuristic utility in separating them out analytically. Such distinctions may provide a framework for conceptually mapping any particular local configuration onto a comparative landscape, and for exploring what contribution, if any, local concepts make to the shape and texture of personal, cultural, and social senses of identity in any community (Poole 1991). It must be noted, nevertheless, that our analytic notions of person, self, and individual will inevitably bear a problematic and at most approximate relationship to local concepts of identity. Moreover, cultural schemata of identity in any society will variously draw upon a broad range of other culturally embedded ideas, both explicit and implicit.

Personhood

Following Mauss (1938), Fortes (1973), and Harris (1989), the notion of personhood refers to those culturally constituted and socially conferred attributes, capacities, and signs that mark a moral career and its jural entitlements in a particular society. An analytic concern with personhood focuses on those cultural forms and social forces that together confer on the individual a public presence, in the sense of a human nature which is socially encompassed, and place him or her in an array of social positions that establish the contexts, entitlements and emblems for the enactment and achievement of particular kinds and degrees of social agency. Indeed, social personhood endows the culturally recognized individual as a social being with those powers or capacities upon which agency depends, makes possible and constrains his or her proper actions, casts him or her as possessed of understanding and judgement and, thus, of responsibility, and renders him or her accountable as an actor in a socio-moral order.

Although the capacities of personhood may be anchored to the powers and limitations of the human body, they consist fundamentally of the cognitive, emotional, motivational, evaluative and behavioural abilities that are entailed in becoming an actor in community life. Thus, the person is essentially a social being with a certain moral status, is a legitimate bearer of rights and obligations, and is endowed with those characteristics of agency that make possible social action. Conversely, certain culturally marked abnormalities or deficiencies in capacity or in action, whatever their locally understood foundations, may lead to the social denial or withdrawal of particular kinds and degrees of personhood.

Yet a person also has, by cultural implication, a sense of self and of individuality, and a notion of past and future. He or she can hold values, perceive goals, experience motivations, recognize resources, acknowledge constraints, make choices and, thus, adopt plans of action. Moreover, these plans are attributable to him or her as a social being with the conscious, reflective capacity to frame culturally appropriate representations of phenomena and to have purposes, desires, and aversions that require judgement and demand accountability. To be a person, or a moral agent, is to be sensitive to certain standards of the socio-moral order of the community and to suffer a sense of shame (or guilt) when a breach of this order may be attributed to one's personal judgement and responsibility. Thus, personhood consists generally in a conceptual adjustment of a culturally constituted sense of human nature to a socially constituted jural and moral order, with entailments concerning both selfhood and individuality.

Selfhood

In the tradition of Hallowell (1955, 1960), selfhood implicates a set of orientations towards the 'culturally constituted behavioural environment', which, in

842

turn, significantly enfolds, informs, and shapes the self. The self refers to the perceiving and experiencing ego as it is known to himself or herself. Thus, it implies an understanding of the human being as a locus of experience, encompassing the experience of being a more or less distinctive 'someone' beyond one's identity as a person. It is that conceptualized self which is the referent of such notions as 'I' (the subject and author of experiential states and processes and, thus, of thoughts, feelings, evaluations, motivations, and behaviours), and 'me' (the cognized and recognized object of my own and others' attention), and which is distinguished from a contrasting set of phenomena experienced and represented as 'other-than-self'.

It appears that the sense of self is bound up, developmentally and otherwise, with the perceptions and interpretations of other people. Understanding the emergence of self-awareness therefore requires some consideration of the ways in which one's actions are interpreted by others. But that the self emerges *vis-à-vis* others also implies a sense of separateness and distinctiveness predicated on some developmental process of individuation, and a sense of those phenomena that confer individuality and mark personal difference.

Perhaps the constitution of the self is best seen as a process of establishing problematic linkages between relatively inward-facing, private self-understandings and outward-facing, public presentations of self, and between images of past, present, and future selves. An enduring question, therefore, concerns whether selfhood should be regarded as singular or multiple, transcendent or context-bound. As Ewing (1990: 274) observes, it is necessary to attend to 'how multiple self-representations are organized, contextualized, and negotiated'. Self-understandings are often experienced, anchored and remembered in particular frames of reference that refer to personally salient and culturally shaped social encounters. Aspects of such understandings may emerge in the course of a process of self-construction that continues throughout the life-cycle. Ever shifting across contexts, they are always being reconfigured by experiences of marked personal significance. On the other hand, cultural and personal representations of selfhood often invoke a more or less cohesive, stable and enduring sense of self. Notions of the unity, stability, and boundedness of certain aspects of selfhood must be placed, nevertheless, against the background of the multiplicity, openness, and fluidity of selfhood as it emerges in contexts of experience and action throughout the life-cycle.

Individuality

Whereas notions of person and self figure frequently in anthropological maps of cultural landscapes, the notion of the individual has come to be seen as problematic. Indeed, the question of how to take account of the individual in a principled way in relation to the character, dynamics, and reproduction of socio-cultural phenomena has long been recognized as a profound problem in anthropology (Emmet 1960, Evens 1977). Although people in all societies seem to recognize the individual as an empirical agent, the ways in which any sense of individuality is culturally inscribed in schemata of person, self, and the activities of social life are enormously varied. With regard to the 'individualism' of the West, Geertz notes that:

> The Western conception of the person as a bounded, unique, more or less integrated motivational and cognitive universe, a dynamic center of awareness, emotion, judgment, and action organized into a distinctive whole and set contrastively both against other such wholes and against its social and natural background, is, however incorrigible it may seem to us, a rather peculiar idea within the context of the world's cultures.
>
> (1984: 126)

Characterized along these lines, Western individualism is now commonly assumed in anthropology to be the biased source of any putatively analytic notions of the individual, individuation, or individuality. Beyond the West, a relational, socio-centric, holistic, or socially embedded understanding of self is said to prevail (Shweder and Bourne 1991, Shweder and Miller 1991), and it is supposed that this latter sense of self pervades non-Western cultural, social, and personal self-understandings. Both logically and empirically, however, this assumption seems unwarranted, on the following grounds.

First, there is ample evidence that, even in the West, concepts of the individual have undergone considerable permutations and transformations, not only on a broad historical scale but also locally (Lukes 1973, Macfarlane 1979, Taylor 1989). Much of the scholarly representation of Western individualism has been drawn from metaphysical or ideological images, variously embedded in diverse economic, moral, political, and other social philosophies. Such images bear a highly problematic relationship to notions of individuality adduced in local cultural contexts, and to the ways in which individuals experience themselves or are seen by others in their socio-cultural environments. To suppose that representations of personal difference or some sense of individuality can exist only in conjunction with a highly elaborated, metaphysically complex, ideologically prominent, and institutionally embedded concept of the individual would be unduly restrictive.

Second, images of identity are unlikely to be only singular, altogether coherent, and pervasively uniform, and, as Geertz (1973: 406) notes, 'patterns counteractive to the primary ones exist as subdominant but nonetheless important themes in . . . any culture'. Within any society, a variety of senses of person, self, and individuality are manifested in diverse contexts. Whatever their cultural elaboration and social prominence, culturally recognized aspects of personal difference are variously marked in a number of non-Western societies (Briggs 1970, 1991, Fajans 1985, Kirkpatrick 1985, McHugh 1989, Poole 1987, 1991). Moreover, a longstanding tradition of thought on the development of the self among Westerners, from a social interactionist perspective, has emphasized the relational character of the 'looking-glass self' (Cooley 1902, Mead 1934); and social psychology has begun to consider the more general applicability of a social-constructionist perspective on identity to any socio-cultural milieu (Gergen 1985a, b). It is probable that in any society, the full range of explicit and implicit cultural ideas about identity, as they are variously interconnected, contextualized, socially embedded, and personally construed, exhibits a complex web of collectivistic and individualistic themes, woven together in different ways and for differing purposes.

Third, if notions of the self, however culturally constituted and socially realized, are also personally constructed, they represent individuality in at least three senses: they are (re)constructed by individuals; they are assembled from and embedded in life experiences of personal salience; and they mark, in part, certain kinds and degrees of personal distinctiveness. Self-understandings seem always to encompass various senses of personal difference, and personhood seems inevitably to entail some recognition of certain kinds and degrees of individuality. Thus, it is in those places and on those occasions where such facets of individuality are most readily imagined to be at issue that account must be taken of the dimensions of recognized personal difference.

Finally, to imagine that whole cultures or societies may be classified in terms of mutually exclusive, monolithic categories, as either individualistic or socio-centric, is simplistic and misreads the ethnographic and historical record. Such a view also inhibits cross-cultural comparison, blunts the subtlety of ethnographic analysis, distorts ethnopsychological understanding, and once again privileges the West as having a uniqueness different in kind from that of other socio-cultural traditions, thus placing it beyond comparison. Anthropology needs to reconsider how to take account not only of the ethnographer's field experience of individuals who cannot readily be assimilated to a view of the generalized 'other', but also of local understandings of the conditions under which certain recognized personal differences become socio-culturally significant.

All societies must come to terms with the problem of individuality, of the presence of the individual in society, or of the differentiation of each person from each and every other, and must recognize the entailments and consequences of such personal differences for maintaining and perpetuating a socio-moral order. Yet the kinds and degrees of cultural emphasis on individuality, its social force, its expressive possibilities and necessary constraints, and its psychological salience, will vary both within and between societies and cultures. In different socio-cultural situations, certain personal differences may be seen, for example, as valued resources, as behavioural propensities requiring constraint, as natural inevitabilities, as pathological signs, or as insignificant dispositions. Whether as figure or ground, individuality is variously articulated within, and qualifies, broader patterns of personal and socio-cultural identity.

An analytic notion of individuality makes no assumption of analogy with the various and shifting historical notions of *individualism* attributed to certain genres of socio-cultural discourse in the West (cf. Dumont 1970, 1977, 1986; see Béteille in this volume, Article 37). Referring to personally construed,

845

culturally recognized, and socially expressed personal differences, individuality may involve various kinds and degrees of unity, separateness, exclusiveness, boundedness, privacy, interiority, autonomy, naturalness, value, power, control, agency, and other distinctive qualities. Nor does a notion of individuality necessarily connote absolute qualities of uniqueness or idiosyncrasy; it may also refer to *relatively* distinctive qualities that could, in principle, be plotted on an ethnopsychological or ethnosociological map.

All of the intertwined senses of identity discussed above are essential to social life because they enable members of a community to identify a particular embodied being as human, normal, cognizant, sentient, intentional, in possession of agential capacities, having a certain history and place in a system of social relations, and bearing a certain responsibility and accountability for action. Such interwoven senses of identity, as they are personally constituted, in turn significantly affect an individual's understandings of, and participation in, the activities of social life. As LeVine and White (1986: 38) note,

> There are concepts of the person and the self in all cultures. Self-awareness and a sense of one's continuity over time are universal in human experience, and all human adults distinguish between actions of the self as opposed to those of another.

THE EMERGENCE OF IDENTITY IN CHILDHOOD

The developmental emergence, elaboration, and perpetuation or transformation of schemata of personhood, selfhood, and individuality through processes of socialization and enculturation among non-Western children has rarely been examined in anthropology. Indeed, in view of the proliferation of studies of culturally constituted constructs of person and self and, to a lesser extent, of individuality in recent anthropological literature, remarkably little attention has been paid not only to how such constructs are socially distributed and embedded, are acquired in socio-cultural contexts, and are personally construed and deployed, but also to local ethnopsychological portrayals of children or childhood (Poole 1985, 1987, Reisman 1992). How various aspects of identity are developmentally formed, consolidated, contextualized, perpetuated, or transformed over the early life-cycle with respect to socio-cultural forms and forces remains largely unknown terrain, waiting to be ethnographically mapped. Such understanding, however, is essential to the development of theories of socialization and enculturation, as well as to the theories of society and culture upon which they are founded. As I have already noted, cultural schemata of person, self, and individuality, particularly to the extent that they are personally acquired and internalized, are central to how an individual finds his or her orientation, place, significance, and purpose in the community. They are possibly among the most complex of acquired schemata, of perhaps the greatest centrality and generality, and of the greatest personal significance and psychological force. Consequently, it might be expected that the processes of continually both perpetuating and (re)constructing such senses of identity, and of interconnecting them with other salient schemata, are channelled through socialization and enculturation in critically important ways.

Infancy and early childhood

Explorations of the enculturation and socialization of infants from a cross-cultural perspective remain few and far between (Field *et al.* 1981, Leiderman *et al.* 1977, Super 1981). Most ethnographic attention has been directed toward adults' values, understandings, expectations, and actions *vis-à-vis* infants, for prelinguistic children are not considered to be readily accessible to ordinary modes of ethnographic inquiry. In developmental psychology, however, it is now recognized that well before the end of the first year of life, infants exhibit an incipient capacity to form images and concepts, to express emotions and perhaps intentions, and to engage in reciprocities of interaction (Mandler 1990). Indeed, not only does a family-centred social world envelop the infant interactively, but the infant also soon begins to participate in those interactions in a more or less patterned way (Kaye 1982, Stern 1985). In the course of such early development, the rudiments of what might be termed a 'proto-self' begin to emerge.

From infancy onwards, beliefs held by parents and others about the nature and capacity of the child significantly shape the character of their interactions with the child (Kaye 1991, Sigel 1985). There is considerable cross-cultural variation in such beliefs (LeVine 1974, Poole 1985, Whiting 1974). The cultural construction of images of the developing child, and their consequences for socialization and enculturation, are complex (Gergen *et al.* 1990). In the first year of life, however, infants begin to respond to and to accommodate the actions directed towards them and gradually to transform such actions into increasingly intricate *inter*actions (Poole 1985). They also begin to construct what will become more and more contoured maps of their 'developmental niche' (Super and Harkness 1986), which they play an increasing part in constituting.

After a few months, the mutual accommodation and co-ordination of certain caretaking activities begins to take on a more interactive character, and modifications of routines in regard to the everyday patterns of family, household, and community seem to become integrated into infants' expectations. At about two and a half months, infant development comes to be marked by signs of anticipation and aversion, retention of learning between interactions, increased attention span and focus, more visual acuity and scanning of the environment, smiling as a means of social elicitation or response, reduction of diffuse or generalized signals of distress, and, thus, a new quality of contact with caretakers. Increased complexity in reaching, grasping, and later loco-motive capacities, allows the infant to explore both its own body and nearby objects, persons, and situations, as well as to attempt to repeat and extend motoric skills that are often encompassed and shaped by early socialization and enculturation. Such advances set the stage for certain rudimentary sensitivities to, and recognitions of, facets of what will become a more integrated sense of selfhood.

By seven to nine months, however, attachment behaviours to mothers and significant other persons begin to be manifested in various forms of ensuring contact, protesting against separation, and expressing wariness of unfamiliar persons and strange situations (Ainsworth 1967, Lamb 1982). Although the character, onset, foci, strength, security, and duration of varying kinds of attachment seem to differ in some respects, depending on how they are shaped by socialization and enculturation and by the qualities of relations with multiple caretakers, they all involve social relationships with significant others, are invested with personal significance and psychological force, and imply incipient abilities to categorize and remember persons. Attachment behaviours are bound up with expanding communicative abilities involving not only bodily expression and social referencing but also instrumental vocalizations and understandings of simple expressions.

After the end of the first year, naming and more complex categorization begin to emerge and to be directed, in part, towards an early mapping of persons, places, things, and activities in community life. Aspects of the environment are manipulated in elementary puzzle-solving, and play facilitates more fluid forms of experimenting with, and imitating, environmental knowledge. In various contexts, infants appear to acquire implicit knowledge of the scripts of routine events, as we can infer from their signs of anticipation or recognition of such events, and from their reactions of surprise and protest when ordinary expectations are confounded and habitual routines altered. The ability to represent everyday scripts explicitly, and outside their ordinary and immediate contexts, emerges in rudimentary form at the end of the first year (Bates et al. 1979). Thereafter, there often appears to be a growing ability to construct increasingly complex pretend representations of everyday persons, roles, and actions – representations that entail decentering, individuation, and recognition that the world consists of objects and agents other than the self. Collaborative play, in turn, requires not only the metacommunicative framing of action (in Bateson's (1972a) sense) among children, but also some sharing of scripts of the social activities enacted.

In infancy and early childhood, the role of the family and of a relatively intimate and stable sphere of significant caretakers, however this may be bounded, is particularly significant in processes of socialization and enculturation. Dunn (1988), Hess and Handel (1985), and Reiss (1981) variously argue that the psycho-social interior of the family serves to mediate and to interpret for the child the latter's encounters with, and understandings of, socio-cultural phenomena beyond its realm. Indeed, the family often provides a gateway for contact between a child and the wider community. Although much attention has been focused on the importance of mother–child attachments and interactions within the family, there is now greater realization of the significance of the roles of fathers (Hewlett 1992, Katz and Konner 1981), of siblings (Dunn 1988, Mendelson 1990), and of other important persons in early socialization and enculturation within the domestic–familial realm of social life.

As infancy merges into early childhood, there is often a marked decline in expressions of distress at separation, an expansion of exploration, and the emergence of a more elaborated sense of a distinctive self in a world of other persons. The child exhibits a growing sensitivity to social standards and a greater capacity to judge actions, to influence others, and to control or modify its own behaviour with respect to them, and such perceived standards become inscribed in the scripts of play activities. Utterances reveal an incipient sense of agency in self-descriptions, which are also increasingly elaborated in other respects. The qualities of social interaction become not only more complex and differentiated, but also more co-ordinated and sensitive to person, activity, and context. Folk models of child development in many societies indicate a broad recognition that the child is now on a threshold of new understandings and competences in its expanding realm, and processes of socialization and enculturation are often adjusted in consequence of such recognition.

In early childhood (from about two to four years), however, linguistic competence advances rapidly and, through its developing conversational abilities, the child is increasingly able to encounter and to understand what is of significance in the socio-cultural environment and to bring such understandings to bear on its expanding realms of interaction. Yet linguistic ability does not merely imply greater and more sophisticated access to cultural knowledge. As Schieffelin (1990) demonstrates, acquiring a language is profoundly affected by the process of becoming a competent social actor, which in turn is significantly realized through language (see also DeBernardi's discussion of this point in the next article). Conversational capacity, requiring some recognition of distinctions between self and other, categories of other persons, interactive contexts, and socio-linguistic patterns of interaction, is established as early as the age of two.

This advance is marked in two especially significant ways in regard to the child's understanding of personhood, selfhood, and individuality. First, as Bates (1990) notes, a child's acquisition of the linguistic features of person-marking and pronominal referencing illuminates some aspects of an emerging self-concept in the transition from infancy to early childhood. By the age of three to four years, the child appears to have learned to map certain understandings of self onto a complex set of lexical and grammatical forms, and to use these forms conversationally in socially appropriate ways (Mühlhäusler and Harré 1990). Second, as the mastery of speech proceeds, the child develops the ability to construct narratives of increasing complexity, and, as Bruner (1990), Kerby (1991), and Schafer (1992) propose, much that can be glimpsed of self-understandings is cast in narrative constructions about the self – stories about self and others both in everyday events and contexts and in salient life experiences. Such self-narratives include not only auto-biographical portraits, but also a variety of less complex but none the less revealing requests, refusals, excuses, and other comments, interpretations, and explanations that implicate the child as subject or object in social encounters and experiences.

Early childhood also marks the appearance of a more elaborated map of persons in an experientially expanding sense of community. Self-identification of and with other persons through observation, differentiation, imitation, and affiliation involves a complex array of processes of perception, categorization, appraisal, and comparison. Gender comes to figure prominently in under-standings of person and self, and to inflect the character of social interaction. Of particular importance to the development of perceptions and under-standings of persons other than the self, and of the child's senses of its own personhood, selfhood, and individuality, however, is its acquisition of a 'theory of mind' (Astington *et al.* 1988, Frye and Moore 1991, Wellman 1990). Drawing on ethnopsychological schemata of 'mind' encountered in the inter-active contexts of socialization and enculturation, a child begins to develop senses of sensitivity (Light 1979) and empathy (Eisenberg and Strayer 1987) in regard to other persons, and to acquire a subtler sense of the ethnopsycho-logical contours of interactive contexts involving self and other. Under-standings and representations of other persons and of the self become at once more richly connected and distinguished in diverse respects (Shields and Duveen 1986).

Beginning in the second year, as Kagan (1981a) notes, self-awareness and self-understanding, with implications for how the child conceives its person-hood and individuality, become increasingly marked in self-descriptions which reflect more elaborated senses of social standards, agency, mastery, control, evaluation, and so on, coupled to the child's perceptions of its own thoughts, feelings, expectations, intentions, competence, and actions. Various phen-omena come to possess meanings which are significant in socio-cultural con-texts of morally shaped interaction, and which are thus of relevance to other persons besides oneself. In the context of an expanding awareness of its ability to initiate, cease, and reflexively monitor its own actions, the child acquires greater sensitivity to its own capacity to generate goal-directed activity, and to the resources and constraints affecting the attainment of goals. As the child's own awareness of its qualities, capacities, competences, agential powers, and abilities to affect other persons in contexts of social interaction proceeds, its experience of its environment and of its domain of community life becomes significantly organized in terms of its senses of being a person, a self, and an individual in a socio-cultural world.

Middle childhood

It is at the point in early to middle childhood when self-understanding is consolidated, deployed, and elaborated that folk models of childhood in most societies also establish the beginnings of social personhood. The bestowal of personhood, coupled to a recognition of a child's advancing cognitive, emotional, motivational, and behavioural capacities in various arenas of social interaction, implies an attribution of judgemental ability appropriate to the assumption of responsibility and, thus, of social accountability as an incipient actor. In consequence, as social horizons expand and interactions begin to pervade newly experienced domains of community life, children come to know much about the statuses they occupy, the roles they are expected to enact, how to act accordingly, how to control expressions of socially inappropriate feelings, and how to respect the rights of other persons. They develop richer understandings of the socio-cultural perspectives of other persons – especially in contexts of friendship – and of the implications of such perspectives for the course of social interaction and in the management of co-operation and conflict. Their recognition of the social significance of self-control, and of strategies and tactics for controlling others in interaction, becomes more elaborate. Their play, now more and more in the contexts of peer interaction, is infused with understandings of socio-moral rules and conventions, of the consequences of their breach, and of the cultural values of various genres of co-operation and conflict.

On the threshold of middle childhood, a child's notions of its own personhood, selfhood, and individuality become increasingly infused with experiential anchorages in interactive contexts and with personal investments of significant psychological force. Various emotions and motivations come to be personally bound up with understandings of both the outward-facing and the inward-facing aspects of these senses of identity. In this context, the role of shame (and guilt) may be particularly important (Epstein 1992: 198–247, Lewis 1992), and an understanding of shame seems to be acquired by the time of the transition from early to middle childhood. Although shame, in its varying guises, is a cultural construct that operates as a sanction in social control, it is manifested not only in public arenas of social interaction, but also in a more intimate way in experiences of one's own personhood, selfhood, and individuality. The experiential sense of shame, sometimes verging on guilt, is less visible socially but may perhaps affect more profoundly one's senses of identity, to the extent that such senses are forged in contexts of social interaction. Indeed, the effectiveness of shame as a mechanism of social control depends upon the way in which the cultural schemata of shame are linked, in the course of their acquisition and internalization, to schemata of person, self, and individuality, thereby taking on personal significance and psychological force. However, the ways in which shame and other emotional complexes come to be shaped by and connected to the schemata of person, self, and

851

individuality, through socialization and enculturation, are largely unknown for any culture and society.

The period of middle childhood is culturally marked at its inception (about five to seven years) in most societies by the recognition of a dramatic advance in social competence. As middle childhood begins to unfold, children are seen in almost every society to possess a different cognitive, emotional, evaluative, motivational, and agential capacity and, thus, a new order of independence, action, responsibility, and accountability. This transformation is recognized not only in local ethnopsychological portrayals of personhood, selfhood, and individuality at the inception of middle childhood, but also in developmental psychological characterizations of intellectual (Piaget 1954), moral (Kohlberg 1981, 1984) and other social advances in understanding. Processes of socialization and enculturation often involve taking significant account of such changes in articulating expectations, demands, and sanctions in regard to an expanding sphere of social opportunities, responsibilities, and interactions.

As middle childhood advances towards the brink of adolescence, senses of personhood, selfhood, and individuality are increasingly manifested in the interactions of a more or less distinctive world of peers, which is often segregated by gender. It is in this context that the distinctive 'societies' and 'cultures' of children take significant shape (Poole 1987, Tuzin 1990), while relationships with adults – both within the family and beyond – are transformed from emphasizing the dependence, management, and control of children to a greater stress on the mutual negotiation of independence and interdependence. Yet however segregated the child–centred and adult–centred milieux may be in social space, what is learned and experienced in each is brought to bear on the other. Earlier fantasy play tends to give way to games involving more complex understandings of moral rules, social conventions, reciprocal responsibilities, resource distributions, and co-ordinations of personal orientations in the regulation of social interaction. Relations of friendship come to involve increasing emphasis on the sharing of interests, the construction of mutual understandings, and the creation of senses of mutual sensitivity, responsibility, and trust. As social horizons widen, socio-cultural knowledge expands across increasingly diverse contexts, and social relationships and interaction become more extensive and complicated.

CONCLUSION

Although these brief sketches of aspects of early through middle childhood only partially portray the myriad complexities of this time of life in any culture or society, they do indicate some of the largely untapped potential for an ethnographic exploration of the formation of identity in processes of socialization and enculturation. An approach to the anthropological study of socialization and enculturation focused on the character of personal construals of cultural schemata of personhood, selfhood, and individuality, as they are variously experienced, apprehended, and rendered salient in and through the social interactions shaping a child's emerging sense of everyday community life, and of its locus in its socio-cultural milieu, holds considerable promise for theoretical understanding on several fronts.

First, it adopts a perspective that considers, in an integrated and principled manner, the developmental interconnections of the cultural, the social, and the individual over time. This perspective is centred on how the personal apprehension and appropriation of socio-cultural understandings, acquired in various ways and with variable psychological significance and force, are bound up with interactive processes of learning in the varied contexts of community life.

Second, the approach is not predicated, as are more orthodox accounts, on a view of culture as a largely seamless and shared web of significance somehow descending upon and altogether encompassing the individual, who often appears to vanish in the notion of the cultural constitution of phenomena. From the present perspective, culture is rather seen to be organized and experienced in various contextually embedded ways that exhibit inconsistencies, contradictions, ambiguities, lacunae and loose interconnections, to be socially distributed and problematically shared, and to be personally construed or constituted.

Third, the approach is also predicated on a view of society as consisting in pragmatically organized and contextualized events of patterned interaction involving the negotiation of mutual understandings about, and co-ordinations of, such interactions by individual actors whose knowledge of what is going on and what is at stake is incompletely shared. For the individual actor's understandings are not automatically congruent with those of others, nor are the interactions that flow from them necessarily co-ordinated. Cultural models of the proper patterning of social interaction do not translate unproblematically, by way of individual understandings of them, into actual patterns of interaction.

Fourth, the approach recognizes the individual as the proper locus of culture, as the actor in social interaction, and as the bearer of senses of identity that inform the apprehension and appropriation of culture and the engagement in social interaction. In so doing, it denies that an analytic construct of the *individual* is merely, or must necessarily be, an artefact of some Western tradition of *individualism*. To the contrary, it posits an analytic sense of individuality by attending not only to the individual as an empirical agent, but also to how that agent is at once culturally constituted, interactively realized, and personally constructed in the ebb and flow of the varied situations of community life. Thus, it attends to how personal differences, constituted in various ways, do or do not become culturally, socially, and personally significant in different ways in different communities.

Fifth, the approach makes possible a developmental, person-centred, context-embedded appreciation of person and self, agency and emotion, as well as of local ideologies, philosophies, and worldviews, in a manner that explores how what is culturally constituted and socially negotiated can become personally significant and endowed with psychological force. For it is not enough simply to assert that this or that phenomenon is culturally constituted or socially negotiated. We need to attend also to the theoretical and epistemological implications of our notions of 'constitution' and 'negotiation', and to probe the interactive contexts wherein the social and the cultural are woven, through socialization and enculturation, into the life-histories of individuals.

Finally, the approach suggests that certain interlinked schemata of identity – of personhood, selfhood, and individuality – are centrally involved in the processes whereby personally apprehended realms of socio-cultural knowledge are variously acquired, (re)constructed, comprehended, rendered significant, and sometimes internalized and imbued with psychological force as they affect the thoughts, feelings, orientations, evaluations, intentions, plans, and actions of individuals in the course of their continual socialization and enculturation in the contexts of community life. Anthropological theorizing about socialization and enculturation still remains in its infancy. As Benthall (1992) suggests, however, ethnographic study of the socialization and enculturation of children may hold the promise of recasting anthropological perspectives not only on the distinctiveness of children's socio-cultural worlds and of children's images of the adult-centred socio-cultural realm, but also on how socio-cultural worlds in general are learned by individuals and constituted in and through such learning. This article represents but a modest proposal in that direction.

REFERENCES

Ainsworth, M. D. S. (1967) *Infancy in Uganda*, Baltimore: Johns Hopkins University Press.

Asher, S. R. and Gottman, J. M. (eds) (1981) *The Development of Children's Friendships*, Cambridge: Cambridge University Press.

Astington, J. W., Harris, P. L. and Olson, D. R. (eds) (1988) *Developing Theories of Mind*, Cambridge: Cambridge University Press.

Bates, E. (1990) 'Language about me and you: pronominal reference and the emerging concept of self', in D. Cicchetti and M. Beeghly (eds) *The Self in Transition*, Chicago: University of Chicago Press.

Bates, E., Benigni, L., Bretherton, I., Camaioni, L. and Volterra, V. (1979) *The Emergence of Symbols*, New York: Academic Press.

Bateson, G. (1972a) 'A theory of play and fantasy', in G. Bateson *Steps to an Ecology of Mind*, New York: Ballantine Books.

—— (1972b) 'Social planning and the concept of deutero-learning', in G. Bateson *Steps to an Ecology of Mind*, New York: Ballantine Books.

Benthall, J. (1992) 'A late developer? the ethnography of children', *Anthropology Today* 8(2): 1.

Bornstein, M. H. (1987) 'Sensitive periods in development: interdisciplinary perspectives', in M. H. Bornstein (ed.) *Sensitive Periods in Development*, Hillsdale, NJ: Lawrence Erlbaum.

Brauth, S. E., Hall, W. S. and Dooling, R. J. (1991) 'Epilogue', in S. E. Brauth, W. S. Hall and R. J. Dooling (eds) *Plasticity of Development*, Cambridge, Mass.: MIT Press.

Briggs, J. L. (1970) *Never in Anger*, Cambridge, Mass.: Harvard University Press.

—— (1991) 'Mazes of meaning: the exploration of individuality in culture and of culture through individual constructs', *The Psychoanalytic Study of Society* 16: 111–53.

Bronfenbrenner, U. (1979) *The Ecology of Human Development*, Cambridge, Mass.: Harvard University Press.

Bruner, J. S. (1986) 'Value presuppositions of developmental theory', in L. Cirillo and S. Wapner (eds) *Value Presuppositions in Theories of Human Development*, Hillsdale, NJ: Lawrence Erlbaum.

—— (1990) 'Autobiography and self', in J. S. Bruner, *Acts of meaning*, Cambridge, Mass.: Harvard University Press.

Bruner, J. S. and Bornstein, M. H. (1989) 'On interaction', in M. H. Bornstein and J. S. Bruner (eds) *Interaction in Human Development*, Hillsdale, NJ: Lawrence Erlbaum.

Clarke, A. M. and Clarke, A. D. B. (1976) *Early Experience*, New York: Free Press.

Cooley, C. H. (1902) *Human Nature and the Social Order*, New York: Charles Scribner's Sons.

D'Andrade, R. G. (1981) 'The cultural part of cognition', *Cognitive Science* 5: 179–95.

—— (1984) 'Cultural meaning systems', in R. A. Shweder and R. A. LeVine (eds) *Culture Theory*, Cambridge: Cambridge University Press.

—— (1990) 'Culture and personality: a false dichotomy', in D. K. Jordan and M. J. Swartz (eds) *Personality and the Cultural Construction of Society*, Tuscaloosa: University of Alabama Press.

—— (1992) 'Schemas and motivation', in R. G. D'Andrade and C. Strauss (eds) *Human Motives and Cultural Models*, Cambridge: Cambridge University Press.

Dumont, L. (1970) *Homo Hierarchicus*, Chicago: University of Chicago Press.

—— (1977) *From Mandeville to Marx*, Chicago: University of Chicago Press.

—— (1986) *Essays on Individualism*, Chicago: University of Chicago Press.

Dunn, J. (1988) *The Beginnings of Social Understanding*, Cambridge, Mass.: Harvard University Press.

Eisenberg, N. and Strayer, J. (1987) *Empathy and Its Development*, Cambridge: Cambridge University Press.

Emde, R. N. and Harmon, R. J. (1984) 'Entering a new era in the search for developmental continuities', in R. N. Emde and R. J. Harmon (eds) *Continuities and Discontinuities in Development*, New York: Plenum Press.

Emmet, D. (1960) 'How far can structural studies take account of individuals?', *Journal of the Royal Anthropological Institute* 90: 191–200.

Epstein, A. L. (1992) *In the Midst of Life*, Berkeley: University of California Press.

Evens, T. M. (1977) 'The predication of the individual in anthropological interactionism', *American Anthropologist* 79: 579–97.

Ewing, K. P. (1990) 'The illusion of wholeness: culture and the experience of inconsistency', *Ethos* 18: 251–78.

Fajans, J. (1985) 'The person in social context: the social character of Baining "psychology"', in G. M. White and J. Kirkpatrick (eds) *Person, Self, and Experience*, Berkeley: University of California Press.

Feldman, C. and Bruner J. S. (1987) 'Varieties of perspective: an overview', in J. Russell (ed.) *Philosophical Perspectives on Developmental Psychology*, Oxford: Blackwell.

Field, T. M., Sostek, A. M., Vietze, P. and Leiderman, P. H. (eds) (1981) *Culture and Early Interactions*, Hillsdale, NJ: Lawrence Erlbaum.

Fogelson, R. (1982) 'Person, self and identity: some anthropological retrospects, circumspects and prospects', in B. Lee (ed.) *Psychosocial Theories of the Self*, New York: Plenum Press.

Fortes, M. (1973) 'On the concept of the person among the Tallensi', in G. Dieterlen (ed.) *La Notion de personne en afrique noire*, Paris: Centre National de la Recherche Scientifique.

Frye, D. and Moore, C. (eds) (1991) *Children's Theories of Mind*, Hillsdale, NJ: Lawrence Erlbaum.

Geertz, C. (1973) 'Person, time, and conduct in Bali', in *The Interpretation of Cultures*, New York: Basic Books.

—— (1984) '"From the native's point of view": on the nature of anthropological understanding', in R. A. Shweder and R. A. LeVine (eds) *Culture Theory*, Cambridge: Cambridge University Press.

Gergen, K. J. (1985a) 'Social constructionist inquiry: context and implications', in K. J. Gergen and K. E. Davis (eds) *The Social Construction of the Person*, New York: Springer.

—— (1985b) 'Theory of the self: impasse and evolution', in L. Berkowitz (ed.) *Advances in Experimental Social Psychology*, vol. 17, New York: Academic Press.

Gergen, K. J., Gloger-Tippelt, G. and Berkowitz, P. (1990) 'The cultural construction of the developing child', in G. R. Semin and K. J. Gergen (eds) *Everyday Understanding*, London: Sage.

Giddens, A. (1979) *Central Problems in Social Theory*, Berkeley: University of California Press.

Gollin, E. S. (1981) 'Development and plasticity', in E. S. Gollin (ed.) *Developmental Plasticity*, New York: Academic Press.

Goodwin, C. and Duranti, A. (1992) 'Rethinking context: an introduction', in A. Duranti and C. Goodwin (eds) *Rethinking Context*, Cambridge: Cambridge University Press.

Hallowell, A. I. (1955) 'The self and its behavioral environment', in A. I. Hallowell *Culture and Experience*, Philadelphia: University of Pennsylvania Press.

—— (1960) 'Self, society and culture in phylogenetic perspective', in S. Tax (ed.) *Evolution After Darwin*, vol. 2, Chicago: University of Chicago Press.

Harris, G. G. (1989) 'Concepts of individual, self, and person in description and analysis', *American Anthropologist* 91: 599–612.

Hartup, W. W. (1983) 'Peer relations', in E. M. Hetherington (ed.) *Handbook of Child Psychology*, vol. 4, New York: John Wiley.

Herskovits, M. J. (1948) *Man and His Works*, New York: Alfred A. Knopf.

Hess, R. D. and Handel, G. (1983) 'The family as a psychosocial organization', in G. Handel (ed.) *The Psychosocial Interior of the Family*, 3rd edn, New York: Aldine de Gruyter.

Hewlett, B. S. (ed.) (1992) *Father–Child Relations*, New York: Aldine de Gruyter.

Hutchins, E. (1980) *Culture and Inference*, Cambridge, Mass.: Harvard University Press.

Kagan, J. (1980) 'Perspectives on continuity', in O. G. Brim Jr and J. Kagan (eds) *Constancy and Change in Human Development*, Cambridge: Harvard University Press.

—— (1981a) *The Second Year*, Cambridge, Mass.: Harvard University Press.

—— (1981b) 'Universals in human development', in R. H. Munroe, R. L. Munroe and B. B. Whiting (eds) *Handbook of Cross-Cultural Human Development*, New York: Garland STPM Press.

—— (1983) 'Developmental categories and the premise of connectivity', in R. M. Lerner (ed.) *Developmental Psychology*, Hillsdale, NJ: Lawrence Erlbaum.

—— (1984) 'Continuity and change in the opening years of life', in R. N. Emde and R. J. Harmon (eds) *Continuities and Discontinuities in Development*, New York: Plenum Press.

—— (1986) 'Presuppositions in developmental inquiry', in L. Cirillo and S. Wapner (eds) *Value Presuppositions in Theories of Human Development*, Hillsdale, NJ: Lawrence Erlbaum.

Katz, M. M. and Konner, M. J. (1981) 'The role of the father: an anthropological perspective', in M. E. Lamb (ed.) *The Role of the Father in Child Development*, 2nd edn, New York: John Wiley.

Kaye, K. (1982) *The Mental and Social Life of Babies*, Chicago: University of Chicago Press.

—— (1991) 'The parental frame', in M. Woodhead, R. Carr and P. Light (eds) *Becoming a Person*, London: Routledge.

Kerby, P. (1991) *Narrative and the Self*, Bloomington: Indiana University Press.

Kirkpatrick, J. (1985) 'How personal differences can make a difference', in K. J. Gergen and K. E. Davis (eds) *The Social Construction of the Person*, New York: Springer.

Kohlberg, L. (1981) *Essays on Moral Development*, vol. 1, New York: Harper & Row.

—— (1984) *Essays on Moral Development*, vol. 2, New York: Harper & Row.

Konner, M. J. (1981) 'Evolution of human behavior development', in R. H. Munroe, R. L. Munroe and B. B. Whiting (eds) *Handbook of Cross-Cultural Human Development*, New York: Garland STPM Press.

La Fontaine, J. S. (1985) 'Person and individual: some anthropological reflections', in M. Carrithers, S. Collins and S. Lukes (eds) *The Category of the Person*, Cambridge: Cambridge University Press.

Lamb, M. E. (1982) 'Parent-infant interaction, attachment, and socio-emotional development', in R. N. Emde and R. J. Harmon (eds) *The Development of Attachment and Affiliative Systems*, New York: Plenum Press.

Lee, B. and Hickman, M. (1983) 'Language, thought and self in Vygotsky's developmental theory', in B. Lee and G. G. Noam (eds) *Developmental Approaches to the Self*, New York: Plenum Press.

Lee, B., Wertsch, J. V. and Stone, A. (1983) 'Towards a Vygotskian theory of the self', in B. Lee and G. G. Noam (eds) *Developmental Approaches to the Self*, New York: Plenum Press.

Leiderman, P. H., Tulkin, S. R. and Rosenfeld, A. (eds) (1977) *Culture and Infancy*, New York: Academic Press.

Lerner, R. M. (1984) *On the Nature of Human Plasticity*, Cambridge: Cambridge University Press.

LeVine, R. A. (1969) 'Culture, personality and socialization: an evolutionary view', in D. Goslin (ed.) *Handbook of Socialization Theory and Research*, Chicago: Rand McNally.

—— (1974) 'Parental goals: a cross-cultural view', *Teachers College Record* 76: 52–65.

—— (1977) 'Child rearing as cultural adaptation', in P. H. Leiderman, S. E. Tulkin and R. Rosenfeld (eds) *Culture and Infancy*, New York: Academic Press.

—— (1982) *Culture, Behavior, and Personality*, 2nd edn, New York: Aldine.

LeVine, R. A. and White, M. (1986) *Human Conditions*, London: Routledge & Kegan Paul.

Lewis, M. (1992) *Shame*, New York: Free Press.

Light, P. (1979) *The Development of Social Sensitivity*, Cambridge: Cambridge University Press.

Lukes, S. (1973) *Individualism*, Oxford: Blackwell.

Macfarlane, A. (1979) *The Origins of English Individualism*, Cambridge: Cambridge University Press.

Mandler, J. M. (1990) 'A new perspective on cognitive development in infancy', *American Scientist* 79: 236–43.

Mauss, M. (1938) 'Une catégorie de l'esprit humain: la notion de personne, celle de "moi"', *Journal of the Royal Anthropological Institute* 68: 263–282.

McHugh, E. L. (1989) 'Concepts of the person among the Gurungs of Nepal', *American Ethnologist* 16: 75–86.

Mead, G. H. (1934) *Mind, Self and Society*, Chicago: University of Chicago Press.

Mead, M. (1963) 'Socialization and enculturation', *Current Anthropology* 4: 184–8.

Mendelson, M. J. (1990) *Becoming a Brother*, Cambridge: MIT Press.

Mühlhäusler, P. and Harré, R. (1990) *Pronouns and People*, Oxford: Blackwell.

Nelson, K. (1985) *Making Sense*, Orlando: Academic Press.

Piaget, J. (1954) *The Construction of Reality in the Child*, New York: Basic Books.

Poole, F. J. P. (1985) 'Coming into social being: cultural images of infants in Bimin-Kuskusmin folk psychology', in G. M. White and J. Kirkpatrick (eds) *Person, Self, and Experience*, Berkeley: University of California Press.

—— (1987) 'Personal experience and cultural representation in children's "personal symbols" among Bimin-Kuskusmin', *Ethos* 15: 104–35.

—— (1991) 'Cultural schemas and experiences of the self among the Bimin-Kuskusmin of Papua New Guinea', *Psychoanalytic Study of Society* 16: 55–85.

Quinn, N. (1992) 'The motivational force of self-understanding: evidence from wives' inner conflicts', in R. D'Andrade and C. Strauss (eds) *Human motives and cultural models*, Cambridge: Cambridge University Press.

Reisman, P. (1992) *First Find your Child a Good Mother*, New Brunswick, NJ: Rutgers University Press.

Reiss, D. (1981) *The Family's Construction of Reality*, Cambridge, Mass.: Harvard University Press.

Roberts, J. M. (1951) *Three Navaho Households: a Comparative Study of Small Group Culture*, Peabody Museum of America Archaeology and Anthropology Papers vol. 40(3).

Rogoff, B. (1981) 'Adults and peers as agents of socialization: a highland Guatemala profile', *Ethos* 9: 18–36.

—— (1990) *Apprenticeship in Thinking*, New York: Oxford University Press.

Sapir, E. (1949) *Selected writings of Edward Sapir in Language, Culture and Personality*, ed. D. G. Mandelbaum, Berkeley: University of California Press.

Schafer, R. (1992) 'Narratives of the self', in R. Schafer, *Retelling a Life*, New York: Basic Books.

Schieffelin, B. B. (1990) *The Give and Take of Everyday Life*, Cambridge: Cambridge University Press.

Schwartz, T. (1976) 'Introduction', in T. Schwartz (ed.) *Socialization as Cultural Communication*, Berkeley: University of California Press.

—— (1978) 'Where is culture? personality as the distributive locus of culture', in G. D. Spindler (ed.) *The Making of Psychological Anthropology*, Berkeley: University of California Press.

—— (1981) 'The acquisition of culture', *Ethos* 9: 4–17.

Shields, M. M. and Duveen, G. M. (1986) 'The young child's image of the person and the social world: some aspects of the child's representation of persons', in J. Cook-Gumperz, W. A. Corsaro and J. Streeck (eds) *Children's Worlds and Children's Language*, New York: Mouton de Gruyter.

Shweder, R. A. (1991) 'Rethinking culture and personality theory', in R. A. Shweder, *Thinking Through Cultures*, Cambridge, Mass.: Harvard University Press.

Shweder, R. A. and Bourne, E. J. (1991) 'Does the concept of the person vary cross-culturally?', in R. A. Shweder, *Thinking Through Cultures*, Cambridge, Mass.: Harvard University Press.

Shweder, R. A. and Miller, J. G. (1991) 'The social construction of the person: how is it possible?', in R. A. Shweder, *Thinking Through Cultures*, Cambridge, Mass.: Harvard University Press.

Sigel, I. E. (1985) 'Introduction', in I. E. Sigel, *Parental Belief Systems*, Hillsdale, NJ: Lawrence Erlbaum.

Spiro, M. E. (1982) 'Collective representations and mental representations in religious symbol systems', in J. Maquet (ed.) *On Symbols in Anthropology*, Malibu: Udena.

Stern, D. N. (1985) *The Interpersonal World of the Infant*, New York: Basic Books.

Strauss, C. (1992) 'What makes Tony run? Schemas as motives reconsidered', in R. D'Andrade and C. Strauss (eds) *Human Motives and Cultural Models*, Cambridge: Cambridge University Press.

Super, C. M. (1981) 'Behavioral development in infancy', in R. H. Munroe, R. L. Munroe and B. B. Whiting (eds) *Handbook of Cross-Cultural Human Development*, New York: Garland STPM Press.

Super, C. M. and Harkness, S. (1986) 'The developmental niche: a conceptualization at the interface of the child and culture', *International Journal of Behavioral Development* 9: 545–69.

Swartz, M. J. (1991) *The Way the World Is*, Berkeley: University of California Press.

Taylor, C. (1989) *Sources of the Self*, Cambridge, Mass.: Harvard University Press.

Toulmin, S. (1981) 'Epistemology and developmental psychology', in E. S. Gollin (ed.) *Developmental Plasticity*, New York: Academic Press.

Tuzin, D. F. (1990) 'Of the resemblance of fathers to their children: the roots of primitivism in middle-childhood enculturation', *The Psychoanalytic Study of Society* 15: 69–103.

Vygotsky, L. S. (1978) *Mind in Society*, Cambridge, Mass.: Harvard University Press.

Wallace, A. F. C. (1970) *Culture and Personality*, 2nd edn, New York: Random House.

Weisner, T. S. and Gallimore, R. (1977) 'My brother's keeper: child and sibling caretaking', *Current Anthropology* 18: 169–91.

Wellman, H. M. (1990) *The Child's Theory of Mind*, Cambridge, Mass.: MIT Press.

Wentworth, W. M. (1980) *Context and Understanding*, New York: Elsevier North Holland.

White, S. H. (1983) 'The idea of development in developmental psychology', in R. M. Lerner (ed.) *Developmental Psychology*, Hillsdale, NJ: Lawrence Erlbaum.

Whiting, B. B. (1974) 'Folk wisdom and child rearing', *Merrill-Palmer Quarterly of Behavior and Development* 20: 9–19.

Whiting, B. B. and Edwards, C. P. (1988) *Children of Different Worlds*, Cambridge, Mass.: Harvard University Press.

Whiting, B. B. and Whiting, J. W. M. (1975) *Children of Six Cultures*, Cambridge, Mass.: Harvard University Press.

Whittaker, E. (1992) 'The birth of the anthropological self and its career', *Ethos* 20: 191–219.

Youniss, J. (1980) *Parents and Peers in Social Development*, Chicago: University of Chicago Press.

FURTHER READING

Ainsworth, M. D. S. (1967) *Infancy in Uganda*, Baltimore, Md.: Johns Hopkins University Press.

Briggs, J. L. (1970) *Never in Anger*, Cambridge: Harvard University Press.

Chisholm, J. S. (1983) *Navajo Infancy*, New York: Aldine.
Dunn, J. (1988) *The Beginnings of Social Understanding*, Cambridge, Mass.: Harvard University Press.
Erchak, G. M. (1992) *The Anthropology of Self and Behavior*, New Brunswick, NJ: Rutgers University Press.
Field, T. M., Sostek, A. M., Vietze, P. and Leiderman, P. H. (eds) (1981) *Culture and Early Interactions*, Hillsdale, NJ: Lawrence Erlbaum.
Hewlett, B. S. (1991) *Intimate Fathers*, Ann Arbor: University of Michigan Press.
Kelly–Byrne, D. (1989) *A Child's Play Life*, New York: Teachers College Press.
Leiderman, P. H., Tulkin, S. R. and Rosenfeld, A. (eds) (1977) *Culture and Infancy*, New York: Academic Press.
LeVine, R. A. (1982) *Culture, Behavior and Personality*, New York: Aldine Publishing Company.
Munroe, R. H., Munroe, R. L. and Whiting, B. B. (eds) (1981) *Handbook of Cross-Cultural Human Development*, New York: Garland STPM Press.
Reisman, P. (1992) *First Find Your Child a Good Mother*, New Brunswick, NJ: Rutgers University Press.
Rogoff, B. (1990) *Apprenticeship in Thinking*, New York: Oxford University Press.
Whiting, B. B. and Edwards, C. P. (1988) *Children of Different Worlds*, Cambridge, Mass.: Harvard University Press.

31

SOCIAL ASPECTS OF LANGUAGE USE

Jean DeBernardi

Language use is fundamental to the creation and expression of social identity and difference, and the translation of cultures has always depended on understanding the complexities of language use in other social worlds. Such understanding is crucial even in the work of anthropologists who would not describe themselves as 'linguists': the analysis of kinship systems, for example, depends on a sophisticated understanding of the way that terms of reference and address both classify social relationships and pattern social interaction. Even Radcliffe-Brown's work (1965 [1952]) on joking relationships, though defined as a study in social structure, is in fact a concise statement of the social meaning of certain norms of linguistic interaction.

Contemporary ethnographic linguists are driven by functional questions regarding the role of linguistic interaction in expressing social identity and shaping value. Research into the pragmatics of language use suggests that people not only speak about the world 'out there'; they also create a good deal of their social reality in the very act of speaking (Silverstein 1979: 194). Thus the acquisition of a language is not only the internalization of a linguistic code, but also entails the learning of status and role, of appropriate social affect, and (ultimately) of a worldview. Language provides both the foundation of a shared cultural identity and the means for the reproduction of social difference.

Early cross-cultural research on language use emphasized the shared dimensions of language, attending to the role of language in constraining thought, revealing worldview, and determining social action, and these theoretical premises have had a deep influence on the work of both linguists and anthropologists. Malinowski (himself highly sensitive to the 'verbal contour of native thought' (1922: 23)) was among the first to shift theoretical attention to questions about social aspects of language use (1978 [1935]) in

861

work that influenced the development of the field of functional linguistics (see for example J. R. Firth (1957) and Halliday (1978)). The emergence of the approach known as the 'ethnography of speaking' and its application to the cross-cultural study of language use was an important step in the establishment of an interdisciplinary sociolinguistics, and gave impetus to the growth of both ethnopoetics and 'dialogic anthropology'. Interdisciplinary interest in the relationship between language, ideology, and power has also had a significant impact in the field, and anthropologists have made important contributions to research on the politics of language use.

While much recent work places theoretical emphasis on performance and choice rather than system and code (Luong 1990), in practice the cross-cultural analysis of language in society must explore the interaction between the particular and the general. Thus Abu-Lughod (1986) interprets a Bedouin poetic performance in the light both of the personal history of the singer and of a shared cultural code governing the social expression of affect; Scotton (1988) explains an instance of code-switching in Kenya in terms both of the strategic aims of the speaker and of the shared social meaning of two linguistic varieties. With this dialectic in mind, between individual circumstance and common code, let me begin with a discussion of the social nature of the linguistic sign.

THE LINGUISTIC SIGN

Languages in their variability and diversity are profoundly social. Sapir emphasized this fact when he defined language as 'a purely human and non-instinctive method of communicating ideas, emotions, and desires by means of a system of voluntarily produced symbols' (1949a [1921]: 8), and as 'the most massive and inclusive art we know, a mountainous and anonymous work of unconscious generations' (1949a: 220). Since, ultimately, each language is both an abstraction from and a classification of experience, each gives 'predetermined form' to the symbolic expression of its speakers.

Consider, then, the nature of the linguistic sign. De Saussure made the arbitrariness of the association between signifier and signified fundamental to his theory of language (1959 [1915]: 67–9). On the foundation of the arbitrary association between sounds and meanings, a diverse range of linguistic codes may be constructed. Within those codes, by contrast, arbitrariness is relative (de Saussure 1959: 131–4), limited for example by the use of metaphor to construct chains of association. To illustrate the relativity of arbitrariness, examine the word 'tree,' which clearly has no necessary relationship with the branched plants that we so label. But 'tree-diagrams', 'shoe trees', and 'family trees' all bear an iconic relationship to a prototypical tree, and are non-arbitrarily named (Benveniste 1971, Friedrich 1979).

Many scholars would assent to the proposition that 'all language is almost totally tropological' (Friedrich 1991: 24). Nietzsche noted that 'every concept originates through our equating what is unequal', and ironically characterized 'truth' as a 'mobile army of metaphors, metonyms, anthropomorphisms' (1954: 46–7). In a development of this insight, the linguists Lakoff and Johnson assert that 'our ordinary conceptual system, in terms of which we both think and act, is fundamentally metaphorical in nature' (1980: 3). In their study of American English they explore conceptual metaphors such as 'time is money' by detailing the expressions that build on it: 'You're wasting my time', 'You're running out of time', 'You must budget your time' (Lakoff and Johnson 1980: 7).

Cross-cultural comparison foregrounds the intimate relationship between society, language, and concept. Time is money for us because of the way that work is accomplished and rewarded (Thompson 1967). In contrast, Nuer pastoralists of the Southern Sudan are said to live by a 'cattle clock', with activities co-ordinated by events rather than by an abstract system (Evans-Pritchard 1940: 103). The Nuer have no concept of time comparable to our own, and Evans-Pritchard (whom Ardener (1971: lix) credits with securing a place for language in British social anthropology) described the difference in these terms:

> The Nuer have no expression equivalent to 'time' in our language, and they cannot, therefore, as we can, speak of time as though it were something actual, which passes, can be wasted, can be saved, and so forth. I do not think that they ever experience the same feeling of fighting against time or of having to co-ordinate activities with an abstract passage of time, because their points of reference are mainly the activities themselves, which are generally of a leisurely character. Events follow a logical order, but they are not controlled by an abstract system.
>
> (1940: 103)

Indeed, as Evans-Pritchard wistfully concluded, 'Nuer are fortunate'. (See, however, Adam in this volume, Article 18, for a critical commentary on Evans-Pritchard's analysis of Nuer time.)

Metaphoric and conceptual elaboration are thus keys to areas of socio-cultural importance (and difference). While the Nuer may not elaborate temporal metaphors, they do have a highly developed vocabulary with which to discuss another key concern – their cattle. Cattle are not only a source of food but also a medium of exchange in bridewealth payments and bloodfeud settlements. The vocabulary that describes and names them is rich and detailed, and songs that praise them also praise their owners – young men who take their names from their cattle. Finally, the tribe itself is metaphorically construed as a cattle camp (Evans-Pritchard 1940: 16–50).

LANGUAGE AND WORLDVIEW

The first generation of American ethnographic linguists asserted strong links between language and worldview. They suggested not only that language channels perception, but also that it contains the 'genius' of the people who use it as their means of verbal expression. The view that language was essential to the continuation of the unique identity and destiny of a group was fundamental to the German Romanticism of the late eighteenth and early nineteenth centuries (Edwards 1985: 23–7). Divorced from its evolutionist and nationalist matrix, this perspective influenced the formation of Boasian anthropology, with its emphasis on the mastery of American Indian languages (ironically, in a period of widespread language extinction). In particular, the argument that a language shapes its speakers more than its speakers shape language (that 'language speaks man' in Heidegger's felicitous expression) is one that recurs repeatedly in studies of language and worldview. The emphasis given to language by Boas and his students led to the establishment of 'linguistic anthropology' in North American universities as one of the four basic subfields of the discipline, together with cultural anthropology, archaeology, and physical anthropology.

Sapir (1949a [1921], 1949b) and Whorf (1964) were among those who developed a linguistic relativism based on the premiss that language shaped worldview, while rejecting the assumption that the languages used by members of technologically less advanced and non-literate societies were inferior vehicles for conception. Sapir, for example, argued that:

> Both simple and complex types of language of an indefinite number of varieties may be found spoken at any desired level of cultural advance. When it comes to linguistic form, Plato walks with the Macedonian swineherd, Confucius with the head-hunting savage of Assam.
>
> (1949a [1921]: 219)

In a relativistic inversion of earlier evolutionist arguments, Boas (1966), Sapir (1949a [1921], 1949b), Reichard (1951), and Whorf (1964) promoted an appreciation of the formal elegance of non-Western languages as vehicles for thought, and Whorf reversed evolutionist schemes when he praised Hopi representations of time as truer analyses of temporal experience than the objectifications of 'Standard Average European' (1964: 151–5; see also Lucy 1985).

Basic to studies of language and worldview is the attention they give to the detail of linguistic structure, particularly in so far as that structure provides a classification of experience. As Sapir observed, 'the world of our experiences must be enormously simplified and generalized before it is possible to make a symbolic inventory of all our experiences of things and relations and this inventory is imperative before we can convey ideas' (1949a [1921]: 12). A community of speakers must agree tacitly to a classification of experience if they are to communicate, and this classification forms a foundation for their worldview.

Not surprisingly, anthropologists often analyse society and culture through the prism of language. Much work in the field of symbolic anthropology in fact entails analysis of the linguistic metaphors that inform classification, ritual practice, and concepts of the person. Metaphor and metonymy, for example, figured as key tropes in Lévi-Strauss's (1966) characterization of primitive thought (*la pensée sauvage*), and interpretive anthropologists explored 'key' or 'root' metaphors (also described as 'key cultural ideas' or 'key symbols') in order to gain insight into cultural values (Turner 1974, Ortner 1973). The translation of culture cannot proceed without exploration of the associational base that natural languages provide to their speakers.

To take a single example, Mary Black (1984) analysed Hopi corn metaphors using a model drawn from the work of Lakoff and Johnson (1980). She explored a small number of 'conceptual metaphors' summarized as 'people are corn' and 'maidens are corn.' The implications of these analogies are part of ordinary language, in which the same terms apply to both people and corn, and the analogy receives further elaboration in ritual speeches and song. This example richly illustrates the relation between language and poetry: the associations implicit in the Hopi language linking the life-cycle of humans and the life-cycle of corn are developed in poetic form in the public performances of ritual. Language gives shape to the individual imagination, and poetic performance realizes the implicit in an aesthetic form.

The classificatory implications of linguistic structure continue to be a source of insight into the relationship between language and culture. Witherspoon, for example, in his studies of Navaho 'language in culture and culture in language', gives careful consideration to the translation of Navaho words such as *hozho* ('beauty', but also 'goodness'), with their penumbra of associations, as he seeks to elucidate essential cultural values (1977: 23–46). Moreover, he delves into the classificatory implications of syntactic structure, and associates these with aspects of worldview. For example, he explores the use of 'subject–object' inversion in Navaho, and demonstrates that restrictions on the use of this syntactic form are enmeshed with assumptions about who may act upon whom in a society in which beings are implicitly ranked in terms of their ability to shape outcomes by their will (Witherspoon 1980: 8). Cultural ideas constrain linguistic form, and linguistic form attests to the depth and tenacity of cultural ideas.

FROM STRUCTURE TO PROCESS

In his *Course in General Linguistics*, de Saussure emphasized the code-like properties of language, and provided the founding statement for a semiotics of society. He suggested that language was but one of many human sign systems, and proposed a new science of semiology to study the 'life of signs within society' (1959 [1915]: 16). His proposal for the synchronic study of language as *langue*, organized as a system of differences, inspired the development of structuralist anthropology. Building on this insight, and inspired by Jakobson's breakthroughs in the understanding of phonological codes, Lévi-Strauss inferred semiotic codes (or structures) from the data of kinship systems and mythologies (1963, 1966, 1969a, b; see also Leach 1970). He claimed that through these cross-cultural studies of structure, he could elucidate aspects of the organization of the human mind. Ultimately, the theoretical base of his model was cognitive, and it gave linguistic theory a new prominence in anthropological analysis. However, with its focus on the analysis of abstract structures, the theory did not address questions dealing with social action and language use in context.

By contrast, recent studies of language in society emphasize social process rather than structure, and performance rather than code. The development of the interdisciplinary field of sociolinguistics was an important step in the move from structure to process, and major theoretical and methodological contributions include the works of Fishman (1986), Gumperz (1982), Gumperz and Hymes (1986 [1972]), Hymes (1974), and Labov (1972a, b). The 'ethnography of speaking' (see below) laid stress on the cross-cultural study of language use, and has contributed an important comparative dimension to the formation of a socially constituted linguistics. The turn towards the study of language use in social process has been given further impetus by an interdisciplinary interest in 'discourse analysis', which seeks to interpret the diversity of discursive practices in the light of unequal socio-economic conditions.

THE ETHNOGRAPHY OF SPEAKING

The study of linguistic performance in relation to social process has important roots in the 'ethnography of speaking', an approach developed by American linguistic anthropologists and folklorists. The approach was given early theoretical definition by Hymes (1974) and Gumperz and Hymes (1986 [1972]), and has been developed by Basso (1979, 1984, 1990), Bauman (1977, 1983), Bauman and Sherzer (1974), and others. Articulated here is a forceful challenge to linguistic models that emphasize formal structure to the exclusion of practice. Hymes (1974), for example, opposed the Chomskyan emphasis on 'competence' (often equated with de Saussure's concept of *langue*) and the concomitant exclusion of 'performance' (corresponding to de Saussure's *parole*), arguing that a fundamental aspect of linguistic competence is *communicative* competence, i.e. the ability to produce utterances that are appropriate to the occasion. Linguistic skills entail more than mastery of a linguistic code that allows the speaker to produce grammatical sentences; they also involve knowing how to speak appropriately in different social settings.

Important theoretical sources for the ethnography of speaking were the works of the Prague School, including (most importantly) Jakobson (see Caton 1987) and Mukarovsky (1977). The Prague School theorists developed a model for understanding the structure of the communicative act that has been foundational for study of the social use of language. A key statement of this theoretical programme is Roman Jakobson's (1960) 'Closing statement: linguistics and poetics', in which he outlines a model of the major components of a communicative situation and their associated functions. In this model, the linguistic code is but one of six components or 'aspects' into which the speech event may be analysed. Other aspects include the addresser, the addressee, the channel, the message, and the context. The functions associated with these aspects of the speech event include the expressive (focus on the speaker), the conative (focus on the audience), the phatic (focus on establishing social contact rather than communicating ideas), the poetic (elaboration of the message form using linguistic parallelism), and the referential (focus on the context) (1960: 353–7). Any one or more of these functions might be emphasized in a given speech event.

This model provides the starting point for more recent discussion and analysis of situated language use. With the aim of analysing 'linguistic competence', Hymes (1974: 54–62) developed a model rooted in Jakobson's work on the speech event, which he summed up with the mnemonic 'SPEAKING' (setting and scene; participants; ends; acts; key; instrumentalities; norms of interaction and interpretation; genres). These terms are used in the description of speech events, and Hymes sets himself the analytic goal of creating a taxonomy to classify the range of cross-cultural variation in language use in context (1974: 33–5).

Basso's studies of Western Apache language and culture illustrate Hymes's claims regarding cross-cultural variability in language use. Basso observes that Western Apache norms of interaction are fundamentally different from 'Anglo-American' norms. For example, silence is enjoined in a number of social situations: when strangers meet, when two young people court, when children come home (from college, say), and when someone is drunk or in deep mourning (and thus likely to be emotionally volatile). He concludes that silence is a response 'to uncertainty and unpredictability in social relations' (1972: 83). Unfortunately, the Apache response easily leads to cross-cultural misunderstanding in situations such as job interviews, where reticence might be interpreted as sullen defensiveness. For their part, the Western Apache caricature Anglo-American assertiveness in joking performances that are themselves a mocking inventory of contrasting communicative norms (Basso 1979).

A development of this insight, and a convergence of interest with folklore studies, appears in the approach to performance of Bauman and others (Bauman 1977, Bauman and Sherzer 1974). The approach entails a critique of genre studies of the kind which elicit folklore items in the artificial setting of the interview and, in analysis, abstract these items from their social context. By contrast, ethnographers of speaking emphasize the importance of studying language and the genres of verbal art that interest the folklorist in the social context of performance. At the same time, Bauman and Briggs (1990: 74) observe that an important feature of works of verbal art is that they are often created as texts that may be detached from the context of their creation without significant loss of meaning (see also Hanks 1989).

Abraham's (1977) analysis of tea meetings in the West Indies provides a good illustration of the importance of a focus on the social context of performance. Members of the community concerned recognize two contrasting styles of speaking: the 'rude' (associated with young men, and street corner society), and the 'behaved' (associated with women, home, and church). The two styles confront one another in the 'tea meeting', a speech contest in which the speechmaker, who is the master of an elevated style of speaking that combines Latin with erudite English, is challenged to continue despite rude (and comic) heckling from the audience (1977: 117–19). Attention to genre conventions of the speech alone would fail to convey the social meaning and humour of the event.

The ethnographic approach to verbal art persuasively demonstrates that meaning is often only completed in the context of the speech event. The contexts in which people live their lives are themselves endowed with meaning, and a full understanding depends on our comprehension of meanings associated with physical settings and community history. In the Western Apache practice of 'shooting with stories,' reprimands or didactic messages are conveyed indirectly by moralistic stories that are linked to physical locations where memorable past events took place. Retelling the story, or mentioning the name of the story ('It happened at "men stand above here and there"'), invites the hearers to search for analogies between their own behaviour and the disapproved behaviour of the anti-hero of the tale. Moreover, the place itself is a constant reminder of the values and judgements that emerge from the tale. As Basso puts it:

> After stories and storytellers have served this beneficial purpose [to make the listener think about his life], features of the physical landscape take over and perpetuate it. Mountains and arroyos step in symbolically for grandmothers and uncles.
> (1984: 43)

Words condense a community's recollections of its experiences within a unique environment, and the environment in turn evokes a community's memories of its past (see also DeBernardi 1993).

One of the more fruitful developments in the field of the ethnography of speaking has been cross-cultural work on language socialization (Ochs and Schieffelin 1983, Schieffelin and Ochs 1986). Following Vygotsky (1978, see also Wertsch 1985), Ochs suggests that the genesis of thought and language must be placed within the context of social interaction, a point that is also central to Poole's discussion of socialization and enculturation in the previous article. Invoking Sapir and Whorf, she further proposes that 'children acquire a worldview as they acquire a language' (1986: 3). In her view, children acquire performance competence through participation in social interactions that are in part constructed as an 'interactional display (covert or overt) to a novice of expected ways of thinking, feeling, and acting' (1986: 2).

In a formulation that recalls Hymes's emphasis on competence in performance, Ochs emphasizes the fact that the child learning a language is also acquiring 'social competence', which entails 'the ability to recognize/interpret what social activity/event is taking place and to speak and act in ways sensitive to the context' (1986: 3). Types of knowledge acquired in language socialization include the ability to express status and role through language use, and to recognize and express feelings in context. For example, in Kaluli society, teasing and shaming are assertive interactive strategies that are important modes of social control in adult life. Schieffelin demonstrates that both are a systematic component of interactions with children, and are used extensively 'to teach children how to be part of Kaluli society' (1986: 179).

Recent anthropological research challenges the premiss that emotions are psychobiologically universal, and relativizes different kinds of affect as sociocultural constructs that are, like kinship systems or concepts of time, cross-culturally variable (Besnier 1990, Lutz and Abu-Lughod 1990, Lutz and White 1986). The key to this research has proven to be the study of discourse, defined as 'the situated social practices of people speaking, singing, orating, or writing to and about each other' (Abu-Lughod and Lutz 1990: 10). In the view of Abu-Lughod and Lutz, discourse does not merely carry emotion; rather emotional discourse is viewed as a learned 'form of social action that creates effects in the world' (1990: 12). Emotion is both content and effect; hence the expressive and conative functions of language (to use Jakobson's terms) are uppermost here.

Abu-Lughod thus determined to study sentiment through the observation of emotion talk (Abu-Lughod and Lutz 1990: 15). In her study of the Bedouin use of poetic form in social life, she observes that there are two basic codes governing the expression of emotion in Bedouin life, a 'code of honour' that precludes expressions of vulnerability and weakness, and a 'code of modesty' that women realize in their conduct through self-restraint and effacement – or what Abu-Lughod calls 'the honour of the weak' (1986: 108). Bedouin women contravene both codes in singing poetic couplets that express love, attachment, and loss. These set poetic forms express standard sentiments; but at the same time, they are interpreted in the light of the life histories of their singers, whose inner emotions are inferred from their songs. For example, a woman responded with anger when her husband took a second wife, but communicated sadness and grief through song (1986: 189–94). As with linguistic etiquette (discussed below), poetic discourse is a strategy of indirectness, and Abu-Lughod concludes that 'individuals are shielded from the consequences of making statements and expressing sentiments that contravene the moral system if they do so in poetry' (1986: 248).

ETHNOGRAPHIC POETICS

Linguistic anthropologists have recently established the new subfield of 'ethnopoetics', focused on the cross-cultural study of poetic language and performance (Friedrich 1991, Hymes 1981, Sherzer and Woodbury 1987, Tedlock 1983). This emphasis on the poetic is in part justified by the philosophical view that language is, in its essence, tropological – a 'work of art' – and studies often emphasize the creative and emergent qualities of poetic performance (see Weiner in this volume, Article 21). For example, in a recent statement that Sapir would surely have endorsed, Friedrich has forcefully argued that 'language, whether at the individual, sociocultural, or some universal level, is inherently, pervasively, and powerfully poetic' (1986: 17). Language (and culture) influence the imagination, but the imagination of the individual speaker, particularly the more poetic person, remains relatively unconstrained, and is thus able to innovate and reorder cultural and linguistic materials (1986: 17).

The poetic also assumes prominence in the work of scholars who advocate the study of performance as a means of gaining insight into social life (Abu-Lughod 1986, Bauman 1977, Caton 1990, Sherzer 1983). Frequently the poetic elaboration of language is an element of socio-cultural performance, from political oratory to magical invocation. While the aesthetic qualities of these performances may be difficult to convey in translation, the social use of the poetic is a topic of continuing relevance and importance.

Intensified poetic forms are often displayed in formal and public contexts (see for example Fox 1977, Sherzer 1983), a fact that led Bloch to examine their different social functions. In his consideration of Merina oratory, he concluded that such poetic ways of speaking were in fact designed to further the goals of power-holders, since the formal elegance of the words and the contexts in which they were spoken made them inaccessible to debate and challenge (1975, 1989). Bloch's interpretation has however been questioned by others who, finding his perspective over-reductionistic, have in turn refocused on the aesthetic qualities of verbal art forms. Nonetheless, the debate has drawn attention to the cross-cultural importance and centrality of poetic language in public (and often political) contexts.

Caton (1990) explores the poetry of Yemeni men as cultural practice, enmeshed in the history and public life of a tribal society. For Khawlani tribesmen, the art of composing poetry and the rhetoric of public persuasion are closely connected, making politics and poetics inseparable (1990: 155). The poet has 'the power to enter into a discourse in which honour is created or defended... and persuasion is exercised' (1990: 178), at weddings for example (pp. 65–71), or in the mediation of disputes (pp. 71–4). These rhetorical outcomes are only possible if the poet can exhibit skill in the manipulation of poetic form, and Caton concludes that verbal skill gives the poet power in the constitution of social reality (1990: 268). As Gal describes the force of language in politics, 'power is more than an authoritative voice in decision-making; its strongest form may well be the ability to define social reality, to impose visions of the world. Such visions are inscribed in language and enacted in interaction' (Gal 1989: 26).

While ethnopoetics is a relatively new subfield, it has deep roots in the discipline. Many anthropologists would agree with Victor Turner, who summed up a fundamental premiss of his anthropology when he stated:

> Experience always seeks its 'best', i.e. most aesthetic expression in performance . . . .
> Cultures, I hold, are better compared through their rituals, theatres, tales, ballads, epics, operas than through their habits.
>
> (Turner and Bruner 1986: 13)

In this view, aesthetic expression is inseparable from social use, and art becomes a window on the most fundamental values in a society (in Article 22 of this volume, Schechner develops this idea at greater length).

DIALOGIC ANTHROPOLOGY

The turn towards an analytical focus on speaking and dialogue coincides with a critique of totalizing concepts of culture (or ideology) that leave no place for variation or the individual voice. Ideally, in a dialogic study many voices, both generic and individual, are represented. By contrast, structural accounts capture the system at the expense of a nuanced understanding both of creative and emergent cultural or linguistic forms (metaphor, for example), and of the development of personal or subcultural symbols. The writings of the Russian literary critic Mikhael Bakhtin (1981, 1984) on the 'dialogic imagination' in literature have provided a point of departure in the formulation of this dialogic critique. From the Bakhtinian perspective, culture is:

> an open-ended, creative dialogue of subcultures, of insiders and outsiders, of diverse factions. A 'language' is the interplay and struggle of regional dialects, professional jargons, generic commonplaces, the speech of different age groups, individuals, and so forth.
>
> (Clifford 1988: 46)

This reworked concept of culture shifts the analytic focus away from system and towards the study of the diversity of human practice. In addition, it takes discourse and dialogue as keys to understanding human experience (see Bruner 1984).

The dialogic approach, with roots in Bakhtinian literary criticism and the ethnography of speaking, has also had a pronounced impact on the writing of ethnography (Marcus and Fischer 1986: 67–73). The discourse of fieldwork has itself become the object of critical analysis (Briggs 1986, Moerman 1988), and the recognition that ethnographic knowledge is the product of a dialogue between researcher and informants has led to criticism of standard styles of

representation in ethnographic writing. Anthropologists are seeking alternatives to an 'ethnographic authority' constructed through third-person objective
reporting (Clifford 1988), and have explored ways of using the first-person
voice and of presenting data in the form of a dialogue between ethnographer
and informant (Tedlock 1979, 1987, Tedlock and Mannheim 1994).

THE POLITICS OF LANGUAGE USE

Linguistic varieties or ways of speaking may be conscious or unconscious
markers of personal and social identity, and through these markers language
finds an important function. Linguistic usage expresses and creates social difference, and language realizes the power structure of society in so far as it
expresses, symbolizes, and maintains the social order (Halliday 1978: 172).
The social prestige or stigma attached to linguistic varieties often supports and
expresses the value attached to social identities.

That a linguistic item or variety may function as a badge of identity is
beyond dispute. Linguistic varieties are associated with national identities (see
Smith in this volume, Article 25), class differences, ethnic differences, subcultural differences, gender and generational differences. Distinctive aspects of
language use range from pronunciation to syntax, from the use of slang to
norms of interaction: speakers may use virtually any aspect of the linguistic
code as a vehicle for identity (Hudson 1980, Trudgill 1974). LePage and
Tabouret-Keller (1985: 14) argue provocatively that linguistic behaviour 'is a
series of *acts of identity* in which speakers reveal both their personal identity
and their search for social roles.'

While the relativistic anthropologist might argue that all languages are equal
in so far as they are adequate to the communicative needs of their speakers,
the social fact is that linguistic varieties are stratified (Grillo 1989a, b, Wolfson
and Manes 1985). The question then arises as to how certain linguistic varieties come to be socially ranked as more prestigious than others. The response
most frequently encountered is that the most prestigious form will be that of
the most powerful group in society, because it is this group that controls such
channels of influence as educational institutions and the media.

Often (though not always) the prestige form is the standard language.
Standardized linguistic varieties are typically the creations of modern nation
states that seek to use language to unify populations and promote literacy (see
Article 19). As Haugen observes, a national language has the two-fold potential to create internal cohesion and to foster external distinction – a duality that
forms a powerful base for national identity (1972: 245). While political goals
may have led to the establishment of national languages, economic factors
often motivate their acceptance. Frequently, material advancement depends
on mastery of the national language, and language shift (and sometimes the
'death' of minority languages) is not an uncommon outcome (Edwards 1985:
91–6, Dorian 1989).

The abandonment of a minority language in favour of the dominant language may be the pragmatic choice from an economic perspective. Minority languages often persist, however, despite the lack of institutional support for their transmission. These languages may serve to mark off ethnic differences within multi-ethnic societies, but loyalty to or revival of marginalized languages may also express the political aspirations of their speakers.

The case of modern Chinese (Mandarin) well illustrates the political aspects of language. Prior to the twentieth century, China was united by a shared written language, but divided into eight distinct major 'dialect' areas whose speakers in fact spoke topolects as different from one another as French is from Italian. Each topolect had its 'reading pronunciation' for characters, which meant that shared literacy did not confer a shared spoken language. High-ranking scholar–literati who left their regions for national service compensated for this diversity by learning *guan hua*, literally 'official language', a lingua franca based in Northern Chinese.

In the early part of the twentieth century, the republican leaders of China recognized the potential political and economic value of a shared national language, and the Ministry of Education called a Conference on Unification of Pronunciation. In a spirit of compromise, the new national language, based in Mandarin, incorporated elements of southern dialects (and indeed was called 'Blue–green Mandarin' because of its mixed quality (DeFrancis 1972: 66)). 'Blue–green Mandarin' failed, however, to be adopted in use, since the new national language had no pre-existing community of speakers (Ramsey 1987: 9). In 1932, standard pronunciations were normalized to reflect those in use in Beijing, in an important step that some feared would 'force the south to follow the north' (Ramsey 1987: 11). Significant progress in the adoption of the national language was not made until after the Second World War, when the communists actively promoted the use of Mandarin as well as the simplification of characters as a means towards widespread literacy. Because they followed the Soviet model of toleration of topolects, China shifted from being a diglossic nation to become a nation of bilingual speakers (DeFrancis 1972, 1984, Norman 1988: 249–53).

The pragmatic usefulness of the shared national language does not always guarantee that it should enjoy an exclusively prestigious status (Norman 1988: 245–9). Regional languages continue to be spoken in China and Taiwan in informal contexts, and in Taiwan, 'Southern Min' (or 'Taiwanese', as it is known) is now promoted in certain quarters as a symbol of the desire for independent nationhood. The promotion of Taiwanese involves reclaiming the reading pronunciation of characters, as well as devising original ways to create a written standard for the language, since it is a topolect with much vocabulary that is non-cognate with Northern Chinese (DeBernardi 1991).

Economic power as well as political aspiration may allow the promotion of regional languages at the expense of national ones. Barcelona, for example, is a community that is economically powerful but politically peripheral to the

Spanish state. Castilian is the language of the nation, but it has been marginalized in Barcelona owing to the social configuration of that urban community, in which Castilian is the language of an emigrant working population and Catalan the language associated with élite social standing (Woolard 1989).

The restoration of a language in decline may also be undertaken as an aspect of 'ethnic revival'. In Ireland, for example, English policies of settlement and education (many of them begun as early as the mid-sixteenth century) led to the decline of Irish. As language shift occurred, English became the language of social prestige, while Irish became a language maintained primarily among the poor. In the mid-nineteenth century an Irish nationalist movement emerged that sought to encourage and revive the original language. This effort at language restoration was part of a larger national movement, which culminated in the founding of the Irish Free State (Edwards 1985: 53–5).

With the founding of that state Irish became its first official language, and support for its revival now exists in the form of compulsory education in the language, the standard use of Irish in bilingual government publications, and the establishment of a government board to promote its use (Edwards 1985: 56–9). Edwards observes that 'in daily Irish life there are places for the language but almost all are either ceremonial or trivial, or exist only in tandem with English' (1985: 59–60). The effort to revive Irish as a spoken language has failed, and Edwards concludes that the original language that romantic nationalists so ardently defended is not, after all, essential to the maintenance of a strong Irish identity (1985: 64).

For multi-lingual speakers, linguistic varieties may index aspects of identity, and a number of close-grained studies of code-switching have demonstrated that language choice is both systematic and socially meaningful (Breitborde 1983, Gal 1979, 1988, Gumperz 1982, Gumperz and Hymes 1986, Heller 1988, Hill and Hill 1986, Urciuoli 1991). Code-switching often involves the use of both the state-supported language (with associations of power and prestige) and ones used by minority groups (perhaps stigmatized). The choice of code is often strategic, and as Gal notes, it is used in conversation 'to establish, cross or destroy group boundaries; to create, evoke or change interpersonal relations with their accompanying rights and obligations' (1988: 247).

In Kenya, for example, use of the official language indexes membership in a multi-ethnic élite (Scotton 1988: 162). There are contexts, however, in which minority languages have greater social value, and Scotton (1988: 169) describes an interaction in Kenya in which a young woman switches from Swahili, an ethnically neutral lingua franca, to a shared tribal language, in an attempt to smooth over a minor conflict with the gatekeeper at her club. In this context, the minority language is used to establish ethnic co-identity and to negotiate a different (more solidary) relationship. In multi-ethnic Kenya, minority languages may also function to ensure privacy, excluding outsiders from comprehension (Scotton 1988: 174–5).

ACTS OF IDENTITY: LINGUISTIC STYLES

Even within a national or regional language variation exists, which may range from regional or local dialects to registers (varieties according to use), from subcultural or social class or ethnic styles to gender differences. For many years, of course, scholars have noted that any 'language' will vary in use, and what a transformational grammarian might dismiss as idiosyncratic aspects of performance, or 'free variation', is of central concern to those who study the linguistic expression of social identity. As a technique of the body, language use in this instance is an aspect of *habitus*, defined by Bourdieu as 'the system of structured, structuring dispositions... which is constituted in practice and is always oriented towards practical functions' (1990: 52). One practical function of the linguistic habitus is the communication of identity through linguistic style. As a form of 'linguistic capital', style may express and confirm the speaker's position in society, and mastery of what Bourdieu terms the 'authorized language' may yield a profit in terms of authority or distinction, since language 'represents, manifests, and symbolizes authority' (1982: 103–5; see also Irvine 1985).

In the United States, for example, consistent use of the double negative ('He don't know nothing') is characteristic of a linguistic variety termed 'black English vernacular' (BEV), and associated with African American speakers. In the 1960s, this linguistic form came to be stigmatized by educators as 'bad grammar', or as an expression of illogicality, a judgement made from the standpoint of standard English. William Labov, however, has argued for the grammatical integrity of BEV, observing with characteristic acuteness that although the double negative (termed by him 'negative concord') is employed in Russian, Spanish, French, and Hungarian, those languages are not stigmatized as 'illogical' (1972a: 226). Bolinger sums up the situation thus:

> Attitudes toward a form of speech are hardly other than attitudes towards the speakers. Inferior people speak in inferior ways. Naturally. And the differences that mark their speech tend to be stigmatized.
>
> (1980: 45)

Or as Halliday puts the matter: 'the conscious motif of "I don't like their vowels" symbolizes an underlying motif of "I don't like their values"' (1978: 179).

There may be an objective basis for the social usefulness and prestige of a language such as Standard English, which is a highly 'developed' language with a wide range of functions (Halliday 1978: 194). However, advocates of the standard language (and in America, proponents of an 'English-only' policy) have often been ideologically driven. Silverstein observes (1987: 3) that 'the culture of Standard is aggressively hegemonic, dominating... linguistic situations with an understanding of other linguistic usages as locatable only in terms of Standard.'

Deep differences between Standard and non-Standard speakers have been inferred on the basis of patterns of language use. In an influential formulation, Bernstein (1972) suggested that class differences in the use of language in social interaction could explain differences in academic achievement in Britain. He proposed that the middle class had achieved mastery of a form of speech that he termed an 'elaborated code', verbally explicit and relatively independent of context, a way of speaking that 'maintained social distance, demanded individuated responses, and made no assumptions about the hearer's intent' (Halliday 1978: 87). The speech of the English working class, by contrast, was limited to a 'restricted code', which Bernstein described as socially and situationally bounded, and particularistic rather than universalistic. The restricted code was a more verbally implicit and context-dependent, but also a more socially intimate form of speech in which meaning was 'tied to a local relationship and to a local social structure' (Bernstein 1972: 164). The educational system demanded an elaborated code, and children who – due to the manner of their socialization – did not wholly master this code were put at a disadvantage.

In the United States, Bernstein's model was (mis)applied by researchers in the field of education to explain the poor academic performances of lower-class black children. Labov has singled out for critique the work of Bereiter, who described the speech of pre-school African American children as a series of emotional cries amounting to 'a nonlogical mode of expressive behaviour' (Bereiter, cited in Labov 1972a: 205). Labov questioned the research methods that produced these conclusions, pointing out that the structure of the testing situation itself had an inhibiting effect on the verbal performance of the children tested (1972a: 205–13). He also reviewed the criteria used to define 'elaborated' and 'restricted' codes, and observed that the 'elaborated code' used by educated speakers was often merely an elaborated style, and was no more logically incisive or conceptually universalistic than the 'restricted code' of BEV speakers (1972a: 216–20).

'Women's language', as it is termed, also demonstrates the relationship between linguistic style, identity, and prestige. Gender identity and gender attitudes find expression in both linguistic form and style, and in studies of gender and language, the interaction of system and use, representation and choice, is perhaps more fully explored than in other areas of linguistic anthropology (McConnell-Ginet 1988). Lakoff long ago pointed out that 'language uses us as much as we use language' (1975: 3), and interdisciplinary feminist scholarship has explored the implications of representations of male and female implicit in the very structure of language. Use of 'man' as a generic term for 'men and women' has been criticized as 'sexist' for example, as has use of 'he' as the pronoun of indefinite reference. In the history of the English language, gender-related vocabulary has undergone a process in which terms associated with men tend to retain connotations of high social standing ('master', 'lord', 'king'), while those associated with women have acquired derogatory, negative (and often sexual) connotations ('mistress', 'lady', 'queen') (Graddol and Swann 1989: 112–18). Like linguistic relativists, feminist scholars argue that language shapes worldview, and conclude that linguistic practice must change if society is to change.

Gender differences in language use have also been documented, to the extent that Tannen can confidently assert that 'male–female conversation is cross-cultural communication' (1986: 133). Lakoff observed that American women are taught 'women's language', which she describes as consisting of polite and deferential ways of speaking which ultimately subordinate women in society (1975: 6–8). Supporting Lakoff's contention that women are more deferential than men in conversation, research on middle-class Americans has shown that men take longer conversational turns, and interrupt more frequently in order to take the floor from the current speaker (West and Zimmerman 1983). Women, by contrast, do a disproportionate amount of 'maintenance work', by providing encouraging responses, asking questions, and listening (Fishman 1983). At the same time, however, it has been questioned whether women's language really exists in English (by comparison with Japanese, where women use special terms of self-reference and address; Jorden 1974, see also Shibamoto 1985, 1987), or whether the variety of speech described by Lakoff is not rather a 'powerless script' used by both men and women who are in socially subordinate positions (O'Barr and Atkins 1980). Cross-cultural research also suggests that the association of women with greater politeness is not universal: in Malagasy women are seen as direct and abrupt, while men are seen as speaking with care and indirectness (Keenan 1974).

Words, too, have value. As Bakhtin stated, words have 'owners', and 'each word tastes of the context and contexts in which it has lived its socially charged life; all words and forms are populated by intentions' (1981: 293). Variability in language creates and embodies different social lives and intentions, which is one reason why dislike of a person's vowels, syntax, or choice of words may in fact, to recapitulate Halliday's point (1978: 179), be symbolic of dislike or disregard of their values.

Slang, for example, is a linguistic style that is associated with young speakers, and has low value when compared with the formal language of academic or legal discourse. In a study of Zuni, Newman (1964) observed that the sacred language used in the ceremonial house (*kiva*) carried high social prestige, whereas slang language (while metaphorical and witty) carried low prestige. The two varieties of Zuni were used by different speakers in distinct contexts: community elders used sacred language in the *kiva*, while young people used slang in informal settings. The use of slang terms like 'cotton-wood' for 'Anglo-American' was prohibited in the *kiva*, and the Zuni compared the use of slang in that setting to bringing a radio into the sacred precincts. Newman observes that 'status differentiation is applied to age groups, and the speech peculiar to young people is low-valued, while that associated with old people is prestigeful.' He concluded that 'words acquire connotative gradations in accordance with the cultural values assigned to ideas, status groups, and situations' (1964: 402).

The elaboration of linguistic style in the defence of identity is often a characteristic of subcultural groups. Durkheim classically suggested that the social contract was inscribed in linguistic categories (1965 [1915]: 482–7), and those who stand outside the norms of the social contract frequently reshape language to express their values. Such cases are illuminating, since they illustrate vividly the claim that conversation creates and sustains inter-subjective reality. Attention to the creative dimensions of language use also serves as a reminder that 'it is people who retain the power to name, entitle, and objectify others, who determine the terms of discourse' (Parkin 1984: 359).

Halliday coined the term 'anti-language' to describe the argots of socially marginal persons (primarily thieves) who refashion the language's lexicon in order to have a secret code in which to speak of such things as criminal acts, the tools of their trade, their opponents (the police), their victims, and the penalties for their crimes. Halliday observed that such persons need anti-languages in order to 'act out a distinctive social structure' wherein is inscribed an 'alternative social reality' (1978: 165, see also DeBernardi 1987).

David Maurer's classic study of the 'Whiz Mob' provides a rich example of an anti-language. In the technical argot of pickpockets, victims of their trade are 'beats', 'clips', 'clouts', and 'nails' (1964: 49). By contrast, pickpockets are 'class cannons', 'careful tools', or 'bangup operators' (1964: 95). As Halliday observes (1978: 167), those of whom society at large disapproves can respond to the negativity of their disapprobation by themselves redefining positive and negative values. The argot of pickpockets also contains a vocabulary of disap-probation: a pickpocket who is too careful is a 'centre fielder' or 'sneeze shy'; one who is small-time is a 'doormat thief', and a 'forty-second street thief' is one who will not leave New York (Maurer 1964: 96–7). In Halliday's terms, 'an anti-language is the means of realization of a subjective reality: not merely expressing it, but actively creating and maintaining it' (1978: 172).

IDENTITY IN INTERACTION

Social distinctions are also constructed and expressed in interaction through the use of 'indexical' linguistic items. Indexicals are items that mark features of the speaker's and/or the hearer's identity, and they include pronouns, kin-ship terms and titles, and the differential use of speech levels. In social use, indexicals often create and sustain a relational social identity, and thus have a performative function. As Silverstein notes, 'social indexes such as deference vocabularies and constructions... are examples of maximally creative or per-formative devices, which, by their very use, make the social parameters of speaker and hearer explicit' (1976: 34).

The model developed by Brown and Levinson (1987) to discuss linguistic etiquette is a useful starting-point. They approach politeness from the perspective of a 'model person' who desires to secure the co-operation of others while avoiding the appearance of imposition. 'Politeness', therefore, involves linguistic strategies of indirectness that are understandable in the light of human 'face wants'. They define 'face' as:

> the public self-image that every member wants to claim for himself, consisting of two related aspects:
>
> (a) negative face: the basic claim to territories, personal preserves, rights to non-distraction − i.e. to freedom of action and freedom from imposition
> (b) positive face: the positive consistent self-image or 'personality' (crucially including the desire that this self-image be appreciated and approved of) claimed by interactants.
>
> (1987: 61)

Brown and Levinson assume that all competent adult members of society have both 'face', and the rationality to devise means (including strategies of politeness) to achieve their ends (1987: 61).

While in the short run direct communication would be a more efficient way to accomplish interactional work, it would threaten the 'face needs' of others by imposing demands on them. Forms of politeness, however, communicate through strategies of indirectness that invite the addressee to draw implications from non-explicit speech. Brown and Levinson suggest that all languages employ two primary strategies of politeness, which involve 'negative politeness' (or respect and distance), and 'positive politeness' (or familiarity) (1987: 2).

These strategies correspond to the axes of power and solidarity often employed in analyses of pronoun use in European languages. In a classic study, Brown and Gilman (1960) detailed the development and contemporary use of pronouns in European languages that employ two forms of the second-person pronoun 'you' (e.g., French *vous* and *tu*; Spanish, *usted* and *tu*; German *Sie* and *du*). In these pairs of pronouns, the first (which is in fact the plural 'you') is formal and distant, while the second is informal and familiar. Use of the familiar form expresses solidarity with a peer, but will express condescension when used to a social inferior, while use of the plural 'you' marks respect to the addressee or social distance. When the forms are used non-reciprocally, an asymmetric power semantic is set up in which the higher-status speaker condescends to the lower-status hearer with the familiar form, while the lower-status speaker shows respect to the higher-status hearer with use of the plural form.

For Brown and Levinson, honorific forms, broadly defined to include such linguistic phenomena as pronoun use, are a case of 'frozen conversational implicature' (1987: 23). In the case of the second-person pronoun, reciprocal use of the familiar form marks an assumption of 'positive politeness', while reciprocal use of the formal form implies the social distance of 'negative politeness'. The power semantic established through non-reciprocal pronoun use implies a social difference: to borrow a Wolof expression, 'one person has shame, the other has glory' (Irvine 1974: 175).

The social structural assumptions embedded in such linguistic forms surface when they are contested, as occurred when seventeenth-century Quakers refashioned their linguistic practices to express radical social ideals. The Quakers sought to replace the socio-religious dominance of Anglican ministers with the authority of persons 'speaking in the light' of divine revelation. In pursuit of this goal they eliminated mannered and polite ways of speaking, and substituted 'plain speech', which for them was literal speech. Use of the informal 'thee' replaced the asymmetric pronominal semantic of 'you' and 'thee', and they reasoned that use of the plural 'you' to address a single person was untruthful. Against the backdrop of conventional norms, the Quakers' use of 'thee' to address their social superiors was however interpreted as insolent behaviour, and was considered deeply offensive (Bauman 1983). A contemporary observer wrote in 1655 that:

> We maintain that Thou from superiors to inferiors is proper, as a sign of command; from equals to equals is passable, as a note of familiarity, but from inferiors to superiors, if proceeding from ignorance, hath a smack of clownishness; if from affectation, a tang of contempt.... Such who now quarrel at the honour will hereafter question the wealth of others.
>
> (cited in Hill 1972: 247)

Clearly the 'frozen implicature' of pronoun use functions as part of a linguistic habitus that is both structured and structuring: consequently, a change in that habitus is a threat to structural continuity. The observer whose words are cited above did not err when he interpreted the Quaker challenge to linguistic norms as a challenge to the social structure itself.

Occasionally social and political élites have attempted to transform social structure through language planning. During the French revolution, for example, the Committee for the Public Safety banned use of the aristocratic *vous* as a feudal remnant, and promoted adoption of mutual *tu* and the egalitarian *Citoyen* (Brown and Gilman 1960: 266). More recently, the Chinese equivalent of *Citoyen*, *Tongzhi* (literally, 'with a common will'), was promoted to replace inegalitarian titles with the goal of remaking Chinese society through a reworking of linguistic norms (Scotton and Zhu 1983).

As in France, in China linguistic asymmetry persisted, and *Tongzhi* ('Comrade') came to be used primarily in situations where the status title of the addressee was unknown. In circumstances of status inequality, use of 'Comrade' took on marked meanings. When a social inferior addressed a social superior as 'Comrade', the meaning invoked was one of solidarity, and most often the term was used when making a request. When a social superior addressed a social inferior as 'Comrade', then most often the superior implied a rebuke (Scotton and Zhu 1983: 483–4).

While social hierarchy persists in China, the social system has nevertheless changed dramatically, and terms of address such as 'Comrade' are one index of this change. Halliday has observed that:

> semantic style is a function of social relationships and situation types generated by the social structure. If it changes, this is not so much because of what people are now speaking about as because of who they are speaking to, in what circumstances, through what media, and so on. A shift in the fashion of speaking will be better understood by reference to changing patterns of social interaction and social relationships than by the search for a direct link between the language and the material culture.
>
> (1978: 77)

Linguistic style may indeed be a function of social structure, but social structure is realized only in social activity, including, conspicuously, the activity of discourse.

Asian languages provide a good illustration of the realization of social structure in discourse. A number of East and South-east Asian languages make extensive use of speech levels and honorific vocabulary, and the relative statuses of speaker and hearer find linguistic expression in these forms. Like pronoun use in European languages, the use of these forms of politeness is often expressive of identity within a social hierarchy.

For speakers of Japanese, choice from a variety of speech levels indicating formality and politeness is basic to all communication (Shibamoto 1987: 269). The choice of plain, polite, or deferential style depends on the speaker's attitude towards the person(s) addressed. Within each of these styles, Japanese speakers also have the choice of humble, neutral, or exalted expressions, depending on their attitude towards the subject of the expression (Martin 1964: 408–9). Age difference, gender difference, social position, and group membership are all factors in the choice of speech levels and the degree of politeness. A study of Japanese concluded that 'politeness of usage seems to be in inverse proportion to feeling that one has the upper hand in a situation' (Martin 1964: 411).

Traditionally, strict codes of etiquette ruled the Thai court and the Malay sultanates, and the use of polite language was one aspect of the enactment of social hierarchy. Politeness entailed the correct use of formal modes of addressing royalty with linguistic terms that exalted royalty and humbled those of lower status. These terms often gave vivid expression to social difference. For example, one Sanskrit-derived term of address for Malay royalty is *paduka*, literally 'shoe', defined by Coope as 'a royal title derived from the fact that the subject addresses the raja's feet, being unworthy to address the prince himself'. Common people were *pacal*, meaning 'slave of a slave, the humblest of the humble' (Coope 1976: 197). This highly self-deprecatory term was used as a first-person pronoun when non-royalty addressed royalty, and ministers also referred to their family members as 'slaves of slaves' when they addressed their *raja* (Ghazali 1977: 275).

In Thailand a palace language also existed, which was primarily derived from Sanksrit (with some vocabulary from Khmer). As Wales describes the Thai court, 'it was taboo to use words of the common language, or common modes of address, when speaking to or about the King and princes' (1931: 39). The first-person pronoun used when addressing the King meant 'I, the slave of the Lord Buddha'; the second-person pronoun meant 'the dust beneath the sole of your august feet', meaning that the speaker did not dare to address the king directly, and directed his comments instead to the dirt on the floor (1931: 40). A range of lexical items also had a court form, including terms for body parts, articles used by royal persons, food and drink, kinship relationships, verbs of bodily action, and names of certain animals, fish, fruit, and flowers (1931: 39–40).

In contemporary Javanese, the norms governing linguistic etiquette are basic to correct language use, and Javanese provides a complex illustration of the use of language in the construction of identity in interaction (Keeler 1984). Geertz noted as follows:

> In Javanese it is nearly impossible to say anything without indicating the social relationship between the speaker and the listener in terms of status and familiarity. Status is determined by many things – wealth, descent, education, occupation, age, kinship, and nationality, among others, but the important point is that the choice of linguistic forms as well as speech style is in every case partly determined by the relative status (or familiarity) of the conversers.
>
> (1960: 248)

Speech levels, however, are but one complex and nuanced aspect of Javanese etiquette, an etiquette that governs not only speaking but also 'sitting, standing, pointing, composing one's countenance, and so on' (Errington 1988: 11) – in short, what Bourdieu would term the *habitus* of Javanese society.

In a study of the speech levels of the Javanese élite (*priyayi*), Errington cites an elderly Javanese who instructed him thus:

> Whenever two people meet they should ask themselves: 'Who is this person? Who am I? What is this person to me?' (Here he held out his hands, palms up, as if they were pans of a scale.) That's 'relative value' (*unggah-ungguh*).
>
> (1988: 11)

Speakers of Javanese choose among lexical variants, and 'the system is based on sets of precisely ranked, or style-coded morphemes that are semantically equivalent but stylistically contrastive' (Wolfowitz 1991: 121). Most basic to the system is the distinction between ordinary and polite vocabulary, but speakers draw on these to create a continuum of stylistic mixes (Wolfowitz 1991: 123). Also important is an honorific vocabulary referring to the 'possessions, attributes, states, and actions of persons', a vocabulary that includes honorific kin terms (since kin may be regarded as attributes of persons (Errington 1988: 139)).

CONCLUSION

Anthropologists involved in the cross-cultural study of language use have contributed to the formation of a socially grounded linguistics that has great relevance for socio-cultural analysis. The structure of language and norms for language use are basic to the matrix of social life, and a wide range of anthropological questions cannot be addressed without taking account of the data provided by linguistic form and function.

The analysis of 'discourse' holds a central place in contemporary scholarship, comparable to that once held by structural analysis or hermeneutics, and anthropologists have also made essential contributions to interdisciplinary dialogues on this topic. For many scholars, the study of discourse is closely linked to questions of social power and ideological control, and those who study the 'political economy' of language use argue that discourse is a fundamental means through which hegemonic ideas are imposed or contested, and social differences reproduced (Eagleton 1991: 193–220). The cross-cultural study of language use provides discourse analysis with essential comparative insight into the conceptual and practical ordering of social life, and underscores the importance of the unconscious ideological dimensions of language use. At the same time, however, the close focus on the relationship between language and power should not be allowed to overshadow the other manifold uses to which speakers put language, including (most notably) the aesthetic.

Socio-cultural anthropologists of various theoretical persuasions have explored the role of language in the construction of social thought and practice. As demonstrated above, language use shapes the formation of the conceptual systems shared by speakers of a language, and at the same time constitutes diverse social identities in interaction. In speaking, these two aspects of language use converge, as when metaphorically derived polite terms of address simultaneously image hierarchy and index identity: the Thai noble who addresses his comments to the dirt beneath his king's shoe is invoking a cultural image of 'low' status, but he is also indexing relative identity in the social interaction of discourse. Language is profoundly social, and language use both constitutes shared worlds and realizes social diversity in practice.

REFERENCES

Abrahams, R. D. (1977) 'The training of the man of words in talking sweet', in R. Bauman (ed.) *Verbal Art as Performance*, Prospect Heights, Ill.: Waveland Press.
Abu-Lughod, L. (1986) *Veiled Sentiments: Honor and Poetry in a Bedouin Society*, Berkeley: University of California Press.

Abu-Lughod, L. and Lutz, C. A. (1990) 'Introduction', in C. A. Lutz and L. Abu-Lughod (eds) *Language and the Politics of Emotion*, Cambridge: Cambridge University Press.

Ardener, E. (ed.) (1971) *Social Anthropology and Language*, A.S.A. Monographs no. 10, London: Tavistock.

Bakhtin, M. (1981) *The Dialogic Imagination*, ed. M. Holquist, trans. C. Emerson and M. Holquist, Austin: University of Texas Press.

—— (1984) *Problems of Dostoevsky's Poetics*, ed. and trans. C. Emerson, Minneapolis: University of Minnesota Press.

Basso, K. (1972) '"To give up on words": silence in Western Apache culture', in P. P. Giglioli (ed.) *Language and Social Context*, New York: Penguin (reprinted in Basso 1990).

—— (1979) *Portraits of the 'Whiteman': Linguistic Play and Cultural Symbols Among the Western Apache*, Cambridge: Cambridge University Press.

—— (1984) '"Stalking with stories": names, places, and moral narratives among the Western Apache', in E. M. Bruner (ed.) *Text, Play, and Story: The Construction and Reconstruction of Self and Society*, Prospect Heights, Ill.: Waveland Press (reprinted in Basso 1990).

—— (1990) *Western Apache Language and Culture: Essays in Linguistic Anthropology*, Tucson: University of Arizona Press.

Bauman, R. (ed.) (1977) *Verbal Art as Performance*, Rowley: Newbury House .

—— (1983) *Let Your Words be Few*, Cambridge: Cambridge University Press.

Bauman, R. and Briggs, C. L. (1990) 'Poetics and performance as critical perspectives on language and social life', *Annual Review of Anthropology* 19: 59–88.

Bauman, R. and Sherzer, J. (eds) (1974) *Explorations in the Ethnography of Speaking*, Cambridge: Cambridge University Press.

Benveniste, E. (1971 [1966]) 'The nature of the linguistic sign', in *Problems in General Linguistics*, trans. M. E. Meek, Coral Gables, Fla.: University of Miami Press.

Bernstein, B. (1972) 'Social class, language and socialization', in P. P. Giglioli (ed.) *Language and Social Context*, New York: Penguin.

Besnier, N. (1990) 'Language and affect', *Annual Review of Anthropology* 19: (419–51).

Black, M. E. (1984) 'Maidens and mothers: an analysis of Hopi corn metaphors', *Ethnology* 23(4): 279–88.

Bloch, M. (1975) 'Introduction', in M. Bloch (ed.) *Political Language and Oratory in Traditional Society*, London: Academic Press.

—— (1989) 'Symbols, song, dance and features of articulation: is religion an extreme form of traditional authority?', in M. Bloch, *Ritual, History and Power: Selected Papers in Anthropology*, London: Athlone Press.

Boas, F. (1966 [1911]) *Introduction to the Handbook of American Indian Languages*, Washington, D.C.: Georgetown University Press Reprint.

Bolinger, D. (1980) *Language, The Loaded Weapon. The Use and Abuse of Language Today*, London: Longman.

Bourdieu, P. (1982) *Ce que Parler veut dire: l'economie des échanges linguistiques*, Paris: Fayard.

—— (1990 [1980]) *The Logic of Practice*, Stanford, Cal.: Stanford University Press.

Breitborde, L. B. (1983) 'Levels of analysis in sociolinguistic explanation: bilingual code switching, social relations, and domain theory', *International Journal of the Sociology of Language* 39: 5–43.

Briggs, C. L. (1986) *Learning How to Ask: A Sociolinguistic Appraisal of the Role of the Interview in Social Science Research*, Cambridge: Cambridge University Press.

Brown, P. and Levinson, S. (1987) *Politeness: Some Universals in Language Usage*, Cambridge: Cambridge University Press.

Brown, R. and Gilman, A. (1960) 'The pronouns of power and solidarity', in T. A. Sebeok (ed.) *Style in Language*, Cambridge, Mass.: MIT Press.

Bruner, E. M. (ed.) (1984) *Text, Play, and Story: The Construction and Reconstruction of Self and Society*, Prospect Heights, Illinois: Waveland Press.

Caton, S. C. (1987) 'Contributions of Roman Jakobson', *Annual Review of Anthropology* 16: 223–60.

—— (1990) *'Peaks of Yemen I Summon': Poetry as Cultural Practice in a North Yemeni Tribe*, Berkeley: University of California Press.

Clifford, J. (1988) 'On ethnographic authority', in *The Predicament of Culture: Twentieth-Century Ethnography, Literature, and Art*, Harvard: Harvard University Press.

Coope, A. E. (1976) *A Malay-English Dictionary*, Kuala Lumpur: Macmillan Malaysia.

DeBernardi, J. (1987) 'The god of war and the vagabond Buddha', *Modern China* 13(3): 310–32.

—— (1991) 'Linguistic nationalism: the case of southern Min', in V. Mair (ed.) *Sino-Platonic Papers*, University of Pennsylvania.

—— (1993) 'Historical allusion and the defense of identity: Malaysian Chinese popular religion,' in H. Hardacre, C. Keyes and L. Kendall (eds) *Asian Visions of Authority*, Honolulu: University of Hawaii Press.

DeFrancis, J. (1972 [1950]). *Nationalism and Language Reform in China*, New York: Octagon Books.

—— (1984) *The Chinese Language: Fact and Fantasy*, Honolulu: University of Hawaii Press.

Dorian, N. (ed.) (1989) *Investigating Obsolescence: Studies in Language Contraction and Death*, Cambridge: Cambridge University Press.

Durkheim, E. (1965 [1915]) *The Elementary Forms of the Religious Life*, New York: Free Press.

Eagleton, T. (1991) *Ideology: An Introduction*, London: Verso.

Edwards, J. (1985) *Language, Society, and Identity*, Oxford: Blackwell.

Errington, J. J. (1988) *Structure and Style in Javanese: A Semiotic View of Linguistic Etiquette*, Philadelphia: University of Pennsylvania Press.

Evans-Pritchard, E. E. (1940) *The Nuer*, Oxford: Oxford University Press.

Firth, J. R. (1957) *Papers in Linguistics 1934–1951*, Oxford: Oxford University Press.

Fishman, J. A. (1986 [1972]) 'Domains and the relationship between micro- and macrosociolinguistics', in J. J. Gumperz and D. Hymes (eds) *Directions in Sociolinguistics*, Oxford: Blackwell.

Fishman, P. M. (1983) 'Interaction: the work women do', in B. Thorne, C. Kramarae and N. Henley (eds) *Language, Gender, and Society*, Rowley, Mass.: Newbury House.

Fox, J. J. (1977) 'Roman Jakobson and the comparative study of parallelism', in C. H. van Schooneveld and D. Armstrong (eds) *Roman Jakobson: Echoes of his Scholarship*, Lisse, The Netherlands: Peter de Ridder Press.

Friedrich, P. (1979) 'The symbol and its relative non-arbitrariness', in *Language. Context, and the Imagination*, Stanford, Cal.: Stanford University Press.

—— (1986) *The Language Parallax: Linguistic Relativism and Poetic Indeterminacy*, Austin: University of Texas Press.

—— (1991) 'Polytropy' in J. W. Fernandez (ed.) *Beyond Metaphor: The Theory of Tropes in Anthropology*, Stanford, Cal.: Stanford University Press.

Gal, S. (1979) *Language Shift: Social Determinants of Linguistic Change in Bilingual Austria*, New York: Academic Press.

—— (1988) 'The political economy of code choice', in M. Heller (ed.) *Codeswitching: Anthropological and Sociolinguistic Perspectives*, Berlin: Mouton de Gruyter.

—— (1989) 'Between speech and silence: the problematics of research on language and gender' *IPrA Papers in Pragmatics* 3(1): 1–38.

Geertz, C. (1960) *The Religion of Java*, Chicago: University of Chicago Press.

Ghazali, D. M. (1977 [1933]) 'Court language and the etiquette of the Malays', *Malaysian Branch of the Royal Asiatic Society Reprint no. 4: A Centenary Volume*, Singapore: Times Printers.

Graddoll, D. and Swann, J. (1989) *Gender Voices*, Oxford: Blackwell.

Grillo, R. (ed.) (1989a) *Social Anthropology and the Politics of Language*, London: Routledge.

—— (1989b) *Dominant Languages: Language and Hierarchy in Britain and France*, Cambridge: Cambridge University Press.

Gumperz, J. J. (1982) *Discourse Strategies*, Cambridge: Cambridge University Press.

Gumperz, J. J. and Hymes, D. (eds) (1986 [1972]) *Directions in Sociolinguistics: The Ethnography of Communication*, Oxford: Blackwell.

Halliday, M. A. K. (1978) *Language as Social Semiotic: The Social Interpretation of Language and Meaning*, Baltimore, Md.: University Park Press.

Hanks, W. F. (1989) 'Text and textuality', *Annual Review of Anthropology* 18: 95–127.

Haugen, E. (1972) 'Dialect, language, nation', in A. S. Dil (ed.) *The Ecology of Language*, Stanford, Calif.: Stanford University Press.

Heller, M. (ed.) (1988) *Codeswitching: Anthropological and Sociolinguistic Perspectives*, Berlin: Mouton de Gruyter.

Hill, J. C. (1972) *The World Turned Upside Down: Radical Ideas During the English Revolution*, New York: Viking Press.

Hill, J. H. and Hill, K. C. (1986) *Speaking Mexicano: Dynamics of Syncretic Language in Central Mexico*, Tucson: University of Arizona Press.

Hudson, R. A. (1980) *Sociolinguistics*, Cambridge: Cambridge University Press.

Hymes, D. (1974) *Foundations in Sociolinguistics: An Ethnographic Approach*, Philadelphia: University of Pennsylvania Press.

—— (1981) *'In Vain I Tried to Tell You': Essays in Native American Ethnopoetics*, Philadelphia: University of Pennsylvania Press.

Irvine, J. T. (1974) 'Strategies of status manipulation in the Wolof greeting', in R. Bauman and J. Sherzer (eds) *Explorations in the Ethnography of Speaking*, Cambridge: Cambridge University Press.

—— (1985) 'Status and style in language', *Annual Review of Anthropology* 14: 557–81.

Jakobson, R. (1960) 'Closing statement: linguistics and poetics', in T. A. Sebeok (ed.) *Style in Language*, Cambridge, Mass.: MIT Press.

Jorden, E. H. (1974) 'Female speech: persisting myth and persisting reality', in *Report of the Second U.S. Japan Joint Sociolinguistics Conference*, Tokyo: Japanese Society for the Promotion of Social Science.

Keeler, W. (1984) *Javanese: A Cultural Approach*, Athens: Ohio University Monographs in International Studies.

Keenan, E. (1974) 'Norm-makers, norm-breakers: uses of speech by men and women in a Malagasy community', in R. Bauman and J. Sherzer (eds) *Explorations in the Ethnography of Speaking*, Cambridge: Cambridge University Press.

Labov, W. (1972a) *Language in the Inner City*, Philadelphia: University of Pennsylvania Press.

—— (1972b) *Sociolinguistic Patterns*, Philadelphia: University of Pennsylvania Press.

Lakoff, G. and Johnson, M. (1980) *Metaphors We Live By*, Chicago: University of Chicago Press.

Lakoff, R. (1975) *Language and Woman's Place*, New York: Harper & Row.

Leach, E. R. (1970) *Claude Lévi-Strauss*, Harmondsworth: Penguin.

LePage, R. and Tabouret-Keller, A. (1985) *Acts of Identity: Creole-based Approaches to Language and Identity*, Cambridge: Cambridge University Press.

Lévi-Strauss, C. (1963 [1958]) *Structural Anthropology*, trans. C. Jacobson and B. Grundfest Schoepf, New York: Basic Books.

—— (1966 [1962]) *The Savage Mind*, Chicago: The University of Chicago Press.

—— (1969a [1949]) *The Elementary Structures of Kinship*, trans. J. H. Bell, J. R. von Sturmer, ed. R. Needham, Boston: Beacon Press.

—— (1969b [1964]) *The Raw and the Cooked: Introduction to a Science of Mythology*, vol. 1, trans. J. and D. Weightman, Chicago: The University of Chicago Press.

Lucy, J. A. (1985) 'Whorf's view of the linguistic mediation of thought' in E. Mertz and R. J. Parmentier (eds) *Semiotic Mediation: Sociocultural and Psychological Perspectives*, New York: Academic Press.

Luong, H. V. (1990) *Discursive Practices and Linguistic Meanings*, Amsterdam and Philadelphia: John Benjamins.

Lutz, C. and Abu-Lughod, L. (eds) (1990) *Language and the Politics of Emotion*, Cambridge: Cambridge University Press.

Lutz, C. and White, G. M. (1986) 'The anthropology of emotions', *Annual Review of Anthropology* 15: 405–36.

McConnell-Ginet, S. (1988) 'Language and gender' in F. J. Newmeyer, (ed.) *Linguistics: The Cambridge Survey*, vol. 4, *Language: the Sociocultural Context*, Cambridge: Cambridge University Press.

Malinowski, B. (1922) *Argonauts of the Western Pacific*, London: Routledge & Kegan Paul.

—— (1978 [1935]) *Coral Gardens and Their Magic*, vol. 2: *The Language of Magic and Gardening*, New York: Dover.

Marcus, G. E. and Fischer, M. M. J. (1986) *Anthropology as Cultural Critique: An Experimental Moment in the Human Sciences*, Chicago: University of Chicago Press.

Martin, S. E. (1964) 'Speech levels in Japan and Korea', in D. Hymes (ed.) *Language in Culture and Society: A Reader in Linguistics and Anthropology*, New York: Harper & Row.

Maurer, D. W. (1964 [1955]) *Whiz Mob: A Correlation of the Technical Argot of Pickpockets with Their Behavioral Pattern*, New Haven: College and University Press.

Moerman, M. (1988) *Talking Culture: Ethnography and Conversational Analysis*, Philadelphia: University of Pennsylvania Press.

Mukarovsky, J. (1977) *The Word and Verbal Art. Selected Essays by Jan Mukarovsky*, trans. and ed. J. Burbank and P. Steiner, New Haven: Yale University Press.

Newman, S. (1964) 'Zuni sacred and slang usage', in D. Hymes (ed.) *Language in Culture and Society: A Reader in Linguistics and Anthropology*, New York: Harper & Row.

Nietzsche, F. (1954) 'On truth and lie in an extramoral sense', in W. Kaufmann (ed.) *The Portable Nietzsche*, New York: Viking.

Norman, J. (1988) *Chinese*, Cambridge: Cambridge University Press.

O'Barr, W. and Atkins, B. K. (1980) '"Women's language" or "powerless language"?', in S. McConnell-Ginet, R. A. Borker and N. Furman (eds) *Women and Language in Literature and Society*, New York: Praeger.

Ochs, E. (1986) 'Introduction', in B. B. Schieffelin and E. Ochs (eds) *Language Socialization Across Cultures*, Cambridge: Cambridge University Press.

Ochs, E. and Schieffelin, B. B. (eds) (1983) *Acquiring Conversational Competence*, London: Routledge & Kegan Paul.

Ortner, S. B. (1973) 'On key symbols', *American Anthropologist* 75: 1338–46.

Parkin, D. (1984) 'Political language', in *Annual Review of Anthropology* 13: 345–65.

Radcliffe-Brown, A. R. (1965 [1952]) 'On joking relationships', in *Structure and Function in Primitive Society: Essays and Addresses*, New York: Free Press.

Ramsey, S. R. (1987) *The Languages of China*, Princeton: Princeton University Press.

Reichard, G. (1951) *Navaho Grammar*, New York: J. J. Augustin.

Sapir, E. (1949a [1921]) *Language: An Introduction to the Study of Speech*, New York: Harcourt Brace Jovanovich.

—— (1949b) *Selected Writings of Edward Sapir*, ed. D. G. Mandelbaum, Berkeley: University of California Press.

Sapir, J. D. and Crocker, C. (eds) (1977) *The Social Use of Metaphor*, Philadelphia: University of Pennsylvania Press.

Saussure, F. de (1959 [1915]) *Course in General Linguistics*, ed. C. Bally and A. Sechehaye, trans. W. Baskin, New York: McGraw-Hill.

Schieffelin, B. B. (1986) 'Teasing and shaming in Kaluli children's interactions', in B. B. Schieffelin and Ochs, E. (eds) *Language Socialization Across Cultures*, Cambridge: Cambridge University Press.

Schieffelin, B. B. and Ochs, E. (eds) (1986) *Language Socialization Across Cultures*, Cambridge: Cambridge University Press.

Scotton, C. M. (1988) 'Code switching as indexical of social negotiations', in M. Heller (ed.) *Codeswitching: Anthropological and Sociolinguistic Perspectives*, Berlin: Mouton de Gruyter.

Scotton, C. M. and Zhu, W. (1983) 'Tongzhi in China', *Language in Society* 12: 477–94.

Sherzer, J. (1983) *Kuna Ways of Speaking: An Ethnographic Perspective*, Austin: University of Texas Press.

Sherzer, J. and Woodbury, A. C. (eds) (1987) *Native American Discourse: Poetics and Rhetoric*, Cambridge: Cambridge University Press.

Shibamoto, J. S. (1985) *Japanese Women's Language*, New York: Academic Press.

—— (1987) 'Japanese sociolinguistics', *Annual Review of Anthropology* 16: 261–78.

Silverstein, M. (1976) 'Shifters, linguistic categories, and cultural description', in K. H. Basso and H. A. Selby (eds) *Meaning in Anthropology*, Albuquerque: University of New Mexico Press.

—— (1979) 'Language structure and linguistic ideology', in P. R. Clyne, W. F. Hanks and C. L. Hofbauer (eds) *The Elements: A Parasession on Linguistic Units and Levels*, Chicago: Chicago Linguistic Society.

—— (1987) *Monoglot 'Standard' in America*, Working Papers and Proceedings of the Center for Psychosocial Studies no. 13, eds R. J. Parmentier and G. Urban, Chicago: Center for Psychosocial Studies.

Tannen, D. (1986) *That's Not What I Meant! How Conversational Style Makes or Breaks Your Relationships*, New York: William Morrow.

Tedlock, D. (1979) 'The analogical tradition and the emergence of a dialogical anthropology', *Journal of Anthropological Research* 35(4): 387–400.

—— (1983) *The Spoken Word and the Work of Interpretation*, Philadelphia: University of Pennsylvania Press.

—— (1987) 'Questions concerning dialogical anthropology', *Journal of Anthropological Research* 43(4): 325–44.

Tedlock, D. and Mannheim, B. (eds) (1994) *The Dialogic Emergence of Culture*, Urbana: University of Illinois Press.

Thompson, E. P. (1967) 'Time, work-discipline, and industrial capitalism', *Past and Present* 38: 56–97.

Trudgill, P. (1974) *Sociolinguistics: An Introduction*, Harmondsworth: Penguin.

Turner, V. (1974) *Dramas, Fields, and Metaphors*, Ithaca: Cornell University Press.

Turner, V. W. and Bruner, E. M. (eds) (1986) *The Anthropology of Experience*, Urbana: University of Illinois Press.

Urciuoli, B. (1991) 'The political topography of Spanish and English: the view from a New York Puerto Rican neighborhood', *American Ethnologist* 18(2): 295–310.

Vygotsky, L. (1978) *Mind in Society. The Development of Higher Psychological Processes*, eds M. Cole, V. John-Steiner, S. Scribner and E. Souberman. Cambridge, Mass.: Harvard University Press.

Wales, H. G. Q. (1931) *Siamese State Ceremonies: Their History and Function*, London: Bernard Quaritch.

Wertsch, J. V. (1985) *Vygotsky and the Social Formation of Mind*. Cambridge, Mass.: Harvard University Press.

West, C. and Zimmerman, D. (1983) 'Small insults: a study of interruptions in cross-sex conversations between unacquainted persons', in B. Thorne, C. Kramarae, and N. Henley (eds) *Language, Gender, and Society*, Rowley, Mass.: Newbury House.

Whorf, B. L. (1964) *Language, Thought, and Reality*, ed. J. Carroll, Cambridge, Mass.: MIT Press.

Witherspoon, G. (1977) *Language and Art in the Navaho Universe*. Ann Arbor: University of Michigan Press.

—— (1980) 'Language in culture and culture in language', *International Journal of American Linguistics* 46: 1–13.

Wolfowitz, C. (1991) *Language Style and Social Space: Stylistic Choice in Suriname Javanese*, Urbana: University of Illinois Press.

Wolfson, N. and Manes, J. (eds) (1985) *Languages of Inequality*, Berlin: Walter de Gruyter.

Woolard, K. (1989) *Doubletalk: Bilingualism and the Politics of Ethnicity in Catalonia*, Stanford: Stanford University Press.

FURTHER READING

Basso, K. (1990) *Western Apache Language and Culture: Essays in Linguistic Anthropology*, Tucson: University of Arizona Press.

Bauman, R. and Sherzer, J. (eds) (1974) *Explorations in the Ethnography of Speaking*, Cambridge: Cambridge University Press.

Bourdieu, P. (1982) *Ce que Parler veut dire: l'economie des echanges linguistiques*, Paris: Fayard.

Brown, P. and Levinson, S. (1987) *Politeness: Some Universals in Language Usage*, Cambridge: Cambridge University Press.

Brown, R. and Gilman, A. (1960) 'The pronouns of power and solidarity', in T. A. Sebeok (ed.) *Style in Language*, Cambridge, Mass.: MIT Press.

Edwards, J. (1985) *Language, Society, and Identity*, Oxford: Blackwell.

Fernandez, J. W. (1991) *Beyond Metaphor: The Theory of Tropes in Anthropology*, Stanford, Calif.: Stanford University Press.

Friedrich, P. (1986) *The Language Parallax: Linguistic Relativism and Poetic Indeterminacy*, Austin: University of Texas Press.

Grillo, R. (ed.) (1989) *Social Anthropology and the Politics of Language*, London: Routledge.

Heller, M. (ed.) (1988) *Codeswitching: Anthropological and Sociolinguistic Perspectives*, Berlin: Mouton de Gruyter.

Hudson, R. A. (1980) *Sociolinguistics*, Cambridge: Cambridge University Press.

Hymes, D. (1974) *Foundations in Sociolinguistics: an Ethnographic Approach*. Philadelphia: University of Pennsylvania Press.

Mertz, E. and Parmentier, R. J. (1985) *Semiotic Mediation: Sociocultural and Psychological Perspectives*, New York: Academic Press.

Newmeyer, F. J. (ed.) (1988) *Linguistics: The Cambridge Survey*, vol. 4, *Language: The Socio-cultural Context*, Cambridge: Cambridge University Press.

Sapir, E. (1949 [1921]) *Language: An Introduction to the Study of Speech*, New York: Harcourt Brace Jovanovich.

Schieffelin, B. B. and Ochs, E. (eds) (1986) *Language Socialization Across Cultures*, Cambridge: Cambridge University Press.

32

WORK, THE DIVISION OF LABOUR AND CO-OPERATION

Sutti Ortiz

WORK, LABOUR AND LEISURE

Farmers, factory workers, housewives, hunters, secretaries and children spend part of their days working, studying, training, and then enjoying themselves. We use different terms to describe these various activities, even though what is done in leisure time and work time may be very similar. A weekend gardener tending his tomatoes in his backyard is performing an activity comparable to what a coffee farmer does when he plants tomatoes among the immature coffee trees. A young person spending his day in a trade school toils in the same way as a young apprentice learning a trade. Yet, we think of home gardeners as enjoying themselves while farmers work; of students as applying themselves to acquire knowledge, while apprentices work to receive instruction in a trade.

Why do we use different words? What is the significance attached to the term 'work' that renders it inapplicable to the student and weekend gardener? Adam Smith pointed to a crucial distinction in the various uses of the term in his book of 1776, *The Wealth of Nations* (Smith 1982 [1776]). He would have answered our question by pointing out that the tomatoes of the farmers, in being exchanged in the market, would have become commodities that generated capital, whereas the tomatoes of the gardener would have been likely only to generate pleasure. The significant difference was not in the quality of the effort but in how the product of the effort was used. Since the effort of the farmer yielded wealth and capital it could be called 'productive' effort or 'work'. The gardener, on the other hand, was engaged in an 'unproductive' effort since the products were consumed. Likewise, the work of servants 'seldom leaves any trace of value behind' (Smith 1982: 430) since nothing exchangeable is produced by their effort.

Economists since Adam Smith have narrowed the meanings of the concept of work, focusing on what they have called 'productive labour' – a labour that produces commodities with exchange value – and disregarding efforts that they regard as unproductive or activities that they consider to represent leisure. They argue that the growth of an economy depends, in part, on the willingness of the suppliers of labour to give up leisure time, and on the capacity of the economy to absorb the labour supplied. By plotting the flows of labour, the income it can offer to those who provide it, and the capital it can generate to those who purchase it, economists are indeed able to uncover some of the dynamics of economic systems. Since productivity is the cornerstone of the definition of labour, its productive potential must be one of the determinants of the wage rate. The capability of skilled or educated labourers to produce either more items within a unit of time or items with higher market value – that is, their ability to generate more capital – is remunerated with higher wages. A tractor driver is paid more than a field hand; piece rate payments ensure that the more experience harvester receives the higher remuneration. A more complex reformulation of this argument, incorporating conditions of supply and demand, has permitted economists to construct elaborate models to describe and predict the movement of wages, trends in the economy, and the behaviour of firms and farmers. But to do so they have had not only to rely on Adam Smith's narrower meaning of the term 'productive labour', but also to quantify it in terms of its market value and the units of time required.

By concentrating on the narrower analytical definition of labour, economists have excluded from their analysis, until recently, the impact of other work efforts that make the availability of a given quantity of productive labour possible. For example, the time spent by the wives and daughters of the wage labourers preparing their meals and washing their clothes – effort that allows the labourer to spent more time working for wages and that ensures the reproduction of the labour force – is often ignored. Likewise, the 'unproductive' labour of the service sector has remained on the sidelines of most economic models.

There are other, less obvious aspects of work effort that should not be ignored, as they reveal important social meanings affecting the performance and the form of remuneration. For example, a wife who spends much of her time doing 'housework' is said to be a 'housewife'. Her work is considered a duty, not a remunerable service. It is a duty assumed at marriage and reciprocated with consideration and financial support. Her work not only allows for the reproduction of the domestic unit, but also helps to strengthen the marital bond. She helps her man. The time she spends on housework is not simply motivated by the need to feed and care for the family, but rests also on the nature of the marital bond and the prestige associated with a particular style of demonstrating one's dedication to the family. Not surprisingly, when a wife of some means pays someone to come and help her discharge these duties, she is said to contract 'household help' rather than household workers.

Work can help both to strengthen existing social relationships, and to generate new ones. The farmer who helps his brother with the harvest through an exchange-of-hands agreement is reasserting a moral obligation, while at the same time solving a harvest-labour problem and overcoming a cash constraint. When he helps a neighbour under a similar arrangement he gives new meaning to that neighbourly relationship. Simmel argued, in 1907, that a gift always brings forth a counter-exchange which is constrained by morality (Simmel 1971: 43–69). Mauss (1967), using examples from Melanesia and Polynesia, suggested that it was because a gift contains some part of the spiritual essence of the giver that the recipient is moved to make a return; a new relationship is sealed and gifts and counter-gifts flow endlessly.

When a Colombian Paez Indian decides to clear a large field to plant his food crops, he calls a *minga* or labour party, inviting his close kinsmen and intimate friends. The work day ends in celebration, not of what has been accomplished, but of what was ascertained: the communal bond of the participants. The feast serves as an initial and only partial retribution for help received. It has to be followed by the collaboration of the host in the future *minga*s called by his guests; only then will the obligation be fully reciprocated and the host's social debt cancelled. This cancellation, in turn, makes the initial guest indebted; he is now the one who must reciprocate with a feast and return help. Prestations and counter-prestations follow one another as a set of social debt and credit relations, permanently linking friends and kinsmen to each other.

The central theme of the exchange is the significance of the obligation shared by related families, rather than the quantity of food that is produced in this or that field and the cost of producing it. Thus, there is no point in keeping track of how much work was done by each participant, nor of the cost of labour in beer, meat and tubers. Instead, the Paez farmer remembers who comes, and who are the close friends and kinsmen who consistently, and without reason, shirk invitations to *minga*s and other requests for help. In fact, all Paez agree that a *minga* working party is neither the most efficient nor the cheapest way to go about clearing a large field. However, if there is enough cane to prepare beer and enough money to buy meat, the Paez farmer prefers to call a *minga* in order to reassert his social commitments, while clearing a large enough field to assure the survival of his family (Ortiz 1979). After all, if the crops fail to grow and not enough food is produced to feed the family, the farmer will have no alternative but to approach his kinsmen. It is significant that work parties are not used to clear fields for commercially grown crops, for in the case of such crops, costs and productivity are the key concerns – indeed it is only in these terms that their cultivation can be justified.

Work is also an activity that can bring an individual closer to supernatural deities. In the Polynesian island of Tikopia, the sago palm is not just a food-producing tree but represents one of their gods. When a chief is about to cut down a tree, a number of activities requiring some effort must be performed.

Because they are endowed with religious symbolism, we are inclined to regard them as ritual activities. Yet the effort is similar to that involved in productive activities. In fact, it is expected to yield two outcomes: the collaboration of the deity, and the successful production of starch. The intertwining of productive pursuits and religious activities in Tikopia was so intense that Firth (1967a) adopted the phrase 'work of the gods' to describe the religious cycle he observed in that island in 1928, and again in 1952. The rites are obligatory, and involve the production and presentation of food to gods and spirits, food that is eventually put into circulation and consumed.

Cutting the trees, scraping the pith and processing the sago not only bring Tikopian men and gods closer to one another but also, as with the Paez, bring a work party of kinsmen together (Firth 1967b: 269–83). This joint co-operative effort is regarded as a social obligation: 'Anything done in the house of a brother-in-law, I rise and go after it' (Firth 1967a: 147). The kinsman who responds in such a manner is also mindful of the complexities of the social bond and will be careful to acknowledge symbolically the important differences of status and role. If the chief is the one who has invited others to work for him, he must offer a more elaborate feast than a host of lower rank. If a senior individual helps in the production of starch, he must receive a bowl of starch as well as the customary amount of flour.

In some cases, the offering and receipt of help can be used to formalize status differences. In England, large staffs of cooks, gardeners and cleaners allowed the gentry to keep well-manicured gardens, entertain with great formality and assume a style of life becoming to their social status. However, just as significant was the demeanour adopted by the managing butler when discharging his duties. He had to act in a dignified manner, never revealing his emotion or anxieties, and had to speak eloquently with a good accent on appropriate topics. This professionalism was attributed to the squire, who was thereby freed to act in a more relaxed manner. In other words, the work effort of the butler allowed upper-class gentlemen to mark their class difference by a particular style, without having overly to constrain their behaviour. The butler's ability to enhance the status of his master put him in a class apart from the manservants, housekeepers and domestic help hired by middle-class housewives.

Relations forged while labouring are both complex and delicate. In the case of the butler, he must distance himself from the squire whose status he enhances, and from other members of the staff, in order not to demean the symbolism of his pose. All social aspects of the work relation are brought to bear on the forging of rules of conduct among co-workers. In turn, the patterns of conduct, as well as pervasive social conflicts, class antagonisms, or more ramifying loyalties, are likely to affect performance. This is most striking in rural areas and in small-scale societies, where there is little separation between domestic tasks, farming tasks at home and work on the farms of neighbours and kinsmen. Class differences are said to have a negative effect on the work performance of field hands in England. Farm owners, concerned with productivity, try to offset the impact of class differences by relating to their workers as informally and as supportively as possible. They drink together in pubs and work along with the labourers as often as they can. In this way, farm owners foster the loyalty, commitment and deference of their workmen, and attempt to transform the contractual tie into a socially meaningful work relation (Newby 1977: 303).

The social significance of work extends beyond the conveyance of symbolic information. Work involves the transformation of nature into objects which then become identified with the people who produced them. As Marx long ago observed, it is through labour, through the transformation of nature into commodities, that human beings define themselves (see also Miller in this volume, Article 15). The exercise of care and ability, as demonstrated by the quality of workmanship, further enhances their stature. Well-tended fields, smooth and delicious cubes of uncentrifuged sugar and tightly woven cloth all bring prestige to a Paez Indian and many of them are willing to give up leisure time to gain the recognition attained through such products. Some of these carefully manufactured craft objects become so identified with the producer that it is not easy to convince them to part with them (Ortiz 1979). Even in societies where crafts are readily sold in the market the identification of the object with the person who made it or designed it is retained (Annis 1987). Much has been written about the existential significance of work, how and when it serves to integrate a person, to give him or her a sense of satisfaction and identity, or alternatively leads to a sense of insignificance and alienation. Chinoy's classical study of automobile workers (Chinoy 1965) has set some useful guidelines for the analysis of the significance of wage work in the life of labourers.

By transforming nature through their work, individuals can establish a claim over what they produce. In most pre-capitalist societies work serves to establish rights of use over fields, trees or crops. Territories may belong to certain clans, but individual members of a clan can carve out sections for themselves and their families by clearing them and planting them with crops. Although the recognition that work generates rights of use or disposition is most common in pre-capitalist societies, it is not unknown in market economies. In Colombia, individuals can claim rights over unused land by clearing it and using two thirds of the claimed territory. The disastrous fate of the forest of Amazonia is in part rooted in that fundamental notion, which has received formal legal recognition in most Latin American countries.

The recognition that labour is a force that serves to link commodities to their producers is probably what induced Ricardo (1911: 5–18) and Marx (1965: 48–54) to think of labour as a value-endowing process. For example, they supposed that in non-market economies, the value of the hunt could be measured by the time spent tracking animals, plus the time spent making the spear used to kill them (in proportion to the durability of the tool). Marx introduced the qualification that this was likely to be the case only in economies in which producers controlled the means of production, and in which capital requirements were similar among industries. Morishima (1973) has added another condition: that the mobility of labour should not be impeded sociologically or geographically.

Some anthropologists have adopted Marx's proposition that the exchange value of a commodity rests on the labour expended in producing it, in order to explain the rates at which commodities were exchanged, as well as the rigidity of such rates, in pre-capitalist economies. However, in an analysis of the exchange of salt blocks for bark capes among the Baruya of Highland New Guinea, Godelier (1971) found that although there was a certain correspondence between the rate of exchange and the proportional input of labour required, on average, to manufacture these two kinds of goods, the Baruya themselves justify the terms of this exchange with different arguments. The request for a specific number of bark capes in exchange for a given quantity of salt is initially backed by arguments of need. Only when the trading partner remains unmoved does the Baruya salt producer bring up the issue of the work required for the item offered in exchange. Godelier concludes that the rate of exchange is determined not by the relative amounts of labour 'congealed' in the items exchanged, but by the relative social need of the trading partners for these items (Godelier, 1971: 66–7; see also Gregory's discussion of the Baruya case in Article 33). Cook (1976) has attempted a rather similar type of analysis to determine whether the exchange value of *metate*s (grinding stones) produced by Zapotec peasants in Mexico is pegged – allowing for seasonal fluctuations in supply and demand – around a value fixed by the labour cost of their production. He concludes that the *metate* producers are indeed concerned to ensure that they receive an appropriate compensation for their labour. In other words, in this peasant economy, labour time *is* adduced as one factor in assigning value to commodities, but only after excluding certain costs (such as the time spent at the quarry to extract the stone, and the time and money required to maintain and replace the required tools).

Thus, the meanings of work and labour are multiple. Work is an activity that can generate or strengthen social relations. As a social process it reflects and symbolizes all other conditions: rank differences, role characteristics, kinship obligations. On ritual occasions, work acquires a religious connotation. It is because work evolves in this social context that it can serve to link the individual to the produce of his or her labour, but only if that labour has not been sold as a commodity to another party (the employer). In the latter situation, for example in modern factory production, the relation that individuals retain with the commodities they produce is extremely tenuous. The meaning of their work then shifts from the items produced to the status of their job and to social relations within the factory.

More importantly, work in industry and commercial agriculture generates capital for the owner of the means of production or for the buyer of the labour. This is the meaning of work to which economists draw most attention. It is of course an important meaning. Yet, since the production of capital is affected by the social context of labour, it is wrong to disregard the other meanings of work alluded to in this section. To do so would render our explanations incomplete, and our arguments only partial.

None of these meanings is *intrinsic* to work. Rather, the significance of work is drawn from, and reflects, the social contexts of production and exchange. An individual who sells his labour-power enters into a contract. It is the contract, and the socio-economic relations implied by it, that gives to work its particular tenor. Moreover, all of these diverse meanings are learned: workers must be socialized, for example, into the experience of factory employment. Once socialization is achieved, the experience becomes generalized and is often reified as a code of work ethics and of job characterizations.

MEASURING LABOUR AND WORK

These different meanings and significances are sometimes conveyed by using separate terms. Domestic helpers may be referred to as domestics, servants, cleaning women, household helpers, or housewives, rather than – say – home labourers. Servants are said to produce 'services' instead of capital. Kinsmen in a working party are known as 'guests' rather than 'workers'.

A Paez farmer distinguishes linguistically between the various social and economic meanings of his work effort. He describes his participation in a *minga* as 'accepting an invitation', and his several hours' walk in taking salt to his cattle – raised as an insurance against starvation – as a 'visit' to the animal. When a Paez sells his energy for money, however, he 'works'. He also 'works', as does his wife and children, when clearing his field and planting his crops. Work is seen as what generates capital and sustenance. *Mingas*, of course, also generate sustenance, but more importantly, they generate sociability and future work resources (Ortiz 1979).

The context of the work experience affects the way that experience is recalled. A farmer who has helped a kinsman does not keep track of the number of hours spent at each task; when he returns home, he thinks about his relationship to his kinsman. Likewise, his collaboration is remembered not with a figure but as an affective gesture. To keep an exact account of time expenditure may signal a disinterest in the social obligation. Loathing to convey such a message, the farmer may undervalue or even overvalue the extent of his contribution. When however the work is provided under contract and a wage is paid, farmers are more likely to keep track of time spent at a job, and to evaluate financially the wage received.

I noticed that Paez farmers did not include, in their estimates of labour time expenditure, the contribution of guests at a *minga*, or the time spent visiting their cattle. They can give some very rough estimates of work requirements for a field planted with subsistence crops, since they are labouring at this task. But this work effort is clouded by the social significance of subsistence crops, and a strict accounting of time spent cannot convey what the effort is all about: the ability to care for a family. This ability, in the view of the farmers themselves, is more clearly demonstrated by bountiful dinners and feasts, than by individual expenditure of effort. Hence, time accounting seems to them to be somewhat irrelevant. This finding accords with those cited earlier, concerning the relative inaccuracy, in terms of labour costs, of the evaluation of *metates* by Zapotec stone workers and of salt blocks by Baruya. Time spent working becomes more crucial when the effort is vested in planting cash crops, because the question then present in the mind of a Paez farmer is whether the alternative of wage work may not be a better solution to the problem of meeting his cash needs.

The introduction of time accounting (see Adam in this volume, Article 18) does not automatically follow from the commercialization of labour, nor from industrialization. 'Rather, time in relation to work has been continuously shaped, defined and contested by workers and employers in the context of changing structural pressures contained within the spheres of production and social reproduction' (Whipp, 1987: 211). Even as late as 1940, accounts of labour costs in pottery production were not kept by most factories in Britain. Instead of using time to regulate labour costs, the factory owner divided the production process into tasks and paid by task completed. Whipp quotes a moulder as saying: 'We have no set time for stopping and starting here, that is in regard to moulded work, should any job be given out, a piece-work rate is at once fixed on. So the Boss troubles no more about one's comings and goings' (Whipp 1987: 226). In this way pottery employees could mix domestic work with productive work. The first was called play, the second work.

These uneven patterns of labour-time accounting in farming and industry undermine the economists' attempts to evaluate the relative significance of different factors of production. They can represent labour inputs by payments made for labour, but only when the payments correspond to the quantity and quality of effort vested in the production process.

Anthropologists should be even more careful when gathering estimates of labour input in non-market economies. Data cannot be obtained through recall of past events, but must instead be carefully adduced from daily observations and time budgets. The field observer should not ask 'what *work* did the informant carry out on that day?' but 'what did she or he *do* on that day?' In this way one can avoid the risk of failing to attend to tasks that may be classed, whether in the conventions of the observer or in those of the local people, as other than work (Johnson 1975).

DIVISION OF LABOUR

In all societies there are some tasks that require training and experience. But most other tasks could, in principle, be performed by just about anyone. Yet in practice this is rarely the case. Tasks tend to be categorized as appropriate for certain sets of individuals rather than others. Young men are often the warriors, women the ones to prepare food, and older men are the political managers. To some extent one can account for specialization and the division of labour as responses to technical requirements and time constraints.

For example, some activities are very time-consuming and need exclusive attention in locations distant from where other activities must be performed. This and other conflicting demands can be resolved by differential allocation of responsibilities among individuals who recognize their social interdependence and who share the proceeds of work. Thus, it is most often within households composed of close kinsmen that one can note task specialization and interdependence. It is understandable, within this setting, that women who must nurse children, and who are thus more limited in their mobility, should take on tasks that can be performed within or near the household. Tending the fire, processing staples, caring for domestic animals, preparing the food and tilling nearby gardens are jobs often assigned to women. These are tasks that can readily be combined with the responsibilities of child care. Men can more easily assume responsibilities that take them further away from their homes: going to war, hunting large animals that must be followed for days, herding and trading in faraway territories. In fact, women are likely to assume a major responsibility for agriculture in societies where men are called away by war or must tend distant herds of livestock (Ember 1983: 297–99). This pattern is replicated when wage labour is introduced and men must go away to work (Burton and White 1984: 580). The intermittent yet interminable daily task of fetching water and wood can be left to children who have little else to do.

Long dry seasons, followed by short periods of rain, skew work rhythms in ways that are difficult to manage. Agricultural tasks have to be completed within short periods of time, while working very intensively. Men may be in a better position to handle such work cycles (Burton and White 1984: 579). Alternatively, some of the agricultural activities that have to be completed within a short period of time can be subdivided into tasks that are each judiciously allocated to either men or women. By so doing, and by also taking into account the domestic constraints on women, time pressures can be at least partially resolved. When the Bemba have to clear a field before the rains come, the men are assigned to pollarding the trees and cutting the underbrush. The women pile the branches that men will later burn (Richards 1939: 289–94).

The problems posed by uneven seasonal demands can also be resolved through co-operation rather than specialization. The production of salt from grasses, as practised by the Baruya of New Guinea, requires a number of operations, some of which cannot be carried out by a single individual within the short dry periods. The grass must be cut, transported, dried for two weeks, and burned before the rains come. Baruya men with rights over grassland solve their problem by enlisting the help of other kinsmen who lack such rights, or by working co-operatively with other salt producers. Once the grass is burned, the ash residues have to be soaked and filtered, and the sediment extracted by heat-induced evaporation of the water. This second stage requires much time but only limited attention; it can be carried out by a single individual with free time to spare – time he can make available to other salt producers. Altogether, the production of one bar of salt requires 21 person-days, but this labour requirement can be selectively distributed among a group of co-operating men (Godelier 1971: 55–8).

Work rhythms, however, are not simply dictated by the demands of growing crops. Before cocoa farming was introduced into West Africa, important Beti men were able to mobilize enough labour to clear large tracts of land. They took advantage of this opportunity to instigate not only an intensive period of land preparation, but also a subsequent season of intensive planting. Women, clients and junior men who lacked access to a large labour force had to content themselves with cultivating land previously used; they also had to avoid practices requiring peak labour periods (Guyer 1988: 256). Even today, Beti women are limited to growing crops that can be combined in such a way that periods requiring intensive inputs of labour are avoided (Guyer 1984: 381).

Thus technological arguments, though relevant, cannot fully explain seasonal work rhythms, nor can they explain why certain tasks, in specific societies, are performed by women. If it is more rational and efficient for women to concentrate on jobs that can be performed near their dwellings, why is it that in New Guinea their gardens are often so far from the village? According to Salisbury (1962: 49–52), the men go to their fields every third day and spend about four hours a week travelling, while women go every day and spend twelve hours a week on their return trips. Technological arguments also fail to explain why, among the Baruya of New Guinea, women are allowed to help with the cutting and piling of the grass, yet they are excluded from helping in the collective task of wrapping the salt bars. The explanation, in this case, is cultural: women can pollute salt bars (Godelier 1971: 56). Carlstein (1982: 339) has depicted diagrammatically the daily routine of members of a Gusii agropastoralist household in East Africa, illustrating the imbalances in the time invested by husband, wives, daughters and sons in their respective tasks, and the locations of such tasks (Figure 1). Men spend more time around their dwellings than women do. Johnson (1975: 639) estimated that among the Machiguenga – slash-and-burn horticulturalists in Peru – men spend $4\frac{1}{2}$ hours daily in agriculture and foraging and about 15 to 20 minutes helping with childcare and cooking. When other productive tasks are included, men work a total of 6 hours per day. Women spend more time on food processing and

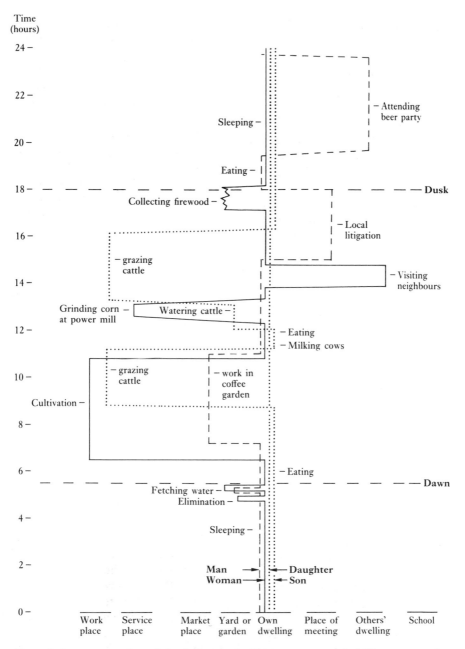

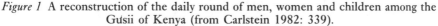

Figure 1 A reconstruction of the daily round of men, women and children among the Gusii of Kenya (from Carlstein 1982: 339).

childcare, and less time in agricultural and gathering activities, adding up to a total of 7.3 hours of work per day.

To understand how labour is allocated among members of a household, and how these allocations correspond to social categories (males, females, parents, adolescents and younger children), one must consider the social as well as the technical aspects of work. Since work can generate power and prestige, establish relationships and symbolize status, the allocation of tasks is likely to reflect both the prevailing social organization and the politico-economic context within which the labour process unfolds.

If only some people are allowed, or are in a position, to produce an item which is basic for survival, others must become dependent on those people. When the goods produced can be used to gain other assets, the control so conferred can yield significant political and economic power. Among the Lele of West Africa, the elders reserve the right to produce the decorated bark cloth that circulates as part of bridewealth payments (Douglas, 1963: 54–61). When new cash crops are introduced, it is often the men who reserve to themselves the right to plant them, and by so doing they retain control over capital assets, thus ensuring their own economic ascendancy.

However, the planting of staples can only bring power to producers when they control the means of production. For example, in New Guinea, it is the women who produce the yams. Their specialization in this activity has not, however, enhanced their position because, while controlling the production of a basic staple, they remain dependent on their husbands for the land on which to plant the yams and for the clearing of their fields (Salisbury 1962: 46).

For power to be gained through control over the production process, the producer must not only control the means of production, but also be in command of his or her own efforts. A Paez woman in Colombia may gain considerable prestige by producing a well-designed and tightly woven *ruana* or poncho; in theory she could also make non-weavers dependent on her effort. But before a wife sets a loom she must ask for her husband's permission. He has a prior claim over her labour and may prefer that she works in the family field, rather than remain at home weaving a blanket. More importantly, and because he has a claim over her labour, the cloth she produces, even when she uses the wool of her own sheep, has to be committed to a family member. Her bargaining powers are, thus, limited.

The power and status that may potentially be achieved through specialization can also be contained by controlling the distribution of commodities. In Guatemala, women are often the weavers of blankets, but seldom do they sell what they themselves produce. The explanation given is that the markets, and tourist craft buyers, are too far away (Bossen 1984). The question remains as to whether men are not also trying to link themselves to a work activity that is profitable and that might, if left totally in the hands of women, allow them to build considerable bargaining power within the domestic circle. Thus power can only be gained by specialists when they have free access to the means of production or to capital assets, total claim to their own labour and the freedom to distribute what they produce.

Since producers are often identified with the fruits of their labours, specialists can gain stature, as well as power, when their products are significant luxuries or prestigious staples. In India, activities are ranked according to a scale of religious purity, with professions at the top of the list and defiling activities, like those of street sweepers, at the bottom — restricted to the lowest untouchable castes. Any activity connected with dead things or bodily emissions pollutes, and is reserved for the lowest castes and subcastes. But other, less polluting occupations are also evaluated according to how degrading it is to perform them and hence whether they should be avoided by higher-ranked castes. Occupations thus serve as indices of the social rank of castes.

A more subtle illustration of occupational stratification is to be found with the emergence of guilds and the nineteenth-century artisan societies. Elaborate technologies do of course account for the institution of apprenticeship, through which novices were enabled to acquire the required skills. However, the training was often overly protracted in order both to limit entry and to enhance the prestige of the trade. The Amalgamated Society of Engineers insisted that for a man to be recognized as a member of the trade, he had to serve a five-year apprenticeship. The knowledge thus acquired became the artisan's personal capital, marking him as an adult, a special individual in society and a member of a prestigious social group (McClelland 1987: 191). Prestige rested not only on the importance of the trade, but also on a well established code of behaviour. A shipwright who came to work on Mondays unshaven and wearing a dirty shirt was likely to be fined (McClelland 1987: 193). A labourer who worked alongside a mason was often physically chastised by being struck hard with the mason's leather apron, as a way of symbolically humiliating him (Rule 1987: 109). In fact, most trades were ranked in terms of how 'honourable' or 'dishonourable' they were.

Because, as we have seen, work is an activity that links individuals to commodities, services, communities and gods, and because it can create relations of debt and power, it is a social as much as a technological process. Hence, the division of labour must always be closely connected with political structures and must lie at the heart of any process of stratification. Indeed, Godelier argues that the division of labour emerges *alongside* social hierarchies rather than being the prior cause of them (Godelier 1980).

With this in mind, we should re-examine Durkheim's visionary portrayal of the evolution of societies from those of a simple and undifferentiated kind, held together by shared values that were routinely obeyed, ritually reinforced and communally sanctioned, to larger and more secular societies where specialization prevailed, fostering social interdependence. He characterized the former as integrated through mechanical solidarity, and the latter as integrated through organic solidarity (Durkheim, 1933: 129–32). In Tikopia, for example, the ritual cycle brings each clan together and links it to the three other clans. Likewise, the feasts that end the labour parties of the Colombian Indians help to reassert the significance of social bonds. In these and many other small-scale societies, solidarity rests in the routinized performance of communal acts.

Once specialization makes interdependence a more constant and pervasive reality, the ritual re-enactment of solidarity becomes less crucial. Societies become secularized, new codes of conduct are forged, and new sanctions are established to ensure the smooth operation of society. The division of labour, Durkheim argued, allows individuals to strive for equal opportunity, to have greater autonomy and to be constrained not so much by tradition as by contractual obligation (Durkheim 1933: 147–56).

Inter-caste exchanges illustrate how specialization can bring interdependence and solidarity, much as Durkheim suggested. However, they also highlight another point made by Durkheim: that specialization can lead to hierarchical and exploitative social arrangements, and that religion can buttress some of these unbalanced relationship. The exchanges of rice and services between carpenters and landlord, for example, are fixed by tradition. At times, these exchanges may be balanced, but the fact is that the carpenter cannot hold land and that the landlord, who is a member of the dominant caste, controls the distribution of rice and services. This is a right that is sanctioned by religion and renders the landlord more powerful, despite his dependence on a number of specialists (Dumont 1972: 138–48). It is important to note that, in this example, it is not so much individuals who become interdependent as social groups, which remain in such a position generation after generation.

It becomes clear that the emerging division of labour can be accompanied by, and can consolidate, class stratification. Durkheim himself drew attention to this in his admission that neither America nor Western Europe had achieved true organic solidarity. He characterized these as transitional capitalist societies, in which workers who would otherwise be unemployed are often forced to enter into contractual agreements that benefit only industrialists, and in which a state of anomie prevails. Only in societies that offer equal opportunities to all, where entry to certain occupations is determined by ability and capacity rather than by birth, can a division of labour generate organic solidarity. In these (ideal) societies no hidden power structures determine how people use their time and what occupation they can practise. The state is supposed to protect individual freedoms and to ensure access to education and other important resources for the acquisition of skills.

The division of labour has not yet given us the utopian society that Durkheim wished for. If anything, the consequences of this social process have been more accurately described by Marx. Specialization, when one class retains control over the means of production and circulation, often leads to domination. Short of remaining unemployed, the factory worker has no choice but to abide by the contractual terms imposed by the capitalist employer. His occupation is specified by the technical engineer who designs the machinery that he will operate, and is manipulated by the foreman who allocates tasks and schedules times. Concerns other than those of mechanical efficiency are also present in the minds of these designers and managers. These are concerns about how to hold down the costs of production, either by controlling wage payments, or by increasing the intensity of the labour process, or by minimizing the possibilities of industrial action. Reorganizations of the division of labour often reflect management concerns as well as technical problems; together they deeply affect the structure of wage labour markets.

THE DIVISION OF LABOUR AND THE STRUCTURE OF LABOUR MARKETS

Durkheim was correct in pointing out that the division of labour became more pervasive with the expansions of capitalism. For it is this that locks a large sector of the population into an exchange of labour for wages and of money for subsistence needs. A new set of social classes emerged against the background of already existing social hierarchies, and within each a shared consciousness began to be formulated. The division of labour took on a strongly political dimension.

It also became more spatially defined. Work was removed from the domestic circle, creating, in factories and plantations, new social relations of production. The differentiation between labour and leisure began to be acknowledged more categorically. Clock time started to regulate labour, taking away from the individual the management of his or her own work effort. Labour, more often than not, began to be sold by units of clock time rather than by tasks completed (Thompson 1967, Adam, this volume, Article 18). Legal contracts emerged as the mode for negotiating the sale and exchange of labour. These transformations in the organization of production thus began to create new divisions of labour: between jobs in the family that are unremunerated, wage jobs that may vary according to what is being produced, manual jobs, and administrative jobs.

Analysts of Marxist persuasion point to another parallel development with industrialization: de-skilling, the degradation of work and the resulting homogenization of the labour force (Braverman 1974). This transformation of the production process became possible, it is argued, with technification. It represents a counter-move against the division of labour that had been fostered by the system of craft guilds. Artisans hoping to safeguard their interests had drawn sharp lines around their professions, tightening entry conditions and requiring ever lengthier apprenticeship. Capitalists, who had to rely on skilled workers for a large part of the production process, were at the mercy of the regulations that limited the supply of competent labourers and augmented the cost of their labour. De-skilling has to be considered as part of the rationalization process employed by capitalists to reduce the costs of production. Once achieved, capitalist producers could tap much cheaper sources of labour: the unskilled, women and children. Alternatively, they could bypass the skills of the artisans by simply allowing the production of cruder produce (Rule 1987: 101).

It was partly through de-skilling that capitalists were able to gain control over the labour process and open up the labour market to a vast sector of the population. Gordon *et al.* (1982) have rephrased the same historical trajectory, adding that only certain industries had enough available capital to achieve almost complete de-skilling. Eventually, these industries were the only ones that could advance technologically and thereby increase productivity and returns so as to be able to offer better wages. Other enterprises, constrained by access to capital, were unable to achieve high productivity through mechanization, and had to retain a labour force with lower wages. They had to rely on a supply of workers who were socially rejected by the core industries: above all, women and members of ethnic minorities. This process of differentiation differs from the division of labour in that it does not categorize prestige, quality of work and payment by the type of task, but by the type of firm and the social type of labourer it prefers to recruit. It has been given a new label: the segmentation of labour markets.

Neoclassical economists countered that there is no real segmentation of the labour market. In free-market economies, specialization is a rational response to both technical problems and management issues. Jobs are open to anyone who is qualified, and remuneration is based on the cost of acquiring the required skills, productivity and the supply of labour. The division of labour within the market sector, they argued, is based solely on an open network for achievement and promotion (Cain 1975).

While this may be the case for some sectors of the labour market, it is hard to believe that social processes of differentiation, empowerment and stratification, which had operated until the emergence of industrial society, would have suddenly ceased to influence the organization of the economy. The neoclassical argument also fails to explain certain historical patterns of recruitment and wage rates. When the Dutch engine loom was introduced by large manufacturers in 1815, only men were hired to operate them, relegating women weavers to the more unskilled tasks of operating the single-hand looms. Neither technology, nor mechanization, nor skill could explain this segmentation of the labour market along gender lines. Women had worked in the weaving industry and would have probably been perfectly able to work with the new looms, had they been allowed to operate them. What probably kept women from these looms was a combination of cultural notions about the kinds of work that are appropriate to different categories of people (in this case, men and women), and the wish to prevent the empowerment of women through their admission to relatively prestigious and financially rewarding occupations. In fact women, off and on, had alternately participated in, and then again been barred from, the weaving trade in Spitalfield (Berg 1987). When they did participate in trades along with men, as in nail manufacturing,

906

they received much lower wages. When women and ethnic minorities consistently concentrate on more marginal industries, we may expect to find causes for this other than the requirements of training, competence and scheduling. Given what has been said about the social significance of work, it seems much more plausible that this segmentation is akin to a gender division of labour.

More conscious subsequent resegmentations of the market, targeting particular categories of individuals for newly defined skills, have been associated with strategic attempts by farmers and industrialists to subvert protest, to control the labour force, and to lower wages. Redefining certain tasks as requiring experience and skill that are gender-specific, contractors can control the recruitment process to avoid labour conflicts, and to influence pay scales. By praising the dexterity of women as lettuce wrappers, lettuce growers in California, fearful of the spread of unions, targeted a population of supposedly less troublesome workers as the suppliers of labour for their crews. The task of cutting, leafing, wrapping and crating the lettuce in the field used to be done by an undifferentiated crew of individuals. When the process became partly mechanized, men, women and machines had to move in unison, but since the job was redefined as consisting of three different tasks, a different type of individual could be hired for each. By assigning different modes and levels of remuneration to each task, the lettuce-growers were able to lower the costs of production. While migrant male cutters and packers received a piece-rate payment, the women who followed the cutters were paid by the hour. Thomas (1985) calculates that the wages thus earned by women were much lower than those earned by men, though the skill required did not differ.

By ranking occupations in terms of prestige, growers also affect the sources of labour. Whether intentionally or not, farmers often downgrade certain tasks, allowing entrepreneurial contractors to set a cap on wages and to seek out sources of supply willing to provide it: usually the most vulnerable sectors of the population. Florida cane growers insist that Americans are not used to hard work and would not apply for cane-cutting jobs. With this argument in hand they petition for special immigration licences to bring in foreign labourers for a season at a time (Martin 1988). In fact, crops seem to be ranked by a scale of prestige, and workers are loath to move from the 'ladder crops' to the less esteemed jobs in cotton, grapes and potatoes, or in the still lower status crops that require stooping. With industrialization in manufacture and agriculture we find a new redivision of tasks that combines with other processes of gender, ethnic and social differentiation, once again to generate closed occupational groups. This is a response on the part of management to the escalating costs of production, the demands from workers who are unionized, and the difficulty in asserting a work ethic that is profitable to capital.

With the spread of wage work there is also a shift in the way that the labour relationship is defined, from the exchange of labour as a gift, or as part of a social obligation, to exchange with remuneration. The shift was gradual as it entailed the sanctioning of contracts, and the freedom of both parties to initiate or terminate them. In England, labourers did not gain such freedom until late in the nineteenth century. Labour relations then became bureaucratized, the traditional base of pre-existing relations between labourers and employers was weakened and the force of the supply–demand tension began to be felt in full. Only then did the new forms of redivision of labour, alluded to above, begin to take shape.

Although in principle this shift has now been completed, a large part of the agricultural produce consumed, or of manufactured goods purchased, in modern societies is nevertheless *not* produced by individuals who work in plantations, workshops or factories, and who enter freely into clearly defined contractual agreements. Much food is still produced by self-employed farmers, or sharecroppers, or labourers who offer their services either to repay a loan or in exchange for access to land. Although some of these arrangements are not necessarily exploitative, they are not always explicitly negotiated. Robertson (1987), in a survey of sharecropping contracts in Africa, points out that the terms of the contracts are often implicit, and are negotiated over a number of occasions. Many informants, upon hearing Robertson's summary of his findings, were struck by the unfairness of some of the contracts into which they themselves had entered, and were inspired to drive a harder bargain on future occasions. In the highly commercialized sector of Colombian coffee agriculture, many labourers are not at present certain of what pay they are going to receive at the end of the week. When negotiations are not open, wages cannot reflect market conditions. They are more likely to reflect other capital costs of the enterprise and the landlord's or manufacturer's perception of what is an appropriate standard of living for the labourer. Such perceptions are coloured by class and ethnic differences and are likely to perpetuate them. When contractual agreements are unclear and negotiations not bureaucratized, a labour market may be more readily segmented along social lines than along task-specific lines. Thus the nature of the division of labour also rests on the nature of the wage negotiating process.

REFERENCES

Annis, S. (1987) *God and Production in a Guatemalan Town*, Austin, Tex.: University of Texas Press.

Bossen, L. (1984) *The Redivision of Labour: Women and Economic Choice in Four Guatemalan Communities*, Albany: State University of New York Press.

Berg, M. (1987) 'Women's work, mechanisation and the early phases of industrialisation in England', in P. Joyce (ed.) *The Historical Meanings of Work*, Cambridge: Cambridge University Press.

Braverman, H. (1974) *Labour and Monopoly Capital*, New York: Monthly Review Press.

Burton, M. and White, D. R. (1984) 'Sexual division of labor in agriculture', *American Anthropologist* 86: 568–83.

Cain, G. G. (1975) 'The challenge of dual and radical theories of the labor market to orthodox theory', *American Economic Review* 65: 16–22.

Carlstein, T. (1982) *Time Resources, Society and Economy*, vol. 1, *Pre-industrial Societies*, London: Allen & Unwin.

Chinoy, E. (1965) *The Automobile Worker and the American Dream*, Garden City, N.Y.: Doubleday.

Cook, S. (1976) 'Value, price and simple commodity production: Zapotec stone workers', *Journal of Peasant Studies* 3: 395–428.

Douglas, M. (1963) *The Lele of Kasai*, London: Oxford University Press.

Dumont, L. (1972) *Homo Hierarchicus*, London: Palladin.

Durkheim, E. (1933) *The Division of Labour in Society*, New York: Free Press.

Ember, C. (1983) 'The relative decline in women's contribution to agriculture with intensification', *American Anthropologist* 86: 285–304.

Firth, R. (1967a) *The Work of the Gods in Tikopia*, London School of Economics, Monographs in Social Anthropology, vols 1 and 2, London: Athlone Press.

—— (1967b) *Tikopia Ritual and Belief*, London: Allen & Unwin.

Godelier, M. (1971) 'Salt currency and the circulation of commodities among the Baruya of New Guinea', in G. Dalton (ed.) *Studies in Economic Anthropology*, Anthropological Studies no. 7, Washington DC: American Anthropological Association.

—— (1980) 'Work and its representation: a research proposal', *History Workshop* 10: 164–74.

Gordon, D., Edwards, R. and Reich, M. (1982) *Segmented Work, Divided Workers, The Historical Transformation of Labor in the United States*, Cambridge: Cambridge University Press.

Guyer, J. (1984) 'Naturalism in models of African production', *Man* (N.S.) 19: 371–88.

—— (1988) 'The multiplication of labour: historical methods in the study of gender and agricultural change in modern Africa', *Current Anthropology* 29: 247–72.

Johnson, A. (1975) 'Time allocation in a Machiguenga community', *Ethnology* 14: 301–10.

Martin, P. L. (1988) *Harvest of Confusion, Migrant Workers in U.S. Agriculture*, Boulder, Colo.: Westview Press.

Marx, K. (1965 [1906]) *Capital, A Critique of Political Economy*, ed. F. Engels, New York: Random House.

Mauss, M. (1967 [1925]) *The Gift, Forms and Functions of Exchange in Archaic Societies*, New York: W. W. Norton.

McClelland, K. (1987) 'Time to work and time to live: some aspects of work and the re-formation of class in Britain, 1850–1880', in P. Joyce (ed.) *The Historical Meanings of Work*, Cambridge: Cambridge University Press.

Morishima, M. (1973) *Marx's Economics: a Dual Theory of Value and Growth*, Cambridge: Cambridge University Press.

Newby, H. (1977) *The Deferential Worker*, Harmondsworth: Penguin.

Ortiz, S. (1979) 'The estimation of work: labour and value amongst Paez farmers', in S. Wallman (ed.) *Social Anthropology of Work*, London: Academic Press.

Ricardo, D. (1911) *The Principles of Political Economy and Taxation*, Dutton, NY: Everyman's Library.

Richards, A. (1939) *Land, Labour and Diet in Northern Rhodesia*, Oxford: Oxford University Press.

Robertson, A. F. (1987) *The Dynamics of Productive Relationships: African Share Contracts in Comparative Perspective*, Cambridge: Cambridge University Press.

Rule, J. (1987) 'The property of skill in the period of manufacture', in P. Joyce (ed.) *The Historical Meanings of Work*, Cambridge: Cambridge University Press.

Salisbury, R. (1962) *From Stone to Steel; Economic Consequences of Technological Change in New Guinea*, Cambridge: Cambridge University Press.

Simmel, G. (1971) *On Individuality and Social Forms: Selected Writings*, ed. D. N. Levine, Chicago: University of Chicago Press.

Smith, A. (1982 [1776]) *The Wealth of Nations*, Harmondsworth: Penguin.

Thomas, R. J. (1985) *Citizenship, Gender and Work: Social Organization of Industrial Agriculture*, Berkeley: University of California Press.

Thompson, E. P. (1967) 'Time, work discipline, and industrial capitalism', *Past and Present* 38: 56–97.

Whipp, R. (1987) '"A time to every purpose": an essay on time and work', in P. Joyce (ed.) *The Historical Meanings of Work*, Cambridge: Cambridge University Press.

FURTHER READING

Bossen, L. (1984) *The Redivision of Labour: Women and Economic Choice in Four Guatemalan Communities*, Albany: State University of New York Press.

Braverman, H. (1974) *Labour and Monopoly Capital: The Degradation of Work in the Twentieth Century*, New York: Monthly Review Press.

Burawoy, M. (1979) *Manufacturing Consent: Changes in the Labour Process Under Monopoly Capitalism*, Chicago: University of Chicago Press.

Burton, M. L. and White, D. (1984) 'Sexual division of labor in agriculture', *American Anthropologist* 86: 568–83.

Gill, L. (1990) 'Painted faces: conflict and ambiguity in domestic servant–employer relations in La Paz, 1930–1988', *Latin American Research Review* 25: 119–36.

Guyer, J. (1984) 'Naturalism in models of African production', *Man* (N.S.) 19: 371–88.

Joyce, P. (ed.) (1987) *The Historical Meanings of Work*, Cambridge: Cambridge University Press.

Kahn, J. S. (1981) 'Mercantilism and the emergence of servile labour in colonial Indonesia', in J. S. Kahn and R. Llobera (eds) *The Anthropology of Pre-Capitalist Societies*, London: Macmillan.

Newby, H. (1977) *The Deferential Worker*, Harmondsworth: Penguin.

Ortiz, S. (1992) 'Market, power and culture as agencies in the transformation of labor contracts in agriculture', in S. Ortiz and S. Lees (eds) *Economy as Process*, Lanham, Md.: University Press of America.

Pahl, R. E. (1984) *Divisions of Labour*, Oxford: Blackwell.

Richards, A. (1939) *Land, Labour and Diet in Northern Rhodesia*, London: Oxford University Press.

Robertson, A. F. (1987) *The Dynamics of Productive Relations, African Share Contracts in Comparative Perspective*, Cambridge: Cambridge University Press.

Rueschemeyer, D. (1986) *Power and the Divisions of Labour*, Stanford, Calif.: Standford University Press.

Scott, J. W. and Tilly, L. A. (1975) 'Women's work and the family in nineteenth century Europe', *Comparative Studies in Society and History* 17: 36–64.

Thomas, R. J. (1985) *Citizenship, Gender and Work: Social Organization of Industrial Agriculture*, Berkeley: University of California Press.

Wallman, S. (1979) *Social Anthropology of Work*, London: Academic Press.

33

EXCHANGE AND RECIPROCITY

C. A. Gregory

The concepts of 'exchange' and 'reciprocity' are closely related. This much is clear from the *Oxford English Dictionary*, which defines exchange as 'the action, or act of, reciprocal giving and receiving', and reciprocity as 'mutual action, influence, giving and taking'. Indeed the words are often used as synonyms. However, in the anthropological literature over the past century the term 'reciprocity' has acquired a special meaning, and a distinction between exchange and reciprocity of great theoretical importance has arisen. The distinction turns on fine differences in meaning between the words 'mutuality', 'giving', 'receiving' and 'taking', and to understand these nuances it is necessary to situate the anthropological theory of exchange in the broader historical and theoretical context from which it has emerged.

The general theory of exchange is concerned with analysing acts of exchanging things, people, blows, words, etc. Exchange is a 'total social phenomenon', to use Mauss's (1990 [1925]: 3) famous expression, and, as such, its study involves the fields not only of economics but also of law, linguistics, kinship and politics, among others. Most anthropological theorizing about exchange, however, has been restricted to exchanges of wealth. But what is 'wealth'? The answers to this question fall into three broad categories. For economists of the nineteenth century wealth consisted in *commodities*, whereas for those of the twentieth, it consists in *goods*. Either way, it is stuff which is valued by the market. For anthropologists, on the other hand, wealth consists above all in *gifts*, products that are valued according to the non-market principle of reciprocity. The notion of reciprocity, then, is at the heart of theoretical debates concerning the distinction between market and non-market forms of valuation. But ethnographers have also found the principle of reciprocity operating in tribal trading systems and peasant markets, and these findings have led to a revision of the theory of commodity exchange itself.

To understand the anthropological concept of reciprocity, it is necessary to compare and contrast economic and anthropological theories of the exchange of wealth. I propose to do this under the following five headings. Under the first, 'Commodities as wealth', I briefly discuss the nineteenth-century political economy approach to exchange. This is followed, under the heading, 'Goods as wealth', by a discussion of twentieth-century economic theories of exchange. In the third section, 'Gifts as wealth', I provide an overview of the anthropological notion of reciprocity. This is followed by a discussion of 'Barter and other forms of counter-trade', in which I introduce some anthropological revisions to the theory of the commodity. In the final section, on 'Market-place trade', I show how anthropological work also requires certain revisions to the theory of market exchange.

COMMODITIES AS WEALTH

'The wealth of those societies in which the capitalist mode of production prevails', Marx (1954 [1867]: 43) declares in the first sentence of *Capital*, 'presents itself as an immense accumulation of commodities.' This notion of wealth was part of the conventional orthodoxy of eighteenth- and early nineteenth-century European thought, and all the leading theorists of the time – Quesnay, Smith, Ricardo – developed their particular conceptions of the principles regulating the market within this general paradigm. The truly radical break came in the 1870s with the development of the theory of *goods* and, with it, a new set of answers to the fundamental questions of market exchange: What is profit? What determines relative prices? What determines the level of wages? In this section I present, in very general terms, the answers developed within the commodity-theory paradigm; in the next section these will be set in contrast to the answers given by the goods-theory paradigm.

The notion of a commodity has its origins in the Aristotelian idea that a product has two distinct values: a value in use and a value in exchange. Shoes, for example, are useful because they protect one's feet when walking over rough ground. This value is called 'use-value' and is quite distinct from the value shown on the price-tag of a pair of shoes displayed in a shop window. The price-tag value is called 'exchange-value', and it was value in this sense that pre-twentieth-century commodity theorists sought to explain; the study of the useful properties of objects, and that of the manner in which they satisfy human wants, were regarded as falling outside the scope of political economy (Marx 1954 [1867]: 43). Within the overall commodity-theory paradigm many different theories of exchange-value were formulated. Quesnay, the eighteenth-century French physiocrat, found the answer in the natural productivity of land; Adam Smith, the so-called father of economics, opposed this theory and developed a labour theory of value in its place; this theory was developed, in turn, by Ricardo and Marx, among others.

Marx's contribution to the theory of the commodity, though it hinged upon the labour theory of value, gave it a new twist. Marx (1954 [1867]: 53) claimed that he was the first to point out that labour, too, possesses a use-value and an exchange-value. To make shoes, for example, requires a certain quality of effort, a particular kind of skilled technical practice. The use-value of the shoemaker's labour lies in these qualitative aspects of his performance. As such, it differs from the use-value of the labour of the farmer in growing wheat. If, however, we 'abstract out' the particular, technical *qualities* of the shoemaker's and the farmer's labour, reducing both to their lowest common denominator, then they may both be regarded as representing certain *quantities* of labour, which may be measured and compared in terms of identical units of (chronological) time. As a commodity measured in these terms, and exchangeable for other things, labour has exchange-value. Now suppose that the shoemaker exchanges one pair of shoes for, say, ten kilograms of wheat. In quality and hence in their respective use-values, shoes and wheat are quite different. How come, then, that they are equated in exchange? Marx's answer was that they are equated because an identical amount of 'abstract human labour' was expended in the production, respectively, of the pair of shoes and the ten kilos of wheat. Or more generally, the equation in exchange of heterogeneous commodities comes about by virtue of the equality in the amounts of homogeneous, abstract labour which they embody.

Marx distinguished between a number of different historical forms of the commodity. Following Aristotle, he speculated that commodities emerged on the boundaries of tribal communities where people would enter into transactions with strangers and exchange products for which they had no use in return for those which they desired. Following its birth in these marginal regions the commodity form, Marx argued, began to grow like a cell, developing ever more complex manifestations as it divided and multiplied. Initially, on the boundaries of the community, exchange took the form of the barter of one commodity (C) directly for another ($C-C$). With the development of peasant markets, and the need for a generalized medium of exchange – namely money (M) – to facilitate trade, barter gave way to selling ($C-M$) in order to buy ($M-C$), and the tribal community disappeared under the corrosive influence of the new commodity form. The subsequent development of mercantile capitalism – buying ($M-C$) in order to sell at a profit ($C-M'$) – and of moneylending at interest ($M-M'$), further eroded the agrarian pre-capitalist society. Following a series of bloody struggles involving the emerging capitalist class and the pre-capitalist peasants and landlords, a new class of propertyless wage-labourers was born and the commodity assumed its most generalized form, $C=c+v+s$, where c is constant capital, v variable capital, and s surplus value, these values corresponding to the quantities of abstract labour embodied in raw materials, wages and profit respectively.

The historical prerequisite for the emergence of capitalism, and of the $C=c+v+s$ form of the commodity, was, according to Marx, the emergence of a proletariat. With this, labour-power became a commodity with an exchange-value like any other. But this historical development gave rise to a new problem: What determines the exchange-value of labour-power?

Marx's answer is long and involved but is based on a simple idea. He observed that under feudalism the rate of exploitation, i.e. the ratio of surplus labour to necessary labour, is expressed in a simple and direct form. Suppose, for example, that a serf farms three days per week for his own benefit and that he gives his landlord three days of labour per week as rent for the land he uses. The former is called 'necessary labour' and the latter 'surplus labour'. This relation, Marx argues, did not disappear with the development of capitalism; it merely changed its form as rent was transformed, firstly, into a share of the physical output (e.g. half the harvest) and then into money (e.g. half the money profits or a fixed rent per acre of land used). With the emergence of labour-power as a commodity, necessary labour assumed the abstract form of variable capital (v), corresponding to the amount of money paid as wages, while the profit over and above this amount – corresponding to the product of surplus labour – was shared between the capitalist and the landlord.

Marx's immediate concern was to analyse the principles governing the production, consumption, distribution and exchange of this most generalized form of the commodity; pre-capitalist forms of commodity exchange were of interest to him only to the extent that they illuminated the social preconditions of the capitalist form. In any case, his understanding of the pre-capitalist and non-commodity forms of exchange was severely constrained by the absence, at the time, of reliable ethnographic and historical data.

Apart from the distinction between use-value and exchange-value, two other defining characteristics of the commodity-theory paradigm deserve mention. One of these concerns the prominence given to the notion of reproduction. Exchange was not seen as an isolated act but as a phase in a reproductive cycle consisting of successive acts of production, exchange and distribution. This conception of the economy was first developed in 1759 by Quesnay, in his *Tableau Économique* (1962 [1759]), and it has provided the conceptual framework for all discussions of commodity-value theory ever since. The notion has been refined over the years, the most recent and logically sophisticated being the version found in Sraffa's (1960) *Production of Commodities by Means of Commodities*. As the title of this book suggests, a commodity is both an output and an input, and Sraffa argues that these input–output ratios, combined with a given distribution of income, determine the exchange-values of commodities.

The other defining characteristic of the commodity-theory paradigm is the focus on class relations. Even though some of the early commodity theorists espoused naturalistic theories of wealth, they all addressed the problem of the principles governing the distribution of surplus among competing classes. Quesnay's theory, for example, distinguished three classes – the landlords, the peasant farmers and the artisans – a division that captured the essence of the social organization of the eighteenth-century French countryside; Ricardo based his theory of value on the opposition between landlords and capitalists, a key social conflict in the England of his time; and Marx, as is well known, based his theory on the opposition between wage-labour and capital. These class relations of production were seen to be crucial because they gave exchange relations their particular form and content. In other words, the classical political economists conceptualized exchange as an expression of underlying power relations.

GOODS AS WEALTH

Following the marginalist revolution of the 1870s, which saw the fall of the theory of commodities and the rise to dominance of the theory of goods, exchange came to be seen as an expression of the subjective preferences of individuals rather than of underlying power relations. This change in thinking was reflected in a new concept of wealth. The marginalists, or 'neoclassicals', as they are sometimes called, no longer saw the unit of wealth as a commodity but as a good whose magnitude was measured by its subjectively attributed 'utility'. In other words, the concept of a commodity, with its distinction between use-value and exchange-value, was replaced by the concept of a good with an undifferentiated utility value.

This new concept of wealth quite literally affected the way people viewed the world. Emphasis was placed on consumption and scarcity rather than on reproduction, and on choice and subjective preferences rather than on objective class relations of production. The new paradigm also provided a novel conceptual framework for posing, and answering, the old questions concerning wages, prices and profit. This can be seen by examining, in a little more detail, the notion of a good.

Despite appearances to the contrary, the word 'utility' does not mean the same as use-value. Use-values refer to the objective properties of things and are a function of the technological and scientific knowledge available to a society at a given point in its history. For example, the discovery of photography in the nineteenth century meant that silver acquired a new use-value to complement its other uses as a store of value, as jewellery, as cutlery, and so on. Utility, on the other hand, refers back to the subjective preferences of an individual consumer. A cup of tea, for example, has positive utility to a thirsty person, but that utility will be less for each additional cup consumed. Thus the marginal utility of the tea declines, until the point is reached when the consumer's thirst is quenched and she desires no more; at this point the tea ceases to be a 'good' and, logically speaking, becomes a 'bad' – although this term is rarely used.

The utility of a good, then, derives from its ability to yield subjective satisfaction. It refers to individual psychological feelings about scarce objects and not to the objective properties of different things. As Robbins (1932: 47) has

915

noted, 'Wealth is not wealth because of its substantial qualities. It is wealth because it is scarce.' This conception of wealth is obviously very different from its classical precursor. Among other things it contains the paradoxical implication that wealth, because it is the subjective sum of enjoyments, might increase as material abundance declines (Heilbroner 1987: 882).

This new theory of wealth opened up a new angle on ancient problems. Consider the water–diamond paradox which was concerned with the following question: Why does water have a high use-value and negligible exchange-value while diamonds have a high exchange-value and negligible use-value? The classical economists regarded this problem as peripheral and answered it in terms of a highly technical theory of rent. The neoclassical theorists, on the other hand, regarded it as central and made it the basis for an alternative theory of price. Their answer, in a word, was *scarcity*. The marginal utility of water is low because of its great abundance, the marginal utility of diamonds is high because of their scarcity, and the ratio of the marginal utility of water to that of diamonds determines their relative prices.

This proposition applies to the prices of all goods, according to an argument that runs as follows. Suppose water became scarce because of a drought. In this case its marginal utility would rise relative to the marginal utility of diamonds and a price for water would emerge; if the drought was particularly severe the price of water would rise even further and it may even become more valuable than diamonds. Thus all exchanges, and hence prices, are expressions of relative scarcity as manifested in the ratios of marginal utility.

The great appeal of this theory of exchange and price lies in its generality. Indeed, it is difficult to imagine a form of exchange to which it cannot be applied. Take, for example, the well-known exchange of *kula* valuables – armbands and necklaces of polished shell – that are traded by the people of the Trobriand Islands off the eastern tip of Papua New Guinea (described by Malinowski 1922). Traders obviously prefer the scarce, high-ranking shells to the relatively abundant, low-ranking shells. Thus it is possible to conceptualize *kula* exchange in terms of marginal utilities. Furthermore, it could be argued that the paradoxical conception of wealth contained in the theory of goods is just what is needed to explain the notorious destruction of wealth that occurs in the potlatch ceremonies of the Kwakiutl and other indigenous peoples of the Northwest Coast of North America (Codere 1950). In the face of a superabundance of material goods, their worth is effectively eroded.

It is not without some justification, then, that Jevons, one of the founding fathers of marginalism, could claim in 1871 that the science of economics is in some degree peculiar, owing to the fact 'that its ultimate laws are known to us immediately by intuition', and that from the notion of utility it is possible to reason deductively to theories of value and exchange (Jevons 1970 [1871]: 18). The leading figures in the theory-of-goods paradigm today – Nobel prizewinners such as Samuelson (1947), Debreu (1959) and Friedman (1962)

916

– have all developed highly complicated theories of value by reasoning deductively in this way.

Like the theory of commodities, the theory of goods has many internal divisions. However, these are mere dialectal variations of the one language. The language of the theory of goods shares a common grammar and lexicon which have nothing in common with those of the language of the theory of commodities. The terms 'good' and 'commodity' epitomize this difference, the etymology of the former suggesting a subjective approach to value, the latter an objective approach.

The new language in which economists began to talk around the 1870s can be likened to Esperanto, and the old language of the commodity theorists to, say, German. This is not to say that one is better than another. Indeed, there is no meta-theory by which they can be compared and evaluated. The two paradigms have different consequences for understanding human life which can only be evaluated in specific contexts. This implies some notion of adequacy in relation to practical aims. To pursue the language analogy, do we try to overcome the communication problems of the world by teaching people Esperanto or do we try to learn some particular languages in order to develop our general ideas from a comparative analysis of them? Needless to say, anthropologists have tended to find the latter path more attractive, and few have embraced the Esperanto of the theory of goods.

In this sense, then, anthropologists took up the implicit questions left unanswered by the commodity theorists: What, in positive terms, does non-commodity exchange mean, and by what principles is it governed? What principles govern the circulation of commodities on the periphery of tribal communities? Is commodity exchange the end of an evolutionary sequence? Does it have a corrosive influence on other forms of exchange? And are these the right questions to be asking anyway?

The fieldwork tradition pioneered by Malinowski, Boas and others has provided us with the means to answer these questions. It is ironic that at the very time that these means were becoming available – in the era of European capitalist imperialism (1870–1914) – economists ceased to be interested in the concrete problems posed by the theory of commodities and turned instead to the abstract and formal problems posed by the new paradigm of goods. Many of the theories formulated within the latter paradigm contained ill-considered assumptions about the workings of tribal economies, and these provided ethnographers such as Malinowski (1922) with easy targets to criticize in the course of developing their own ideas. But fieldwork anthropologists, for the most part, remained ignorant of the classical tradition of economic thought and of the challenging questions that lay waiting to be answered. (It was not until the 1970s, when neo-Marxist anthropology flourished, that anthropologists took the theory of commodities seriously.) But it is now possible, with the benefit of hindsight, to see that anthropologists have provided implicit answers to the questions posed by the commodity theorists and, in the process, have laid the foundations for a whole new approach to the theory of exchange of wealth by posing many new questions.

GIFTS AS WEALTH

Though the terms 'wealth' and 'valuables' are often used in anthropological literature in the common dictionary sense of 'riches' and 'abundance', they also take a more precise and anthropologically specific meaning. The word 'gift' captures this meaning in a very general way and, like the words 'commodity' and 'goods', it signifies a distinct paradigm (see Belshaw 1965, Sahlins 1972, Gregory 1982, Strathern 1988 and Weiner 1992 for analytical overviews of the literature).

The notion of gifts as wealth has assumed a variety of concrete forms, most of which are now very familiar: the celebrated coppers and blankets of the Kwakiutl, the armshells and necklaces of the Trobriand Islanders, the brass rods and cowrie shells of the Tiv of Nigeria, the pigs and pearlshells of the peoples of the Papua New Guinea Highlands, and so on. Many of these objects are nowadays valuable in conventional money terms. In the Trobriand Islands, for example, a vigorous trade in real and counterfeit (plastic) necklaces goes on outside the tourist centres. However, the most highly prized shells are quite literally priceless, and have remained in circulation in the *kula* ring throughout the colonial period despite the attempts of outsiders to buy them (Campbell 1983). The reasons for this are complex, but it would seem that they have as much to do with the intricacies of local-level politics as with subjective preferences. What is clear, though, is that these objects, when exchanged as gifts, are valued by transactors according to a standard that has quality rather than quantity as its basis.

Consider Campbell's (1983) discussion of the ranking criteria used for Trobriand armshells (*mwari*). Five named categories are distinguished and these are ordered according to their personal history, personal name, colour, and size. Shells of the top category, *mwarikau*, have personal names and histories; they have red striations and are the largest of all. Shells of the lowest category, *gibwagibwa*, have neither names nor personal histories; they are white, unpolished and small in size. Necklaces (*vaiguwa*) are ranked in a similar way. The ranking system, then, is ordinal rather than cardinal.

Ordinal ranking systems are ethnographically widespread and their character is commonly captured in anthropological literature by the expression 'spheres of exchange'. Bohannan (1959), for example, uses this expression to describe the ranking system of the Nigerian Tiv. Among the Tiv objects are classified as belonging to one of three spheres. The first, and lowest sphere, is what the Tiv call *yiagh*. This includes locally produced foodstuffs, some tools, and raw materials which are traded at the markets. The second sphere comprises items of a kind that carry prestige (*shagba*) and whose transaction is independent of the markets. Slaves, cattle, horses, white (*tugudu*) cloth, and brass rods circulate within this sphere. The third sphere, considered 'supreme', contains a single item: rights in human beings, especially women and children.

The theoretical significance of this distinction between quality and quantity has, by and large, escaped the notice of twentieth-century economists. J. M. Keynes (1982) was the prominent exception. Unlike many of his contemporaries, he had an interest in comparative economy and, during the 1920s, studied the monetary system of the ancient Greeks. In a remarkable essay, not published until 1982, he noted that cows, corn, iron and bronze, which were the principal materials of exchange, had 'a conventional *order* of value and even a conventional *relation* of value for customary purposes' (1982: 256, original emphasis). He argued that 'three types of monetary or quasi-monetary practice' coexisted: (1) a cow–sheep standard for purposes of ostentation, religion, reward and punishment; (2) a corn standard for agricultural rents, wages and loans; and (3) an iron or bronze standard for market purposes.

It is not surprising that Keynes and Bohannan independently developed the notion of spheres of exchange, since the ethnographic and historical evidence repeatedly posed a question for which this theory was the answer. This question took many forms, one of which was to explicate the puzzling notion of 'equivalence' which Malinowski (1922: 355), among others, used to describe the relationship between objects of gift exchange. This notion is broadly similar to, but nevertheless subtly different from, the notion of 'equality' which holds in a price relation. For example if a loaf of bread costs two dollars, then this relation can be expressed as an equation of the type $2 = 1$ loaf of bread. But if a *kula bagiriku* necklace is held to be equivalent to a *mwarikau* armshell, then this relation cannot be put in the form of an equation because to do so would be to reduce a qualitative relation to one of quantity.

An analogy with playing cards helps to clarify this point. The four aces constitute an equivalent set superior in rank to the set of four kings; the set of kings, in turn, constitutes an equivalent set superior in rank to the four queens, and so on. This relation can be expressed using the 'greater than' sign ($>$) as follows: aces $>$ kings $>$ queens $>$ jacks $>$ tens $>$ nines $>$ etc. These relationships are ordinal and cannot be expressed in equations of the type '1 ten $= 2$ fives'. Within equivalent sets ordinal relations also hold. An ace of hearts, for example, is of a higher rank than an ace of clubs. Objects of gift exchange are similarly ranked, though the analogy should not be pushed too far. The ranking of gifts is a serious matter of politics rather than a mere game, and the ordering is often disputed, especially at the lower end of the scale.

The existence of these qualitative standards poses new questions concerning the principles governing the exchange and distribution of wealth items. It was the great achievement of Mauss, in his classic essay on *The Gift*, first published in 1925, to pose these questions in a precise way. What, he asked, is the basis of the obligations to give, to receive, and to return gifts? His answer – implied in one of the ways he phrased the question: 'What power resides in the object given that causes its recipient to pay it back?' (1990 [1925]: 3) – can be criticized for its implicit objectification of power relations, by which a property of the relations between persons is made to appear as though residing in things. Nevertheless, his comparative analysis of the ethnographic evidence, which demonstrated the widespread importance of inalienable bonds between persons and things, was an extremely valuable contribution to the theory of exchange. Among other things, it replaced the vacuity of Marx's theory of the 'non-commodity' with a *positive* theory of the gift. Mauss makes no reference to Marx in his essay, but his ghost haunts its every page as a kind of invisible antithesis. Mauss's method was, like Marx's, dialectical, evolutionary, comparative and political. Dialectics enabled Mauss to see that even though gifts appear voluntary they are, in reality, repaid under obligation; his evolutionary approach led him to suggest the primacy of gift exchange over barter; and his comparative method enabled him to see the significance of the distinctions between stranger and relative and between the alienable and the inalienable in terms that were the mirror-image of those employed by Marx.

Mauss's essay on the gift is also very much a political tract. Indeed, it could be argued that the essay is primarily about early-twentieth-century France. In the last chapter he discusses the implications of his survey of 'archaic' economies for the France of his day. Mauss, it must be remembered, was a socialist but not a communist revolutionary, and his conclusion offers a gift theory of capitalism to counter Marx's surplus-value theory. He likens the wage-labour contract to a gift exchange, notes that the worker is giving his time and life, and that he wishes to be rewarded for this gift (1990 [1925]: 77). He favours a form of welfare capitalism because, as he put it (1990 [1925]: 69), 'Overgenerosity, or communism, would be as harmful to himself [the worker] and to society as the egoism of our contemporaries and the individualism of our laws.'

Mauss's theory of the gift owed much to the ethnographic work of Malinowski and a limited number of other scholars. Since Malinowski's time the number of high-quality ethnographic reports on exchange has been increasing apace. These detailed first-hand accounts have been synthesized and generalized by, among others, Polanyi (1944), Lévi-Strauss (1969 [1949]) and Sahlins (1972). The significant logical and conceptual developments which anthropologists have made to the theory of exchange can be identified by comparing the approaches of these three authors.

Polanyi, an economic historian, first became interested in the theory of gift exchange in order to understand the 'extraordinary assumptions' underlying the market economy of Europe, the principal subject of his magnum opus, *The Great Transformation* (1944). For him the market economy was a system of self-regulating markets in which the prices of commodities organized the whole of economic life. The basis of this system was seen to lie in the profit motive and in the existence of commodities in the form of land, labour and money. The non-market economy, he noted, is the very opposite of this: the

Principle of economic behaviour	Form of social organization	Institutional pattern
Reciprocity	Kinship	Symmetry
Redistribution	Polity	Centricity
Householding	Household	Autarky

Table 1 Relations between principles of economic behaviour, forms of social organization and institutional arrangements, according to Polanyi (1944).

motive of gain is absent, there is no wage-labour, and no distinctively economic institutions. How then, he asked, is production, exchange and distribution organized? His argument rests on the identification of three principles of economic behaviour – 'reciprocity', 'redistribution', and 'householding' – which are 'a mere function of social organization' (1944: 49) and which, in turn, are associated with distinct institutional patterns. Polanyi's argument is summarized in Table 1.

Reciprocity has family and kinship as its basis. The reciprocal obligations that parents and children, brothers and sisters, and husbands and wives have towards each other 'help safeguard production and family sustenance' (1944: 48). Exchange between groups of kin is facilitated by the symmetry inherent in the principle of duality upon which many tribal societies are based. The subdivision of a tribe into moieties, the pairing of villages in different ecological niches, alliances of individuals from different communities, and other expressions of the duality principle lend themselves to the creation of exchange partnerships which personalize the relation of reciprocity and make long-term exchanges possible.

Redistribution refers to the process by which a substantial part of the annual produce of a society is delivered to a central figure of authority, who keeps it in storage for subsequent disposal on special occasions such as annual feasts, the ceremonial visit of neighbouring tribes, and so on. The social basis of this form of exchange is a political organization headed by village elders, a chief, king or despot. It was practised, says Polanyi, in ancient China, the empire of the Incas, the kingdoms of India, by Hammurabi of Babylonia, in the feudal society of Europe and in the stratified societies of Africa and the Pacific.

The third principle, householding or production-for-use, is based on the closed, self-sufficient and territorial household group. The internal organization and size of the group is a matter of indifference – Polanyi lists the European peasant farming household and the Carolingian magnates as examples – because the principle is always the same, namely, 'that of producing and storing for the satisfaction of the wants of the members of the group' (1944: 53).

For Polanyi, then, the comparative economic history of humanity is characterized by a great divide: on one side is the self-regulating market; on the other, economies based on the principles of reciprocity, redistribution and householding (or some combination of these three principles). This is just another way of saying that the capitalist economy that emerged at the end of the eighteenth century ushered in a radically new form of economic organization, which was unique in world history.

This is a bold generalization, but it is still a great advance on the mistaken idea that there was no divide at all – that all economies were commodity economies. This fallacy, which lay at the base of the writings of Adam Smith, was uncritically accepted by many twentieth-century economists, and Polanyi – like Malinowski – was concerned to challenge it. Like Marx, Polanyi started with Aristotle's distinction between householding and money-making – 'probably the most prophetic pointer ever made in the realm of the social sciences' (1944: 53) – but was able to develop the distinction much further. Marx, we have seen, developed the category of production-for-exchange by calling it 'commodity exchange' and distinguishing between its various forms: barter $(C–C)$; selling-in-order-to-buy in peasant markets $(C–M–C)$; buying-in-order-to-sell for mercantile profit $(M–C–M')$, usurious money lending $(M–M')$, and industrial capitalism $(M–C–M')$ where labour-power is the principal commodity. Polanyi's 'great divide' is not between the presence and absence of commodities but between industrial capitalist exchange and all other forms. Thus Polanyi was not claiming, any more than was Marx, that commodity exchange did not exist prior to the emergence of capitalism. His claim was rather that prior to capitalism, commodity exchange was subordinate to the principles of reciprocity and redistribution; in other words that it was socially embedded and hence regulated rather than self-regulating.

Perhaps the most enduring legacy of Polanyi's work was the equation of 'reciprocity' with 'gift exchange'. However, this usage is something of a coded shorthand because the adjective 'positive' is elided. Thus it is *positive* reciprocity which is being equated with gift exchange. The logical corollary of this formulation was that *negative* reciprocity came to be synonymous with commodity exchange. This much is clear from Sahlins's well-known essay 'On the sociology of primitive exchange' (first published in 1965 and reprinted in Sahlins 1972: ch. 5), which revises Polanyi's arguments in the light of new ethnographic data.

Sahlins does not use the term 'positive reciprocity', but it is implicit in his notion of a kind of reciprocity that he called 'generalized' (as opposed to 'negative'). Generalized reciprocity and negative reciprocity are defined, respectively, as the 'solidary' and 'unsociable' extremes in a spectrum of reciprocities. Negative reciprocity is 'the attempt to get something for nothing with impunity' (Sahlins 1972: 195): haggling, barter, gambling, chicanery, theft, and other varieties of seizure are examples. Generalized reciprocity 'refers to transactions that are putatively altruistic, transactions on the line of assistance given and, if possible and necessary, assistance returned' (1972: 194): examples include food-sharing, the suckling of children, help and generosity.

	Remittance			*Admittance*
Positive reciprocity	Giving	← Converse →	Receiving
	↑	←	↑
	Contrary	Contradictory	Contrary
	↓		↓
Negative reciprocity	Losing	← Converse →	Taking

Table 2

The distinction between positive (generalized) and negative reciprocity that Sahlins proposes here is really an application of Aristotelian logic to the oppositions giving–receiving and losing–taking. Giving, for example, is the converse of receiving and the contradictory of taking; losing, the contrary of giving, is the converse of taking and the contradictory of receiving. This logic defines two modes of mutuality between the transactors, positive reciprocity (giving–receiving) and negative reciprocity (losing–taking), and two positions in relation to the transmission of objects, remittance (giving–losing) and admittance (receiving–taking). These logical relations are summarized in Table 2.

This table clarifies, at least in a formal sense, the distinction between reciprocity and exchange. Exchange is the transmission of wealth from one transactor to another, whereas reciprocity refers to the specific *quality* of the relationship between the transactors. This relationship is characterized by mutual friendship at one extreme (positive reciprocity) or mutual hostility at the other (negative reciprocity). Thus specification of the qualitative form of reciprocity enables particular forms of exchange to be distinguished from exchange in general. Where wealth is defined as either commodities or gifts this specification of the quality of the relationship necessarily involves a concrete investigation into the spatio-temporal forms of social and political organization of the economy in question. This much is common to the approaches of Smith, Ricardo, Marx, Mauss and Polanyi, notwithstanding the great differences between them.

Sahlins places positive and negative reciprocity at two ends of a continuum whose mid-point specifies a third type which he calls 'balanced' reciprocity. This form of reciprocity is 'less personal' than generalized reciprocity and 'more economic' (in the Western sense of the term). It expresses the need to transcend hostility in favour of mutuality, to strike a balance in a relationship. Examples include formal friendship or kinship involving compacts of solidarity and pledges of brotherhood, and the affirmation of corporate alliances in the form of feasts, peace-making ceremonies and marital exchanges.

Sahlins summarizes his argument in terms of a diagram (Figure 1) in which kinship distance is correlated with reciprocity. Kinship distance, he argues, is defined by the intersection of consanguinity and territoriality. This defines a

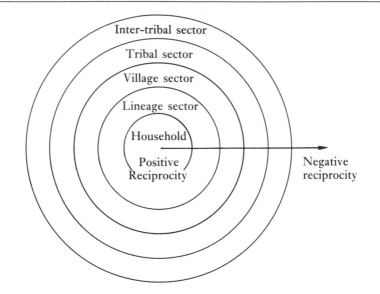

Figure 1 Reciprocity and kinship residential sectors. (After Sahlins 1972: 199)

set of ever-widening spheres of co-membership – household, lineage, village, etc. – such that as one moves out through these spheres positive reciprocity is gradually counteracted by a negative charge. Each sector is, therefore, characterized by the dominance of a certain type of exchange, with the purest form of gift exchange occurring in the closest sphere and the purest form of commodity exchange in the most distant – i.e. in the inter-tribal sector.

This model of exchange has been modified and developed by Ingold (1986), who has noted that the negativity of reciprocity is independent of kinship distance. Ethnographic reports on contemporary hunter–gatherer economies show that negative reciprocity, in the form of 'demand sharing' (Peterson, in press), exists at the very core of the system; it also exists on the outermost periphery in the form of theft and burglary. Likewise, positive reciprocity exists not only at the core, as sharing in which the donor takes the initiative, but also on the periphery, in the form of haggling and barter. Thus, as kinship distance increases it is not that positive reciprocity gradually becomes negative but rather that one form of positive (or negative) reciprocity is transformed into another form of positive (or negative) reciprocity. Figure 2 illustrates Ingold's argument; intermediate cases have been omitted for ease of exposition.

Sahlins's neat model – and Ingold's variation – is of course complicated by the presence of 'other factors'. The most important of these is political rank, which can be thought of as a vertical axis that intersects, and interacts with, the horizontal axis of kinship distance. This vertical axis is associated with

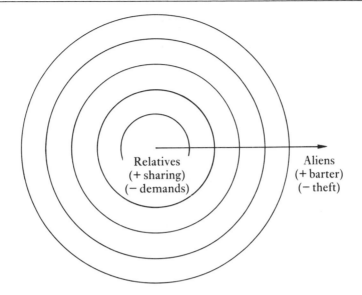

Figure 2 Modified model of reciprocity and residential sectors. (After Ingold 1986: 232)

what Sahlins calls a system of reciprocities. Under this system products are pooled in a many-to-one and a one-to-many pattern of exchange.

Sahlins's conceptual framework, which has Mauss's theory as its basis (Sahlins 1972: ch. 4), provides an answer to Mauss's question about the obligation to return gifts. As Figure 1 illustrates, this answer is given in terms of the social organization of kinship and rank typical of tribal societies. Like Polanyi, Sahlins was more concerned to examine the implications of this proposition than to investigate its philosophical basis. Furthermore, there is a sense in which he considered such a task to lie beyond the scope of his analysis, for it had already been undertaken by Lévi-Strauss in his great work, *The Elementary Structures of Kinship* (1969 [1949]).

One of the innovations of Lévi-Strauss's book was to conceptualize marriage as the *gift* exchange of sisters (daughters) by brothers (fathers). This notion, as Sahlins (1972: 181) observed, provoked a reaction from British and American anthropologists who 'recoiled at once from the idea, refusing for their part to "treat women as *commodities*"' (emphasis added). Such a reaction, as Sahlins correctly noted, betrayed a misunderstanding of the comparative theory of exchange and an inability to distinguish gifts from commodities.

Lévi-Strauss's conceptualization of marriage as gift exchange enabled him to develop a definition of reciprocity of great generality and rigour; this, in turn, enabled him to synthesize a vast amount of data from Oceania and Asia and to find patterns of exchange where others had found none. His primary distinction is between elementary and complex structures of kinship; the former, the focus of his analytical attention, are further subdivided into structures of *restricted* and *generalized* exchange.

Restricted exchange, his theoretical starting point, takes the following general dyadic form:

$$A \longleftrightarrow B$$

Lévi-Strauss shows that alliance relations based on the bilateral marriage rule, that a man should marry a woman in the combined kinship category of mother's brother's daughter and father's sister's daughter, take this form. The notion of 'sister exchange', which is often used to describe this form of reciprocity, precisely captures the essence of restricted exchange. The perspective is, of course, from the male point of view (compare Strathern 1988 and Weiner 1992), but this is as much the indigenous male's point of view as it is the ethnographer's. In other words, Lévi-Strauss's perspective on exchange is that of the powerful men who do the exchanging, rather than that of the women whose place of residence is usually changed as a result of marriage. He draws illustrative examples from ethnographic studies of the Australian Aborigines, among whom dual organization is widespread. This conception of restricted exchange corresponds exactly with Polanyi's correlation of reciprocity with a symmetrical kinship structure, the difference being only that Polanyi was mainly concerned with the exchange of objects rather than the exchange of persons (i.e. sisters or daughters).

By contrast to restricted exchange, generalized exchange takes the following form:

This form of exchange

> establishes a system of operations conducted on credit. A surrenders a daughter or a sister to B, who surrenders one to C, who, in turn, will surrender one to A. This is its simplest formula. Consequently, generalized exchange always contains an element of trust.... There must be the confidence that the cycle will close again, and that after a period of time a woman will eventually be received in compensation for the woman initially surrendered.
>
> (Lévi-Strauss 1969 [1949]: 265)

Generalized exchange is another way of expressing the matrilateral marriage rule that a man should marry a woman in the kinship category of mother's brother's daughter, and it is associated with a long cycle of reciprocity.

These two systems of exchange are conceived of as extremes between which lies a third form of exchange, delayed exchange, which establishes a short cycle of reciprocity of the following form:

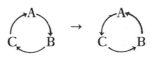

Marriage with the father's sister's daughter, the patrilateral rule, is consistent with exchanges of this type, in which the direction of exchange is reversed rather than repeated in each successive generation.

These three forms of exchange are all of the 'elementary' type. Lévi-Strauss sees in such elementary structures of kinship the basis for the gift exchange of things. A bridewealth exchange, for example, is 'a process whereby the woman provided as a counterpart is replaced by a symbolical equivalent' (1969 [1949]: 470). A transformation such as this can only occur, however, if the marriage is of the generalized or delayed kind. All three elementary forms, in Lévi-Strauss's scheme, are then opposed to complex structures which leave 'the determination of the spouse to other mechanisms, economic or psychological' (Lévi-Strauss 1969 [1949]: xxiii). Lévi-Strauss's 'great divide', between elementary and complex structures of kinship, can be mapped onto Polanyi's between non-market and market exchange. The fit is by no means perfect, but the degree of correlation is high.

These different forms of exchange, argues Lévi-Strauss, are an expression of the incest taboo, the 'supreme rule of the gift' (1969 [1949]: 22). As he put it, the 'prohibition of incest is less a rule prohibiting marriage with the mother, daughter or sister, than a rule obliging the mother, sister, or daughter to be given to others' (1969 [1949]: 22). This is not only Lévi-Strauss's answer to Mauss's question about the basis of the obligation to give, it also underwrites his theory of cultural evolution. Lévi-Strauss argues (1969 [1949]: ch. 28) that it was man's desire to maximize the kinship distance between himself and his wife that saw society progress through different evolutionary stages of development.

There is, in sum, a sense in which the theories of Mauss, Lévi-Strauss, Polanyi and Sahlins, taken together, provide a conceptual framework which is the mirror image of Marx's. Whereas the gift theorists begin their analyses with the direct gift exchange of people and then progress through various mediating forms to the generalized gift exchange of things, commodity theorists like Marx begin with the direct commodity exchange of things and progress to the generalized commodity exchange of labour (Gregory 1982: 68). This method of analysis is 'evolutionary' to the extent that it is making claims about actual historical processes, but it can also be seen as a 'logical historical' method (Meek 1967), a mode of reasoning employed in the process of developing an abstract conceptual framework. This distinction is important because the logical historical method makes no claims about actual historical processes. Thus, an evolutionary theory can be rejected without affecting the legitimacy of the logical historical method. The importance of this distinction should become clear in the course of the following discussion of barter and other forms of counter-trade.

BARTER AND OTHER FORMS OF COUNTER-TRADE

Counter-trade is the general form of non-monetized commodity exchange. Barter, the simultaneous exchange of commodities $(C-C)$, is the best known example of counter-trade, but there are many other non-simultaneous forms (e.g. delayed barter exchange). The latter necessarily involve a time element and, in consequence, some notion of credit. In formal terms they are analogous to delayed exchanges of gifts, and in practice it is often impossible to distinguish between gift and commodity components of a counter-trade transaction.

The phenomenon of counter-trade poses two questions: What is the evolutionary status of barter? And what determines the rate of exchange?

For both classical and neoclassical economists barter is the origin of all exchange. They believe that the original economy was a 'natural' one based on an elementary division of labour and lacking any form of money. This inefficient system gave way to money-based exchanges with the progressive division of labour and the development of markets. Thus the invention of money was the answer to the 'problem' of barter. This 'origin myth', as Hart (1987) has aptly called it, is based on a priori logical reasoning about an imagined past rather than on contemporary ethnographic evidence. The myth was repeatedly attacked by early anthropologists as ethnographic evidence on actual barter exchanges began to accumulate. The evidence shows that different forms of exchange co-exist rather than following one another in a temporal sequence. An object can participate in many different forms of exchange in the course of a day. For example, a pig may begin the day by being sold in a market for cash, then be bartered for another commodity, later resold at a profit, then given away as a gift, and finally consumed as a good.

The first reliable evidence to point along these lines came from Malinowski's (1922) classic study of the tribal economics of the Trobriand Islanders. From a comprehensive list of gifts, payments and commercial transactions he distinguished seven types of exchange, and showed how they were interrelated in the concrete ecological and social context of the Trobriand Islands in the early part of this century. His study showed that much geographically based barter trade took place within the framework of the annual *kula* gift-exchange ritual. Recent studies from the Milne Bay area show that these gift exchanges continue to take place today under the umbrella of the world market economy. This complexity poses few problems for indigenous transactors in the region, who know exactly what type of transaction they are entering into, but it has posed many theoretical problems for anthropologists who have tried to comprehend what is going on.

Mauss was one of the early synthesizers. He recognized the implications of Malinowski's data for the economists' theory of barter and developed the alternative thesis that gift exchange preceded commodity exchange. He proposed a three-stage theory: first came the restricted exchange of gifts within a tribe, next came generalized gift exchange, and finally the money economy originated when the ancient Semitic societies 'invented the means of detaching... precious things from groups' (1954 [1925]: 94).

It is interesting to note, in passing, that barter exchange is re-emerging in the heartland of international financial capitalism as the hegemony of the United States wanes and with it the value of the dollar. Barter has long been a major component of international trade between East and West (i.e. on the boundaries of United States power), but now many multi-national companies are resorting to it to safeguard losses from deals involving a declining dollar; within the United States the rise of computerized exchange, where debts can be cancelled without the aid of money, has begun to worry the Internal Revenue Service (Hart 1987: 197).

The ethnographic and historical evidence, then, does not support any simplistic theory of the evolution of economic forms. This is not to say that the logical historical method, which organizes concepts in a sequence from simple to complex, is invalid. To the contrary, as the above discussion has shown, it has underlain all the significant conceptual developments in the theory of exchange over the past two centuries.

Let me now turn to consider the question of exchange-rate determination.

Classical political economy, as we have seen, proposed the labour theory of value as the key to understanding the exchange-rate of commodities. It was argued that two heterogeneous commodities can be equated in value because of the equality of the labour time contained therein. Neoclassical economists, on the other hand, proposed that scarcity and utility determine the prices of goods. What contribution have anthropologists been able to make to this debate?

The controversy has been uppermost in the minds of many ethnographers as they observed and collected quantitative data on tribal systems of barter and counter-trade. Godelier (1977), for example, explicitly addressed the debate on the theory of value in his article on ' "Salt money" and the circulation of commodities among the Baruya of New Guinea'.

The Baruya are a people of the Eastern Highlands of Papua New Guinea for whom the production of sweet potatoes is the principal economic activity. They are also specialists in the production of vegetable salt which is redistributed among relatives within the tribe and bartered for various products and services beyond its borders. The latter exchanges were conducted in pre-colonial times by daring individuals who made contact with hostile neighbours and managed to establish 'trade and protection' pacts with certain members of the host groups. Trading partners would feed and protect their guests and do their best to find the merchandise which the latter desired. Salt was a highly desired prestige item which was stored above the hearth to be used on ceremonial occasions involving the exchange and consumption of gifts. Baruya traders bartered their salt for a range of commodities, one of which was bark cloth obtained from the Youndouyé, long-time friendly neighbours. Godelier noted that the exchange rate was one bar of salt (average weight 2 kg) for 6 bark cloths, and he calculated the labour time required to make the two products. A single bar of Baruya salt entailed, on average, $1\frac{1}{2}$ days of labour, whereas 6 bark cloths entailed 4 days of labour. In other words, the exchange rate was imbalanced in labour terms, with the Baruya receiving the equivalent of almost three times more labour than they gave.

Godelier denies, however, that the Baruya exploit other people's labour. 'What counts', he argues

is the reciprocal satisfaction of their need and not a well-kept balance of their labour expenditure. For this reason, the inequality of exchange expresses the comparative social utility of exchanged products, their unequal importance in the scale of social needs and the diverse monopolist positions of exchange groups.

(1977: 150)

Godelier's conclusion is based on an interpretation of the statement of one of his informants, who declared that 'If we receive enough, then work belongs to the past, it is forgotten.'

This looks like a victory for neoclassical theory. However, it could also be argued that the unequal exchange reflects a difference in the *quality* of the labour because the skills required to produce salt are much more highly specialized than those involved in making bark cloth. The labour theory of value requires that differences of quality be reduced to those of quantity, and if the reduction factor was such that three hours of Baruya labour is equivalent to one hour of Youndouyé labour, then it could be argued that the exchange is indeed equal.

The conclusion that both theories are valid is, perhaps, to be preferred, because evidence such as this cannot resolve the fundamental problems of the theory of value. What is at issue are different methods of apprehending the world. If we conceptualize Baruya salt as a commodity certain implications follow; if we conceptualize it as a good different implications follow. They are incommensurable paradigms and, as such, no way of comparing them exists. Furthermore, accurate accounting of utility value and labour value is impossible, even in the Baruya's own terms. How does one reduce skilled labour time to unskilled? How does one measure marginal utility and make interpersonal comparisons? There are no satisfactory answers to these hotly debated questions.

The labour-value and utility-value paradigms do not exhaust the universe of possibilities, and there is room for other theories of value. Sahlins's essay, 'Exchange value and the diplomacy of primitive trade' (in Sahlins 1972), can be seen as an attempt to develop an alternative. He begins by noting that the 'characteristic fact of primitive exchange is indeterminacy of the rates' (1972: 278). By this he means that similar commodities move against each other in different proportions in different transactions. He addresses the usual explanations, finds them wanting, and argues that, in partnership trade, the rates are set by social tact, 'by the diplomacy of good measure appropriate to a confrontation between comparative strangers' (1972: 302). Sahlins maintains that in times of scarcity when, according to neoclassical theory, prices are supposed to rise, the partnership absorbs the pressure and the exchange rate remains undisturbed. In other words, the 'flexibility of the system depends on the social structure of the trade relation' (1972: 313).

This theory moves the focus of attention from the economic value of objects to the political value of the trade partnership. In this regard, it invites comparison with Marx's (1954 [1867]: 76) theory of the 'fetishism' of commodities, which argues that in a world of generalized commodity circulation, relations between people assume the fantastic form of relations between things. Sahlins, by way of contrast, argues that in the highly particularized world of countertrade, relations between people always appear *as such*.

MARKET PLACE TRADE

In the discussion of market exchange, it is essential to distinguish between market *principles* and market *places*. The former have to do with the abstract principles that determine the formation of wages, prices and profit. Market places, by contrast, are the loci where concrete exchanges take place. Marketing systems are organized frameworks for the purchase and sale of commodities; their features include customary market centres and a calendar of market days so that buyers and sellers can meet in regular and predictable ways.

Economists have shown little interest in market places, confining themselves almost exclusively to the analysis of abstract principles. Most research on market places has been carried out by geographers and anthropologists, the former concentrating on their spatial aspects and the latter on their social and cultural aspects (as Bromley's (1979) comprehensive bibliography illustrates).

Anthropological studies of markets mainly take the form of ethnographic accounts of particular local regions. General and comparative studies of the kind that Mauss, Polanyi, Sahlins and others made of gift exchange are rare. However, while all the classic ethnographic studies – Skinner (1964–5) on China, Mintz (1959, 1961) on the Caribbean, Dewey (1962a) on Indonesia, Malinowski and Fuente (1982 [1957]) on Mexico, Geertz (1979) on Morocco – are concerned with the analysis of particular situations, they do contain many important general analytical points. Some of these have been drawn out by Bohannan and Dalton (1962) in their introduction to an important collection of essays on African rural markets.

Markets can be classified by the types of commodities transacted, by the forms of trade, by the roles of traders, and by the mode of spatio-temporal organization.

The commodities traded in markets can be divided into those of the 'vertical' and those of the 'horizontal' type (Mintz 1959). Vertical commodities are either 'upwardly mobile' or 'downwardly mobile' (Skinner 1964–5). Upwardly mobile commodities are those which are produced in a rural area and exported from it by wholesalers. They usually consist of agricultural products, but may also include products of artisanship such as ceramic pots, basketware, iron tools, folk art, and so on. These products will ascend through a hierarchy of wholesalers and eventually become the downwardly mobile commodities of another area, usually urban and possibly overseas, where they will be consumed. For a rural area, downwardly mobile commodities usually consist of manufactured commodities of urban provenance such as clothing or jewellery. They are brought into a marketing area by wholesalers who resell them to retailers who, in turn, offer them for sale at the market place. The image of a vertical commodity, then, captures the nested hierarchy of markets that characterizes many peasant marketing systems, and locates them in a system that incorporates local economies into the regional, national and international economy. By contrast with vertical commodities, horizontal commodities move across a limited local space. They are usually sold direct to the final consumer by the producer at the market place, without the mediation of wholesalers.

This distinction, then, provides the first means of classifying markets: some will be characterized by a predominance of vertical commodities (e.g. China), others by a predominance of horizontal commodities (e.g. West Africa – see Hill 1966: 298).

A second method of classifying markets is by the form of trade. All the forms of commodity trade discussed above – barter $C-C$, selling in order to buy $C-M-C$, buying in order to sell $M-C-M'$, and moneylending $M-M'$ – are found in rural peasant markets. Barter trade is extremely rare. I observed barter transactions in the markets I studied in Central India, but they accounted for a negligible proportion of total commerce. Reports exist of Andean markets operating almost exclusively by barter (Mintz 1959: 29), but the vast majority of transactions are of the $C-M-C$ and $M-C-M'$ variety. In Central India selling in order to buy is the basis of the system from the farmer's perspective. Farmers, or rather the female members of farming households, bring small loads of agricultural produce to sell at weekly markets in order to purchase kerosene, cloth, ornaments or other items. Selling is obviously more intense at the end of the harvest, but so too is buying. I was struck by the difference in the trading patterns of markets in the more prosperous areas of northern India. Here markets are solely of the $M-C-M'$ variety, as farmers only go to the markets to buy. Their produce, which is grown using more capital-intensive techniques, is not brought to the market but sold through other channels in a manner similar to that found in the rich capitalist countries.

Classification by the roles of traders is yet a third way to characterize different market place systems. Traders fall into two main categories: the mobile trader and the settled shopkeeper. Mobile traders include pedlars, who wander from place to place hawking commodities in an unsystematic, opportunistic way. They may be artisans who provide a service or add value to a product, or they may be pure merchants who buy in order to sell at a profit. Pedlars of this type usually possess a very small trading capital and travel by foot, but there are also relatively wealthy individuals who possess motorized transport. Thus pedlars can be distinguished by the type of trade they do, by the size of their capital and by their means of transport.

Pedlars are only one kind of mobile trader, and they should be distinguished from periodic market place traders. These traders have a set round of places, which are visited on specified weekly market days. A cloth trader I interviewed in India, for example, would set up his ten thousand rupees'-worth of stock at the big market in his home town of Kondagaon on Sunday, travel 20 km by jeep to Sampur on Monday, 50 km to Makdi on Tuesday, 70 km to Randha on Wednesday, rest on Thursday, travel 80 km to Bare Dongar on Friday, and 50 km to Mardapal on Saturday – and so on in this way for 52 weeks of the year. Like the pedlars, traders in this category can be divided into artisans and merchants and ranked in terms of their capital (which for many is often less than a hundred rupees); they can also be divided into wholesalers and retailers. In addition, traders who attend periodic markets can be distinguished by the particular locations in the market where they set up shop. Rich traders usually have a fixed establishment (e.g. a thatched-roof stall covering a small piece of cleared ground), poor traders will crouch in the dust under an umbrella, while the pedlar will wander around the market place hawking his or her commodities.

Mobile traders of all kinds are to be distinguished from shopkeepers. Again, this category can be subdivided along a variety of axes: wholesaler–retailer, rich–poor, and so on, all of which are salient in rural areas. They usually surround the central market place. In Western European countries the relative importance of the periodic market trader has declined significantly over the past two centuries as shopkeeping has emerged as the dominant form of exchange. Nowadays the large department stores reign supreme as the central loci of exchange. In many non-European countries, however, periodic market traders are still the key merchants in most rural areas. They capture almost all of the trade and customers only go to stores for emergency purchases or to buy insignificant items such as a toothbrush, a pencil, or a packet of biscuits.

It is obvious that the distinct ways of characterizing markets outlined above, according to types of commodities, forms of trade and roles of traders, are interrelated. But it is also obvious that they allow for very diverse combinations of features, and hence for a great variety of possible market place systems. The task of the observer, looking at such systems in their empirical manifestations, is to identify the principal tendencies and to account for them. But before we examine some of the factors which have been used to explain the observed patterns (such as the predominance of periodic market traders in the rural areas of poor countries, of hierarchical markets in China, of C–M–C markets in Central India, and so on), it is necessary to consider some of the many different types of spatio-temporal organization found in periodic markets.

Periodicity concentrates the demand for a product to a certain place on a specified day between set hours. A trader can, by repositioning him or herself at regular intervals, tap the demand of a market area and obtain an income from commerce that is adequate for survival. From the point of view of farming households the periodicity of markets reduces the distance they must travel in order to sell their produce and to buy goods for consumption. In effect, periodicity disperses the central market-town throughout the countryside and converts sleepy backwaters into thriving commercial centres for a few hours each week. This pattern of dispersal is a function of the availability of transport: for rich market-town traders there is a limit to how far they are prepared to drive each day, and for poor farmers there is a limit to how far they are prepared to walk.

The distribution of periodic markets over time and space poses a problem that can be expressed in mathematical terms. Christaller's (1966 [1933]) classic application of central place theory is one such expression that has proved very influential with geographers and with some anthropologists (e.g. Skinner 1964–5). However, rather than elaborating on formal models of this kind, it is more appropriate here to give some indication of the actual variations found in the spatio-temporal organization of marketing systems.

In China market schedules are usually based on a ten- or twelve-day week. This structure allows for the development of cyclical systems of great complexity. For example, the 12-day cycle yields three regular cycles of 12-day, 6-day and 3-day market weeks; within these cycles many further possibilities for scheduling are found. Six different schedules make up the 6-day week for example: the first consists of the 1st and 7th day of the cycle, the second of the 2nd and 8th day, the third of the 3rd and 9th day, and so on. If town A chooses the first schedule, town B the second, town C the third and so on, then it can be seen that a farming household living equidistant from these three towns has 3 markets close by on 6 of the 12 days of the market week; towns D, E, F, G, etc. will provide the household with a range of more distant markets to choose from on the other days of the week.

In Central India the system is comparatively simple. The market week is a 7-day one. The major market is held on Sundays at the central market town; intermediate level centres hold their markets on Fridays, Saturdays and Mondays; and small centres hold their markets on the remaining days. In West Africa there is a standard market week of 3, 4, 5, 6, 7 or 8 days in length, such that all markets in a given locality are based on the same cycle.

In areas where vertical commodities predominate, space becomes ordered in a hierarchical way with market centres of various sizes constituting the nodal points. Skinner (1964–5) proposes a multi-level typology of central places, ranging from the local minor marketing area, based on a central village, to the major regional trading area based on a regional city. He finds that the arrangement of minor market areas in China approximates to a honeycomb pattern and that this hexagonal spatial grid is reproduced at the higher levels. Abstract models like this are useful heuristic devices for understanding the empirical complexity of market systems and have stimulated much geographical research (Smith 1978), but it is the social organization of markets that has been the anthropologists' prime concern.

A persistent theme of anthropological literature is the ubiquity of economic and social differentiation in periodic market places. Mintz (1959), for example, notes that in Haiti horizontal exchange occurs among class equals, while vertical exchange occurs between class unequals. In other words, as we move up the hierarchy of vertical commodities we also move up through a class hierarchy. Dewey (1962b) found a similar situation in Java. Here Javanese farmers dominate the small-scale trade, Chinese, Arabs and Indians dominate the large-scale inter-market trade, and Europeans retain control over the really large-scale economic enterprises. This pattern, she claims, is found throughout South-east Asia. In India the marketing system is entirely in the hands of Indians, but the general correlation of class and ethnicity is still to be found. The élite traders found in almost all market areas of India are the Marwaris. They are migrants from Marwar in Rajasthan and, as a group, control a disproportionate share of the industrial and mercantile wealth of the country.

Explaining this social differentiation has been a central concern for anthropologists. How is it, they ask, that markets that are the closest known approximation to the economists' ideal of free competition are nevertheless characterized by such gross social and economic inequalities? Many explanations have been put forward. Investigations have focused, among other things, on culture, ecology, population pressure, the labour-intensive technology of poor farmers, and systems of land tenure.

One paradox that anthropologists have identified is that the competitive market system is backed by a 'strong personalistic element which affects the nature of internal marketing activity' (Mintz 1959: 25). In Haiti this personal relationship is called *pratik*. It means that buyer and seller emphasize 'the *reciprocal* nature of relationships' (1961: 55, my emphasis). Women who buy and sell on these terms call each other *bel me* ('stepmother') or *matelot* ('concubine of the same man'). Reciprocity of this kind between buyer and seller is called 'goodwill' in European countries, where it has been converted into a commodity: shopkeepers and sellers of professional services (e.g. doctors, lawyers, dentists) pay huge sums for it.

Another important kind of reciprocity in market systems is that obtaining between sellers of a given type of vertical commodity. As we have seen, these merchants tend to belong to families or ethnic groups whose members identify with each other in opposition to the world at large. These groups, Dewey (1962b) notes, develop a social structure that enables them to bring informal sanctions to bear on their members. In these localized power systems coercion and collaboration create solidary relations which bring benefits to the in-group and problems for the out-group. One of the greatest benefits to the in-group is access to credit. This provides members of the in-group with initial capital and the ability to accumulate more. Whereas debt can enchain a consumer, for merchants it is their lifeblood, for without it they cannot expand their capital. It is obvious that credit will not be extended where there is neither trust nor sanction and, in periodic market systems, this marks the boundary between the in-group and the out-group. Thus we find that credit for merchant capital expansion flows upon the foundations laid by consanguinity and territoriality. Here, then, is an important factor behind the observed hierarchies found in market places and, when considered in the light of the particular history of a merchant class, it goes some way towards explaining the wealth of some and the poverty of others. Dewey's argument, for which a wide range of supporting evidence can be marshalled, amounts to the claim that positive reciprocity asserts itself in unique ways in the heartland of negative reciprocity, the market place.

This argument seems to contradict Sahlins's theory of positive and negative reciprocity. However a distinction must be maintained between the analysis of abstract principles of exchange and the analysis of exchange in concrete situations. The theories developed by scholars such as Smith, Ricardo, Marx, Malinowski, Mauss, Polanyi and Sahlins are abstractions which must be recognized as such and applied with caution to the analysis of concrete reality. The message of Dewey's argument – and of the growing body of literature concerned with applying the theory of the gift to European history (White 1988), literature (Hyde 1984), economy (Zelizer 1989) and culture (Agnew 1986) – is that concrete reality is riddled with contradictions. This means that any attempt, say, to characterize the European economy as a commodity economy and the Melanesian economy as a gift economy, is bound to fail because positive and negative reciprocity is at work in both economies. The notion of reciprocity, then, can be defined in the abstract but its real meaning will always depend on the concrete political context.

REFERENCES

Agnew, J-C. (1986) *Worlds Apart: The Market and the Theater in Anglo-American Thought, 1550–1750*, Cambridge: Cambridge University Press.

Belshaw, C. S. (1965) *Traditional and Modern Markets*, Englewood Cliffs, NJ: Prentice-Hall.

Bohannan, P. (1959) 'The impact of money on an African subsistence economy', *The Journal of Economic History* 19: 491–503.

Bohannan, P. and Dalton, G. (eds) (1962) *Markets in Africa*, Evanston, Ill.: Northwestern University Press.

Bromley, R. (1979) *Periodic Markets, Daily Markets, and Fairs: A Bibliography Supplement to 1979*, Centre for Development Studies Monographs no. 5, University of Swansea.

Campbell, S. (1983) 'Attaining rank: a classification of shell valuables', in J. Leach and E. R. Leach (eds) *The Kula: New Perspectives on Massim Exchange*, Cambridge: Cambridge University Press.

Christaller, W. (1966 [1933]) *Central Places in Southern Germany*, Englewood Cliffs, N.J.: Prentice-Hall.

Codere, H. (1950) *Fighting with Property*, New York: J. J. Augustin.

Debreu, G. (1959) *Theory of Value: An Axiomatic Analysis of Economic Equilibrium*, New Haven: Yale University Press.

Dewey, A. (1962a) *Peasanting Marketing in Java*, New York: Free Press.

—— (1962b) 'Trade and social control in Java', *Journal of the Royal Anthropological Institute* 92: 177–90.

Friedman, M. (1962) *Price Theory: A Provisional Text*, Chicago: Aldine.

Geertz, C. (1979) 'Suq: the bazaar economy in Sefrou', in C. Geertz, H. Geertz and L. Rosen, *Meaning and Order in Moroccan Society*, Cambridge: Cambridge University Press.

Godelier, M. (1977) *Perspectives in Marxist Anthropology*, Cambridge: Cambridge University Press.

Gregory, C. A. (1982) *Gifts and Commodities*, London: Academic Press.

Hart, K. (1987) 'Barter', in J. Eatwell, M. Milgate and P. Newman (eds) *The New Palgrave: A Dictionary of Economics*, New York: Macmillan.

Heilbroner, R. L. (1987) 'Wealth', in J. Eatwell, M. Milgate and P. Newman (eds) *The New Palgrave: A Dictionary of Economics*, New York: Macmillan.

Hill, P. (1966) 'Notes on traditional market authority and market periodicity in West Africa', *Journal of African History* 7: 295–311.

Hyde, L. (1984) *The Gift: Imagination and the Erotic Life of Property*, London: Vintage.

Ingold, T. (1986) *The Appropriation of Nature: Essays on Human Ecology and Social Relations*, Manchester: Manchester University Press.

Jevons, W. (1970 [1871]) *The Theory of Political Economy*, Harmondsworth: Penguin.

Keynes, J. M. (1982) 'Ancient currencies', in D. Moggridge (ed.) *Collected Writings*, New York: Macmillan.

Lévi-Strauss, C. (1969 [1949]) *The Elementary Structures of Kinship*, London: Eyre & Spottiswoode.

Malinowski, B. (1922) *Argonauts of the Western Pacific*, London: Routledge & Kegan Paul.

Malinowski, B. and de la Fuente, J. (1982 [1957]) *Malinowski in Mexico: The Economics of a Mexican Market System*, ed. S. Drucker-Brown, London: Routledge & Kegan Paul.

Marx, K. (1954 [1867]) *Capital, vol. I: A Critical Analysis of Capitalist Production*, Moscow: Progress.

Mauss, M. (1954 [1925]) *The Gift: Forms and Functions of Exchange in Archaic Societies*, trans. I. Cunnison, London: Routledge & Kegan Paul.

—— (1990 [1925]) *The Gift: The Form and Reason for Exchange in Archaic Societies*, trans. W. D. Halls, London: Routledge.

Meek, R. L. (1967) *Economics and Ideology and Other Essays*, New York: Chapman.

Mintz, S. W. (1959) 'Internal market systems as mechanisms of social articulation', *Proceedings of the 1959 Annual Spring Meeting of the American Ethnological Society*, ed. V. F. Ray, Seattle: Washington University Press.

—— (1961) 'Pratik: Haitian personal economic relationships', *Proceedings of the 1961 Annual Spring Meeting of the American Ethnological Society*, ed. V. E. Garfield, Seattle: Washington University Press.

Peterson, N. (in press) 'Demand sharing: reciprocity and the pressure for generosity among foragers', *American Anthropologist*.

Polanyi, K. (1944) *The Great Transformation*, New York: Rinehart.

Quesnay, F. (1962 [1759]) 'The tableau economique', in R. Meek (ed.) *The Economics of Physiocracy*, London: George Allen.

Robbins, L. (1932) *An Essay on the Nature and Significance of Economic Science*, London: Macmillan.

Sahlins, M. (1972) *Stone Age Economics*, London: Tavistock.

Samuelson, P. (1947) *Foundations of Economic Analysis*, Cambridge, Mass.: Harvard University Press.

Skinner, G. W. (1964–5) 'Marketing and social structure in rural China', *Journal of Asian Studies* 24: 3–43, 195–228, 363–99.

Smith, R. H. T. (ed.) (1978) *Market-Place Trade: Periodic Markets, Hawkers, and Traders in Africa, Asia, and Latin America*, Vancouver: University of British Columbia Press.

Sraffa, P. (1960) *Production of Commodities by Means of Commodities: Prelude to a Critique of Economic Theory*, Cambridge: Cambridge University Press.

Strathern, M. (1988) *The Gender of the Gift*, Berkeley: University of California Press.

Weiner, A. B. (1992) *Inalienable Possessions: The Paradox of Keeping-While-Giving*, Berkeley: University of California Press.

White, S. D. (1988) *Custom, Kinship, and Gifts to Saints: The Laudatio Parentum in Western France, 1050–1150*, University of North Carolina Press: Chapel Hill.

Zelizer, V. (1989) 'The social meaning of money: "Special monies"', *American Journal of Sociology* 95: 342–77.

FURTHER READING

Belshaw, C. S. (1965) *Traditional and Modern Markets*, Englewood Cliffs, NJ: Prentice-Hall.

Bohannan, P. and Dalton, G. (eds) (1962) *Markets in Africa*, Evanston, Ill.: Northwestern University Press.

Dalton, G. (ed.) (1967) *Tribal and Peasant Economies*, Austin: University of Texas Press.

Geertz, C. (1963) *Peddlars and Princes: Social Change and Economic Modernization in Two Indonesian Towns*, Chicago: University of Chicago Press.

Godelier, M. (1977) *Perspectives in Marxist Anthropology*, Cambridge: Cambridge University Press.

Gouldner, A. (1960) 'The norm of reciprocity: a preliminary statement', *American Sociological Review* 25: 161–78.

Gregory, C. A. (1982) *Gifts and Commodities*, London: Academic Press.

Gregory, C. A. and Altman, J. C. (1990) *Observing the Economy* (ASA Research Methods in Social Anthropology, 3), London: Routledge.

Humphrey, C. and Hugh-Jones, S. (eds) (1992) *Barter, Exchange and Value: an Anthropological Approach*, Cambridge: Cambridge University Press.

Leach, J. and Leach, E. R. (eds) (1983) *The Kula: New Perspectives on Massim Exchange*, Cambridge: Cambridge University Press.

Lévi-Strauss, C. (1969) *The Elementary Structures of Kinship*, London: Eyre & Spottiswoode.

Malinowski, B. (1921) 'The primitive economics of the Trobriand Islanders', *Economic Journal* 31: 1–16.

Mauss, M. (1990) *The Gift: the Form and Reason for Exchange in Archaic Societies*, trans. W. D. Halls, London: Routledge.

Parry, J. P. and Bloch, M. (eds) (1989) *Money and the Morality of Exchange*, Cambridge: Cambridge University Press.

Polanyi, K. (1944) *The Great Transformation*, New York: Rinehart.

Polanyi, K., Arensberg, C. and Pearson, H. (eds) (1957) *Trade and Markets in the Early Empires*, New York: The Free Press.

Sahlins, M. (1972) *Stone Age Economics*, London: Tavistock.

Skinner, G. W. (1964–5) 'Marketing and social structure in rural China', *Journal of Asian Studies* 24: 3–43, 195–228, 363–99.

Strathern, M. (1988) *The Gender of the Gift*, Berkeley: University of California Press.

34

POLITICAL DOMINATION AND SOCIAL EVOLUTION

Timothy Earle

The evolution of societies from small-scale intimate groups to large and complex urban states is a fact of human history. To explain the processes responsible for this evolution has been a challenge for social philosophers, sociologists, and anthropologists.[1] In this article, I argue that the evolution of social complexity needs to be understood first and foremost as a political process. Fundamental is the issue of control: how emerging leadership establishes and extends control over the labour of a non-kin support group (Earle 1989, Webster 1990).

Control is essential to mobilize the resources needed to finance emerging institutions. It is grounded in different sources of power: military, ideological and economic; but these different sources of power are not of equal use to an emerging élite. To construct the hierarchical power structure that is the backbone of a complex society, access to power must itself be controllable, and the different sources of power vary considerably in their ability to be thus controlled. As I argue here, it is the grounding of each source of power in controllable economic systems that becomes the critical factor for the evolution of socially stratified and politically centralized societies.

In this article, I proceed in two steps. First, I summarize briefly the evolutionary typologies for human society that have proliferated in the last century or so. My goal is to clarify the key variables in these typologies as they relate to different mechanisms of change. Second, I propose a synthetic model for the evolution of complex societies that draws extensively on existing formulations, but focuses on the political processes tied to different sources of power.

TYPOLOGIES OF CULTURAL EVOLUTION

The proliferation of evolutionary typologies in the literature has been greeted by scholars with some dismay (Feinman and Neitzel 1984, Kristiansen 1991). In the sections that follow, I review the most important typological schemes that have been proposed, their diagnostic variables, and their respective engines for change. Table 1 summarizes the main stages in the various schemes and indicates how they intersect typologically.

Although the authors of these various schemes have been at great pains to recognize the complicated and multi-causal nature of societal change, three rather distinct schools of thought emerge. One emphasizes technology, another stresses the scale of integration, and the third singles out social structure as the most significant dimension of variability.

Technology and social evolution

According to the 'technological' theories of social evolution, human beings solve problems of living by developing material culture, and in the course of time they gradually accumulate knowledge of how to adapt better to their environments. Each successful, novel solution increases the effectiveness of subsistence practices, allows for population growth, and has many social consequences both foreseen and unforeseen.

A dominant influence in this school of evolutionary thought has been that of Marx. Based on a common, nineteenth-century belief in technological progress (see Morgan 1877), Marx (1904) and Engels (1972 [1884]) constructed their seminal theory that human history has been propelled by complicated interplays between developing forces of production and the social relations within which these forces have been worked out. During the

Table 1 Some common anthropological typologies of social evolution

Childe (1936)	Service (1962) Johnson and Earle (1987)	Sahlins (1963) Earle (1978)	Fried (1967)
Hunter–gatherers	Band (family level)	Head man	Egalitarian society
Farmers	Tribe (local group)	Big man	Ranked society
Civilization	Chiefdom	Simple	
		Complex	Stratified society
	State	State	State

twentieth century, an eclectic mix of Marxist, Weberian, and functionalist theoreticians have emphasized the role of technology in social evolution (Childe 1936, White 1959, Lenski 1966, Glassman 1986).

The evolution of social complexity, according to this view, is tied to the development of effective technologies that permit human populations to grow, to establish permanent settlements and eventually to generate a surplus that supports administrators, merchants, priests, artists, and craftsmen. The major technological stages are adduced from Morgan's (1877) tripartite division into hunter–gatherer societies (savagery), agricultural societies (barbarism), and complex specialized societies (civilization).

Such a tripartite division is a common feature of many evolutionary schemes. Perhaps most influential have been the writings of the archaeologist V. Gordon Childe (1936, 1951). Childe conceived of two major revolutions in human history – the Neolithic Revolution and the Urban Revolution. In Childe's scheme, *hunter–gatherers* were wanderers, eking out an existence from foods available in nature. Following the domestication of plants and animals, *farmers* were able to settle down and create a village life with permanent houses, a richer material culture, and a more reliable subsistence. Then, further technological advances, especially the beginnings of metallurgy, brought into being a specialized and highly efficient economy from which the urban life of *civilization* could flourish.

The primary engine for change, according to these theories, is the dynamic relationship between technology and human population. In order to survive and prosper, human groups must solve critical problems of making a living; technology is the means to solve these problems of subsistence. This 'vulgar' form of Marxism (cf. Friedman 1974, Johnson and Earle 1987: 9) emphasizes how technology's most basic function is to extract energy and materials used to support human populations. The dynamic relationship between technology and population has been conceived in both a positive and a negative light.

Following nineteenth-century optimism, technological development has been seen as the means to liberate human societies from the bondage of nature, allowing a growing and settled human world. This was Childe's position in *Man Makes Himself* (1936), in which he emphasized the successful revolutions in human technology. Leslie White (1943) elaborated and systematized this view of technological development as increasing the efficiency of energy capture and thus permitting the evolution of more complex societies. By contrast, a more pessimistic view, which goes back to Malthus (1798) and his followers, turns the equation around. Human populations, like those of any other animal species, have the biological potential for sustained growth, and will expand until that growth is curtailed by disease, starvation and war.

Unique to human beings is the capability to increase by technological means the environment's productivity, and thus to permit the population to expand. Boserup (1966) thus shows how agricultural technology developed in response to the population-driven need to intensify subsistence production. Following this logic, Cohen (1977) argues that the origins of agriculture in different regions of the globe resulted from sustained population growth that led to the peopling of the world and pressed against the availability of wild resources in a hunter–gatherer economy (see also Cohen's contribution to this volume, Article 10).

This is a classic chicken-and-egg debate: on the one hand, an inherent growth in human technology is said to have permitted population growth (Childe and White); on the other hand, inherent growth in human population is said to have caused hardships that either limited growth (Malthus), or caused technological and social innovations that permitted further growth (Boserup). Most probably the two suggested prime movers – demographic expansion and progressive technological innovation – are inexorably bound together (Johnson and Earle 1987). The reproductive potential of human populations and the cultural capability to enhance the productivity of environmental resources together generate a growth-oriented system of a kind hitherto unknown. But a further implication of this interpretation is that technological change did not result in a 'better world' with higher per capita consumption; rather, the result was simply a greater population.

The positive feedback between population growth and technological innovation is linked to social modes of production which provide the material basis for social differentiation. Marxist analyses of capitalism, for example, describe how the ownership of industrial technology conferred control over the productive process and exclusive rights to the profits derived therefrom. Several recent evolutionary schemes, Marxist in conception, emphasize how the characteristics of the new technologies and economies affect the political and social character of life. Major syntheses include those of Lenski (1966), who distinguishes between hunting and gathering societies, simple horticultural societies, advanced horticultural societies, agricultural societies, and industrial societies; and Glassman (1986), who separates the stages of democracy in hunting–gathering band society, democracy in hunting–horticultural or herding–hunting tribal society, and despotism in horticultural village society or nomadic herding society. On the basis of this separation into stages, Glassman attempts to show how gender and political relations derive from the way in which persons stand, *vis-à-vis* each other, with regard to their respective labour roles in subsistence production.

Clearly, what is needed is a systematic way to link the processes of technological elaboration and population growth with the development of more complex societies. The next school of social evolutionary thought to be considered deals with this linkage explicitly.

Scale of integration and social evolution

The scale of integration in human society expands through the creation of overarching levels of organization that embed pre-existing structures. The school of thought that emphasizes this aspect of social evolution holds that institutional mechanisms develop to integrate the larger and more complex sociopolitical groups needed to solve economic problems. Such institutions include central leadership, social hierarchies, and related features, such as writing, state religions and bureaucracies, that are characteristic of complex societies. Why new levels of integration are created is still a matter of debate between those who emphasize, respectively, *managerial* and *political* causes.

Evolutionary schemes based on levels of integration have a long pedigree. The original conquest theories of the origins of the state, for example, explained the creation of large-scale societies as resulting from conquest and incorporation. In the nineteenth century, Spencer (1967) conceived of social evolution as the political process by which stronger societies expanded to dominate politically weaker ones. In recent anthropology, Steward (1955) regarded the development of new levels of social integration as a solution to problems of adaptation. This perspective from cultural ecology was popularized in the influential evolutionary typology of Elman Service (1962), who distinguished the successive levels of band, tribe, chiefdom, and state.

This scheme, based on four levels and mechanisms of integration, has been recast in the recent synthesis by Johnson and Earle (1987), as follows.

Family level society (the band)

Describing them as the 'most rudimentary form of social organization', Service (1962: 107) envisions bands as exemplars of the primordial human social form. The band was originally thought to consist of a small, patrilineal, exogamous group organized for effective hunting. Subsequent studies, notably those included in the symposium volume *Man the Hunter* (Lee and DeVore 1968; cf. Williams 1974), forced a significant modification of the band concept. Gathering is now recognized as a primary source of food in many hunter–gatherer societies, and residential groups are seen as small and flexible in composition, allowing people to respond to changing opportunities in their environments. By renaming this level of integration 'the family level', Johnson and Earle (1987) emphasize the informal and intimate character of the small social groups that are based on close kinship relationships (compare Steward 1977).

The local group (the tribal level)

The local group forms by organizing and embedding several extended families into a village-sized group of a few hundred. Originally, Service (1962: 113) emphasized the importance of pan-tribal sodalities, such as clans and warrior societies, that create a regional, decentralized organization integrating many villages. Criticizing this concept, Fried (1967: 154) argued that tribes as regional organizations were largely constructs of colonial governments, designed for administrative purposes. Sahlins (1968) then reconceived the tribal level of integration as inherently fragmented into local villages. Lacking regional political institutions that could resolve conflict, villages in tribal societies constantly fight with each other. Johnson and Earle (1987) describe these regionally fragmented social systems, organized politically at the village level and extended regionally only through shifting political alliances and ritual cycles.

Leadership within a local group varies considerably in terms of the degree and concentration of political power (Johnson and Earle 1987). It is not, however, formalized in political offices (see Sahlins 1963; cf. Earle 1987).

The chiefdom: simple and complex

The primary distinguishing characteristic of the chiefdom is the extension of the polity to incorporate and integrate multiple communities within a region (Carneiro 1981). For Service (1962), chiefdoms are redistributive societies in which a formalized central agency, personified as the chief, emerges to co-ordinate the distribution of specialized goods within the regional polity. Johnson and Earle (1987) emphasize the inherent social inequality and control that emerge with chiefdoms. They differentiate between simple chiefdoms – polities of a few thousand people with modest social differentiation, and complex chiefdoms – polities of tens of thousands with marked social stratification. Integration is provided by a highly generalized and undifferentiated hierarchy of chiefly roles (Earle 1978, Wright 1984).

The state

State societies are complex and internally differentiated by class, economic specialization, and ethnicity. The expansion in scale, in comparison to chiefdoms, is connected to various institutions of integration: military, religious and bureaucratic. As Wright (1984) emphasizes, the centralization of leadership is based on the formalization of decision-making hierarchies. In contrast to chiefdoms, in which a leadership stratum remains generalized, state bureaucracies are internally specialized with a differentiation of decision-making and control functions. Special characteristics of states may include writing systems, which are important for record-keeping, and elaborate systems of transportation and communication. The economies of states are based either on a system of pooling and redistribution or on market exchange, or on a combination of the two.

In the schemes presented above, which classify societies by their levels of integration, the main engine for change must be one that leads human societies to increase in scale. When it comes to specifying this engine for change, two competing approaches are evident (Service 1978). The first stresses issues of adaptation, arguing that central leadership is a social technology developed to solve problems of survival. The second approach stresses the political dimension, arguing that central leadership is an outcome of expanding domination.

The adaptationist approach of Steward (1955) and Service (1962) envisaged a simple dynamic for the evolution of human society. Human institutions are organizational solutions to critical problems of adaptation. Directly analogous to technological advance, the evolution of central leadership was conceived as the development of administrative forms designed to manage the economy for the benefit of the collectivity. More recently scholars have emphasized the role of population growth in creating new problems, which in turn call forth novel social solutions (see Johnson and Earle 1987).

Examples in which the evolution of social forms is seen to have a managerial basis abound in the literature. The flexible organization of family-level society is seen as an adaptation to the fluctuating resource base of a gathering economy (Yellen and Harpending 1972). The decentralized organization at the local-group level could be similarly appropriate to the management of intergroup relations, including those of exchange, insurance against risk, military co-ordination, and exogamy (see Dalton 1977, Braun and Plog 1982). Service (1962) envisioned chiefdoms as having evolved through the adaptation of expanding populations to a settled life in diverse environments requiring local specialization. The possibility this opened up for a more productive and secure agriculture based on irrigation encouraged groups to accept despotic leaders responsible for co-ordinating the construction and maintenance of irrigation works. These leaders then created the bureaucratic state (Wittfogel 1957). In all of these cases, the logic is quite similar: the 'need' to adopt a particular solution for collective survival, or the advantage it confers, encourages the group to accept a leader's central direction.

The alternative approach emphasizes the political basis for the evolution of central authority and corresponding social stratification. In a view derived loosely from nineteenth-century Marxism, the social stratification of chiefdoms and states is seen to emerge from the material conditions of control. In his oft-quoted preface to *A Contribution to the Critique of Political Economy*, Marx (1904: 12) argued that:

> The sum total of these relations of production constitutes the economic structure of society – the real foundation, on which rise legal and political superstructures and to which correspond definite forms of social consciousness. The mode of production in material life determines the general character of the social, political and spiritual processes of life.

Anthropologists have returned to this basic materialism, emphasizing the importance of economic control, rather than management, in the evolution of stratification and related social complexity. Carneiro (1970), attributing his approach to Spencer, has argued that complexity derives from conquest. Where geographical or 'social' (i.e. demographic) circumscription exists, a subjugated population has no escape from its conquerors. Similarly, irrigation and intensive agriculture act to circumscribe a population by tethering it to improved lands; ownership of these lands by élites confers the control on which stratification can emerge (Earle 1978, Gilman 1981). The redistributive and market systems of chiefdoms and states are viewed as mechanisms of institutional finance, rather than of ecological adaptation (Brumfiel 1976, 1980, Earle 1977). In an elegant argument, Haas (1982) shows that systems of resource extraction rely on a balance whereby the cost to a commoner of his compliance with an élite's demand for labour and resources must remain less than the cost of refusal. The commoner is caught in an asymmetrical power relationship; the greater the asymmetry in the relationship the more likely is the commoner to comply.

A peasant will give labour and resources to his lord as long as his options for refusal are limited. But what limits the options available to the commoner? The answer to this question should solve the dilemma of how complex systems evolve. One obvious limitation is structural, as I shall now show.

Social structure and social evolution

The basic premise of evolutionary schemes emphasizing structural change is that a historical transformation in the nature of social relationships and resource ownership underlies the evolution of human society. For example, what Polanyi (1944) called the 'great transformation' refers essentially to a change in how people are structurally related to one another. In nineteenth-century writings, Maine (1861) distinguished between the structuring of societies by status and by contract, and Engels (1972 [1884]) distinguished between societies based on kinship and those based on territory. From an economic standpoint, Durkheim (1933 [1893]) contrasted divisions of labour based respectively on mechanical and organic solidarity, while Mauss (1954 [1925]) saw an evolution from societies characterized by gift exchange to societies in which the exchange of commodities prevailed. Moreover, many anthropologists have drawn a structural division, albeit non-evolutionary in conception, between stateless and state societies (Evans-Pritchard and Fortes 1940, Mair 1962). All such formulations envisage a fundamental contrast in the structural basis of society: on the one hand are traditional societies integrated by social relations, and on the other are modern societies organized by a combination of codified laws and the economic relations of the market.

The most clearly elaborated evolutionary synthesis deriving from this intellectual tradition is to be found in the work of Fried (1967). His four stages are those of egalitarian, ranked, stratified and state societies. In many respects these social stages may readily be identified with those posited by Service, but Fried emphasizes the structural transformations involved.

947

Egalitarian society

Equated with family-level integration and with local groups with headmen, this has 'as many positions of prestige in any given age–sex grade as there are people capable of filling them' (Fried 1967: 33). These societies are structured traditionally by kin relationships and by the universal criteria of age and sex.

Ranked society

Equated with Big Man polities and simple chiefdoms, this has a limited number of positions of valued status such that 'not all those of sufficient talent to occupy such statuses actually achieve them' (Fried 1967: 109). Local polities have ritual and political leaders who acquire their positions on the basis of traditional principles that rank individuals with respect to each other. Fried believed that such positions were not based on economic power or privilege. Leadership carried traditional rights of obedience and obligations to manage economic projects such as the construction of irrigation systems and the redistribution of specialized goods (compare Service 1962).

Stratified society

Equated loosely with complex chiefdoms, this 'is one in which members of the same sex and equivalent age status do not have equal access to the basic resources that sustain life' (Fried 1967: 186). This stage is poorly defined ethnographically, and its separation from that of ranked society seems to be based only on the structural transformation from communal to private property.

My impression, though disputed by some (Kristiansen 1991), is that ranked and stratified societies are not qualitatively different. Rather, in both, leaders attempt to maximize their political advantage, but their ability to do this varies according to the available systems of control and finance; the outcome is quantitative variation in the strength and extent of political centrality and in the resulting developmental dynamics (Sanders and Webster 1978, Earle 1989).

State society

This is identified as having 'specialized institutions and agencies . . . that maintain an order of stratification' (Fried 1967: 235). Thus states simply represent the expansion and institutionalization of the structural changes underwriting the emergence of stratified society, and Fried explains the rarity of the prototypical stratified society on the grounds that once the critical structural transformation giving rise to stratification has occurred, the state will necessarily develop quickly to solidify it.

Friedman and Rowlands (1977) significantly expand on Fried's formulation by looking at the inherent developmental characteristics of non-stratified 'tribal' society, including both local groups and chiefdoms. Leaders seek to enhance their positions of eminence by manipulating prestige goods, exchange ties and linked social relationships involving political marriages and alliances. Asiatic states, based on the replacement of kinship by territorial principles, develop as chiefs control systems of redistribution that are grounded in ownership of productive resources (i.e. agricultural lands). Perhaps the most important element of Friedman and Rowlands's model is that the society is seen as having its own, growth-oriented dynamic based both on its internal structure (compare Earle 1978) and on its regional and long-distance articulation with world economic systems. Thus development can be understood in terms of broad political interactions that link together the internal changes taking place within individual societies.

The important point to note is that social systems have *internal* dynamics responsible for change. This idea is, of course, a direct intellectual descendent of Marx's view of social evolution as a working out of the internal contradictions in historically specific modes of production. Thus the inherent conflicts between feudal lord and merchant underlay the developments that took European societies out of feudalism. But what causes this transformation? So-called structural Marxists, such as Godelier (1977) and Friedman (1974, 1975, Friedman and Rowlands 1977), take the weight off Marx's original insistence that social relationships derive ultimately from economic relationships, and off the corresponding character of power. The structural Marxists' view of the dynamic character of human social relations must, however, be extended to consider what is *practical* under varying material conditions.

TOWARDS A SYNTHETIC THEORY OF SOCIAL EVOLUTION

In what follows, I argue that the three schools of thought outlined above each have important contributions to make to a synthetic theory of social evolution (see Johnson and Earle 1987). These contributions and some of the unanswered questions to which they give rise, are summarized below:

1 The 'technological' schemes identify a dynamic interrelationship between human population expansion and technological development. But why should this lead to the development of more complex societies?

2a The 'integrationist' schemes that invoke processes of adaptation identify the ways in which human organizations function to solve critical problems of survival. But for any particular problem, multiple organizational solutions seem practicable. The difficulty with these arguments is *not* that central leadership, for example, might not meet the needs of local populations, but that there is no a priori reason why these needs should be fundamentally different from those of people in decentralized societies.

949

Adaptationist theories of evolutionary integration have by now been extensively criticized, and it has been shown that, by and large, the adaptive advantage of central management, by contrast to other social solutions, is unclear (see Earle 1987).

2b The 'integrationist' schemes that invoke political processes emphasize that control over populations is the basis for the development of more integrated systems. But why would a political system expand in the first place, and why should different political systems, all operated by equally sophisticated strategists, vary in their capacity to expand and dominate?

3 The 'social structuralist' schemes emphasize that different social systems have fundamentally different organizational structures and thus have contrasting developmental dynamics and trajectories. But whence come these different structures? Are they simply the outcome of historical differences?

A synthetic theory can draw on the strengths of each theoretical scheme, which complement each other in many respects. To construct such a theory, we should recognize that every human society depends on a conjunction of subsistence economy and political economy (Earle 1978, Johnson and Earle 1987: 11–15). The differences emphasized in the 'social structural' schemes do not, I argue, represent qualitative differences in society, but rather represent different properties of the two economic spheres of subsistence and politics.

The *subsistence economy* meets the direct survival needs of a population. Its character depends on the scale of these needs (reflecting largely the population's size) and on the availability of resources in its environment which may be transformed by the human productive process. The dynamic relationship between technology and population growth underlies the gradual expansion in the subsistence economy, subject however to environmental constraints on technological intensification. Problems of survival may require the establishment of social networks and group leaders backed by traditional reciprocal rules of aid and support.

The *political economy* provides the finance to support emerging élites and their related institutions. As I have argued for the Hawaiian case (Earle 1978), unlike the subsistence economy, the political economy is inherently growth-oriented. In essence, competition for positions of leadership puts a premium on the mobilization of resources used to support contending factions. Growth in a political economy can be very rapid, constrained only by the ability to mobilize resources from a commoner population. But what confers and limits this ability? Local élites will actively seek to develop means of control, but control can also be seen as derived fundamentally from the character of the subsistence economy.

Long-term intensification of the subsistence economy, of a kind that might require local management, also creates conditions of control in the political economy (Johnson and Earle 1987). As Lenski (1966) argues, the institutionalization of privilege that underlies social complexity derives from a balance of power and need. Although state coercion never lies far below the surface, stable systems of domination depend upon the ruling élite's ability to provide (or deny) essential products or services. To show how this works we need to examine the varying sources of power in chiefdoms and states, and how these sources offer potentially conflicting and complementary bases for control.

Sources of power

In this section, I argue that four sources of power exist: social, military, ideological, and economic (compare Mann 1986, Earle 1987). A person's political position depends on using one or more of these power sources. The political process involves the selective application of power to control access to these power sources and thus to weaken potential opposition.

Power relationships, either overt or thinly disguised, underlie the dynamics of all societies; however, an ability to control access to power can be realized in the mobilization of resources to finance those institutions of rule on which complex societies rest (Johnson and Earle 1987). I shall first summarize briefly the literature on the alternative sources of power and then go on to argue that the economy is primary, in that it alone permits control over all other sources of power.

Social power

Characterizing all societies, social power derives from the ability to draw political support and resources from close kin, and most probably takes its strength from the intimacy of such kinship bonds. In Yanomamö axe fights, for example, when interpersonal confrontations arise, factions of close kin form such that brothers and cousins side with each respective combatant (Chagnon 1983). Similarly, in the political machinations of Big Men, critical to a man's initial success is the size of his immediate kindred on which he can rely for support (Oliver 1955). In their model of tribal society, Friedman and Rowlands (1977) emphasize its kin-based character and the chief's political strategy to extend his power through marriage. Each marriage unites a leader with an affinal group from which he can draw politically. Among the Trobriand Islanders, the wives that a chief takes enable him to collect affinal gifts which become a rudimentary form of tribute (Johnson and Earle 1987: 216–23; see Malinowski 1935). Webster (1990) offers a recent review of power relations in the chiefdoms of Africa and prehistoric Europe, which also emphasizes their personal, kin-based nature.

Military power

Military power is based on might and intimidation. Gilman (1987) characterizes this as a protection racket in which commoners must give to the élites what they demand, or face reprisal. Certainly military might both maintains and extends political control. In the complex Hawaiian chiefdoms, a military cadre was supported by the paramount chief, who used it to conquer new lands and peoples and to retain control internally (Earle 1978). The warriors of the Polynesian chiefdoms (Sahlins 1958), and of European medieval society, were the most direct instruments of oppression. Control over the manufacture and ownership of the weapons of war could form a basis for political domination (Childe 1951). Traditional African chiefdoms and states, for example, show how control over the technology of war can translate into a monopoly of force (Goody 1971).

Ideological power

Another important source of power is a society's ideology. Chiefs and kings maintain domination through perpetuating the belief that their superiority is part of the natural order, sanctioned by superhuman powers and authority. This is done by hosting ceremonies that present the legitimate ascendancy of the leaders, frequently grounding that ascendent position in history and gene-alogy. For example, in the Merina state of Madagascar (Bloch 1989) and the Mapuche chiefdoms of Chile (Dillehay 1990), leaders use ceremonial occa-sions at burial monuments to proclaim the legitimate genealogical basis for their rule. One is drawn to the parallels in Neolithic and Bronze Age Europe, where the monumental burial grounds of chiefs dominated both the physical and the political landscape. In the complex Hawaiian chiefdoms, rulers were not simply leaders; they were gods who ruled by religiously sanctioned authority (Earle 1978, 1991). Through dress and ceremony, chiefs identified their status with that of the gods. Most impressively, in chiefdoms and states, ceremonial and political spaces were organized according to a cosmic order that created a celestial stage on which leaders acted out their sanctified roles (see Krupp 1983). This theme is exemplified in Geertz's (1980) notion of the nineteenth-century Balinese state as a theatre, and by Fritz's (1986) analysis of spatial organization in a medieval Indian capital. Individuals thus ruled not by might but by their sanctified place in a universal order.

Economic power

Economic power derives from control over the production and distribution of necessary goods. These goods may be either staple supplies or valuables. Staples, such as food and clothing, are goods required by all for subsistence; by contrast, a society's valuables, such as the items used in marriage payments or political displays, are necessary for establishing personal (and group) standing.

The actual sources of economic power are quite variable, depending on how control is exercised by a ruling élite. In the establishment of institutions supporting political integration, leaders must assemble the goods needed to compensate political supporters and others who work for them. Essentially this is a problem of institutional finance for which goods must be mobilized and distributed strategically. In traditional societies, I have distinguished two forms of mobilization – staple finance and wealth finance (D'Altroy and Earle 1985, Brumfiel and Earle 1987). *Staple finance* involves the mobilization of foods, typically by virtue of ownership of the land, followed by their disbursement to provide subsistence for supporters. *Wealth finance* involves procuring valuables through exchange or sponsored manufacture, which are then distributed as a political currency.

Staple and wealth finance are linked to strategies of economic manipulation involving, respectively, feasting and resource ownership, and long-distance exchange. Each strategy has characteristics of stability and centrality that affect the dynamics of political evolution.

Feasting is, to different degrees, important in societies of highly variable social complexity. Friedman and Rowlands (1977) show how leaders in 'tribal' societies amass foods to host feasts. The success of an individual leader and his supporters is measured by the scale of the feast and its associated gift exchanges. Thus among the Mae Enga of New Guinea, a Big Man builds his political position by hosting feasts in the regional *te* exchange cycle; success in these feasts establishes an individual's prestige and translates directly into his ability to attract additional political supporters, marriage partners, and allies (Johnson and Earle 1987: 183–6, Meggitt 1974).

What is described as the redistributional economy of chiefdoms characteristically involves the mobilization and distribution of food and wealth in annual ceremonies (see, for example, Sahlins 1958 on Polynesian chiefdoms). Even in complex states, like the Inca empire, major annual ceremonies were among the most prominent and economically significant of the events staged at political centres.

These feasts are a rudimentary and often composite form of institutional finance. Subsistence goods are mobilized through various means such as personal ties to Big Men, first-fruit obligations to chiefs, and more directly controlled systems of staple production. Wealth items are most commonly obtained through intergroup exchange dominated by leaders and channelled through ceremonial exchange. For example, a Trobriand chief collects goods through extended kin relationships and political patronage, and then invests these goods by hosting competitive feasts that reflect directly on both his prestige and the renown of his political supporters (Johnson and Earle 1987). Payment to supporters is thus direct, in the form of ceremonial food and wealth distributions, and indirect, in the form of increased personal status deriving from association with a successful leader.

One way to stabilize economic control is through the assertion of ownership of the means of subsistence production. In simpler chiefdoms this is often manifested as an overarching system of land tenure in which the chief is considered to be ultimately the owner of all lands by virtue of his religiously sanctioned position as the focal point for the polity. This is the case, for example, among the Bemba of Central Africa (Richards 1939). Social anthropologists frequently emphasize that chiefs control labour by calling on kin relationships. However, although the kinship structure is certainly a basis for the recruitment of support, the ability to centralize kinship responsibilities around the chief (as opposed to anyone else in the society) is based on reputed ownership and rights to allocate productive resources (*contra* Sahlins 1972). For example, the ceremonial and burial monuments of the European Neolithic and Early Bronze Ages can be interpreted as chiefly assertions of ownership over political territories (Earle 1991). By funding the construction of monuments, chiefs transformed the landscape into spaces associated with particular genealogical lines and with the performance of ceremonies that they themselves financed. Thus, chiefs ground their structural power (derived from a hierarchical kinship system represented by the burials) and their ideological power (derived from imputed connections to superhuman forces) in a constructed and owned landscape.

Direct ownership by a ruling élite, however, becomes most explicit in situations where the landscape is developed and divided, as for example in the case of irrigated lands. In the complex protohistoric chiefdoms of the Hawaiian Islands, chiefs developed tracts of irrigated land and then bestowed use rights in specific plots upon commoners in return for the latter's labour on land producing directly for the chief (Earle 1978). In this example of a system of staple finance, ownership is used to mobilize subsistence goods that were then used to support the chiefs, their specialists, and feasts.

Staple finance, based on ownership of irrigated and other developed field systems, probably supports many complex societies. Gilman (1981, 1987) suggests that the evolution of chiefdoms in prehistoric Europe was based on ownership of developed lands, especially in south-eastern Spain, where irrigation was practised. Where social complexity has already emerged, the subsequent abandonment of ceremonial monuments and the development of elaborately laid-out field systems may indicate the establishment of direct land ownership by a ruling élite (Earle 1991). By establishing direct control over subsistence production, élites trade off access to land for corvée labour or a proportion of commoner production.

After feasting and resource ownership, a third source of economic power lies in control over exchange. Exchange in wealth objects (social valuables) is facilitated by the fact that the objects are easily moved over great distances. This is because, in comparison to staples, they have a very high value for their bulk and weight. Therefore, the production and movement of wealth can be centralized and controlled over a broader region (D'Altroy and Earle 1985). In addition to their use in marriage payments and similar social transactions, wealth objects – if they come from afar – may bespeak exotic and esoteric knowledge not available to local commoner populations (Helms 1979). Thus foreign wealth is associated with special ritual knowledge that legitimizes the elevated status of chiefs and links them with the gods.

Chiefs and kings control exchange in wealth by virtue of their foreign contacts (Friedman and Rowlands 1977). In their role as foreign diplomats, chiefs can maintain the trade partnerships through which their wealth is obtained. Through ownership of the means of transportation, chiefs can also monopolize participation in foreign exchanges. For example, the Trobriand chiefs were able to dominate the exchange of *kula* objects by virtue of their ownership of sea-going canoes. Burton (1975) argues that the unusual development of social complexity in the Trobriand Islands, by comparison with neighbouring Melanesian societies, is an outcome of the Islands' marginal position in the *kula* exchange system. This system connects many islands off the eastern tip of New Guinea; most of these islands are relatively close to each other such that inter-island trade is comparatively easy for anyone to engage in, and thus difficult to control. The Trobriand Islands, by contrast, are more isolated than others in the system, and large sea-going canoes are needed to participate in the competitive external exchanges. By owning these canoes, chiefs can control the exchange.

A synthetic model of power and control

Are the four sources of power alternative foundations for political development? To some degree, they are. From my review of the emergence of complexity in chiefdoms, it is evident that different societies have maintained comparable levels of political complexity on the basis of quite different sources of power (Earle 1987, 1989). In his archaeological comparison of the development of chiefdoms in Colombia, Panama, highland Mexico, and coastal Veracruz in Mexico, Drennan (1991) emphasizes the individual character of each sequence; power is manifested quite differently in each case, and these differences are reflected in the developmental trajectories involved. Sociopolitical change can, in at least some situations, be seen as an outcome of factional competition, in which each faction draws its power from a different source (Bradley 1991).

The different sources of power are, however, not equivalent, and they cannot be conceived to be independent of one another. They are not equivalent because emerging élites cannot control them equally. Thus it is not power *per se*, but the ability to control potential power, that is the crucial factor in understanding the evolution of social complexity.

Social relationships constitute a web in which any individual is in the centre of his or her personal network. To try to extend your social support group is thus to draw on relations of increasing genealogical distance, in which the kinship bond is progressively weaker. Any polity based on kinship will harbour a constant tendency towards fission (Sahlins 1958). This was the case, for example, with Polynesian chiefdoms, which were structured on the basis of kinship ranking. When these chiefdoms expanded, they split into independent polities. One would hardly expect a junior line to have retained its allegiance to a senior line, when the expansion of the latter structurally undermined the former's rank and political position. Consequently, it was common for a junior line to break away and to form its own polity (Sahlins 1958, Earle 1978). It is difficult to see, then, how kinship could form the bedrock of a stable arrangement of political power.

Military power, in its application, is manifested as naked force. Although no complex society can exist without it, military force is inherently difficult to control. As proverbial wisdom has it, 'He who lives by the sword dies by the sword.' The military cadre on which a leader depends is often his greatest threat because its force can be quickly turned against him. What gives a monopoly of force and allows that force to be controlled?

Ideological power derives from an accepted notion of order, characteristically backed by religious sanction. But what limits access to esoteric knowledge and religious sanctity? Cannot anyone – a new shaman, priest, prophet, or a man on a soapbox – claim to have direct communication with the gods and create a new religious order? Tradition may constrain what can be done and said, but in this respect it can be used as much against centralizing power as to support it.

Power can be an equalizing force. It is used not only to dominate, but also to resist domination. Complex societies are especially complicated because the competing sources of power are continually dissolving centralization (Mann 1986). Modern state society may actually 'devolve' as the multiplicity of the sources of power makes political centralization impractical.

The evolution of complex social systems, while certainly encompassing complicated and conflicting power relationships, is fundamentally based on control over material conditions, which in turn permits control over the other sources of power. Economic power alone provides the stability that allows for the creation and extension of politically centralized societies. It does this because of the ease with which economic processes can be controlled and used to control the other sources of power.

Economic forces can be controlled by restricting access to the means of production and distribution. In evolutionary development, the intensification of production increases the ease with which control can be established, by gradually replacing labour with technology as the critical limiting factor. For example, with a shift to irrigated agriculture, improved lands become centrally important, and access to these improvements can be regulated by an emerging élite (see Earle 1978). Economic power becomes increasingly centralized as income from owned facilities is used to finance further economic development with the construction of agricultural facilities, the attachment of specialists, and the development of transport technology.

The products of the economic system can also be reinvested materially in control over the other sources of power. A chief's kinship network is extended by polygamous marriages secured through rich gift exchanges (Friedman and Rowlands 1977). Military forces are controlled by providing material support to the cadre and by control over the manufacture and importation of their weaponry (Goody 1971). Ideological power is controlled by the substantial capital required to finance religious institutions and the spectacular ceremonies of legitimation.

The primary dynamic in the evolution of complex society lies in an intensely competitive political arena (Earle 1978, Johnson and Earle 1987). Survival in that arena depends on astute strategies on the part of individual leaders in manipulating their investments in the alternative sources of power and in mechanisms for establishing control. Thus within the political arena there is a social process of leadership selection; at times a leader's success centralizes his polity, but miscalculation can as quickly lead to collapse.

Chiefdoms are characteristically cyclical. For example, the prehistoric Mississippian chiefdoms of the South-eastern United States were never stable; they expanded and declined rapidly as different localities rose and fell from political dominance (Anderson 1990). The different bases of political power were continually tested and the ability to maintain and extend domination formed the foundation for political development. With the emergence of states, the frequency of cycling may be reduced by increasingly centralized and institutionalized control; nevertheless the rise of states anticipates their eventual fall (see, for example, Khazanov 1984).

Élites must continuously seek out mechanisms of domination. These may include the establishment of a police force and of religious institutions. The economy may be systematically manipulated to increase the dependency of the peasantry. However, stability in control may equally be the outcome of long-term changes in the subsistence economy that make commoners dependent on the ruling élite for necessary goods and services that cannot be obtained independently.

Successful systems of domination are characterized by the intertwining of the sources of power and control. Income from a growth-oriented political economy is invested in economic expansion, political alliances, military support, and religious extravaganzas. Thus economic dependence, social relationships, naked force, and sacred legitimacy are continually bound up with one another. The binding thread is the economic flow of resources. Material wealth begets both more wealth and political control.

NOTE

1   Major syntheses abound, including Morgan (1977), Marx (1904), Engels (1972 [1884]), Spencer (1967), Childe (1936, 1951), Steward (1955), Service (1962), Wittfogel (1957), Lenski (1966), Carneiro (1970), Fried (1967), Harris (1977), Glassman (1986), Mann (1986), and Johnson and Earle (1987). Some

excellent histories of social evolutionary theory are also available, among them Lenski (1966), Harris (1968), Service (1975, 1978).

REFERENCES

Anderson, D. (1990) 'Political change in chiefdom societies: cycling in the late prehistoric Southeastern United States'. PhD dissertation, Department of Anthropology, University of Michigan.

Bloch, M. (1989) *Ritual, History and Power*, London: Athlone Press.

Boserup, E. (1966) *The Conditions of Agricultural Growth: the Economics of Agrarian Change Under Population Pressure*, Chicago: Aldine.

Bradley, R. (1991) 'Ideology and economy in the prehistory of Southern England', in T. Earle (ed.) *Chiefdoms: Power, Economy, and Ideology*, Cambridge: Cambridge University Press.

Braun, D. and Plog, S. (1982) 'Evolution of "tribal" social networks theory and prehistoric North American evidence', *American Antiquity* 43: 504–25.

Brumfiel, E. (1976) 'Regional growth in the eastern Valley of Mexico: a test of the "population pressure" hypothesis', in K. Flannery (ed.) *The Early Mesoamerican Village*, New York: Academic Press.

—— (1980) 'Specialization, exchange and the Aztec state', *Current Anthropology* 21: 459–78.

Brumfiel, E. and Earle, T. (1987) 'Introduction', in E. M. Brumfiel and T. K. Earle (eds) *Specialization, Exchange, and Complex Societies*, Cambridge: Cambridge University Press.

Burton, R. (1975) 'Why do the Trobriands have chiefs?', *Man* (N.S.) 10: 544–58.

Carneiro, R. L. (1970) 'A theory of the origin of the state', *Science* 169: 733–8.

—— (1981) 'The chiefdom as precursor of the state', in G. Jones and R. Kautz (eds) *The Transition to Statehood in the New World*, Cambridge: Cambridge University Press.

Chagnon, N. (1983) *Yanomamö: the Fierce People*, New York: Holt, Rinehart & Winston.

Childe, V. G. (1936) *Man Makes Himself*, London: Watts.

—— (1951) *Social Evolution*, London: Watts.

Cohen, M. N. (1977) *The Food Crisis in Prehistory: Overpopulation and the Origins of Agriculture*, New Haven: Yale University Press.

D'Altroy, T. and Earle, T. (1985) 'Staple finance, wealth finance, and storage in the Inca political economy', *Current Anthropology* 26: 187–206.

Dalton, G. (1977) 'Aboriginal economies in stateless societies', in T. Earle and J. Ericson (eds) *Exchange Systems in Prehistory*, New York: Academic Press.

Dillehay, T. (1990) 'Mapuche ceremonial landscape, social recruitment and resource rights', *World Archaeology* 22: 223–41.

Drennan, R. (1991) 'Prehispanic chiefdom trajectories in Mesoamerica, Central America, and Northern South America', in T. Earle (ed.) *Chiefdoms: Power, Economy, and Ideology*, Cambridge: Cambridge University Press.

Durkheim, E. (1933 [1893]) *The Division of Labor in Society*, New York: Free Press.

Earle, T. (1977) 'A reappraisal of redistribution: complex Hawaiian chiefdoms', in T. Earle and J. Ericson (eds) *Exchange Systems in Prehistory*, New York: Academic Press.

—— (1978) *Economic and Social Organization of a Complex Chiefdom: the Halelea District, Kaua'i, Hawaii*, University of Michigan, Anthropological Papers, vol. 63, Ann Arbor: University of Michigan.

—— (1987) 'Chiefdoms in archaeological and ethnohistorical perspective', *Annual Review of Anthropology* 16: 279–308.

—— (1989) 'The evolution of chiefdoms', *Current Anthropology* 30: 84–8.

—— (1991) 'Property rights and the evolution of chiefdoms', in T. Earle (ed.) *Chiefdoms: Power, Economy, and Ideology*, Cambridge: Cambridge University Press.

Engels, F. (1972 [1884]) 'The origin of the family, private property and the state', in K. Marx and F. Engels (eds) *Selected Works in One Volume*, New York: International Publishers.

Evans-Pritchard, E. E. and Fortes, M. (eds) (1940) *African Political Systems*, London: Oxford University Press.

Feinman, G. M. and Neitzel, J. (1984) 'Too many types: an overview of sedentary prestate societies in the Americas', in M. Schiffer (ed.) *Advances in Archaeological Method and Theory*, vol. 7, New York: Academic Press.

Fried, M. H. (1967) *The Evolution of Political Society: an Essay in Political Economy*, New York: Random House.

Friedman, J. (1974) 'Marxism, structuralism and vulgar materialism', *Man* (N.S.) 9: 444–69.

—— (1975) 'Tribes, states and transformations', in M. Bloch (ed.) *Marxist Analyses and Social Anthropology*, New York: Malaby Press.

Friedman, J. and Rowlands, M. J. (1977) 'Notes towards an epigenetic model of the evolution of "civilization"', in J. Friedman and M. Rowlands (eds) *The Evolution of Social Systems*, London: Duckworth.

Fritz, J. (1986) 'Vijayanagara: authority and meaning of a South Indian imperial capital', *American Anthropologist* 88: 44–55.

Geertz, C. (1980) *Negara: the Theater State in Nineteenth-Century Bali*, Princeton: Princeton University Press.

Gilman, A. (1981) 'The development of social stratification in Bronze Age Europe', *Current Anthropology* 22: 1–24.

—— (1987) 'Unequal development in Copper Age Iberia', in E. M. Brumfiel and T. K. Earle (eds) *Specialization, Exchange, and Complex Societies*, Cambridge: Cambridge University Press.

Glassman, R. (1986) *Democracy and Despotism in Primitive Societies: a Neo-Weberian Approach to Political Theory*, New York: Associated Faculty Press.

Godelier, M. (1977) *Perspectives in Marxist Anthropology*, Cambridge: Cambridge University Press.

Goody, J. (1971) *Technology, Tradition and the State in Africa*, Oxford: Oxford University Press.

Haas, J. (1982) *The Evolution of the Prehistoric State*, New York: Columbia University Press.

Harris, M. (1968) *The Rise of Anthropological Theory: a History of Theories of Culture*, New York: Random House.

—— (1977) *Cannibals and Kings: the Origins of Cultures*, New York: Vintage Books.

Helms, M. W. (1979) *Ancient Panama: Chiefs in Search of Power*, Austin: University of Texas Press.

Johnson, A. and Earle, T. (1987) *The Evolution of Human Societies: From Foraging Group to Agrarian State*, Stanford: Stanford University Press.

Khazanov, A. M. (1984) *Nomads and the Outside World*, trans. J. Crookenden, Cambridge: Cambridge University Press.

Kristiansen, K. (1991) 'Chiefdoms, states and systems of social evolution in Northern Europe', in T. Earle (ed.) *Chiefdoms: Power, Economy, and Ideology*, Cambridge: Cambridge University Press.

Krupp, E. C. (1983) *Echoes of the Ancient Skies: the Astronomy of Lost Civilizations*, New York: Harper & Row.

Lee, R. B. and DeVore, I. (eds) (1968) *Man the Hunter*, Chicago: Aldine.

Lenski, G. E. (1966) *Power and Privilege: a Theory of Social Stratification*, New York: McGraw-Hill.

Maine, H. S. (1861) *Ancient Law*, London: John Murray.

Mair, L. (1962) *Primitive Government*, Harmondsworth: Penguin.

Malinowski, B. (1935) *Coral Gardens and their Magic: a Study of the Methods of Tilling the Soil and of Agricultural Rites in the Trobriand Islands*, New York: American Book Co.

Malthus, T. (1798) *An Essay on the Principle of Population*, London: Johnson.

Mann, M. (1986) *The Sources of Social Power*, vol 1: *A History of Power from the Beginning to A.D. 1760*, Cambridge: Cambridge University Press.

Marx, K. (1904) *A Contribution to the Critique of Political Economy*, trans. N. I. Stone, Chicago: Charles H. Kerr.

Mauss, M. (1954) *The Gift: Forms and Functions of Exchange in Archaic Societies*, London: Cohen & West.

Meggitt, M. (1974) 'Pigs are our hearts!: the *te* exchange cycle among the Mae Enga of New Guinea', *Oceania* 44: 165–203.

Morgan, L. H. (1877) *Ancient Society*, Chicago: Charles H. Kerr.

Oliver, D. L. (1955) *A Solomon Island Society: Kinship and Leadership Among the Siuai of Bougainville*, Cambridge, Mass.: Harvard University Press.

Polanyi, K. (1944) *The Great Transformation*, New York: Farrar & Rinehart.

Richards, A. I. (1939) *Land, Labour and Diet in Northern Rhodesia*, London: Oxford University Press.

Sahlins, M. (1958) *Social Stratification in Polynesia*, Seattle: University of Washington Press.

—— (1963) 'Poor man, rich man, big man, chief: political types in Melanesia and Polynesia', *Comparative Studies in Society and History* 5: 285–303.

—— (1968) *Tribesmen*, Englewood Cliffs, NJ: Prentice-Hall.

—— (1972) *Stone Age Economics*, London: Tavistock.

Sanders, W. T. and Webster, D. (1978) 'Unilinealism, multilinealism, and the evolution of complex societies', in C. L. Redman, M. J. Berman, E. V. Curtin, W. T. Langhorne, Jr, N. M. Versaggi and J. C. Wanser (eds) *Social Archaeology: Beyond Subsistence and Dating*, New York: Academic Press.

Service, E. (1962) *Primitive Social Organization: an Evolutionary Perspective*, New York: Random House.

—— (1975) *Origins of the State and Civilization: the Process of Cultural Evolution*, New York: Norton.

—— (1978) 'Classical and modern theories of the origins of government', in R. Cohen and E. Service (eds) *Origins of the State: the Anthropology of Political Evolution*, Philadelphia: Institute for the Study of Human Issues.

Spencer, H. (1967) *The Evolution of Society: Selections from Herbert Spencer's Principles of Sociology*, ed. R. L. Carneiro, Chicago: University of Chicago Press.

Steward, J. (1955) *Theory of Culture Change*, Urbana: University of Illinois Press.

—— (1977) 'The foundations of Basin–Plateau Shohonean society', in J. Steward and R. Murphy (eds) *Evolution and Ecology*, Urbana: University of Illinois Press.

Webster, G. (1990) 'Labor control and emergent stratification in prehistoric Europe', *Current Anthropology* 31: 337–66.

White, L. (1943) Energy and the evolution of culture, *American Anthropologist* 45: 335–56.

—— (1959) *The Evolution of Culture*, New York: McGraw-Hill.

Williams, B. J. (1974) 'A model of band society', *Society for American Archaeology Memoirs* no. 29, Washington, DC: Society for American Archaeology.

Wittfogel, K. (1957) *Oriental Despotism*, New Haven: Yale University Press.

Wright, H. (1984) 'Prestate political formations', in T. Earle (ed.) *On the Evolution of Complex Societies*, Malibu: Undena Publications.

Yellen, J. and Harpending, H. (1972) 'Hunter–gatherer populations and archaeological inference', *World Archaeology* 4: 244–53.

FURTHER READING

Carneiro, R. L. (1981) 'The chiefdom as precursor of the state', in G. Jones and R. Kautz (eds) *The Transition to Statehood in the New World*, Cambridge: Cambridge University Press.

Cohen, R. and Service, E. (eds) (1978) *Origins of the State: the Anthropology of Political Evolution*, Philadelphia: Institute for the Study of Human Issues.

Earle, T. (ed.) (1991) *Chiefdoms: Power, Economy, and Ideology*, Cambridge: Cambridge University Press.

Fried, M. H. (1967) *The Evolution of Political Society: an Essay in Political Economy*, New York: Random House.

Friedman, J. and Rowlands, M. (eds) (1977) *The Evolution of Social Systems*, London: Duckworth.

Glassman, R. (1986) *Democracy and Despotism in Primitive Societies: a Neo-Weberian Approach to Political Theory*, New York: Associated Faculty Press.

Goody, J. (1971) *Technology, Tradition and the State in Africa*, Oxford: Oxford University Press.

Johnson, A. and Earle, T. (1987) *The Evolution of Human Societies: from Foraging Group to Agrarian State*, Stanford, Cal.: Stanford University Press.

Kirch, P. V. (1984) *The Evolution of Polynesian Chiefdoms*, Cambridge: Cambridge University Press.

Lenski, G. E. (1966) *Power and Privilege: a Theory of Social Stratification*, New York: McGraw-Hill.

Mann, M. (1986) *The Sources of Social Power*, vol 1: *A History of Power from the Beginning to A.D. 1760*, vol. 1, Cambridge: Cambridge University Press.

Sahlins, M. D. (1972) *Stone Age Economics*, London: Tavistock.

Service, E. (1962) *Primitive Social Organization: an Evolutionary Perspective*, New York: Random House.

—— (1975) *Origins of the State and Civilization: the Process of Cultural Evolution*, New York: W. W. Norton.

Steward, J. H. (1955) *Theory of Culture Change*, Urbana: University of Illinois Press.

Upham, S. (ed.) (1990) *The Evolution of Political Systems: Sociopolitics in Small-Scale Sedentary Societies*, Cambridge: Cambridge University Press.

Webster, G. (1990) 'Labor control and emergent stratification in prehistoric Europe', *Current Anthropology* 31: 337–66.

White, L. A. (1959) *The Evolution of Culture*, New York: McGraw-Hill.

Wright, H. (1984) 'Prestate political formations', in T. Earle (ed.) *On the Evolution of Complex Societies*, Malibu: Undena Publications.

35

LAW AND DISPUTE PROCESSES

Simon Roberts

INTRODUCTION

A sociology of those specialized, differentiated arrangements which we would unambiguously label 'law' in the contemporary West is in itself problematic. Law lays claim to a dual character: it furnishes the normative 'map' informing the life-world of a society's members as they experience it; and it provides one of the central means through which government exercises a steering role. Hence a sociology of law must be concerned with commonly accepted standards and with imposed regulation, with the domains of 'order' and of 'domination'. Thus the ambition must be to keep these domains analytically distinct, without losing sight of the strands which undoubtedly connect them.

Whatever these difficulties, law's robustly self-defined character at least provides the 'folk' categories upon which a sociological analysis of 'norms' and of 'government' can be brought to bear. But this quality at once poses a problem when we try to imagine what an *anthropology* of law might be. The very concept of 'law', with its claimed separation of the cognitive and normative domains, its identification with a discrete sphere of the 'ought', may not always find counterparts in the small-scale and technologically simple societies which anthropologists have traditionally studied. The institutional arrangements which we associate with law in the West — the differentiation of legal norms; a specialized judiciary within a compartmentalized, self-conscious governmental structure; the emergence of a legal profession — are all specific to a particular socio-political context. Even in functional terms, law's almost inextricable identification with 'government', the exercise of a steering role, raises problems as soon as we move beyond the bounds of the sovereign state.

These concerns, which are surely of a different order from those associated with marking out such broad, general categories as kinship, politics, economics and religion, have not inhibited the growth of legal anthropology. Despite an important shift in perspective, the interest of nineteenth-century scholars in 'primitive law' survived the transition into modern anthropology through

Malinowski's early monograph, *Crime and Custom in Savage Society* (1926). At the same time, Radcliffe-Brown confidently identified 'law' as one of the principal compartments into which anthropological studies should be divided, and in his important essay 'On social structure' (1940) law appears as a separate and privileged element in the proposed 'social physiology'. Subsequently, some of the leading Anglo-American anthropologists of the next generation made their names with books about law; and today, the writings of legal anthropologists provide one inspiration for a new jurisprudence in the West, enlarging the realm of legal studies to embrace formerly 'suppressed discourses' of 'non-state law' (Cotterrell 1983, Fitzpatrick 1992, Teubner 1992).

While 'law' has thus provided a durable label, the appearance of continuity in anthropological interest is deceptive. Looking back, what we see is an unbroken succession of quite different 'anthropologies of law'. In the mid- and later nineteenth century 'primitive law' featured prominently in efforts to characterize, and provide an ancestry for, 'modernity'. Under Malinowski and Radcliffe-Brown, these evolutionary studies were replaced by an anthropology of 'order'. After the Second World War, legal anthropology became the study of dispute processes. This focus gave way in turn to a new legal anthropology which examined the part played by law in the imposition of colonial domination, and which has now itself been transformed into a 'legal pluralism' which cuts across boundaries between the anthropologies and sociologies of law. Obviously, the above compartments have not been watertight, and the sediments of these successive anthropologics of law may suggest the elements of what legal anthropology might become. In what follows, however, I attend to them individually, in the order of their appearance.

PRIMITIVE LAW AND THE CHARACTERIZATION OF MODERNITY

An enduring source of interest in 'primitive law' lay in the ambition of classical and recent social theorists to characterize the condition of modernity. In the course of this project, 'tradition' was invoked both as a means of highlighting modernity through contrast and as an aid in reconstructing the route along which we (in the West) have travelled to the present. The widespread invocation of an opposition between 'tradition' and 'modernity' may also conceal shifting levels of focus: upon differences between traditional and modern persons; upon the diverse ways in which traditional and modern societies 'hold together'; upon contrasting features of traditional and modern authority. Thus the opposition may be located at the levels of action, order or domination and these levels may be mutually entangled. At the level of domination, a major focus of interest has been on the origin and development of the state. In these studies, 'law' is deployed in varied ways; sometimes it is itself the focus of attention, as it was for Maine in *Ancient Law* (1861), sometimes it is invoked as a means of understanding society, as in Durkheim's *De la Division du travail social* (1893).

In *Ancient Law*, and in his later *Dissertations on Early Law and Custom* (1883), Maine mapped out a broad transition from small, kin-based groups to larger, territorial units. While the famous 'status to contract' formulation suggests a concern with different foundations of social solidarity, his history is one of 'government' rather than 'order'. For Maine, the story of society is a story of decision-making. The very origin of social life is identified in the steering role exercised within a group of kin by the senior male agnate. These old patriarchs made decisions on an *ad hoc* basis; no consistent rules underpinned the decisions they took, yet government was supposed to be by adjudication by the senior male, before whom all disputes were brought.

In the form of society that followed, collections of these small groups of agnates became clustered together under chiefs, but the (sometimes fictional) assumption of shared kinship remained the basic organizing principle. Then came the territorial stage, in which members identified themselves through their common occupation of a defined tract of land, rather than through kinship. Around the end of the second stage and the beginning of the third, 'law' developed as rulers began to pronounce the same judgments in similar situations, providing their decision-making with an underlying set of rules. Later in the development of territorially based societies, the settlement of disputes fell into the hands of a specialized élite, who alone had access to the principles to be followed in their resolution. As Maine wrote: 'What the juristical oligarchy now claims is to monopolize the *knowledge* of the laws, to have the exclusive possession of the principles by which quarrels are decided' (1861: 7). There followed the 'era of codes', and so on, but we can leave the developmental process at this stage.

Several important features are clear from this summary. First, for Maine there were no structural changes in the process of dispute settlement over the three fundamental stages of societal development. From the senior male agnate onwards, disputes were resolved by decision, handed down by a third party; there was no suggestion of negotiatory modes of settlement giving way to processes of third-party adjudication. Secondly, the presence of a normative basis for decision-making was the key attribute of law for Maine, and the emergence of this feature heralded the transition from the pre-legal to the legal world. Thirdly, there was the later development of specialization as legal rules became separated off from other rules operating in society. Thus for Maine, social life is the product of 'government', law develops in the course of that process, and the fundamental way in which kingly power is revealed is through adjudication.

In examining the foundations of social order the classical sociologists, writing towards the close of the nineteenth century, continued to make use of explicit oppositions between 'tradition' and 'modernity'. On one level the writings of Durkheim and Weber can be seen as a bridge between scholars like

Maine and Morgan on the one hand, and modern social anthropology on the other. They posed a 'problem of order' in terms which are recognizably the same as those in which it was addressed by Radcliffe-Brown and Malinowski. But they remain remote in that their central interest, like that of their predecessors, was in understanding modernity; the past, along with contemporary examples of the primitive, was still invoked in the project of getting to grips with the present. They are also remote in their partly concealed presupposition, reinforced by the poor quality of the ethnography then available, that governmental action is an inevitable concomitant of life in a social world.

In opposing 'mechanical' and 'organic' solidarity in *De la Division du travail social* (1893), Durkheim purports to elucidate the different ways in which traditional and modern societies hold together rather than to examine the nature of governmental action. But the use he makes of law in this discussion reveals a conflation of the problems of order and of domination. In arguing that the predominance of 'repressive' sanctions can provide us with a criterion for identifying societies characterized by mechanical solidarity, and by similarly linking 'restitutive' sanctions with organic solidarity, primitive societies were credited with regimes of criminal law, and hence with mechanisms of adjudication and coercive governmental action.

In his *Economy and Society* (1978 [1917]) Weber invokes an opposition between tradition and modernity primarily at the level of government, rather than at the level of society. This opposition is used to elucidate the different kinds of legitimacy claims made by traditional and modern (rational–legal) authorities, and in an examination of the underpinnings of traditional and modern forms of adjudication. For Weber, 'law' was a creature of the modern world, linked to the application of general rules, and served to differentiate bureaucratic government and specialized, rule-based adjudication from their 'traditional' forerunners.

Although an assumption that developed law is an achievement of the modern world is implicit in a great deal of English legal anthropological writing, explicit interest in legal evolution had fallen away by the 1920s. In North America, on the other hand, this interest was sustained in such works as Hoebel's *Law of Primitive Man* (1954), Redfield's influential essay on 'Primitive Law' (1967) and Newman's *Law and Economic Organisation* (1983). All three works search through the ethnographic record for the pre-legal and the proto-legal, mapping out with anthropological findings the path along which law has evolved.

While processes of state formation have now become a source of renewed interest among social theorists (see Giddens 1986, Mann 1986), 'law' has not yet found a prominent place in these discussions. It is perhaps surprising that no one has pursued in detail Maine's tantalizing aside, in his *Dissertations on Early Law and Custom*, to the effect that the origins of adjudication are intimately linked to those of kingship (1883: 160). But Bloch's recent account of the formation and expansion of the Merina kingdom in Madagascar is entirely consistent with the idea that 'law', as a differentiated corpus of regulations, is best seen as a by-product of the business of rule (Bloch 1971). Initially brought into being as 'custom', in the sense of an undifferentiated repertoire of communal understandings, it is co-opted by rulers seeking to establish and consolidate their ascendancy. Bloch presents a scenario of would-be kings seeking to associate themselves with the traditional norms of the acephalous rice-growing Merina communities of the valleys, and ultimately presenting themselves as the source of these norms, at the same time seeking to play an adjudicatory role in local-level dispute processes.

THE PROBLEM OF ORDER

From the 1920s, a second anthropology of law began to develop. It appeared as part of the general changes which were noticeable in anthropology at that time, with a shift in attention away from invoking 'the primitive' as a means of characterizing modernity, and away from interest in larger questions having to do with change and historical development. There was also an explicit reaction against attempts to understand particular features of the culture under observation in terms of survivals from some earlier 'stage'; every institution was rather to be understood in terms of its contemporary 'function'.

Once sustained attention came to be directed, at close quarters, to those small-scale, relatively simple societies which were found right across the colonial world, some new questions arose. It quickly became clear that many of these societies had no obvious centralized authority, let alone the differentiated institutional arrangements associated with government in the West. For observers coming from cultures where 'order' had become linked to the accomplishments of kingship or some other form of self-conscious administration, this seemed problematic. Here were societies without 'kings, courts and constables', as Malinowski put it (1934: lxii); and yet they were not the savage anarchies which Hobbes had postulated as the inevitable alternative to the presence of a sovereign. How were the evident coherence and regularity of these groups to be explained? What held them together? The absence of explicit governmental arrangements, and of anything looking like a legal system, placed the 'problem of order' at the top of the agenda. It also raised a difficulty for observers interested in law. Did these societies have 'law'? If so, what form did it take and what were its central attributes?

Malinowski's response to the problem of order, at least so far as the Trobriand Islanders whom he had studied were concerned, was that compliance with socially approved norms was ensured through the complex of reciprocal economic obligations which bound members of the society to each other. Among these relationships the simplest bound together the group of fishermen who shared a boat on the lagoon. Each of these men carried out a particular task in manning the boat and the net, and through its performance acquired a right to a share in the catch. Repeated failure to accompany the fishing expeditions of 'his' boat would deprive a man of his share of the fish. Another relationship bound the fisherman on the lagoon with an inland partner, the yam grower. (Both fish and yams were staples of the Trobriand diet.) The fisherman supplied the inland farmer with fish, and the farmer supplied the fisherman with yams. If either party persistently failed to honour his side of the arrangement, he would soon find himself without an essential element in his overall subsistence budget: no fish, no yams. Malinowski suggested that while a breakdown of this kind could possibly be endured for a while, it would over time have such a destructive effect on other relationships that in the end the recalcitrant partner would be forced back into line or obliged to live elsewhere. One of the other relationships which could be directly affected was that between husband and wife. In Trobriand society, instead of being responsible for feeding his own household – himself, his wife and children – a man's efforts are directed towards providing for his sister and her husband and their children, while his own needs in this respect are met by his wife's brother. It is not hard to see how the breakdown of any one of these relationships will immediately place the remaining strands in jeopardy. Under such circumstances the mechanism of enforcement lies within the complex of relationships itself, and no external sanction is necessary.

Malinowski presented this account of the forces securing the coherence of the Trobriand social world in the form of an explicit attack on what he saw as the conventional view, as represented in the work of Durkheim. In *De la Division du travail*, Durkheim had claimed that in societies characterized by 'mechanical solidarity' order is secured primarily through a shared repertoire of common understandings which are comprehensively internalized by the societies' members – a position which Durkheim partially reiterated in his last book, *Les Formes élémentaires de la vie religieuse* (1912), where he described the inhabitants of the primitive world as more embedded in society than their modern counterparts. Malinowski ridicules Durkheim for envisaging people in primitive societies as virtual automata, blindly and unthinkingly complying with long-standing customs. His vigorous polemic appears to set up an exciting argument, but the issue is never really joined since Durkheim's discussion is located at the level of rules and structure, whereas Malinowski's eye is on the actions and motivations of persons.

Malinowski's contemporary, Radcliffe-Brown, adopted a position much closer to that of Durkheim. His early *The Andaman Islanders* (1922) had a 'rule-centred' quality; and although he stressed the need for 'sanctions' to ensure compliance with rule, implying attention to motivation, his theoretical work (see especially Radcliffe-Brown 1952) was largely focused at the level of structure. At first glance, the argument here seems polemical and capable of ready solution, but while subsequent ethnographies have struggled to achieve a multi-dimensional quality, they have on the whole revealed the clear imprint of either a Radcliffe-Brownian or a Malinowskian approach. Overall, it has proved difficult to achieve a satisfactory balance of 'rule' and 'practice', to articulate the level of 'order' with the level of 'action' (Comaroff and Roberts 1981).

In retrospect, a striking quality of *Crime and Custom in Savage Society* is that Malinowski seems to escape effortlessly from longstanding presuppositions in social, political and legal theory about the need for certain actors to occupy positions of command if stability is to be sustained in social life. But these assumptions were not easily abandoned in legal anthropology. In *Kapauku Papuans and their Law* (1958), for example, Pospisil reasserted the idea that the presence of authorities playing command roles is an essential feature of human association, and he has subsequently sought to reinterpret the ethnography which appears to cast doubt upon this proposition. While it would be absurd to underplay the importance which 'government' – in the form of self-conscious steering mechanisms – assumes in contemporary polities, questions of 'order', in the sense of the reproduction of pattern in the social world, remain all too easily conflated with those of command and domination.

While *Crime and Custom* inaugurated an anthropology of law which embraced broad questions of order and social control, and so by-passed potentially troubling questions about the nature of law and its institutional location in stateless societies, arguments about the definition of law and the conditions under which it is to be found have continued. On the whole, the working definitions of law offered by anthropologists have been influenced strongly by the predominantly imperative and positivist orientation of Anglo-American legal theory. In his entry on 'law' in the 1933 edition of the *Encyclopedia of the Social Sciences*, Radcliffe-Brown explicitly followed Roscoe Pound, the American jurist, in identifying law as 'social control through the systematic application of force in politically organized society' (1933: 202). Malinowski immediately responded, in his Introduction to Hogbin's *Law and Order in Polynesia* (1934), by reasserting the position he had adopted in *Crime and Custom*. Subsequently a divide has remained between those who have held to institutional definitions derived from Western legal and political theory, those who have followed Malinowski in adopting a conception of law which does not distinguish it from social control in general, and those who have declined to talk about 'law' at all outside the context of the modern state.

These disagreements surfaced in a different form in the 1950s, in the context of a celebrated debate between Max Gluckman and Paul Bohannan (see Nader 1969: 337–418). In *The Judicial Process among the Barotse* (1955), Gluckman, following Schapera (1938), had made deliberate use of the linguistic, conceptual and institutional categories of Western law. Bohannan, for his part, in his study of *Justice and Judgment among the Tiv* (1957), claimed that such Western categories are inappropriate for understanding the legal concepts, procedures and rules of a non-Western culture. Ultimately, however, the argument raised worries as to the extent to which it is proper to talk about 'law' at all in a cross-cultural context (Bohannan 1957: 4–6, Moore 1978: 135–48).

AN ANTHROPOLOGY OF LAW AS THE STUDY OF DISPUTE PROCESSES

The 1950s saw the appearance of a number of major ethnographies built around case histories of 'dispute', and for a couple of decades this work became a central concern of leading anthropologists in Britain and North America. Bailey (1960), Bohannan (1957), Fallers (1969), Gluckman (1955), Gulliver (1963, 1971), Pospisil (1958) and Turner (1957), major figures in post-war social anthropology, all made or consolidated their reputations with such ethnographies.

At first glance it would appear that this shift from an anthropology of law focused on the problem of order to an anthropology of law as the study of dispute process took place rather abruptly. Yet there was an undercurrent of continuity. The 'processual' emphasis in most of these studies builds directly on strands present in Malinowski's work. 'Dispute' also became an obvious focus in the context of sustained participant observation; the very accessibility of public quarrels made it likely that they would become the centrepieces of the research. Disputes were also topical at this moment for another reason. In Africa, at least, dispute management was one of the main tasks of the traditional and neotraditional authorities established under 'indirect rule'. Whether or not the agency under observation was directly drawn into colonial local government, 'disputes' were flagged for special attention by that system.

For a majority of the authors mentioned above, a conscious decision to focus on disputes was also influenced by the example of an earlier work, *The Cheyenne Way* (1941). This book, on a North American Indian group, was the product of a collaboration between Karl Llewellyn, a law professor, and Adamson Hoebel, a social anthropologist. Their focus on 'trouble cases' flowed from Llewellyn's commercial law teaching and research at Columbia Law School. A member of what is now labelled the Realist School, Llewellyn thought that law was best approached and understood from the study of superior court litigation: the 'cases' which were the product of such processes were the central materials with which law teachers and their students worked. Confronted with Hoebel's desire to study Cheyenne law, it seemed natural to suggest that he should look for the equivalents of these cases in the Cheyenne context. In the end, the book they wrote together was constructed around remembered case histories from the Cheyenne past, recalled for Hoebel by elderly Cheyenne informants. According to Llewellyn and Hoebel, it initially proved difficult to get their informants to understand what it was they wanted from them; but in the end a series of 'trouble cases' was assembled, from which, in true lawyerly manner, the two researchers managed to extract what they saw as some fundamental principles of Cheyenne law. This work is

969

vividly and confidently written, and it is easy to recognize the possibilities which anthropologists immediately saw in it. Malinowski (1942) himself reviewed it favourably just before he died.

Looking back, it does seem that *The Cheyenne Way* is vulnerable to the criticism that Llewellyn's lawyerly preoccupation with superior court litigation obtruded too strongly into this attempt to understand conflict in another culture. There must be some question as to just how much of Cheyenne culture survived accommodation within the format of an American law school text. But that kind of criticism cannot be made of the rich and wide-ranging studies which followed. These made advances in at least four important directions: freedom from a rigid adjudicatory model of decision-making; escape from a narrow view of conflict as necessarily pathological and linked to rule breach; progress towards a more sophisticated understanding of the relationship between rules and outcomes; and rejection of an inflexible 'law–war' dichotomy.

In *Ancient Law* and in subsequent writings, Maine had treated third-party decision-making as the basic means of resolving disputes across all known societies. From the old patriarchs who stood at the head of the earliest social groups to Victorian High Court judges, he saw the mode of resolution as one of imposed decision; it was just that as different stages of civilization were reached, different kinds of people made the decisions and new criteria underpinned their judgments. Today, now that we recognize the possibility of 'order' without 'command', and are thus no longer constrained to invoke the necessity of the king and the judge (although in the West still expecting to find them somewhere in the picture), it becomes possible to characterize the range of dispute-processing institutions in a far less restricted way.

On the basis of the ethnographies of dispute which appeared in the 1950s and 1960s a number of tentative typologies of dispute institutions were put forward (Gulliver 1963, Abel 1974, Koch 1974). These emphasized various features, such as the presence or absence of third-party intervention, or the form which such intervention might take in those cases where it was to be found. A measure of agreement also began to emerge as regards the essential range of variation which empirical studies disclosed. At the heart of these variations appear to lie three basic forms which settlement-directed discourse may take: the disputants may feel their way towards a settlement through bilateral negotiation; they may try to resolve the matter with the help of a neutral mediator; or they may submit the quarrel to an umpire for decision. My discussion of these alternatives in the following paragraphs conforms closely to Roberts (1979: 69–71).

Bilateral negotiation represents the least complex form of settlement process. Here the rival disputants approach each other without the intervention of third parties and try to bring the dispute to an end through discussion. No intermediaries or supporters are involved; the achievement of communication and the subsequent process of settlement lie in the hands of the two parties alone. A variation of this mode of settlement occurs when partisans align themselves in support of one or other of the disputants; but while the 'strength' of the respective sides may be altered by this procedure, the structural form of the encounter remains unchanged.

In each of the remaining modes of settlement this bilateral element is removed by the intervention of third parties in some intermediate position. Where this role is mediatory, the third party helps the disputants towards their own solution rather than imposing a solution upon them. The most limited form of mediation arises where the third party acts as a 'go-between'. His role is passive in the sense that while he operates as a bridge or a conduit between the two disputants, he does no more than carry messages backwards and forwards between them. Through this means of communication the disputants themselves reach some kind of settlement. The go-between has not actively contributed by tendering advice or urging particular avenues of conduct; but he has enabled the disputants to communicate with each other. This form of mediation may be contrasted with a more active one, in which the third party takes a positive part in promoting a settlement. His intervention may take the form of advice, suggested solutions, reasoned pleas, or even impassioned cajoling, threats and bullying. Unlike the go-between, he actively pursues a settlement, while remaining ostensibly neutral and without seeking to impose an outcome.

Under the third mode of settlement the neutral party seeks to resolve the dispute by making a decision, rather than by assisting the disputants towards their own solution. Within this broad category we can distinguish two types of umpire, whom I shall call the arbitrator and the adjudicator. The arbitrator derives his authority to decide the dispute from the invitation of the disputants themselves, who have voluntarily submitted to his decision. The adjudicator, by contrast, derives his authority from some office in the community, and intervenes to impose a decision by virtue of that office rather than by the invitation of the disputants. In some respects this last distinction is of limited importance, as both kinds of umpire possess the authority to resolve a dispute in the face of competing claims by imposing a decision. Nevertheless, the distinct sources from which this authority is derived may (as we shall see later in this section) be of critical importance.

This typology underlines some of the important variables which affect these different processes: the achievement of a solution by negotiated agreement or imposed decision; the presence or absence of third-party involvement; the nature of the intervener as either partisan or neutral; and the derivation of authority in decision-making. It also points to what may be considered the crucial feature of any dispute process, namely the location of the power to decide the outcome.

The lawyer's 'folk' view of conflict as pathological, as arising out of rule breach and requiring remedial intervention, is central to the analysis in *The Cheyenne Way*. Underlying this view is a determination to keep the 'legal' and the 'political' apart, to treat disputes associated with departures from commonly accepted understandings as somehow different from those associated with competitive processes in which there is a struggle for a scarce resource which one may win and another lose without either departing from mutually accepted standards of conduct. Although this distinction is deeply rooted in Anglo-American legal ideology, it does not provide a safe point of departure for the study of dispute processes in other cultures. One of the strengths of Turner's discussion, in his *Schism and Continuity in an African Society* (1957), of the cyclical processes through which the headship of Ndembu villages devolves, lies in his demonstration of the way in which claims about 'wrong doing' are closely interwoven with struggles for political ascendancy and competition for resources.

Conventional accounts of judicial decision-making in Anglo-American courts postulate a clear-cut relationship between rule and decision: the facts adduced by the parties identify for the judge the relevant rule which is then invoked as determining the outcome. This seemingly mechanical process is little more than a caricature of judicial decision-making, even in the superior courts; but while it may provide an ideal model of how things should be done in a particular legal culture, it is not a model which provides a safe starting point in understanding the dispute processes of other societies. The legal ethnographies produced since the 1950s reveal wide differences from one society to another in the nature of the normative repertoire and in the manner in which the repertoire is invoked in the context of dispute. Norms may be vague and general, seldom explicitly invoked, but none the less implicitly shaping the contours of claim and argument; or they may be clear-cut and detailed, exposed to explicit discussion and scrutiny in the context of dispute, and seen as determinative of the outcome. Or alternatively, while regarded as important, norms may be treated as but one kind among many of the resources that can be invoked.

Another durable strand in legal ideology is the time-honoured idea that fighting and talking are opposed – in the sense that talking tends to be rule-governed whereas fighting does not. Introducing a volume of papers on *Law and Warfare*, Bohannan (1967) promotes this idea in his comment that there are 'basically two forms of conflict resolution: administered rules and fighting, Law and War' (1967: xiii). A number of carefully observed accounts of intercommunal fighting in New Guinea indicate that this formulation should be treated with caution. They reveal that such fighting almost invariably takes on an institutionalized form, in some cases constituting elaborate set-piece encounters (e.g. Rappaport 1967). Elsewhere conflict is taken even further into the sphere of ritual, as in the Eskimo *nith*-songs, where the participants 'fight' with words (Weyer 1932). Here, fighting *is* talking, rather than being opposed to it.

One ground on which anthropological studies of dispute processes have been fairly criticized is their tendency to present disputes in very much the way that lawyers do, as typically involving the clash of two relatively evenly matched individuals. It is argued that the implications of stratification and the presence of control from the centre have frequently been ignored (Cain and Kulcsar 1981). This neglect can perhaps be partially explained as a consequence of the kind of society which anthropologists have typically studied; but as soon as we move away from small-scale, relatively egalitarian cultures, at least three broad categories of dispute have to be distinguished:

1 Disputes between parties in relationships of relative equality.
2 Disputes which cross lines of stratification (e.g. confrontations between lord and villein; between employer and employee).
3 Disputes which arise directly out of a ruler's efforts to govern and in which the ruler himself or his agents will be directly involved.

Dispute processes within each category may be expected to take a different shape; and variations in institutional structure may be observable, as also in the criteria invoked by the disputants and by those attempting to achieve an outcome.

AN ANTHROPOLOGY OF LAW AS THE STUDY OF LAW IN THE COLONIAL CONTEXT

The anthropologies of law as the study of order and of dispute processes tended to focus upon small, local communities, cut away from the larger colonial context within which nearly all of them had become encapsulated by the time the studies discussed above were carried out. This excision was typically a conscious choice, taken because it was the uniqueness of the society in question that was of central interest. But from the 1970s – and in a few cases from much earlier – this fiction tended to be dropped: the implications of 'contact' were foregrounded and the points of contact of small local communities with the larger encapsulating colonial order became the explicit focus of interest. Thus a historical dimension and an interest in change were restored to legal anthropology. The important questions became: What was the link between the governmental arrangements and normative understandings of the pre-colonial world, and those prevailing in the same localities in the post-colonial present? What was 'customary law', and what was its relationship to the colonial project? What was the relationship between the colonial legal order and life in the localities?

In jural terms what happened is largely uncontested. Across Africa, Asia and the Pacific, overarching, territorially based legal orders were imposed, founded on the metropolitan law of whichever happened to be the colonial power concerned – Britain, France, Germany, Holland, or Portugal. Subject to that dominant legal order, the pre-existing normative orders of local encapsulated groups enjoyed qualified, parallel survival. At the same time, in many territories, 'traditional authorities' became ever more caught up in the project of colonial rule. In the case of Britain, this was first a matter of necessity — there were simply not enough expatriates to go round; later, a virtue was made out of necessity, as native intermediaries were employed under the policies of 'indirect rule'. The provenance of these authorities was rather varied: in some instances they had occupied apical positions in pre-colonial polities; in others they were virtually the creations of the colonial power. This led, in formal terms, to the development of a 'dual system' of government, of which the 'native' (later 'local' or 'customary') courts became part. The national law provided the regime of norms in the superior courts and the magistrates' courts; and 'native' or 'customary' law provided it in the local courts. In general terms, these arrangements survived to the end of the colonial period; and in some countries they still survive today.

The way in which this process has been regarded by scholars has undergone considerable modification, in line with changing views concerning both the nature of the pre-colonial world onto which the colonial legal order was superimposed, and the character and effects of the colonial project itself.

In general, older accounts offer a picture of order and continuity, later ones of abrupt transformation. The earlier view depicted an imposition of colonial rule upon a stable egalitarian consensus. Life in most encapsulated communities was said to have altered little: at first, because the colonial power lacked the resources to bring about rapid, ameliorating change; later, because the survival and continuity of 'traditional' life was deliberately fostered under the policies of 'indirect rule'.

Later accounts (e.g. Chanock 1985, Ranger 1983, Snyder 1981, Woodman 1983) tend to contradict this picture rather sharply. They tell a story of discontinuity and abrupt transition which left members of encapsulated communities exposed to the arbitrary rule of neotraditional authorities, and drawn to their disadvantage into new forms of economic relations. Colonial local government is now presented as having had few links with the past: authorities had to be 'found' and placed in charge of formerly acephalous groups, or, at best, holders of existing offices were made to perform roles quite different from their accustomed ones. The 'customary law' which was recognized in colonial legislation, and developed and 'applied' in the newly established 'native' courts, was a tendentious montage with only a superficial connection with the past, supportive of the project of colonial rule, and entrenching the position of elders over juniors, men over women. Some have even called it an 'invented tradition' (Ranger 1983).

Overall, this revision is a valuable one, a necessary antidote to earlier accounts which had postulated a deceptively harmonious and egalitarian precolonial context, and which had overemphasized the extent to which longstanding indigenous institutions had been there in the first place and then survived. There is no doubt, either, of the coercive nature of 'indirect rule', or about the disruption to the lives of colonized peoples resulting from their association, often involuntary, with European economic operations.

974

Nevertheless, the new picture is arguably still an incomplete one, and care must now be taken to avoid distortions of an opposite kind to those present in the earlier accounts. There are real difficulties with seeing 'customary law' solely in terms of domination. Similarly there are problems in regarding it as of entirely recent manufacture. Lastly, there must be doubt as to how far 'colonial customary law' was successfully transmitted into, and assimilated within, the life-worlds of most colonized peoples.

First, while it was important, as a counter to the consensus implied in earlier writings, to reveal the extent and nature of colonial domination, this is by no means the whole story. Even if we freely concede the coercive nature of local government in the colonial period, and the ideological quality of what passed for 'customary law', an exclusively one-way, top–down view of the colonial encounter would be misleading. There is no need to repeat here the now well-articulated and generally accepted concerns about placing too literal a reliance upon a conception of 'sovereign' power (Foucault 1984). 'Power' resides at different levels, takes on diverse forms, and runs in all directions (Giddens 1985). Thus while 'customary law', in the sense of the repertoire of rules applied in the colonial courts, *did* provide an instrument of rule, it also offered avenues of escape and resistance for the ruled. Similarly, 'customary law' in the different sense of the meanings and commitments which furnished the life-worlds of indigenous peoples, while subject to covert penetration and co-option (de Sousa Santos 1980), also provided the means to achieve qualified autonomy.

The insistence of scholars like Chanock, Snyder and Ranger that 'customary law' is of recent manufacture, a creature of the colonial period rather than the pre-colonial past, is helpful in a number of ways. It is essential to recognize that the relationship between contemporary and past forms is, at the very least, problematic. Moreover the association between 'custom' and a supposedly egalitarian context must be questioned. Further, the specific idea of 'invention' restores and gives prominence to a conception of agency, the essential notion that custom is linked to the affairs of living men and women – that it is both at the root of action and the product of it. But there are difficulties in pressing this view of customary law too far. First, it risks conflating two separate, if interlinked spheres: the 'customary law' of the colonial and post-colonial courts, and that which furnishes the everyday life-world of local people. Second, the connotation of novelty, of a clean break, which 'invention' carries, draws attention *away* from crucial aspects of what was happening. The very strength of customary law, the source of its supposedly coercive power, lay in the links it could claim with a past, established and approved state of affairs. Foreign novelties do not lay claim through existing commitments; yet that – if anything – is what custom does. Thus we should be looking not for novelty but for the exploitation of an existing repertoire, or the artificial sustaining of ancient forms, with detrimental, constraining effects upon the ruled.

The idea of an 'invented' tradition seems also to imply an impoverished and grossly simplistic understanding of the operation of ideology. It calls up a vision of the manufacture, transmission and assimilation, intact, of some new worldview, and the corresponding destruction of the pre-existing cognitive and normative foundations of the life-world. Much more persuasive is an account of ideology as working with what is already to hand, covertly upon and within an existing life-world, transforming without eradicating. Such an account seems to me to be essentially that suggested by Althusser (1977), and in the specific context of customary law, by de Sousa Santos (1980). But even here we must not neglect the very significant extent to which some cultures are resistant to transformation through co-option. Empirical observations reveal wide and interesting variations in the response of encapsulated groups to the experience of colonial rule.

The problem of transmission and assimilation raises a final concern over recent revisions. How far, in fact, *were* colonial subjects affected in their everyday lives by colonial 'customary law'? It would be foolish to underestimate the consequences of economic changes during and following the colonial period, and the operation of colonial customary law was undoubtedly in some respects supportive of those changes. But we should nevertheless keep an open mind as to the extent to which the worldviews of those in power came to the attention of the ruled. Even where they did, there is a question over how far they ever came to be shared. As Weber indicated in *Economy and Society*, the importance of ideology may lie more in supporting the agents of those in power than in engendering commitments among the ruled. Recent writings, including those with a direct focus upon the colonial period, offer confirmation of this view (see Hobsbawm and Ranger 1983).

THE ANTHROPOLOGY OF LAW AS LEGAL PLURALISM

The shift to a focus on the operation of law in the colonial context brought with it a number of important gains. First, it reinforced the recognition that law had a political dimension, in the sense of its implication in processes of domination. Thus, 'power' remained in the centre of the picture, to which it had already been drawn in the more sophisticated discussions of dispute processes (Starr and Collier 1989: 1–25). As a result, attention inevitably moved to the role which 'the rule of law' and the process of adjudication might play in the legitimation of particular forms of government. Accordingly, the ideological aspects of law achieved a new prominence, as did the nature of legal ritual. Secondly, the focus upon the operation of law in the colonial context forced scholars to give much more careful thought to the nature of indigenous governmental arrangements and normative understandings in the pre-colonial world, and to the transformation which these subsequently underwent (for an important example, see von Benda-Beckman 1979). In this respect, the process of incorporation of the 'traditional authorities' into regimes of colonial and post-colonial government was of central interest (Mann and Roberts 1991).

All of this posed some troubling questions, which ultimately resolved them-selves into a single problem: with the imposition of a national, formally dominant legal order upon the diversity of pre-colonial indigenous communi-ties, how can we best conceptualize the relationship between what was going on at the centre, in 'the secretariat'; and what was happening on the periphery, in the localities? One way of looking at this is in terms of what Kidder (1979) has vividly called 'the static hypodermic model'. This involved a vertical, top–down, command view of the operation of law in the colonial world. Rules enacted by government at the centre were transmitted to the localities, where they produced direct, matching changes in behaviour, resulting in 'develop-ment' or progress towards modernity. 'Law', made at the centre, superseded existing 'customary' regimes.

Pospisil, in his early work, *Kapauku Papuans and their Law* (1958), rejected this extreme positivism. 'Law' should be located at different points in the social world, wherever 'authorities' could be found imposing normatively based deci-sions. Accordingly, whether you looked at the developed West, or at the terri-tories then undergoing colonial encapsulation, 'law' should be seen as residing at a number of hierarchically ranged, more or less discrete, 'legal levels'. In so far as these levels were connected, the linkage was still seen to be vertical, with change being transmitted down from the top. Most important, perhaps, was Pospisil's rejection of an exclusive focus upon state law, allowing as much attention to be given to other normative fields. Why, he asked, should national law be privileged: should we not treat as 'law' the normative understandings prevailing within local groups at *any* level? For Pospisil, norms operative at the village level were just as much 'law' as those enacted at the centre.

A more flexible approach was proposed by Moore in her seminal essay, 'Law and change: the semi-autonomous social field as an appropriate area of study' (1973). Here, Moore substitutes the concept of 'social field' for that of 'legal level'. Normative orders, including that presented by the national legal system, are best seen as partially discrete, but nevertheless overlapping and interpenetrating social fields, within which meaning is communicated on a two-way, interactive basis. The social field is identified in terms of its 'semi-autonomy', by 'the fact that it can generate rules and customs and symbols internally, but . . . is also vulnerable to rules and decisions and other forces emanating from the larger world by which it is surrounded' (Moore 1978: 55).

Moore was not talking exclusively about 'law', but rather about 'normative fields' in general; nevertheless her approach proved immediately congenial to legal anthropologists. She depicted change as a fluid, interactive process, full of imponderables and unintended consequences.

Pospisil's insistence that in examining the 'legal' we should not focus on the level of national law alone, and Moore's lead in turning attention to the *rela-tionship* between coexisting normative fields, together constituted the principal agenda and approach for the anthropology of law during the latter part of the 1970s and the 1980s. Under the label of 'legal pluralism' the anthropology of

977

law virtually became the study of how several normative regimes may coexist in the same social field. Legal anthropologists formed themselves into a professional association under the grandiose title of the 'Commission on Folk Law and Legal Pluralism'; the journal *African Law Studies* re-emerged as the *Journal of Legal Pluralism and Unofficial Law*; a conference was held at Bellagio in 1981 to inaugurate this movement, and a large literature emerged which sought to re-present the anthropology of law as legal pluralism and to delimit this new field (see specially, Griffiths 1986, Merry 1988, Allott and Woodman 1985). Following Moore's lead, societies of the West became as much a focus of attention as did those of the post-colonial world.

In retrospect, this new anthropology of law brought important insights. First, the move away from 'legal centralism' (Griffiths 1986), from according privileged attention to national law, and from treating it as unproblematically determinative of social forms, represented something of a release for legal scholars. Equally significant was the way in which the relationship between adjacent, semi-autonomous fields came to be perceived – as fluid, interactive and imponderable. The very focus of lawyers' attention on a wider slice of the social world, which legal pluralism implied, was in itself welcome; as was a new openness to social and anthropological theory.

But there are also costs entailed in 'melting it all together as "law"' (Moore 1978: 81). As Merry notes (1988: 878), to extend the term law to forms of ordering that are not state law may lead to a loss of analytic rigour. Depending upon the focus of analysis, while 'recognizing the existence of and common character of binding rules at all levels, it may be of importance to distinguish the sources of the rules and the sources of effective inducement and coercion' (Moore 1978: 81). The distinctive character of state law in the West derives from its implication in the growth of a particular form of government; this provenance accounts for crucial differences between it and other normative orders. Correspondingly, in labelling other normative orders as 'law', it is important to avoid the trap of investing them with the attributes of state law. This seems to be exactly the trap into which Pospisil himself had fallen. Insisting that 'Kapauku law' takes the form of norms derived from legal decisions, which have to enjoy the attributes of 'authority' and 'intention of universal application' in order to have a legal quality, he imputes an adjudicative, command character to Kapauku processes which seriously distorts their nature. While most advocates of the approach of legal pluralism are entirely conscious of the hazards of distorting non-state processes through investing them with a framework derived from Western law, the designation of the approach as one of *legal* pluralism should perhaps sound a warning note.

It is significant that the field of the anthropology of law has become almost exclusively occupied by lawyers rather than anthropologists. Until the 1960s it was occupied almost entirely by anthropologists, with lawyers showing relatively little interest; but since then the position has been entirely reversed. And because it has been colonized by lawyers, it has inevitably been treated as an area of 'legal' scholarship. Overall, it is difficult to avoid the impression that the invocation of 'legal pluralism' has more to do with the entrenchment of an academic discipline than with the struggle to understand the social world.

CONCLUSION

The potential gains in understanding to be achieved with the rejection of 'legal centralism' were made clear in the writings of Malinowski more than sixty years ago; it is good that these should now be recognized by lawyers working within a pluralist paradigm. These gains can be consolidated by giving equal attention to different normative orders, and by sensitivity to the ways in which these orders intersect and are interwoven.

Inevitably this extension of the legal gaze brings with it renewed, agonized attempts to delineate the 'legal'. Teubner's proposal that this boundary should be marked by the use of 'the binary code of legal communication' (1992: 1451) is the latest in a heroic line; but it is hard to forecast a wider consensus for this effort than for any of its predecessors. More worrying is the fact that sociological understanding is immediately imperilled once we impose an imprint of 'law' across plural normative fields. Merry (1988: 878) senses this in reflecting upon the boundary problems and renewed struggles for definition which a 'legal' pluralism involves:

> Why is it so difficult to find a word for nonstate law? It is clearly difficult to define and circumscribe these forms of ordering. Where do we stop speaking of law and find ourselves simply describing social life? Is it useful to call these forms of ordering law? In writing about legal pluralism, I find that once legal centralism has been vanquished, calling all forms of ordering that are not state law by the term law confounds the analysis. The literature in this field has not yet clearly demarcated a boundary between normative orders that can and cannot be called law.

These difficulties are self-imposed, inherent in the project of *legal* pluralism. In the context of such a project they are inevitable, given the extent to which our ideas about law are bound up with Judaeo-Christian beliefs on the one hand, and the development of secular government in Europe on the other. The specific, situated character of those roots should be enough to warn us against the enlargement of the realm of law which legal pluralism demands. Looking forward, the anthropology of law should be content to resolve itself into the respective anthropologies of norms and of government, attentive to the distinct but nevertheless related problems of 'order' and 'domination'. Within the ambit of these general enquiries, 'law' is best viewed as an interesting folk category, encountered under specific and limited conditions.

REFERENCES

Abel, R. L. (1974) 'A comparative theory of dispute institutions in society', *Law and Society Review* 8(2): 218–347.

Allott, A. N. and Woodman, G. (eds) (1985) *People's Law and State Law*, Dordrecht: Foris.

Althusser, L. (1977) 'Ideology and the ideological state apparatus', in *Lenin and Philosophy and Other Essays*, London.

Bailey, F. G. (1960) *Tribe, Caste and Nation*, Manchester: Manchester University Press.

von Benda-Beckmann, F. (1979) *Property in Social Continuity: Continuity and Change in the Maintenance of Property Relationships in Minangkabau, West Sumatra*. The Hague: Nijhoff.

Bloch, M. (1971) 'Decision-making in councils among the Merina of Madagascar', in A. Richards and A. Kuper (eds) *Councils in Action*, Cambridge: Cambridge University Press.

Bohannan, P. (1957) *Justice and Judgment among the Tiv*, London: Oxford University Press for the International African Institute.

—— (1967) 'Introduction', in P. Bohannan (ed.) *Law and Warfare*, New York: Natural History Press.

Cain, M. and Kulcsar, K. (1981) 'Thinking disputes: an essay on the origins of the dispute industry', *Law and Society Review* 16: 375–402.

Chanock, M. (1985) *Law, Custom and Social Order*, Cambridge: Cambridge University Press.

Comaroff, J. L. and Roberts, S. A. (1981) *Rules and Processes: the Cultural Logic of Dispute in an African Context*, Chicago: University of Chicago Press.

Cotterrell, R. M. B. (1983) 'The sociological concept of law', *Journal of Law and Society* 10: 241–55.

de Sousa Santos, B. (1980) 'Law and community: the changing nature of state power in late capitalism', *International Journal of the Sociology of Law* 8: 379–97.

Durkheim, E. (1893) *De la Division du travail social*, Paris: Alcan.

—— (1912) *Les Formes élémentaires de la vie religieuse*, Paris: Alcan.

Fallers, L. (1969) *Law Without Precedent*, Chicago: University of Chicago Press.

Fitzpatrick, P. (1992) *The Mythology of Law*, London: Routledge.

Foucault, M. (1984) *The History of Sexuality*, vol. 1, Harmondsworth: Penguin.

Giddens, A. (1985) *The Nation-State and Violence*, Cambridge: Polity Press.

—— (1986) *The Constitution of Society*, Cambridge: Polity Press.

Gluckman, M. (1955) *The Judicial Process Among the Barotse of Northern Rhodesia*, Manchester: Manchester University Press.

Griffiths, J. (1986) 'What is legal pluralism?', *Journal of Legal Pluralism* 24: 1.

Gulliver, P. H. (1963) *Social Control in an African Society*, London: Routledge & Kegan Paul.

—— (1971) *Neighbours and Networks*, Berkeley: University of California Press.

Hobsbawm, E. J. and Ranger, T. O. (eds) (1983) *The Invention of Tradition*, Cambridge: Cambridge University Press.

Hoebel, E. A. (1954) *The Law of Primitive Man*, Cambridge, Mass.: Harvard University Press.

Kidder, R. L. (1979) 'Toward an integrated theory of imposed law', in S. B. Burman and B. Harrell-Bond (eds) *The Imposition of Law*, New York: Academic Press.

Koch, K. F. (1974) *War and Peace in Jalemo*, Cambridge, Mass.: Harvard University Press.

Llewellyn, K. N. and Hoebel, E. A. (1941) *The Cheyenne Way*, Norman: University of Oklahoma Press.

Maine, H. S. (1861) *Ancient Law*, London: John Murray.

—— (1883) *Dissertations on Early Law and Custom*, London: John Murray.

Malinowski, B. (1926) *Crime and Custom in Savage Society*, London: Kegan Paul, Trench & Trubner.
—— (1934) 'Introduction', in H. I. Hogbin, *Law and Order in Polynesia*, New York: Harcourt Brace.
—— (1942) 'A new instrument for the study of law – especially primitive', *Yale Law Journal* 51: 1237–54.
Mann, K. and Roberts, R. (eds) (1991) *Law in Colonial Africa*, Portsmouth, NH: Heinemann.
Mann, M. (1986) *The Sources of Social Power*, vol. 1, Cambridge: Cambridge University Press.
Merry, S. E. (1988) 'Legal pluralism', *Law and Society Review* 22: 869–96.
Moore, S. F. (1973) 'Law and change: the semi-autonomous social field as an appropriate area of study', *Law and Society Review* 7: 719–46.
—— (1978) *Law as Process*, London: Routledge & Kegan Paul.
Nader, L. (1969) *Law in Culture and Society*, Chicago: Aldine.
Newman, K. (1983) *Law and Economic Organisation*, Cambridge: Cambridge University Press.
Pospisil, L. (1958) *Kapauku Papuans and their Law*, New Haven: Yale University Publications in Anthropology no. 54.
Radcliffe-Brown, A. R. (1922) *The Andaman Islanders*, Cambridge: Cambridge University Press.
—— (1933) 'Primitive law', in *Encyclopedia of the Social Sciences* 9: 202–6. New York.
—— (1940) 'On social structure', *Journal of the Royal Anthropological Institute* 70: 1–12.
—— (1952) *Structure and Function in Primitive Society*, London: Cohen & West.
Ranger, T. O. (1983) 'The invention of tradition in colonial Africa', in E. Hobsbawm and T. O. Ranger (eds) *The Invention of Tradition*, Cambridge: Cambridge University Press.
Rappaport, R. A. (1967) *Pigs for the Ancestors*, New Haven: Yale University Press.
Redfield, R. (1967) 'Primitive Law', in P. Bohannan (ed.) *Law and Warfare*, New York: Natural History Press.
Roberts, S. (1979) *Order and Dispute*, Harmondsworth: Penguin.
Schapera, I. (1938) *A Handbook of Tswana Law and Custom*, London: Oxford University Press.
Snyder, F. G. (1981) 'Colonialism and legal form', *Journal of Legal Pluralism* 19: 49–90.
Starr, J. and Collier, J. F. (eds) (1989) *History and Power in the Study of Law*, Ithaca, NY: Cornell University Press.
Teubner, G. (1992) 'The two faces of legal pluralism', *Cardozo Law Review* 13: 1443–62.
Turner, V. (1957) *Schism and Continuity in an African Society*, Manchester: Manchester University Press.
Weber, M. (1978 [1917]) *Economy and Society*, trans. and ed. G. Roth and C. Wittich, Berkeley: University of California Press.
Weyer, E. M. (1932) *The Eskimos*, New Haven: Yale University Press.
Woodman, G. R. (1983) 'How state courts create customary law in Ghana and Nigeria', in H. W. Finkler (compiler) *Papers of the Symposia on Folk Law and Legal Pluralism, XIth International Congress of Anthropological and Ethnological Sciences*, Vancouver, Canada, 19–23 August 1983.

FURTHER READING

Abel, R. L. (1974) 'A comparative theory of dispute institutions in society', *Law and Society Review* 8(2): 218–347.

Bohannan, P. (1957) *Justice and Judgment among the Tiv*, London: Oxford University Press for the International African Institute.

Cain, M. and Kulcsar, K. (1981) 'Thinking disputes: an essay on the origins of the dispute industry', *Law and Society Review* 16: 375–402.

Fallers, L. (1969) *Law without Precedent*, Chicago: University of Chicago Press.

Gluckman, M. (1955) *The Judicial Process among the Barotse of Northern Rhodesia*, Manchester: Manchester University Press.

Griffiths, J. (1986) 'What is legal pluralism?', *Journal of Legal Pluralism* 24: 1.

Gulliver, P. H. (1963) *Social Control in an African Society*, London: Routledge & Kegan Paul.

Hamnett, I. (ed.) (1977) *Social Anthropology and Law*, New York: Academic Press.

Hoebel, E. A. (1954) *The Law of Primitive Man*, Cambridge, Mass.: Harvard University Press.

Koch, K. F. (1974) *War and Peace in Jalemo*, Cambridge, Mass.: Harvard University Press.

Llewellyn, K. N. and Hoebel, E. A. (1941) *The Cheyenne Way*, Norman: University of Oklahoma Press.

Malinowski, B. (1926) *Crime and Custom in Savage Society*, London: Kegan Paul, Trench & Trubner.

Merry, S. E. (1988) 'Legal pluralism', *Law and Society Review* 22: 869–96.

Moore, S. F. (1978) *Law as Process*, London: Routledge & Kegan Paul.

Nader, L. (1969) *Law in Culture and Society*, Chicago: Aldine.

Newman, K. (1983) *Law and Economic Organisation*, Cambridge: Cambridge University Press.

Pospisil, L. (1958) *Kapauku Papuans and their Law*, New Haven: Yale University Publications in Anthropology no. 54.

Roberts, S. (1979) *Order and Dispute*, Harmondsworth: Penguin.

Turner, V. (1957) *Schism and Continuity in an African Society*, Manchester: Manchester University Press.

36

COLLECTIVE VIOLENCE AND COMMON SECURITY

Robert A. Rubinstein

Anthropologists have taken a long and varied interest in studying armed conflict and aggression. Acts of collective violence, however, have relatively rarely been a principal topic of anthropological concern. Instead, descriptions of collective violence have been embedded in ethnographies or in theoretical discussions focused primarily on such other topics as social organization, legal systems, or political evolution (see the previous two articles in this volume). Moreover, this attention has most often been paid within the context of studies of small, well-bounded 'preliterate' or 'primitive' societies – the traditional subjects of anthropological study.

Although collective violence is usually considered only incidentally, and in the context of small-scale societies, it has occasionally formed the main subject of anthropological study. This shift of focus has often occurred at times of major international crisis – like the Second World War, the Vietnam War, or the threat of nuclear war – when anthropologists have sought to bring their knowledge to bear on contemporary circumstances (see, for example, Malinowski 1941, Swanton 1943, Fried *et al.* 1968, Worsley and Hadjor 1987).

As a result of the direct and indirect anthropological study of collective violence, many approaches to the topic have been elaborated and the relevant literature is large. It would be impossible to review it all. In this article, therefore, I have selected for review those anthropological materials relevant to the understanding of collective violence and security in the modern world. I focus primarily on how anthropological data and theory can contribute to contemporary discussions of collective violence and security, as these are carried out by the various professional communities – of diplomats, analysts and politicians – which are charged with deciding related policy issues. I argue that during the last forty years these communities have been dominated by methods and topics of analysis which produce too narrow an understanding of the social and cultural phenomena involved.

The article is divided into four general sections. First I present a brief overview of some of the concerns that anthropologists have traditionally brought to the study of violence and security. This first section is highly schematic, intended simply to indicate the range of approaches that anthropologists have taken, and to direct the interested reader to the relevant literature. The second section describes the tenor of contemporary discussions of collective violence and security. The assumptions underlying the dominant forms of analysis are presented and some examples are given to illustrate the results of applying these assumptions. The third section focuses on how the introduction of anthropological materials forces us to enlarge our understanding of two key concepts: 'power' and 'collective violence'. The fourth discusses how anthropology can directly contribute to avoiding, managing, and resolving collective violence by attending to cultural aspects of negotiations.

SOME THEMES IN THE ANTHROPOLOGICAL STUDY OF VIOLENCE

Several broad themes characterize the anthropological literature on violence and aggression. Perhaps the most frequent is the discussion of the biological basis of human aggression. At various times during this century theorists have asserted that individual and collective violence is a necessary result of the circumstances of human biological evolution. Early claims to this effect were grounded in a relatively crude biological determinism, while later claims have been based in more sophisticated elaborations of biological theory.

For instance, basing his work on ethology and a general understanding of the evolution of aggressive behaviour in non-human species, Lorenz (1963, also Ardrey 1966, Morris 1967) argued that humans have a heritage of intraspecific aggression. This heritage, he further argued, is especially troublesome because it is linked to the rapid development of weapons and yet is unconditioned by biological mechanisms of restraint, as are aggressive drives in other species. Thus he writes (1963: 42):

> It is more than probable that the destructive intensity of the aggression drive, still a hereditary evil of mankind, is the consequence of a process of intraspecific selection which worked on our forefathers for roughly forty thousand years, that is, throughout the Early Stone Age. When man reached the stage of having weapons, clothing, and social organization, and so overcoming the dangers of starvation, freezing and being eaten by wild animals, and these dangers ceased to be the essential factors influencing selection, an evil intraspecific selection must have set in. The factor influencing selection was now the wars waged between hostile neighbouring tribes.

This view of the biological basis of human aggression has been widely criticized as based on faulty inference, and especially on inappropriate and oversimplified analogies between the behaviour of modern humans and that of non-human animals (see Dunbar in this volume, Article 27). More recently, the growth of sociobiology has raised anew the issue of the biological basis of human aggression (Wilson 1975, 1978). Chagnon (1988: 985), for instance, recently reported that among the Yanomamö Indians of Brazil, 'men who have killed have more wives and offspring than men who have not killed', and he went on to argue, on these grounds, that reproductive variables were critical to understanding tribal violence.

Such sociobiological attempts to account for human aggression in genetic and evolutionary terms have, however, been as vulnerable as their ethological precursors to the charge of depending upon faulty inference. Moreover they fail to specify a mechanism of action (Sahlins 1976), and are ultimately unhelpful in accounting for *specific* forms of violence.

The general consensus currently is that attempts to understand violent human action in terms of some hereditary load are misconceived, especially when an innate tendency towards aggression is invoked in order to attribute collective violent action to an essential human nature (Hinde 1988). Indeed, as Koch has observed:

> It really does not matter whether or not one assumes an innate drive toward aggression. History and comparative anthropology show that people fight not because they need to satisfy some instinct, but because their interests clash with those of others. The recognition, scope, and relative value of these interests are culturally defined.
> (Koch 1974: 52–5)

A second approach widely adopted in the anthropological analysis of human collective violence views it in ecological terms, as serving to preserve a viable relationship between a population and the environmental resources available to it (Vayda 1968, 1974, Tefft 1974). For example, in a study of the Maring of Highland New Guinea, Rappaport (1967) attempts to show that population pressure leads to conflicts whose effect is to redistribute human population over available land.

Although such ecological accounts have been proposed independently of the biologically deterministic views of human aggression reviewed above, the two approaches are often contrasted. This contrast is particularly evident in anthropological discussions of warfare in Amazonia. Anthropologists dispute among themselves whether Amazonian warfare is best accounted for by reference to protein scarcity, reproductive fitness, or something else altogether (see Gross 1975). Those who take an ecological view argue that game animals are relatively scarce in the area and that protein shortage is therefore a limiting aspect of the environment (e.g. Ross 1980: 38–39, Ross and Ross 1980). Their opponents, however, argue that rather than being due to limitations of the area's carrying capacity, Amazonian warfare results either from pressures of the socio-political environment (Chagnon 1967), or from the reproductive benefit it confers (Chagnon 1988; see Chagnon and Hames 1979). Although attempts have been made to reconcile these positions (Ferguson n.d.), warfare in Amazonia remains to be adequately accounted for.

Anthropological concern with collective violence, and especially with understanding and defining war, has in part been motivated by the objective of interpreting the growth and evolution of human societies. Many analysts view warfare as having been particularly important for the growth of states as centralized political systems (Sahlins 1968, Cohen 1983, 1986, Ember and Ember 1988, Vincent 1990: 90–2). Political evolution is treated in detail by Earle, in Article 34 of this volume. Here I merely note that whatever positive role it may have played in the development of 'early' states, collective violence no longer supports the stability of states in the contemporary world (Foster and Rubinstein 1986, Beeman 1989).

More generally, as anthropologists have gained more experience in the analysis of collective violence, it has become clear that human violence and aggression cannot adequately be accounted for in terms of relatively simple models, and that it is essential to appreciate their complex and multi-causal nature (Foster and Rubinstein 1986, Rubinstein and Foster 1988). In this light, Vayda (n.d.) has reconsidered his earlier attempts at an ecological explanation of primitive war, and finds them inadequate. He argues that his previous accounts placed too much of an explanatory burden on the annexation of territory. By contrast, he now concludes that 'we need to be more aware of the context-relatedness of human behavior and of how answers to "why-questions" differ depending upon differences in assumptions'.

Finally, the anthropological literature reflects a concern with the definition of war. Anthropologists have sought to distinguish warfare as a unique form of collective violence. Yet because collective violence is a complex social phenomenon, a single definition of warfare necessarily proves inadequate. As Koch (1974: 52–3) put it, 'linguistic distinctions between raids, feuds, and war tend to obscure rather than elucidate the problem of explaining why people resort to violent methods of confrontation in pursuit of their interests'.

It is principally because collective violence is resorted to as a means by which groups pursue their own perceived interests (Wright 1968, Herran 1988, Foster 1989), which are patterned by socially and culturally based symbolic forms, that attempts at all-encompassing definitions and explanations of war and collective violence necessarily fail. In place of global explanations of war, a more particularistic approach, one that adequately deals with the multiple levels – from small scale to large scale – on which collective violence occurs, yields greater understanding. In addition to the economic, ecological, and material concerns that are routinely included in attempts to define and understand collective violence, it is also necessary to consider culturally specific symbolic and organizational systems. Anthropological enquiry is particularly well suited to the identification of such systems (Foster and

Rubinstein 1986, Rubinstein and Foster 1988, Turner and Pitt 1989), and I focus on these in the remainder of this article.

ETHNOCENTRISM, VIOLENCE AND SECURITY IN INTERNATIONAL AFFAIRS

Recent critiques of anthropological writing have argued that despite the claim of the discipline to present a view of other societies and cultures 'from the inside', the images of the 'other' which it presents are distorted by their passage through the warped lenses of Western, logocentric discourse. It is therefore somewhat out of fashion to offer anthropological descriptions of other societies and cultures as possible correctives to ethnocentrism. But while no description of another culture can be perfect, some conceptions of culture, and the descriptions that derive from them, are for some purposes more adequate than others (Rubinstein 1992). This is especially the case when we come to consider approaches to violence and collective security.

Despite the lively intellectual debate surrounding this topic, discussion has been dominated during the past forty years by a single and widely held approach, often called 'political realism'. The vigour of the debate tends to obscure the fact that this approach continues to furnish the context within which issues of collective violence and security are presented and evaluated. Furthermore, it forms the symbolic matrix that shapes discourse about these issues in contemporary circumstances (Cohn 1987, Brasset 1988). Political realism places a premium on the production of information that is characterized as 'objective', 'rational' (in a logical sense), amenable to formal modelling, and derived from 'correct scientific methods' (Beeman 1986, Rubinstein and Foster 1988: 3–7). In an important sense, the role accorded to such information in the analysis of social and cultural life derives from, and perpetuates, a pervasive ethnocentrism.

A few examples can illustrate how an ethnocentric hegemony is reinforced in discussions of violence and collective security. Although 'culture' has become a category of some concern in diplomacy, attempts to understand its role in negotiations tend to rely on caricatures of national negotiating and decision-making styles. These attempts seek to specify how the national culture affects negotiations in order that diplomats may be advised about what to expect in their dealings with representatives of different countries. In contrast to anthropological descriptions of the dynamic and symbolic nature of social and cultural life, the resulting accounts treat culture as homogeneous and stable. They discover 'cultural patterns' by collecting the impressions of diplomatic and military personnel of 'what it was like to deal with *them*', or by gathering impressions from the personnel of a third country. Because of the elements of self-presentation or national self-interest that generally permeate these accounts, the descriptions they provide are highly unreliable (see, for example, Fahmy 1983). Nevertheless, they form the basis of the

987

caricatures of culture that inform most discussions of world affairs. Thus, for example, interviews with Polish personnel have been used to reveal the cultural basis of Soviet negotiation strategies (Checinski 1981), and Middle Eastern negotiation styles are portrayed as deriving from the haggling behaviour sometimes observed in bazaars (Binnendijk 1987).

In discussions of collective violence and security in the Third World, the local-level concerns that motivate less powerful nations and local groups tend to fall from view. Instead, a privileged position is accorded to the interests and interpretations of the superpowers, and diplomatic and military initiatives are treated from the perspective of ideological, political, and economic superpower contests. A recent study of constraints on United States policy in relation to Third World conflicts (Hosmer 1985; see also Record 1985) reflects this excessively narrow-minded view of global affairs. This report considers United States involvement in the Third World almost entirely from the perspective of military concerns. It treats that involvement primarily in relation to the Soviet Union, for the most part ignoring the specific interests and concerns of Third World countries and groups. This preoccupation with East–West relations, to the exclusion of numerous regional concerns around the world, is revealed in the fact that in his study, Hosmer makes *explicit* reference to the Soviet Union on no fewer than 90 of the monograph's 130 pages, and on those pages where he does not do so, it is only because he dwells instead on Chinese communist interests or actions.

This kind of ethnocentrism continues to hold sway despite the recent superpower détente, and the collapse of the Soviet Union. An otherwise instructive, recent three-volume analysis of the *Lessons of Modern War* examines wars fought mainly in and by Third World actors principally from the perspective of relations with great powers outside the Third World, and by emphasizing military technology. Local-level political, social and cultural factors are neglected, being considered 'only to the extent necessary to understand military events' (Cordesman and Wagner 1990: xv). This neglect is remarkable because, especially during the last decade, many anthropological studies have appeared which show how analyses that ignore cultural and symbolic factors are bound to fail (Foster and Rubinstein 1986, Worsley and Hadjor 1987, Rubinstein and Foster 1988, Turner and Pitt 1989). To the extent that attention has been paid to the human arrangements underlying the formulation and implementation of policy, it has largely been by resort to formal, econometric or game-theoretic models of behaviour, decision-making, and negotiation (Brams 1985, Ball and Richelson 1986). And for the most part, the sociocultural processes which qualify the application of these models have not been considered (Rubinstein 1988a: 23–31). Worsley's (1982, 1986, 1987) discussions of the Third World, and of the consequences of excluding cultural considerations from analysis, provide a more general perspective on this issue.

POWER AND COLLECTIVE VIOLENCE IN
ANTHROPOLOGICAL PERSPECTIVE

The perspective of political realism, embodied both in the aforementioned examples and in most contemporary discussions of violence and security, depends, as anthropologists especially have pointed out, on a number of unwarranted assumptions (see, for example, Foster and Rubinstein 1986, Rubinstein and Foster 1988, Kim 1983, Beeman 1986, 1989, Myrdal 1969). Here I wish to draw attention to three assumptions, in particular, that anthropological work has seriously questioned: that actions in relation to collective violence and security are based on objective social scientific knowledge; that they are rational to the extent that they conform to formal models of econometric analysis or game theory; and that the proper unit of concern for understanding such action in the contemporary world is the nation state.

As regards the first point, it is rarely acknowledged by advocates of the realist approach that it is the approach itself that determines what counts as analytically relevant information. Thus the local-level meanings and symbolic significance entailed in conflict situations are dismissed out of hand (Kim 1983: 9). Yet facts, of course, are never 'just facts'. They depend upon value judgements that can be consciously presented and explored or, for whatever reasons, hidden. As Myrdal (1969: 51–2) has observed:

> Biases in social science cannot be erased simply by 'keeping to the facts' and refining the methods of dealing with statistical data. Indeed data and the handling of data are often more susceptible to tendencies toward bias than 'pure thought'. . . . Biases are thus not confined to the practical and political conclusions drawn from research. They are more deeply seated than that. They are the unfortunate results of concealed valuations that insinuate themselves into research at all stages, from its planning to its final presentation. As a result of their concealment, they are not properly sorted out and can thus be kept undefined and vague.

When it comes to rationality, the realist approach assumes that both decision-making and action are mechanical processes: once a group has the 'objective facts' at its disposal, it (through its leaders) will act rationally, according to the predictions of formal models. For a typical example, we could cite the philosophy and methods used by the RAND Corporation Strategy Assessment Center. The work of the Center is based on automated war games in which rule-guided decision models for managing behaviour and for co-ordinating responses are substituted for human decision-makers. RAND representatives argue that

> the power of the approach is due in large part to its emphasis on realism (relative to more standard approaches) and to the use of artificial intelligence and force modelling techniques that make behaviour rules and other key variables transparent and interactively variable.

> (Davis and Winnefeld 1983: vii)

The rationality implied here is of a purely 'technical' kind, which excludes any consideration of substantive cultural and social influences (Simon 1983). It might perhaps be more appropriately described as logical rather than rational.

A corollary of the realist approach is that decisions and actions are attributed to corporate groups, and especially in the last twenty-five years or so these have generally been taken to be nation states. As a result, local or indigenous views of intergroup relations are simply disregarded (Rubinstein and Foster 1988). Anthropological analyses, to the contrary, are most often concerned with interactions below the level of the nation state. In one such analysis, Beeman (1986, 1989) demonstrates how United States foreign policy decisions regarding the Middle East operate on the assumption that the world consists only of nation states, and he shows that this leads analysts to ignore crucially relevant information.

In general, political realism presents us with a telling example of what can happen when the original reasons for adopting particular approaches, forms of evaluation, or indices of measurement are ignored or forgotten, such that these techniques become ends in themselves, regardless of their applicability in actual contexts of human affairs. When this takes place in any field of inquiry, the result is to narrow the perspective to the point at which it must ultimately fail to yield a convincing account (Rubinstein et al. 1984). Yet it is just this kind of process that has characterized discussions of power, violence and security.

Power

Discussions of the relationships among political groupings often focus on disparities in access to advanced military technologies. For the most part, power is taken in these discussions to refer to the range of measurable military, technological or other such outcomes that can be effected by one group in its relations with other groups (cf. Thibault and Kelly 1959, Cordesman and Wagner 1990). In this sense, power is the ability to coerce other individuals or groups to change their behaviour in some intended direction (Dahl 1969, Zartman 1974). The result of this kind of reasoning is that power has come to be measured in terms of such indicators as concession rates, economic or military pay-offs, and the like.

When policies are developed on the basis of such realist assumptions, groups that control the disposition of material resources tend to be regarded as powerful. Groups that do not control these resources are taken to be powerless. Only physical and material resources are included in calculations of relative power. Kim (1983: 9) notes that 'the concept of "power" in mainstream realism is excessively narrow and limited. This realism respects only material and physical power and is contemptuous of "normative power".... It denies the existence of the world normative system.' By taking power as resting only on material strengths, the domain of activities that are considered legitimately to represent power is artificially restricted. This narrow view is indeed thoroughly *un*realistic, for it ignores the entire range of traditional and non-Western conceptions of power. These alternative conceptions are much like what Kim (1983: 44) calls *normative* power, which 'is the ability to define, control and transform the agenda'.

By explicating how this normative dimension of power works through studies of actions below the level of the nation state, anthropologists have focused on areas of experience that, at first glance, might appear to have little to do with collective violence and security. Of course, they have not ignored the material and technological aspects of power, for to do so would be naïve (sec Otterbein 1973). However, anthropological work recognizes that normative power can work even in the face of apparently superior power, as measured in material terms. According to Wahrhaftig and Lukens-Wahrhaftig (1977: 231), the Cherokee conceive of this power as

> sacred, not secular. It is an aspect of permanence granted each people at creation. Autonomy and self-government are inseparable attributes of primordial power; these are in the created nature of peoples, for each of the many distinct peoples set forth at creation, of which Cherokees are one, was created self-governing. In Cherokee myth, even animals and plants meet in council to determine their own course of action – often with greater wisdom than humans. Such power *is*; it cannot be gained.

More generally, this power can be said to accrue to a person through the experience of leading a morally good life, which is marked by dealing with other people through social relations that are considerate and mutually respectful. It is the *process* of living according to principle, not material force, that produces power. 'To live according to one's laws is to be powerful' (Wahrhaftig and Lukens-Wahrhaftig 1977: 231).

The hardships experienced by Native Americans in the United States as a result of military defeat, disease, external political control, and other kinds of disasters and deprivations have been accompanied by material powerlessness. In the face of such material hardships the focus of Indian groups on *how* things are done rather than on *what* is done has allowed them to retain a sense of the continuity of their ways of life and thus to retain their normative power. As the case of the Cherokee demonstrates in particular, this normative power has consequences in the political arena. It is their concept of, and respect for, normative power that has enabled the Cherokee to build autonomous social, political, and economic institutions, despite the repeated exercise of secular, material power by whites (Gearing 1958, Wahrhaftig and Lukens-Wahrhaftig 1977). Indeed, normative power is rarely the inconsequential factor that it is sometimes made out to be. To the contrary, normative power is an important force which must be understood and counted in any reckoning of the 'balance of power'.

Anthropological descriptions of normative power and its consequences show that actions based in such conceptions of power can successfully challenge materially more powerful groups. For example, the Dené (Kehoe 1988) have successfully opposed uranium mining and other nuclear-related actions, and the Cherokee have successfully resisted their economic and cultural extinction (Rubinstein and Tax 1985). The Palestinian *intifada* is also an example of the force of such non-materially based power (Schiff and Ya'ari 1990). The *intifada*, like the actions of the Dené, the Cherokee, and of other indigenous peoples, or of people in Iran (Bateson 1988; see also Beeman 1986) and China (Potter 1988), shows how power grounded in non-material, symbolic, normative aspects of social and cultural life can achieve very real effects which, although they cannot be neatly estimated by some quantitative index, make a significant difference in the political arena.

Collective violence

Just as conceptions of power are culturally patterned, so conceptions of collective violence have been channelled by cultural understandings, both lay and professional. For the most part, discussions of collective violence have focused on observable acts of violence launched by one group against another, on the size and relations of military forces and on technological aspects of fighting capabilities. Collective violence is described in terms of its intensity as this is defined by battlefield deaths or the military technology used in a dispute. Thus, for example, in deciding what to consider as 'war', only those conflicts in which some critical number of deaths directly results from combat are included (Cohen 1986). The 'Correlates of War' Project undertaken at the University of Michigan, for instance, defines a conflict as war only if it involved at least 1,000 battlefield deaths. And a 'conflict spectrum' (Sarkesian 1986: 116) has been defined in terms of the destructive capabilities of the armaments employed or in terms of the number of deaths directly resulting from combat.

It is obvious, however, that collective violence extends well beyond the range of military aggression. War and violence, as contemporary political realities, are nowadays very different from the conventional wars of other eras of human history. Combat between opposing armies is now infrequent. In its place, 'war is focused on the Third World, and pits guerrilla insurgencies against state governments and states against indigenous nations' (Nietschmann 1987: 1). The direct killing and maiming of combatants is the unfortunate goal of war. But civilians also die: in the Middle East, for example, since the Second World War 1.1 million deaths have resulted directly from wars and civil conflicts in the region.

A less obvious effect is of the loss of this human power for society – the loss of teachers, engineers, and manual workers to carry on the daily business of keeping a society going. In the aftermath of war the society must support and care for disabled veterans, and suffers the effects of angry men in its midst who have been trained to kill. Some researchers have suggested that people maturing in a society at war may suffer a form of moral and social retardation.

These people, and others, may develop long-term personality difficulties resulting from the abnormal conditions in which they have grown up. Moreover, war can profoundly affect civilian health. The civilians need not be members of an enemy group; war may provide an excuse for the genocide of a national minority population. Examples of such genocide are numerous, from the German Holocaust of European Jews to the 'ethnic cleansing' of Bosnian Muslims and the Guatemalan extermination of the indigenous Indian peasants (Carmack 1988). Direct health effects on civilian enemies are also numerous, but these are often ignored since the people killed are typically women, children, and elders.

Less obvious effects of war on civilian health are the disruption of food distribution and the breakdown of health care. In Sudan, the largest country in Africa, the brutal civil war between the Moslem North and non-Moslem South has undone much of the progress achieved by past development efforts, and has reduced the prospects for development in the future. For example, for the South the war has meant the near cessation, since 1985, of the drilling of boreholes for fresh water, an exceptionally high infant mortality rate of 180 per thousand, prevalent malnutrition among children of twelve years and below, and the decimation of the infrastructure for primary and secondary health care in the region.

There are no reliable estimates of how many children may have died in the Sudanese war from 1983 to 1989. However, donor officials estimate that in 1988 alone a total of 250,000 Southerners died from starvation and related illnesses, when both the SPLA and government troops bombed and threatened to destroy food convoys. Roughly half of the Sudanese population is below 16 years of age, but reports indicate that many more than half of the 250,000 dead were children. Reports prepared by Médecins Sans Frontières, who were working in the southern town of El Meiram, indicate that about two times as many children died as adults. Extrapolating from this proportion, some 165,000 children may have died in one year of the war. In some areas the rate of child mortality may have been even higher. A United States congressional fact-finding committee reported that in the Abiye refugee camp in Southern Sudan, every child under the age of two years and six months died. One factor contributing to the higher death rate in children was a measles epidemic that struck the malnourished and unimmunized child population in the summer of 1988. A UNICEF report on children in nine Southern African countries found that war contributed directly to 20 per cent of the mortality of children under the age of five.

In Zimbabwe from 1978 to 1980 the military carried out Operation Turkey, destroying crops, livestock, and food supplies in order to starve the guerrillas. The unfortunate consequence of this strategy was widespread malnutrition of rural children and increased infant and childhood mortality. In Nicaragua the Contra forces explicitly targeted health workers and health institutions. From 1981 to 1985, 38 health workers were killed and 28 kidnapped while they were performing medical duties; 61 health units were destroyed and 37 others forced to close due to Contra activity. Because of the reduced availability of health services, immunization, sanitation, nutrition and other health programmes have been curtailed, and the health, especially of the rural peasants, has suffered.

That the devotion of a disproportionate share of a nation's economy to maintaining a military effort has negative effects on human services and on social supports in that nation has been well documented (Melman 1965, 1986, Pinxten 1986). Furthermore, the devotion of resources to the procurement of arms has worldwide effects, causing distortions both within and between national economies. Indeed, much of the inability of Third World countries, and even some industrialized countries, to provide a basic level of food, housing, and health care to their peoples can be traced directly to the distorting effects of military expenditures.

Wars and civil conflicts over issues of ethnicity, self-determination, access to resources and equity directly involve massive civilian populations. Violent disruptions in a society disproportionately affect the most vulnerable: the poor, women, and children. Like most pathogenic conditions, for every mortality there are many more who are injured or suffer permanent disability. War affects people, perhaps especially children, directly through death, disabling injury, and psychological stress; indirect effects are disruption of health services and education, impeded food distribution, family disruption and displacement, destruction of housing, water and sanitation facilities, and diversion of national funds for military needs (Zwi and Uglade 1989).

CULTURE AND NEGOTIATION

Negotiations are those communicative processes through which individuals or groups try to resolve the disagreements that exist among them. Nearly every human communicative interaction involves negotiation. Sometimes the negotiation process is explicit. At other times it is taken for granted, and takes place without the participants recognizing that they are involved in negotiation at all. Whether explicit or not, negotiation is a shared process that occurs within a social and cultural matrix that shapes both how problems are defined and what solutions are conceivable. In general, negotiators seek to resolve disagreements, which may involve eliminating the source of controversy. Resolution may also result from reframing items under discussion, so that there is no longer disagreement, or so that whatever disagreement persists is no longer considered meaningful by those involved. In any event, negotiators work within the boundaries of their cultural expectations and symbolic frameworks to judge the outcomes of their efforts.

When negotiators come from a common background many fundamental aspects of the negotiation process are part of their shared tacit knowledge – like whether a proposal should be made with blunt straightforwardness or instead with artful indirection. When negotiation involves actors with sensibilities, understandings, and expectations grounded in different cultural backgrounds, additional complexities are involved. In such instances, structures of understanding and patterns of behaviour and communication that might otherwise be effective, and thus taken for granted, may produce paradoxical results – such as unintended insult or confusion where clarity was intended.

In this section I sketch some of the ways in which culture provides the context for negotiation and the control of collective violence. For illustration I show how matters of culture and communication impinge on negotiations between Arabs and Israelis. (Because discussions among residents of the region are sometimes referred to as taking place between Arabs and Israelis, it is easy to suppose that all Arabs share a single culture and set of metacommunicative rules. It is important to recognize that just as differences exist between and within the Palestinian and Israeli communities, there are also cultural and metacommunicative differences among and between Palestinians and other Arabs.) The literature concerning negotiation and conflict resolution is large. It is not my intention to survey that literature here. Rather, I merely wish to illustrate how symbolic repertoires and cultural traditions shape, and are in turn shaped by, processes of negotiation.

Studying negotiation

Communicating with others in order to arrive at a resolution of differences is the essence of negotiation. It 'is a basic means of getting what you want from others. It is a back-and-forth communication designed to reach an agreement when you and the other side have some interests that are shared and others that are opposed' (Fisher and Ury 1981: xi). Like many other processes that are ubiquitous in social life, negotiation ranges from the mundane and taken-for-granted to the elaborately formal and institutionalized.

The process and patterns of various kinds of negotiations have been studied in some depth. In general, such studies have had two very different emphases. The first is most evident in analyses of institutionalized forms of negotiation, like bargaining in the context of labour relations or in arms control talks. These analyses have tended to study negotiation through one or more of three general strategies: (1) through laboratory experiments, (2) in terms of abstract mathematical decision and game theoretic models, or (3) through qualitative analysis of the recollections of participants in particularly important negotiations, like the Cuban Missile Crisis (Janis 1983) or the Camp David negotiations (Raiffa 1982). Especially when laboratory analyses and mathematical modelling have been used, this approach to the study of institutionalized negotiations has sought to describe their formal characteristics.

The second and less commonly adopted approach examines the implicit negotiations in daily life. The aim of these studies is to understand how agreement is reached through the interaction of individuals. Anselm Strauss (1978), for instance, argues that all social orders *are* to some degree negotiated orders. To understand the forms that negotiation takes, researchers focus on the effects of the larger social context on the ways in which people in particular societies actually resolve their differences. Much of this study of mundane negotiation is to be found embedded in anthropological accounts of conflict resolution. Greenhouse (1986: 54–8), for example, describes how the resolution of significant differences among the inhabitants of a small American town depends upon a calm, negative attitude towards conflict. By contrast, in Egyptian popular culture one form of negotiation involves a ritual pantomime – a *dowsha* – in which sham gestures of violence are used to focus attention on a dispute, and to attract and justify the intervention of third parties with a view to resolving the dispute and re-establishing harmony (Rugh 1982: xvi). By explicating episodes of mundane negotiation these studies help to reveal the cultural and symbolic components that contribute to successful negotiations in particular societies.

Lessons from formal negotiations

Studies of institutionalized negotiation have been of central concern to students of international affairs (e.g. Ikle 1964, Schellenberg 1982), and have provided considerable insight into its formal aspects. By examining how groups and individuals resolve disputes in controlled settings, these studies have explicated the structural stages in the process of achieving agreement and the formal properties of decision-making in bargaining situations. The resulting literature mainly develops two lines of thinking. The first often describes both actual and possible negotiations (i.e. those simulated in laboratory settings) as instances of '*n*-player games', and analyses how decisions conform to models of rational decision-making (e.g. Raiffa 1982). The second, related approach is to consider how prospects for negotiations can be improved, for example by creating situations in which both sides can win or by developing a variety of confidence-building mechanisms. This line of work has resulted in several guidebooks which describe how to negotiate successfully and fairly (e.g. Fisher and Ury 1981). Both approaches provide useful starting points for thinking about negotiation and peacemaking.

Studies of this general kind began in the 1940s with the analysis of two-player, single-choice games. The field rapidly developed, however, into one in which sophisticated analyses are made of ongoing, multiple-player negotiations. According to these analyses a number of structural features are critical to the success of negotiation, including: (1) the number of negotiating parties involved; (2) the degree of consensus existing within each negotiating group; (3) whether the negotiation is ongoing or discrete; (4) the number of issues being considered and the connections between them; (5) the linkage of the negotiations to other issues; (6) whether discussions are held in public or in private; and (7) how agreements reached through the negotiation will be enforced (Raiffa 1982: 11–19).

For instance in the context of negotiations between Israelis and Palestinians, neither of the parties can be taken to be single actors. Each represents a diverse constituency and any negotiating team contains internal divisions. Furthermore, there are variations among Palestinians in their perceptions of the land of Palestine and the possibilities for satisfactory settlement, and these run along the lines of regional and religious–ideological identity (Lesch and Tessler 1989, Grossman 1988). Between Palestinians living in the Occupied Territories of the West Bank and Gaza, Arabs living within Israel and Palestinians living in Jordan, there exist differences in the perception of the nature of the 'problem' and possible solutions to it. Shehadeh (1982), who chose to remain in the West Bank as a *samid* – one who resists Israeli occupation by leading a life of principled non-co-operation and non-acquiesence in Israeli authority – describes how his perceptions of political action and of his attachments to the land came to differ markedly from those of his cousin residing in Jordan, and how he felt almost alienated from Arabs in Acre (Shehadeh 1982: 7–11, 20–3). In addition, there are ideological loyalties that cross-cut and confuse this variation: the scorn of the freedom fighter and political prisoner for the *samidin* is keenly felt, as is the frustration felt by the *samidin* in response to the romanticization of the conflict by Palestinians living abroad (Shehadeh 1982: 23–6, 56–8).

The Israeli community is similarly divided in opinion and perception, depending upon religious–ideological and regional factors. Views on the nature and possible resolution of the 'problem' of the Occupied Territories are shaped by political affiliations, religious commitments, and personal experience, among other factors. Benvenisti (1989) describes the range of these variations, and Shavit (1991) describes the variety of reactions to military service in a Gaza Strip internment camp. The divisions internal to Israeli society are evident in the diversity of political parties, both religious and ideologically based, and of social movements like *Peace Now* and *Gush Emunim* (the latter of which seeks to develop Israeli settlements in the West Bank).

Under such circumstances, presenting a united front in negotiations is an extremely difficult task for each party. Privately and in public, both must negotiate among themselves in order to arrive at bargaining positions that can be put forward, and considerable intra-group negotiation is needed in order to arrive at responses to proposals made by their interlocutors. These intra-group negotiations, moreover, may themselves be explicit or tacit, conducted in public or in private. In addition, negotiators must continually touch base with their constituencies. All of these tasks are difficult, and failure in either group's internal negotiations may place in jeopardy the possibilities and potentials for intergroup negotiations (Fahmy 1983, Maksoud 1985, Eban 1985, Grossman 1988, Friedman 1989, Schiff and Ya'ari 1990, PASSIA 1991, Alternative Information Centre n.d.).

997

In addition to identifying the structural characteristics of negotiations, some analysts have attempted to explicate the role of different techniques within negotiation settings. Ikle (1968: 117–18), for instance, describes the techniques of threat and commitment. In the former, one of the negotiating parties asserts its intention to cause the other party the loss of some valued asset should the other party not comply. Threat, of course, may be credible or bluff. Commitment, on the other hand, imposes constraints on the party making it. By making a commitment a negotiating party makes it difficult for itself to renege on a position it has advanced. Because such limitation is self-imposed, the act of commitment is a move to convince the other negotiating parties of the sincerity of the position advanced.

Other researchers have sought to transform the information derived from analytic studies of negotiation into practical and straightforward advice for improving negotiation practice (Karrass 1970, Coffin 1976, Fisher and Ury 1981). Some of the books in this genre offer useful suggestions about how to conduct negotiations. Fisher and Ury (1981: 11), for instance, develop a method they call 'principled negotiation' or 'negotiation on the merits', which is really concerned with meta-negotiation. Each move is to be made with the awareness that it 'helps structure the rules of the game you are playing' (Fisher and Ury 1981: 10). They contrast this to the more usual kind of account which regards negotiation as a process of 'positional bargaining' in which negotiators define and defend their respective positions. The parties, however, are inclined to adopt these positions as their own *raison d'être*, and this can easily cause their underlying interests to be overshadowed.

The method of principled negotiation depends upon four general strategies for ensuring good negotiations, which Fisher and Ury (1981: 11) sum up as follows:

> Separate the people from the problem. Focus on interests not positions. Generate a variety of possibilities before deciding what to do. Insist that results be based on some objective standard.

The method is intended to have very practical results; to produce wise agreements, to do so efficiently, and to allow the parties to separate on amicable terms. Fisher and Ury (1981: 14) claim that

> in contrast to positional bargaining, the principled negotiation method of focusing on basic interests, mutually satisfying options, and fair standards typically results in a *wise* agreement. The method permits you to reach a gradual consensus with a joint decision *efficiently* without all the transactional costs of digging into positions only to have to dig yourself out of them. And separating the people from the problem allows you to deal directly and empathetically with the other negotiator as a human being, thus making possible an *amicable* agreement.

The method of principled negotiation has been put to very good use. Its directives are admirable and productive, especially in situations where negotiators share tacit understandings of the general nature and purpose of negotiation.

998

Like other methods of understanding negotiation, however, its application encounters a unique set of obstacles when applied in cross-cultural contexts.

Culture and negotiation

Once a method of understanding or action is developed which is said to be universally applicable, it is easy to become over-optimistic about the possibilities for using it to solve previously intractable problems. This is especially prone to happen in the context of international and intercommunal disputes (Rubinstein 1988a, Rubinstein and Foster 1988).

An example of the complexities involved in real international disputes can be drawn from the Camp David negotiations between Egypt and Israel. After a long and difficult process of negotiation, Egypt and Israel signed the Camp David peace accords in September 1978. It is widely acknowledged, however, that the successful conclusion of this accord did not result in an equally successful peace. Israeli and Egyptian accounts and interpretations of the course of their post-accord relations vary widely, and each side has found that its expectations have not been met (Lesch and Tessler 1989, Fahmy 1983, Cohen 1990). For these reasons, the peace between the two countries has been described as a 'cold peace.'

Fisher and Ury's (1981: 4) view is that a good negotiation method 'should produce a wise agreement if agreement is possible. It should be efficient. And it should improve or at least not damage the relationship between the parties.' By these criteria negotiations between Egypt and Israel over the Camp David accords and subsequently must be judged as wanting: resolutions have been achieved, but with each subsequent negotiation the relationship between the two countries appears to have deteriorated (see Cohen 1990). However, negotiators whose tacit cultural knowledge leads them to see efficiency and the improvement of interpersonal relations as mutually exclusive may not view these criteria so positively. More obviously, the search for objective standards for use in resolving disputes may produce greatly varying responses: what one person takes to be neutral objectivity is not infrequently taken by another to be biased in the extreme (Rubinstein 1989: 52–6). In the Egyptian–Israeli case, for instance, the record seems to indicate that each side would view its conduct in negotiations as principled. Yet, each views the other as having dealt with it in bad faith (Fahmy 1983, Cohen 1990).

Dealing with longstanding problems in cross-cultural negotiations reveals a variety of pitfalls that guides to negotiation technique and formal models of the negotiating process are unable to overcome. In order to deal successfully with the problems presented by cross-cultural negotiation, it is necessary to have an understanding of culture as a dynamic, symbolically based system through which people construct and enact meaning (Kertzer 1988). One of the most salient symbolically based aspects of the Israeli–Palestinian issue is the way in which the devotion to the land of Israel/Palestine has become invested

with multiple meanings and emotions. Both Palestinian and Israeli interlocutors bring to their discussions a *symbolic* understanding which frames their
discourse. The Palestinian concept of 'the preserving' (*samid*), and the Israeli
conception of a special homeland (*moledet*) exert powerful emotional and cognitive influences on those who hold them (Shehadeh 1982, Benvenisti 1989).

Successful cross-cultural negotiation depends, therefore, upon integrating
the results of formal studies of negotiation with contextual information about
the role of culture in mundane negotiation processes. The following section
of this article considers the importance of intra-cultural variability and the role
of symbols in political discourse.

Culture and internal variability

In part because negotiating cross-culturally introduces new difficulties,
interest in the formal aspects of negotiations has been supplemented by
attempts to characterize national negotiating and decision-making styles. It is,
however, misguided to rely on stereotyped characterizations of cultural
negotiating styles, since this is to assume that cultures are homogeneous and
stable, and that once described the patterns stay intact. The cultural characterization of patterns of behaviour, belief, and interaction is not in itself fallacious. Such characterizations can be useful if they are clearly anchored in
specific circumstances. But it is always misguided and unhelpful to treat them
as though they had a permanent existence, outside time and history. To do
so is to commit what I call the 'fallacy of detached cultural descriptions'.

Anthropological work shows that cultural norms and preferences, such as
for social harmony or directness, do indeed exist, but that not all individuals
from a particular society will hold or behave according to a single set of norms.
And, of course, such norms are constantly affected by social, political, economic, and other processes and contradictions within the society. Thus, cultural styles are not stable, even if they may be clearly discerned in relation to
a particular problem or situation. This is because societies always contain
within themselves a variety of styles, some of which will be in direct tension
with each other.

Ismail Fahmy, former Egyptian Minister of Foreign Affairs and Deputy
Premier, recalls (1983: 124) that,

> It takes time to learn to deal with the Soviets and understand their tactics. For
> example, the Russian negotiator never answers 'da' (yes) at the outset. The answer
> is always 'niet'. Often the first 'niet' means 'da', but at other times 'niet' is 'niet.' The
> problem is to learn to tell the difference. Once I learned, I enjoyed tremendously
> negotiating with the Soviets. It was always tough, but they could be outmanoeuvred
> once their tactics were understood.

Yet during the period in which Minister Fahmy was dealing with the Soviets,
their interests in the region shifted many times, as did the constraints on their

actions. As even the record of missed opportunities and misunderstandings reported in his own memoirs shows, Fahmy's view that once understood, Soviet negotiators could henceforth be handled with aplomb, was in fact a chimera.

Beeman (1986, 1989) and Bateson (1988), for example, describe how the assumptions of United States negotiators about Iranian political styles proved inaccurate, precisely because they failed to be aware of cultural heterogeneity. Bateson and her colleagues (see Bateson 1988) isolated two distinct forms of political discourse in Iran — the opportunistic and the absolute. At the time of the Iranian revolution public rhetoric and public policy changed in ways that baffled United States analysts. Yet, Beeman and Bateson argue, when it is recognized that contrasting themes generally coexist in any culture, these events are more readily understandable. As Bateson (1988: 39) puts it,

> Iranian public policy and public rhetoric, both domestically and internationally, went through an apparent radical change at the time of the revolution into a style that appeared totally different and therefore unpredictable, but we would argue that the two styles — and more significantly the tendency to think of them as alternatives facing individuals and societies — were and still are both implicit in Iranian culture.

Understanding that opposing styles exist in any society, and being aware of which styles are ascendant in a particular situation, requires that the analyst be aware of the different contexts in which negotiators frame their work, and further requires them to understand how the give-and-take of social process in these situations keeps the cultural matrix in which actions are situated in a constant state of flux. Indeed, 'the truth of the matter is that people have mixed feelings and confused opinions, and are subject to contradictory expectations and outcomes, in every sphere of experience' (Levine 1985: 8–9).

In sum, it is as misleading to attend exclusively to autobiographical recollections of formal negotiations as it is to rely on laboratory simulations or on the mathematical modelling of decision-making processes. Studies that rest on such analyses direct our attention towards a limited number of characteristics of negotiations, and away from other less easily explained or measured, but nevertheless equally critical, aspects of the negotiation process (Rubinstein 1989).

Culture, symbols, and negotiation

The elements of negotiating competence in one culture may ensure failure in negotiation in another. This is because metacommunicative rules of negotiation are culturally specific. Egyptian communicative competence places a high value on maintaining face agreement and a smooth and harmonious social order. As a result negotiations are often structured in a way that is cyclical in form, incorporating within them a large amount of repetition. Once a point is put forward, in a relatively indirect way, it is discussed until a sense of closure appears imminent. At this stage, the discussion might return to consider the point anew. Again closure is approached, and again discussion is reopened. This next episode of discussion may be briefer than its predecessor; this process continuing until all parties have had a chance to speak fully to the point and consensus is presumed. Each of these episodes of discussion may be quite animated, and important information may be conveyed in an indirect fashion. All of this might well strike a Western observer as wasteful of both time and energy. It is true that this pattern of negotiation is not efficient in reaching a conclusion – but it is efficient for maintaining social harmony. (Descriptions of Egyptian communicative styles derive from my own work and from that of Cohen (1990). The analysis of Israeli negotiating styles presented in this section is based primarily on Cohen.)

The rules of communicative competence characterizing Israeli negotiations are very different. There, according to Cohen (1990), little care is taken to sugarcoat positions that may be unpalatable to an interlocutor. Rather the emphasis is on direct, forthright, 'clear' communication. Thus, negotiating positions tend to be put forward directly, and little attention is paid to the human side of the social transaction. On the other hand, when every word is listened to, analysed, and taken seriously, as it is by Israeli negotiators, the use of artful ambiguity and hyperbole, often employed by Egyptian negotiators, rankles and insults just as deeply as does blunt disregard for social niceties.

Communication, of course, is more than just the content of a message. Language, like all symbols, is essentially ambiguous. There is nothing novel in the observation that the same words, spoken in different ways or in different contexts, may convey a range of different meanings (on this, see DeBernardi in this volume, Article 31). Indeed, Cohen (1990) shows that Israeli and Egyptian interlocutors repeatedly misunderstand one another, and take insult from their interaction, precisely because their metacommunicative expectations are not mutually consistent.

Among the many examples that Cohen offers, his description of the first meeting between Boutros Boutros-Ghali and Moshe Dayan, who at the time were acting as foreign ministers of Egypt and Israel respectively, is instructive. Cohen (1990: 57–58) observes:

> Within hours of President Sadat's historic arrival in Israel, on the evening of 19 November 1977, with nerves at a high pitch of anticipation, Israeli diplomacy made its first tactless and maladroit overture.... Without trying to soften the blow in any way, Dayan brusquely informed Boutros-Ghali, with astonishing insensitivity, that since there was no chance of Jordan or the Palestinians' joining in the negotiations – as Sadat hoped at that point, anxious to avoid isolation in the Arab world – Egypt had to be ready to sign a peace treaty with us [Israel] even if she were not joined by others.
>
> Boutros-Ghali was profoundly shocked by Dayan's ill-timed proposal of a separate peace, as was Sadat when it was reported to him. At issue was not the idea itself, which was based on an objective analysis of the situation.... It was the

unsubtle directness of the approach that was utterly repellent to the Egyptian minister. This first conversation with an Israeli leader rankled in Boutros-Ghali's mind for years afterward.

The value placed on directness is not the only communicative expectation over which Egyptians (and other Arabs) and their Israeli counterparts diverge. Israeli negotiators often appear to be immediately concerned with working out the details of an agreement. By contrast, Arab diplomats have tended to seek frameworks for solution, leaving aside the details. For the Israeli actor attention to the precise wording of an agreement is considered an expression of good faith, whereas for the Egyptian negotiator good faith is displayed by agreement to a broad conceptual framework; the details are left to be worked out at a future time (see Carter 1982: 342, Fahmy 1983: 285–308).

Raymond Cohen (1990) traces these and other obstacles to negotiations between the Israelis and the Egyptians, and other Arabs. Such obstacles all belong outside the structural character of formal negotiations. Indeed, both the Israeli and the Egyptian negotiators understand and seek to adhere to the structural features of negotiations, as these are understood by the international diplomatic community. The stumbling blocks that remain are the result of conflicting metacommunicative expectations.

CONCLUSION

Expectations about what is proper and good are *cultural*, and they are encoded in a society's symbolic forms. Most importantly, symbols are ambiguous in that they may have several meanings – being often imprecisely defined – and they may invoke emotional responses. As Abner Cohen (1979: 89; see also Kertzer 1988) notes, cultural symbols have great political impact because they allow political relationships to be 'objectified, developed, maintained, expressed, or camouflaged by means of symbolic forms and patterns of symbolic action'. Such symbolic forms include, among other things, the repetitive, ritual organization of negotiations (Rubinstein 1988b), the public rhetoric of political leaders (Cohen 1990: 45–8), and the literature of resistance (Lesch and Tessler 1989: 125–39). Because symbolic forms have both an ambiguous cognitive component and a strong emotional load they are powerful factors in structuring political perceptions.

Such cultural factors affect the patterning of collective violence both direct and indirect, and of conceptions of power and security. Moreover, the cultural factors that affect negotiation, such as metacommunicative expectations, are encoded in symbols. These cultural factors structure the way that negotiators respond to their interlocutors, they affect the perception of what is fair and objective, and of how to begin and end discussions. Especially when disagreement is emotionally laden and rich in symbolic elements, it is all the more necessary to appreciate the role of culture in the dynamics of negotiation, if we are to gain a better understanding of collective violence, an understanding that is vital to present and future security.

ACKNOWLEDGEMENT

Preparation of this article was supported in part by a grant from the Ploughshares Fund, which I gratefully acknowledge. I thank Mary LeCron Foster and Sandra D. Lane for comments on an earlier draft. Many colleagues responded to my circular letter requesting references to pertinent literature. I am grateful for their helpful replies. Much of the substance of this article is drawn from my earlier published papers, especially Rubinstein 1988a, 1989, and 1992.

REFERENCES

Alternative Information Centre (n.d.) *Three Years of Intifada. News from Within from December 1987 to the Gulf Crisis*, Jerusalem: Alternative Information Centre.
Ardrey, R. (1966) *African Genesis*, New York: Doubleday.
Ball, D. and Jeffrey R. (eds) (1986) *Strategic Nuclear Thinking*, Ithaca, NY: Cornell University Press.
Bateson, M. C. (1988) 'Compromise and the rhetoric of good and evil', in R. A. Rubinstein and M. L. Foster (eds) *The Social Dynamics of Peace and Conflict. Culture in International Affairs*, Boulder, Colo.: Westview Press.
Beeman, W. O. (1986) 'Conflict and belief in American foreign policy', in M. L. Foster and R. A. Rubinstein (eds) *Peace and War: Cross-Cultural Perspectives*, New Brunswick, NJ: Transaction Books.
—— (1989) 'Anthropology and the myths of American foreign policy', in P. R. Turner and D. Pitt (eds) *The Anthropology of War and Peace. Perspectives on the Nuclear Age*, Granby, Mass.: Bergin and Garvey.
Benvenisti, M. (1989) *Conflicts and Contradictions*, New York: Eshel Books.
Binnendijk, H. (ed.) (1987) *National Negotiating Styles*, Washington, DC: United States Department of State.
Brams, S. J. (1985) *Superpower Games: Applying Game Theory to Superpower Conflict*, New Haven: Yale University Press.
Brasset, D. (1988) 'Values and the exercise of power: military elites', in R. A. Rubinstein and M. L. Foster (eds) *The Social Dynamics of Peace and Conflict: Culture in International Security*, Boulder, Colo.: Westview Press.
Carmack, R. M. (ed.) (1988) *Harvest of Violence. The Maya Indians and the Guatemala Crisis*, Norman: University of Oklahoma Press.
Carter, J. (1982) *Keeping Faith: Memoirs of a President*, New York: Bantam.
Chagnon, N. (1967) *The Fierce People*, New York: Prentice-Hall.
—— (1988) 'Life histories, blood revenge, and warfare in a tribal population', *Science* 239: 985–92.
Chagnon, N. and Hames, R. (1979) 'Protein deficiency and tribal warfare in Amazonia: New data', *Science* 203: 910–13.
Checinski, M. (1981) *A Comparison of the Polish and Soviet Armaments Decisionmaking Systems*, Santa Monica: RAND Corporation.
Coffin, R. A. (1976) *Negotiator: A Manual for Winners*, New York: Everyday Handbook Service.

Cohen, A. (1979) 'Political symbolism', *Annual Review of Anthropology* 8: 87–113.

Cohen, Raymond (1990) *Culture and Conflict in Egyptian-Israeli Relations*, Bloomington: Indiana University Press.

Cohen, Ronald (1983) 'War, war machines, and state formation in pre- and post-industrial states', paper presented at the International Congress of Anthropological and Ethnological Sciences, Vancouver, BC, Canada, August 1983.

—— (1986) 'War and war proneness in pre- and postindustrial states', in M. L. Foster and R. A. Rubinstein (eds) *Peace and War: Cross-Cultural Perspectives*, New Brunswick: Transaction Books.

Cohn, C. (1987) 'Sex and death in the rational world of defense intellectuals', *Signs* 12(4): 687–718.

Cordesman, A. and Wagner, A. (1990) *The Lessons of Modern War*, vol. 1, Boulder, Colo.: Westview Press.

Dahl, R. (1969) 'The concept of power', in R. Bell, D. Edwards and R. Wagner (eds) *Political Power*, New York: The Free Press.

Davis, P. K. and Winnefeld, J. A. (1983) *The RAND Strategy Assessment Center: An Overview and Interim Conclusions about Utility and Development Options*, Santa Monica, Cal.: RAND Corporation.

Eban, A. (1985) 'Multilateral diplomacy in the Arab-Israeli conflict', in A. Lall (ed.) *Multilateral Negotiation and Mediation. Instruments and Methods*, New York: Pergamon Press.

Ember, M. and Ember, C. (1988) 'Fear of disasters as an engine of history: resource crises, warfare, and interpersonal aggression', paper prepared for the conference 'What is the Engine of History?', Texas A&M University, 27–29 October 1988.

Fahmy, I. (1983) *Negotiating for Peace in the Middle East*, London: Croom Helm.

Ferguson, R. B. (n.d.) 'Game wars? Ecology and conflict in Amazonia', manuscript, Department of Anthropology, Rutgers University, Newark, NJ.

Fisher, R. and Ury, W. (1981) *Getting to Yes*, Boston: Houghton Mifflin.

Foster, M. L. (1989) 'The causes of conflict', paper prepared for the World Affairs Council of Northern California, 14 July.

Foster, M. L. and Rubinstein, R. A. (eds) (1986) *Peace and War: Cross-Cultural Perspectives*, New Brunswick, NJ: Transaction Books.

Fried, M., Harris, M. and Murphy, R. (eds) (1968) *War: The Anthropology of Armed Conflict and Aggression*, Garden City, NY: Natural History Press.

Friedman, T. (1989) *From Beirut to Jerusalem*, New York: Farrar Straus Giroux.

Gearing, F. (1958) 'The structural poses of 18th century Cherokee villages', *American Anthropologist* 60: 1148–57.

Greenhouse, C. (1986) 'Fighting for peace', in M. L. Foster and R. A. Rubinstein (eds) *Peace and War: Cross-Cultural Perspectives*, New Brunswick: Transaction Books.

Gross, D. (1975) 'Protein capture and cultural development in the Amazon Basin', *American Anthropologist* 77: 526–49.

Grossman, D. (1988) *The Yellow Wind*, London: Jonathan Cape.

Herran, F. (1988) 'Conclusions of a transdisciplinary investigation of the causes of war and the conditions of peace', manuscript, Universidad Nacional de Salta, Argentina.

Hinde, R. A. (1988) *Aggression: Integrating Ethology and the Social Sciences. Medicine and War*, New York: John Wiley.

Hosmer, S. (1985) *Constraints on U.S. Strategy in Third World Conflict*, Santa Monica, Calif.: RAND Corporation.

Ikle, F. (1964) *How Nations Negotiate*, New York: Harper.

—— (1968) 'Negotiation: A definition', in D. Sills (ed) *International Encyclopedia of the Social Sciences*, New York: Free Press, Macmillan.

Janis, I. (1983) *Groupthink. Psychological Studies of Policy Decisions and Fiascoes*, 2nd edn, Boston: Houghton Mifflin.

Karrass, C. L. (1970) *The Negotiating Game: How to Get What you Want*, New York: Crowell.

Kehoe, A. B. (1988) 'Fourth world responses to external threats: the Dené', in R. A. Rubinstein and M. L. Foster (eds) *The Social Dynamics of Peace and Conflict: Culture in International Security*, Boulder: Westview Press.

Kertzer, D.(1988) *Ritual, Politics, and Power*, New Haven: Yale University Press.

Kim, S. (1983) *The Quest for a Just World Order*, Boulder, Colo.: Westview Press.

Koch, K.-F. (1974) *The Anthropology of Warfare*, Addison-Wesley Modules in Anthropology no. 52, Reading, Mass.: Addison-Wesley.

Lesch, A. and Tessler, M. (1989) *Israel, Egypt, and the Palestinians. From Camp David to the Intifada*, Bloomington: Indiana University Press.

Levine, D. N. (1985) *The Flight from Ambiguity: Essays in Social and Cultural Theory*, Chicago: University of Chicago Press.

Lorenz, K. (1963) *On Aggression*, New York: Harcourt, Brace and World.

Maksoud, C. (1985) 'Arab League negotiations', in A. Lall (ed.) *Multilateral Negotiation and Mediation. Instruments and Methods*, New York: Pergamon Press.

Malinowski, B. (1941) 'An anthropological analysis of war', *American Journal of Sociology* 46(4): 521–50.

Melman, S. (1965) *The Permanent War Economy*, New York: Simon & Schuster.

—— (1986) 'The war-making institutions', in M. L. Foster and R. A. Rubinstein (eds) *Peace and War: Cross-Cultural Perspectives*, New Brunswick, NJ: Transaction Books.

Morris, D. (1967) *The Naked Ape*, New York: Doubleday.

Myrdal, G. (1969) *Objectivity in Social Research*, Middletown, Conn.: Wesleyan University Press.

Nietschmann, B. (1987) 'Militarization and indigenous people', *Cultural Survival Quarterly* 11(3): 1–16..

Otterbein, K. (1973) 'The anthropology of war', in J. J. Honigmann (ed.) *Handbook of Social and Cultural Anthropology*, Chicago: Rand McNally.

PASSIA (Palestinian Academic Society for the Study of International Affairs) (1991) *Palestinian Assessments of the Gulf War and its Aftermath*, East Jerusalem: PASSIA Publications.

Pinxten, R. (1986) 'The developmental dynamics of peace', in M. L. Foster and R. A. Rubinstein (eds) *Peace and War: Cross-Cultural Perspectives*, New Brunswick NJ: Transaction Books.

Potter, J. (1988) 'The communist ethic and the spirit of China's party cadres', in R. A. Rubinstein and M. L. Foster (eds) *The Social Dynamics of Peace and Conflict: Culture in International Security*, Boulder, Colo.: Westview Press.

Raiffa, H. (1982) *The Art and Science of Negotiation*, Cambridge, Mass.: Harvard University Press.

Rappaport, R. (1967) *Pigs for the Ancestors*, New Haven, Conn.: Yale University Press.

Record, J. (1985) 'Third world conflicts: implications for US security and force structure', in K. A. Dunn and W. O. Staudenmaier (eds) *Alternative Military Strategies for the Future*, Boulder, Colo.: Westview Press.

Ross, J. (1980) 'Ecology and the problem of tribe: A critique of the Hobbesian model of preindustrial warfare', in E. Ross (ed.) *Beyond the Myths of Culture: Essays in Cultural Materialism*, New York: Academic Press.

Ross, E. and Ross, J. (1980) 'Amazon warfare', *Science* 207: 590–1.

Rubinstein, R. A. (1988a) 'Cultural analysis and international security', *Alternatives* 13(4): 529–42.

—— (1988b) 'Ritual process and images of the other in arms control negotiations', *Human Peace* 6(2): 3–7.

—— (1989) 'Culture, international affairs and peacekeeping: confusing process and pattern', *Cultural Dynamics* 2(1): 41–61.

—— (1992) 'Culture and negotiation', in E. Fernea and Mary Hocking (eds) *The Struggle for Peace: Israelis and Palestinians*, Austin: University of Texas Press.

Rubinstein, R. A. and Foster, M. L. (eds) (1988) *The Social Dynamics of Peace and Conflict: Culture in International Security*, Boulder, Colo.: Westview Press.

Rubinstein, R. A. and Tax, S. (1985) 'Power, powerlessness, and the failure of political realism', in Jens Brosted *et al.* (eds) *Native Power*, Bergen: Universitetsforlaget.

Rubinstein, R. A., Laughlin, C. and McManus, J. (1984) *Science as Cognitive Process*, Philadelphia: University of Pennsylvania Press.

Rugh, A. (1982) 'Foreword', in *Khul-Khaal. Five Egyptian Women Tell Their Stories*, Nayra Atiya, Syracuse: Syracuse University Press.

Sahlins, M. (1968) *Tribesmen*, Englewood Cliffs, NJ: Prentice-Hall.

—— (1976) *The Use and Abuse of Biology*, Ann Arbor: University of Michigan Press.

Sarkesian, S. (1986) 'The nature of war and the American military profession', in M. L. Foster and R. A. Rubinstein (eds) *Peace and War: Cross-Cultural Perspectives*, New Brunswick, NJ: Transaction Books.

Schellenberg, J. (1982) *The Science of Conflict*, Oxford: Oxford University Press.

Schiff, Z. and Ya'ari, E. (1990) *Intifada: The Palestinian Uprising – Israel's Third Front*, New York: Simon & Schuster.

Shavit, A. (1991) On Gaza Beach, *The New York Review of Books* 38(13): 3–5.

Shehadeh, R. (1982) *The Third Way: A Journal of Life in the West Bank*, London: Quartet Books.

Simon, H. A. (1983) *Reason in Human Affairs*, Stanford, Cal.: Stanford University Press.

Strauss, A. (1978) *Negotiations*, San Francisco: Jossey-Bass.

Swanton, J. R. (1943) *Are Wars Inevitable?*, Washington, DC: Smithsonian Institution.

Tefft, S. K. (1974) 'Warfare regulation: a cross-cultural test of hypotheses', in M. Nettleship, R. D. Givens and A. Nettleship (eds) *War: Its Causes and Correlates*, The Hague: Mouton.

Thibault, J. and Kelly, H. (1959) *The Social Psychology of Groups*, New York: John Wiley.

Turner, P. and Pitt, D. (eds) (1989) *The Anthropology of War and Peace. Perspectives on the Nuclear Age*, Granby, Mass.: Bergin and Garvey.

Vayda, A. P. (n.d.) 'Explaining why Marings fought', manuscript, Department of Anthropology, Rutgers University, New Brunswick, NJ.

—— (1974) 'Warfare in ecological perspective', *Annual Review of Ecology and Systematics* 5: 183–93.

—— (1968) 'Hypotheses about the functions of war', in M. Fried, M. Harris and R. Murphy (eds) *War: The Anthropology of Armed Conflict and Aggression*, Garden City, NY: Natural History Press.

Vincent, J. (1990) *Anthropology and Politics: Visions, Traditions, and Trends*, Tucson: University of Arizona Press.

Wahrhaftig, A. and Lukens-Wahrhaftig, J. (1977) 'The thrice powerless: Cherokee Indians in Oklahoma', in R. Fogelson and R. Adams (eds) *The Anthropology of Power: Ethnographic Studies from Asia Oceania and the New World*, New York: Academic Press.

Wilson, E. O. (1975) *Sociobiology*, Cambridge, Mass.: Harvard University Press.
—— (1978) 'What is sociobiology?', in M. Gregory, A. Silvers and D. Sutch (eds) *Sociobiology and Human Nature*, San Francisco: Jossey-Bass.
Worsley, P. (1982) 'Non-western medical systems', *Annual Review of Anthropology* 11: 315–48.
—— (1986) 'The superpowers and the tribes', in M. L. Foster and R. A. Rubinstein (eds) *Peace and War: Cross-Cultural Perspectives*, New Brunswick, NJ: Transaction Books.
—— (1987) 'Introduction', in P. Worsley and K. B. Hadjor (eds) *On the Brink: Nuclear Proliferation and the Third World*, London: Third World Books.
Worsley, P. and Hadjor, K. B. (eds) (1987) *On the Brink: Nuclear Proliferation and the Third World*, London: Third World Books.
Wright, Q. (1968) 'War', in D. Sills (ed.) *International Encyclopedia of the Social Sciences*, vol. 16, New York: Free Press, Macmillan.
Zartman, W. (1974) 'The political analysis of negotiations', *World Politics* 26: 385–99.
Zwi, A. and Uglade, A. (1989) 'Towards an epidemiology of political violence in the Third World', *Social Science and Medicine* 28(7): 633–42.

FURTHER READING

Beer, F. (1981) *Peace Against War: The Ecology of International Violence*, San Francisco: W. H. Freeman.
Bramson, L. and Goethals, G. (eds) (1964) *War: Studies from Psychology, Sociology, Anthropology*, New York: Basic Books.
Cohen, R. (1990) *Culture and Conflict in Egyptian–Israeli Relations: A Dialogue of the Deaf*, Bloomington: Indiana University Press.
Coser, L. (1956) *The Functions of Social Conflict*, New York: Free Press.
Eibl-Eibesfeldt, I. (1979) *The Biology of Peace and War: Men, Animals, and Aggression*, New York: Viking Press.
Falk, R. and Kim, S. (eds) (1980) *The War System: An Interdisciplinary Approach*, Boulder, Colo.: Westview Press.
Ferguson, R. B. (ed) (1984) *Warfare, Culture and Environment*, New York: Academic Press.
Foster, M. L. and Rubinstein, R. (eds) (1986) *Peace and War: Cross-Cultural Perspectives*, New Brunswick: Transaction Books.
Fried, M., Harris, M. and Murphy, R. (eds) (1967) *War: The Anthropology of Armed Conflict and Aggression*, Garden City: Natural History Press.
Kertzer, D. I. (1988) *Ritual, Politics and Power*, New Haven: Yale University Press.
Koch, K.-F. (1974) *The Anthropology of Warfare*, Addison-Wesley Modules in Anthropology no. 52, Reading, Mass.: Addison-Wesley.
Nettleship, M., Givens, R. D. and Nettleship, A. (eds) (1974) *War: Its Causes and Correlates*, The Hague: Mouton.
Nordstrom, C. and Martin, J.-A. (eds) (1992) *The Paths to Domination, Resistance and Terror*, Berkeley: University of California Press.
Otterbein, K. (1970) *The Evolution of War*, New Haven: HRAF Press.
Riches, D. (ed.) (1986) *The Anthropology of Violence*, Oxford: Blackwell.
Rubinstein, R. A. and Foster, M. L. (eds) (1988) *The Social Dynamics of Peace and Conflict: Culture in International Security*, Boulder, Colo.: Westview Press.
Turner, P. and Pitt, D.(eds) (1989) *The Anthropology of War and Peace: Perspectives on the Nuclear Age*, Granby, Mass.: Bergin & Harvey.

Turney-High, H. (1971) *Primitive War: Its Practice and Concepts*, Columbia: University of South Carolina Press.

Väyrynen, R. (ed.) (1987) *The Quest for Peace*, London: Sage.

Worsley, P. and Hadjor, K. B. (eds) (1987) *On the Brink: Nuclear Proliferation and the Third World*, London: Third World Books.

Wright, Q. (1965) *A Study of War*, 2nd edn, Chicago: University of Chicago Press.

37

INEQUALITY AND EQUALITY

André Béteille

EVOLUTIONARY PERSPECTIVES AND THE COMPARATIVE METHOD

A striking feature of the modern world is the deep and pervasive disjunction between the ideal of equality and the reality of inequality. The ideal of equality is widely endorsed and, as Isaiah Berlin has put it, 'The assumption is that equality needs no reasons, only inequality does so' (1978: 84). At the same time, there is extensive and sometimes extreme inequality in the distribution of material and other resources, and in the relations between individuals, groups and categories of every conceivable kind.

In studying inequality systematically we have to keep in mind the fact that inequalities differ not only in degree but also in kind. Inequalities in the distribution of income or of wealth are difficult to compare directly with inequalities in the distribution of power, or with inequalities of status, prestige or esteem. Moreover, the idea of equality is not a simple or a homogeneous one, so that when people say they value equality, they may not all mean the same thing. There are striking differences of orientation and perception between those who emphasize competitive equality or equality of opportunity, and those who stress distributive equality or equality of results. For these reasons it may be misleading to argue about the nature and forms of inequality without keeping in mind the various meanings of equality which, in our age, is both an ideal and a value.

While social theorists are agreed that the societies in which they live are marked by many forms of inequality, there is disagreement about whether inequality is inevitable. Perhaps the majority believe that inequality is inherent in the very nature of collective life, and some would go even further and argue not only that inequality or stratification is inevitable but also that it has a definite social function (Davis and Moore 1945; see Bendix and Lipset 1966). Others maintain that inequality or stratification is not inevitable, and that an egalitarian society is possible as a reality and not merely as an ideal. Most of the latter would probably concede that it is possible to attain only what Tawney (1964 [1931]) described as 'practical equality' rather than absolute or perfect equality.

Those who argue that in spite of the wide prevalence of inequality, egalitarian societies are in fact possible, have sought to demonstrate either that such societies have existed in the past or that they can be constructed in the future, or both. Characteristically, the faith in the possibility of constructing such a society in the future has been sustained by the belief that equality and not inequality was the original condition of human life.

Among modern social and political philosophers, Rousseau was one of the first to argue that equality or near-equality was the original or natural condition of humanity, although Hobbes and Locke had put forward similar arguments before him (Béteille 1980). Rousseau did not deny the existence of natural or physical inequalities, but he believed these to be slight or insignificant. The inequalities that really mattered were political or moral inequalities which, being based on a kind of convention, could in principle be abolished or at least diminished by a different convention. Rousseau's views were considered radical in his time and they left a lasting impact on succeeding generations, both in Europe and elsewhere.[1]

The writings of Marx and Engels gave rise to the doctrine that the first stage of social evolution was one of 'primitive communism' and that the final stage would also be one of communism, both stages being marked, despite many differences, by the absence of classes. However, there was a difference in approach and method between Rousseau and the nineteenth-century proponents of the theory of primitive communism. Rousseau constructed his model from first principles, observing, 'Let us begin then by laying facts aside, as they do not affect the question' (1938 [1762]: 175). Marx, and more particularly Engels (1948 [1884]), on the other hand, turned to the available evidence from primitive societies to demonstrate that classless societies existed in reality.

The second half of the nineteenth century saw the emergence of the new science of ethnography, based largely on accounts of primitive societies by explorers, missionaries, traders and administrators. A whole new world was opened up for systematic enquiry. The early ethnographers were enthusiastic advocates of the comparative method, by which contemporary primitive societies were likened to those that were supposed to have existed at earlier stages in the development of more advanced civilizations, and they used it to construct ambitious evolutionary schemes. Perhaps the most famous among these, and one which had a lasting influence in the Soviet Union, was formulated in 1877 by Lewis Henry Morgan (1964). According to Morgan, the first stage of evolution, designated as 'savagery' and represented by a number of surviving primitive societies, was marked by an absence of inequality and class.

The theory of primitive communism aroused great interest in the late nineteenth and early twentieth centuries. Inevitably, the discussion turned around the presence or absence of individual property in the early stages of evolution. The predominant view was that the concept of property – and indeed of the individual – was absent in primitive societies; and it was tacitly assumed that where there was no individual property, there could be no classes, no strata, and no significant inequality. This view was challenged in a landmark study published in 1921 by the American anthropologist Robert Lowie (1960). Through a meticulous examination of the ethnographic record, he showed that primitive societies were far more varied and far more differentiated than had been allowed for in the theories of his predecessors. It is fair to say that most anthropologists are nowadays sceptical about the existence of a universal stage of primitive communism.

This scepticism does not of course mean that anthropologists altogether reject the view that primitive societies, or at least *some* primitive societies, may be genuinely egalitarian in their constitution. Recently the characterization 'egalitarian' has been applied to a number of societies in which 'equalities of power, equalities of wealth and equalities of prestige or rank are not merely sought but are, with certain limited exceptions, genuinely realized' (Woodburn 1982). The use of the term 'egalitarian' in the case of these societies is justified on the grounds 'that the "equality" that is present is not neutral, the mere absence of inequality or hierarchy, but is *asserted*' (1982: 431–2). Examples of such societies include the Mbuti Pygmies of Zaire, the !Kung Bushmen of Botswana and Namibia, the Pandaram and Paliyan of South India, the Batek Negritos of Malaysia and the Hadza of Tanzania.

The egalitarian societies referred to above are all based on a foraging or hunting-and-gathering economy. Indeed according to Woodburn, not all hunter-gatherer societies are egalitarian, but only those characterized by 'immediate-return' as against 'delayed-return' systems of production (1982: 431). An immediate-return system is one in which there is no time-lag, or only a small one, between the investment of labour in production and the realization of the product, so that no complex chain of rights and obligations is entailed in production, whereas such a chain is a necessary part of delayed-return systems. Hunter-gatherers with immediate-return systems live and move about in very small groups which have no fixed membership and only a very rudimentary division of labour, a condition that comes close to the outer limit of organized social life. It is very difficult to draw any significant conclusion from their study for the future of equality in more organized societies.

Although evolutionary theories are no longer as popular as they were in the past, those engaged in the comparative study of equality and inequality often adopt an evolutionary perspective, either implicitly or explicitly. A characteristic expression of the evolutionary perspective on the subject is to be found in a recent essay by Gellner. Commenting on the work of a well-known

American author, Gerhard Lenski (1966), he observed that:

> The pattern of human history, when plotted against the axis of equality, displays a steady progression towards increasing *in*equality, up to a certain mysterious point in time, at which the trend goes into reverse, and we then witness that equalisation of conditions which preoccupied Tocqueville.
>
> (Gellner 1979: 27)

This view of the course of human history is very widely held, and it merits a brief discussion.

Implicit in the evolutionary scheme outlined above is a classification of societies into three broad types: (1) primitive societies, (2) agrarian civilizations, and (3) industrial states. Primitive societies, including bands, segmentary tribes as well as tribal chiefdoms, are small in scale and relatively undifferentiated; though few of them are egalitarian in every sense, they are generally not divided into distinct classes or strata. Agrarian civilizations of the kind that prevailed in Europe, India or China are or were hierarchical both by design and in fact; their characteristic divisions were into castes or estates whose boundaries were relatively clear and acknowledged by custom and law. Industrial states, whether of the capitalist or the socialist type, have a formal commitment to equality rather than hierarchy; their characteristic divisions are classes and strata[2] which must accommodate themselves to the ideals of democratic citizenship and equality of opportunity. It is not that inequalities are unknown or even uncommon in industrial societies, but rather that they depend, or are believed to depend, on achievement rather than ascription.

The distinction between 'aristocratic' and 'democratic' societies, and the historical passage from the former to the latter, were described in memorable prose by Alexis de Tocqueville in 1835. He wrote:

> In running over the pages of our history, we shall scarcely find a single great event of the last seven hundred years that has not promoted equality of condition.

And again,

> The gradual development of the principle of equality is, therefore, a providential fact. It has all the chief characteristics of such a fact: it is universal, it is lasting, it constantly eludes all human interference, and all events as well as all men contribute to its progress.
>
> (1956, I: 5–6)

De Tocqueville set out to demonstrate the progress of equality in every sphere of life: in the material conditions of human beings, in the pattern of their social relations, and in their ideas, beliefs and values.

It must be remembered that de Tocqueville's argument about 'aristocratic' and 'democratic' societies was an historical one, intended to bring out the continuity as well as the contrast between the two. The contrast has been extensively applied, both to different historical phases in the life of the same society and to different societies independently of historical connections. The second kind of contrast does not have any necessary link with the evolutionary perspective, and might in fact be accompanied by an explicit rejection of such a perspective.

Western scholars have long been fascinated by the Indian caste system, which has often been represented as the prototype of rigid hierarchy. Some of them have seen in it an extreme form of tendencies present in their own society, while others have viewed it as a qualitatively different, if not an altogether unique, system. The French anthropologist Louis Dumont (1966, 1977) has developed a body of work in which the contrast between traditional Indian society and the modern West is presented in the sharpest possible terms, epitomized in the respective notions of *Homo hierarchicus* and *Homo aequalis*. The contrast, as he draws it, is confined largely to the plane of values, to what people believe or say they believe rather than to what they do or practise. When Dumont talks about *Homo aequalis*, what he means is that modern societies have an egalitarian ideology – that they are egalitarian in intention – not that they have attained or are likely to attain equality in the distribution of material resources. I discuss some of these issues more fully below (p. 1028ff.), and note here only that it may be misleading to characterise whole societies as either 'egalitarian' or 'hierarchical'.

How tangled the question is can easily be seen by returning briefly to de Tocqueville. When he spoke of the providential advance of equality, de Tocqueville clearly believed that equality was, in his own lifetime, advancing simultaneously on all fronts. But that, plainly, was an illusion. We have no reason to believe that equality of condition, or equality in the distribution of material resources, always advances simultaneously with equality as a moral or philosophical value.

An important aspect of inequality in all modern societies is inequality in the distribution of income. Now it is a well-established truth that there was an *increase* rather than a decrease in inequality of income in the early stages of economic growth in most, if not all Western countries (Kuznets 1955). In other words, inequality in one significant sense was increasing during precisely that period when the modern egalitarian ideology was spreading rapidly in the West. Not all societies have had, or can be expected to have, the same historical experience in every respect. But it is obvious that 'legal equality' and 'economic equality' do not have the same rhythms of change and might, arguably, change in opposite directions.

An additional difficulty arises from the fact that different concrete forms of inequality may coexist in the same society: for instance, an open class system and a rigid system of racial stratification. This was noted by de Tocqueville for the United States (1956 [1835, 1840], I: ch. 18). Lack of internal consistency makes comparison difficult, and the difficulty is compounded when the units being compared differ vastly in scale – for instance, a small foraging band and a large nation state. A society on a large scale with a complex pattern of stratification may contain within it component units which have an appearance of remarkable homogeneity and equality, as indeed was the case in traditional India; and a small-scale egalitarian community, enjoying a degree of isolation and autonomy, may depend for its survival on its articulation with a large and complex system of stratification.

The inadequacy of treating the nation state as an irreducible unit in the study of equality and inequality has become increasingly apparent. Societies are at all levels in continuous interaction with each other, and modern anthropologists no longer regard them as isolated or self-sufficient units with fixed and rigid boundaries. Recent studies have shown how the rise of European societies from the seventeenth century onwards was often at the cost of smaller or less developed or less powerful societies in Asia, Africa and Latin America which they oppressed and exploited (Wolf 1982). One must not be too quick to characterize the former as egalitarian societies by looking only at the ideals they set for themselves while looking away from their actual treatment of others.

APPROACHES TO THE STUDY OF INEQUALITY

It is clear that when we compare different societies, we are dealing with inequalities that differ not only in degree but also in kind. There is no universally accepted criterion which enables us to conclude that a given society corresponds more closely than another to some general standard of equality; and common sense is not always a very reliable guide. Economists often single out a specific aspect of the problem, namely inequality in the distribution of income, on the grounds that it lends itself most easily to quantitative treatment. But even here they find it difficult to judge unequivocally whether a given distribution shows more or less inequality than another (Sen 1973). And inequality of income has to be viewed alongside other aspects of inequality which differ significantly among themselves.

The conclusion we reach from a comparison of different patterns of inequality will depend in part on our method and approach. Of the several approaches to the study of inequality, two are of particular importance. The point of departure for the first approach lies in the inequalities inherent in the distribution of abilities among the individual members of a society; for the second, it lies in the inequalities inherent in their arrangement into an organized whole. The first approach stresses that individuals are unequal to begin with, and that their unequal abilities will be bound to show up no matter how or where they are initially placed; the second maintains that since individuals are unequally placed from the start, they develop and display unequal abilities.

Individual variations are a matter of common observation, and they are to be found in every society. No two individuals are exactly alike, and identical twins are the exception that proves the rule. However, we must be careful to distinguish between difference and inequality – an obvious distinction that is easily overlooked by proponents of the theory of natural inequality (Béteille 1980). Two individuals may be quite different from each other without being in any meaningful sense unequal.

Do individuals differ to the same extent in all societies? It is difficult to give an unequivocal answer to this question. One might like to distinguish between variations in purely physical or biological traits and those in mental or 'moral' characteristics, or between 'natural differences of kind' and 'social differentiation of positions' (Dahrendorf 1968); but the distinction is by no means easy to sustain. Comparison of the degrees of individual variation becomes difficult where societies differ very greatly in scale. Moreover, variations among individuals of one's own kind always appear greater than among individuals of a different kind. Explorers, missionaries and colonial administrators systematically underestimated individual variations, even in physical characteristics, among the natives whom they observed and described.

Some anthropologists take the view that the stress on individual variation, if not the very fact of it, is unique to modern societies, being undeveloped or weakly developed in primitive or traditional societies. Émile Durkheim, whose work has left a lasting impression on the French school of sociology, put forward this view in his very first book, *The Division of Labour in Society* (1982 [1893]), in which he argued that primitive societies (conceived in a very broad way) were held together by mechanical solidarity which was based on 'likeness' as against 'complementary difference'. He believed that people in these societies lacked individuality to such an extent that even the differences between men and women, including their physical differences, were weakly expressed or rudimentary in them. This is an extreme position to which few would assent today.

While individual differences are present in all societies, they may be culturally restrained in some cases and encouraged in others. They tend to be encouraged to such an extent in modern societies that individualism has come to be regarded as the dominant ideology of these societies (Dumont 1977, 1983). De Tocqueville believed that there was a close connection between individualism and equality (1956, 2: 98–100). But individualism has more than one implication, just as equality has more than one meaning (Béteille 1986). To the extent that individualism stresses the autonomy and the dignity of the individual, it places itself against all forms of ascribed inequality. But to the extent that it stresses competition and achievement, it justifies and promotes inequality in other forms.

The preoccupation with individual achievement (and with individual quality on which it is presumably based) has given a distinctive character to contemporary debates on equality and inequality. The logic of capitalism is that opportunities are *in principle* equally available to all individuals who, nevertheless, do not all benefit from them to the same extent because they differ in their endowments and fortunes. For many, this difference in individual endowments and individual fortunes lies at the heart of the problem of inequality in modern societies (Hayek 1960: ch. 6, Eysenck 1973). Such a view reveals a bias in favour of methodological individualism, seen most commonly in writings on inequality by economists and psychologists.

Methodological individualism, or the procedure which treats the individual as the basic and irreducible unit in social analysis, faces many difficulties in the study of variation and change in patterns of inequality. It can perhaps account for the ranks assigned to individuals on a given scale, but it cannot as easily account for the scale itself. An issue that all students of social inequality must face is what may be called the passage from difference to inequality. It is a truism that not all differences count as inequalities. Why, then, do only some differences count as inequalities, and not others? Do the same differences count as inequalities in all places, at all times? What is actually involved when a set of differences is transformed into a system of inequalities? These questions cannot be addressed without considering some of the constitutive features of human society and culture.

The majority of sociologists and anthropologists take as their point of departure not the individual agent, but the framework of collective life within which he acts (Bendix and Lipset 1966, Heller 1969, Béteille 1969). Every individual acts within a framework of society and culture which both provides him with facilities and, at the same time, imposes constraints. The language he speaks, the technology he uses, the division of labour within which he works, all exist to some extent independently of his exertions. The regularities governing language, technology and division of labour are of a different kind from those governing individual action.

Language provides us with a convenient example of the place of collective representations in human life. Without language, human life as we know it would be impossible, and human language, in its turn, would not exist in the absence of collective life. But collective representations include much more than language. They consist of the full range of beliefs and values shared by individuals as members of society. At this point it will be enough to say that collective representations include both cognitive and evaluative elements − which are, moreover, closely intertwined − so that the individual members of a society share not only common modes of thought but also common standards of evaluation. Indeed, it is difficult to see how collective life would be possible in the complete absence of shared beliefs and shared values.

Durkheim stressed the contrast between the fullness and variety of the collective representations of a society and what it is possible for any individual mind to create or comprehend on its own. Subsequent investigations by anthropologists in the field have fully confirmed the truth of Durkheim's insight. People with a simple Neolithic technology, such as the Bororo or the Nambikwara Indians of the Amazon basin, show a richness and complexity in their collective representations that seem to surpass what even Durkheim might have expected. The luxuriance of expressive life commonly encountered in the primitive world at the level of cosmology and taxonomy can scarcely be explained by the practical requirements of material existence (Lévi-Strauss 1966).

A seminal paper published by Durkheim and Mauss in 1903 opened up a new field of cultural anthropology devoted to the study of systems of classification (Durkheim and Mauss 1963). We now know that such systems, which are sometimes extraordinarily elaborate, are present in all societies, even those of the smallest scale. They not only arrange the vast multitude of culturally recognized items into broad classes but also order them according to principles that may be implicit or explicit. This means that as well as there being socially preferred items of food, dress, adornment, and so on, there are also recognized preferences in regard to colours and other attributes of nature. These preferences reveal the aesthetic and moral categories of a society. Once again, it is difficult to see how a human society could exist in their absence.

Now, it would be strange in a culture to have standards of evaluation that apply to food, dress, adornment, plants and animals, but none that apply to human beings and their activities. In other words, where people are able to discriminate between good and bad food, they will also discriminate between good and bad cooks; where they judge some gardens to be superior to others, they will also judge some gardeners to be superior to others; where there are preferences as between artefacts, there are likely to be preferences also as between artisans. I am of course talking now of culturally prescribed, or at least culturally recognized, preferences, and not the personal preferences of particular individuals.

Every culture, no matter how rudimentary, has its own bias, not only for certain types of human performance but also for certain types of human quality. Quality and performance are closely related in the minds of people, but they may be given different priorities in different cultures. Men and women may be believed to have different qualities, and where these qualities are themselves ranked, as they often are, men and women will also be ranked (for further discussion of this point, see Article 29). Even where qualities are assigned priority, there is always room to take performances into account. For instance, women may be considered to excel in gardening and men in hunting, but then hunting may rate higher than gardening, in which case men will be ranked higher than women. The stress on quality tends to be associated with the segregation of distinct sections of society into separate fields of activity, so that their members do not compete with each other on a common ground. Where the stress is on performance, men and women — or, to vary the example, whites and blacks — may be allowed to compete for the same prizes and then ranked according to their performance, irrespective of gender (or race). But here again, success or failure will be attributed, at least in part, to the presence or absence of some quality such as intelligence. Moreover, the fact that whites and blacks (or men and women) may in certain spheres compete on equal terms, and be judged on merit, does not mean that they will not in other spheres be treated differently or even unequally.

Thus, it is clear that what transforms differences into inequalities are scales of evaluation. A scale of evaluation is not a gift of nature; to speak in the language of Rousseau, 'it depends on a kind of convention, and is established, or at least authorized by the consent of men' (1938: 174). Even while invoking the name of Rousseau, however, it is important to guard against the dangers of a constructivist argument. The conventions by which human beings rank each other – their qualities and their performances – are rarely the outcome of conscious design. Most people use these scales as they use language, without a clear awareness of their structure.

Once we realize that scales of evaluation are not usually the products of conscious design and are not always clearly recognized for what they are, we have to turn to consider the coexistence of a multiplicity of scales and the problem of their mutual consistency. It is a common experience that where A ranks higher than B in scholastic ability, B may rank higher than A in athletic ability, leaving open the question of the overall rank of A in relation to B. Some occupations are more remunerative, others permit greater freedom of individual action; how are they to be ranked in relation to each other? How complicated the general problem is may be seen from a glance at the voluminous literature that has grown around so specific a topic as the social grading of occupations (see Goldthorpe and Hope 1974).

To assign a central place to evaluation in the explanation of inequality is not to deny that different values coexist in the same society. One can go further and argue that different values tend to predominate in different sectors of the same society. Manual workers and professionals may not rank occupations in the same way; blacks and whites may not assign the same significance to colour in social ranking; and men and women may show different kinds of bias in the personal qualities they value. While this is true, it should not lead to the conclusion that there can be as many scales of evaluation as there are individual members of society, for no society can endure without some coherence in the domain of values.

Advocates of the so-called 'structural-functional' approach in social theory tend to stress the integration of values in the societies about which they write (Parsons 1954). One form of the functionalist argument is that, although there may be different scales of evaluation in the same society, these scales themselves can be arranged in a hierarchy, since every society has a 'paramount value' which determines the alignment of all its other values (Dumont 1980, 1987). This is a tendentious argument which should not be allowed to divert attention from the empirical investigation of the actual extent to which different values reinforce or subvert each other in concrete historical situations.

Where there are competing or conflicting values in a society, each associated with a particular section of it, they do not always rest in a state of stable equilibrium. Of course, the discordance may be reduced through reflection, argument and self-correction, and accommodation may be achieved on the plane of beliefs and values itself. But this is not the only or even the most typical way in which the problem of value conflict is resolved. Differences that cannot be resolved on the plane of values are typically resolved on the plane of power. Or, to put it plainly, 'Between equal rights force decides' (Marx 1954 [1867]: 225).

The resolution of conflict (including the disagreement over values) through the exercise of power brings to our attention a second important source of inequality in collective life. The importance of force (as against common values) in maintaining order and stability in society has been noted by many, and there are some who would say that it is not only important but decisive (Dahrendorf 1968). This is particularly true of those who deal with the place of the state in human affairs. As Hobbes wrote in his *Leviathan* of 1651, 'And Covenants, without the Sword, are but Words, and of no strength to secure a man at all' (1973: 87).

The state provides the most striking example of inequalities in the distribution of power, but by no means the only one. Such inequalities are commonly found in many domains, including the domestic domain, that are a part of society but not, strictly speaking, of the state. No doubt it can be argued that where the state exists it provides sustenance to inequalities of power in every domain and that with the collapse of the state, those inequalities should also collapse. This has been a familiar argument among Marxists who have found support for it in a work published by Engels a century ago (Engels 1948 [1884]). At that time it was hoped that the argument would be confirmed by the imminent collapse of the bourgeois state. The bourgeois state, however, has collapsed many times over, but the end of the inequality of power is nowhere in sight.

There is, besides, plenty of evidence for inequality of power in what are commonly described as 'stateless societies' (Tapper 1983; see also this volume, Article 34). There are, firstly, the chiefdoms, varying greatly in size and degree of organization, with tribal or clan chiefs who might exercise considerable, though intermittent authority in organizing people for collective activities. Much depends on the scale and importance of the collective activities that have to be organized. Pastoral tribes have leaders whose voice carries considerable authority in matters concerning the movement of people and animals, and in conducting and coping with raids.

There are then the segmentary systems proper – segmentary tribes as against tribal chiefdoms, to follow the terminology of Sahlins (1968) – which do not have chiefs in the accepted sense of the term. Here the system works not so much through a hierarchical distribution of power as through the balance of power between groups at different levels of segmentation (see Evans-Pritchard 1940 for a classic account). Two kinds of groups are especially significant in such societies: descent groups and local groups. Where descent groups are corporations – whether among the patrilineal Tallensi (Fortes 1945, 1949) or the matrilineal Truk (Goodenough 1951) – the senior male members have a decisive say in the disposal of the productive and reproductive resources of the corporation, mainly land, livestock and women. This is particularly true at the lower levels of segmentation where the descent group is functionally most effective as a corporation.

It is on the level of the local group rather than the descent group, however, that the crucial evidence for the kind of argument that I am trying to make will have to be found. The evidence seems to me to be clear, though perhaps not decisive. Evans-Pritchard, whose book on the Nuer of southern Sudan (1940) was a turning point in the study of tribal political systems, deliberately excluded the internal organization of the village from his consideration of Nuer political structure. We can nevertheless say something about the exercise of power in maintaining the stability of such groups, even while conceding that this stability is itself a matter of degree.

The problem is of the following kind. Every stable group has a division of labour, no matter how rudimentary, which is regulated by rules regarding the rights and obligations of its individual members. It is in the nature of human life that these rules do not operate mechanically, with clock-like regularity and precision. They are occasionally, if not frequently, violated, if only because individuals have different perceptions of the rules themselves, as well as divergent interests. These divergences, which are found in even the simplest local groups, may appear trivial in scale by comparison with those that occur in industrial societies, but they are nevertheless important in their own context. Disputes have to be settled, decisions that are binding on all have to be made, and this provides the basis for the exercise of power by some individuals over others. To be sure, matters may be settled from one situation to another by all the members of the group acting together so that no individual accumulates more power or authority than any other. But that would be the *limiting* case and not the *typical* one.

We may recall at this point the egalitarian society based on an 'immediate-return' economy of hunting and gathering. It will be a little more clear now why I regard it as a limiting case. It stands at one extreme, the other extreme being represented by the monolithic and authoritarian industrial state with its massive apparatus of coercion and manipulation which reached perfection, or near perfection, in the Soviet Union under Stalin, and, more briefly, in Germany under Hitler. We can learn a great deal about equality and inequality from both social types, although it is my judgement, which I cannot substantiate here, that they are both highly unstable.

SOME COMMON HISTORICAL FORMS OF INEQUALITY

In an important essay on the origin of inequality, Ralf Dahrendorf (1968) distinguished, on the one hand, between natural differences of kind and natural differences of rank, and on the other, between the latter and social stratification. We shall set aside for the moment the significance of 'natural differences of rank', or what is more commonly called natural inequality (Béteille 1980). The relation between natural difference and social inequality is a very important one, although it is by no means as simple as might at first sight appear. Natural differences do not present themselves to us directly, but are perceived in a highly selective manner, through the lenses of socially established systems of classification (Lévi-Strauss 1966). What needs to be stressed is that not merely the evaluation of differences, but to some extent their very recognition, is a social process.

Differences that are assigned cardinal significance in one society may be ignored or overlooked in another. The differences between men and women are, however, taken into account in all human societies, and it is difficult to see how it could be otherwise. This does not of course mean that they are taken into account in the same way or to the same extent in every society. Where men and women are given distinct social roles, they develop differences, and sometimes marked differences, in temperament and ability; these differences in temperament and ability are then taken – by women as well as by men – to be the reason for their being given different roles. It is clear that much of this rests on convention which varies from one society to another (see the classic but controversial account in Mead 1963 [1935]). What is not clear is whether, outside of procreation and parturition, there have been or can be conventions for the social division of labour that ignore altogether the differences of gender.

Leaving aside the question of what is possible, we have to consider how far the differences of gender are in fact treated as inequalities. This is a vexed question where the facts are confusing and are open to conflicting interpretations. There is a vast literature on the position of women in primitive societies which it is impossible to summarize here. In a lecture delivered on the subject in 1955 and first published in 1965, Evans-Pritchard, then Britain's foremost anthropologist, observed that the acrimonious debates on the subject belonged to the past and that it could at last be discussed with scholarly detachment (Evans-Pritchard 1965: ch. 2). That has turned out to be a monumental error of judgement, for no field of anthropology is more deeply embattled today than the one that deals with gender and inequality (Ardener 1975, MacCormack and Strathern 1980; see also Moore in this volume, Article 29).

The historical record of the development of the subject is roughly as follows. Early anthropologists commonly subscribed to the theory of the primitive matriarchate or the view that the first stage of social evolution was marked uniformly by the prevalence of matriarchy or mother-right. This view gradually became obsolete, particularly after Lowie's critique of it in *Primitive Society* (1960 [1921]). At about the same time, Rivers (1924: ch. 5) also pointed out that power lay generally in the hands of men, irrespective of the form of descent, and that there was no uniform relationship between the position of women on the one hand and forms of descent, inheritance and succession on the other. The considerable body of empirical material that was

1022

available when Evans-Pritchard wrote his lecture seems to have borne out Rivers's basic point that women were in general subordinated to men in public life, and that parity between men and women was unusual if not unknown.

The whole subject has now been thrown open once again, mainly through the recent spate of feminist studies (see, for example, Leacock 1978). New dimensions have been brought to light which were not perceived by even the most acute minds among the earlier anthropologists. These studies have implications, only now beginning to be explored, for understanding not just the disparity between the sexes but inequality in general. I here merely touch upon two such issues, one relating to power and the other to values.

Those who have stressed the subordination of women to men have tended to dwell mainly upon the politico-jural domain rather than the domestic domain. Clearly, in even the most strongly 'patriarchal' societies, women sometimes play an important, not to say a crucial, role in domestic affairs. They may play the major part in everything concerned with food, health and nurture, and exercise independent initiative in all these regards. As against the 'jural' inferiority of the wife to the husband or the sister to the brother, there might be a 'psychological' dominance of the son by the mother. A contemporary Indian psychologist has indeed argued with regard to his own society, which is to all appearances strongly patrilineal, that 'the Indian lives in his inner world less with a feared father than with a powerful, aggressive and unreliable mother' (Nandy 1980: 107; see also Kakar 1978). All this, however, would require a reconsideration of the concepts of power and dominance as conventionally used in the social sciences to an extent that would take us far beyond the scope of the present article.

Just as it may be unreasonable to assume the existence of a single homogeneous domain in which some individuals invariably exercise power over others, it may also be unrealistic to assume the existence of a homogeneous conceptual or moral universe whose categories of classification and evaluation are accepted in the same way by all. The important contribution of women's studies has been to draw attention to the existence of alternative beliefs and values whose implications for the *social* ranking of persons have yet to be fully explored.

Distinctions of race, though also marked by physical or biological traits, differ significantly from those of gender. They are less clear and less fixed, and are not universally present. Only some societies have or recognize them while others do not. Within a given society racial differences exist and are perpetuated because they have cultural significance. If people simply ignored those distinctions in their social interactions and married without any regard for them, the distinctions themselves would cease to exist or become substantially different (Béteille 1977, ch. 5). The same can hardly be said about gender.

There is a very wide range of variation of physical features in the human species, much wider than in most other animal species. However, variation by itself does not give us distinct races; the variation has to be clustered in a particular way for races to become visibly apparent. That can happen in either of two ways: when populations are territorially dispersed to an extent which practically rules out interbreeding; or when, though sharing the same territory, they are prevented or discouraged from interbreeding by law, custom and convention. The continued presence of distinct races in a society and their social segregation are, in a sense, two sides of the same coin.

Racial discrimination in its characteristic modern form is a feature of societies that owe their origin to historical circumstances of a particular kind. These are circumstances of sudden and violent encounter between populations differing sharply in physical appearance, language and material culture, associated with the European conquest of Africa and the New World (and to a much lesser extent of Asia). This is not to say that the violent penetration by people of one physical type into the territories of another never took place in the past. But the European penetration of Africa and the New World in the seventeenth and eighteenth centuries was unique in its global character, in its swiftness and violence, and in the scale on which it led to the dislocation of populations (Wolf 1982).

We find today two distinct patterns of racial inequality, both involving whites and blacks, one in the United States and the other in South Africa (Béteille 1977). In the United States racial inequality survives under a liberal democratic regime which has shown some commitment to affirmative action; in South Africa it holds its own under a minority racist regime committed to a policy of apartheid (i.e. 'apartness').[3] Apart from differences in constitutional history and background, there is an important demographic difference between the two countries. In the United States the whites are not only politically dominant, they are also in a majority, having overwhelmed other races on account of their superior firepower, the devastating impacts of introduced diseases on indigenous populations (see Article 11), and sheer strength of numbers. In South Africa the whites are politically dominant but numerically in a minority, being surrounded, moreover, by states which are totally hostile to white-minority rule. What is notable in the United States is the ambivalence of the blacks, whereas what is striking in South Africa is the anxiety of the whites.

Even where two distinct races are initially brought together by the use of force, and are then kept at least partially segregated also by the use or the threat of force, their coexistence over successive generations can lead them to share certain common values. To be sure, these 'common' values are largely the values of the dominant race, but the point is that they tend to be internalized, at least to some degree, also by the subordinate race. A striking example of this may be found in the extent to which upwardly mobile blacks in the United States have internalized white values and standards in regard to personal beauty, elegant dress and refined speech (Frazier 1957). Where, on the other hand, the subordinate race fails or refuses to internalize the 'common' values of the dominant race, we have an unstable and a potentially explosive situation, as exists in South Africa.

We have seen that the inequality of races is, in the typical case, established by the exercise of power and maintained by the hold of a common culture which assigns higher values to the traits characteristic of one race as against those characteristic of another. There is nothing 'natural' about either of these processes. Indeed, if the present population of either the United States or South Africa were allowed to revert to its 'natural' state, all distinctions of race, or at least those distinctions now considered significant, would disappear with the passage of time. This is quite apart from the fact that no matter what we might think of 'domination', evaluation cannot in any meaningful sense be regarded as a natural phenomenon.

Caste and race are sometimes considered together as they are both regarded as extreme forms of rigid social stratification maintained by strict rules of endogamy. Both Lloyd Warner, who pioneered the empirical study of social stratification in the United States (Warner 1941), and Gunnar Myrdal, who conducted a monumental study of the blacks in the same country (Myrdal 1944, 1: ch. 31), found it convenient to use the concept – and not merely the metaphor – of caste in analysing stratification by race. They both pointed out that neither the blacks nor the whites were a race in the scientific sense, that the whole system rested on social conventions, and that, therefore, to represent it in a biological idiom was misleading. They also felt that the barriers separating blacks and whites were qualitatively different from those between classes within each of these populations. Thus, the choice of the term 'caste' was to some extent dictated by negative considerations, since neither 'race' nor 'class' seemed appropriate.

But other anthropologists, too, have pointed to certain fundamental similarities between the Indian caste system and the colour-caste system of the United States (Berreman 1960, 1966). One of these similarities relates to attitudes towards women. Both white males in the United States and upper-caste males in India have shown an obsessive concern with the 'purity' of their own women while engaging freely in the sexual exploitation of black or untouchable women. All of this can be related to ideas about bodily substance and the conditions appropriate for its exchange. The general importance of these ideas in American culture has been stressed by Schneider (1968), and in the Hindu caste system by Marriott and Inden (1974). In other words, inequalities of caste are illuminated in the same way as those of race by a consideration of gender (Béteille 1990).

There are of course differences between caste and race, and the tendency among contemporary anthropologists is to stress the differences more than the similarities (Dumont 1961, de Reuck and Knight 1968). At any rate, the Hindu caste system is a sufficiently important historical example of inequality to deserve attention in its own right. Recent writers on caste, notably Dumont (1966), have seen in it the most complete example of a hierarchical society, one which in its traditional form was hierarchical not only in fact but also by design, and in which the hierarchical principle animated every sphere of life. Viewed in this light, the Hindu caste system had its analogue in the European system of estates which was also governed by the 'hierarchic conception of society' (Huizinga 1924: ch. 3).

The caste system may be viewed at two levels, those of *varna* and *jati*, for both of which the same English word 'caste' has been commonly used (Srinivas 1962). *Varna* represents the formal order of caste, the 'thought-out' rather than the 'lived-in' system, and the traditional discourse on caste has been typically in the idiom of *varna*. All humankind and, indeed, all created beings were in principle divided into four *varnas* which were both exclusive and exhaustive. The *Manusmriti* declares that Brahman, Kshatriya, Vaishya and Shudra are the four *varnas* and that there is no fifth. The same four *varnas*, in the same order of precedence, were acknowledged by Hindus throughout India for more than two millennia until disowned by the new constitutional and legal order.

The *varna* order is expounded in detail in the classical socio–legal literature known as the *Dharmashastra*, particularly in the *Manusmriti* or the *Manavadharmashastra*, which dates back roughly two thousand years (Kane 1974). Anyone who reads this literature will be struck by the elaborate and comprehensive manner in which human beings – their qualities and actions – and all things around them are classified and ordered. To take a well-known example, it is decreed that the sons of a male Brahman shall inherit property in the following proportions: the son of the Brahman mother, four parts; the son of the Kshatriya mother, three parts; the son of the Vaishya mother, two parts; and the son of the Shudra mother, one part only. To be sure, the classification and the ordering are highly schematic, and present us with models rather than descriptions.

The invariance and fixity characteristic of the *varna* model are reduced to some extent when we move down to the plane of *jatis*. *Jati* is a regional rather than a national system, and the number of *jatis*, as well as their names, vary from one part of the country to another. Moreover, there is reason to believe that old *jatis* have disappeared and that new ones have come into being with the passage of time in each and every region. Although Hindu theory states that the whole of humankind is embraced by the *varna* order, *jatis* have in fact freely existed outside of that order, among Muslims, among Christians and, to some extent, also among so-called 'tribals' (Bose 1975 [1949]). The problem of the correspondence between *varna* and *jati* is a difficult one (Srinivas 1962, Lingat 1973), although the assumption of such a correspondence was a part of Hindu beliefs about caste.

Whereas the *varnas* are only four in number, the *jatis* in each region are very many; exactly how many is difficult to say, because they are frequently segmented in a manner that has baffled census takers over the distinction between caste and subcaste (Béteille 1964). Suffice it to say that there may be in a single village as many as 30 to 35 subcastes (Béteille 1965). The *jatis* in a region are not merely differentiated from each other; they are also mutually ranked. This ranking manifests itself in a variety of social contexts through transactions of different kinds (Marriott 1959, 1968). Traditionally, a very large social distance had to be maintained between the Brahmans at one extreme and the Harijans or Untouchables at the other.

The ranking of *jatis* differs, and has always differed, from the ranking of *varnas* in a number of important ways. There is no clear linear order of *jatis* as there is of *varnas*. It is no doubt true that the Brahmans are at the top and the Harijans at the bottom, but each of these two categories is made up of a number of distinct *jatis*, which themselves cannot be readily placed in a linear order. This ambiguity has always left some room for mobility among castes and subcastes (Srinivas 1968). An upwardly mobile *jati* not uncommonly phrased its claim to superior status in the idiom of *varna*.

While there is general agreement that the ranking of *jatis* is very elaborate and, compared with other systems of social ranking, also very rigid, there is considerable disagreement about the sources of caste rank. The actual ranks enjoyed by the different castes arise from a variety of factors, although the idiom in which caste ranking is phrased is typically a ritual one, more specifically the idiom of purity and pollution. This had led some observers to exaggerate the importance of ritual factors, giving the system an appearance of mechanical rigidity without any room for freedom of action.

Despite the impressive stability and continuity of the caste structure, Hindu ideas behind the ranking of persons are fluid and complex, and perhaps heterogeneous. *Varna*, which may loosely be rendered as 'order' or 'kind', provides an overall framework, but it does not stand by itself. Besides the four *varnas* detailed in the *Dharmashastras*, there are the three *gunas* or 'qualities' discussed elsewhere, particularly in the *Samkhya* texts (Rege 1984, 1988, Larson and Bhattacharya 1987). The three *gunas* are: *sattva* (signifying light, purity, intellect), *rajas* (energy, valour), and *tamas* (darkness, inertness). The *gunas* enter as constituents into the make-up of different persons. In addition to *guna*, there is also *karma*, which refers to action or works: what a person does rather than what he or she is.

Guna and *karma* are commonly discussed in relation to persons rather than groups, although they may also be linked more or less explicitly to the four *varnas*. In the *Bhagavadgita*, Lord Krishna declares, '*caturvarnyam mayam sristam, guna-karma-vibhagasah*' ('the four *varnas* did I create, dividing (or distributing) the *gunas* and the *karmas*')(Zaehner 1969: 4/13). Some modern interpreters of the *Gita*, including the great nationalist leaders B. G. Tilak and M. K. Gandhi, have tried to argue that it represents an activist philosophy; however, it cannot be too strongly emphasized that throughout the long course of Indian history individual action has been severely constrained by the social framework of caste.

Some contemporary anthropologists (e.g. Dumont 1964) have overstressed the hierarchical completeness of Hindu society in order to bring out the distinctive features of their own. Modern societies do indeed have a number of distinctive features, both in their organizational structures and in their value patterns. These features stand out when we contrast the modern West not only with traditional India but also with its own medieval past (Béteille 1986, Dumont 1987).

In the context of our present theme, perhaps the most striking feature of modern societies is the notion of equality before the law. As an explicit principle governing the relations between persons, it has found its fullest expression only in modern times. It developed first in the West, in England, France and the United States, and came to be widely adopted in the present century so that there are very few parts of the world today where it is not acknowledged. The far-reaching implications of this should not be overlooked, for equality before the law requires equality not only between the rich and the poor or the high- and the low-born, but also between blacks and whites and between men and women. Medieval European society and, to an even greater extent, traditional Indian society, was a society of privileges and disabilities; by contrast we now have a society of citizens entitled to, if not actually enjoying, the equal protection of laws.

The acceptance in principle of equality before the law or of equality of opportunity does not mean, of course, that inequalities of status and power have ceased to exist. There is a vast body of sociological literature showing beyond a shadow of doubt that such inequalities do exist in all modern industrial societies (Bendix and Lipset 1966, Heller 1969, Béteille 1969). There is, as one would expect, a polemical side to this. Socialist writers from the Soviet Union and from East European countries have argued that since such inequalities derive primarily from the private ownership of property, they are to be found in their most extreme form in capitalist countries, notably the United States. Liberal writers from the West, on the other hand, have asserted that the truly oppressive forms of inequality are those arising from the monolithic concentration of power in the apparatus of state and party, as exemplified in countries like the Soviet Union.[4]

We might begin on neutral ground with a consideration of the occupational structure of modern societies. It would be difficult to exaggerate the importance of that structure in industrial societies, whether of the capitalist or the socialist type. Occupations have become highly specialized, and the occupational system has become more elaborate, more complex and more autonomous than in any society previously known to history. Industrialization is accompanied not only by a new attitude to work but also by a new organization of work (see this volume, article 32). Much of a person's adult life is spent in his or her occupational role, and early life is largely a preparation for it.

The hundreds of named occupations present in an industrial society are classified and ranked. The principles of occupational ranking have been discussed even more exhaustively by sociologists than have those of caste ranking by anthropologists (Goldthorpe and Hope 1974). Studies in the United States have shown that, although new occupations displace old ones with great rapidity, the *structure* of occupational ranking shows a high degree of stability. Moreover, comparative studies of occupational ranking in different industrial societies, of the capitalist as well as the socialist types, have shown that this structure is not only remarkably stable but also relatively invariant (Hodge *et al.* 1966a, b).

In general, non-manual occupations rank higher than manual ones, not only in the United States, but also in the Soviet Union in spite of official theory which assigns pride of place to manual work in the creation of value in the form of material products. Doctors rank higher than typists, not only in the United States where they are independent professionals, but also in the Soviet Union where, like typists, they are state employees. Soviet attempts to level out differences of income between occupations had limited success, despite strong pressures from the state. They eventually had to be abandoned, and were later condemned by Stalin (Lane 1971).

The question of why some occupations are consistently ranked higher than others is in some ways as difficult to answer as the question of why some castes are always ranked higher than others. It no more suffices to say that space scientists rank higher than plumbers because they receive higher earnings, than it does to say that Brahmans rank higher than Oilpressers because they have greater purity. One might just as well ask why the space scientist should earn more than the plumber. Various kinds of explanations, none of them very satisfactory, have been offered, in terms of 'scarcity', 'function' and so on (Bendix and Lipset 1966). It is quite clear, as Parsons (1954) consistently stressed, that occupational ranking is governed by the value system of a society, and the more fully a given occupation embodies or expresses its core values, the more highly it is likely to be ranked. There are only two qualifications to be added: first, occupations alone do not express the core values of a society; and secondly, their ranking is also governed, at least in part, by considerations of power which are different from those of esteem.

Although occupational ranking may be as elaborate as caste ranking, the nature of occupational status differs from that of caste status. Caste status is ascribed whereas occupational status is, at least in principle, achieved. There is no guarantee that an individual will have the same occupation, or even the same occupational level, as his father, and the same individual may in fact move considerably from one occupational level to another in his own lifetime. Therefore, sociologists who study occupational structure and occupational ranking also study occupational mobility. Indeed, the enormous literature on the social grading of occupations has grown largely in response to the problems of describing, analysing and measuring occupational mobility (Goldthorpe 1980: ch. 1).

The literature on occupational mobility in industrial societies is not only very large but in parts highly technical (Blau and Duncan 1968), so that casual inferences drawn from it are likely to be misleading. But some of the studies have come to conclusions that at first sight appear surprising. In a pioneering study made in the 1950s, Lipset and Bendix emphasized at the outset that 'the overall pattern of social mobility appears to be much the same in the industrial societies of various Western countries' (Lipset and Bendix 1967: 13). They found their own conclusions 'startling' in view of the universal assumption that the United States had much higher rates of mobility than European countries like Britain and France. The earlier studies operated with such broad differences of level as between 'manual' and 'non-manual' workers; more refined analyses have naturally revealed variations in rates of mobility within the same overall pattern.

An important issue in the study of social mobility relates to its implications for the formation and stability of classes (Goldthorpe 1980). Sociologists who deal with this question tend to approach it from two different points of view. There are those who maintain that the multiplicity of occupational levels together with high rates of individual mobility renders the formation of distinct and stable social classes difficult if not impossible in advanced industrial societies. Blau and Duncan (1968) argued in an influential book that high rates of mobility make most individual positions impermanent to such an extent that few individuals are likely to develop a lifelong commitment to any particular class. 'Class' then becomes a statistical construct rather than a socially significant category.

The second approach is a Marxian one. Marxists have traditionally held an ambivalent attitude towards individual mobility. On the one hand, they have questioned whether capitalist societies have high or even rising rates of mobility. On the other hand, they have maintained that rates of mobility have little, if anything, to do with the polarization of classes – which they see as an historical tendency generated by contradictions within capitalism (Poulantzas 1976). A reasonable position would seem to be that, while rising rates of individual mobility do alter the context of class conflict, they do not abolish class identity as such, certainly not the identity of the working class (Goldthorpe 1980).

Marxists, as is well known, contrast class with occupation (Dahrendorf 1959: pt. I), and assign far more importance to the former than to the latter, at least in the analysis of capitalist societies. The importance that we assign to class in industrial societies in general, as against the capitalist variant alone, will depend on what we mean by class. In the Marxian scheme, the inequality of classes is much less a matter of status and esteem than of unequal power in the economic domain. The inequality of power is itself seen to be rooted in the particular historical institution of private property. Thus, in this scheme, although inequalities of power are crucial and quite large in capitalist societies, they can, at least in principle, be greatly reduced, if not eliminated, by the abolition of private property.

Others argue that property is only one of the bases of power, and that power has other bases that would survive the abolition of property and might even be strengthened in consequence. These writers also tend to subordinate esteem or status to power in their analytical schemes, but in a way that is different from that of the Marxists (Dahrendorf 1968). In their view power is a universal and inescapable source of inequality which permeates all forms of human life, particularly in societies organized on a large scale. To be sure, there are variations in the patterns of its distribution, and the resulting inequalities can be controlled or regulated to some extent, but never eliminated altogether.

Some have taken the further step of trying to redefine class by substituting power (or more narrowly, authority) for property. Thus, for Dahrendorf (1959: 204), 'the term "class" signifies conflict groups that are generated by the differential distribution of authority in imperatively co-ordinated associations'. The presumption behind this definition (like the one behind the definition it seeks to supersede) is that inequality of power (like inequality of property) generates conflict. Whether it does so or not, and under what conditions, to what extent and in what forms, are important questions on which there is much disagreement and some confusion among sociologists. Some regard 'class' as an aspect of 'stratification', being primarily an expression of the economic ranking of groups. Others regard 'stratification' and 'class' as fundamentally different; according to them, 'stratification' relates to the ranking of groups, whereas 'class' relates to the conflict of interests between them (Dahrendorf 1959).

EQUALITY AS CONCEPT AND IDEAL

We are now in a position to return to a consideration of equality as a concept and an ideal. There is no doubt that inequalities of status and power exist everywhere in the modern world, but they now exist in a greatly altered legal and moral environment.

'Hierarchy', wrote Marx and Engels, 'is the ideal form of feudalism' (1968: 190), and it was also the ideal form of other past civilizations. This is not the case today. People live with inequality, they may seek to explain or even to justify it, but they no longer idealize it. This is true not only of England, France and the United States, where the modern ideal of equality first took shape, but also of countries like India to which it later spread.

But the ideal of equality is no less confusing a subject than the reality of inequality, and the confusion is compounded when we seek to consider it in a comparative perspective. Two questions may be asked at this point: first, whether the ideal of equality is indeed unique to modern ideology and, if so, in what sense; and, second, whether the ideal, or rather the concept behind it, is a coherent one.

Some scholars believe that egalitarian values have not only originated in the West but are, moreover, somehow incompatible with non-Western societies

1031

and cultures. Others maintain that they are neither uniquely Western nor uniquely modern. I have already alluded to Woodburn's (1982) argument about the 'egalitarian societies' of certain hunting and gathering peoples. References to egalitarian values are not uncommon in the comparative anthropological literature on tribal societies including those of pastoralists and agriculturalists. On a larger scale, Islamic civilization was in many respects more markedly egalitarian than medieval Christianity, not to speak of medieval Hinduism (Gellner 1981). However, Islamic egalitarianism lacked the universality characteristic of modern egalitarianism: it denied equality, even in the formal sense, to women as well as to adherents of other faiths. In the case of most tribal societies as well, this lack of universality also qualifies such commitment to equality as there is.

Although modern societies have universalized the *idea of equality* and have elaborated it in moral, legal and political discourse to an unparalleled degree, they have not come anywhere near to the *equality of condition* said to be common in many tribal communities, including those adhering to Islam. The modern idea of equality arose under specific historical conditions, in response to a society where hierarchy was deeply and firmly entrenched. It was under such conditions that 'equality of opportunity' – or, in Napoleon's famous phrase, 'careers open to talent' – became a powerful slogan. Equality of opportunity could hardly be a forceful idea in a tribal society where equality of condition, or near-equality of condition, is an established datum of experience.

The idea of equality of opportunity, which was a new one in Napoleon's time, had already lost its shine a century later. R. H. Tawney, one of the strongest advocates of equality in the inter-war years, saw clearly that in a society marked by acquisitiveness and untempered competition, equality of opportunity by itself could do little to reduce the gap between the rich and the poor, and might in fact increase it (Tawney 1964). Thus he contrasted equality of opportunity with what he called 'practical equality', and sought to make the latter the central focus of social policy.

It is through considerations of social policy rather than abstract speculation that the ambiguities in the concept of equality have become manifest. We know today that legal equality, equality of opportunity and even rising rates of mobility can coexist with increasing inequality in the distribution of income. As we have seen, equality of opportunity can be of significance only in a society based on the competition of individuals. But this means that there can be equality only *before* the competition, and not *after* it. From this it may be argued that the commitment to equality requires not only that the competition itself should be free, but also that the rewards of success should not be too lavish nor the penalties of failure too severe.

Thus, equality may signify equality of opportunity, or it may signify equality in the distribution of things (Béteille 1985). If it is true that modern ideology sets a high value on equality, it is also true that it is deeply divided

1032

between these two conceptions of what equality is. Several positions may be taken on this. One may argue that there is no real contradiction between the two, that the contradiction is only apparent. If we take equality of opportunity to mean an equality that is 'fair' and not merely 'formal', then we can more easily reconcile it with equality, or at least equalization, in the distribution of things (Rawls 1972: 83–9, 298–303).

Others would maintain that the idea of a 'fair' equality of opportunity is subjective and arbitrary, and that the ideal of equality cannot be tested against any preconceived model of distribution. This being so, substantive equality is a kind of mirage whose pursuit is bound to be self-defeating. More importantly, it can subvert the ideal of formal equality, or equality before the law, which in this view is where the essence of equality lies (Hayek 1960: ch. 6, Joseph and Sumption 1979).

If we now look back on the transition from the 'aristocratic' to the 'democratic' type of society, or from the 'hierarchical' to the 'egalitarian' type, we realize how complex the issues are. When we look at that transition in Europe, and also elsewhere, we cannot but be struck by the crucial part played in it by the forces of the 'self-regulating market'. These forces broke down old barriers and created new cleavages. In Europe the old distinctions of estate, guild and parish yielded before the expanding forces of the market to the extent that the latter took less account of social origin than of individual ability.

However, the market did not dissolve all the old distinctions, some of which survived, although in altered forms, and accommodated themselves to it. First of all, there are countries like India where market forces have not penetrated far enough and where so-called 'semi-feudal' arrangements, based on caste and patronage, are still well entrenched. It can of course be argued that what survives from the past will inevitably decay as and when the market takes full command. But this argument loses much of its force when we see that distinctions of race and ethnicity, and sometimes marked disparities based on them, flourish even in such a mature capitalist society as the United States.

The market also sharpens old distinctions, and creates new ones, the most important being the distinction between capital and labour. The widening gap between capital and labour, and the simultaneous enrichment of the few and impoverishment of the many in mid-nineteenth-century England, were noted not only by Marx and Engels but also by many others who witnessed the expansion of market forces at first hand. It is true that the worst excesses of this phase of capitalism have to some extent been corrected, at least in the advanced capitalist societies, but it is not true that they have all been corrected solely by the 'self-regulating market'. Few of those who are witnessing the expansion of market forces and the accompanying rise in economic disparity in India and other Third World countries can seriously believe that they should wait for the market itself to correct these disparities in the long run.

The belief that the inequalities inherited from the past and those being generated at present can and should be corrected by some form of social intervention is widely, if not universally, held in countries like India, and is also held by varying and fluctuating sections of society in countries like Britain and the United States. Of course, such intervention can be of many different kinds, and opinion is naturally divided on who should intervene, to what extent and in which areas of social life. A certain consensus on these issues, however fragile and momentary, was embodied in the institutions of the welfare state created in a number of West European countries in the wake of the Second World War.

Given the full range of historical possibility and experience, the welfare state of post-war Western Europe appears as a relatively mild instrument for the containment of inequality. Far more powerful apparatuses of state and government have been devised in the Soviet Union and elsewhere, at least in part with the objective of reducing inequality. Nor should we underestimate their achievements. There were notable successes in controlling unemployment, in giving workers a better deal and in reducing income differentials between 'mental' and 'manual' workers. Some advances were also made since the Bolshevik Revolution in reducing disparities between the different ethnic groups and nationalities, but many disparities still remain, as is becoming evident in the rising tide of ethnic conflicts.

The notable gains in equality mentioned above were achieved at some cost, which, by any reasonable account, was at times exceedingly high. A consideration of this cost at once reveals one of the paradoxes of equality. The very attempt to regulate and reduce inequality through direct intervention in social and economic processes led, some would say inevitably, to a tremendous concentration of power in the apparatuses of state and party. In other words, the instruments for the suppression of inequality are not neutral, but generate their own inequalities. One could then ask whether, in moving from the inequalities of estate prevalent until the eighteenth century to the inequalities of class about which Marx wrote, and from those again to the inequalities of power of the twentieth century, any real or demonstrable gain was made in the achievement of equality.

A monolithic structure of power imposes constraints on the realization not only of equality but also of other social values, notably liberty. It may be possible in principle to envisage an ideal world where liberty and equality would complement rather than contradict each other; but such an ideal world is not yet within reach, and perhaps for most, not even within sight. Libertarians do not question the principle of equality before the law, or even of equality of opportunity to the extent that it is consistent with the former. But they do question the 'legitimacy of altering social institutions to achieve greater equality of material condition' (Nozick 1980: 232), whether in the name of distributive equality or of 'fair equality of opportunity'.

The stress on distributive equality may be viewed as a threat not only to liberty but also to efficiency. Few people would place efficiency on the same plane as equality and liberty in their hierarchy of values. It is nevertheless true that efficiency has a central place in the economic ideology that dominates much of modern life. Some of the most crucial debates in the realm of social and economic policy relate to the comparative advantages of market and plan as two alternative forms of rationality (Dahrendorf 1968). A major test of these advantages, even for those who believe that the two alternatives cannot be mutually exclusive, is the degree of efficiency attainable under each, either singly or in combination with some elements of the other.

Modern egalitarians have always argued that an order that tolerates extremes of inequality is not only socially unjust but also economically wasteful and inefficient. But the considerable experience now available of centrally-regulated economies has shown up the other side of the coin. In the socialist countries, the market was for decades held responsible for both generating and sustaining economic inequality, and one of the main objectives of centralized planning was precisely to restrict that role. If the market is viewed with less suspicion in these countries today, it is not because its role in sustaining inequality has been completely lost to sight, but rather because people are now a little better prepared to accept some economic inequality as a price to pay for the efficiency guaranteed by a measure of competition.

Thus, although equality is undoubtedly an important value in modern societies, there is a considerable distance between a minimal definition of it as equality before the law and a definition that also tries to take into account the distribution of income, wealth and various social services, such as health and education. One must always keep in mind that there are not only strong advocates of equality in these societies but also critics of it (Letwin 1983). These critics point not only to the high political and economic costs of realizing equality, but also to the conceptual ambiguity inherent in the very idea of equality. 'The central argument for Equality', a contemporary political philosopher has written, 'is a muddle' (Lucas 1965: 299). And even of the more specific ideal of 'equality of opportunity', a distinguished American educationist has written, seemingly in despair, that it is 'a false ideal' (Coleman 1973: 135).

Perhaps equality is not so much a false ideal as one which cannot be meaningfully conceived in an historical vacuum. It can only make sense in the context of, and in response to, the specific challenge that a given society presents to its reflective members. Sometimes the challenge comes from an order established by age-old religious tradition, such as that of caste; sometimes it comes from a recklessly competitive economic system such as that of free-enterprise capitalism; or again, it may come from a monolithic political apparatus itself designed to solve the problem of inequality once and for all. Equality is today too powerful an idea to be set aside simply because it cannot be precisely defined. It is like the djinn which, once released from the bottle, cannot be put back into it again.

NOTES

1 To take an example from outside the West, Rousseau influenced the great nineteenth-century Bengali writer Bankimchandra Chattopadhyay, who published a tract on equality entitled *Samya* in 1879; for an English translation, see Haldar (1977); see also Ganguli (1975).

2 Soviet writers have generally preferred the term 'strata' to 'classes' to describe the characteristic divisions of their own society which, according to them, was marked by an absence of 'contradiction' or, at least, of 'antagonistic contradiction'.

3 This article was completed in 1989. No account is taken of political developments in South Africa since that time.

4 The collapse of the Soviet Union, which took place after this article was written, has rendered much of this polemic at least temporarily obsolete. In what follows, references to the Soviet Union specify conditions predating the collapse.

REFERENCES

Ardener, S. (ed.) (1975) *Perceiving Women*, London: Dent.

Bendix, R. and Lipset S. M. (eds) (1966) *Class, Status and Power*, New York: Free Press.

Berlin, I. (1978) *Concepts and Categories*, London: Hogarth Press.

Berreman, G. D. (1960) 'Caste in India and the United States', *American Journal of Sociology* 66: 120–7.

—— (1966) 'Caste in cross-cultural perspective', in G. De Vos and H. Wagatsuma (eds) *Japan's Invisible Race*, Berkeley: University of California Press.

Béteille, A. (1964) 'A note on the referents of caste', *European Journal of Sociology*, 5: 130–4.

—— (1965) *Caste, Class and Power*, Berkeley: University of California Press.

—— (1977) *Inequality Among Men*, Oxford: Blackwell.

—— (1980) *The Idea of Natural Inequality*, London: London School of Economics.

—— (1985) *Equality of Opportunity and the Equal Distribution of Benefits*, Pune: Gokhale Institute.

—— (1986) 'Individualism and equality', *Current Anthropology* 27(2): 121–54.

—— (1990) 'Race, caste and gender', *Man* (N.S.) 25: 489–504.

—— (ed.) (1969) *Social Inequality*, Harmondsworth: Penguin.

Blau, P. M. and Duncan, O. D. (1968) *The American Occupational Structure*, New York: Free Press.

Bose, N. K. (1975 [1949]) *The Structure of Hindu Society*, Delhi: Orient Longman.

Coleman, J. S. (1973) 'Equality of opportunity and equality of results', *Harvard Educational Review* 43(1): 129–37.

Dahrendorf, R. (1959) *Class and Class Conflict in Industrial Society*, London: Routledge & Kegan Paul.

—— (1968) *Essays in the Theory of Society*, Stanford, Cal.: Stanford University Press.

Davis, K. and Moore, W. E. (1945) 'Some principles of stratification', *American Sociological Review* 10(2): 242–9.

de Reuck, A. and Knight, J. (eds) (1968) *Caste and Race*. London: J. & A. Churchill.

de Tocqueville, A. (1956 [1835, 1840]). *Democracy in America*, 2 vols, New York: Alfred Knopf.

Dumont, L. (1961) 'Caste, racism and "stratification"', *Contributions to Indian Sociology* 5: 20–43.

—— (1964) *La Civilization indienne et nous*, Paris: Armand Colin.

—— (1966) *Homo hierarchicus*, Paris: Gallimard.
—— (1977) *Homo aequalis*, Paris: Gallimard.
—— (1980) *On Value*, London: British Academy.
—— (1983) *Essais sur l'Individualisme*, Paris: Seuil.
—— (1987) 'On individualism and equality', *Current Anthropology*, 28(5): 669–77.
Durkheim, E. (1982 [1893]) *The Division of Labour in Society*, London: Macmillan.
Durkheim, E. and Mauss, M. (1963 [1903]) *Primitive Classification*, London: Cohen & West.
Engels, F. (1948 [1884]) *The Origin of the Family, Private Property and the State*, Moscow: Progress Publishers.
Evans-Pritchard, E. E. (1940) *The Nuer*, Oxford: Clarendon Press.
—— (1965) *The Position of Women in Primitive Societies, and Other Essays in Social Anthropology*, London: Faber & Faber.
Eysenck, H. J. (1973) *The Inequality of Man*, London: Temple Smith.
Fortes, M. (1945) *The Dynamics of Clanship Among the Tallensi*, London: Oxford University Press.
—— (1949) *The Web of Kinship Among the Tallensi*, London: Oxford University Press.
Frazier, E. F. (1957) *Black Bourgeoisie*, New York: Free Press.
Ganguli, B. N. (1975) *Concept of Equality*, Simla: Indian Institute of Advanced Study.
Gellner, E. (1979) 'The social roots of egalitarianism', *Dialectics and Humanism* 4: 27–43.
—— (1981) *Muslim Society*, Cambridge: Cambridge University Press.
Goldthorpe, J. H. (1980) *Social Mobility and Class Structure in Modern Britain*, Oxford: Clarendon Press.
Goldthorpe, J. H. and Hope, K. (1974) *The Social Grading of Occupations*, Oxford: Clarendon Press.
Goodenough, W. H. (1951) *Property, Kin and Community on Truk*, New Haven: Yale University Press.
Haldar, M. K. (1977) *Renaissance and Reaction in Nineteenth Century Bengal*, Calcutta: Minerva Associates.
Hayek, F. A. (1960) *The Constitution of Liberty*, London: Routledge & Kegan Paul.
Heller, C. S. (ed.) (1969) *Structured Social Inequality*, London: Macmillan.
Hobbes, T. (1973 [1651]) *Leviathan*, London: Dent.
Hodge, R. W., Siegel, P. M. and Rossi, P. H. (1966a) 'Occupational prestige in the United States: 1925–63', in R. Bendix and S. M. Lipset (eds) *Class, Status and Power*, New York: Free Press.
Hodge, R. W., Trieman, D. H. and Rossi, P. H. (1966b) 'A comparative study of occupational prestige', in R. Bendix and S. M. Lipset (eds) *Class, Status and Power*, New York: Free Press.
Huizinga, J. (1924) *The Waning of the Middle Ages*, London: Edward Arnold.
Joseph, K. and Sumption, J. (1979) *Equality*, London: John Murray.
Kakar, S. (1978) *The Inner World*, Delhi: Oxford University Press.
Kane, P. V. (1974) *History of Dharmasastra*, vol. 2, pt. 1, Poona: Bhandarkar Oriental Research Institute.
Kuznets, S. (1955) 'Economic growth and income inequality', *American Economic Review* 45(1).
Lane, D. (1971) *The End of Inequality?* Harmondsworth: Penguin.
Larson, G. J. and Bhattacharya, R. S. (eds) (1987) *Encyclopedia of Indian Philosophy: Samkhya*, Princeton: Princeton University Press.
Leacock, E. (1978) 'Women's status in egalitarian societies', *Current Anthropology* 19(2): 247–75.
Lenski, G. (1966) *Power and Privilege*, New York: McGraw-Hill.

Letwin, W. (ed.) (1983) *Against Equality*, London: Macmillan.

Lévi-Strauss, C. (1966) *The Savage Mind*, London: Weidenfeld & Nicolson.

Lingat, R. (1973) *The Classical Law of India*, Berkeley: University of California Press.

Lipset, S. M. and Bendix, R. (1967) *Social Mobility in Industrial Society*, Berkeley: University of California Press.

Lowie, R. (1960 [1921]) *Primitive Society*, London: Routledge & Kegan Paul.

Lucas, J. R. (1965) 'Against Equality', *Philosophy* 40(154): 296–307.

MacCormack, C. and Strathern, M. (eds) (1980) *Nature, Culture and Gender*, Cambridge: Cambridge University Press.

Marriott, M. (1959) 'Interactional and attributional theories of caste ranking', *Man in India* 39(2): 92–107.

—— (1968) 'Caste ranking and food transaction', in M. Singer and B. S. Cohn (eds) *Structure and Change in Indian Society*, Chicago: Aldine.

Marriott, M. and Inden, R. B. (1974) 'Caste systems', *Encyclopaedia Britannica* (Macropaedia), vol. 3.

Marx, K. (1954 [1867]) *Capital*, vol. 1, Moscow: Progress Publishers.

Marx, K. and Engels, F. (1968) *The German Ideology*, Moscow: Progress Publishers.

Mead, M. (1963 [1935]) *Sex and Temperament in Three Primitive Societies*, New York: Morrow.

Morgan, L. H. (1964 [1877]) *Ancient Society*, Cambridge, Mass.: Harvard University (Belknap) Press.

Myrdal, G. (1944) *An American Dilemma*, New York: Harper.

Nandy, A. (1980) *At the Edge of Psychology*, Delhi: Oxford University Press.

Nozick, R. (1980) *Anarchy, State and Utopia*, Oxford: Blackwell.

Parsons, T. (1954) *Essays in Sociological Theory*, New York: Free Press.

Poulantzas, N. (1976) *Les Classes sociales dans le capitalisme aujourd'hui*, Paris: Seuil.

Rawls, J. (1972) *A Theory of Justice*, London: Oxford University Press.

Rege, M. P. (1984) *Concepts of Justice and Equality in the Indian Tradition*, Pune: Gokhale Institute.

—— (1988) 'Dharma: man, society and polity', *New Quest* 69: 133–40.

Rivers, W. H. R. (1924) *Social Organization*, London: Kegan Paul.

Rousseau, J-J. (1938 [1782]) *The Social Contract and Discourses*, London: J. M. Dent.

Sahlins, M. D. (1968) *Tribesmen*, Englewood Cliffs, NJ: Prentice-Hall.

Schneider, D. M. (1968) *American Kinship*, Englewood Cliffs, NJ: Prentice-Hall.

Sen, A. (1973) *On Economic Inequality*, Oxford: Blackwell.

Srinivas, M. N. (1962) *Caste in Modern India and Other Essays*, Bombay: Asia Publishing House.

Srinivas, M. N. (1968) 'Mobility in the caste system', in M. Singer and B. S. Cohn (eds) *Structure and Change in Indian Society*, Chicago: Aldine.

Tapper, R. (ed.) (1983) *The Conflict of Tribe and State in Iran and Afghanistan*, London: Croom Helm.

Tawney, R. H. (1964 [1931]) *Equality*, London: Unwin.

Warner, W. L. (1941) 'Introduction', in A. Davis, B. B. Gardner and M. R. Gardner, *Deep South*, Chicago: University of Chicago Press.

Wolf, E. R. (1982) *Europe and the People Without History*, Berkeley: University of California Press.

Woodburn, J. (1982) 'Egalitarian societies', *Man* (N.S.) 17: 431–51.

Zaehner, R. C. (ed.) (1969) *The Bhagvad-Gita*, London: Oxford University Press.

FURTHER READING

Bendix, R. and Lipset, S. M. (eds) (1966) *Class, Status and Power*, New York: Free Press.

Béteille, A. (1977) *Inequality Among Men*, Oxford: Blackwell.

—— (1987) *The Idea of Natural Inequality and Other Essays*, Delhi: Oxford University Press.

Bourdieu, P. (1985) *Distinction*, London: Routledge & Kegan Paul.

Duby, G. (1980) *The Three Orders*, Chicago: University of Chicago Press.

Dumont, L. (1980) *Homo hierarchicus*, Chicago: University of Chicago Press.

Eysenck, H. J. (1973) *The Inequality of Man*, London: Temple Smith.

Franklin, J. H. (ed.) (1968) *Color and Race*, Boston: Houghton Mifflin.

Goldthorpe, J. H. (1980) *Social Mobility and Class Structure in Modern Britain*, Oxford: Clarendon Press.

Jencks, C. (1973) *Inequality*, Harmondsworth: Penguin.

Leach, E. R. (1970) *Political Systems of Highland Burma*, London: Athlone Press.

Letwin, W. (ed.) (1983) *Against Equality*, London: Macmillan.

Marshall, T. H. (1977) *Class, Citizenship and Social Development*, Chicago: University of Chicago Press.

Ossowski, S. (1963) *Class Structure in the Social Consciousness*, London: Routledge & Kegan Paul.

Sen, A. (1973) *On Economic Inequality*, Oxford: Blackwell.

Strathern, M. (ed.) (1987) *Dealing with Inequality*, Cambridge: Cambridge University Press.

Tawney, R. H. (1964) *Equality*, London: Unwin Books.

Treimann, D. J. (1977) *Occupational Prestige in Comparative Perspective*, Orlando: Academic Press.

Tumin, M. M. (1985) *Social Stratification*, Englewood Cliffs, NJ: Prentice-Hall.

Wesolowski, W. (1979) *Classes, Strata and Power*, London: Routledge & Kegan Paul.

38

THE NATION STATE, COLONIAL EXPANSION AND THE CONTEMPORARY WORLD ORDER

Peter Worsley

THE RISE OF THE NATION STATE

The rise of the nation state is a modern phenomenon. Its origins, in Europe, date back only two centuries. The earlier rise of the centralized state entailed three interrelated processes: the concentration of political power, economic centralization, and cultural hegemony.

The establishment of monarchical supremacy over hitherto vigorously self-assertive aristocracies – especially the great feudal magnates whose vast estates provided them with strong regional bases of power – was a long-drawn-out struggle. The new absolutist monarchs also had to construct their states out of feudal polities in which the consent of the traditional estates had to be gained for major taxation (Anderson 1973: chs 1 and 2). The creation of a system of centralized taxation through which money was directly available to the monarch made it possible to raise military forces that came immediately under the sovereign's command. 'A prince', Machiavelli wrote, 'should... have no other thought or aim than war.' The new armies and navies were used, not just to bring the magnates to heel, but to expand the economic system by protecting the domestic market and stepping-up overseas trade.

Culturally, the consolidation of the absolutist monarchy led to the domination of the culture of the victorious heartland over provincial cultures: for example, the transformation of the dialect of the Isle de France around Paris into a 'national' French, and of the East Midlands dialect into 'Standard English'. But thorough-going cultural standardization was not achieved by any Absolutist state. 'The ideological conceptions of "nationalism"', Anderson has remarked, 'were foreign to the inborn nature of absolutism' (Anderson 1973: 38). It was the bourgeoisies that inherited the centralized polities created by the absolutist monarchs who instituted national systems of education to meet the requirements of industrial society and to integrate the citizen with the state (Gellner 1983) – a model that was subsequently exported to the rest of the world (see this volume, Article 25).

NON-EUROPEAN POLITIES AT THE TIME OF EUROPEAN COLONIAL EXPANSION

Empires and states

The societies encountered by Europeans during the expansion of the West varied enormously, from the 'stateless' societies Columbus found in the Caribbean to the great empires of Turkey and China. The latter were far greater in size and wealth than any European state. To the Ottomans, rulers of fifty million people at a time when Queen Elizabeth inherited a state with only five million, the inferiority of Europe was self-evident: in 1666, the Grand Vizier of the Ottoman court addressed the French Ambassador as a '*Giaour* [unbeliever], a hogge, a dogge, a turde eater'. Fifty years later, Oliver Cromwell's grandson, Governor of Fort William (Calcutta), was expected to make obeisance to the Moghul Emperor 'with the reverence due from a slave' (Stavrianos 1981: 157).

Technologically, Europe had no great superiority over Asian economies, whose industries ranged from large-scale ship-building to sophisticated textiles. Superior military equipment had proved decisive in the conquest by Europeans of the Aztec and Inca Empires, and their superiority in sea power and in naval tactics enabled them to establish small coastal trading-posts. But for the two and a half centuries after Da Gama, they were effectively excluded from the Indian subcontinent. Even at their height, the Portuguese in Asia as a whole were merely middlemen in a purely intra-Asian trade in which European goods were unimportant (Stavrianos 1981: 158, 230, van Leur 1955: 281).

Asia was also the centre from which most of the great 'world-religions' (Weber 1956) reached the adjoining regions: Hinduism spread into South India and South-east Asia (Fuller 1984); Buddhism spread from North India southwards, reaching present-day Sri Lanka several centuries before the birth of Christ (Geiger 1986, Gunawardana 1979), as well as northwards into the Himalayan zone and China, and into countries south and east of the subcontinent. The spread of Chinese influence over Korea, Japan and Indo-China was as much cultural as political. In these countries, where religious 'Great Traditions' (Tambiah 1970) flourished, resistance to European culture was correspondingly stronger.

Yet not all the societies encountered by Europeans were large empires. Many states did not conform to Weber's 'rational–legal' ideal type, with monopoly of the legitimate use of physical force within a given territory, a centralized bureaucracy, and an effective system of state economic organization (Weber 1961: 249–58). China, the 'world's largest enduring state' (Elvin 1973: 15), certainly possessed, in the mandarinate, a highly organized administrative apparatus. Yet the political articulation and integration of the provinces varied with the vicissitudes of power at the centre: at times of weak central control, the empire would divide into lower-level regions. Similarly, the range of economic articulation and integration of the different levels of marketing system fluctuated over the centuries (Chi 1936, Skinner 1964–5).

But many states were endemically weak. The authority of the ruler was often little more than the acceptance of the loose suzerainty, often largely ritual, of one political grouping – an aristocratic house or tribal group – over others equally noble or powerful. Hence succession was often determined less by clear rules than by civil war between followers of rival royal or noble houses. In lieu of a 'rational–legal' system of administration, noble representatives of tribal houses or conquered tribes were made to serve at court. Random levies, patronage, or campaigns to secure booty abroad took the place of a 'rational' system of securing income for the state.

Weak states of this kind were therefore often segmentary in structure rather than centralized (Southall 1956). The prime focus of individual loyalty was not the state but local authority-figures and communities; the first allegiance was to one's lord, or to clan and tribe, or to religious communities – the 'little traditions' of earth and ancestor-cults.

These variations of state structure and civil society were of major consequence when the Europeans arrived. Even the great empires contained serious structural weaknesses, visible to Europeans, which Sir Walter Raleigh summed up as a 'void of libertie' and a 'want of Nobilitie' – the absence of any checks on the sovereign's power, especially on the part of an independent land-owning class; a state of affairs which Montesquieu was later to designate as 'Asiatic Despotism' (Anderson 1973: 462ff.). Weak state structures were susceptible to division and manipulation by determined invaders. Thus Cortés, with only 600 Spaniards under his command, was able to conquer Mexico because he was assisted by tens of thousands of traditional enemies of the Aztecs from Tlaxcala and Texcoco; Pizarro, in Peru, was able to exploit divisions resulting from a very recent succession war. Clive's victory at Plassey in 1757 turned, in the end, on the defection of one of the enemy's generals.

Stateless societies

By no means all of the world penetrated by Europeans was inhabited by populations living in states, let alone empires. Large parts of Amazonian South America and virtually all of North America, as well as Australia and many other parts of the globe, were occupied by societies without a state apparatus. The social and political institutions of 'stateless' societies, however, were very varied. There were societies with chiefs and hereditary aristocracies, even with slaves, as well as societies where age and sex were the primary bases of status, rank and authority (see Article 34). Using such political criteria, societies of this kind have often been called 'tribes' or 'bands', and on the grounds of techno-economic criteria, these have been associated respectively with 'agricultural' and 'hunting and gathering' economies. Whichever criteria are adopted, whether political or techno-economic, such designations ignore the profound differences between peoples around the world whose cultures are as dissimilar as the languages they speak.

Terms such as 'stateless', or 'acephalous', are in any case only negative, residual categories; they tell us what these societies are *not*. In an attempt to provide a positive designation of their common attributes, Wolf has called them societies based on a 'kin-ordered' mode of production (Wolf 1982: 88–100). Kinship systems, he accepts, may be of many kinds; moreover kinship is neither equally salient in all stateless societies, nor does it fulfil the same functions. But in so far as it is used to regulate descent and marriage, it does affect the deployment of economic and political power.

However exiguous the material equipment of such peoples, their systems of religious belief are rich and complex, and the empirical knowledge they possess of their environments, in particular of the plants and animals on which they depend, is both wide-ranging and intellectually highly organized (Waddy 1988). In such societies, it is people and their knowledge, rather than things or capital, that are the crucial social resource: their labour-power, their skills and, in the case of women, their capacity to produce more people. They are not, as nineteenth-century ethnologists thought, 'primitive communists': there is institutionalized differentiation, particularly of sex and age, which recurs generation after generation – inequalities, for instance, as between the original settlers of the land and newcomers, or between senior and junior lines of descent (see Article 37).

Even stateless polities, lacking kings or chiefs and specialized military forces, were capable of co-ordinated and steady campaigns of resistance or aggression against neighbouring peoples. For example, the segmentary lineage organization of such tribal peoples as the Nuer of the southern Sudan was pre-adapted to a process of what Sahlins (1961) has called 'predatory expansion'. Such polities were also capable of radical political innovation. The arrival of British colonial forces in Nuerland, for instance, resulted in the rise of religious prophets who were able to mobilize very large numbers of people (Evans-Pritchard 1937). Similarly, in Melanesia, individuals and communities who believed in the other-worldly source of material commodities, and in a future apocalypse, followed prophets who foretold the imminent end of the world – one in which the whites would be defeated and their goods would fall into the hands of the natives (Worsley 1957).

The establishment of European rule was not necessarily accomplished suddenly, as in South America. In North America, the struggle between Britain and France for control of the fur trade and for political domination of the region sucked different Amerindian peoples into a succession of wars. In the process, institutions which had brought separate groups together, often for ritual purposes, were transformed. The Iroquois Confederacy, for example, established initially for the peaceable settlement of disputes between the five 'nations', and for co-ordinating defence against outsiders, became a mechanism for organizing war against their neighbours and was increasingly wracked by violent internal battles for hegemony. The alliance of the Iroquois with the losing side, the British, during the American War of Independence, proved to be their final undoing. Subsequent movements among the Iroquois, notably the Handsome Lake prophetic movement around the beginning of the nineteenth century, focused on personal spiritual revival and revelation and were staunchly opposed to war (Kehoe 1981: 244–50).

THE BEGINNINGS OF EUROPEAN EXPANSION

In pre-capitalist Europe, state power was agrarian power, consisting in control over land and over the labour which produced wealth from the land.

In classical antiquity, trade had been both predominantly seaborne, due to the geographical location of the Mediterranean countries, and largely confined to luxury commodities, notably spices, silks and fine cottons imported from the Orient. But by the late medieval period, the centre of European trade had moved to the north of the continent. This was a trade not in luxuries but in necessities, notably the export, on a massive scale, of timber and grain from Eastern Europe to Western Europe. The states of Western Europe could only solve the resulting negative balance of payments by exporting gold and silver.

Beginning in the fifteenth century, the trading relations of the largest Eastern European state, Russia, shifted eastwards. In 1584 the Cossacks began crossing the Urals, and by 1637 the Russians had reached Okhotsk on the Pacific, having traversed a distance half as far again as that between the Atlantic and Pacific coasts of the United States, and at a time when the English colonists in America had not yet crossed the Alleghany mountains (Stavrianos 1981: 69). This orientation to the Asian hinterland deflected Russia from colonial adventure outside the Euro-Asian landmass, while the preservation of a social structure founded on serfdom at the bottom and autocracy at the top became the principal preoccupation of the Tsars. The nobility exchanged power over the state for power over their serfs, while trade passed into the hands of foreign middlemen. These developments also cut the Russian Empire off from the technological and economic advances that were taking place in the West. Despite periodic attempts of autocrats like Peter the Great and Catherine to imitate the West, Russia and the other states of Eastern Europe increasingly became an underdeveloped agrarian region.

In Western Europe, by contrast, the rise of the absolutist monarchies led to a quite different organization and geographical orientation of trade, based on co-operation between monarchical rulers and the rising mercantile bourgeoisies which undertook overseas ventures in which the state invested funds and provided military and political backing.

International trade within Western Europe, especially in textiles, was growing steadily and was based in towns where merchants had acquired immunities from arbitrary state action. Increasingly, they involved themselves in trade outside Europe, above all in the spice trade.

THE GROWTH OF THE SPICE TRADE

Eastern spices were needed in medieval times to preserve meat or to disguise the taste. But spices such as nutmeg and cloves were also valued as medicaments, even as aphrodisiacs, or simply for their flavours or scents. Their importance was reflected in the immense social value placed upon them: in the conspicuous consumption of a year's supply of cinnamon which Nero burned at the funeral of his wife, or in the payment of 1,200 kilograms of pepper to the Gothic king, Alaric, in return for his undertaking (later broken) not to sack Rome. As early as the first century AD, the Romans had sailed as far as the Malabar Coast of South India in their search for pepper, and to present-day Sri Lanka for cinnamon, deliberately spreading economic 'disinformation' as to where the spices were actually produced and who produced them.

The trade with Europe was to become the most fateful for the world. It had been pioneered by Indonesian traders who had taken spices over 6,500 kilometres of ocean to Madagascar, whence Arabs or perhaps Phoenicians had shipped them via the Red Sea, or overland up the Nile Valley, to the Mediterranean. But with the establishment of Arab domination over the Eastern Mediterranean, control over the spice trade gradually became a stranglehold. The Arab conquest of Cairo (Abu-Lughod 1971) signalled the beginning of Muslim control over the land routes to China and the sea routes to the East, which even the later capture of Constantinople by the Crusaders in 1204 could not break. Though the spice trade within Europe became a Venetian monopoly, Venice was dependent on Arab compliance for access to the sources of the spices. And even at the height of Venetian power gold continued to flow eastwards to pay for the spices. When the Ottomans took Constantinople in 1453, control of trade between the Mediterranean and the Orient seemed to have fallen irrevocably into Muslim hands.

But within only a few years, Da Gama had rounded the Cape and Magellan had circumnavigated the globe. European explorer-traders now poured into the Indian and Pacific Oceans.

The possibility of defeating the Saracens now seemed on the cards. After the Crusades, Christians in Europe had realized that they were only a minority in the world, and could not hope to defeat Islam on their own (Southern 1962: 27–31). The idea of establishing alliances against the Turk with non-Muslim empires in the East was canvassed as early as the thirteenth century. Some of these projects – like the idea of making contact with the legendary Prester

John in Abyssinia, or with the Nestorian Christians in China – were fantasies; others, especially the attempt to build an alliance with the Mongols, were more realistic. Between 1245 and 1253, no less than four missions were sent to the Mongol Khan by the Papacy alone, visits which were reciprocated by Mongol embassies to Rome (Southern 1962: 39–65).

But the dream of breaking the power of Islam only began to seem realizable after the Arabs had been driven out of the Iberian peninsula and following the conquests in America. Spanish confidence now knew no bounds. Muslim resistance, some thought, could be broken by diverting the Nile to the Red Sea or by raiding Mecca and seizing the Prophet's body; five thousand Spaniards, it was even suggested, could take China. Thus inspired, Spanish and Portuguese 'discoverers' set out on voyages that were to end with the unification of the entire globe. The central purpose of these expeditions was unambiguous: Magellan's first round-the-world voyage, westwards, was an expedition to reach the Spice Islands; the eastwards route, round the Cape, was aimed at securing the sources of pepper on the Malabar Coast.

THE CONQUEST OF SOUTH AMERICA: GOLD, SILVER, SUGAR AND SLAVERY

In order to avoid head-on confrontation, Spain and Portugal accepted the Papal division of the New World under which all lands west of a line near Cape Verde were allocated to Spain, while those to the east went to Portugal. But an attempt to define similar spheres of influence in the Spice Islands themselves, where the Spaniards had established themselves in Tidore and the Portuguese in Ternate, was only resolved by bitter warfare between the colonizers and their respective local allies (Spate 1979: 99–100).

The absence of spices in the Americas was a bitter disappointment to Columbus, but the gold ornaments of the Carib Indians suggested another source of profit. Since there was not much gold to be had locally, the Spaniards were encouraged to invade the mainland. Gold rapidly became the main driving-force of the Spanish Conquest: 'We Spaniards', Cortés wrote, 'suffer from an affliction of the heart which can only be cured by gold'. To a priest who criticized his lack of concern with saving Indian souls, Pizzaro replied: 'I have not come for any such reasons. I have come to take away from them their gold'.

The initial looting of Mexico – what Weber termed 'booty capitalism' (Bendix 1960: 306) – soon exhausted the gold available. The conquerors were forced into organizing the production of gold themselves on a massively expanded scale. By the end of the sixteenth century, bullion, mainly silver, came to constitute more than 95 per cent of all colonial exports, tripling the supply of silver in Europe, a flow so gigantic that when Drake returned from 34 months of piracy in the Spanish Main, Queen Elizabeth was able to pay off the whole of England's foreign debt and finance the Levant Company, the predecessor of the East India Company (Spate 1979: 263). The line between legitimate trade (always accompanied by ruthless violence) and buccaneering – whether private enterprise, directly state-financed, or financed indirectly by the state through the grant of 'letters of marque' – was often hard to perceive. Such was the continuing wealth of the Americas, though, that in the mid-seventeenth century, the prostitute-filled silver centre of Potosí could boast 14 dance-halls, 80 churches, 36 gaming-houses and seven or eight hundred professional gamblers. On his round-the-world voyage of 1770–4, Anson captured only one large Spanish silver vessel. But 32 wagon-loads of Spanish treasure were conveyed in triumphant procession to the Tower of London (Spate 1983: 256–65).

In the process, the indigenous population was decimated: partly worked to death, but in the main succumbing to disease (see this volume, Article 11). The population of Mexico declined from some 25 million in 1519 to 5.3 million in 1548 and 1.05 million by 1605; in Peru, from possibly 7 million to 1.8 million by 1580.

The imperial connection also proved fatal for the Spanish economy, intensifying the relative economic backwardness and the social ossification of that country *vis-à-vis* its more dynamic northern neighbours. The abundance of bullion inhibited investment in manufacturing industry and encouraged costly wars of expansion. Eventually, the Spanish empire became chronically bankrupt, the Spanish imperial system little more than a mechanism for transferring the wealth of America to pay for the manufactured goods it had to buy from northern Europe. By the end of the sixteenth century, only 3.8 per cent of the goods carried to the New World in Spanish ships were products of Spain (Spate 1983: 335). Portugal became a client state of England.

Where gold and silver were absent or became worked out, sugar became the major source of colonial profit. During the Crusades, the Christians had become acquainted with sugar and with the technology which the Arabs had developed to produce it. Arab production, and the industry which the Portuguese and the Spaniards implanted on their new Atlantic island possessions off the West African coast, had been based on a mixture of free labour, indentured labour and slave labour. Slavery had not been the dominant form of labour, nor – as the world 'slave', derived from the name '*Sclavus*' ('Slav'), indicates – had slavery been confined to Africans. But in the New World, production came to be organized entirely on the basis of plantations worked by African slave labour (Mintz 1986: 28–32). The sugar plantation was an agro-*industry*, in which centralized discipline and a concern to achieve maximum economy in the use of time constituted in many ways the prototype for the factories of the subsequent Industrial Revolution (Patterson 1982).

England and France now came into head-on conflict for control of the sugar trade in the Caribbean. By the end of the century, William Pitt the Younger estimated that four-fifths of British overseas income derived from the West Indies, while two-thirds of French external commerce was with one island,

Saint-Domingue (Haiti). Holland exchanged New York for the far more important sugar-fields of Surinam, while France let Britain have Canada rather than lose Guadeloupe.

Whichever power ran the plantations, new and larger supplies of slave labour were needed. A whole continent, Africa, was converted into the major source of supply. Thirty-six million people died without reaching the Americas; perhaps twelve millions got there: together, nearly fifty million human beings were transported. In the process, the indigenous economies of Africa were destroyed; powerful kingdoms were broken or converted into machines for capturing slaves, and new slave-raiding and slave-trading states were brought into being.

FROM COLONIALISM TO IMPERIALISM

The decline of Spain and Portugal opened up a struggle between England, France and Holland for global mastery. Once independent of Spain, the Dutch turned their attention to supplanting their former imperial masters and the Portuguese in colonial trade.

The location of the Spice Islands and the routes to them had been subjects of the tightest security. The Portuguese had probed southwards along the cost of West Africa and rounded the Cape of Good Hope in 1487. To protect the slave trade, Manoel I, King of Kongo, had forbidden the inclusion in maps of the route southwards to the Cape. But neither this nor subsequent Portuguese attempts to keep these secrets to themselves succeeded. Da Gama was able to reach Calicut, in India, thanks to an Arab pilot. (Drake's method of acquiring navigational intelligence had been simple and direct: 'kidnap a local pilot' (Spate 1983: 298 n. 1, and ch. 9).) In 1595, van Linschoten, a Dutchman who had lived in Goa, published the sailing instructions for the Cape route in his *Itinerario*. Immediately, a Dutch fleet set out for the Indies. By the middle of the seventeenth century, they had conquered Ceylon, captured Malacca, and finally seized the ultimate prize: the Spice Islands themselves. They were also implanted in Recife in Brazil and were raiding the west coast of South America.

Military conquest led to the replacement of trading-posts, or 'factories', by colonies. Direct political power now allowed the Dutch to dominate the production process itself. For more than a century they enforced the most rigorous control over the production of spices. The island of Banda, the only source of nutmegs, was depopulated and the entire council of headmen butchered in order to break indigenous resistance. In the Moluccas, where cloves grew widely, native people were exterminated on every island except Amboyna, where the guns of the colonial forts ensured that no one grew, transported or possessed a single seedling of cloves (Greenberg and Ortiz 1983: 17, 20, 61).

Other European colonizing states did the same. The historic pattern of mercantile competition now gave way to global struggle between these

European states for the direct and permanent conquest of colonies. The power of the historic trading companies was replaced, step by step, with that of representatives of the metropolitan state. By 1778, a new principle of bourgeois political economy was introduced even in the Spanish Empire: free trade within and between the Spanish colonies, and with the metropolis. In 1790, the Casa de Contratación, in Seville, which had controlled trade with the Americas since the Conquest, was abolished. The consequent increase in both the production and the trade of the colonies resulted in a new realization that the economic interests of the colonies were not necessarily identical with those of Spain. It led, in other words, to the strengthening of a sense of nationalism.

In 1830, the Dutch replaced the system under which the Dutch East India Company had managed trade with the Indies for over two centuries with a new 'Culture [Cultivation] System'. This established incentives designed to stimulate peasant production for the market: those who produced export crops on a fifth of their land had their taxes remitted. Java was soon transformed into a 'mammoth state plantation' (Geertz 1963: 53) for the production of coffee and sugar; 'a whole people...converted into a nation of...estate coolies, with their own natural aristocracy reduced to the position of foremen and superintendents' (Panikkar 1959: 88).

Despite the measures taken by the Dutch to preserve their monopoly of spices, they failed. In any case, spices and sugar were fast becoming less important as the major sources of colonial wealth. The monopoly over the plants themselves was broken by British 'botanic imperialism', as seedlings of cocoa, tea and rubber plants, and of cinchona (for the production of quinine), were smuggled, often by agents of the British, including diplomats, from the East Indies, Brazil and Peru, and disseminated from Kew Gardens to new colonial Botanic Gardens in Kingston (Jamaica), Peredeniya (Ceylon) and Raffles Gardens (Singapore), where they became the bases of new and immensely profitable tropical agro-industries (Brockway 1979).

The struggle between Britain and France for control of North America and India had left India as the jewel in Britain's crown. One major consequence of the subsequent desperate attempt to throw off the British yoke, the 'Mutiny' of 1857, was the final abolition of the (by then) weakened British East India Company, and its replacement by a regime of direct control of both the polity and the economy by the colonial state.

Agriculture and industrial revolution in the West now led to a new pattern of economic relations between the metropoles and the colonies. In India, traditional industries, notably shipbuilding and textiles, were destroyed. In their place, a new division of international labour arose: Indian agriculture supplied the raw material for Lancashire's new cotton mills, whose products were then exported back to India. The wealth extracted from the colonies thus went to fuel the British agricultural and industrial revolutions. Liverpool, the world's leading slave port, survived the ending of the trade by converting itself into a centre of international commerce and industry.

There was also a revolution in consumption: a near-doubling of wages in Western countries after the middle of the nineteenth century stimulated a mass demand for tropical commodities like sugar and fruits which had once been supreme luxuries, so valuable that sculptures in sugar were conspicuously displayed on royal banqueting tables in the Middle Ages (Mintz 1986: ch. 3). In 1815–44, the average Briton still consumed less than 20 pounds of sugar per year; by the 1890s, this had risen to between 80 and 90 pounds (Hobsbawm 1969: 74).

THE CONSOLIDATION OF GLOBAL IMPERIALISM

India became the springboard for Britain's onslaught upon the most populous country on earth, China. When Lord Macartney had proposed the opening of China to foreign trade and to Christian missionizing in 1793, the response from the Chinese Emperor had been one of polite incredulity. His respectful spirit of submission was appreciated, Macartney was told, but China had no need of the manufactures of 'barbarians'. Plainly, however, *they* needed Chinese products, so would be allowed to establish small trading-posts on the coast, under strict supervision. The notion that they might proselytize Christianity, however, was dismissed as 'utterly unreasonable'.

One commodity introduced by the Europeans from India soon outstripped all others: opium. Within a few decades, millions of Chinese had been turned into drug addicts and in two Opium Wars all barriers to trade were destroyed. A joint British–French force took advantage of the Taiping Rebellion (1848–64) to impose its will on the enfeebled imperial government, burning the Summer Palace and opening the country's trade to foreigners. By the end of the century, China had been divided into British, French, Japanese and German 'spheres of influence'.

The final act in the establishment of modern imperialist control over virtually the entire world came with the Berlin African Conference of 1884–5, when Africa was divided between a handful of industrialized European powers.

The establishment of virtually global European rule depended not just on technological superiority in general, but on one specific kind of production: armaments. The technological edge in the Spanish conquest of South America – armour, swords, muskets, horses and dogs – had not been very great. But by the nineteenth century, European industry provided its armed forces with new weapons of terrible destructive power. Nevertheless, people continued to resist. In early clashes in New South Wales, between 2,000 and 2,500 settlers were killed by Aborigines armed only with spears; however, settlers and the military wiped out upwards of 20,000 Aborigines (Hughes 1988: 277). In well-organized empires and states with large armies, resistance was more effective: the Ashanti wiped out a British army in 1824. So did the Mahdi in the Sudan and the Zulu in 1879, while Abyssinian forces destroyed an Italian army as late as 1896, at Adowa.

THE COLONIAL POLITY

European conquest also depended, as in the Americas, on using local forces. In West Africa, for instance, an army of 1,200 men, most of whom were Africans, had defeated 30,000 of their enemies at Sokoto. Colonial troops from countries outside Africa were also used.

The consolidation of military victory entailed the construction of new states that were entirely subordinate to the mother state back in Europe. Administration was designed to cost as little as possible. Sir Harry Johnston governed Nyasaland with his own salary plus £10,000 a year, one British officer and 75 Indian soldiers. Lord Lugard had an annual budget of just over £100,000, five European administrators and one African regiment to govern ten million people. Hence administration necessarily depended on co-opting indigenous political authorities and dividing any possible indigenous opposition. The Dutch in the East Indies, likewise, governed with only a small European administrative staff.

'Divide and rule' involved more than the elimination of any potentially threatening physical force that might have remained in the hands of others. In India, the British organized their army recruitment on the basis of obsessional divisions of the population not only into castes and subcastes, but even into sub-subcastes, in their racist search for uncontaminated 'martial' stock (Mason 1974: 350–61).

In post-Mutiny India, a cultural offensive was launched to persuade the conquered that their future lay in joining the British in building a new imperial order. The Queen now became monarch of both Britain and India, and in 1877 she was restyled Empress of India. Indian princes and notables were won over not just by showering them with material rewards, but by the award of honours and an elaborate series of durbars in which an act of incorporation was the central ritual.

New 'traditions' were invented to incorporate and divide India's old aristocrats and new civil servants. Competition and division between the princes was instilled by creating fine distinctions according to their new positions in the imperial hierarchy: distinctions of title; of clothing and uniform; in the numbers of retainers and soldiers that princes were allowed, and so on. A whole array of new orders, escutcheons, armorial bearings, robes, banners, etc. was created – a bizarre iconic mix of 'Victorian feudal', Mughal, Hindu, imperial Roman, Sikh and Rajput elements (Cohn 1983: 165–209).

'Indirect rule' was much older than Lugard's subsequent formulation of the idea; it had been used for centuries in territories where populations were numbered in tens, even hundreds of millions, and it continued to the end of the colonial epoch. On the eve of the Second World War the Dutch East Indies were divided into directly administered areas and areas of indirect rule with 269 'native states'; India's constitution was similarly heavily weighted in favour of the princely states.

The principal task of the colonial authorities in India was the collection of taxes to pay for the costs of administration, as the title of the Indian administrative official – the 'Collector' – indicated. In the sphere of production, the promotion of capitalism was the major economic priority. The pioneer transformation of colonial land-holding and taxation systems was the Permanent Settlement of 1793 in Bengal, whereby 3,000 zamindars and jaghirdars who, until then, had possessed rights over labour and the products of that labour on lands granted to them by the Moghuls, were made absolute owners of the land – which they had never been before. Their loyalty was assured by allocating to them one-tenth of the taxes collected.

The same basic principles informed policy a century later, in a quite different kind of colony. In Kenya, a white settler colony, Africans were forced to become wage-labourers on lands allocated to Europeans. Even so, in 1914 more than 70 per cent of exports were still coming from African peasant smallholdings. European farmers were now given a vast range of government services – railways, roads, schools, hospitals, extension services, etc. – together with subsidies built into the customs tariffs. Africans were forced to pay head and hut taxes, in cash, and each individual had to carry a *kipande* which recorded their tax payments and labour-history, and which had to be presented on demand by employers and officials. A Masters and Servants Ordinance bound the African to serve out a contract on pain of imprisonment. For those Africans who stayed on lands allotted to white settlers, the Resident Labourers Ordinance permitted them a small subsistence plot, on condition that they put in 180 days of work a year for the settler-owner. By 1920, more than half of the men of the Kikuyu and Luo, the largest agricultural tribes, were working for Europeans. These economic measures were reinforced by a colour-bar excluding Africans from legislative and other public bodies and prohibiting African trade unions, together with a whole social apartheid of separate schools, separate residential areas, exclusive access for whites to hotels and recreational facilities, and 'whites only' seats in buses and public places (Leys 1975: 30–4).

CULTURAL HEGEMONY AND CULTURAL RESISTANCE

Political and economic domination was reinforced by the dissemination of values and institutions designed to promote the acceptance, by the colonized, of their place in the colonial order. To the European colonizers, the superiority of their culture was a *total* superiority: not just one of technology and productive systems, but also of ideas and values. If material pre-eminence was based on modern science, the spiritual superiority of European culture over all forms of indigenous culture, including even the religions of Asia, was equally unquestioned.

Missionaries of all denominations now flocked to the colonies. In inter-war Papua, 15 per cent of Europeans were missionaries belonging to eleven different missionary societies. The colonial state was so thin on the ground that the missions often carried out functions which would elsewhere be the business of the state. Schools run by missions, not by the state, were the main vehicles for the dissemination of European culture. But even where paganism was stamped out, as in Latin America, and Christianity became the religion of the people, it was still informed by indigenous ideas (Wachtel 1971). The quintessence of European culture, it seemed, was religious rather than secular. In a society where all positions of power and wealth were monopolized by whites, the missions were often the only available avenues of social mobility open to the more enterprising and ambitious individuals. Some – whom Asians called 'rice Christians' – 'converted' in order to learn to read and write, or because the missionaries provided them with free health services or food in times of scarcity. Innovators and entrepreneurs seeking to carve out a place in commerce and market agriculture found the Protestant ethic as attractive as did their European predecessors during the Reformation (Long 1968).

For those who resented white authority, interpretations of Christian doctrine which emphasized fraternity, hope and charity, and the righteousness of the meek and the humble as against the arrogance of the mighty, provided a 'critical' ideology of social dissent. The more radical found Biblical authority for deviant, even apocalyptic ideas, or developed syncretic mixtures of Christianity and indigenous belief, organizing their followers into new churches independent of white missionaries. In South Africa, where blacks were kept out of even Christian churches, the formation of their own, 'Zionist' and 'Ethiopian' separatist churches was one of the principal outlets for the intelligent and the ambitious. These churches were also extraordinarily fissiparous, since would-be leaders constantly broke away from the parent body to found their own sects (Sundkler 1948).

A tiny minority, normally sons of the aristocracy, went on to higher levels of European education designed to fit them for positions of responsibility in systems of indirect rule, or, in the economic field, as supervisors on estates or as managers in urban business. But for the vast majority without capital, there was little hope of rising above the level of the small farm or the small shop, and even these niches were often occupied by people from immigrant business cultures, such as Ismaili Muslims in East Africa (Morris 1968).

An even tinier minority had access to literature which was critical of European society or informed them about the values and institutions of their own pre-colonial legacies. Given their socially privileged backgrounds, most of them were not disposed to respond to such ideas.

But eventually, secularism, liberalism and nationalism did filter through:

first the Enlightenment ideas of Rousseau, Locke and Voltaire, and later the positivism of Comte and Saint-Simon and the liberalism of Mill and Spencer. The classical cultures of Mediterranean antiquity had inspired the thinkers of the Enlightenment in Europe; a century later, they still inspired pioneer Egyptian nationalists like Ahmad Lutfi al-Sayyid. Others, like Ram Mohan Roy in India, struggled to modernize their own cultural traditions by combining elements of Hinduism and of Western thought. Early nationalists were also naturally inspired not only by philosophers, but also by their counterparts in Europe: liberal, positivist, radical, revolutionary, and utopian political activists from Mazzini and Cavour to Tolstoy, Kossuth and Parnell.

Today, at a time when it is uncritically assumed that what is labelled 'fundamentalism' (in fact, modern interpretations of Muslim belief) is the authentic and immanent essence of Islam, it is worth remembering that nationalists in Turkey, for instance, had been predominantly secularist since as far back as the epoch of the Tanzimat (1839) right through into the period when Ataturk abolished the Caliphate in 1924 (Zubaida 1989).

But a religious heritage going back thousands of years and deeply imbricated in the institutions of everyday life, especially in rural areas, was not to be overthrown by secularist modernizers, even less by a few European missionaries. In particular, the great religions rendered believers impervious to the message of Christianity. The priority of the colonizing state, however, was not the saving of souls but the exploitation of the colonies in the interests of the Motherland. Whatever the degree of cultural resistance and persistence, therefore, the colonial impact could not be prevented from transforming secular life.

ECONOMIC TRANSFORMATION

The colonial powers crushed early attempts by non-European states to develop modern Western-style industries, especially armaments industries. Periodic requests from Ethiopia, from 1520 through to the nineteenth century, for the technology with which to manufacture European-style swords, muskets, textiles and books, were refused. Other African projects – to import foreign tailors, smiths and carpenters into Dahomey in the 1720s; to develop cotton production among the Fante; to establish sugar refineries in Calabar – were all blocked. In Egypt, Mohammed Ali was more successful in developing the cultivation and processing of cotton, and he used the profits to set up state factories for the manufacture of cotton, woollen, silk and linen textiles, as well as sugar, paper, glass, leather, sulphuric acid, and guns and gunpowder. Palmerston thereupon invaded Egypt and imposed a 'capitulation' treaty under which Egypt's internal trade was opened to foreigners, the state monopolies were abolished, and Egyptian finances were plundered (Stavrianos 1981: 118–19, 215–16).

Even after the abolition of the slave trade in the British Empire – as a result not only of the growth of Abolitionist sentiment in Europe and the growing costs of slavery, but also of the major armed slave rebellions in Saint Domingue and Jamaica (Blackburn 1988) – slavery continued to expand in the USA, Brazil and Cuba. Nor did the abolition of slavery mean the end of the plantation system. Rather, it became the main method of organizing the production of tea, coffee, sisal and rubber, involving the transporting of large populations, often overseas, to plantations where the intensity of work and the methods of control over the workforce amounted to instances of what Goffman has called 'total institutions' (Goffman 1968). The system of indentured labour in Burma has been described as a 'new system of slavery' (Tinker 1974). In the South Pacific, nineteenth-century 'blackbirders' recruited islanders – often by force or deceit – for labour in the Queensland or Fiji plantations, whence as many as 750 out of every thousand failed to return (Belshaw 1954: 39–40).

Large-scale agro-industry was not the only mode of capitalist production, however. The purchase of peasant produce by large trading companies was an alternative way of securing the volume of raw material needed by modern industry in the West. What was destined to become one of the largest of modern multinational corporations, Unilever, built its fortunes, initially, upon the basis of the West African peasant production of palm oil. In 1810, West Africa exported a mere 1,000 tons of oil; by 1860, it was exporting up to 50,000 tons annually. The peasant was now intimately affected by the ups and downs of world prices.

In the first major continent to be colonized, another productive system had flourished for centuries: the large estate or hacienda, based upon the use of tied Indian labour, often living in communities bordering on the large estates, or, like the 'squatters' of Kenya, living off the produce of small plots of land belonging to the hacienda in return for so many days' obligatory labour on the estate. Alternatively, rent might be paid to landlords in cash or in kind. 'Free' labourers, without any land on which to produce their families' subsistence, could only sell their labour-power. Whatever the labour-regime, the upshot was the same: dependence and debt which could last beyond a person's lifetime. Even in the twentieth century a child in the Andes could be born inheriting its father's debts to the landlord (Redclift 1978, Zamosc 1986). Yet because peasant ideology was based on norms of reciprocity which included the legitimacy of obligations to the landlord, and which distinguished good landlords from bad, and because the expectations of peasants rarely aspired beyond ensuring a bare subsistence, they did not become revolutionaries (Scott 1976).

The new imperialism also transformed the city. In China, pre-capitalist cities had often been large centres of craft production centuries before the 'urban revolution' of the eleventh century AD. By the thirteenth century, Hang-chou, which Marco Polo described as 'without doubt the finest and most splendid city in the world', probably had between five and seven million inhabitants and was forty miles in circumference. Yet Chinese cities did not play the same historic role as their smaller medieval counterparts in Europe. The towns were places where rural produce was marketed, and merchants lacked the privileges, and craftsmen the guilds, which provided their European contemporaries with a crucial measure of protection from the whims of kings. Imperial power remained unchallenged for millennia: there was no bourgeois revolution. It was the market towns which grew in the eighteenth and nineteenth centuries, not the cities. By 1900, only about 4 per cent of the Chinese population lived in cities of 100,000 inhabitants or more; *less* than in the thirteenth century (Elvin 1973: 175–8).

But once connected to the world market, cities, some old but most quite new, began to expand rapidly, usually in coastal locations like Bombay and Calcutta, Lima, Valparaiso or Buenos Aires, Canton and Shanghai. As they grew, they sucked in huge supplies of labour from the rural hinterland or, if that supply was lacking, from further afield. Regions with vast populations, like India and China, supplied less-populated but growing countries around the Pacific rim – Ceylon, Fiji, Malaya, Hawaii, California, Australia – and the West Indies with labour. After the abolition of slavery in Brazil in 1885, immigrant labour flooded in to replace the slaves on the coffee plantations. The growth of a city like Buenos Aires, based on the export of wheat, wool and sugar, and later the centre of a world trade in meat, generated the rapid expansion of construction, service and other industries such as the railways and the docks which serviced the export trade. Later, the city became an industrial centre supplying the growing internal market, and also producing for export to adjoining regions. By 1914, Buenos Aires had one and a half million inhabitants, a fifth of the total national population. With only a thinly-populated rural interior, the new labour force was predominantly an immigrant one: three out of four inhabitants of the city were born abroad (Roberts 1978: 49–56).

The rise of industry in the West led to a vastly expanded demand for new kinds of raw materials from the colonial world, such as petroleum. The expansion of world commerce, too, called for new supplies of gold on an unprecedented scale. The whole of southern Africa now became a vast reservoir of labour servicing the mines of the Rand and the Copperbelt. The African village, denuded of its menfolk, was inhabited by children, the elderly, and by women upon whom the responsibility now fell for working the land, bringing up the children, and taking care of the old people. Consumption increasingly included purchased imports of foreign manufacture, from kerosene lamps and bicycles to medicines and clothing. To pay for these, cash crops had to be cultivated alongside subsistence produce. But the major source of cash with which to satisfy these new wants consisted in the remittances sent by men from the mining areas. Rather then constituting a 'dual' economy, then, mine and village were by now integral parts of a single economic network (van Onselen 1976).

Most of the wealth from the mines did not go to Africans at all: only a third of the value of the output from the mines of Northern Rhodesia, for instance, even stayed in the country; of this, European mineworkers, who monopolized the skilled and supervisory jobs, received twice as much as a member of the much larger African labour force (Epstein 1958). But though African miners only earned an average of around £40 a year, this was far superior to wages on European-owned farms or what could be earned by producing cash crops.

The internal market in a country of this size was limited by the earning power and by the size of the population. In countries with much larger populations, not only was the internal market of a far greater scale, but there were also indigenous classes in possession of wealth which could now be invested not just in commerce or light industry but eventually, in the case of India, in modern heavy industry and manufacturing. Thus the coal mines and iron works of Jamshedpur in Orissa were built up, not by British capitalists, but by the Tata dynasty. Modern industry therefore generated two new classes which were to play important parts in ending British imperial rule: an indigenous bourgeoisie and an urban working class. The main financial support for the Indian Congress party was to come from the Tatas.

THE IDEA OF THE NATION

Modern conceptions of the nation, and the linking of the nation to the state, were novel ideas, pioneered principally by Herder and Kant (see this volume, Article 25). Before the rise of the absolutist state, individuals had identities ascribed to them, horizontally, as belonging to a certain rank: in feudal Europe, as members of an estate, as nobles or commoners; in Hindu India, as members of a caste. Relationships to the state were mediated by vertical ties to superior groupings in a hierarchy of dependence and authority; in medieval Europe, through ties to one's lord (Worsley 1984: 252 ff.).

Absolutism meant the concentration of internal sovereignty in the hands of the monarch by breaking the power of the magnates and by refusing to recognize claims to universalistic Papal authority over secular monarchs.

In the subsequent bourgeois revolutions of the seventeenth century, the rights of lower-level corporate groups, especially the propertied, were entrenched. There had been too much sovereignty; now what was needed were the checks and balances of constitutional government. By the time of the French Revolution and the first successful revolt against European colonialism, namely the American War of Independence, civic rights had been widened and defined as the Rights of *Man* − not just the propertied. The unit of civil society was the individual, not the group. Corporate interests intermediate between the individual and the public weal were a constraint on freedom. The interests of society were to be decided by the general will: the aggregate of the individual wills of all citizens. But for these choices to be

1057

based on reason, education was needed. Under Napoleon's corporatist version of equality of education, the ideal was *étatiste* uniformity: every French school-child would turn over the same page in the same authorized textbook at the same time on the same day of the year.

Equality, the atomic relationship to the state, and the supersession of older identities of ethnic group and nationality, contained no collective element, however. The gap was filled by formulating a new, supplementary kind of identity: not just that of citizen (of the state), but a national identity – that of Frenchman.

But when these ideas were transferred to the colonies, national identity was an attribute which set off the indigenous population from their foreign rulers. Members of the indigenous upper classes who collaborated with the colonialists, by serving as administrators, were dubbed traitors; in the economic field, indigenous intermediaries in the export trade with the metropoles were branded pejoratively, in China, as 'compradores'.

Initial resistance to European penetration drew upon both indigenous and new foreign sources in developing analyses of imperialism and in devising programmes for creating a more modern and improved society. The ideology of the biggest revolution of the nineteenth century, the Taiping 'Rebellion' in China, which lasted nearly two decades and in which between twenty and thirty millions died, was not exclusively Chinese in inspiration: many of its ideas and social ideals had been borrowed from Protestant missionaries in Canton. But they were combined with radical social ideals and modes of organization taken from the perennial secret societies (Chesneaux 1971, 1973), and with beliefs that had flourished for centuries in unorthodox schools of Mahayana Buddhism. The Rebellion had been a revolt, in the first place, not against Western imperialism but against the rule of the foreign Manchus. But the support given to the imperial counter-revolution by the Western powers, which was decisive in crushing the revolutionary regime, ensured that the next major revolt, the 'Boxer Rebellion', would be virulently anti-European.

In Latin America likewise, the first movements of resistance against colonial rule drew heavily on indigenous sources. Despite enforced Christianization, the Indian heritage was still strong. Messianic and millenarian movements occurred throughout the colonial period, from the Andes to Yucatán, cul-minating in the revolt, under Tupac Amaru in 1780–83, to recover Indian land and Indian cultural identity. The 'American' nationalism that sub-sequently developed, largely among mestizo strata, during the struggle for independence, was a quite different phenomenon.

By 1848, liberal nationalism had been crushed in Europe, especially in Austria-Hungary and Russia. Thereafter, new and much more radical creeds, notably socialism and eventually Marxism, were to challenge liberalism and give rise to new kinds of mass movements and organized parties. From then on, the removal of foreign rule and the removal of their own indigenous ruling classes were two sides of the same coin for social revolutionaries.

The first successful revolts against colonial rule occurred in the Americas in the eighteenth century: the establishment of the 'First New Nation' in the thirteen colonies (Lipset 1964), followed by the winning of independence by Haiti despite savage British and French repression (Blackburn 1988). But a revolution of black slaves was not to be tolerated, even if it could not be undone. Haiti was therefore strangled economically and was totally isolated politically by the outside world (James 1963). Whatever happened in Europe, the principles of the French Revolution were not to be applied anywhere in the French or Dutch colonies. Thus in South Africa, where two small towns, Swellendam and Graff-Reinet, declared themselves independent, liberty, equality and fraternity were to apply only to whites (De Kiewiet 1941).

The compliance of the colonized could often be ensured without recourse to direct intervention. Britain controlled South America mainly by economic and financial pressures or by using surrogates to crush troublesome regimes. But Britain's successor converted the Monroe Doctrine into a new wave of interventionism in the Teddy Roosevelt epoch: revolt against Spain in the Philippines was hijacked, and the much bloodier revolt against both Spain and slavery in Cuba ended with *de facto* American domination of the new states. Both were policed by a strong US military presence. Thenceforth, the United States intervened regularly in the 'banana republics' of the Caribbean. The Mexican Revolution of 1910 – in which one in three of the population of the state of Morelos died – was not repeated in neighbouring countries; and even here the edge of peasant discontent was blunted by the *ejido* land-reform, while capitalism took off in the cities (Womack 1969).

THE GROWTH OF NATIONALISM

1885, the year in which the great European powers dismembered Africa, had seemed to Lenin, in his study of imperialism (Lenin 1915), an appropriate date from which to reckon the consolidation of the new world system. True, Latin America had been politically independent, with the exception of one or two small countries, for most of the nineteenth century, and a few countries had never fallen into European hands at all: Siam, Afghanistan, China, Persia and Turkey, and Abyssinia (until the 1930s). Their formal political autonomy, however, deceived no one, least of all their indigenous populations, about their true status: that of 'semi-colonies'. By 1914, China, for instance, had been divided into 'spheres of influence' of no less than fourteen foreign powers, based on 'concessions' in the modern cities on the coast.

At the time of the First World War, nationalist movements in Asia were too weak to take advantage of the rivalries between the imperial powers. Rather it was a new, Asian imperialism, that of Japan, which snapped up colonial territories. Those that had belonged to Germany were everywhere simply transferred to the victors.

But within three years of the outbreak of the First World War, a new threat to world capitalism had emerged, with the victory of the Bolsheviks in Russia. Nationalists had long made common cause both with their brothers in other colonial countries and with those in the metropoles themselves – liberals and socialists for the most part – who opposed the imperialist policies of their own governments. But for those who saw the struggle for national independence as entailing social revolution as well, the USSR presented a new and impressive model. The prestige of that revolution, too, ensured that Lenin's theory of imperialism quickly eclipsed both J. A. Hobson's liberal analysis and Hilferding's earlier Austro-Marxist one, and became the dominant global revolutionary theory. Yet the ideological inspiration provided by the infant USSR was not matched by the provision of material assistance to the tiny groups of communists in the colonies. Even in China, where the communists had emerged as a significant armed force, Soviet assistance was limited to a few military advisors. The Chinese communists were wiped out in the cities and forced to retreat to a remote rural base in Yenan, where they developed their revolution on the basis not of the proletariat, but of the peasantry.

The experience of China, however, was different from that of other major Asian colonized countries. Between the wars, nationalist movements arose practically everywhere in Asia. But in India, the largest country after China, the rapid growth of Congress did not eventuate in armed struggle. Elsewhere, the colonial powers remained entrenched for the entire inter-war period. In Southern Africa, white power was in the saddle; in East and West Africa nationalist movements only emerged on the eve of the Second World War. When pressed, colonial governments displayed consummate skill in fobbing off nationalist pressure by interminable discussions about gradual instalments of self-government and the necessity of ensuring the slow internalization of the key values – accountability, impartiality, and so on – of Western civic culture.

It was not until the whites were actually defeated in Asia, by Japan in the Second World War, and the subsequent defeat of the Japanese themselves by the Allies, that the opportunity arose for nationalists to seize power themselves through armed revolution, notably in Indonesia.

The Western powers were able to crush communist-led revolution in Malaya, to contain the communists in Indo-China, and to restore themselves in Hong Kong. But in China they met with a world-historic defeat from which all that could be rescued was the quarantining of the new revolution, and the separation off of Taiwan – into which country foreign capital, mainly Japanese, flowed on such a scale that the island grew to be a far larger industrial power than mainland China itself. Korea was divided between a capitalist South and a North that achieved Soviet-style modernization of agriculture and industry, but which was faced, by the 1990s, with the same problems that undermined the economy of the Soviet Union. In India, the transfer of power took place peacefully before the continent could explode. With the 'Green Revolution' in agriculture, and the creation of a large industrial sector, India was to become a 'regional superpower' in Asia. In most of Asia, then, the survival of capitalism was ensured. The second major defeat of the West – the triumph of a nation of peasants, Vietnam, over the greatest military power in world history – was followed by a period of stagnation, in which the organizational structures which had won the war proved incapable of developing the peacetime economy.

NATION-BUILDING

In 1960 alone, seventeen new African countries appeared on the world scene. Most of them were colonial constructs, entities such as 'Nigeria' or 'Kenya', much less than a century old. Within (and sometimes across) their boundaries, people commonly identified much more strongly with their ethnic group – an identification reinforced by colonial policies of using the 'tribe' as the favoured unit of administration – than with their class or nation. The priorities of the new rulers who were catapulted into power were therefore to divest their society and their culture of European influence, and to build a new state based upon a new national identity, 'Tribalism' was henceforth seen as a sin, as were any other identities or groupings which threatened to divide the nation. Thus, according to the new populist ideologies of 'African socialism', class struggle was a foreign ideology which had no place in the new Africa. Classes were colonial phenomena and had never been part of the authentic pre-colonial past (Worsley 1964: ch. 4, Ionescu and Gellner 1969). Given the power of the state, and despite attempts by outside powers to foment divisions, nation-building proved effective enough in most countries – especially where there were a large number of different ethnic groups – to avert the kinds of internal confrontations which, in Nigeria, resulted in the attempted secession of Biafra and civil war.

The movements which came to power with great popular support embarked upon programmes of nationalization. Politically, nationalization meant placing nationals in all the positions of state legislative and administrative power, both central and local. In Europe, 'nationalization' had meant state-ownership, and indeed 'parastatals' were also created in the new states, notably the marketing boards which monopolized the purchase of peasant cash-crop produce and then sold it on the world market, making a profit for the state. New oil industries were commonly developed under state control, and in some countries older mining industries too. But foreign companies operating outside the field of mineral exploitation were normally left untouched, though they were pressured to appoint African directors to their boards. The state also provided generous assistance to would-be indigenous entrepreneurs. In the process, two new classes were created: a political 'new class' which controlled the state, including the parastatals, and a new national bourgeoisie in the private sector, brought into being through the provision of capital (and sometimes of land) by the state and society.

The dominant parties proceeded, step by step, to concentrate power in their hands, by destroying rival parties and bringing the whole of civil society under their control. The logical end-product was the single-party state. Once that had been brought into being, it was open to whosoever could mobilize enough power to take over the state and society. Increasingly, that meant not those who could mobilize votes, but those who wielded military power. Within two decades, military coups had taken place in a majority of black African states. Outside powers – often the former colonial rulers – were able to manipulate this situation to restore *de facto* economic control, and even at times to intervene militarily.

Whatever the nationalist rhetoric and intent, key economic resources often remained in foreign hands. Massive borrowing by the new states also increased their vulnerability to outside economic control. So long as prices for their primary goods remained buoyant, as they did in the 1960s and 1970s, the problem of repaying the debt was deferred. But when export prices fell, increased output often proved insufficient to service interest payments, let alone to pay off the capital. Even those countries which had aimed at self-reliance found that they were at the mercy of large corporations, since the latter could charge high prices for manufactured goods. On the other hand, demand for Third World commodities was inelastic, or could be undercut by competitors, or even eliminated by substituting man-made materials. More importantly, the 'impersonal' power of the market was such that it was controlled, collectively, by the giant corporations which produced what the Third World needed and which purchased Third World commodities.

In 1974, it seemed that there was one major exception to all this, when the OPEC oil cartel raised its prices to the outside world. This looked like a model which could be applied across the board: all that was needed was for the producers to act in concert, and the West could be held to ransom. Even with such a strategic commodity as oil, however, the panic created resulted in the rapid development of alternative modes of energy use in the West, and to a consequent reduction in world demand for petroleum relative to its increased production. The economies of non-oil states in the Third World itself also suffered severely. And when attempts were made to create a banana producers' cartel, for example, they failed: in part because the West did not need bananas as much as it needed oil; in part because it was easily able to break the solidarity of the suppliers.

Before the 1950s, there had been no such entity as the 'Third World'. But the common interests of the new ex-colonies increasingly brought them together, firstly in a series of regional conferences in Asia and Africa, then in Afro-Asian conferences, of which the Bandung Conference of 1955 was the most important, and culminating in the establishment of the Non-Aligned

Movement. Initially, its major preoccupations were with political decolonization, both domestically and in the remaining colonies, and – as the name of the Movement indicates – with the attempt, in the epoch of the Cold War, to create a global grouping which would not itself be a bloc, but would be independent of both superpowers. But by the 1980s, the major problems had turned out to be economic ones: unequal terms of trade on the world market, and the rising tide of debt. It was Third World pressure which forced the United Nations to establish the UNCTAD conferences on trade and development.

The Third World also found that it had to deal not just with the political power of foreign states, but also with the economic power of giant multinational corporations, which were now organized on the basis of a global division of labour (Henderson 1989). Within this 'new international division of labour', even some Third World countries – notably the 'four little tigers' (South Korea, Hong Kong, Taiwan and Singapore), Mexico, Brazil and other states – became 'newly industrializing countries'. By 1990, the majority of the world's population was living in towns and cities.

Yet in the 1980s, black Africa had slipped backwards in terms of production while its debts increased. Countries like India and Brazil still contain huge rural sectors comprising tens of millions of people mired in agrarian poverty. The evolutionist notion, based on the experience of the minority of 'newly industrializing' countries, that the Third World is 'disappearing' (Harris 1987) therefore seems premature; indeed, those countries where famine is rife appear to be 'underdeveloping'. The older Marxist evolutionary notion, still strongly held in some parts of the Third World, that communism is the 'wave of the future', seems equally destined to disappear as the collapse of the Soviet bloc begins to have its impact on communist regimes in the Third World.

Academic debate about the causes of underdevelopment, and the search for international remedies, continues. But it would be naïve to neglect popular conceptions of the Third World; these include racist views that people in poor countries are simply lacking in intellectual ability. Others attribute their backwardness to cultural beliefs and institutions, such as fatalistic 'other-worldly' religions; while yet others see 'traditional', 'pre-modern' social structures as the problem: aid from the developed world is considered a waste of resources, because corrupt rulers will simply pocket it or use it inefficiently. Finally, the whole notion of 'development', along with the assumption that Western production-systems and patterns of consumption are models to be imitated, has come into increasing question in the era of 'Green' politics (Redclift 1984).

REFERENCES

Abu-Lughod, J. L. (1971) *Cairo: 1001 Years of the City Victorious*, Princeton, Princeton University Press.
Anderson, P. (1973) *Lineages of the Absolutist State*, London: New Left Books.

Belshaw, C. S. (1954) *Changing Melanesia*, Melbourne: Oxford University Press.

Bendix, R. (1960) *Max Weber: an Intellectual Portrait*, New York: Doubleday.

Blackburn, R. (1988) *The Overthrow of Colonial Slavery, 1776–1848*, London: Verso.

Brockway, L. H. (1979) *Science and Colonial Expansion: the Role of the British Royal Botanic Gardens*, New York: Academic Press.

Chesneaux, J. (1971) *Secret Societies in China in the 19th and 20th Centuries*, London: Heinemann.

—— (1973) *Peasant Revolts in China 1840–1949*, London: Thames & Hudson.

Chi Ch'ao-ting (1936) *Key Economic Areas in Chinese History as Revealed in the Development of Public Works for Water-Control*, London: Allen & Unwin.

Cohn, B. S. (1983) 'Representing authority in Victorian India', in E. Hobsbawm and T. Ranger (eds), *The Invention of Tradition*, Cambridge: Cambridge University Press.

De Kiewiet, C. W. (1941) *A History of South Africa – Social and Economic*, Oxford: Oxford University Press.

Elvin, M. (1973) *The Pattern of the Chinese Past*, London: Eyre Methuen.

Epstein, A. L. (1958) *Politics in an Urban African Community*, Manchester: Manchester University Press.

Evans-Pritchard, E. E. (1937) *The Nuer: a Description of the Modes of Livelihood and Political Institutions of a Nilotic People*, Oxford: Clarendon Press.

Fuller, C. J. (1984) *Servants of the Goddess: the Priests of a South Indian Temple*, Cambridge: Cambridge University Press.

Geertz, C. (1963) *Agricultural Involution: the Process of Ecological Change in Indonesia*, Berkeley, University of California Press.

Geiger, W. (1986) *The Mahāvaṃsa or the Great Chronicles of Ceylon*, New Delhi, Asian Educational Services.

Gellner, E. (1983) *Nations and Nationalism*, Oxford: Blackwell.

Goffman, E. (1968) *Asylums: Essays on the Social Situation of Mental Patients and Other Inmates*, Harmondsworth: Penguin.

Greenberg, S. and Ortiz, E. L. (1983) *The Spice of Life*, London: Michael Joseph.

Gunawardana, R. A. L. H. (1979) *Robe and Plough: Monasticism and Economic Interest in Early Medieval Sri Lanka*, Tucson, Arizona: Association for Asian Studies.

Harris, N. (1987) *The End of the Third World: Newly Industrializing Countries and the Decline of an Ideology*, Harmondsworth: Penguin.

Henderson, J. (1989) *The Globalization of High Technology Production: Society, Space and Semi-conductors in the Restructuring of the Modern World*, London: Routledge.

Hobsbawm, E. J. (1969) *Industry and Empire*, Harmondsworth: Penguin.

Hughes, R. (1988) *The Fatal Shore: a History of the Transportation of Convicts to Australia 1787–1868*, London: Pan Books.

Ionescu, G. and Gellner, E. (eds) (1969) *Populism, Its Meanings and National Characteristics*, London: Weidenfeld & Nicolson.

James, C. L. R. (1963) *The Black Jacobins: Toussaint L'Ouverture and the San Domingo Revolution*, New York: Vintage Books.

Kehoe, A. B. (1981) *North American Indians: a Comprehensive Account*, Englewood Cliffs, NJ: Prentice-Hall.

Lenin, V. I. (1915) *Imperialism: the Highest Stage of Capitalism* (many editions).

van Leur, J. C. (1955) *Indonesian Trade and Society: Essays in Social and Economic History*, The Hague: van Hoeve.

Leys, C. (1975) *Underdevelopment in Kenya: the Political Economy of Neo-colonialism, 1964–1971*, London: Heinemann.

Lipset, S. M. (1964) *The First New Nation: the United States in Historical and Comparative Perspective*, London: Heinemann.

Long, N. (1968) *Social Change and the Individual: a Study of the Social and Religious Responses to Innovation in a Zambian Rural Community*, Manchester: Manchester University Press.

Mason, P. (1974) *A Matter of Honour: an Account of the Indian Army, its Officers and Men*, London: Cape.

Mintz, S. W. (1986) *Sweetness and Power: the Place of Sugar in Modern History*, Harmondsworth: Penguin.

Morris, H. S. (1968) *The Indians in Uganda*, London: Weidenfeld & Nicolson.

van Onselen, C. (1976) *Chibaro: African Mine Labour in Southern Rhodesia, 1900–1933*, London: Pluto Press.

Panikkar, K. M. (1959) *Asia and Western Dominance*, London: George Allen & Unwin.

Patterson, O. (1982) *Slavery and Social Death: a Comparative Study*, Cambridge, Mass.: Harvard University Press.

Redclift, M. (1978) *Agrarian Reform and Peasant Organization on the Ecuadorian Coast*, London: Athlone Press.

—— (1984) *Development and the Environmental Crisis: Red or Green Alternatives?*, London: Methuen.

Roberts, B. (1978) *Cities of Peasants: the Political Economy of Urbanization in the Third World*, London: Edward Arnold.

Sahlins, M. (1961) 'The segmentary lineage: an organization of predatory expansion', *American Anthropologist* 63(2): 332–45.

Scott, J. C. (1976) *The Moral Economy of the Peasant: Rebellion and Subsistence in Southeast Asia*, London: Yale University Press.

Skinner, G. W. (1964–5) 'Marketing and social structure in rural China', *Journal of Asian Studies* 34(1–3): 3–43, 195–227, 363–99.

Southall, A. (1956) *Alur Society: a Study in Processes and Types of Domination*, Cambridge: Heffer.

Southern, R. W. (1962) *Western Views of Islam in the Middle Ages*, Cambridge: Mass.: Harvard University Press.

Spate, O. H. K. (1979) *The Spanish Lake*, London: Croom Helm.

—— (1983) *Monopolists and Freebooters*, London: Croom Helm.

Stavrianos, L. S. (1981) *Global Rift: the Third World Comes of Age*, New York: Morrow.

Sundkler, B. G. M. (1948) *Bantu Prophets in South Africa*, London: Lutterworth Press.

Tambiah, S. J. (1970) *Buddhism and Spirit Cults in North-east Thailand*, Cambridge: Cambridge University Press.

Tinker, H. (1974) *A New System of Slavery: the Export of Indian Labour Overseas, 1830–1920*, Oxford University Press.

Wachtel, N. (1971) *La Vision des vaincus: les Indiens du Pérou devant la Conquête espagnole*, Paris: Gallimard.

Waddy, J. A. (1988) *Classification of Plants and Animals from a Groote Eylandt Aboriginal Point of View*, 2 vols, Darwin: Australian National University.

Weber, M. (1956) *The Sociology of Religion*, London: Methuen.

—— (1961) *General Economic History*, New York: Collier.

Wolf, E. R. (1982) *Europe and the People without History*, Berkeley: University of California Press.

Womack, J. (1969) *Zapata and the Mexican Revolution*, Harmondsworth: Penguin.

Worsley, P. (1957) *The Trumpet Shall Sound: a Study of 'Cargo' Cults in Melanesia*, London: MacGibbon & Kee.

—— (1964) *The Third World: a Vital New Force in International Affairs*, London: Weidenfeld & Nicolson.

—— (1984) *The Three Worlds: Culture and World Development*, London: Weidenfeld & Nicolson.

Zamosc, L. (1986) *The Agrarian Question and the Peasant Movement in Colombia: Struggles of the National Peasant Association, 1967–1981*, Cambridge: Cambridge University Press.

Zubaida, S. (1989) *Islam, the People and the State: Essays on Political Ideas and Movements in the Middle East*, London: Routledge.

FURTHER READING

Blackburn, R. (1988) *The Overthrow of Colonial Slavery, 1776–1848*, London: Verso.

Brockway, L. H. (1979) *Science and Colonial Expansion: the Role of the British Royal Botanic Gardens*, New York: Academic Press.

Cohn, B. S. (1983) 'Representing authority in Victorian India', in E. Hobsbawm and T. Ranger (eds) *The Invention of Tradition*, Cambridge: Cambridge University Press.

Geertz, C. (1963) *Agricultural Involution: the Process of Ecological Change in Indonesia*, Berkeley: University of California.

Gellner, E. (1983) *Nations and Nationalism*, London: Blackwell.

Hughes, R. (1988) *The Fatal Shore: a History of the Transportation of Convicts to Australia, 1787–1868*, London: Pan Books.

Kehoe, A. B. (1981) *North American Indians: a Comprehensive Account*, Englewood Cliffs, NJ: Prentice-Hall.

Lenin, V. I. (1915) *Imperialism: the Highest Stage of Capitalism* (many editions).

van Leur, J. C. (1955) *Indonesian Trade and Society: Essays in Social and Economic History*, The Hague: van Hoeve.

Mason, P. (1974) *A Matter of Honour: an Account of the Indian Army, its Officers and Men*, London: Cape.

van Onselen, C. (1976) *Chibaro: African Mine Labour in Southern Rhodesia, 1900–1933*, London: Pluto Press.

Pannikar, K. M. (1959) *Asia and Western Dominance*, London: George Allen & Unwin.

Redclift, M. (1978) *Agrarian Reform and Peasant Organization on the Ecuadorian Coast*, London: Athlone Press.

Roberts, B. (1978) *Cities of Peasants: the Political Economy of Urbanization in the Third World*, London: Edward Arnold.

Skinner, G. W. (1964–5) 'Marketing and social structure in rural China', *Journal of Asian Studies* 34(1–3): 3–43, 195–227, 363–99.

Spate, O. H. K. (1979) *The Spanish Lake*, London: Croom Helm.

Stavrianos, L. S. (1981) *Global Rift: the Third World Comes of Age*, New York: Morrow.

Wolf, E. R. (1982) *Europe and the People Without History*, Berkeley: University of California Press.

Worsley, P. (1984) *The Three Worlds: Culture and World Development*, London: Weidenfeld & Nicolson.

Zubaida, S. (1989) *Islam, the People and the State: Essays on Political Ideas and Movements in the Middle East*, London: Routledge.

INDEX

environment (*continued*)
  shared 164–5
  socialization 832
  spatial organization 330, 337,
    460–97
  symbolism 381
  tool-use 133
environment-behaviour studies
  spatial organization 480
Eoanthropus
  early hominid evolution 37
epidemics *see* disease
episodic high mortality
  population debate 286–8
epizootics *see* disease
equality
  concept of 1031–5
  education 1058
equivalence
  gift exchange 919
Errington, J. J. 882
Errington, S. 815, 817–18
Espinas, A. 448
essentialism
  social life 738
ethics
  spatial organization 481
ethnic categories
  nationalism 709
ethnic election
  politics 712–13
ethnic minorities
  division of labour 907
  industrialization 906
ethnicism
  politics 709–10
ethnicity
  cultural significance 346–8
  dissolution 711–13
  politics 706–28
  survival 711–13
ethnie
  lateral/vertical 713–17
  modern nations 721–5
  politics 709–10
ethnoarchaeology
  spatial organization 481
ethnocentrism
  art analysis 655, 656
  belief systems 582
  human uniqueness debate 28, **29**, 30
  violence 987–8

ethnochoreology 688
ethnogenesis
  politics 711
ethnography
  anthropological role 370–1
  dialogic anthropology 871–2
  dispute processes 969
  inequality 1011–12
  infancy 847
  law 965, 968, 972
  literacy 550
  person-centred 832, 834
  personhood 841
  poetics 870–1
  sex 822
  socialization 837
  speaking 862, 866, 866–9
  verbal art 868
Ethnological Society 142
ethnology
  dance 688, 690, 692
  symbolism 375
  technology 446
ethnomusicology
  anthropological theory 331
  comparative study 687
  technological development 690, 692
ethnopoetics
  language 862, 870–1
ethology
  animality/humanity comparison 22
  definition 480
  displacement activities 622
  primates 440
etic models
  built environment 463, 481
etiquette
  language 879, 881–2
euphoria
  music 696
Europe
  see also Old World
  colonial expansion 1041–2, 1044–5
  colonization 4, 297–9
  evolution debate 79–80
  Neanderthals 84–5
  Upper Palaeolithic 92, 94
evaluation
  scales of 1019
Evans-Pritchard, E. E.
  inequality 1020, 1021–3
  language 863

housework (*continued*)
  political economy 747
housing
  Third World 723
  warfare 994
Howell, Nancy 285, 288, 289
Howiesons Poort industry
  South Africa 94
Hoxne (England)
  cultural traditions 84
Hrdlicka, A.
  art 98
  colonization 101, 102
  evolution debate 80
Hubert, H. 575–6
Huffman, M. 139–40
Hugh-Jones, Stephen 602–3, 604
Hughes, A. 774–5
human ecology
  definition 480
human evolution
  see also evolution
  subsistence 10–13
human geography
  definition 480
human hands *see* hands
human populations
  see also populations
  calorie requirements 232
  diet and nutrition 226–56
  protein requirements 229
human sciences
  infrastructure 187–90
humans
  anthropocentrism 15, 25–30
  classification debate 39
  concept of 23–4, 26
  condition definition 15, 19–25
  disease 4
  evolution 3
  H. s. sapiens 3–5
  language 20, 63–4
  molecular biology 38
  sociality 756–77
  species definition 15–19
  spoken language 3
  theoretical debate 14–30
  tool-use 3
humming
  non-verbal communication debate 64
Hunsgi (India)
  Acheulean 84

Hunt, George 593
hunter-gatherers
  bands 944
  behaviour debate 275–6
  categorization 442
  ceremonial centres 616–17, **618,**
    619–20
  colonization 102
  definition 200–1
  demand sharing 924
  disease 285, 298
  efficiency studies 279
  egalitarianism 1012
  famine 287–8
  fertility rates 289–91
  food production debate 10
  food-collecting populations
    200–4
  group size 770
  hunting debate 86
  incest 800
  nutrition 233–4
  Palaeolithic 7
  population debate 284–6
  population growth 271
  population size 11
  social evolution 942, 943
  social order 752
  spatial organization 469
  subsistence modes 197–221
hunting
  animal behaviour 765, 766
  behaviour comparison 228
  definition 199
  H. erectus 85–6
  performance 620–2
  prefrontal cortex 119
  residence rules 796
  Upper Palaeolithic 204, 209
husbandry
  see also animal husbandry
  domestication comparison 11
Hutchins, E. 577
Huxley, Thomas 28
hygiene
  social structure 403
Hylobatinae
  early hominid evolution 37
Hymes, D. 866, 867
hypertension
  disease 12
  Pacific island societies 315

Makapansgat (South Africa)
  fossil records 56, **57**
maktab literacy
  Iran 541
malaria
  colonization policy 300, 302, 307, 308
  natural selection 167
Malaysia
  sex 826–7
Malinowski, Bronislaw
  belief systems 576
  economics 928–9
  equivalence 919
  fatherhood 789, 793
  food 226
  gift exchange 920
  kula exchange 916
  language 861
  law 963, 965, 966–8, 969, 970
  myth 592, 608–9
  non-commodity exchange 917
  technology 445
malnutrition
  disease 12
  food selection 237–8
  warfare 993, 994
Malthus, Thomas 269, 943
mammals
  animal behaviour 766
  mimicry 368, 391
  reproduction 765, 774
  sociality 757
  symbolic behaviour 382–3
mammoth
  hunting debate 85, 86
'Man the Hunter' paradigm 203
man-made disease
  see also disease effects 12
mana
  concept of 575–6
Mantoux, P. 442
Maori
  belief systems 576
maps
  spatial organization 468, 484
marginalism
  political economy 748
  wealth 916
markets
  classification 931–6
  social order 752–3

trading 931–6
weaving 902
Marquesas
  double-headed club 662, **663**
marriage
  definition 798–803
  gift exchange 925–8
  housework 892
  lateral *ethnie* 714
  prescriptive 801–3
  templates 379
Marshack, A. 99
Martin, Debra 283
Marx, Karl
  belief systems 583
  division of labour 904
  equality 1011
  fetishism 931
  forces of production 141
  hierarchy 1031
  industrial revolution 442
  inequality 1020, 1030–1
  instrumentalism 707
  labour 895–6
  modes of production 204
  non-commodity exchange 920
  religion 632
  small-scale societies 416
  social evolution 941, 942, 946
  technology 143, 441
  wealth 912–15, 922, 928
Marxism
  structural 949
Marzke, M. 145, 440
masks
  art analysis 663, 666–7, 676
  structuralist study 401
Mason, O. T. 423, 446
mass consumption
  freedom 414, 417
  material culture 405–6
Mass Observation 411–12
mass production
  political economy 747
massacres
  ethnicity 714
Matenkupkum cave (Pacific)
  fossil records 94
material culture
  aesthetics 673
  art analysis 656
  definition 334–5, 398–9